HANDBOOK OF ENVIRONMENTAL PSYCHOLOGY

Volume One

HANDBOOK OF
ENVIRONMENTAL PSYCHOLOGY

V. 1 —

Edited by

DANIEL STOKOLS
University of California, Irvine

IRWIN ALTMAN
University of Utah

A Wiley-Interscience Publication

JOHN WILEY & SONS

New York / Chichester / Brisbane / Toronto / Singapore

Library of Congress Cataloging in Publication Data:

Handbook of environmental psychology.

   "A Wiley-Interscience publication."
   Includes bibliographies and indexes.
   1. Environmental psychology.   I. Stokols, Daniel.
II. Altman, Irwin.   [DNLM: 1. Behavior.   2. Environment.
3. Psychology.   BF 353 H236]

BF353.H26   1987   155.9   86–19081
ISBN 0-471-63016-0 (v. I)
ISBN 0-471-86631-8 (Two-volume set)

Printed in the United States of America

10 9 8 7 6 5 4 3 2 1

EDITORIAL BOARD

CONTRIBUTORS

JOHN AIELLO
Department of Psychology
Douglass College
New Brunswick, New Jersey

IRWIN ALTMAN
Department of Psychology
University of Utah
Salt Lake City, Utah

ROGER G. BARKER
Department of Psychology
University of Kansas
Oskaloosa, Kansas

ANDREW BAUM
Department of Medical Psychology
Uniformed Services University of the
    Health Sciences
Bethesda, Maryland

BARBARA B. BROWN
Department of Family and Consumer Studies
University of Utah
Salt Lake City, Utah

DAVID CANTER
Department of Psychology
University of Surrey
Guildford, Surrey
United Kingdom

FRANCES CARP
Wright Institute
Berkeley, California

JANET REIZENSTEIN CARPMAN
Carpman Grant Associates
Ann Arbor, Michigan

SHELDON COHEN
Department of Psychology
Carnegie-Mellon University
Pittsburgh, Pennsylvania

KENNETH CRAIK
Institute of Personality Assessment and Research
University of California
Berkeley, California

KAREN CRONICK
Instituto de Psicologia
Universidad Central de Venezuela
Caracas, Venezuela

IAN DONALD
Department of Psychology
University of Surrey
Guildford, Surrey
United Kingdom

GARY W. EVANS
Program in Social Ecology
University of California
Irvine, California

PETER B. EVERETT
College of Human Development
Pennsylvania State University
University Park, Pennsylvania

NICKOLAUS FEIMER
The Quaker Oats Company
Chicago, Illinois

BARUCH FISCHHOFF
Decision Research
Eugene, Oregon

E. SCOTT GELLER
Department of Psychology
Virginia Tech
Blacksburg, Virginia

REGINALD G. GOLLEDGE
Department of Geography
University of California
Santa Barbara, California

CARL F. GRAUMANN
Psychologisches Institut
Universitat Heidelberg
Heidelberg, Federal Republic of Germany

PAUL V. GUMP
Department of Psychology
University of Kansas
Lawrence, Kansas

CONTRIBUTORS

GENICHI HAGINO
Department of Psychology
Komazawa University
Tokyo, Japan

ROB HALL
School of Behavioral Sciences
Macquarie University
North Ryde, New South Wales, Australia

HARRY HEFT
Department of Psychology
Denison University
Granville, Ohio

MATI HEIDMETS
Department of Psychology
Tallinn Pedagogic Institute
Tallinn, Estonian S.S.R., U.S.S.R.

CHARLES J. HOLAHAN
Department of Psychology
University of Texas
Austin, Texas

DENISE JODELET
Laboratoire de Psychologie Sociale
Ecole des Hautes Etudes en Sciences Sociale
Paris, France

RICHARD KNOPF
Arizona State University
Phoenix, Arizona

ANDRÉ KREMER
Psychologish Laboratorium
Katholieke Universiteit
Nijmegen, The Netherlands

LENELIS KRUSE
Schwerpunkt Okologische Psychologie
Fern Universitat
Hagen, Federal Republic of Germany

JURI KRUUSVALL
Environmental Psychology Research Unit
Tallinn Pedagogic Institute
Tallinn, Estonian S.S.R., U.S.S.R.

RIKARD KÜLLER
Lund Institute of Technology
School of Architecture
Lund, Sweden

BRIAN R. LITTLE
Department of Psychology
Carleton University
Ottawa, Ontario, Canada

WILLIAM MICHELSON
Department of Sociology
University of Toronto
Toronto, Ontario, Canada

MAMORU MOCHIZUKI
School of Liberal Arts
International College of Commerce and Economics
Saitama, Japan

GARY T. MOORE
School of Architecture and Urban Planning
University of Wisconsin
Milwaukee, Wisconsin

TOOMAS NIIT
Department of Sociology
Institute of History
Tallinn, Estonian S.S.R., U.S.S.R.

STUART OSKAMP
Department of Psychology
Claremont Graduate School
Claremont, California

PAUL PAULUS
Department of Psychology
University of Texas
Arlington, Texas

DAVID PITT
Department of Horticulture
University of Maryland
College Park, Maryland

HAROLD M. PROSHANSKY
Graduate School and University Center
City University of New York
New York, New York

BARBARA ROGOFF
Department of Psychology
University of Utah
Salt Lake City, Utah

JAMES A. RUSSELL
Department of Psychology
University of British Columbia
Vancouver, British Columbia, Canada

SUSAN SAEGERT
Environmental Psychology Program
Graduate School and University Center
City University of New York
New York, New York

EUCLIDES SÁNCHEZ
Instituto de Psicologia
Universidad Central de Venezuela
Caracas, Venezuela

PAUL SLOVIC
Decision Research
Eugene, Oregon

JACALYN SNODGRASS
Department of Psychology
University of British Columbia
Vancouver, British Columbia, Canada

ROBERT SOMMER
Department of Psychology
University of California
Davis, California

PAUL C. STERN
National Academy of Sciences
Washington, D.C.

DANIEL STOKOLS
Program in Social Ecology
University of California
Irvine, California

PETER STRINGER
The Queen's University of Belfast
Belfast, Northern Ireland

PETER SUEDFELD
Psychology Department
University of British Columbia
Vancouver, British Columbia, Canada

ERIC SUNDSTROM
Department of Psychology
University of Tennessee
Knoxville, Tennessee

OLA SVENSON
Department of Psychology
University of Stockholm
Stockholm, Sweden

RALPH B. TAYLOR
Criminal Justice Department
Temple University
Philadelphia, Pennsylvania

ROSS THORNE
School of Architecture
The University of Sydney
Sydney, New South Wales, Australia

JEROME TOGNOLI
C.W. Post Center
Long Island University
Brooklyn, New York

ABRAHAM WANDERSMAN
Department of Psychology
University of South Carolina
Columbia, South Carolina

SEYMOUR WAPNER
Department of Psychology
Clark University
Worcester, Massachusetts

BARRY G. WATSON
Toronto Transit Commission
Toronto, Ontario, Canada

ESTHER WIESENFELD
Instituto de Psicologia
Universidad Central de Venezuela
Caracas, Venezuela

ALLAN W. WICKER
Department of Psychology
Claremont Graduate School
Claremont, California

GARY H. WINKEL
Environmental Psychology Program
Graduate School and University Center
City University of New York
New York, New York

JOACHIM F. WOHLWILL
Department of Individual and Family Studies
College of Human Development
Pennsylvania State University
University Park, Pennsylvania

TAKIJI YAMAMOTO
Hiroshima University
Hiroshima, Japan

CRAIG ZIMRING
College of Architecture
Georgia Institute of Technology
Atlanta, Georgia

ERVIN ZUBE
School for Renewable Natural Resources
University of Arizona
Tucson, Arizona

PREFACE

The relationships between people and their everyday environments received only sporadic attention from behavioral scientists prior to the mid-1960s. However, several circumstances converged during the late 1960s to move environment–behavior research from the background to the forefront of social science. Concerns about environmental degradation and urban violence, shortages of natural resources, and the impacts of environmental pollution on health increased sharply during this period. At the same time, behavioral scientists had few theoretical or methodological guidelines for studying the psychological, performance, and health impacts of these complex environmental problems. Owing to this heightened awareness of community–environment crises and the existence of major scientific gaps in our understanding of these problems, the multidisciplinary field of environment and behavior expanded rapidly after 1970. During this period, psychologists and their colleagues from several related disciplines embraced the challenge of developing new scientific approaches for studying human behavior and well-being from an interdisciplinary and ecological perspective.

Between 1970 and 1980, several coherent paradigms of environment–behavior research emerged, focusing on topics such as personal space, crowding, and territoriality; environmental attitudes and assessment; spatial cognition, resource conservation, and behavior settings analysis; individuals' reactions to environmental stressors; small group ecology; and the influence of urban and cultural factors on the vitality of neighborhoods and community groups. New theoretical and methodological approaches evolved within each paradigm, and the rapidly growing body of empirical findings spurred the establishment of new journals, professional organizations, and conference series, as well as the publication of several textbooks and monographs in environmental psychology and related areas of environment–behavior research.

We first considered the possibility of editing a *Handbook of Environmental Psychology* during the

fall of 1980. The potential usefulness of such a volume was suggested by the rapid growth of the field, by the uniqueness and increasing coherence of the field's conceptual, methodological, and empirical directions, by the international scope and practical significance of environment–behavior research, and by the prospects for continued growth and scientific innovation within environmental psychology and the broader environment–behavior field. Considering these trends, we concluded that the development of this volume could prove valuable in several respects.

First, we wanted to develop a comprehensive volume that would offer a representative and detailed overview of environmental psychology in terms of its major theoretical, methodological, and empirical contributions. Equally comprehensive coverage of the field is typically precluded by the space limitations of review articles and the more restrictive focus of research monographs.

Second, we wanted the *Handbook* to highlight novel directions of inquiry and to identify recent and prospective linkages among diverse research paradigms. As of the early 1980s, several integrative or "cross-paradigm" research programs were underway. By emphasizing the integrative and interdisciplinary aspects of the field, we hope that this volume will facilitate future progress toward conceptual and methodological integration within environment–behavior research.

Third, considering the applicability of environment–behavior concepts, methods, and findings to the analysis and resolution of community problems (e.g., resource conservation, facilities design, health promotion), we wanted this volume to reflect the previous and potential contributions of environmental psychology to community planning and public policy. Part 4 of this volume, for example, provides a valuable sourcebook for practitioners interested in applying psychological perspectives to a broad range of community–environment problems. Thus the *Handbook* is oriented not only toward researchers and graduate students in environmental psychology, but also toward a broad spectrum of environmental practitioners and professional groups, including architects, interior designers, facilities managers, natural resource managers, transportation analysts, urban planners, and health care providers.

Fourth, in view of the increasingly international scope of environmental psychology (as reflected in the establishment of international organizations, journals, and conference series for the support and dissemination of environment–behavior research), we wanted this book to highlight the distinctive theoretical and methodological perspectives that have evolved within various countries and regions of the world. Thus Part 5 of the *Handbook* is devoted to an analysis and comparison of environment–behavior research developments within ten different countries or geographical regions. A comparison of the scientific perspectives presented in these chapters reveals the striking influence of geographic, political, and cultural forces on the directions of environment–behavior research.

Fifth, we wanted this volume to trace the scientific–historical context in which environmental psychology evolved and the ecological and demographic trends that are likely to influence the course of future research. Thus the first section of the *Handbook* focuses on the social and intellectual origins of environmental psychology while the last explores several potential directions for future research in this field. In addition, all of the chapters in other parts of the volume describe the historical development of specific research areas and examine potentially important directions for future work.

These five major goals guided our assumptions about the selection and sequencing of chapter topics and about the overall organization of the book. (The organizational assumptions and structure of this volume are discussed in greater detail in the Introduction.) The structure and development of this volume also was guided by the insightful and expert advice offered by 35 of our colleagues in environmental psychology from around the world, who served as members of the Editorial Board for the *Handbook*. These individuals were asked to comment on our prospectus for the *Handbook* and to provide suggestions regarding the selection of chapter topics, authors, and

the general themes to be emphasized within each part of the volume. In developing the initial prospectus for the volume and in the reviews of authors' chapter outlines, we were assisted by Edwin Willems of the University of Houston and through our discussions with Thurman Poston at John Wiley & Sons. In subsequent stages of the *Handbook's* production, we received invaluable assistance from Herb Reich, Valda Aldzeris, Sheck Cho, and Michael Flaherty at John Wiley & Sons. The complex and incremental process of developing the *Handbook* over the past seven years was greatly facilitated by the gracious and competent assistance we received from the editorial and production staff at John Wiley & Sons.

The planning and eventual production of the *Handbook* was very much a collaborative effort and we are deeply grateful to the numerous individuals who have assisted us throughout all stages of the project. We thank the members of the Editorial Board, who provided extremely detailed and constructive reviews of chapter outlines and chapter drafts. We also appreciate the dedication and persistence of chapter authors, who painstakingly prepared their manuscripts and graciously responded to the suggestions of the editors and additional reviewers in preparing the revised and final versions of their chapters. Our respective universities (the University of California, Irvine, and the University of Utah) provided us with continuing assistance in the form of staff support, facilities, and sabbatical leave during the period in which we edited this volume. We thank Fran Renner, Jill Vidas, and Carol Wyatt for their able assistance in typing various sections of the manuscript. And last but not least, we want to thank our wives, Jeanne and Gloria, and our children, Eli, David, and William, who provided support and encouragement throughout the seven years that we worked on this project.

DANIEL STOKOLS
IRWIN ALTMAN

Irvine, California
Salt Lake City, Utah
January 1987

CONTENTS OF VOLUME ONE

CONTENTS OF VOLUME TWO

HANDBOOK OF ENVIRONMENTAL PSYCHOLOGY

Volume One

INTRODUCTION

Daniel Stokols, *University of California, Irvine, California*

Irwin Altman, *University of Utah, Salt Lake City, Utah*

Environmental psychology, or the study of human behavior and well-being in relation to the sociophysical environment, emerged during the 1960s as the result of both scientific and societal concerns. At the societal level, increased awareness of community problems such as overcrowding, the shrinkage of natural resources, and the deterioration of environmental quality prompted widespread concern about the constraints of the ecological environment. Yet as psychologists turned their attention to the study of the relationships between the large-scale physical environment and behavior they encountered several conceptual and methodological issues that had been left unresolved by the mainstream of behavioral science. Most important, traditional psychological theories had neglected the molar physical environment while focusing more narrowly on the links between microlevel stimuli and intrapersonal processes such as perception, cognition, learning, and development. Theoretical and methodological guidelines for charting the ecological context of behavior remained to be established. Thus the environmental dilemmas of the 1960s and 1970s and the scientific agenda posed by these problems facilitated the coalescence and rapid growth of environmental psychology.

The rapid expansion of environmental psychology during the past decades is reflected in the appearance of numerous textbooks and research monographs, the establishment of new journals (*Environment and Behavior,* 1969; *Population and Environment,* 1978; the *Journal of Environmental Psychology,* 1981; *Journal of Architectural Planning and Research,* 1984), and the development of several professional organizations (e.g., the Environmental Design Research Association and the environmental sections of the American Psychological Association, American

Sociological Association, and the International Association of Applied Psychology). The *Annual Review of Psychology* now incorporates chapters on environmental psychology at regular intervals. Since 1973, four such chapters have appeared (Craik, 1973; Holahan, 1986; Russell & Ward, 1982; Stokols, 1978). Moreover, the increasingly international scope of the field is evident from the recent professional meetings that have been held in Australia, Ecuador, France, West Germany, Great Britain, Israel, Japan, Mexico, the Netherlands, the Soviet Union, the United States, Turkey, Venezuela, and Scandinavia, and the establishment of graduate training programs in environmental psychology at universities around the world.

Sheer quantity of publication and the vigorous level of professional activity within environmental psychology were not in themselves sufficient reasons for developing the present handbook. This volume, the first large-scale compendium of knowledge on environmental psychology, is warranted only to the degree that these indications of quantitative growth coincide with evidence of the scientific maturity, practical utility, and future viability of the field.

SALIENT FEATURES OF ENVIRONMENTAL PSYCHOLOGY

Our objective in developing a comprehensive, scholarly *Handbook of Environmental Psychology* was closely linked to four major features of contemporary research on environment and behavior. First, the high levels of research and professional activity, noted earlier, have yielded substantial scientific achievements. An earlier review of the field concluded that:

Environmental psychology is no mere fad of the 1960's — a short-lived product of environmentalist and political activism. Instead, this field has taken hold both conceptually and empirically and is now comprised of several active and focused research domains....The scientific vitality of environmental psychology is reflected in the substantial theoretical and empirical progress that has been made within many of its major subareas. (Stokols, 1978, p. 278)

Second, recent research indicates an increasing emphasis on theoretical integration and coherence. Progress toward conceptual and methodological integration is reflected in the linkages that have been drawn between various research paradigms within the field (e.g., the combination of environmental cognition and operant perspectives in the analysis of energy conservation and community use of public transit systems; applications of behavior-setting analysis to issues of environmental assessment, human development, and stress). Moreover, several programs of research reflect novel lines of inquiry, the results of which may contribute to a clearer delineation of the unique, theoretical underpinnings of the field.

Third, the accumulation and consolidation of scientific knowledge have been accompanied by several effective applications of environment–behavioral research to issues of community planning and environmental design. The development of certain research areas within environmental psychology (e.g., environmental assessment, environmental stress), in fact, reflects a direct response to applied concerns. The community problems orientation and proven practical utility of environmental psychology are among its most distinctive and desirable features.

Fourth, prospects for the continued vitality and viability of environmental psychology are favorable. On the one hand, environmental psychologists have discovered several engaging scientific questions within diverse areas of the field that are likely to stimulate new theoretical, methodological, and empirical advances in the years to come. At the same time, the persisting (and in many instances worsening) environmental dilemmas of the present and future decades should provide an additional impetus for the continued development of the field.

Furthermore, owing to the complexity of environmental problems and the necessity of approaching them from different perspectives and levels of analysis, contemporary research on environment and behavior is interdisciplinary in scope. Researchers and practitioners in the fields of geography, urban sociology, public health, natural resources management,

architecture, organizational behavior, facilities management, and urban planning constitute a broad base of professional support for environmental psychology. In view of the interdisciplinary orientation of the field, it is likely that these scholarly and professional groups will continue to collaborate with psychologists in the analysis of community problems and to utilize the conceptual and methodological tools of environmental psychology.

ORGANIZATION OF THE HANDBOOK

The six sections of this volume, true to the nature of the field of environmental psychology, are not organized around neatly circumscribed, nonoverlapping content areas. Possible analogies for the organization of chapters and sections include a mosaic of overlapping but distinctive units, a pattern of somewhat inseparable parts, a multidimensional figure that can be viewed from any of several perspectives, or a series of overlay maps, each of which contains different qualities of the terrain. As such, there are many ways to approach the material in this volume, and the organization of chapters and sections could have taken any of several forms.

It might be best to imagine the volume as a series of cartographic maps, each of which describes different qualities of a geographic region. One traditional form of map emphasizes highway and road routes; another describes terrain configurations and contours; another depicts vegetation and climatic conditions; another focuses on distributions of agricultural products and mineral resources. Each map is incomplete in respect to the whole, but each is valid in relationship to its specific focus. This volume can be seen to reflect a series of overlapping maps, and one can proceed through the volume on any of several "intellectual journeys."

The requirement to produce a single map bound between hard covers results in only one representation of the field of environmental psychology when, in fact, it is possible to work through the volume using any of several paths or maps. Following is our "guide" to the handbook through several of its organizational maps.

The visible organization of the volume is reflected in its Table of Contents and six sections. Briefly, Part 1, "Origins and Scope of Environmental Psychology," traces the societal and intellectual origins of environmental psychology, the scientific structure of the field, and recent theoretical and methodological trends.

Parts 2, 3, and 4 contain chapters that focus on the conceptual and empirical substance of the field, albeit from different perspectives. One can treat these sections as reflecting a three-dimensional matrix. A major focus of the chapters in Part 2, "Processes of Person–Environment Transactions," is basic psychological processes such as cognition, personality, emotion, life-stage development, and territoriality as they relate to people's day-to-day transactions with the large-scale environment. Here, authors examine the major research paradigms of environmental psychology and the psychological processes emphasized within these areas. Individual chapters review important theoretical, methodological, and empirical developments within particular research areas. Authors also were invited to deal with unresolved theoretical and methodological issues, potentially fruitful lines of inquiry, and the practical significance of previous and current work within their topical area.

A second dimension of these chapters deals with the environmental contexts or settings in which psychological processes are embedded such as homes, neighborhoods, educational settings, medical treatment centers, recreational areas, and work environments. Thus, Part 3, "Levels of Environmental Analysis: Situations, Settings, and Places," focuses on various categories and scales of environments and the psychological processes embedded in those settings. The study of places (and the psychological processes manifested in places) is a unique hallmark of environmental psychology, and the chapters of this part deal with some of the more heavily researched environmental settings.

A third facet of research in this field concerns environmental change, intervention, and a broad range of applications. In Part 4, "Applications of Environmental Psychology to Community Problems," psychological processes and environmental settings are examined from the perspective of a problem solving and action–research orientation. Thus the chapters of Part 4 deal with potential applications of environmental psychology to community problems such as crime prevention, depletion of natural resources, pollution, inefficient public transit systems, urban stress, and environmental degradation. Chapters examine instances in which psychological theory and/or research methods have been utilized in the analysis and amelioration of environmental problems. Authors also discuss factors influencing the effectiveness of collaboration among environmental researchers and practitioners and the development of criteria for judging the cost-effectiveness of alternative community interventions. In summary, Parts 2, 3, and 4 form a diverse yet overlapping set of chapters, each adopting a different focus on the fundamental subject matter, research and theory of environmental psychology.

Part 5, "International Perspectives on Environmental Psychology," is a unique approach to the subject matter of the field. Environmental psychology is not only an interdisciplinary field; it is international in scope. Given its substantive concerns, the theories and research problems of environmental psychology are intimately linked to local cultural and physical circumstances. Because of the vigorous and energetic international activity in this field we decided to include a set of chapters that explicitly examine trends in environmental research and theory in different parts of the world. These chapters also portray the historical, cultural, and geographical factors associated with the development of environmental psychology around the world.

Part 6, "Prospects for the Future," contains chapters by pioneers in environmental psychology. Authors were invited to present their views of the field—its history and prospects for the future, as well as a retrospective and prospective look at their own work. These chapters capstone the volume and are based on the contributions of those who have participated in and observed the field for over three decades.

Embedded within the volume are a number of themes and topics, analogous to the multiple maps of a geographical region. Following are some thematic guidelines for various intellectual trips through the complex region of environmental psychology.

How does one gain a sense of the history of the field? Environmental psychology is too new and too diverse to expect a singular, standardized, and all-encompassing chapter on the history of the field, as one might find in a traditional textbook or handbook. For that reason, and because we think it is important to place contemporary work in perspective, we asked authors to include some historical background in their chapters. Thus almost every chapter includes some form of historical commentary.

The international chapters of Part 5 are especially rich in historical perspective, and one might begin with this cluster of contributions. The philosophically oriented chapters of Part 1 all adopt a historical perspective on the development of the field, as do the chapters of Part 6 by pioneers in the field. And the chapters of Parts 2, 3, and 4, focusing on psychological processes, settings, and applications, respectively, usually place their subject matter in historical perspective. Because there was no way to achieve a single all-encompassing history of the field, we asked all authors to address history from the perspective of their topical area.

How does one obtain an overview of the subject matter of the field? Here again, one will find such information in all chapters. But the best starting point is the chapters of Parts 2, 3, and 4. These chapters deal with research and theory on psychological processes, physical settings, and applications, respectively. If one is interested in particular places, then one should begin with the chapters of Parts 3 and 4 and then trace back into the chapters of Part 2, which deal with psychological processes. If one is interested primarily in fundamental psychological processes, one should begin with the relevant chapters of Part 2 and then work through the chapters of Parts 3 and 4. And, to round out one's view of subject matter, it will be helpful to examine parts of the international chapters of Part 5, because they deal with research and theory on psychological processes, settings, and applications in particular regions of the world. Also, some substantive research is discussed in the first and last parts of the volume, albeit from historical, theoretical, methodological, and philosophical perspectives.

How does one gain a sense of the future of environmental psychology and opportunities for promising directions of research and theory? Here too, the diversity of the field did not permit a single chapter or two on this topic. Instead, we asked each author to conclude his or her chapter with an analysis of potentially fruitful directions for future research and theory. Proposals for further research consistently appear in the main substantive chapters of Parts 2, 3, and 4, which address research and theory on psychological processes, places, and applications of environmental psychology. The chapters in Parts 1 and 6, which address broad philosophical, historical, and methodological issues, also contain many suggestions for future research, as well as projections of the future directions of the field.

How does one explore methodological issues of environmental psychology? Here we pursued a mixed strategy. In Part 1, "Origins and Structure of Environmental Psychology," Chapter 3 by Winkel is devoted specifically to methodological issues. The other chapters in Part 1 also deal with methodological questions at a broad strategic level, as do the chapters in Part 6, "Environmental Psychology: Prospects for the Future." We also asked authors in all of the other parts of the volume to include issues of research methodology in relationship to their topics, as appropriate.

Forty-three chapters, written by authors from different parts of the world, dealing with a multidisciplinary and overlapping subject matter that can be approached from several vantage points and perspectives, cannot possibly yield a singular and simplified representation of the field. Although we editors have attempted to coordinate the diverse material presented in this handbook, the sheer volume and diversity of material made it impossible to avoid some overlap and redundancy across individual chapters. We trust, however, that the richness and comprehensiveness of the material, the enthusiasm and competence of the authors, and the untold possibilities for new and exciting research in environmental psychology will help foster the continued scientific vitality and societal contributions of this field.

REFERENCES

Craik, K.H. (1973). Environmental psychology. *Annual Review of Psychology, 24,* 403–422.

Holahan, C.J. (1986). Environmental psychology. *Annual Review of Psychology, 37,* 381–407.

Russell, J.A., & Ward, L.M. (1982). Environmental psychology. *Annual Review of Psychology, 33,* 651–688.

Stokols, D. (1978). Environmental psychology. *Annual Reviews of Psychology, 29,* 253–295.

PART 1

ORIGINS AND SCOPE OF ENVIRONMENTAL PSYCHOLOGY

WORLD VIEWS IN PSYCHOLOGY: TRAIT, INTERACTIONAL, ORGANISMIC, AND TRANSACTIONAL PERSPECTIVES

Irwin Altman, *University of Utah, Salt Lake City, Utah*

Barbara Rogoff, *University of Utah, Salt Lake City, Utah*

1.1. INTRODUCTION

This chapter examines world views or philosophical approaches that presently and historically underlie research and theory in psychology. These world views, termed *trait, interactional, organismic,* and *transactional,* are associated with different definitions of psychology and its units of study, different assumptions about the nature of person–environment relationships, varying conceptions about the philosophy and goals of science, and potentially different theories, methods, and strategies of research. Because environmental psychology is emerging as a full-fledged discipline but has not yet fully explored its implicit and explicit philosophical underpinnings, it is crucial to engage in self-reflection and introspection regarding its basic values. In order to facilitate the process of self-examination, we will present a taxonomy of world views of person–environment relationships and their associated conceptual and philosophical assumptions.

As background to the idea that present-day environmental psychology is an emergent field, it may be helpful to summarize aspects of its historical and sociological underpinnings (see also Moore, Chapter 39, Proshansky, Chapter 42, Sommer, Chapter 43, this volume). The origins of environmental psychology are rooted in a variety of social and scientific issues that came to the forefront in the 1960s and 1970s. These included a worldwide concern with the environment and the ecological movement, a call for psychology and other social sciences to contribute to the solution of social problems, increasing criticism of laboratory methods and advancement of naturalistic research, an interdisciplinary ethos (involving especially environmental design fields), a focus on molar, global units of analysis, and a plea for new theoretical approaches.

This array of values has been associated with certain tensions as environmental psychologists attempt to bridge traditional and unorthodox ways of thinking. Alongside a social problem orientation are an interest in basic theory and the discovery of knowledge for its own sake. And the call for a molar perspective coexists with the desire to explain and account for psychological processes in an analytic and dimensional fashion. Furthermore, the value of working in natural settings is accompanied by a traditional scientific requirement to conduct research in controlled situations so that one can attribute variations in psychological processes to known conditions. In addition to the goal of establishing new theories uniquely appropriate to environmental phenomena, there is a desire to translate and apply existing theories from other established fields in psychology. So environmental psychologists are and will continue to be subject to oppositional forces deriving from their disciplinary heritage and their aspiration to find a new path appropriate to the study of person–environment issues.

These tensions and directions ultimately concern psychology's orientation to the relationship between persons and environments, the relationship of time and change to psychological processes, and issues associated with philosophy of science, theory, and research methodology. These issues are not unique to environmental psychology. Indeed, they have begun to be addressed in many fields of psychology. For example, Tyler (1981) portrayed how psychology has begun to extend its boundaries in recent years by emphasizing the role of context and holistic aspects of human activity. She described mounting interest in the idea of multiple directions of causation and relations between variables, systems approaches involving complex sets of variables, appreciation of the importance of understanding single events, theoretical approaches that emphasize contextualism and that view phenomena as historical events, theories centered around ideas of interactionism, holism, and reciprocity, and cross-cultural analyses that link behavior to environments and situations. The writings of Gergen (1982), Harre and Secord (1972), Riegel (1976), Rosnow (1981), and others also raise fundamental issues about alternative philosophical approaches to the study of psychological phenomena.

It is a propitious time, therefore, for psychology in general and environmental psychology in particular to examine their philosophical substrates and to explore alternative assumptions and approaches to the study of psychological phenomena. By proposing a taxonomy of world views and describing their associated properties, we hope to contribute to the process of self-reflection and choice of philosophical strategies in environmental psychology.

The following section examines the roots of our taxonomy in the writings of Dewey and Bentley (1949) and Pepper (1942, 1967). The main body of the chapter describes historical and contemporary approaches in psychology and environmental psychology in terms of our fourfold classification of world views: trait, interactional, organismic, and transactional perspectives.

1.2. THE PHILOSOPHICAL FRAMEWORKS OF DEWEY AND BENTLEY (1949) AND PEPPER (1942, 1967)

Dewey and Bentley (1949) and Pepper (1942, 1967) examined philosophical and metatheoretical assumptions implicit in the research and theories of the physical, biological, and social sciences. They reflected on the dramatic changes in physics associated with the Newtonian and Einsteinian perspectives, pondered the state of knowledge and epistemology of the biological and social sciences, and analyzed alternative approaches and assumptions regarding scholarly inquiry.

1.2.1. Dewey and Bentley (1949)

These authors distinguished three approaches to the pursuit of knowledge—self-action, interaction, and transaction—corresponding to early or prescientific approaches, the Newtonian perspective, and the Einsteinian view of science, respectively.

Self-action assumes that the functioning of physical and social phenomena is governed by internal *essences, self-powers, forces,* or intrinsic qualities that are inherent in objects, organisms, or phenomena. Aristotle's system of physics involved a self-action approach in its assumption that substances inherently possessed *being* that produced self-initiated actions. In biology, the notion of vitalism implied inner, self-directing biological forces that gave rise to and guided organismic functioning. In psychology, the early concepts of *soul, mind,* and *instinct* reflected the self-action perspective. These orientations imply that physical or psychological phenomena are defined and operate more or less independently of settings and environments. Self-action approaches do not usually emphasize temporal processes or change, except as manifestations of the essence of a phenomenon. As noted in Table 1.1, Dewey and Bentley's self-action

Table 1.1. Philosophical Approaches to Psychological Phenomena

Dewey and Bentley	Pepper	Altman and Rogoff	Definition of Psychology
Self-action	Formism	Trait	The study of the individual, mind, or mental and psychological processes
Interaction	Mechanism	Interactional	The study of the prediction and control of behavior and psychological processes
	Organicism	Organismic	The study of dynamic and holistic psychological systems in which person and environment components exhibit complex, reciprocal, and mutual relationships and influences
Transaction	Contextualism Selectivism	Transactional	The study of the changing relations among psychological and environmental aspects of holistic unities

category overlaps with Pepper's formism and our trait perspective.

Dewey and Bentley stated that interaction and transaction approaches are more characteristic of modern science than are self-action perspectives. The interaction orientation is epitomized by Newtonian principles of classical physics, in which particles are assumed to exist as separate elements that act on and react to one another; that is, they *interact* to yield a phenomenon with causally linked and interdependent components. This approach assumes that physical and psychological elements exist independently of one another and possess certain intrinsic qualities, although their functioning may be affected by interaction with other elements.

According to Dewey and Bentley the interaction perspective assumes that temporal factors are not integral aspects of a phenomenon, since time and the properties of a phenomenon are defined independently of one another. Furthermore, psychological phenomena are treated as fundamentally static, although changes in states occur when elements interact. Put in another way, the interaction perspective reflects a "billiard ball" conception of phenomena. The balls—physical and psychological components—exist as separate entities with their own characteristics, and they act and react to influences from each other over time. As described in the next section, Dewey and Bentley's interactionist category shares many features with Pepper's mechanist approach and our interactional world view.

The *transaction* approach assumes an inseparability of contexts, temporal factors, and physical and psychological phenomena. Unlike interaction approaches, where phenomena interact with and are in-

fluenced by contexts, transaction orientations treat context, time, and processes as aspects of an integrated unity. Thus one is not dealing with separate elements of a system. Instead, a transaction approach defines aspects of phenomena in terms of their mutual functioning. Persons, processes, and environments are conceived of as aspects of a whole, not as independent components that combine additively to make up a whole. For example, present-day biology conceptualizes cells and genes as intrinsic aspects of a complex and unified whole, whose properties and functioning are based neither on their fundamental "essences" nor on their functioning as independent elements.

Dewey and Bentley also emphasize that transactional orientations study *processes* and *activities,* or people doing things in relation to the social and physical environment. Thus temporal qualities are inherent aspects of phenomena and embody the flow and dynamics of people's relations to social and physical settings. This treatment of time is different from that adopted in the interaction approach, where time is a separate dimension and only provides a backdrop against which to observe the phenomenon. Moreover, the emphasis on activity and process requires attention to the dynamic and often emergent qualities of phenomena. Dewey and Bentley's transactional approach is very similar to Pepper's contextual and our transactional world view.

1.2.2. Pepper (1942, 1967)

Pepper (1942) undertook a philosophical analysis of four major "world hypotheses" that characterize scholarly approaches to knowledge. He termed these *formism, mechanism, organicism,* and *contextualism.*

Formism assumes that knowledge accrues from delineation of similarities and differences between phenomena, grouping together like things and distinguishing them from unlike things. Formist approaches are analytic and search for dimensional properties of phenomena as a basis for comparison and categorization.

Pepper's formist world hypothesis, Dewey and Bentley's self-action orientation, and our trait category are very similar, since all three approaches attempt to identify the "essences" of phenomena, without direct attention to their temporal aspects or to the contexts within which they are embedded. In self-action, formist, and trait orientations the intrinsic and stable properties of phenomena determine their functioning.

Pepper's second world hypothesis, *mechanism,* uses the machine, for example, a watch or dynamo, as its root metaphor, with discrete parts responding to stimulation in a static system. Mechanist orientations, like formist approaches, are analytic and attempt to identify the dimensions of phenomena. However, mechanist perspectives assume that the functioning of physical or psychological phenomena is based on the interplay of a variety of elements that interact and influence one another (like mechanical parts that work together). One understands phenomena by describing their parts or elements and by discovering the lawful relationships between elements. Pepper's mechanist perspective, Dewey and Bentley's interaction approach, and our interactional world view are similar in their common assumption that phenomena are composed of independent elements that interact according to certain laws or principles. Although context and time can be included in these approaches, they are usually treated as independent domains, not as intrinsic parts of psychological phenomena. Thus space and time are "locations" of phenomena and are external to their functioning.

Organicism uses the integrated organism as its root metaphor. Organicist world hypotheses are holistic and synthesizing and treat a whole unity, not its parts, as the focus of understanding. According to Pepper, organicist world hypotheses consider phenomena to reflect underlying organic processes that can eventually be understood through the integration of facts. That is, the elements of a system are assumed to be bound to the unity by a limited number of underlying organic principles. The task is, therefore, to work with the whole, to search for the underlying principles that govern the system, and to treat each element in its relationship with other elements as parts contributing to the holistic unity. The whole system is the unit of study, although one approaches it through the characteristics of its elements and, most important, through the relationships between them.

A teleological predilection characterizes the organicist approach, with the system directed toward an ideal end state through the operation of underlying organic principles that link parts of the whole. In this sense time and change are intrinsic aspects of organicist approaches, although once the ideal is achieved change theoretically no longer occurs. Our organismic approach is similar to Pepper's organicist world hypothesis.

Contextualism is similar in many respects to the transaction orientation described by Dewey and Bentley, particularly in its assumption that contextual and temporal processes are fundamental aspects of phenomena. The root metaphor of contextualism is the historical event, which is intrinsically embedded in its surrounding context and which unfolds in time. To paraphrase Pepper, the historical event is a complex and holistic phenomenon whose parts interpenetrate and are connected in an inseparable fashion. Although one can focus on events from different angles, a full understanding requires recognition of the interpenetration of the different viewpoints. One must study the whole event as a unity; studying its elements is not sufficient to understand the whole, since the whole is not "a sort of added part, like a clamp that holds together a number of blocks" (Pepper, 1942, p. 237).

The contextualist world hypothesis assumes that temporal processes are inherent features of events. To understand phenomena from a contextualist view requires description of their changing features and temporal processes. "Change goes on continuously and never stops. It is a categorical feature of all events; and since in this [contextualist] world theory all the world is events, all the world is continually changing in this manner" (Pepper, 1942, p. 243).

Unlike organicist approaches, contextualist world hypotheses do not emphasize universal and/or teleological principles that govern the functioning of phenomena. Contextualist orientations allow for the possibility of unique events that are not necessarily progressing toward any specified ideal state. And the event may or may not function in accord with an ultimate "law" of nature. While it is assumed that examination of a particular event will be instructive for understanding nature in the general sense, it is not necessarily the aim of a contextualist world hypothesis to describe all events according to the same principles.

In a later analysis, Pepper (1967) proposed a fifth world view, *selectivism,* which he described as either an extension of contextualism or a totally new world hypothesis. The root metaphor of contextualism is the "purposive act," which Pepper considered to be a fundamental feature of human functioning. The purposive act assumes that behavior is goal directed and intentional in a pragmatic and functional way; however, no assumptions are made about teleological or ingrained purposes that govern functioning. The concept of purposiveness also emphasizes meaning, intention, and experiential processes, and an active organism that exhibits volition, agency, and control over its functioning.

Selectivism, like contextualism, adopts a holistic unit of analysis of psychological phenomena and rejects the idea of isolated and separate person and environment elements. Instead, purposive behavior consists of integrated acts associated with physical and social environments, with change and process being central features of the whole. There is, therefore, a unity of psychological processes, space, and time. As will be evident later, Pepper's contextualist and selectivist world hypotheses jointly reflect our transactional world view.

1.3. TRAIT, INTERACTIONAL, ORGANISMIC, AND TRANSACTIONAL WORLD VIEWS

This section of the chapter describes the fourfold taxonomy of world views that we use to describe research and theory in psychology and environmental psychology. Our framework, which integrates and extends the analyses of Pepper, Dewey, and Bentley, will examine assumptions of each world view regarding units of analysis, the role of the environment, temporal factors, philosophies of science (especially concepts of causation), and the role of observers in relation to describing psychological functioning. Table 1.2 summarizes similarities and differences in world views in respect to some of these factors.

Several caveats to the discussion are in order. First, trait approaches are described only briefly, with successively more attention given to interactional, organismic, and transactional world views, respectively. Trait world views are rarely employed in a pure form in modern psychology. Furthermore, they have minimal relevance to environmental psychology, given their deemphasis of the role of environments, contexts, and settings. Interactional orientations are prevalent in modern psychology and thus do not require extensive elaboration. Because organismic and especially transactional world views are particularly relevant to environmental psychology, but at the same time are not widely used, more attention is devoted to them, especially to transactional approaches.

A second caveat is that no research example, theory, or theorist can be exclusively pigeonholed into one or another world view. Indeed, theories in psychology often contain ideas from more than one world view. The examples we cite, therefore, only illustrate qualities of world views and are not rigid categorizations of particular theories.

Third, no world view is intrinsically better than any other. They are different approaches to the study of psychological phenomena and they each may have unique value in different circumstances. However, our bias is to encourage greater use of organismic and especially transactional world views. Psychology and environmental psychology have thus far neglected or not wholly understood these approaches, and these orientations, especially the transactional, can enhance our understanding of psychological phenomena.

1.3.1. Trait World Views

Trait approaches in psychology are very similar to Dewey and Bentley's self-action and Pepper's formist perspectives in several assumptions: (1) The fundamental units of study are psychological processes, cognitive characteristics, and personality qualities. These person-oriented characteristics are considered to be the primary determinants of psychological functioning and to operate more or less independently of physical and social contexts. (2) Temporal processes are given only a minimal role in relation to psychological functioning, since personal characteristics are presumed to be somewhat impervious to situational factors, or are treated teleologically, with a preestablished course of development and ideal end state.

Unit of Analysis

For trait world views, a typical definition of psychology is *the study of the individual, the mind, or mental and psychological processes.* The focus is on individuals or psychological processes as self-contained phenomena, with environments and contexts playing a secondary or supplementary role. Classical instinct theories exemplify the trait orientation; however, one finds few examples of pure trait approaches in modern psychology. Present-day theories usually assume that environmental and situational factors play an im-

Table 1.2. General Comparison of Trait, Interactional, Organismic, and Transactional World Views

	Unit of Analysis	Time and Change	Causation	Observers	Other
				Selected Goals and Philosophy of Science	
Trait	Person, psychological qualities of persons.	Usually assume stability; change infrequent in present operation; change often occurs according to preestablished teleological mechanisms and developmental stages.	Emphasizes *material causes*, i.e., cause internal to phenomena.	Observers are separate, objective, and detached from phenomena; equivalent observations by different observers.	Focus on trait and seek universal laws of psychological functioning according to few principles associated with person qualities; study predictions and manifestations of trait in various psychological domains.
Interactional	Psychological qualities of person and social or physical environment treated as separate underlying entities, with interaction between parts.	Change results from interaction of separate person and environment entities; change sometimes occurs in accord with underlying regulatory mechanisms, e.g., homeostasis; time and change not intrinsic to phenomena.	Emphasizes *efficient causes*, i.e., antecedent-consequent relations, "push" ideas of causation.	Observers are separate, objective, and detached from phenomena; equivalent observations by different observers.	Focus on elements and relations between elements; seek laws of relations between variables and parts of system; understand system by prediction and control and by cumulating additive information about relations between elements.

Organismic	Holistic entities composed of separate person and environment components, elements or parts whose relations and interactions yield qualities of the whole that are "more than the sum of the parts."	Change results from interaction of person and environment entities. Change usually occurs in accord with underlying regulatory mechanisms, e.g., homeostasis and long-range directional teleological mechanisms, i.e., ideal developmental states. Change irrelevant once ideal state is reached; assumes that system stability is goal.	Emphasizes *final causes*, i.e., teleology, "pull" toward ideal state.	Observers are separate, objective, and detached from phenomena; equivalent observations by different observers.	Focus on principles that govern the whole; emphasize unity of knowledge, principles of holistic systems and hierarchy of subsystems; identify principles and laws of whole system.
Transactional	Holistic entities composed of "aspects," not separate parts or elements; aspects are mutually defining; temporal qualities are intrinsic features of wholes.	Stability/change are intrinsic and defining features of psychological phenomena; change occurs continuously; directions of change emergent and not preestablished.	Emphasizes *formal causes*, i.e., description and understanding of patterns, shapes, and form of phenomena.	Relative: Observers are aspects of phenomena; observers in different "locations" (physical and psychological) yield different information about phenomena.	Focus on event, i.e., confluence of people, space, and time; describe and understand patterning and form of events; openness to seeking general principles, but primary interest in accounting for event; pragmatic application of principles and laws as appropriate to situation; openness to emergent explanatory principles; prediction acceptable but not necessary.

portant role in human activity, often in combination with person qualities. Some contemporary personality theories, for example, authoritarianism, locus of control, and Type A–Type B characteristics, are not really trait approaches in the strict sense, because they usually consider situational factors in interaction with personal qualities as determinants of psychological functioning. Thus pure trait approaches are a rarity in contemporary psychology and have been supplanted by interactional world views.

Classic trait approaches often assumed a biological basis to personal qualities; however, that is not a requirement. One can assume a history of situational and environmental experiences, especially in childhood and early years, that results in stable personal qualities. Once formed, they govern contemporary functioning, are unchanging, and are more or less independent of present contexts and environments. It is the assumption that personal qualities are primary determinants of contemporaneous behavior that defines a trait approach, not the assumption of an underlying biological predisposition.

Time and Change

Trait approaches handle temporal factors and change either by assuming stability of the personal characteristic or by portraying change as following an internal predetermined timetable independent of environmental influence. For example, characteristics such as authoritarianism, Type A–Type B personalities, and introversion–extroversion are usually not examined with respect to ongoing temporal variation or change. Rather, emphasis is put on their correlates and manifestations. On the other hand, some trait world views incorporate change in relation to stages of development of a personal quality. In so doing, they often emphasize predetermined patterns of development that are relatively independent of environmental factors. For example, Freudian, Eriksonian, and some other theories of social development postulate fixed and predetermined stages in which development is not emergent and does not result from the interaction of persons and environments. Such changes are analogous to the metamorphosis of caterpillars into butterflies, where change is preprogrammed and occurs in a fixed sequence. Similarly, in some trait approaches psychological functioning may be described as progressing in a predetermined way toward some ideal or ultimate end state.

Traitlike theories of change and development do not necessarily ignore the influence of environments and contexts, although they are treated as secondary considerations. Psychological development may be facilitated or retarded by unusual environmental factors, in the same way that adverse environmental conditions may interfere with the normal metamorphosis from caterpillar to butterfly. Such conditions are presumed, however, to be out of the ordinary, although they are worthy of study insofar as they reveal the nature of the underlying traits.

Philosophy of Science

Contemporary theories that have traitlike features, for example, theories of intelligence and aptitudes, certain personality theories that adopt a psychometric orientation, and so on, usually adhere to principles of rigorous operational definition of concepts, testability, generalizability, and replicability of findings and theories. For example, assessing the predictive validity of a trait or psychological quality is crucial, since it enables the researcher to examine the manifestation of the personal quality and/or depict the "causal" influence of the trait on other aspects of psychological functioning.

In accordance with traditional values of philosophy of science, trait approaches treat observers or researchers as separate from phenomena. The trait or personal quality and its manifestations can be observed "scientifically" by an objective, detached, and independent observer whose position or personal qualities do not affect the manifestations or qualities of the phenomenon. Indeed, two or more separate observers may be employed in order to assess and correct for errors of observation and to obtain an objective judgment. The psychological quality of interest is located, therefore, in the person or group, not in the relation of the observer to the phenomenon. As a result, the phenomenon is assumed to be describable in objective terms by any trained observer or observational agent.

Trait, interactional, and organismic world views share the values of objectivity, replicability, and generalization of findings and theories, and the separateness of observers from phenomena. However, trait perspectives differ from the other world views in terms of general issues of causation. To appreciate this issue, it is useful to compare briefly the four world views in respect to cause–effect relations. Table 1.2 summarizes their differences, based in part on Rychlak's (1977) application of Aristotle's fourfold classification of causation in natural phenomena.

The first type of cause, *material causation*, is central to trait perspectives. A material cause involves the idea that there is some "underlying matter or universal palpability, which lends the essential meaning to an object or event in experience" (Rychlak, 1977, p. 5). Material cause involves "a substance [such as genes] having certain qualities that set limits on behavior" (Rychlak, 1977, p. 245). Consistent with material causation, trait approaches assume that psychological causes are self-contained in the phenomenon itself and are ingrained qualities or material "essences."

Aristotle's concept of *efficient cause* is based on antecedent–consequent relations between variables, whereby it is presumed that an antecedent variable is a "cause" if it is systematically associated with variations in a consequent variable. This conception of causation is central to contemporary science and is associated with an interactional world view.

The third Aristotelean conception of causation, *final cause,* emphasizes predetermined directions, goals, or end states toward which phenomena gravitate. As Buss (1979) and Bates (1979) suggest, final causation is teleological, with a phenomenon operating in accordance with a preestablished end or purpose toward which it is pulled. Organismic world views emphasize this approach to causation, as do certain trait orientations that include final cause conceptions to account for growth.

The fourth Aristotelean approach to causation is *formal cause,* which focuses on the pattern, shape, or organization of a phenomenon in a given set of circumstances (Rychlak, 1977). An example of formal explanation is Bates's (1979) observation that the spherical form of a bubble is not "caused" by the material qualities of air, water, and soap, by the antecedent influence of someone blowing the bubble, or by the intentions of the bubble blower. In essence, the "cause" of the bubble's spherical form is a formal one; that is, "roundness is the only possible solution to achieving maximal volume with minimal surface" (Bates, 1979, p. 129). Formal causation can also involve analysis of the pattern or configuration of a phenomenon in a given context without use of universal explanatory principles. The concepts of formal causation are consistent with a transactional world view.

Although the four world views emphasize different Aristotelean concepts of causation, they do not do so in a categorical or exclusive way. Perhaps more important, the ideal description, understanding, and explanation of a phenomenon require that it be studied in terms of all four concepts of causation (Bates, 1969).

1.3.2. Interactional World Views

Unit of Analysis
The interactional world view builds on the mechanist orientation described by Pepper and the interaction approach described by Dewey and Bentley (see Table 1.1, Table 1.2). It adopts a definition of psychology as a field that studies *the prediction and control of behavior and psychological processes.*

Interactional world views, which have been the dominant approaches in contemporary psychology, treat psychological processes, environmental settings, and contextual factors as independently defined and operating entities. Moreover, the emphasis on prediction and control in the definition implies that antecedent factors affect or produce variations in psychological processes, typically in a unidirectional fashion. Thus behavior and psychological processes are usually treated as dependent variables, whereas environmental factors (and sometimes person qualities or other psychological processes) are treated as independent variables or causal influences on psychological functioning. To use an analogy from Dewey and Bentley (1949), interactional world views treat psychological phenomena like Newtonian particles or like billiard balls. Each particle or ball exists separately from the others and has its own independent qualities. The balls or particles interact as one ball bangs into another ball, thereby altering their locations. The goal of interactional research is to study the impact of certain particles and balls (environmental and situational qualities) on other particles and balls (psychological processes and behaviors).

Although interactional approaches sometimes study reciprocal relationships between variables, they usually focus on relationships between antecedent predictor variables and consequent behavioral and psychological outcomes. Findings and theories usually involve linear theoretical models that vary from single antecedent–consequent links to lengthy chains of cause–effect relationships involving intermediate and ultimate dependent variables.

Interactional world views vary from those that emphasize singular social or physical situational determinants of psychological processes to those that incorporate combinations of situational and personal qualities as "causes" of psychological functioning. Examples that emphasize the influence of physical or social factors on psychological functioning include situational orientations to personality and leadership, radical operant approaches that focus on stimulus situations as determinants of behavior, studies of parental effects on children's behavior, and research on the direct impact of environmental factors such as density, noise, or climate on psychological functioning. However, even the most extreme situational approaches usually take some account of the contribution of person variables (e.g., motive and drive states, personality factors, mediating psychological processes) to variations in psychological outcomes.

The dominant world view in current psychological research and theory is an interactional perspective that treats psychological functioning as a joint and interactive product of situational and personal factors. A first step in this approach is to identify separate and independent situational and person or psychological entities and describe their characteristics and properties. The next step is to study their independent and interactive effects on psychological outcomes and functioning, in much the same logic that underlies analysis of variance statistical models, with main effects and interactions. Although substantive and theoretical debates often center around the relative contributions of individual and interacting variables to behavioral and psychological outcomes, the underlying philosophical structure and assumptions of different theories are fundamentally compatible and fall within an interactional world view.

There are numerous examples of complex interactional world views in modern psychology. In personality theory and research. Frederiksen (1972), Lewis (1978), Pervin (1978), and others call for separate definitions and taxonomies of person and situation units, in order to examine the "processes through which the effects of one are tied to the operations of the other" (Pervin & Lewis, 1978, p. 20). Contingency theories of leadership are based on the idea that leader effectiveness and group performance result from the interaction of separate personal qualities of leaders (task orientation vs. social orientation) and characteristics of tasks and group situations (task structure, leader power, leader–member relationships) (Fiedler & Chemers, 1974).

Other examples of interactional approaches include cognitive dissonance, social comparison, and altruism theories. For example, cognitive dissonance research has studied the separate and interactive effects of cognitive states of persons, characteristics of social situations, and other factors on the nature and extent of cognitive dissonance and modes of reducing dissonance. The traditional strategy of altruism research and theory has likewise been to examine independently defined properties of social situations, for instance, group size, presence of others, potential costs and rewards to the helper, and so on, in combination with personal characteristics of helpers and victims. Such research is addressed to the study of the separate and interacting effects of independently defined person and environment entities on psychological outcomes.

Historically, research and theory in many fields of psychology often initially adopted a trait world view that was eventually replaced by an increasingly complex interactional orientation. For example, personality theorists examined personal qualities of authoritarianism in the 1940s and 1950s, locus of control in the 1960s and 1970s, and Type A and Type B personalities in the 1970s and 1980s. The pattern of research on these theories first involved a trait orientation, as investigators sought to identify behavioral and psychological manifestations of the personality quality, on the assumption that the quality was an internally based determinant of psychological functioning. These traitlike orientations usually shifted to an interactional perspective in which the *joint* contributions of separately defined situational and personality qualities were examined as determinants of behavior.

Time and Change

Interactional world views treat temporal factors as distinct from psychological processes and describe change as a result of the interaction of variables, not as an intrinsic aspect of phenomena. That is, interactional world views in psychology refer to time in much the same way that Newtonian physics relates time to physical matter. Capra (1976) stated:

> All changes in the physical world (in the Newtonian system) were described in terms of a separate dimension, called time, which again was absolute, having no connection with the material world and flowing smoothly from the past, through the present, to the future. "Absolute, true, and mathematical time," said Newton, "of itself and by its own nature, flows uniformly, without regard to anything external." (p. 43)

Although time is treated as an independent dimension, interactional world views do study change and assume temporal variations in psychological functioning. Problem solving, performance, and social interaction are charted over time; long- and short-term effects of persuasive communications are investigated; the effectiveness of antilitter and energy conservation programs is studied at different points in history; short- and long-term effects of population density are researched; and so on. However, change in the interactional perspective has several distinguishing qualities. First, change is presumed to result from the interaction of independent person and environment entities. The properties of these entities, in combination, determine the psychological result. Change is determined, therefore, by the preestablished properties of the interacting entities. Second, in accordance with the idea that time is not an intrinsic aspect of the phenomenon, change in psychological functioning is usually marked by arbitrary chronological units, not by natural psychological units. Thus changes in psychological functioning are described in terms of absolute chronological units of time that are imposed on phenomena—seconds, hours, and years. In a sense, time is treated as a *location,* and the phenomenon is examined as a snapshot, frozen in time, or as repeated snapshots, with time locating the phenomenon in two or more places. Change is treated, therefore, as the difference between the state and structure of the phenomenon at time 1 and the state and structure at time 2, time 3, and so forth.

The imposition of absolute chronological units may encourage treatment of psychological phenomena as states, with change viewed as the difference between the state and structure of the phenomenon at two or more times. Actual processes of change are usually inferred from changes in status from one time to the next, rather than being examined directly as the phenomenon unfolds and shifts. In contrast, transactional approaches, described later, focus on "event" organized sequences that unitize and describe phenomena on the basis of inherent changes in the directions, purposes, and functioning of the phenomenon, rather than through externally imposed or arbitrary chronological units.

A third feature of change in interactional approaches is that change is not teleological. Unlike trait and organismic approaches, interactional perspectives do not assume that phenomena are pulled or directed toward some ultimate or final state of being. Although interactional approaches sometimes assume underlying governing mechanisms, such as homeostasis or drive reduction, they rarely adopt teleological regulators that control the ultimate directions and goals of system change and movement. Instead, change is determined by the preestablished properties of the interacting entities.

Philosophy of Science

The philosophy of science of interactional world views has been the cornerstone of psychological thinking for most of the present century. These values have been derived from the scientific revolution and the associated philosophies of Hume, Bacon, and others, and the culmination of these ideas in the twentieth century logical positivist perspective on scientific inquiry. For example, as described next, interactional approaches are distinguished by an analytic orientation to psychological phenomena, an emphasis on Aristotle's concept of efficient causation with a search for antecedent–consequent relationships between variables, and a belief in the importance and possibility of independent and objective observations of psychological events. In addition, interactional world views value precise and rigorous operational definitions of variables and consider important the testability, generalizability, and replicability of findings and concepts. They also assume that it is possible and necessary to develop universal or general laws and principles of psychological functioning.

Kitchener (1982), in a comparison of holistic models (our organismic and transactional perspectives) and mechanistic models (our interactional approaches), described the latter as analytic and dimensional in orientation. According to Kitchener, mechanistic approaches, which grew out of the scientific revolution, use the *method of analysis* to investigate phenomena. This method involves three steps: (1) "the analysis of a whole into its basic, irreducible àtomic' parts" (p. 234); (2) the specification of the properties of these elements or parts, and their interaction; and (3) the statement of so-called composition laws that describe principles according to which the elements interact.

Through an analytic strategy, therefore, separately existing elements or building blocks are determined, and the whole is constructed in an additive fashion. The whole is reducible ultimately to its separately existing elements and to the laws that relate them to one another. It is assumed that the properties of the elements (person qualities and situational qualities) and of composition laws can be precisely described, tested, and replicated. It is further assumed that these qualities and laws are generalizable and universal, and that the goal of research and theory is to search for broad principles of psychological phenomena.

As an aspect of the preceding strategy, interactional world views rely heavily on Aristotle's efficient concept of causation. In describing efficient causation, Rychlak (1977) stated:

> An *efficient cause* rests on the notion that an antecedent event invariably and necessarily causes a consequent event which is called an 'effect.' Thanks to natural science, most people immediately think of *this* meaning of cause when we use the term. (p. 5)

Associated with the idea that causes and effects are different entities, interactional world views assume that observers are separable from the phenomenon of interest. Much as do trait approaches, interactional world views treat the observer as separate and detached from the phenomenon and believe that the search for knowledge can be objective, replicable, and independent of the observer's biases or status with respect to the phenomenon. Whereas transactional perspectives, exemplified by relativity and quantum theories in physics, consider the position and rate of movement of observers to be part of the phenomenon, interactional perspectives (including the Newtonian approach in physics) assume that observers are separate from the phenomenon and that observation can be done without the observer's influencing or altering the phenomenon. In summary, the philosophy of science of the interactional world view, dominant in contemporary psychology, emphasizes analysis, objectivity, testability, replicability, generalizability, prediction, and universal principles and laws.

Interactional Approaches in Environmental Psychology

Much as it is with the field of psychology as a whole, research and theory in environmental psychology are dominated by the interactional world view. Early research adopted an interactional perspective that focused on straightforward unidirectional effects of environments on behavior. For example, the first studies of crowding examined the direct impact of different forms of population density on psychological functioning, that is, social and spatial density, people-per-room ratios, people per acre, and so on (Epstein & Baum, 1978; Baum & Paulus, Chapter 14, this volume). Eventually, research on crowding examined the joint and interactive effects of physical density, person qualities (age, sex, psychological abnormality, etc.), and interpersonal qualities (attraction, group cohesion, social networks and support systems, etc.) on psychological outcomes. Likewise, studies of spatial proximity shifted from analyses of situational and personal factors as separate determinants of spatial behavior to examination of person and setting qualities as interacting variables (see Aiello, Chapter 12). Thus demographic factors, cultural differences, and personality dispositions were examined in interaction with situational characteristics such as formality and location of settings, nature and quality of intrusions by strangers or friends.

A great deal of the research on environmental perception and cognition of large-scale built and natural environments also reflects a complex interactional world view (see Golledge, Chapter 5, Knopf, Chapter 20, Wohlwill & Heft, Chapter 9). Early work identified properties of the environment presumed to influence directly perceptions and cognitions, for example, environmental simplicity and complexity, environmental coherence, and physical dimensions of environments such as paths and landmarks. Very

quickly, however, research began to study the interactions of environmental, person, and group variables, such as cultural background, experience in certain types of environments, personal predispositions, social class, and a variety of demographic factors. A similar pattern of research activity occurred in studies of cognition, attitudes and perceptions toward work settings, neighborhoods and communities, institutional environments, and other places.

Another tradition of research in environmental psychology that adopts an interactional perspective involves the application of an operant learning theory perspective to environmental phenomena (see Cone & Hayes, 1980; Geller, 1982; Everett & Watson, Chapter 26, Geller, Chapter 11). This research studies techniques for changing behavior in a number of environmentally relevant areas—littering, recycling of wastes, transportation, and water and energy conservation. The basic approach involves application of environmental contingencies, reinforcement schedules, information and feedback, and other ideas from operant theories to environmental behavior. Although necessarily incorporating personal variables, for instance, motives and drives, this research emphasizes manipulation of separate environmental contingencies to produce variations in outcomes.

Another example is research on postoccupancy evaluation of housing developments, workplaces, and other settings, which examines how personal and group factors interact with physical design characteristics directly to affect attitudes, satisfaction, performance, and other outcomes. Similarly, research on certain aspects of territorial behavior and defensible space (Brown, Chapter 13, Taylor, Chapter 25) is based on the assumption that person and group factors interact with environmental variables, for example, design of exteriors and interiors of dwellings, communities, and neighborhoods, to produce different degrees of perceived and actual territorial control and spatial defensibility.

In most of this research, environmental factors, person or group qualities, and psychological processes are defined in terms of different dimensions, with each factor considered as an independent entity. While some of this research examined short-term and delayed impacts of environmental factors on psychological functioning, time was treated as independent of the phenomenon and served primarily as a locational device to mark the state of a psychological process undergoing the interactive influence of environmental and person/group variables.

In summary, interactional world views emphasize the separate existence of contexts and settings, person factors, psychological processes, and temporal variables. Interactional research and theory are analytic, describe dimensions of separate entities, examine their interactions, and attempt to understand antecedent–consequent causal relationships between variables. Environments are usually treated as independent predictor variables; psychological functioning is treated as a dependent or outcome variable; and time serves as a mechanism for locating and describing changes in the state of psychological systems. For the interactional world view the goal of research and theory is to develop general principles of psychological phenomena. This is to be accomplished by means of an analytic perspective in which knowledge about antecedent–consequent relationships of person and environmental variables is accrued in a systematic, objective, and parametric fashion.

1.3.3. Organismic World Views

This approach corresponds most closely with Pepper's organicist orientation and shares certain features with Dewey and Bentley's interaction and transaction approaches (see Table 1.1, Table 1.2). Organismic orientations define psychology as *the study of dynamic and holistic psychological systems in which person and environment components exhibit complex, reciprocal relationships and influences.*

Unit of Analysis
The emphasis on holistic units of study in organismic world views was concisely stated by Reese and Overton (1973):

> The basic metaphor in the organismic model is the living organism, an organized whole. The whole is organic rather than mechanic, and rather than being the sum of its parts, the whole is presupposed by the parts and gives meaning to parts. (p. 69)

Unlike interactional approaches, which focus on the elements of a phenomenon, organismic approaches take as their unit of study the integrated system. And the holistic system is, to use a frequently cited phrase, "more than the sum of its parts." An exploration of this catchphrase in the writings of systems theorists (Kitchener, 1982; Laszlo, 1972; Miller, 1978; Von Bertalanffy 1968) reveals several aspects of the organismic view. Most important is the idea that the qualities of the whole cannot be understood strictly on the basis of knowledge about the qualities of the elements or parts that comprise the whole, especially if those parts are studied in iso-

lation or in simple relations with other parts. Rather, it is the complex set of relationships between elements that is important to comprehend, including the relations among subsets of the whole. As Kitchener (1982) stated, the whole places constraints on the parts, since it is the relations among parts that determines their functioning. Thus the elements are subordinate to the purposes or relations that govern the whole. Miller (1978) pointed out that holistic systems can be described in terms of levels or hierarchies, with any system being a subsystem or part of a higher-level system and at the same time being a holistic system itself composed of subsystems and parts. Superordinate systems cannot be described solely in terms of the qualities of their subsystems or parts; understanding them requires principles of organization that apply uniquely to the configuration of subsystems and parts. As a result, the parts are subordinated to the principles and laws that govern the whole, and the parts exist in a relation of dependency to one another and to the whole (Kitchener, 1982).

It is important to note that organismic approaches, like interactional orientations, conceive of wholes or systems as composed of separate elements or parts. Although the whole cannot be completely described in terms of its parts—that is, one could not predict the nature of the whole in advance from knowledge of the properties of its parts—an eventual understanding of the whole does permit a better understanding of its parts and of the relation of the parts to the whole. For example, Laszlo (1972) stated that a hydrogen atom is more than the sum of its neutron, proton, and electron parts; the same parts in different configurations would result in different outcomes. The relations between its parts plus the qualities of the parts yield the unique configuration of the hydrogen element. Von Bertalanffy (1968) summarized these themes as follows:

> The whole is more than the sum of its parts.... If, however, we know the total of the parts contained in a system and the relations between them, the behavior of the system may be derived from the behavior of the parts. (p. 55)

In summary, organismic world views consider the whole and certain part–whole relationships to be the proper unit of analysis of psychological phenomena, and they view the whole to possess distinctive properties that are not directly derived from the properties of the elements that comprise the whole. On the other hand, they view elements as independently definable and functioning, as do interactional approaches. However, in contrast to interactional perspectives, organismic approaches require an appreciation of how elements fit together in terms of system-wide principles of organization. Organismic perspectives also examine system parts within the context of the whole, not solely as separate entities, whereas interactional approaches view the whole from the vantage of its parts and treat the whole as an additive outcome of the relations of its parts.

The relationships between elements in organismic wholes and between elements and the whole can be quite complex. Unlike interactional perspectives, which tend to emphasize unidirectional relations between independent and dependent variables, organismic orientations focus on reciprocal and complex patterns of relationships between variables. Any variable in the system can, theoretically, function either as an independent or dependent variable, and causality can operate in multiple paths and directions. Furthermore, changes in one part of the organismic whole may reverberate in complex ways throughout the system, and the direction and nature of reverberations may vary with circumstances. Thus organismic world views emphasize dynamic, reciprocal, and complex relationships between the elements of holistic systems.

Most organismic approaches assume that system functioning is governed by a limited set of laws or principles. In Pepper's (1942) terms, the goal of research and theory in the organismic world view is to discover underlying "organic" principles that regulate the operation of the system and that are universal for a class of phenomena. Homeostasis and its offshoots of balance and consistency, need reduction and reinforcement, and progression through fixed stages toward adult cognitive functioning are examples of underlying organicist principles. In the organismic world view the goal of the science of psychology is to discover general and universal principles of human behavior and to achieve a unity of knowledge. Organismic approaches assume, therefore, the potential for attaining a "grand synthesis" or general theory of psychological functioning.

Time and Change
The nature of change and the role of temporal factors in organismic perspectives are closely linked with assumptions about underlying organicist principles that control system operation and with assumptions about concepts of causation. Systems are often conceived of as striving to maintain or move toward ideal states, with organic processes directing the system in the direction of the ideal. Theories based on concepts of homeostasis, balance, and consistency fit this model, as do those that postulate stages of cognitive and personality development through which the person inevitably progresses. Miller (1978) stated:

> All living systems tend to maintain steady states (or homeostasis) of many variables, keeping an orderly balance among subsystems which process matter-energy or information. Not only are subsystems usually kept in equilibrium, but systems also ordinarily maintain steady states with their environments and supra-systems, which have outputs to the systems and inputs from them.... (p. 34)

Organismic systems that seek stability are posited to use deviation-countering mechanisms or negative feedback processes. These processes involve adjustive and compensatory responses by the whole system and/or some of its parts and subsystems, and they serve to ensure stability and keep the system on an even keel. Biological mechanisms of temperature control, oxygen maintenance, hormonal balances, and so forth exemplify negative feedback processes (Cannon, 1932). Thus system change and temporal factors are conceived of in terms of maintenance processes that operate under the governance of integrative organicist principles.

System change away from stability or toward new levels of stability can result from positive feedback or deviation-amplifying processes as, for example, in permanent ecological, internal, or externally imposed events that impinge on a stable system (Laszlo, 1972; Miller 1978). In such cases the organismic whole may undergo a radical transformation of its organization as it establishes a new level of stable functioning or, if a new equilibrium cannot be achieved, the system may undergo irreversible entropic processes.

As noted previously, system change can also be linked to teleological processes (Laszlo, 1972), whereby a person progresses through preestablished stages of development or maturation toward some ideal end state. Some processes of physical, moral, and cognitive development reflect these change dynamics, which function in accordance with teleological principles that "pull" the system toward an ideal state, often through specified stages of development.

Although change and temporal processes are central to organismic perspectives, as systems strive to maintain stability and/or move toward an ideal end state, the endpoint of organismic functioning involves total stability and the absence of change. Thus Pepper (1942) noted that if and when an organismic system achieved its teleological ideal, admittedly a hypothetical event, it would no longer change, but would function in a totally smooth and harmonious fashion. So temporal change operates in the service of system maintenance or a teleological goal but would cease if the system achieved its ideal condition. In this respect, change and temporal factors are markers that reflect the state and location of systems in relation to present stability–instability and/or an ultimate end state.

Since change in organismic wholes can result from the influence and interaction of system components on one another as well as from external factors that impinge on the system or on its parts, organismic and interactional perspectives are similar. However, organismic approaches are concerned with changes at the level of the whole system, as well as with changes in subsystems and parts, whereas interactional approaches emphasize changes in separate parts of phenomena.

Philosophy of Science
Organismic and interactional perspectives share many of the same values of philosophy of science, although they differ in some respects. These world views uphold principles of objectivity, replicability, and testability and argue for the importance of uncovering universal and general laws of psychological functioning. Some organismic theorists are more expansive than most interactional approaches, however, and argue for the unity of scientific principles and laws throughout the entire range of physical and psychological phenomena—from small-scale subatomic physical phenomena through biological processes and psychological phenomena to larger-scale social and geopolitical systems (Miller, 1978).

Organismic world views also overlap with interactional perspectives in their use of concepts of efficient causation. They accept the idea of efficient causation in that changes in one part of a system can affect other parts of the system, and external factors can be antecedents of change in system functioning. However, the complexity of organismic wholes makes it difficult to pinpoint singular antecedent–consequent relations. Furthermore, the fact that any part of the system can be an antecedent or consequent variable mitigates against an approach based primarily on simple notions of efficient causation and requires consideration of the complex relations between variables. Perhaps more important, the focus on teleological changes in the system as a whole deemphasizes the search for specific antecedent–consequent relations between variables as sufficient explanation of phenomena.

As indicated in Table 1.2, organismic approaches seem to rely heavily on Aristotle's concept of *final causation*. Rychlak (1977) defined final causation as

> that, for the sake of which something happens or comes about. Is there a reason, purpose, intention or premising meaning that acts as that for the sake of which a substance is formed into some recognizable shape...? The emphasis on the direction, goal or end of events is why theories that employ final cause meanings are called "telic" or "teleological" descriptive accounts. (p. 6)

The emphasis on organicist principles that underly phenomena, for example, homeostasis, or movement through predetermined stages, reflects teleological concepts that "pull" organismic systems toward some ideal state of functioning.

Organismic Approaches in Psychology
Exemplars of organismic world views include general systems theory, discussed previously (Laszlo, 1972; Miller, 1978; Von Bertalanffy, 1968; and others), Heider's balance theory (1958), Bandura's model of reciprocal determinism (1977, 1978), research and theory on reciprocity of self-disclosure and interpersonal exchange (Altman, 1973; Altman & Taylor, 1973), family systems theory (Haley, 1966; Watzlawick, Beavin, & Jackson, 1967), aspects of Piaget's (1952) theory of cognitive development, and research on parent–child interaction (Lewis & Lee-Painter, 1974).

Heider's (1958) social–psychological balance theory reflects an organismic orientation in its analysis of the relationship between elements of a cognitive system—an attitude or opinion held by a person about an object, issue, or other person, and corresponding attitudes or opinions actually or presumed to be held by another individual. The cognitive system is assumed to strive toward a balanced state of the positive and negative valences between elements in the system. Imbalances that result from inconsistencies among system elements are presumed to cause stress, leading to a readjustment of relations between elements. The elements in the system, although interrelated to form a unified and distinctive whole, exist as separate entities that have their own properties. Heider's theory does not explicitly postulate a long-range teleological direction of system functioning, but it focuses on the maintenance of momentary psychological balance or consistency.

Bandura (1977, 1978) recently proposed an organismic model of *reciprocal determinism,* with the parts of the holistic system composed of person factors, such as beliefs and perceptions, overt behavioral acts, and physical and social environmental factors. Bandura postulated that these variables function as a unified system, with changes potentially initiated from any component, and with reciprocal influences between system components. Although Bandura articulated the independence of the components of the holistic system, the whole involves a unique pattern of relationships of its parts. Although he is not precise with respect to organicist principles that regulate the operation of the system, ideas of balance and reinforcement are implicit in Bandura's writings. In addition, Bandura's model does not contain any specific statement regarding teleological end states, although he hypothesizes that reciprocally deterministic systems move toward increased efficiency and efficacy.

Certain aspects of Piaget's (1952) theory of development also illustrate an organismic world view. Although the concepts of assimilation and accommodation seem to fit best in a transactional orientation, as discussed later, his description of children's progress through stages of cognitive development has organismic qualities. Mental structures are hypothesized to fit together in an integrated system in which the organism strives for equilibrium between the mental structures and reality. The equilibrium is not static because the organism transforms in successive attempts to adapt cognitive structures and information from the environment into a unified organization. Development of cognitive processes is described by Piaget as progressing through a fixed sequence of stages, culminating in the ideal state corresponding to adult cognition (formal operations). Thus cognitive development acts in accordance with an underlying teleological principle that directs its movement toward a predetermined, increasingly well adapted structure of cognitive functioning.

Some research on parent–child interaction reflects a transition from an interactionist to an organismic perspective (Lewis & Lee-Painter, 1974). Early research focused on the unidirectional impact of situational and parental influences on child behavior, with parents serving as social environments independent of the child, and with temporal processes handled in a static "snapshot" fashion rather than as ongoing, or flowing. However, recent work reflects an organismic perspective, with an emphasis on the reciprocal relationships and holistic quality of parent–child interaction. For example, Lewis and Lee-Painter (1974) demonstrated reciprocal patterns of smiling and vocalization between parents and children and instances where children's behavior tripped off parental behavior and vice versa. However, in this and related research, child and parent behaviors are still defined independently of each other, although a unique holistic parent–child system emerges from the distinctive pattern of the participants' actions and reactions to one another. Lewis and Lee-Painter noted the organismic quality of such research and suggested the need for incorporating a transactional approach:

> In all the models we have presented there have been "elements" [individual parents and infants]....What we need to develop are models dealing...with interaction independent of elements. This is by no means an easy task. Although many investigators have attempted this...the elements rather than the relationship constantly reappear. This...also requires that we not consider the static quality of these interactions. Rather, it is necessary to study their flow with time. While proponents of static theory state that their models can approximate flow through a series of still photographs, it is not at all obvious that such a technique is valid and does not seriously distort that which is being studied. Thus, relationship and flow must somehow find a way into our models independent of the elements. (p. 47)

Aspects of some family systems approaches to psychotherapy also illustrate an organismic world view (Haley, 1966; Minuchin, 1974; Watzlawick et al., 1967). These approaches take many different forms and often have both organismic and transactional properties; however, they consistently treat families as holistic units. Family systems are composed of components (family members) who influence and interact with one another in complex ways. The pattern of their interactions and relationships yields a system with emergent and unique properties that transcends the characteristics of the family members considered singly or in their separate relationships with one another. Problems and solutions to family system imbalances are based on reciprocal patterns of influence and communication, with reverberating effects throughout the system. Thus marital conflict and parent–child difficulties are treated as family system problems, not as problems of individuals. These approaches also assume underlying systems principles that govern families, for example, homeostasis, negative and positive feedback, and equifinality. The goal of therapy is to help families achieve a mode of operation that involves stable and balanced relationships between family members.

Organismic Approaches in Environmental Psychology

Organismic perspectives have also begun to be developed in environmental psychology. Moos applied a general systems framework to hospitals, schools, dormitories, and other settings (see, e.g., Moos & Lemke, 1984). Each of these settings contains a number of subsystems: an environmental subsystem that includes characteristics of the natural and designed physical environment, and organizational factors such as size, management control, social climate; a personal subsystem that includes demographic variables and personal characteristics such as expectations, personality, and coping skills of participants. Environmental and personal subsystems interact and influence one another and together set in motion an array of psychological processes, including efforts to cope with and adapt to the setting. These mutual influences result in a degree of adjustment, stability, and change that can also feed back and produce alterations in the environmental and personal subsystems. Thus Moos envisions holistic systems to be composed of interacting but separate elements whose influence on one another is multifaceted and multidirectional.

Several models of crowding also illustrate an organismic perspective (Altman, 1975; Bell, Fisher, & Loomis, 1978; Sundstrom, 1978). These models treat crowding as a complex system composed of separate antecedent elements, including personal and interpersonal variables, and physical factors, especially density. These factors affect intervening processes such as psychological appraisal of the situation and stress, which, in turn, result in coping responses and short- and long-term psychological, physical, and physiological consequences of crowding. Included in these models are complex feedback loops involving many combinations of system components. These models are classic examples of organismic perspectives in several ways. They are holistic frameworks, and they treat crowding as a complex and organized system composed of components that exhibit reciprocal influences on one another, with a change in one part of the system capable of reverberating in complex ways throughout the system. Although differing in the exact linkages of variables, these models all contain feedback loops that reflect reciprocal influences and a system in dynamic motion. In accordance with organismic perspectives, they also portray crowding as governed by an underlying organicist principle of homeostasis, such that system balance that is disrupted by density in interaction with other factors leads to coping responses designed to restore or establish an acceptable equilibrium.

In an ecological analysis of the relation between transportation and human well-being, Stokols and

Novaco (1981) developed a holistic model that also fits an organismic perspective. They described psychological aspects of transportation as involving a variety of components, including mode of travel, travel aims or goals, and travel stressors (congestion, vehicle characteristics, distance, travel time), and psychological well-being based on perceptions of the situation, affect and stress, physiological arousal, cognitive and behavioral functioning, attitudes, adaptations, and coping responses. These component factors are assumed to have reciprocal and multidirectional causal relationships with one another, are described and defined independently, and are linked together in terms of person–environment "fit" or "congruence." Well-being or psychological adjustment is considered to be associated with the degree to which personal and interpersonal goals and activities are congruent with qualities of the physical environment. As well as describing holistic, multidirectional causal connections between variables, this approach adopts an organicist notion of homeostasis or balance in the form of person–environment congruence.

In summary, organismic perspectives focus on holistic, molar systems as the proper unit of study in psychology. Although they emphasize holistic units of analysis, organismic approaches treat systems as made up of elements, components, or parts that are interrelated in complex ways. Thus organismic, interactional, and trait approaches are similar in their assumption that components or elements make up the whole. On the other hand, organismic perspectives emphasize the idea that the system components are related to one another in complex ways and that it is the overall pattern of relationships between elements that is crucial, not the characteristics of the elements considered in isolation or in specific relationships with other elements. System relationships are mutual and reciprocal, such that any component can potentially influence and serve as a cause of variation in other components.

Organismic approaches are sensitive to the role of temporal factors, as they postulate a dynamic quality to holistic systems and describe feedback loops and ongoing reciprocal and mutual influences within the system. However, change is linked to underlying regulatory principles such as homeostasis, and/or teleological principles, that is, final causes that direct the system toward some ultimate, ideal, and stable state of functioning. As a result, change is usually associated with system movement toward an ideal state and reflects the "location" of a system in respect to an ideal stable condition.

Organismic world views also emphasize the goal of achieving a "grand synthesis" or unity of knowledge whereby many levels and forms of psychological functioning can be understood in terms of a limited number of causal factors, laws, or principles. Finally, organismic world views share with trait and interactional perspectives an emphasis on traditional scientific approaches to the study of psychological phenomena, including detached and objective observations of events.

1.3.4. Transactional World Views

The transactional approach is a synthesis of Pepper's (1942, 1967) contextualist and selectivist orientations and Dewey and Bentley's (1949) transactional perspective. A prototype definition of psychology for transactional approaches is *the study of the changing relations among psychological and environmental aspects of holistic unities.* According to this definition, the unit of psychological analysis is holistic entities such as events involving persons, psychological processes, and environments. The transactional whole is not composed of separate elements but is a *confluence* of inseparable factors that depend on one another for their very definition and meaning. Furthermore, transactional approaches focus on the *changing* relationships among aspects of the whole, both as a tool for understanding a phenomenon and because temporal processes are an integral feature of the person–environment whole.

Unit of Analysis
Although both transactional and organismic orientations emphasize the study of holistic person–environment units of analysis, they differ in their conceptions of how holistic systems are composed and operate. Organismic orientations view the system as made up of separate elements whose patterns of relationships comprise the whole. The relations between elements are constituents of the whole; in fact, they constitute a form of element that contributes to the nature of the whole system. In the transactional view there are no separate elements or sets of discrete relationships into which the system is ultimately divisible. Instead, the whole is composed of inseparable aspects that simultaneously and conjointly define the whole.[1]

As Pepper (1942) stated, the root metaphor of contextualism is the historical event—a spatial and temporal confluence of people, settings, and activities that constitutes a complex organized unity. There are no separate actors in an event; instead,

there are acting relationships, such that the actions of one person can only be described and understood in relation to the actions of other persons, and in relation to the situational and temporal circumstances in which the actors are involved. Furthermore, the aspects of an event are mutually defining and lend meaning to one another, since the same actor in a different setting (or the same setting with different actors) would yield a different confluence of people and contexts. The aspects of an event are so intermeshed that the definition or understanding of one aspect requires simultaneous inclusion of other aspects in the analysis. To put this in another way, the transactional world view does not deal with the relationship *between elements,* in the sense that one independent element may cause changes in, affect, or influence another element. Instead, a transactional approach assumes that the *aspects* of a system, that is, person and context, coexist and jointly define one another and contribute to the meaning and nature of a holistic event.

An example of relations among aspects of transactional unities appears in sociological and psychological concepts of norms, rules, and roles. These qualities define and govern the functioning of actors in physical and social contexts in relation to one another and in changing circumstances. It is these relational qualities that are of interest to a transactional approach, not the characteristics of elements considered one at a time, as independent entities, or in subsets. For example, a transactional world view would focus on the actions and context involved in orchestrating a symphony, rather than the separate characteristics of the conductor, the string section, the score, or the concert hall. The actions of the participants, the rules and norms that bind them together, their relationship to the physical setting and to the qualities of the audience, and the temporal flow of the event are of interest in a transactional orientation.

The inseparability and holistic nature of aspects of psychological phenomena were expressed by a number of early writers in the field of personality:

We cannot define the situation operationally except in reference to the specific organism which is involved. We cannot define the organism operationally, in such a way as to obtain predictive power for behavior, except in reference to the situation. Each serves to define the other; they are definable operationally while in the organism/situation field. (Murphy, 1947, p. 891)

The organism is entirely permeated by the environment which insinuates itself in every part of it. On the other hand, the organism does not end at the body surface but penetrates into its environment. (Angyal, 1958, p. 97).

Although transactional and organismic world views both focus on holistic units of psychological phenomena, they differ in how they approach wholes. Whereas organismic approaches consider wholes to be composed of separate components and relations between components, transactional perspectives assume that wholes are composed of inseparably existing actors engaged in dynamic psychological processes (actions and intrapsychic processes) in social and physical contexts. Transactional approaches reject the use of separate components or parts; instead, the preceding features are necessary and intrinsic definitional qualities of all psychological phenomena and collectively constitute an event, whole, or unity. Whereas organismic world views define each component of a system separately and examine their relationships in order to understand the whole system, transactional world views define every aspect of psychological wholes in terms of one another, not as separate elements. The relations among aspects of the whole exist, therefore, in their very definition, not in the influences of separate variables on one another. Relations among the aspects of a whole are not conceived of as involving mutual influences or antecedent–consequent causation. Instead, the different aspects of wholes coexist as intrinsic and inseparable qualities of the whole.

Time and Change
In addition to its focus on intertwined aspects of an event, the transactional world view incorporates temporal processes in the very definition of events. The transactional view shifts from analysis of the causes of change to the idea that change is inherent in the system and the study of its transformations is necessary to understand the phenomenon. In the transactional perspective the changing configuration itself is the focus of analysis. Regularities and predictive patterns of change may be found, but not by separating elements of an event from each other in order to localize what exactly "caused" the change. Change is viewed more as an ongoing, intrinsic aspect of an event than as the outcome of the influence of separate elements on each other.

These views of temporal processes and change contrast with interactional and organismic perspectives, where time is treated as a separate dimension and is used to "mark" or "locate" the state of a phenomenon at a given instance or series of instances. Interactional approaches assume that change results from the interaction of separate en

tities, with some entities treated as independent variables that cause change in dependent variable entities. Organismic approaches consider change to result from complex reciprocal interactions between elements of the system, with a given element potentially being an independent or dependent variable on different occasions. While time and change in organismic perspectives are associated with deviations from an ideal state or attempts to achieve some long-range predetermined teleological goal, transactional approaches do not assume that change is associated with a predetermined ideal state. Rather, change is treated as an intrinsic property of holistic unities, without regard to movement toward some ideal that, if achieved, involves no further change.

Crude parallels may be drawn between the transactional view in psychology and quantum and relativity theory in physics. In contrast with a Newtonian interactional view, which examines the qualities of particles as sources of change, modern theories in physics focus on the "field" or changing configurations of energy. Modern studies of subatomic and high-velocity phenomena suggest that mass and energy are interchangeable, and that many things called particles can be viewed as momentary and changing nexuses of energy and activity. In this view, there are no "real" particles. Instead, patterns of energy are distributed and redistributed in different configurations. In a similar way, the transactional view in psychology focuses on changing configurations of persons, psychological processes, and contexts. Rather than focusing on the static qualities of psychological entities or "particles," the transactional view emphasizes changing processes in different person–environment configurations. To use Dewey and Bentley's (1949) analogy, transactional world views use action verbs in describing psychological phenomena—acting, doing, talking, thinking—in contrast to studying states, structures, and static entities.

Change in the transactional model may result in psychological outcomes that are variable, emergent, and novel. That is, configurations of people, psychological processes, and contexts can be temporally and spatially distinctive and not always wholly predictable from knowledge of the separate aspects of the system. Transactional approaches differ markedly in this respect from the other world views. In the trait approach, the variety of psychological outcomes is limited by the predetermined qualities of the person. The interactional world view assumes that psychological outcomes are predictable from the interaction of elements with known qualities. In the or ganismic world view teleological principles guide or pull the system toward a predetermined ideal state, with the nature and outcomes of change highly predictable. The fact that transactional views permit variability and novelty in the pattern and direction of change does not mean that these approaches eschew prediction and general principles of psychological functioning. The dynamics of psychological events, while variable, may form general patterns across similar events. Although phenomena are intrinsically changing, the change is not necessarily random or idiosyncratic. Thus consistencies and patterns in the flow of similar events may or may not allow for general statements and theories. In summary, both unique events and patterns across similar events are of interest in transactional perspective.

Transactional approaches, in contrast with organismic orientations, deemphasize the operation of universal regulatory principles that predetermine the course of development of a phenomenon, although they accept the idea that psychological events are purposive, intentional, and goal directed. Goals and purposes are based on short- and long-term motives, social norms, emergent qualities of phenomena, and other factors. However, goals are flexible and are not assumed to be undergirded by a limited number of all-encompassing organicist principles. They may shift as the confluence of people, places, and processes changes, as outside events impinge on the configuration, and as people and cultures change in their day-to-day lives and over longer-term historical periods. And there often are multiple goals at work in the same transactional configuration.

Philosophy of Science

The philosophy of science of transactional world views differs in several respects from the philosophies of trait, interactional, and organismic approaches. Transactional world views rely heavily on Aristotle's fourth conception of causation, *formal cause,* which Rychlak (1977) described as

> a pattern, shape, outline, or recognizable organization in the flow of events or in the way that objects are constituted....Natural objects and behavioral sequences are clearly patterned outlines, recognizable styles of this or that significance to the viewer, who comes to know them as much by these features as by their substantial nature (material cause) or the fact that they are assembled (efficient cause). (Rychlak, 1977, p. 6)

The focus of formal causation on patterns, forms, and flow is compatible with the transactional approach, in which one attempts to discern the nature of the whole without emphasis on antecedent and consequent relationships among variables, without analysis of the whole into its elements, and without identification of monolithic teleological or other mechanisms that inevitably govern the phenomenon.

Formal causation and transactional approaches do not rule out the value of applying existing general principles or laws to understand an event. Thus to account for the physical basis of an event such as a rock breaking a window one might draw on a combination of laws of materials, trajectories, forces, tensions, and so on (Bates, 1969). In such instances the goal is to understand a specific event, and general principles or laws are applied, as appropriate, in order to explain the event. Transactional approaches are also open to the possibility that new or emergent principles might be necessary to account for an event, or that some combination of existing and new principles may be needed.

In summary, transactional approaches begin with the phenomenon—a confluence of psychological processes, environmental qualities, and temporal features—and employ all necessary principles and combinations of principles, including emergent ones, to account for it. Instead of only invoking specific preestablished explanatory principles to account for phenomena, transactional approaches include hypothesis-generating as well as hypothesis-testing strategies and eclectic rather than monolithic applications of explanatory principles.

The other world views seek to discover the few key underlying principles that govern the functioning of all psychological phenomena and, in so doing, proceed toward an ultimate synthesis and unity of knowledge. In contrast, transactional world views, although interested in principles and laws that may apply broadly, set their sights on accounting for specific events in terms of whatever theoretical principles may apply. The focus is, therefore, on the event, with acceptance of the possibility that different configurations of principles may be necessary to understand different events. Transactionalism adopts, therefore, a pragmatic, eclectic, and relativistic approach to studying psychological phenomena.

Transactional world views also stress the value of studying unique events. As Pepper noted, the contextualist approach allows for the possibility that the workings of an event are not predictable or repeatable (in addition to the possibility that they are). Although the development of broad-ranging principles is a possibility, transactional approaches also appreciate and give attention to unique, nonrecurring, novel events. Understanding idiosyncratic events is valuable because it allows for examination of an event from several perspectives and facilitates an appreciation of the variety of factors that contribute to the fabric of a phenomenon. In addition, the study of single events may lead to new ideas, principles, and approaches or confirm the operation of principles and theory developed in other research.

The role of observers and the nature of observation in transactional world views are also distinct from those of the other perspectives. Trait, interactional, and organismic orientations adopt a classic Newtonian perspective with respect to the role of observers. That is, the phenomenon is treated as "out there," independent of the physical location and movement of the observer. On the other hand, relativity and quantum theory in physics consider the position and rate of movement of the observer to be literally an aspect of the phenomenon itself. Two observers at different locations and moving at different velocities will provide different but accurate descriptions of the same phenomenon. As such, a phenomenon is partly defined by the qualities of the observer, making the observer an aspect of the event. In the same way, a transactional approach calls for the study of how observers in different "locations" with differing characteristics and perspectives view and interpret the same event. Observers are, therefore, inseparable from phenomena, and their role, perspective, and "location" must be understood as an aspect of an event. The methodological implications of this approach to observation are discussed in a later section of the chapter.

In summary, transactional world views emphasize the study of holistic units of analysis, with phenomena defined in terms of inseparable psychological, contextual, and temporal facets. Unlike other orientations, transactional approaches include temporal qualities and change as intrinsic aspects of psychological phenomena. Furthermore, origins and directions of change are presumed not to be governed by singular or monolithic organicist or deterministic principles, but to occur as a result of shifting goals, purposes, and motives that are part of the psychological and contextual properties of specific events. Moreover, the goal of transactional approaches is to understand the pattern and flow of particular events, by means of existing and emergent principles that apply to the event.

Transactional Approaches in Psychology

Theories and research in several areas of psychology incorporate transactional ideas. In experimental psychology, Gibson's theory of perception (Gibson, 1979; Michaels & Carello, 1981) uses the event as a basic unit of psychological analysis and focuses on the animal–environment system of adaptation, with change assumed to be inherent in events. Transformation and change are not regarded as following a fixed, unidimensional course toward a predetermined end point. Rather, the organism and environment uniquely differentiate to fit one another, thereby forming a distinctive ecological niche. Furthermore, the animal and the environment are defined and change in a wholly mutual way:

> An animal's wings, gills, snout, or hands describe that animal's environment. Likewise, a complete description of a niche describes the animal that occupies it. For example, if we specify in detail the niche of a fish (its medium, its predators and prey, its nest, etc.), we have in a way described the fish. Thus, just as the structure and functioning of an animal implies the environment, the particulars of the niche imply the structure and activities of its animal. (Michaels & Carello, 1981, p. 14)

Thus Gibson and his associates reject the separateness of contexts and psychological processes and treat them as aspects of a holistic unity. This theme is further elaborated in the concept of environmental *affordances*, which reflects the psychological and behavioral utility of the environment for the organism. People do not perceive chairs and pencils in physical terms; rather, they see them in functional, utilitarian ways. They perceive places to sit, things to write with, or aspects of the environment that relate to actions, process, flow, and activity. The environment is conceived of, therefore, as an aspect of ongoing behavior and psychological functioning. Psychological processes, context, and time are inseparably fused.

In some respects, Piaget's (1952) theory of development fits with a transactional world view. Although his description of progression through stages of development relates to an organismic perspective, Piaget expresses the mutuality of organism and environment in his discussion of assimilation and accommodation:

> The organism and the environment form an indissoluble entity, that is to say...there are adaptational variations simultaneously involving a structuring of the organism and an action of the environment, the two being inseparable from one another. (Piaget, 1952, p. 16)

Soviet activity theory, as originally stated in Vygotsky's developmental theory (1962,1978), focuses on the concept of activity to reflect the mutual involvement of the individual and the social context. According to Leont'ev (1981) an activity is

> [not] an aggregate of reactions, but a system with its own structure, its own internal transformations, and its own development....If we removed human activity from the system of social relationships and social life, it would not exist and would have no structure. With all its varied forms, the human individual's activity is a system in the system of social relations. (pp. 46–47)

Soviet activity theory also emphasizes analysis of change in order to understand developmental phenomena, as illustrated in studies of long-term individual development (ontogenesis), analyses of transformations occurring over short periods of learning (microgenesis), phylogenetic studies, and analyses of the development of cultural history. Vygotsky (1978) argued for the value of developmental or "genetic" explanations of psychological phenomena, since the goals of theory and research are to examine process as opposed to object and to study dynamic relations rather than "fossilized" behavior. An emphasis on holistic units of analysis, the study of process and change, and the inseparability of aspects of psychological systems are firm transactional underpinnings of this approach.

Certain features of Riegel's dialectical approach to social and cognitive development, particularly his analysis of developmental change, are congruent with a transactional orientation (Riegel, 1976, 1979). He described human development as a continual and lifelong interplay of biological, psychological, sociocultural, and physical processes. A central feature of this approach is its emphasis on change as an intrinsic feature of development:

> As soon as a developmental task is completed...new questions, doubts and contradictions arise within the individual and within the society. A dialectic theory places less emphasis on stable plateaus of balance and more emphasis on the contradictions and questions raised by each achievement because it is...profoundly concerned with the process of change and the conditions that keep it moving. (Riegel, 1976, p. 398)

In social psychology, Lewin's theorizing (1936, 1964) exemplifies many aspects of a transactional perspective. Lewin considered psychological processes to be embedded in physical and social situations, forming a "life space" or psychological "field." That is, the life space is a momentary confluence of person qualities and properties of the psychological environment. The psychological environment involves those features of situations that are relevant to the present motives, needs, and characteristics of the person, thereby fusing persons and environments. As well as emphasizing holistic units of analysis, Lewin described the life space as a dynamic field made up of continually changing person–environment regions and relationships. In the same way that fields in modern physics represent changing energy configurations, the life space exhibits continual activity and flow.

Lewin departed from a strict transactional perspective by assuming quasi-stationary equilibrium states toward which life spaces gravitate. However, he also noted that an ultimate state of perfect equilibrium is unattainable. Furthermore, except for the concept of quasi-stationary equilibrium processes, Lewin explicitly rejected teleology as an explanation of the dynamics of the life space since it implies that the "future causes the present" (Lewin, 1964, pp. 26–27). He also deemphasized the concept of efficient causation, that is, antecedent–consequent relationships between variables. Instead, he focused on the understanding of patterns and dynamics of current life spaces. In this respect, Lewin adhered to Aristotle's "formal" causation approach to psychological phenomena.

Another exemplar of a transactional approach is the ethogenic or situated-action approach to social psychological phenomena (Ginsberg, 1980; Harre, 1978; Harre & Secord, 1972), which examines the rules or norms of social events. Emphasis is placed on ongoing and active relations among participants and settings, not on actors or settings as separate entities. Actors and settings are linked by rules or norms that permit considerable latitude for variation and novelty in how events are played out. Because social actions occur in the context of prior actions and have implications for future actions, the understanding of events requires attention to dynamic and emergent processes that are not wholly predictable from separate knowledge of the setting or its participants.

The purpose of an ethogenic orientation is to understand the structure and pattern of a flowing event and treat it as a unique occurrence. The capstone to Ginsberg's (1980) approach to understanding lies in his essentially articulating Aristotle's concept of formal cause:

> [One tries] to identify relationships among component parts and processes—but none of the components is "caused" by the prior occurrence of another component; and even more important, none of the components "causes" the action or act of which they are components. The identity of the components is a functional identity which derives from the larger

unit of which they are components, such as the act which the component actions are in a process of producing. (p. 307)

The ethogenic perspective is similar to several other transactional orientations, including Sarbin's (1976) contextualist approach, the ethnomethodological tradition (Cicourel, 1974; Garfinkel, 1967), and Goffman's dramaturgical analyses of social situations (1959, 1963, 1971). All of these approaches are holistic, focus on unfolding and changing facets of events, and seek to describe and account for the oftentimes unique patterns and qualities of events.

Gergen (1982) also called for a transactional approach, emphasizing the need to treat psychological phenomena as dynamic processes, not as stable, enduring entities. And, in accordance with a transactional perspective, he portrayed change as an *aleatory* process, that is, exhibiting emergence and spontaneity, and not following a fixed teleological or preestablished path and direction. Moreover, Gergen emphasized the holistic quality of psychological phenomena and how they are embedded in historical, situational, and physical contexts. He proposed that psychology adopt a formal cause orientation, not bound by efficient, final, or material conceptions of causation. To support this proposal, Gergen drew on Wilhelm Wundt's nineteenth century treatise on *Volkerpsychologie* (folk psychology or social psychology):

> For Wundt, the guiding metaphor for social psychology was not that of natural science, but rather that of historical analysis....Rather than searching for general laws of psychological functioning, the task of a social psychologist was to render an account of contemporary behavior patterns as developed from the culture's history....The method for social psychology was to lie in the documentation and explanation of historical patterns as they emerged over time. The function of social psychology was not that of making predictions....Rather than prediction, the goal of the social psychologist was to render the world of human affairs intelligible. And, like Darwin, this task was to be carried out by examining the etymology of contemporary patterns. (p. 174)

The Transactional Approach in Environmental Psychology

The transactional world view might be expected to have broad appeal to environmental psychologists, given that field's emphasis on the molar physical environment in relation to human behavior. Transactional thinking was salient in the writings of the pioneers in the field:

> [There is] absolute integrity of person/physical setting events....Understanding the mutual relationship between human behavior and experience and the dimensions of physical settings is necessarily rooted in the methodology which preserves the *integrity* of these events. (Proshansky, 1976, p. 63)

> Man is never concretely encountered independent of the situation through which he acts, nor is the environment ever encountered independent of the encountering individual. It is meaningless to speak of either as existing apart from the situation in which it is encountered. (Ittelson, 1973, p. 19)

Although readily accepted in principle, these ideas have not always been translated into theoretical and empirical work. An exception, however, is the ecological research of Barker and his associates (Barker, 1968, 1978; see also Barker, Chapter 40, Wicker, Chapter 16). For several decades, Barker has examined psychological processes in a variety of environmental settings—small towns, schools, churches, grocery stores—in accordance with the thesis that behavior is inextricably linked with the physical and social environment in a continuous flow. For Barker, the tasks of the ecological psychologist are to understand the stream of behavior and to describe the natural units of psychological functioning in physical settings, as they unfold and change direction.

A central concept for understanding the dynamic quality of person–environment relationships is the *behavior setting*: "A bounded, self-regulated and ordered system composed of replaceable human and non-human components that interact in a synchronized fashion to carry out an ordered sequence of events called the *setting program*" (Wicker, 1979, p. 12). Thus a behavior setting is a confluence of actions in relation to places and things; these actions are organized in systematic temporal sequences and patterns. Behavior, places, and temporal dynamics are mutually interlocked such that behavior gains meaning by virtue of its location in a particular spatial and temporal context, and the context gains meaning by virtue of the actors and actions that exist within it. Thus aspects of the behavior setting are defined by and define one another and lend a collective unity to the stream of behavior within the setting. Barker used the game of baseball as an analogy, where understanding the game requires that instead of focusing on elements or attributes taken out of context, for example, one player's skill or the speed of the pitched ball, one must study the game as a behavior setting or series of behavior settings, in which patterns of behavior become understandable only when viewed in the context of the places, things, and times that constitute the whole setting.

Although transactional in most respects, Barker

does assume the operation of generic homeostatic mechanisms that regulate behavior settings, maintain the program of the setting, and smooth their functioning. Thus deviation-countering mechanisms redirect the system or bring it in line with its ideal functioning, and vetoing mechanisms sometimes reject the source of disruption and eliminate it from the setting. For example, small schools are often undermanned and require students to take on many jobs and assignments so that they can maintain their programs. An overmanned system with too many participants exhibits the opposite qualities, screening out certain participants to maintain its program with an optimum number of individuals. Although these mechanisms reflect homeostatic principles that regulate ongoing behavior, there is no indication of a longer-range teleological conception in Barker's framework. On the contrary, behavior settings seem to be capable of changing in many ways, rather than being directed toward some predetermined long-term ideal condition. Finally, in accord with a transactional orientation, Barker's framework does not emphasize prediction and forecasting, but it attempts to describe and understand behavior settings as complex patterns of psychological functioning, without isolation of specific cause–effect relationships.

In a recent statement, Wicker (Chapter 16) added a substantial transactional quality to the ecological psychology approach by describing the *life history* of behavior settings. His analysis emphasizes the dynamic and changing quality of settings as they proceed from formative or convergence phases through operating phases to dissolution or divergent phases. Behavior settings are conceived of, therefore, as configurations of actors, activities, and physical and social contexts that change in emergent and contextually linked ways. Although Barker's theorizing over the decades has illustrated many transactional themes, Wicker's analysis of the changing qualities of behavior settings places this theory even more squarely within a transactional world view.

The writings of Wapner (Wapner, 1981; Wapner, Kaplan, & Cohen, 1973; Wapner, Chapter 41) reflect aspects of both organismic and transactional orientations. On the one hand, Wapner explicitly adopts Pepper's organicist world hypothesis, and he specifies his own key principles as follows:

1) The person-in-environment is the unit to be analyzed;

2) The person-in-environment system operates in dynamic equilibrium directed toward long- and short-term goals;

3) Disturbance in one part of the person-in-environment system affects other parts in the transactional system as a whole. (Wapner, 1981, p. 224)

Wapner's approach makes several other assumptions, for example, that aspects of the person–environment system include cognitive, affective, and behavioral domains, that humans are active and vigorous initiators of events, and that the environment is a complex part of systems and includes physical features, sociocultural rules and norms, and other people. These principles contain or imply the organismic emphasis on holism, equilibrium, and multiple influences among separately existing components of the system.

In order to understand systems under conditions of disruption and adjustment, Wapner has recently studied various life transitions, such as retirement, graduation from college, or changing schools (Wapner, 1981; Wapner, Chapter 41). This newer work has a decided transactional quality in that temporal features are part and parcel of psychological phenomena, with person–environment systems as holistic unities that contain environmental, psychological, *and* temporal features. Other aspects of his writings are also transactional. For example, although Wapner sometimes acknowledges the possibility of examining the components or parts of systems, he also sometimes rejects the idea that components can be treated as isolated entities with fixed or separate characteristics. Rather, as called for by a transactional approach, components or parts are mutually defined in terms of one another, and their meaning and operation are closely linked with other aspects of the whole. Moreover, although Wapner explicitly accepts intentions, goals, and purposes, he does not adopt monolithic organicist principles that inevitably direct or pull behavior in specific directions. Like many transactional theorists, Wapner seems to use a pragmatic, functional, and eclectic approach to goals and purposes. (Indeed, he uses the term *multiple intentionality* to describe goal-oriented functioning; see Chapter 41.) On the other hand, he does explicate the assumption that person–environment systems generally gravitate toward states of equilibrium. In short, although Wapner adopts an organismic world view in some facets of his theorizing, there are other parts of his thinking that reflect a transactional perspective. Indeed, Wapner's theorizing and research represent an interesting bridge between organismic and transactional world views.

Transactional concepts are also evident in anthropologically oriented environmental research and theory. Rapoport (1977, 1982) defined *environment* as a complex and systematic organization of *space, time, meaning,* and *communication.* These four facets of environments occur simultaneously in a variety of configurations. For example, various physical settings in different cultures, such as a street corner, water well, or coffee house, may involve different patterns of use by different types of people, different flows of communication and meanings to participants, variations in events at different times of day, and so forth. Understanding the places and their events requires a holistic perspective that recognizes the inseparability of their different aspects. In all such cases there is a unity of temporal flow, types of participants, rules of communication, and psychological meanings of the interaction.

Transactional perspectives are salient in cross-cultural studies in which homes are conceptualized as inseparable unities of people, places, and psychological and social processes that exhibit different qualities of change. For example, Saile (1977, 1985) found that rituals associated with the building and restoration of homes of the Pueblo cultures of the southwestern United States embed the home in an array of cultural and religious beliefs, link the home with the past, present, and future, and renew ties between members of the community and their ancestral values.

In another analysis, Altman and Gauvain (1981) described homes in a variety of cultures in terms of two dimensions that involve inseparable linkages of psychological processes and physical features of homes: identity/communality and openness/closedness. The first dimension indicates that homes reflect unique and distinctive qualities of occupants through their design, decorations, and use of siting, front facades, entranceways, thresholds, and interior spaces and objects. At the same time, people display social bonds to their community and culture through the physical features of homes. Altman and Gauvain also described how homes are used to regulate openness/closedness to others, permitting control over privacy. This analysis is transactional in that openness/closedness and identity/communality contribute, in part, to the definition and meaning of homes, and these psychological processes are themselves defined in part by the physical qualities of homes. In a subsequent analysis, Gauvain, Altman, and Fahim (1983a, 1983b) introduced a temporal dimension to the analysis of homes by examining how rapid and gradual changes in cultures were manifested in the design and use of homes. Certain forms of rapid and pervasive social change altered an established config-

uration of psychological processes and places, and Gauvain et al. (1983a, 1983b) described how cultures attempted to restore the prior harmony or develop new integrations of psychological processes and homes.

Phenomenological approaches to person–environment relationships are transactional in many respects (Dovey, 1985; Korosec-Serfaty, 1985; Norberg-Shulz, 1972; Relph, 1976; Seamon, 1979, 1982; Tuan, 1973, 1977, 1980). The phenomenological approach focuses on subjective and experiential aspects of person–environment relationships and is concerned with meanings, feelings of attachment, and affective orientations of people to places: "People are their place and the place is its people, and however readily these may be separated in conceptual terms, in experience they are not easily differentiated" (Relph, 1976, p. 34).

An example of this approach is Tuan's (1973, 1977, 1980) description of homes, buildings, cities, and regions as inseparable confluences of environmental and psychological experiences. Thus a physical environment or space becomes a place when psychological experiences involving meanings, actions, and feelings become attached to it. In our terms, spaces become places when they are attached to people, gain psychological meaning, and involve ongoing activities.

Furthermore, time and change are inseparable aspects of places, as they reflect the past, present, and future and involve the lives and activities of residents. Werner, Altman, and Oxley (1985) described the ways in which temporal features of homes are intrinsically linked with psychological, social, cultural, and physical qualities of homes. They proposed a temporal framework that included linear and cyclical (past, present, and future) dimensions and associated properties of temporal salience, temporal scale, pace, and rhythm. These features of time and change were applied to psychological processes, objects, and places in the homes of many cultures.

Another application of the phenomenological perspective appears in research on "environmental autobiographies" and residential histories (Cooper-Marcus, 1978; Korosec-Serfaty, 1982; Rowles, 1980, 1981a, 1981b, 1984). This research reflects a transactional perspective in that people, psychological processes, places, and temporal flow form intrinsic aspects of a whole and do not exist as separate elements. For example, Rowles (1980, 1981) interviewed elderly residents of a small Appalachian town about their present and long-term attitudes, feelings, perceptions, and attachments to their homes and town; he examined how people interacted with one another on a regular basis, at certain times, and in specific places; he studied how specific places were linked with social relationships and activities in different stages of their lives.

Altman's dialectic analysis of privacy regulation also illustrates the transactional approach (Altman, 1975, 1977; Altman & Chemers, 1980; Altman, Vinsel, & Brown, 1981). Change is a central feature of this theory, with social interaction treated as a dynamic interplay of openness/closedness to others, and with the particular level of openness/closedness varying from circumstance to circumstance. Furthermore, Altman described privacy regulation as a holistic, multimechanism process in which verbal, nonverbal, and environmental (personal space and territorial behavior) mechanisms are brought into play in a unified fashion. Altman's theory also explicitly discounts teleological views of privacy, arguing that privacy does not function in accordance with fixed short- or long-range ideal levels of openness/closedness but is linked to contexts and social circumstances. Although privacy regulation is hypothesized to be a culturally pervasive process, unique mixes of verbal, nonverbal, and environmental privacy mechanisms are often associated with particular individual and cultural contexts.

The recent research and theorizing of Stokols and his associates also illustrates the transactional world view (Jacobi & Stokols, 1983; Stokols, 1981; Stokols & Shumaker, 1981; see also Stokols, Chapter 2). For example, Stokols and Shumaker (1982) developed a holistic taxonomy of places that weaves together their geographical and physical properties with participants, psychological processes, and sociocultural meanings. This analysis was complemented by Stokols's (1981) use of the concept of *subjective life stage* of settings (spatially and temporally bounded periods associated with particular goals, activities, and processes), thereby highlighting temporal qualities of person–environment functioning. Complex relationships within and between temporal stages yield a dynamic, flowing, holistic orientation to person–environment relationships.

In another analysis, Jacobi and Stokols (1983) emphasized some broad-ranging temporal qualities of group functioning in relation to physical settings. For example, present-focused orientations involve situations where individuals and groups relate to the physical environment in terms of its functional significance for achieving certain immediate goals and plans; traditional orientations involve configurations of people, objects, and places, and affective feelings

that link them to the past; futuristic temporal perspectives focus on people, places, things, and events yet to come; a coordinated temporal perspective involves a balanced person–environment orientation to past, present, and future.

Congruent with other transactional world views, Stokols and his associates do not hypothesize organicist and teleological principles that regulate the operation of person–environment unities or direct them toward a particular end state. Instead, they imply self-initiated, qualitative transformations of settings, the possibility of different phases in their history, and variations in temporal processes from circumstance to circumstance. Furthermore, Stokols does not emphasize identification of antecedent–consequent causal mechanisms between isolated sets of variables. Rather, he and other transactionally oriented environmental psychologists attempt to understand and describe holistic networks of person–environment configurations in terms of a formal causation perspective. Although seeking broad-ranging principles of person–environment relationships, transactional researchers such as Stokols seem to accept the idea that psychological functioning may involve unique configurations of actors, settings, and cultures.

In summary, transactional orientations are unique approaches to the study of psychological phenomena in several respects. They are holistic and treat the confluence of psychological processes and environmental contexts as the fundamental unit of analysis. Persons, processes, and contexts mutually define one another and serve as aspects of the whole, not as separate elements. These aspects do not combine to yield the whole; they *are* the whole and are defined by and define one another. In addition, temporal factors are intrinsic aspects of the transactional unity, with degrees of stability and change being fundamental properties of phenomena. Also, although they may attempt to establish general principles of psychological functioning, transactional world views do not necessarily seek universal principles that are presumed to govern all facets of a phenomenon. Different explanatory principles may emerge in different circumstances; change may evolve from unique confluences of psychological processes and environments; long-range directional and teleological principles are not assumed; and variability of psychological functioning is expected. And transactional views emphasize a formal cause approach to understanding, wherein the goal of research and theory is to account for, describe, and understand the pattern of relationships among people, places, and psychological processes.

1.4. IMPLICATIONS, ISSUES, AND PROSPECTS

The discussion in this chapter has been based on the theme that psychology in general, and environmental psychology in particular, can profit from an examination of underlying philosophical assumptions regarding *units of analysis* and *temporal aspects* of psychological phenomena. Our analysis suggested that contemporary psychology stresses interactional world views, wherein psychological functioning is assumed to result from the interaction of separate person and environment entities. We have advocated greater attention to transactional approaches because their unique philosophical perspective has promise for enhancing research and theory and has been underutilized to date. Although many psychologists have advocated a transactional world view, implementation has usually occurred only at a very general theoretical level, and only occasionally in empirical research. In order to facilitate empirical application, the next section of the chapter outlines some broad methodological principles associated with a transactional world view.

1.4.1. Principles of Methodology

Beliefs about research methodology and approaches to science share much in common with social stereotypes. They contain an element of truth, they are convenient descriptors, and they lend a sense of order to the stereotyper's life. However, social and methodological stereotypes can distort, do not apply to all cases, and may involve inappropriate value judgments. For example, trait world views are easy to stereotype as necessarily adopting correlational methods, such that traits are correlated with other traits and behaviors in a nonexperimental study design. And interactional approaches are prone to be characterized as relying almost solely on experimental laboratory methods, because these methods are useful in working with analytic dimensions of phenomena and because they permit clear delineation of antecedent–consequent relationships between variables. Furthermore, those who adopt an interactional orientation often avoid nonexperimental methods, believing that they are inherently flawed, primitive, and inconclusive. If nonexperimental methods are used, interactional researchers tend to be apologetic and tentative regarding their value. Organismic and transactional approaches, given their holistic emphasis, are prone to be portrayed as relying solely on "descriptive" methods, naturalistic observations, and other nonexperimental procedures.

Although there is, in fact, a general fit between world views and methodological approaches along the lines just stated, overly absolutistic stereotypes distort the fact that a range of methodologies can be employed with any of these orientations. We next illustrate this thesis by considering some methodological principles that apply to the transactional world view.

Transactional Research Takes Settings and Contexts into Account

Transactional approaches treat "events" as the fundamental unit of study. Events are composed of psychological, temporal, and environmental aspects and therefore require methodologies that tap these facets of the unity. Because it is important to study how psychological processes are embedded in physical and social contexts, transactional researchers are inclined to work in natural settings of homes, schools, workplaces, playgrounds, and so on. However, laboratories, observation rooms, and other less "natural" situations are also real settings and contexts. *Any* situation, laboratory or otherwise, is a context, and any psychological process always occurs in some context. A psychological process exhibited in the laboratory is not context free, and neither is psychological functioning in any other setting, however familiar or unfamiliar it may be. Therefore, the researcher must always treat the process as embedded in a context, and no context can be assumed to be widely generalizable. So denying the laboratory experiment as a relevant method for transactional approaches is fallacious. In the same way, arguing for sole reliance on laboratory experiments as the only appropriate way to study psychological functioning is equally fallacious. Instead, investigators must keep the context in mind in interpreting data. And the field benefits from attempts to sample settings broadly, a point emphasized by Brunswick (1947).

What do we mean by context? Contexts and settings include the qualities of the physical and social environment that may be psychologically relevant, the nature of tasks and instructions, the flow of events, how the setting relates to other aspects of a person's life, the "meaning" and interpretation of the situation by participants, and the familiarity of the participants with the setting. Such factors apply to the laboratory experiment and naturalistic setting alike, and transactional researchers attend to these and related issues when using any specific method. In summary, all research settings, including laboratories, have value to a transactional approach, as long as psychological phenomena are treated as occurring within, being defined by, and linked with temporal and contextual aspects of a setting.

Transactional Research Seeks to Understand the Perspective of the Participants in an Event

People come to familiar settings with knowledge, expectations, norms, and behavioral styles. In any setting they attempt to discern its demands and figure out how to behave. For a transactional orientation to succeed, the researcher should attempt to discover the "meanings" of the events to participants. Too often, investigators have preconceptions of the meaning of an event and determine only whether or not the results of a study are in accord with those preconceptions. Although such a strategy is appropriate for some purposes, it is also useful to incorporate the perspective of participants in the interpretation and analysis of an event. For example, the presence of a mother in an experiment or observational setting may be essential to ensure involvement of an infant, while her presence may be a distraction for an older child. Thus the mother's presence may not be equivalent in meaning from the perspective of the infant versus the perspective of the child. However, given cultural uniformities in experience and interpretation of events, there are regularities in the meanings with which people approach certain situations, so that descriptions of events may often rely on normative situational definitions and expectations rather than requiring individualistic and unique descriptions. This methodological requirement is not inconsistent with use of objective measures but instead stresses that one must attend to aspects of the context that are often overlooked.

Transactional Research Attempts to Understand the Observer as an Aspect of Events

In trait, interactional, and organismic orientations observers are treated as independent of the phenomenon. In contrast, transactional approaches consider the position and role of the observer to be an aspect of the phenomenon. Different observers may provide varying but equally accurate descriptions of the same phenomenon, depending on their locations, roles, and perspectives, as the observer plays a part in the event.

The so-called experimenter bias effect studied in the 1960s and 1970s demonstrated that different qualities of experimenters affected behavior in otherwise standardized situations, often resulting in nonreplicability of findings (Rosnow, 1981). This was interpreted as a serious methodological "problem" on the grounds that psychological phenomena were assumed to operate and be capable of observation independent of the investigator studying them. In contrast, the transactional researcher interprets such findings as evidence that the location, attitudes, and behavior of the observer are aspects of the phenomenon, and that the very process of observation affects and alters the event. Obviously, one can standardize observations, ensure that observers always adopt a certain perspective, and develop rigid rules for instructions and data collection procedures. Although appropriate, this does not eliminate the observer as part of the phenomenon, but merely fixes the location of the observer and restricts the findings to a particular configuration of observer, participant, and setting.

A transactional approach advocates study of how observers interpret events. Rather than assuming that reliability across observers indicates closeness to the "truth," transactional approaches require more explicit attention to the evidence used by observers to make inferences about the phenomenon. This requires that the investigator include knowledge about the characteristics and orientations of observers.

A transactional perspective calls for use of a variety of research methods, including those that emphasize careful analysis of the context and of understandings shown by participants, for example, ethnographic or ethnomethodological techniques (Cicourel, 1974). In such methods observers attempt to understand psychological processes in relation to the context and norms of the setting and its participants. Transactional approaches may, therefore, require use of traditional and nontraditional psychological research methods to analyze the structure and pattern of events. In so doing, the stereotype that "true" explanation and understanding of psychological functioning comes about only through particular methods is rejected.

Transactional Research Emphasizes the Study of Process and Change

Transactional orientations treat the event as a confluence of temporal, contextual, and psychological processes. This necessitates development of procedures to describe the flow and dynamics of events, that is, people's ongoing actions in relation to one another and the environment. Thus the personal qualities or cognitive structure of actors taken alone is of less interest than are the dynamic transactions of people with one another and with the environment.

Methods are required to study process and change and to examine what Dewey and Bentley (1949) described as active verb indicators of psychological functioning—doing, thinking, behaving, feeling—rather than methods that only emphasize states, static structures, and fixed conditions. We hasten to add that this methodological principle does not rule out the use of measures of states, but one is required to link these qualities to activities, processes, and changes.

An emphasis on transformation and change also requires identification of "natural" beginnings and endings of events. Traditional psychological research usually employs temporal indicators that are independent of the phenomenon, in accord with conceptions of time as a separate dimension that "marches on" by itself. Seconds, minutes, and stimulus time intervals are typical temporal units that are imposed on psychological processes to mark their course. Transactional approaches attempt to bound events by means of temporal qualities that are intrinsic to phenomena. Thus Barker (1968) circumscribes events in terms of changes in configurations of actors, consistent behavior patterns, and foci of attention. In this way, an event is defined in psychological and functional terms, not in chronological clock terms.

Finally, a transactional orientation attempts to track simultaneously a variety of ongoing psychological processes that are relevant to a question, and it does not focus on only a single facet of psychological functioning. Within a theme of inquiry, it is important to understand how aspects of a question are woven together. That is, the multitude of associated goals of participants in an event can be examined as they relate to each other. For example, in instructional communication between a parent and child, an adult often simultaneously maintains a child's attention, evaluates the pace of instruction, ensures appropriate social status relative to the child, and provides information on a specific component of a task. The child may also engage in a variety of actions, including seeking approval from the parent, attempting to shift the focus of attention, and working on the task. Ideally, a transactional perspective attempts to track the array of ongoing interactions related to the theme of the inquiry without being restricted to a particular isolated bit of behavior. In so doing, one can generate a sense of the whole and how subordinate activities fit into the total event.

Transactional Approaches Accept the Relativity of Indicators and Measures of Psychological Functioning.

Much of the research conducted according to trait, interactional, and organismic orientations attempts to develop measures of psychological phenomena that can be used over a range of situations and partici-pants, in order to achieve standardization and generality of indicators of psychological processes. Thus performance tasks and measures of performance, personality and attitude instruments, and so on are used from situation to situation and as universally as possible.

For the transactional researcher, rigid standardization of measures across settings may result in an artificial fragmentation of the phenomenon or an imposition of psychological indicators that are not appropriate to the social, physical, and temporal qualities of the setting. Ideally, a transactional approach would first analyze the situation or event of interest, including characteristics of participants, the environment, and norms and rules that link people and context together. Then one might use standard measures that are suited to aspects of the event. However, indicators and measures unique to the event may also be required—and perhaps not used again in other situations. This does not rule out the use of standardized procedures, but it emphasizes the importance of not being rigidly bound to them and makes salient the need for sensitivity to idiosyncratic indicators of a phenomenon. For example, the study of stress in high-density transportation systems may profitably use standard measures such as blood pressure or self-reports as well as measures of stress that do not readily apply elsewhere, for example, patterns of accelerator pressing in automobiles or nonverbal indicators of agitation.

This is a challenging methodological task because it requires sensitivity to each situation and to each case, a strong linkage between theoretical constructs and measures, and an "artistic" ability to identify indicators that are embedded in situations. It also requires consideration of the function of any particular act in the setting in which it is observed, as well as the goal(s) that the participants are attempting to meet. Ideally, therefore, a transactional approach does not unilaterally impose measures on an event, but it derives them from the event. What generalizes from study to study is not the measure, procedure, or technique but the construct and theory that underlies the research.

Transactional Approaches Emphasize Methodological Eclecticism

A transactional perspective calls for research designs and procedures that are tailored to the problem and questions investigated, and to the state of knowledge about a phenomenon. Sole reliance on a single method at all stages of knowledge, or the belief that certain methods are inherently better than others, is incompatible with a transactional perspective. Qualitative descriptions may yield the best information in some circumstances; laboratory experiments may be fruitful in other circumstances; systematic interview and questionnaire analyses may be most appropriate elsewhere. When, how, and where to adopt a particular research strategy depend on one's conception of the particular confluence of psychological processes, contextual factors, and temporal dynamics for a given question and the state of knowledge about a phenomenon. Therefore, those who adopt a transactional approach should be receptive to using a wide range of research methods.

Furthermore, a particular methodological strategy or a particular study may not satisfy all the ideals of a transactional orientation. For example, it may not be feasible to examine temporal processes in a particular study even though time and change are intrinsic features of psychological phenomena. What is important is that such an omission be recognized, and that the larger program of research and theory eventually encompass the full transactional perspective.

1.5. SOME FINAL WORDS

Before concluding it is necessary to address the question: Which of the four world views is the "best," "correct," or "most fruitful" approach to the study of psychological phenomena? Although we have advocated more attention to a transactional approach, our answer to this question is nevertheless unequivocal: *None* of these world views provides the "best" or "correct" approach. They simply result in different forms of inquiry, understanding, and theory. We have called for more use of a transactional perspective because it has been neglected in psychology and because it provides a different and potentially fruitful vantage point from which to understand psychological processes. We also advocate complementary use of alternative world views, that is, adding the transactional to the other more traditional approaches in psychology, in order to avoid a doctrinaire, often ideological stance that there is an ultimately true, best, and correct way to study psychological functioning.

This position has been stated in clear terms by Dewey and Bentley (1949) and Pepper (1942):

> Our assertion is the right to see in union what becomes important to see in union; together with a right to see in separation what is important to see in separation—each in its own time and place; and it is this right, when we judge that we require it for our own needs, for which we find strong support in the

recent history of physics. (Dewey & Bentley, 1949, p. 112)

> We believe that at the present time there are four world hypotheses of about equal adequacy....Now, the very statement that these are relatively adequate hypotheses means that they are capable of presenting credible interpretations of any facts, whatever, in terms of their several sets of categories. (Pepper, 1942, p. 99)

These statements endorse the notion that different world views are acceptable and serve different purposes. Furthermore, the proof of a theory associated with one world view does not necessarily disprove one derived from another world view. For example, Newtonian mechanics accounts for phenomena involving large numbers of atoms operating at relatively low velocities, with objects or atoms conceptualized as stable and indestructible material entities. At the subatomic level, however, quantum theory is more appropriate. In lieu of stable entities or objects, quantum theory conceives of dynamic, changing concentrations of energy that appear as particles or mass. When dealing with speeds approaching that of light, the Newtonian model is best replaced by relativity theory, in which a phenomenon is described in terms of the relative positions and movements of observers, and where time is an intrinsic aspect of the phenomenon. Although major steps have been taken toward unification of these theories in physics, the theme stated by Pepper and by Dewey and Bentley remains valid, namely, that there can be value in using alternative world views to understand different aspects of psychological phenomena.

The central theme of this chapter has been that psychology is presently engaged in a process of self-inquiry concerning its philosophical underpinnings, particularly with respect to its units of analysis and approaches to temporal factors and change. Our discussion of trait, interactional, organismic, and transactional world views emphasized the idea that assumptions about units of analysis and temporal factors relate to the nature of concepts regarding contexts and settings, philosophy of science, and methodological strategies.

We described how earlier periods in the history of psychology emphasized a trait world view, how present-day psychology adheres to an interactional perspective, and how there is a mounting interest in organismic and transactional perspectives. The last two approaches have strong appeal for many psychologists who deal with complex, molar phenomena. Transactional approaches are particularly relevant to environmental psychology, given that field's intrinsic interest in holistic, changing aspects of person–environment relationships.

The lure of the transactional approach is simultaneously coupled with a sense of uncertainty. How does one build a theory of holistic, changing phenomena? What methods can be use to study phenomena at a holistic level? How do we incorporate change and temporal factors as part of psychological phenomena? For the most part, psychology is comfortable with an interactional perspective; indeed, it is an automatic and ingrained aspect of the thinking of many contemporary researchers and theorists, so it is difficult to conceive of working out of a different framework. Furthermore, the mechanics of working with the transactional approach are not as well articulated in psychology as are those of the more traditional approaches; we do not yet quite know "how to do it." Yet there has been a significant beginning, as exemplified by the writings of theorists and researchers cited in this chapter, and numerous others, who have incorporated aspects of the transactional world view in psychology.

We have written this essay with the hope that a description of the properties and assumptions of different world views may enhance our perspective on psychological phenomena. Enhancement of perspective means expansion, not constriction or rejection; psychology can simultaneously view its phenomena from different perspectives without sacrificing inquiry according to one world view for that of another. We hope that this chapter encourages scholars in the field to broaden their approach and begin to examine psychological phenomena from different perspectives, especially the transactional world view.

Acknowledgments

We are indebted to the following colleagues who commented on earlier drafts of the manuscript: James Alexander, David Altman, William Altman, Martin Chemers, Mary Gauvain, Kenneth Gergen, David Grant, Robert Hays, Joseph McGrath, Diana Oxley, Fred Rhodewalt, Seymour Rosenberg, Ralph Rosnow, Daniel Stokols, Charles Turner, Abraham Wandersman, Seymour Wapner, Carol Werner, Jack White, and Jay Wysocki.

NOTE

1. We use the term *aspects* to mean features of a system that may be focused on separately but that require consideration of other features of a system for their definition and for an understanding of their functioning. In contrast, we use the terms *parts, elements,* and *components* to refer to independently existing entities that may contribute to a whole, as in the organismic world view.

REFERENCES

Aiello, J. (1987). Personal space. In D. Stokols & I. Altman (Eds.), *Handbook of environmental psychology.* New York: Wiley.

Altman, I. (1973). Reciprocity of interpersonal exchange. *Journal for the Theory of Social Behavior, 3,* 249–261.

Altman, I. (1977). Privacy regulation: Culturally universal or culturally specific? *Journal of Social Issues, 33,* 66–84.

Altman, I. (1981). *The environment and social behavior: Privacy, personal space, territory and crowding.* New York: Irvington. (Original work published 1975)

Altman, I., & Chemers, M.M. (1983). *Culture and environment.* New York: Cambridge University Press. (Original work published 1980)

Altman, I., & Gauvain, M. (1981). A cross-cultural and dialectic analysis of homes. In L. Liben, A. Patterson, & N. Newcombe (Eds.), *Spatial representation and behavior across the life span: Theory and application* (pp. 283–319). New York: Academic.

Altman, I., & Taylor, D.A. (1981). *Social penetration: The development of interpersonal relationships.* New York: Irvington. (Original work published 1973)

Altman, I., Vinsel, A., & Brown, B.B. (1981). Dialectic conceptions in social psychology: An application to social penetration and privacy regulation. In L. Berkowitz (Ed.), *Advances in experimental social psychology* (Vol. 14, pp. 108–160). New York: Academic.

Angyal, A. (1958). *Foundations for a science of personality.* Cambridge, MA: Harvard University Press.

Bandura, A. (1977). *Social learning theory.* Englewood Cliffs, NJ: Prentice-Hall.

Bandura, A. (1978). The self system in reciprocal determinism. *American Psychologist, 33,* 344–358.

Barker, R.G. (1968). *Ecological psychology: Concepts and methods for studying the environment of human behavior.* Stanford, CA: Stanford University Press.

Barker, R.G. & Associates. (1978). *Habitats, environments and human behavior.* San Francisco: Jossey-Bass.

Barker, R.G. (1987). Prospecting in environmental psychology: Oskaloosa revisited. In D. Stokols & I. Altman (Eds.), *Handbook of environmental psychology.* New York: Wiley.

Bates, E. (1979). Brainerd versus Aristotle with Piaget looking on. *The Behavioral and Brain Sciences, 1,* 138–139.

Baum, A., & Epstein, Y.M. (Eds.). (1978). *Human response to crowding.* Hillsdale, NJ: Erlbaum.

Baum, A., & Paulus, P. (1987). Crowding. In D. Stokols & I. Altman (Eds.), *Handbook of environmental psychology*. New York: Wiley.

Bell, P.A., Fisher, J.D., & Loomis, R.J. (1978). *Environmental psychology*. Philadelphia: Saunders.

Brown, B.B. (1987). Territoriality. In D. Stokols & I. Altman (Eds.), *Handbook of environmental psychology*. New York: Wiley.

Brunswick, E. (1955). Representative design and probabilistic theory in a functional psychology. *Psychological Review, 3*, 193–217.

Buss, A.R. (1979). *A dialectical psychology*. New York: Halsted.

Buss, A.R. (1979). On the four kinds of causality. *The Behavioral and Brain Sciences, 1,* 39.

Cannon, W.B. (1932). *The wisdom of the body*. London: Kegan.

Capra, F. (1977). *The tao of physics*. New York: Bantam.

Cicourel, A.V. (1974). *Cognitive sociology: Language and meaning in social interaction*. New York: Free Press.

Cone, J.D., & Hayes, S.C. (1982). *Environmental problems/behavioral solutions*. New York: Cambridge University Press. (Original work published 1980)

Cooper-Marcus, C. (1978). Remembrance of landscapes past. *Landscape, 22,* 35–43.

Dewey, J., & Bentley, A.F. (1949). *Knowing and the known*. Boston: Beacon.

Dovey, K. (1985). Home and homelessness. In I. Altman & C.M. Werner (Eds.), *Home environments: Vol. 8, Human behavior and environment: Advances in theory and research* (pp. 33–64). New York: Plenum.

Everett, P.B., & Watson, B.G. (1987). Psychological contributions to transportation. In D. Stokols & I. Altman (Eds.), *Handbook of environmental psychology*. New York: Wiley.

Fiedler, F.E., & Chemers, M.M. (1974). *Leadership and effective management*. Glenview, IL: Scott, Foresman.

Garfinkel, H. (1967). *Studies in ethnomethodology*. Englewood Cliffs, NJ: Prentice-Hall.

Gauvain, M., Altman, I., & Fahim, J. (1983). Homes and social change: A cross cultural analysis. In N.R. Feimer & E.S. Geller (Eds.), *Environmental psychology: Directions and perspectives* (pp. 180–218). New York: Praeger.

Geller, E.S. (1987). Applied and behavior analysis and environmental psychology. In D. Stokols & I. Altman (Eds.), *Handbook of environmental psychology*. New York: Wiley.

Geller, E.S., Winett, R.A., & Everett, P.B. (1982). *Preserving the environment: New strategies for behavior change*. Elmsford, NY: Pergamon.

Gergen, K.J. (1982). *Toward transformation in social knowledge*. New York: Springer-Verlag.

Gibson, J.J. (1979). *An ecological approach to visual perception*. Boston: Houghton Mifflin.

Ginsburg, G.P. (1980). Situated action: An emerging paradigm. In L. Wheeler (Eds.), *Review of personality and social psychology* (Vol. I, pp. 295–325). Beverly Hills, CA: Sage.

Goffman, E. (1959). *The presentation of self in everyday life*. New York: Doubleday, Anchor.

Goffman, E. (1963). *Behavior in public places*. New York: Free Press.

Goffman, E. (1971). *Relations in public*. New York: Basic Books.

Golledge, R.G. (1987). *Environmental cognition*. In D. Stokols & I. Altman (Eds.), *Handbook of environmental psychology*. New York: Wiley.

Haley, J. (1963). *Strategies of psychotherapy*. New York: Grune & Stratton.

Harre, R. (1977). The ethogenic approach: Theory and practice. In L. Berkowitz (Ed.), *Advances in experimental social psychology* (Vol. 10, pp. 284–314). New York: Academic.

Harre, R., & Secord, P.F. (1972). *The explanation of social behavior*. Totowa, NJ: Rowman & Littlefield.

Heider, F. (1958). *The psychology of interpersonal relations*. New York: Wiley.

Ittelson, W.H. (1973). Environment perception and contemporary conceptual theory. In W.H. Ittelson (Ed.), *Environment and cognition* (pp. 1–19). New York: Seminar.

Jacobi, M., & Stokols, D. (1983). The role of tradition in group-environment relations. In N.R. Feimer & E.S. Geller (Eds.), *Environmental psychology: Directions and perspectives* (pp. 157–190). New York: Praeger.

Kitchener, R.F. (1982). Holism and the organismic model in developmental psychology. *Human Development, 25,* 233–249.

Knopf, R.C. (1987). Human behavior, cognition, and affect in the natural environment. In D. Stokols & I. Altman (Eds.), *Handbook of environmental psychology*. New York: Wiley.

Korosec-Serfaty, P. (1985). Experiences and uses of the dwelling. In I. Altman & C.M. Werner (Eds.), *Home environments: Vol. 8, Human behavior and environment: Advances in theory and research* (pp. 65–86). New York: Plenum.

Laszlo, E. (1972). *The systems view of the world*. New York: Braziller.

Leont'ev, A.N. (1981). The problem of activity in psychology. In J.V. Wertsch (Ed.), *The concept of activity in soviet psychology*. Armonk, NY: Sharpe.

Lewin, K. (1936). *Principles of topological psychology*. New York: McGraw-Hill.

Lewin, K. (1964). *Field theory in social science*. New York: Harper.

Lewis, M., & Lee-Painer, S. (1974). An interactional approach to the mother-infant dyad. In M. Lewis & L.A. Rosenblum (Eds.), *The effect of the infant on its caretaker* (pp. 21–48). New York: Wiley.

Magnusson, D., & Endler, N.S. (Eds.) (1977). *Personality at the crossroads: Current issues in interactional psychology.* Hillsdale, NJ: Erlbaum.

Michaels, C.F., & Carello, C. (1981). *Direct perception.* Englewood Cliffs, NJ: Prentice-Hall.

Miller, J.G. (1978). *Living systems.* New York: McGraw-Hill.

Minuchin, S. (1974). *Families and family therapy.* Cambridge, MA: Harvard University Press.

Moore, G. (1987). Environment and behavior research in North America. In D. Stokols & I. Altman (Eds.), *Handbook of environmental psychology* New York: Wiley.

Moos, R.H., & Lemke, S. (1984). Supportive residential settings for older people. In I. Altman, M.P. Lawton, & J.F. Wohlwill (Eds.), *Elderly People and the Environment: Vol. 7. Human behavior and environment: Advances in theory and research* (pp. 159–190). New York: Plenum.

Murphy, G. (1947). *Personality: A biosocial approach to origins and structure.* New York: Harper.

Norberg-Schulz, C. (1971). *Existence, space and architecture.* New York: Praeger.

Overton, W.F., & Reese, H.W. (1973). Models of development: Methodological implications. In J.R. Nesselroade & H.W. Reese (Eds.), *Lifespan developmental psychology: Methodological issues* (pp. 65–86). New York: Academic.

Pepper, S.C. (1942). *World hypotheses: A study in evidence.* Berkeley: University of California Press.

Pepper, S.C. (1967). *Concept and quality: A world hypothesis.* La Salle, IL: Open Court.

Pervin, L.A., & Lewis, M. (Eds.) (1977). *Perspectives in interactional psychology.* New York: Plenum.

Piaget, J. (1952). *The origins of intelligence in children.* New York: Norton.

Proshansky, H.M. (1976). *Environmental psychology: A methodological orientation.* In H.M. Proshansky, W.H. Ittelson, & L.G. Rivlin (Eds.), *Environmental psychology: People and their physical settings* (pp. 59–69). New York: Holt, Rinehart & Winston.

Proshansky, H.M. (1987). The field of environmental psychology: Securing its future. In D. Stokols & I. Altman (Eds.), *Handbook of environmental psychology.* New York: Wiley.

Rapoport, A. (1977). *Human aspects of urban form.* Oxford, England: Pergammon.

Rapoport, A. (1982). *The meaning of the built environment.* Beverly Hills, CA: Sage.

Relph, E.C. (1976). *Place and placelessness.* London: Pion.

Riegel, K.F. (1976). From traits and equilibrium toward developmental dialectics. In W.J. Arnold (Ed.), *Nebraska Symposium on Motivation* (pp. 349–407). Lincoln: University of Nebraska Press.

Riegel, K.F. (1979). *Foundations of dialectic psychology.* New York: Academic.

Rosnow, R.L. (1981). *Paradigms in transition: The methodology of social inquiry.* New York: Oxford University Press.

Rowles, G.D. (1980). Growing old "inside": Aging and attachment to place in an Appalachian community. In N. Datan & A. Lahmann (Eds.), *Transitions of aging* (pp. 153–170). New York: Academic.

Rowles, G.D. (1984). Aging in rural environments. In I. Altman, M.P. Lawton, & J.F. Wohlwill (Eds.), *Elderly People And The Environment: Vol. 7, Human behavior and environment: Advances in theory and research* (pp. 129–157). New York: Plenum.

Rychlak, J.F. (1977). *The psychology of rigorous humanism.* New York: Wiley.

Saile, D.G. (1977). Building rituals and spatial concepts in the Pueblo Indian world: Making a house. *Architectural Association Quarterly, 9* (2), 72–81.

Saile, D.G. (1985). The ritual establishment of home. In I. Altman & C.M. Werner (Ed.), *Home Environments: Vol. 8, Human behavior and environment: Advances in theory and research* (pp. 87–112). New York: Plenum.

Sarbin, T.R. (1977). Contextualism: A world view for modern psychology. In A.W. Landfield (Ed.), *Nebraska Symposium On Motivation* (Vol. 24, pp. 1–41). Lincoln: University of Nebraska Press.

Seamon, D. (1979). *A geography of the life world.* New York: St. Martin's.

Seamon, D. (1982). The phenomenological contribution to environmental psychology. *Journal of Environmental Psychology, 2,* 119–140.

Sommer, R. (1987). Dreams, reality, and the future of environmental psychology. In D. Stokols & I. Altman (Eds.), *Handbook of environmental psychology.* New York: Wiley.

Stokols, D. (1981). Group x place transactions: Some neglected issues in psychological research on settings. In D. Magnusson (Eds.), *Toward a psychology of situations: An interactional perspective* (pp. 393–415). Hillsdale, NJ: Erlbaum.

Stokols, D. (1987). Scientific and policy challenges of a contextually-oriented psychology. In D. Stokols & I. Altman (Eds.), *Handbook of environmental psychology* New York: Wiley.

Stokols, D., & Novaco, R.W. (1981). Transportation and well-being: An ecological perspective. In I. Altman, J.F. Wohlwill & P.B. Everett (Eds.), *Transportation environment: Advances in therapy and research* (pp. 85–130). New York: Plenum.

Stokols, D., & Shumaker, S.A. (1981). People in places: A transactional view of settings. In J. Harvey (Ed.), *Cognition, social behavior and the environment* (pp. 441–488). Hillsdale, NJ: Erlbaum.

Sundstrom, E. (1978). Crowding as a sequential process: Review of research on the effects of population density on humans. In A. Baum & Y.M. Epstein (Eds.), *Human response to crowding* (pp. 32–116). Hillsdale, NJ: Erlbaum.

Taylor, R.B. (1987). Toward an environmental psychology of disorder: Delinquency, crime and fear of crime. In D. Stokols & I. Altman (Eds.), *Handbook of environmental psychology.* New York: Wiley.

Tuan, Y.F. (1974). *Topophilia: A study of environmental perception, attitude and values.* Englewood Cliffs, NJ: Prentice-Hall.

Tuan, Y.F. (1977). *Space and place: The perspective of experience.* Minneapolis: University of Minnesota Press.

Tuan, Y.F. (1982). *Segmented worlds and self: Group life and individual consciousness.* Minneapolis: University of Minnesota Press.

Tyler, L.E. (1981). More stately mansions— Psychology extends its boundaries. In M.R. Rosezweig & L.W. Porter (Eds.), *Annual Review of Psychology* (Vol. 32, pp. 1–20). Palo Alto, CA: Annual Reviews.

Von Bertalanffy, L. (1968). *General system theory.* New York: Braziller.

Vygotsky, L.S. (1978). *Mind in society: The development of higher psychological processes.* Cambridge: MA: Harvard University Press.

Wapner, S. (1981). Transactions of persons-in-environments: Some critical transitions. *Journal of Environmental Psychology, 1,* 223–239.

Wapner, S. (1987). A holistic, developmental, systems-oriented environmental psychology: Some beginnings. In D. Stokols & I. Altman (Eds.), *Handbook of environmental psychology.* New York: Wiley.

Wapner, S., Kaplan, B., & Cohen, S.B. (1973). An organismic-developmental perspective for understanding transactions of men and environments. *Environment and Behavior, 5,* 255–289.

Watzlawick, P., Beavin, J.H., & Jackson, D.D. (1967). *The pragmatics of human communication.* New York: Norton.

Werner, C.M., Altman, I., & Oxley, D. (1985). Temporal aspects of homes: A transactional perspective. In I. Altman & C.M. Werner (Eds.), *Home Environments: Vol. 8, Human behavior and environment: Advances in theory and research* (pp. 1–32). New York: Plenum.

Wicker, A.W. (1982). *An introduction to ecological psychology.* New York: Cambridge University Press. (Original work published 1979)

Wicker, A.W. (1987). An expanded conceptual framework for analyzing behavior settings. In D. Stokols & I. Altman (Eds.), *Handbook of environmental psychology.* New York: Wiley.

Wohlwill, J.F., & Heft, H. (1987). The physical environment and the development of the child. In D. Stokols & I. Altman (Eds.), *Handbook of environmental psychology.* New York: Wiley.

Chapter 2

CONCEPTUAL STRATEGIES OF ENVIRONMENTAL PSYCHOLOGY

Daniel Stokols, *Program in Social Ecology, University of California, Irvine, California*

2.1. INTRODUCTION

In Chapter 1, Altman and Rogoff traced the historical development of four philosophical world views within psychology: trait, interactionist, organismic, and transactional perspectives. They suggest that, while trait and interactionist analyses have received most attention to date, recent work reflects an emerging trend toward the development of organismic and, particularly, transactional models of behavior. Altman and Rogoff conclude their chapter with the following cautionary note:

> The lure of the transactional approach is simultaneously coupled with a sense of uncertainty. How does one build a theory of holistic, changing phenomena? What methods can we use to study phenomena at a holistic level? How do we incorpo-

rate change and temporal factors as part of psychological phenomena? (p. 37)

These questions pose an ambitious but promising agenda for future work in environmental psychology: namely, *the translation of a transactional world view into operational strategies for theory development and research.* Whereas some researchers have characterized environmental psychology as a "problem-centered rather than theory-centered set of activities" organized around the solution of community problems (Darley & Gilbert, 1985, p. 949), it is clear that much of the work in this field has focused on more basic theoretical tasks such as the development of new concepts and methods for understanding the ecological context of behavior and the transactions between people and places (cf. Barker, 1968; Holahan, 1986; Ittelson, 1973; Stokols, 1983; Winkel,

Chapter 3, Wapner, Chapter 41, this volume). Future elaborations of this work may well succeed in achieving the kind of comprehensive scientific expression of transactionalism called for by Altman and Rogoff, Barker, Wapner, Winkel, and others in the environment and behavior field.

A fundamental feature of transactional research is its emphasis on the dynamic interplay between people and their everyday environmental settings, or "contexts." This chapter offers certain conceptual strategies for organizing *contextual* theorizing and research. It should be noted at the outset that this chapter does not review the numerous theoretical paradigms that have emerged within the field of environmental psychology over the past two decades; comprehensive coverage of these developments is provided in Section 2 of this volume. Rather the chapter focuses on some of the more general, metatheoretical issues that are inherent in the development of contextually oriented analyses of environment and behavior.

2.2. EMERGENCE OF A CONTEXTUAL PERSPECTIVE IN PSYCHOLOGY

During the 1970s and early 1980s, a growing interest in contextualism occurred within several areas of psychological research. Psychologists within every major area of the discipline noted the deficiencies of decontextualized research and called for more holistic and ecologically grounded approaches to the study of behavior. In the fields of clinical, biological, and health psychology, for example, Schwartz (1982) proposed a *biopsychosocial* view of health and illness, which replaces "single-cause, single-effect" models with those that address the complex interactions among physiological, psychological, and social dimensions of well-being. Similarly the volumes by Magnusson and Allen (1983) and by Wapner and Kaplan (1983) call for holistic approaches to the study of human development and are part of an ever widening stream of ecologically oriented research in developmental psychology (cf. earlier discussions of this research by Bronfenbrenner, 1979; Scarr, 1979). Within the fields of cognitive, personality, and social psychology, the volumes by Gergen (1982), Kaplan and Kaplan (1982), and Neisser (1982) and the articles by Georgoudi and Rosnow (1985), Kelley (1983), Little (1983), McGuire (1983), Smith (1983), and Veroff (1983) are indicative of an increasing trend toward contextual analyses of cognition and social behavior. Altman (1982), in his Presidential Address to the Di-

vision of Population and Environmental Psychology, contended that we are in the midst of a full-fledged scientific revolution across all areas of psychology, involving a shift from unidirectional, mechanistic analyses of environment and behavior toward transactional and contextually oriented models. Little (Chapter 7, this volume) has referred to these developments as the "contextual revolution" in psychology.

The terms *ecological* and *contextual* are certainly not new to psychologists. Explicit concern for the ecological context of behavior was evident in the writings of Koffka (1935), Lewin (1936), Murray (1938) and Tolman and Brunswik (1935), during the mid-1930s and in the subsequent work of Barker (1968), Chein (1954), Gibson (1960), Jessor (1958), and Kohler (1947). But the emergence of areas such as population, community, and environmental psychology during the sixties and seventies signaled a surge of interest in ecological issues that in recent years has begun to pervade more established areas of the field as well (cf. Barker & Schoggen, 1973; Craik, 1973; Fawcett, 1973; Heller & Monahan, 1977; Kelly, 1985; Proshansky, Ittelson, & Rivlin, 1976; Russell & Ward, 1982; Saegert, 1985; Sarason, 1976; Stokols, 1978a).

The current popularity of contextual approaches in psychology appears to be rooted in both societal and intellectual developments. At the community level, concerns about global population growth, resource shortages, and environmental decay have increased the salience of ecological constraints on behavior. And, at a more academic level, the growing emphasis on contextual theorizing and research in psychology can be viewed as part of a conceptual shift within the behavioral sciences away from exclusively intrapersonal explanations of behavior, toward those that encompass not only the immediate social environment but also the broader cultural, historical, and geographic milieu of people's day-to-day activities (cf. Cronbach, 1975; Gergen & Gergen, 1984; Manicas & Secord, 1983).

Whatever its sources and the differences in terminology that surface among its proponents, the contextual perspective in psychology seems to be associated with certain widely shared core assumptions. Among these assumptions are: (1) that psychological phenomena should be viewed in relation to the spatial, temporal, and sociocultural milieu in which they occur; (2) that a focus on individuals' responses to discrete stimuli and events in the short run should be supplemented by more molar and longitudinal analyses of people's everyday activities and settings; (3) that the search for lawful and generalizable relationships between environment and behavior should be balanced by a sensitivity to, and analysis of, the situation specificity of psychological phenomena (cf. Cronbach, 1975; Gergen, 1973); and (4) that the criteria of ecological and external validity should be explicitly considered (along with the internal validity of the research) not only when designing behavioral studies but also when judging the applicability of research findings to the development of public policies and community interventions (cf. Brinberg & McGrath, 1985; Cook & Campbell, 1979; Winkel, Chapter 3, this volume).

While there have been much discussion about the virtues of contextualism and some agreement about its general assumptions, considerably less progress has been made in translating these assumptions into more specific guidelines for theory development and empirical research (for notable exceptions to this trend see Barker & Schoggen, 1973; Bronfenbrenner, 1979; Little, Chapter 7, Wicker, Chapter 16, this volume). Lest contextualism become an empty buzzword, several difficult questions must be addressed. First, what are the distinguishing features of contextual theorizing and research? *Specifically, what features differentiate a contextual analysis from a noncontextual one?* Second, are psychological research questions differentially suited to a contextual approach? That is, *for which psychological phenomena is a contextual analysis warranted and for which is it not?* And, third, in those instances where a contextual perspective is adopted, what criteria determine the scope and content of the variables included in the analysis? *What particular considerations should guide the researcher's decisions about how broadly to draw the contextual boundaries of a phenomenon, and which concepts and methods to use in analyzing the relationships between the phenomenon at hand and the specific contexts in which it is observed?*

The complexity of these questions suggests the value of adopting a more systematic approach to contextual theorizing than has usually been taken. What has been lacking in earlier studies of environment and behavior is a set of programmatic guidelines for contextual theorizing and research. As an initial foundation for establishing this more systematic approach, the following sections of the chapter outline certain distinctive features of contextual research and offer a set of dimensions for mapping important sources of situational influence on behavior. The proposed dimensions include the spatial, temporal, and sociocultural scope of an analysis; the integration of objective and subjective perspectives on environment and behavior; the use of both individual and aggregate levels of analysis; and the

partitive or composite representation of situations. Taken together, these dimensions provide a framework for developing contextual theories, or those that account for the cross-situational variability of psychological and behavioral events.

The construction of psychological theories is often regarded as a strictly intuitive matter rather than as a process that can be systematically described and enhanced. Furthermore many researchers contend that efforts to develop behavioral theories are best postponed until a substantial body of empirical facts about a phenomenon has been amassed across several studies. By contrast, this chapter assumes that the application of theoretical strategies for mapping the context of behavior can be valuable, especially during the early stages of research, as a tool for discovering the situational boundaries of psychological phenomena, specifying the dimensions on which diverse settings can be meaningfully compared, and estimating the applied utility of our theories and policy recommendations before these ideas and interventions are implemented in a costly and sometimes ineffective manner.

A subsequent section of the chapter examines some of the ways in which the proposed strategies of contextual analysis can contribute to the policy relevance of psychological research. It is suggested that the applied utility of psychological research depends not only on the scientific validity of our theories and data but also on the complexity of the settings toward which our policy recommendations are targeted. In particular, the use of contextual analysis in identifying leverage points for community interventions and criteria for judging their cost-effectiveness is discussed.

2.3. STRATEGIES OF CONTEXTUAL ANALYSIS

2.3.1. Contextual and Noncontextual Research

A fundamental idea underlying the notion of contextual research is the concept of embeddedness. That is, a particular phenomenon is thought to be embedded in (and influenced by) a surrounding set of events. The first task of contextual research is to identify the central or *target phenomenon* to be examined. Once the target variables have been specified, the next step is to define a set of situational or *contextual variables* that are thought to exert an important influence on the form and occurrence of the target phenomenon.

Figure 2.1. The everyday environment of a hypothetical individual as it exists in three-dimensional space. (*Source:* "A Time-Geographic Simulation Model of Individual Activity Programmes" by B. Lenntorp, in *Human Activity and Time Geography* by T. Carlstein, D. Parkes, and N. Thrift(Eds.), Halsted Press, 1978, copyright 1978 by John Wiley & Sons. Adapted by permission.)

For example, Figure 2.1 depicts the everyday environment of a hypothetical individual as it exists in three-dimensional space. Suppose that we are interested in the relationship between automobile commuting and stress, and that our main target variables are the distance of the commute between the individual's dwelling and workplace and his or her average blood pressure levels on arrival at work. Having specified these target predictor and outcome variables, we might suspect that their relationship is qualified by other aspects of the commute such as the size and luxuriousness of the individual's vehicle and the typical levels of traffic congestion encountered along the route (e.g., perhaps the commuter drives to and from work through the center of town or, alternatively, takes a longer but less congested route through the countryside). Also we might hypothesize that the relationship between driving distance and blood pressure on arrival at work is moderated by certain life circumstances extending beyond the immediate commuting situation such as the overall quality of a person's residential situation and the extent to which the inconveniences of a long commute are offset by attractive neighborhood amenities, or the degree to which the commuter is satisfied with and involved in his or her job (cf. Stokols & Novaco, 1981). These additional variables are "contextual" in the sense that they surround (or are connected in time and space with) the individual's experience of the commute to work and are thought to influence the quality and intensity of that experience.

If we hypothesize that the relationship between the target variables of commuting distance and blood pressure is not influenced by surrounding events, then there is no need to complicate our analysis by incorporating additional measures of the individual's driving, residential, and work situations. For example, we might predict that long commuting distances (e.g., 25 miles or longer) invariably raise systolic and diastolic blood pressure levels, regardless of the context in which these variables are observed. If this hypothesis is correct, then the inclusion of contextual variables in our analysis would not add appreciably to our understanding of the target phenomenon.

If, on the other hand, we suspect that the relationship between commuting distance and blood pressure *is* significantly qualified by situational factors, then it becomes important to include these factors in our analyses of the target variables. For if we hypothesize and find that the stressfulness of automobile commuting is moderated by the perceived quality of one's residential and work environments then we have learned more about the relationship between commuting and stress than if we had focused exclusively on the links between commuting distance and blood pressure (irrespective of home and job satisfaction levels).

To summarize, *noncontextual research* focuses entirely on the relationships between target predictor and outcome variables (e.g., commuting distance and blood pressure levels). *Contextual research*, on the other hand, incorporates supplementary predictor variables drawn from the immediate situation (e.g., levels of traffic congestion encountered along the route, size and amenities of one's vehicle) or from other areas of a person's life situation (e.g., levels of residential and job satisfaction) that presumably qualify the relationship between the target variables.

With respect to criterion (outcome) measures, a contextual analysis might incorporate not only blood pressure measurements on arrival at work but also cross-setting assessments of emotional stress, coping strategies, and behavioral problems observed within the commuter's residential and recreational domains. A contextual approach thereby widens the scope of analysis to include not only the target variables of commuting distance and blood pressure but also supplementary indexes of environment and behavior that qualify the relationship among these variables.

2.3.2. Distinguishing Features of Contextual Theories

Given a particular set of target variables, the selection of contextual variables for empirical analysis can proceed either in an exploratory and atheoretical fashion or on the basis of theoretically derived assumptions about the target phenomenon. Lacking a well-developed theory, the researcher may begin with a tentative hunch about one or more situational moderators of the target variables. If the relevant data on these situational factors can be conveniently gathered, the researcher may pursue his or her hunch by examining the empirical relationships among the contextual and target variables. These exploratory analyses can play a useful role in the early stages of theory development by revealing situational factors that significantly influence the target variables and by excluding from further consideration those that do not.

A more systematic and powerful form of contextual analysis occurs when the research design and the empirical assessments of situational and target variables are explicitly guided by a *contextual theory*. A distinguishing feature of contextual theories is that they specify a pattern of cross-situational variation in the target phenomenon (cf. Stokols, 1983). If, for example, the target variables are commuting distance and blood pressure, then a contextual hypothesis explicitly predicts a change in the relationship between these variables, depending on the presence or absence of certain situational factors. And a contextual theory goes on to explain *why* the hypothesized cross-situational variations in the target phenomenon occur.

In contrast, *noncontextual theories* do not predict or explain cross-situational variation in the relationships among target variables. For instance, *environmental or situationist theories* construe behavior simply as a function of the immediate target situation (e.g., "Routine exposure to long-distance commutes invariably raises commuters' blood pressure."). *Trait theories* account for individual behavior entirely

in terms of personal dispositions (e.g., "Type A or coronary-prone commuters exhibit higher blood pressure upon arrival at work than Type B individuals, regardless of the distance of their commutes."). And *interactionist theories* account for behavior in terms of the joint influence of situational and intrapersonal factors.[1] For instance, Stokols and Novaco (1981) observed that commuters' blood pressure and task performance were jointly influenced by the physical distance of their commutes and by their personal dispositions toward coronary-prone behavior. In this instance, the relationship between commuting distance and behavior was moderated by an intrapersonal attribute rather than by a contextual factor. The focus of contextual theories, on the other hand, is clearly on situational rather than intrapersonal moderators of environment–behavior relationships. Thus, in contrast to environmental, trait, and interactional models, contextual theories specify a set of situational boundary conditions that qualify the relationship among target predictor and response variables.

The distinction between contextual and noncontextual theories is important, as it suggests a programmatic strategy for future research in environmental psychology: namely the development of theories that explicitly account for the situational specificity of environment–behavior relationships. Often the discovery of contextual moderators of environment–behavior relationships is treated as an "afterthought" of empirical analyses. The identification of important contextual factors tends to occur through post hoc rather than deductive assessments of external validity, or the extent to which research findings generalize across different groups of people, settings, and times (cf. Campbell & Stanley, 1963; Cook & Campbell, 1979; Mook, 1983; Petrinovich, 1979). Consequently information about contextual factors is acquired in a nonprogrammatic, happenstance manner as researchers gradually compare the findings from their separate and independently conducted studies. For example, early formulations of human response to crowding and noise treated these phenomena in a decontextualized manner, as if they could be understood apart from the contexts in which they occur. Accordingly, empirical studies were designed to test universalistic, transsituational hypotheses about the effects of these environmental conditions on behavior and well-being. The pattern of results from these early studies, however, was far more complex than had been anticipated, revealing striking differences in people's reactions to crowding and noise depending on the situational contexts in which these events were experienced. Eventually, more contextually oriented formulations of crowding and noise were developed to account for the diverse and often contradictory findings obtained across multiple programs of research (cf. Cohen & Spacapan, 1984; Evans, 1982; Stokols, 1979).

Considering the progression of research on crowding and noise, it seems reasonable to suggest that future studies of environment and behavior could be designed more efficiently and programmatically if contextual theories were developed prior to, or as an intended outcome of, empirical research. By making the explicit consideration of contextual factors a routine part of the research process, important aspects of the target phenomenon might be revealed that otherwise would have been neglected. And oversimplified assumptions about the cross-situational generality of the phenomenon might be recognized and abandoned during the early rather than later phases of investigation.

As a general guideline for future research, an effort should be made to identify plausible contextual moderators of environment–behavior relationships in a predictive rather than post hoc fashion. This is not to suggest, however, that all target phenomena will be equally amenable to contextual analysis. For instance, many studies conducted across a wide range of settings indicate that exposure to extremely high levels of noise invariably elevates cardiovascular arousal (cf. Cohen & Weinstein, 1981). Apparently once a certain threshold of noise intensity is exceeded, the impact of this environmental factor becomes relatively uniform across individuals and settings. Also, although the behavioral and emotional effects of certain drugs are mediated by situational factors (cf. Schachter & Singer, 1962; Whalen & Henker, 1980), other pharmacological processes may be more exclusively dependent on intrapersonal factors and the type of drug introduced than on more remote aspects of the individual's spatial and social environment. Thus certain psychophysiological phenomena may be relatively invariant across a wide array of situations.

The researcher's decision to adopt or not adopt a contextual view of a given problem is therefore likely to be influenced by several considerations such as existing empirical evidence for either the cross-situational variability or the stability of the target phenomenon and the theoretical objectives of the research (e.g., whether the investigator is attempting to test hypotheses about intrapersonal or situational moderators of the target phenomenon). Moreover whether or not a contextual perspective is actually translated into an operational research design may ultimately depend on more pragmatic considerations — especially the availability of sufficient research funding, personnel, and time to permit empirical study of the phenomenon across different environmental settings.

2.3.3. Criteria for Evaluating Contextual Theories

Having mentioned some of the distinctive features of contextual theories, it is important to specify criteria for evaluating their scientific and practical value. Contextual analyses of environment and behavior can have significant advantages over noncontextual approaches, particularly when there is reason to expect that the behavior or health effects of an environmental condition are mediated by situational factors. But once the researcher has opted for a contextual approach, the question then arises: Which set of contextual variables affords the greatest analytic leverage for understanding the target phenomenon?

The Effective Context

Clearly any phenomenon can be analyzed in relation to multiple and alternative contextual factors. The key challenge in developing contextual theories is to identify from among the myriad of potentially relevant situational factors those that are most crucial for understanding the form and occurrence of the target phenomenon. I will refer to that subset of influential situational factors as the *effective context* of the target phenomenon (cf. Stokols, 1983).

The effective context for a given set of target variables is never completely knowable or specifiable, because the range of situational factors that affect a phenomenon is potentially infinite, and future environmental conditions that may impinge on individuals and groups can only be estimated rather than predicted unequivocally (cf. Manicas & Secord, 1983). Nonetheless the hypothetical notion of an effective context is useful in prompting researchers to consider the *plausible range* of situational factors that are likely to influence a phenomenon as it occurs within a particular time and place, and to distinguish (on the basis of prior theory, research, and intuition) among those factors in terms of their relative impact on the target variables.

The concept of effective context raises certain fundamental questions about the scientific and practical adequacy of contextual theories. First, how accurately does a theory specify the relationships between a set of target variables and a particular contextual variable? Second, how completely does the theory represent the full range of important contextual moderators of the target variables? Even if a theory accurately represents the relationships between the target variables and one or more situational factors, it may fail to identify other (and perhaps more important) contextual moderators of the target phenomenon. And, third, what is the generative potential of the theory, or its capacity to provoke new insights about important contextual moderators of a target phenomenon that were not explicitly stated in the initial version of the theory? A theory may offer an incomplete account of the effective context of a phenomenon but in so doing may prompt researchers to discover new relationships between the target variables and additional contextual factors that had been overlooked in prior theorizing and research.

The questions discussed suggest certain key criteria for comparing and evaluating contextual theories, as described in the following.

Contextual Validity

The term *contextual validity* refers to the accuracy of a theory in specifying the pattern of relations among a set of target variables and one or more situational factors. For example, if a theory predicts that poststressor performance decrements are more likely to occur when the stressor is uncontrollable than when it is controllable, and the available evidence from several research programs fits the predicted pattern (cf. Cohen, 1980; Glass & Singer, 1972; Lazarus, 1966), then the theory is assumed to be valid over the range of contextual circumstances that it specifies. The contextual validity of a theory is low to the extent that it incorporates situational factors that have no influence on the occurrence and form of the target phenomenon, or those that affect the target variables in a manner that is contrary to the predicted pattern.

As mentioned earlier, many theories fail to specify the contextual moderators of a phenomenon altogether. These noncontextual theories are exemplified by statements like: "Exposure to high levels of noise invariably leads to negative aftereffects on task performance." Such statements assume that the hypothesized relations among target variables are universally valid across all situations. Any evidence of change in the target phenomenon as a function of one or more situational factors necessarily undermines the contextual validity of the original theory.

A basic question raised by the proposed concept of contextual validity concerns its potential redundancy or overlap with the related criteria of predic-

tive, external, ecological, and construct validity. Although contextual validity bears certain similarities to these concepts, it can be differentiated from them in some important respects. First, contextual validity can be defined as a subcategory of predictive validity. Contextual validity explicitly pertains to the accuracy with which a theory specifies the *cross-situational* variations in a phenomenon. Predictive validity, as it is typically defined, does not require cross-situational analysis (cf. Carmines & Zeller, 1979). A noncontextual theory might demonstrate a high degree of predictive validity within a single setting but fail to specify important moderators of the phenomenon that would only become evident in alternative and as yet unobserved settings. Thus high predictive validity of a theory within a particular setting is a necessary but not sufficient condition for contextual validity. Contextual validity specifically requires that a theory be valid in its predictions about the cross-situational variation of a target phenomenon.

Also, though the concepts of contextual, external, and ecological validity share certain similarities, they are not entirely overlapping. External validity refers to the generalizability of research findings or a proposed causal relation across populations of persons, settings, and times (cf. Campbell & Stanley, 1963; Cook & Campbell, 1979). Definitions of ecological validity are more diverse, but most emphasize Brunswik's (1956) original notion of *representativeness*—that is, the extent to which an existing event or situation is similar to, or representative of, another (cf. Bronfenbrenner, 1979; Petrinovich, 1979; Wohlwill, 1978; Winkel, Chapter 3, this volume). Contextual validity, as defined earlier, also involves an assessment of the cross-situational generalizability of theories and an appraisal of the similarity among different settings. But the present analysis of contextual validity diverges from earlier treatments of external and ecological validity in the following respects. First, although Cook and Campbell (1979) and others (e.g., Wohlwill, 1978) have distinguished between inductive and deductive analyses of external validity, recent reviews of research within several areas of psychology reveal that assessments of external validity are usually conducted in a post hoc rather than a priori fashion (cf. Dipboye & Flanagan, 1979; Mook, 1983; Winkel, Chapter 3, this volume). These atheoretical assessments of external validity often reflect what Mook (1983) has referred to as "count 'em mechanics"—the comparison of two or more situations on the basis of a haphazard rather than theoretically derived checklist of their immediately obvious differences. By contrast, contextual validity can be assessed only in relation to those theories that explicitly posit cross-situational variations in a target phenomenon as functions of one or more contextual factors.

Another difference between the proposed concept of contextual validity and certain earlier treatments of external and ecological validity pertains to the types of situational factors invoked as evidence for the similarity of settings and for the generalizability of theories and findings across those settings. Assessments of external and ecological validity often have focused entirely on objective and readily observable attributes of places and people such as the degree of physical naturalism evident in field versus laboratory settings or the demographic similarities among individuals comprising different populations (cf. Berkowitz & Donnerstein, 1982; Brunswik, 1956; Dipboye & Flanagan, 1979; Mook, 1983). This overemphasis on objective or naturalistic criteria of external and ecological validity is unfortunate, as it has led to the neglect of more subtle, transactional dimensions of settings that impinge on individual and collective behavior. The present analysis of contextual validity, however, gives explicit attention to transactional and subjective (as well as objective) representations of settings and emphasizes their relevance to appraisals of the cross-situational generality of psychological theories.

The criterion of contextual validity is most similar to Winkel's (Chapter 3, this volume) conceptualization of ecological validity. Winkel explicitly links the assessment of ecological validity to a theoretical and empirical modeling process in which the researcher attempts to identify those aspects of situations that exert an important influence on psychological and behavioral phenomena. He defines ecological validity as:

> The extent to which the overall design of the research plan and the specific measuring instruments that are employed yield accurate estimates of the multiple dimensionality of the phenomenon that is the focus of study and those components of the context that may be expected to influence variation in the phenomenon. (p. 83)

Winkel further states that his definition of ecological validity refers not only to the adequacy of the methods and procedures incorporated within the research plan but also to the explanatory system that is advanced to account for the findings.

The proposed criterion of contextual validity diverges from Winkel's conception of ecological validity in two important respects. First, the former concept focuses in a more limited way on the adequacy of theoretical formulations, rather than research techniques, in identifying cross-situational variations in the target phenomenon. A theory may accurately specify the contextual moderators of a phenomenon, yet the methods chosen to assess the theory may themselves be unreliable and/or invalid. The present analysis, therefore, treats the contextual validity of theories and the construct validity of methods (cf. Cook & Campbell, 1979) as two separate, albeit closely related, issues, whereas Winkel's analysis subsumes these issues under the broader concept of ecological validity.

Second, as an alternative to the post hoc, atheoretical assessments of ecological validity that are prevalent in behavioral research, the present analysis of contextual validity emphasizes the value of a priori theorizing about the situational moderators of target phenomena. This perspective is not meant to deny the usefulness of inductive, exploratory studies as a basis for developing empirically grounded explanations of the relations between target and contextual variables (cf. Glaser & Strauss, 1967; Winkel, Chapter 3, this volume). Nevertheless the present analysis gives relatively greater attention to the theory development (vs. data collection) phase of contextual research and underscores the scientific value of developing predictive (vs. post hoc) theories about the situational moderators of target phenomena.

Finally it is important to note certain divergencies between earlier discussions of construct validity (cf. Cook & Campbell, 1979) and the proposed criterion of contextual validity. *Construct validity* generally refers to the degree of match between research operations and theoretical constructs—that is, the extent to which the former adequately represent the latter. From the perspective of construct validity, contextual factors that alter the relationships among target variables are viewed as situational *confoundings* of the presumed causes and effects (i.e., the target predictor and outcome variables). Many of the threats to construct validity discussed by Cook and Campbell (e.g., the interaction between testing situations and treatment; restricted sampling of treatment and response levels and of testing intervals) relate to sources of situational confounding that can distort the researcher's assessments of the target variables. From the perspective of contextual theorizing, however, the identification of situational sources of variation in the target phenomenon becomes important, not as a means for achieving a clean or unconfounded representation of the target phenomenon, but rather as the basis for developing a broader theoretical understanding of the relationships between target phenomena and their situational contexts (for further discussions of this perspective see also Petrinovich, 1979; Winkel, Chapter 3, this volume). Thus whereas the construct validity perspective is oriented toward identifying sources of situational confounding and eliminating them from research assessments of the target phenomenon, the goal of contextual theorizing is to incorporate potential sources of situational variability into more integrative and environmentally contingent explanations of behavior.

In summary, the concept of contextual validity is distinguishable from several related validity criteria and offers a practical guideline for encouraging the development of theories that are sensitive to cross-situational variations in environment–behavior relationships. Although the criterion of contextual validity can be applied as an "absolute" standard for evaluating individual theories, its utility as a tool for theorizing and research becomes most apparent when one is attempting to choose among alternative theories of the same phenomenon. In the earlier-mentioned example of commuting and stress, one theory might predict that high levels of social support among co-workers *intensify* the cardiovascular strains of long-distance commuting because the individual is eager to arrive at the workplace each day and therefore is likely to be frustrated by travel delays that impede the journey to work. On the other hand, an alternative theory might predict that high levels of social support at work *buffer* the stressful effects of long-distance commuting by providing psychological "compensation" for the inconveniences experienced during the daily drive to work (cf. Campbell, 1983). And a third theory might suggest that the availability of social support at work has *no influence* on the relationships between commuting distance and blood pressure, but that other situational factors such as the crowdedness of one's home and neighborhood moderate the effects of driving distance on commuters' blood pressure. Each of these theories makes a different prediction about the role of social support among co-workers in moderating the relationship between commuting and stress. Thus the three theories can be evaluated in terms of their relative accuracy in predicting the empirically observed pattern of covariation among the target and contextual variables.

Relative Power and Efficiency of Contextual Theories

An additional criterion for gauging the adequacy of contextual theories is their *relative power*, or the extent to which they encompass the full range of situational factors that qualify a particular phenomenon. A contextual analysis may correctly identify some of those conditions but may exclude several others. For example, a theory may accurately account for the influence of social support at work on the relationship between commuting distance and stress. But if other contextual variables such as dwelling and neighborhood crowding are also important in explaining the target variable relationships, then a theory that focuses only on the moderating role of social support at work would be less powerful than one that explains the contextual influence of residential crowding, as well.

Alternatively a contextual analysis may be too inclusive, incorporating situational factors that are negligibly related to the target variables. This case suggests another criterion for evaluating contextual theories, namely, their *efficiency*. A contextual analysis is efficient to the extent that it includes those and only those situational factors that exert a significant influence on the target variables. In the preceding example, if we determine empirically that social support at work, but not home and neighborhood crowding, qualifies the relationships between commuting distance and blood pressure, then the theory that focuses only on the moderating role of social support would be more efficient than the one that also incorporates the variables of home and neighborhood crowding. The theories may be equally powerful in explaining the moderating role of social support at work, but the former is more efficient or parsimonious than the latter because it omits the trivial variables of residential and neighborhood crowding.

Thus it is possible to evaluate theories not only in terms of their accuracy in specifying the relationships between a particular contextual factor and the target variables but also with respect to their power and efficiency in representing the full range of situational factors that collectively exert the greatest influence on the target phenomenon. In short, the power and efficiency of a contextual theory increase to the extent that it accounts for a large rather than small proportion of the effective context, while excluding those situational factors that are negligibly related to the target variables.

The criteria of relative power and efficiency are directly relevant to the questions raised earlier about which phenomena are amenable to contextual analysis and, for those that are, how broadly the effective context should be drawn. Because the range of influential contextual factors varies across psychological phenomena (with some being impervious to situational influence and others being highly dependent on the context in which they occur), it is important for researchers to give careful consideration to the effective context of the target phenomenon during the early stages of theorizing, and to be as selective as possible in deciding which contextual variables should be incorporated into their theories and research designs.

Generativity of Contextual Theories

Ideally theories of environment and behavior should demonstrate high levels of contextual validity, relative power, and efficiency. However, certain theories that are inadequate according to these criteria may still be valuable in sensitizing researchers to important situational moderators of psychological phenomena. Following Gergen's (1973, 1978) and Cronbach's (1975) discussions of the sensitization functions of theory, the generativity of contextual theories is defined here as their capacity to provoke new insights about important contextual moderators of a target phenomenon that were not explicitly stated in the initial version of the theory or in earlier theoretical and empirical work.

The generative potency of a theory is difficult to evaluate in the short run and requires a prospective analysis of the theory's impact on subsequent conceptualizations of a phenomenon. Nonetheless the generativity criterion is useful in that it underscores the importance of the sensitization functions of contextual theorizing and the potential contributions of preliminary yet provocative theories to the evolution of more valid, powerful, and efficient explanations of environment and behavior.

As an illustration of the generativity of contextual theories, consider the issue of environmental stress. A contextually narrow theory of stress might focus on the controllability or uncontrollability of the immediate stressor, without considering the moderating influence of other factors in the immediate situation, or of events occurring outside the situation within other life domains. A broader contextual analysis, however, would examine individuals' reactions to an environmental stressor as they are moderated by events both within and outside the immediate stressor situation. The mapping of stress phenomena in relation to one's overall life situation, for example, might suggest hypotheses about the ways in which uncontrollable stressors in one life domain are offset by highly desirable events within another (cf. Campbell, 1983; Jacobi, 1984); or about life-style factors associated with the temporal and spatial organi-

zation of one's life situation that may be promotive of Type A behavior, chronic stress, and health problems (cf. Cullen, 1978; Michelson, 1985). Thus the process of contextually mapping the phenomena of stress and well-being across the major settings of one's life may generate new insights about these phenomena that would be missed by a contextually narrower analysis.

This section has focused on evaluative criteria that are especially appropriate for judging the scientific value of contextual theories (see Table 2.1). There are, of course, several other criteria that apply equally well to assessments of noncontextual as well as contextual theories such as the theory's testability, its consistency with available empirical evidence, and its utility or applicability to everyday problem solving. The utility criterion is discussed in a subsequent section of this chapter pertaining to the policy relevance of contextual theorizing and research. For more general discussions of criteria for evaluating psychological theories, see Cook and Campbell (1979), Cronbach (1975), Gergen (1978), Platt (1964), and Shaw and Costanzo (1970).

2.3.4. Modeling the Effective Context of the Target Phenomenon

Faced with a multitude of potentially relevant situational factors, the process of identifying the effective context of various environment–behavior phenomena can be challenging and complex. One strategy for reducing the complexity of this task is to organize the search for situational moderators of the target phenomenon around certain basic dimensions of contextual analysis: namely, (1) the *contextual scope* of the analysis, as reflected in the range of spatial, temporal, and sociocultural factors that are thought to influence the target variable relationships; (2) the joint use of both *objective and subjective representations* of the target and contextual variables; (3) the *individual or aggregate level* at which contextual and target variable relationships are examined; and (4) the representation of people and environments in

Table 2.1. Criteria for Developing and Evaluating Contextual Theories

1. Contextual validity
2. Relative power
3. Efficiency
4. Generativity
5. Applied Utility

Table 2.2. Dimensions of Contextual Representation

1. Spatial, temporal, and cultural *scope*
2. Individual or aggregate *level*
3. Objective or subjective *focus*
4. Partitive or composite *structure*

terms of their independent or *partitive characteristics*, or in terms of higher-order, *composite concepts* (e.g., person–environment fit, place identity) that reflect the interdependence among people and their surroundings.

Any target phenomenon can be modeled in relation to these general contextual dimensions (see Table 2.2). The ensuing discussion examines each of the four mapping dimensions and the ways in which their systematic application can enhance the researcher's efforts to identify and operationally measure the effective context of the target phenomenon.

Contextual Scope: Spatial, Temporal, and Sociocultural Dimensions

The environmental contexts of people's day-to-day activities can be described in terms of their scale or complexity. The scale of environmental units ranges from the specific stimuli and situations that occur within a given setting to the more complex life domains that comprise multiple situations and settings. *Situations* are sequences of individual or group activities that occur at a particular time and place (cf. Forgas, 1979; Pervin, 1978). *Settings* are geographic locations in which various personal or interpersonal situations recur on a regular basis (cf. Stokols & Shumaker, 1981; Barker, Chapter 40, Wicker, Chapter 16, this volume). *Life domains* are different spheres of a person's life such as family, education, spiritual activities, recreation, employment, and commuting (cf. Campbell, 1981; Stokols & Novaco, 1981). An even broader unit of contextual analysis is the individual's *overall life situation* (cf. Magnusson, 1981), consisting of the major life domains in which a person is involved during a particular period of his or her life.

Just as environmental units can be arrayed with respect to their scale or complexity, contextual analyses can be compared in terms of their relative scope. The *contextual scope* of research refers to the scale of the contextual units included in the analysis. A set of target variables can be examined in relation to the immediate situation in which they occur, or in relation to broader and more remote segments of the

individual's life situation and life history. Moreover a contextual analysis may exclude any reference to the social–structural or cultural context of the target phenomenon or, alternatively, may encompass sociocultural conditions within the immediate target situation and those whose influence extends beyond that setting. Thus theoretical and empirical analyses of environment and behavior can be compared on at least three different dimensions of contextual scope: namely, spatial, temporal, and sociocultural scope.

The dimensions of contextual scope suggest an important distinction between the ecological environment as it exists in reality and the environment as it is modeled in relation to a particular individual or group. For example, Figure 2.1 offers a detailed geographic overview of a person's major life domains as they are arrayed in three-dimensional space. In Figure 2.2, however, the environment is represented more abstractly in terms of a daily activity program— that is, a record of the individual's distribution of daily activities and allocation of time across residential, transportation, employment, and commercial settings (cf. Lenntorp, 1978). The time-geographic simulation of an activity program is a highly selective representation of the individual's relationship to his or her environment because it describes only certain facets of that relationship—namely, the temporal and spatial distribution of one's daily activities. Thus even as the scale of the environmental units included in an analysis increases (e.g., from a focus on single situations to a broader analysis of multiple life domains) the actual number of contextual variables chosen to represent the relevant environmental dimensions might remain relatively small.

The *spatial scope* of an analysis increases to the extent that it represents places, processes, and events occurring within a broad rather than narrow region of the individual's (or group's) geographical environment. In Figure 2.2, the activity program encompasses a geographically broader range of settings (e.g., the home, workplace, commute to work, commercial areas) than a more limited record of one's behaviors within the dwelling alone. Similarly the *temporal scope* of an analysis increases to the extent that it represents places, processes, and events experienced by the individual or group within an extended rather than narrow time frame. For instance, a time budget summarizing the individual's typical allocation of activities over a calendar year would be of broader temporal scope than one compiled in relation to a single 24-hour period. Finally the *sociocultural scope* of an analysis increases to the extent that it de-

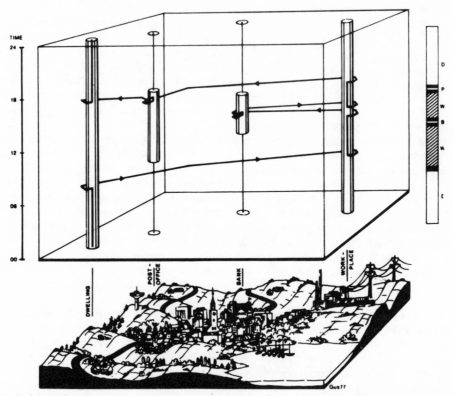

Figure 2.2. A time-geographic analysis of the individual's daily activity patterns. (*Source:* "A Time-Geographic Simulation Model of Individual Activity Programmes" by B. Lenntorp, in *Human Activity and Time Geography* by T. Carlstein, D. Parkes, and N. Thrift(Eds.), Halsted Press, 1978, copyright 1978 by John Wiley & Sons. Reprinted by permission.)

scribes behaviorally relevant dimensions of an individual's or group's sociocultural environment. To understand extreme departures from a person's typical activity patterns, for example, it may be necessary to consider the influence of national or religious holidays and other public events that impinge on people's regular activities. Thus a time-geographic analysis that accounts for such events would be of broader sociocultural scope than one that excludes them.

The above dimensions suggest a continuum of research ranging from narrow to broad contextual scope. At the "narrow" end of the continuum are those analyses that are conceptually and methodologically reductionistic. That is, the conceptualization and measurement of the phenomena under study are limited to target events that occur within a spatially, temporally, and socioculturally restricted situation. Located at the "broad" end of the continuum are analyses in which the target predictor and criterion variables are examined in relation to conditions occurring within a wide rather than restricted region of the

individual's geographical and sociocultural environment, and within an extended rather than narrow interval of the individual's life experience.[2]

Any attempt to discover the effective context of a phenomenon begins with some preliminary deliberation about the appropriate scope and content of the analysis. The researcher must decide how broadly to construe the relevant context of the phenomenon and which contextual factors exert a significant rather than trivial influence on the phenomenon. The broader and more complex the contextual units of analysis, the greater the potential range of factors—psychological, sociocultural, architectural, and geographic—that can affect a person's relationships with his or her surroundings. For any phenomenon, the researcher must try to determine at what point increasing or decreasing the scope of the contextual variables brings diminishing returns in terms of the explanatory power of the analysis.

When the researcher has access to extensive prior information about the situational variability of a

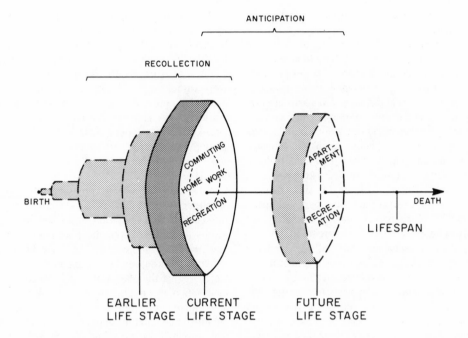

ANTICIPATION

RECOLLECTION

BIRTH

COMMUTING

HOME WORK

RECREATION

APART-MENT

RECRE-ATION

DEATH

LIFESPAN

EARLIER
LIFE STAGE

CURRENT
LIFE STAGE

FUTURE
LIFE STAGE

INTER-STAGE CONTEXT OF ENVIRONMENTAL EXPERIENCE

Figure 2.3. Individuals' judgements about the quality of past and future life stages have been found to play an important role in moderating the health consequences of residential change. (*Source:* "Environmental Psychology: A Coming of Age" by D. Stokols, in *G. Stanley Hall Lecture Series* (Vol. 2), by A. G. Kraut (Ed.), copyright 1982 by American Psychological Association. Reprinted by permission.)

phenomenon, decisions regarding the appropriate scope of the analysis become relatively straightforward. When one is lacking such information, however, it may be useful to adopt a broad contextual orientation during the early phases of an investigation (e.g., during the theorizing that often occurs prior to the design and implementation of the research). This approach avoids a premature narrowing of contextual scope while permitting the gradual deletion of irrelevant situational dimensions as additional insights and information about the phenomenon are acquired. Adopting a contextually narrow perspective at the outset may unduly limit the possibilities for discovering the situational moderators of the target phenomenon as the research proceeds.

Consider, for example, the relationship between residential mobility and health. On the one hand, it is possible to construe relocation as an acute, short-term life event whose effects on health depend primarily on conditions directly associated with the move and are manifested during the period immediately preceding and following the move. Alternatively the health effects of mobility could be examined within a broader spatial and temporal context encompassing one's feelings about previous residential situations, the current dwelling, and anticipated housing options for the future; they could be assessed longitudinally as they unfold across a spatially extended range of life domains including home, work, commuting, and recreation. In keeping with the latter perspective, a study by Stokols, Shumaker, and Martinez (1983) explicitly examined the temporal and spatial context of mobility and personal well-being. The links between mobility and health were assessed in relation to individuals' judgments about the quality of previous and future residential stages as well as their current job and residential situations (see Figure 2.3). Our findings suggested that an understanding of relocation and health can be enhanced by considering these phenomena not only in relation to the immediate circumstances surrounding a move, but also within the broader context of the individual's residential history, current life situation, and aspirations for the future.

The relative power and generativity of contextual analyses also depend on their capacity to identify important sociocultural moderators of target phenomena. Several areas of environmental research suggest that social–structural and cultural processes are crucial to an understanding of person–environment transactions. Studies of crowding, for example, indicate that group structure, composition, and cohesion moderate the intensity of stress reactions to high-density settings (cf. Cassel, 1974; Epstein & Karlin, 1975; Baum & Paulus, Chapter 14, this volume). Also, research on territoriality and personal space suggests that cultural norms influence the nature and intensity of people's reactions to territorial infringements and interpersonal proximity with strangers (cf. Altman & Chemers, 1979; Aiello, Chapter 12, Brown, Chapter 13, this volume). Thus it is important for environmental psychologists to consider sufficiently the possible links between the target phenomenon and various aspects of the sociocultural environment over the course of their theorizing and research.

The systematic assessment of spatial, temporal, and sociocultural scope does not ensure that the key contextual moderators of a phenomenon will be discovered. Nonetheless these dimensions of contextual scope are useful in that they offer a set of analytical coordinates for mapping diverse phenomena in relation to alternate clusters of contextual variables. This exploratory mapping process often can enhance efforts to discover the effective context of a phenomenon by highlighting important geographic, temporal, and cultural aspects of the phenomenon that might otherwise be overlooked.

Having delimited the scope of analysis and selected certain contextual variables for further assessment, the researcher may then consider how best to represent those variables in operational terms.

Objective and Subjective Representations of Contextual and Target Variables

Contextual and target variables can be represented in objective terms irrespective of the individual's perception and cognition or, alternatively, from the subjective vantage point of the individual or group. For example, the commute between home and work can be represented objectively in terms of its physical distance and duration or in terms of the driver's perception of traffic congestion along the route. Also

levels of overcrowding in the commuter's home or neighborhood can be described in terms of actual density levels or through measures of perceived residential and neighborhood crowding. Similarly the commuter's stress reactions can be assessed objectively through physiological recordings of arousal (e.g., blood pressure measures; biochemical assays of urinary adrenaline levels) and observations of overt behavior (e.g., task performance at work) or subjectively through self-report measures of stress symptoms such as negative mood states and perceived time demands.

Whereas many research programs rely exclusively on either an objectivist or a subjectivist approach, the contextual orientation described here underscores the value of combining both perspectives in research on environment and behavior. For instance, research on automobile commuting and stress suggests that the effects of long-distance driving on measures of mood, physiology, and task performance at work are not uniform across individuals but instead depend on commuters' appraisals of their residential and employment domains (cf. Stokols, Novaco, Stokols & Campbell, 1978; Stokols & Novaco, 1981). Among long-distance commuters, those reporting high levels of job involvement and choice in selecting their current residence exhibited lower stress across a variety of measures. Only by examining commuters' subjective reports of their home and work environments was it possible to detect the influence of these domains in qualifying the behavioral effects of commuting distance, an objective feature of a person's everyday environment (see Figure 2.4).

An important methodological reason for combining objective and subjective representations of environment and behavior within the same analysis is to counterbalance the respective strengths and weaknesses of these measurement approaches (cf. Cohen, Kamarck, & Mermelstein, 1983). For instance, subjective measures of environment and behavior share common method variance (e.g., attributable to response sets, memory distortions, denial, and/or other psychological defense mechanisms). Therefore the degree of spurious correlation between these predictor and criterion variables is likely to be greater than among a "mixed" set of objective and subjective measures (cf. Derogatis, 1982; Guski & Rohrmann, 1981). The strategy of combining objective and subjective measures of predictor and response variables can enable the researcher to offset the relative weaknesses of the two separate approaches and to assess the degree of convergence and divergence among the various measures included

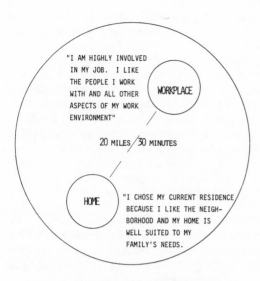

"I AM HIGHLY INVOLVED IN MY JOB. I LIKE THE PEOPLE I WORK WITH AND ALL OTHER ASPECTS OF MY WORK ENVIRONMENT"

WORKPLACE

20 MILES / 30 MINUTES

HOME

"I CHOSE MY CURRENT RESIDENCE BECAUSE I LIKE THE NEIGHBORHOOD AND MY HOME IS WELL SUITED TO MY FAMILY'S NEEDS.

OBJECTIVE AND SUBJECTIVE REPRESENTATIONS OF LIFE DOMAINS

Figure 2.4. The combined use of objective and subjective representations of the individual's commute between home and work.

in the analysis (cf. Campbell & Fiske, 1959; Cohen, Evans, Stokols, & Krantz, 1986; Webb, Campbell, Schwartz, Sechrest, & Grove, 1981).

Individual and Aggregate Levels of Analysis

The distinction between contextual and noncontextual features of the environment depends partly on whether the focus of analysis is on an individual or some aggregate of individuals. The term *contextual* applies not to any and all attributes of real settings but only to those conditions that constitute the external environment of a particular individual or group. Conditions of crowding and noise at work, for example, are aspects of the individual's job environment that may influence his or her job satisfaction and productivity. But if the focal unit of analysis is the work organization as a whole, then the exposure of workers to crowding and noise would be viewed as an intrasystem factor rather than as a condition of the company's external environment. Accordingly, if we were interested in estimating the long-term viability of the company, it might be necessary to look beyond the physical and social conditions within the organization to more remote, external events such as government monetary policies and competition from other corporations — all of which may affect the long-range survival of the firm.

The decision to represent an environment from the perspective of an individual or a group of individuals depends on the target issues we are attempting to explain. In research on spatial cognition, the analysis of individual sketch maps may reveal the geographic and architectural features of environments that contribute to their physical imageability. Yet if we want to understand the influence of cultural and historical factors on the imageability of urban areas then it becomes necessary to aggregate the data from individual maps and to identify those areas of the environment that are collectively recognized or remembered among a sample of their residents and users. In their research on cognitive maps of Paris, for example, Milgram and Jodelet (1976) analyzed cognitive maps from both an individual and an aggregate perspective and were able to show that the imageability of various locations in a city is influenced not only by the architectural and geographical characteristics of those places but also by their historical and cultural significance for the city's residents.

An additional reason for linking individual and aggregate levels of analysis is that the relationship between specific environmental conditions and a person's behavior may be mediated by his or her membership in various demographic groups (e.g., age cohorts, dual-career families, single-parent households). In research on work environments, for example, individuals belonging to different age and developmental cohorts have been found to vary considerably in their values and expectations about their jobs and their sensitivities to physical conditions of the workplace such as natural lighting, ergonomic amenities of workstations, and noise (cf. Cakir, Hart, & Stewart, 1980; Jones & Davies, 1984; Wurtman, 1975). Also the multiple family roles and activities performed by the members of dual-career and single-parent groups may increase the vulnerability of those individuals to the stressful consequences of environmental demands at work (cf. Everly & Feldman, 1985; Jacobi, 1984; Michelson, 1985). To the extent that studies focus exclusively on individuals' performance and health, subgroup variations in response to the work environment will be overlooked. At the same time, however, an entirely aggregate level of analysis ignores the important role of personal dispositions and risk factors in moderating individuals' performance and health, given a particular set of environmental conditions (cf. Caplan, 1983; Glass, 1977; Hedge, 1984; Kobasa, 1979). Therefore the limitations inherent in purely individual or aggregate analyses can be offset by adopting a more integrative, cross-level approach to the conceptualization and measurement of environmental conditions and their impacts on performance and health.

Partitive and Composite Representations of People and Environments

Partitive analyses view places and their occupants as independent entities and emphasize the interactive effects of environmental and personal attributes on various criteria of behavior and well-being (e.g., the effects of workstation enclosure on task performance, as mediated by individual preferences for high or low levels of arousal; cf. Mehrabian & Russell, 1974). Composite analyses, on the other hand, treat people and places as closely interrelated within a common behavioral setting or system (cf. Barker, 1968). A major goal of composite analyses is to develop concepts for representing the varieties of interdependence that can exist among people and their sociophysical surroundings (e.g., the notions of person–environment fit, social climate, place identity, and place dependence; cf. Caplan, 1983; Kaplan, 1983; Moos, 1979; Proshansky, Fabian, & Kaminoff, 1983; Stokols & Shumaker, 1981). An additional goal of composite analyses is to explain how the relationships among specific environmental and behavioral variables (e.g., degree of workstation enclosure and task performance) are qualified by the situational contexts in which they are observed (e.g., loosely structured groups whose members collaborate closely on common tasks). Thus composite analyses treat structured situations as the primary units of analysis and provide theoretical terms for describing and classifying diverse environmental settings.

The distinction between partitive and composite theories is important for several reasons. First, it reveals that the contextual boundaries of psychological phenomena do not always reside in the observable features of settings or in the demographic characteristics of their occupants. Instead, the effective context of certain phenomena may be better represented in terms of more covert, abstract dimensions of the relationships between people and their surroundings. Consider for example the two places depicted in Figure 2.5a and 2.5b. The first is a street corner in Las Vegas, Nevada. The second is the Wailing Wall in Jerusalem. A partitive analysis would differentiate these two areas on the basis of several situational elements including the cultural attributes of the occupants, age of the buildings in the area, the kinds of activities that go on in the location, and the relative historical continuity and significance of the area (see Fig. 2.6a). A composite analysis, however,

might distinguish these settings in terms of the degree to which each constitutes a *traditional* or *nontraditional behavior setting*. As defined by Jacobi and Stokols (1983), a traditional behavior setting is an environment where the activities of its occupants directly reinforce the historical continuity of the place and the perceived ties between past, present, and future generations of occupants (see Fig. 2.6b). The Wailing Wall in Jerusalem exemplifies a traditional behavior setting in the sense that it holds deep religious significance for a particular cultural group who have performed the same (or similar) traditional activities in the place over several generations. Rather than treating people, places, and recurring activities as independent parts of the situation, the composite construct portrays them as interdependent and consolidates or "chunks" these components into a new summary concept—in this case, the concept of a traditional behavior setting (see Fig. 2.6b).

The distinction between traditional and nontraditional behavior settings provides a theoretical basis for comparing diverse environments and also suggests a set of boundary conditions that may qualify existing psychological theories. Analyses of social support, for example, often ignore the role of the physical environment in conveying indirect or noninteractional forms of support. The notion of a traditional behavior setting, however, suggests that the physical elements of these places acquire a high degree of symbolic significance to the group, and that a vicarious sense of social support may accrue to the individual group member by virtue of his or her mere presence in the area. Also, in relation to a different substantive concern, environmental degradation, the traditional behavior-setting notion suggests that the occurrence of littering and other forms of defacement may be restricted in traditional settings, and that the influence of situational factors (such as large group size and visibility of prior litter) that would otherwise promote degradation in a nontraditional area may be offset by the strong tendencies toward environmental preservation within traditional settings.

An advantage of composite analyses is that they often reveal previously neglected processes by which target phenomena are contextually moderated. A common approach to representing person–environment relationships is to view them in terms of statistical interactions among multiple predictor variables. This approach is typified by statistical analyses of trait-by-situation interactions (cf. Endler & Magnusson, 1976). It is also reflected in the earlier-mentioned analysis of commuting distance and the coronary-prone behavior pattern as joint predictors of blood pressure. Yet contextual factors also may qualify target phenomena by precluding their occurrence or by changing their perceived meaning. For instance, phenomena such as noise and crowding stress may be prevalent within settings such as urban transit or commercial districts, but relatively atypical within libraries or wilderness areas. These instances, in which the occurrence of the target variables is either restricted or precluded by contextual factors, are not adequately represented in terms of the statistical interactions among independent variables.

An illustration of how contextual factors can alter the meaning of target variables is provided by the now famous Hawthorne studies of environmental conditions at work and employee productivity (cf. Roethlisberger & Dickson, 1939). In this research, increases as well as decreases in illumination levels within workstations were associated with improved performance. These initially unexpected findings were later explained in terms of the symbolic significance of the

environmental changes and the fact that both interventions, either to increase or to decrease illumination, were viewed by employees as being part of a larger research program implemented by the management to improve working conditions. In this instance, the composite dimension of management concern, rather than interacting statistically with levels of illumination, altered the basic meaning of the physical stimulus to the workers (see Fig. 2.7). Within the context of a less structured social situation or, alternatively, one in which the management appeared to be unconcerned about workers' welfare, the meaning of the physical intervention and its impact on productivity might have been different (cf. Merton, 1968).

The utility of partitive versus composite perspectives depends largely on the level of interdependence that exists among people and their environments. While transactional analyses of situations (e.g., Barker, 1968; Altman & Rogoff, Chapter 1, Wapner, Chapter 41, this volume) treat interdependence as a

Figure 2.5.(a) A street corner in Las Vegas, Nevada. (*Source: The Complete Nevada Traveler: A Guide to the State* by D. Toll, copyright 1981 by Gold Hill Publishing Co. Reprinted by permission.)

Figure 2.5.(*b*) The Wailing Wall in Jerusalem. (*Source: Jerusalem, Sacred City of Mankind: A History of Forty Centuries* by T. Kollek and M. Perlman, copyright 1968 by Steimatzky's Ltd. Reprinted by permission.)

constant or a given, the present discussion of contextual theorizing views interdependence as a variable (cf. Weick, 1979). For instance, many person–environment encounters such as those that occur in temporary, short-term situations (e.g., public transportation environments) involve less interdependence among individuals and the physical and social features of the setting than those that occur within the context of more structured settings (e.g., within home, school, or workplace). In transitory and unstructured situations, composite concepts of situational structure might be irrelevant and superfluous. In these instances, environmental and personal characteristics could be viewed as relatively independent elements of the setting. In more complex and organized settings, however, composite terms can provide a powerful and efficient representation of environment and behavior since they consolidate multiple situational and personal attributes into a smaller number of unifying constructs, each of which describes a theoretically significant form of interdependence among people and their surroundings.

2.3.5 Research Biases Resulting from Inadequate Modeling of the Effective Context

The dimensions of contextual representation outlined previously offer a framework for organizing conceptual and empirical research on environment and behavior. Rather than focusing prematurely on either pole of each dimension (e.g., narrow *vs.* broad contextual scope, and the use of objective *or* subjective measures at either an individual *or* aggregate level), the researcher can exploratively "map" a set of target variables at multiple points along all four continua. This exploratory mapping process can be useful in suggesting hypotheses about the range and content of contextual factors that significantly influence the target phenomenon.

CONTEXTUAL COMPONENTS:

PEOPLE	ENVIRONMENT	ACTIVITIES	TIME
NORTH AMERICAN VS. MIDDLE EASTERN CULTURES	MODERN VS. OLD ARCHITECTURE	DRIVING, WALKING, GAMBLING VS. PRAYING, OBSERVING	LOW VS. HIGH DEGREE OF HISTORICAL PRESERVATION

(a)

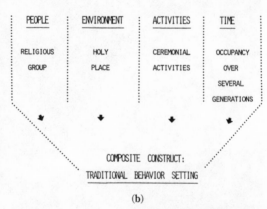

CONTEXTUAL COMPONENTS

PEOPLE	ENVIRONMENT	ACTIVITIES	TIME
RELIGIOUS GROUP	HOLY PLACE	CEREMONIAL ACTIVITIES	OCCUPANCY OVER SEVERAL GENERATIONS

COMPOSITE CONSTRUCT:
TRADITIONAL BEHAVIOR SETTING

(b)

Figure 2.6.(*a*) A partitive analysis of the differences between the Las Vegas and Jerusalem locations. (*b*) The concept of traditional behavior setting consolidates multiple features of the Wailing Wall area into a composite construct.

To the extent that the scope, level, and content of contextual analyses encompass those situational factors most relevant to the phenomenon under study, the scientific and practical value of our theories is enhanced. On the other hand, premature selection of inadequately drawn constructs can lead to a variety of research biases that obscure important theoretical and policy questions. Figure 2.8a–2.8d summarizes eight types of research bias that can result from inadequate modeling of the effective context of a particular phenomenon. Each of these biases stems from a mismatch between the scope, level, or content of a contextual analysis and the inherent qualities of the target phenomenon itself (e.g., whether the phenomenon is actually influenced by a narrow as opposed to a wide range of contextual factors, at both individual and aggregate levels of analysis, and irrespective of the complexity of situational structure).

The dimensions of spatial, temporal, and sociocultural scope suggest at least two types of bias that can occur in environment–behavior research. For those target phenomena that are influenced by a wide range of contextual factors, analyses of narrow scope will have low explanatory power because they fail to encompass a significant portion of the effective context of the phenomena. Alternatively for those environment–behavior relationships that are relatively invariant across a wide range of situations (e.g., the frequently observed link between exposure to high-intensity noise and elevated blood pressure), analyses of broad contextual scope are inefficient since they incorporate situational factors that have a negligible influence on the target phenomenon (see Fig. 2.8a). These potential sources of bias suggest a basic guideline for theory development and research design; that is, every effort should be made by researchers to match the contextual scope of their analysis with the range of spatial, temporal, and sociocultural factors that are thought to exert a significant influence on the target phenomenon.

An exclusive reliance on either objective or subjective representations of target and contextual variables can lead to at least two additional types of bias: environmental determinism, or the tendency to interpret behavior entirely in relation to the objective properties of the physical and social environment (cf. Franck, 1984); and extreme subjectivism, whereby the direct (nonpsychologically mediated) effects of environmental conditions on behavior are ignored (cf. Sampson, 1981; Wohlwill, 1973). The integration of objective and subjective perspectives, particularly during the early stages of theoretical and empirical work, can reduce these sources of bias (see Fig. 2.8b).

Also it was noted earlier that an emphasis on cross-level analyses, linking both individual and aggregate perspectives, can serve as a useful strategy for reducing two additional sources of research bias: namely an insensitivity to subgroup variations in people's response to the environment resulting from an exclusive focus on the individual level of analysis; and the neglect of intrapersonal moderators of environment–behavior relationships (e.g., life history, personality, health status) that typifies much aggregate-oriented research (see Fig. 2.8c). The avoidance of these individualist and collectivist biases requires that the levels of analysis chosen to represent the relations between people and their environments be commensurate with both the individual and the aggregate processes inherent in the target phenomena.

Finally the use of partitive or composite constructs that are inadequately matched with the structure of the target situation can introduce at least two other forms of research bias: namely an overemphasis on either the systemic or the mechanistic qualities of environment–behavior relationships (see Fig. 2.8d). In the former case, composite concepts attribute a greater degree of organization and structure to the target situation than actually exists. In the latter case, partitive terms fail to represent the systemic qualities of organized settings, thereby conveying an overly mechanistic view of the transactions

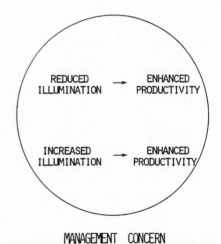

MANAGEMENT CONCERN

Figure 2.7. In the Hawthorne Studies by Roethlisberger & Dickson (1939), the contextual factor of management concern altered the meaning of the physical stimulus to the employees participating in the research.

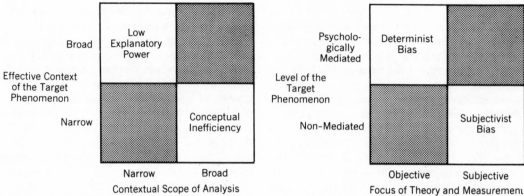

(a)The biases of low explanatory power and inefficiency of conceptualization.

(b)The biases of environmental determinism and extreme subjectivism.

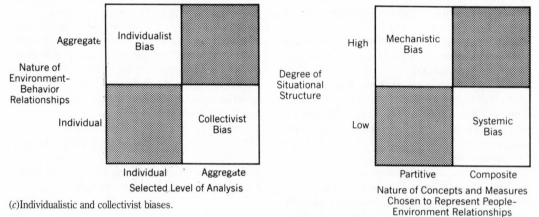

(c)Individualistic and collectivist biases.

(d)Mechanistic and systemic biases.

Figure 2.8. Research biases resulting from a mismatch between the scope, level, and focus of contextual analysis and the range of situational factors affecting the target phenomenon. The shaded cells denote low levels of bias and high congruence between the type of analysis chosen and the complexity of the target phenomenon.

between people and their surroundings (cf. Altman & Rogoff, Chapter 1, this volume).

The four dimensions of contextual analysis and the corresponding categories of bias summarized in Figure 2.8 suggest certain general strategies of theorizing for enhancing the scientific and practical value of environment and behavior research. These conceptual and procedural strategies are outlined below.

2.3.6. Summary of Strategies for Developing Contextual Theories and Research

Contextual theorizing, as described in the preceding sections of the chapter, is a process involving two basic phases: (1) a *contextual mapping phase*, in which environmental and behavioral target variables are examined within increasingly broad segments of the individual's (or group's) spatial, temporal, and cultural milieu; and (2) a *contextual specification phase*, in which the researcher attempts to define, on the basis of the initial exploratory phase, those situational dimensions that are most crucial for understanding the target phenomenon. The major goal of the first stage is to discover potentially important contextual moderators of the target variables. The major goal of the second phase is to delimit and define, as specifically as possible, the effective context of the target phenomenon.

Too often in psychological research, the exploratory mapping phase of contextual theorizing is bypassed. In an effort to maximize the construct validity and clear operationalization of research variables, investigators may prematurely narrow the contextual scope of their analysis and move too quickly to a specification of predictor variables and response criteria. The present discussion suggests, however, that the validity, power, efficiency, and generativity of our theories are highly dependent on the effectiveness of the contextual mapping process, whereby a particular phenomenon is analytically rotated or charted in relation to several dimensions of contextual representation.

Having considered some of the distinguishing features of contextual theories and criteria for evaluating them, it is possible at this point to specify a number of programmatic assumptions that can serve as *guidelines for developing contextual theories and research*:

1. The specification of contextual moderator variables should become an inherent part of psychological theorizing. The contextual mapping and specification stages of theorizing, when coupled with cross-setting empirical research, can provide a broader understanding of the generalizability of our theories and research than can strictly inductive assessments of external validity alone.

2. It is important for psychologists to shift their focus from an exclusive emphasis on people's reactions to discrete stimuli and events to the ways in which these phenomena are qualified by the behavior settings, life domains, and overall life situations in which they occur. An advantage of adopting contextually broader units of analysis is that they permit an assessment of the interrelationships among environmental conditions, activities, and experiences that occur within and across different life domains.

3. Psychological phenomena should routinely be examined in relation to temporal dimensions of context. This temporal mapping process should involve a consideration of the ways in which the history of an individual or group and its anticipation of the future qualify their experience of, and response to, immediate environmental conditions.

4. It is important to avoid the tendency toward psychological reductionism (cf. Sampson, 1981) that characterizes many behavioral theories and to consider systematically the sociocultural dimensions of individual and collective behavior.

5. It is useful to examine the effective context of a target phenomenon from the perspective of both individuals and groups. In many instances, the combined use of individual and aggregate representations

of context can provide the basis for a broader understanding of the target phenomenon.

6. The combined use of objective and subjective representations of context can reduce two sources of biases in psychological research: the tendency to interpret people's behavior entirely in relation to the objective features of their physical and social environments; or, at the other extreme, the failure to consider the direct (or nonpsychologically mediated) effects of environmental conditions on behavior. A systematic analysis of the objective features of the environment as well as people's subjective appraisals of their surroundings can contribute to the development of theories that are sensitive to two types of contextual effects on behavior: those that are mediated by cognitive or interpretive processes, and those that are not.

7. It is important that our representation of contextual factors in either partitive or composite terms be commensurate with the degree and quality of interdependence that exists among people, their activities, and places. In certain loosely organized situations, the relationships between environment and behavior may be represented most usefully in terms of the interactions among independent variables. In other situations, however, the form and occurrence of environment–behavior relationships may be more dependent on the composite or structural features of the setting. The selective and appropriate use of partitive and composite constructs can help avoid a haphazard, atheoretical approach to the description of environments and can encourage, instead, a more systematic, theoretically based assessment of the cross-situational generality of our theories and research.

I now turn to a consideration of the ways in which these strategies of contextual theorizing can contribute to the policy relevance and applied utility of environment and behavior research.

2.4. USING STRATEGIES OF CONTEXTUAL THEORIZING TO ENHANCE THE EFFECTIVENESS OF COMMUNITY INTERVENTIONS

An additional criterion for evaluating contextual theories that has not yet been discussed is their *applied utility,* or the degree to which they contribute to an understanding of community problems and suggest guidelines for developing effective policy interventions. The applied utility of a theory depends fundamentally on the criteria of contextual validity, relative power, and generativity, discussed earlier.

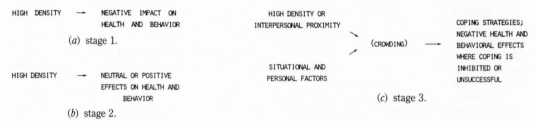

Figure 2.9. Different theoretical orientations of three stages reflected in the research literature on crowding and behavior.

But the utility of a theory is also influenced by the complexity of the policy-making process and the structure of the situations in which the interventions derived from the theory will be implemented. To be useful, then, a theory must validly specify the situational conditions under which a particular set of environment–behavior relationships will hold. But the contextual conditions specified by the theory also must be relevant to the structure of the intervention setting.

To illustrate the relationship between the contextual validity and utility of a theory, consider some examples drawn from the research literature on crowding. Elsewhere (Stokols, 1978b) I have suggested that the research on human crowding during the 1960s and 1970s can be characterized in terms of three conceptual stages. The earliest stage of crowding research consisted primarily of naturalistic studies of animal populations living under conditions of extremely high density (e.g., Calhoun, 1962; Christian, Flyger, & Davis, 1960), and sociological analyses of the relationships among levels of density, crime, suicide, and disease within different urban areas (e.g., Schmitt, 1957; Winsborough, 1965). Both lines of research indicated a significant relationship between high levels of density and behavioral pathology. Thus studies conducted during the first stage of research supported the deterministic position that high density is invariably harmful to human well-being (see Fig. 2.9a).

The second stage of crowding research commenced with a series of experiments conducted by Freedman and colleagues (Freedman, 1975; Freedman, Klevansky, & Ehrlich, 1971). In these experiments, groups of people were exposed to either large or small laboratory rooms while their task performance and social behavior were observed. The consistent finding from this research was that high density did not affect task performance and altered social behavior only slightly, with female group members showing a higher tolerance for spatial limitation than males. This line of research, along with addi-

tional survey research that controlled for socioeconomic confounds with census tract density (e.g., Mitchell, 1972), supported a different conclusion than the one suggested by the first research stage: namely, that high density, when isolated from other situational circumstances that often accompany it (e.g., poverty, heat, noise, unpleasant odors), does not lead to stress among people (see Fig. 2.9b).

Despite the optimistic conclusions of these social psychological and survey studies, the fact that people often regard high density as unpleasant suggested that a still more detailed analysis was required to determine when and where people experience stress under conditions of limited space. Thus the third stage of crowding research was marked by the development of theoretical models that distinguished between the physical condition of density, or limited space, and crowding, a type of stress that arises when proximity with other people creates distracting stimulation or infringements on one's privacy and behavioral freedom (cf. Altman, 1975; Baum & Epstein, 1978; Stokols, 1976). These contextually oriented theories attempted to specify the conditions under which high density does or does not lead to negative impacts on health and behavior. Both the theories and the findings from this third stage of research supported the nondeterministic view that high density (or proximity with other people) does not necessarily impair health and behavior. Only to the extent that density, in conjunction with other situational and personal factors, leads to the experience of crowding will it have negative effects on health and behavior (see Fig. 2.9c).

The policy implications of these three stages of research were, of course, different. The message conveyed to community planners by the first stage of research was: "Avoid high-density buildings and neighborhoods at all costs." By contrast, the design implication of studies from the second stage was: "High density has very little impact on people and, therefore, can be regarded as an unimportant factor in urban planning." And findings from the third stage of research conveyed yet another message to planners, namely: "High density sometimes affects people adversely and sometimes favorably. The particular effects of density in any given situation will depend on the type of environment being designed and the psychological and social attributes of its prospective users."

These examples illustrate that *the effectiveness of public policies depends largely on the adequacy of the theoretical assumptions from which they are derived.* Theories that fail to specify the contextual qualifiers of a phenomenon may appeal to policymakers by virtue of their simplicity. But the low contextual validity of such theories jeopardizes their effectiveness to the extent that they are applied within settings that exceed the situational boundaries of the proposed target variable relations.

The present analysis of the applied utility of theories further suggests that contextual theorizing can help not only to specify the situational moderators of a particular phenomenon, but also to understand the complexity of the intervention situation itself. There are at least two aspects of this complexity that can be usefully approached from a contextual perspective. The first concerns the relative efficacy of alternative leverage points for environmental and behavioral interventions with a particular setting and time interval. The second concerns the identification of appropriate criteria for judging the cost-effectiveness of the proposed intervention.

An excellent example of the applied utility of contextual analysis is provided by Stern and Gardner's (1981) discussion of psychological research and energy policy (see also Stern & Oskamp, Chapter 28, this volume). A unique feature of Stern and Gardner's analysis was their assessment of national energy consumption across household, industrial, commercial, and other sectors and across different energy uses within the household domain. They also identified the kinds of behaviors (e.g., the purchase of a fuel-efficient car) that have the greatest impact on the amount of energy consumed by a household. And by moving from an individual to an aggregate level of analysis, Stern and Gardner were able to identify potential targets for energy conservation programs other than the individuals comprising a household such as government leaders within a community and the executive boards of large corporations. Stern and Gardner's description of the context of energy consumption indicated that the majority of national energy use occurs outside the household sector and that, within the household, transportation-related and space-heating uses account for the largest pro-

portion of energy expenditure. Thus by examining energy consumption in relation to different sectors of the economy and from the perspective of individual and aggregate systems Stern and Gardner were able to suggest a variety of intervention points at the community level that would have been missed by a contextually narrower analysis.

The specification of criteria for judging the cost-effectiveness of community interventions also can be enhanced through the application of contextual mapping strategies. Consider, for example, the development of corporate ride-sharing programs to alleviate commuter stress and to improve organizational effectiveness. Again the proposed intervention can be analyzed in relation to alternative representations of the environment as viewed from the perspective of individuals, aggregates, or both. The cost-effectiveness of corporate vanpooling programs might be evaluated differently depending on whether the target phenomenon of interest was commuter stress and well-being, organizational effectiveness and profitability, or the quality of life at a community level. At the first level, an evaluation of the proposed program would involve an individually oriented analysis of the travel conditions and stress levels experienced by participants in the vanpooling program and among a comparable sample of automobile commuters. At an organizational level of analysis, the cost-effectiveness of the vanpooling program might be assessed in relation to aggregate levels of employee morale, productivity, illness-related absence from work, and attrition. And at the community level, the effectiveness of the program could be measured in terms of its impact on residents' aggregate perceptions of traffic congestion and ambient noise levels in their neighborhood (cf. Appleyard, 1981). Only by considering the proposed intervention in relation to individual as well as aggregate levels and subjective as well as objective descriptors of the environment can the appropriate criteria of cost-effectiveness be identified and understood.

The present discussion of the applied utility of contextual theories and research neglects several important issues such as the political, legislative, and economic forces that impinge on the policy-making process and thereby influence the effectiveness and implementability of our proposed interventions (cf. DiMento, 1981; Kantrowitz & Seidel, 1985; Wohlwill, 1981; Zube, 1980). Nonetheless the preceding examples illustrate several of the advantages that can accrue from the systematic application of contextual theorizing and research to an analysis of policy issues.

2.5. DIRECTIONS FOR FUTURE THEORIZING AND RESEARCH

The preceding sections of the chapter have described several strategies for developing contextual theories and for evaluating their scientific and practical utility. All of these strategies rest on a basic assumption: that the usefulness of our theories and research depends on the extent to which they correctly identify the effective (or influential) context of the target phenomenon. Under certain circumstances, however, the goal of identifying the effective context of a phenomenon may be unwarranted. It is important at this point in the chapter to mention some critical qualifications of the proposed strategies of contextual analysis, and to consider certain priorities for future theorizing and research that are raised by these issues.

One factor that limits the usefulness of the proposed strategies is the *relative stability (or instability) of the relationships between the target and contextual variables*. Because the transactions between people and their surroundings are intrinsically dynamic rather than static, the effective context of environment—behavior phenomena is never perfectly stable—that is, the important situational moderators of a phenomenon can be expected to shift across time, places, and cultures. The key question, however, is how rapidly and predictably these changes in the effective context occur. For those phenomena that are relatively stable, efforts to identify generalizable relationships between the target and contextual variables would be warranted on both scientific and practical grounds. But for those forms of person–environment transaction that are characterized by very rapid rates of change, efforts to specify the effective context of the target phenomena might prove to be highly impractical.

For example, earlier research on commuting and stress suggests that the relationships between travel distance and various measures of physiological and emotional well-being are moderated by situational factors such as the level of overcrowding when passengers first board their train (cf. Singer, Lundberg, & Frankenhaeuser, 1978); or the degree to which automobile commuters are satisfied with their residential and work domains (Stokols & Novaco, 1981). To the extent that contemporary patterns of commuting in urban areas continue into the future, the observed links between the target variables of travel distance and stress and the above-mentioned contextual factors would be expected to remain relatively stable. If, on the other hand, current commuting patterns are substantially transformed by the growing trends toward "telecommuting" and doing work at home (Olson & Primps, 1985), the provision of child-care facilities within corporate settings (cf. Michelson, 1985; Naisbitt & Aburdene, 1985), and the availability of mobile telephone systems that permit direct communication between the commuting and destination points (Toffler, 1980), then the previously recorded links between travel distance, situational factors, and stress are likely to change as well.

Thus an important direction for future research is the development of *transformational theories*, or those that suggest the circumstances under which people–environment transactions are likely to undergo fundamental and rapid change (cf. Stokols, 1986). Examples of transformational analyses are recent discussions of the geographical, social, and psychological factors that encourage the formation, modification, or termination of behavior settings (cf. Stokols & Shumaker, 1981; Wicker, Chapter 16, this volume) and Saegert's (Chapter 4, this volume) analysis of the ways in which researchers contribute to fundamental social change through the very process of studying the relations between people and their environments. Each of these analyses focuses directly on the sources and rates of change in people–environment transactions. To the extent that we develop a better understanding of how, when, and why human environments change, we will be able to estimate the relative stability of the hypothesized (or observed) relationships between a particular set of target and contextual variables.

A related factor that qualifies the proposed strategies of contextual analysis is the *varying influence of chance factors on environment–behavior phenomena*. Whereas it might be possible to predict the timing and direction of certain changes in the relations between people and their environments, other changes will occur in a much more spontaneous or random fashion. Given that many facets of person–environment transaction are *chance-dependent* (Gergen, 1982; Maruyama, 1963), does it make any sense to develop contextual theories that posit generalizable links between a target phenomenon and one or more situational factors? The answer to this question depends on the presumed likelihood that chance factors will exert a relatively major (or minor) influence on some facet of environment and behavior, within a given temporal, spatial, or cultural context.

Although the exact nature and timing of chance factors cannot be reliably predicted, it may be possible to identify certain forms or phases of person–environment transaction that are especially susceptible to influence by such factors. For example, the impact of chance factors on environment and behavior may be particularly great during periods of geographic relocation, especially when such moves coincide with major life transitions (cf. Wapner, Chapter 41, this volume). Acutely stressful events that restructure a person's overall life situation (e.g., death of spouse and subsequent residential and employment change) may instigate numerous chance encounters with new settings and people that profoundly affect the future course of the individual's life (cf. Aldwin & Stokols, in press). If, in fact, the relative influence of chance factors varies across certain forms, phases, and contexts of person–environment transaction in some systematic fashion, then a potentially useful direction for future research is suggested: namely the development of theories that account for the situations in which chance factors play a major or minor role in shifting the course of environment–behavior relations.

A third set of issues that should be considered when using the proposed strategies of contextual analysis concerns the *importance of matching one's theoretical approach to the predominant goals and objectives of the research at hand*. The development of contextual theories that offer testable predictions about the links between target variables and situational factors makes most sense when the researcher is conducting inferential, comparative studies of two or more settings. On the other hand, the inferential (or *specification*) phase of contextual analysis may be less appropriate when a study is being conducted within a single setting to compile an in-depth, empirical description of environment–behavior relationships within that setting, alone; and for the purposes of developing new research questions or situation–specific proposals for environmental intervention. In both of these instances, the exploratory–mapping phase of contextual analysis could provide a useful framework for organizing one's research. But the more specific tasks of developing contextual theories and evaluating their validity, power, efficiency, and utility would be less appropriate within the context of single-setting, descriptive research. These aspects of contextual theorizing would be most powerful as a basis for multisetting, inferential research, especially where the relationship between the target and contextual variables can be expected to remain relatively stable within certain geographic, historical, and cultural boundaries.

A fourth set of issues that has received little attention in previous work is that group of *processes by which researchers develop hunches, hypotheses, and theories about the sources of situational influence on environment and behavior*. The proposed strategies of contextual analysis can help organize the search for the situational moderators of a phenomenon, but they do not account for the creative connections that researchers make between the exploratory-mapping phase of their work and the subsequent framing of new concepts and relationships. The success of the researcher's efforts to develop a valid and powerful theory may depend not only on his or her personal characteristics (e.g., degree of familiarity with the phenomenon under study; creativity and insight), but also on a variety of situational factors that influence the theorizing process itself (cf. Gergen, 1985; Wicker, 1985; Weick, 1979). Future research on the process of contextual theorizing could address the following questions: (1) What aspects of the researcher's environmental experiences and social relations affect his or her selection of topics for theoretical and empirical study? (2) What contextual factors enhance the creativity and generativity of the theory development process? And (3) how might research and educational settings be organized to encourage creative and generative theorizing about environment and behavior?

2.6. SUMMARY AND CONCLUSIONS

In this chapter, I have examined several dimensions for representing the context of individual and group behavior that together offer a descriptive framework for developing theoretical constructs and community interventions. I have noted some of the distinctive features of contextual theories and have proposed criteria for evaluating their validity, power, efficiency, generativity, and applied utility. I also have characterized contextual theorizing as a two-phase process involving an initial exploratory or mapping phase and a subsequent specification and inferential phase. I have suggested several strategies by which these processes of theory development can be used to broaden our understanding of the contextual moderators of individual and collective behavior and to sharpen our assessments of the potential effectiveness of public policy proposals. Finally I have noted certain limitations of the proposed strategies and some related directions for future research.

The strategies of contextual analysis described in this chapter provide a descriptive framework to facilitate the discovery of potentially important constructs rather than a "surefire" set of formulas that guarantee the development of powerful and generative theories. Nonetheless, when applied to a wide range of environment and behavior issues, they can serve as a valuable tool for enhancing the validity and utility of our theoretical work, and for translating a broad contextual perspective into operational guidelines for theory development, research, and community intervention.

Acknowledgments

Portions of this chapter were presented as part of the author's Presidential Address to Division 34 of the American Psychological Association (Stokols, 1983). The author thanks the following colleagues who provided valuable suggestions on earlier versions of the chapter: Carolyn Aldwin, Irwin Altman, Barbara Brown, Dorwin Cartwright, Sheldon Cohen, Gary Evans, Kenneth Gergen, Maryann Jacobi, Gerhard Kaminski, David Krantz, Joseph McGrath, Patricia Parmelee, Tracey Revenson, Sally Shumaker, Brewster Smith, Ralph Taylor, Allan Wicker, and the social ecology graduate students enrolled in my Seminar on Strategies of Theory Development during fall 1984.

NOTES

1. See Endler and Magnusson (1976) for a more detailed discussion of situationist, trait, and interactionist theories.

2. See, for example, the critiques of conceptual and methodological reductionism in behavioral research, presented by Gergen (1973, 1982) and Schwartz (1982). See also McGuire's (1983) distinction between *convergent* and *divergent* research styles.

Note that the spatial, temporal, and sociocultural dimensions of contextual scope can be considered separately for predictor and outcome variables. That is, the scope of the predictor variables might be wide while that of the criterion variables is narrow, or vice versa. Alternatively the scopes of both sets of variables might be broad or narrow.

REFERENCES

Aldwin, C., & Stokols, D. (in press). The effects of environmental change on individuals and groups: Some neglected issues in stress research. In D. Jodelet & P. Stringer (Eds.), *Towards a social psychology of the environment*. Cambridge, England: Cambridge University Press.

Altman, I. (1975). *The environment and social behavior*. Monterey, CA: Brooks/Cole.

Altman, I. (1982). *Problems and prospects of environmental psychology*. Presidential address to the Division of Population and Environmental Psychology, American Psychological Association, Annual Conference of the American Psychological Association, Washington, DC.

Altman, I., & Chemers, M.M. (1979). *Culture and environment*. Monterey, CA: Brooks/Cole.

Appleyard, D. (1981). *Livable streets*. Berkeley: University of California Press.

Barker, R.G. (1968). *Ecological psychology: Concepts and methods for studying the environment of human behavior*. Stanford, CA: Stanford University Press.

Barker, R.G., & Schoggen, P. (1973). *Qualities of community life*. San Francisco: Jossey-Bass.

Berkowitz, L., & Donnerstein, E. (1982). External validity is more than skin deep: Some answers to criticisms of laboratory experiments. *American Psychologist, 37*, 245–257.

Brinberg, D., & McGrath, J.E. (1985). *Validity and the research process*. Beverly Hills, CA: Sage.

Bronfenbrenner, U. (1979). *The ecology of human development*. Cambridge, MA: Harvard University Press.

Brunswik, E. (1956). *Perception and the representative design of experiments*. Berkeley: University of California Press.

Cakir, A., Hart, D.J., & Stewart, T.F.M. (1980). *Visual display terminals*. New York: Wiley.

Calhoun, J.B. (1962). Population density and social pathology. *Scientific American, 206*, 139–148.

Campbell, A. (1981). *The sense of well-being in America*. New York: McGraw-Hill.

Campbell, D.T., & Fiske, D.W. (1959). Convergent and discriminant validation by the multitrait-multimethod matrix. *Psychological Bulletin, 56*, 81–105.

Campbell, D.T., & Stanley, J.C. (1963). *Experimental and quasi-experimental designs for research*. Chicago: Rand McNally.

Campbell, J.M. (1983). Ambient stressors. *Environment and Behavior, 15*, 355–380.

Caplan, R.D. (1983). Person-environment fit: Past, present, and future. In C.L. Cooper (Ed.), *Stress research: Issues for the eighties*. New York: Wiley, 35–78.

Carmines, E.G., & Zeller, R.A. (1979). *Reliability and validity assessment*. Beverly Hills, CA: Sage.

Cassel, J. (1974). Psychosocial processes and "stress": Theoretical formulation. *International Journal of Health Services, 4*, 471-482.

Chein, I. (1954). The environment as a determinant of behavior. *Journal of Social Psychology, 39*, 115–127.

Christian, J.J., Flyger, V., & Davis, D.E. (1960). Factors in the mass mortality of a herd of Sika Deer, *Cervus nippon. Chesapeake Science, 1*, 79–95.

Cohen, S. (1980). After-effects of stress on human performance and social behavior: A review of research and theory. *Psychological Bulletin, 88*, 82–108.

Cohen, S., Evans, G.W., Stokols, D., & Krantz, D.S. (1986). *Behavior, health, and environmental stress*. New York: Plenum.

Cohen, S., Kamarck, T., & Mermelstein, R. (1983). A global measure of perceived stress. *Journal of Health and Social Behavior, 24*, 385–396.

Cohen, S., & Spacapan, S. (1984). The social psychology of noise. In D.M. Jones & A.J. Chapman (Eds.), *Noise and society*. Chichester: Wiley. 221–245.

Cohen, S., & Weinstein, N. (1981).Nonauditory effects of noise on behavior and health. *Journal of Social Issues, 37*, 36–70.

Cook, T.D., & Campbell, D.T. (1979). *Quasi-experimentation: Design and analysis issues for field settings*. Chicago: Rand McNally.

Craik, K.H. (1973). Environmental psychology. *Annual Review of Psychology, 24*, 403–422.

Cronbach, L.J. (1975). Beyond the two disciplines of scientific psychology. *American Psychologist, 30*, 116–127.

Cullen, I.G. (1978). The treatment of time in the explanations of spatial behavior. In T. Carlstein, D. Parkes, & V. Thrift (Eds.), *Human activity and time geography*. New York: Wiley. 27–38.

Darley, J.M., & Gilbert, D.T. (1985). Social psychological aspects of environmental psychology. In G. Lindzey & E. Aronson (Eds.), *The Handbook of Social Psychology* (Vol. 2, 3rd ed.), Reading, MA: Addison-Wesley. 949–991.

Derogatis, L.R. (1982). Self-report measures of stress. In L. Goldberger & S. Bresnitz (Eds.), *Handbook of stress: Theoretical and clinical aspects*. New York: Free Press. 270–294.

DiMento, J.F. (1981). Making usable information on environmental stressors: Opportunities for the research and policy communities. *Journal of Social Issues, 37*, 172–204.

Dipboye, R.L., & Flanagan, M.F. (1979). Research settings in industrial and organizational psychology: Are findings in the field more generalizable than in the laboratory? *American Psychologist, 34*, 141–150.

Endler, N.S., & Magnusson, D. (Eds.). (1976). *Interactional psychology and personality*. Washington, DC: Hemisphere.

Epstein, Y.M., & Karlin, R.A. (1975). Effects of acute experimental crowding. *Journal of Applied Social Psychology, 5*, 34–53.

Evans, G.W. (Ed.). (1982). *Environmental stress*. New York: Cambridge University Press.

Everly, G.S., & Feldman, R.H.L. (1985). *Occupational health promotion: Health behavior in the workplace*. New York: Wiley.

Fawcett, J.T. (Ed.). (1973). *Psychological perspectives on population*. New York: Basic.

Forgas, J.P. (1979). *Social episodes: The study of interaction routines*. New York: Academic.

Franck, K.A. (1984). Exorcizing the ghost of physical determinism. *Environment and Behavior, 16*, 411–435.

Freedman, J.L. (1975). *Crowding and behavior*. San Francisco: Freeman.

Freedman, J.L., Klevansky, S., & Ehrlich, P. (1971). The effect of crowding on human task performance. *Journal of Applied Social Psychology, 1*, 7–25.

Georgoudi, M., & Rosnow, R.L. (1985). Notes toward a contextualist understanding of social psychology. *Personality and Social Psychology Bulletin, 11*, 5–22.

Gergen, K.J. (1973). Social psychology as history. *Journal of Personality and Social Psychology, 26*, 309–320.

Gergen, K.J. (1978). Toward generative theory. *Journal of Personality and Social Psychology, 36*, 1344–1360.

Gergen, K.J. (1982). *Toward transformation in social knowledge*. New York: Springer-Verlag.

Gergen, K.J. (1985). The social constructionist movement in modern psychology. *American Psychologist, 40*, 266–275.

Gergen, K.J., & Gergen, M.M. (1984). *Historical social psychology*. Hillsdale, NJ: Erlbaum.

Gibson, J.J. (1960). The concept of the stimulus in psychology. *American Psychologist, 15*, 694–703.

Glaser, B.G., & Strauss, A.L. (1967). *The discovery of grounded theory*. Chicago: Aldine.

Glass, D.C. (1977). *Behavior patterns, stress, and coronary disease*. Hillsdale, NJ: Erlbaum.

Glass, D.C., & Singer, J.E. (1972). *Urban stress*. New York: Academic.

Guski, R., & Rohrmann, B. (1981). Psychological aspects of environmental noise. *Journal of Environmental Policy, 2*, 183–212.

Hedge, A. (1984). Evidence of a relationship between office design and self-reports of ill health among office workers in the United Kingdom. *Journal of Architectural Planning and Research, 1*, 163–174.

Heller, K., & Monahan, J. (1977). *Psychology and community change*. Homewood, IL: Dorsey.

Holahan, C.J. (1986). Environmental psychology. *Annual Review of Psychology, 37*. 381–407.

Ittelson, W.H. (1973). Environment perception and contemporary perceptual theory. In W.H. Ittelson (Ed.), *Environment and cognition*. New York: Seminar. 1–19.

Jacobi, M. (1984). *A contextual analysis of stress and health among re-entry women to college*. Unpublished doctoral dissertation, University of California, Irvine.

Jacobi, M., & Stokols, D. (1983). The role of tradition in group-environment relations. In N.R. Feimer & E.S. Geller (Eds.), *Environmental psychology: Directions and perspectives*. New York: Praeger. 157–179.

Jessor, R. (1958). The problem of reductionism in psychology. *Psychological Review, 65*, 170–178.

Jones, D.M., & Davies, D.R. (1984). Individual and group differences in the response to noise. In D.M. Jones & A.J. Chapman (Eds.), *Noise and society*. New York: Wiley. 125–154.

Kantrowitz, M., & Seidel, A.D. (Eds.). (1985). Applications of environment and behavior research [Special issue]. *Environment and Behavior, 17.* 3–144.

Kaplan, S., & Kaplan, R. (1982). *Cognition and environment.* New York: Praeger.

Kaplan, S. (1983). A model of person-environment compatibility. *Environment and Behavior, 15,* 311–332.

Kelley, H.H. (1983). The situational origins of human tendencies: A further reason for the formal analysis of structures. *Personality and Social Psychology Bulletin, 9,* 8–30.

Kelly, J.G. (1985). *Context and process: An ecological view of the interdependence of practice and research.* Paper presented at the American Psychological Association Conference, Los Angeles, CA.

Kobasa, S.C. (1979). Stressful life events, personality, and health: An inquiry into hardiness. *Journal of Personality and Social Psychology, 37,* 1–11.

Koffka, J. (1935). *Principles of gestalt psychology.* New York: Harcourt, Brace, and World.

Kohler, W. (1947). *Gestalt psychology.* New York: Liveright.

Lazarus, R.S. (1966). *Psychological stress and the coping process.* New York: McGraw-Hill.

Lenntorp, B. (1978). A time-geographic simulation model of individual activity programmes. In T. Carlstein, D. Parkes, & N. Thrift (Eds.), *Human activity and time geography.* New York: Wiley. 162–180.

Lewin, K. (1936). *Principles of topological psychology.* New York: McGraw-Hill.

Little, B. (1983). Personal projects: A rationale and method for investigation. *Environment and Behavior, 15,* 273–310.

Magnusson, D. (1981). Wanted: A psychology of situations. In D. Magnusson (Ed.), *Toward a psychology of situations: An interactional perspective.* Hillsdale, NJ: Erlbaum. 9–32.

Magnusson, D., & Allen, V.P. (Eds.). (1983). *Human development: An interactional perspective.* New York: Academic.

Manicas, P.T., & Secord, P.F. (1983). Implications for psychology of the new philosophy of science. *American Psychologist, 38,* 399–413.

Maruyama, M. (1963). The second cybernetics: Deviation-amplifying mutual causal processes. *American Scientist, 51,* 164–179.

McGuire, W.J. (1983). A contextualist theory of knowledge: Its implications for innovation and reform in psychological research. In L. Berkowitz (Ed.), *Advances in experimental social psychology* (Vol. 16) (pp. 1–47). New York: Academic.

Mehrabian, A., & Russell, J.A. (1974). *An approach to environmental psychology.* Cambridge, MA: MIT Press.

Merton, R.K. (1968). Manifest and latent functions. In R.K. Merton (Ed.), *Social theory and social structure.* New York: Free Press. 73–138.

Michelson, W. (1985). *From sun to sun: Contextual dimensions and personal implications of maternal employment.* New York: Rowman & Allanheld.

Milgram, S., & Jodelet, D. (1976). Psychological maps of Paris. In H. Proshansky, W. Ittelson, & L. Rivlin (Eds.), *Environmental psychology* (2nd ed.) (pp. 104–124). New York: Holt, Rinehart & Winston.

Mitchell, R.E. (1972). Some social implications of high-density housing. *American Sociological Review, 36,* 18–29.

Mook, D.G. (1983). In defense of external invalidity. *American Psychologist, 38,* 379–387.

Moos, R.H. (1979). Social ecological perspectives on health. In G.C. Stone, F. Cohen, N.E. Adler, & Associates (Eds.), *Health psychology: A handbook.* San Francisco: Jossey-Bass. 523–547.

Murray, H.A. (1938). *Explorations in personality.* New York: Oxford University Press.

Naisbitt, J., & Aburdene, P. (1985). *Reinventing the corporation.* New York: Warner.

Neisser, U. (1982). *Memory observed: Remembering in natural contexts.* San Francisco: Freeman.

Olson, M.H., & Primps, S.B. (1985). Working at home with computers: Work and nonwork issues. *Journal of Social Issues, 40,* 97–112.

Pervin, L.A. (1978). Definitions, measurements, and classifications of stimuli, situations, and environments. *Human Ecology, 6,* 71–105.

Petrinovich, L. (1979). Probabilistic functionalism: A conception of research method. *American Psychologist, 34,* 373–390.

Platt, J.R. (1964). Strong inference. *Science, 146,* 347–353.

Proshansky, H., Ittelson, W., & Rivlin, L. (Eds.). (1976). *Environmental psychology: People and their physical settings* (2nd ed.). New York: Holt, Rinehart & Winston.

Proshansky, M.M., Fabian, A.K., & Kaminoff, R. (1983). Place identity: Physical world socialization of the self. *Journal of Environmental Psychology, 3,* 57–83.

Roethlisberger, F., & Dickson, W. (1939). *Management and the worker.* Cambridge, MA: Harvard University Press.

Russell, J.A., & Ward, L.M. (1982). Environmental psychology. *Annual Review of Psychology, 33,* 651–688.

Saegert, S. (1985). *Environmental psychology and the world beyond the mind.* G. Stanley Hall Lecture presented at the American Psychological Association Conference, Los Angeles, CA.

Sampson, E.E. (1981). Cognitive psychology as ideology. *American Psychologist, 36,* 730–743.

Sarason, S.B. (1976). *The psychological sense of community: Prospects for a community psychology.* San Francisco: Jossey-Bass.

Scarr, S. (1979). Psychology and children: Current research and practice. *American Psychologist, 34,* 809–811.

Schachter, S., & Singer, J.E. (1962). Cognitive, social, and physiological determinants of emotional state. *Psychological Review, 69,* 379–399.

Schmitt, R.C. (1957). Density, delinquency, and crime in Honolulu. *Sociology and Social Research, 41,* 274–276.

Schwartz, G.E. (1982). Testing the biopsychosocial model: The ultimate challenge facing behavioral medicine? *Journal of Consulting and Clinical Psychology, 50,* 1040–1053.

Shaw, M.E., & Costanzo, P.R. (1970). *Theories of social psychology.* New York: McGraw-Hill.

Singer, J.E., Lundberg, U., & Frankenhaeuser, M. (1978). Stress on the train: A study of urban commuting. In A. Baum, J.E. Singer, and S. Valins (Eds.), *Advances in environmental psychology* (Vol. 1). Hillsdale, NJ: Erlbaum. 41–56.

Smith, M.B. (1983). The shaping of American social psychology: A personal perspective from the periphery. *Personality and Social Psychology Bulletin, 9,* 165–180.

Stern, P.C., & Gardner, G.T. (1981). Psychological research and energy policy. *American Psychologist, 36,* 329–342.

Stokols, D. (1978a). Environmental psychology. *Annual Review of Psychology, 29,* 253–295.

Stokols, D. (1978b). A typology of crowding experiences. In A. Baum & Y. Epstein (Eds.), *Human response to crowding.* Hillsdale, NJ: Erlbaum. 219–255.

Stokols, D. (1979). A congruence analysis of human stress. In I.G. Sarason & C.D. Spielberger (Eds.), *Stress and anxiety* (Vol. 6.) (pp. 27–53) New York: Wiley.

Stokols, D. (1981). Group *x* place transactions: Some neglected issues in psychological research on settings. In D. Magnusson (Ed.), *Toward a psychology of situations: An interactional perspective* (pp. 393–415). Hillsdale, NJ: Erlbaum.

Stokols, D. (1982). Environmental psychology: A coming of age. In A.G. Kraut (Ed.), *The G. Stanley Hall Lecture Series* (Vol. 2) (pp. 155–205). Washington, DC: American Psychological Association.

Stokols, D. (1983). *Scientific and policy challenges of a contextually-oriented psychology.* Presidential address to the Division of Population and Environmental Psychology of the American Psychology Association, Annual Conference of the American Psychological Association, Anaheim, CA.

Stokols, D. (1986). Transformational perspectives on environment and behavior: An agenda for future research. In W.H. Ittelson, M. Asai, & M. Ker (Eds.), *Cross-cultural research in environment and behavior: Proceedings of the Second United States—Japan Seminar on Environment and Behavior.* Tucson: University of Arizona, 243–260.

Stokols, D., & Jacobi, M. (1984). Traditional, present oriented, and futuristic modes of group-environment relations. In K. Gergen & M. Gergen (Eds.), *Historical social psychology.* Hillsdale, NJ: Erlbaum. 303–324.

Stokols, D., & Novaco, R.W. (1981). Transportation and well-being: An ecological perspective. In J. Wohlwill, P. Everett, & I. Altman (Eds.), *Human behavior and environment—Advances in theory and research: Vol. 5. Transportation environments* (pp. 85–130). New York: Plenum.

Stokols, D., Novaco, R.W., Stokols, J., & Campbell, J. (1978). Traffic congestion, Type-A behavior, and stress. *Journal of Applied Psychology, 63,* 467–480.

Stokols, D., & Shumaker, S.A. (1981). People in places: A transactional view of settings. In J. Harvey (Ed.), *Cognition, social behavior and the environment.* Hillsdale, NJ: Erlbaum. 441–488.

Stokols, D., Shumaker, S.A., & Martinez, J. (1983). Residential mobility and personal well-being. *Journal of Environmental Psychology, 3,* 5–19.

Toffler, A. (1980). *The Third Wave.* New York: Bantam.

Tolman, E.C., & Brunswik, E. (1935). The organism and the causal texture of the environment. *Psychological Review, 42,* 43–77.

Veroff, J. (1983). Contextual determinants of personality. *Personality and Social Psychology Bulletin, 9,* 331–343.

Wapner, S., & Kaplan, B. (1983). *Toward a holistic developmental psychology.* Hillsdale, NJ: Erlbaum.

Webb, E.J., Campbell, D.T., Schwartz, R.D., Sechrest, L., & Grove, J.B. (1981). *Nonreactive measures in the social sciences.* Boston: Houghton Mifflin.

Weick, K.E. (1979). *The social psychology of organizing* (2nd ed.). Reading, MA: Addison-Wesley.

Whalen, C.K., & Henker, B. (1980). *Hyperactive children: The social ecology of identification and treatment.* New York: Academic.

Wicker, A.W. (1985). Getting out of our conceptual ruts: Strategies for expanding conceptual frameworks. *American Psychologist, 40,* 1094–1103.

Winkel, G. (1985). Ecological validity issues in field research settings. In A. Baum & J.E. Singer, (Eds.), *Advances in environmental psychology: Vol. 5. Methods of environmental investigation.* Hillsdale, NJ: Erlbaum. 1–41.

Winsborough, H.H. (1965). The social consequences of high population density. *Law and Contemporary Problems, 30,* 120–126.

Wohlwill, J.F. (1973). The environment is not in the head! In W.F. Preiser (Ed.), *Environmental design research: Vol. 2. Symposia and Workshops. Proceedings of the 4th Annual Environmental Design Research Association Conference* (pp. 166–181). Stroudsburg, PA: Dowden, Hutchinson, & Ross.

Wohlwill, J.F. (1978, November). *Ecological representativeness in developmental research: A critical view.* Paper presented at the Institute of Psychology of the Technological University of Berlin.

Wohlwill, J.F. (1981). Environmental psychology and environmental problems. *Journal of Environmental Policy,* 2, 157–182.

Wurtman, R.J. (1975). The effects of light on the human body. *Scientific American, 233,* 68–77.

Zube, E. (1980). *Environmental evaluation: Perception and public policy.* Monterey, CA: Brooks/Cole.

IMPLICATIONS OF ENVIRONMENTAL CONTEXT FOR VALIDITY ASSESSMENTS

Gary H. Winkel, *Graduate School and University Center, City University of New York, New York*

3.1. INTRODUCTION

Over the past 20 years, efforts by psychologists to move research studies into field settings have raised questions about the match between the requirements of traditional research designs and the complexities of people's activities in everyday environments. Many of those who have expressed the need for a reexamination of the rules that have been developed for the assessment of claims regarding the validity of research findings have been motivated by a desire to address so-called real world problems in the settings in which they may be found rather than attempting to simulate them within the laboratory (Bronfenbrenner, 1977; Ellsworth, 1977; Ittelson, Proshansky, Rivlin, & Winkel, 1974; Petrinovich, 1979; Proshansky, 1976; Winkel, 1977). Concerns for field-relevant research design have also been a result of the growth of social, behavioral, economic, and political evaluations of various policies and programs designed to bring about change in important arenas of public life.

While broader social forces have provided extrinsic motivation for a reevaluation of methodological problems by environmental researchers, there are some intrinsic forces that make field settings an important locale for the investigation of person–environment relations. The differential functioning of people in environments constitutes a central explanatory focus for environmentalists. As such, the field and its operating characteristics represent a challenge both for theory development and for research design.

The purpose of this chapter is to examine some conceptual and practical issues associated with proposals advanced for the determination of validity claims offered by investigators who conduct field research. I will suggest some alternatives that might be considered when thinking about validity. These alternatives represent a departure from the recommendations of those who do not consider environmental issues theoretically relevant to their concerns.

Within the perspective being advanced in this chapter, field sites are viewed as relatively bounded physical systems in which people pursue goal-directed activities. The nature and expression of goals are affected by a complex set of personal, social, and situationally based variables. Some of these factors generalize across settings while others may be unique to a particular time and place. There are many occasions in which people's personal histories, demographic backgrounds, values, symbolic associations to settings, and social structures represent important textural elements that are essential to understanding the progressive accommodations of people to environments. In addition to these person-related aspects of environmental accommodation, there are social contexts in which personal goals and actions represent negotiated compromises based on the needs and aspirations of others. Settings themselves are often the focus of idiosyncratic and socially determined evaluations that affect the structure and organization of the environments within which research is conducted.

Depending on the stance that an investigator adopts regarding the nature of valid knowledge about human actions and experiences, differences among people and environments within which they function may be conceptualized in either of two ways. Either they represent a potential for multiple challenges to the validity of research results or they are possible sources of information that would be relevant to theory generation and assessment. For reasons to be pursued later in this chapter, I will argue that variations in person–setting characteristics can often be of theoretical relevance to environmentalists. Other investigators, however, may be inclined to believe that the complexities associated with efforts to accommodate to different environments are more likely to create "threats" to validity (Campbell & Stanley, 1963; Cook & Campbell, 1979; Judd & Kenny, 1981).

If potential threats to validity assessments can be traced to the functional characteristics of field settings, there are two tasks that must be undertaken by environmental researchers. The first involves a reevaluation of different formulations of the validity question. If in the process of this reevaluation the social forces that lead to the differential uses and evaluations of environments require a conceptual framework in which they are considered relevant to theoretical explanations of person–environment transactions, the second step requires approaches to research design and analysis that would incorporate these factors into the study plan.

I think that such a reevaluation is necessary at this point in the field's development. In the material that follows, I hope to build on the insights of those who have addressed field research questions from a tradition that emphasizes the use of experimental and quasi-experimental designs (Cook & Campbell, 1979; Judd & Kenny, 1981). Although the positions espoused by these authors are not representative of the many perspectives taken by those who write about research design from other philosophical orientations (Bogdan & Taylor, 1975; Filstead, 1970; Glaser & Strauss, 1967; Lofland, 1971; McCall & Simmons, 1969; Schatzman & Strauss, 1973), it is clear that the experimental tradition from which their work springs has played an important role in shaping our thinking and actions regarding the planning, conduct, and evaluation of research strategies. I intend to use these contributions as a basis for some alternatives that may provide a more holistically oriented approach to people in environments.

This chapter is organized in the following manner. I plan first to examine briefly the structure and aims of classically oriented approaches to theory construction and research design. I will then suggest that classical experimental design encounters some fundamental difficulties when efforts are made to determine the generality of research findings to different settings. These difficulties arise because of the proposals that have been advanced by environmental researchers who adopt a more complex and dynamically oriented framework regarding explanations of people's relationships to the environment. Next, I discuss the implications of field characteristics for the assessment of the different types of validities that have been used in the literature on experimental and quasi-experimental design. This discussion leads to a proposal for the use of the concept of ecological validity to describe the influence of field characteristics in research planning and design. An effort is then made to link the ecological validity concept to other forms of validity that have been discussed in the methodological literature. Finally, I suggest a series of steps that might be taken to improve the ecological design of field studies.

3.2. AN ENVIRONMENTAL PERSPECTIVE ON CLASSICAL THEORY AND RESEARCH DESIGN

Within the classical approach to theory development and testing (Marx & Hillix, 1973, discuss major systems and theories in psychology), theories purporting to explain human behavior are communicated in a formal verbal and/or quantitative framework. The explanatory systems are generally not grounded directly in any particular setting, time, or historical context. The theory's terms are usually phrased in such a way that its concepts are general enough to allow a range of operational measurements. This range, however, is not necessarily tied to any particular setting, nor is it intended to be so (Mook, 1983). The aim of those who work within this tradition is the creation of generalizations regarding human experience and behavior that are transsituational, transtemporal, and transenvironmental and will cover the widest possible range of individual and group characteristics.

The scope of the intended generalizations is gradually extended through the use of methodologies that take temporally, spatially, and socially correlated events and disentangle them systematically. The analytic decomposition or disaggregation of multiple variables into components that are subsequently studied in relative isolation from one another is considered to be a necessary prelude to the task of synthetic reconstruction into formal theory. The research designs and procedures that have been developed to facilitate the analytic phase of research are a direct consequence of the desire to formulate cause and effect statements of maximum generality.

Through the appropriate use of control and comparison conditions, along with randomization procedures, it becomes possible to study various processes in a systematic and segmental fashion. If complexity is introduced into the research design, it is done so additively. The anticipation is that over the course of such work it should be possible to construct an explanatory system that will ultimately mirror the complexity of human behavior.

To make the theory's components credible, the researcher must, at a bare minimum, demonstrate that the variable(s) asserted to be causal produces variation in factors that are assumed to be dependent on it. If such covariation occurs, attention is then focused on the question of whether the putatively causal variable(s) is indeed responsible for any observed effects.

This issue is resolved in two steps. First, the investigator must establish that the causal variable temporally preceded the effect variable. Second, he or she must provide convincing evidence that observed variation in the effect was due solely to the causal factor and not to something that was unmeasured, unknown, and/or uncontrolled.

The establishment of the conceptual purity of the explanatory variable(s) involves the identification of what are called competing alternative hypotheses that might account for observed outcomes. If these can be identified, they may be ruled out of contention by means of appropriate controls or, under certain conditions, by statistical adjustments. If they cannot be identified, the use of randomization procedures for assignment to different comparisons may reduce the likelihood that plausible alternatives can account for the observed results of the study.

The process of explanation is further enhanced if the causal variable(s) can be manipulated systematically and actively under the investigator's control. The utilization of systematic treatments, interventions, or experimental changes is assumed to be a powerful and efficient means for determining whether there are any regular and, one hopes, theoretically meaningful relationships among independent and dependent measures. If there are, and rival explanations have been eliminated, the investigator has established the internal validity of the study (Cook & Campbell, 1979).

From Cook and Campbell's perspective, the internal validity of a study is the sine qua non for its possible contribution to understanding interrelationships among variables. While necessary, however, internal validity is not sufficient for the ultimate determination of a study's value in any theoretical or practical sense. The analyst must also assess the generality of findings across settings, individuals, occasions, and alternate measures of the cause and effect variables to establish what these authors call external validity.

The determination of external validity is not an easy task. As Cook and Campbell point out through numerous examples, the types of experimental treatments that are administered in most behavioral and social science studies may interact with different people in different settings at different times. To the extent that such interactions occur, the plausibility of any straightforward statements regarding the noncontingent nature of relationships between or among variables is compromised (Cook & Campbell, 1979, pp. 74–80). Establishing external validity is clearly an issue of major importance for environmental researchers. This is because the nature of a setting's operation is ultimately linked to the nature of the theoretical constructs that can be used to account for the diverse activities that occur in the locales under investigation.

3.2.1. Limits of Generalization Are Defined by Theoretical Issues

The definition of external validity provided by Cook and Campbell refers not just to generalizations across person, setting, and time but also to generalizations "to and across alternative measures of the cause and effect" (Cook & Campbell, 1979, p. 37).

When we consider alternate measures of cause and effect relationships, we are really discussing different *indicators* of the constructs that are employed in a study. An assessment of construct indicators and their relationships to one another is a central problem for the establishment of construct validity (Cronbach & Meehl, 1955). If an investigator wishes to evaluate the transferability of constructs used in one setting to another, he or she must advance a *theoretical* rationale that would support the linkage between construct indicators employed at different research sites. For example, if the construct of interest involves the provision of voluntary aid to another person, to what extent is willingness to help an experimenter pretest some arithmetic problems in a laboratory comparable to helping a person pick up a package that has fallen to the ground?

One way of approaching this question involves the development of a set of somewhat more abstract categories that would allow the investigator to dimensionalize the voluntary aid construct. For example, Amato (1983) describes a scheme he developed with Pearce in which various helping behavior indicators were classified in terms of the seriousness of the assistance requested, whether the aid required the person to give something or do something for the other person, and whether the help involved a spontaneous or planned act.

From an environmental perspective, there is an even more fundamental set of issues that requires consideration. For a setting to be considered a candidate for the investigation of possible generalizations and extensions of research findings, the researcher must provide some evidence that the behaviors to be used as indicators of theoretical constructs are likely to be exhibited in the place chosen for the research, that the indicator(s) of both causal and outcome variables will demonstrate variability that will allow the examination of functional relationships among them, and that aspects of the setting's sociophysical organization can help to illuminate the nature of the phenomenon in which the investigator is interested.

To gain a better appreciation of these aspects of the theoretical issues that are raised when considering external validity questions, the following examples suggest that external validity concerns have ramifications that extend beyond purely technical considerations.

In a recent paper, Levine (1982) describes some theoretical issues that have implications for the construction of two-dimensional maps designed to assist a person who wishes to locate himself or herself in a geographical space whose area may be so large and irregular that it cannot be viewed in its entirety. In particular, Levine is interested in the conditions under which maps indicating that "You Are Here" (YAH maps) will aid or hinder orientation.

Levine correctly notes that there are instances in which such maps, although designed to be helpful, are actually counterproductive for way finding. To facilitate orientation, Levine suggests that there are five factors that are essential to the design and location of YAH maps. First, the map should illustrate a link between the YAH indicator and at least one feature of the space itself. Second, it should be placed near an asymetrical part of the terrain (e.g., not in the center of a group of buildings surrounding the map). Third, it should be aligned with the terrain so that the map's top is equivalent to looking forward. Fourth, the map should indicate where it is located relative to the person's position, and fifth, the cues of the YAH map should be redundant (i.e., the maps and their locations should be designed using various combinations of the first four recommendations listed above).

It should be clear that the conditions hypothesized by Levine could be manipulated independently and in combination to determine the differential and combined effectiveness of those factors he claims will improve way finding. Although Levine did not suggest that a laboratory study should be conducted, it would be possible to test his hypotheses under controlled conditions.

A hypothetical investigator could select a suitably large room and erect partitions simulating different locations and arrange them in different configurations relative to the information contained in the YAH maps. An appropriate group of research participants could be assembled and various subgroups could be formed through random assignment to different combinations of map conditions and partition alignments (e.g., a circular vs. irregular vs. rectangular arrangement). The participant's task would then involve locating partitions that are labeled on the maps and matching them to their location in the room.

If in this hypothetical study support was found for Levine's hypotheses, the use of randomization procedures ensures that factors other than those connected to the different types of YAH maps that were assessed would be unlikely candidates to account for the study's outcomes. If the researcher then attempted to study different YAH maps and their effects on way finding in settings outside the laboratory, the choice of conditions under which this investigation might be undertaken would be somewhat more problematic. For example, dissimilar configurations of buildings will be characteristic of different sites. The number of people present at any place may be expected to vary over the course of the day. If other people are present, they may communicate with one another in ways that might influence way finding choices. Factors that are relevant to way finding such as the presence of individuals who may be expected to know the environment (e.g., security guards), alternative sources of information (e.g., signs), and spatial layouts that are more or less easy to grasp, might all have to temper any judgments regarding the generality of the findings obtained in the laboratory (i.e., in external validity assessments).

What is more, these factors may represent potential "threats" to internal validity. To the extent that these aspects of the research locale are associated with variations in YAH maps in ways that are unknown to the investigator, it would be very difficult to attribute differences in wayfinding ability to the YAH maps only. Yet many of these conditions are very likely to be representative of and relevant to the everyday cognitive processes that are germane to orientation. It is therefore possible to argue that, since they are relevant to the theoretical understanding of orientation processes, it would be inappropriate to try to devise a research design that would necessarily eliminate them in favor of the YAH maps alone. Efforts to model these aspects of the various locales in which research generality is sought would expand the theoretical understanding of way finding and improve external validity.

In this hypothetical example, the transference from laboratory to field, while potentially problematic in its execution and consequences, was at least conceptually easy to accomplish. There are many settings outside the laboratory in which orientation is an issue and setting characteristics may be expected to expand the theoretical range of the way-finding construct. A much more complicated problem arises when generalization based on constructs that have been employed in one setting have a somewhat tenuous link to constructs that may be important to understanding of the range of behaviors in the place to which the research findings are to be generalized.

For example, in work on helping behavior conducted outside the laboratory, two complex construct systems are often used (Korte & Grant, 1980; Page, 1977; Schneider, Lesko, & Garrett, 1980). The first of these involves the notion of information overload (Milgram, 1970). The basic idea is that aversive stimuli in the environment lead to a condition in which the competing behavioral demands of these stimuli interfere with expression of indicators of the second construct system—voluntary aid to another person.

In the papers just cited, the behaviors studied involved the provision of various forms of assistance to others in different public places (streets in or near commercial areas). In Page's (1977) study, it was hypothesized that ambient environmental noise levels would be sufficiently aversive that pedestrians would avoid taking the time to assist someone who had dropped a package or would be unwilling to provide ·change to make a telephone call. In Schneider and colleagues' (1980) research, four types of aid were examined: helping a person on crutches pick up a book, helping a pedestrian who had dropped some groceries, aiding someone looking for a lost contact lens, and agreeing to answer a questionnaire. The authors wished to test the effects of different levels of ambient temperature on willingness to help.

Variations in noise levels in the laboratory had been shown to affect indicators of both anti- and prosocial behavior (Page, 1977). In the research cited by Page, prosocial behavior was operationalized as the provision of low-commitment assistance (pretesting some arithmetic problems) to an experimenter who asked the research subject for this help. Since assistance in picking up packages and providing change for a telephone call involve relatively low degrees of commitment, it was at least plausible to assume that these indicators of prosocial behavior in the field might be affected by differences in noise levels.

Laboratory findings on the behavioral effects of temperature differences, however, were not as extensive as those for variations in noise levels. Temperatures were examined in a range that extended from moderate to hot. The outcome measures used in the laboratory studies involved willingness to administer electric shocks to another person (Baron & Bell, 1975, 1976) or ratings of a hypothetical person whose opinions either agreed or disagreed with those of the research subject (Griffitt, 1970; Griffitt & Veitch, 1971). In the laboratory work cited by Schneider and colleagues, no instances of temperature effects on willingness to provide assistance were reported. Schneider and colleagues, however, argued that the generic construct that was potentially applicable in both the laboratory and the streets in which their study was conducted was propensity to express prosocial behaviors. Their theoretical rationale was based on the proposition that if willingness to administer electric shocks was an expression of antisocial behavior the stress associated with high and low temperatures should reduce the likelihood that prosocial behaviors would be expressed.

Schneider and colleagues' choice of indicators of helping behavior was at least plausible in the context of the settings within which the study was conducted (streets near a commercial area). Yet the outcomes of Schneider and colleagues' study did not support the hypotheses advanced by these authors while the data from Page's research were congruent with his hypotheses.

If we examine the factors that might have influenced these results, it is possible to identify problems with the comparability of indicators employed in the laboratory and field settings as well as theoretical variables associated with the environmental contexts.

Three potentially important theoretical variables pertinent to the laboratory and field settings should be noted in the work cited by Schneider et al.: freedom of behavioral choice in the two research sites, expectancies created by the arrangement of research conditions in the laboratory studies cited by Schneider et al. (demand characteristics), and the degree of exposure to the stressors being studied.

As far as can be determined, in none of the laboratory studies referenced by Schneider and his colleagues were there any indications that the experimental subjects were informed that they could choose to leave the laboratory if they wished to terminate the study. What is more, those researchers whose main outcome variable involved the administration of shocks by experimental subjects to other "subjects" (in fact, confederates of the experimenter) made it clear to the research participants that the purpose of the study was to investigate the role that temperature differences played in affecting the behaviors of interest (Baron & Bell, 1975, 1976).

Resentments that might have been created by a restriction in the freedom to leave the laboratory along with expectancies created by telling the participants that temperature differences were being investigated led Schneider and colleagues to conclude that demand characteristics might have led to the positive findings on the effects of temperature in the laboratory. This suggestion by Schneider and colleagues raises the possibility that field sites in which possibilities of escape into cooler climates are reduced would be better candidates for studies of temperature effects on behavior than would city streets.

A reduction in the freedom to choose to leave a setting has further implications for the degree to which research participants are exposed to those variables whose effects are being investigated. In the laboratory research on temperature, conditions were arranged so that each research subject was given an exposure period sufficient to bring about behavioral changes. Since in the field study no information was available regarding the degree to which passersby had been differentially exposed to the ambient temperatures in different comparisons, it is not clear that field conditions necessarily matched those in the laboratory. The problems of insufficient variation in and exposure to stressor conditions in the field have been addressed by Saegert (1978) in her discussion of environmental stress.

The orientation, noise, and temperature studies just discussed indicate that questions concerning the generalization of research findings from setting to setting are very closely tied to theoretical variables that characterize the operation of settings and to theoretical issues that are raised as a consequence of the decisions that are made regarding the procedures that are employed when attempting to study the transfer of results. Failures to generalize can most often be traced to poorly defined and/or inadequately grounded theoretical constructs.

3.2.2. Generalization as a Problem of Inadequately Grounded Constructs

With what has been said thus far, I hope to have persuaded the reader that external validity problems can often be traced to efforts to develop theoretical constructs that bear little or no explicit connections to persons, places, or times. When the linkage between theoretical constructs and place-situated variables is ambiguous, the investigator is often forced to rely on *implicit* theories that guide the choice of a setting within which to pursue a research question. I refer to this problem as the paradox of contextualizing a decontextualized construct.

An insistence on the embedded nature of person–environment relationships does not preclude the search for general relationships among variables. It does alert the investigator, however, to the possibility that generality may vary along a dimension of increasing contingency. Contingent or warranted generalizations are a reflection of the diversity encountered when doing research in settings that are characterized by different configurations of people, physical structures, and normative codes. It is the understanding of the potentially contingent and multiple determinants of observed behavior that, ultimately, will yield the range and scope of theoretical understanding required for the diverse phenomena in which we are interested.

It would not be appropriate to pursue these theoretical issues here since they are discussed in other chapters of this handbook. It is relevant, however, to consider those aspects of various theoretical approaches to person–environment relationships that have direct implications for validity problems.

3.3 PERSON–SETTING CHARACTERISTICS HAVING IMPLICATIONS FOR VALIDITY

3.3.1. Settings and Their Social Structures Are Dynamically Organized

One of the central tenets of most systems proposed to account for people's actions in environments is that human activity systems and the settings within which these are expressed possess different organizational structures. These structures may be weakly or strongly related both within and among different settings (Stokols & Shumaker, 1981; Wicker, 1979). It is further assumed that people as well as settings pass through historical transitions. Hence settings come into being, maintain themselves for varying periods of time, and pass out of existence (Sarason, 1972; Stokols & Shumaker, 1981; Wicker, Chapter 16, this volume).

In Barker's ecological psychology, behavior settings represent integrated patterns of human and nonhuman components that interact to carry out the setting's "program" within a bounded, self-regulated, and ordered system (Barker, 1963, 1968; Barker & Gump, 1968; Barker & Wright, 1949, 1951.) Behavior in the setting is ordered sequentially and follows definite rules.

Ittelson and colleagues (1974) have suggested that environmental settings include not only the physical components that are present, but also the social and individual behaviors that occur within them. In this sense, environmental settings represent a process defined by their participants and the nature of their interactions.

The boundaries of a particular setting are defined not only by the setting's physical properties but also through its interactive relationships with other physical and social systems. The environment in this sense is an open system. Bronfenbrenner (1977) carries this point further and suggests that the *ecological environment* may be thought of in terms of "nested arrangements of structures, each contained within the next" (p. 514). At the level of the individual behavior setting (which Bronfenbrenner calls the *microsystem*), people engage in activities in particular role relationships to one another for particular periods of time. At any point in the person's development, there is a complex of microsystems that constitute what Bronfenbrenner refers to as the *mesosystem*. It is assumed that microsystems have varying degrees of relationships to one another depending on the person's developmental sequence. The organizational structures of settings, the temporally based experiences of their inhabitants, and the "programs" that guide their operations provide the frames for different affective–cognitive patterns that may or may not be expressed behaviorally.

Among the most immediate implications of these propositions for research planning and design is that both people and environments have *histories* and pass through different *maturational* phases. These developmental aspects of persons and settings represent "threats" to validity only if they affect the variables in which the investigator is interested and have not been conceptualized as part of the construct system used to guide the research plan.

3.3.2. Activities Are Goal Directed

Simple observation of humans in environments can easily establish the integrated nature of behavior. Most theoretical orientations descriptive of person–environment transactions contain an assumption that the person's capacities to think, feel, sense, interpret, and act are interrelated and that people are "dynamically organized systems whose behaviors and experiences express the interactive consequences of these processes and functions" (Ittelson et al., 1974, p. 83). Within this framework, our concerns lie in understanding the nature of individual and social behaviors and experiences in the context of multiple physical settings.

For those who conceive of behavior and experience in these terms, it is generally agreed that the goal-directed character of such behavior appears to provide a potential basis for the explanation of the unity and integrity of human action in settings. This goal-directed intentionality of behavior has direct implications for the assessment of environments in terms of their abilities to accommodate the goals that people bring to them.

Environmental evaluations that are organized around the setting's abilities to accommodate goals have behavioral possibilities. One of the most obvious of these is that people will selectively choose to enter and leave environments. Within the constraints set by social, political, and economic structures, the methodological implications of selective entry and exit from settings lead directly to the realization that people self-select into environments and, depending on the conditions they encounter, choose either to stay or to leave. These aspects of environmental experience have been referred to in the methodological literature as *self-selection into conditions* and *mortality* (or the loss of persons from conditions).

If the social, political, and/or economic arrangements of a society lead to differential restrictions or opportunities regarding the freedom to choose the environments within which a person may operate, the researcher must evaluate the role that assignment rules play in determining who may be found in a setting at the time the research is undertaken and over the course of the study. More importantly, do the correlates of assignment rules have implications for the interpretations that are attached to the findings generated from the research?

3.3.3. Settings Are Guided by Rules or Programs

Environmental settings are frequently conceived of in terms of the rules or programs that guide their operation (Wicker, 1979). From Ittelson and colleagues' (1974) perspective, rule structures are a consequence of a setting's natural history of use and, in many instances, are a direct result of formal planning that guides the behavior sequences observed in the setting. When no formal plan can be identified, implicit normative structures are evolved and communicated by those who are familiar with the setting's natural history of use. For example, there may be no formal rules guiding behavior in a place of worship. Yet the nature of the activities observed there is clearly the result of some type of "program" that defines the limits of acceptable and unacceptable behavior. If behavioral events depart from the "program" efforts are made to reestablish behavior-program conformity. The control mechanisms that may be employed include social actions and/or physical alterations in the setting. If these efforts fail, the persons responsible for the program deviations may be ejected from the setting.

Within the environmental frameworks employed by Barker and his colleagues and by Ittelson and his colleagues, the rules that guide the operation of settings grow out of the prevailing ideologies and behavioral transactions of setting users. Thus the program is often considered to be generated within the setting rather than from outside the setting. Bronfenbrenner (1977), however, suggests that there are institutional structures that govern the nature and organization of activities such as work, neighborhood relations, the distribution of goods and services, governmental services, the mass media, and so on that do not affect individual behavior directly but set the standard against which behavior in microenvironments or behavior settings may be assessed. At an even broader level (the macrosystem), there are "overarching institutional patterns of the culture and subculture" (p. 515) that are expressed concretely at the level of the micro-, meso-, and exosystem. These components of the macrosystem appear to be driven primarily by what Bronfenbrenner calls the prevailing ideology of the society within which the nested structures occur. The theoretical, methodological, and analytic implications of these broader contextual aspects of settings can be found in the work of Blalock (1984) and Boyd and Iversen (1979).

For our purposes, the nature of a setting's program has direct implications for the external validity of a study. When an investigator must decide on the choice of setting within which to generalize research finding, he or she must determine whether the behaviors observed in one setting are compatible with the program of the setting to which generalization is to be made. If, for example, the researcher is concerned about the factors that influence the regulation of information about the self to others, a setting must be chosen in which this aspect of human experience is salient. The setting's program provides guidelines regarding the likelihood that self-disclosing behavior is expected, tolerated, ignored, encouraged, or discouraged. One of the major tasks for setting analysis involves the mapping of setting programs, which in turn involves the identification of the behavioral-social rules that determine the nature of the programs themselves (Wicker, 1979).

3.3.4. Setting Relationships Are Mediated by Social Agents and Symbolic Associations

A significant aspect of all ecologically oriented analyses of behavior in spatial settings involves an understanding of the linkages that exist among the varying environments that are experienced by the organism over the course of its development. It is assumed that the integrated and goal-directed nature of human action can best be understood through an analysis of the interrelationships that exist among different levels of environmental encounters.

The ecological psychologists have tended to stress the behavioral linkages among settings. This methodological decision to confine the analysis to direct observations of the settings that people use is based on Barker's belief that it is difficult to obtain reliable information about a person's inner states compared to the data gathered on what people actually do. As a consequence, it is rare to find any information about the subjective interpretations that people attach to settings, their uses, and their programs (Wicker, 1979).

The frameworks advanced by Ittelson and colleagues (1974) and Bronfenbrenner (1977) provide for the direct observation of action sequences. But these authors also give greater latitude to the possibility that overt action is guided not only by the immediate demand characteristics of the setting program but also by the symbolic associations attached to the locales that people frequent. These symbolic associations may be linked to the institutional structures that Bronfenbrenner mentions but are also guided by the goals that people bring to their choices and uses of particular

places. Overt behavior, then, is multiply determined not only by the immediate demand characteristics growing out of the setting's program but also by people's personal and socially mediated interpretations of the particular setting and its relationships to other locales.

The fact that information about different settings can be mediated both directly (through direct experience or communications with others) and vicariously (through symbolic associations) means that people will differ in terms of the nature and range of their environmental experiences. While these differences represent integral aspects of people's environmental transactions, they can create problems for the investigator who wishes to obtain information about a particular locale "uncontaminated" by knowledge of and exposure to environmental conditions elsewhere. The difficulty becomes acute in those situations in which changes or interventions are to be compared to one another. If the comparisons are made in the field, there is every reason to anticipate that people may be exposed directly and/or vicariously to intervention conditions other than those to which they may have been assigned. This situation has been described generically as the *diffusion of treatments* phenomenon (Cook & Campbell, 1979). Although Cook and Campbell use this term to refer primarily to cases in which research participants are exposed directly to treatment conditions that the researcher did not intend them to experience (i.e., the treatment conditions are diffused rather than focused), it is clear that people can learn about comparison conditions from a variety of sources. Obviously, failure to gather information about diffusion renders the interpretations associated with research findings problematic.

3.4. A PROPOSAL FOR THE REINTERPRETATION OF THE MEANING OF VALIDITY

My abbreviated summary of field-oriented theoretical systems has focused on those aspects of people in relation to the organization of the environment that have direct implications for validity assessments of research designs. These characteristics have usually been framed as potential "threats" to internal validity (Cook & Campbell, 1979; Judd & Kenny, 1981). Although it may be implicitly recognized that issues such as history, maturation, self-selection, mortality, treatment diffusion, reactivity of measuring instruments, and so on are essentially theoretical issues, these factors are more commonly represented as methodological artifacts and dismissed from further substantive consideration. If these factors are expected to influence research outcomes, attention is directed to the technical procedures that might be used to remove their effects. From a theoretical perspective, however, I have already suggested that the elimination of these issues becomes problematic. When potential "threats" are theoretically relevant to variability in the phenomena in which we are interested, the time may have come when, for environmentalists, at least, problems of internal validity should be reinterpreted as issues relevant to the validity of the theoretical constructs that are employed by environmental researchers.

The remainder of this chapter is directed toward some proposals for such a reinterpretation and a more integrated approach to the validity question.

3.4.1. A Field-Oriented Approach to Validity Assessment

When designing a research plan that is sensitive to the systemic qualities of the setting or settings within which a study is to be conducted, there are two major groups of variables that are of interest. The first represents the focal concerns of the investigator. Broadly speaking, these include the explanatory and outcome variables of immediate concern to the researcher. The indicators for the variables of focal interest are based on theoretical and/or practical considerations and do not require further comment.

The second set of variables is of potentially greater significance for environmentalists. These may be referred to as the contextual mediators of the focal set of variables. For my purposes, the context refers to sets of variables that operate either independently or conjointly to affect the behavior of the independent and/or the dependent variables of focal concern. The meaning or interpretation that is attached to variations in the independent and dependent variables depends directly on the operation of these contextual variables. The latter may, depending on the problem in which the investigator is interested, include factors that have been identified as threats to internal and external validity.

Stokols (Chapter 2, this volume) approaches the problem of designing research within this framework within what he calls the contextual scope of research. For him, contextual scope involves target variables (i.e., those of direct concern), supplementary predictors and mediators, and criterion variables that occur in relative proximity in time and space. Both spatial and temporal dimensions of the research

problem can vary independently of one another. For example, a research project possessing a broad spatial scope might involve the investigation of some criterion variable in a number of different settings to determine how events that occur in one place carry over and influence behavior in a different locale.

Empirical examples of these types of carryover effects may be found in the work of Baum, Gatchel, Aiello, and Thompson (1981). These authors showed that the adoption of competitive, cooperative, or withdrawal behaviors in a prisoner's dilemma game conducted in a laboratory was a function of behavioral strategies learned when dealing with the differential amounts of social interaction prompted by the architectural designs of the dormitories within which the students lived. Saegert (1982) has also demonstrated how density factors associated with a child's home environment influence both children's scores on standardized achievement tests in school and the behavioral disturbance ratings given by their teachers. In Saegert's study, behaviors that were adaptive in higher-density home settings interfered with school behaviors.

Stokols goes on to suggest that it is possible to distinguish between two theoretical approaches to the understanding of context. In the first, the environment is conceptualized as a set of uncorrelated variables that interactively affect one or more criterion variables. This so-called partitive approach to analysis is very much similar to classical analysis of variance models in which the "independent" variables are orthogonal to one another. Partitive approaches to the environment expand the analysis of some phenomenon numerically through the inclusion of supplementary situational predictors of criterion measures. Criterion measures are presumed to operate independently of the situation in which the research is conducted.

The second orientation to environmental research is much more sensitive to contextual issues. This so-called composite representation of the environment involves predictor variables that are interdependently related to one another (i.e., correlated). These composite measures essentially reduce the number of independent predictor variables through the use of "chunked" variables and concepts that represent the interdependence or organization of environmental and personal components that comprise the environment.

In composite approaches, the choice of criterion measures is based on those aspects of the context or situation that presumably impact on the criterion measures. For example, the degree of person–environment fit may very well influence the degree of stress that the person experiences, thus affecting any one of a number of outcome measures that might have been of interest (Stern, 1974; Wicker, 1974). Person–environment fit is not a unidimensional construct but represents the interdependence among multiple parts of the situation (i.e., personal goals and relevant environmental supports and constraints).

According to Stokols, composite measures become useful when the investigator wishes to link one setting to another utilizing theoretical constructs (i.e., when attempting to establish external validity). Composite concepts are based on a format that summarizes the dimensions descriptive of one or more situational aspects of environments, thus allowing comparisons among phenotypically diverse settings. This form of categorization becomes the basis for the determination of the ecological representativeness of a study. Stokols also suggests that the scheme he is proposing will permit an assessment of the degree of interdependence that may exist between or among environments. Elements that can form the basis of composite descriptions of settings have been discussed by Stokols and Shumaker (1981).

The suggestion of Stokols that the ecological representativeness of a study may be guided by the use of composite theoretical constructs bears a certain correspondence to an approach to ecologically representative research design first proposed by Brunswik (1956). Brunswik's contributions to representative research can be traced to his insistence that methodology must be field relevant and also to his notion of ecological validity.

3.4.2. Ecological Validity and the Causal Texture of the Environment

There can be little doubt that Brunswik played a central role in early conceptualizations of the environment and its relationship to the organism's behavior (Brunswik, 1937, 1943, 1952, 1956, 1957; Hammond, 1966; Ittelson et al., 1974; Petrinovich, 1979).

Brunswik argued forcibly that psychology must be a science of "organism–environment relationships" but that lamentably it had become confined to a "science of organisms" (Brunswik, 1957, p. 6). Since Brunswik was primarily concerned with perceptual problems, he had an understandable interest in the question of how one went about conceptualizing stimuli from the external environment that the or-

ganism used in making perceptual judgments. One of his important advances was his realization that stimuli function not only as sensory data for the organism but also as sources of information from and about the environment (Ittelson et al., 1974).

From Brunswik's perspective, environmentally driven information can be divided into what he called the *distal variables* in the environment (or information about its organization) and their *proximal cues*. The latter constituted the sensory data available to the organism that allowed it to "perceive correctly, (i.e., to achieve) the intended object" (Hammond, 1966, p. 26).

Although distal variables and proximal cues are related, the connection is not unequivocal. Different environments present different configurations of distal variables relevant to a particular act or perceptual judgment. As a consequence, the proximal cues will also vary. The cues impinging on the organism are considered to be "local representatives of distal objects or variables" (Hammond, 1966, p. 27). Brunswik argued that the correlations among a distal variable and its proximal cues represented the latter's ecological validities. Thus different cues possess different ecological validities. Cue validities also shift from environment to environment. As the organism moves through its world, it encounters different settings (in Barker's terminology) or microsystems (in Bronfenbrenner's approach) possessing varying patterns of correlations among distal variables and proximal cues. It is these informational irregularities that give the environment its causal texture.

Gradually, the organism learns to assign validities to these configurations and acts in accordance with its "best bet" regarding those variables that are relevant to the judgment that is to be made. To the extent that the actions taken by the organism confirm the accuracy of its perceptions, a probability system is established that guides subsequent transactions with the environment (Ittelson et al., 1974, p. 73).

Working with Brunswik, Tolman extended Brunswik's model to take into account the equivocality of different "means–objects" that would enable the organism to achieve its ends (Tolman & Brunswik, 1935, p. 44). The environment possesses different means or tools that will enable the organism to meet its goals, and they, along with the organism's conception of their use, also will demonstrate varying degrees of validity in terms of achieving the organism's intentions.

Petrinovich (1979) has carried Brunswik's probabilistic functionalism further. In his paper, he expands on the distinction that can be drawn between the ecological and functional validity and reliability of environmental cues. Functional reliability is meant to take into account the probability that the organism will not necessarily exhibit stability in its cue assessments. If the cues are not used in a consistent manner, they possess low functional reliability. At the same time, the organism may assign different weights to the significance of cues in terms of meeting its goals. Hence the functional validity of cues will vary.

Using this definitional system, Petrinovich defines ecological validity as "the structure of the environment and the functional validity of the organism's use of that structure" (Petrinovich, 1979, p. 381). Petrinovich further argues that functional validity must be considered in terms of the ways in which stimuli are used, different means are used (to achieve some goal) as well as the link that exists between distal stimulus events and achievement (the actions taken by the organism).

3.4.3. Methodological Implications of Probabilistic Functionalism

Because of Brunswik's insistence on the shifting patterns of cue validities across environments, one of the most immediate methodological implications of this position is that, while it is necessary to sample people who differ on various organismic factors that may be expected to affect a study's outcomes, it is equally necessary to sample environments in a systematic fashion. In his book *Perception and the Representative Design of Experiments*, Brunswik makes a concerted effort to develop a framework for such representative design through sampling different settings. Although this work has been criticized by Hochberg (1966) because Brunswik and his colleagues used photographs of different environments to establish variation in the distal variables and their cues that would be relevant to various perceptual judgments, Brunswik's central point is still well taken. As Petrinovich suggests, a methodology that is sensitive to the *distributional properties* of cues and behaviors in the environment will require the development of "natural histories of the species in order to understand and catalog the range of environmental contexts in which the particular class of behaviors in which we are interested occur" (Petrinovich, 1979, pp. 383–384). Once the range has been identified, efforts would be made to sample both organisms and environments within the settings to determine the linkages that exist between distal variables and functional achievements or outcomes.

3.4.4. An Evaluation of Brunswik's Contributions to Research Design

Although Brunswik made many contributions to the development of what has come to be known as environmental psychology, only those that are directly relevant to the validity problem will be considered here.

The notion of the representative sampling of environments and Petrinovich's suggestions regarding the development of natural histories of species represent a valuable addition to our views of research design. I have argued elsewhere that when attempting to understand a phenomenon that is embedded in a range of sociophysical contexts it is often essential to consider the use of various holistically oriented reconnaissance studies that will provide guides to the possible variables that may affect the phenomenon (Winkel, 1985). The purpose of such holistic study is not necessarily to test hypotheses but to discover those aspects of the sociophysical contexts in which we conduct our research that may be expected to affect variability in the phenomenon. This task is very much akin to the discovery of those qualitatively different contextual elements of a setting that have differential impacts on the focal issues of concern to the investigator. To adapt an observation by Heider (1958, p. 296), it is necessary to be prepared for the likelihood that people are separated from the contents of the distal environment by the qualitatively varying manifold of events that *mediate* the relationship between distal variables and outcomes. For example, it would not be expected that the material resources a person possesses would serve as a direct cue for density perceptions. If crowding, however, is considered to be aversive, material resources might serve as a mediator for the threshold at which a particular density level would lead to a judgment that a setting was crowded.

The notion of mediating variables is especially important for ecologically relevant research planning. Since Burnswik's work was left unfinished at his early death, it is not clear how he might have handled these mediating variables. With regard to research planning in field settings, however, the role of mediators is often very clear, and they may be expected to affect the cue validities of distal variables in ways that extend beyond the distal variables themselves. For example, if we wish to understand those factors in housing environments that affect decisions to provide various forms of assistance to neighbors, there are different aspects of density levels within and among buildings that will help us understand whether help is likely to be forthcoming (Saegert,

1978). There can be little doubt, however, that variables that influence decisions regarding the type of building in which a person chooses or is selected to live might very well influence help giving as well. If it was found that those living in high-rise buildings chose to live there and they were also less likely to provide assistance than residents of lower-density buildings, variables connected with the person's choice of residence (e.g., a desire for anonymity) might be considered plausible candidates for the observed differences. This factor, however, has been identified as a threat to the internal validity of a study (Cook & Campbell, 1979; Judd & Kenny, 1981). As suggested earlier, in my review of various theoretical approaches that have been taken to understanding the forces that affect people in environments, there may be many occasions when issues that have been discussed as instances of one form of validity (e.g., external validity) may relate significantly to the ecological arrangements characteristic of field settings and hence may be considered equally relevant to another form of validity (e.g., construct validity).

Petrinovich (1979) appears to suggest that there are interrelationships among different types of validity at the individual level when he introduces the concepts of functional reliability and validity. People will not always use the cues that would help them attain their goals in either a reliable or a valid fashion. This situation may be traced to the person's history and/or to the press of existing social arrangements within which individual behavior is organized. As a consequence, probability judgments are not confined solely to the pattern of existing information relevant to a particular distal variable but must be sought from a broader range of contextual data.

In summary, then, Brunswik's introduction of an ecologically oriented framework for the consideration of both organismic adaptation to the environment and the representative design of research provides opportunities for thinking about validity issues in a more integrated fashion. I would propose that one approach that may be taken to such an integration would involve a focus on the ecological validity of research design itself.

3.4.5. A Methodologically Oriented Definition of Ecological Validity

Brunswik described the process of organismic achievement in terms of what he called a *lens model*, in which information from the environment is filtered through the sensory lenses that each organism uses in its environmental transactions (Brunswik, 1952; Petrinovich, 1979, p. 379). The processing of environmental information is in turn linked to a set of possible actions that might be taken to achieve the organism's goals. The arc that exists between distal stimuli and distal achievement refers to the ecological validity of the link between environmental information and subsequent behavior.

It does not require much imagination to realize that a similar model applies to the activities of the researcher. He or she seeks to understand how others transact in various settings (the researcher's goal) and employs different measuring instruments to assess distal and proximal cues as well as proximal and distal achievements. The choice and use of the measurement instruments and the structure of the research design itself (e.g., experimental, quasi-experimental, etc.) are guided by a set of hypotheses that stem from theoretical and/or practical questions. The information that is generated from the research must then be analyzed, reported, and evaluated. These steps constitute the researcher's distal achievement.

This double lens model of research in which the investigator attempts to link his or her activities to those of the organism leads directly to a distinction that may be drawn between the ecological validity of the environmental cues that influence the organism's behavior and the ecological validity of the research designs that are devised to understand people's environmental transactions.

The ecological validity of the research design refers to the extent to which the overall design of the research plan and the specific measuring instruments that are employed yield accurate estimates of the multiple dimensionality of the phenomenon that is the focus of study and those components of the context that may be expected to influence variation in the phenomenon.

The ecological validity of a research design is based on the likelihood that the research design employed, the construct system introduced or induced to account for some phenomenon, and/or the intervention(s) utilized are capable of yielding information regarding systematic variation in the parameters that define those components of the setting that affect the phenomenon of interest.

It is important to realize that this definition of ecological validity refers both to those factors that have been identified as potentially relevant to the evaluation of the research design itself (i.e., the structure of the design and the techniques and procedures that are actually used) *and* to the explanatory system that is advanced to account for the findings. If either or both of these aspects of the investigation cannot be linked to the phenomenon and those setting-related contextual factors that affect the phenomenon, its ecological validity is jeopardized.

In the remainder of this chapter, I shall discuss the assumptions that lie behind the use of the ecological validity concept, suggest ways in which it can be used to extend and clarify the criteria that are used to evaluate research designs, and consider steps that can be taken to improve the ecological design of research.

3.4.6. Assumptions Underlying Ecological Validity

One of the primary assumptions underlying my definition of ecological validity is that research is primarily driven by the desire to account for different phenomena that have been identified by environmental social scientists.

Phenomena (defined here as comprising events of interest that are susceptible to scientific description and explanation) are *distributionally organized* in the range of settings that constitute the physical world that is the focus of our research. As Petrinovich (1979) correctly notes, behaviors are embedded in environmental textures that display different patterns of correlation depending on the setting. These patterns of correlation among variables in the environment influence the expression of behaviors of interest. The significance of variables that may affect some phenomenon of interest can only be determined if the variables "appear, both individually and in interaction, with a natural distribution density" (Petrinovich, 1979, pp. 374–375). It is only when we are able to look at behaviors as they are distributed in settings that it is possible to determine the *probable* as against the *possible* importance of setting-based variables as they influence the phenomena in which we are interested.

To assume that phenomena and the variables that affect phenomena are distributionally arranged in different settings does not necessarily require that all aspects of the sociophysical setting be investigated in their totality. Within the framework advanced by the ecological psychologists, behaviors are hierarchically nested within a particular setting (Wicker, 1979). These behavioral systems may be linked to one another to various degrees and for various reasons, some manifest and some latent or symbolic. A significant aspect of research planning, then, involves the development of models descriptive of such linkages. As I have attempted to detail elsewhere, it often does not take a great deal of effort to ascertain the degree of centrality or marginality of various subsystems within some locale of interest (Winkel, 1985).

By the *centrality* of behavioral subsystems in a setting I am referring to the extent to which some group of behaviors comprises the major organizing feature of the setting selected for research. Apparently different subsystems may be organized around the central behavioral subsystem and are designed to achieve an overarchingly important goal or set of goals to various participants in the setting. For example, in a hospital emergency room, primary behavioral emphasis is given to the treatment of patients. This represents the manifest goal of the emergency room staff. There are many stresses that staff encounter during the course of treatment delivery, and stress management and/or reduction for the staff, patients, and visitors becomes a secondary but still powerful latent goal. Thus information transmission, organization of work and waiting spaces, control mechanisms over access to treatment areas, and the location and visibility of nursing stations are not necessarily guided totally by the desire to ease the delivery of treatment. The nursing station may be oriented so that patients are not always visible but those in the waiting area are, since disputes between those waiting for treatment and the admitting staff have been known to occur. For security reasons, therefore, the nursing station is located as it is. Hence each behavioral subsystem has its own internal dynamic, but these can be understood only in the context of a broader set of organizational goals in the emergency room.

In other settings, behaviors may be integrated with but marginal to the environment's total organization. For instance, in a museum, the ability to orient oneself may involve integrated patterns of search behaviors by visitors. Different staff members may have as one of their functions visitor orientation. The wayfinding process itself, however, may not be assigned a high priority in terms of the enjoyment one has in going to the museum, whether experienced by a visitor or an administrator of the facility.

If, however, orientation is an important goal for both visitors and staff, recognition that other components of the museum's operation may impinge on way finding then becomes a relevant ecological concern. For example, different visitor density levels may alter the effectiveness of various orientational aids. If density is construed solely as behavioral interference, it may not have much direct theoretical import for the construct system relevant to way finding. If density is viewed more broadly as influencing the ability to process information from and about the environment, the behavioral activities designed to handle crowd control may have a very direct impact on the cognitive and behavioral requirements for effective way finding. In this example, the ecological validity of the distal variables directly relevant to orientation (i.e., the orientational aids) can only be understood in terms of the mediating effects of different density levels. Density levels in and of themselves may not be expected to affect orientation directly. Thus, the ecological validity of the research design must be evaluated in terms of its ability to account for differences in density levels and their effects on information process and way finding.

A second assumption regarding the establishment of ecological validity involves the necessity of finding instances in which it is possible to observe *variation* in those factors that are presumed to have an influence on the multiple dimensions of the phenomena in which we are interested. This variation may occur either within a particular setting or across different settings. For example, in the museum, it may be reasonable to expect to find variability in the density levels over the course of a day or during the course of a week.

One of the keys to the determination of ecological validity rests on the need to seek out variations in environments that may serve as the basis for systematic comparisons among the conditions that the investigator finds. This assumption of variation in setting conditions is very much congruent with the emphases that are placed on the use of comparative research designs in which selective and systematic contrasts are made among the conditions of interest (Cook & Campbell, 1979; Judd & Kenny, 1981).

If the comparisons are selectively planned and under the control of the investigator, they are usually regarded as experimental designs. If different interventions or treatments are administered to pre-existing groups to which members are not randomly assigned, we are dealing with what are called quasi-experiments (Campbell & Stanley, 1963; Cook & Campbell, 1979). Descriptive—observational studies of some ongoing process generally involve observations of differences that stem from naturally occurring variations within a setting.

The systemic approaches advocated by Barker (1963), Bronfenbrenner (1977), Brunswik (1956), Ittelson and colleagues (1974), and Petrinovich (1979) would tend to suggest that descriptive–observational designs would be most sensitive to the identification of process parameters that characterize people's environmental transactions. And indeed, much of the research growing out of these field-oriented perspectives has involved observational studies in which comparisons are made of different types of person–environment configurations (Bechtel, 1977; Ittelson, Proshansky, & Rivlin, 1970; Wicker, 1979).

It should be clear that this assumption regarding variation in setting conditions is essential for the establishment of functional relationships among variables that can, in turn, be used to develop systemic models of person–environment relationships.

Setting variations are also important when the investigator must confront the problem of correlated explanatory variables. To illustrate this issue briefly, consider the museum example again. If the researcher inadvertently introduced one orientational aid at a low density level and a different device at a high density level, there would be a perfect correlation between density level and type of orienting device. It would be impossible to distinguish the effects of density and type of device without allowing both variables to be either uncorrelated or partially correlated depending on the patterns of observed densities in the setting.

The final assumption lying behind my definition of ecological validity is that major emphasis should be placed on understanding the meanings or interpretations that people provide for the environments they encounter over the course of their development. The relevance of meanings and interpretations to the understanding of observed behavior has been discussed in the context of many different environmental issues (Evans, 1981; Gans, 1962; Ittelson et al., 1974; Michelson, 1970; Rossi, 1955; Schorr, 1963; Saegert & Winkel, 1980; Winkel & Holahan, 1985).

One of the most immediate methodological implications of this assumption is that investigators should employ the full range of research techniques that are available for understanding person–environment relationships. Reliance on one technique alone is unlikely to yield sufficient information about the nature of interpretations that mediate people's evaluations of different settings (Ittelson et al., 1974; Winkel, 1985). Even those ecological psychologists who are sympathetic to Barker's methodological preference for behavioral observation have expressed some misgivings about the limitations that this decision places on some important problems in behavior-setting analysis (Wicker, 1979).

3.4.7. Ecological Validity in Relation to Other Forms of Validity

Between the publication of the first monograph on quasi-experimentation (Campbell & Stanley, 1963) and the most recent expositions of those factors that must be considered in the evaluation of research findings, the number of different types of validity has increased markedly (Cook & Campbell, 1979; Seriven, 1972; Wortman, 1975). Although this is the case, it is clear that problems of internal, external, and construct validity continue to occupy a central place in research planning, execution, and the interpretation of findings. What, then, is the relationship of these forms of validity to ecological validity?

Earlier in this chapter, I discussed some of the problems that are encountered when attempting to determine the degree to which research findings obtained in one setting can be transferred to other locales. As Petrinovich (1979) has suggested, the understanding of some phenomenon of interest to an investigator requires evidence regarding the distribution of the phenomenon in different settings. For example, it is reasonable to suppose that there are various physical and social cues that are relevant to judgments regarding how safe any particular environment may be for the person using it. To ascertain the validity of different cues relevant to safety, it would be necessary to determine the range of settings in which these cues are differentially distributed so that cue configurations could be related to variations in safety judgments. Once the cue validities had been determined, measurements of the presence of these cues in a "new" environment should allow a prediction of the likely safety associated with that setting. The success of the prediction represents a measure of the external validity of findings obtained in settings in which the prediction equation has been developed.

The establishment of external validity is, as Cook and Campbell (1979) have pointed out, not confined to a representative sample of persons, places, and research procedures. It is also linked to the existence of a set of theoretical constructs that guides the investigator in his or her choice of those settings within which safety problems may be assessed. In this sense, external validity is closely related to the construct validity of the measures that are employed in the investigation of safety concerns.

This approach to external validity is very much congruent with my use of the ecological validity concept. In my definition, I suggested that it is necessary to have both a construct system that is relevant to the phenomenon in which the investigator is interested *and* a set of measuring instruments that captures the dimensionality of the constructs that are hypothesized as being able to account for observed variation in behavior.

The development and assessment of construct validity have been described by Cronbach and Meehl (1955). Although their original article was oriented around the theoretical meaning of scores obtained in various psychological testing situations, the notion has been extended to a wide variety of concepts that are employed in psychological research. In an earlier example, I reviewed research directed toward understanding how environmental stressors affected various indicators of pro- and antisocial behavior. When an investigator chooses indicators (i.e., operationalizations) of a construct and asks about the meaning of the scores that have been observed on these indicators, he or she is interested in the construct validity of these indicators. As Cronbach and Meehl (1955) argued, an indicator's meaning must be determined on the basis of its place in a theoretical system. In the earlier example on helping behavior, we do not measure pro- or antisocial behavior directly. The investigator chooses observable behaviors that are considered outcroppings or expressions of the construct of interest. Thus providing various forms of assistance to a person represents a subset of indicators that are presumably relevant to prosocial behavior as an abstract concept. One of the goals of those who wish to determine a construct's validity involves the development of a theoretical system (or *nomological network* in the terminology of Cronbach and Meehl, 1955) within which various indicators are related to one another and to the indicators of other constructs. An introduction to the modeling procedures that are involved in this process may be found in Long (1983).

There is a close set of relationships between construct validity and ecological validity as I have defined this term. I assume that the investigator who is interested in a phenomenon has been able to generate information about the parameters that are relevant to some phenomenon of interest. As I have suggested elsewhere (Winkel, 1985), the range of factors that is devised to account for phenomenon variability may be taken from existing literature, qualitatively based field projects, and/or personal experience with the problem. For each of the constructs that are used to account for the investigator's focal concerns *and those contextual features of the setting that influence the phenomenon of interest*, indicators must be devised and measuring instruments developed. If comparison groups are to be employed, these must be orchestrated into the overall research design. If the construct system is reasonably well articulated, ecologically valid research design implies that construct indicators are matched to both the research design and the techniques.

It is not necessary, however, to have a well-developed theory in order to do ecologically valid research. The purpose of a study may involve the generation of data grounded in the ongoing operation of a setting that may be used to propose a possible theory to account for what was observed (Glaser & Strauss,

1967). The ecological validity of the investigation in this case rests on the identification and attempted modeling of those parameters that are presumed to affect the phenomenon of interest to the researcher. Efforts at parameter identification and modeling may be thought of as the minimal conditions for the establishment of ecological validity.

If, in the analysis of setting conditions, the investigator becomes aware that issues such as self-selection into environments, mortality, reactivity of measuring instruments, past history, diffusion of treatment effects, maturation, differential assignment rules to environments, and so on affect or may be expected to affect observed differences in behavior, how are these aspects of field conditions to be handled within an ecological framework? The answer to this question goes to the core of the internal validity problem.

By the term *internal validity* Cook and Campbell (1979, p. 50) refer broadly to the action of so-called *third-variable* alternative explanations of presumed two-variable relationships. While this is the simplest of situations, these authors go on to point out how there may be multiple sources of internal validity threats operating in any study. Generally, these threats are assumed to account for postintervention group differences (within a comparison groups research design) because people in the different conditions differed systematically from one another prior to the intervention (either as planned by the investigator or as occurred naturally within the environment under study) and/or experienced events other than the intervention(s) of interest. Prior differences among groups and/or extraintervention experiences may be assumed to be plausible alternatives that can account for a study's outcomes rather than those variables hypothesized by the investigator.

One of the problems with this formulation of the validity question is based on my brief review of some of the organizing themes that characterize theoretical approaches to person–environment relations. In Section 3.3 of this chapter, I suggested that many of the threats to internal validity may represent enduring and systematic aspects of people's activities in environments. To the extent that this is the case in any study, problems of internal validity appear to be better conceptualized as issues pertinent to construct validity.

A second difficulty with this way of thinking about plausible alternatives (i.e., as threats) can be traced to the manner in which these third-variable factors are to be treated in designing research. Often, the investigator is advised to focus on techniques that will remove these threats. As I have attempted to show,

this advice is based on a conception of theory formation that involves the decontextualization of variable relationships in the search for "general laws" of behavior. The problem for us as environmentalists involves the preservation of the context, since it is often that very context the operation of which we seek to explain. This intent suggests the following reconsideration of internal validity threats.

When attempting to design ecologically valid research, are the plausible alternative variables identified by Cook and Campbell (1979) and others:

1. Important to our understanding of how people organize their activities and experiences in the settings in which research is to be conducted? For example, if we are working with people who are sympathetic to the need for research, we might not have to be as concerned about problems of noncooperativeness as we would for people who are suspicious of research and researchers (the problem of mortality or selective participation).

If variables that may threaten internal validity are presumed to be present at the research site(s) do they:

2. Distribute themselves differentially between or among whatever comparison groups are to be included in the study?
3. Affect the mediating and outcome variables selected as indicators of the constructs that we wish to study?
4. Represent potentially theoretically relevant issues that should be incorporated into the explanatory system advanced to account for the phenomenon of interest?

To the extent that the sociophysical characteristics of a field setting may be expected to contribute to our theoretical understanding of the phenomena in which we are interested, then, internal validity issues may be more properly considered challenges to construct validity and efforts should be made to model them accordingly. Some suggestions in this regard will be offered at the end of this chapter.

3.4.8. An Alternative Approach to Ecological Validity

The perspective being advanced in this chapter is congruent at many points with the position adopted by Bronfenbrenner in his 1977 paper "Toward an Experimental Ecology of Human Development." He adapts the term *validity* as it is conventionally defined (i.e., the extent to which one actually measures what one purports to measure) by suggesting that the environment as experienced by those who are participants in a study must have the same "properties it is supposed or assumed to have by the investigator" (Bronfenbrenner, 1977, p. 516). He goes on to point out that ecological validity is not necessarily defined by the setting within which one conducts the research. Thus a field setting does not guarantee ecological validity any more than does a laboratory. The question of ecological validity rests on the problem of concern to the researcher.

I would tend to agree with Bronfenbrenner's rejection of efforts to equate ecological validity with field research in general. While Bronfenbrenner would consider ecological validity in terms of the problem of concern to the researcher, I am more interested in the phenomenon as it may be expressed in multiple settings. It is not so much that the environment as experienced by the research participant is the same as that experienced by the researcher, even though I agree with the importance of experiential understanding. For example, there may be instances in which there is relatively good correspondence between the environment as understood by the participant and the environment as it is understood by the researcher. The issue is not the understanding of the environment as much as it is the understanding of the phenomenon as it is embedded in different environments. Since I am primarily concerned with phenomena as they operate in environmental contexts, I do not require any necessary correspondence between the researcher's conception of the environment (or even of the problem) and that of the research participant. We are all aware that the manner in which a research participant understands that his or her environment and/or what he or she is doing in it may not match those variables that appear to account better for the observed behavior (Kahneman, Slovic, & Tversky, 1982; Nisbett & Wilson, 1977).

What my definition of ecological validity does require is that the investigator understand the phenomenon using whatever information may be drawn from the experiences of those who are part of the research process. In many instances, I suspect that the participants in various settings have a better grasp of the phenomenon than does the investigator. That this may be the case, however, cannot be taken as a foregone conclusion.

Bronfenbrenner goes on to suggest that the principal methodological consequence of his definition of ecological validity is what he calls the *ecological exper-*

iment. The ecological experiment is placed within a developmental framework. It represents the means whereby the investigator comes to understand the "progressive accommodation between the growing human organism and its environment." To accomplish this task, there must be systematic contrasts between "two or more environmental systems or their structural components." At the same time, however, "other sources of influence" must be controlled through the use of random assignment or matching strategies (Bronfenbrenner, 1977, p. 517).

Along with demanding rigor, Bronfenbrenner suggests that controlled experimentation should be undertaken in the early phases of research not for the purpose of testing hypotheses but rather for what he calls the systematic understanding of the nature of the accommodation between organism and environment. Thus the ecological experiment is designed to aid in discovery rather than in formalistic hypothesis testing. At the same time, however, such research must be sensitive to the operation of environmental structures and processes that are interdependent and "must be analyzed in systems terms" (Bronfenbrenner, 1977, p. 518).

Bronfenbrenner's recommendations for the use of the ecological experiment are not meant to preclude the use of other research strategies such as naturalistic observation, case studies, field surveys, and so on. Rather, he seems to argue that it is primarily through the use of controlled experimentation in natural field settings that the investigator will be able to identify systems properties. This argument is based on Bronfenbrenner's belief that, if we wish to "understand how something works, [we must] try to change it" (p. 517).

It is entirely possible that the strategy being proposed by Bronfenbrenner can be successfully adopted in developmental psychology, which certainly has a longer history and a richer set of theoretical perspectives from which to draw organizing frames for research. I am not as convinced that the ecological experiment could be used in environmental psychology. In many instances, we are still trying to identify the range of phenomena that would constitute the substantive content for environmental psychology. While progress has been made, and this handbook is a compendium of these advances, I am inclined to believe that the utilization of holistic research procedures will be more fruitful for the establishment of the systems parameters that are likely to be influential in our understanding of persons in environments.

Other impediments to the use of the ecological

experiment concern the problem of changing environments. The first has to do with knowing what it is that we would change. Those decisions must often grow out of our holistic understanding of how the phenomenon in which we are interested is situated within a sociophysical framework and/or a theoretical perspective that would guide our choices.

The second difficulty concerns the obvious impossibility of imposing ourselves on a situation and believing that we can have sole responsibility for deciding what changes are to be made. More often it is the case that we must negotiate our entry into settings, and any changes that occur are a function of our ability both to negotiate and to manage change in a context in which many other persons must participate. For a discussion of the constraints and opportunities that exist when introducing environmental change into various settings the reader should consult Saegert (Chapter 4, this volume).

The possibilities for more ecologically valid research design that grow out of Bronfenbrenner's work and the suggestions contained in this chapter lend themselves to a discussion of the factors that might be considered when designing research projects in field settings.

3.5. PLANNING AND DESIGNING RESEARCH TO IMPROVE ECOLOGICAL VALIDITY

3.5.1. Search for Variability

In Section 3.4.5 I summarized the key assumptions that lay behind my definition of ecological validity. One of these assumptions concerned the necessity for discovering opportunities for variations in those components of a field setting that could be presumed to have a potential for clarifying the nature of some phenomenon of interest. Two key issues are involved in this phase of research planning. The first has to do with the identification of explanatory variables that may be expected to show change over the course of the study. The second concerns the problem of intercorrelations that exist among different explanatory variables. The latter issue has been described as the *confounding* problem.

One of the major impediments to conducting field research involves the correlations that often may be found between conceptually distinct facets of the field setting. For example, in office settings, the "quality" of the work space is frequently correlated with a person's job title. For a researcher who is interested in understanding how different spatial arrangements affect various job performance and satisfaction measures, the person's job title is associated with differing amounts of support services and rewards (e.g., income and promotional opportunities as well as the "quality" of the physical work space). Clearly all these aspects of the work environment should have some bearing on the phenomenon of interest. Yet for both theoretical and practical reasons the researcher may think that the relative combinations of these factors should shift from setting to setting. Three possible outcomes suggest themselves in this example.

In the first, financial and promotional rewards may be much more influential in affecting job performance than is the design of the work spaces. In the second, the investigator may believe that, while reimbursement and promotion possibilities may set a floor on job performance, improvements in environmental "amenities" will be most beneficial for work output. In the third, the possibility is that these factors interrelate with one another and affect performance both directly and indirectly. Neither conceptually nor practically are these aspects of the work environment the same. If the researcher is to evaluate these three scenarios, clearly it is necessary to choose a site, or preferably sites, in which differing combinations of job titles, work activities, incentives, and work spaces may be found.

Even when considering a single site, initial reconnaissance should be undertaken to determine whether it is possible to find the degree of variability among the factors hypothesized to affect job performance that would be required to test different variable combinations on outcomes of interest. For example, if initial data were available that showed how individuals who were expected to engage in different job activities were located in different types of environments (e.g., private offices, shared offices, cubicles accommodating different numbers of employees, and large open work areas), a sampling frame could be developed that stratifies employees on the basis of both work requirements and setting type. Depending on the number of individuals in each person–environment configuration, the sampling frame would be constructed so that a sufficient number of cases appeared in each cell of the design to allow quantitative comparisons among conditions. This might mean, of course, that certain cells would be oversampled if the condition represented by that cell was important conceptually. For example, the majority of supervisors might have private offices. A not insignificant number of them might also be assigned to shared offices. Supervisors in the latter condition might be oversampled so that the effects of work space, holding job title constant, could be determined.

This example illustrates how a selective sampling strategy may be used both to establish variation in explanatory variables and to decrease the degree of correlation that may exist among these variables.

In other field settings, there may be a sufficient amount of change occurring in the setting as part of its ongoing operation that variation among explanatory variables is more likely to be expected. For example, many public settings such as museums, transportation stations, parks, playgrounds, and so on are used by different groups of people, and the programs within these environments may also be expected to change over time. When there are naturally occurring changes in a place, the researcher should be aware of the possibilities that these variations offer for systematic comparisons. For example, suppose a researcher was interested in studying the effects of differing density levels on the expression of aggressive behaviors in children. The investigator might be interested in using the frustration–aggression hypothesis as the theoretical framework for the study (Dollard & Miller, 1950). In this example, frustration is defined operationally as some form of person–environment configuration that blocks the goal of gaining access to play resources. When such goal blockage occurs, the researcher hypothesizes that aggressive behavior will occur.

The setting chosen for the study may be one in which the children are exposed to different density levels in the play environment. That is, some of the play groups contain many children while others contain very few. The physical play spaces themselves differ in the amount of play space available. As part of the research design, the investigator hopes to examine differences between physical density (i.e., given a constant number of people, the amount of space varies) and social density (i.e., given a constant amount of space, the number of people varies) assuming these conditions set the stage for possible frustrations for the children. Given programmatic considerations, however, it is not possible to manipulate these variables. What can be done is to observe the children's behavior as they and their playmates negotiate different parts of the play environment. The only variable that can be manipulated by the investigator is the number of toys available to the children in the different play spaces.

Even with this limited amount of freedom to intervene in an ongoing social system, the researcher may be able to find a sufficient amount of variability in density levels combined with systematic changes in

available resources that the appropriate comparisons may be made. Once again, however, careful preliminary reconnaissance should be undertaken to ensure that a sufficient range of contrasts is available to allow tests of the hypotheses that are being advanced.

This example can be used to illustrate another point with regard to the problem of finding contrasts within a setting for comparison purposes. Assume now that the investigator observes that variations in social density and resource availability are linked to one another in such a way that increasing density levels combined with fewer resources lead to an increase in aggressive outbursts. If the researcher attempted to argue that he or she found support for the role that the mediating variable of frustration plays in aggressive behavior, the argument would not necessarily be convincing even though the researcher had been able to make the appropriate comparisons among conditions. It could be claimed that the children in the larger groups were more likely to be prone to aggression regardless of any frustrating circumstances that might have been created. According to this plausible alternative hypothesis, observed differences in behavior might be due to some form of conscious or unconscious assignment of children to the different density configurations, and it is that factor that could account for the observed differences.

Being aware of this possibility, the investigator decides to take advantage of the fact that at the end of each semester changes in the play group supervisors and their schedules necessitate changes in the sizes of the play groups and their composition. To lessen the effects of differential assignment, the researcher might attempt to persuade the school administrators to assign children randomly to groups within the constraints that are dictated by the children's schedules and other programmatic considerations. While not achieving full random assignment, these efforts have the result that some of the groups now consist of children who have not played together while others consist of children who have. When the observations are repeated, the researcher discovers that in those groups in which children have been randomly assigned more aggressive outbursts occur than in groups of children who have played together before. The density effects that were observed earlier also continue to hold. Higher densities with fewer resources generally lead to greater numbers of aggressive incidents. These results, while surprising, have been hypothesized by Saegert (1981) in her discussion of the role that social support networks play in mediating density effects. In that paper, Saegert argued that random assignment can have the effect of shattering existing ecological arrangements among people, thus exacerbating the deleterious consequences associated with different density levels. In this example, then, the technique of randomization has actually become a variable that is relevant to outcome.

Judd and Kenny (1981) discuss the question of randomization in the context of various rules that are used to assign people to conditions and to settings. From the ecological validity perspective being advanced in this paper, the *consequences* of assignment rules become of most interest to the researcher who wishes to model those aspects of the setting that are relevant to some phenomenon of interest. In the play example, the investigator would be advised to include a variable that reflected the consequences of the assignment rule that was used in placing children in groups as part of the explanatory model advanced to explain the observed results.

The major point to be made in the search for variation in setting conditions that can serve as possible comparison conditions is that contrasts should always be evaluated for their potentialities for generating a broader theoretical perspective that can be used to illustrate a phenomenon of some interest. In the play example, a potential internal validity problem may be reconceptualized as an issue of construct validity that ultimately affects the study's ecological validity.

3.5.2. Determination of Setting Boundaries

Once the researcher has been able to locate possible contrast conditions in a setting, it is necessary to determine what boundaries should be set on the locale that is chosen for study. Initially, the investigator may have only a vague notion of what boundaries exist for the research site since behaviors of interest may occur in many locations. For example, work-related activities in an office can occur in many different locations. Non-work-related behaviors that may impinge on work functions may also occur in many different locations. As the ecological psychologists have noted, the behavioral agenda for a behavior setting has its own integrity. The factors that influence a behavioral agenda in one locale may be different from those occurring only a few feet away (Wicker, 1979). This observation suggests that preliminary field reconnaissance is required to identify the various behavioral agendas that may require measurement within the research design. Obviously, physical boundaries in and of themselves will not necessarily firmly establish the psychological boundaries for the behavioral agendas that can be recognized.

The operation of different agendas is important to decisions regarding ecologically valid research designs because of the potential permeability that exists between and among different agendas and that may affect a study's outcomes.

3.5.3. Boundary Permeability

Once it has been possible to locate tentative or fixed boundaries for the research site, the investigator must assess the degree of direct and indirect permeability that exists at the boundary faces. Here I am referring to possible informational exchanges between and among the users of different locales. These exchanges may be both intended and unintended as well as congruent and incongruent with different behavioral agendas. These informational exchanges may create problems when designing research, particularly when contrasts are to be made among different settings.

For example, in a park or playground, teenagers may appropriate a particular area for themselves. The area may also be used by younger children. This use of space may have been unintended but still congruent with the setting. If the areas overlap there may be considerable permeability between different behavioral agendas that interferes with the activities of one or both groups of users.

A bowling green for the elderly may have been placed in an area away from children so that the elderly would not be disturbed. Suppose, however, that the elderly wish to have children near them since the children's parents provide a sense of security. As a consequence of its location, the green either is not used or is underutilized. This would represent an intended but incongruent loss of informational exchange possibilities that directly impacted on the recreational quality of the bowling green.

Junkies and winos might appropriate a corner of the park where picnic benches and tables have been provided for park users. At least from the picknickers' perspective, the presence of socially undesirable people constitutes an unintended and incongruent use of the park.

Finally, the children's play area is found to be located near a seating area for parents. Thus the parents' and children's behavioral agendas intermix.

These types of interrelationships have a direct bearing on the question of assessing the effects of cross-setting communications that may influence any type of "experimental" treatment of different types of spaces designed for different user groups. Within a more conventional approach to research design, such cross-setting communication might be considered a potential contaminating element in an evaluation of the interventions of interest. From the perspective being advanced in this chapter, however, boundary permeability becomes a potential explanatory factor required for the ecological validity of the study.

In the determination of boundary permeability, it is important to establish the directionality of cross-setting communication over time. Much environmental research is cross-sectional in nature. As such, it is difficult to know whether behavioral system X influences system Y, Y influences X, or the two are reciprocally related to one another. Thus in the park example the activities of the junkies and winos are much more likely to influence the activities of parents and children than vice versa. In the children's play area, informational exchanges among children and their caretakers would tend to be bidirectional and reciprocal. Informational exchanges such as these may have the effect of mediating the influence of various changes that might be introduced into the setting. Cook and Campbell (1979) refer to this as the diffusion of treatment problem.

Thus far, we have been discussing cross-setting communication as if this occurs only verbally among the users of subareas of an environment. Obviously such exchanges may occur verbally. For example, office workers may discuss experimental changes in office layout with workers who are experiencing this change. Communication may also result from actual movement from environment to environment. For example, students from a dormitory with a very institutional library reading area may use a redesigned library reading room that allows greater flexibility of furniture arrangements, more comfortable seating, better lighting, and so on. A researcher interested in comparing the user's evaluations of these two places may encounter problems if he or she is not aware of such mutual use patterns. If it is assumed that such cross-setting experiences do occur, the researcher must describe these behavioral patterns. This may be accomplished by actual observation of activities (Ittelson et al., 1970; Wicker, 1979) and/or verbal accounts of such movement.

Such cross-setting or across-conditions events might represent grounds for suggesting that any comparisons between or among different places will yield equivocal results. For example, a comparison of changes made in the design of three playgrounds in neighborhoods that are closely contiguous to one another may require the investigator to assume that the users of each playground have not experienced any of the others. If cross-setting use occurred, any assertions about the effects of any individual playground might be dismissed because this assumption was violated. From an ecological validity perspective, however, the extent to which children might have made use of more than one playground should be considered as an outcome variable in its own right, included as part of the research design, and entered as part of the data analysis to determine how cross-setting use patterns influenced subsequent outcome measures.

If information is available on play patterns prior to the introduction of changes and/or one of the playgrounds is not redesigned, such prechange information can be very useful in a comparison study. If the investigator has gathered data on prechange use patterns across sites and can assume that not all children will necessarily use the "experimental" play areas, the conditions are ripe for expanding the conceptual scope of the study. In this example, self-selection into the environment can be used as a potentially valuable outcome measure in its own right.

The main point to be made about cross-setting informational exchanges is that these are an important aspect of both Barker's descriptive system and the perspective advanced by Ittelson and colleagues (1974). The development of indicators and measures that reflect this component of the field's operation may be used to increase the ecological validity of the research design.

3.5.4. Participant Familiarity with Setting Characteristics

As is not the case in many laboratory studies of phenomena, the participants in everyday environments possess varying degrees of familiarity with the places they encounter, with other participants, and with the range of transactions that occur there.

When planning ecologically valid research, it is necessary to examine carefully any contribution familiarity may make to variations in dependent measures that goes beyond the influences associated with the focal variables of interest to the investigator. I have already mentioned the paper by Saegert (1981) in which she points out that the existence of social support networks (person-to-person familiarity) may offset some of the negative effects associated with higher densities. If a researcher finds less social exchange under higher-density conditions, a portion of the variation in social exchange may be related to the fact that people did not know one another in the first place as a result of the manner in which they were assigned to the comparison conditions. Higher densities may then hinder the development of social support networks. In this particular instance, then, familiarity has theoretical relevance for the density construct.

The possibility of communication among research

participants has already been discussed but is obviously more likely to occur when people know one another. This creates problems in the analysis of outcome variables that are influenced by group communications. Should this occur, certain forms of statistical analysis may not be possible. This is particularly true if the statistical test rests on the assumption that the observations are independent of one another (which is clearly unlikely to be the case in a group consensus situation). Under these circumstances, it may be necessary to use group rather than individual data as the unit of analysis (Schiffenbauer, Schulman, & Poe, 1978).

The effects of differential amounts of familiarity with a setting and with other setting participants can also be valuable when attempting to understand the consequences associated with the introduction of change into the setting. Lack of familiarity may be equally problematic. For example, Klein and colleagues (1978) questioned the assumption that patients who were recovering from myocardial infarctions would benefit from a transfer from a coronary care unit to a less stressful recovery area. These investigators found that patients often showed intense anxiety about such transfers because they assumed that the absence of proper equipment in the recovery area might be life threatening should another episode occur. Information provided about the operation of the recovery unit and its accessibility to all necessary support equipment provided sufficient reassurance to reduce anxiety.

3.5.5. Self- and Other-Directed Assignments to Environments

People may be found in different environments because they chose to be there, were assigned to go there, or some combination of the two. If the setting's characteristics and/or what Judd and Kenny (1981) call the *assignment rule* to setting have some relationship to the various outcome measures utilized in an investigation, provision must be made for these factors in both research design and data analysis.

In very many practical situations, assignment rules are related to internal characteristics of the person and/or to external environmental circumstances. For example, people who are homeless or who are living in deteriorated slums may be assigned to public housing precisely because of their current situations. Children who have been culturally deprived may be given preferential assignment to special remedial programs and environments designed to improve their performance. For a researcher who is interested in ecological validity issues, such conditions are certainly relevant to as-

signment rules, and they may also be expected to affect the outcomes of interest in a study. Conceptually, the problem becomes one of determining whether and how the factors that influenced assignment compare to the particular changes that result from the assignment as they affect a set of outcomes. It is often the case that the conditions that lead to a person's assignment to a particular environment are of theoretical interest. For example, how does a new housing environment affect people who have lived in a slum compared to people who have had to move into the housing because their financial circumstances have suddenly deteriorated (as might be the case for a mother of two young children who was recently divorced and has no job skills)?

Obviously the researcher must take special pains to ensure that knowledge is generated that might have a bearing on the conditions that led to and are associated with the assignment rule for some program and/or setting. Judd and Kenny (1981) have discussed various strategies that can be adopted when such information exists and the investigator must somehow incorporate these data into his or her data analysis plan. To illustrate the nature of the problem, consider the continuing debate over the merits of Head Start experience. If the relevant outcome measure is the child's first-grade achievement (and this is clearly one of many possible outcomes of interest), than a number of factors other than Head Start experience may be expected to affect performance. For example, children in Head Start classes may be expected to have lived in settings having fewer educational and cultural opportunities than would comparison children. Any differences in first-grade achievement levels might be a consequence of these initial differences rather than Head Start training. Judd and Kenny recount how the initial evaluation of Head Start made use of covariance analysis in an effort to remove the effects of prior educational and cultural experiences. Aside from the questionable nature of this effort to remove what may be considered ecologically valid information, the results revealed that Head Start appeared to lead to worse performance in the first grade. Campbell and Boruch (1975) have shown how the use of covariance analysis with covariates that are measured with error (i.e., are unreliable) can lead to the underestimation of the effects of programs such as Head Start. Reanalysis of the Head Start data in which the unreliability of the covariates was consciously modeled as part of the analysis revealed that Head Start actually had a small but positive effect on children's first-grade achievement (Bentler & Woodward, 1978; Linn & Werts, 1977; Magidson, 1978). Rindskopf (1981) has subsequently shown how it is possible to model data of these kinds either through the incorporation of the assignment rule variables into the model or through the simultaneous comparison of the treatment and control groups as separate units but considered as a whole. In both approaches, the unreliability of the covariates is removed before estimating the effects of the intervention and the assignment rule variables. This analysis was accomplished through the use of the structural modeling technique developed by Jöreskog (Jöreskog & Sörbom, 1979) and is particularly appropriate if the assignment rule itself constitutes a valid aspect of a setting's functioning.

3.5.6. Factors Relevant to Research Participation

This aspect of research design is obviously geared to increasing participation in an investigation and minimizing losses in the research sample over the course of the investigation. Unfortunately, there are no simple rules that can be followed to deal with these problems.

In planning field research, the investigator must give careful consideration to those conditions under which it is anticipated that participants will cooperate with the researcher and the expectations, beliefs, and commitments they bring to the research endeavor. It should be obvious that those who choose to participate in a project often bring multiple agendas with them when they agree to participate. These can range from the desire to be cooperative and "do good" to beliefs that the research results will somehow contribute to or interfere with a set of intentions and purposes they have for being at the research site in the first place. Many useful suggestions for entering field settings can be found in the work of those who do participant observation studies (Bogdan & Taylor, 1975, Chapters 2 & 3; Filstead, 1970; Miller 1977, Pt. 2; Schatzman & Strauss, 1973). Even these investigators admit, however, that not much has been written on this subject.

Although these guides exist, it is important to be clear regarding the mutual expectations that all persons in the research enterprise have regarding one another. This is particularly true when the sociopolitical context of the situation under study may lead to expectations on the part of participants that the research will be used either for or against their interests. Under these circumstances, the field researcher must often literally negotiate a contract with the participants regarding their mutual beliefs concerning research outcomes. Such a contract should also include a clear statement about what uses, if any, the research findings will be put to.

On those occasions when the research project is conducted in an atmosphere in which there are conflicts among the research participants, the investigator must be particularly aware of the problem that reactivity of research instruments may create. Wherever possible, a search should be undertaken for data sources that are germane to the outcomes but that would not be as subject to potential distortion, no matter how well or ill intentioned the study participants may be in their communications with the investigator.

From an ecological perspective, advice regarding the use of multiple sources of information is obviously desirable (Campbell & Fiske, 1959). We often want to know more than just what people think, feel, and verbally communicate to us. We also want to know what they do. For example, in community conflicts, participants may report a range of feelings about whatever the source of the conflicts may be. These verbally reported evaluations should be compared to actions that may have been taken such as writing letters to public officials, participation in community meetings, organization of community residents, and so on. For example, Amir (1972) has focused on protests against highway construction and has drawn upon multiple sources of information in an effort to identify those factors that contribute to successful protest activities.

3.6. CONCLUSIONS AND IMPLICATIONS

One of the major purposes of this chapter has been to show that environmental social scientists have advanced theoretical perspectives regarding person–environment transactions that are organized around a systemic understanding of the settings that comprise people's spheres of activity. The variables that constitute a setting's operation may have both direct and mediating effects on those issues that are of central interest to an investigator pursuing a particular research question.

An important subset of potential mediating variables in many locales has been identified in the methodological literature as potential threats to research validity. The majority of the recommendations that have been advanced to deal with these threats involve strategies that might be used to remove their effects on the focal variables that presumably are of central interest to the investigator. This approach to the treatment of validity, however, tends to ignore the possibility that plausible alternatives both may be substantively relevant to a setting's operation and, as such, can serve to expand the construct validity of variables of primary concern to the investigator. A perspective that emphasizes the minimization of the role of plausible alternatives creates a situation in which environmental investigators encounter conflicts in their efforts to design research that both is sensitive to the systemic qualities of settings and yields results that are not to be dismissed simply as artifacts.

In my discussion of these problems, I have suggested that a possible resolution of some of these conflicts may be sought in a reexamination of the validity question and its meaning for systemically oriented research design. The resolution might involve three steps. First, we should make an effort to redirect our attention away from potential problems in research design so that we might concentrate on the ecological processes characteristic of field settings that could substantively affect a set of research outcomes. In the course of this activity, it may be possible to reconceptualize internal validity issues as problems of construct validity that are relevant to the ecological functioning of the settings within which we choose to pursue research questions. The factors that have been identified as potential sources of ambiguity in the evaluation of the validity of research claims would not be ignored in this process. They would simply be reinterpreted as requiring explanation themselves.

The process of reinterpretation would be facilitated by reliance on existing theory (e.g., models that have been proposed to account for differential selection into various environments), systematically designed holistic research whose purpose it is to identify the parameters that can account for how a setting "works" (Winkel, 1985), and/or firsthand experience with a setting's operation and the phenomena in which the researcher is interested. If a tentative model can be devised for the operation of these variables, the research design and analysis strategies could incorporate these factors as part of the endeavor. At that point, the investigator is primarily oriented around problems of ecological validity as discussed in this chapter.

To the extent that these efforts are successful, the researcher will have moved toward the maximization of external validity and the minimization of possible internal validity problems. The central question then concerns the adequacy of the theoretical system that has been devised to account for the phenomena of interest.

There can be little doubt that the resulting models will be considerably more complex than those that have been advanced in the work that has been accomplished thus far. While we possess the tools that are necessary to design such complex research, the analysis of the data that would be generated from such ecologically oriented research designs has not kept pace. Unfortunately, space does not allow a discussion of these issues. It is in this area that there are considerable opportunities for the development of a more unified approach to person–environment transactions.

REFERENCES

Amato, P. (1983). Helping behavior in urban and rural environments: Field studies based on a taxonomic organization of helping behavior. *Journal of Personality and Social Psychology, 45,* 571–586.

Amir, S. (1972). Highway location and public opposition. *Environment and Behavior, 4,* 413–436.

Barker, R. (1963). *The stream of behavior.* New York: Appleton-Century-Crofts.

Barker, R. (1968). *Ecological Psychology.* Stanford, CA: Stanford University Press.

Barker, R., & Gump, P. (1964). *Big school, small school.* Stanford, CA: Stanford University Press.

Barker, R., & Wright, H. (1949). Psychological ecology and the problem of psychosocial development. *Child Development, 20,* 131–143.

Barker, R., & Wright, H. (1951). *One boy's day.* New York: Harper & Row.

Baron, R., & Bell, P. (1975). Aggression and heat: Mediating effects of prior provocation and exposure to an aggressive model. *Journal of Personality and Social Psychology, 31,* 825–832.

Baron, R., & Bell, P. (1976). Aggression and heat: The influence of ambient temperature, negative affect, and a cooling drink on physical aggression. *Journal of Personality and Social Psychology, 33,* 245–255.

Baum, A., Gatchel, R., Aiello, J., & Thompson, D. (1981). Cognitive mediation of environmental stress. In J. Harvey (Ed.), *Cognition, social behavior and the environment.* Hillsdale, NJ: Erlbaum.

Bechtel, R. (1977). *Enclosing behavior.* Stroudsberg, PA: Dowden, Hutchinson, & Ross.

Bentler, P., & Woodward, J. (1978). A Head Start reevaluation: Positive effects are not yet demonstrable. *Evaluation Quarterly, 2,* 493–510.

Blalock, H. (1984). Contextual-effects models: Theoretical and methodological issues. *Annual Review of Sociology* (Vol. 10). Palo Alto, CA: Annual Reviews.

Bogdan, R., & Taylor, S. (1975). *Introduction to qualitative research methods.* New York: Wiley.

Boyd, L., & Iversen, G. (1979). *Contextual analysis: Concepts and statistical techniques*. Belmont, CA: Wadsworth.

Bronfenbrenner, U. (1977). Toward an experimental ecology of human development. *American Psychologist, 32*, 513–531.

Brunswik, E. (1937). Psychology as a science of objective relations. *Philosophy of Science, 4*, 227–260.

Brunswik, E. (1943). Organismic achievement and environmental probability. *Psychological Review, 50*, 255–272.

Brunswik, E. (1952). The conceptual framework of psychology. In *International encyclopedia of united science* (Vol. 1). Chicago: University of Chicago Press.

Cronbach, L., & Meehl, P. (1955). Construct validity in psychological tests. *Psychological Bulletin, 52*, 281–302.

Dollard, J., & Miller, N. (1950). *Personality and psychotherapy: An analysis in terms of learning, thinking and culture*. New York: McGraw-Hill.

Ellsworth, P. (1977). From abstract ideas to concrete instances: Some guidelines for choosing natural research settings. *American Psychologist, 32*, 604–615.

Evans, G. (1981). *Environmental stress*. New York: Cambridge University Press.

Filstead, W. (1970). *Qualitative methodology: Firsthand involvement with the social world*. Chicago: Markham.

Gans, H. (1962). *The urban villagers*. New York: Free Press.

Glaser, B., & Strauss, A. (1967). *The discovery of grounded theory: Strategies for qualitative research*. Chicago: Aldine.

Griffitt, W. (1970). Environmental effects on interpersonal affective behavior: Ambient effective temperature and attraction. *Journal of Personality and Social Psychology, 15*, 240–244.

Griffitt, W., & Veitch, R. (1971). Hot and crowded: Influence of population density and temperature on interpersonal affective behavior. *Journal of Personality and Social Psychology, 17*, 92–98.

Hammond, K.R. (1966). Probabilistic functionalism: Egon Brunswik's integration of the history, theory and method of psychology. In K.R. Hammond (Ed.), *The psychology of Egon Brunswik*. New York: Holt, Rinehart & Winston.

Heider, F. (1958). *The psychology of interpersonal relations*. New York: Wiley.

Hochberg, J. (1966). Representative sampling and the purposes of perceptual research: Pictures of the world and the world of pictures. In K.R. Hammond (Ed.), *The psychology of Egon Brunswik*. New York: Holt, Rinehart & Winston.

Ittelson, W., Proshansky, H., & Rivlin, L. (1970). The use of behavioral maps in environmental psychology. In H. Proshansky, W. Ittelson, & L. Rivlin (Eds.), *Environmental psychology: Man and his physical setting*. New York: Holt, Rinehart & Winston.

Ittelson, W., Proshansky, H., Rivlin, L., & Winkel, G. (1974). *An introduction to environmental psychology*. New York: Holt, Rinehart & Winston.

Joreskog, K., & Sorbom, D. (1979). *Advances in factor analysis and structural equation models*. Cambridge, MA: Abt Books.

Judd, C., & Kenny, D. (1981). *Estimating the effects of social interventions*. Cambridge, MA: Cambridge University Press.

Kahneman, D., Slovic, P., & Tversky, A. (1982). *Judgment under uncertainty: Heuristics and biases*. Cambridge, MA: Cambridge University Press.

Klein, R., et al. (1968). Transfer from a coronary care unit. *Archives of Internal Medicine, 122*, 104–112.

Korte, C., & Grant, R. (1980). Traffic noise, environmental awareness, and pedestrian behavior. *Environment and Behavior, 12*, 408–420.

Levine, M. (1982). You-are-here maps: Psychological considerations. *Environment and Behavior, 14*, 221–237.

Linn, R., & Werts, C. (1977). Analysis implications of the choice of structural models in the nonequivalent control group design. *Psychological Bulletin, 84*, 229–234.

Lofland, J. (1971). *Analyzing social settings*. Belmont, CA: Wadsworth.

Long, J. (1983). *Covariance structure models: An introduction to LISREL*. Beverly Hills, CA: Sage.

Magidson, J. (1978). Reply to Bentler and Woodward: The .05 significance level is not all-powerful. *Evaluation Quarterly, 2*, 511–520.

Marx, M., & Hillix, W. (1973). *Systems and theories in psychology*. New York: McGraw-Hill.

McCall, G., & Simmons, J. (1969). *Issues in participant observation*. Reading, MA: Addison-Wesley.

Milgram, S. (1970). The experience of living in cities. *Science, 167*, 1461–1468.

Miller, D. (1977). *Handbook of research design and social measurement* (3rd Ed.). New York: Longman.

Mook, D. (1983). In defense of external invalidity. *American Psychologist, 38*, 379–387.

Nisbett, R., & Wilson, I. (1977). Telling more than we know: Verbal reports on mental processes. *Psychological Review, 84*, 231–259.

Page, R. (1977). Noise and helping behavior. *Environment and Behavior, 9*, 311–334.

Petrinovich, L. (1979). Probabilistic functionalism: A conception of research method. *American Psychologist, 34*, 373–390.

Proshansky, H. (1976). Environmental psychology and the real world. *American Psychologist, 31*, 303–314.

Rindskopf, D. (1981). Using structural equation models in evaluation research. In R. Boruch, P. Wortman, & D. Cordrat (Eds.), *Reanalyzing program evaluations*. San Francisco: Jossey-Bass.

Rossi, P. (1955). *Why families move: A study in the social psychology of urban residential mobility.* New York: Free Press.

Saegert, S. (1978). High density environments: Their personal and social consequences. In A. Baum & Y. Epstein (Eds.), *Human response to crowding.* Hillsdale, NJ: Erlbaum.

Saegert, S. (1981). Crowding and cognitive limits. In J. Harvey (Ed.), *Cognition, social behavior and the environment.* Hillsdale, NJ: Erlbaum.

Saegert, S. (1982). Environment and children's mental health: Residential density and low income children. In A. Baum & J. Singer (Eds.), *Handbook of psychology and health* (Vol. 2). Hillsdale, NJ: Erlbaum.

Saegert, S., & Winkel, G. (1980). The home: A critical problem for changing sex roles. In G. Wekerle, R. Peterson, & D. Morley (Eds.), *New spaces for women.* Boulder, CO: Westview.

Sarason, S. (1972). *The creating of settings and the future societies.* San Francisco: Jossey-Bass.

Schatzman, L., & Strauss, A. (1973). *Field research: Strategies for a natural sociology.* Englewood Cliffs, NJ: Prentice-Hall.

Schiffenbauer, A., Schulman, R., & Poe, D. (1978). A nested analysis for data collected from groups: Making crowding research more efficient. *Environment and Behavior, 10,* 127–132.

Schneider, F., Lesko, W., & Garrett, W. (1980). Helping behavior in hot, comfortable, and cold temperatures. *Environment and Behavior, 12,* 231–240.

Schorr, A. (1966). *Slums and social insecurity.* Washington, DC: U.S. Government Printing Office.

Scriven, M. (1972). The methodology of evaluation. In C. Weiss (Ed.), *Evaluating action programs: Readings in social action and education.* Boston: Allyn & Bacon.

Stern, G. (1974). B = f (P, E). In R. Moos & P. Insel (Eds.), *Issues in social ecology.* Palo Alto, CA: National Press.

Tolman, E., & Brunswik, E. (1935). The organism and the causal texture of the environment. *Psychological Review, 42,* 43–77.

Wicker, A. (1974). Processes which mediate behavior–environment congruence. In R. Moos & P. Insel (Eds.), *Issues in social ecology.* Palo Alto, CA: National Press.

Wicker, A. (1979). *An introduction to ecological psychology.* Monterey, CA: Brooks-Cole.

Winkel, G. (1977). The role of ecological validity in environmental research. In L. Van Ryzin (Ed.), *Behavior-environment research methods.* Madison, WI: University of Wisconsin, Institute for Environmental Studies.

Winkel, G. (1985). Ecological validity issues in field research settings. In A. Baum & J. Singer (Eds.), *Advances in environmental psychology: Vol. 5. Methods and environmental psychology.* Hillsdale, NJ: Erlbaum.

Winkel, G., & Holahan, C. (1985). The environmental psychology of the hospital: Is the cure worse than the illness? *Prevention in the Human Services, 4,* 11–33.

Wortman, P. (1975). Evaluation research: A psychological perspective. *American Psychologist, 30,* 562–575.

Chapter **4**

ENVIRONMENTAL PSYCHOLOGY AND SOCIAL CHANGE

Susan Saegert, *City University of New York, New York, New York*

Environmental psychology as a field is in itself a kind of social change, as perhaps are all new areas of inquiry. It can be seen as an unintended consequence of other social changes such as increased human exploitation of the natural environment and high levels of technological innovation. Widespread public perception of deterioration in the quality of urban life also gave momentum to the new field, as did concern among some design professionals and psychologists about the effects of the built environment on human well-being and satisfaction. These concerns raised conceptual and methodological problems that could not comfortably be assimilated by existing subfields of psychology, nor by other social sciences. All social sciences tended to define the environment mainly in terms of social transactions and institutions (includ-

ing financial and political transactions and institutions). The everyday physical world of buildings and parks, automobiles and subways was at best a shadowy backdrop for the drama of social life and psychological processes. Conversely, design theory said much about sculptural form and aesthetic traditions but little about the everyday experience of using designed spaces. Planning theory combined elements of economics, political science, geography, and sociology but mainly overlooked the psychological level of analysis.

To some extent, as a consequence of these antecedents, environmental psychologists tend to see their work as self-consciously, if vaguely, related to changing the relationship of people as individuals and in groups with their environments so that "fit" would be improved. This intent has also been expressed as a desire to optimize person–environment transactions. These formulations recognize the reciprocal nature of person–environment relationships, thus implying plasticity and mutual definition. Thus the environment exists in the psychological experience of the individual, in the social relationships of people, and in the physical environment of time, space, and matter (c.f. Ittelson, 1973; Proshansky, 1976; Proshansky, Ittelson, Rivlin, & Winkel, 1974; Wapner, Kaplan, & Cohen, 1973). Many chapters in this handbook deal with the complexities of understanding person–environment interdependence. This paper will attempt to clarify the connections among psychological change, social change, and physical change when all are seen as aspects of the environment.

The transactional analysis of person–environment relations has implications for our understanding of social change. The person is conceptualized as always simultaneously embedded in the environment and actively defining and giving form to it. The environment as we can know it presents psychological, social, and physical possibilities and barriers to action. We know these not by some moment-to-moment process of perception, but through historical and personal development of expectations and systems of meaning. From this perspective, systems of expectation and meaning are in some senses general and in others always particular and specific. Because they are shaped by the physically and socially possible actions and experiences presented by an already existing set of physical conditions and social practices, they are general. Because these meanings develop historically and throughout life, they are unique. The idea of social change has the same compound quality. It implies a shared and rather general drift in human experience and relationships. At the same time social change points to the development of previously nonexistent conditions and experiences. *Thus the problem for a social scientist interested in social change becomes one of testing the limits of certain generalities in the interest of bringing about new ones.* From a transactional perspective, change must always involve new definitions of self and others in environment. New definitions are inextricably, though plastically, bound to new conditions for action which in turn must have some physical components in order to support new actions. I think that this emphasis on the continuity of the physical, social, and psychological self and environment can advance social science, especially psychological, understanding of social change. By *psychological* I mean the aspects of motives, goals, interpretations, concepts, and individual behavior. Of course these interface with social and physical entities but are not subsumed by them. By *social* I mean interpersonal communications, joint activities, subcultural and cultural definitions of interpretations and concepts, standing patterns of interaction and exchange, and individual behavior governed by group or institutional norms and regulations. These social entities are not only partially psychological but also physical. By *physical* I mean bodies, buildings, physical resources, locations, and organizations of matter in time and space. The distinctions among the three kinds of entities are observed implicitly by the social and natural sciences. In daily life they are normally understood and experienced as interdependent aspects of people's relationships with each other and the nonhuman world.

The following discussion of the relationship between environmental psychology and social change derives from three premises. First, social change always involves physical change and vice versa. This first point may appear controversial and empirical rather than logically derived from the adoption of a transactional perspective. The premise follows from a view of the psychological self as dependent on the social and physical environment for its particular existence. Because any transactions that warrant the label *social* involve transactions among people in which the behaving people are aspects of the environment for others, any social change is also a physical environmental change. Even if one made the unwarranted distinction between people as parts of the environment and everything else, it is hard to imagine behavior so independent of props as to separate change in one from change in the other. Second, the environment is always defined from a particular point of view. In part I am emphasizing again the fact that each person will be from another's point of view part of the environment. Third, we can more fully understand the relationship between knowledge generated by environmental psychologists and social change if we analyze the physical, temporal, spatial, and material social and psychological location of the environmental psychologists concerned and their intents. This point derives from the view that knowledge and action are historically and geographically specific (even when global). Three models based on different intents in bringing about change will be described. I have called these three models of change the *technological*, the *interpretive*, and the *transformative* (Saegert, in press). An environmental psychologist is likely to function in all three models, sometimes sequentially, sometimes simultaneously. The main difference involves the way the researcher–

consultant thinks about his or her endeavors. Because we are social scientists, most of the ways we think about ourselves in applied settings emphasize the separation between the researcher and the problem. In this model basic research leads to the discovery of general truths. The traditional applied researcher takes these truths, analyzes specific situations in terms of the concepts and relationships developed in basic research, perhaps takes some measurements to establish the level of different variables, and then conducts an investigation that reveals how the processes derived from basic research are being expressed in this situation. Within this model the social scientist sometimes serves as a translator to inform nonspecialist audiences, be they the public or a particular group of professionals and decision makers, about the way social science concepts and findings can be used to analyze a particular situation or to change the definition of a particular problem. Training in psychological research does not usually stress the extent to which the researcher acts to define what a situation is, what aspects are most salient, when something should be considered an antecedent, when an outcome, from whose perspective, and so on.

4.1. MODELS OF ENVIRONMENTAL PSYCHOLOGY AND SOCIAL CHANGE

4.1.1. Technological Model

The technological model of change is probably the most common one in American discussions of social science (especially psychology) and social change. In this model the social scientist intends to prescribe the means to a foreseen change based on social science knowledge. This model assumes that a consensus about the definition of the conditions to be changed and the goals of change exists (or at least can be developed). The consensus must include those with sufficient authority and control of resources to effect a change, those with the responsibility for understanding the nature of the conditions to be changed and the means by which they can be changed, and those responsible for implementing the change. Social science research is supposed also to lead to one more or less consensually accepted answer or truth about the situation. This model implicitly separates decision makers, researchers, implementors, and, for want of a better term, the public. Thus it carries with it the notion that one group of people defines the problem and brings about a

change that affects another group. The experience of the change makers does not enter into consideration, nor is attention given to the effects of the change on them. Many of the contexts in which environmental psychologists have worked are defined by this implicit contract. For example, a study of the impact of design changes on patients in a mental hospital ward does not examine the impact on the agency that funded the changes, the hospital administration, nor the researchers (c.f. Holahan & Saegert, 1973).

While much social science research loosely accepts a technological model of social change in that it attempts to establish causes of particular outcomes within clearly specified conditions, the many steps between the discovery of a general scientific "truth" and the development of a technically successful means to an end are usually short-circuited. Gerard (1982) faults the use of social science research in the landmark *Brown v. the Board of Education* school desegregation decision because the social scientists involved did not follow all the steps from the scattered findings in theoretically oriented research through the stages of research and development that could eventually lead to successful school desegregation. One of the missing links he identifies bears on the goals of environmental psychology in that he states that the conditions of the setting in which desegregation was to be attempted differed from the conditions ideally specified in the Social Science Statement as necessary preconditions for successful change. Gerard's recommendations in hindsight help explicate some of the conditions for successful application of the technological model. However, he ignores the preconditions for operating in a technological model: the existence of a sufficient consensus about goals and means among those controlling necessary resources to bring about the technological change. The resources and complex cooperative relationships that would have been required to undertake the research and development of effective school desegregation most likely could not have been mustered. Therefore, one might more appropriately view the social scientists in the case as operating in an interpretive model of social change. From this viewpoint they were not predicting the success of school desegregation but rather were interpreting the experience of segregation for black children as incompatible with basic constitutional rights of American citizens.

Exclusive reliance on a technological model violates some transactional assumptions. A system of analysis that depends on identifying clearly separable aspects of people as individuals and groups and of environments cannot recognize constant mutual definition of person and environment leading to qualitative change and new interdependencies. Because of the historical separation of physical and social sciences, technological changes derived from either branch almost always ignore the human–environment interdependencies. Using the school desegregation issue, we can see that the analysis of social psychological processes out of context in no way took into account the embeddedness of school segregation in geographic racial segregation and the possible consequences for the future of cities and suburbs of the busing decision.

The consequences of busing well illustrate the interwoven nature of social and psychological processes, historical political and economic changes, and the physical form of the environment. When we look at technological changes thought to be physical, two points become immediately evident. First, the specific technology, for example, increased production of energy, generally addresses one goal. Ecological ramifications beyond the achievement of the goal are ignored by those developing the technology and adopting it unless specific social–political pressures call attention to these issues. Second, the social, psychological, political, and cultural nature of the technology and expected changes in these domains in relation to the technology tend not to be addressed as part of the development and adoption of the technology.

When we accept that qualitative changes in person–environment relationships will emerge in historical contexts, the limits of prediction as well as the limits of generalization become apparent. Practitioners in the scientific technological model are aware of these limits. Yet that does not lead them to develop alternative models. Because of the premium placed on a certain kind of scientific and technological knowledge, the implications of areas of genuine uncertainty tend to be ignored. Nontechnological debates concerning moral choice, personal or group interest, and differences in interpretation of both problems and goals are seen as separate from technological discussions. A scientist or technocrat may warn decision makers that the actions being contemplated go beyond scientific knowledge or that the situation under consideration may not meet certain assumptions that are required to generalize from existing knowledge. Within the technological model, this warning defines the limits of the scientist–technocrat's responsibility. The researcher in this model has no interest in the political and social consequences of his or her warning or in the use to which the informa-

tion supplied may be put. The warning of limitations on the information is not accompanied by informed analysis of what the limitations mean for the situation at hand. That type of application is seen as falling in the domain of other specialists. When the technological model fails, when research is distorted, ignored, controverted by other research, and dismissed as too idealistic or impractical, that model itself does not help us understand what has happened. The aim of providing the other two models is to place the researcher more fully in the context in which his or her research emerges, is conducted, and has its effects. A second goal is to raise the question of the extent to which social change entails environmental and psychological change, and each of these also requires the other two.

4.1.2. Interpretive Model

The second model, the interpretive mode, of the relationship between environmental psychology and social change focuses on the process whereby people define the environment and the environment defines people. In this model, social change is not brought about directly. Rather, change and obstacles to change in person–environment transactions are identified. This model also lends itself to an analysis of the perspectives different individuals and groups have of the environment. It recognizes explicitly that the physical and conceptual form of the environment reflects the intentions and actions of specific people and interacting groups. The interpretive model draws our attention to the process of mutual definition in which people who are subjects in their own experience are objects and environments in the experience of others. The intent of the social scientist operating within this model is to communicate with others to achieve shared understanding of self and others in environment.

Research in the interpretive model depends more on analysis and example than on hypothesis and experiment, although careful examination of the two models shows the distinction between them in human sciences to be somewhat blurry. Descriptive research aims primarily at interpretation. While participant observation and intensive interviewing are more frequently practiced by researchers operating in the interpretive model, it is not the method or type of data that differentiates research in one mode from that in another. The intent in interpretive research is to tell a story about the activities of particular people in particular situations that makes their actions intelligible and meaningful to the audience. Tests of the validity of interpretation center on their fidelity to the understandings and meanings attributed to actions and circumstances by the actors in the situations observed. The actors themselves may not be able to verbalize these meanings, yet the test for the researcher involves developing a system of interpretation that does not violate the rules of conduct and interpretation practiced by the actors. Glaser and Strauss (1967) provide an account of the discovery of grounded theory that gives a sense of this method of interpretation. Harre and Secord (1973) present a more thorough and formal analysis of a theoretical and methodological approach to developing valid explanations of social behavior. Since neither of these pairs of authors shares the concern of environmental psychologists with the physical context of behavior, both focus on linguistic practices and rule-governed interaction sequences. As sociologists, Glaser and Strauss pay somewhat more attention to context than do Harre and Secord, who mainly address their work to social psychologists. Some recent examples of interpretive research in environmental psychology include Rivlin's (1982) study of a Hasidic community's attachment to place using a participant observation and interview method and Altman and Gauvain's (1981) discussion of symbolism in the physical forms and decorations of homes.

None of the authors just mentioned is explicitly concerned with social change. Indeed, the descriptive nature of such research sometimes seems at odds with an orientation toward change. Yet some authors do employ this approach to understand the nature of different groups' experience of social change, or to point to needed changes. This understanding can reveal that current policy directions create more harm than good or are at least in conflict with the groups they are ostensibly intended to benefit. Such research can also lead to a new awareness of social needs that in turn can lead to change. For example, Fried and Gleicher's (1976) and Gans's (1962) research in the West End in Boston and Rainwater's (1970) study of Pruitt-Igo both affected thinking about urban renewal and housing for low-income people. The work of Rowles and Ohta (1978) on the elderly shows the needs of a significant portion of the population in a new light and makes clearer the meaning of the experience of aging.

While the examples provided thus far have used participant observation and intensive interviewing as primary methods, more traditional survey research can be employed for interpretive purposes. For example, Otway, Maurer, and Thomas's (1978) work differentiating the core values of opponents and pro-

ponents of nuclear power interprets the meaning of different groups' relationships with a particular aspect of the environment. While this example seems to me to fit within the category of interpretive research, the authors do not address the tests of validity involving fidelity to participants' experience. Because of shared experience, common cultural values of previous research, the categories employed by the researchers may capture the experience of those being described. However, they may also reify researchers' stereotypes and reinforce subcultural or societal divisions supported by existing social, political, and economic arrangements.

One of the limits of interpretive research for contributing to social change arises from the limits of language and communication. While the researchers may immerse themselves in the milieu of those they study, the audience will have to rely on the description of the experience. The meaning of particular phenomena depends to some extent on the sensory and affective experience embedded in the nonverbal assumptions of particular groups. Whatever cannot be or has not been conveyed by the researchers about the phenomena will be assimilated to categories of experience available to the audience. These lacunae will limit the change in ways of thinking about people and situations under discussion. Thus, to the extent that changes in categories of thought provoke different responses to people and situations, change will not occur. Second, just as in the case of the technological model, social change will only occur to the extent that a consensus concerning values, priorities, and actions exists among those with sufficient control over resources to bring about change. Interpretive research can contribute to the formation of such a consensus by increasing understanding and appealing to shared values or societal laws and customs. It can point out potential resources and strategies for change existing in the populations and situations studied or conversely identify previously unrecognized barriers to change. For a researcher operating in the interpretive model, the main goal is to increase communication and develop a wide and more sensitive dialogue to achieve shared understanding of self and others in environment. To the extent that actions to change conditions are discussed it will be with the intent of exploring differences and similarities in interpretation, value, and interests embedded in these actions and in the conditions seen to exist and new conditions to be brought about.

This model emphasizes the importance for the researcher of letting the subject of research speak for himself or herself. Because of the communicative goal of this research, attention may be turned away from the physical environment. While this need not be true, the traditions of social science that direct attention away from the temporal, spatial, and material aspects of experience require that the researcher take special pains to include them. Sociological, anthropological, and even some psychological research follow the interpretive model. Almost no research in ecology or the hard sciences pursues this approach. Thus bringing human knowledge of and relationship with the physical world into discourse about social change provides a central challenge for environmental psychologists working in the interpretive model.

Finally, even if consensus about goals and access to resources for change can be achieved, the existing interpretations may not provide adequate direction for bringing about the intended changes. Thus the third model combines both technical and interpretive approaches to research for social change with an active seeking of the conditions that make change possible.

4.1.3. Transformative Synthesis

The third model contrasts with the previous two in that it places the environmental psychologist as a specific individual in a specific context in the process of both knowing and changing person–environment transactions. Thus the structural relations, intents, and actions that give form and movement to the transactions of other people with the environment and each other in the interpretive model come to include those of the researcher. The models can be seen as a progression toward embeddedness. As this embeddedness increases, the need for theoretical and methodological practices that acknowledge the historical and material nature of people and environments becomes more pressing. We become aware of our boundaries in time and space and of the specificity of our geographic, economic, social, political, biological, and psychological realities.

The first way that the transformative model of research I am proposing differs from the other models, and indeed violates some canons of accepted scientific practice, involves a recognition that the researcher has specific interests. Academics widely accept the proposition that the answer one obtains in research depends on the question one asks. Yet the process of question asking is shrouded in claims of personal curiosity or assertions that a particular problem dominates a field or that a particular theory is "most fruitful." Since Kuhn's (1962) analysis of the structure of scientific revolutions, the possibility that

research direction and scientific theories progress through changes in the social organization of knowledge production has gained credibility. Others have gone further and identified specific economic interests motivating the direction of research efforts at particular points in time (c.f. Rose & Rose, 1969). The social and economic channeling of research questions into specific forms, topics, theories, and methods depends on the same conditions that limit technologically and interpretively oriented research: (1) social consensus about the definition of problems and the desirable directions for change and (2) control of resource bases sufficient to support research and action directed toward change.

A researcher working in the transformation model critically examines the interests and assumptions leading to particular question formulations and methods. The type of criticism differs from the purely scholarly tradition of asking whether these assumptions are logically defensible. In addition, we ask what patterns of domination are assumed in the structure of the question and whose interests are served by pursuing its answers. Often the answers to such questions are far from clear. Many groups of people with specific interests have not contributed to the dialogue that gives rise to the question. Because of this situation, interpretive research usually provides the starting point for work in the transformative model. However, the starting point differs from that of purely interpretive research in that the researcher seeks to interpret his or her own position in relationship to that of others and to existing conditions seen from different points of view. The researcher must analyze the context of research and the sources of consensual definition of the problem and method of study and of the direction of actions. Thus we have to take seriously and be able to answer the questions that participants in research often ask: Why are you doing this study? What is it about? Why would you study that? What do you intend to do with the research? Why should I cooperate with you?

The key difference in the transformative approach and the technological model involves an awareness of the relevant forms of life in which an analysis of a problem and actions to be taken are based. Successful work in this model requires changes in ideas rather than merely demonstration of the adequacy or correctness of a particular formulation, given a specific assumptive system. A researcher acting in the transformative mode may move back and forth between a technological analysis of a problem, courses of action, and limitations of a particular assumptive system, and interpretation of the assumptive system in relationship to other points of view. Since the researcher is interested in the course of change, she or he will not rest content with describing the limits of technological knowledge but will enter into communicative relationships with others and actions directed toward the physical world to change the consensus and command of resources and authority directing change. If the communication is successfully multisided, the researcher will also change in the process. To some extent the technologically oriented researcher acts similarly but without giving systematic attention to these actions and without feeling a responsibility to make an account of these communications and actions as part of the analysis of the problem.

The researcher will act differently depending on the kind of model being employed. In the technological mode, research involves organization of research methods and procedures within a specific context, the gathering of measures, and their analysis. The only communication between the researcher and other people that has to be intersubjectively validated involves communications among the research team and communication with the audience for the results. In contrast, interpretive research necessitates communication among researchers, the subjects of research, and the audience. Thus the people the researcher spends time with change and the methods of communication change. The sources employed in formulating analyses are likely to expand to include sources relied on by all of those in the communicative circle. Thus professional journals and channels of communication lose their primary status.

Actions in the transformative mode move the researcher from the world of professionals and subjects of study into the arena of decision making. When this occurs, different sources of analysis again come into play. The legal, historical, economic, and political context of the problem become crucial. An awareness of issues in these contexts as well as awareness of the researchers' and other participants' context and interests is required. Thus transformative research and practice become not only interdisciplinary but also antidisciplinary. No particular analysis has automatic precedence. But even beyond this condition of pluralism we must assume that analysis and action leading to and establishing viable change will require new definitions of physical, social, and psychological reality. The existing specializations of disciplines are very likely to be outgrown.

The transformative model also denies the priority of the researcher's definition as a professional or scientist. Instead the researcher acts as a person first;

thus moral and subjective criteria for evaluating research activities become the context for judging professional actions. I am inclined to view criteria for notions of truth, evidence, and causality as moral decisions.

Finally, the transformative model does not place abstract analysis and solutions on a higher plane than specific instances. Thus if a set of relationships should hold in principle but existing conditions always violate some of the assumptions required for the relationship to hold then the principle should be seen as a possible but not actual description of reality. When definitional fiat gives way to lived experience, the continuity between knowing a situation and changing it becomes clear, as do the continuity of social change and environmental change and the role of psychological change in both.

4.2. ENVIRONMENTAL PSYCHOLOGY AND SOCIAL CHANGE IN PRACTICE

These three models are not equally represented in the approaches environmental psychologists have taken toward social change, particularly as reported in professional journals and books. As in most of the social sciences, environmental psychologists usually describe their work within the technological model even though much of their actual experience of arriving at a problem, conceptualizing their work, and carrying it out is excluded through the conventions of such description. The following section briefly recounts some of the historical and conceptual developments within environmental psychology that provide the background for the emergence of challenges to largely unexamined acceptance of a technological model.

4.2.1. Social Science Context

Environmental psychology came on the scene during a period preoccupied with the relationship between social science and social change. During the 1960s and 1970s a cohort of social scientists and other professionals emerged who had been trained during the social conflicts of the civil rights movement, the Vietnam War, the student movement, the feminist movement, the ambitious social programs of Johnson's War on Poverty and Great Society, and a growing alarm about environmental degradation. These impossible-to-ignore social phenomena can be characterized by several attitudes that involve often passionate commitments to social change and at the same time conflictual attitudes toward the possibility and desirability of professionally guided, planned change. One of these involved an attack on the naturalistic, positivistic view of social science research.

Philosophical skepticism toward such an attitude was not new. As Altman (1976) points out, the new cohort was met by older professionals disenchanted with the mechanistic and formalistic models and methods of their disciplines. However, during this period blacks, women, and other discontented groups began to assert that the picture presented of them by social scientists and the plans made for them by decision makers reflected the biases of the dominant social groups and were intended to promote and justify an economic and social structure in which they would remain disadvantaged. On the one hand, these groups asserted that a false picture of reality was being drawn. On the other hand, the argument is made that consensually "real" social and physical arrangements promulgate conditions in which certain groups are demonstrably disadvantaged. The belief that valid definitions must arise from the people experiencing the conditions of concern has become associated with participatory approaches to knowledge and decision making, or with an approach that sees social reality as emerging from the struggle of disadvantaged sectors of society against dominant institutions. The belief in objectively determined outcomes lends itself to a model of change in which the contingencies that lead to certain groups being disadvantaged are scientifically and rationally identified, programs are developed to correct the problem, and then the programs are evaluated, adjustments are made if necessary, and the cycle is continued.

American psychology in the early 1960s was vulnerable to criticisms of conceptual bias and those alleging inattention to pressing social issues and reality outside the laboratory. Early work in environmental psychology emerged in part as a response to these criticisms. Before examining the genesis of the field in relationship to social change, it should be noted that other branches of psychology have developed in the same time periods that also demonstrate greater concern with context and with the interdependence of the individual and the social, economic, and political world. Evaluation research, organizational psychology, and community psychology provide some examples of areas that developed rapidly between 1960 and 1980.

This movement toward greater awareness of context still did not address the nature of the relationship of people with the physical environment at an explicitly theoretical level. The emphasis remained on mental and social processes regarded as general and presented without any specific context.

Several theoretical approaches did take more explicit account of the setting in which behavior occurred, though these approaches often glossed over the physical characteristics of settings and experiences. Ecological psychology portrays the environment primarily as a series of behavior settings characterized by standing patterns of behavior with physical aspects seen as props and backdrops. Lewin's field theory has provided inspiration for psychologists who have investigated the interdependence of people and the environment (c.f. Baum & Valins, 1977; Festinger, Schachter, & Back, 1950). But it is inexplicit about the nature of the physical world, except as represented in the psychologically present life space. Brunswik criticized field theory for being postperceptual and prebehavioral, thus disconnecting the life space from what we usually think of as the physical world (Hammond, 1966). In the area of perception both Brunswik (1952) and Gibson (1966) emphasized the importance of the physical environment for understanding perceptual processes.

Two areas of psychological investigation appeared in this 20-year span that did treat people as embodied. The first of these, following Hall's book *The Hidden Dimension* (1966), studied the use of interpersonal spacing as a method of communication. This line of study is closely related to the study of nonverbal behavior. While these areas of research bring into awareness the physicality and spatiality of human behavior, the interacting individuals are described in short observational periods, in isolated contexts, and without a conceptual analysis of the physical environment.

More recently health psychology or behavioral medicine has begun explicitly to examine the relationship among individuals' psychological, social, and physical states (though not usually the environment). The human significance of research in this area suggests the power of such an approach. Yet this area also lacks a coherent analysis of the physical, social (including economic and political), and psychological environment in relationship to the physical, social, and psychological individual.

4.2.2. Environmental Psychology Emerges

The early efforts of environmental psychologists to initiate change in person–environment transactions more or less followed a technological model. From the beginning, environmental psychologists did not distinguish between basic and applied research. The first journal in the area, *Environment and Behavior*, attracted authors from practice-oriented professions such as urban design, city planning, regional planning, architecture, and forestry. Many of the questions they asked were intended to develop basic knowledge of psychological and social processes that affected use and experience of the environment. For example, in the first issue of the journal *Southworth* (1969), a city planner influenced by Lynch's famous work on city images (Lynch, 1960) reported an investigation of sonic perception of the urban environment. The study addressed a topic untouched by psychologists. At the same time, the paper ended with recommendations for ameliorating unwanted noise in the locale studied and with suggestions for increasing the delightfulness of the sonic environment. Psychologists and other social scientists who published in the journal usually formulated their questions and research designs so as to lead to both potentially general statements about person–environment transactions and practical approaches to a problem. These articles differed from those in most psychology journals in that: (1) they were explicitly concerned with the physical environment, (2) they made clear what setting or environmentally related human process was being studied and how it might be improved, and (3) they were usually not designed to achieve general statements about psychological and social process, regardless of context.

At about the same time that *Environment and Behavior* began to appear, the Environmental Design Research Association (EDRA) was formed. This organization's membership drew heavily on design professionals and on social scientists who saw themselves as participating in the creation of a new field rather than as operating within their parent disciplines.

Environmental change (or more frequently the building of new environments) was seen as the central issue, more or less separate from changes in psychological or social processes. Most of the work presented looked either at the ways that design or larger-scale environmental characteristics influenced individual or group behavior *or* at cognitive processes by which the environment was perceived and experienced. Mixed in with these dominant approaches, a smattering of other perspectives can be found. Cross-cultural and ethological studies and theoretical statements aim at the traditional academic pursuit of understanding a phenomenon without necessary consideration of its implications for either social or environmental change (c.f. Rapoport, 1972; Von Furster, 1973). Descriptive studies of people behaving in environments as designers, users, protestors, ad-

ministrators, and so on have also appeared. These fit more appropriately into the interpretive model of the relationship between environmental psychologists and social change than into the technological model underlying the dominant approaches (c.f. Holland, 1972; Jobes, 1976; King-Ming New, Hessler, Hemnitzy, & Kemnitzer, 1972; Leff & Deutsch, 1973).

The sixth EDRA conference took as its theme "Responding to Social Change," a title that suggests a perspective virtually unchanged since EDRA's inception. Many of the papers identify the environmental and social changes to which a response is required: population growth, worldwide unemployment, starvation in many developing countries, an increasing gap between the rich and the poor, environmental degradation, bureaucratization and centralization, energy shortages, social conflict at all levels, increased communication, and speed of change (Blumenfeld, 1975; Brill, 1975; Hershberger, 1975; Sanoff, 1975; Shelley, 1975). The list of concerns, the evidence for them, and the political and moral goals and remedies echoed the debates about growth set forth in the early 1970s (Forrester, 1971; Meadows, Meadows, Randers, & Behrens, 1972; Schumacher, 1972). While the growth ethic was questioned (Blumenfeld, 1975; Lynch, 1975), no one addressed a fundamental moral reunderstanding of economics. Lynch elaborates a gentle, appealing, and ecologically respectful utopia that skips over the fundamental conflict between dominant social, political, and economic assumptions and structures and his vision. Perin (1975) makes conflict the centerpiece of her paper on social governance and environmental design. In doing so, she arrives at an understanding of the necessity for a transformative model of social change:

> In my better world, scientists' selves and their work are at one. For example, each published article would contain, besides its key words and abstracts, an "excursus," in which the scientist would discuss briefly two matters: First, why this question was chosen for study, in light of his/her working-life history; and second, what implications it is seen to have both for research in other disciplines and for issues of importance in society....It seems to me to go without saying that social sciences in general are, by definition "critical studies" in that they identify the locations of society's buried utilities, so to speak, and make explicit their power connections. That very function is the reason for a persistent lack of political support for social science research....(Perin, 1975, p. 53)

Of the papers compiled in the companion volume to the conference, Perin alone links personal identity and social/environmental transformation. In the other papers, two models of approaching social change emerge: the multidisciplinary research–design–policy team in close communication with clients and bureaucratic–governmental officials (Archea, 1975; Brill, 1975; Ventre, 1975) and a model of citizen participation in design, planning, decision making, construction, and management of environments (Goodey, 1975; Grant, 1975; Hartman, 1975). The first model emphasizes the need for academic institutions to train, support, and respect researchers who are competent in interdisciplinary work and who choose to do it. The problems of adjusting to highly demanding and unpredictable time frames for research and the problems of quality control and adequate knowledge base are identified as critical issues to be resolved (Archea, 1975; Brill, 1975; Sanoff, 1975). The second model also acknowledges the lack of support in academic institutions for the model they present. However, a more overt political analysis places the main locus of opposition in larger social and economic trends and institutions. The major calls for reform within professions center on increasing the ease and simplicity of communication between professionals and the public (a concern shared with those presenting the interdisciplinary model) and the development of tools for transferring research, planning, design, decision making, and implementation functions to the public (Goodey, 1975; Grant, 1975). This approach rejects an objectified understanding of people's experiences of the environment and seeks to replace it with a process of research that allows people to share the uniqueness of their experience as part of the process of arriving at socially shared visions of environmental change and conservation.

The interdisciplinary team approach works within the assumptions of the technological model and continues to account for a sizable proportion of activity within EDRA. For the most part, the approach continues to emphasize *responses* to social change. Thus in the economic climate of the mid-1980s fewer presentations address theoretical and research solutions, educational changes, and public information (c.f. Archea, 1975; Blake, 1978; Brill, 1975; Cohen, 1978; Clarke, 1975; Danford, 1978; Francescoto, Weidemann, Anderson, & Chenowith, 1976; Murtha, 1978; Sanoff, 1975; Wandersman, 1976; Wandersman, Murday, & Wadsworth, 1979), and more papers and workshops view environments and behavior research as a product or service to be sold to different markets (Anthony, 1982; Ellis, Duffy, & Jockusch, 1983; Seidel, 1982; Welch, 1983a, 1983b). The participatory model has evolved toward increasing awareness of both the politics of participation and the political context that limits and shapes the nature of participation (Hart, 1976; Jobes, 1976; Sanoff, 1978; Schwartz, 1978). At the same time, some mixing of different models has been occurring. For example, Wandersman and others have established a research thrust examining citizen participation in environmental issues (Giamartino, Ferrell, & Wandersman, 1979; Giamartino & Peabody, 1978). At the same time, reports from those working in a participatory way and those relying on the expert–client model have begun to appear (c.f. Ellis, Duffy, & Jockusch, 1983; Francis, Rivlin, Stone, & Carr, 1983; Marcus, 1983). Most recently, discussions of participatory planning have included reflections on problems of economic survival for participation-oriented environmental researchers and practitioners together with scrutiny of the successes and failures of an advocacy and confrontation style of participation (Moore, 1983). More consideration of worker participation experiments and movements appears to be one direction growing out of a serious consideration of the political and economic constraints on participation. This more self-conscious linking of oneself as a practitioner to the economic context of participation shows continuous growth of participatory planning and design toward a transformative model.

Feminist researchers and practitioners within EDRA have also consciously addressed themselves to social change. Beginning in 1976, workshops and papers have attempted to share women's experiences of environments and of the processes by which environments are created (Niculescu, 1976; Pollowy, 1978; Rothenberg & Hart, 1976; Saegert, 1976). After the creation of a Women's Network in EDRA, meetings continue to nurture a feminist perspective in environmental research and design, as can be seen by recent student papers (c.f. Ahrentzen, Jacobi, Skorpanich, & Ross, 1982; Gelfond, 1982) and workshops (Peterson, 1983). Indeed, the EDRA board's 1983 sponsorship of a symposium entitled "The Gender Gap: Does It Exist in Environmental Design and Research?" with an all-female panel demonstrates interest in women's perspectives in this context at the same time that research on women's roles and participation in the organization show women to be less well represented and less likely to occupy higher status positions (Ahrentzen et al., 1982). The feminist perspective has foreshadowed a transformative model in environmental research in that the link between personal identity, intellectual analysis, research methods and practice, and the larger sociopolitical context has been made explicit from the beginning. Much of the early feminist work was aimed at providing a space in which women could share their experience and research. At that time the male audience for such events was small and women were mainly concerned with articulating what the questions and issues were for themselves. As contact between women increased and work accumulated, it has become possible to put forward a different perspective on person–environment relations that derives from female experience but speaks to male-defined categories and approaches.

Two changes in direction seem to me to characterize the published proceedings over the 14 years of EDRA conferences. Both are of central importance to the discussion. First, theorizing about the relationship among people as physical beings, environments as physical habitats, and the psychological, social, economic, cultural, and political systems through which we know and act in the world has tended increasingly to exclude the physical emphasis and/or the economic and political components except in the work of participatory planners and feminists. Second, the number of studies carried out in conjunction with the planning, design, construction, policy-making, evaluation, and retrofitting of real environments has greatly increased. These trends seem to me to suggest that environmental design researchers have found to some extent the niches in which it is possible to increase the fit between at least some human needs and the environment or in which it is at least politically and socially acceptable to point out the existing problems. This development has significance for an analysis of the relationship between environmental psychology and social change in that it points to areas of social consensus in which the use of a technological or modified technological model of social change may in fact have utility. It also suggests that the dialogue and collaboration that have occurred over the years have given rise to linguistic and procedural practices that to some extent bridge the oft-bemoaned gap between research and application.

While the more interdisciplinary branches of environmental psychology were developing, the area was also being incorporated into psychology as a subfield (c.f. Craik, 1973; Russell & Ward, 1980; Stokols, 1978). Within this tradition, research on environmental stress has appeared as one area with implications for social change. Some of the stressful conditions studied have been topics of frequent political dispute such as aircraft noise (Cohen, Evans, Krantz, & Stokols, 1980) or a nuclear power plant accident (c.f. Baum, Gatchel, Streufert, Baum, Fleming, & Singer, 1980; Bromet, 1980; Houts & Disabella, 1983). Some have been the topic of litigation (c.f. crowding in prison). Many of the conditions studied could potentially be subject to regulation by various governmental entities (c.f. air pollution, Evans, Jacobs, & Frager, 1982; the density and scale of public housing, McCarthy & Saegert, 1978; Saegert, 1982).

DiMento (1981) attempts to outline the ways in which environmental stress research can have implications for public policy. In this article he identifies both the technological and the interpretive functions of environmental psychological research. In pointing out the conflicting modes of operating in the research and policy communities, he makes suggestions for ways in which researchers can have a more direct (technological) bearing on policy and describes certain conditions that augur well for a technological approach. He discusses several types of influences social science research can have: (1) instrumental influence (as in demonstration or regulatory programs), (2) conceptual influence whereby an idea enters public dialogue (perhaps the dominant form of influence of stress research at this time), (3) use of research findings to justify a decision made on political grounds, and (4) use of research to justify the importance of an agency mandate. Beyond these, DiMento suggests a type of influence that goes beyond the technological model, one that "is not calibrated according to impact on policy, but rather according to the extent that information defines the decision-making environment of the society" (p. 184). Nonetheless, the approach he outlines to understanding problems and prospects for policy-relevant research emphasizes a regulatory model in which a governmental body or other controlling authority acts to restrict the quantity of a particular condition associated with human stress (c.f. air and noise pollution, design dysfunction, etc.).

DiMento makes some valuable recommendations for establishing closer links between research and public policy. The research community is advised to formulate questions and methods in such a way as to synthesize different issues. Collaboration among researchers and professionals from different disciplines is recommended at the stage of conceptualizing and designing the research. Scientist–citizen exchanges are advocated as ways of making policies more acceptable and of possibly generating new policies. DiMento suggests that participation by social scientists in committee hearings, advisory boards, and informal contexts can decrease resistance to social science input. Field research is an essential component of all these strategies.

Because of the complexity and changing contingencies that shape dissemination of information, DiMento foresees the need for a formal boundary-spanning role that is professionally recognized and distinct from research. To facilitate this goal, he suggests that social scientists examine the genesis, vicissitudes, and fate of social science knowledge as well as of the latent and manifest functions of the knowledge in its social context. He also suggests that social scientists monitor the uses of their work and use examples of unintended uses to develop dissemination techniques for future efforts. Internships and other practicum experiences are recommended as a part of training as well as modification of curriculum to include more information about divergent perspectives on social problems and research. The recommendations are similar to ones often voiced in discussions about ways to improve the utilization of environmental psychological research in design and planning decisions. DiMento's analysis has led us to the edge of the transformative model in directing us to develop group self-reflection. It stops halfway between a sort of disengaged sociology of knowledge and a position that would require the social scientist to identify himself or herself as a person with intents, goals, and values. I would argue that if social science were to change in the direction of becoming more effective in policy formation it would radically alter our self-understanding and the understanding of what social science is, in the eyes of both practitioners and the rest of society.

4.2.3. Personal and Ethical Dimension

The relationships of individuals and groups with the environment are the basic components of society and of daily experience. Therefore to the extent that environmental psychologists shed new light on these relationships we will change society by bringing into awareness aspects of person–environment transactions that were previously hidden. If these relationships are problematic, they can be rationally, technically, or politically addressed. The question then is not to do research that is "relevant" but to do work in which concepts and methods do justice to the depth and breadth of phenomena studied. Our traditional approaches to research bring with them conceptual and methodological limitations that lead us to do work that lacks relevance because we sidestep basic decisions about the work we undertake. Habermas (1971), who inspired the three models previously described, points out that the way in which knowledge is sought, generated, evaluated, and employed depends on the intent of the knowledge. From this point of view, then, one question we should ask is: Why do I choose to do this work? Habermas asserts

that human knowledge can have three intents: (1) to control and predict, (2) to communicate, and (3) to liberate. I have argued elsewhere (Saegert, in press) that each mode relates the individual to the environment in a different way and involves the researcher in different social and physical practices and relationships. Thus once one has determined why the research is being undertaken one can choose the most appropriate ways and place for going about it.

As psychologists, we may be more familiar with thinking about intent as an individual issue. For example, we might say, "I undertook this work because I was curious about the relationship between X and Y. My intent was to satisfy my curiosity." This kind of answer avoids certain questions. For example, in what context did X and Y come to seem to you to be concepts and to be related? What are the continuities and discontinuities in the context that brought you to this conceptualization, the context in which you explored the question, and the context in which you think it has implications? While these questions stated abstractly sound grand and philosophical, I do not mean to raise them in that way. Rather, I have in mind looking at the concrete world of daily life. Who or what do you talk to, read, observe, and have you talked to, read, observed? Who is outside your experience? Who addresses you directly, seeks you out, sets the conditions for your employment, daily routines, place of residence, and so on? Where have you lived, worked, investigated, traveled, and where not? Such questions are crucial from a transformative perspective. This perspective does not invalidate the inchoate curiosity and fascination that often bring a researcher to a topic. Rather, it suggests that the researcher ask at once: What is going on here, and what am I doing here?

I stress the personal aspect of transformative work because it is the aspect of research and scholarship that our training in social science most distances us from. Yet I think that commitment to bringing about social change and the ability to see into possibilities other than the status quo usually go hand in hand with a desire for personal liberation and the seeking of personal change in relation to others.

Habermas uses as his example of liberating knowledge the self-transforming insights a person gains in a therapeutic dialogue. This definition removes liberation from the social, physical, and historical context and limits it to an understanding of the individual as separate from context and as primarily a psychological self. It seems to stop short of a full recognition of the social and physical nature of self and environment. However, one implication of this central metaphor stands as a hallmark of liberating knowledge and liberating dialogue: There must be an intimate responsive relationship between the general knowledge and practices that inform the discourse and the personal experience, language, and self-understanding of the person who experiences the knowledge of liberating. I would add that the dialogue and liberation must occur in a shared social and physical world that nurtures and shapes the liberated self.

Seeing self, society, and the physical world as inseparable directs the environmental psychologist interested in social change to take all three into account in the development of projects. The idea that we can not ignore parts of the world in the service of other parts implies a certain ethical stance of concern for the continued viability of other people and the nonhuman world. I think most environmental psychologists interested in social change share some common values: (1) that individuals should act so as to nurture the nurturing capacity of the environment, (2) that the physical and social environment should be shaped to nurture the full human development of the individual, (3) that existing individuals and groups should not deplete beyond regeneration the capacity of the environment to nurture future generations, and (4) that environments should not extract from existing individuals and groups such costs that their physical and social continuity are extinguished.

In practice these values require interpretation. I do not think most environmental psychologists would agree on the specifics. Nor do I think that agreement would come through abstract discussion. All these value issues have both empirical–technological content and interpretive elements. Any particular issue will arise in a historical context and particular locale that ties it to the broader ecology in specific ways. In the following sections, I will explore two issues involving environmental and social change that have been addressed by social scientists interested in the direction of the change. These examples will illustrate some common conceptual issues highlighted by a transactional perspective, yet in most other ways they will primarily suggest the differences among different issues as they arise historically. In the first case, a problem is originally conceptualized as requiring a technological change in the physical environment having only limited and unproblematic social and psychological implications. As the technological change is implemented the problematic social and psychological dimensions emerge and move the technology into a politically controversial position. In the other case, a particular group begins to articulate a desire for certain social and psychological changes

in their lives and only later come to an awareness of the role of the physical environment in impeding or facilitating that change.

4.3. NUCLEAR POWER: AN UNEXPECTED SOCIAL PROBLEM

The accident at Three Mile Island (TMI) in Pennsylvania that occurred in spring 1979 brought behavioral and psychological responses to nuclear power into the public eye. After several days of uncertainty as to the severity of the accident in the nuclear plant, pregnant women and young children were advised to evacuate the area. If this group had complied and all others had gone about their regular lives, 2,500 people approximately would have left the area (Ziegler, Brunn, & Johnson, 1981). Instead, an estimated 144,000 evacuated.

Slovic and his colleagues (1979) frequently cite the following statement made by Weinberg in the *American Scientist*:

> As I compare the issue we perceived during the infancy of nuclear energy with those that have emerged during its maturity, the public perception and acceptance of nuclear energy appears to be the question that we missed rather badly....This issue has emerged as the most critical question concerning the future of nuclear energy. (cited in Slovic et al., 1979, p. 224)

Research on TMI expands on this theme. The operating practices of the nuclear industry were established largely through the judgments of engineers of various kinds in interaction with producers of nuclear power. The safety of the public was to be guaranteed primarily through the design of fail-safe facilities. At the time of the TMI incident, nuclear facilities were required to do only minimal planning for a possible accident that might affect people outside the plant and its immediate surroundings. How the public would respond to an accident had not really been considered, even in terms of direct physical health effects (Macleod, 1981). Today it is widely conceded that the main effects of TMI were behavioral and psychological, even those that might involve impaired physical health. Of course the data are not yet in on the possible long-term effects of low-level releases of radiation. Yet when they are obtained the interaction of the effects of radiation directly will have to be considered in the context of the chronic stress associated with the accident (Baum, Gatchel, & Schaeffer, 1980; McLeod, 1981).

The research conducted after the accident provides an example of a case in which social scientists participated extensively in advising policymakers how to manage the aftermath of the incident. Approximately half a dozen research teams studied behavioral and psychological reactions to the incident, several of them sponsored by the Nuclear Regulatory Commission (NRC) (Baum, Gatchel, & Shaeffer, 1981; Dohrenwend et al., 1981; Flynn, 1979; Golhaber & Lehman, 1982; Houts, Miller, Tokuhata, & Ham, 1980; Ziegler et al., 1981). These studies concurred in finding that considerable self-reported stress accompanied the accident. The much-greater-than-expected level of evacuation was attributable to the ambiguity surrounding the accident. Over three-fourths of the evacuees gave as a reason for leaving the fact that information about the existence of danger was confusing. A substantial proportion of those who did not evacuate also gave this as their reason (Flynn, 1979; Goldhaber et al., 1982). Not only did people evacuate in great numbers, they went much further than would seem required if one were to look at industry standards of safety (Rogovin & Frampton, 1979). The median evacuation estimates in the different studies range from 85 to 100 miles. The documentation of these responses played a major role in leading the NRC to develop new standards for emergency preparedness in the area of planning for a radiological emergency (Chenault, Hilbert & Reichlin, 1979; Nuclear Regulatory Commission, 1981).

Up to this point, both nuclear scientists and engineers had proceeded within a technological model, at least ostensibly. The physical scientists had taken as their mandate the task of developing nuclear power to provide new sources of energy for the country. The federal government had nurtured the industry from its inception, indeed, had played a key role in launching nuclear power first as a scientific discovery and then as a commercial enterprise. When something went wrong that revealed a previously ignored set of human problems to be solved, social scientists were brought in to fix it. Yet over the course of the next few years it became more apparent to the nuclear industry, the Nuclear Regulatory Commission, and the social scientists involved that nuclear power was not a simple technological solution to a widely accepted problem. Furthermore, social scientists by explicating the psychological and social aspects of nuclear power acceptance helped open the door to a wider debate about the political, moral, and ecological consequences of technology. While protest against nuclear power predated 1978, only after that year were the consensus to pursue nuclear power

and the provision of adequate resources to do so thrown into question. Since that time, numerous nuclear power plants have been canceled in the design stages, several have been abandoned during construction, and the future of others remains in dispute.

Social science research documents the fissures that began to develop in the national consensus about nuclear power. One of the most significant identified problems during and after the crisis involved lack of trust in official sources of information, particularly the power company and the local government (Dohrenwend et al., 1981; Flynn, 1979).

The NRC rulings regarding evacuation planning opened the way for forms of political conflict that had no legitimate outlet previously. Because local governments are charged with ensuring the health and welfare of their populations, the way was opened for local authorities to oppose the opening or continued operation of plants that might not be amenable to safe and timely evacuation. Rockland County near the Indian Point plant and Suffolk County, site of the Shoreham plant, have refused to participate in evacuation drills on the grounds that a safe and timely evacuation could not be carried out due to geographic and population density characteristics. These contentions are matters of ongoing litigation before various political and regulatory bodies.

The actions of governmental entities in planning and implementing the restored functioning of the TMI plant have been influenced in complex ways. Baum and colleagues were requested by the NRC to advise the body on the psychological consequences of venting the damaged reactor as part of restoring its safety. On the basis of a preliminary review, the researchers advised that relatively immediate venting of the gas would be preferable to more delayed forms of response. The advantages of the delayed responses would be that they would decrease skin dosage of radiation. However, the psychologists reasoned that the chronic stress their studies revealed would continue until the venting. While the venting might occasion a peak in stress, it would be followed by diminished psychological and physiological signs of stress. The skin dosage associated with venting was projected to be well within safe limits. The NRC acted in keeping with these recommendations. A longitudinal study of reported symptoms, anxiety and depression, performance measures of stress, and biochemical indicators supported their hypotheses although of course no comparison of alternative procedures was possible. Interestingly, however, the only measure that appeared to be attaining comparability with the control group 80 miles away was the self-report of depression.

The NRC ruling was not the only political consequence of these findings. Suit was brought by citizen groups opposed to nuclear power to prevent the restart of the undamaged TMI reactor on the grounds, in part, that such an action would increase stress among the residents. The court ruled that psychological stress was not an admissible part of an environmental impact statement in this case. Yet the wording of the decision does not definitively close the door on consideration of stress in other instances.

The researchers in this instance seem to have been working simultaneously in all three models. At one level, they obtained information that would allow them to predict and control responses of the public, the information was acted on by a body with sufficient authority and control of resources to bring the action about, and the results were more or less what had been predicted. At another level, one of the researchers explained his involvement in the research as an effort to represent aspects of experience that were important to the public in a forum in which that kind of data was traditionally absent (Baum, A., personal communication, 1982). Thus the event was interpreted differently when the research was used as one aspect of event interpretation. Finally, the following section from the epilogue of a report on this research indicated that the authors experienced the research as a personally transforming event:

> It is impossible to come away from this kind of research without gaining insight into the basic stuff of which we are made and without a long-term concern for the people you have tried to help. Following these people, hoping that our recommendations were the right ones, and watching to see if we have been of any help—these kinds of things will never be boring. (Baum et al., 1981, p. 246)

Further work by these researchers (Fleming, Baum, Gisriel, & Gatchel, undated) contributes to a theoretical understanding that links environmental circumstances, psychological responses, behavior, and physiological states. Baum and colleagues found that emotionally-focused coping helped reduce symptom reporting and emotional distress as well as errors on a proofreading task and level of catecholamine excretion. Problem-focused coping was less effective, for reasons the authors believe have to do with the difficulty of an individual's successfully changing the situation. To the extent that this finding becomes public knowledge, it may go from a technologically understood finding (i.e., if you are stressed by the accident at TMI, cope emotionally)

to an interpretive one (i.e., see how resistant the situation is to your individual control). Taken together, these two interpretations can confront an individual or group with significant value and action choices (i.e., will you support and accept policies and corporate actions that reduce your healthy sphere of action to emotional coping?).

Nuclear power provides a wonderful example of the transactional nature of human environment relationships for the following reasons:

1. It has emerged as a resource and a danger through intense human intellectual, social, and physical effort.

2. It has been and remains an uncertain commodity. Both its potential uses and the hazard it poses to human life are constantly being reassessed with no end to the debate in sight.

3. The language and belief systems members of different groups bring to bear on the topic lead to very different assessments of opportunities and danger and to very different mandates for action (c.f. Hohenesmer, Kasperson, & Kates, 1977).

Yet the consequences of action will have to be shared. The whole society, indeed, the world, will be shaped by the exploitation of this vast energy resource through the commitment of capital and social organization to this form of energy. Power and economic relations among nations, among different levels of government within nations, and among individuals, groups, economic organizations, and governments will also be shaped. In addition, the health and genetic composition of an unknown number of people and other living beings may be affected in unknown and possibly irreversible ways.

On the other hand, a particular society that forgoes the nuclear power option faces large behavioral challenges. Either current trends toward high levels of per capita energy consumption in developed nations would have to be reversed through conservation and energy-saving inventions or alternative energy sources, some with serious consequences for environmental exploitation and pollution, would have to be developed and the society would have to face possible disadvantage in competition with other nations as well as possible slower rates of development. Another option that somewhat deflates any long-run ecological or moral goals related to forgoing the nuclear option involves buying nuclear power from nations willing to produce it while attempting to protect citizens of the buying nation from having the hazard in their own backyard. Yet no nation can isolate itself from possible global impacts of the long-term intensive development of nuclear power. Transportation of wastes, storage for periods of time beyond human imagination, and long-term accumulation pose possible threats that are difficult convincingly to bound.

The economic investment, governmental policies, and public opposition surrounding nuclear power on the one hand and energy supply and demand, location of plants, incidents of accidents, physical scientific innovations, and development of long-term health effects (or their absence) illustrate the tension between human social psychological processes (including economic and political ones) and "physical" manifestations of nuclear power in the human ecology. At the same time these tensions dramatize the way in which the physical, social, and psychological aspects of human ecologies shape each other. The historical and the developmental nature of knowledge about human transactions with the environment are underlined as debate, decisions, actions, and consequences continue to change.

Clearly a comprehensive understanding of the role of nuclear power is beyond the scope of environmental psychology or a particular individual. Therefore I will turn to identifying issues and questions environmental psychology can address. First, by looking at nuclear power with an interest in how people understand it, act toward different manifestations of it, and feel about it, and what they expect from it, we make the social and psychological processes involved in its development and use visible. The negotiated and plastic quality of different groups' relationships to nuclear power seen from this perspective contrasts with much of the discussion among technical experts, industry personnel, and policymakers. This way of viewing nuclear power raises questions to be addressed within the technological model, the interpretive model, and the transformative.

Decision makers have set an agenda full of technological questions for behavioral scientists. Some of these are as follows:

1. How can we get people to understand that nuclear power is really safe so that they will accept it (or alternately, how can we get people to understand enough of the technological information about nuclear power to allow them to make rational judgments about its safety)?
2. How can we be sure that people will do their jobs in nuclear power plants so as not to endanger public safety?
3. How can we handle emergencies so as to protect the public?

4. What can be done to mitigate the stress associated with an accident like that at TMI?
5. How can we successfully plan for an emergency?
6. What behavioral issues have to be understood in recovering from an accident?

Civic groups raise other questions: How can we get technical experts to explain their positions in such a way that we understand *and* can relate the information to decisions we have to make? How can we affect decision making about nuclear power or some particular aspect of it? These groups turn to behavioral scientists for useful advice on how to solve the problems within a technological model. When the answer is not at hand, we can pursue research that will address the problem. This is not to say that a technological solution will be possible. The other requirements for a successful technological resolution may be and in this case are likely to be missing: consensus on the definition of the problem and a desirable resolution and a unified authority structure in control of resources and decisions necessary to solve the problem.

Whether such a consensus and control of resources should exist raises important questions for a researcher acting in the transformative mode. In the absence of controversy validating the nature of nuclear power as a human endeavor, the social scientist is likely to be dropped from the roll of necessary experts. To the extent that corporate and governmental funding and action support nuclear power plant development, the less well funded and voluntary actions of citizens may begin to fade away.

The public's reaction to nuclear power has been assessed through surveys spanning the last decade (Rankin, Melber, Overcast, & Nealy, 1981). The results of these surveys provide a good example of the tragedy of the commons (Hardin, 1968) and also illustrate why Hardin's solution of individual ownership and responsibility enforced by public authorities is so hard to implement. The majority of citizens do not want the United States to forgo the nuclear option. At the same time, opposition to a power plant in *one's own area of residence* has steadily increased. In 1971 almost 60% of the public favored local nuclear power plant construction with only 25% opposed. By 1978 opposition exceeded support. Since the incident at TMI in 1979, about twice as many people have opposed construction of nuclear plants within 5 or 10 miles of their own homes as have supported it.

The contradictions and divisions in public attitudes toward nuclear power raise a multitude of questions. The work of the Decision Research group provides one example of how a psychological model can be brought to bear conceptually on problems of environmental and social change in relation to nuclear power. Working within behavioral decision theory, these researchers have produced the most general description of how people perceive the risks of nuclear power (Slovic, Lichtenstein, & Fischhoff, 1979). The most striking finding regarding perceptions of risk from nuclear power concerns the wide discrepancy between the public's perception of risk and that of experts in the nuclear industry and its regulatory bodies. Politically the public's opposition to nuclear power has emerged as the biggest obstacle faced by the industry, an obstacle so large that some argue the nuclear option is not viable in the United States (c.f. Cook, 1982). Typically, this discrepancy is treated by experts and decision makers as an example of the public's faulty understanding of nuclear power (c.f. Yankelovitch, Skelly, White, Inc. 1983). This misunderstanding results in unreasonable fear of an accident and is complicated by lack of trust in official and industry sources of information. Slovic and colleagues (1979) offer insights into the causes of such a discrepancy. In one study, respondents to a questionnaire assessing the risks and benefits of 30 activities and technologies viewed nuclear power as having relatively slight benefits (fewer, e.g., than the bicycle) and rather high risks, second only to motor vehicles (Fischhoff, Slovic, Lichtenstein, Read, & Combs, 1978). The authors concluded that nuclear power had a unique risk profile. It was seen as particularly "involuntary, unknown to those exposed or to science, uncontrollable, unfamiliar, potentially catastrophic, severe (likely to be fatal rather than injurious), and dreaded" (Slovic, et al., 1979, p. 225). These findings may be interpreted by experts as signs that more public education about the safety of nuclear power is required. Given this conclusion, the role of the psychologist would be to recommend ways to educate or convince the public of the safety of nuclear power. Elsewhere Fischhoff has noted that experts bring in psychologists as advisers when they perceive that "the public is crazy. Let's bring in some psychologists to solve this clinical problem" (Fischhoff, 1981, p. 181).

Slovic and colleagues (1979) resist this conclusion. Instead they make an argument that if accepted would have far-reaching political consequences. They state that the problem of assessing the risk of nuclear accidents exceeds our technological capacity, pointing to the important subjective decisions that must be made in any fault-free analysis. For example, someone must decide what failures might occur, what failures might be related or independent, which are more important, and so on. The authors suggest that, while the expert calculations of the chance of nuclear power fatalities result in incomprehensibly low probabilities, the error bounds of these calculations are large and uncertain themselves. Slovic and colleagues implicate the same cognitive limitations and resultant reliance on biases and heuristics in the confidence of the expert and the suspicion of the layperson.

The conditions for public acceptance of nuclear power, Slovic and colleagues speculate, would be different from those that exist at the moment. They include a clear record of plant safety, an administering agency that is trusted and respected, and a clear appreciation by the public of the benefit of nuclear power as well as relative risks/costs associated with other energy alternatives. Finally, the authors raise what they call the big question: What kind of political institutions can ensure democratic freedom and participation and at the same time reach decisions involving extreme technological complexity, catastrophic risk, and high levels of uncertainty?

Such a program of research helps us see the tasks of psychology in another light. Clearly the determinants of the public and the expert's understanding of nuclear power are only partially psychological. The history of nuclear power safety, the transactions between different groups in the society with regard to nuclear power, cultural attitudes toward regulation and political participation, expectations for standards of living, and so on, as well as the availability of energy, will all contribute to perceptions of nuclear power as well as to the amount of concern and attention the topic receives. For example, Hohenesmer and colleagues describe the correlations between fear of nuclear war and opposition to nuclear power that seem later to be replaced by a correlation between environmental concern and opposition to nuclear power. Cook (1982) in reviewing the status of nuclear power in Canada and the United States contrasts the greater acceptance of nuclear power in Canada with public opposition in the United States. Cross-cultural research like that done by Decision Research could illuminate some sources of this difference as they are experienced by individuals. Cook's approach of looking at the political regulatory and technological history of nuclear power could suggest issues for comparison other than perceived risk of fatalities due to accidents. Cook concludes his study by observing that all nations fear nuclear energy to some extent, but some fear other things more.

The Decision Research work employed methods that require the subject to respond to the array of issues the researcher deems relevant. This strategy has paid off in that the trade-offs relevant in policy circles and among risk assessment professionals are brought into contact with the data by having been included in the researcher's formulation. Yet at the same time other avenues are closed that might also bear investigation. Concerns about the disposal of nuclear waste, its long decay time, and the possibility of genetic changes associated with nonfatal exposure to radiation all could have influenced responses. Questions concerning future generations also need to be considered. Research that looked at perceptions of nuclear power over the entire cycle and in historical perspective, including fears and expectations of the future, would enhance our understanding of people's perceptions. It could also be useful in helping decision makers, advocates on both sides, and the public get a better sense of the nature of the decisions to be made. On the other hand, the policy-making process in this country tends to isolate these issues. The decisions about citing, licensing, or opening a specific power plant are not linked to decisions about waste disposal. The design, conduct, and dissemination of research examining nuclear power in a broader context would contribute to a reinterpretation of the problem. To the extent that the new interpretations gave rise to new approaches and pressures in decision making about nuclear power, the research would transform the nature of the problem.

Psychological research on nuclear power occupies a strange place on the borderline between consciousness and unconsciousness of the dangers involved. Slovic and colleagues (1979) caution that efforts to educate the public about the relative risks of nuclear power may well cause increased anxiety rather than increased agreement with experts. The realization of the technological complexity and the numerous possible causes of problems, even if they are unlikely, may leave the recipient more impressed by the possibility of danger (a vivid image) than by its unlikeliness (a statistical concept). Janis and Mann (1977) have similarly suggested that information about possible dangers may be avoided because thinking about the emergency is psychologically threatening. In the case of nuclear power, disagreement among experts, the technical complexity of the issue, the long time spans involved, the difficult-to-comprehend smallness of many of the numbers involved, and the yet-unknown nature of possible low-level radiation effects and transgenerational effects all make it doubtful that information is the best prescription for allaying fears.

Thus, one effect of bringing into awareness people's perceptions of nuclear power may be to increase the likelihood that a decision about nuclear power will be viewed as a political and ethical decision rather than a technological one. Nelkin (1977), in a study of public participation in decision making about nuclear power in Sweden, the Netherlands, and Austria, found that the Swedish program, while lengthy and thorough, increased uncertainty and confusion with negative consequences for the government in power. Efforts to accommodate public participation in the two other countries reflected a clear awareness that the research on which the information was based would tend to portray the problem from a particular set of assumptions, thus requiring participation in question formation as well as facilitation of communication between experts of different persuasions and the public.

In another study, Nelkin (1974) examined the role of experts in a controversy about siting a nuclear power plant on Cayuga Lake in upstate New York. Nelkin argues that the technical information provided by each side did not seriously weigh in the decision making of the power company, the local officials or the opposition organizations, and concerned citizen groups. Rather she concludes that the access of the public and advocacy organizations to scientific expertise allowed political forces to operate on a more equitable basis.

Clearly the technological model fails to apply in this situation, although parts of the scientific knowledge base of psychology can suggest parts of answers. Truly useful research must move to an interpretive stance toward the psychological and social aspects of the technology and policy bases of the production and management of nuclear power. This research should reveal the moral and political assumptions underlying technologies and policies. Thus, the possibilities for transformative work would be opened up.

4.3.1. Summary of Implications for Understanding Environmental Psychology and Social Change

1. Thinking about human environments transactions should focus particularly on uncertainty. Brunswik's lens model and his methodological and theoretical treatment of the organism in the environment identified uncertainty as a critical and necessary part of the individual's relationship with the environment (Brunswik, 1952; Hammond, 1966). The studies described earlier illustrate this conclusion well. Furthermore, changes in people, societies, and the physical environ-

ment are most likely to occur in aspects of human–environment transactions that are not highly determined rather than in those that are.

2. Research that is to be politically and socially significant must address fundamental aspects of person–environment transactions and cut across psychological, social, and physical variables within the individual and the environment. Health, reproduction, economic transactions, and political processes are basic aspects of human–environment transactions that psychologists should try to understand.

3. New thinking and models are needed to understand transactions in human ecologies. Human ecologists offer some clues with their emphasis on calorie and energy transfer as an alternative to dollar flow in measuring the well-being of a society. But their approach does not encompass the tension between symbolic representations (c.f. Gergen, 1982) and empirically defined concepts, nor does it provide an understanding of the translation of experience and action at the individual level into higher levels of social organization and vice versa. Here research on power structures, community organization, and citizen participation as well as new approaches is needed.

4. Choice of concepts, problems, theoretical paradigms, and methods comes about in the context of the researchers' experiences with particular traditions, languages, rules of procedure and inference, and personal fascinations (to name but a few factors). The concepts and practices employed may challenge dominant concepts and practices, but a real challenge involves some level of engagement. To deal with the requirements of relating to other disciplines, professions, and kinds of people, time must be allocated to learning the rudiments of new problems and ways of thought. More than that, time must be spent in social interactions and situations outside the domain of normal academic routines. These ways of spending time help overcome some obstacles to interdisciplinary research that Fischhoff identified: lack of training and lack of rewards. We must also accept uncertainty in our own experience. As Fischhoff (1981) states, a realistic goal in interdisciplinary work (and I would add in work

aimed toward social and environmental change) is not to get the answer right, but to avoid getting the wrong answer, with each discipline helping avoid particular types of errors.

5. The story of the role of social scientists in the history of nuclear power is still unfolding. This acceptance of the historical nature of research in this context does not entirely reject the idea of what Gergen (1982) calls enduring fundamentals. The focus on uncertainty in human–environment transactions that may alter the habitability of the planet or the viability of the populace leads to a concern for knowledge of regularities and contingencies. But the acceptance of uncertainty as a fundamental quality of human life leads to a similar rejection of positivist assumptions. As in Gergen's book *Toward Transformation in Social Knowledge*, social scientists are directed to search for new visions and to recognize action as moral choice. The search for regularities and predictability thus is seen as an effort to overcome limitations on human and community development rather than as an effort to predict and control development. To understand the relationship between social scientific thought and research and social change we need continued historical investigation and reflection on different social science practices and their context and consequences.

4.4. WOMEN'S WORLDS: A CHALLENGE TO THE ENVIRONMENT

Women activists have approached an understanding of women's transactions with the environment with the goals of liberating themselves and constructing a more liberating world. The participation of psychologists in these efforts at social change contrast in many ways with the case of psychologists and nuclear power: (1) we were not invited as professionals to participate in an ongoing debate, but rather we challenge the way our professions as well as other political, economic, and social institutions operate, (2) whereas social scientists have added a psychological and social perspective to the physical science monopoly of the nuclear debate, feminist claims have been publicly debated in psychological and social terms that ignored the physical environment, (3) the building of a community advocating changes in women's conditions across class, race, and occupational lines has been part of the work of developing a problem analysis and recommendations for solutions, and (4) social shifts like greater female employment and changes in household form contribute to an awareness of the need for changes in the physical environment. However, as has not been the case with nuclear power, it has been clear from the outset that commitment to environmental change involves social choice, as for example in the social debate and policies related to funding day-care centers.

Much of the impetus to consider women's relationship to the environment came in the 1970s from the women's movement. I feel that my understanding of my life and of the world I lived in was changed by reading feminist writers, participating in consciousness raising, and engaging in the struggles of the feminist movement. The intellectual questions raised by these experiences were not defined by disciplinary boundaries, nor did any particular discipline seem to have really useful conceptual tools. During the 1970s women in psychology and in other academic and professional disciplines formed caucuses to set their own research agendas and to examine their relationships to their professional groups. The fact of entering a profession at a time when women were just beginning to make that choice in significant numbers enforced an awareness of oneself as a woman. Yet it was too early for women to have shaped the discourse and practices of their fields. For feminist psychologists the task seemed to be to question the stereotypes of women as dependent, passive, lacking in confidence, poor at problem solving, lacking independent judgment, unaggressive, and valuing affiliation over achievement (to name but a few) while at the same time to excel professionally in what were thought of as male-typed competencies. To do research not only on women but sympathetic to women's own experiences was to choose an untraveled and treacherous path. Within psychology, questions about differences between women and men were formulated in the following ways: (1) Are there really any differences (c.f. Maccoby & Jacklin, 1974)? (2) To the extent that differences exist, are they attributable to physiology or to socialization? (3) Do women suffer more and benefit less from social institutions and practices? And (4), if they benefit less and suffer more, are the causes attributable to their innate or learned qualities or to social practices that promote discrimination?

Efforts to answer these questions raised the question of what kind of a category sex was, anyway. Maccoby & Jacklin (1974) describe the difference between their experience of women and the portraits provided by psychological generalizations. Kessler &

McKenna (1978) among others systematized the notion that the use of sex as a salient social category is not inherent in the biological differences between men and women, but rather reflects particular social practices, rules, values, and institutions. Yet even with these insights the category *woman* does not go away. Indeed, the recent feminization of poverty in the United States emphasizes the significance of being born female.

However, I do not pursue feminist interests in my work as an environmental psychologist only because I am concerned about women as a social problem. The feminist slogan that the personal is political led me to understand that the intellectual is both personal and political. When I began being a psychologist I did not combine my personal interest in women's liberation with my professional public presentation, nor do I always find it easy or possible to do so now. In coming to terms with writing this chapter I have had to face the split and try to make sense of it. The problem as I see it lies in the category *woman* as it now stands. Thus all research that would really contribute to solving women's problems must reinterpret or cast doubt on existing interpretations of the term *women*. Seeing things this way also led me to think about the conditions in which reinterpretation is possible: Ways of living and experience must also change.

Within the models of social science practice that I absorbed in my training, efforts to change the conditions of life and my own experience seemed to have no place. I chose social psychology as a field after doing my undergraduate work in government because the nexus between individual experience and society seemed critical to me for understanding both politics and individuals. The empirical nature of the field and the existence of consensual rules of argument also attracted me. The tension between individual experience and empirically regular patterns of existence struck me particularly when I thought about what kind of life I could make. Being a woman seemed like a big part of the puzzle.

Laboratory social psychological research gave me a professional respite from being a woman. The bracketing of history, geography, and researchers' and subjects' individual development that occurs in laboratory research allowed me to take the knowledge I had through my participation in the shared language and practices of my place and time and reveal regularity (Saegert, in press). When I could not get the effect I thought would occur, I could comb over my understanding of the minutiae of language, behavior, and timing looking for the missing ingredient. This experience was intellectually bracing and challenging.

It clarified what and how I thought. Two aspects of that practice of social science began to bother me, however: (1) How could one ever really make clear the principles of staging predictable human behavior? And (2) how can one justify using words in a categorical sense (like *crowding*) when the circumstances studied are not only specific but dependent on a very unusual situation, the laboratory? In addition, spending time in laboratory research did not bring me into contact with the world as given nor with different conceptualizations of that world.

This state of affairs forced me to return to the questions of who I was and what I was doing, anyway. I was still interested in how people shaped and were shaped by their transactions with the physical, social, and psychological environment. The addition of the physical dimension came both from my experience of living in a place very different from any I had previously known and from my exposure to the environmental psychology program at CUNY Graduate Center. The program emphasized the study of people's daily lives as they went about their activities in specific places. I did not immediately switch to this practice, but the experience legitimated for me the intellectual question of my own experience, not as an example of human nature but as the experience of a specific person in specific times and places.

Being a woman was a pervasive aspect of life outside the lab and presented problems, challenges, and rewards. Yet despite its greater emphasis on "grounded theory" (Glazer & Strauss, 1967) environmental psychology had nothing to say about women. This field, like others, was about "the person," and the person did not seem to be a woman nor to be identified overtly as a man.

Many feminist writers have argued that the way women were thought about reflected not women's experience, but men's experience of women. Thus women appear as a special category and men as the general person (c.f. de Beauvoir, 1968; Rowbotham, 1973; Weisstein 1971). The extent to which women are disadvantaged by existing conditions has been taken as evidence that women live in a world men have built both physically and institutionally (c.f. Hapgood & Getzels, 1974; Rowbotham, 1973). Another line of argument contends that women live, in a meaningful sense, in another world from that inhabited by men (c.f. Bernard, 1981). A growing body of research and theory suggests a complex reality. Research has revealed the extent to which women have contributed to the building of environments and of social institutions. For example, Hayden (1980) has unearthed a tradition of feminist architects and activists who planned, organized, built and ran collec-

tive housing, kitchens, and domestic workplaces. Birch (1978) documents the pivotal role of women in the development of public housing in the United States. Numerous scholars have examined the role of women in urban reform programs and voluntary associations (c.f. Gittell & Shtob, 1980; Leavitt, 1980). Recently it has been noted by researchers that women are very often the leaders in tenant and neighborhood organizations (c.f. Lawson, Barton, & Joselit, 1980; McCourt, 1977; Wekerle, 1980). Yet it has been documented that women experience more difficult trade-offs in trying to go about their lives in the environment as it now exists (c.f. review by Wekerle, 1980). For example, during the period in which public policies and private market forces led to the construction of primarily residential suburbs, women were entering the work force and living without children or with fewer children in greater and greater numbers. Female-headed households were increasing. The pattern of segregation of workplace and residence has been shown to conflict with women's needs, preferences, and economic advancement (c.f. Mackintosh, 1982; Michelson, 1973; Rothblatt, Garr, & Sprague, 1979; Saegert, 1980; Wekerle, 1980). Women's greater dependence on public transportation, which is increased by greater labor force participation, coupled with their lower earnings and the declining quality and investment in public transportation, provides another example of inequity (c.f. Madden & White, 1978; Wekerle, 1980).

Between the early 1970s and 1980, works concerned with women's relationship to the environment grew from almost nothing into a small mountain. In 1980 two collections of work on women and the environment (Stimpson, Nelson, & Yaktrakis; Wekerle, Peterson, & Morley) as well as two significant books of feminist architectural history (Hayden; Wright) appeared. Because the work was done by individuals, mainly women, in many different fields, working in relative isolation, those of us working in the field were surprised at the richness and volume of the work. The next year, the first comprehensive effort to evaluate community development from a woman's perspective appeared with the title *Women and the Social Costs of Economic Development* (Moen, Boulding, Lillydahl, & Palm, 1981).

Wekerle's (1980) excellent review of research on women and urban environments identifies three main themes:

(1) an emphasis on the dichotomy between private and public spheres under industrial capitalism, the importance of the private world of the family and the necessity of integrating the private/personal and public/political...(2)...(an) emphasis on the "fit" be-

tween women's activities and the environments of home, neighborhood and city and how users of environments might participate more fully in their planning and design...(3) the environmental equity model (that focuses) primarily on the women's right to equal access to public goods and services such as transportation, housing and social services. (p. 186)

She goes on to review the main problems and proposed solutions under each of these themes. Research and theory concerned with the public–private dichotomy focus frequently on the single-family home and on housework. Solutions take the form of suggestions for: (1) industrializing housework through an expanded service sector of the economy, (2) the formation of federally funded neighborhood service houses to do what housewives and women have traditionally done from supervising children's play to cleaning homes for disabled or sick people to providing meals for working people to take home (attributed to Glazer, Majka, Acker, & Bose, 1976), and (3) collectivization of housework. The three alternatives go from those that require little social change and challenge only in a minor way the physical form of the environment to those requiring much greater changes in both. Work on women's experience of and integration into the public domain has been sketchier. The dominance of the male-centered public domain makes research the more challenging and routes to change more difficult. Researchers working within the environment–behavior fit paradigm have concentrated on the contradictions between women's needs and experiences and current land use patterns and planning practices. The policy recommendations in this work focus on changes in zoning, suggestions for participatory planning, and recommendations for new patterns of residential, commercial, and industrial development as well as public amenities. Wekerle notes that these solutions do not address the women's position in a class society nor the link between planning practices and the political and economic forces that determine the eventual form of the environment. The equity model documents the degree to which women as a group have less access to resources like transportation and housing as well as to political power over decisions that shape their homes and communities. Few solutions and no comprehensive models for solving women's transportation problems have been offered. Legislation to increase women's access to credit has been the major policy assault on women's housing access problems. Solutions to problems with rental housing have not been developed. Housing for single parents has given rise to innovative thinking and some experimentation. Overall,

Wekerle concludes that scholarship on women and the environment poses radical challenges to accepted social science theories and to social and environmental planning and development. In addition, at present the work does not link research and findings to other social and feminist theory.

Some changes in the state of affairs are already being revealed. Both professional organizations and feminist scholars show signs of interest in women's transactions with the environment. The annual Barnard conference, the Feminist and the Scholar, chose as its topic for 1983 "Women and Technology." The 1983 special event for the Environmental Design and Research Association Conference was entitled "Bridging the Gender Gap in Environmental Design." The spring 1983 issue of the *Journal of the American Planning Association* featured a special section on planning and the changing family. Many of the contributors wrote from a background of feminist consciousness. In the following section I will speculate on certain theoretical directions that might facilitate further change both intellectually and in practice.

First, I would like to go back to my earlier statement that the central issue in understanding women's transactions with the environment concerns reinterpreting the category *women*. MacKinnon (1983) states that "Feminism affirms women's point of view by revealing, criticizing and explaining its impossibility" (p. 637). To the extent that we use a language, think through our intellectual traditions, and live in a physical and social world formed by male domination, women cannot fully explain their own experience, nor can the consequences for women of the world as given be adequately measured. Thus the way we as social scientists go about understanding the differences in women's and men's transactions with the environment has a political content. Feminist research on women and environments has enstated a greater richness of perspectives on these transactions. To go forward with a valid and liberating understanding of both sexes' relationship with the environment (and with each other), we must pursue variety both in people's understanding of the environment and in their transactions with it until gender categories no longer enforce intellectual, subconscious, social, or physical regularities. This process is likely to reveal greater gender-enforced regularity before we can achieve an androgynous future (Saegert, 1982).

Nor would all androgynous futures necessarily be good. Some of the political, economic, and social forces that have propelled women into the work force and increased the number of people living alone and the number of single parents have also been linked to increased unemployment and underemployment of workers generally, and to the higher cost of home owning and of services to replace those of homemakers, wives, and mothers. Research on the concept of psychological androgyny has revealed two androgynous types: those with high scores on male and female traits and those with low scores on both. The latter group does not bear out the high hopes feminists have for human development in the androgynous mode, nor would a community that failed to nourish both men and women physically, psychologically, and socially reach the positive ideal of an androgynous community. Yet the androgynous community differs from the ideal of an androgynous individual. It places the balance of experiences of nurturance, affiliation, and embeddedness with experiences of aggressive assertion, achievement, and independence in the physical, social, and cultural community. Thus the community weaves together individuals who exemplify different levels of nurturance, independence, achievement, emotionality, and so on.

Second, we must develop a theoretical and value framework within which trivial variety can be distinguished from important variety and oppressive diversity from liberating diversity. An androgynous community that promoted full human and social development would encompass the resources and social–political consensus necessary to produce and distribute the physical, social, and psychological goods of the world. Moen and colleagues (1981) explore the problems faced by women when development is defined primarily as economic. In a straightforward manner, these authors illustrate the extent to which women tend not to benefit financially from economic development. But they also show the myriad life-supporting transactions and arrangements women have developed that fall outside, indeed often stand in opposition to, the definition of development that can be measured by volume of dollars flowing through a community. Those of us who have been thinking, writing, and talking about women and the environment have frequently experienced an evaporation of the topic. All women's problems seem at moments to reduce to economic inequality. But if one pursues that inequality to the roots, the relationship between dollars and women is seen to be far from arbitrary. Many of the values, practices, experiences, and relationships women inherit with their sex tie them to transactions with the environment that keep them poor in the world as given. They tend to be involved with economically unrewarding activities like childbirth, housework, child care, listening to others, visiting with friends, and so

on. The world could not easily get along without these activities, but the rewards are not monetary. In pursuing these questions we would do well to remember that Adam Smith espoused a system of value. I am not taking sides here in a debate concerning wages for housework. Rather, I want to retain a focus on the many person–environment transactions that produce and maintain life in the world and that rate low in a male-dominated economic structure. No one would suppose that paid housekeepers or child-care providers would earn as much as corporate executives or heads of socialist bureaucracies or even as workers in "vital" industries. Changing such a state of affairs would involve unraveling the psychological, social, and physical practices that place a higher value in all senses of the word on the aspects of making and supporting life that men control and define.

One of the changes in linguistic practice that a reader may note in the above passage involves the shift from the term *environment* to the term *community*. If we evolve practices of relating to other people that allow us really to understand their experiences of living in the world and that support positive human development in the world, the physicalistic and distanced notion of environment will be replaced by an understanding that encompasses the psychological, social, and physical self and world. Shared and communicable understanding and respect for the unknown in any difference are the qualities that bind individuals in specific times and places to geographic and cultural communities. Research with these goals in mind departs from the technological model—indeed, from the scientific model. A great deal of time must be spent in communication with the people one seeks to know in the places and circumstances one seeks to know. Time and thought must be spent on the historical, cultural, political, and physical context of a selection of problem, research methods, population to study, mode of analysis, and method of presentation. Working in this mode makes you realize that to a large extent you are yourself the research method as well as many of the artifacts. Thus research aimed at binding people to a community and a social purpose requires self-knowledge, the ability to listen and communicate fully and openly, and the willingness to be revealed as an individual, not just an exemplar of social science in action. These requirements do not work like the list of assumptions to be met before applying a statistical test. They go back to an older understanding of knowledge that recognized the struggle with personal limits as part of its substance.

When one pursues knowledge in this way it becomes difficult to know to what extent one has changed and to what extent the world has changed. This confusion is not merely intellectual or delusional. In the process of trying to understand particular person–environment transactions, one organizes daily life differently, knows different people, reads different books and periodicals, and becomes a different actor in other people's environments.

4.5. SOCIAL AND ENVIRONMENTAL CHANGE AND DIRECTIONS FOR ENVIRONMENTAL PSYCHOLOGY

Scientific and technological ways of understanding the world have demonstrated power to bring into view regularities in the world firm enough to serve as a ground for action. We can do amazing things, like sending people into space and smashing atoms. This heritage of abstract formulations and empirical demonstrations shapes our thinking about other people and ourselves in the world. Yet many social scientists realize secretly or publicly that this mode of thought is not complete when we look at human beings knowing each other in history. Gergen (1982) suggests that what we really have to offer are novel, even audacious interpretations, thus revealing the socially constructed rather than given nature of knowledge. Gergen invites psychologists to abandon the idea of testing hypotheses "to consider ways of using methods in the service of intellectual expression in the service of his or her vision of the good" (p. 208). While I join him in this, I also invite new and clearer thinking about the girders of generality. For the most part, Gergen locates these in linguistic and social conventions. When stated in that way the appearance of generality seems mainly a product of conformity and an intellectual matter. Gergen's perspective pays insufficient attention to the physical self and environment and the extent to which ways of speaking and understanding are embedded in forms of life. Both should be pushed to new limits of understanding. We should recognize that it is particularly in the domain of what we understand as the physical self and environment that science in the positivist tradition made its greatest strides.

Our shared physicality and our language anchor us in the past and present. The physical environment reifies our social categories, especially as it is buttressed by historically developed institutional and economic practices. Thus when we attempt to bring about social change we must continue our social scientific practices of measuring conditions and testing statements in this tradition. However, certain changes in these practices are warranted: (1) We must expand the relationship between what we measure and test and the relevant physical, economic, and political or institutional conditions as they are measured and analyzed within the relevant disciplines. (2) One of our main tasks would become a search for contradictions between different systems of measurement and analysis and within each as well as for uncertainty within systems. Contradictions indicate a tension in the state of affairs (be it at a psychological, social, or physical level), and this contradiction and uncertainty are significant in determining the potential for social change. (3) We need to develop a more adequate and sophisticated analysis of the relationship among verbal, numerical, and visual symbol systems (for examples of this effort, see Winkel, 1977). (4) We need to investigate and understand the forms of life in which the various symbol systems are anchored and the conflicts and misunderstandings involved in using symbol systems in contexts that differ from the forms of life in which they developed. (5) We must question and explore the relationship between our own forms of life and symbol systems and those we purport to describe or desire to change.

These directions for change would require a differently constituted and organized academic community. The inclusion of diverse populations would be seen not as affirmative action to redress a social wrong, but as a necessary condition for the pursuit of valid knowledge. A similar attitude would be taken toward cross-cultural communication and study. The strength of disciplinary divisions could not continue in its present form. The existing links of the university to the society would be better understood, and new links would be forged. New methods of teaching, socializing, and evaluating scholars would have to be evolved, on the one hand, to train us in the disciplined and demanding forms of analysis that are required to face complexity and bring forth new understanding and new grounds for action, and, on the other hand, to prevent a rigid insistence on the correctness and superiority of one's own training, methods, and thematization of life. Finally, the kind of dialogue and soul-searching that lead to individual growth and social development must be reintegrated into all curricula, even the most mathematical and technical or conversely the most poetic and artistic. I am not calling for some kind of social realism, a gloomy and prejudged approach to knowledge; rather, I advocate a placing of the knower in the human condition regardless of the form of knowledge sought.

Would some core of environmental psychology remain if these directions were to be pursued? Yes, I think that the psychological perspective will prove a fresh and useful one in the analysis of social and physical systems when the nonpsychological organization of these systems is adequately confronted.

REFERENCES

Ahrentzen, S., Jacobi, M., Skorpanich, M.A., & Ross, R. (1982). Women researchers in environment-behavior research. In P. Bart, A. Chen, & G. Francescoto (Eds.), *Knowledge for design, EDRA 13 Proceedings*, College Park, MD (pp. 48–61). Washington, DC: Environmental Design Research Association.

Altman, I. (1976). Environmental psychology and social psychology. *Personality and Social Psychology Bulletin, 2*, 96–113.

Altman, I., & Gauvain, M. (1981). A cross-cultural and dialectic analysis of homes. In L.S. Liben, A.H. Patterson, & N. Newcombe (Eds.), *Spatial representation and behavior across the life span* (pp. 283–320). New York: Academic.

Anthony, K.H. (1982) Creating the professional mystique: Marketing environmental psychology. In P. Bart, A. Chen, & G. Francescoto (Eds.), *Knowledge for design: EDRA 13 Proceedings*, College Park, MD. Washington, DC: Environmental Design Research Association.

Archea, J. (1975). Establishing an interdisciplinary commitment. In B. Honikman (Ed.), *Responding to social change* (pp. 285–302). Stroudsburg, PA: Dowden, Hutchinson, & Ross.

Baum, A., Gatchel, R.J., & Schaeffer M.A. (1980). *Psychological stress for alternatives of decontamination of Three Mile Island-2 reactor building atmosphere*. (Report No. NUREG/CR-1584). Washington, DC: Nuclear Regulatory Commission.

Baum, A., Gatchel, R.J., & Schaeffer, M.A. (1981). *Emotional, behavioral, and physiological effects of chronic stress at Three Mile Island*. (Report No. CO7216 and Report No. NRC-03-81-135). Uniformed Services University of the Health Sciences and U.S. Nuclear Regulatory Commission. Washington, DC: Government Printing Office.

Baum, A., Gatchel, R.J., Streufert, S., Baum, C.S., Fleming, R., & Singer, J.E. (1980, August). *Psychological stress for alternatives of decontamination of Three Mile Island-2 reactor building atmosphere*. (Report No. NUREG/CR-1584). Washington, DC: Nuclear Regulatory Commission.

Baum, A., & Singer, J.E. (Eds.). (1981). *Advances in environmental psychology: Vol. 3. Energy: Psychological perspectives*. Hillsdale, NJ: Erlbaum.

Baum, A., & Valins, S. (1977). *Architecture and social behavior: Psychological studies of social density*. Hillsdale, NJ: Erlbaum.

Beauvoir, S. de. (1968). *The second sex*. H.M. Parshley (Ed. and Trans.). New York: Knopf. (Original work published 1952)

Bernard, J.S. (1981). *The female world*. Glencoe, IL: Free Press.

Birch, E. (1978). Women-made America: The case of early public housing policy. *Journal of the American Institute of Planners, 44*, 130–144.

Blake, T. (1978). We are what we study: Priorities for environmental design research. In S. Weidemann, & J.R. Anderson, (Eds), *Priorities for environmental design research: Part 1, EDRA 8* (pp. 7–9). Washington, DC.

Blumenfeld, H. (1975). The changing urban environment of North America. In B. Honikman (Ed.), *Responding to social change* (pp. 9–26). Stroudsburg, PA: Dowden, Hutchinson, & Ross.

Brill, M. (1975). BOSTI: A working model of education through research. In B. Honikman (Ed.), *Responding to social change* (pp. 242–251). Stroudsburg, PA: Dowden, Hutchinson, & Ross.

Bromet, E. (1980, May). *Psychological, behavioral, and social aspects of the Three Mile Island nuclear incident*. Pittsburg, PA: Western Psychiatric Institute, University of Pittsburg.

Brunswik, E. (1952). *The conceptual framework of psychology*. Chicago: University of Chicago Press.

Chenault, W.W., Hilbert, G.D., & Reichlin, S.D. (1979). *Evacuation planning in the Three Mile Island accident*. Washington, DC: Federal Emergency Management Agency.

Clarke, D. (1975). Man-environment humanities. In B. Honikman (Ed.), *Responding to social change* (pp 235–242). Stroudsburg, PA: Dowden, Hutchinson, & Ross.

Cohen V. (1978). Environment-behavior research and architecture programming: An example of design application to unfamiliar settings. In S. Weidemann & J.R. Anderson, (Eds). *Priorities for environmental design research: Part 1, EDRA 8*, Washington, DC.

Cohen, S., Evans, G.W., Krantz, D.S., & Stokols, D. (1980). Physiological, motivational, and cognitive effects of aircraft noise on children: Moving from the laboratory to the field. *American Psychologist, 35*, 231–243.

Cook, E. (1982). The role of history in the acceptance of nuclear power. *Social Science Quarterly, 63*, 3–15.

Craik, K.H. (1973). Environmental psychology. In P.H. Mussen & M.R. Rosenzweig (Eds.), *Annual Review of Psychology* (pp. 403–422). Palo Alto, CA: Annual Reviews.

Danford, S. (1978, April). Design for the elderly: From research to application. In S. Danford (Chair), *Design for the elderly: From research to application*. Symposium conducted at the meeting of the Environmental Design Research Association, Tucson, AZ.

DiMento, J.F. (1981). Making usable information on environmental stressors: Opportunities for the research and policy communities. *Journal of Social Issues, 37,* 172–202.

Dohrenwend, B.P., Dohrenwend, B.S., Warheit, G.J., Bartlett, G.S., Goldstein, R.L., Goldstein, K., & Martin, J.L. (1981). Stress in the community: A report to the President's Commission on the accident at Three Mile Island. *Annals of the New York Academy of Science, 365,* 159–174.

Ellis, P., Duffy, F., & Jockusch, P. (1983). Information technology and office design. In D. Amadeo, J.B. Griffin, & J.J. Potter, (Eds.), *EDRA: 1983: Proceedings of the Fourteenth International Conference of the Environmental Design Association* (pp. 266–267), Lincoln: University of Nebraska. Washington, DC: Environmental Design Research Association.

Evans, G.W., Jacobs, S., & Frager, N. (1982). Behavioral responses to air pollution. In A. Baum & J. Singer (Eds.), *Advances in Environmental Psychology.* Hillsdale, NJ: Erlbaum.

Festinger, L., Schacter, S., & Back, K. (1950). *Social pressures in informal groups.* Stanford, CA: Stanford University Press.

Fischhoff, B. (1981). Hot air: The psychology of CO_2-induced climatic change. In J.H. Harvey (Ed.), *Cognition, social behavior, and the environment.* Hillsdale, NJ: Erlbaum.

Fischhoff, B., Slovic, P., Lichtenstein, S., Read, S., & Combs, B. (1978). How safe is safe enough? A psychometric study of attitudes towards technological risks and benefits. *Policy Studies, 9,* 127–152.

Fleming, R., Baum, A., Gisriel, M.M., & Gatchel, R.J. *Mediating influences of social support on stress at Three Mile Island.* Bethesda, MD: Uniformed Services University of the Health Sciences.

Flynn, C.B. (1979). Three Mile Island telephone survey: Preliminary report on procedure and findings (NUREG/CR.1093). Washington, DC: Nuclear Regulatory Commission.

Forrester, J.W. (1971). *World Dynamics.* Cambridge, MA: Wright-Allen.

Francescoto, G., Weidemann, S., Anderson, J., & Chenowith, R. (1976). Impossible dreams, unrealizable hopes? In P. Suedfeld & J.A. Russell (Eds.), *The behavioral basis of design, Book 1, Selected Papers, Proceedings of the Seventh International Conference of the Environmental Design Research Association* (pp. 5–8). Stroudsburg, PA: Dowden, Hutchinson, & Ross.

Francis, M., Rivlin, L.A., Stone, A., & Carr, S. (1983). Workshop on the assessment of public open space. *EDRA: 1983: Proceedings of the Fourteenth International Conference of the Environmental Design Association* (pp. 261–262). Lincoln: University of Nebraska. Washington, DC: Environmental Design Research Association.

Fried, M., & Gleicher, P. (1976). Some sources of residential satisfaction in an urban slum. In H.M. Proshansky, W.H. Ittelson & L.G. Rivlin (Eds.) *Environmental psychology: People and their physical settings* (2nd ed.) (pp. 550–563). New York: Holt, Rinehart, & Winston.

Gans, H.J. (1962). *The urban villagers.* Glencoe, IL: Free Press.

Gelfond, M. (1982). Agoraphobia in women and the meaning of home. In P. Bart, A. Chen, & G. Francescoto, (Eds.), *Knowledge for design: EDRA 13 Proceedings,* College Park, MD (pp. 348–353). Washington, DC: Environmental Design Research Association.

Gerard, H.B. (1982). School desegregation: The social science role. *American Psychologist, 38,* 869–877.

Gergen, K. (1982). *Towards transformation in social knowledge.* New York: Springer-Verlag.

Giamartino, G.A., Ferrell, M., & Wandersman, A. (1979). Who participates in block organizations and why: Some demographic considerations. In A.D. Seidel & S. Danford (Eds.), *Proceedings of the Tenth Annual Conference of the Environmental Design Research Association,* Buffalo, NY: State University of New York (pp. 83–90). Washington, DC: Environmental Design Research Association.

Gibson, J.J. (1966). *The senses considered as perceptual systems.* Boston: Houghton Mifflin.

Gittell, M., & Shtob, T. (1980). Changing women's roles in political volunteerism and reform in the city. *Signs: Journal of Women in Culture and Society, 5*(3), 64–75.

Glaser, B.G. & Strauss, A.L. (1967). *The discovery of grounded theory: Strategies for qualitative research.* Chicago: Aldine.

Glazer, N., Majka, L., Acker, J., & Bose, C. (1976). *The homemaker, the family, and employment: Some interrelationships.* (Mimeo. Prepared for the American Women in a Full Employment Economy. A compendium for the use of the Joint Economic Committee of Congress.)

Goldhaber, M.K. & Lehman, J.E. (1982, November 16). Crisis evaluation during the Three Mile Island nuclear accident. Three Mile Island population registry paper for the annual meeting of the American Public Health Association, Montreal, Quebec.

Goodey, B. (1975). Spatial behavior and environmental imagery: Lines on the public face. In B. Honikman (Ed.), *Responding to social change* (pp. 189–199). Stroudsburg, PA: Dowden, Hutchinson, & Ross.

Grant, D.P. (1975). Aims and potentials of design methodology. In B. Honikman (Ed.), *Responding to social change* (pp. 96–108). Stroudsburg, PA: Dowden, Hutchinson, & Ross.

Habermas, J. (1971). *Knowledge and human interests.* (J.J. Shapiro, trans.). Boston: Beacon.

Hall, E.T. (1966). *The Hidden Dimension.* Garden City, NY: Doubleday.

Hammond, K.R. (1966). *The psychology of Egon Brunswik.* New York: Holt, Rinehart & Winston.

Hapgood, K., & Getzels, J. (Eds.). (1974). *Women, planning, and change.* Chicago: American Society of Planning Officials.

Hardin, G. (1968). The tragedy of the commons. *Science, 162,* 1243–1248.

Harre, R., & Secord, P.F. (1973). *The explanation of human behavior.* Totowa, NJ: Littlefield, Adams.

Hart, R. (1976). Children and youth as planners and designers. In P. Suedfeld & J.A. Russell (Eds.), *The behavioral basis of design, Book 1. Selected Papers, Proceedings of the Seventh International Conference of the Environmental Design Research Association* (pp. 361–362). Stroudsburg, PA: Dowden, Hutchinson & Ross.

Hartman, C. (1975). Commentary on context. In B. Honikman (Ed.), *Responding to social change* (pp. 55–57). Stroudsburg, PA: Dowden, Hutchinson, & Ross.

Hayden, D. (1980). What would a non-sexist city be like? Speculations on housing, urban design, and human work. *Signs: Journal of Women in Culture and Society, 5*(3), 167–184.

Hershberger, R.G. (1975). The representation and evaluation of environments. In B. Honikman (Ed.), *Responding to social change* (pp. 109–116). Stroudsburg, PA: Dowden, Hutchinson, & Ross.

Hohenesmer, C., Kasperson, R., & Kates, R. (1977). The distrust of nuclear power. *Science, 196,* 25–34.

Holland, V. (1972, January). Cognitive persuasions: Assumptions and presumptions (Sec. 17.4). In W.J. Michaelson (Ed.), *Environmental design: Research and practice, Proceedings of the Third Annual Environmental Research Design Association,* Los Angeles, CA: University of California.

Holahan, C.J., & Saegert, S. (1973). The psychological impact of planned environmental change: Remodeling a psychiatric ward in an urban hospital. *Journal of Abnormal Psychology 82,* 454–462.

Houts, P.S., & Disabella, R. (1983). Moving after the crisis: A prospective study of the Three Mile Island area population mobility. *Environment and Behavior, 15,* 93–120.

Houts, P.S., Miller, R.W., Tokuhata, G.K., & Ham, K.S. (1980, April). *Health-related behavioral impact of the Three Mile Island nuclear incident* (Pt. 1). Report submitted to the TMI Advisory Panel on Health Research Studies, Pennsylvania Department of Health.

Ittelson, W.H. (1973). Environmental perception and contemporary perceptual theory. In W.H. Ittelson (Ed.), *Environment and Cognition.* New York: Seminar.

Janis, I., & Mann, L. (1977). *Decision making: A psychological analysis of conflict, choice and commitment.* Glencoe, IL: Free Press.

Jobes, P.C. (1976). The right to participate: Attitudes regarding land use and development in Southeastern Montana. In P. Suedfeld & J.A. Russell (Eds.), *Proceedings of the Seventh International Conference of the Environmental Design Research Association* (Vol. 7), Stroudsburg, PA: Dowden, Hutchinson, & Ross.

Johnson, J.H., Jr., & Zigler, D.J. (1982). Further analysis and interpretation of the Shoreham Evacuation Survey. In Social Data Analysts, Inc. (Eds.), *Suffolk County radiological emergency response plan: Draft for review by Suffolk County Legislature.* Long Island, NY: Author.

Kessler, S.J., & McKenna, W. (1978). *Gender: An ethnomethodological approach.* New York: Wiley.

King-Ming New, P., Hessler, R.M., Hemnitzy, L.S., & Kemnitzer, L.S. (1972). Community research. Research commune (Sec. 18.4). In W.J. Michaelson (Ed.), *Environmental design: Research and practice. Proceedings of the Third Annual Environmental Research Design Association.* Los Angeles, CA: University of California.

Kuhn, T.S. (1962). *The structure of scientific revolutions.* Chicago: University of Chicago Press.

Lawson, R., Barton, S., & Joselit, J.W. (1980). From kitchen to storefront: Women in the tenant movement. In G.R. Wekerle, R. Peterson and D. Morley (Eds.) *New space for women.* Boulder, CO: Westview.

Leavitt, J. (1980). The history, status, and concerns of women planners. *Signs: Journal of Women in Culture and Society, 5*(3), 223–227.

Leff, H.S., and Deutsch, D.S. (1973). Construing the physical environment: Differences between environment professional and lay persons. In W.E. Dreiser (Ed.), *Environmental design research: Vol. 1. Fourth International Environmental Design Research Association Conference* (pp. 286–297). Stroudsburg, PA: Dowden, Hutchinson, & Ross.

Lifton, R.J. (1976). Nuclear energy and the wisdom of the body. *The Bulletin of the Atomic Scientists, 32,* 16–20.

Lynch, K. (1960). *The image of the city.* Cambridge, MA: MIT Press.

Lynch, K. (1975). Grounds for utopia. In B. Honikman (Ed.), *Responding to social change* (pp. 27–46). Stroudsburg, PA: Dowden, Hutchinson, & Ross.

Maccoby, E., & Jacklin C.N. (1974). *The psychology of sex differences.* Stanford, CA: Stanford University Press.

MacKinnon, C.A. (1983). Feminism, marxism, method, and the state: Toward feminist jurisprudence. *Signs: A Journal of Women in Culture and Society, 8,* 635–658.

MacKintosh, E.A. (1981). The meaning and effects of high-rise living for the middle income family: A study of three high-rise sites in New York City (Doctoral dissertation, City University of New York Graduate School, 1981). *Dissertation Abstracts International, 42,* 4971B.

MacKintosh, E.A. (1982). High in the city. In P. Bart, A. Chen, & G. Francescoto, (Eds.), *Knowledge for design: EDRA 13 proceedings.* College Park, MD (pp. 426–434). Washington, DC: Environmental Design Research Association.

Macleod, G.K. (1981). Some public health lessons from Three Mile Island: A case study in chaos. *Ambio, 10*, 18–23.

Madden, J.F. & White, M.J. (1978, September). *Women's work trips: An empirical and theoretical overview.* Paper presented at Conference on Women's Travel Issues, U.S. Department of Transportation, Washington, DC.

Marcus, C.C. (1983). Success stories: Case studies of researcher-designer-user collaboration. *EDRA: 1983: Proceedings of the Fourteenth International Conference of the Environmental Design Association.* Lincoln: University of Nebraska. Washington, DC: Environmental Design Research Association.

McCarthy, D., & Saegert, S. (1978). Residential density, social overload and social withdrawal. *Human Ecology, 6*(3), 253–271.

McCourt, K. (1977). *Working class women and grassroots politics.* Bloomington: Indiana University Press.

Meadows, D.H., Meadows, D., Randers, J., & Behrens, W.W. (1972). *The limits to growth.* New York: Universe.

Metropolitan Edison Co. et al. v. People Against Nuclear Energy et al. (1983, April 19). U.S. Supreme Court decision No. 81-2399.

Michelson, W. (1973). *The place of time in longitudinal evaluation of spatial structures by women* (Research Paper No. 61). Toronto: University of Toronto, Center for Urban and Community Studies.

Moen, E., Boulding, E., Lillydahl, J., & Palm, R. (1981). *Women and the social costs of economic development: Two Colorado case studies.* Boulder, CO: Westview.

Moore, G.C. (1983). Participation in environmental planning, design, and management. *EDRA: 1983: Proceedings of the Fourteenth International Conference of the Environmental Design Research Association* (p. 67). Lincoln: University of Nebraska. Washington, DC: Environmental Design Research Association.

Nelkin, D. (1974). The role of experts in a nuclear siting controversy. *The Bulletin of the Atomic Scientists, 30*(9), 29–36.

Nelkin, D. (1977). Technological decisions and democracy: European experiments in public participation. Beverly Hills, CA: Sage.

Niculescu, S. (1976). Women as creators of environments [Summary]. In P. Suedfeld & J.A. Russell (Eds.), *Proceedings of the Seventh International Conference of the Environmental Design Research Association* (Vol. 7). (pp. 201–206) Stroudsburg, PA: Dowden, Hutchinson, & Ross.

Nuclear Regulatory Commission. (1981, March). Report to Congress on status of emergency response planning for nuclear power plants (Report No. NUREG-0755). Washington, DC: Author.

Otway, H.J., Maurer, D.M., and Thomas, K. (1978). Nuclear power: The question of public acceptance. *Futures, 10*, 109–118.

Perin, C. (1975). Social governance and environmental de-sign. In B. Honikman (Ed.), *Responding to social change* (pp. 47–54). Stroudsburg, PA: Dowden, Hutchinson, & Ross.

Peterson, R. (1983). Workshop on environmental design issues affecting women: An agenda for the eighties. *EDRA: 1983: Proceedings of the Fourteenth International Conference of the Environmental Design Research Association* (p. 265). Lincoln: University of Nebraska. Washington, DC: Environmental Design Research Association.

Pollowy, A.M. (1978). Women and environmental issues. In S. Weidemann, & J.R. Anderson, (Eds.), *Priorities for environmental design research: Pt. 1, EDRA 8.* Washington, DC: Environmental Design Research Association.

Proshansky, H.M. (1976). Environmental psychology and the real world. *American Psychologist, 31*, 303–310.

Proshansky, H.M., Ittelson, W.H., Rivlin, L.A., & Winkel, G.H. (1974). *An introduction to environmental psychology.* New York: Holt, Rinehart, & Winston.

Rainwater, L. (1970). *Behind ghetto walls: Black families in a federal slum.* Chicago: Aldine.

Rankin, W.W., Melber, B.D., Overcast, T.D., & Nealy, S.M. (1981). *Nuclear power and the public: An update of collected survey research on nuclear power* (Report No. BHARC-400/81/027). Seattle, WA: Battelle Memorial Institute Human Affairs Research Center.

Rapoport, A. (1972). Australian aboriginies and the definition of place (sec. 3.3). In W.J. Michaelson (Ed.), *Environmental design: Research and practice. Proceedings of the Third Annual Environmental Design Research Association.* Los Angeles, CA: University of California at Los Angeles.

Rivlin, L.G. (1982). Group membership and place meanings in an urban neighborhood. *Journal of Social Issues, 38*(3), 75–94.

Rogovin, M., & Frampton, G.T., Jr. (1979). *Three Mile Island: A report to the Commissioners and to the public* (Vol. 2, Pts. 2 & 3). Nuclear Regulatory Commission Special Inquiry Group. Springfield, VA: National Technical Information Service.

Rose, H., & Rose, S. (1969). *Science and Society.* Harmonsworth, Middlesex, England: Penguin.

Rothblatt, D.N., Garr, D.J., & Sprague, J. (Eds.). (1979). *The suburban environment and women.* New York: Praeger.

Rothenberg, M. & Hart, R. (1976). Developmental sex differences in learning environments (Summary). In P. Suedfeld & J.A. Russell (Eds.), *Proceedings of the Seventh International Conference of the Environmental Design Research Association* (370). Stroudsburg, PA: Dowden, Hutchinson, & Ross.

Rowbotham, S. (1973). *Woman's consciousness, man's world.* New York: Penguin.

Rowles, G.D. (1978). *Prisoners of space? Exploring the geo-*

graphical experience of older people. Boulder, CO: Westview.

Russell, J.A., & Ward, L.M. (1982). Environmental psychology. In M.R. Rosenzweig & L.W. Porter (Eds.), *Annual Review of Psychology* (Vol. 33). Palo Alto, CA: Annual Reviews.

Saegert, S. (1976). Towards better person-environment relations: The changing relationships of women and men to the environment. In P. Suedfeld & J.A. Russell (Eds.), *Proceedings of the Seventh International Conference of the Environmental Research Design Research Association, 7*, 370. Stroudsburg, PA: Dowden, Hutchinson, & Ross.

Saegert, S. (1980, Summer). Masculine cities and feminine suburbs: polarized ideas, contradictory realities. *Signs: An Interdisciplinary Journal of Women and Culture,* pp. 96–111.

Saegert, S. (1982). Towards an androgynous city. In G. Gappert & D. Knight (Eds.), *Cities of the twenty-first century.* Beverly Hills, CA: Sage.

Saegert, S. (in press). Environment as material, artifact and matrix. In D. Springer & D. Jodelet (Eds.), *Toward a social psychology of the environment.* Cambridge, England: Cambridge University Press.

Sanoff, H. (1975). Son of rationality. In B. Honikman (Ed.), *Responding to social change* (pp. 225–234). Stroudsburg, PA: Dowden, Hutchinson, & Ross.

Sanoff, H. (1978). Teaching environmental awareness to young children. In S. Weidemann & J.R. Anderson (Eds.), *Priorities for environmental design research: Pt. 1, EDRA 8* (pp. 347–349). Washington, DC: Environmental Design Research Association.

Schumacher, E.F. (1972). *Small is beautiful: Economics as if people mattered.* New York: Harper & Row.

Schwartz, S. (1978). User participation in environmental change. In S. Weidemann, & J.R. Anderson, (Eds.), *Priorities for environmental design research: Pt. 1, EDRA 8* (pp. 16–25). Washington, DC: Environmental Design Research Association.

Seidel, A. (1982). Usable EBR: What can we learn from other fields. In P. Bart, A. Chen, & G. Francescato, (Eds.), *Knowledge for design: EDRA 13 proceedings.* College Park, MD (pp. 16–25). Washington, DC: Environmental Design Research Association.

Shelley, M.W. (1975). Possible future worlds. In B. Honikman (Ed.), *Responding to social change* (pp. 252–268). Stroudsburg, PA: Dowden, Hutchinson, & Ross.

Slovic, P., Lichtenstein, S., & Fischhoff, B. (1979). Images of disaster: Perception and acceptance of risks from nuclear power. In G.T. Goodman & W.D. Rowe (Eds.), *Energy risk management.* New York: Academic.

Social Data Analysts (1983, January 23). Testimony before the Suffolk County Legislature in the matter of the Shoreham Nuclear Station emergency planning procedures. New York: Author.

Southworth, M. (1969). The sonic environment of cities. *Environment and Behavior, 1*, 49–70.

Stimpson, K., Nelson, M., & Yaktrakis, G. (1980). *Women in the American city.* Chicago: University of Chicago Press.

Stokols, D. (1978). Environmental psychology. In M.R. Rosenzweig & L.W. Porter (Eds.), *Annual review of psychology* (Vol. 29) (253–295). Palo Alto, CA: Annual Reviews.

Ventre, F.T. (1975). Transforming environmental research into regulatory policy. In B. Honikman (Ed.), *Responding to social change* (pp. 277–284). Stroudsburg, PA: Dowden, Hutchinson, & Ross.

Von Furster, H. (1973). On constructing a reality. In W.E. Dreiser (Ed.), *Environmental design research: Vol. 1, Proceedings of the Fourth International Environmental Design Research Association Conference* (pp. 36–46). Stroudsburg, PA: Dowden, Hutchinson, and Ross.

Wandersman, A. (1976). Applying humanism, behaviorism, and a broader social developmental view to understanding and researching the design process. In P. Suedfeld & J.A. Russell (Eds.), *Proceedings of the Seventh International Conference of the Environmental Design Research Association* (Vol. 7) (9–12). Stroudsburg, PA: Dowden, Hutchinson & Ross.

Wandersman, A., Giamartino, G. & Peabody, G. (1978, April). Factors influencing participation: A study of two block organizations [Summary]. *Proceedings of the Ninth Annual Conference of the Environmental Design Research Association, 9*, 453.

Wandersman, A., Murday, D., & Wadsworth, J.C. (1979). The environment-behavior-person relationship: Implications for research. In A.D. Seidel & S. Danford (Eds.) *Proceedings of the Tenth Annual Conference of the Environmental Design Research Association* (pp. 162–174). Buffalo: State University of New York.

Wapner, S., Kaplan, B., & Cohen S. (1973). An organismic developmental perspective for understanding transactions of men (sic) and environments. *Environment and Behavior, 5*, 255–289.

Weisstein, N. (1971). Psychology constructs the female. In V. Gornick & B.K. Moran, (Eds.), *Woman in sexist society* (pp. 207–224). New York: Basic Books. (Original work published 1969)

Wekerle, G.R. (1980). Women in the urban environment. *Signs: Journal of Women in Culture and Society, 5*(3), 185–211.

Wekerle, G., Peterson, R., & Morley, D. (1980). *New space for women.* Boulder, CO: Westview.

Welch, P. (1983a). Programming and the federal client. *EDRA: 1983: Proceedings of the Fourteenth International Conference of the Environmental Design Research Association.* Lincoln: University of Nebraska (p. 258). Washington, DC: Environmental Design Research Association.

Welch, P. (1983b). The business of doing environmental design. *EDRA: 1983: Proceedings of the Fourteenth International Conference of the Environmental Design Research Association*. Lincoln: University of Nebraska (p. 258). Washington, DC: Environmental Design Research Association.

Winkel, G.H. (1977). The role of ecological validity in environmental research (Paper No. 77-7). New York: City University of New York, Center for Human Environments.

Wright, G. (1980). *Moralism and the model home*. Chicago: University of Chicago Press.

Yankelovitch, Skelley, White, Inc. (1983, July). *Status report on public response to emergency planning efforts*. New York: Author.

Ziegler, D.J., Brunn, S.D., & Johnson, J.H., Jr. (1981). Evacuation from a nuclear technological disaster. *Geographical Review, 71*, 1–16.

PROCESSES OF PERSON–ENVIRONMENT TRANSACTION

Chapter **5**

ENVIRONMENTAL COGNITION

Reginald G. Golledge, *Department of Geography, University of California,*
Santa Barbara, California

5.1. INTRODUCTION

Rarely are we completely lost. Even at times of considerable uncertainty we have a reasonable knowledge of the state of our existence at some spatial scale. We may only know that we are in the United States as opposed to Mexico, Canada, Nigeria, or New Zealand. Or we may know we are in Arizona and not in Connecticut or Texas. We may know we are in an urban rather than in a rural environment. But sometimes we do not know precisely where we are, and even a prolonged search of information stored in long-term memory may give us few clues as to our location. However, we constantly search for input from the environment, using all of our different senses, to help us solve our locational and relational problems.

The ability to store and access information about different environments is generally taken for granted. Those interested in studying environmental cognition, however, seek to understand a series of questions related to this ability such as: *How* do we abstract information from the environment? How do we store it? Recover it? Use it? *What* information is extracted from the environment? What spatial properties of external environments do we understand

and use? Is it possible to recover specific subsets of spatial knowledge and represent them in a conventional format that has meaning and significance to others? How is environmental cognition related to planning and policy making? What relationships exist between environmental cognition and spatial behavior? These and many other questions of a similar nature provide the basic stimulus for exploring that interdisciplinary area known as environmental cognition.

Environmental cognition is now firmly established as a subfield of the general area of environmental psychology, but it also has subfield status in fields such as geography, architecture, design, and planning, and concepts, theories, and empirical evidence from each of these other areas will be freely used in this chapter.

As Russell and Ward (1982) point out, environmental psychology generally is that segment of psychology concerned with the systematic accounting of the relationship between person and environment. Obviously this attention to environment is not new nor unique, for researchers in perception, cognition, developmental psychology, and so on have all paid some attention to the role of environment and its relation to behavior. Craik (1970), however, described the task area of environmental psychology as providing a study of the physical setting of molar behavior; this extended the previous boundaries of the subject beyond the study of an immediate response to an immediate stimulus to include the study of behavior as organized over a larger span of time and, in particular, in relation to the multidimensional spatial setting external to human mind.

While rejecting environmental determinism as a major underlying theory, researchers admit that many behaviors are place specific—that is, behavior plans are devised not necessarily just on the basis of the nature of the currently occupied environment, but perhaps also on the image of other places with which one has to interact (Canter, 1977; Gärling, Lindberg, & Mantyla, 1983). This image is based on information previously obtained from both primary and secondary sources. Thus an arrival at a particular place is usually accompanied by some a priori expectations about the type of behavior that could take place in such a place and some a priori notion of what behavior path will be followed while occupying that place.

Environments can be treated as more than antecedents to behavior. They afford opportunities for present and future actions. As one recognizes different orders or levels in the organization of the environ-

ment, so too does one recognize that variation can occur in the types of associated expected behaviors. Obviously the concept *environment* as treated here is multidimensional in nature, and, as Wohlwill (1973) points out, it is not entirely in the head.

Although much of the theory underlying environmental cognition research is culled from psychology, there is little doubt that the area has developed with an interdisciplinary focus, and that a variety of seminal works appeared in disciplines such as geography (e.g., Gulliver, 1908; Kirk, 1947; Trowbridge, 1913; White, 1954; Wright, 1947), economics (Boulding, 1956), sociology (Firey, 1945; Strauss, 1961), and planning (Lynch, 1960). In psychology, there are multiple connections to past research. For example, the influence of Brunswik (1944) is seen in the recent work by Baird and his students (1972), where the authors attempt to differentiate between objects sampled directly from the objective environment and objects sampled from an individual's visual field. Hebb's (1949) neural net models influenced the ideas of Kaplan (1973); Lee (1964) adopted the idea of schema and schemata as developed by Bartlet (1932) and Head (1920) Piaget and Inhelder (1967) heavily influenced the important paper by Hart and Moore (1973) as well as a large volume of work by researchers such as Acredolo (1976) and Pick (1972). Piagetian developmental hypotheses similarly underlie the theories of Siegel and White (1975), while the general models of Shemyakin (1963) and Tolman (1948) are evident in much of the developmentally based literature. Ittelson (1960) followed earlier theorizing of Bruner (1957), Lewin (1936), and Mead (1934). Even psychotherapy spawned a set of disciples as Kelly's personal construct theory (1955) influenced work by Bannister (1970), Downs (1970, 1976), Honikman (1976), and others.

As more and more research is undertaken in the area of environmental cognition, more and more links have been made obvious to prior theorizing. For example, a recent paper by S. Kaplan (1983) develops the concept of *plan* originally developed by Miller, Galanter, and Pribram (1960). A plan refers to any organized pattern of action about which an individual thinks; it may include alternatives to a specific action that is undertaken and must be considered as part of the cognitive component of decision making. An obvious further link is made between Miller and colleagues' concept of image and the current interpretation of the term *cognitive map*. Thus in addition to the importance of perception and cognition Kaplan stresses the significance of internal processes such as meditating, or simply "sitting and thinking." In other work Kaplan and Kaplan (1982) summarize efforts toward user-oriented interpretations of environmental cognition process by examining the fundamental question related to comprehension of and willingness to participate in environmental decision-making situations (e.g., the preparation of environmental impact statements).

Although environmental cognition research can still be characterized as being in its infancy, a number of excellent reviews, texts, and edited books exist that thoroughly document the development of the research knowledge of this area. Examples of comprehensive reviews include those by Craik (1970), Evans (1980), Moore (1975, 1979), Saarinen (1976), Saarinen and Sell (1981), Stokols (1979), and Ward and Russell (1982). Relevant texts include those by Canter (1977), Downs and Stea (1977), Gold (1979), Ittelson, Proshansky, Rivlin, and Winkel (1974), Kaplan and Kaplan (1982), Lynch (1960), and Saarinen (1976). Relevant edited collections include Altman and Wohlwill (1977), Cohen (1982), Cox and Golledge (1969, 1982), Downs and Stea (1973), Harvey (1981), Ittelson (1973a), Liben, Moore and Golledge (1976a), Patterson and Newcombe (1981), Proshansky, Ittelson, and Rivlin (1970), and so on. In addition, the annual proceedings of the Environmental Design and Research Association (EDRA), published under a variety of titles, contains many valuable papers and symposia. Journals such as *Environment and Behavior* and *Journal of Environmental Psychology* have been spawned to handle the increasing volume of theoretical and applied research emanating from the many fields supporting environmental cognition research.

Given the richness and recency of this literature source, it is not necessary again to review the history and development of environmental cognition research for this volume. Rather, the reader is referred to the literature just cited in which both intra- and interdisciplinary surveys are readily available.

5.2. EPISTEMOLOGICAL BASES OF ENVIRONMENTAL COGNITION RESEARCH

5.2.1. Influence of Positivism

Throughout much of the history of experimental psychology, perhaps the most central problem has been the epistemological question of how we obtain knowledge of the external world.

There is little doubt that, in the early stages of the interdisciplinary work on environmental cognition, philosophies of empiricism, positivism, and neopositivism heavily influenced developments. While positivist philosophy was conceived holistically with both an *epistemology* and an *analytic methodology* (scientific method), it has often been decomposed into its component parts. *Epistemologically*, positivism accepted a world of atomistic facts. This was a physicalist view of reality that argued that values and beliefs were metaphysical and not scientific, and that the scientist was a passive observer of an a priori given world—a world of objective reality. At the heart of positivist thought was the search for process theory. This search was conducted through a hypothesis-testing procedure (or methodology) that insisted on reliable and publicly verifiable results.

While being perfectly suited to a scientific examination of an a priori given reality, the *epistemological base* of positivism was often found wanting in research that accepted cognition as a significant factor mediating the dialectical relationship between man and environment. The *analytical methodology* of positivism has, however, survived, and it continues to underlie much ongoing experimental work. In particular, the use of scientific method in hypothesis-testing contexts, the use of logico-mathematical languages and reasoning processes, the need for public verifiability of results, and the search for generalization are essential components of much experimental research in environmental cognition. (Couclelis & Golledge, 1983).

Epistemologically, then, while much of the early research leaned heavily on the positivist tradition, parts of this tradition were selectively abandoned as the study of cognition became a central theme of man–environment research. For example, a falling-out took place with the original positivist doctrine as it became more evident that information from the "a priori given world" was mediated by sets of values, beliefs, and meanings that had both idiosyncratic and general significance and that heavily influenced the probability that a bit of information emanating from an element or thing was received, stored, and potentially used by people.

Of critical importance in early research work was the influence of the Kantian theory of knowledge (i.e., there is no way to comprehend the nature of reality except through the human being). The role this theory played in early environmental cognition research is detailed in Moore and Golledge (1976, chapter 1). While it is unnecessary to reproduce those arguments again, Kant's influence can be seen in the work of neo-Kantian philosophers such as Cassirer

(1944) and psychologists like Werner and Kaplan (1963) and in the early works of Piaget (1950). This position argued that reality in general and the environment in particular are grasped through the effort of mind as the subject enters into a creative interaction with the environment. Thus the position evolves that human behavior should be examined in the context of an organism-in-environment situation and as a function of the ongoing transactions between the two. Obviously, this transaction includes referencing to past events as well as to expected outcomes.

5.2.2 Interactionalist Approaches

With the recognition that mental reality could be a primary object of study, further positivist principles (e.g., physicalist and reductionist interpretations of human behavior) lost much of their strength. Likewise, the positivist image of the experimenter as the passive observer of an objectively given reality was altered as an increasing number of studies came to be based on a living interaction between researcher and conscious human subject. Thus an "interactionalist" approach was coupled with the pure research on cognition, and these two inflicted what many philosophers saw as a decisive blow to remaining objectivist beliefs in a human behavioral context. What cognitive researchers focused their attention on was not some a priori object (e.g., a fully structured cartographically rendered mental map) existing in their subjects' minds, but the result of the subtle interaction between analytic methodology and conscious decision making and behavior.

Once one accepted an assumption that human beings respond to their environment as it is perceived and interpreted through previous experience and knowledge, fundamental questions of what information is filtered through the senses, how it is stored and accessed, how it is used, and how it can be represented became a necessary part of the environmental cognition research arena. (An overview of the transactional perspective can be found in Wapner, Kaplan, & Cohen, 1973, and the interactional/constructivist perspective is summarized extensively in Hart & Moore, 1973, and Moore & Golledge, 1976b).

Of course it soon became obvious that interpretation, experience, and even knowledge are clearly a function of social and cultural values and constraints, memory, affect, emotion, fears, beliefs, prejudices, misconceptions, mental capacities, habits, expectations, and other idiosyncratic values along with all the institutional, economic, and physical factors that not only characterize the public (objective) environment but are an essential part of the flow of information from it. For example, a house is not necessarily the "same" house when perceived by different people. It is imbued with meaning and significance with respect to factors such as its location, its naturalistic setting, its size and preeminence, its neighborhood, its integration with or protection from the outside world, and so on. Location and facade both conceal and reveal volumes of information that may be misinterpreted or misrepresented by those sensing the messages that emanate from a given environment.

The acceptance of an interactionalist approach allows the investigation of situations mediating direct relations between person and environment. In other words, while an individual may have a preferred behavioral response to a given situation, the response may be inhibited by the presence of other people or societal or cultural constraints or taboos. Many researchers now recognize the importance of differences in cultural parameters on problem-solving activities. For example, choosing the appropriate algorithm to solve a mathematical problem depends on the types of procedures to which one has been exposed through an educational system. Recognizing the significance of numbers (e.g., 1492, 1776) is also generally culturally specific, as is recognizing names of people and places. Variations in cultural background can result in much longer response times and more extensive searching of long-term memory storage for a clue to the meaning of a particular stimulus. As has been pointed out by researchers such as Rapoport (1969, 1977), there are also significant cultural differences in the way that environments and space generally are cognized. It is suggested that as problems become more culturally specific problem solvers use more and more general strategies (the so-called weak methods) in their attempts to identify and understand the general strategy required to solve problems (Newell & Simon, 1972). It is in part due to the effects of society and culture that we expect the commonalities in environmental cognition that allow aggregation and/or generalization to occur.

Interactional theories of person–environment relationships also posit that individuals differentially interpret and perceive their environment, and in fact it may be impossible to separate the environment from the person perceiving it (Bowers, 1973). They also argue that individuals by their overt behaviors create, select, and maintain environments with properties congenial to their own cognitive, motivational, and behavioral states (Altman, 1975). Thus in some respect the information filtered from the environment is consistent with an individual's purposes and intentions.

5.2.3. Humanist and Analytical Approaches

The continued debate between humanist (e.g., phenomenological) and analytical (e.g., positivist) researchers is primarily of limited academic interest, but the fact the debate occurs at all is evidence of a growing concern for a wider epistemological base for continued environmental cognition research (Seamon, 1982). Although there is some sentiment that the world of affect and the world of cognition should be kept separate, with different theories, methods, and matters of concern clearly focused on each, the area of environmental cognition is one in which such distinctions and differences appear difficult to make. Thus interactional views appear to merge aspects of phenomenology and positivism, literature and science, human feelings, emotions, and objective measurement to a degree that is not apparent in other epistemologies. As more and more researchers bring their interests to bear on environmental cognition problems, the turmoil, however, appears to grow. There is increased uncertainty as to whether or not the use of a priori theories and a consequent search for generalization are necessary components of research in this area. The opposite question, of course, is whether or not the uniqueness component of individual–environment relations and their phenomenological interpretation are useful, or indeed whether activities of this type can legitimately be regarded as part of the meaningful research in this area. Questions such as these reflect the relative newness of the field, the uncertainty with respect to its concepts and contexts, and the general lack of theory, concepts, core, and periphery for ongoing research.

5.3. CONCEPTS AND THEORIES

While recognizing that much of the existing theory used in environmental cognition research has its origins in psychology, we must also realize that a variety of concepts and embryonic theories have filtered in from other disciplines. In this section several of the more widely referenced bases will be reviewed regardless of origin. These bases include development theory, information-processing theory, theories of spatial knowledge acquisition, and principles of hierarchical ordering.

5.3.1. Development

During the 1970s there was a rapid increase in the quantity of research associated with the development of spatial representations. Studies focused on topics ranging from search strategies to map reading and memory for spatial layout. For the most part, such studies concentrated on preoperational and concrete operational stages of development (i.e., the years from 3 to 11). In the late 1970s and early 1980s there developed a different focus, with attention being directed to the development of spatial representation during infancy. As they have for other areas of spatial cognition, Piaget's developmental theories have provided the seminal base for much of this work. Now, several embryonic developmentally based theories that are powerful in their own right and that with continued modification and refinement could conceivably provide a productive theoretical basis, do exist (Golledge, 1975, 1978; Shemyakin, 1963; Siegel & White, 1975).

The dominant theoretical position with respect to the role of development in environmental cognition derives from Piaget's work. The essence of his theory is that knowledge progresses through different stages, and considerable research in different environments (e.g., Evans, 1980; Hazen, Lockman, & Pick, 1978) supports this theory by positing a developmental sequence consisting of an *egocentric* stage, an *allocentric* stage, and a *geocentric* stage. At the egocentric stage all spatial knowledge is referred to self; at the next stage a relative space is constructed that is independent of self and that has critical elements of sequence, directionality, and some simple relational concepts associated with it; the third stage involves the construction of an absolute space independent of self and specific objects in which people, places, and things can be related one to another through general spatial principles such as proximity, closeness, separateness, and so on. These developmental sequences also follow the early hypotheses of Hart and Moore (1973), and can be graphically summarized (Fig. 5.1).

However, some evidence perhaps inconsistent with this framework has also appeared (Spencer & Darvizeh, 1981). This evidence argues that there is a developmental progress in the use of different types of spatial elements (self, landmark, route, frame of reference, etc.) in addition to the developmental sequence from the use of one type to another. Thus

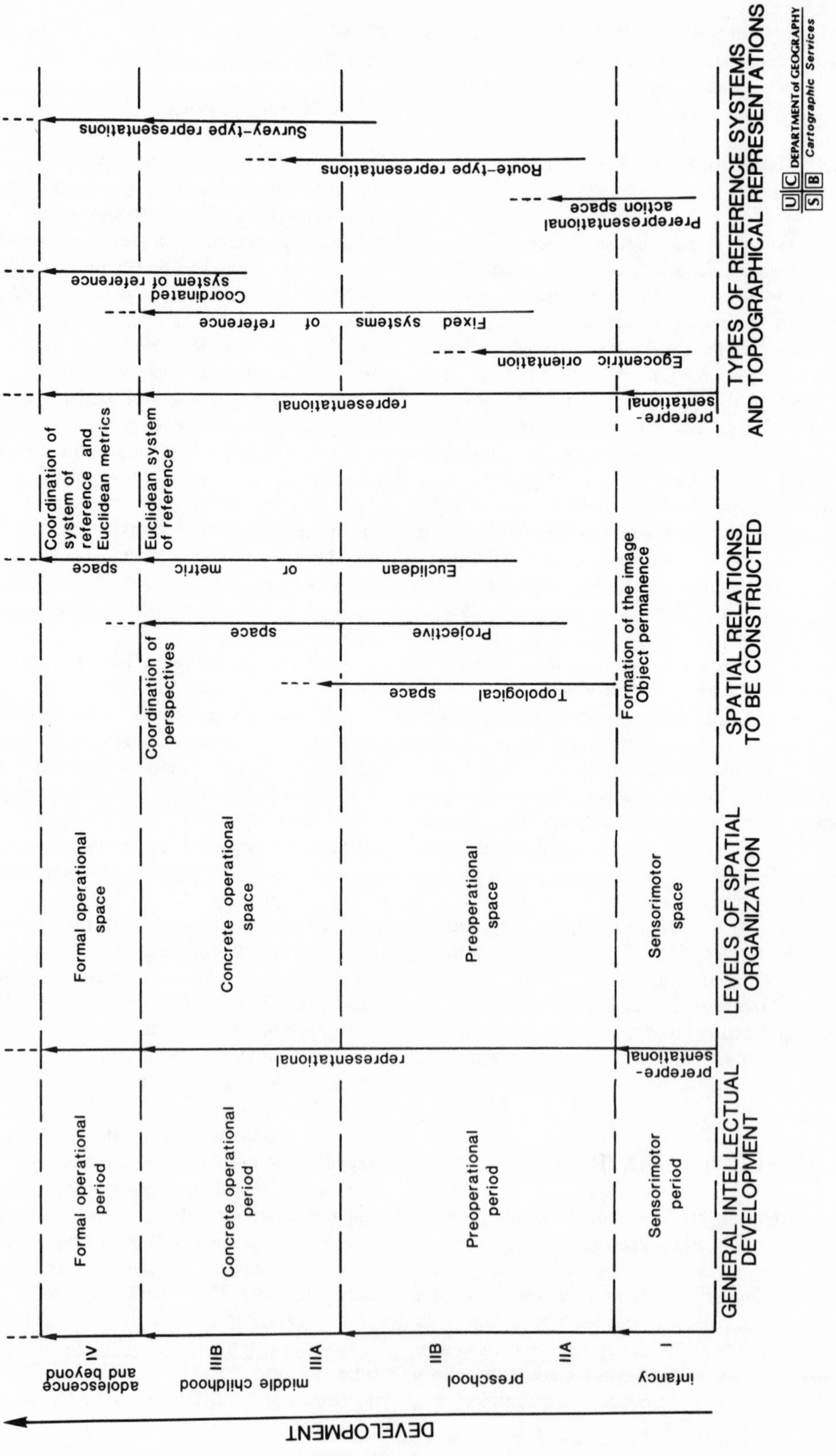

136

Figure 5.1. Hart and Moore's development schema.

there are both naive and sophisticated ways of using, say, a reference point or landmark. As pointed out in the various works of Pick and other researchers (e.g., Flavell, 1977; Pick & Lockman, 1981; Pick & Reisser, 1981; Siegel, Kirasic, & Kail, 1978), an "immature" way to use landmarks is simply to tie successive landmarks one to another in a strict one-on-one sequencing manner, whereas a "mature" way would be to use a relational space consisting of a series of landmarks as spatial structure. Research by Acredolo (1976, 1977, 1978, 1979, 1983) indicates that some young children have the ability to use external cues if they are made salient enough. Other researchers investigating children's way-finding activity describe perspective taking and conservation competencies at levels well before they appear in the Piagetian schema. Disparity between competence and performance levels reinforces this feeling of uncertainty with respect to the general applicability of Piaget's hypotheses.

Yet another alternative to Piaget's schema emphasizes the constraints of anchorpoints on developing cognitive representations. Both Golledge (Golledge 1978; Golledge, Parnicky, & Rayner, 1980) and Evans (Evans, Marrero, & Butler, 1981; Evans & Pezdek, 1980) have found empirically that the developmental changes that occur *with age* are strikingly similar to those found in experiments with various subjects *over time*. As experience increases, locational and relational accuracy increases. As more information about a task situation is accumulated, and as more interconnections can be made among a limited set of environmental cues, metric precision emerges and increases as a result of reductions in the variance associated with possible cue locations. Thus knowledge (and accuracy) of spatial relations may be a function of the stage of learning about a system and may occur more completely at each of the Piagetian levels than is usually hypothesized. This appears to hold until aging results in a tendency not to use organizational frameworks when recalling information (Craik, 1975; Evans, Brennan, Skorpanich, & Held, 1984).

Since the nature of children's environmental cognition has been covered in a separate chapter of this handbook, we need not venture far into this topic here. However, because of its relevance to work with adults it is necessary simply to restate Piaget's genetic epistemology. The essence of this is that spatial knowledge has its origins in development and proceeds from overt and motor to covert and allocentric in its structural orientation and organization. As greater facility is obtained in symbolic and abstract

thinking, there is an increased ability to recognize relationships between environmental features distinct from self. This understanding of the geographic environment independently of one's own self or point of view represents the type of spatial knowledge attributed to older children (from the concrete operational stage onward) and all adults. Both topological and structured geometrical concepts become incorporated into the environmental cognition process as development proceeds through the allocentric stage. The understanding of how places are linked together to form coherent wholes (e.g., urban places) and the development of an understanding of how to travel between two places that were previously unconnected by any sequential or pathfinding activities represent important stages in the general development of spatial understanding.

In addition to the Piagetian hypothesis, Siegel and White (1975) have suggested a three-phase developmental sequence for environmental cognition. Starting with the identification of landmarks as representing reference points in navigation, they posit a progression to route and then configurational representations. They argue that this model accounts for both ontogenetic and microgenetic changes and that each stage is related to another in a hierarchical manner. While the Piagetian and Siegel and White hypotheses are reasonably compatible, some specific differences occur, particularly with respect to the utility of landmarks and paths in developing the sequencing of spatial knowledge.

5.3.2. Information Processing

Within the cognitive mapping literature, the information-processing approaches of Steven and Rachel Kaplan have attracted significant attention. S. Kaplan (1973) stressed the *functionalist* nature of information processing, in that survival in any "hostile" environment would involve object recognition, past experience, anticipation of future events, and spatial abstraction and generalization. Drawing on the network theory of Hebb (1949, 1963), and to some extent on Gibson's theoretical perspectives on ecological perception (Gibson, 1946, 1966), S. Kaplan emphasized both the spatial and the nonspatial relevance of principles such as contiguity, proximity, sequence, and representation. In contexts ranging from neighborhood traverses in naturalistic and/or urban settings to holistic knowledge of larger regions or urban places, S. and R. Kaplan and their students explored the information-processing mechanisms that helped people (and animals) cope with everyday life experiences (Devlin, 1976; R. Kaplan, 1976; S. Kaplan, 1973, 1976; Peters, 1973). Throughout, this work emphasizes the metaphorical nature of the cognitive map and an overlapping network, intersecting sequencing, and noncontinuous structuring process for pattern matching and representation purposes. The parallelism between Kaplan's theories and some early information-processing work in cognitive science and artificial intelligence modeling is now obvious, although the two streams of research existed largely independently of each other (Klatsky, 1980).

Gibson's innovative theories of the senses as perceptual systems (1966, 1979) also emphasized the critical importance of information processing as a means for extracting, storing, and using information from external environments. In particular, his concept of *affordance—physical* associated with objects and places, *social* associated with interpersonal interactions and social or cultural situations—has been extended in the works of Evans (1980; Evans et al., 1984) and Stokols (1981; Stokols & Shumaker, 1981).

In recent years an increasing amount of attention has focused on the development of knowledge structures and the importance of central information-processing mechanisms as critical elements of environmental cognition. This has been accompanied by a move to build sets of linked computer models (*computational process models*) that translate various theories of knowledge storage, acquisition, and use into symbolic terms such that specific task situations can be programmed and performed by computers (Hayes-Roth, 1977, 1979; Kuipers, 1978, 1979, 1980, 1983; Smith, Pellegrino, & Golledge, 1982). Based in part on the work of Simon (1970) and Newell and Simon (1972), adoption of positions such as that suggested by Kahneman (1973) (i.e., that the amount of central processing capacity available at any given moment is limited) has spawned a volume of research that has focused on people's abilities to undertake orientation or locomotion tasks both in laboratory and real world settings in the presence or absence of disturbances. In particular, the extensive work by Gärling and colleagues (1975, 1981, 1982, 1983, 1984) in Sweden should be noted in this area. In one paper, for example, Lindberg and Gärling (1982) examine the difficulty associated with performing a task when one increases the processing demands of the task itself. Thus they develop a series of experiments requiring locomotion along an unknown path through a complex environment while subjects are free either to concentrate on the task itself or to undertake a difficult concurrent task. Results certainly bear out Kahneman's suggestions that

the availability of central information-processing capacity during locomotion appears to be of particular importance.

The emphasis on artificial intelligence modeling has been concentrated in the cognitive science literature, where psychologists, computer scientists, electrical engineers, and others have been seeking to model knowledge acquisition and use. Within cognitive science generally, it is common to distinguish between declarative and procedural knowledge structures. Abstractly, a knowledge structure is viewed as a set of symbol structures representing certain aspects of an individual and the individual's environment. Declarative knowledge (knowing what) is generally regarded to be more context free than procedural knowledge (knowing how). Declarative knowledge consists of places, things, meanings, and symbols. Such knowledge structures have been examined from both a conceptual and a cognitive point of view and include semantic networks, frames, and episodes. Semantic networks typically involve sets of nodes representing concepts and sets of links represented by relationships (Brachman, 1979). Simple inferential processes can be carried out on semantic networks; for example, joining the concepts *place* and *town* by an *is a* link so that if an individual knows that X is a town, the individual may immediately infer that X is also a place. Anderson (1978) argues that propositions about the world may also be represented in this manner.

An alternative to the use of semantic nets as a general structure for representing knowledge is the concept of the frame (Minski, 1975). This is basically a knowledge template applicable in a given context. In essence, the position held here is that if a frame is evoked in some environment a large quantity of standard information is made available. A semantic network evoked in the same environment would generally require significant amounts of search in order to access all the relevant information (Schank & Abelson, 1977). The structure and use of frames is well exemplified in Kuipers's (1978) model of how individuals represent spatial knowledge. Kuipers assumes that an individual's map is composed of a collection of stereotypical elements and that as spatial learning occurs various properties of the frames are given values and new frames are added to the representation (see also Kuipers, 1979, 1980, 1982). Concepts similar to the frame have been defined in other contexts and include *scripts* for stereotypical time sequences of occurrence (Schank & Abelson, 1977) and *stereotypes and schemata* (Bobrow & Norman, 1975). Such structures are assumed to be evoked by individuals when dealing with contexts that arise with great frequency. Apart from semantic nets and frames another declarative knowledge structure is termed an *episode*—this may be conceived of as a record of some previous experience (Kintsch, 1980; Schank, 1980).

While it is recognized that declarative knowledge is fundamental to all humans, it is also recognized that a great deal of human knowledge is procedural in nature. Newell and Simon (1972), for instance, hypothesized that much human knowledge is stored in procedural form and that simple structures known as production rules provide good models of this knowledge.

Both Kuipers's model of spatial knowledge representation and Hayes-Roth's (1978) models of multipurpose trip making make extensive use of productions in their representation of individual, procedural knowledge structures. In the Kuipers model the individual responds to instructions from the environment and to the current state of knowledge concerning the environment by accessing rules that take the form of productions. In the Hayes-Roth model the knowledge specialists interact to produce plans that are sets of heuristic rules for dealing with specific tasks in specific situations. These also take the form of collections of production rules.

Many of the above information-processing concepts are being linked into what is called a *computational process model* (CPM). Such an activity permits the construction of general models of individual performance in given task domains, and it helps to calibrate the models so constructed so that they represent the behavior of specific individuals. In particular, emphasis has been placed on constructing and calibrating models of "experts." Recently, Smith and colleagues (1982) have specifically focused on the relevance of CPM in the general area of spatial cognition. It is assumed that an individual's knowledge of the environment is a function of accumulated and organized perceptual experiences representing interactions between the organism and environment. The knowledge acquisition process is thus based on episodes from which a more generalized and context-independent knowledge structure emerges that is capable of sustaining a wide range of spatial behaviors.

As an alternative to these procedures, Kosslyn (1980) developed a computational theory of imagery that posits that visual mental images are transitory data structures that occur in an analog spatial medium. Surface representations, of which these mental images are typical, are generated from more abstract deep representations in long-term memory.

Once formed, such deep representations can be used in a variety of spatial contexts. Kosslyn also suggests that there are two critical kinds of structures in a cognitive account of imagery. The first of these is *data structures*, which can be specified by reference to three properties—format, content, and organization. The second consists of *the media*, which are specified by referencing their formatting and accessibility. Two other general kinds of processes exist: *comparison* processes, which are used to compare two data structures or parts thereof, returning a match/mismatch decision or a measure of similarity between them, and *transformation* processes, which are either alteration transformations, changing the content of a given data structure, or production transformations, which either replace or supplement existing data structures with new data structures.

Using a similar conceptual base, Gärling, Böök, and Ergezen (1982) posit that a cognitive map is a representation of information supported by several different internal structures. Representation in short-term memory may proceed in either analog or visual image format or may occur in a procedural format in language. A cognitive map, however, appears in essence to be more of a semantic long-term memory structure and may be organized in a manner similar to that assumed by network models of long-term memory.

Given that human knowledge structures are extremely large and that relevant knowledge must be accessed in a timely manner and updated as the world changes, it is essential to have some understanding of the processes underlying the control of information processing and to know how knowledge restructuring takes place. Two of the more frequently mentioned processes to achieve these goals are *pattern matching* and *activation spread*. Pattern matching processes determine the similarity of two or more symbol structures. They are capable of operating on either declarative or procedural knowledge. Activation spread relies on the notion that specific parts of a knowledge structure can be activated. *Activation* refers to a state of excitation, and the levels of activation determine which parts of the basic knowledge structure are available for access and use. Activation spreads from activated to unactivated parts of a knowledge structure so that linkages can occur between bits of knowledge. Bower and Cohen (1981) have suggested that the basic process of thought in humans is, in fact, the activation of a proposition and its concepts. McClellan (1979) has examined the spread of activation in the context of networks. Here a node is primed or activated in response times and measured in relation to the recall of related and unrelated concepts.

In a recent review of interdisciplinary work on images, Lloyd (1982) summarized various approaches to the internal representation of spatial phenomena into classes such as *radical image theory* (e.g., Kosslyn & Pomerantz, 1977), including various scaling studies, rotation studies, and reaction time studies); *conceptual–propositional* approaches (Anderson & Bower, 1973); and the *dual coding* approach (Paivio, 1969, 1971). Basic differences in these classes relate to how information is coded and stored.

Regardless of which aspect of this debate one focuses on, it is obvious that no definitive answers exist at this stage and that it may be possible to define research that contests any specific hypotheses concerning the processing of spatial information. However, the use of information-processing theories to examine the selection, storage, reconstruction, and use of cognitive information appears to be a potentially fertile topic for cartographers, behavioral researchers, environmental psychologists, and cognitive scientists generally.

5.3.3. Acquisition of Spatial Knowledge: Nodes, Paths, and Configurations

Until recently little detailed empirical work has been carried out on temporal aspects of the process of acquiring spatial knowledge. Golledge (1978) reports on a year-long experiment in Columbus, Ohio, in which new, intermediate, and long-term residents were studied to show how cognitive maps changed over time (see Golledge, Rayner, & Rivizzigno, 1975b). These studies indicated that over time people tended to converge to asymptotically stable cognitive maps that were good approximations of existing spatial relations among points, paths, and areas. Later work by Spector (1977) and Golledge and Spector (1978) focused on the information sources that are used in acquiring knowledge about elements in the environment. Spector (1978) also undertook a detailed path analysis of individual regressions (one for each subject and each cue used in the experiment) to show that the frequency of interaction appeared to be the greatest factor influencing the amount of locational error associated with a given cue. Other researchers (Evans & Pezdek, 1980; Hintzman, O'Dell, & Arndt, 1981; Thorndyke & Stasz, 1980) have specifically examined the problem of acquiring spatial information from maps and have compared it to acquisition of spatial information by direct observation in a given environment.

Acquiring spatial information by direct observation

is a much more frequently used procedure (Gibson, 1966, 1979; Kozlowski & Bryant, 1977; Kuipers, 1978, 1979, 1980, 1982; Siegel & White, 1975). For the most part, research has focused on using individuals who have lived for varying amounts of time in a given environment while comparing the complexities of their cognitive maps one with another. Some researchers have used conventional learning paradigms involving subjects touring through known or familiar environments. Lindberg and Gärling (1981, 1982) used the novel experiment of taking subjects through complex featureless passages underneath a hospital and asking them to learn paths and remember reference points. Using errors and response latencies of estimates of direction and distances to designated reference points from stopping points, they indicated that locations were less accurately estimated and response latencies longer for subjects that were given a backward counting task than for subjects whose walking was unimpeded by any intrusive activities.

Building on some initial work by Miller and colleagues (1960), Leff (1978), and Russell and Ward (1982) utilize the concept of an *action plan* as an important codeterminant of behavior in the everyday social and physical environment. Travel plans are integrated into many action plans, and while many travel plans are likely to be routine (because of the importance of developing habitual travel patterns between frequently connected end points) some spatial movement requires accessing stored information about the environment prior to undertaking a trip. Various information sources such as direct experience, mass media, and stored memory can be accessed in order to form such travel plans (Gärling et al., 1984).

A critical part of most actions is the path chosen. Fundamentally, paths consist of an origin and destination connected by sets of procedural rules that are translated into spatial components such as distance, direction, and orientation (Kozlowski & Bryant, 1977). To learn a path is to learn the procedural rules that prevent one from becoming lost when traveling between the origin and destination (Golledge, Smith, Pellegrino, Doherty, & Marshall, 1985). Between any pair of locations in space there are an infinite number of possible routes. Criteria such as efficiency, cost, time, least effort, maximum aesthetics, and so on can be used by an individual traversing the space between two points, and the formalization of such criteria on successive route-finding exercises delineates the path selected and used from the infinite possible array of alternatives. Travel can, therefore, be undertaken in a purely search phase—as between an experienced origin and an unknown destination—

or it can be preplanned in terms of taking place between known or experienced origins and destinations. Selecting a criterion for controlling movement and translating this into practice by traversing a specific route constitute the planning and implementation phases of pathfinding. Once particular origins and destinations have been connected by some plan, the operational section of the plan then heavily influences the type of information gleaned from the total environment in which the origin, destination, and path segments are located. Obviously, path selection and implementation become critical components of cognitive maps. They limit the potential mapping process and help account for variations, distortions, disturbances, and errors that may creep into the knowledge structure of a particular segment of space.

Sadalla, Burroughs, and Staplin (1980) have reported several experiments showing that landmarks have a cognitive status different from that of other points in space. They pointed out that people tend to underestimate the distance from an arbitrarily chosen point to a landmark, but not from a landmark to such an arbitrarily chosen point. Their paper also indicated that, by examining response latencies, estimates of interpoint distances involving landmarks were completed faster than those not involving landmarks. In another study related to the significance of landmarks, Golledge and Spector (1978) examined cognitive configurations recovered from multidimensional scaling analysis of proximity judgments among sets of well-known places in the city of Columbus, Ohio. Some significant results from this analysis showed that there were important intersubject differences due in large part to their travel behavior and general interaction patterns with the environment. Within areas heavily utilized by a subject (i.e., contained within a daily activity space), well-coordinated configurations emerged. The goodness of fit between cognitive configuration and objective reality increased with length of residence and level of interaction with the areas. For nodes other than primary nodes that may be located at the periphery of (or outside) an individual's activity space, there is only sufficient information to access such nodes from well-known (higher-order) nodes or paths.

Other research suggests that a memory representation of the spatial layout of large-scale environment may be acquired very quickly (Gärling, Böök, Ergezen, & Lindberg, 1981; Gärling, Böök, Lindberg, & Nilsson, 1981). Adult subjects taken on tours through a residential area with which they were familiar found that memory for the path traversed was almost perfect after the first trial. This evaluation was indicated by almost perfect recall of the order of a number of designated landmarks along the route. Asymptotic levels of memory for landmark location appeared to have been reached after three trials. Significant results were that acquisition rates were faster for subjects driven in cars than for those who walked, men tended to improve slightly faster than women, and the memory representation required was resistant to forgetting.

These results appeared to have some significant implications for the order in which different types of spatial information (landmarks, paths, and locations) are acquired. Gärling and colleagues addressed a question raised by Siegel and White (1975) and Herman and Siegel (1979) concerning the order in which landmark and path knowledge accumulates. Both the Gärling, Böök, Lindberg, and Nilsson (1981) and the Evans and Pezdek (1980) research support the hypothesis that locations of landmarks are learned before paths. When paths or systems of paths have been learned, the location of landmarks can be recalled more exactly because the paths reduce the number of possible locations that a given landmark could potentially occupy. This seems to be consistent with the idea that landmarks function as anchorpoints in spatial representations of the environment (Golledge, 1978; Golledge & Spector, 1978).

In a temporal sense, Gärling and colleagues (1981) found that the location of landmarks in an average Swedish town were remembered accurately in less than 4 months of residence, while during the same time period path systems were much less accurately remembered. A fine distinction was drawn, however, between learning the location of individual paths linking the location of landmarks and the process of learning systems of paths. The Gärling, Böök, Lindberg, and Nilsson studies also indicated that distortions in the memory representation of landmarks or paths can persist for a long time. This may be because of low levels of motivation to learn, the existence of concurrent or distracting tasks hindering the acquisition of knowledge, or the type of travel mode used to navigate the environment. In addition, individuals with higher spatial abilities tended to acquire information faster. Distortions in all subjects may be produced by forgetting. This latter factor is tied in to the interactional component with the landscape; since every part of an area may not be visited with equal frequency, an individual will have different schedules for reviewing and retaining some landmark/path information but not other. Other work by the Swedish researchers has shown that distance estimates were less accurate than direction estimates, so some distortion of cognitive configurations may result from an emphasis on the former rather than the latter. Testing the specific hypothesis that paths are learned faster than locations has produced varying results (Gärling, Böök, & Lindberg, 1982; Siegel & White, 1975). However, since it can readily be assumed that paths are anchored at each end by an origin and destination, there is commonsense reason to expect that a minimal set of primary nodes or landmarks that define the end points of any given path system not only anchor a cognitive configuration but also precede path learning, and that they similarly define a given path segment. More research is needed to investigate these hypotheses, for the results have some implications for theories of the development of spatial knowledge (e.g., see Smith and colleagues, 1982).

5.3.4. The Hierarchical Ordering of Spatial Knowledge

Much research in environmental cognition has as a basis a hierarchical model, whether this is the developmental sequence posited by Hart and Moore (1973), the path-node sequence suggested in Siegel and White (1975), the node-path (anchorpoint) hypothesis suggested by Golledge (1975), the route-to-survey progression of Shemyakin (1963), or the spatial orientation theories embedded in different navigational systems (Pick & Acredolo, 1983). In the context of developmentally based work, Siegel and Cousins (1982) point out that with the exception of work by Newcombe and Liben (summarized in Cohen, 1982) previous research had not accessed children's environmental way-finding competence in the same environment in which their cognitive mapping competence was accessed. Thus neither developmental sequencing nor hierarchical ordering principles had been definitively established. While not formalizing experience in as rigid a manner as Newcombe and Liben, geographers Blaut, McCleary, and Blaut (1970) and Hart (1973) had previously experimented with this same problem. Current work by Smith and colleagues (1982) specifically addresses the question of hierarchical ordering and adds a further dimension by trying to develop a CPM of the way-finding activities of selected children based on such principles. The CPM consists of a comprehensive computer model of the actual environment in which way-finding takes place, along with models of the individual and the process and procedures used in a way-finding task, and it relies on hierarchical orderings in both the environmental and the decision-making models.

bodied in the ideas put forward initially by Briggs (1972) and Golledge and Zannaras (1973), who hypothesized that the hierarchical structuring of information *necessarily* results in some places obtaining a status as primary nodes or reference points. These primary nodes or reference points anchor segments of space and dominate spatial relations in that segment of space. For example, other places are referred to in terms of proximity to a major primary node; paths are accessed by reference to the closest primary path; areas are discussed in terms of proximity to well-known primary areas. Thus even though precise details of the spatial location of a place need not be known its proximal relations may be understood well, and this substantially reduces the potential search space for someone who is seeking that location in space. The expansion of reference points and the systems of references (Acredolo, 1976; Pick, 1976) also appear to have significance for spatial orientation, even at the earliest stages of infancy, where early evidence of hierarchical order is embodied in the egocentive reference phase of spatial understanding. The significance of hierarchical order to the propositional versus analog arguments regarding the logical basis of cognitive representations is as yet not fully explored and could be an interesting way to differentiate the relative worth of these theories.

One of the most common distinctions in the literature on spatial cognition is that between route knowledge and survey knowledge (Shemyakin, 1962). Theoretically and empirically there appears support for the notion that knowledge progresses from landmarks to specific path knowledge to an integrated frame of reference system for structuring spatial information, and at each level hierarchical orderings appear to exist.

The exact nature of the transition from route knowledge to survey knowledge appears largely unknown. There is, however, a volume of work that argues for the importance of the role of attention processes in selecting spatial sensory information for further processing in way-finding tasks (Böök & Gärling, 1978a, 1978b; Gärling, 1975; Gärling et al., 1975). Of critical importance appears to be information such as whether or not a reference point is visible from the origin, destination, or some intermediate decision point (see also Appleyard, 1976). Visibility and consequent interaction potential then become key aspects for integrating information about individual cues into short-term and/or long-term memory storage, and for determining linkages and orders among such cues. For example, if an individual is undertaking a way-finding task, and if a reference point cannot be directly perceived during locomotion along a path, then short-term memory must be further processed to yield its possible location and the locations of other reference points. This is an essential part of planning movement along a route. The deduced information about nonvisible anchorpoints is probably stored in long-term memory with a hierarchical ordering being superimposed depending on the task situation (Böök & Gärling, 1980).

The progression from route knowledge to survey knowledge, a progression from one-dimensional to two-dimensional knowledge, necessarily incorporates the concept of angle orientation and direction. Thus it is also argued that a good "sense of direction" is important in the structuring of cognitive representations (Kozlowski & Bryant, 1977).

An integral part of route knowledge, survey knowledge, and the transition between them is some type of *hierarchical ordering* of reference nodes or anchorpoints. Thus anchorpoints represent the organizational nodes of a representation and, together with the path connections between them, define the skeletal structure of a representation (Golledge, 1978). Anchorpoints also facilitate clumping or clustering of information, thus allowing greater efficiency in coding, storage, and recall than would otherwise be possible under the simple hypotheses of procedural descriptions, or coordinate or undifferentiated frames of reference.

5.4. SUBSTANTIVE AREAS: EMPIRICAL RESEARCH

Despite its relative recency, environmental cognition research is extremely diverse. Any attempt to review all its many facets must inevitably fall short. In this section, therefore, we will concentrate on a limited set of examples, briefly summarizing some past and current projects and highlighting what appears to be state-of-the-art knowledge. Areas to be covered include cognitive mapping, city images, route and survey knowledge, spatial cognition of disadvantaged populations, cognitive distance, spatial abilities, spatial orientation, and some cross-cultural comparisons involving environmental cognition.

5.4.1. Cognitive Mapping and Cognitive Maps

Investigations of the process of cognitive mapping generally begin with a model including four elements: an actor; an external situation or environment; a set of outputs from situation to actor called *environmental cognition*, and a set of outputs from actor to situation called *environmental response behavior*. This general schema assumes that spatial behavior cannot be explained in terms of stimulus and response alone, but that such behavior requires an intervening variable—an internal mechanism that reorders, recodes, and in some sense transforms the stimuli in a way that is novel or creative.

The basic question asked then is: What kinds of information must be coded, stored, and decoded if one is to engage successfully in environmental behavior? One possible framework is to regard the cognitive map as a set of stored propositions about the environment, each having been assigned a truth value or salience by an actor. In this sense, the process of cognitive mapping consists of a set of operations designed to code environmental information and subsequently decode it to allow spatial behavior to take place. Three of the most fundamental skills involved in this transformation process are the acquisition of shape constancy, size constancy, and a generalized pattern recognition ability related to concept formation and stimulus generalization (Gibson, 1966). Here shape constancy through rotation is homologous to the control of projection, size constancy is homologous to control of scale, and pattern recognition is homologous to the symbolic reference of map sign and legend.

Even tasks as simple as going from home to work or to a store, directing newcomers to places that they do not know, or suggesting travel routes and choosing them oneself all require information to be stored, accessed, and used in a convenient and quick way. The memory representation of spatial information in particular has been called a *cognitive map*, and some of the central questions in environmental cognition concern the nature of these cognitive maps, the process of acquiring and forming such maps, and the use of cognitive maps in processes such as way finding or other spatial behaviors. In general, the process of acquiring spatial knowledge is denoted as the *cognitive mapping process*. The product, the sum total of environmental information stored in memory, is called a *cognitive map*.

Although the notion of cognitive maps has been in the literature of various fields for the best part of this century (e.g., Tolman, 1932; Trowbridge, 1913), it was a series of pioneering studies by researchers such as Lynch (1960), De Jonge (1962), Gulick (1963), Appleyard (1969, 1970), Stea (1969), and Downs (1970) that served to focus a considerable volume of cross-disciplinary attention on the notion of the cognitive map and helped solidify this area of environmental cognition research. While many of the pioneers were more interested in showing the difference between images of reality and objective reconstructions of reality, there has been an increasing focus on the analysis of cognitive maps as a problem in cognitive structure, per se.

The process of cognitive mapping is a means of structuring, making sense of, and coping with the complexities of environments external to mind. These include not only the observable physical environment but also the many and varied social and cultural environments that impinge on our lives and behaviors (Stokols & Shumaker, 1981). Each individual goes through a cognitive taxonomic process that is culturally constrained and that results in the filtering of masses of "to whom it may concern" messages from the multitude of environments in which we live. The result is the development of some form of internal representation of the information contained in these messages. The term *cognitive map* has been developed to refer to these internal representations. A cognitive map, therefore, is an individual's model of the world. As simply pointed out by Downs (1981), the term *map* as used here should be interpreted more as a metaphor than as a strict analogy. There appears to be no sound reason that we should expect people to carry information in their minds in terms of scaled-down maps of environment, or indeed that one should store information in terms of Cartesian coordinates or in other pseudocartographic formats. Foley and Cohen (1984), however, argue that "working representations" of short-term memory may indeed have some maplike properties.

There is an ongoing discussion as to whether cognitive information is most likely to be represented and stored as holistic images, propositional strings, analogs, or other storage devices (Anderson, 1978; Hayes-Roth & Hayes-Roth, 1979; Kosslyn, 1981). In the context of developing cognitive maps it is possible to suggest some general principles by which information is selected, stored, and used without confining oneself to a particular storage hypothesis.

The literature on cognitive mapping basically is concerned with describing and understanding people's awareness of the physical phenomena surrounding them. It is a comment on the completeness, degree of schematization, and types of augmentation found in the information sets that people collect about their environments. Geographers, for example, have focused on the relative locational attributes of various phenomena including site, proximity, orientation, direction, fuzziness in location, distortion, and so on. This literature appears to demonstrate that a person's knowledge of an environment is at least partially influenced by his or her interactions

with it and the extent, organization, and efficiency of those interactions. Continued repetitive interaction patterns appear to result in the development of stable images over time, with the image and the individual's spatial behavior being inextricably linked one to the other (Golledge, 1978; Golledge & Spector, 1978). The behavioral relevance of cognitive images has been recognized for some time in the geography and planning literature (e.g., Chapin, 1969; Horton & Reynolds, 1970). Thus it is suggested that the space–time locus of individual behavior (activity space, action space, or, as Hagerstrand, 1970, calls it, the *time path prism*) contains all but a small part of the environmental transactions initiated by people. Similarly, distortions and disturbances occur in cognitive maps in those places where environmental transactions are avoided—either because the places are well outside the space–time locus of an individual's activity pattern or because a considerable quantity of stress would be felt if an interaction with a place was forced on an individual. Thus people may have images of supposed high-crime areas, or areas dangerous to personal safety, or a negative image of an area dominated by a different subgroup, and each of these will produce distortions in the cognitive representation of the place or area (Golledge & Rayner, 1977; Nyerges, 1976).

Familiarity with elements of the environment that are within or adjacent to activity spaces is uniformly highest, and this space most frequently contains the principal anchorpoints of one's cognitive mappings of an environment. Thus individual cognitive maps may be most accurate in widely disparate places. A change in emphasis from local to more distant areas to anchor a cognitive map appears to be part of the process of maturing, aging, and passing through successive life cycle stages. As Golant (1983) and Evans and colleagues (1984) point out, there is no shortage of evidence either in the literature on children or in the gerontological literature that demonstrates that both very young and very old people assign the most important material and symbolic significance to their proximate environments—including their dwellings and immediate neighborhoods (see also Rowles & Ohta, 1983).

While a considerable effort has been expended on trying to develop methodologies to externalize what an individual knows about a given environment, the data recovered from these procedures indicate that spatial knowledge is incomplete, partial, and disconnected (Golledge & Hubert, 1982; Kosslyn, Pick, & Fariello, 1974). When the information recovered from an individual is represented in real or pseudocartographic form, the results are often seen to have distortions such as holes, folds, tears, and cracks. Examples of different ways of cartographically representing cognitive information are shown in Figure 5.2 (Gale, 1982). These distortions could also be the results of researchers trying to represent information metrically that cannot be so represented (Baird, Wagner, & Noma, 1981; Richardson, 1981b). Depending on the history of experience with an environment and degree of familiarity with its features, it may only be possible to represent specific features of an individual's knowledge structure in terms of formal metric relations among locations. In such cases the metric information allows one to recover approximate distance, directional, and orientational information. However, even in such cases problems arise with asymmetric distance judgments (Siegel, Allen, & Kirasic, 1979a), nonlinear distance transforms (Baird et al., 1981; Cadwallader, 1979), and the hierarchical nature of node–path connections that may cause substantial distortions in a spatial knowledge structure (Golledge, 1978).

Distortions may occur for distance judgments either along a single route or within a larger configuration (Stevens & Coupe, 1978). The nature of errors uncovered in various cognitive configurations has been presumed to reflect a hierarchically organized knowledge structure in both route and configurational terms (Chase & Chi, 1981; Golledge, 1978). Tversky (1981) has argued that such errors and distortions are a fundamental characteristic of any individual's representation of geographical maps and cognitive maps of areas (such as cities or regions). The hierarchical nature of stored spatial knowledge is also used to account for different speeds of access and activation spread (Lehito, Poikonen, & Tuunainen, 1980).

Siegel and Cousins (1983) present a number of "basic assumptions" that appear to underlie the cognitive mapping processes and further stress the need for researchers to be extremely sensitive to the characteristic of the settings in which behaviors are studied and from which environmental cognitions are derived. They point to the difference in research results as children are changed from familiar to novel settings, from settings in context to isolated settings, and so on.

In another important paper, Gärling and colleagues (1983) assume that there are three interrelated properties of cognitive maps: *places, spatial relations*, and *travel plans*. Places have obvious properties such as spatial scale, names, perceptual characteristics, and function, and psychological attributes such as attractiveness, affectiveness, and so on.

Obviously, they also have location and properties of distance, direction, and orientation with respect to other places. Places are made specific by providing them with names or verbal labels. It has also been shown (Golledge & Spector, 1978; Pezdek & Evans, 1979) that the function a place performs and its role in human activity patterns are critical differentiating characteristics that help identify them. A considerable volume of work in environmental psychology has focused on determining the most appropriate attributes of places. *Spatial relations* are characteristics related to two or more places. They can include proximity relations (e.g., among pairs of points), metric relations with respect to distance and direction (among sets of points), and topological relations (such as inclusion, ordinal and other nonmetric characteristics). *Metric relations* include both general Minkowskian and various curvilinear geometric properties (Baird et al., 1981; Golledge & Hubert, 1982; Golledge, Parnicky, & Rayner, 1979a; Richardson, 1981). Although some attention has been focused on the question of whether or not spatial knowledge can be represented at all metrically (Baird et al., 1981), there is some evidence that metric properties exist among the most familiar points, lines, and areas or nodes, paths, and areas contained within a cognitive map (Golledge, 1982). As Gärling, Böök, Lindberg, and Nilsson (1982) point out, however, the lack of a formal geometry in a segment of a cognitive map may simply be a function of the degree of knowledge acquisition, the quality of the information acquired, or the nature of the simplifying rules for storage.

It has been a common practice since Lynch's pioneer work to attempt to recover the critical cue structure of cities by the process of simply asking people for a list of best-known places and then compiling composite scores based on the frequency with which particular places are mentioned (see Figure 5.3). In this next section we shall discuss some of the ways of representing spatial information and illustrations of how this information can be represented both in terms of simple warped grids and as modified street maps. In addition some comments will be made on some of the classes of distortions that can be easily identified in sets of such map phenomena. To be consistent with our earlier arguments on the nature of recovering stored information, we construct these configurations from responses individuals give about the relative proximity of pairs of places in the city; they do not represent actual hand-drawn maps of the individuals themselves.

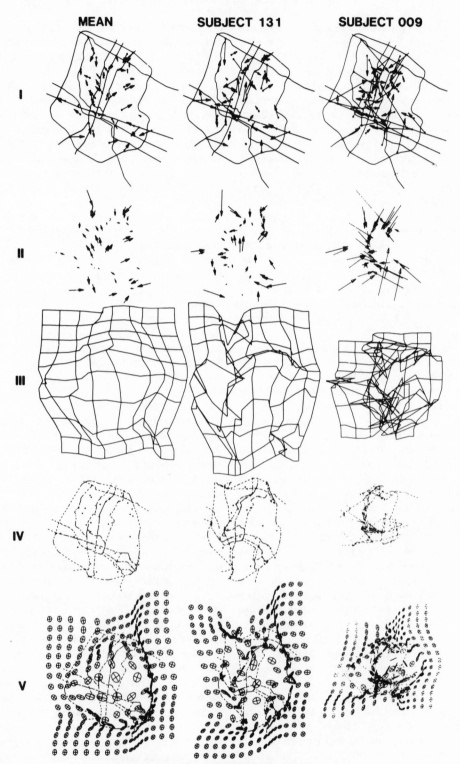

MEAN **SUBJECT 131** **SUBJECT 009**

I

II

III

IV

V

Figure 5.2. Sample cartographic representations of cognitive maps.

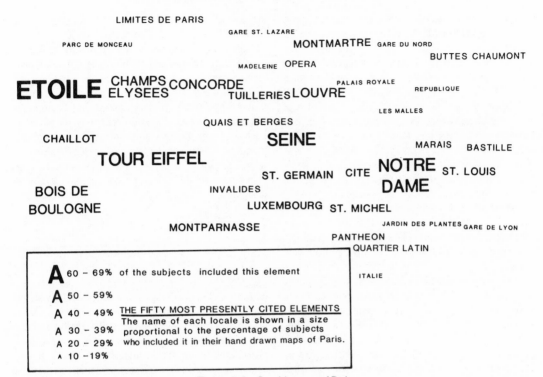

Figure 5.3. Cognitive map of Paris.

Other fundamental questions that appear to be the focus of architectural, planning, and design speculations about cognitive maps concentrate on finding whether some particular environments are more imageable and more easily and accurately represented than others. Questions asked include: How complex need the environment be before it becomes overwhelming? How do variations in the physical landscape or changing land use patterns affect images? What are the critical affective components of environment that influence the degree to which information is selected and stored? Obviously these and a host of other questions relating to the selection and use of environmental information as well as to the appropriateness of externally representing it require much more research activity.

Siegel and Cousins raise a number of critical issues regarding the notion of accuracy in cognitive maps, including: How are the maps of children and adults different? What developmental differences are found between younger and older children? In what ways do the maps change across age or experience? And what should be the standard against which performances are assessed? With respect to what might be an appropriate standard, Siegel and White, like

Downs (1981), Downs and Stea (1973), Golledge (1978), and Kuipers (1978), question the validity of "cartographic reality" as the most appropriate standard against which to measure cognitive configurations. This research implies that over time and as information about an environment mounts there are shifts in the spatial relations among cues such that a relatively stable configuration, anchored by a number of critical common points, gives an interpretable and communicable common structure to a given environment and perhaps represents an asymptotic mapping of this objective reality. However, as Gale and Costanzo (1982) point out, when one changes focus from the major anchorpoints to include other elements of an informational hierarchy, disturbances and distortions appear with increasing frequency. These distortions and disturbances may be caused by misrepresentation or mislocation of a key anchoring node or path, such that entire segments of space are consequently misaligned in terms of their "real" spatial properties. A major anchorpoint in an area perceived to be stressful or antithetical to one's goals or lifestyle (e.g., an anchorpoint to a high-crime area, an anchorpoint in a major ghetto area, or conversely one in an exclusive residential neighborhood) can be mentally pushed away such that entire segments of space become distorted. Further information on the distorting influence of mislocated anchors and their contribution toward errors of both the individual and the group level has been examined by Gale and Costanzo (1982). While not producing overwhelming conclusive results, their work does support the importance of the major anchorpoints in a configuration, and they show, by eliminating less familiar cues or cues that occur lower in the hierarchy, that an overall goodness of fit criterion improves and the fuzziness and distortion components of error significantly decrease the more one focuses on the "primary" cues.

It does seem that the accuracy of cognitive maps improves throughout the ages of childhood into adulthood (Evans et al., 1981). The interesting question that this raises is what persons of any age do when they are required to locate items with which they are unfamiliar or whose position in relation to well-known anchorpoints or landmarks is fuzzy or unknown.

It is generally assumed that cognitive maps are represented uniformly across adult populations. Recent work by Golledge (1983), Golledge, Parnicky, and Rayner (1980), and Richardson (1982), however, shows that this assumption holds primarily for what are known as *normal* adult populations. Mildly and moderately retarded adults may not hold more than sequentially ordered information in memory, and they have great difficulty producing external representations of two-dimensional information that can be differentiated from random responses. Similarly, the literature on environmental learning indicates that in the early stages of learning about an environment an individual's cognitive map may be confined to topological or sequentially ordered information. Even though a subject may have the inherent ability to work at a more abstract level connecting landmarks or nodes by paths not previously traveled, a more cautious and less risky process of relating places to the nearest major anchoring nodes and paths seems to be a feasible way of operating.

The positive relationship between length of residence and environmental familiarity is supported by a variety of psychological and geographical evidence (Golledge, 1978; Golledge & Zannaras, 1973; Milgram, 1970; Moore, 1979). Through direct participation, observation, or access to instructional information gleaned from individuals or from the mass media, a greater likelihood exists that individuals have learned to discriminate efficiently an environment's physical objects that are salient to them. When the cognized environment reaches a relatively

stable state then environmental transactions should be more predictable and less stressful in a decision-making context. Obviously, all information that passes through the perceptual filters is not readily recalled over time, and some diminution of knowledge takes place as residents try to cope with the information overload of everyday life, as individual maturation takes place, or as changes occur in one's life cycle such that previously significant environmental elements no longer occupy the same place in one's cognitive mapping. Examples of this process can be seen in recent work on the cognitive mapping of the elderly (Evans et al., 1984).

5.4.2. Cognitive Images of the City

Much has been written over the last two decades about people's images of cities. Apart from references to the development of some key concepts, definitions, and methodologies, we will not survey all this literature. Instead we offer a brief introduction on early research on the images of cities. Thereafter the current state of the art is summarized in terms of recovering and representing city images. This latter task is achieved by example, that is, constructing cognitive mappings of a sample city from a variety of subject populations. Errors in the matching of subjective and objective configuration are examined by referring to notions of distortion and fuzziness in the maps so produced.

A considerable volume of attention has focused on developments emanating from Lynch's seminal work *The Image of the City*. Initially fundamental concepts from the psychology of perception were incorporated into the city image— for example, figure–background clarity, singularity or dominance of visible form, closure, and so on (De Jonge, 1962; Gulick, 1963). Further work in this area abstracted from the perceptual characteristics of the physical environment to add in values relating to meaning and significance in the cultural and societal sense as well as focusing on the location of cues and interaction patterns between individual and environment. One of the more widely quoted examples of work in this tradition is that of Appleyard (1969) whose focus on why buildings are known included discussion of characteristics such as intensity, singularity, level of visibility, community significance, and so on. Appleyard also focused on critical spatial properties such as their topological, positional, sequential, configurational, and spatial characteristics (see Figure 5.4). Even at this early stage, evidence indicated that city images were likely

MAP TYPES

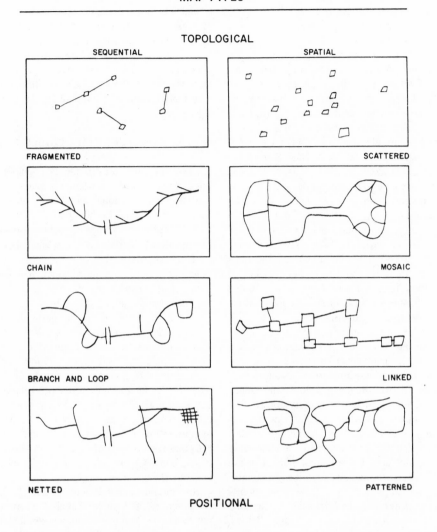

Figure 5.4. Appleyard's map types. (*Source: Planning Urban Growth and Regional Development* by L. Rodwin and Associates, copyright 1969 by MIT Press. Reprinted by permission.)

to be schematic, disjointed, and simplified rather than one-to-one mappings of any objectively defined reality. Research in the early 1970s in particular focused on finding reasons for departure from "accuracy" and included things such as residential history, place familiarity, travel mode, and ethnic and cultural differences (Ladd, 1970; Maurer & Baxter, 1972; Milgram, Greenwald, Keesler, McKenna, & Waters, 1972; Milgram & Jodelet, 1975; Orleans & Schmidt,

1973). Parallel to this were ongoing attempts to refine the modes of externally representing cognitive spatial information other than by sketch maps and verbal descriptions (e.g., Golledge & Zannaras, 1973; Golledge, Rivizzigno, & Spector, 1975).

It is obvious that city images can be recovered and represented in a variety of ways. Lynch (1960) originally proposed a five-element classification system for examining cognitive maps. Regardless of how information about the environment is stored in the mind, Lynch pointed out that one can obtain an external representation of stored knowledge about a place (such as a city). By examining several representative modes (such as sketch mappings, verbal descriptions, and information lists), he inferred that there were five elements that could be considered fundamental components of cognitive imagery and that, if recovered with a suitable level of rigor, could be used to construct a map summary of that stored knowledge. The five elements were defined as *paths, edges, districts, nodes,* and *landmarks.* Paths were basically channels along which an observer would customarily, occasionally, or potentially move as he or she conducted a set of spatial activities in the urban area. Edges were conceived of more as barriers that could be either permeable or impenetrable and that tended to mark off or differentiate one segment of space from another. Districts were the areas delineated by the edges and were seen as having some common identifying characteristics. Nodes were strategic spots acting as intensive foci that anchored the behavioral patterns of each individual. Landmarks were easily identified elements of the physical landscape and could be drawn from the entire range of urban functions or structures.

Following Lynch's innovative work, planners such as Appleyard (1969), De Jonge (1962), and Gulick (1963) conducted research in Venezuela, the Netherlands, and Lebanon (respectively) identifying reasons that certain nodes of landmarks may be expected to be incorporated into cognitive images, defining more clearly the point, line, and areal component of the basic Lynch structure, and investigating the connective and relational properties of these fundamental components. Other work by Carr (1967), Carr and Schissler (1969), Downs (1969), Golledge, Briggs, and Demko (1969), Golledge and Zannaras (1973), Ladd (1970), Lee (1963), and Magana (1978) all further investigated possible components of city images and helped develop the belief that cognitive mapping could be viewed as an essential component of human adaptation and use of particular environments. The argument was made that the success of everyday behaviors (such as journey to work, trips to a grocery store, giving directions to a lost stranger) is at least in part dependent on the cognitive transformation of that environment and the type and quality of stored information that could be accessed once a given task situation is faced. These various researchers indicated that, as the completeness and accuracy of this stored information varied, so too did individual behaviors depart from what one might objectively

consider to be optimal—in the spatial, economic, social, psychological, political, or other sense. Thus it was argued that in order to understand relations between persons and environment one needed to discover the information base on which activities are overlain. On this conceptual and empirical base the surge of interdisciplinary literature on cognitive images has been building for the last two decades.

5.4.3. Cross-Cultural Characteristics

An essential part of environmental cognition is knowledge of place. Such knowledge is generally explicitly spatial (i.e., locational, relational, and configurational), but it may be nonspatial and be culturally coded in terms of symbolism, values, beliefs, and so on (Appleyard, 1979; Stokols and Shumaker, 1981).

Place knowledge has been investigated from the point of view of finding fundamental dimensions along which people can localize places. Researchers such as Tuan (1977) imply that part of environmental meaning is symbolic (i.e., that particular places can stand for an idea). From a cross-cultural perspective this characteristic of environmental meaning has been emphasized by Rapoport (1980), particularly with respect to the religious significance of place. The Navajo, for example, attribute religious significance to both the location and the orientation of a house. Similarly, Saegert and Winkel (1981) point to a symbolization of home by many women in terms of the importance of self, family, and social relationships; home for men may in turn symbolize ownership of childhood memories.

In a seminal paper Blaut and Stea (1971) defined the functions of cognitive mapping in terms of a simple communication model and tested their model in a cross-cultural context. The cross-cultural component of the study focused on two test groups, consisting of 107 children beginning first grade in Worcester County, Massachusetts, and 20 in Rio Piedras, Puerto Rico, who were asked to interpret aerial photographs by naming and pointing to features that they recognized. In a second study with first graders, 19 Worcester children were tested to determine their ability to handle two other mapping problems: first, to draw meaningful map signs and understand the meanings of these signs, and second, to perform a simulated map use task such as way finding. Although some problems exist in the experimental design of these papers, the results indicated that children know the skills of map reading and map using when they enter school. They can read an aerial photograph and can perceive a reduced rotated image of the earth's surface. They can trace a simple map from a photograph and abstract semi-iconic map signs. They can solve a simple navigation problem by tracing signs overlaying an aerial photograph.

The main results of this work indicated that regardless of cultural context preliterate children of school-entering age can interpret vertical aerial photographs and hence perform the mapping transformations of scale reduction and projective rotation (see also Hart, 1977). Regardless of cultural context, they were also able to abstract from the photographic image to a system of highly iconic map signs and use the reduced rotated abstracted presentation in solving a simulated route planning problem.

One of the most quoted instances of cross-cultural implications of environmental cognition focuses on way-finding activities—particularly on the use of navigational systems that are not conventionally cartographic in nature (Gladwin, 1970). In such a system, orientation occurs with respect to a fixed reference system such as an island or star position, direction of currents, or wave formations that is claimed to be noncartographic. However, like other navigational systems described by Rapoport (1980, 1983), each of these systems conforms to an anchor-point theory. The anchorpoints (e.g., current direction) may be more dynamic than the ones on which we usually focus, but, once an anchorpoint is perceived, critical information is relayed to the senses about position with respect to origin and destination, and with respect to the types of choices and decisions that have to be made before a journey can be completed. While not all cultures have the equivalent of a reproducible cartographic map, their navigational structure appears to have many map-like properties. Whether these maplike properties are reduced to information chunks or to strings with critical decision points anchoring or defining end points, the underlying process appears to be the same. This underlying process implies a hierarchical ordering of information with critical elements of the real environment triggering meaningful associations and initiating decisions that may involve repetition of behavior or change of behavior (Pick & Acredolo, 1983).

In another recent cross-cultural comparison paper, Kearins (1981) investigated visual spatial memory in Australian aboriginal children of desert origin. Aboriginal children from 6 to 17 years were found to perform at significantly higher levels than white Australian children on particular skills related to survival habitats. This work is again typical of a growing concern with cross-cultural characteristics of environmental cognition and reflects to some extent the increasing importance of such comparisons.

5.4.4. Transition from Route to Survey Knowledge

Route knowledge is characterized as a series of procedural descriptions involving a sequential record of the starting points, subsequent landmarks, and destination points related to a given path. An individual needs to know how to get from one point to another via an intervening space and in the process of getting between the places must be able to use cues from the environment to tell whether or not he or she is proceeding in such a manner as to be able to solve the way-finding task. Essential elements of route knowledge include the ability to identify decision points where changes of orientation or direction are required, the ability to identify transition points between different transport modes, and the ability to identify whether a subject is on or off the chosen route (Golledge, Smith, Pellegrino, Doherty, & Marshall, 1983). Simple way-finding knowledge in complex environments emerges in preschool children.

The knowledge structure developed and used by an individual to assist in daily interactions with an environment is termed by Kuipers (1983) a *commonsense knowledge structure*. Such a structure consists of a limited number of associations that relate perceptual views to actions that have to be taken at places covered by the given view. To the degree that expectations are not included in the knowledge structure and to the extent that a current view must act as a retrieval key for associative links required to review a route or to anticipate perceptions or behavior, this commonsense knowledge structure may be considered partial. As familiarity increases with a route, however, it may become more complete and efficient while at the same time becoming streamlined so that only critical features will be activated in any given problem situation. As particular routes are learned they represent in a sense a knowledge structure created by aggregating views, actions, associations, and expectations with a given goal context.

Thus Kuipers argues that cognitive spatial description is not a single representation but a number of distant representations that are metrical, topological, procedural, and sensorimotor in character. The original "map in the head" metaphor does not, he argues, capture some of the critical intuitions about spatial knowledge, but he is able to retain this metaphor within the context of a much wider interpretation of the concept of a spatial knowledge structure.

In a study of Parisian cabdrivers, Pailhous (1970) argues that their knowledge structure of Paris consists of two complementary elements—the basic network and the secondary network. The basic network contains up to 10% of the streets, is relatively well integrated and well known, and constitutes the skeleton of the cognitive map. When traveling in it, drivers frequently select optimal or near optimal routes. A secondary network is accessed from selected points in the basic network. A typical route involves the selection of a route from a pickup point to the nearest place on the basic network, use of the basic network until one is close to the vicinity of the destination point, and the use of local information in the secondary network to arrive at specific destinations. As did Carr and Schissler in their seminal work (1969) on commuters and less regular travelers in Boston, Pailhous found that a web of efficient routes emerges along which the regular traveler's information set far exceeds that of passengers or part-time travelers. This route structure, anchored by key landmarks at entrance and exit points that provide gateways to secondary paths and areas, provides a skeleton structure that can be recovered and represented in interpretable cartographic format.

Perhaps the most extensive experiments on wayfinding have taken place at Umea, Sweden, and are summarized in the various work of Gärling and his collaborators. In one experiment (Böök & Gärling, 1978) two sets of subjects were assigned task situations that involved locomoting through space from a given starting point with either visible or invisible access to the destination. In some cases the destination was visible throughout the entire period of locomotion and in others it was visible only from the starting point or not at all until immediately before termination. With invisible end points, the distance estimates were less differentiated and the visible errors larger.

In another paper the same authors (Gärling & Böök, 1981) focused on the relationship between memory and representation of the spatial layout of cities and towns and different types of travel behavior (e.g., to shops, business offices, and restaurants). Results indicated that accuracy of performance decreased with the number of places in the set while latency times increased in an exponential manner. Results also indicated that memory load affected performance negatively, more so than did the difficulty of the planning task. Some support was found for the possibility that the subjects used a heuristic that

minimized distances locally rather than globally in their search for the shortest paths.

Gärling and Böök hypothesized that, for general episodic behaviors such as the one they investigated, it may be difficult to find the shortest route between places simply because the number of possible alternative routes is extremely large. While recognizing that subjects may not achieve an optimal short path route, they did argue that heuristics are used that tend to approximate optimal routes in many cases, although there was some confusion between the definition of optimal route and that of short path in distance and time terms. They suggested that both individual and situational differences occur in task situations and that different people will trade off different aspects (e.g., accuracy against effort) as critical elements of the task environment (e.g., time pressure or mental fatigue) dominate.

In this and other work, Gärling and his associates have found that most research on memory for the spatial layout of environments shows that spatial locations are not necessarily accurately remembered. They quote work by Byrne (1979), Canter and Tagg (1975), Stevens and Coupe (1978), and Tversky (1981), who argue that memory representations acquired by people are schematized and clustered simply because this makes it possible to remember a vast amount of information. Such schematization facilitates the planning of trips and may be in part responsible for large errors associated with spatial representations of specific environment cues (e.g., because of a tendency to cluster cues in spatially linked sequences or groups). They suggest that planning is assumed to impose a load on short-term working memory and thus, even if there is no distortion in long-term memory, temporary representation of that information in short-term memory as the planning process is executed may be an unreliable representation and could cause errors.

The current status of research on the topic of landmark information accumulation can be summarized as follows. The Siegel and White hypothesis implies that landmarks are learned before paths and that paths are learned before relative locations. Herman and Siegel (1978) provide some support for this implication but they also found that memory representations of the relative locations of the landmarks were acquired very rapidly. Byrne (1979) showed that memory for the lengths of routes and the angles between crossing routes was systematically distorted. He assumes that a network of paths is remembered accurately wheras memory for the relative location of places and the like may be systematically in error. By contrast, Evans and colleagues (1981) argue that the initial learning consists of learning landmarks and their relative locations, then the paths, and finally, as a result of learning the paths, the memory representation of the relative locations becomes more precise. Other researchers such as Golledge (1978) posit landmarks as the initial places learned in an environment. Then the paths connecting them are learned; the paths provide information on the relative location of places, and then a spread effect occurs in the vicinity of places and paths to develop areal or regional knowledge of place (e.g., concepts of neighborhood and community).

5.4.5. Environmental Cognitions of Special Populations

Although the bulk of research on environmental cognition has focused on normal adults, students, or children, there has been a steadily growing literature involving special populations such as the elderly, the physically handicapped, and the mentally retarded. The importance of environmental cognition for groups such as the blind, the hearing impaired, the wheelchair bound, the aged, and the mentally retarded has been stressed in past and recent colloquia at the Environmental Design and Research Association (e.g., EDRA Proceedings, 1983), or in recent books on spatial abilities (e.g., Pick & Acredolo, 1983; Potegal, 1982). The recent book by Potegal (1982), for example, covers topics such as the sensory bases of spatial abilities in which orientation within and without vision is considered and in which special emphasis is placed on selected handicapped populations such as the blind. In addition, the rapidly growing literature on the development of spatial abilities from infancy to adulthood is covered from both a developmental and a physiological point of view. Sex-related differences in spatial ability, spatial abilities in the brain damaged, and the behavioral and neurological bases of spatial knowledge are all examined.

Obviously, the process of environmental cognition is not a simple one that can be covered from a single and narrow perspective. The complexity of the area is evidenced by the number of chapters in this handbook that could have been subsumed under the general title "Environmental Cognition" with different population subgroups such as children, the aged, the infirm, or the physiologically handicapped. However, the problem of investigating the cognitive representations of the environment held by special populations is a particularly important one. As an example of a relatively underdeveloped segment of this work, let us focus on some recent work with mentally retarded subjects.

With government cutbacks in mental health budgets and with an emergent programming stressing the right of the retarded to live among the rest of society, the process of deinstitutionalizing the mentally retarded raises several questions about their ability to comprehend their spatial environment and navigate within it. Some of these questions include: What aspects of existing adaptive behavior scales are related to retarded individuals' cognitive mapping abilities? Since spatial and navigational concepts are markedly absent from current behavior (or competency) scales, what fundamental concepts and principles about spatial cognition might be incorporated into such assessment scales? Can knowledge about the cognitive mapping process be used to develop more sophisticated programs for training the mentally retarded to navigate within the environment? Do the current theories of spatial cognition generalize to individuals at subnormal levels of cognitive abilities (i.e., the mentally retarded)?

While these questions have yet to be fully answered, research efforts at the University of California at Santa Barbara and the Ohio State University have focused on the cognitive mapping abilities of the mentally retarded. The reader is referred to Golledge (1983), Golledge, Parnicky, and Rayner (1979a, 1979b, 1980), Golledge, Richardson, Rayner, and Parnicky (1983), and Richardson (1982) for complete details of the research, but a brief overview is relevant.

An experimental group and a contrast group of subjects from Columbus, Ohio, and Santa Barbara, California, participated in a series of experiments aimed at assessing the degree of spatial knowledge about neighborhoods in which the subject resided. The experimental group consisted of young adults who were classified as either severely, moderately, mildly, or borderline retarded. The mean IQ score for the experimental group was 56.6. Each member of the experimental group had been living in the community either in a group home or in an individual apartment for a period of at least 6 months before the start of the experiment. Additionally, each experimental subject was physically able to travel throughout the environment. The contrast subjects were socioeconomically deprived normal adults with lengths of residence in the same two neighborhoods roughly equivalent to those of the experimental group.

Two experiments were used to assess the level of

spatial knowledge held by each subject. First, a map model methodology was used to assess survey knowledge. This consisted of each subject's placing 2-inch by 3-inch Kodachrome pictures of 19 neighborhood landmarks on a plywood board marked with tape to depict the bordering streets and two major crossroads of the defined neighborhood. The second experiment, aimed at representing route knowledge, was a route-sequencing task. Each subject was told to consider a yard-long stick as a route to a particular destination (e.g., neighborhood grocery store, local theater, downtown department store, local shopping mall). The researcher placed a picture of the subjects's residence at one end of the stick and a picture of a particular destination at the other end. Each subject was then given pictures of six landmarks occurring along the route and was asked to locate the pictures at their appropriate place along the stick. Information was collected on the accuracy of sequencing as well as location and distance apart.

In the map board experiment, the location of landmarks as placed by each subject (the so-called cognitive configuration) can be related to the landmark locations as they should actually appear on the map board (the objective configuration) using a bidimensional correlation coefficient (Tobler, 1965, 1976, 1977). Based on this measure the normal adult subjects from Columbus and Santa Barbara performed much better on the map model task than did the experimental subjects, the vast majority of whom located the pictures on the map board in configurations bearing little resemblance to the objective configuration.

In the route-sequencing task, the contrast subjects' estimates of landmark locations along each route were also far superior to the locational estimates of the experimental subjects. The average rank correlation between cognitive and objective landmark locations was .525 for the experimental (retarded) subjects and .900 for the contrast (normal) subjects. The experimental subjects, however, did *not* locate landmarks along all routes in a random fashion, all achieving a statistically significant sequencing of cues.

The level of cognitive development reached by a person can be evaluated via a selection of IQ, adaptive behavior, motivational, personal independence, and other performance tasks. For these subjects, the level of development was examined in relation to whether or not the experimental subjects had progressed to the stage of two-dimensional (survey-level) spatial knowledge. For example, significant positive correlations were found between the performance on the map board task and IQ scores, the cognitive portion (but not personal and social motivational domain, personal independence domain, or physical development domain) of the Adaptive Behavior Scale, and Wide Range Achievement tests (Richardson, 1982). These results suggest that individuals in the upper levels (mild or borderline) of retardation may have the mental capacity to construct survey knowledge cognitively from experiencing and interacting with the environment. The severely and moderately retarded subjects did not appear to have the ability to code, construct, and represent spatial experiences cognitively as survey knowledge. None of the severely or moderately retarded had map board cognitive configurations that were significantly congruent with objective reality, despite the fact that some of these subjects had lived in the neighborhood for as long as 2½ years.

5.4.6. Cognitive Distance

In the process of cognitive mapping, not only are the locational and connective properties of landmarks and paths learned, but information is also accumulated about their *relative* locations and connectivities. A critical component of relative location is spatial separation; this concept has generally become known by the term *cognitive distance* or *subject distance*. Examining the properties of cognitive distance has become a major research thrust in environmental cognition research.

Some of the earliest work on cognitive distances was undertaken in the consumer behavior area (Thompson, 1963). The aim of such work was to increase the power to explain store choice, and this effort usually took the form of incorporating a subjective distance estimate in a conventional gravity-type predictive model. Later research by Briggs (1969, 1973), Cadwallader (1975, 1981), Golledge (1967), Golledge et al., (1969), Lowrey (1973), and MacKay, Olshavsky, and Sentell (1975) confirmed the significance of the subjective evaluation of distance or proximity. Obviously, a critical component of this work concerned the type of transformation used to estimate subjective distance or to convert objective to subjective distance. Many studies (Allen, Kirasic, Siegel, & Herman (1979); Briggs, 1972; Ericksen, 1975; Lowery, 1973; Thorndyke, 1981) supported Stevens's (1957) contention that a power function was the most appropriate transformation. Both Day (1976) and Cadwallader (1979), however, argue that the type of function found was significantly influenced by the measurement procedure used to elicit the subjective estimates. Of further importance was whether the objective and subjective distances were measured in metric or nonmetric units (e.g., linear measures vs. proximity judgments) and the type of criterion used in the estimation process, particularly whether spatial, temporal, social, or functional separation was being considered (Brown & Longbrake, 1969; Brown, Odland, & Golledge, 1972; Golledge et al., 1969).

Early investigations of cognitive distance produced some apparently contradictory results. For example, Lee (1962) found that outward distances from the center of the city of Dundee were overestimated more than inward distances, while Briggs (1972), Erickson (1975), and Golledge et al. (1969) found that distances *toward* downtown were overestimated while those toward the periphery were *underestimated*. Reasons for the apparent differences were related to the size and functional complexity of the cities in question—that is, they varied with qualities of the built environment.

Other research has focused on sex differences in the cognition of distance (Lee, 1970), the effect of intervening barriers (Lowrey, 1973), the influence of curves or bends (Briggs, 1972), and asymmetries in distance estimates (Burroughs & Sadalla, 1979; Sadalla & Staplin, 1980a). The use of noneuclidean metrics to represent spatial separation has been investigated by Richardson (1980) and Spector (1978), while Baird et al. (1981), Golledge and Hubert, (1982), and Tobler (1976) have speculated on the so-called "impossible" cognitive spaces and various curved and elliptical spaces. Like Briggs (1972) and Böök and Gärling (1980), Sadalla and Staplin (1980a) considered distance estimates under conditions of visible or invisible end points, and line lengths around curves, 90° turns, and along straightaways between well-known or less well-known end points. In this latter context, Golledge (1978) suggests that the cognitive distance between points in space will depend on their position in a hierarchical ordering of knowledge. For example, the distance between two primary nodes in a person's knowledge structure may be well known and adequately represented in standard metric terms. The distance between lower-order nodes tied to a single primary node may also be well represented. However, the distances between minor-order nodes that are tied to separate primary nodes may become substantially distorted; this is more likely to be the case if the primary nodes themselves are distorted or not adequately represented one in relation to the other.

In the continuing tradition of research on cognitive distance, Thorndyke (1981) had subjects estimate distances between pairs of points on memorized maps. He found that the estimation of distances between pairs of points increased with the linear function of the number of intervening points along the route. The results verified earlier empirical work (Briggs, 1973; Lowrey, 1973) demonstrating that a power function (relating true to estimated distance) is an appropriate one. Similar results can be found in Allen (1981), MacEachren (1980), and Sadalla and Magel (1980). An up-to-date review of research in this area is also contained in Gärling (1983).

Since cognitive distance has always been considered a critical component of cognitive mapping, it is important to realize that this measure frequently violates one or more of the standard axioms of metricity. That is,

1. $a_{ii} = 0$ (identity or reflexivity)
2. $a_{ij} = a_{ji}$ (symmetry)
3. $a_{ij} \leq a_{ik} + a_{jk}$ (triangle inequality)

Following suggestions by Tobler (1976), Cadwallader (1979) and Burroughs and Sadalla (1979) have focused on problems of triangle inequality, translation invariance, and asymmetry (respectively) (axioms 2 and 3 above). The significance of cognitive distance and its role in estimates of angular direction and orientation knowledge will be covered in a later section. Other topics of continued research importance in this area include examining the cultural context of distance estimates, the effect of development on interpoint distance estimation, and the metric bases of such estimates.

5.4.7. Orientation and Frames of Reference

Human spatial orientation implies an ability to recognize self in relation to sets of points or reference systems existing in the general cognitive map of an area (Howard & Templeton, 1966). In other words, human spatial orientation is defined as "the perception of one's position relative to the environment" (Gärling, Böök, & Lindberg, 1982, p. 43). Note particularly that in spatial orientation the reference points may or may not occur within a visual perceptual field. Thus a distinction is drawn between the process of space perception and environmental orientation (Beaumont, Gray, More, & Robinson, 1974; More, 1975b). Although Attneave and Pierce (1978) found no important differences between space perception and environmental orientation at small scales, this lack of difference may not hold as the spatial scale of a task situation changes. If, for example, one assumes that both the environmental orientation and the perceptual space are metrically euclidean, one need not expect to find major differences between experiments focusing on either procedure. The uncertainty as to whether the two cognitive spaces generally are either metric or euclidean, however, makes one less likely to accept the validity of this equivalence as spatial scale changes (Pick & Acredolo, 1983).

There is a fundamental dispute in the literature on environmental knowing and cognitive representations as to whether mental representations of space are propositional or analog in nature (see Norman & Rummelhart, 1975; Pylyshyn, 1973, 1979, 1981). Regardless of position, a most important question concerns the operations that can be carried out on mental representations and whether these operations are like those that can be carried out in perception. Pick (undated) points out a distinction in mental representations between perceptual relevant representations and motor relevant representations. Motor relevant representations would be equivalent to sets of directions for getting around a space and would be sequential in nature. It might be difficult to make spatial inferences on the basis of such representations. Mental rotation would be more difficult but reversibility would be possible. It seems likely that motor relevant representations would be generated when perceptual orientation was maintained by an egocentric reference system and perceptual relevant representations could be constructed on the basis of orientation through geographical reference systems. To the extent that children seemed to orient themselves in an environment on the basis of increasingly remote geographical frames of reference, they would over time be developing more perceptual relevant representations. Generally, the more remote the frame of reference the more stable it is likely to be, for example, chairs in a room (micro-) as opposed to houses on a block, or street intersections in a city (macro-spatial representations).

A critical aspect of environmental cognition then is the problem of how we keep track of the location of things when our body coordinates continually undergo change. Some recent research in cognitive theory suggests that locations of objects with respect to one's body coordinates are represented directly in propositional form. In this situation, however, even a simple rotation of self in environment would require many of the propositions to be changed in order to keep up with the internal representation of data. Continual movements would consequently require the continuous monitoring of all such spatial propositions. Hintzman and colleagues (1981) suggest that orientation with respect to body coordinates would seem to be an unlikely mechanism for keeping track of where things are.

With respect to orientation, Hintzman and colleagues (1981) offer a hypothesis that assumes that subjects directly locate the origin and the target in memory, activate the shortest route between them, and then sequentially span this potential route to determine a correct response. They also point to the unsatisfactory nature of some theories in that they do not account for mechanisms whereby spatial relations not already directly represented by memory can be inferred from other relations—a critical part of survey-level knowledge. Other articles by Briggs (1972), Byrne (1979), and Stevens and Coupe (1978) tend to support the Hintzman and colleagues observations.

When a person moves in space, all parts of the environment simultaneously undergo changes in direction and distance to and from her or him according to a family of transformation functions determined by his or her locomotion path. While much of the literature on environmental cognition focuses on the relative stability of key elements of this ever-changing environment (anchorpoints) that are probably well remembered and whose spatial relations are probably well understood, one must also posit that mechanisms exist that update internally represented locations by compensating for movement and rotation. Otherwise, a person could not in general relate to out-of-sight locations even if it was possible to remember how these locations were related to himself or herself. This problem is exacerbated in situations of unfamiliar environments (Böök & Gärling, 1978; Gärling et al., 1983; Lindberg & Gärling, 1977).

In the context of cognitive mapping and orientation, Böök and Gärling (1980) pointed out that an important function of a cognitive map is simply to make it possible to infer the location of reference points not in sight. They argued, therefore, that one way of studying the acquisition of such information would be to investigate to what extent maintenance of orientation relative to such points improves with repeated exposure to an initially unfamiliar path environment. In general their report emphasizes that acquisition of a cognitive map of any particular environment through which one moves repeatedly can be defined as the increase in long-term stored information that improves the ability of a subject to recognize reference points in sight (e.g., landmarks) and allows him or her to implement direction changes associated with locomoting through the environment even though new destination points or reference points are not in sight.

5.5 METHODOLOGIES

5.5.1. Overview of Methods

The literature on environmental cognition abounds with tasks that have been used to collect information (see Figure 5.5). As early as 1894, Binet asked subjects to introspect; Brown (1932) required maze learning, as did Tolman (1932, 1948); Lynch (1960) suggested the use of sketch map techniques; Appleyard (1969) used sketch map procedures and some resulting topological clusterings to categorize such mappings; Piaget and Inhelder (1967) asked subjects to image scenes from different perspectives; Milgram and colleagues (1972) asked subjects to recognize city scenes; Golledge and colleagues (1969) used multidimensional scaling of paired interpoint distance judgments; Briggs (1972) used the linear scaling of interpoint distance judgments; Attneave and Farrah (1977) asked subjects to judge locations and orientation of objects placed behind the head; Kozlowski and Bryant (1977) required subjects to image unseen objects; Byrne (1979) asked for estimates for lengths of streets and the angles for intersections; Golledge and Spector (1976) combined scaling and category grouping methods to obtain judgments of interpoint proximities; Baird (1979) required subjects to interact with a computer in order to develop configurations of places; Blaut and colleagues (1970) used toy play with children; Golledge, Parnicky, and Rayner (1980) used photos of places located on a map board by both borderline retarded and normal subjects, and so on.

Regardless of the particular task environment, most researchers experience situations in which there is a transition of information from declarative knowledge of discrete places, things, or events to node and path sequencing and to more or less completely integrated spatial representations including characteristics such as distance, direction, orientation, proximity, clustering, and hierarchial order.

The search for the most appropriate way to represent stored spatial information externally has occupied many researchers over the past decade. Building on the sketch maps and verbal protocols of spatial experience used in early research (Appleyard, 1970; Ladd, 1970; Lynch, 1960; Piaget, Inhelder, &

Czeminska, 1960), researchers began experimenting with a host of other representational forms as they realized that developmental differences in spatial abilities and differences in verbal and drawing skills were confounding such tasks. Alternative methods include the constructive use of models and toy play with children (Blaut & Stea, 1970; Siegel & Schadler, 1977) and the use of two- and three-dimensional models with normal and borderline retarded adults (Golledge, Parnicky & Rayner, 1980; Richardson, 1982; Zannaras, 1973, 1976).

The initial problems associated with sketch mapping procedures, which later attempts were designed to overcome, were: (1) the assumption that the subject—whether child, adult, or retarded person—understood the abstract notion of a model and its relation to the real world and (2) the initial difficulty of translating cognized spatial information from large to small scales (Siegel, Herman, Allen, & Kirasic, 1979). Recent research by Golledge, Smith, Pellegrino, Doherty, and Marshall (1983) has emphasized the relative advantages of on-site recall and slide identification (in a mobile laboratory) over sketch mapping by showing considerable lags between the trial in which a feature is first remembered or recognized and the trial in which it first appears on sketches.

5.5.2 Task Environments—Natural and Laboratory

While it is now possible to recover with a great deal of confidence the different types of directional and distance error that appear on externalized representations (Gale, 1980, 1983; Golledge & Tobler, 1982), the question of what exactly produces the distortion (e.g., lack of knowledge, inappropriate internal referencing, scale transformation difficulty) has not been fully explored. Herman and Siegel (1978) conducted experiments in which task environment and model were both experienced and reconstructed at the same scale. Again, however, problems are evident in terms of removing the task environment from the larger one in which it is imbedded. Recent innovative attempts by researchers such as Evans (1982) have used an environmental simulator as the model of the task environment. Experiments with children's and adults' way-finding activities in natural environments coupled with on-site mobile laboratory testing and off-site laboratory testing of cue recognition and sequencing (Doherty, 1984; Golledge, Smith, Pellegrino, Doherty, & Marshall, 1983; Shute, 1984) appear to throw important light on these processes by

METHOD	TASK ENVIRONMENT	PROCEDURE	EXTERNAL REPRESENTATION FORM	EXAMPLES
EXPERIMENTER OBSERVATION OF ACTUAL SUBJECT RESPONSES	NATURALISTIC OR RURAL SETTINGS	EXPERIMENTER OBSERVES OR TRACKS MOVEMENTS THROUGH ACTUAL ENVIRONMENTS - WILDERNESS, RURAL, NATIONAL PARKS, URBAN NATURE AREAS.	VERBAL REPORTS; SLIDES; VIDEO TAPES; SKETCH MAPS, ANALYTICAL TABLES.	R. KAPLAN (1976, 1983) DEVLIN (1976) HERZOG ET. AL (1982) STANKEY (1973) HART (1979) HAMMITT (1980, 1982)
	NATURALISTIC AND BUILT URBAN SETTINGS	EXPERIMENTER OBSERVES OR TRACKS MOVEMENTS THROUGH ACTUAL URBAN ENVIRONMENTS - USING DIFFERENT TRANSPORT MODES, LAND USE MODES, LAND USE TYPES AND TRIP PURPOSES.	WAY FINDING MAPS; SKETCHES; VERBAL RECALL; DISTANCE AND/OR DIRECTIONAL SCALINGS; ANALYTICAL TABLES.	JONES (1972) ZANNARAS (1973) DOHERTY (1984) SHUTE (1984)
	LABORATORY SETTINGS BASED ON ACTUAL ENVIRONMENTS	EXAMINATION OF RECOGNITION FREQUENCY, RESPONSE TIMES, PRIMING AND CONTEXT EFFECTS OF SLIDES, VIDEO TAPES, MOVIES, VIDEO DISKS; SKETCHES OF CUE LOCATION; ENVIRONMENTAL SIMULATORS.	REPONSE LATENCIES; CUE RECALL FREQUENCIES; PATHS AND STRUCTURES IDENTIFICATION; VERBAL INSTRUCTIONS REGARDING CONTENT OR ACTIONS.	EVANS (1981) GOLLEDGE ET. AL (1984) FOLEY (1979) THORNDYKE (1980)
	MAP OR BOARD MODELS OF REAL, IDEAL, OR HYPOTHETICAL ENVIRONMENTS.	SUBJECT CREATES PATTERN ON A MODEL; SUBJECT INTERPRETS OR USES PATTERN GIVEN IN EXPERIMENTAL MODEL; SEQUENCES AND/OR CONNECTIVITIES; IDEAL STATES.	2 OR 3 DIMENSIONAL MODEL OF TASK SITUATION; ABSTRACT AND/OR SYMBOLIC REPRESENTATION OF ENVIRONMENTAL ELEMENTS AND STRUCTURES; BASE MAP OVERLAYS.	ACREDOLO (1978) BLAUT AND STEA (1969) ZANNARAS (1973) GOLLEDGE ET. AL. (1979;1980) MARK AND SILVERMAN (1971) HART (1976)
INDIRECT JUDGEMENTS	LABORATORY OR IN-HOME	ELICITING VERBAL CONSTRUCTS; ADJECTIVAL CHECK LISTS; SEMANTIC DIFFERENTIALS.	FACTOR OR COMPONENT SCORES; CONSTRUCT FREQUENCIES; REPERTORY GRIDS.	BANNISTER (1973) HONIKMAN (1976) WARD AND RUSSELL (1981) RUSSELL ET. AL. (1981)
		PROXIMITY JUDGEMENTS; LINEAR SEQUENCES; TOPOLOGICAL CLUSTERINGS; DEFINITION OF LATENT SPATIAL STRUCTURES.	COGNITIVE CONFIGURATIONS; MDS MAPPINGS; RANKED SEQUENCES; SIMILARITY AND CONFUSION MATRICES; COGNITIVE DISTANCE MEASURES.	GOLLEDGE ET. AL. (1975) GOLLEDGE (1978) RIVIZZIGNO (1976) SPECTOR (1978) PEZDEK AND EVANS (1979) EVANS AND MARRERO (1981) BAIRD (1979) BRIGGS (1973) STEVENS AND COUPE (1978)
		PROJECTIVE TESTS -- T.A.T.; ENVIRONMENTAL RESPONSE INVENTORY; CLINICAL TESTING.	VERBAL DESCRIPTIONS; ERI SCORES; SUBJECT PERFORMANCE PROFILES AND CHARTS.	SAARINEN (1973) MCKECKNIE (1977)
	LABORATORY OR NATURALISTIC SETTINGS	INFERENCES FROM EXPERIMENTS ON ANIMALS; MACHINE SIMULATION; COMPUTER MAPPING	MAZE OR PATH FINDING BEHAVIOR; LOCOMOTION THROUGH SIMULATED ENVIRONMENTS.	TOLMAN (1948) BAIRD ET. AL. (1979) EVANS ET. AL. (1983) PETERS (1973) KUIPERS (1980)

Figure 5.5. Table showing some of the tasks that have been used to collect information.

158

METHOD	TASK ENVIRONMENT	PROCEDURE	EXTERNAL REPRESENTATION FORM	EXAMPLES
HISTORICAL RECONSTRUCTION	LIBRARIES, ARCHIVES, PERSONAL SPECIAL COLLECTIONS.	EXAMINATION OF WRITTEN DOCUMENTS, ART, NOVELS, POETRY, FILMS, STATISTICAL MATERIAL OR OTHER ARCHIVED SOURCES.	PAINTINGS; POEMS; NOVELS; LETTERS; GOVERNMENT DOCUMENTS; MOVIES.	TUAN (1976, 1978) SEAMON (1980) LOWENTHAL AND PRINCE (1964) HEATHCOTE (1965) BOWDEN (1975)
		PERSONAL, ORAL, WRITTEN OR SKETCHED RECONSTRUCTIONS BASED ON MEMORY AND EXPERIENCE OF ACTUAL OR IMAGINED ENVIRONMENTS.	ITEM AND CONTENT ANALYSES; MAPPINGS; CREATIVE OR ANALYTICAL WRITINGS.	TROWBRIDGE (1913) WRIGHT (1968) LOWENTHAL (1960) LYNCH AND RIVKIN (1959)
SUBJECT PARTICIPATION	WITHIN BUILDINGS	WAYFINDING, LOCATIONAL AND DIRECTIONAL/ ORIENTATION TASKS; ROLE PLAYING; TOY PLAY AND MODEL BUILDING.	ROUTE MAPS; YAH MAPS AND POINTERS; VERBAL PROTOCOLS; 3-D MODELS; TOY CONFIGURATIONS.	THORNDYKE (1980) GARLING ET. AL. (1979) ITTELSON (1960) SAEGERT (1973)
	NEIGHBORHOOD	WAYFINDING, LOCATION OF CUES; HOME RANGE DEFINITION; PROXIMITY JUDGEMENTS; DISTANCE COGNITION; MAP OR BOARD MODELLING.	ROUTE MAPS; PERCEPTUAL NEIGHBORHOODS; MDS CONFIGURATIONS OF CUES; SUBJECTIVE-OBJECTIVE DISTANCE TRANSFORMS; VERBAL PROTOCOLS; NEIGHBORHOOD MODELS IN 2 OR 3-D.	ZANNARAS (1969) T. LEE (1964) LADD (1970) GOLLEDGE ET. AL. (1984) SHEMYAKIN (1963) BRIGGS (1973) OHTA AND KRAUSSE (1978) EVANS ET. AL. (1984)
	CITIES	WAYFINDING; CUE PROXIMITY JUDGEMENTS; SKETCH MAPPING; CARTOGRAPHIC CONSTRUCTION; VERBAL DESCRIPTIONS; GROUPING/ SORTING CUES; MODEL BUILDING OR USE.	TIME-SPACE PRISMS; SKETCHES; SETS OF TRAVEL DIRECTIONS; MDS CONFIGURATIONS; TOPOLOGICAL OR METRIC REPRESENTATION OF KEY ELEMENTS; DISTORTION VECTORS, ERROR ELLIPSES; CPM AND AI COMPUTER PROGRAMS; MAPBOARD MODELS; WAYFINDING MOVIES.	CARR AND SCHISSLER (1969) HAGERSTRAND (1970) APPLEYARD (1969,1970) GOLLEDGE ET. AL. (1978,1980) GALE (1980) RICHARDSON (1982) TOBLER (1976, 1977) T. SMITH ET. AL. (1982) SPECTOR (1978) RIVIZZIGNO (1976)
	REGIONS AND LARGER SCALES	LOCATION AND DISTANCE ESTIMATES; PAIRED OR OTHER COMPARISONS; SKETCHES; SIMILARITY AND FAMILIARITY RATINGS; STEREOTYPING; CROSS CULTURAL COMPARISONS.	MDS CONFIGURATIONS; SPACE TRANSFORMS (EG VIEW OF THE US); NATIONAL STEREOTYPING; STRUCTURAL GROUPINGS OR CLUSTERINGS.	COX AND ZANNARAS (1973) BRATFISH (1969) RIVIZZIGNO (1976)

Figure 5.5. (*Continued*)

examining the effects of context and priming on cue recognition tasks.

Photographic simulation, usually consisting of single slides or pairs of slides, has also been used successfully in both a route and a survey context (Allen, Siegel, & Rosinski, 1978; Golledge, Parnicky, & Rayner, 1979b; Zannaras, 1973). In conjunction with photographic presentation, techniques such as paired comparisons, category sorting, similarity judgments, proximity judgments, and triadic comparisons have been used in environmental cognition research. Analytically, both metric and nonmetric multidimensional scaling procedures have proved feasible and valuable (Baird, 1979; Briggs, 1972; Golledge, 1975, 1976, 1977, 1978; Golledge & Rushton, 1973; Golledge & Spector, 1978; Golledge & Zannaras, 1973; Kosslyn et al., 1974; Rivizzigno, 1975; Sadalla & Burroughs, 1980; Spector, 1978; etc.). Other multidimensional techniques such as cluster analysis (Golledge et al., 1975a; Rivizzigno, 1975), two-dimensional spectral analysis (Golledge, Rayner, & Rivizzigno, 1982), and trilateration (Gale & Costanzo, 1982; Golledge & Rushton, 1973; Tobler, 1967), have all been used to represent cognitive spatial information externally. In the context of orientation experiments, triangulation (Hardwick, McIntyre, & Pick, 1976)—a technique used in geography, cartography, and surveying for several centuries (Tobler,

1982)—has recently been utilized in the context of obtaining directional estimates from three set locations to multiple targets in a small scale task environment.

In a procedure similar to the imaginative toy play procedures used by Blaut and Stea (1971) and Hart (1977), Baird and Wagner (1983) asked students to move pieces labeled with building names around a board in such a way as to represent on the board the spatial relations of buildings on a campus. Map distances between locations were averaged across the entire student set to produce a data matrix of interpoint distances that was then analyzed via multidimensional scaling and cluster analysis to produce a generalized cognitive map for the entire sample population (Sheppard, 1972; Sheppard & Romney, 1972).

In other types of experiments, Baird, Deguman, Paris, and Noma (1972) had previously showed that students were very accurate in their judgment of spatial relations among campus buildings. Nagy and Baird (1978) indicated that sixth graders were adept at reconstructing model configurations of items in their playground. Sherman, Croxton, and Giovanatto (1979) found that the exponent of the power function relating judged distances to actual distances is greater when the experiment is based on paired estimates (magnitude estimation) than when based on map board-type experiments, although the experiments of Baird and colleagues (1979) do not support these generalizations. Siegel and Schadler (1977) report that kindergarten children were capable of locating objects in their classroom from memory but tended to cluster subgroups of objects, and while the internal spatial relational developments of the clusters were consistent with reality, the positioning and relations of the clusters one to another were not as well conceptualized.

5.5.3. Analysis of Spatial and Structural Properties

While Lynch and Appleyard in particular focused on the content and some *elemental* properties of cognitive maps, there was, for a long period of time, little emphasis on their peculiar spatial and structural properties. The last decade, however, has seen geographers, and psychologists in particular, applying a range of sophisticated methodologies to help analyze spatial data recovered from the knowledge structure of individuals (Baird, 1979; Baird et al., 1972; Golledge, 1975, 1976, 1977; Tobler, 1976). Such methodologies have supported the fact that strong inferences can be made about the spatial properties of cognitive maps although there is increasing evidence that any given representation may encompass a variety of metric and nonmetric sets of information. For example, some people prove to be amazingly accurate in remembering essential elements of the spatial layout of large-scale environments with which they are familiar (Evans et al., 1981; Gärling, Böök, & Ergezen, 1982; Golledge et al., 1969; Golledge & Spector, 1978). However, a considerable quantity of evidence also indicates that at least some parts of cognitive maps are usually spatially distorted (Byrne, 1979; Canter & Tagg, 1975; Gale, 1980; Golledge & Hubert, 1982; Golledge, Parnicky, & Rayner, 1980; Golledge & Tobler, 1983; Richardson, 1981). Thus, depending on the task situation, familiarity of the subject with the task environment, the degree of interaction between the individual and environment, and so on, cognitive maps may be more or less schematized and may incorporate fully metric knowledge to a greater or lesser extent. As Tversky (1981) argues, there is an extremely large quantity of information that is stored about any given environment, and at this stage we can only imagine that simplifying heuristics condition the way we access and externally represent our spatial knowledge structures. What seems to be needed is the use of converging methods that both help understand environmental cognition processes and help overcome some of the limitations inherent in each separate methodology (e.g., see Evans, 1980; Golledge & Rushton 1976).

5.5.4. Error

While one segment of the literature in this area continues to argue about the way information is stored, represented, and accessed (see earlier sections on information processing and artificial intelligence), another segment of the literature assumes that spatial information is stored "in some way" and concentrates on externally representing such information. In other words, the main problem is directly or indirectly to obtain information about spatial knowledge from individuals, to represent that information in an appropriate form, and thence to examine properties such as location, distance, or directional errors.

The whole question of error is still very much an open one, and for the most part it is tied to specific representational formats. For example, Golledge and Spector (1978) examined error in the general configuration sense by using bidimensional correlation (Tobler, 1976) to compare configurations from multidimensional scaling analysis with configurations of actual locations plotted in two-dimensional euclidean space. They also examined location errors associated with each particular cue, where location was measured purely as a distance displacement vector and regressed against individual characteristics of subjects, their activity spaces, and environmental and locational characteristics. MacKay (1976) pointed to the general complexity of the question of error, thus echoing earlier sentiments expressed by psychologists such as Spence, Young, and Green at an interdisciplinary seminar in 1975 (see Golledge & Rayner, 1982) and geographers such as Tobler (1976). Recent work by Gale (1980, 1983) has distinguished between distortion and fuzziness components of error, with distortion being defined as the deviation of a cognized location from an actual location, while fuzziness is interpreted as the variance in the set of cognized locations of a cue across a population subgroup (see Figure 5.6). Thus distortion is seen as an accuracy component and fuzziness is seen as a precision component of error.

There appears to be substantial evidence (Golledge & Rayner, 1976; Golledge, Parnicky, & Rayner, 1979a, 1979b, 1980) that error varies differentially across a cognized area and that one may expect disruptions to occur in the knowledge fabric of a place. Such interruptions appear to be almost a logical outcome of things such as asymmetric distance judgments (Sadalla & Staplin, 1980), spatial applications of the power function for distance distortion (Briggs, 1972), and translation invariance and triangle equality violations (Cadwallader, 1979; Burroughs & Sadalla, 1979). In addition there appears to be some conflict over the preservation of fully metric properties of cognitive information (Golledge & Spector, 1978; Kosslyn, Bowle, & Reiser, 1978; Richardson, 1981) with varying evidence supporting hypotheses of euclidean properties, other Minkowskian properties (e.g., city block metric), hyperbolic spaces (Baird et al., 1981), and various nonmetric spaces (Golledge & Hubert, 1982; Tobler, 1976). However, assuming a euclidean metric allows one to summarize peculiar properties of individual and group configurations by using simple warped grids to illustrate the nature of distortion that occurs on a given cognitive representation (Beck & Wood, 1976a, 1976b; Golledge et al., 1975a).

Obviously, some of the finer displacements and distortions cannot be shown on the relatively coarse grids used in these experiments. Although each simplified grid has its own distinctive pattern of distortion. Rivizzigno (1976) found that there were sev-

eral striking similarities that were repeated among many group members. For example, many grids indicate a pronounced exaggeration of shorter distances; for many others, there is a sectoral exaggeration of interpoint distances; others show a typical "fish-eye lens" type of distortion (see Figure 5.2, example III). All these distortions may result at least in part from the representational mode chosen for eliciting information from individuals, and of course may be repudiated by subjects if they were faced with such a map and asked, "Is this what your city image really looks like?"

Like other studies of city images, the results described provide evidence that people's knowledge structures are much as we expected—incomplete, schematized, having holes representing places of little or no knowledge, and with places of greatest interaction being represented most confidently and most faithfully. Most of the maps reflect some common characteristics of spatial cognitions such as overestimation of close or well-known distances and underestimation of the distances apart of places that are further away or less known. The information contained in the maps also indicates that there are pronounced local effects (in that knowledge peaks exist around well-known places), and that a "knowledge surface" declines exponentially away from these places—but not equally in all directions. Obviously, also, there are more precise measures of distortion, disturbance, or error than can be encompassed by these simple grid distortions and street map transformations.

5.5.5. Matching Objective and Subjective Configurations

Given that it is possible to obtain an externalized configuration that is assumed to reflect an internal representation of the location of certain phenomena in the environment, it then becomes of interest to ask how such a configuration relates to an objective or "real" configuration. In other words, is there any correspondence between what is "out there" (as measured and portrayed by conventional techniques) and what can be reconstructed from the image of the world inside an individual's mind?

To answer this question one may take several approaches and use a variety of analytical techniques. Obviously the method chosen in any given problem situation depends on how the task is defined by the researcher and what output is expected. There is abundant evidence that carefully controlled experiments will provide valid and reliable data and will

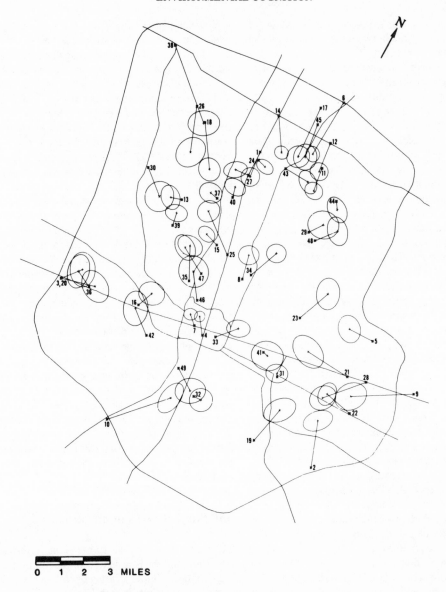

0 1 2 3 MILES

* **MAP LOCATION**
\+ **MEAN CENTER OF ESTIMATES**

Figure 5.6. Composite cognitive configuration with vectors representing average landmark displacements and error ellipses representing locational variances.

allow the researcher to choose the most appropriate analytical tools for obtaining and interpreting results. Methods of scientific experimentation and consequent statistical analysis appear to be giving useful information on what properties of mappings, judgments, toy play, recall, or other methods are commonly interpretable. The use of parallel experiments and converging methodologies have provided hard scientific evidence of cognitive map properties and have laid the foundations for many of the commonly accepted generalizations about the environmental cognition process. Future researchers should be aware that controversy still exists over the relative merits of different methods for representing and interpreting cognitive information, and researchers should be prepared to defend the appropriateness of whatever method(s) they select.

5.6. SUMMARY: PROBLEMS AND PROSPECTS

Although almost two decades of research have passed since the publication of Lynch's seminal work on city images, the academic investigation of environmental cognition is still in its infancy. This is not surprising since, while many of the cognitive variables examined by researchers interested in things such as the city of the mind had been developed, defined, and measured at a microscale or in a laboratory context in fields such as psychology or economics, their verification, validation, and measurement at large scale such as the uncontrolled, complex internal–external environments with which other disciplines traditionally deal, had not been achieved. In a very real sense, most researchers have had to start from scratch. Starting from scratch involved examining cognitive concepts to see whether they had spatial relevance; examining existing behavioral theory to see whether it contributed to the understanding of environmental knowing; attempting to see whether information about complex large-scale environments could possibly be recovered from individuals, developing appropriate experimental designs for the collection of meaningful data concerning environmental cognitions, and developing or adapting existing methodologies for the external representation of subjective information and for analyzing its properties. While all these problems have not been effectively solved, many of them have been given substantial attention. For example, while the concept of a mental map was raised originally by Tolman in the psychology literature in 1948, it had, until the development of behavioral research in geography, no geographic or cartographic counterpart. Whether or not cognitive images were maplike in form and propositional in content, and whether people could externalize cognitive information in schematic maplike form, were completely unknown.

It has taken a substantial number of isolated individual studies of these phenomena to get to the point where some general conclusions can be drawn about the external representation of cognitive information and some degree of confidence can be given to the nature of the information so represented (Downs &

Stea, 1973, 1977; Evans, 1980; Kuipers, 1978). For example, focusing on "image" is a part of the process of explaining spatial behavior. If one cannot define, measure, or represent an image, one cannot include it in any way in an explanatory schema. Therefore, before one can accept a premise that "image" is a relevant concept, one has to have confidence in the attempts to obtain data on it, measure it, and/or represent it. The last decade in particular has seen numerous attempts to measure and represent such images via means such as sketch mapping, verbal descriptions, model manipulation, interpoint distance judgments, and so on. There still appears at this stage to be no consensus as to the most appropriate way of externally representing image information, but there is increasing evidence of the close coincidence of many techniques (Baird, 1979; Richardson, 1981).

While this chapter has concentrated to a large extent on showing that it appears possible to access and to represent cognitive information externally, it is also apparent that we may not have reached the stage of being able to recover the full meaning of such a cognitive representation. For example, many of the problems associated with representing cognitive information in cartographic form are the same problems that surfaced in interpreting the original sketch maps suggested by early researchers. Just as the sketches may be incomplete, have holes, folds, cracks, tears, and so on, or may in part incorporate ordinal information whereas in other parts they may be fully metric, the attempt to represent cognitive information cartographically can suffer from the same problems. Recent investigations of cognitive images have focused on questions such as the suitability of using euclidean distance measures in *any* representational device (Golledge & Hubert, 1982; Richardson, 1979; Tobler, 1976). Obviously, the question of how best to represent cognitive information has not been solved. Recent experiments in cognitive science and artificial intelligence are even now suggesting alternate ways for representing such information (Hayes-Roth, 1979; Smith et al., 1982). Other problems that occur with considerable frequency in analyzing cognitive images are things such as asymmetry of distance relations, incompleteness of information sets, lack of metricity, a mixture of topological and full metric information within the same broad area, unreliability of data obtained from subjects, poor validation of methods for extracting data, and selection of the most appropriate experiments/designs and analytic methods for working with subjective data.

The problems mentioned in the preceding paragraphs are primarily oriented to the extraction and/or representation of image data. There are many other unsolved problems associated with work in this area, and these unsolved problems should provide exciting prospects for future work. For example, the nature of the relationship between cognitive images and actual spatial behavior still remains a vastly underresearched area. A growing mass of work in psychology and some work in geography have indicated that the two appear to be strongly connected. But more evidence needs to be collected before we have sufficient faith that this type of premise is suitable as a base for explanations and understandings of spatial phenomena. A second problem, which again details an existing area for future research, concerns the process of acquiring spatial knowledge. At this stage there is considerable speculation concerning how information is selected, attended to, coded, structured, stored, and represented in the mind. Relevant questions concern the role of experience, familiarity, and environmental interaction in the construction and maintenance of this basic knowledge structure.

Another important research question has recently been raised by Kuipers (1983), who suggests that cognitive spatial information may be more like an atlas than a map. At each scale and within each separate frame of reference, different metric information may be stored. Thus a range of different types of distortions may be present, some of which are related to conventional measurement properties such as distance and direction, some of which can only be related through topological properties, and some of which must go through extensive transformations before any type of comparison or matching process might take place.

Kuipers argues that a major aim of current research should be to find a common basis for expressing the mechanism that produces different kinds of behaviors. He suggests that computational process models may be a productive way of viewing cognitive processing because they are based on the strong analogy between cognitive processes and computational processes. Thus he suggests that research in artificial intelligence, the home of computational process model, is an appropriate way to describe both complex data structure and sets of associated procedures that together make up the full description of decision processes and consequent behaviors. Other researchers see continued explorations into the possibility of hemispheric control of spatial activities as a fruitful line of research, while many others would argue that the most pressing problem is to explicate fully the relationship of cognition and affect.

Perhaps the fundamental question that all researchers would raise and that has barely been touched is: How do variations in the environment itself influence the nature of cue selection and the storage of environmental information (see Evans et al., 1981; Wohlwill, 1973)? Are some environments more imageable than others? How complex need the environment be before it becomes overwhelming? And how do variations in the physical landscape or changing land use patterns affect cognitive images? Along with such questions is the fact that we have not adequately researched the problem of how variations of personal, social, and cultural characteristics of individuals affect cognitive images. We have had some evidence on the nature and role of historical, social, and cultural features on the selection of environmental information, but the general problem of determining the role of values and beliefs in forming environmental images has not been examined in great detail. Given the discussion of problems and prospects, one can see that there is much work still to be done on many aspects of environmental cognition. This should make it one of the more exciting areas of future interdisciplinary research.

Acknowledgments

The final draft of this chapter was completed after the author had lost his sight. He wishes gratefully to acknowledge the assistance of Nathan D. Gale, postdoctoral researcher in geography at U.C.S.B., for his willing and able assistance in editing the final draft of the manuscript and incorporating editorial and referees' suggestions into the final draft.

REFERENCES

Acredolo, L.P. (1976). Frames of reference used by children for orientation in unfamiliar spaces. In G.T. Moore & R.G. Golledge (Eds.). *Environmental knowing,* Stroudsburg, PA: Dowden, Hutchinson, & Ross.

Acredolo, L.P. (1977). Developmental changes in the ability to coordinate perspectives of a large-scale space. *Developmental Psychology, 13,* 1–8.

Acredolo, L.P. (1978). Development of spatial orientation in infancy. *Developmental Psychology, 14,* 224–234.

Acredolo, L.P. (1979, May). *Small and large scale spatial concepts in infancy and childhood.* Paper presented at the Conference in Spatial Representation and Behavior Across a Life Span, Pennsylvania State University, University Park.

Acredolo, L.P. (1981). Small- and large-scale spatial concepts in infancy and childhood. In L. Liben, A. Patterson, & N. Newcombe (Eds.), *Spatial representations and behavior across the life span: Theory and application.* New York: Academic.

Acredolo, L.P. (1982, March). The familiarity factor in spatial research. In R. Cohen (Ed.), *New directions for child development: Children's conception of spatial relationships* (No. 15). San Francisco: Jossey-Bass.

Acredolo, L.P. (1983). Coordinating perspectives on infant spatial orientation. In R. Cohen (Ed.), *Development of spatial cognition.* Hillsdale, NJ: Earlbaum.

Acredolo, L.P., Pick, H.L., & Olsen, M.G. (1975). Environmental differentiation and familiarity as determinants of children's memory for spatial location. *Developmental Psychology, 11,* 495–501.

Allen, G.E., Kirasic, K.C., Siegel, A.W., & Herman, J.F., (1979). Developmental issues in cognitive mapping: The selection and utilization of environmental landmarks. *Child Development, 50,* 1062–1070.

Allen, G.L. (1981). A developmental perspective on the effects of subdividing macrospatial experience. *Journal of Experimental Psychology: Human Learning and Theory, 7,* 120–152.

Allen, G.L., Siegel, A.W., & Rosinski, R.R. The role of perceptual context in structuring spatial knowledge. *Journal of Experimental Psychology: Human Learning & Memory, 4.*

Altman, I. (1975). *The environment and social behavior.* Monterey, CA: Brooks/Cole.

Altman, I., & Wohlwill, J.F. (1977). *Human behavior and environment* (Vol. 2). New York: Plenum.

Amedeo, D., & Golledge, R.G. (1975). *An introduction to scientific reasoning in geography.* New York: Wiley.

Anderson, J.R. (1978). Arguments concerning representations for mental imagery. *Psychological Review, 85,* 249–277.

Appleyard, D. (1969). Why buildings are known. *Environment and Behavior, 1,* 131.

Appleyard, D. (1970). Styles and methods of structuring a city. *Environment and Behavior, 2,* 100–118.

Appleyard, D. (1976). *Planning a pluralistic city.* Cambridge, MA: MIT Press.

Appleyard, D. (1979). The environment as a social symbol. *Journal of the American Planning Association, 45,* 143–153.

Attneave, F., & Pierce, C.R. (1978). Accuracy of extrapolating a pointer into perceived and imaged space. *American Journal of Psychology, 91,* 371–387.

Baird, J.C. (1979). Studies of the cognitive representation of spatial relations: An overview. *Journal of Experimental Psychology General, 108,* 90–91.

Baird, J.C., Degerman, R., Paris, R., & Noma, E. (1972). Student planning of town configurations. *Environment and Behavior, 4,* 159–188.

Baird, J.C., & Wagner, M. (1983). Modeling the creation of cognitive maps. In H. Pick and L. Acredolo (Eds.), *Spatial orientation.* New York: Plenum.

Baird, J.C., Wagner, M., & Noma, E. (1981). Impossible cognitive spaces. *Geographical Analysis, 14*(3), 204–216.

Bartlett, F. (1932). *Remembering.* Cambridge, England: Cambridge University Press.

Beaumont, P., Gray, J., Moore, G., & Robinson, B. (1984). Orientation and way-finding in the Tauranga department building: A focused post-occupancy evaluation. In *EDRA 1984, Proceedings of the Fifteenth International Conference of the Environmental Design Research Association* (pp. 77–90). San Luis Obispo, CA.

Beck, R.J., & Wood, D. (1976a). Cognitive transformation from urban geographic fields to mental maps. *Environment and Behavior, 8,* 199–238.

Beck, R.J., & Wood, D. (1976b). Comparative developmental analysis of individual and aggregated cognitive maps of London. In G.T. Moore and R.G. Golledge (Eds.), *Environmental knowing* (pp. 173–189). Stroudsburg, PA: Dowden, Hutchinson, & Ross.

Binet, M.A. (1894). Reverse illusions of orientation. *Psychology Review, 1,* 337–350.

Blaut, J.M., McCleary, G., & Blaut, A. (1970). Environmental mapping in young children. *Environment and Behavior, 2,* 335–349.

Blaut, J.M., & Stea, D. (1971). Studies of geographic learning. *Annals of the Association of American Geographers, 61*(2), 387–393.

Bobrow, D.A., & Norman, D.A. (1975). Some principles of memory schemata. In D.A. Bobrow & A. Collins (Eds.), *Representation and understanding.* New York: Academic.

Böök, A., & Gärling, T. (1978a). *Processing of information about location during locomotion: Effects of a concurrent task and locomotion patterns* (Umea Psychological Reports, No. 135). Umea, Sweden: University of Umea, Department of Psychology.

Böök, A., & Gärling, T. (1978b). *Processing of information about location during locomotion: Effects of amount of visual information about the location pattern* (Umea Psychological Reports, Vol. 136). Umea, Sweden: University of Umea, Department of Psychology.

Böök, A., & Gärling, T. (1980). Processing of information about location during locomotion: Effects of concurrent task and locomotion patterns. *Scandinavian Journal of Psychology, 21,* 185–192.

Böök, A., Gärling, T., & Lindberg, E. (1975). *Speed and accuracy of orientation performance in verbally presented two-segment route tasks as a function of directions of routes, length of route segments and angle of turn.* (Umea Psychological Reports, Vol. 92). Umea, Sweden: University of Umea, Department of Psychology.

Bower, G.H., & Cohen, P.R. (1981). *Emotional influences in memory and thinking.* Unpublished manuscript, Stanford University, Stanford, CA.

Bowers, D.S. (1973). Situationism in psychology: An analysis and a critique. *Psychological Review, 5,* 307–337.

Brachman, R.J. (1979). On the epistemological status of semantic networks. In N.J. Findler (Ed.), *Associative networks* (pp. 3–50). New York: Academic.

Briggs, R. (1969). Scaling of preferences for spatial locations: An example using shopping centers. Unpublished master's thesis, Ohio State University, Columbus.

Briggs, R. (1972). cognitive distance in urban space. Unpublished doctoral dissertation. Ohio State University, Columbus.

Briggs, R. (1973a). On the relationship between cognitive and objective distance. In W.F.E. Preiser (Ed.), *Environmental design research* (Vol. 2, p. 187) Stroudsburg, PA: Dowden, Hutchinson and Ross.

Briggs, R. (1973b). Urban cognitive distance. In R.M. Downs & D. Stea (Eds.), *Image and environment: Cognitive mapping and spatial behavior* (pp. 361–388). Chicago: Aldine.

Briggs, R. (1976). Methodologies for the measurement of cognitive distance. In G.T. Moore & R.G. Golledge (Eds.), *Environmental knowing.* Stroudsburg, PA: Dowden, Hutchinson, & Ross.

Brown, L.A., & Longbrake, D. (1970). Migration flows in intra-urban space: Place utility consideration. *Annals AA6, 60,* 368–389.

Brown, L.A., Odland, J., & Golledge, R.G. (1970). Migration functional distance of the urban hierarchy. *Economic Geography, 46*(3), 472–485.

Brown, W. (1932). Spatial integrations in a human maze. *University of California Publications in Psychology, 5,* 123–134.

Bruner, J.S. (1957). On going beyond the information given. In J.S. Burner (Ed.), *Contemporary approaches to cognition: A symposium* (pp. 41–69). Cambridge, MA: Harvard University Press.

Brunswik, E. (1944). Distal focusing of perception. *Psychological Monographs, 56,* 1–48.

Burroughs, W.J., and Sadalla, E.K. (1979). Asymmetries in distance cognition. *Geographical Analysis, 11*(14), 414–421.

Byrne, R. (1979). Memory for urban geography. *Quarterly Journal of Experimental Psychology, 31,* 147–154.

Cadwallader, M. (1975). A behavioral model of consumer spatial decision making. *Economic Geography, 51,* 339–349.

Cadwallader, M. (1976). Cognitive distance in intraurban space. In G.T. Moore & R.G. Golledge (Eds.), *Environmental knowing* (pp. 316–324). Stroudsburg, PA: Dowden, Hutchinson, & Ross.

Cadwallader, M. (1979). Problems in cognitive distance and their implications for cognitive mapping. *Environment and Behavior, 11,* 559–576.

Cadwallader, M. (1981). Towards a cognitive gravity model: The case of consumer spatial behavior. *Regional Studies, 15,* 275–284.

Canter, D.V. (1977). *The psychology of place.* London: Architectural Press.

Canter, D.V., & Tagg, S.K. (1975). Distance estimation in cities. *Environment and Behavior, 7,* 59–80.

Carr, S. (1967). The city of the mind. In W.R. Ewald, Jr. (Ed.), *Environment and man: The next fifty years* (pp. 197–231). Bloomington: Indiana University Press.

Carr, S., & Schissler, D. (1969). The city as a trip: Perceptual selection and memory in the view from the road. *Environment and Behavior, 1,* 7–35.

Cassirer, E. (1944). *An essay on man: An introduction to the philosophy of human culture.* New Haven, CT: Yale University Press.

Chapin, F.S., & Brail, R.K. (1969). Human activity systems in the metropolitan United States. *Environment and Behavior, 1,* 107–130.

Chase, W.G., & Chi, M.T.H. (1980). Cognitive skill: Implications for spatial skill in large-scale environments. In J. Harvey (Ed.), *Cognition, social behavior, and the environment.* Potomac, MD: Erlbaum.

Cohen, R. (Ed.). (1982). *The development of spatial cognition.* Hillsdale, NJ: Earlbaum.

Couclelis, H., & Golledge, R.G. (1983). Analytic research, positivism, and behavioral geography. *Annals of the Association of American Geographers, 73*(3), 331–339.

Cox, K.R., & Golledge, R.G. (Eds.). (1969). *Behavioral problems in geography: A symposium* (pp. 169–196). Evanston, IL: Northwestern University.

Cox, K.R., & Golledge, R.G. (Eds.). (1981). *Behavioral problems in geography revisited.* New York: Methuen.

Craik, K.H. (1970). Environmental psychology. In K.H. Craik et al. (Eds.), *New directions in psychology* (Vol. 4, pp. 1–121). New York: Holt, Rinehart & Winston.

Craik, K.H. (1973). Environmental psychology. *Annual Review of Psychology, 24,* 403–422.

Day, R.A. (1976). Urban distance cognition: Review and contribution. *Australian Geographer, 13,* 193–200.

De Jonge, D. (1962). Images of urban areas: Their structure and psychological foundations. *Journal of American Institute of Planners, 28,* 266–276.

Devlin, A. (1976). The small town cognitive map: Adjusting to a new environment. In G.T. Moore & R.G. Golledge (Eds.), *Environmental knowing* (pp. 58–66). Stroudsburg, PA: Dowden, Hutchinson, & Ross.

Doherty, S.E. (1984). *Developmental differences in cue recognition at spatial decision points.* Doctoral dissertation proposal, University of California, Santa Barbara.

Downs, R.M. (1970). The cognitive structure of an urban shopping center. *Environment and Behavior, 2,* 13–39.

Downs, R.M. (1976). Personal constructs of personal construct theory. In G.T. Moore & R.G. Golledge (Eds.), *Environmental knowing* (pp. 72–87). Stroudsburg, PA: Dowden, Hutchinson, & Ross.

Downs, R.M. (1981a). Maps and metaphors. *The Professional Geographer, 33*(3), 287–293.

Downs, R.M. (1981b). Maps and mappings as metaphors for spatial representation. In L. Liben, A. Patterson, &

N. Newcombe (Eds.), *Spatial representation and behavior across the life span: Theory and applications.* New York: Academic.

Downs, R.M. (1982). Cognitive mapping: A thematic analysis. In K.R. Cox & R.G. Golledge (Eds.), *Behavioral problems in geography revisited* (pp. 95–122). New York: Methuen.

Downs, R., & Meyer, J. (1978). Geography and the mind: An exploration of perceptual geography. *American Behavioral Scientist, 22,* 59–77.

Downs, R.M., & Stea, D. (Eds.). (1973). *Image and environment: Cognitive mapping and spatial behavior.* Chicago: Aldine.

Downs, R.M., & Stea, D. (1977). *Maps in minds: reflections of cognitive mapping.* New York: Harper & Row.

Ericksen, R.H. (1975). *The effects of perceived place attributes on cognition of urban residents.* (Discussion Paper No. 23). University of Iowa, Department of Geography.

Evans, G.W. (1980). Environmental cognition. *Psychological Bulletin, 88,* 259–287.

Evans, G.W., Fellows, J., Zorn, M., & Doty, K. (1982). Cognitive mapping and architecture. *Journal of Applied Psychology, 65,* 474–478.

Evans, G.W., Marrero, D.G., & Butler, P.A. (1981). Environmental learning and cognitive mapping. *Environment and Behavior, 13,* 83–104.

Evans, G.W., & Pezdek, K. (1980). Cognitive mapping: Knowledge of real world distance and location information. *Journal of Experimental Psychology: Human Learning and Memory, 6,* 13–24.

Evans, G.W., Smith, C., & Pezdek, K. (1982). Cognitive maps and urban form. *Journal of the American Planning Association, 48,* 232–244.

Evans, G.W., Brennan, P., Skorpanich, M.A., & Held, D. (1984). Cognitive mapping and elderly adults: Verbal and location memory for urban landmarks. *Journal of Gerontology, 39,* 452–457.

Firey, W. (1945). Sentiment and symbolism as ecological variables. *American Sociological Review, 10,* 140–148.

Flavell, J.H. (1977). *Cognitive development.* Englewood Cliffs, NJ: Prentice-Hall.

Foley, J.E., & Cohen, R.A.J. (1984). Working mental representation of the environment. *Environment and Behavior, 16,* 713–729.

Gale, N. (1980). *An analysis of the distortion and fuzziness of cognitive maps by location* (Discussion Paper No. 2). Santa Barbara: University of California, Department of Geography.

Gale, N. (1982). Bidimensional regression and the study of cognitive configurations. In R.G. Golledge & W.R. Tobler (Eds.), *An examination of the spatial variation in the distortion of fuzziness of cognitive maps* (National Science Foundation, Grant #SES81-10253, Final Report). Santa Barbara: University of California, Department of Geography.

Gale, N. (1983). Measuring cognitive maps: Methodological considerations from a cartographic perspective. In D. Amedeo, J.B. Griffin, & J.J. Potter (Eds.), *EDRA 1983. Proceedings of the Fourteenth International Conference of the Environmental Design Research Association* (pp. 65–72). Lincoln: University of Nebraska.

Gale, N., & Costanzo, C.M. (1982). Anchors and errors in cognitive images. In R.G. Golledge & W.R. Tobler (Eds.), *An examination of the spatial variation and the distortion and fuzziness of cognitive maps* (National Science Foundation Grant #SES81-10253. Final Report). Department of Geography, University of California. Santa Barbara.

Gärling, T. (1975). *Cognitive representation of the spatial environment as related to movement regulation* (Project Report No. 2). Umea, Sweden: University of Umea. Department of Psychology.

Gärling, T., & Böök, A. (1981). *The spaciotemporal sequencing of everyday activities: How people manage to find the shortest route to travel between places in their hometown.* Unpublished manuscript, Umea, Sweden. University of Umea, Department of Psychology.

Gärling, T., Böök, A., & Ergezen, N. (1982). Memory for the spatial layout of the everyday physical environment: Differential rates of acquisition of different types of information. *Scandinavian Journal of Psychology, 23,* 23–35.

Gärling, T., Böök, A., Ergezen, N., & Lindberg, E. (1981). Memory for the spatial layout of the everyday physical environment: Empirical findings and their theoretical implications. In A.E. Osterberg, C.P. Teirman, & R.A. Findlay (Eds.), *Design Research Interactions. Proceedings of the Environmental Design Research Association 12 Conference.* Ames, IA.

Gärling, T., Böök, A., & Lindberg, E. (1975). *Orientation performance in two-segment and three-segment route tasks during blindfolded and sighted walking* (Umea Psychological Reports, Vol. 94). Umea, Sweden: University of Umea, Department of Psychology.

Gärling, T., Böök, A., Lindberg, E., & Nilsson, T. (1981). Memory for the spatial layout of the everyday physical environment: Factors affecting the rate of acquisition. *Journal of Experimental Psychology, 1,* 263–277.

Gärling, T., Böök, A., Lindberg, A., & Nilsson, T. (1981). Memory for the spatial layout of the everyday physical environment: Factors affecting the rate of acquisition. *Journal of Experimental Psychology, 1,* 263–277.

Gärling, T., Lindberg, E., & Mantyla, T. (1983). Orientation in buildings: Effects of familiarity, visual access, and orientation aids. *Journal of Applied Psychology, 68*(1), 177–186.

Gärling, T., Böök, A., & Lindberg, E. (1984). Cognitive mapping of large-scale environments, action plans, orientation and their interrelationships. *Environment and Behavior, 16,* 3–34.

Gibson, E. (1969). *Principles of perceptual learning and development.* New York: Appleton-Century-Crofts.

Gibson, J.J. (1958). Perception of distance and space in the open air. In D.C. Beardslee & M. Wertheimer (Eds.), *Readings in perception* (pp. 415–431). New York: Van Nostrand Reinhold. (Reprinted from *Motion Picture Testing and Research*, 1946, AAF Program Report No. 7, 181–195.

Gibson, J.J. (1966). *The senses considered as perceptual systems*. Boston: Houghton Mifflin.

Gibson, J.J. (1979). *The ecological approach to visual perception*. Boston: Houghton Mifflin.

Golant, S.M. (1983). Individual differences underlying the dwelling satisfaction of the elderly. *Journal of Social Issues, 38*, 121–133.

Gold, J.R. (1980). *An introduction to behavioral geography*. New York: Oxford University Press.

Golledge, R.G. (1967). Conceptualizing the market decision processes. *Journal of Regional Science, 7* (Suppl.), 239–258.

Golledge, R.G. (1975). *On determining cognitive configurations of a city*. Columbus: Ohio State University Research Foundation, Department of Geography. National Science Foundation Report #6S-37969.

Golledge, R.G. (1976). Method and methodological issues in environmental cognition research. In G.T. Moore & R.G. Golledge (Eds.), *Environmental knowing* (pp. 300–314). Stroudsburg, PA: Dowden, Hutchinson, & Ross.

Golledge, R.G. (1977). Multidimensional analysis in the study of environmental behavior and environmental design. In I. Altman and J.F. Wohlwill (Eds.), *Human behavior and environment: Advances in theory and research* (Vol. 2) (pp. 1–42). New York: Plenum.

Golledge, R.G. (1978). Learning about urban environments. In T. Carlstein, D. Parkes, & N. Thrift (Eds.), *Timing space and spacing time* (Vol. 1). London: Edward Arnold.

Golledge, R.G. (1982). Misconceptions, misinterpretations, and misrepresentations of behavioral approaches in human geography. *Environment and Planning A, 13*, 1325–1344.

Golledge, R.G. (1983, April). *The spatial competence of the borderline retarded*. Paper presented at Environmental Design Research Association Conference, Lincoln, NB.

Golledge, R.G., Briggs, R., & Demko, D. (1969). The configuration of distances in intra-urban space. *Proceedings of the Association of American Geographers, 1*, 60–65.

Golledge, R.G., & Hubert, L.J. (1982). Some comments on non-Euclidean mental maps. *Environment and Planning A, 14*, 107–118.

Golledge, R.G., Parnicky, J.J., & Rayner, J.N. (1979a). *The spatial competence of selected populations* (Vols. 1 & 2). Columbus: Ohio State University Research Foundation.

Golledge, R.G., Parnicky, J.J., & Rayner, J.N. (1979b). An experimental design for assessing the spatial competence of mildly retarded populations. *Social Science and Medicine, 13*, 291–295.

Golledge, R.G., Parnicky, J.J., & Rayner, J.N. (1980). *The spatial competence of selected populations*. Columbus: Ohio State University Research Foundation.

Golledge, R.G., & Rayner, J.N. (1976). *Cognitive configurations of a city* (Vol. 2). Columbus: Ohio State University Research Foundation.

Golledge, R.G., & Rayner, J.N. (1982). *Proximity and preference: Problems in the multidimensional analysis of large data sets*. Minneapolis: University of Minnesota Press.

Golledge, R.G., Rayner, J.N., & Rivizzigno, V.L. (1982). Comparing objective and cognitive representations of environmental cues. In R.G. Golledge & J.N. Rayner (Eds.), *Proximity and preference: Problems in the multidimensional analysis of large data sets* (pp. 233–266). Minneapolis: University of Minnesota Press.

Golledge, R.G., Richardson, G.D., Rayner, J.N., & Parnicky, J.J. (1983). The spatial competence of selected mentally retarded populations. In H.L. Pick and L. Acredolo (Eds.), *Spatial orientation and spatial representation*, Hillsdale, NJ: Earlbaum.

Golledge, R.G., Rivizzigno, V.L., & Spector, A. (1975a). Learning about a city: Analysis by multidimensional scaling. In R.G. Golledge and G. Rushton (Eds.), *Spatial choice and spatial preference*. Columbus: Ohio State University Press.

Golledge, R.G., Rivizzigno, V.L., & Spector, A. (1975b). Learning about a city: Analysis by multidimensional scaling. In R.G. Golledge (Ed.), *On determining cognitive configurations of a city* (Vol. 1). Columbus: Ohio State University Research Foundation, Department of Geography.

Golledge, R.G., & Rushton, G. (1973). Multidimensional scaling review and geographical applications (Tech. Paper No. 10). Washington, DC: *Problems in the multidimensional analysis of large data sets*. Minneapolis: University of Minnesota Press.

Golledge, R.G., & Rushton, G. (Eds.). (1976). *Spatial choice and spatial behavior*. Columbus: Ohio State University Press.

Golledge, R.G., Smith, T.R., Pellegrino, J.W., Doherty, S., & Marshall, S.P. (1983, July). *The acquisition of spatial knowledge: Empirical results and computer models of path finding processes*. Paper presented at the 19th Inter-American Congress of Psychology, Quito, Ecuador.

Golledge, R.G., Smith, T.R., Pellegrino, J.W., Doherty, S., & Marshall, S.P. (1985). A conceptual model and empirical analysis of children's acquisition of spatial knowledge. *Journal of Environmental Psychology, 5*, 125–152.

Golledge, R.G., & Spector, A.N. (1978). Comprehending the urban environment: Theory and practice. *Geographical Analysis, 10*, 403–426.

Golledge, R.G., & Tobler, W.R. (1982). *Spatial variation in the distortion and fuzziness of cognitive maps* (National

Science Foundation, Grant No. SES81-10253, Final Report). Santa Barbara: University of California, Department of Geography.

Golledge, R.G., & Zannaras, G. (1973). Cognitive approaches to the analysis of human spatial behavior. In W.H. Ittelson (Eds.), *Environment and cognition* (pp. 59–94). New York: Seminar.

Green, R.S. (1982). Suggestions for identifying sources of unreliability in multidimensional scaling analysis. In R.G. Golledge & J.N. Rayner (Eds.), *Proximity and preference: Problems in the multidimensional analysis of large data sets* (pp. 289–304). Minneapolis: University of Minnesota Press.

Gulick, J. (1963). Images of an arab city. *Journal of the American Institute of Planners, 29*, 179–198.

Gulliver, F.P. (1908). Orientation of maps. *Journal of Geography, 7*, 55–58.

Hagerstrand, T. (1970). What about people in regional science? *Papers of the Regional Science Association, 24*, 7–21.

Hardwick, D.A., McIntyre, C.W., & Pick, H.L., Jr. (1976). The content and manipulation of cognitive maps in children and adults. *Monograph of the Society for Research in Child Development, 41*(3, Serial No. 166).

Hart, R.A. (1978). *Children's experience of place: A developmental study*. New York: Halsted.

Harvey, D. (1969). *Explanation in geography*. London: Edward Arnold.

Hayes-Roth, B. (1977). Evolution of cognitive structures and processes. *Psychological Review, 84*, 260–278.

Hayes-Roth, B. (1978). The role of partial and best matches. In D.A. Waterman & F. Hayes-Roth (Eds.), *Pattern-directed inference systems* (pp. 557–576). New York: Academic.

Hayes-Roth, F. (1979). Distinguishing theories of representation: A critique of Anderson's "arguments concerning mental imagery." *Psychological Review, 86*, 376–382.

Hayes-Roth, B., & Hayes-Roth, F. (1979). A cognitive model of planning. *Cognitive Science, 4*, 275–318.

Hazen, N.L., Lockman, J.J., & Pick, H.L., Jr. (1978). The development of children's representations of large-scale environments. *Child Development, 4*, 71–115.

Head, H. (1920). *Studies in neurology*. Oxford, England: Oxford University Press.

Hebb, D.O. (1949). *The organization of behavior*. New York: Wiley.

Hebb, D.O. (1963). The semi-autonomous process: Its nature and nurture. *American Psychologist, 18*, 16–27.

Herman, J.F., & Siegel, A.W. (1978). The development of spatial representations of large-scale environments. *Journal of Experimental Child Psychology, 26*, 389–406.

Hintzman, D.L., O'Dell, C.S., & Arndt, D.R. (1981). Orientation in cognitive maps. *Cognitive Psychology, 13*, 149–206.

Honikman, B. (1976). Personal construct theory and environmental meaning: Applications to urban design. In G.T. Moore & R.G. Golledge (Eds.), *Environmental knowing* (pp. 88–98). Stroudsburg, PA: Dowden, Hutchinson, & Ross.

Howard, I.P., & Templeton, W.B. (1966). *Human spatial orientation*. Chichester: Wiley.

Howard, I.P., & Templeton, W.B. (1979). *Human spatial orientation*. New York: Wiley.

Hubert, L.J., & Golledge, R.G. (1981). A heuristic method for the comparison of related structures. *Journal of Mathematical Psychology, 23*(3), 214–226.

Ittelson, W.H. (1951). The constancies in perceptual theory. *Psychological Review, 58*, 285–294.

Ittelson, W.H. (1973). Environmental perception and contemporary perceptual theory. In W.H. Ittelson (Ed.), *Environment and cognition* (p. 1–19). New York: Seminar.

Ittelson, W.H., Proshansky, H.M., Rivlin, L.G., & Winkel, G.H. (1974). *An introduction to environmental psychology*. New York: Holt, Rinehart & Winston.

Kahneman, D. (1973). *Attention effort*. Englewood Cliffs, NJ: Prentice-Hall.

Kaplan, R. (1976). Way-finding in the natural environment. In G.T. Moore & R.G. Golledge (Eds.), *Environmental knowing* (pp. 46–57). Stroudsburg, PA: Dowden, Hutchinson, & Ross.

Kaplan, R. (1983). The impact of urban nature: A theoretical analysis. *Urban Ecology*.

Kaplan, S. (1973). Cognitive maps in perception and thought. In R. Downs & D. Stea (Eds.), *Image and environment: Cognitive mappings and spatial behavior*. Chicago: Aldine.

Kaplan, S. (1976). Adaptation, structure, and knowledge. In G.T. Moore & R.G. Golledge (Eds.), *Environmental knowing* (pp. 32–45). Stroudsburg, PA: Dowden, Hutchinson, & Ross.

Kaplan, S. (1983). A model of human/environment compatibility. *Environment and Behavior, 15*, 311–332.

Kaplan, S., & Kaplan, R. (1982). *Cognition and environment*. New York: Praeger.

Kearins, J.M. (1981). Visual spatial memory in Australian aboriginal children of desert regions. *Cognitive Psychology, 13*, 434–460.

Kelley, G.A. (1955). *The psychology of personal constructs* (Vols. 1 & 2). New York: Norton.

Kintsch, W. (1980). Semantic memory: A tutorial. In R.S. Nickerson (Ed.), *Attention and performance* (Vol. 8) (pp. 595–620). Hillsdale, NJ: Erlbaum.

Kirk, W. (1951). Historical geography and the concept of the behavioral environment. In G. Kuriyan (Ed.), *Indian geographical journal* (Silver Jubilee ed.) (pp. 152–160). Madras, India: Indian Geographical Society.

Klatzky, R.L. (1980). *Human memory* (2nd ed.). San Francisco: Freeman.

Kosslyn, S.M. (1975). Information representation in visual images. *Cognitive Psychology, 7*, 341–370.

Kosslyn, S.M. (1980). *Image and mind.* Cambridge, MA: Harvard University Press.

Kosslyn, S.M. (1981). The medium and the message in mental imagery: A theory. *Psychological Review, 88*, 46–66.

Kosslyn, S.M., Bowle, T.M., & Reiser, B.J. (1978). Visual images preserve metric spatial information: Evidence from studies of image scanning. *Journal of Experimental Psychology: Human Perception and Performance, 4*, 47–80.

Kosslyn, S.M., Pick, H.L., Jr., & Fariello, G.R. (1974). Cognitive maps in children and men. *Child Development, 45*, 707–716.

Kosslyn, S.M., & Pomerantz, J.R. (1977). Imagery, propositions and the form of internal representations. *Cognitive Psychology, 9*, 52–76.

Kosslyn, S.M., Reiser, B.J., & Ball, T.M. (1978). Visual images preserve metric spatial information: Evidence from studies of image scanning. *Journal of Experimental Psychology: Human Perception and Performance, 4*, 47–60.

Kozlowski, L.T., & Bryant, K.J. (1977). Sense of direction, spatial orientation and cognitive maps. *Journal of Experimental Psychology: Human Perception and Performance, 3*, 590–598.

Kuipers, B. (1978). Modeling spatial knowledge. *Cognitive Science, 2*, 129–153.

Kuipers, B. (1979, April). Commonsense knowledge of space: Learning from experience (Cognitive Science Working Papers). Medford, MA: Tufts University, Dept. of Mathematics.

Kuipers, B. (1980). A model of the acquisition of spatial knowledge. In L. Bowl (Ed.), *Models of dialogue: Theory and application.* London: McMillan.

Kuipers, B. (1982). The "map in the head" metaphor. *Environment and Behavior, 4*, 202–220.

Kuipers, B. (1983). The cognitive map: Could it have been any other way? In H.L. Pick, Jr. and L.P. Acredolo (Eds.), *Spatial orientation, theory, research and application* (p. 345–360). New York: Plenum.

Lee, T. (1962). Brennan's law of shopping behavior. *Psychological Reports, 2*, 662.

Lee, T. (1964). Psychology and living space. *Transactions of the Bartlett Society, 2*, 11–36.

Lee, T. (1967). The psychology of spatial orientation. *Architecture Association Quarterly, 1*(3), 11–15.

Lee, T. (1968). Urban neighborhood as a socio-spatial schema. *Human Relations, 21*, 241–268.

Lee, T. (1970). Perceived distance as a function of direction in the city. *Environment and Behavior, 2*, 40–51.

Leff, H. (1978). *Experience, environment and human potentials.* New York: Oxford University Press.

Lehito, P.K., Poikonen, L., & Tuunainen, K. (1980). Retrieval of information from a mental map. In R.S. Nickerson (Ed.), *Attention and performance* (Vol. 8). Hillsdale, NJ: Erlbaum.

Liben, L., Lindberg, E., & Gärling, T. (1977). *Speed and accuracy of performance in geographical orientation tasks for different modes of presentation of information about routes as a function of number of route segments.* (Umea Psychological Reports, Vol. 111). Umea, Sweden: University of Umea, Department of Psychology.

Liben, L.S., Patterson, A.H., & Newcombe, N. (1981). *Spatial representation and behavior across the life span: Theory and application.* New York: Academic.

Lindberg, E., & Gärling, T. (1981). Acquisition of locational information about reference points during locomotion with and without a concurrent task: Effects of number of reference points. *Scandinavian Journal of Psychology, 22*, 109–115.

Lindberg, E., & Gärling, T. (1982, July). Cognitive mapping: The role of central information processing. Paper presented at 20th International Congress of Applied Psychology, Edinburgh, Scotland.

Lloyd, R.E. (1976). Cognition, preference and behavior in space: An examination of the structural linkages. *Economic Geography, 52*, 241–253.

Lloyd, R.E. (1982). A look at images. *Annals of the Association of American Geographers, 72*(4), 532–548.

Lowrey, R.A. (1970). Distance concepts of urban residents. *Environment and Behavior, 2*, 52–73.

Lowrey, R.A. (1973). A method for analyzing distance concepts of urban residents. In R.M. Downs & D. Stea (Eds.), *Image and environment: Cognitive mapping and spatial behavior* (pp. 338–360). Chicago: Aldine.

Lynch, K. (1960). *Image of the city.* Cambridge, MA: MIT Press.

MacEachren, A.M. (1980). Travel time as the basis of cognitive distance. *The Professional Geographer, 32*, 30–36.

MacKay, D.B. (1976). The effect of spatial stimuli on the estimation of cognitive maps. *Geographical Analysis, 8*, 439–452.

MacKay, D.B., Olshavsky, R.W., & Sentell, G. (1975). Cognitive maps and spatial behavior of consumers. *Geographical Analysis, 7*, 19–34.

Magana, J.R. (1978). An empirical and interdisciplinary test of a theory of urban perception. *Dissertation Abstracts International, 39*, 1460B. (University Microfilms No. 78-15,840).

Magana, J.R., Evans, G.W., & Romney, A.K. (1981). Scaling techniques in the analysis of environmental cognition data. *Professional Geographer, 33*(3), 294–301.

Marx, L. (1964). *The machine and the garden: Technology and the pastoral ideal in America.* New York: Oxford University Press.

Maurer, R., & Baxter, J. (1972). Images of neighborhood

among black, anglo and Mexican-American children. *Environment and Behavior, 4*, 351–388.

McClelland, J.L. (1979). On the time relations of mental process: An examination of systems of processes in cascade. *Psychological Review, 86*, 287–330.

Mead, G.H. (1934). *Mind, self, and society*. Chicago: University of Chicago Press.

Milgram, S. (1970). The experience of living in cities. *Science, 167*, 1461–1468.

Milgram, S., Greenwald, J., Keesler, S., McKenna, W., & Waters, J. (1972). A psychological map of New York city. *American Scientist, 60*, 194–200.

Milgram, S., & Jodelet, D. (1976). Psychological maps of Paris. In H.M. Proshansky, W.H. Ittelson, & L. Rivlin, *Environmental psychology* (2nd Ed.). New York: Holt, Rinehart, Winston, Inc.

Miller, G.A., Galanter, E., & Pribram, K.H. (1960). *Plans and the structure of behavior*. New York: Holt, Rinehart & Winston, Inc.

Minsky, M.A. (1975). A framework for representing knowledge. In P.H. Winston (Ed.), *The psychology of computer vision*. New York: McGraw-Hill.

Moore, G.T. (1975a). The development of environmental knowing: An overview. In D. Canter and T. Lee (Eds.), *Psychology and the built environment*. London: Architectural Press.

Moore, G.T. (1975b). Spatial relations ability and developmental levels of urban cognitive mapping. *Man-Environment Systems, 5*, 247–248.

Moore, G.T. (1979). Knowing about environmental knowing: The current state of theory and research on environmental cognition. *Environment and Behavior, 11*, 33–70.

Moore, G.T., & Golledge, R.G. (1976a). *Environmental knowing: Theories, research, and methods*. Stroudsburg, PA: Dowden, Hutchinson, & Ross.

Moore, G.T., & Golledge, R.G. (1976b). Environmental knowing: Concepts and theories. In G.T. Moore & R.G. Golledge (Eds.), *Environmental knowing*. Stroudsburg, PA: Dowden, Hutchinson, & Ross.

Muller, J-C. (1982). Non-Euclidean geographic space: Mapping functional distances. *Geographical Analysis, 14*(3), 189–203.

Nagy, J., & Baird, J.C. (1978). Children as environmental planners. In I. Altman & J.F. Wohlwill (Eds.), *Children and the environment* (pp. 291–294). New York: Plenum.

Newell, A., & Simon, H.A. (1972). *Human problem solving*. Englewood Cliffs, NJ: Prentice-Hall.

Norman, D.A., & Rummelhart, D.E. (1975). *Explorations in cognition*. San Francisco: Freeman.

Olivier, D. (1970). *Metric for comparison of multidimensional scaling*. Unpublished manuscript.

Orleans, P. (1973). Differential cognition of urban residents: Effects of social scale on mapping. In R.M. Downs & D. Stea (Eds.), *Image and environment: Cognitive mapping and spatial behavior* (pp. 115–130). Chicago: Aldine.

Orleans, P., & Schmidt, S. (1972). Mapping the city: Environmental cognition of urban residents. In W.J. Mitchell (Ed.), *Environmental design: Research and Practice* (Vol. 1) (pp. 1-4-1–1-4-9). Los Angeles: University of California, School of Architecture and Urban Planning.

Pailhous, J. (1970). *La représentation de l'espace urbain: L'exemple du chauffeur de taxi*. Paris: Presses Universitaires de France.

Paivio, A. (1969). Mental imagery in associative learning and memory. *Psychological Review, 76*, 241–263.

Paivio, A. (1971). *Imagery and verbal processes*. New York: Holt, Rinehart, & Winston.

Peters, R.P. (1973). Cognitive maps in wolves and men. In W.F.E. Preiser (Ed.), *Environmental design research* (Vol. 2) (pp. 247–253). Stroudsburg, PA: Dowden, Hutchinson, & Ross.

Pezdek, K., & Evans, G.W. (1979). Visual and verbal memory for objects and their spatial locations. *Journal of Experimental Psychology: Human Learning and Memory, 5*, 360–373.

Piaget, J. (1950). *The psychology of intelligence*. (M. Piercy & D. Berlyne, Trans.) (orig. French ed. 1947). London: Routledge and Kegan Paul; New York: Harcourt Brace; Totowa, NJ: Littlefield Adams, 1963.

Piaget, J., & Inhelder, B. (1967). *The child's conception of space*. New York: Norton.

Piaget, J., Inhelder, B., & Czeminska, A. (1960). *The child's conception of geometry*. New York: Basic.

Pick, H.L., Jr. (1972). Mapping children—mapping space. Paper presented at the meeting of the American Psychological Association, Honolulu, HI.

Pick, H.L., Jr. (1976). Transactional-constructivist approach to environmental knowing: A commentary. In G.T. Moore & R.G. Golledge (Eds.), *Environmental knowing* (pp. 185–188). Stroudsburg, PA: Dowden, Hutchinson, & Ross.

Pick, H.L., Jr., & Acredolo, L. (1981). *Spatial orientation and spatial representation*. Hillsdale, NJ: Erlbaum.

Pick, H.L., Jr., & Acredolo, L. (1983). *Spatial orientation: Theory, research and application*. New York: Plenum.

Pick, H.L., Jr., & Lockman, J.J. (1981). From frames of reference to spatial representations. In L.S. Liben, A.H. Patterson, & N. Newcombe. *Spatial representation and behavior across the lifespan: Theory and applications*. New York: Academic.

Potegal, M. (1982). *Spatial abilities: Development and physiological foundations*. New York: Academic.

Proshansky, H.M., Ittelson, W.H., & Rivlin, L.G. (Eds.).

(1970). *Environmental psychology.* New York: Holt, Rinehart & Winston.

Pylyshyn, Z.W. (1973). What the mind's eye tells the mind's brain: A critique of mental imagery. *Psychological Bulletin, 18,* 1–24.

Pylyshyn, Z.W. (1979). The rate of "mental rotation" of images: A test of holistic analogue hypothesis. *Memory and Cognition, 7:* 19–28.

Pylyshyn, Z.W. (1981). The imagery debate: Analogue media vs. tacit knowledge. *Psychological Review, 88,* 16–45.

Rapoport, A. (1969). *House, form and culture.* Englewood Cliffs, NJ: Prentice-Hall.

Rapoport, A. (1975). Socio-cultural aspects of man–environment studies. In A. Rapoport (Ed.), *The mutual interaction of people and their built environment: A cross-cultural perspective.* The Hague, Netherlands: Mouton.

Rapoport, A. (1976). Environmental cognition in cross-cultural perspective. In G.T. Moore & R.G. Golledge (Eds.), *Environmental knowing* (pp. 220–234). Stroudsburg, PA: Dowden, Hutchinson, & Ross.

Rapoport, A. (1977). *Human aspects of urban form.* New York: Pergamon.

Richardson, G.D. (1981a). Comparing two cognitive mapping methodologies. *Area, 13,* 325–331.

Richardson, G.D. (1981b). The appropriateness of using various minkowskian metrics for representing cognitive configurations. *Environment and Planning A, 13,* 475–485.

Richardson, G.D. (1982). Spatial cognition. Doctoral Dissertation, University of California, Santa Barbara.

Rivizzigno, V.L. (1975). Individual differences in the cognitive structuring of an urban area. In R.G. Golledge (Ed.), *On determining cognitive configuration of a city* (Vol. 1) (pp. 471–482). Columbus: Ohio State University Research Foundation.

Rivizzigno, V.L. (1976). *Cognitive representations of an urban area.* Columbus. Ohio State University, Doctoral Dissertation.

Rivizzigno, V.L., & Golledge, R.G. (1974). A method for recovering cognitive information about a city. In D.H. Carson (Ed.), *Man-environment interactions* (Pt. 2). (pp. 9–18) Milwaukee: University of Wisconsin, School of Architecture and Urban Planning.

Romney, A.K., & D'Andrade, R.G. (1964). Transcultural studies in cognition. *American Anthropologist, 66.*

Rowles, G., & Ohta, R. (1983). *Aging and milieux.* New York: Academic.

Russell, J.A., & Ward, L.M. (1982). Environmental psychology. *Annual Review of Psychology, 33,* 651–688.

Saarinen, T. (1966). *Perception of the drought hazard on the great plains* (Research Paper No. 106). Chicago: University of Chicago, Department of Geography.

Saarinen, T. (1976). *Environmental planning: Perception and behavior.* Boston: Houghton Mifflin.

Saarinen, T., & Sell, J.L. (1980). Environmental perception. *Progress in Human Geography, 5*(4), 525–548.

Sadalla, E.K., Burroughs, W.J., & Staplin, L.J. (1980). Reference points in spatial cognition. *Journal of Experimental Psychology: Human Learning and Memory, 6,* 516–528.

Sadalla, E.K., & Magel, S.G. (1980). The perception of traversed distance. *Environment and Behavior, 12,* 65–79.

Sadalla, E.K., & Staplin, L.J. (1980a). The perception of traversed distance: Intersections. *Environment and Behavior, 12,* 167–182.

Sadalla, E.K., & Staplin, L.J. (1980b). An information storage model for distance cognition. *Environment and Behavior, 12,* 183–193.

Schank, R.C. (1980a). Language and memory. *Cognitive Science, 4,* 209–241.

Schank, R.C. (1980b). Comments on "minds, brains, and programs" (J.R. Searle). *Behavioral and Brain Sciences, 3,* 417–457.

Schank, R., & Abelson, R. (1977). *Scripts, plans, goals, and understanding.* Hillsdale, NJ: Erlbaum.

Seamon, D. (1982). The phenomenological contribution to environmental psychology. *Journal of Environmental Psychology, 2,* 2119–2140.

Shemyakin, F.N. (1962). General problems of orientation in space and space representations. In B.G. Ananyev (Ed.), *Psychological science in the USSR* (Vol. 1). (NTIS No. TT62-11083). Washington, DC: U.S. Office of Technical Reports.

Sheppard, R.N. (1978). The mental image. *American Psychologist, 33,* 125–137.

Sherman, R.C. (1979). Investigating cognitive representations of spatial relationships. *Environment and Behavior, 11,* 209–226.

Sherman, R.C., Croxton, J., & Giovanatto, J. (1979). Investigating cognitive representations of spatial relationships. *Environment and Behavior, 11,* 209–226.

Siegel, A.W. (1981). The externalization of cognitive maps by children and adults: In search of ways to ask better questions. In L. Liben, A. Patterson, & N. Newcombe (Eds.), *Spatial representation and behavior across the life span: Theory and application.* New York: Academic.

Siegel, A.W., Allen, G.L., & Kirasic, K.C. (1979a). Children's ability to make bi-directional distance comparisons: The advantage of thinking ahead. *Developmental Psychology, 15,* 656–665.

Siegel, A.W., Allen, G.L., & Kirasic, K.C. (1979b). The development of cognitive maps of large- and small-scale open spaces. *Child Development, 50,* 582–585.

Siegel, A.W., & Cousins, J.H. (1983). The symbolizing and symbolized child in the enterprise of cognitive mapping. In R. Cohen (Ed.), *The development of spatial cognition.* Hillsdale, NJ: Erlbaum.

Siegel, A.W., Kirasic, K.C., & Kail, R.V. (1978). Stalking

the elusive cognitive map: The development of children's representations of geographic space. In J.F. Wohlwill & I. Altman (Eds.), *Human behavior and environment* (Vol. 3). New York: Plenum.

Siegel, A.W., & Schadler, M. (1977). Young children's cognitive maps of their classrooms. *Child Development, 48*, 388–394.

Siegel, A.W., & White, S.H. (1975). The development of spatial representations of large-scale environments. In H.W. Reese (Ed.), *Advances in child development and behavior* (Vol. 10). New York: Academic.

Simon, H.A. (1957). *Models of man.* New York: Wiley.

Simon, H.A. (1969). *The sciences of the artificial.* Cambridge, MA: MIT Press.

Simon, H.A. (1979). *Models of thought.* New Haven, CT: Yale University Press.

Simon, H.A. (1981). Studying human intelligence by creating artificial intelligence. *American Scientist, 69*, 300–309.

Slovic, P., Fischhoff, B., & Lichtenstein, S.C. (1977). Behavioral decision theory. *Annual Review of Psychology, 28*, 1–39.

Smith, T.R., Pellegrino, J.Q., & Golledge, R.G. (1982). Computational process modeling of spatial cognition and behavior. *Geographical Analysis, 14*, 305–325.

Spector, A.N. (1978). *An analysis of urban spatial imagery.* Columbus. Ohio State University, Unpublished doctoral dissertation.

Spence, I. (1982). Incomplete experimental designs for multidimensional scaling. In R.G. Golledge & J.N. Rayner (Eds.), *Proximity and Preference.* Minneapolis: University of Minnesota Press.

Spencer, C., & Darvizeh, C. (1981). The case for developing a cognitive psychology that does not underestimate the abilities of young children. *Journal of Environmental Psychology, 1*, 21–31.

Sperry, R. (1982). Some effects of disconnecting the cerebral hemispheres. *Science, 217*(24), 1223–1226.

Staplin, L.J., & Sadalla, E.K. (1981). Distance cognition in urban environments. *Professional Geographer, 33*(3), 302–310.

Stea, D. (1969). The measurement of mental maps: An experimental model for studying conceptual spaces. In K.R. Cox & R.G. Golledge (Eds.), *Behavioral problems in geography: A symposium.* Evanston, IL: Northwestern University.

Stea, D., Blaut, J.M., & Kasnitz, D. (1970). *Toy geography: A study of environmental modeling in Puerto Rican children ages 5–8* (Place Perception Research Reports, No. 6). Worcester, MA: Clark University.

Stevens, A., & Coupe, P. (1978). Distortions in judged spatial relations. *Cognitive Psychology, 10*, 422–437.

Stokols, D. (1978). Environmental psychology. *Annual Review of Psychology, 29*, 253–295.

Stokols, D., & Shumaker, S.A. (1981). People in places: A

transactional view of settings. In J.H. Harvey (Ed.), *Cognition, social behavior, and the environment.* Hillsdale, NJ: Erlbaum.

Strauss, A.L. (1961). *Images of the American city.* New York: Free Press.

Thorndyke, P.W. (1981a). Distance estimation from cognitive maps. *Cognitive Psychology, 13*, 526–550.

Thorndyke, P.W. (1981b). Spatial cognition and reasoning. In J. Harvey (Ed.), *Cognition, social behavior and the environment.* Hillsdale, NJ: Erlbaum.

Thorndyke, P.W., & Stasz, C. (1980). Individual differences in knowledge acquisition from maps. *Cognitive Psychology, 12*, 137–175.

Thorndyke, P.W., & Hayes-Roth, B. (1980). *Differences in spatial knowledge acquired from maps and navigation* (Research Rep.). Santa Monica, CA: Rand.

Tobler, W.R. (1965). Computation of the correspondence of geographical patterns. *Papers and Proceedings of the Regional Science Association, 15*, 131–139.

Tobler, W.R. (1976). The geometry of mental maps. In G. Rushton & R.G. Golledge (Eds.), *Spatial choice and spatial behavior.* Columbus: Ohio State University Press.

Tobler, W.R. (1977). *Bidimensional regression.* Unpublished manuscript, University of California, Department of Geography, Santa Barbara.

Tobler, W.R. (1982). Surveying multidimensional measurement. In R.G. Golledge & J.N. Rayner (Eds.), *Proximity and Preference.* Minneapolis: University of Minnesota.

Tolman, E.C. (1932). *Purposive behavior in animals and men.* New York: Appleton-Century-Crofts.

Tolman, E.C. (1948). Cognitive maps in rats and men. *Psychological Review, 55*, 189–208.

Trowbridge, C.C. (1948). *Comparative psychology of mental development.* New York: International Universities Press.

Tuan, Y-F. (1975). Images and mental maps. *Annals of the Association of American Geographers, 65*, 213.

Tuan, Y-F. (1976). Literature, experience, and environmental knowing. In G.T. Moore & R.G. Golledge (Eds.), *Environmental knowing.* Stroudsburg, PA: Dowden, Hutchinson, & Ross.

Tuan, Y-F. (1977). *Space and place: The perspective of experience.* Minneapolis: University of Minnesota Press.

Tversky, B. (1981). Distortions in memory for maps. *Cognitive Psychology, 13*, 407–433.

Wapner, S., Kaplan, B., & Cohen, S.B. (1973). An organismic–developmental perspective for understanding transactions of men in environment. *Environment and Behavior, 5*, 255–289.

Wapner, S., & Werner, H. (1957). *Perceptual development.* Worcester, MA: Clark University Press.

Werner, H., & Kaplan, B. (1963). *Symbol information: An*

organismic-developmental approach to language and the expression of thought. New York: Wiley.

White, G. (1945), *Human adjustments to floods* (Research Paper No. 29). Chicago: University of Chicago, Department of Geography.

Wohlwill, J. (1973). The environment is not in the head. In W. Preiser (Ed.), *Environmental design research* (Vol. 2). Stroudsburg, PA: Dowden, Hutchinson, & Ross.

Wright, J.K. (1947). Terrae incognitae: The place of imagination in geography. *Annals of the Association of American Geographers, 37,* 1–15.

Young, F.W., Null, C.H., Sarle, W.S., & Hoffman, D.L. (1982). Interactively ordering the similarities among a large set of stimuli. In R.G. Golledge & J.N. Rayner

(Eds.), *Proximity and preference.* Minneapolis: University of Minnesota Press.

Zannaras, G. (1968). *An empirical analysis of urban neighborhood perception.* Columbus: Ohio State University. Unpublished master's thesis.

Zannaras, G. (1973). *An analysis of cognitive and objective characteristics of the city: Their influence on movements to the city center.* Columbus: Ohio State University. Unpublished doctoral dissertation.

Zannaras, G. (1976). The relation between cognitive structure and urban form. In G.T. Moore & R.G. Golledge (Eds.), *Environmental knowing* (pp. 336–350). Stroudsburg, PA: Dowden, Hutchinson, & Ross.

Chapter 6

ENVIRONMENTAL COGNITION IN CHILDREN

Harry Heft, *Department of Psychology, Denison University, Granville, Ohio*

Joachim F. Wohlwill, *Department of Individual and Family Studies, Pennsylvania State University, University Park, Pennsylvania*

During the past decade we have witnessed considerable interest in the nature and development of environmental cognition in infancy and childhood. Inquiries into this issue represent a significant point of contact between environmental psychologists, geographers, and planners on the one hand and developmental psychologists on the other (see, e.g., Baird & Lutkus, 1982). The convergence of these two domains can be accounted for in part by a shared interest on both sides in the ideas of Piaget as they relate to environment–behavior concerns, although, as we shall see, the current theoretical focus in this area is by no means derived solely from Piagetian theory. The result has been a theoretically inspired research effort

and, as a consequence, a clear sense of direction and of progress in the area.[1]

At the outset we should attempt to be clearer about the specific focus of this chapter. We are concerned here with children's knowledge of environmental layout, including knowledge of its overall spatial configuration, of paths or routes to particular places, and of the functional significance or *affordances* of places. The last two types of environmental knowledge place considerable emphasis on the perceptual activities of the child; accordingly, the concerns of the chapter should be seen to include both perceptual and cognitive processes as they relate to the acquisition and development of environmental knowledge. The research to be examined addresses the environment at several different scales, from classrooms to school campuses and neighborhoods, and considers these settings both as they are directly experienced and as they are represented by models and maps.

We begin our treatment of environmental cognition by considering several theoretical approaches, before moving to a review of the research literature. Section 6.1 is a brief examination of two theoretical approaches to environmental cognition, the constructivist models of Piaget and of Siegel and White, and also a consideration of the ecological theory of perception of J.J. Gibson, as it pertains to issues in this research area. Section 6.2 is a review of research concerning environmental cognition in children. This section begins with a brief discussion of several conceptual issues, presented as three preliminary questions (Section 6.2.1) that will provide a framework for evaluating this research. These questions, derived in part from our examination of theoretical alternatives, concern the manner in which environmental knowledge may be conceptualized, the relationship between environmental knowledge and exploration, and the influence of affective and motivational processes on environmental cognition. Following this discussion, we examine research directed at environmental cognition in infancy (Section 6.2.2) and in childhood (Section 6.3.2); among the topics included in this latter discussion will be a consideration of the role of environmental features, topological and configurational reference systems, route learning, exploratory activity, environmental affordances and environmental knowledge, the influence of affective state and preference on environmental knowledge, and map-reading skills. We conclude the chapter (Section 6.3) with a reassessment of the issues raised by the preliminary set of questions in the light of the research review and a consideration of significant methodological issues in the area.

6.1. THEORETICAL APPROACHES TO THE DEVELOPMENT OF ENVIRONMENTAL KNOWLEDGE

In spite of its generality and diverse uses, *cognitive map* is perhaps the central concept in the area of environmental cognition, and it is the theoretical term that is most readily associated with this topic by those working outside of the area. Tolman (1948) introduced the concept of cognitive map to psychology in order to explain characteristics of the spatial *behavior* of rats under particular maze conditions. Although this concept has regained some prominence in recent years, with the establishment of environmental cognition as a research area its role in psychological models has changed considerably since its initial introduction. Instead of serving as an intervening variable to explain spatial behavior, the term *cognitive map* now stands for psychological processes that are investigated for their own sake (e.g., Lynch, 1960; Neisser, 1976)—a shift in orientation that reflects the more general emergence of cognitive psychology as a dominant perspective in the discipline. Particularly influential in this shift of focus, especially as regards the development of spatial representation, has been the work of Piaget on the development of the child's understanding of space (e.g., Piaget & Inhelder, 1967).

Most theoretical approaches to the development of spatial knowledge have been influenced directly or indirectly by Piaget's constructivist theory. At a minimum, most investigators assume with Piaget that a cognitive representation of space, or of spatial relationships, underlies spatial thinking and spatial behavior (Mandler, 1983).[2] These spatial relationships include those between places on the body (e.g., the location of the mouth relative to the thumb), those between the body and objects (manifested in reaching for and grasping an object), and those between objects (revealed in locomotion between objects or places; see Pick & Lockman, 1981).

A number of investigators have explicitly adopted Piaget's analysis of spatial representation as a set of distinguishable, developmental stages in the comprehension of spatial relations (Piaget & Inhelder, 1967). Rather than viewing Piaget's framework in detail, we will summarize the derivation of it presented by Hart and Moore (1973), who have attempted to synthesize this approach with other pertinent ones, most notably that of Werner (1948). In this chapter we will refer to their derivation as the Piagetian model since it conveys the essential character of the initial formulation and since it has served to introduce this model to many investigators in the field.

From the perspective of Piaget's genetic epistemology, knowledge has its origins in the child's sensorimotor actions on the environment. As cognitive development proceeds these actions become covert and symbolic. For example, the overt action of moving an object in one direction and then back to its original location is a primitive form of the logical operation of reversibility, the latter operation emerging only after the onset of symbolic thought. Because the earliest forms of environmental knowledge consist of overt activities directed at features of the environment [i.e., a practical sensorimotor form of intelligence (Piaget, 1970)], children understand the location of features and the structure of the environment with reference to their own bodies. That is, the body is the frame of reference for interacting with the environment, and the location and orientation of objects are understood relative to the child's position in the environment. This *egocentric reference system* is considered to characterize infancy and early childhood (i.e., the sensorimotor and the early preoperational periods).

Although initially the child's cognitive representations of the environment are tied directly to sensorimotor operations, according to Piaget, as the child gains greater facility in symbolic and abstract thinking, gradually these representations begin to reflect a recognition of the relationships *among* environmental features. For example, from the perspective of the egocentric reference system, the relationship between environmental features might be understood solely in terms of the order in which the child encounters them. Understanding the reverse order of a succession of environmental features requires a perspective independent of the child's immediate encounters with these features. It is the emergence of an *allocentric reference system* that provides the basis for understanding the organization or layout of the environment independent of one's own point of view. The environment has an intrinsic structure that is distinct from the individual's experience with the environment, and an allocentric frame of reference permits the comprehension of this independent structure.

Allocentricity develops during the preoperational period, and it undergoes several transformations. Initially, the positional relationships among environmental features are conceptualized *topologically*. In this context, topological relationships include proximity of features ("near"), separation of features ("far"), order, and enclosure (Hunt, 1961). Hence environmental features are conceptualized as being, for example, near or far with respect to the body or other environmental features, without any sense of either metric distance or configurational structure.[3]

This topological reference system is superseded by a *fixed system* of reference with the emergence of concrete operational thought. Children can orient themselves with respect to certain regions in the environment, and as a result they can view their own location in the environment or the location of other features with reference to these fixed regions. However, all of the known features of the environment are not systematically coordinated with each other; rather, coordination of features is limited within these fixed regions, and these regions serve as reference points for the other features. To take an example, for the concrete operational child the relationships among those environmental features immediately adjacent to the home may be well understood. However, the location of more distant places can be comprehended only with reference to this home region, and the relationships among these "distant" places are poorly coordinated. Thus in contrast to an egocentric system the child's environmental frame of reference corresponds to some permanent features of the environment; and in contrast to the topological system the environment becomes differentiated into distinguishable but only partially coordinated regions.

This fixed system in turn gives way to a *coordinated system of reference*. At this more advanced level of understanding, the known features and regions of the environment become fully coordinated, and as a result the directional and distance relationships between these various features become articulated. The child understands how to reach any place in the environment from any other and how far these places are from one another. In other words, the child imposes an essentially euclidean geometric framework on interactions with the environment. The transition from a fixed to a coordinated system is seen to entail the following:

> The child decenters from each of the partially coordinated fixed systems of reference of the previous stage. Thereafter, through processes of reciprocal assimilation among the reference systems and reflective abstraction between them, he intercoordinates these structures and advances to a higher plane of thought. (Hart & Moore, 1973, p. 282.)

To summarize, then, the child's cognitive representation of the environment is seen as shifting from an egocentric frame of reference to an allocentric representation, first with a reliance on topological relations, followed by a differentiation of the environment into a few fixed regions that eventually become fully coordinated with veridical distance and directional relationships established between these regions.

Siegel and White (1975) offer an alternative model of the development of environmental cognition. Their analysis has been influenced by diverse sources, perhaps most prominently by Piaget and Werner. Siegel and White's model has stimulated a great deal of research in environmental cognition; in fact, it has more directly stimulated research activities in the area than has Piagetian theory, which instead has influenced the field more through its general perspective—a perspective conveyed through conceptual work such as that of Siegel and White. Their common orientation includes the constructivist assumption that a spatial representation underlies all spatial thought and behavior, and further the view that this representation undergoes several stagelike transformations. The precise nature of the stages presented in the Siegel and White model, however, differs from that of the stages of the Piagetian framework, reflecting in part the fact that Siegel and White are more concerned with spatial *behavior* than Piaget, whose interests in this area were primarily focused on the structure of thought. Also, unlike Piaget's stages, those proposed by Siegel and White are conceived of as applying to both ontogenesis and microgenesis (i.e., the structure of adult learning), the latter reflecting Werner's influence. Finally, it should be noted that Siegel and White do not attempt to offer a formal theory of spatial cognitive development as in the manner of Piaget, but rather their model is a more general account that, according to them, emerged from their review of the research literature.

In the first of Siegel and White's three stages, *landmarks* are identified primarily as reference points in navigating. Landmarks can be selected to mark the beginning point and end point of a journey, as well as serving to guide navigation as intermediate markers between these terminal foci. Landmarks can also serve as a frame of reference from which other landmarks can be located (Siegel, Kirasic, & Kail, 1978). Second, when one is in the process of finding one's way with the aid of landmarks, routes connecting these landmarks become established. Whereas identification of landmarks is seen largely to involve a process of visual discrimination, *route learning* is considered to be a sensorimotor process that results in expectations of the sequence of landmarks to be encountered along a route. Finally, learned routes in the environment become integrated into a *configurational representation*. In this phase, the relationships between various landmarks and routes become coordinated into a pattern that may be understood as an overview of some region of the environment. The possibility of orientation with respect to cardinal directions arises with the environment represented in a configurational manner.

Although the Piagetian and the Siegel and White models differ in many respects, some of which were noted previously, in broad outline their respective accounts are reasonably compatible. They are both con-

structivist approaches, and both posit a reliance on environmental features such as landmarks at an early point in knowledge acquisition within an allocentric frame of reference. Furthermore, both consider attainment of configurational knowledge as the final level of achievement, with a fully coordinated, euclidean spatial representation reflecting at once the ideal cognitive structure and the standard against which all other forms of environmental knowledge are judged. On the other hand, knowledge of the sequence of landmarks along the route, as suggested by Siegel and White (1975), does not find a direct parallel in the Piagetian framework, and, as noted above, this difference reflects the greater emphasis by the former on the utility of environmental knowledge for way-finding.

As for the conception of stages that characterizes each of these theoretical models, they differ in important respects, as already noted. Yet they share certain common features that are revealed in their mutual compatibility with the account of spatial representation offered by Shemyakin (1962). He distinguishes between two types of representations: *route maps*, which reflect the sequence of features in the environment that the individual encountered when previously experiencing a particular route, and *survey maps*, which represent configurational knowledge of the environment. Appleyard (1970) reports evidence from map drawings of adults that is consistent with this distinction. The enactive quality of a route map representation corresponds to the action-based, egocentric frame of reference in Piaget's theory that precedes allocentric, configurational representations of the environment. Similarly, the distinction between route and survey map representations is consistent with Siegel and White's successive stages of route knowledge and configurational knowledge.

As we have seen, the approaches discussed thus far share common intellectual roots that include the assumption that spatial thinking and spatial behavior are based on a cognitive representation. Within the fields of perception and cognition generally, this assumption has been challenged through the ecological theory of perception developed by J.J. Gibson (1966, 1979). Gibson argues that environmental features are perceived directly without the intervention of cognitive processes. Although Gibson's ecological approach has not as yet served as the source of much environmental cognition research, some recent work to be reviewed later points in directions consistent with this perspective. Further, and perhaps most significantly, Gibson's ecological approach suggests some new directions for work in the field (see Heft,

1981). For these reasons, we will briefly introduce this theoretical perspective here.

Gibson's ecological approach to perception focuses on the stimulus information that supports the individual's ongoing transactions with the environment. In the case of visual perception, an analysis of this information begins with a consideration of the way in which light interacts with the surfaces of the environment. Light from a radiant source reflects off the surfaces of objects and the ground filling the medium (i.e., the air) with reflected light structured by those surfaces. Perceiving is a process of picking up this structure in the ambient array of reflected light, and as we will see, movements of the perceiver play an essential role in this process.

Two kinds of structures are available to be perceived in the ambient array. As the perceiver moves eyes, head, and body in the course of perceiving, some aspects of the array undergo change, and other aspects do not. There is a flowing or streaming of the array that accompanies the perceiver's movements, as for example when walking along a path in the environment. This flowing *perspective structure* is visual information about locomotion. There is also nonchange or *invariant structure* in the ambient array that is revealed in the context of the changing perspective structure accompanying the perceiver's movements. Invariant structure is information that specifies persisting features of the environment such as objects. Both perspective structure and invariant structure are picked up concurrently *over time* as the perceiver explores the environment.

Applying this approach to the problem of spatial knowledge, the flowing perspective structure provides more than an indication that the perceiver is moving; in addition, the particular course of the information flow specifies a particular path of locomotion. This temporal flow of information is picked up as the perceiver locomotes along a given route, and reciprocally, it guides the direction of locomotion along the route (see Heft, 1983). Moreover, an invariant is revealed through the changing perspective structure along paths of locomotion through the environment, and this invariant information specifies the layout of the environment. That is, in the course of perceiving the flow of information that specifies paths of locomotion, the invariant structure of the environment is gradually apprehended as well.

Let us briefly contrast this analysis with the constructivist approach considered previously. From this latter perspective, perception of routes and the overall layout of the environment *necessarily* depends on a cognitive representation of the environment because perception is assumed to be limited in significant ways. For example, many investigators adopt the view that visual input consists of temporally discrete glimpses, or "retinal snapshots," of the environment, that perception is limited to what can be seen at any given moment (e.g., Allen, Siegel, & Rosinski, 1978). In order to account for the apparent temporal continuity and spatial extension of our environmental experience, cognitive operations are required that assemble and integrate these fragmented inputs. Hence perception of the environment, as a product of these cognitive operations, is mediated and indirect. From the ecological perspective, as we have seen, visual information is picked up over time as the perceiver moves through the environment. Perception is direct inasmuch as this information unequivocally specifies the routes and the layout of the environment. Supplemental, mediating cognitive processes are not required in this account of environmental perception.

The ecological perspective suggests a reformulation of the standard view of the relationship between perception and cognition. Instead of considering perception to be a lower-level process, which is subordinate to cognition (e.g., Bruner, 1957; Piaget, 1969), both can be seen as autonomous processes serving different *complex* functions in the environment (Newtson, 1980). Environmental conditions, or *contextual* factors, as well as the goals of the person, will determine whether perceptual or cognitive processes are required in particular circumstances. In this light, way-finding may be viewed as a form of environmental *perception*, considering perception as involving the pickup of information over time, and as such it would not rely on a cognitive representation of the environment. On the other hand, tasks such as constructing maps or models of an environment, or imagining new routes through a familiar setting, may draw directly on *conceptual knowledge*.

A second aspect of Gibson's formulation that is pertinent here concerns his emphasis, in his later work, on the perception of the *affordances* of the environment, that is, of the functional significance or meaning of environmental features (Gibson, 1979, Chapter 8; E.J. Gibson, 1982; E.J. Gibson & Spelke, 1983; see also the discussion of affordances in Heft, 1985, and Wohlwill & Heft, Chapter 9, this volume). With respect to the child's development of knowledge of particular places, it could be suggested that the child learns originally the affordances of places, that is, the kinds of activities that a place permits or, more positively, encourages. We will return to this point in Section 6.2.3, where we will examine some evidence that children readily learn what activities and resources particular places afford, (e.g., playgrounds, toy stores). A consideration of this issue raises questions about the way in which this kind of environmental knowledge is acquired, how the process of identifying place affordances differs from the acquisition of configurational knowledge, and how perceptual knowledge of place affordances plays a role in the development of environmental cognition generally. By drawing attention to the affordances of places in the environment, the ecological perspective thus adds a significant new dimension to the study of environmental knowledge.

6.2. EMPIRICAL INVESTIGATIONS OF THE DEVELOPMENT OF ENVIRONMENTAL COGNITION

6.2.1. Three Preliminary Questions

In this section we will briefly consider several conceptual issues in the area of environmental cognition. While some of these issues grow out of the preceding theoretical discussion, for the most part they anticipate matters that emerge from the literature review that is to follow. We will consider these issues in the form of three questions, with the intent of providing a preliminary framework for our subsequent consideration of the research literature. These questions are:

1. What is the nature of environmental knowledge?
2. What is the relationship between environmental knowledge and exploration?
3. What is the influence of affective and motivational processes on environmental cognition?

Consideration of specific aspects of each of these issues will, for the most part, be reserved for the succeeding literature review, and a reassessment of these issues in light of the research will be presented in the concluding section (Section 6.3).

What Is the Nature of Environmental Knowledge?

How do we conceptualize the psychological processes that underlie spatial behavior? The intellectual tradition from Kant to Piaget approaches spatial knowledge as a unitary, conceptual category. Accordingly, most contemporary investigators of environmental cognition, because of their Piagetian orientation, accept this assumption implicitly. Research is typically designed to reveal the underlying cognitive representation of space, and findings of investigations employing different types of tasks in different types of settings converge to articulate the character of this cognitive capacity. Furthermore, the Piagetian emphasis on the logical–mathematical structure of thought has directly influenced the research focus in the area; this can be seen in the concern of many investigators with the geometry of spatial thinking, with euclidean geometry as the standard against which to assess performance. The recent studies of configurational knowledge of environmental layout and of distance estimation between environmental features reflect this perspective (see Sections 6.2.2 & 6.2.3).

Alternatively, environmental knowledge can be viewed as a set of distinguishable functions or skills rather than as a single psychological capacity, and in addition there may be ways to characterize environmental knowledge that capture features that a geometrical–logical analysis leaves out. With regard to the former, spatial functions may be specified with reference to the specific requirements of particular tasks or particular settings. Thus, for example, whereas the different tasks such as building models of a town and finding one's way in the environment have sometimes been treated as revealing a common spatial capacity, it may be more appropriate to view them as distinguishable functions that need to be examined somewhat independently. In other words, instead of viewing environmental cognition as a single, abstract process, we may need to consider this term as referring to several distinguishable skills that are specifiable with respect to specific goals in relation to particular environmental contexts. Such an alternative orientation to psychological phenomena, which emphasizes contextual factors, has been offered in recent years as a theoretical alternative to more process-oriented approaches with respect to a variety of problem areas (e.g., Jenkins, 1977; Proshansky, 1976; Rogoff & Lave, 1984; Wohlwill, 1981).

Along similar lines, a description of environmental knowledge in terms of an abstract, geometrical formalism may omit other features of such knowledge, such as the *significance* or meaning of particular environmental features. As we have suggested, what the child knows about a particular environmental setting is not only its configurational layout, but also what kinds of opportunities are afforded in the setting. Further, there are certain forms of environmental knowledge that may require something other than a euclidean–geometrical conceptualization of spatial layout. *Finding one's way* along a route through the environment may be more appropriately described in terms of a temporal sequence of information than with reference to the spatialized and atemporal euclidean framework. Still other forms of environmental knowledge such as *geographical* orientation may require different descriptive systems (e.g., Baker, 1980; see also Gould & Able, 1981). Our research review will point to a variety of spatial skills, and we will need to consider the most appropriate ways to characterize the psychological structures that support these skills.

What Is the Relationship Between Environmental Cognition and Exploration?

In the theoretical approaches considered previously, actions of the individual are viewed as playing a fundamental role in the acquisition of knowledge generally (although the specific role of action in knowledge acquisition differs across these theoretical formulations). At the same time, we can ask more specifically about the relationship between exploration of an environmental setting and acquisition of knowledge about that setting. In the following literature review, it will be important to note the extent and manner in which attention to exploratory activities has been incorporated into empirical investigations. In the process we may want to keep in mind at least two related issues. First, it would seem that environmental knowledge and exploration are reciprocally related: The extent of knowledge about environmental layout will constrain exploratory activities, and inversely, knowledge about layout will be extended through environmental exploration. Precisely how these factors interact, however, will need to be more clearly understood. Second, we will need to consider the *type* of exploratory activity the child engages in. For example, a child may explore a setting on his or her own (self-directed exploration) or may be guided by another (passive exploration). Are these two types of exploration comparable with respect to what is learned about the environment by the child? Or is learning facilitated by self-directed exploration? Research directed at these questions will have implications for our understanding the relationship between exploration and environmental cognition.

What Is the Influence of Affective and Motivational Processes on Environmental Cognition?

Perceptual and cognitive processes do not operate in isolation from other psychological processes, such as

affective experience, and indeed, the latter are likely to interact with these epistemic functions. For instance, as we will see, the child's affective state can influence responsiveness to information in the environment. Thus performance on a task assessing environmental knowledge may need to be examined with respect to factors that contribute to affect, such as the familiarity of the setting (see Section 6.2.2). Similarly, preferences for particular types of settings or places (Section 6.2.3) may determine the extent to which an individual explores a setting and learns about its layout. Hilgard (1980) has argued that the recent emphasis on cognitive processes in psychology generally has been to the neglect of the two other traditional subdivisions of mental activity, affect and conation (i.e., will, motive). We should note in reviewing the literature whether this claim is applicable to the environmental cognition area as well, such that cognitive processes tend to be examined in isolation from other significant psychological processes.

6.2.2. Environmental Cognition in Infancy

Having considered some broad conceptual issues, we will now proceed to an examination of the research literature in the area, in which some of these issues will be found to recur as themes. Our analysis will consider first research concerning infants, and then we will examine the more extensive literature on environmental cognition in childhood. The treatment of infant research will primarily focus on the issue of the transition from an egocentric to an allocentric reference system, and in the process we will consider the role of environmental landmarks, the infant's affective state, and task demands in spatial performance. The relevant studies are summarized in Table 6.1.

The study by Acredolo (1978) may be taken as prototypical of this body of research. The investigator tested 24 infants longitudinally at 6 months, 11 months, and 16 months[4] in a 10-ft-by-10-ft curtained enclosure with windows in two opposite walls. At the sound of a buzzer, located in the center of the room, the experimenter appeared in one of the windows and interacted with the infant. For half the subjects this target window was surrounded by a yellow star (the landmark condition). Once the infant could correctly anticipate the location of the experimenter at the sound of the buzzer, she was rotated 180° and moved to the opposite end of the enclosure. An infant employing an allocentric reference system should tend to look in the direction of the target window at the sound of the buzzer, even after rotation and relo-

Table 6.1. Major Empirical Studies of Environmental Cognition in Infancy

Author(s)	Ages	Task or Situation	Major Findings
Acredolo (1978)	6,11,16 months (long)	Locating target window with and without landmark; infant rotated 180° following original learning and placed at opposite end of room	Decrease in egocentric responses with age; at 11 months, presence of landmarks reduced egocentric responding
Acredolo & Evans (1980)	6,9,11 months (x-sec)	As above; landmarks more prominent	Landmarks increased allocentric responses at 9 and 11 months; decreased egocentrism at 6 months
Bremner & Bryant (1977)	9 months	Locating object under cloth following 180° rotation	Egocentric responding
Bremner (1978)	9 months	As above; cloth distinctively marked	Reduction in egocentric responding as a result of markings
Acredolo (1979)	9 months	As in Bremner & Bryant; subjects tested in offices with and without landmarks, and in their homes	Egocentric responding in office, independent of landmarks; decreased in home
Acredolo (1982)	9 months	As in Acredolo (1978); interaction between infant, mother, and experimenter preceding testing	Prior interaction with mother and experimenter reduced egocentric responses from 65% (in Acredolo, 1978) to 19%
Rieser (1979)	6 months	As in Acredolo (1978) but subject only rotated 90° without being displaced to other end of room	More allocentric responding than found by Acredolo, provided landmarks available as orienting cues
Presson & Ihrig (1982)	9 months	As in Acredolo (1978); mothers either moved with infant for transfer trials or remained in place	Mother functions as landmark when present; seeming egocentric responses may be allocentrically based responses to this "landmark"

cation in the enclosure, reflecting a sensitivity to the spatial framework of the environmental setting independent of her own bodily position. In contrast, an egocentric reference system would result in responses to the same side of the body as the target window during the training. Acredolo found that at 6 months the infants consistently responded in an egocentric manner, even in presence of the landmark, but by 16 months very few egocentric responses were in evidence in either condition. At 11 months, responses in the no-landmark condition resembled those at 6 months; however, when a landmark was present, this age group was significantly less egocentric in learning spatial location. This finding of the use of an egocentric system of reference at 6 and 11 months is consistent with Bremner and Bryant's (1977) report that 9-month-old infants, having learned to locate an object under a cloth to one side, continue to choose a cloth on that same side even after having been rotated 180° to the other side of a table.

As shown in Table 6.1, Acredolo and Evans (1980) replicated these findings but found in addition that allocentric responding, which had been virtually absent at 6 months in the previous study, could be facilitated at this age, and at 9 and 11 months as well, by making the landmarks more salient. The role of distinctive environmental cues in reducing egocentric responding was likewise brought out by Bremner (1978), though only at one age level (9 months). Acredolo (1981) has suggested that this evidence for both egocentric and allocentric responding among the youngest age group indicates a competition between these two systems of reference during infancy.

The results of Acredolo and Evans (1980) point out that findings concerning cognitive abilities must be evaluated with regard to the environmental conditions in which those abilities were assessed. Based on the results of Acredolo (1978) and Bremner and Bryant (1977), it would appear that infants during the first year are primarily limited to an egocentric frame of reference; however, we have seen that under conditions where the environment is distinctively differentiated infants do not consistently respond egocentrically, but to varying degrees appear to employ an allocentric frame of reference. The system of reference employed by the infant apparently depends to a considerable degree on the salience of environmental features in relation to developmental status. In a related vein, Presson and Ihrig (1982) present evidence that suggests that apparent instances of egocentric responding may in fact have involved allocentric responding, with infants utilizing their mothers as an environmental landmark. According to these investigators, what changes developmentally is the environmental information that is used in orientation rather than a spatial frame of reference. We will return to this point.

Two other factors that may influence which reference system is employed are the child's affective state and task demands. First, with regard to affect, Acredolo (1979) found that 9-month-old infants, though responding egocentrically in an unfamiliar office environment, with or without landmarks, showed a sharp reduction in the incidence of egocentric responding when tested in their own homes. Acredolo (1982) suggested that the more positive affective state of the infant in her own home was the factor responsible for this improvement in performance, presumably because "feelings of security allowed the child to attend to the spatial information being presented in the task" (p. 27). A similar effect might be expected if the infant was allowed to interact freely with the mother and the experimenter in the laboratory prior to testing, and that was indeed what was found in a subsequent study (reported in Acredolo, 1982). This finding indicates that neither the degree of differentiation of the setting nor affective factors can be treated in isolation. It is likely that these factors interact such that positive affect (e.g., feelings of security) facilitates the use of available environmental features and consequently promotes allocentricity. A further way in which this interaction may be manifested is in terms of competence in environmental exploration: Feelings of security may lead to greater utilization of environmental features and in so doing may facilitate the development of exploratory skills. In this regard, Hazen and Durrett (1982) found that security of attachment to the caretaker at 12 months of age was positively related to degree of independent exploration and measures of spatial behavior at 30 to 34 months (see Section 6.2.3).

The results of Reiser's (1979) study point to yet another determinant of the extent of allocentric responses to be found in infancy: the task demands placed on the infant. Instead of displacing the infant to the opposite end of the room following original learning, and in the process rotating him or her 180° as well, Reiser confined himself to rotating the infant (6 months) without any change in spatial location. Under this less demanding condition there was clear evidence of allocentric responding, even at this very young age (see also Presson & Somerville, 1985). As we will see in our examination of the research with children (Section 6.2.3), this issue of the effects of experimental task demands on subjects' responses and its subsequent influence on data interpretation is critical.

In summary, the hypothesis that environmental cognition during infancy is characterized by a fixed, developmental progression from an egocentric to an allocentric frame of reference can be accepted only with qualification. If a setting is sufficiently differentiated through salient features, if there is a feeling of security in familiar surroundings, and if task demands are not too high, then even young infants reveal a sensitivity to the spatial relationships among environmental features independent of their own bodily position in the setting. (Most settings that infants find themselves in during the course of a typical day, e.g., settings in the home, will probably meet these three criteria.) For this reason, investigators should be cautious in generalizing findings obtained under one set of circumstances to other settings (Acredolo, 1982).

Rather than viewing egocentricity and allocentricity as developmentally successive reference systems, we may need to see them as reflecting different spatial skills for engaging the environment, with environmental conditions, affective states, and task demands determining in large measure which mode of performance is employed at a particular time. The most significant developmental change during this time may be the child's ability to shift to the most adaptive reference system given the immediate, situational demands (Hazen & Pick, 1985; Wohlwill, 1981).

A somewhat different assessment of spatial cognition in infancy has recently been offered by Presson and Somerville (1985), who argue that there is only one spatial reference system, an allocentric one, which is employed by the individual in a gradually expanding range of ways over the course of development. They interpret the evidence in support of an egocentric system as attributable in part to task demands, but also as instances when the infant attempts (sometimes unsuccessfully) to respond allocentrically. The ways in which the use of spatial knowledge may change with age include an increased sensitivity to a wider range of environmental features for maintaining orientation (e.g., from proximal to more distal features), and a shift from employing this knowledge solely for orienting and navigating to its symbolic expression as well, as reflected, for example, in the drawing and reading of maps.

6.2.3. Environmental Cognition in Childhood

Turning now to the literature dealing with children, we will examine several issues that were introduced in our consideration of the different theoretical approaches (Section 6.1). We will consider research pertinent to the transition from topological to configurational knowledge posited by Piaget, and route-learning and way-finding research, much of which was stimulated by Siegel and White's analysis, and then we will briefly review distance estimation studies. Our discussion will then turn to two issues especially prominent in Gibson's approach, although not necessarily exclusive to it, namely, the role of environmental exploration and the role of the functional significance of places in environmental learning. Finally, we will take up two issues that did not come up earlier but are pertinent to environmental cognition: the relationship between environmental preference and environmental cognition, and map-reading skills in children. In the course of examining all of these topics, we will consider a number of significant methodological issues.

From Topological to Configurational Knowledge

In our consideration of the theoretical approaches to the development of environmental cognition, we noted that the Piagetian and the Siegel-White models both hold that development proceeds from a landmark-oriented, noncoordinated representation of the environment to a configurational representation in which distance and positional relationships in the environment are preserved. In this section we will re-

view research that examines this hypothesized progression. The major studies relevant to this question are summarized in Table 6.2.

In one of the first investigations designed to address this issue, Acredolo, Pick, and Olsen (1975) assessed the spatial cognition skills of 3-year-olds and 8-year-olds in either an undifferentiated setting (an unfamiliar hallway) or a differentiated setting (the same hallway with the addition of two chairs serving as potential landmarks). Subjects were walked through one of these settings and at the conclusion of the walk were asked to return to the hallway location where the experimenter had previously dropped a key ring. If the child has available a configurational representation of the setting, that is, a representation with euclidean–metric properties, then he or she should be able to carry out this task in the absence of salient landmarks. On the other hand, with potential landmarks present, the child could utilize a topologically based representation to recover the key ring. The investigators reasoned that, if configurational knowledge succeeds topological knowledge developmentally, then a performance difference should be found across these two age groups in the undifferentiated setting, which required configurational representation for accurate performance, whereas no age-related differences should be found in the differentiated setting with potential landmarks present. These hypotheses were supported. Further, the performance of the 3-year-olds improved over trials in the differentiated setting, and this improvement in performance demonstrates their reliance on a topological framework, since the presence of landmarks enabled them to utilize proximity relations.

As Herman and Siegel (1978) pointed out, however, Acredolo and colleagues (1975) may have failed to uncover configurational knowledge in their younger subjects because these children had very limited exposure to the setting prior to testing. This is a significant limitation of their study, for children as young as kindergarten age not only improve in the accuracy of their placement of objects in a tabletop model of a setting (e.g., their classroom) as a function of continued exposure to the setting (Siegel & Schadler, 1977), but they also evince increasing sensitivity to the location of objects in a model of a town through which they have walked repeatedly (Herman & Siegel, 1978, Experiment 1). On the basis of this last-mentioned finding, Herman and Siegel were led to emphasize the important role of experience in determining young children's ability to structure space configurationally rather than merely on a topological basis. Yet in a second experiment these investigators were unable to replicate this effect of experience in an un-

Table 6.2. Major Empirical Studies of Topological and Configurational Representation in Early Childhood

Author(s)	Ages	Task or Situation	Major Findings
Acredolo et al. (1975)	3 and 8 years	To find previously traversed location in either differentiated or undifferentiated spatial layout	Marked age difference in undifferentiated setting; none in differentiated one
Siegel & Schadler (1977)	5.5 years	Placing items of furniture, etc., in models of classroom, with and without landmarks, and after 1 to 2 months vs. 8 months experience in classroom	Experience improved absolute accuracy of positioning of items; landmarks improved positioning of items in regard to their spatial interrelationship to one another
Herman & Siegel (1978)	6, 8, 11 years	Reconstructing layout of model town following experience in either walking through the town or viewing it repeatedly. Model town presented in either bounded space (boundaries close by) or unbounded (boundaries far away)	Accuracy increased with both age and experience with layout; viewing layout as effective as walking through it; near framework provided in bounded condition markedly improved accuracy for younger children
Liben, Moore, & Golbeck (1982)	4.5 years	Reconstructing layout of familiar classroom based on either scale model or actual classroom; also placing specific items in their proper locations	Accuracy better in full-scale than in reduced-scale environment; placement of individual items relied on topological information
Hardwick, McIntyre, & Pick (1976)	6.5, 10 years and adults	Cognitive maps of a room (school library) studied via triangulation procedure, involving pointing tube at fixed objects from different positions within room either directly experienced (walking to points) or represented in imagination	Cognitive maps generally accurate at all age levels under direct experience condition; errors increased markedly with age under imaginal representation
Curtis, Siegel, & Furlong (1981)	7, 11, 14 years	Direction and distance judgments of points in school building	Judgments generally accurate at all ages for points along a line of sight from subject; youngest children made large errors in estimating distances between points not along a line of sight, suggesting lack of configurational knowledge
Biel (1982)	6 years	Judgments of relative distance from one point in child's neighborhood to two others, the points being verbally indicated	Children generally accurate; distances from home judged with greater accuracy than from other points
Cousins, Siegel, & Maxwell (1983)	7, 10, 13 years	Assessment of landmark, route, and configurational knowledge, based on walks over terrain near school	Accuracy and configurational knowledge increased with age

bounded rather than a bounded setting: When the model town was placed in the center of a large gymnasium floor rather than in a room whose walls were in close proximity to the edges of the model, the effect of experience was no longer observed. Apparently, with repeated exposures to the bounded setting, the children were uncovering topological relations rather than learning abstract euclidean positions.

In combination, the findings of Acredolo and colleagues (1975) and Herman and Siegel (1978), along with those of Liben, Moore, and Golbeck (1982), support the theoretical claim that a topological representation of the environment precedes a configurational representation. This suggestion derives added plausibility from the confirmation by Cousins, Siegel, and Maxwell (1983) of a progression from landmark to route to configurational knowledge over the period of 7 to 14 years, in accordance with the developmental model of Siegel and White (1973). At the same time, the findings are inconsistent with an evident fact: Young children do not tend to lose their way in actuality to the extent one might predict from an exclusive reliance on topological relations, which would generally be insufficient for effective orientation and way-finding. This inconsistency may be resolved by recognizing that outside of the laboratory most settings are typically filled with a wealth of potential landmarks and environmental features, which can provide sufficient environmental information for children with a topologically based spatial representation. Where, on the other hand, settings are in fact lacking in differentiation through landmarks, or are unbounded (e.g., in the woods), spatial orientation will indeed become a problem for children, as it may for adults as well (Heft, 1979). Further discussion of the value of topological relationships in spatial knowledge can be found in Mandler (1983).

The study by Liben and colleagues (1982) cited in the preceding paragraph, besides providing further evidence on younger children's tendency to rely on topological referents, illuminates two additional and significant methodological issues. These investigators found, first, that task performance (placing items of furniture contained in the child's classroom) was more accurate in the classroom itself than when the room was only simulated via the use of a model. This finding is revealing since numerous investigations (e.g., Herman & Siegel, 1978; Siegel & Schadler, 1977) have employed model construction as a procedure for assessing cognitive abilities. In reconstructing a model of a larger-scale setting, the child must contend not only with the problem of spatial positioning of features, but also with scale reduc-

tion.[5] Second, the placement accuracy with the model was higher when the model was located in the classroom than when it was located in a separate testing room. This finding suggests that a further task demand of the typical model construction procedure is that subjects are required to *remember* the spatial position of environmental features since testing is typically done out of sight of the reference setting. In short, model construction may place significant task demands on the young child because it requires scale reduction and memory for location. Thus the results of studies adopting such an approach confound spatial representation abilities with these two additional task requirements, and consequently these findings may underestimate cognitive spatial abilities.

One procedure that obviates a need for models is the triangulation technique introduced by Hardwick, McIntyre, and Pick (1976). In this task subjects are asked to align a sighting tube or a pointer from several station points around a setting in the direction of particular fixed objects. The intersection of the directional "lines of sight" for a given object is used as an estimate of its perceived location for the subject, and collectively these intersections provide an overall estimate of the subject's configurational knowledge of the setting. The accuracy of the spatial representation can be evaluated with respect to mean angle error in sighting attempts, locational accuracy based on sighting intersections, and locational consistency of sightings (see Hardwick et al., 1976, for more details). Also, utilizing a multidimensional scaling procedure, the congruence between the estimate of configurational knowledge and a projective coordinate map of the setting can be assessed (see Curtis, Siegel, & Furlong, 1981).

Employing this triangulation method, Hardwick and colleagues (1976, Experiment 1) found that while performance measures tended to improve with age (6:5, 10:4, 21:9) the youngest subjects' cognitive representation of the setting was reasonably accurate and coherent. These findings have been replicated (Anooshian & Young, 1981). Curtis and colleagues (1981), on the other hand, found accurate directional and distance estimates only for points along a line of sight for the subject. When the children were asked to estimate distances between points that did not lie along the sighting line, first-grade children showed relatively large errors. The investigators interpret these findings to mean that young children have accurate route knowledge (here defined as knowledge of distances between sites during navigation), but their knowledge of configuration is not well articulated. By fifth grade, however, this knowledge is substantially established. In evaluating Curtis and colleague's (1981) conclusions, it is important to remember that their configurational congruence measure relies on multidimensional scaling. According to a recent study by Kirasic, Siegel, and Furlong (cited in Siegel & Cousins, 1985), this technique may underestimate accuracy of spatial representation (see also Baird, Merrill, & Tannenbaum, 1979).

An issue that has come up in several places in this discussion is that research findings to date may have underestimated children's cognitive representation skills. Two other studies of configurational knowledge are relevant to this point. Biel (1982) asked 6-year-olds to make pairwise distance comparisons between five sites in their neighborhood. These judgments were found to be internally consistent (i.e., the relative distance judgment was consistent with the location of each site relative to all others), and the interpair distance estimates corresponded to the actual distances. Biel suggests that this superior performance may be attributable to the fact that the children were making assessments relative to their own very familiar neighborhood, but the investigator's limitation to judgments of *relative* distance render his results moot with regard to their basis in a true euclidean–configurational representation.

Landau, Gleitman, and Spelke (1981) report rather more dramatic evidence, though based on a single case, for the early development of configurational knowledge. They examined the ability of a 34-month-old congenitally blind girl to walk a route between pairs of sites in a room after having only experienced the location of each from a third site. Although the paths she took between the three pairings of sites were at times circuitous, overall her performance was reasonably accurate. The investigators concluded that these results indicate at least a basic appreciation for the euclidean properties of space at this age, although they correctly point out that their findings do not speak to the issue of the origin of this knowledge.[6]

In summary, the evidence for the most part supports the developmental progression from topological or landmark knowledge to configurational knowledge posited according to both the Piagetian and the Siegel-White framework. At the same time, it seems clear that the research methods employed (e.g., map drawings, models, multidimensional scaling procedures) and the settings in which research is often carried out (e.g., unbounded settings) may lead us to underestimate children's cognitive abilities. Furthermore, most of the studies reviewed assessed children's environmental knowledge of settings in which they had limited familiarity. From Biel's (1982) findings, as well as from Acredolo's (1982) examination of the role of familiarity in infant performance, it appears that children's environmental knowledge of thoroughly explored and familiar places (e.g., the home and neighboring environs) may be relatively well developed. We will take up this issue again in considering the role of exploration in the development of environmental cognition.

Route Learning and Way Finding in Children

Common observation indicates that children are efficient travelers in their familiar environment. Happily, this casual observation is now supported by more systematically gathered data. Cousins and colleagues' (1983) assessed the ability of 7-, 10-, and 13-year-olds to find their way along three routes on their school campus. Performance at all age levels was virtually perfect: Of the entire sample, only 3 of the 16 first graders tested made any errors at all.

What is the nature of route learning and subsequent way-finding? Siegel and White (1975) and Gibson (1966, 1979) have suggested theoretical models, but only with regard to the former has research with children been carried out. In Siegel and White's (1975) model, route learning depends on an initial selection of landmarks, particularly those features located at points of navigational change; further, because landmark recognition and route learning are posited to precede configurational knowledge, way finding should be possible in the absence of knowledge of configuration.

Several studies have been conducted to test different facets of this model. In an investigation conducted by Hazen, Lockman, and Pick (1978), an experimenter taught children (ages 3 to 6) a path through a four-room or a six-room enclosure situated in a laboratory with a landmark (a toy animal) placed at the center of each room. Children at each age level had little difficulty traveling the route in reverse, or naming the landmarks in reverse order, except for the youngest group on the latter task. In contrast, inferences about the relative location between places not previously traveled were poor for the younger two groups, who were otherwise adept at route reversal.[7] These results broadly support the view that route learning precedes configurational knowledge. At the same time, however, the finding of age differences in performance on the landmark reversal task, without comparable age differences on the route reversal task, suggests the possibility that route knowledge can be differentiated into at least two components: knowledge of sequence of turns and knowledge of the landmarks to be encountered along that route. This finding, in fact, reverses the order in which landmarks and routes are thought to be learned according to Siegel and White (1975), in that route learning without apparent attention to landmarks seemed to precede landmark learning.[8] The presence of route knowledge without the subject's having learned the sequence of landmarks suggests that such knowledge should be conceived of as a "motor map of a route, which probably does not require much, if any symbolic representation, occurring largely on a sensorimotor level" (Hazen et al., 1978, pp. 628–629).

Siegel, Allen, and Kirasic (1979) also report evidence for the gradual emergence of route knowledge in children. Second graders (mean age = 7:4), fifth graders (10:7), and college students were shown a series of slides taken along a route through a commercial neighborhood and then were asked to make distance rankings among a subset of these slides. The investigators hypothesized that with the onset of route knowledge there should be an asymmetric direction effect such that distance judgments in the direction that the route (i.e., the slide sequence) was experienced should be more accurate than judgments in the reverse direction. This hypothesis was supported by the findings of a grade by direction interaction.

Starting from Siegel and White's (1975) premise that landmark identification is an important component of route learning, Allen, Kirasic, Siegel, and Herman (1979) investigated possible age-related differences in responsiveness to landmarks along a route. Second graders (mean age = 7:4), fifth graders (10:7), and college students (age unspecified) were shown a series of slides taken at varying intervals along a route through a commercial neighborhood and were asked to select the nine slides that would be most helpful in finding one's way. All subjects tended to select slides designated a priori as presenting critical information, although this tendency increased with age. A second study by Allen and colleagues (1979) showed that children's ability to *select* information scenes lags behind their ability to *utilize* such information for route learning. Cohen and Schuepfer (1980) provide further evidence for the reliance on landmarks at navigational decision points in route learning, especially among younger children, as well as support for the route learning–configurational knowledge progression hypothesized by the Siegel-White model.

It is important to note that several of the studies of route learning just reviewed employed a simulation of a route in the form of a slide presentation, and two issues need to be raised concerning this procedure.

First, those studies examining the role of landmarks variously describe the information presented to subjects as environmental landmarks, environmental features with landmark value, and scenes having potential landmark value (e.g., Allen et al., 1979). Inasmuch as subjects view entire scenes (i.e., prints made from slides) rather than specific features, only the latter designation seems appropriate. If particular features were salient landmarks, this factor is not revealed by the methodology. This largely semantic point raises a broader and more significant (and as yet unanswered) question, namely, what environmental features are selected as landmarks in way-finding.

Second, while this methodology permits the control and manipulation of environmental information, at the same time it differs from the experience of traveling a route in at least three ways. First, a route is experienced continuously over time rather than as a series of segmented and temporally frozen arrays, as is the case with a slide presentation such as employed by Siegel and his colleagues; other investigators (e.g., Cohen & Schuepfer, 1980) have utilized even more fragmented modes of presentation. An alternative procedure for presenting route information that preserves the continuity of the route is through videotape (Heft, 1979) or film (Heft, 1983).[9] Second, any purely visual simulation of a route omits other nonvisual information that may prove to be significant (Southworth, 1969). Third, in a simulated presentation of a route the subject plays a minimal role in selecting information, in contrast to the experience of actual travel along a route, where the individual can move and look around in selectively attending to environmental information. The extent to which such factors serve to confound the study of route learning remains for future research to determine.

Distance Estimation in Childhood

There is a growing body of research that examines the development of distance estimation and the effects of environmental conditions and experience on this ability. This work is related conceptually to investigations of distance conservation that grew out of the Piagetian research program, and as such, the study of this problem can be linked more broadly to the development of concrete operational thinking in children. At the same time, although this latter topic is certainly pertinent to the problem of cognitive representation of configurations and routes, as Newcombe (1982) points out, these issues have typically been treated separately.

In a relatively early study of distance estimation, Kosslyn, Pick, and Fariello (1974) asked preschoolers (median age = 4:11) and college students (21 years) to make distance judgments between 10 locations in an experimental space, subdivided into four quadrants. Two of the barriers creating the quadrant were opaque, and the other two were transparent. Through an examination of the distance judgments, the investigators found that, while the adults' configurational representation of the setting was more accurate, the children's representation was reasonably accurate as well. More significantly, children made larger relative distance judgment errors between locations separated by a barrier than between those locations that were unobstructed. These results suggest that the *functional distance* between places has a greater effect on children's as compared to adults' distance judgments, which, in turn, were most affected by obstructions to visible distance (i.e., opaque barriers).

Similarly, Anooshian and Wilson (1977) found that kindergartners overestimated the relative distance between locations connected by circuitous routes (i.e., longer functional distances). Consistent with these results, Cohen, Baldwin, and Sherman (1978) reported that the presence of hills and buildings, that is, features that would create a greater functional distance, resulted in overestimated distance judgments for 9- to 10-year-olds and adults. Surprisingly, the absence of these features seemed to have the opposite effect. A further interesting demonstration of the effect of functional distance on distance estimates was revealed in a study by Lockman (cited in Pick & Lockman, 1981) in which adult subjects ranked distances between pairings of 20 locations in a two-story house, the locations equally divided between floors. Lockman found that distances between locations on different floors were overestimated relative to locations on the same floor separated by a comparable distance.

As Cohen and Weatherford (1980) point out, in spite of the fact that the research of Kosslyn and colleagues (1974) and Cohen and colleagues (1978) highlights the significance of functional distance, neither investigation considered the effects of actually walking the paths between sites on distance estimations. Accordingly, Cohen and Weatherford (1980) obtained distance estimates from second graders (mean age = 7:6), sixth graders (11:6), and college students (20:2) for seven sites in an experimental room after the subjects had walked a designated path connecting those sites. Consistent with Kosslyn and colleagues and Cohen and colleagues the presence of barriers between locations resulted in distance overestimation. At the same time, however, the overestimation effect was reduced for those paths between locations that were previously walked by subjects,

and this pattern of results was consistent across age levels. More recently, Cohen and Weatherford (1981) replicated these findings using a different setting design. It appears then that, although barriers creating longer functional distances may result in overestimation of distance, the opportunity to walk between sites may compensate for this effect.

An additional factor that may affect distance estimates, particularly among young children, is task demands. Cohen, Weatherford, and Byrd (1980) found that when the nature of the training and that of the testing procedures are not congruent—that is, when training involved walking but testing did not, or vice versa—there is a greater tendency for younger children to overestimate distances. Similarly, Cohen, Weatherford, Lomenick, and Koeller (1979) report that first graders' distance judgments were adversely affected by constraints imposed through measurement procedures. As we have seen at several earlier points in our discussion, task demands play a critical role in performance and consequently need to be carefully considered when evaluating research findings (see Section 6.3.1).

Exploration and the Development of Environmental Cognition

Direct knowledge about the environment is obtained through exploration, although one can learn about the environment indirectly through the use of maps, photographs, and so on. Siegel and White (1975) and Gibson (1966, 1979) stress the importance of exploration, although their views on the subject differ. In this section we will focus on the relationship between exploration and environmental cognition as it is revealed in the research literature, with reference to two aspects of exploration in particular. The first concerns *type* or form of exploration (self-directed, guided by others, or passive transport); the second concerns the *extent* of the environment explored.

TYPE OF EXPLORATION

Based on the theoretical models considered, it would be expected that self-directed exploration would result in more accurate knowledge of environmental layout than would passive exploration. According to the Piagetian and the Siegel-White views, self-directed actions of the individual are critical because knowledge arises from operations on the environment and not from mere exposure to stimulus information. Siegel and White in particular consider cognitive representations of the environment to be fundamentally enactive or figurative systems that are derived from locomotion through the environment. For Gibson, on the other hand, information specifying paths and environmental layout is most readily detected through self-directed activity. Exploring the environment with movements of the eyes, head, or whole body is an essential facet of perceiving. At the same time, the individual can learn about environmental layout to some extent when being passively transported because some invariant information will be revealed in the process. Although the research to be examined does not address the relative merits of each of these views, it does speak to the differences between self-directed and other types of exploration.

Feldman and Acredolo (1979) asked a group of children 3- to 4-years-old and 9- to 10-years-old to locate a site in a series of hallways where they had previously found an object (a cup). At the time of initial exposure to the setting, either the children were led through the hallways to the cup by the experimenter (guided exploration condition) or they were allowed to find their own way with minimal direction from the experimenter (self-directed exploration condition). The performance of the younger children was more accurate in the self-directed exploration condition. The older children did not differ in their performance across these two conditions, although they were more accurate overall in their judgments than the younger group.

Herman (1980) presents data that at first glance appear to contradict this conclusion. Kindergartners (mean age = 5:10) and third graders (8:8) guided through a model town by an experimenter who pointed out each building were more accurate in their subsequent constructions of the town than were subjects who either were guided through the town without commentary, were guided around the perimeter of the model town, or were engaged in self-directed exploration of the model town. The discrepancy between these results and those reported by Feldman and Acredolo (1979) can be attributed, at least in part, to the differences in *scale* of the settings used in the two studies. While Herman's model town was small enough to allow the entire model to be seen from a single vantage point, Feldman and Acredolo's setting was considerably larger, since it enclosed and surrounded the child. The value of self-directed exploration, especially for young children, may be most evident in settings of this latter scale, rather than in those reduced in scale and for which no motor activity is needed in order to perceive the entire layout of the setting. In fact, the relative unimportance of motor activity for learning the layout of these model towns was demonstrated by Herman and Siegel (1978), who found that young children who were led through the model town were no more accurate in

their constructions than children who merely looked at the town from a single vantage point.

An important examination of the relative effectiveness of self-directed versus guided exploration from a different research perspective has recently been reported by Hazen (1982). She treats these types of exploration as consistent and distinctive *individual styles* that generalize across settings, rather than looking at the significance of each exploration type for children in general. In her investigation, the predominant type of exploration utilized by children of two age groups (20 to 28 months and 36 to 44 months) was assessed through observation of their explorations in a natural history museum and among three rooms constructed in the laboratory. An observer recorded the number of moves between exhibits and among the laboratory rooms (quantity of exploration) and whether explorations were self-directed or guided by an adult (quality of exploration). Following these initial observations, the children were taught a route through the laboratory enclosures and then were tested on their knowledge of the route and the configuration of the setting. Hazen found that amount of *self-directed* exploration in the museum and among the laboratory enclosures was positively related to several measures of knowledge about environmental layout, but sheer quantity of exploration was not. This finding suggests that type of exploration (e.g., self-directed vs. passive exploration) may be an individual style that generalizes across settings, since the information concerning quantity and quality of exploration was obtained in one setting (i.e., the museum) and tested in another. Further, style of exploration appears to be relevant to the superior performance of the older children in this study. While both age groups engaged in a similar *amount* of exploration in the museum and in the laboratory, the older children engaged in more self-directed exploration. The studies of Feldman and Acredolo (1979) and Hazen (1982), both of which were carried out in naturalistic settings, thus come to the same conclusion: Self-directed exploration, as compared to guided exploration, facilitates learning about environmental layout.

A further question we can raise is: What might be the source of self-directed exploration as an *individual style* of behavior? Recent research of Hazen and Durrett (1982) addresses this question through an examination of children's exploration style, as well as environmental cognition skills generally, in relation to the nature of their early attachment to their mothers. Children (approximately 32 months of age) who had been previously classified as either securely attached infants, anxious/avoidant infants, or anxious/resistant infants[10] were participants in the study. The investigators observed the children and their mothers exploring a four-room curtained enclosure, and as in Hazen (1982) both the amount of exploration and the type of exploration (guided vs. self-directed) were assessed. Children classified as securely attached engaged in a greater degree of self-directed activity, but not a greater amount of exploration per se, and the anxious/resistant group was less likely to venture outside of the enclosure than were the other two groups. In addition, the securely attached group performed more skillfully than their counterparts on a subsequent route-finding task conducted in the same room. This study is significant in revealing an early predictor of exploratory style; however, it does not indicate the reasons for this relationship between attachment and mode of exploration (see Hazen and Durrett, 1982, for a discussion of several possible explanations). Hazen's work represents an important approach to the study of environmental cognition in its examination of individual differences rather than generalized spatial skills. We will return to this issue in the next section.

EXTENT OF EXPLORATION

The second aspect of exploration to be considered is extent or range of activities, and in particular, the relationship between extent of experience in exploring the environment and the development of knowledge concerning environmental layout. Certainly, children's understanding of environmental layout will influence their environmental explorations; at the same time, opportunities to explore will facilitate the development of environmental cognition (see Wohlwill & Heft, Chapter 9, this volume, for an examination of the more general developmental implications of exploration).

Barker and Wright's (1955) observational studies of the children of the town of Midwest indicate that the amount of time spent outdoors increases steadily with age during childhood, reaching a peak in adolescence. What is the relationship between this increase in outdoor activity and environmental knowledge? Based on some early studies that examined subjects' hand-drawn maps of the environment, it would appear that, with greater exposure to the environment in question, knowledge of the environment improves in accuracy and detail (Appleyard, 1970; Ladd, 1970). More recently, Hart (1979, 1981), as a part of his comprehensive study of the environmental experiences of children in a small New England town, examined the models that children constructed of

their town in relation to information concerning their exploratory activities. He also determined the extent of the town they could explore without permission (free range), with permission, or in the company of other children. Hart found that the extent of the town included in the models was positively correlated with age, free range, and range with permission. In addition, extent of exploration was associated with the degree of sophistication of their models. Using two different measures of level of organization, Hart found that the more advanced models (e.g., those "abstractly coordinated"), tended to be constructed by those children with more extensive free range, range with permission, and range with others. These findings suggest that the development of environmental cognition is directly influenced by opportunities to explore.

This point is made more forcefully by the finding that even the youngest children in this study (4- and 5-year-olds) constructed models that contained some regions with accurately coordinated elements. These regions tended to be home-centered; that is, they constituted that portion of the environment in which the child had the most experience exploring. According to the Piagetian framework, representations at this level of organization are not to be expected by preschoolers (see also Biel, 1982). However, exploration, presumably of the self-directed type, can apparently facilitate the development of sophisticated cognitive representations of environmental layout. Among older children as well, Hart found varying levels of organization of different regions of the model and the level of organization seemed to be associated with the degree of familiarity with the region.

The level of organization of the models was also related to gender. Girls in Hart's sample produced models of the town that were on the average inferior to those of the boys. This difference is most likely attributable to the considerable differences in exploratory activity across sex. The girls had much more restricted parentally defined ranges and less often took trips around town alone (i.e., engaged in self-directed activity). It would appear that the more limited environmental experiences of the girls affected their understanding of the layout of the town, as reflected in the model-building task. In turn, more limited knowledge of the environment may curtail subsequent self-initiated explorations of the environment at older ages; as noted earlier, development of environmental cognition and exploration are likely to be reciprocally related.

This conclusion points more generally to the reciprocal influence between environment and behavior, such that the quality of environmental experience can be viewed at once as a product of the child's behavior and a primary influence on behavioral development. Incipient behavioral differences related to, for example, gender, temperament, and activity level may affect responsivity to environmental stimulation, which may be reflected in early individual differences in exploration (e.g., Hutt, 1972), and as a result, differentially affect the development of environmental cognition across individuals (Wohlwill, 1981).

Distinctive Structural Features, the Affordances of Places, and Environmental Knowledge

Lynch's (1960) seminal work on environmental cognition highlighted the significance of structural characteristics of the environment in adults' knowledge of cities. There have been few attempts to link this work to the development of environmental cognition in children, and the absence of this connection is attributable, in part, to the fact that very few studies with children have been conducted in sufficiently large-scale settings for Lynch's concepts to be applicable. Hart's (1979; 1981) investigation, discussed in the previous section, is exceptional in this regard, and he does report some evidence on the relationship between children's environmental knowledge and distinctive structural features of their town. For example, in his analysis, Hart noted that in the better-organized models of the town the children used the roads as a reference around which to position buildings and other features; in the poorer models, roads were employed primarily to connect landmarks. This finding is in accordance with the route learning/ configurational progression discussed previously, and it also points to the role of *paths*, to use Lynch's terminology, in conceptualizing the environment. Further, Hart found that a particularly distinctive, or "imageable," crossroad (i.e., a *node*) in town was utilized as a reference point by even the youngest children tested. Thus, although younger children may rely on topological relations in the environment, and consequently construct models that reflect a greater knowledge of routes than of configuration, very distinctive structural characteristics of the environment may result in a more sophisticated level of understanding than might be expected at a given age. By focusing on distinctive structural features of the environment, we may view the development of environmental cognition as not merely a transformation in levels of cognitive representation, but also as a changing sensitivity to environmental information. As environmental features become more distinctive

through perceptual differentiation (E.J. Gibson, 1969), these features can be utilized for an increasingly complex conceptualization of environmental layout.

A further potentially significant point is raised by the finding that a crossroad in town was a prominent part of most children's models. A factor that probably made this node especially salient, other than its structure, was the fact that stores selling candy were located on three of its four corners—a feature that would pass by very few children! This finding suggests that the process of learning about the environment may be based to some extent on the functional significance of places. In Hart's study other places in the environment were identified in functional terms. He reports that a young girl (5:11) identified a specific house in her model as "the house with the dog that bites." Hart notes further:

> Similarly, when describing streets or regions the children use the name of the children they play with such as "on Peter Scott's hill" or "it's down Joe Douglas' streetway." When talking with each other, children most commonly use descriptors throughout their elementary school lives. When they use the more general descriptors in talking with adults, such as Plum Hill and North Hill, they frequently get mixed up. (p. 150)

These observations indicate that children may learn the places or regions of the environment in terms of their functional implications; that is, in terms of what they will find there (e.g., "dangerous and scary places"), whom they will find there, what kind of activities are afforded there, and so on. The primacy of functional knowledge is also suggested by findings previously discussed indicating that children's distance estimates are more influenced by functional characteristics (e.g., availability of a path between sites) than are those of adults.

According to Gibson (1979), the environment is experienced primarily in terms of the functional significance of environmental features, that is, in terms of its *affordances*. Affordances are derived from the structural properties of the environment and are perceptual in nature (see Heft, 1985). Consequently, for a feature to qualify as an affordance, its functional meaning must be potentially, at least, specifiable in terms of stimulus information available to the perceiver. The perceived functional character of environmental features has been considered in the work of Barker and his colleagues. In their study *Midwest and Its Children*, Barker and Wright (1955) discuss various sources of behavior–milieu synomorphy (i.e., factors that influence the congruence between standing patterns of behavior and the nonpsychological features of the environment), including *physiognomic perception*. With regard to this latter factor, particular natural or built places in the environment are considered to exert a "coercive influence" on perception and on activity; in other words, these places are perceived in terms of their functional significance, that is, as affordances.

> The children of Midwest appear to see a smooth, level area which is free from obstructions, such as the football field, the Courthouse lawn, the school gymnasium, or the American Legion hall, as places for running and romping in unorganized, exuberant activity. The milieu features of such behavior settings appear via perception to demand this kind of behavior. Open spaces seduce children. The behavior settings of Midwest are loaded with these perceived, seductive characteristics. (p. 55)

In light of this statement from Barker and Wright, it is worth noting that Hart (1979) found that the most popular place among both boys and girls in his study was the town ballfield. Similarly, Lynch (1977) reports a preference for green spaces among children in Cracow, Poland.

Other examples of children's perceiving environmental features as affordances appear in the pioneering research of Martha Muchow (Muchow & Muchow, 1935; see also Wohlwill & Heft, Chapter 9, this volume). In her observations of children playing around a canal loading dock area in Hamburg, Muchow observed that fences separating the area from the street and embankments sloping down to the wharf were focal elements for their activity. While the fence may have been intended to serve as a boundary, it was apparently perceived as an environmental feature to be climbed and to be perched on by the children, and similarly, the embankments were for sliding, running, and climbing as well as for rolling objects down its slopes.

Further, the affordances of environmental features appear as prominent aspects of adults' memories of their childhood in the city (Lukashok & Lynch, 1956). Among the most common references in the subjects' reminiscences were the play opportunities afforded by lawns, sidewalks, and other ground surfaces, and by trees and low buildings (e.g., garages) that one could climb, jump from, and hide in.

If, indeed, the affordances of the landscape are especially salient, as Gibson suggests, it would be interesting to examine the development of environmental cognition with these properties in mind. As we have seen, most studies have focused on structural (e.g. configuration) rather than functional characteristics of the environment. However, closer attention to the perception of the affordances of places in the environment may reveal that such perception can facilitate the development of configurational knowledge. This possibility is suggested by research of Cohen and Cohen (1982), who found that children's knowledge of the distances between sites (i.e., stations established in a classroom) was more accurate following a task that functionally linked those sites, as compared to the knowledge of those children who merely walked routes connecting the sites or who performed independent tasks at each site. This finding held both for paths that were previously walked and paths not walked; a comparison of estimates for walked paths alone was not significant.[11]

It may be that the layout of the environment is learned originally with respect to its affordances, with configurational knowledge coming later as various contextual or task demands require. For example, one may know the configuration of the roads in some region of the environment, but such knowledge could be an abstraction from the more immediate awareness that "this road" leads to the candy stores, for example, and "that road" leads to the school. Such an abstraction might be produced when one needs to determine a new route between places, or when one is asked for configurational information by researchers, for instance. If investigators would begin to examine environmental knowledge in terms of the affordances of places, they might discover not only that such knowledge is basic to children's understanding about their environment, but also that children are more knowledgeable about the environment than has yet been revealed.

Children's Environmental Preference and Environmental Cognition

As noted in the context of our discussion of infant research (Section 6.2.2), cognitive processes have been typically examined in isolation relative to other potentially significant psychological factors such as affective state. However, environmental preferences and affective responses relative to particular aspects of the environment may interact with environmental cognition. Research on children's environmental preference and on their affective or evaluative judgments is virtually nonexistent, the study by Balling and Falk (1982) representing a rare exception (see Wohlwill & Heft, Chapter 9, this volume). Nagy and Baird (1978; see also Baird, 1982) have, however, examined the spatial configurations created by children when asked to plan an *ideal* playground and compared these with their maps of an actual playground. Using a congruence measure between the configurations of the features on either of these two map representations and those in the real environment, they found that fourth and sixth graders' representations of the actual environment showed a much higher degree of congruence with the real one than was the case for their ideal configuration. This finding suggests that the children were not simply assimilating the "ideal" instruction to the task of reproducing a familiar environment; they were creating a new environment. That conclusion, in turn, is relevant to the interpretation of the same authors' findings from a previous study of fourth and twelfth graders' representation of an ideal *town*. In various respects, interesting differences emerged between the two age groups in the latter investigation: For instance, the fourth graders placed the home in a more peripheral location and tended to maximize its distance from the hospital, presumably reflecting real differences in their conception of an ideal town. Nagy and Baird further report that the children's view of the ideal town was related to their sense of aesthetics (i.e., fourth graders' ideal town tended to emphasize balance and symmetry, more so than those of the older subjects).

Nagy and Baird's research represents an interesting attempt to go beyond the veridicality emphasis that has marked virtually all of the research on environmental cognition, and examine children, in their words, as "planners"; that is, to consider budding conceptions of an ideal environment. Their methodology, directed at the assessment of the degree of congruence between the child's conception of both an actual and an ideal environment and the real spatial configuration of that environment, is an interesting one, though the multidimensional scaling technique employed is subject to certain limitations, as noted earlier.

The findings of Nagy and Baird that children do not simply assimilate the environmental configurations they prefer or consider ideal to those that they know are relevant to a conclusion reached by Gould and White (1974), whose work lays major stress on the extent of the child's knowledge and information about a particular location or area as a prime determinant of the child's preference. Their work dealt with environments at a much broader scale than any that we have considered thus far. They mapped both the informational and the preference space corresponding to the child's own region or country, along with adjoining geographic areas among school-age children in Sweden, Norway, and Nigeria. For these geographic areas, experienced vicariously for the most part, children's preferences showed a close re-

lationship to the extent of their knowledge about them (and thus conformed essentially to a random pattern prior to the acquisition of such knowledge). But as Gould and White note themselves, information may act to detract from as well as enhance the preference expressed for a particular locale, depending on the characteristics associated with it, so the relationship between knowledge and preference, though high, is far from perfect.

The work of Nagy and Baird (1978) and of Gould and White (1974) bears out, in any event, the importance of studying preference for environments, and affective responses to them, along with the child's cognitive representation of the environment, for a proper understanding of the way in which the environment is comprehended and experienced by the child, in a broad functional sense.

Children's Map-Reading Skills

The preceding sections have dealt largely with investigations of the processes involved in children's cognitive representation of the environment, in the service of orientation and way-finding. That topic is clearly of direct relevance to a more specific skill that children are called on to acquire in our culture, namely, reading and interpreting actual maps of particular environmental areas. Whereas most of the investigations considered in the previous sections dealt with knowledge about environmental settings obtained through direct, first-hand experience, map reading is an indirect way in which we learn about the environment.

We need to recognize at the outset that map reading involves several different processes. First, there is a strong perceptual component involved in interpreting a map, for instance, in detecting differences in relief, in following contours that may be intersected by other lines, and in integrating information that may be distributed over a considerable area. Second, there is an obvious symbolic element involved in encoding features on a map. Third, the proper reading of a map requires the ability to recognize that it is a scalar projection and that alignment with compass directions is necessary. All of these aspects of map reading, along with spatial orientation and map construction per se, should be of concern both to developmental psychologists and to those involved in geography education. Yet they have received surprisingly little systematic attention on the part of researchers. Thus a brief review of a few significant studies will suffice.

Blaut and his associates (Blaut, McCleary, & Blaut, 1970; Stea & Blaut, 1973) provided an initial impetus to research on this problem through their studies on grade school children's responses to information contained in aerial photographs. Their main finding was that both American and Puerto Rican children, from at least the age of kindergarten on, are able to identify particular features from such photographs, houses, trees, streets, and the like, with some degree of success. Curiously, while there is considerable improvement between kindergarten and the second grade, little further change was found (in the Puerto Rican study) between the second and sixth grades, leaving the latter children still well short of complete success on this task (Stea & Blaut, 1973). The nature of this task, furthermore, appears to be largely perceptual, involving the recognition of an object or environmental feature from a photographic representation of it, albeit from an unusual angle, that is, from the air, and greatly reduced in normal size. Whatever the basis for this skill, it clearly need not involve any process related to the structuring of relationships among environmental features. The same point applies to a task reported by Blaut and colleagues (1970), which was considered to be a measure of way-finding.

The photographs used by Blaut and colleagues differ from standard maps in bearing an iconic relationship to the environment portrayed. That is true similarly of so-called perceptual maps, popular with tourists, in which major features of an area are drawn in to simulate the actual environment, thereby minimizing the purely symbolic relationship between map and environment. Spencer, Harrison, and Darvizeh (1980) have used both aerial photographs and perceptual maps in a study similar to Blaut and colleagues but extending the age range downward to preschool level. They report that even preschoolers are successful in identifying the major features contained in both the photographs and the perceptual maps such as roads, houses, trees, a river, a railway line; however, less differentiated aspects of the natural terrain such as hills and fields proved less readily identifiable. These differences among features serve to reinforce the interpretation of this skill as an essentially perceptual one, based on the detection of distinctive features, much as E.J. Gibson (1969) has discussed in her theory of perceptual learning.

Bluestein and Acredolo (1979) come to a conclusion similar to that of Spencer and colleagues, namely, that map reading in a rudimentary sense can be demonstrated at the preschool level. The focus of their study was children's ability to interpret information on maps representing a single room rather than a large geographical area. They used a simple task in which children had to find a toy hidden in a particular spot in the room designated on a map of the room that was presented to them. When the orientation of the map matched that of the room, even 3-year-olds were able to use the map to find the toy, regardless of whether the map was presented inside the room or outside before the child entered the room (and thereby requiring a representation of the map in memory). Not surprisingly, rotating the map 180° caused a marked drop in performance among both the 3- and the 4-year-olds, but by age 5 the children were able to achieve the necessary mental rotation to use the map even in that condition. Presson (1982), however, found that this ability to use a map presented at an 180° rotation did not develop until age 8; and the same applied to a lesser extent for a 90° rotation. The important difference between the two studies was that Presson's (1982) was limited to a bare room containing but a single landmark that the child could use to align the map, whereas in the earlier study there were a number of features in the room that could serve that function.

These studies indicate, then, that young children are able to achieve a correspondence between a relatively restricted environmental area and a representation of that area through a map, but that, as previous research had shown (Pufall & Shaw, 1973; see also Section 6.2.2), the achievement of a mental rotation of the space presents difficulties, at least in early childhood. None of these studies, however, addresses the question of the extent to which young children are able to utilize a map to orient themselves geographically, or to aid in way-finding. Even research undertaken by those in the field of geographical education does not seem to have answered that question (see review by Rushdoony, 1968; Meyer, 1973).

6.3. A REEXAMINATION OF CONCEPTUAL AND METHODOLOGICAL ISSUES

In this final section we will return to some of the issues raised as a set of preliminary questions earlier (Section 6.2.1) in the light of our research review, and we will also consider other issues that emerged from the review and indicate some directions for future research. The ensuing discussion will be organized around the following four topics: task demands and the problem of externalizing spatial knowledge; environmental scale and the problem of ecological representativeness; the role of environmental features and affective state; and the configurational and cognitive bias in environmental cognition research.

6.3.1. Task Demands and the Problem of Externalizing Spatial Knowledge

There has been growing recognition among investigators in the environmental cognition area that the demands of the testing situation can significantly influence children's task performance. As a result, it is difficult to obtain a clear indication of the child's cognitive representation of the environment independent of the procedures employed in attempting to "externalize" it. To take an obvious and long-recognized example, it is clear that the disorganization and sketchiness typical of children's hand-drawn maps tell us at least as much, if not more, about their rudimentary drawing skills at a particular age as about an underlying spatial representation. To avoid this problem, some researchers (e.g., Siegel & Schadler, 1977) have asked children to construct models of a familiar setting. Again, as we have seen, this task requires more than just "externalizing" a spatial representation since in order to build a model the child is faced with the problem of reconstructing a familiar setting from memory and also of shifting from one scale to another. As Liben and colleagues (1982) found, when the demands presented by changes in memory requirements and in scale are reduced, children's performance improves. Similarly, children's distance estimates are affected by the way in which these judgments are obtained (Cohen et al., 1979). Other approaches such as ordinal distance rankings that are subsequently analyzed through multidimensional scaling techniques are subject to problems of their own. The extrapolated spatial representation that results from this procedure appears to underestimate subjects' knowledge of the environment (Baird et al., 1979: Kirasic et al., 1982, cited in Siegel & Cousins, 1985); furthermore, because various mathematical solutions can be imposed on the data, a number of different derived cognitive representations are possible (Liben, 1982).

As a result of these considerations, two positions seem to be emerging that may influence future research. First, the claim is being presented by a number of investigators that previous research has tended to underestimate children's spatial competencies; that, in fact, the somewhat poor performance often demonstrated by young children in experimental settings is a product of significantly demanding tasks, as well as other setting factors, and as such it belies the high degree of spatial competence that is evidenced in everyday settings (e.g., Landau & Spelke, 1985; Liben et al., 1982; Siegel & Cousins, 1985; Spencer & Darvizeh, 1981; see also Presson & Somerville, 1985, who make a similar argument with regard to infant research in this area). In all likelihood, our research findings to date have underestimated children's spatial abilities; the question that remains is to what degree. At the same time, Liben and colleagues (1982) caution against going too far in the other direction and overestimating these skills. However, at present we are left with an uncertain picture as to children's competence with regard to various aspects of environmental cognition and environmental behavior. In order for future research to clarify this issue, investigators may need to probe children's spatial skills with more careful attention to task demands and in less contrived settings than in the past. We will return to this latter point.

A second related issue concerns the general focus of environmental cognition research, which was recently discussed by Siegel and Cousins (1985). They maintain that while the notion of *competence* in the environmental cognition area (analogous to its use in psycholinguistics) suggests spatial capacities that may be isolated from particular tasks, environmental knowledge and behavior need instead to be studied in relation to particular situations and situational demands. They state:

> Competence implies a context-free capability; ...we suggest that a more appropriate unit for analysis is the action or performance itself in the context of a particular task, rather than the individual's presumed situation-independent capability. (p. 359)

Such a contextualist view follows from the task-dependent nature of performance.

Rather than "externalizing" spatial knowledge in some abstract sense, investigations reveal the forms that spatial knowledge takes as the child attempts to function adaptively in various environmental contexts. Spatial knowledge may not be a structure that can be isolated from the context in which it is expressed. An emphasis on spatial *performance* leads to a view of spatial knowledge as a set of distinct, though related, behavioral skills instead of some underlying, unitary capacity (Wohlwill, 1981). A conceptualization of spatial knowledge as a set of multiple skills that are selectively employed in different environmental circumstances recognizes a greater measure of adaptability and flexibility in spatial behavior than is the case in a unitary view. In addition, a multiple skills approach is consistent with conclusions drawn from some investigations of spatial orientation in animals (Hazen, 1983).

6.3.2. Environmental Scale and the Problem of Ecological Representativeness

In the first few years of research in this area, table top models of settings, large models within which the child could walk, and naturally occurring settings were typically treated as comparable "environments" for revealing the nature of spatial representation. Investigators are now beginning to demonstrate a greater awareness of the significance of environmental scale in their research, and as a result they are beginning to question whether findings obtained through research with one of these types of conditions can be generalized to the other conditions. More specifically, because the vast majority of research in the area has been conducted with model spaces, it has become necessary to consider whether the results of this research can be generalized to processes at work in representative, everyday, large-scale environments.

While the necessary data required to answer these questions definitively are not yet available, it appears at this time that in all likelihood findings derived from model settings are not generalizable to everyday, large-scale environments. We have seen several instances where the findings from research in large-scale settings differ from those derived from the other scale settings (e.g., compare Liben et al., 1982, and Siegel & Schadler, 1977; Acredolo, et al., 1975, and Herman & Siegel, 1978; see also Siegel et al., 1979). The goals of the particular investigation are what is important here. If the primary aim of the research is to understand the nature and development of *environmental* cognition, it may be necessary to select or design conditions that are comparable in scale to naturally occurring settings. On the other hand, if investigators are interested in children's responses to models or to maps of the environment, these experimental conditions are certainly most appropriate for those purposes. Scaled-down models of naturally occurring settings (e.g., a model town) and maps of the environment differ in so many ways from their naturalistic counterparts that it is not at all clear without careful analysis whether psychological processes uncovered in one context are similar to those uncovered in the other. It will not do simply to assume that the processes at work are the same regardless of the scale employed (see Lockman & Pick, 1984).

In their considerations of the environmental scale and the ecological representativeness of research settings, investigators will benefit from an examination of the thoughtful analyses of the environment pre-sented by Gibson (1966, Chapter 1, 1979, Chapter 1) and by Ittelson (1973), bearing in mind that these analyses represent different theoretical approaches to perception. As both of these perceptual psychologists point out, the environment surrounds the individual—the environment is spatially extended, and consequently the individual must actively explore the environment in order to learn about it. Further, they both suggest that the features of the environment are perceived in terms of their functional meaning. In keeping with the abstract, largely geometric orientation derived from the Piagetian approach, much of the research in the area has focused on structural knowledge of spatial layout, with little regard to the functional significance of settings. As we have seen, however, the meaning of places in the environment for children may play an important role in their understanding of the environment.

At the same time it is important to note that real world environments (as opposed to models or maps of the environment) vary in scale, with smaller units of the environment nested within successively larger units. Thus, for example, a child's bedroom might be considered one scale unit, which is nested within the home, which in turn is one feature in the larger neighborhood, and so on. In future investigations we will want to remain sensitive to these scale levels in order to determine whether the psychological processes uncovered within one level are comparable to those required at other levels. These considerations return us to the preceding discussion of the need for considering spatial behavior in context (Section 6.3.1).

6.3.3. The Role of Environmental Features and Affective State

Our review of the research broadly supported the theoretical model offered by Piaget, as extended by Hart and Moore, and the model of Siegel and White. The development of a cognitive representation of the environment seems to be describable in terms of systems of reference, or levels of representation, as suggested by these frameworks. At the same time, however, much of the research indicates that significant revisions of these positions are required. The infancy and childhood research examined previously demonstrates that while particular stages seem to be developmentally prior to others, there is greater precocity and flexibility in cognitive skills than would be predicted in either model. The reference system employed by the child appears to be determined not only by developmental considerations, but also by environmental conditions confronting the child at any particular time. For example, we have seen that the availability of environmental features can support allocentricity in infants (e.g., Acredolo & Evans, 1979) and an accurate conceptualization of positional relations in the setting by young children (e.g., Herman & Siegel, 1978; Hart, 1979).[12]

As pointed out earlier, findings such as these suggest that spatial reference systems reflect alternative skills for adjusting to various conditions as a function of the environmental information available. Development in this domain may largely involve improved facility in selecting the reference system that is most adaptive for a particular setting. Perhaps as the child becomes increasingly sensitive to varieties of environmental information, more advanced levels of conceptualization can be employed with less salient information present. Alternatively, instances when an egocentric spatial reference system seems to have been operating, when examined more closely, may indicate that in fact infants were utilizing environmental information, and responding allocentrically, all along (Presson & Somerville, 1985). Similarly, Landau and Spelke (1985) have recently argued that spatial knowledge itself undergoes little development during childhood; instead, spatial skills improve because the child learns to utilize environmental information as landmarks, as well as to coordinate motor activity with spatial knowledge.

These considerations suggest that a more complete understanding of the development of environmental cognition requires much closer attention to a specification of the environmental information available to the individual in a given situation (see Heft, 1981; Moore, 1979; Wohlwill, 1973, 1976). Additionally, in a developmental context, studies of *perceptual learning* are called for to reveal the increasing sensitivity of the developing child to environmental information as a function of the experience (E.J. Gibson, 1969; E.J. Gibson & Spelke, 1983). Indeed, further progress in our understanding of the developmental processes involved in this realm would seem to require at some point a shift from the essentially descriptive age group comparisons that are the norm in this field of research to attempts through either observational or experimental approaches (or both) to study the effects of particular forms of environmental experiences, both short and long term, on the child's environmental learning.

Affective processes have also been largely excluded from research considerations, but as Acredolo (1982) has shown, these factors could prove to be significant. What is the relationship between affect and environmental performance? Acredolo suggests "that if one is highly aroused, one is consid-

erably less likely to attend to the very spatial information that might make the environment more familiar" (p. 26). In other words, the child's affective state at any particular time may influence perceptual sensitivity to available environmental information.

Further, there is some evidence to indicate that knowledge about places, at least at the scale of countries or regions, influences environmental preferences to some extent (Gould & White, 1974). In turn environmental preferences give rise to the possibility of children's imaginative constructions of ideal or alternative environments (Nagy & Baird, 1978).

A plea to incorporate the role of affective processes into our models for the analysis of environmental knowledge and its development appears particularly relevant for work with children, for whom cognition and affect are not apt to function in the tightly compartmentalized fashion implicit in most experimental research on cognition. Such a plea might well be supplemented by a suggestion to rely to a greater extent than has been done heretofore on observations of children's spontaneous behavior, through analysis of play, games, and exploration of the large-scale environment, to complement evidence from systematic experimental research. In this regard, Hart's (1979) field study of children in a Vermont village stands as a model effort that deserves to be applied and elaborated on a wide scale.

6.3.4. The Configurational and Cognitive Bias in Environmental Cognition Research

In both the Piagetian and the Siegel-White theoretical models, configurational–euclidean knowledge of the environment is seen as the highest level of spatial representation, and as a result, it is typically used as the standard against which performance is evaluated. This form of knowledge has the metric properties of a cartographic survey map, and at least since Tolman investigators have typically taken the survey map as the metaphor for a cognitive representation of the environment.

This emphasis on configurational representations, with the cartographic map serving as metaphor, has generally been accepted all too uncritically by investigators (see Downs, 1981), to the detriment of a more broadly based conceptualization of the psychological processes contributing to the development of environmental knowledge. It should be recognized that Piaget used formal logic, mathematics, and geometry as the basis for describing the structure of thought, and the development of knowledge about the world is seen as involving the progressive approximation of thought to these formalizations. Thus the focus of Piaget's study of spatial knowledge is how children understand the geometry of space. However, environmental knowledge entails more than thinking about the environment; it also involves acting—wayfinding, exploration, orientation—activities that enable the individual to function adaptively in the environment (see Hazen & Pick, 1985). In order to do justice to such processes, we may need to consider alternative models. Some alternatives are available, but only in somewhat undeveloped form (e.g., Gibson, 1966, 1979, see Section 6.1; Neisser, 1976), and to date little attention has been given to these models within the environmental cognition area.

In short, we may need to question our inclination to explain all forms of environmental knowledge in terms of an underlying cognitive representation (Liben, 1982). With a greater appreciation for alternative theoretical models of environmental perception and environmental cognition, a consideration of psychological processes from a more contextualist point of view, and a recognition of the influence of factors such as preference and affect, the next decade of research may reveal a broadening of perspectives in our study of this problem.

Acknowledgments

Work on this chapter was supported in part through a Denison University Professional Development Award to Harry Heft.

NOTES

1. In addition to the research reviewed in this chapter, the reader is referred to several edited volumes of papers, both on environmental cognition generally (Downs & Stea, 1973; Moore & Golledge, 1976; Pick & Acredolo, 1983) and on its developmental aspects in particular (Cohen, 1982, 1985; Liben, Patterson, & Newcombe, 1981), and to a number of of review articles and chapters (Evans, 1980; Golledge, Chapter 5, this volume; Hart & Moore, 1973; Hazen & Pick, 1985; Siegel, Kirasic, & Kail, 1978).

2. Liben (1981) has argued that Piaget did not consider spatial behavior necessarily to be supported by cognitive structures. Instead, actions in space such as solving a detour problem rely on a practical notion of space that is distinguishable from the logical structures underlying spatial thought. However, the spatial behavior made possible by practical structures is limited. It is necessary for symbolic reasoning to develop in order to go "beyond short and rapidly automatized connections between perceptions and responses (habit), and operate at progressively greater distances and by more complex routes, in the direction of mobility and reversibility" (Piaget, 1966, p. 116). Thus within a

strict Piagetian framework the kinds of complex spatial behaviors of concern in the environmental cognition area may indeed require support from cognitive representations.

3. Acredolo (1981) has pointed out that Piaget's use of topological relations may not be in keeping with the standard view of topology in mathematics. Topology lacks any conception of distance, metric or otherwise; therefore, proximity and separation may be inconsistent with this geometric framework. See also Mandler's (1983) discussion of Piaget's topology.

4. This study of Acredolo's (1978) appears to be the only example of the use of a longitudinal design in research on the development of environmental cognition. The predilection of researchers for the cross-sectional shortcut, however understandable for pragmatic reasons, has considerably reduced the value of this body of research, since it has failed to provide any direct information concerning the *changes* in the children's cognitive processes occurring during their development. A fortiori, factors that might relate to these changes, such as conditions of experience, have remained virtually ignored.

5. Siegel, Herman, Allen, and Kirasic (1979) found that, when young children were exposed to a large-scale model town and were then asked to construct either a large-scale or a small-scale model of that town, performance in both cases was comparable. However, Liben and colleagues (1982) point out that levels of performance in this study were relatively low, especially for the youngest children tested—an outcome that might be attributable to the demands of scale reduction. The superior performance of the preschoolers in the classroom relative to the models in Liben and colleagues (1982) supports this contention.

6. See Landau and Spelke (1985) for an account of more recent investigations of spatial cognition with this child.

7. In a recent study, Herman, Shiraki, and Miller (1985) report an improvement in spatial inferences between children 3- and 5-years-old. They account for the discrepancy between these findings and those of Hazen and colleagues (1978) by referring to the size of the experimental settings in each investigation. Herman and colleagues conducted their research in a larger setting (i.e., a nursery school), and the greater demands placed on their subjects as a consequence of this scale factor apparently revealed a difference in spatial reasoning between these age groups not uncovered in the earlier study. More generally, this discrepancy points again to the importance of being sensitive to the environmental scale of settings in designing research and in interpreting findings (see Section 6.3.2).

8. It should be noted, however, that the landmarks in this study, placed as they were in the center of the rooms, may have played little role in guiding way-finding—a role that is important in Siegel and White's model. Thus these findings do not offer a compelling case against the Siegel and White model.

9. The differences in choice of medium, that is, slides versus film, may reflect a deeper issue, namely, the manner in which perceptual processes are conceptualized. As discussed earlier, in the constructivist approach to perception,

manifested, for example, in information-processing models, information to the visual system is considered to be temporally discrete and must be integrated cognitively. Consequently, the choice of a slide presentation may appear to be quite in keeping with the assumed nature of perception. In Gibson's approach, perceiving is assumed to involve the continuous pickup of information over time, and the studies utilizing videotape and film, cited previously, were designed with this theory in mind.

10. The securely attached infant is defined as one who uses the mother as a base for exploration and freely ventures out from her location; the anxious/avoidant infant either explores with little regard for the mother's presence or, conversely, keeps very close tabs on her presence; and the anxious/resistant infant engages in little exploration or proximity-seeking behavior.

11. It is important to note that this investigation by Cohen and Cohen is not a clear-cut test of the claim that affordances in the environment play a role in the development of environmental cognition, nor was it intended to be. The functional significance of the sites was imposed on the setting as a result of the task designed by the investigators; it was not intrinsically related to environmental features. In spite of this, their findings are most suggestive concerning the potential significance of place affordances for the development of configurational knowledge.

12. The results of a study (DeLoache & Brown, 1983) of memory for hidden objects are compatible with the finding that the availability of familiar environmental features in a large-scale setting facilitates spatial cognition performance. These investigators found that the search for hidden objects by 18- to 30-month-olds was virtually error free when common objects were hidden in relation to natural features in the home (e.g., under a cushion, behind a door) as compared to the comparatively lower levels of performance typically reported when objects are hidden in boxes with picture cues.

REFERENCES

Acredolo, L.P. (1978). Development of spatial orientation in infancy. *Developmental Psychology, 13*, 1–8.

Acredolo, L.P. (1979). Laboratory versus home: The effect of the environment on the nine-month-old infant's choice of spatial reference system. *Developmental Psychology, 15*, 224–234.

Acredolo, L.P. (1981). Small and large-scale spatial concepts in infancy and childhood. In L.S. Liben, A.H. Patterson, & N. Newcombe (Eds.), *Spatial representation and behavior across the life span* (pp. 63–83). New York: Academic.

Acredolo, L.P. (1982). The familiarity factor in spatial research. In R. Cohen (Ed.), *Children's conceptions of spatial relationships* (pp. 19–30). San Francisco: Jossey-Bass.

Acredolo, L.P., & Evans, D. (1980). Developmental changes in the effects of landmarks on infant spatial behavior. *Developmental Psychology, 16*, 312–318.

Acredolo, L.P., Pick, H.L., Jr., & Olsen, M.G. (1975). Environmental differentiation and familiarity as determinants of children's memory for spatial location. *Developmental Psychology, 11*, 495–501.

Allen, G.L., Kirasic, K.C., Siegel, A.W., & Herman, J.F. (1979). Developmental issues in cognitive mapping: The selection and utilization of environmental landmarks. *Child Development, 50*, 1062–1070.

Allen, G.L., Siegel, A.W., & Rosinski, R.R. (1978). The role of perceptual context in structuring spatial knowledge. *Journal of Experimental Psychology: Human Learning and Memory, 4*, 617–630.

Anooshian, A.J., & Wilson, K.L. (1977). Distance distortions in memory for spatial locations. *Child Development, 48*, 1704–1707.

Anooshian, A.J., & Young, D. (1981). Developmental changes in cognitive maps of a familiar neighborhood. *Child Development, 52*, 341–348.

Appleyard, D. (1970). Styles and methods of structuring a city. *Environment and Behavior, 2*, 100–118.

Baird, J.C. (1982). Aesthetic factors in adults and child evaluation of visual space. In J.C. Baird & A.D. Lutkus (Eds.), *Mind child architecture* (pp. 89–109). Hanover, NH: University Press of New England.

Baird, J.C., & Lutkus, A.D. (Eds.). (1982). *Mind child architecture*. Hanover, NH: University Press of New England.

Baird, J.C., Merrill, A.A., & Tannenbaum, J. (1979). Cognitive representation of spatial relations: II. A familiar environment. *Journal of Experimental Psychology: General, 31*, 456–469.

Baker, R.R. (1980). Goal orientation by blindfolded humans after long-distance displacement; possible involvement of a magnetic sense. *Science, 210*, 555–557.

Balling, J.D., & Falk, J.H. (1982). Development of visual preference for natural environments. *Environment and Behavior, 14*, 5–28.

Barker, R.G., & Wright, H.F. (1955). *Midwest and its children: The psychological ecology of an American town*. New York: Harper & Row.

Biel, A. (1982). Children's spatial representation of their neighborhood: A step towards a general spatial competence. *Journal of Environmental Psychology, 2*, 193–200.

Blaut, J.M., McCleary, G.S., & Blaut, A.S. (1970). Environmental mapping in young children. *Environment and Behavior, 2*, 335–349.

Bluestein, N., & Acredolo, L. (1979). Developmental changes in map-reading skills. *Child Development, 50*, 691–697.

Bremner, J.G. (1978). Egocentric versus allocentric spatial coding in nine-month-old infants: Factors influencing the choice of code. *Developmental Psychology, 14*, 346–355.

Bremner, J.G., & Bryant, P.E. (1977). Place versus response as the basis of spatial errors made by young infants. *Journal of Experimental Child Psychology, 23*, 162–171.

Bruner, J.S. (1957). On perceptual readiness. *Psychological Review, 64*, 123–152.

Cohen, R. (Ed.). (1982). *Children's conceptions of spatial relationships.* San Francisco: Jossey-Bass.

Cohen, R. (1985). *The development of spatial cognition.* Hillsdale, NJ: Erlbaum.

Cohen, R., Baldwin, L.M., & Sherman, R.C. (1978). Cognitive maps of a naturalistic setting. *Child Development, 49*, 1216–1218.

Cohen, R., & Schuepfer, T. (1980). The representation of landmarks. *Child Development, 51*, 1065–1071.

Cohen, R., & Weatherford, D.L. (1980). Effects of route traveled on distance estimates of children and adults. *Journal of Experimental Child Psychology, 29*, 403–412.

Cohen, R., & Weatherford, D.L. (1981). The effects of barriers on spatial representations. *Child Development, 52*, 1087–1090.

Cohen, R., Weatherford, D.L., & Byrd, D. (1980). Distance estimates as a function of acquisition and response activities. *Journal of Experimental Child Psychology, 30*, 464–472.

Cohen, R., Weatherford, D.L., Lomenick, T., & Koeller, K (1979). Development of spatial representations: Role of task demands and familiarity with the environment. *Child Development, 50*, 1257–1260.

Cohen, S., & Cohen, R. (1982). Distance estimates as a function of type of activity in the environment. *Child Development, 53*, 834–837.

Cousins, J.H., Siegel, A.W., & Maxwell, S.E. (1983). Way finding and cognitive mapping in large scale environments: A test of a developmental model. *Journal of Experimental Child Psychology, 35*, 1–20.

Curtis, L.E., Siegel, A.W., & Furlong, N.E. (1981). Developmental differences in cognitive mapping: Configurational knowledge of familiar large-scale environments. *Journal of Experimental Child Psychology, 31*, 456–469.

DeLoache, J.S., & Brown, A.L. (1983). Very young children's memory for the location of objects in a large-scale environment. *Child Development, 54*, 888–897.

Downs, R. (1981). Maps and mappings as metaphors for spatial representation. In L.S. Liben, A.H. Patterson, & N. Newcombe (Eds.), *Spatial representation and behavior across the life span* (pp. 143–166). New York: Academic.

Downs, R., & Stea, D. (Eds.). (1973). *Image and environment.* Chicago: Aldine.

Evans, G. (1980). Environmental cognition. *Psychological Bulletin, 88*, 259–287.

Feldman, A., & Acredolo, L. (1979). The effect of active versus passive exploration on memory for spatial location in children. *Child Development, 50*, 698–704.

Gibson, E.J. (1969). *Principles of perceptual learning and development.* New York: Appleton-Century-Crofts.

Gibson, E.J. (1982). The concept of affordances: The renascence of functionalism. In W.A. Collins (Ed.), *The concept of development. The Minnesota symposia on child development* (Vol. 15) (pp. 55–81). Hillsdale, NJ: Erlbaum.

Gibson, E.J., & Spelke, E.S. (1983). The development of perception. In J.H. Flavell & E.M. Markman (Eds.), *Handbook of child psychology Vol. 3: Cognitive development* (pp. 1–76). New York: Wiley.

Gibson, J.J. (1966). *The senses considered as perceptual systems.* Boston: Houghton Mifflin.

Gibson, J.J. (1979). *The ecological approach to visual perception.* Boston: Houghton Mifflin.

Gould, J.L., & Able, K. (1981). Human homing: An elusive phenomenon. *Science, 212*, 1061–1063.

Gould, P., & White, R. (1974). *Mental maps.* Baltimore, MD: Penguin.

Hardwick, D.A., McIntyre, C.W., & Pick, H.L., Jr. (1976). The content and manipulation of cognitive maps in children and adults. *Monographs of the Society for Research in Child Development, 41*, (3, Serial No. 166).

Hart, R.A. (1979). *Children's experience of place.* New York: Irvington.

Hart, R.A. (1981). Children's spatial representation of the landscape: Lessons and questions from a field study. In L.S. Liben, A.H. Patterson, & N. Newcombe (Eds.), *Spatial representation and behavior across the life span* (pp. 195–233). New York: Academic.

Hart, R.A., & Moore, G.T. (1973). The development of spatial cognition: A review. In R.M. Downs & D. Stea (Eds.), *Image and Environment.* (pp. 246–288). Chicago: Aldine.

Hazen, N.L. (1982). Spatial exploration and spatial knowledge: Individual and developmental differences in very young children. *Child Development, 53*, 826–833.

Hazen, N.L. (1983). Spatial orientation: A comparative approach. In H.L. Pick, Jr. & L.P. Acredolo (Eds.), *Spatial orientation: Theory, research, and application* (pp. 3–37). New York: Plenum.

Hazen, N.L., & Durrett, M.E. (1982). Relationship of security of attachment to exploration and cognitive mapping abilities in 2-year-olds. *Developmental Psychology, 18*, 751–759.

Hazen, N.L., Lockman, J.J., & Pick, H.L., Jr. (1978). The development of children's representations of large-scale environments. *Child Development, 49*, 623–636.

Hazen, N.L., & Pick, H.L., Jr. (1985). An ecological approach to development of spatial orientation. In T.D. Johnston & A.T. Pietrewicz (Eds.), *Issues in the ecological study of learning* (pp. 201–243). Hillsdale, NJ: Erlbaum.

Heft, H. (1979). The role of environmental features in route learning: Two exploratory studies of way-finding. *Environmental Psychology and Nonverbal Behavior, 3*, 172–185.

Heft, H. (1981). An examination of constructivist and Gibsonian approaches to environmental psychology. *Population and Environment: Behavioral and Social Issues, 4*, 117–245.

Heft, H. (1983). Way-finding as the perception of information over time. *Population and Environment: Behavioral and Social Issues, 6*, 133–150.

Heft, H. (1985). High residential density and perceptual–cognitive development: An examination of the effects of crowding and noise in the home. In J.F. Wohlwill & W. VanVliet (Eds.), *Habitats for children: The impacts of density* (pp. 39–75). Hillsdale, NJ: Erlbaum.

Herman, J.F. (1980). Children's cognitive maps of large-scale spaces: Effects of exploration, direction, and repeated experience. *Journal of Experimental Child Psychology, 29*, 126–143.

Herman, J.F., Shiraki, J.H., & Miller, B.S. (1985). Young children's ability to infer spatial relationships: Evidence from a large, familiar environment. *Child Development, 56*, 1195–1203.

Herman, J.F., & Siegel, A.W. (1978). The development of cognitive mapping of the large-scale environment. *Journal of Experimental Child Psychology, 26*, 389–406.

Hilgard, E.R. (1980). The trilogy of mind: Cognition, affection, and conation. *Journal of the History of the Behavioral Sciences, 16*, 107–117.

Hunt, J. McV. (1961). *Intelligence and experience*. New York: Ronald.

Hutt, C. (1972). Sex differences in human development. *Human Development, 15*, 153–170.

Ittelson, W.H. (1973). Environment perception and contemporary perceptual theory. In W.H. Ittelson (Ed.), *Environment and cognition*. New York: Seminar.

Jenkins, J.J. (1977). Remember that old theory of memory? Well, forget it! In R. Shaw & J. Bransford (Eds.), *Perceiving, acting, and knowing: Toward an ecological psychology.* (pp. 413–429). Hillsdale, NJ: Erlbaum.

Kosslyn, S.M., Pick, H.L., Jr., & Fariello, G.R. (1974). Cognitive maps in children and men. *Child Development, 45*, 707–716.

Ladd, F.C. (1970). Black youths view their neighborhood: Neighborhood maps. *Environment and Behavior, 2*, 64–79.

Landau, B., Gleitman, H., & Spelke, E. (1981). Spatial knowledge and geometric representation in a child blind from birth. *Science, 213*, 1275–1277.

Landau, B., & Spelke, E. (1985). Spatial knowledge and its manifestations. In H.M. Wellman (Ed.), *Children's searching: The development of search skills and spatial representation* (pp. 27–52). Hillsdale, NJ: Erlbaum.

Liben, L.S. (1981). Spatial representation and behavior: Multiple perspectives. In L.S. Liben, A.H. Patterson, & N. Newcombe (Eds.), *Spatial representation across the life span*. New York: Academic.

Liben, L.S. (1982). Children's large-scale spatial cognition: Is the measure the message? In R. Cohen (Ed.), *Children's conceptions of spatial relationships* (pp. 51–65). San Francisco: Jossey-Bass.

Liben, L.S., Moore, M.L., & Golbeck, S.L. (1982). Preschoolers' knowledge of their classroom environment: Evidence from small-scale and life-size spatial tasks. *Child Development, 53*, 1275–1284.

Liben, L.S., Patterson, A.H., & Newcombe, N. (Eds.). (1981). *Spatial representation and behavior across the life span*. New York: Academic.

Lockman, J.J., & Pick, H.L., Jr. (1984). Problems of scale in spatial development. In C. Sophian (Ed.), *Origins of cognitive skill: The eighteenth annual Carnegie symposium on cognition* (pp. 3–26). Hillsdale, NJ: Erlbaum.

Lukashok, A., & Lynch, K. (1956). Some childhood memories of the city. *Journal of American Institute of Planners, 22*, 142–152.

Lynch, K. (1960). *The image of the city*. Cambridge, MA: MIT Press.

Lynch, K. (Ed.). (1977). *Growing up in cities: Studies of adolescence in Cracow, Melbourne, Mexico City, Salta, Toluca, and Warszawa*. Cambridge, MA: MIT Press.

Mandler, J.M. (1983). Representation. In J.H. Flavell & E.M. Markman (Eds.), *Handbook of child psychology, Vol. 3: Cognitive development* (pp. 420–494). New York: Wiley.

Meyer, J.M.W. (1973). Map-skills instruction and the child's developing cognitive ability. *Journal of Geography, 72*, 27–35.

Moore, G.T. (1979). Knowing about environmental knowing: The current state of theory and research on environmental cognition. *Environment and Behavior, 11*, 33–70.

Moore, G.T., & Golledge, R.G. (1976). *Environmental knowing: Theories, research and methods*. Stroudsburg, PA: Dowden, Hutchinson, & Ross.

Muchow, M., & Muchow, H. (1935). *Der Lebensraum des Grosstadtkindes*. (H. Andrews, G.Gad, & J.F. Wohlwill, Trans.). Hamburg, Germany: M. Riegel.

Nagy, J., & Baird, J.C. (1978). Children as environmental planners. In I. Altman & J.F. Wohlwill (Eds.), *Human behavior and environment: Vol. 3, Children and the environment*. (pp. 259–294). New York: Plenum.

Neisser, U. (1976). *Cognition and reality: Principles and implications of cognitive psychology*. San Francisco: Freeman.

Newcombe, N. (1982). The development of spatial cognition and cognitive development. In R. Cohen (Ed.). *Children's conceptions of spatial relationships* (pp. 65–82). San Francisco: Jossey-Bass.

Newtson, D. (1980). An interactionist perspective on social knowing. *Personality and Social Psychology Bulletin, 6*, 520–531.

Piaget, J. (1966). *The psychology of intelligence*. New York: Littlefield, Adams.

Piaget, J. (1969). *The mechanisms of perception.* New York: Basic Books.

Piaget, J. (1970). *Genetic epistemology.* New York: Columbia University Press.

Piaget, J., & Inhelder, B. (1967). *The child's conception of space.* New York: Norton.

Pick, H.L., Jr., & Acredolo, L.P. (Eds.).(1983). *Spatial orientation.* New York: Plenum.

Pick, H.L., Jr., & Lockman, J.J. (1981). From frames of reference to spatial representations. In L.S. Liben, A.H. Patterson, & N. Newcombe (Eds.), *Spatial representation and behavior across the life span* (pp. 39–62). New York: Academic.

Presson, C.C. (1982). The development of map-reading skills. *Child Development, 53,* 196–199.

Presson, C.C., & Ihrig, L.H. (1982). Using mother as a spatial landmark: Evidence against egocentric coding in infancy. *Developmental Psychology, 18,* 699–703.

Presson, C.C., & Somerville, S.C. (1985). Beyond egocentrism: A new look at the beginnings of spatial representation. In H.M. Wellman (Ed.), *Children's searching: The development of search skills and spatial representation* (pp. 1–26). Hillsdale, NJ: Erlbaum.

Proshansky, H.M. (1976). Environmental psychology and the real world. *American Psychologist, 31,* 303–314.

Pufall, P., & Shaw, R. (1973). Analysis of the development of children's spatial reference systems. *Cognitive Psychology, 5,* 171–175.

Rieser, J. (1979). Spatial orientation in six-month-old infants. *Child Development, 50,* 1078–1087.

Rogoff, B., & Lave, J. (1984). *Everyday cognition: Its development in social context.* Cambridge, MA: Harvard University Press.

Rushdoony, H.A. (1968). A child's ability to read maps: Summary of the research. *Journal of Geography, 67,* 213–222.

Shemyakin, F.N. (1962). Orientation in space. In B.G. Ananyev et al. (Eds.), *Psychological sciences in the USSR* (Vol. 1, Report No. 62-11083). Washington, DC: Office of Technical Services.

Siegel, A.W., Allen, G.L., & Kirasic, K.C. (1979). Children's ability to make bidirectional distance comparisons: The advantage of thinking ahead. *Developmental Psychology, 15,* 656–657.

Siegel, A.W., & Cousins, J.H. (1985). The symbolizing and symbolized child in the enterprise of cognitive mapping. In R. Cohen (Ed.), *The development of spatial cognition* (pp. 347–368). Hillsdale, NJ: Erlbaum.

Siegel, A.W., Herman, J.F., Allen, G.L., & Kirasic, K.C. (1979). The development of cognitive maps of large- and small-scale spaces. *Child Development, 50,* 582–585.

Siegel, A.W., Kirasic, K.C., & Kail, R.V. (1978). Stalking the elusive cognitive map: The development of children's representations of geographic space. In I. Altman & J.F. Wohlwill (Eds.), *Human behavior and the environment: Vol. 3: Children and the environment* (pp. 223–258). New York: Plenum.

Siegel, A.W., & Schadler, M. (1977). The development of young children's spatial representations of their classroom. *Child Development, 48,* 388–394.

Siegel, A.W., & White, S.H. (1975). The development of spatial representations of large-scale environments. In H.W. Reese (Ed.), *Advances in child development and behavior* (Vol. 10). New York: Academic.

Southworth, M. (1969). The sonic environment of cities. *Environment and Behavior, 1,* 49–70.

Spencer, C., & Darvizeh, Z. (1981). The case for developing a cognitive environmental psychology that does not underestimate the abilities of young children. *Journal of Environmental Psychology, 1,* 21–31.

Spencer, C., Harrison, N., & Darvizeh, Z. (1980). The development of iconic mapping ability in young children. *International Journal of Early Childhood, 12,* 57–64.

Stea, D., & Blaut, J.M. (1973). Some preliminary observations on spatial learning in school children. In R. Downs & D. Stea (Eds.), *Image and environment* (pp. 226–234). Chicago: Aldine.

Tolman, E.C. (1948). Cognitive maps in rats and men. *Psychological Review, 55,* 189–208.

Werner, H. (1948). *Comparative psychology of mental development.* New York: International Universities Press.

Wohlwill, J.F. (1973). The environment is not in the head! In W.F.E. Preiser (Ed.), *Environmental design research* (Vol. 2) (pp. 166–181). Stroudsburg, PA: Dowden, Hutchinson, & Ross.

Wohlwill, J.F. (1976). Searching for the environment in environmental research: A commentary on research strategy. In G.T. Moore & R.G. Golledge (Eds.), *Environmental knowing: Theories, research, and methods* (pp. 385–392). Stroudsburg, PA: Dowden, Hutchinson, & Ross.

Wohlwill, J.F. (1981). Experimental, developmental, differential: Which way the royal road to knowledge about spatial cognition? In L.S. Liben, A.H. Patterson, & N. Newcombe (Eds.), *Spatial representation and behavior across the life span* (pp. 129–139). New York: Academic.

Chapter 7

PERSONALITY AND THE ENVIRONMENT

Brian R. Little, *Department of Psychology, Carleton University, Ottawa, Ontario, Canada*

7.1. INTRODUCTION AND OVERVIEW

A remarkable little film produced by the National Film Board of Canada begins with a bucolic picture of a boy rowing a boat on the Ottawa River. As the still frame freezes his action, a rapid change of scale and focus occurs and the image shifts from the boy in the boat to the surrounding area, to the city, the region, the continent, and up to a rocket's view of earth, of the outer planets, and eventually to the farthest reaches of galactic space. In a stunning zoom descent, the camera bursts through successive layers of enveloping space to rest once more on the boy in the boat. Then, in a kind of delayed visual counterpoint, the camera focuses on the boy's arm where a mosquito has just pierced the skin. This time a zoom into microspace unfolds. First, we see a small drop of blood and successive layers of cellular material appear, until the elemental particles of life are bared. Finally, a reverse zoom back up to the common scale reveals once more the human organism in its everyday context: the boy in the boat.

In many respects the film can serve as a symbol and sustained image for the present chapter. Like the boy in the boat, whose name I will take to be David Mendon, the joint themes of personality and the environment can span a remarkable number of issues depending on the power of lens we use, and it will be useful at the outset to clarify just what level of resolution is being sought. As two of the most inclusive terms in the social sciences, *personality* and *environment* could be treated so as to subsume much of cultural anthropology and substantial portions of geography, history, and traditional social psychology. At a considerably more focused level, discussion could center primarily on the environmental disposition research carried out at Berkeley, where individual differences in areas such as urbanism or need for privacy are assessed. To a limited extent, themes at the more comprehensive level will be touched on in this chapter, less as substantive topics for review than as organizing rubrics and historical perspectives within which current research might be placed. To a greater extent the Berkeley tradition will be dealt with, both as a major contribution to environmental psychology and as a historical bridge between environmental and personality psychology. In the main, however, this chapter will focus on a middle-range perspective on personality and environment, somewhere between the galactic scope of capital-letter *Personality* and *Environment* and the microscopic analysis of finely honed environmental dispositions. The scale will be that of examining theory and re-

search on the interaction between persons and their everyday physical milieu: a scale, in short, of Davids rowing boats on rivers.

An alternative way of viewing the selection of topics to be discussed is to see it as *charting the common ground between personality and environmental psychology*. Thus among the topics to be covered are the measurement of environmental dispositions, the application of orthodox personality measures to the prediction of environmentally relevant behaviors, the impact of different types of nonhuman environment on personality processes, and the emergence of a molar interactional psychology and its theoretical and methodological implications. To set the stage for this review it will be useful to provide a picture of the historical context from which the current research perspectives have emerged.

7.2. PERSONALITY AND ENVIRONMENT IN HISTORICAL PERSPECTIVE

7.2.1. From Antiquity to Classical Personology

Three Recurring Historical Themes About Person–Environment Relations

The interdependence of human personality and the surrounding milieu is so complete that human thought about environment was most likely coterminous with the emergence of consciousness. Historians, philosophers, and geographers have long speculated on the emergence and course of different conceptions of environment (Glacken, 1967; Sprout & Sprout, 1965; Tuan, 1974), and for the present purpose we can highlight several root themes or historically recurring images concerning the relationship between humans and their physical surround. As Glacken (1967) has so richly documented, three questions have persistently been asked concerning this relationship. The first is *the idea of a designed earth* and involves the question of whether it represents a purposefully made creation. Fostered by mythology, philosophy, and theology, the search for an answer to the teleological significance of the environment has taken different forms throughout the centuries. Of particular significance to the concept of a designed earth was the contrast of nature with artifice. Spiritual harmony was felt to reside in nature, and it would be in the primordial wilderness, not the built environment, that the mysteries of creation would be found. As Glacken (1967) has stressed, the recurring image of the designed earth represented one of western civilization's great attempts to create a holistic concept of nature and to see order and unity within it.[1]

The second root historical issue, *the idea of environmental influence*, asks whether environmental climate and morphology help mold human nature or the character of social institutions. Largely influenced by medicine and voyaging, the question turned on the obvious differences between people living in different climatic regions or geographical enclaves. The impact of nature on human personality is one of the most ancient theories of individual differences. Astrology, in particular, held a central place in ancient accounts of the sources of human behavior (McReynolds, 1975). Indeed, the most elaborate classical precursors to personality psychology were environmental theories stressing the influence of celestial movements on human destiny and the pervasive effect of geographical elements (earth, air, fire, and water) on human personality.[2] The influence credited to the environment has ranged from extreme forms of determinism in which the human being is seen as "a sort of chip in the stream of history...borne along by a current which he is incapable of resisting, within a channel from which he cannot escape" (Sprout & Sprout, 1965, p. 48) to softer forms of determinism where notions of lawful causation gave way to formulations about environmental influence. Buttressed by technological triumphs over nature and environment and by nineteenth century American pragmatism, a less deterministic view of person–environment relationships, possibilism, emerged, emphasizing freedom of choice and the exclusion of strict environmental determinism (Sprout & Sprout, 1965).[3]

The image of humans as active participants in their environmental transactions represents the third historically recurring issue raised in different forms since antiquity. This question concerns *the idea of humans as environmental agents* and asks how wisely humans have acted upon the earth and what gains and losses have accrued during our tenure on the planet. Again, a diversity of answers to the question of human agency has appeared throughout the centuries. Much recent debate has centered on the role of Christian doctrine in encouraging human dominion over nature, with its twin consequences of progress and despoliation,[4] though the temptation to paint the history of such themes in broad strokes should be resisted, if only because of the inordinate degree of variability within historical movements as vast as Christianity. The critical issue here is the centrality of the theme of agency throughout history and the

importance to all ages of knowing whether our victories over nature are pyrrhic ones.

Consider some conceptual camera work that can be done on the boy in the boat with whom we started in order to capture the psychological, as contrasted with purely historical, meaning of the three classic themes. With regard to the question of a designed earth, we might picture the boy rowing until nightfall and experiencing for the first time a sense of awe at the expanse of stars and sheer scale of nature. Or consider another boy whose journey in the boat will end in his suicide. Before slipping over the side he captures a glimpse of stars and skyline and is struck for the last time with its utter absurdity. These contrasting experiences depict the recurring themes of human response to the question of a designed earth: *an affirmative sense of meaning* versus *a sense of the basic incoherence of nature*.

Consider the boy again through the filter of the theme of environment influence. He has dozed off and the boat has slipped into a strong current that is rapidly pulling him to some dangerous rocks. He is helpless to fight against the force of the current and with fear resigns himself to the unknown outcome: a chip in the stream of deterministic nature. The psychological response to the determinism of environment is a *sense of passive vulnerability*. Consider, finally, another version of the last scene. Upon waking up and finding he's been drifting, the boy pulls out his 2½-hp Evinrude motor, slings it over the transom, and purrs across the chop to the calm waters off stream. Here the psychological response to nature is the agentic feeling of *mastery or control*. Even so, his competency is bought at the price of dependence on technical artifact and is more precariously achieved than that of another boy, perhaps from an earlier time, who has learned to pit muscle against milieu and steer the boat to safety on his own.

These three historic themes linking the human condition and the environment within which that condition unfolds can serve as the initial set of conceptual goggles through which to review theory and research on the common ground between personality and environmental psychology.

Elaboration of Themes in Classical Psychology

It is instructive to examine several themes and issues in classical theories of personality that were to influence environmental psychology. This review will necessarily be selective, focusing only on those issues relevant to the major themes discussed in previous sections.

While the nonhuman environment received little explicit attention in orthodox psychoanalytic theory, powerful implicit themes within the theory are concerned with the nature of the human milieu. The very arbitrariness of demarcating a specific aspect of the environment as *physical*, in contrast with the social or intrapersonal, is highlighted by Freudian conceptions of the dynamics of libidinal energy. The capacity of the nonhuman environment to absorb emotional charges directed toward a frustrating social object ensures that the human response to *symbolic* aspects of the environment (e.g., artifacts of loved ones) will display an emotional intensity as powerful as in the domain of the explicitly human. Nowhere has the subtlety of human response to the nonhuman environment from a psychoanalytic perspective been more sensitively portrayed than in Searles's (1960) *The Non-Human Environment: In Normal Development and in Schizophrenia.* Of particular significance to Searles is the persistence of an *unconscious identification of humans with their nonhuman surroundings*, an identification that, while gradually relinquished at the conscious level during ontogenesis, nonetheless threatens to return and swamp the individual during times of stress and emotional disturbance.[5] During psychotic breakdowns symbolic identification with the nonhuman environment can become almost a literal fusion with the mechanical or the inanimate, with Bettelheim's (1959) case of "Joey, the mechanical boy" being perhaps the most famous clinical example.

Certainly within Jungian theory the range of objects deemed to be of emotional significance was increased dramatically and was no longer restricted to those manifesting sexual symbolism. Indeed, the primordial images of nature and the historical recurrence of archetypal geographical and historical themes in independent isolated cultures led Jung (1957) to emphasize the primary, not merely derivative, importance of environmental symbols to the human organism.

Both Freudian and Jungian themes were integrated into the comprehensive program of personological studies begun by Murray at the Harvard Psychological Clinic in the 1930s. Again, while the nonhuman environment was not a focus of classical personology, its role in the determination of human conduct was made explicit:

> Since, at every moment, an organism is within an environment which largely determines its behaviour and since the environment changes—sometimes with radical abruptness—the conduct of an individual

cannot be formulated without a characterization of each confronting situation, *Physical and social.* (italics added, Murray, 1938, p. 39)

Murray (1938), in contrast with psychoanalytic investigators, was concerned with developing techniques for the assessment of individual dispositions as well as techniques for the assessment of the characteristics of environments that satisfy or frustrate human needs. These environmental characteristics, termed *press* by Murray, were further differentiated into *alpha* and *beta* press, the former representing environmental characteristics as objective inquiry might disclose them, the latter being subjective construals of environmental objects and events. Murray also pioneered in the use of life history analysis as a basis for personological investigation. His insistence on the need for temporally extended units of analysis (serials) in the study of lives, together with his innovations in measuring jointly the needs of individuals and the press of their environments, make Murray the most relevant of the classical personality theorists to the concerns of this chapter.

The impact of Lewin (1936) on environmental psychology has been felt more in those areas intersecting with applied social psychology than in the personality domain. However, the linked concepts of life space, foreign hull, and psychological environment were particularly noteworthy as an early representation of person–milieu relations. For Lewin, the life space is the psychologist's primary domain of exploration. It contains the totality of personal and environmental influences on a given individual's conduct at a given point in time. Thus, to return to David in his boat, his life space would comprise David himself and the subjectively salient features of the real world that are influencing him. David's psychological environment thus represents not only environmental objects (e.g., his motor, the family dog) but also purely psychological facts or constructions. The soccer field he is daydreaming about is therefore as much a part of the psychological environment as the river he is rowing in. David's life space is separated by a semipermeable boundary from the foreign hull, an area of reality that is irrelevant to the explanation of his behavior unless it were to penetrate the barrier and become represented in the psychological environment. Thus the deadhead lodged just underneath the water surface belongs to the foreign hull in our rowing example. When the first signs of a leak in the boat are detected by David, however, that which was extrinsic to his life space becomes central: A leaking hull, once detected, is most decidedly not foreign.

The contributions of Murphy (e.g., Murphy, 1947) have not been widely acknowledged, but he was among the first to write in detail about both the economic and historical contexts within which human personality developed. Murphy should be counted among the earliest of those proffering an image of the hierarchical nature of environmental influence.[6]

Kelly's (1955) personal construct theory offered an original and controversial view of the environment from the perspective of personality psychology. Kelly stressed that humans create personal constructs through which they predict and act on their environments and that study of these subjective templates is sufficient for the explanation of human conduct. In contrast to radical environmental theories within general psychology, Kelly's theory offered an alternative that forced psychologists to examine environments from within the idiosyncratic construction systems of the people confronting them, and to eschew misguided attempts to measure the environment objectively.[7]

Finally, the influence of traditional factor or trait models in personality deserves mention. Both Cattell (1979) and Eysenck (1981) expounded major theoretical perspectives emphasizing enduring trait dispositions such as anxiety and extraversion.[8] Trait theorists generated testable hypotheses relating personality to environmental factors. With respect to extraversion, for example, Eysenck postulated individual differences in neocortical arousal that led in turn to predicted differences in preference for stimulating physical environments. While the question of the transsituational generalizability of traits would come to be the major preoccupation of personality psychologists in the 1970s, the influence of orthodox trait models has persisted throughout the early years of environmental psychology, although in a form rather less doctrinaire than before the "trait debate" to be discussed in Section 7.5.1.

The contributions of orthodox or classical personality theories to issues that were to emerge in environmental psychology can be summarized by returning again to David Mendon.

With respect to the issue of whether the environment is seen to be meaningful or meaningless, classical psychodynamic theories would dilate the term *meaning* to include consideration of unconscious determinants of attraction or repulsion toward the milieu. Thus David's rowing may be the acting out of unconscious sexual fantasies or a response to the archetypal power of water symbolism. In a vital sense, he may be drawn to the river by sources beyond his awareness. Murray's conception of beta press,

together with the Lewinian "psychological environment" and Kellian "constructs," emphasize the subjective nature of that milieu and its personally constructed nature and directs us to the cognitive appraisal of David's views of his surroundings. The trait theorists, too, would remind us that there are many for whom anxiety is so great that the achievement of any kind of environmental meaning is highly unlikely.

With respect to the issue of environmental influence, and the boy's sense of power or vulnerability, the concepts of alpha press and foreign hull attest to the physical constraints within which subjective construals are played. The boy in the boat *will* be a victim of the forces of nature if he cannot escape from the eddy, regardless of his subjective construal of invulnerability. Moreover, the milieu also reflects the hierarchical embedding emphasized by Gardner Murphy. David's nautical journey is subject to the economic realities of owning a boat, the local regulations governing launching access on the Ottawa River, and the absence of heavy freighters in those waters—all aspects of the milieu within which the simple act of rowing a boat is embedded. Trait theorists, too, would attempt to account for the boy's explorations in the boat by invoking notions of the stimulus-seeking characteristics of classic extraverts, or his tendency to hug the shoreline by invoking notions of anxiety level or harm avoidance.

Finally with respect to the theme of human agency, classical personology would inquire into the impact of the boy's actions on the milieu by examining the motives underlying his trip and the consequences of those motives for the milieu itself. If he carries with him a 15-hp outboard, for example, and starts this up on his 10-ft pram, the rooster tailing boy (no doubt also throwing Coke cans overboard) becomes not only an active agent vis-à-vis his environment but a potentially destructive one: polluting the river, annoying the old couple paddling near shore, scaring his father, and delighting his dog.

In short, classical theories of personality might fairly be said to have extended and elaborated the historical notions of person–environment relations and to have set the stage for the explicit construction of an environmental personology in the late 1960s.[9]

7.2.2. Two Revolutions in the Psychology of the 1960s

Two revolutions in psychology reached their peak in the 1960s and each had a critical influence on the shaping of theory and research at the intersection of personality and environmental psychology.

The Cognitive Revolution

The cognitive revolution can be traced through virtually all the subdisciplines of behavioral science.[10] During the 1950s and early 1960s, psychological theory witnessed several related shifts in perspective: the Piagetian transformation of a behaviorally dominated developmental psychology, the rise of cognitive models to counterbalance drive-reductive theories of emotion, the shift from a peripheralistic experimental psychology to a central, mediational one, and the gradual domination of social motivational theory by models emphasizing cognitive balance, congruency, and dissonance reduction. Within personality theory itself, the cognitive, information-processing perspective, in areas as far apart as psychoanalytic theory and personal construct theory, began to displace earlier perspectives. Within psychoanalytic theory increased attention was paid to ego-control functions and to the *conflict-free ego sphere* (Hartmann, 1958) in contrast to the more unconsciously determined personality processes. The cognitive revolution might be said to have reached its emotional zenith in the mid to late 1960s when, particularly in the fields of social, personality, and clinical psychology, not only were our theoretical variables transformed but our views of the human condition seemed to shift rapidly and radically. In a fairly short period of time, say, from 1964 to 1970, articles, books, and scholarly discussions about human personality stressed its *active* nature, emphasized its constructive propensities, and endorsed an optimistic view of the human condition. The bête noire of the day was the passive, drive-reductionist model that treated human beings as automatons. Despite the often shrill tone of the polemic, the image of the human personality that emerged during the cognitive revolution was a more active creature than at any other period of this century. Thus when environmental psychologists and personality psychologists began to chart their common ground a particularly sanguine image of personality was already in ascendance; an image that, if it did not serve as the major substantive theory of personality, was at least a pervasive shaper of the issues that were soon to emerge.

The Contextual Revolution

The contextual revolution in psychology can be seen as arising in parallel with the cognitive revolution, and each on occasion served as the implicit, and sometimes explicit, foil to the other. Within theories of perception, Gibson's (1960) call for a more stimulus-centered view of the perceptual process emphasized the characteristics of objective stimulus events, placing less stress on the proximal stimulus patterns detected by the organism. A related development, Brunswik's (1943, 1956) twin contributions of the ecological representativeness of experimental design and his lens model, provided a major impetus toward a more fully contextual theory of behavior. His ecological representativeness argument was based on his concern that the stimulus characteristics used in conventional experiments were unrepresentative of the patterns of stimulation that naturally occur in the organism's ecosystem and that more representative sampling was called for in order to clarify the nature of our perceptual systems. His lens model, which, as Craik (1983) has recently observed, has had the lesser influence of his two major contributions, emphasized the interrelationship between distal and proximal stimuli in perception, and the functional importance of being able to predict distal relationships from patterns of proximal cues. Brunswik's emphasis on the need for psychologists to chart both the proximal *and distal* features of environmental stimulation represented another important precursor to environmental psychology.

If Brunswik's concept of ecological representativeness called attention to the need for more contextually sensitive accounts of perceptual phenomena, Barker's (1968) ecological psychology sounded the call for a full-scale excursion into that context as a major, untapped domain of psychological research. His highly original work on the nature and dynamics of *behavior settings* could be seen as either an immediate precursor to or an early exemplar of environmental psychology. In contrast to perspectives that assumed that the major causal influences on behavior were endogenous to the organism (e.g., motivational state, perceptual set), Barker insisted that the behavior setting itself had a "claim" on the individual that deserved serious psychological examination. When at a bicycle club meeting we behave bicycle club; when we are at a funeral we act funeral; when at a *festschrift* for Barker we wax *festschrift*. Barker's detailed accounts of the content and claim of behavior settings in small towns in the United States and England, in schools and many other locations, opened up a major subfield within what is now regarded as environmental psychology (see Wicker Chapter 16, and Barker, Chapter 40, this volume). Of more relevance to the present chapter, Barker's ecological psychology also contrasted with orthodox personality theories that stressed the intrapsychic determinants of behavior. Ecological psychology stressed the propaedeutic task of gathering extensive naturalistic data on what goes on in different types of settings, including the critical role of the physical milieu in shaping human activities. Thus instead of probing intrapsychic causes for hostility or sociability it sought to determine in what kinds of settings aggressive or hostile acts occur most frequently, or in what natural enclaves sociability flourishes.

In a nutshell, the contextual revolution shifted the search for laws in psychological research from the self-contained individual to the natural milieu within which that individual was located. Moreover, in its extreme form, contextualism stripped personality psychology of the exclusive right to explanatory primacy, making a strong case that the claim of the context was causally significant. Personologists, clinicians, and others were to grapple repeatedly with this contention during the next decade. To capture the essential message of the contextualist position in understanding human action and its personological implications, consider again the boy in the boat. If we observe him over the course of a day, an exercise in hemerography, in Barker's (1968) terms, we might observe a hundred behavioral acts that could be seen as manifestations of his personality, on the one hand, or as behaviors evoked by the particular setting or settings in which he was situated. Thus his rowing, sloppiness, and bare-chestedness could be seen as aspects of his personality or as the kinds of behaviors typically pulled out by the behavior setting known as a fishing trip. As we shall see, as the 1960s were drawing to an end, the contextualist perspective grew stronger and began to stake its claim on the field.

Mischel's Personality and Assessment

If one book could be selected both as representing the twin revolutions of the 1960s and as setting the stage for the next decade of disputation at the interface of personality and environmental psychology, it would be Mischel's tour de force of 1968, *Personality and Assessment*. In essence, Mischel's book was a frontal attack on the dominant personality paradigm that posited stable traits as the determinants of human behavior. Mischel's book had an immediate impact on the field of personality and applied psychology. While the contextual, or situationalist, slant of Mischel's book is often stressed, a less noticed but equally important emphasis within the 1968 book was derived from his advocacy of a personal construct perspective (Kelly, 1955) on human behavior. Thus for Mischel there was a double jeopardy to using

broadly designative trait concepts such as dominance or sociability. First, contextually, he interpreted the empirical research evidence to that date as indicating little cross-situational generality to behavior, a conclusion consistent with ecological psychology's emphasis on the claim of settings on behavior. Second, Mischel's perspective was explicitly cognitive: He envisaged individuals as actively monitoring their behavior and changing it in the light of feedback. Two exemptions from the tyranny of trait-like impulses were thus apparent in Mischel's (1968) view of human personality: An exemption on the grounds of contextual diversity and an exemption based on the cognitive acuity of an active agent. In short, as the 1960s drew to an end both revolutions had crested and had found common outlet in a book that was in many respects the harbinger of the 1970s.

7.2.3. Person–Environment Themes in Other Disciplines

Craik (1970) has shown that the emergence of environmental psychology reflected both internal disciplinary pressures, as reviewed previously, and external forces. Among the latter were questions of a psychological nature raised by researchers and practitioners in ecology, architecture, geography, sociology, and literary history. We can briefly summarize the major issues raised by each of the fields and their relevancy for the study of environmental psychology and personality.

During the 1960s, there was a remarkable increase in the extent and visibility of research in ecology and environmental medicine. Among their concerns were the effects of pollution and overcrowding and the general vulnerability of the human ecosystem. Apart from its direct effect on other areas of environmental psychology, this perspective raised crucial concerns about the kind of life and human personalities we were trying to create, however implicitly, in our theories of personality and the applied programs derived from them. Bartz (1970), for example, captured the essence of the ecological challenge to one of the more popular, if contentious, perspectives in personality theory:

In a recent issue of the *American Psychologist*, Maslow (1969) asserts that in our developing humanistic concern "The first and over-arching Big Problem is to make the Good Person (p. 732)." I would suggest that this is an irrelevant concern if we do not first insure having a *living* person, with enough to eat, room in which to live, and an environment worth living in. To the man who is starving in the street, who has watched his children die of disease and malnutrition and his country collapse in anarchy, questions of what makes a "good person," self-actualization, psychotherapy, interpersonal relations, and our many other humanistic diversions become just so much esoteric bull. (p. 502)

Within architecture and city planning a related concern with designing for enhanced quality of life was being felt. With increasing urgency, designers began to inquire of psychologists what kinds of human needs had to be taken into account in order to enhance the habitability of rooms, houses, neighborhoods, and regions (Perin, 1970). Before 1970, the response was, of necessity, brief. Little systematic research existed on user needs or design criteria for enhanced responsivity to the physical environment.

Similar questions were being asked in the fields of geography and resources management, where the interaction of human agents and their environments had been explored for years, often with ad hoc adoption of psychological assessment devices. Two examples will suffice to convey the psychological aspects of research in this field. A highly productive research program on human adaptation to natural hazards centered on the exploration of motivational and decision-making factors of individuals living in hazardous regions (e.g., Kates, 1976). A second research perspective examined the opposite pole of environmental influence, the salutary effect of recreational settings such as riverine environments and mountains (e.g., Shafer, 1969).

Concern with the physical form of human communities had been a staple of sociology and anthropology for decades; of particular relevance to environmental psychology were studies on the consequences of slum clearance on the well-being of residents in "urban villages" (Gans, 1962; Young & Willmott, 1957). While it had been originally thought by planners that physical relocation from crowded slums to the sanitized high-rise apartments would enhance resident satisfaction, the results established that critical trade-offs were involved. Despite their physical shortcomings, high-density slum areas were found to promote and sustain a critically important set of social ties between individuals, their "extended families," and the neighborhood community. The superficially more hygienic high-rises, by contrast, failed signally in providing the vital source of community and social support.

In both literary and historical scholarship, themes of the interrelation of the human and physical milieu have been pursued for centuries. Representative of

these traditions are three writers who share a common concern with the symbolic potency of the nonhuman environment and the strength of bond between people and their nonhuman environments. The philosopher Bachelard (1964) captured the subtle emotional significance of mundane architectural form in a series of essays on aspects of dwellings such as corners, windows, and so on. French writer and film director Robbe-Grillet (1965) explored the impact of a literary genre called *la chosisme,* or Thingism, in which physical objects were given equal existential standing with persons. In marked contrast to perspectives that treated objects merely as personification of human phenomena, Robbe-Grillet's perspective stressed the primary, unmediated significance of physical objects to humans. Similarly, L. Marx's (1967) *The Machine in the Garden* traces the evocativeness of machine imagery, the train in particular, as juxtaposed to the pastoral images that once had dominated American literature. For our present purpose, what is interesting about these literary and historical examples is the tacit psychological theory, particularly personality theory, that they presupposed. Their common theme, the symbolic richness of nonhuman objects and the physical milieu in human identity, was not to be explored in depth by environmental personologists for another decade.

Relationship of Historic Themes to Issues in Related Disciplines

Together these five areas of research, along with the endogenous movements within psychology itself, characterized the intellectual milieu that greeted those committed to developing an environmental psychology during the late 1960s.

In summarizing these influences, we can discern how they exemplify or expand the historically dominant themes identified earlier. The theme of the designed earth with its contrasting psychological responses of meaning or incoherence is reflected in the study of place attraction in geography, habitability in the design professions, and the symbolic potency of milieu in literary and historical analysis. The historic theme of environmental influence and its consequences for human vulnerability or active exploration is expanded in ecological and geographical research on environmental risks and hazards and in architectural concern with responsive rather than coercive design. With respect to the historical question of human agency, ecological concern with responsible stewardship of natural resources echoes an ancient theme.

The concept of the physical environment as a

creator of *community* from the sociological/anthropological fields can be regarded as a new major dimension at the same level as the other three dimensions.[11]

In short, cognitive and contextual shifts within psychology, together with diverse influences outside it, reflected and elaborated ancient environmental themes. The stage was now set for the systematic, empirical investigation of personality and the environment.

7.2.4. Rise of the Personological Perspective in Environmental Psychology

The personological perspective in environmental psychology was already articulated as early as 1966 and received its clearest exposition in Craik's writings (1966, 1968, 1970). For present purposes we can distinguish three major characteristics of this approach:[12] (1) a historical continuity with the classical personality assessment paradigm summarized in the previous section, (2) delineation of the themes and issues in other disciplines that could provide a conceptual basis for the generating of environmentally relevant scales for personality assessment, and (3) specific guidelines for the development of measures of environmental dispositions.

The Classical Assessment Paradigm and the Beginning of Environmental Personology: The IPAR Connection

The Institute of Personality and Research (IPAR) at Berkeley under the direction of Donald MacKinnon, an emigré from Murray's Harvard Psychological Clinic, carried on the tradition of assessment begun in that clinic in the 1930s.[13] The now-classic series of studies on the assessment of creative individuals provides an intriguing and direct link to the development of a personological perspective in environmental psychology. One of the graduate students at IPAR at the time the creative architects were being studied was Kenneth Craik. MacKinnon (1963) noted that Craik, while perusing the data files, had unearthed an interesting correlate of creativity in architects: the extent to which they had experienced many domestic moves in childhood. This could lay claim to being the first empirical finding at the interface of personality and what was to become environmental psychology. Shortly after this, Craik served as a field observer in a large architectural firm. Not only did this expose the physical context within which creative architects work, it also disclosed many of the assumptions held by designers about human dispositions and needs

vis-à-vis the physical environment. The possibility of exploring this new domain via the framework and methods of classical personology at IPAR proved irresistible.

Conceptual and Methodological Base of Environmental Disposition Measurement

In the earliest writing on environmental personality, Craik (1966, 1968, 1970) outlined the need to study individual differences vis-à-vis the physical environment and to develop individual difference measures tapping a diverse set of environmental themes. He outlined the logic of an environmental trait inventory including the creation of a comprehensive item pool. As Craik noted, there is no coherent field of environmental counseling with cumulative wisdom comparable to that available to the developers of inventories in fields such as clinical psychology. The source of items was to be drawn from those who had direct experience in environmental fields (e.g., naturalists and construction workers) as well as references to literary works dealing with environmental themes such as those discussed in Section 7.2. Craik suggested several specific scales that might be constructed, including a Pastoralism scale, an Urbanite scale, a Luddite scale, and an Ecological Perspective scale.[14]

The psychometric mission of environmental personology was clear: it was to generate a valid set of scalable folk concepts (Gough, 1968) related to a broad range of environmental themes. As Craik has argued, the domain of folk concepts studied prior to the rise of environmental personology was largely restricted to the interpersonal and the intrapersonal domain. An environmental personology would dilate the range of objects about which folk concepts are developed to include the natural and built environments. It would remain for McKechnie (1972) to demonstrate the empirical validity of an environmental disposition inventory.

At the same time as the intellectual path breaking proceeded on the frontier of environmental personology, the whole paradigmatic foundation of orthodox personality psychology was under attack and suffering the first stages of Mischel shock. As dispositions were both a focus of attack in the trait debate and key units of analysis in the new environmental personology, it will clarify discussion of both areas if we pause to examine just what an environmental disposition entails. Consider, for instance, David Mendon's father, Samuel, who was standing on the shore watching his son on the river. It is perhaps more than a little coincidental that Craik (1976) has provided a detailed sketch of this hypothetical Samuel Mendon, who, at the time Craik wrote about him, lived in Massachusetts:

> Mr. Samuel Mendon is a district manager for a nationwide corporation who has recently been reassigned to a branch office in a moderately large American city. He has been offered a choice of offices in several geographic settings and elected the northeastern section of the country. In resettling, did Mr. Mendon and his family decide to live well out into the countryside or in the suburban outskirts or within the older central district? Did they seek a purely residential neighborhood with single-family homes, and a large shopping center nearby, or perhaps, a neighbourhood with assorted dwellings, grocery store, post office, drugstore, physician, churches, elementary schools all located within it?...What recreational use does Mr. Mendon make of the outdoor environment? If his weekend avocation is nautical, does he purchase a motor boat (or sailboat or cabin cruiser or a Monterey fishing boat)? Does he sail along highly used and developed waterfronts with diverse facilities or on remote pastoral lakes? If at vacation time he is a wilderness user, does he stay on the periphery or does he backpack in?...How are his children learning to use, appreciate and understand the physical environment, and how does that learning reflect family activities and values? On weekdays, does Samuel Mendon use his lunch time to explore the city, stroll its streets, sample its restaurants, and browse in its shops, or does he remain in his building at the local cafeteria?...A year after his arrival in his new habitat, has Mr. Mendon adjusted with ease or difficulty to his move? (Craik, 1976, p. 64)

And why, it might be asked, has Mendon recently moved to Canada?

Let's consider some of Samuel Mendon's actions in terms of whether they support the ascription of an environmental disposition. Let's assume that in the choice situations offered by Craik, Mendon has opted to live on a hobby farm 15 miles outside of a medium-sized city, that he chooses to spend recreational periods backpacking in the wilderness, and that he spends his lunch hours walking down by the river, as far away from the office as he can get. We should note at the outset that his cognitive ("deciding"), affective (e.g., "seeking"), and behavioral (e.g., "purchasing," "using lunch time," etc.) characteristics have all been described. Assuming that we continue to list relevant exemplars of his thoughts, feelings, and actions concerning the physical environment, what if any attributions can we make about his relatively enduring environmental dispositions? Or, more importantly at this point, what *allows* us to form such a dispositional predicate about him? In what sense is

it a legitimate enterprise to ascribe traitlike characteristics to people? On the basis of the information provided (assuming we knew which of the choices he opted for), can we say that he is basically an "outdoors person," a snob, a "macho-machine sport type," or a nature lover? And what do these terms, in fact, convey? Are they hypothetical statements enabling us to predict, within certain measurable error limits, Mendon's behavior? Or are they simply verbal summaries of how he's been behaving up till now? Are they predictions or merely ways of conveying the gist of a person's conduct for a given period of time?

Buss and Craik (1983a, 1983b) have given a provocative treatment of these and several other crucial issues in personality and dispositional theory. To illustrate their argument we can contrast four alternative models of dispositions.

Ryle (1949) developed a philosophical account of dispositions that emphasized their status as hypothetical statements. Akin to dispositional terms in physics, such statements entailed an intrinsic characteristic of the object under consideration, a particularly popular example of which was the brittleness of a glass bottle. This intrinsic characteristic (brittleness) would, in conjunction with a given situation (e.g., having a rock thrown at it on a beach), yield a consequent result (shattering). Note that the occasion for the manifestation of the disposition of fragility, the situation or context of having rocks thrown at it, is an essential component for identification of the disposition. Moreover, the dispositional ascription is formally a hypothesis of the form if *a* under conditions *b*, then *c* will follow. As with the bottle, so too with Barry, a high school senior who has been close to a full-blown anxiety attack brought about by a romantic complexity in his life, about which he is now musing while throwing stones on the river shore. Let's assume that his anxiety is posited as a dispositional attribute that, under certain circumstances, will manifest itself in action of a specifiable sort. Further, let's assume that the situation most likely to generate the expression of anxiety is when his macho defenses are down and he has imbibed to excess. If Barry is an anxious sort of individual, then when he's under the influence of alcohol or drugs he'll suffer an anxiety attack. The same logical entailments apply to Barry and the bottle; both shatter when they're stoned.

A major alternative to Ryle's formulation was presented by Hampshire (1953), who argued for a view of dispositions not as hypothetical predictions but rather as summary accounts of an individual's characteristics to date, based on the frequency with which he or she has manifested occurrences of a particular type of action signaling a given dispositional quality.[15] Under this formulation, had Barry not manifested any instances of anxious conduct, the attribution of an anxious disposition would be untenable. And the greater the frequency with which acts codable as anxious are observed in him, the more credence is given to the ascription of the dispositional label of *anxious*. Buss and Craik, in highlighting the contrast between the Rylean and Hampshirean positions, opt clearly for the latter, which, following Alston (1971), they refer to as an act-frequency approach to dispositions in contrast to a *purposive–cognitive* conception. Buss & Craik suggest that, in crucial ways, the frequency and purposive–cognitive concepts may be components of incommensurate approaches. Let's examine this possibility by returning to Samuel Mendon and his environmentally relevant thoughts, feelings, and actions. With respect to his choices of living on a hobby farm and engaging in wilderness activities, for example, can the frequency of such acts serve as an uncontentious basis for the ascription of, say, pastoralism to Sam Mendon?[16] According to the act-frequency perspective this would be so. However, consider whether the following information would make matters more complex. Consider that, from the cognitive–purposive standpoint, each of these choices was made in order to satisfy his most central, preoccupying personal goal, *pleasing his wife, Molly*. Were we to assess how enjoyable he actually found the country life, the backpacking, and canned beans, we might find out that he hated them, that he saw them as being utterly un-Mendonian, and that the only reason for throwing himself to the mortgage holders and mosquitoes was to placate Molly. Is he still a pastoralist? Or more a posturalist? Perhaps a highly empathic person? A wimp? Just what is to count as the attributional home of a natural act when there are multiple alternative constructions of it (Kelly, 1955), each with some claim to ontological purity? As Buss and Craik argue:

> Efforts to clarify the conceptual and empirical interrelations among various middle-level personality approaches to the categorization of acts, and to explanatory systems offer an important road to the revival of theoretical discourse that Maddi (1980) has advocated. Indeed, this endeavor is likely to occupy personality theorists in a profitable fashion during this decade of the 1980s. (1983a, p. 124)

As we proceed with discussing the rise of empirical research on environmental dispositions, it will be helpful to bear in mind these conceptual subtleties. For now, it should be emphasized that a resurgence of interest in dispositional analysis has appeared in recent personality theory and that molar-level acts are seen as the common focus of disparate conceptual frameworks.

7.3. ENVIRONMENTAL DISPOSITIONS

7.3.1. Environmental Dispositions as Differential Orientation

A major task in developing measures of environmental orientation is to demarcate clearly just what aspects of the environment are to be partitioned; in short, the development of an environmental taxonomy is an important component of the development of environmental disposition scales (see Pervin, 1978). In this section, we shall approach the taxonomic task by providing increasingly fine gradations of environmental classifications. We shall start first with dispositional measures that attempt to differentiate global environmental orientation from nonenvironmental orientation and proceed down to scales that differentiate the *type* of environmental object as a basis for dispositional assessment, and finally to the quality of orientation or *type* of action vis-à-vis demarcated aspects of the environment. The global conceptions have a longer history of usage in personality theory and research; the more finely honed measures of environmental dispositions have been the product of more recent research.

Measures Using an Inner–Outer Dichotomy

Though seldom discussed as such, a number of commonly used personality measures can be seen as measuring environmental dispositions as much by default and implication as by design. As Hogan and Cheek (1983) have recently argued, the differentiation of inner and outer is a fundamental one in personality research, and broad-based individual differences in orientation toward the environment or away from the environment (and by implication toward oneself) underlie four of the most frequently used measures of individual differences: measures of extraversion, external locus of control, field dependency, and self-monitoring.

Research on introversion–extraversion is extensive (Eysenck, 1981; Stelmack, 1981; Wilson, 1977) and is based on a multilevel model of personality that spans neurophysiological, psychological, and social domains. It is postulated that extraverts and introverts differ in their chronic levels of cortical arousal, extraverts being chronically understimulated and introverts chronically overstimulated. As a result of these differences, and in order to reach an optimal level of arousal, extraverts require greater environmental stimulation than do introverts. Differences in excitability of reward and punishment centers in the brain have also been postulated, with extraverts being hypersensitive to seeking out reward cues and introverts to avoiding punishment cues in the environment (Gray, 1972). The net result is that, in general, extraverts will be actively engaged in environmental transactions, while introverts will be more likely to avoid them.[17]

While introversion–extraversion appears to derive largely from physiological differences, another major individual difference variable, locus of control, is more clearly the product of socialization and learning experience than of heredity. Internals, relative to externals, are characterized by ascribing greater responsibility to themselves than to their external environments for successes and failures, particularly the former. They seem to adopt a stance toward the environment that is more active, perhaps manipulative, and more goal oriented, than do their external peers. As in extraversion, it is often assumed that there is a homogeneous dimension of environmental (or external) orientation that stands in contrast to internal orientation. Despite the fact that there have been numerous reports on the multidimensionality of external orientation (e.g., Paulhus, 1983; Reid & Ware, 1974), studies continue to be carried out with the singular dimension as a major predictor variable, while few studies have examined the impact of internal versus external locus of control as it relates to specifically environmental variables (see Trigg, Perlman, Perry, & Janisse, 1976; Wolk, 1976; Wolk & Telleen, 1976). It should be expected that, relative to the historic themes outlined earlier, external orientation toward the environment should be one of passive resignation while that of the internal should be one of attempted mastery. We shall see in a later section what the long-term consequences of such orientational differences might be in the light of the *interaction* of personality and environmental characteristics.

Another major dimension of personality used in research has been the dimension of field dependence–field independence (Witkin, Dyk, Faterson, Goodenough, & Karp, 1962), which, while arguably a cognitive abilities trait, is sufficiently broad in scope to warrant treatment as a personality variable. Field-dependent individuals have been found to adopt global perceptual stances to their environments, not differentiating clearly among environmental components, while field-independent individuals are more

likely to articulate their environmental fields. Berry (1977), for example, has shown how field independence and dependence may be based on aspects of the resource ecology within which people live. He showed that Inuit subjects scored high on measures of field independence, while natives of an agricultural society in Africa were more field dependent. Similar links between analytic and global perception of the environment have been reported by Hart (1977) with respect to sex differences. He attributes the greater tendency for males to score high on field independence to their greater latitude in early childhood to explore their environments. The free range of exploration given males is, according to Hart, notably higher than for same-age sisters.

Finally, another dimension that relates an inner with an outer orientation has figured in the studies by Snyder on self-monitoring (Snyder, 1979). Again, a tendency to look inward to one's own feelings and perceptions versus a tendency to look outward for social and environmental cues differentiates the two types. The high self-monitor is one who looks to the outward situation (i.e., monitors his or her social presence) as a guide to correct conduct, while the low self-monitor is more likely to base feelings and judgments on context-free absolutistic judgments.

Each of these dimensions of personality is based on a crude distinction between inner and outer, yet each has generated an impressive corpus of research.[18] They can be seen as forming the first rung of an increasingly variegated taxonomy of environmental dispositions, in which those who look outward at the environment, be it for stimulation, as a source of power, or as a guide to conduct, are differentiated from those who look inward, be it to reduce external stimulation, as a fundamental locus of control, or as the repository of context-independent standards of conduct. While we have briefly noted several examples of the use of these measures in predicting environmental psychological variables, there has been relatively little work done on applying these scales to areas of environmental psychology.

A number of linkages can be postulated theoretically between these individual difference scales and the recurring environmental themes discussed earlier. Thus with respect to the question of environmental meaning versus incoherence we might suggest that introverts and extraverts would differ in their sense of environmental coherence, depending on the level of stimulation to which they were exposed; introverts obtaining a greater sense of coherence from understimulating and extraverts from highly arousing environments. With respect to the question of environmental influence, the dimension of internal versus external locus of control seems particularly relevant. The external is more likely to manifest dispositions of passive vulnerability and the internal more likely to attempt to explore or control. With respect to general environmental competency, it is likely that field-dependent individuals would be less adept at exploratory and way-finding tasks in the environment, while their field-independent colleagues would fare better. With respect to a nurturing versus exploitative orientation toward the environment, it is likely that, given their more aggressive stance toward their milieu, both extraverts and internal locus of control individuals may put their environments at risk.

Such broadband dispositions can guide the questions we ask of events such as Sam Mendon watching his son rowing a boat on a Thursday afternoon. Depending on whether, for example, Sam scores as a field-independent, internal extravert or a field-dependent, external introvert, we might expect different forms of shoreline waiting. The former would be expected to be vigilant, actively pursuing the sight of a boat along the shoreline, perhaps actively pacing along the shore and calling out occasionally. The latter may sit quietly on a log, glancing out to the misty river but essentially lost in revery until his boat comes in.

Psychometrically, these first-order environmental disposition measures can claim relatively high bandwidth but low fidelity with respect to the prediction of environmental criterion variables. More importantly, such measures do not make distinctions between different types of environmental objects; they posit a rather undifferentiated Big Environment that serves as an alternative to a Big Self orientation. As a consequence, attempts to differentiate between selective orientation to, say, social objects in contrast to the physical objects are not illuminated by such measures.

Measures Based on Partitioning the Environmental Component into Primary Elements

One way of moving toward a more environmentally oriented approach to dispositional assessment is to begin the job of taxonomizing the environment into a set of more differentiable objects or focuses. One attempt along these lines began with a philosophical analysis of the primary objects comprising environments (Little, 1972b, 1976a, 1976b). Following Strawson (1964), it was suggested that environments comprise two irreducible objects: material bodies

(things) and persons. Just as Strawson showed that neither of these primitive categories can be reduced to more analytically basic components, that is, that they are primary in a fundamental sense, persons and things as primary environmental objects may have psychological significance as well.

To test the assumption that person orientation and thing orientation might serve as useful dispositional measures linking the personality and environmental domains, a series of studies was begun (Little, 1968) that led to the construction of a thing–person orientation scale (TP Scale) (Little, 1972a). This scale comprises 24 items, of which half are person-oriented items and half thing-oriented items. Individuals are asked their preference for activities, for example, repairing a watch (thing orientation), or interviewing someone for a newspaper column (person orientation).

Person orientation and thing orientation have been shown to be internally consistent, independent, broadband dimensions of environmental orientation that generate a fourfold typology of primary specialist types: nonspecialists, person specialists, thing specialists, and generalists. These groups differ predictably on a number of dimensions related to environmental behavior. For example, person specialists are found more frequently in occupations relating to people (e.g., social work, counseling), while thing specialists are more often found in professions such as chemistry, physics, or engineering (Little, 1976a). When construing urban scenes, person specialists focus primarily on persons and social stimuli, while thing specialists construe more in terms of physical appearance, amenities, and so on. Nonspecialists tend to be more egocentric in their construing, suggesting that they are better regarded as being self-specialists, focusing on their particular goals and projects rather than the environment as such. Finally, generalists were shown to construe in a more complex fashion and to use integrative, aesthetic constructs (Little, 1976a). These differences between individuals in terms of primary orientation may also be applied reflexively to professional groups who make decisions regarding the environment (Murphy, 1978; Sewell & Little, 1973). A detailed summary of person–thing orientation within a framework of environmental psychology has appeared elsewhere (Little, 1976b). In essence, this research extends the work on inner–outer orientations one step further by suggesting that we need to know to what specific elements extraverts extravert themselves, over what kind of objects internals have control, and on what kinds of environmental stimuli field-dependent people depend. Thus the work on person–thing orientation occupies a middle-level position between monolithic environment versus self-dichotomies and the more fine-grained and qualitative distinctions to be discussed later.[19]

7.3.2. McKechnie's Environmental Response Inventory

The first major empirical effort in the development of a multiscale environmental disposition inventory was carried out by McKechnie (1972, 1977, 1978) under the direct aegis of the Berkeley IPAR group.

Using the historical, literary, and other materials prescribed by Craik as his source, McKechnie compiled a provisional item pool covering a comprehensive set of environmental dispositional themes. Then, through a detailed process of factor analysis, rational scaling, and testing of convergent and discriminant validity, a final 184-item Environmental Response Inventory (ERI) was constructed comprising scales of Pastoralism, Urbanism, Environmental Adaptation, Stimulus Seeking, Environmental Trust, Antiquarianism, Need for Privacy, and Mechanical Orientation.

Several studies have documented the utility of the ERI in predicting environmental behavior. Kegel-Flom (1976) showed that optometrists migrated to locations that were highly consistent with Urbanism scale scores on the ERI. Both attitudes (McKechnie, 1977) and planning policy stands (Charns, 1973) have been shown to relate to ERI profiles, and Collins and Hardwick (1974) have created an intriguing map of the Greater Vancouver area, based on the ERI profiles of a 0.1% random sample of residents in the region. Gifford (1980) tested several hypotheses linking ERI scores with evaluative ratings of slides of public buildings. Of particular interest was the effectiveness of the Environmental Adaptation scale in predicting a broad range of preferences, particularly for the big and the new. Gifford suggests that the high scorers on Environmental Adaptation are development oriented, a view consistent with the dominance over nature theme carried by this scale. Corroborative evidence is found in Buss and Craik (1983c), who have developed a measure of two contrasting worldviews and correlated them with ERI and other measures. Scores on worldview A, which emphasizes support for high growth and high technology, showed substantial positive correlation with Environmental Adaptation scores and negative correlation with worldview B, which emphasizes limits to technological growth and less emphasis on materialism.

A clear demonstration of the interrelations between personality and environmental and recreational dispositions was carried out by Phillips (1978) using the ERI, a modification of McKechnie's (1975) Leisure Activities Blank, and a measure of orientation and attentional deployment (Nideffer, 1974). She showed that the ERI scales figured prominently in a set of 10 major clusters linking personality and recreational orientation. For example, a cluster called Extraverted Sociable has very high loadings from the ERI's Environmental Adaptation scale, an All-American cluster is loaded highly by low scores on Need for Privacy, and a cluster called Intellectual Dilettante is largely defined by Urbanism. Finally, Defensive Introvert cluster members score extremely high on Need for Privacy.

As the first major attempt to measure environmental dispositions, the ERI represents a noteworthy research accomplishment. Despite its careful development and its applicability to a broad spectrum of potential applied fields, published studies with the ERI have appeared infrequently (see Stokols, 1982). There are two possible reasons for this. First, the ERI was published at the peak of attacks on the field of personality assessment. One aspect of this attack (Mischel, 1968; Peterson, 1965; Sechrest, 1976) was the contention that simple self-ratings on trait dimensions may have greater validity than the more cumbersome multiitem inventory approach.[20] This view was expressly taken against the ERI in a critical review by Richards (1978).[21] Another possible reason for a relatively low incidence of studies using the ERI is the change in national climate that has occurred in most western industrial democracies, at least during the decade since the ERI was developed. While the physical milieu, as we have seen earlier, was a major focus of the popular consciousness during the early 1970s, it later came to be eclipsed by economic factors, including energy and unemployment, as issues of national concern. Thus, the themes addressed by the ERI may have lost some of their "folk relevancy" over the decade, irrespective of their objective importance. Perhaps the most important contribution of the ERI is that it has provided an essential foundation on which other environmental dispositions, enduring, ephemeral, and emerging, may be constructed.

7.3.3. Other Individual Difference Measures in Environmental Psychology

While McKechnie's ERI represents the most complex and ambitious scale construction research in environmental personology, there have been other individual difference measures concerned with assessing people's responses to the natural and built environments. Some of the more recent of these can be briefly discussed.[22]

Three of McKechnie's scales, Need for Privacy, Stimulus Seeking, and Antiquarianism, have counterparts in the work of other environmental psychologists. Marshall (1970, 1972), in one of the first research studies within the Berkeley tradition, developed a Privacy Preference Scale based on a conceptual analysis of privacy including legal, psychological, and sociological conceptions (e.g., Westin, 1967). Her Privacy Preference Scale (PPS) comprises six factors: Solitude, Intimacy, Anonymity, Reserve, Not Neighboring, and Seclusion. Several derivations of her scale have been reported (e.g., Hunter, Grinnell, & Blanchard, 1978), and others have subsequently examined the issue of the multidimensional versus unidimensional status of the Privacy concept (e.g., Pedersen & Shears, 1973; Wolfram & Wearing, 1982). Wolfram and Wearing (1982), in addressing the issue of multidimensionality, have proposed a hierarchical model of privacy based on their own adaptation of Marshall's scales for an Australian sample. They report an interesting "two-level" hierarchy that they claim is intermediate between a "holistic" view of Privacy, which would posit a single overarching factor, and a reductionist model, which would posit a fairly large number of orthodonal privacy measures.

Stimulus or Sensation Seeking is one of the most thoroughly studied individual difference measures, and its degree of overlap with Extraversion makes it rather arbitrary whether to include it with general personality measures or as a specific environmental disposition measure (e.g., McCarroll, Mitchell, Carpenter, & Anderson, 1967; Schiff, 1971; Zuckerman, 1979; Zuckerman, Kolin, Price, & Zoob, 1964).[23]

With respect to Antiquarianism, two geographers (Taylor & Konrad, 1980) reported a factor-analytic investigation of scales that they developed to tap several dispositions to the past such as historical nostalgia. Four factors emerged (e.g., Conservation, Historical Interest) *each* of which correlated highly and significantly with McKechnie's Antiquarianism scale, suggesting that Antiquarianism subsumes diverse but interrelated aspects of orientation toward the past.

Mehrabian and Russell (Mehrabian, 1977; Mehrabian & Russell, 1974) have also been concerned with developing several measures of individual differences in response to the physical environment. They have constructed tests of arousal-seeking tendency (Mehrabian & Russell, 1973) and the tendency to screen out environmental stimuli and studied the implications of this for stimulus overload and arousability.[24]

A closely related set of scales appears in the work of Nideffer (1974), who has developed a test of attentional and interpersonal style. Nideffer argues that attention can be studied in terms of two broad dimensions: breadth of focus (narrow vs. broad) and direction (inner vs. outer); this yields scales that tap combinations of attentional variables (e.g., broad internal vs. broad external) and also scales for assessing both internal and external stimulus overload and the ability to focus and a scale measuring amount of information process.

7.3.4. Using Conventional Personality Inventories to Predict Environmental Behavior

While the foregoing sections have given details on new measures of individual differences deemed important for the study of person–environment interactions, orthodox inventories have also been used to predict environmentally relevant criterion variables.

Gough's California Psychological Inventory (1975) is an excellent example of a standard personality inventory that focuses primarily on intra- and interpersonal "folk concepts" (Gough, 1968) but that has been adopted for use by environmental psychologists. Borden and Francis (1978), for example, have shown that the CPI Dominance, Capacity for Status, and Sociability scales significantly differentiate individuals high in environmental concern from those low on environmental concern. Bryant (1982) has shown the relationship of CPI scale scores to a sense of direction and geographical orientation, suggesting that individuals scoring high on Capacity for Status, Sociability, and Self-acceptance more actively engage and monitor the environment in their daily transactions.[25]

Gough has taken some interesting steps to adapt his own CPI for use in problems relating to environmental and population concerns. He developed a Personal Values Abstract (Gough, 1972) based on a subset of CPI items that is designed to measure dimensions of relevance to contemporary social and environmental issues. One of these scales, Modernity, is likely to serve as an important moderator variable in predicting the relationship between environmental dispositions (e.g., pastoralism) and criterion variables (e.g., practicing birth control).[26]

7.3.5. Toward an Integrated Model of Environmental Dispositions

Given that systematic empirical work on environmental dispositions is only a decade old, it would be premature to expect a coherent and well-validated taxonomy of such dispositions to have emerged in the literature. There is a need for two types of investigations in order to clarify the domain of environmental dispositions. First, taxonomic studies within the domain of environmental orientations and dispositions should be undertaken (see Pervin, 1978). It would be valuable to examine whether the diverse set of measures discussed previously might be resolved into a circumplex structure similar to that discovered in the interpersonal domain (Wiggins, 1982). For example, environmental dispositions may be structured around two major orthogonal axes representing an active–passive dimension and a nurturance–exploitation dimension, corresponding to similar factors in the social sphere. Second, for research on environmental dispositions to be fully integrated with research on other individual difference domains, it will be necessary for interdomain studies to be carried out in order to determine to what extent environmental dispositions (or what Wiggins refers to as material traits) overlap with dispositions in other primary areas such as the interpersonal, intrapersonal, and character domains. Phillips (1978), as mentioned, has examined the interdomain linkages between environmental dispositions, interpersonal dispositions, and recreational patterns and in general found substantial interrelations.

Our summary of the empirical studies on environmental dispositions has taken us far downstream from our starting point. Lest we forget David and leave him languishing in his boat, let's go back to see just what mutual relevancy, if any, exists between his nautical actions and the research just summarized.

To start, while the intensive study of single cases is an honorable if seldom observed tradition in personology (Carlson, 1971), it has been overshadowed by an even more venerable tradition: the normative analysis of relationships between test scores and criterion measures. Normative analysis resembles what happens when the camera swings upward to get an aerial view of the river. First, David Henry Mendon rowing his white 16-ft clinker-built boat becomes just a kid on the river. Higher still he becomes one of 78 walking (or rowing) blobs discriminable at the level of the village or the municipal subregion. From this perspective, general trends can be detected such as the tendency for people to go inside when it rains, and to come out again when it's sunny. But the individual acts that generate these aggregate patterns are literally lost to sight in aerial photography and conceptually lost to sight in the normative analysis of psychological test scores. Con-

sider the question of how test items relate to natural acts (e.g., item 23 on the ERI and any of David's naturally occurring acts during the week of August 18). Until very recently personologists would have argued that there is *no* necessary relation between them, or, at best, that the relation is only symbolic, tangential, and arbitrary. The act of rowing a boat *might* be loosely linked with the tendency to say "yes" to a test item asking for expressions of interest in, say, outdoor activities or fishing. But adherents of a strict empirical keying approach to test theory (e.g., Bass, 1962; but see Burisch, 1984; Hase & Goldberg, 1967; Wiggins, 1973) would rule out even this degree of correspondence between acts and items. In short, personal acts and psychological test items inhabit two different domains of conceptual discourse. Similarly, it might be thought that the development of empirical scales for the assessment of environmental dispositions is systematically irrelevant to the issues we discussed in Section 7.2.4 about acts and their meaning. But, as we hinted at earlier, the past 5 years have witnessed major strides in personology directed toward bridging the gap between acts and items and providing a sound rationale for conjoining them. So, while David will be left floating for a section or two, we shall return to him before closing. In the meantime, we should resolve not to sell him down the river just yet.

7.4. THE IMPACT OF THE EVERYDAY PHYSICAL ENVIRONMENT ON HUMAN PERSONALITY

7.4.1. Meaning, Structure, and Community as Core Dimensions

While in Section 7.3 we discussed the nature of environmental dispositions—the ways in which individuals differ in their orientations and modes of approaching their environments—in the present section we will examine the impact of the physical environment on human personality. Several of the themes that will concern us here have been anticipated in Section 7.1, where primordial themes of person–environment interaction were introduced. Here we wish to focus in more detail on contemporary research that bears on three major areas of impact of the physical environment. The first area will be referred to as *meaning* and will examine evidence that the physical milieu can contribute to a sense of coherence in individuals by providing a place identity, or contrastingly can provide the grounds for alienation. A second major area will be referred to as environmental *structure* and will concern the extent to which environments constrain, shape, and give structure to our everyday activities. The third area examines the extent to which the physical environment creates and sustains a *sense of community* and the impact this has on human health and well-being.[27] Two additional, oblique dimensions will also be discussed: the impact of environment on stress and competency. Finally, for each of these topic areas we shall illustrate the importance of taking into account the individual differences in environmental dispositions that we have discussed in detail in the past section.

7.4.2. Meaning and Personal Identity: A Sense of Place

There is evidence in both the clinical and the environmental literature that a sense of place is closely related to a sense of personal identity: that we are, in an important sense, the places that we inhabit. Several lines of research can be used to illustrate the kinds of questions asked by those who posit the interrelatedness of place and personal identity.

Searles (1960) provided one of the earliest treatments of the interrelatedness of physical milieu and sense of personal identity. Stressing the essential kinship of individuals and the domain of the inorganic, he postulated that normal development involves movement from global unity with environment, as in the newborn, to increasing differentiation and distancing during the course of development.[28] Searles presents some intriguing examples of how some schizophrenics, moving through periods of rapid transition, may regress to a stage of symbiotic identity with the nonhuman environment, becoming themselves little more than physical artifacts. Thus at the deepest levels of human attachment establishing a sense of oneness with the physical surround appears to be important. In contrast, when there is little opportunity to establish a bond with the physical milieu or to develop a sense of place, normal development appears to be at risk.

While Searles's psychoanalytic treatment of place–person interdependency is primarily Freudian in orientation, Cooper-Marcus (Cooper, 1975) has taken an explicitly Jungian approach to examining the house as symbol of the self. Cooper argues that houses and the spaces within them become symbolic of the different structures postulated by Jung as comprising human personality. For example, she sees living room areas as being the equivalent of the personae, or masks, through which we present ourselves for social consumption. Living rooms provide a particularly sensitive indicator of the self that individuals wish to project to others. Cooper goes on to suggest that other areas of the house are equivalent to the darker, unconscious regions of personality (e.g., private areas within the bedroom) and there are considerable social sanctions imposed against intrusion into such areas in another person's dwelling.[29]

Wapner and his colleagues (e.g., Wapner, 1981; Wapner, Kaplan, & Ciottone, 1981) have presented a perspective on self–world relationships that expands our notion of the interrelatedness of place/space and personal development. By juxtaposing and integrating Wernerian developmental theory with Burke's (1966) dramatistic model of human action, they have generated a program of research on genetic dramatism that provides a sensitive picture of the subtleties of place identity in human development. Space–place entities are seen as being important not only as the mere *setting* for social activities; they may also comprise superordinate values (e.g., the acquisition of property) that direct actions, and, of particular significance to this section, places can also be seen as agents themselves, as when an individual is battling the elements for survival.[30]

Another innovative approach to the area bridging environmental and social psychology is Csikszentmihalyi and Rochberg-Halton's (1981) study of the symbolic importance of domestic objects and the centrality of domestic symbols in self-definition. Noting the absence of systematic empirical research on domestic symbols and household objects, they developed a conceptual framework that emphasizes that

> objects affect what a person can do, either by expanding or restricting the scope of that person's actions and thoughts. And because what a person does is largely what he or she is, objects have a determining effect on the development of the self, which is why understanding the type of relationship that exists between people and things is so crucial. (p. 53)

To explore these relationships, the authors interviewed several hundred individuals about their most cherished household objects and the reasons they were valued. The most frequently cited objects were pieces of furniture, visual arts, and photographs. Reasons for cherishing these objects included past memories and associations, intrinsic qualities, style, and utilitarian and personal values. Physical objects, in short, can be significant across a broad spectrum of meanings, from devices for mere self-gratification, through devices for social memory, up to symbols of enduring traditions and values.

Together, these four representative approaches to the relationship between people and their environment converge on the proposition that our physical surroundings may play an important role in creating a sense of meaning in our lives apart from their function as mere facilitators of social action.

It is likely that the meaningfulness of place and its importance in the development of personal identity are closely related to demographic and individual difference variables. Csikszentmihalyi and Rochberg-Halton (1981) have shown how both age and social class influence what particular type of object is cherished for what kind of reason. Beds, for example, are seen to be particularly important for children, in contrast to other age groups, as objects of personal attachment, while they are valued as heirlooms or for aesthetic reasons by older groups. Among personality variables likely to be important in mediating the environment as a source of positive or negative affect are those identified by McKechnie (1974) as major environmental dispositions. Indeed, perhaps the most useful contribution such variables can make at this stage in the development of environmental personology is to demarcate the major areas where environmental meaning will show wide individual differences. For example, individuals high in Urbanism should find city sights and sounds uplifting and rewarding, while those high on Pastoralism should seek delight in more sylvan settings.

7.4.3. Structure and Environmental Overload: The Vicissitudes of Control

There is a general thesis of considerable popularity within environmental psychology to the effect that humans have limited capacity for processing information, that contemporary environments, particularly urban ones, provide a surfeit of such information, and that this situation in part creates much of the malaise of current living. Certainly the most influential statement of this thesis was Milgram's (1970) elegant formulation of the insidious effects of information input overload in generating urban pathology. While reflecting ideas earlier formulated by the Chicago school of urban sociologists (e.g., Wirth, 1938), Milgram's ability to relate urban indifference and hostility to the vagaries of information processing struck a responsive chord in social psychologists who, no doubt, valued the blend of cognitivism, contextualism, and social relevance in Milgram's perspective. Milgram identified large populations, high density, and social heterogeneity as the major demographic facts generating a state of information input overload in cities. He argued that, in an attempt to reduce such incipient overload, people created a set of adaptive responses, including reduction of quality and quantity of interactions with others, the setting up of preference hierarchies guiding the choice of with whom to interact, and the diverting of certain social responsibilities to more specialized individuals and groups. More insidiously, norms of noninvolvement became institutionalized, so that it became socially unacceptable to be responsive to others. Milgram's model stemmed primarily from a social–environmental perspective, so it is not surprising that individual difference issues were underplayed. However, one obvious dimension that likely moderates the relationship between overload and malaise is that of introversion–extraversion.

For many an extravert, the noise, pace, and complexity of the urban surround are precisely the stimulus conditions most conducive to optimal performance. The demographic conditions that are anathema to the introvert are a major attraction to the extravert. Thus, while the overload–social pathology link has been a highly influential contribution to environmental *social* psychology, it raises one of the most critical issues viewed from the perspective of environmental *personology*. In the presence of ubiquitous interactions between personal characteristics and environmental preference, how can a sound theory of environmental meaning or attraction be advanced?[31]

The Glass and Singer (1972) research paradigm for the study of stress has fostered some of the most elegant experimentation in environmental psychology. The key notion underlying this research has been that noxious stressors such as very loud noise can have deleterious effects on postadaptational behavior; in effect, there may be costs of adaptation to environmental stress. Moreover, one of the key mitigating forces of such costs is the extent to which individuals perceive themselves as having control over the source of stressful stimulation. Not only is the time needed for adaptation to a noise stressor found to be lessened if individuals are told they can turn it off with an escape button, but the psychological costs of adaptation such as lowered frustration tolerance level and efficiency appear to be lessened as well (Glass & Singer, 1973). It is intriguing to note that it is mere *perceived* control that has a potent effect in these studies. Subjects did not, in fact, press the button. Indeed, in some cases the buttons were not even operative. It might be suggested that the emphasis on perceived environmental control so nicely exemplified in the Glass and Singer paradigm meshed perfectly with the burgeoning research on internal locus of control in the personality literature.[32] In both areas there was a tendency to view perceived control over environmental stimulation as a Good Thing, and control lodged in external sources as undesirable. It is legitimate to ask, however, whether the advocacy of an internal orientation could be potentially hazardous, given the vicissitudes of fortune and the pervasive role of chance and circumstance in natural environments (see, e.g., Bandura, 1982). What if internal control expectations are unrealistic? What if Glass and Singer's subjects *had* pushed the button but found it wasn't hooked up? Would they have actually adapted less well to noise stressors than those who had *no* expectations of control at all? What if David's Evinrude motor didn't start up when his boat got caught in the riptide? What happens to internal locus of control individuals if external events conspire to thwart their most cherished goals? A hint of what might happen is contained in an intriguing report by Schultz (1976; see also Schulz & Hanusa, 1978). In a preliminary study he showed that, when elderly people were visited by college students under conditions of either their control (i.e., the elderly) or the students', those who had control reported higher scores on measures of health and well-being. However, on termination of the study (i.e., when control was relinquished by the group previously having control) the results reversed dramatically. The group who had control and then lost it had subsequent declines in both health and well-being. This suggests that both the monolithic view of personality that sees internality as an unmitigated good and monolithic views of environmental design that see control by the inhabitant as a cardinal virtue may be shortsighted. It would appear that the interaction of person with milieu is crucial here. Highly internal individuals may perform better in environments that allow for control, but externals may not. Indeed, externals appear better adjusted than internals in environments that are constraining (see Wolk, 1976; Wolk & Kurtz, 1975; Wolk & Telleen, 1976).[33]

A similar shift away from a simplistic emphasis on the need for control has occurred recently within the field of health psychology. Antonovsky (1979) has put forward the case that one of the key factors influencing human health and well-being is a well-developed *sense of coherence* that he defines as:

a global orientation that expresses the extent to which one has a pervasive, enduring though dynamic feeling of confidence that one's internal and external environments are predictable and that there is a high probability that things will work out as well as can be reasonably expected. (p. 123)

Antonovsky insists that this sense of coherence is *not* simply a sense of control. The latter is a matter of having things under *your* control; the former is perceiving that "things are under control" (p. 155). Kaplan (1983) has also addressed this issue and applied it directly to the field of environmental psychology. He argues that current pressure to design environments for user control is ill conceived; that even if it were desirable, it would be unrealizable in a world of intrinsically limiting and constraining conditions. He goes on to suggest that a more realistic and desirable goal for environmental designers is to design supportive and restorative environments. Supportive environments are high in information availability and in legibility (Lynch, 1960) and they foster a sense of participation. Restorative environments are those that foster repose, stimulate intrinsically enjoyable activities, and capture a person's attention. From the perspective of a coherence model, in contrast to a control model, the ideal milieu is not infinitely flexible or flimsy, but fascinating.

Together, the perspectives of Antonovsky and Kaplan shift our concerns with environmental structure from an emphasis on overload and the need for control to a focus on environmental compatibility and coherence. Not only do we anticipate that there will be important individual differences moderating general environmental models but we see emerging a subtle relevancy of the personological, for the environmental, aspects of psychology. Fine shifts in our understanding of certain personality variables such as problematic aspects of internal locus of control illuminate homologous aspects of environmental variables such as the shift from controllable to supportive environments. A similar parallelism appears in the third of our major dimensions of environmental influence on personality: the sense of community.

7.4.4. The Psychological Sense of Community

One of the most critical dimensions along which environments can vary is that of providing the physical basis of a sense of community. At the microlevel, some environments are sociofugal, pushing people away from each other and fostering social isolation. Others are sociopetal and pull people together (e.g., Altman, 1975; Osmond, 1957; Sommer, 1969). At more of a macrolevel, Moos (1976) had distinguished between environments high on a *relationship* dimension, that is, stimulating interpersonal contacts, while at the neighborhood level we can differentiate those environments that promote a sense of kinship and community from those that engender social disintegration and alienation.[34]

One of the earliest and most innovative treatments of this general theme of the interdependence of personality and a sense of community was Alexander's (1967) model of the "City as a Mechanism for Sustaining Human Contact." Alexander argues that the Industrial Revolution created opportunities for two closely related human characteristics to emerge: autonomy and withdrawal. Autonomy was created as a result of the emancipation of individuals from collective farming due to mechanization. The capacity to earn an independent livelihood led to the migration of individuals to the burgeoning cities. These in turn created sufficient stress that individuals began to withdraw into themselves. Alexander proposed that the long-range effect of industrialized urbanization has been the emotional isolation of individuals and concomitant social disorganization. The central components of the syndrome are seen to be the creation of isolated, inward dwellings that lead to practical difficulties of sustaining intimate contact with friends and neighbors and that have particularly insidious effects on children who, living in isolation, begin to believe in their own self-sufficiency and nondependence on others. This in turn leads to a *desire* to live in isolated, autonomous independence, and the circle closes. Central to Alexander's thesis is the following prescription:

> An individual can be healthy and happy only when his life contains three or four intimate contacts. A society can be a healthy one only if each of its individual members has three or four intimate contacts at every stage of his existence. (pp. 67–68)

He goes on to show that such intimacy requires an urban architecture based on a particular set of geometrical features. These features encourage the formation of frequent, intense, but casual exchanges that are not constrained by role prescriptions. Without our going into the details of Alexander's architectural solution to this design problem, several key implications of his proposal deserve comment. First, it is one of the most clearly articulated models of the impact of architectural form on human personality. Second, it postulates that the lack of correspondence between fundamental human needs and urban form is generating individual and social pathologies. Finally, it proposes that, by judicious architectural change,

human personality can change, and benefits to health and well-being will ensue. The relevancy of this early formulation to social ecological models for the enhancement of human well-being (e.g., Little & Ryan, 1978, 1979; Moos, 1976) is noteworthy.

While Alexander provides some architectural devices for ensuring that individuals have a choice for *when* interaction with others is to be encouraged (through the use of glassed "open for business" areas in the home easily visible from the street), his assumption of the universality of the need for this level of intimate contact is contentious. Again, the individual difference dimensions in the personality field are relevant. There is considerable empirical evidence that extraverts have a higher need for social stimulation than do introverts (Wilson, 1977). Indeed, it is not unlikely that introverts would find the emotional load of "three or four" intimate contacts at each stage of the life cycle sufficient inducement to beat a hasty retreat to the wilderness for a respite from conviviality. In short, personality factors will likely serve as key moderators of the effects of environment on human well-being, and this might mitigate whatever ameliorative effects innovative environmental design might have.

Alexander's paper is a strikingly original contribution to environmental personology, even though it was intended as a critique and guide to architectural planning. In recent years a number of studies have appeared that, while seldom citing Alexander, deal with important aspects of his model. Perhaps the most extensive set of studies has been those concerned with the role of social support networks in sustaining mental and physical health and with the environmental structures that promote this support. It has become commonplace in the community psychology literature, for example, to ascribe salutary effects to the presence of social networks (e.g., Tolsdorf, 1976).[35]

A recent major study in Australia, however, challenges the assumption that the availability of social networks has a direct effect on health and well-being. Henderson, Byrne, and Duncan-Jones (1981) have reported a carefully designed study on the impact of social resources on neurotic behavior. They conclude that it is not so much the availability of social resources but the perception of their usefulness that seems to promote well-being. Moreover, personality factors seem critical in influencing whether resources are evaluated positively or negatively.[36] Even if social networks or intimate Alexandrian quartets exist as potential "cushions" (Butt, 1971) and helping resources, their effectiveness is screened through personality characteristics that serve as critical components of the environment-outcome linkage. While the physical mileu can provide the grounds for community and social support, it cannot extort a sense of community from those who, be it out of confusion or conviction, choose to turn away and seek a life of solitude[37]

7.4.5. Stress and Competency as Environmental Effects on Personality

While environmental meaning, structure, and community are likely to subsume most of the major dimensions of environmental influence, there are two other dimensions that should be briefly mentioned in order to round out our discussion of the impact of environment on personality.

The dimension of environmental stress deserves special comment, particularly in light of the frequency with which it is attracting serious environmental research (e.g., Evans, 1982; see also Evans & Cohen, Chapter 15, this volume). It is at present unclear whether environmental stress should be regarded as simply one aspect of environmental structure, as may have been implied in the last section, or whether it stands as a basic dimension on its own. One of the most valuable contributions of recent work in this area has been clarification of the difference between varieties of environmental stress. Campbell (1983) has distinguished between the concepts of acute stressors, daily hassles, and what she calls *ambient* stressors. The latter are described as being chronic, negatively valued, nonurgent, physically discernible, and intractable to the efforts of *individuals* to change them. While research that has focused primarily on acute stressors and daily hassles has identified a number of relevant personality or coping factors that facilitate adaptation such as perceived control, it is likely that the personality factors that relate to ambient stressors, in terms of both effects and mediators, are of a different sort. Of particular relevance here are units of analysis involving longer temporal spans for their enactment than are characteristic of most personality variables. As Stokols (1983) has recently documented, one of the most noteworthy recent trends in environmental psychology has been the adoption of units of analysis involving temporally extended sequences of person–environment interaction. Once more, an effective parallelism appears to be emerging, with elaboration and articulation of personality constructs both illuminating and reflecting similar distinctions in the domain of environmental attributes.[38]

Another area of environmental influence that cannot be easily subsumed under the major headings is that of competency, the extent to which environments are able to inculcate, sustain, and support feelings of personal efficacy. An excellent example of the impact of the physical environment on a specific area of competency is provided by Cohen, Glass, and Singer (1973), who reported a field study examining how noise in New York City apartment buildings influenced the reading ability of children. They discovered that children living on the lower floors showed poorer auditory discrimination and subsequent reading achievement than did children living on the higher floors. It appears that children, in order to adapt to loud ground noise, learn to screen out auditory cues. By also screening out speech-relevant cues, the children fail to learn some discriminative skills essential for learning to read. It is intriguing but sobering to conjoin this result with evidence on the development of preparedness for speech acquisition in young infants. It has been reported (Condon & Sander, 1974) that a finely coordinated synchronization exists between muscular movements in babies and the pattern of sound stimulation coming from parent speech exchanges. This neuromuscular synchronization may reflect the laying down of a neural substratum necessary for the development of speech acquisition, and for later social interaction. If so, the results of the apartment noise studies are rather ominous. By interfering with synchronized exchanges between developing infants and their parents and peers, environmental noise may block the acquisition of basic interactional skills necessary for both academic and social competency.[39]

7.4.6. Summary and Critique of the Environmental Influence Research

This section has reviewed perspectives supporting the proposition that the physical environment plays a significant role in creating a sense of meaning, structure, and community among its inhabitants, in generating stress, and in providing the context for enhanced competency. We have also, for each of these areas, indicated the key moderating role of personality factors and pointed to the dangers of assuming more homogeneity of need or response than in fact exists. Moreover, we are increasingly able to specify the kinds of personal dispositions most likely to mediate the major classes of environmental effects. An extensive array of potential linkages between individual dispositions and environmental effects can be generated by conjoining the dispositional measures summarized above with the dimensions of influence discussed in the present section. For example, for individuals characterized by a high degree of aesthetic orientation and environmental concern, the physical milieu may be a major, perhaps the prepotent, source of meaning in life. For others, perhaps more person-oriented, dependent, and anxious individuals, the physical milieu may be a bland backdrop against which social figures stand stark and salient. With respect to environmental structure we have argued that urban overload may be a major source of malaise for some and a sought-out source of stimulation for others, and that the social intensity of communal living may be nirvana or nuisance, depending on one's capacity for intimacy.

Clearly a major agenda item for research in environmental personology will be to chart more extensively the empirical linkages between environmental dispositions and dimensions of the physical milieu and their combined impact on human and environmental well-being and adaptation. While the research on physical environments and personality is still relatively underdeveloped, if we dilate the environment to include not only physical but also more broadly based social and situational factors, a large and growing literature on interactional psychology exists that is highly relevant to our theme. We now turn to this.

7.5. PERSONALITY, ENVIRONMENT, AND INTERACTIONAL PSYCHOLOGY

7.5.1. The Trait Debate and the Origins of Interactional Psychology

As discussed earlier, Mischel's (1968) *Personality and Assessment* had a transforming effect on the field of personality and social psychology. The initial impact was to shift attention from trait-like stabilities of human personality to the situational or contextual factors controlling human behavior, a shift that harmonized well with the growing contextual revolution in the ecological, environmental, and behavior modification streams in psychology. Part of the data base on which Mischel had drawn were studies examining the amount of variance attributable to persons, situations, and their interaction in influencing particular behaviors such as stress or anxiety (Endler, Hunt, & Rosenstein, 1962). These studies continued to grow in the late 1960s and early 1970s until a fairly substantial data base existed to examine whether persons, situations, or person-by-situation interactions accounted for the bulk of variance in relevant human behaviors (Argyle & Little, 1972; Endler & Magnusson, 1976; Magnusson & Endler, 1977). Examination of the conceptual and empirical issues concerning the relative contributions of these sources of behavioral variation comprised a new field of research: interactional psychology (Endler & Magnusson, 1976; Furnham & Jaspars, 1983; Hunt, 1975; Magnusson, 1980; Magnusson & Endler, 1977). While this is now a large and diffuse field of its own, several aspects of it bear directly on the present chapter and will be dealt with selectively.

7.5.2. Methodological Issues in P × E Interactionism

A number of important methodological issues have attended the rise of an interactional psychology dealing with the representativeness of situations, the selective exposure of persons to situations, and the nature of the measurement unit in examining person × environment interaction. Each of these can be briefly examined.

Bowers (1973), in surveying 11 studies, concluded that interactions are stronger in their effects than either situation or person effects, while others reached opposing conclusions (e.g., Gifford, 1981; Sarason, Smith, & Diener, 1975). One of the criticisms of the first wave of interaction studies was that the proportion of variance explained by either main or interaction effects could be artificially inflated by sampling extreme cases of either persons or situations. For example, if one measured competency in three similar social situations in a small Icelandic village with three individuals, an Icelander, a unilingual Samoan, and a multilingual but psychotic anthropologist from Cleveland, the chances are great that persons would swamp situations as sources of variation. Similarly, situations would overwhelm persons as sources of variation if one were to measure anxiety level in a group of homogeneous, middle-aged, Rotarian cost accountants observed watching the news at home, driving the Santa Ana Freeway, and being launched from Cape Kennedy. The point is that the early demonstrations of the need for an interactional psychology were unsystematic in their choice of situations or persons so that any attempt to draw substantive conclusions about *the* relative effects of persons and situations or their interaction was indeterminate. Technical criticisms of the models used to test effect sizes were also published (e.g., Golding, 1975; Olweus, 1977). Another criticism of the early treatments of interactionism was that they had overpolarized the positions of the classic personologists and the situationalist. A cursory glance at the history of personality psychology informs us that most of the classical formulations, even those explicitly sympathetic to traits, recognized the role of situational and interactional effects (Ekehammar, 1974; Herrmann, 1980). Indeed, the belief that individual conduct is a joint function of person and situation has long been a truism among personologists. So interactional psychology in its formative period was criticized from one perspective for the inappropriateness of the methodological tools through which it apportioned variance due to persons and contexts, and from another point of view as little more than cliché. What seemed to be required was a clear rationale for sampling the situations presumed to influence human conduct.

A second and related issue hinged on the question of whether in interactional studies the subjects were given a choice in the settings in which they were involved, rather than simply responding to an experimentally created setting. One interpretation of the early evidence supporting situational and interactional effects was that individuals selectively enter settings and situations in accordance with their interests, abilities, and dispositions, a position consistent with a more personological orientation.[40] Thus if Barry is a furtive, romantic fool he likely seeks out settings in which he can wax furtively romantic: skulking along river banks, or lurking on the periphery of "people-places." To expose individuals to the same experimentally contrived situation and to conclude that they all tend to behave in similar ways is to throw out the personological baby with the Barkerian bathwater.[41]

Another methodological issue in many respects subsumes the others and has been raised frequently in recent discussions on the nature of interaction as a psychological concept (e.g., Alker, 1977; Buss, 1978; Endler, 1982; Magnusson, 1982; Overton & Reese, 1977; Ozer, 1982). At the simplest level, we can ask whether we wish to adopt a mechanistic view of person–situation interaction or a systemic interactionism.[42] The former is best exemplified by studies using ANOVA designs in which the interaction between persons and situations is revealed by the *statistical* interaction effect of separately measured person factors and separately measured environment factors. A poignant illustration of the rather passive, unsystemic nature of early mechanistic interactionism in environmental psychology has been sketched recently by Russell and Ward (1982). Commenting on the image of our subjects implicit in the first decade of research in environmental psychology, they suggest:

The subjects who volunteered in the environmental psychology laboratory 10 years ago were fragile crea-

tures.... They didn't really produce their own behavior. They drifted aimlessly about until they encountered a behavior setting. Suddenly they sprang to life, behaving according to the setting's program until, duties completed, the setting ended. Then they fell lifeless again until their next behavior setting. The thought even occurred that we should forget about such puppets and study the behavior setting directly. The creatures were the medium for the behavior setting's message. (p. 681)[43]

But in the mechanical interaction model not all creatures were effective media in all settings; there was preferential selection of certain individuals to particular situations. Thus, Herman, Alice, and David may, if exposed to Pinecrest Public Library and the river on a Thursday morning, show differential patterns of enjoyment or stress. Alice and David prefer the river setting, while Herman finds the greatest pleasure and least stress in the reading room at Pinecrest library. On the basis of many such studies, we might conclude that enjoyment and stress show high interaction effects. We might even measure the subjects on dispositional variables and conclude that those who were more comfortable in the river settings were more pastoralist or sensation seeking in their environmental orientations than those seeking out reading rooms. This would also be consistent with a mechanical interaction research agenda. But such an agenda seems rather like a five-year plan for a behavioral accounting firm, totting up variance payable to one dispositional department here, or to a situational ledger there. One might also say that rather than capturing the essence of person–environment *interaction* one has a whole paradigm in place for the examination of person–environment *interpassivity*. What has happened to that purposive, active creature born during the cognitive revolution? Does it matter, for example, that the *reasons* Alice and David preferred the river setting were very different? Alice may have been actively seeking out rural delights, while David simply needed a place to escape the storms of pubescent politics. Herman, meanwhile, was feeling the swells and sprays of a whale hunt as he walked the deck of the Pequod Public Library, reading *Moby Dick*.

7.5.3. Toward a Systemic Interactional Methodology: Emerging Perspectives

While still at an early stage of development, several new approaches to the assessment of individuals in context have been emerging that, in contrast with the mechanical P × E interaction approaches, focus directly on an interactional unit of analysis. These perspectives appear to offer some possibility of theoretical and empirical integration of issues intersecting the domains of environmental and personality psychology.

Natural Acts and Molar Imperatives

The common point of convergence of these new approaches is the assessment and analysis of molar-level natural acts, actions, or activities. To deal first with the issue of naturalness, a good example of such an interactional unit would be the action of David rowing a boat on the Ottawa River on Thursday afternoon. Such a datum is "natural" in two senses. The act itself is a datable occurrence, one which is grounded in time and place and to which questions such as Where?, With whom?, and When? are appropriately asked.[44] A second sense in which it is natural is that action occurs without coercion from the experimenter. Thus, in contrast with items on orthodox tests and with the raw behaviors studied in traditional experimentation, David's rowing has greater claim to ontological status. The use of such natural units of analysis is extensive, and some exemplars will be briefly sketched.[45]

Klinger (1977; Klinger, Barta, & Maxeiner, 1980) has made creative use of paging devices to sample what he calls the "current concerns" and activities of individuals in situ. Ecologically oriented behavior analysts have undertaken the sampling of naturally occurring acts (Rogers-Warren & Warren, 1977), and Hurlburt (1979) has used paging devices to sample the thoughts occurring at the time of paging (see also Camerson, Stewart, Craig, & Eppelman, 1973).

Another technique used for sampling natural acts and activities is the keeping of logs and diaries of situations experienced over a period of time (e.g., Diener, Larsen, & Emmons, 1984; Pervin, 1983; Sjoberg, 1981). While the sampling of such natural acts is less representative in a statistical sense, the units sampled by diaries and logs allow for a greater amount of personal screening for relevancy (to say nothing of propriety) than do methods involving pagers and beepers.

Mention should also be made of the extensive studies carried out on time budget research (Chapin, 1968; Chapin & Hightower, 1966; Szalai, 1972) that attempt to examine the spatial and temporal characteristics of everyday activity. Like logs and diaries, time budget analysis aims at assessing the full spectrum of daily activities, though typically this is done by asking the respondent to check off time spent in broad normative categories (e.g., social activities, domestic chores) rather than the more idiosyncratic

acts and events recorded in logs and diaries (e.g., seeing Elizabeth; fixing David's torn pants).

Buss & Craik's (1980, 1983a) innovations in measuring dispositions by focusing on topographically independent acts can also be regarded as a contribution to the search for natural units of analysis. Their initial methodology involved having respondents check off whether, during the past 2 years, they had engaged in any of a list of acts that had been nominated by judges as representative of a given trait domain (e.g., the item "pushed ahead of someone in a movie line-up" might be an exemplar of the trait domain of "dominance"). More recently, however, they have started to record act trends based on observer (spouse) reports as well as self-reports (Buss & Craik, 1984; see also Moscowitz & Schwartz, 1982).

It was suggested that these new perspectives seem to offer promise for integration of themes in personality and environmental psychology. It is noteworthy, therefore, that some of the researchers just cited have come primarily from the perspective of environmental design and urban planning (e.g., Chapin's time budget research), while others have approached the same units of analysis as vehicles for trait ascription in personological studies (e.g., Buss & Craik). Another potential area of convergence facilitated by the use of natural acts as units of analysis is that of ethological and evolutionary perspectives on person–environment interaction. For example, within personality psychology, Hogan (1982; Hogan, Jones, & Cheek, 1984) has made the case for a socioanalytic theory based in part on an analysis of the types of fundamental tasks and roles demanded by our evolutionary provenance. Similarly, Kaplan (1972), writing from within an environmental framework, has stressed the adaptive aspects of basic forms of environmental activity.

We may turn now to consider the molarity issue of molar-level natural acts. It should be noted that several different powers of lens have been used by those exploring natural acts. For example, imagine David as a subject in the studies of each of the researchers discussed above. For those employing paging or beeper technology, David might well have been beeped just as he was cutting through the rough chop. One can image him responding to the prompt with the reply that he's in the process of saving his neck, with the nautical nature of his escape left unspecified. Thus his concern with the current (in the hydrological, not temporal, sense) becomes his preeminent current concern and the fishing trip fades into peripheral vision. In a study using logs or diaries, he may simply list "went fishing," adding for the time budget researcher, "2:30–4:08." Much as it was with the zoom lens imagery with which we began, we might ask what is the best level of molarity at which to capture the characteristics of the scene.

Considerable agreement seems to exist that it is necessary to focus on relatively molar-level acts in order to capture patterns of characteristics in both people and their settings. Until recently, however, there was little in the way of methodological agreement as to how such molar imperatives were to be operationalized. However, the work of Rosch (1975, 1978) on the characteristics of natural categories provided an elegant combination of conceptual differentiation and allied methodological techniques for measuring the vertical and horizontal structure of natural categories. *Vertical structure* refers to the nested, hierarchical nature of categories developed by humans for the construing of common objects both physical (e.g., Rosch, 1975, 1978) and social (e.g., Cantor & Mischel, 1979). Rosch, Simpson, and Miller (1976), working with superordinate- (molar), middle-, and subordinate-(molecular) level categories for physical objects, found that middle-level concepts were particularly rich, vivid (imageable), and distinctive relative to the higher and lower levels. Cantor and Mischel (1979), similarly, have shown how middle-level concepts in the social domain optimize information processing. This middle level of molarity is regarded as a "basic level" for information processing. *Horizontal structure* refers to the differentiation of objects into different content categories irrespective of level of abstraction.

A key notion in this literature is that of the prototype of a given domain. Individuals seem readily able to sort objects into those that are and those that are not good exemplars of a given category. Robins and sparrows, for example, are seen as good exemplars or prototypes of the domain of birds; albatrosses are not. In contrast with classical two-valued logic, most everyday categorization involves the use of fuzzy sets organized around such prototypical instances. A great deal of current research is examining both the vertical and the horizontal structure of concepts in the physical and social domains, including the domain of situations (Cantor, Mischel, & Schwartz, 1982) and environments (Tversky & Hemenway, 1983). Given our concern in this section with interactional units of analysis, we might ask to what extent natural acts, like natural objects, can be analyzed in terms of the vertical and horizontal structure features examined in other domains. To date, there has been relatively little work done on the classification of acts or actions. Buss & Craik (1983a), however, have conjoined Roschian analysis of natural categories with

psychometric research on multiple-act criteria and with the previously discussed summary view of traits to generate a new program of research on dispositions. In essence, Buss and Craik see trait domains as natural categories of acts, each with its prototypical exemplars and internal structure. They develop lists of domain-relevant acts, have judges rate each act for its prototypicality for the domain in question, and then get respondents to indicate which of a set of such acts they have engaged in over the past 2 years. In a series of empirical studies across a diversity of trait domains, Buss and Craik have been able to show that orthodox trait measures (e.g., CPI and PRF scales) correlate significantly and highly with the frequency with which individuals report engaging in acts rated as highly prototypical for that domain. A gradient of predictor-criterion correlations is found, such that as the prototypicality of acts diminishes the correlations diminish. Further, the degree of association between acts in one trait domain and acts in adjacent domains (e.g., hostile vs. dominant acts) can be measured, and results to date support a circumplicial ordering of interpersonal traits around two orthogonal dimensions of warmth and dominance (Buss & Craik, 1983d, 1984; Wiggins, 1979).

The shift in the status of acts within the personality paradigm as reflected in the work reported in this section is noteworthy. In the classic personality paradigm, personality tests comprising multiple items were validated against criterion variables that were often single acts of unknown (or at least unverified) prototypicality vis-à-vis the domain under study. By aggregating multiple, molar-level, topographically independent acts of high prototypicality into composite criterion variables, new conceptual life seems to have been breathed into the classical trait paradigm. Equally noteworthy is the convergence on molar-level natural acts by researchers in the cognitive social learning and personological domains (see Little, 1982). Though with different conceptual expectations about temporal and cross-situational generality (Funder & Ozer, 1983; Mischel & Peake, 1982), it is of considerable interest that two fields of research that only a decade ago were engaged in conceptual hostilities now at least have the same acts to grind.

Personal Projects Analysis

While natural molar-level acts serve as a common focus for new personological and cognitive social learning perspectives, the systemic and interactional nature of such acts is central to another recently developed framework, personal projects analysis (Little,

1983). Based on a model of specialization that stresses the selective channeling of individual orientations and competencies (Little, 1972b, 1976b), personal projects analysis provides a methodology within which the social ecological implications of natural acts (Little & Ryan, 1978, 1979; Sundberg, 1977; Sundberg, Snowden, & Reynolds, 1978), as well as their personological relevance, are given due emphasis. A detailed introduction to the methodology appears elsewhere (Little, 1983), but selected aspects can be highlighted in order to show how the approach contributes to the major themes of this chapter. Indeed, in many respects we can use projects analysis as a means for pulling together some of the diverse themes running through our review.

Personal projects are essentially extended sets of personally relevant action. They can include such concerns as "getting my car fixed," "visiting Stowe," "taking David fishing," and "controlling my temper better." Methodologically, they are elicited by asking individuals to write down their current concerns and activities. The respondents are encouraged to make the list as idiosyncratic as they wish. With respect to the issue of the vertical structure of acts, personal projects can range from highly molecular-level acts (e.g., "feed the cat") to highly molar goals and values (e.g., transform western thought). After elicitation is completed, respondents rate each project on a set of 17 dimensions chosen for their relevancy in capturing key individual difference variables (e.g., perceived control over projects) and for their likely association with criterion variables relating to personal, social, and physical well-being (e.g., stress, time adequacy).

. Respondents are also asked to describe where and with whom each project is taking place, and these open columns allow access to the social ecological context within which the individual's projects are embedded. Finally, they complete a cross-impact matrix that examines the impact of each project on the others in terms of conflict, mutual facilitation, and so on. This matrix can also be applied to examining the cross-impact of two or more individuals' project systems.

The result is a set of interrelated measures on the current concerns, activities, problems, pursuits, and commitments of individuals, phrased in their own terms and rated on dimensions currently regarded as critical to the understanding of person–environment interaction. The matrix can be examined ipsatively, that is, within the single case, or normatively. In the former case, we examine the correlations between dimensions for the single case and ask whether, for example, stressful projects for this individual also happen to be those that are low in visibility to other people; or whether projects high in control also happen to be low in difficulty.

Normatively, the project list can be regarded as the functional equivalent of a set of test items, and column scores on, say, perceived control of projects can be treated as scale scores and treated normatively like other individual difference variables. Thus, excluding the open columns, 17 normative scales can be scored for each individual from the standard projects matrix. Personal projects can thus serve as a unit of analysis through which the reciprocal interactions between person and environment can be expressed directly. In a sense, they serve as carrier units for interactional analysis. Rather than examining practical orientation or outdoor interests as person variables, and mean snowfall or inclemency as environmental variables, we look at the spontaneous elicitation of personal projects like "shoveling the driveway" that simultaneously informs us of systemically linked aspects of the person and her milieu. Such projects allow us to determine what salient features of both environment and persons need to be invoked in order to explain their interaction: an inductive analytic procedure which, in Cronbach's (1975) terms, allows us to "pin down the contemporary facts" (p. 126) as a primary task. Several key themes of the chapter can now be drawn together by showing how projects methodology attempts to assess the systemic interaction between persons and environments.

The actual content of personal projects, the *what* of daily concerns, speaks to the first issue raised in this chapter—the enduring, historically dominant themes about people in their environmental settings. The three themes of environmental meaning, control, and stewardship can be seen emerging in such projects as "escape to the cottage for the weekend," "fix the air conditioner," and "start a car pool with Julian," though the themes are screened through the particular social ecological niche within which the individual lives and require knowledge of that niche for their proper interpretation. It is possible also to examine the links between these dominant themes and other personal and environmental variables: What are the project dimension profiles of environmentally responsive projects, for example. Are they more stressful and conflictful than projects that lead to environmental despoliation?

When discussing themes raised by other disciplines, we noted that one way in which they could be incorporated into environmental personology would be their being used as the content for questionnaire items in multiscale inventories as in the ERI. A somewhat different approach to interdisciplinary linkages occurs with projects analysis. The content of the projects can be directly appropriated by other disciplines for direct subsumption within their own professional and scientific construct systems. For example, resource planners can examine spatial aspects of urban design by looking at the relationships between project content and the distance between prime locations within which those projects are enacted (see, e.g., Martensson, 1977). Sociologists with a linguistic orientation can examine the phrasing level of project content as related to social class. It is also possible to create ad hoc columns for analyzing projects on dimensions of particular interest to a given discipline. We have used a column looking at the financial load of projects to explore economic issues, for example, and various elaborations of the "with whom" column have been used to operationalize social network variables of interest to sociologists (Palys & Little, 1983).

Projects methodology can also be used to examine some of the personality variables discussed in Sections 7.2 and 7.3. Variables such as internal versus external locus of control can be assessed with projects methodology by use of the appropriate normative scales. Additionally, content analysis of the projects a la Buss and Craik's approach is possible. Act frequency counts for certain central dispositional domains can be performed. Rapley (1983), for example, analyzed the extent to which personal projects were rated as prototypically person oriented (e.g., "helping Jenny with her problems") and/or thing oriented (e.g., "fixing my universal joint"), thus providing a measure of individual differences tapping the same domain as the Thing–Person Orientation Scale reviewed previously, but using ecologically representative units of analysis instead of rather arbitrary scale items. Each of the personality and environmental dispositions discussed in Section 7.3 could, in principle, be appraised by the process of generating natural acts or personal projects and having them rated for their centrality to different dispositional domains. In some cases it will be necessary to "tune" the elicitation phase of projects analysis to a particular content domain (e.g., to projects relating to recreational activities, or to energy concerns) in order to canvass a sufficiently large number of scalable projects or acts. The main point to be stressed here is that, whereas orthodox test items allow us to ascribe traits to individuals but do not allow access to systemic ecological analysis, natural acts and personal

projects allow *both* functions to be performed. They can serve both as markers for dispositional assessment and as a source of nourishment for the social ecological researchers. With such units you can have your trait and eat it, too.

Each of the major dimensions of environmental influence on personality discussed in Section 7.4 has been operationalized with projects methods. In one study, for example, physical symptomatology was shown to be a joint function of high project hassle (a structure variable) and low social support (a community variable), while project meaning has been a consistent predictor of measures of well-being and life satisfaction (Little, 1983).

With respect to interactional psychology, a key issue we discussed was the hierarchical nature of acts, and the question arose as to whether we could talk about an optimal level of molarity. While the work of Cantor and Mischel suggests that middle-level units will be optimal, projects analysis offers an alternative way of handling the question of molarity level. We assume that individuals adapt to a preferred level of molarity in phrasing their projects to themselves and others, and one of our methodological tasks is to assess the molarity level by a process we call *left* and *right laddering*.

Right laddering involves asking the respondent to answer, for each project, just *how* he or she will be carrying out the project over the next 2 weeks. This generates molecular acts one "ladder rung" down from the level at which the project was originally phrased. This act, in turn, can be laddered and so on until an irreducible act is generated that can be grounded in time and space (i.e., it can literally be scheduled).

Left laddering comprises a parallel process with the question, Why? When this question is asked for each project, several different types of responses can occur. Motives, justifications, general accounts, reasons, perceived causes, and superordinate goals and values can be elicited. When the respondent reaches a terminal point beyond which no further superordinate account is possible, the process stops. This procedure allows us literally to count the ladder steps between the molecular and molar scan of a given project. The level at which a person phrases projects may be shifted in one direction or the other. For example, some persons phrase their projects at a very molecular level (one step removed from a schedulable act), while others may drift into molar abstractions and become lost in semantic hyperspace.[46]

A fundamental difference exists between research

that does not inquire into the superordinate accounts of acts and that which, like projects analysis, takes such accounts as a critical concern. Recall our earlier discussion about Sam Mendon and our puzzling over whether we should see him as a certifiable McKechnie Pastoralist or not. Knowing that the reasons he was engaged in Pastoralist activities was to please his wife, do we still wish to credit him with a disposition based on the outward and visible signs of his actions? This is a surprisingly complex question. Projects analysis would argue that, to the extent an act trend can be discounted by a superordinate account from the respondent, dispositional attribution by mere act frequency is no longer tenable. Buss and Craik's act frequency approach, I believe, would argue otherwise.

To summarize this section, several new approaches in personality and environmental psychology seem to be converging on the analysis of natural acts as units of analysis. While offering alternative, perhaps conflicting, approaches to the appraisal of persons in context, they agree that the proper focus for research and analysis is the naturally occurring molar act. David rowing his boat, then, is not just a convenient symbol for the concerns of this chapter; it comprises the fundamental unit of an emerging interactional psychology. By way of conclusion, let us revisit him, see where we have been, and look at the prospects upstream.

7.6. RETROSPECT AND PROSPECTS FOR THE STUDY OF PERSONALITY AND THE ENVIRONMENT

7.6.1 Retrospect: Pictures at an Exhibition

We began by looking at a boy rowing a boat on the river and noted how he could fade into insignificance either by soaring up into macrospace or by zooming down into microspace. The image is a fitting one to capture the status of research at the interface of environmental and personality psychology. Many different camera angles and lenses can examine his nautical pursuits, and each provides a partial glimpse of an inordinately complex phenomenon. Let's conduct one last tour of these alternative pictures at a conceptual exhibition.

We saw first how his activity can be construed as an exemplification of historic themes about human–environment relations: the search for meaning in the coherent image of a designed universe or the sense

of alienation and homelessness; the sense of control or of futility in the face of natural or built disasters; the pursuit of harmony with, or hegemony over, the physical milieu. This image should remind us that themes about the interpenetration of human personality and its physical surround predate our current psychological concern by centuries, and that the kind of perspective afforded by historical geography is required for those wishing seriously to study the interplay of environment and personality.

We also saw how different perspectives within and outside of psychology have approached the physical environment and its human impact: how the boat trip could variously be seen as embodying an archetypal symbol, as comprising a term in an equation showing behavior to be a joint function of person and environment, as an incipient act of environmental depredation, or as the central plot of a narrative about growing up in contemporary society. We saw, in short, that simple acts of persons in environments can be variously construed, and that these multiple constructions all have equal epistemic claim: their capacity to provide a coherent account of environmental action depending on the disciplinary or personal perspective through which the act is viewed and the goal of observing it in the first place.

While these issues emerged from the fairly lofty vantage point of Sections 7.1 and 7.2, in Section 7.3 we zoomed into the psychological counterpart of microspace and examined a drop of environmental action under the lens of environmental disposition research. In a sense we were searching for the basic anatomy of dispositions toward the physical environment, and we concluded that the outlines of its major components were becoming apparent. However, it was here that we noted that, by viewing the deeper structure of acts through the filter of orthodox trait measurement, we simultaneously blurred the primary subjects of our composition; neither David nor his riverine milieu was visible any more. Orthodox trait inventories were seen to have an ambivalent status and, in an attempt to capture our subjects again, the last two sections shifted lenses once more—back up to the level of mundane activity in its natural context.

In Section 7.4 an attempt was made to show how contemporary research on the impact of environments on personality had suggested that the physical milieu provides for a sense of meaning, of structure, and of community, themes that are contemporary counterparts of the primordial ones discussed in Section 7.2. The role of the physical environment in generating both stress and a sense of competency was also reviewed, showing that themes particularly relevant to the present-day environment join the more traditional themes on our research agenda. Central to the section was the warning that the full effect of these environmental factors could only be seen if individual differences of the kind reviewed in Section 7.3 were taken into account. Just as David got lost at the microlevel of trait measurement, he also disappeared when the viewfinder was fixed on the water. A picture of a raging river evokes different interpretations if, in the lower left-hand corner, one substitutes the grinning face of a sensation-seeking, congenital extravert for the green visage of an overloaded and underconfident introvert.

In the opening parts of Section 7.5, this theme of the interaction of personal and environmental variables was examined in some detail, and it was concluded that the most veridical, if not most evocative, pictures of environmental behavior will involve carefully constructed split screens: one of the person, through the filter of trait variables or other individual difference measures; the other of the situation or environment, again through the filter of climate variables or other measures of environmental characteristics. While acknowledging the legitimacy of such snapshots, the final subsection of Section 7.5 developed the case that for a truly illuminating picture of environmental action a freeze-frame snap was not enough. In arguing the case for the systemic analysis of sequences of natural acts, we were calling for the conceptual equivalent of home movies—where the temporally expanded pictures of mundane acts and their sometimes predictable, sometimes perplexing, sequelae unfold. We concluded that several new perspectives, including the act frequency approach and personal projects analysis, offer different vantage points for attaining such a goal. It remains now to look forward to what seem to be the priorities and prospects for these emerging perspectives on environment and personality.

7.6.2 Prospects and Priorities: A Third Revolution?

The field of environmental personology has gone through an intriguing first decade. While it comprised one of the foundation blocks of environmental psychology, its parent discipline has gone through a difficult period and has emerged with a major reconstruction of its mandate and its research agenda. While the willing suspension of disciplinary faith is difficult to achieve, I think it fair to say that there is a strong current of excitement in contemporary per-

sonology and that its environmental offshoot is feeling its ripples and creating some of its own. In particular, the new emphasis on natural acts as focal variables in personological inquiry sets new priorities for research investment in the next few years. One obvious need is for systematic application of the Buss and Craik act frequency model to the domain of environmental dispositions. Not only should this comprise the creation of act lists of relevant environmental actions and demonstration of their relationship to major inventories like the ERI, but the detailed observation of acts in situ should be high on the priority list of future studies. Similarly, the empirical mapping of relationships between major dispositional domains such as environmental, social, and self-orientations should be expanded.

An important shift in research strategy has been occurring recently in personality psychology, but it has received very little explicit notice. This is the shift from a focus on the measurement of independent, predictor variables via orthodox tests to a detailed concentration on dependent variables (see Buss & Craik, 1983a; Christie, 1978; McClelland, 1981). McClelland has succinctly captured the nature of this reversal of traditional approaches to measurement in personality:

> Traditionally personality theory has started with the person. A lot of different measures are obtained, they are intercorrelated, and a scale for some personality dimension is derived from these correlations. Then we determine whether it gives a reliable estimate of the characteristic and finally we attempt to relate this personality dimension to some transactions with the environment, usually with poor success. Let us reverse the process, start with the transactions with the environment, try to identify the competencies involved and work backwards to the personality measures that will predict them. (1981, pp. 103–104)

It is precisely these transactions with the environment that we have identified as natural acts, and increasingly they are being adopted as units in diverse fields, including personology (Buss & Craik, 1983a), interactional psychology (Little, 1983), and environmental psychology (Russell & Ward, 1982; Stokols, 1982, 1983). Another major priority for environmental personology over the next decade will thus be to clarify and expand research on such units and to show how they link to relevant dimensions of individual and environmental differences.

Another priority area is that of the intensive study of single cases within environmental personology. Particularly if systemic interactionism is analyzable only at the level of individual systems, a position held by those studying personal projects, it becomes essential to track individuals through the temporally and spatially expanded course of daily living and to highlight the prototypic transactions that characterize the individual's projects and pursuits. Then it will be possible inductively to form classificatory systems detailing the modal types of transaction between persons and their environments.

We have been dealing with some new priorities in personology and environmental psychology that may, in fact, reflect larger movements and currents of thought within psychology and related disciplines. It will be fitting, in conclusion, to climb to a somewhat higher vantage point and survey the larger terrain.

The case can be made that a third revolution, a counterpart to the cognitive and contextual revolutions, is under way. While it is difficult to label precisely, there is some merit in considering it to be a *conative* revolution. Conation, of course, refers to purposive action and intentionality, and a conative psychology attempts to account for the genesis of acts, actions, and activities of individuals. Treated classically as independent of cognitive and affective propensities, conative processes appear to subsume aspects of the cognitive, the affective, the behavioral, and even the contextual features of human conduct. MacIntyre (1981) in a trenchant analysis of problems in contemporary accounts of ethics and human action has captured the essence of a contextually sensitive conative analysis: "We cannot...characterise behaviour independently of intentions, and we cannot characterise intentions independently of the settings which make those intentions intelligible both to agents themselves and to others" (p. 192).

A number of perspectives in contemporary philosophy, many of them virtually uncited by researchers in relevant cognate areas, converge on analyzing the nature of intentional action (e.g., Anscombe, 1963; Binkley, Bronaugh, & Marras, 1971; Gould & Shotter, 1977; Harré & Secord, 1972; Hornsby, 1980). The integration of this literature, particularly the analytic philosophy of action, with corresponding areas of psychological research would be of considerable merit. Related studies in hermeneutics and in the theory of narrative (van Dijk, 1976) have concerns that overlap with the systemic interactional perspectives on environmental behavior. Within psychology, research efforts on "personal goals" (Staub, 1980), current concerns (Klinger, 1975, 1977), life tasks (Cantor & Kihlstrom, 1983), activity (Atkinson & Birch, 1970; Snyder, Gangestad, & Simpson, 1983), and scripts (Abelson, 1981) all

have a common focus of looking at the intentions, competencies, and superordinate goals, plans, or projects that guide and gate natural action.

Whether these disparate areas converge to form a new, psychological action theory or whether a conative revolution arises to counterbalance the other major movements of this century (see Hilgard, 1980), there is ample evidence that environmental personology will have company in its quest for a viable theory of human activity in its personal and environmental contexts. While the discovery of convivial intellectual company is a pleasant event, the "more holistic than thou" sentiment that can accompany merging subfields often results in more conceptual sterility than fecundity. Indeed, perspectives within environmental and interactional psychology that seem to hold promise for future research still comprise genuine theoretical alternatives. Recall, for example, Buss and Craik's (1983a) concern that cognitive–purposive and act frequency formulations on dispositions may represent incommensurate approaches. What is exciting, however, is that, even though clear conceptual differences remain and will continue to sharpen our research ventures, fields of research traditionally regarded as speaking different languages are now beginning to talk, and constructive discourse, rather than silence, seems to be beckoning.

The systemic examination of natural acts has accomplished one important thing: Trait psychologists, social learning theorists, environmental psychologists, social psychologists, and diverse groups in related fields are able to focus on a common unit of analysis. Literally, and in the most technical sense, the study of David Mendons rowing boats on Thursdays allows us, at last, to get our acts, together.

Acknowledgments

I wish to thank the editors of this volume for their very constructive suggestions, David Buss, Jim Horley, and Barbara Rodway for comments on an early draft, and Ben Little for assistance with the references. Barbara Watkinson and Susan Phillips deserve major credit for sustaining me through the final stages of project completion.

I also wish to acknowledge my continuing indebtedness to Ken Craik, who first introduced me to environmental personology and who has continued to instruct, correct, challenge, and reform me in my intellectual pursuits. His very detailed comments on an earlier draft were invaluable. I gratefully acknowledge the financial support of the Pickering Foundation, Carleton's Office of Graduate Study and

Research, and the Social Sciences and Humanities Research Council of Canada.

Finally, warm thanks to my students in the Social Ecology Lab at Carleton for being so patient and supportive while I've been absorbed in this project.

NOTES

1. Glacken (1967) makes the intriguing suggestion that the design argument in natural history favored the study of interrelationships of things rather than the study of taxonomies and that the theocentric view of a designed world was the intellectual precursor to current ecological conceptions.

2. It should be noted that as early as fifth century B.C. humoral theory assumed that local environmental conditions could affect the mixture of the humors in the body. Thus humoral theory, far from being a fixed temperament theory as seems often to be depicted, is perhaps better seen as an ancient precursor to a microlevel interactional psychology, or more specifically an environmental psychopharmacology.

3. The later models of explanation within geographic theory, probabilism, cognitive information processing models, and so on are reviewed by Craik (1970) and Sprout and Sprout (1965).

4. See White (1967).

5. Compare also Schachtel (1959).

6. Murphy's (1947) chapters on "Economic Determinism," "History as the Proving Ground," and "Situationism" are particularly interesting as precursors to contemporary topics in environmental psychology, particularly those stressing a social ecological perspective (e.g., Bronfenbrenner, 1979; Little & Ryan, 1979; Moos, 1974, 1979).

7. Research on cognitive perspectives in environmental psychology is dealt with in more detail in Golledge, Chapter 5, this volume. For early treatments of environmental psychology from a Kellian perspective see Little (1968) and Harrison and Sarre (1971). For those bitten by Kelly's bug, an effective antidote for cognitive swelling can be found in Wohlwill's (1973) "The Environment Is Not in the Head."

8. We are referring here primarily to the early writing of both these theorists. Cattell (1979), for example, has recently expanded his trait model to include an *ecometric* component that specifies measurement procedures for capturing environmental aspects of person–environment interaction. This serves as a counterpart to the psychometric component of earlier models. His expanded *econetic model* for measurement of stimulus, situation, observer, personality, and role factors is a major advance over simple trait models (see also Ozer, 1982).

9. It should be noted also that personality theory and research during the late 1950s and 1960s began to abandon broad-based theoretical views and turned instead to more circumscribed ventures, typically dealing with single variables (e.g., locus of control, sensation seeking, etc.). Rather than review this development at length we shall incorporate relevant details into a subsequent section of environmental disposition measures.

10. An early and now classic treatment of the joint movement toward cognitive models in the areas of animal, child, and personality/clinical psychology was White's (1959) theoretical analysis of the concept of competence.

11. Two other dimensions, stress and competency, can also be discerned in this exogenous literature, which, while arguably subthemes of the environmental influence and human agency themes respectively, seem to have attracted sufficient recent attention to be accorded separate status. For details of the early influences on environmental stress see Evans and Cohen, Chapter 15, this volume. Research of the competency-inducing aspects of environmental design was apparent in the education field, particularly interactional educational psychology (Tomlinson, 1981).

12. An additional characteristic of Craik's approach is the application of the orthodox personality paradigm to the assessment of environmental displays via the same assessment strategies used to evaluate human personality. While this may well be the most original contribution of the personological paradigm to environmental psychology, it falls outside the terms of reference for this chapter.

13. The IPAR approach has a number of important defining characteristics and a key literature (not all of it homegrown) well exemplified by Gough (1965), MacKinnon (1963), and Wiggins (1973) (see also Loevinger, 1957). Among the characteristics of the assessment paradigm that were to be incorporated into environmental personology were the use of multiple assessment devices and the use of consensual ratings by expert assessors of individuals observed extensively over several days.

14. A core component of the Berkeley perspective is Gough's assessment approach, best exemplified in the California Psychological Inventory (CPI) (Gough, 1975). Several of Gough's principles for scale construction were incorporated into Craik's program for environmental personology. For example, Craik endorsed the use of environmental folk-concepts, cross-culturally generalizable, functionally important traits through which people coded their own and others' conduct. Also Gough's (1965) tripartite procedure for establishing test validity was to be incorporated into the measurement of environmental dispositions.

15. See also Wiggins (1974) for a particularly helpful treatment of these distinctions.

16. As we shall see in a later section, a pasturalist is one who is disposed toward the enjoyment and conservation of the natural environment in an intellectual and aesthetic fashion.

17. Recent attempts to explore the physiological and neurochemical basis of extraversion should also be noted (see, e.g., Ballenger, Post, Jimerson, Lake, Murphy, Zuckerman, & Cronin, 1983; Stelmack & Wilson, 1982).

18. We are not implying that because these different di-

mensions posit a common distinction between inner and outer orientation they will necessarily intercorrelate as individual difference measures. However, Furnham (1984) provides evidence that extraversion is significantly correlated with a set of measures to be discussed in the next section.

19. Windley (1975) has also presented a searching critique of the logic of environmental disposition research.

20. Mention should also be made of other measures of orientation and interest that, while not explicitly designed for the study of environmental dispositions, are likely to be effective predictors of response to the physical milieu. Both the Strong Campbell Interest Scale (Campbell, 1971) and Holland's work on vocational preferences (Holland, 1966) tap a diversity of environmentally relevant interests (e.g., realistic orientation, artistic orientation, etc.).

21. See also Burisch's (1984) treatment of this issue in the context of an excellent comparative analysis of strategies of personality scale construction.

22. Sonnenfeld (1969) and Winkel, Malek, and Thiel (1969) were among the very earliest of contributors to environmental disposition research. One of Winkel and colleagues' factors pitted those high in need for environmental order against those preferring diversity and ambiguity. Given recent work on the functions of category systems and prototypes in environmental construing (e.g., Cantor, Mischel, & Schwartz, 1982; Tversky & Hemenway, 1983) it is intriguing to note that one of the items defining this scale was "I think a church should look like a church, a school a school, etc."

23. As this chapter was going to press a major publication on sensation seeking appeared (Zuckerman, 1984) that posits central catecholamine neurotransmitter involvement in sensation seeking within a brain-behavior, feedback-loop model. See also the intriguing exploratory study by Ballenger and colleagues (1983) on the positive relation between cerebrospinal fluid calcium ion levels and extraversion.

24. Mehrabian and Russell's (1974) work is notable both for its links with early Russian work on the neurophysiological basis of personality (see, e.g., Gray, 1972) and contemporary extraversion research and for relating these variables to specific environmental characteristics. This encourages a more dynamic and context-sensitive model of environmental dispositions than those perspectives assuming fixed traits.

25. It would be interesting to see whether these same individuals tend spontaneously to adopt different "environmental sets" (Leff, 1978; Leff & Gordon, 1980) than low scorers when engaged in environmental encounters.

26. Driver and Knopf (1977) have also used Jackson's Personality Research Form (Jackson, 1967) to examine environmental criterion variables.

27. It should be noted that meaning, structure, and community have been chosen not only for their broad applicability as theoretical constructs (e.g., Toffler, 1980) but also because they emerge, empirically, as major dimensions of daily activities in personal projects research (Little, 1983) (see Section 7.5.3.).

28. See also the detailed theoretical account of development by Heinz Werner (1948) and the current applications of that perspective to the environmental area by Seymour Wapner and his colleagues (e.g., Wapner, Kaplan, & Ciottone, 1981).

29. It would be intriguing to see whether Snyder's (1979) high self-monitors are particularly likely to differentiate their dwellings in terms of different aspects of self that can be presented, while low self-monitors are content to be Barry whether it's in the bathroom or bedroom. The high self-monitor should also be more likely to experience distress if visitors pop in unannounced, that is, without giving an opportunity for the self-reflective aspects of the house to be tidied up and shoved under the couch.

30. A related perspective is provided by Sarbin (1968, 1976), who was an innovative pioneer on the spatial ecology of self-identity as well as an important influence on the early development of environmental personology at Berkeley. See also his recent comments on the work of Proshansky, Fabian, and Kaminoff (1983) on place identity.

31. It should also be noted that Milgram's model has stimulated critiques about the assumption of differential urban overload above and beyond the role played by individual differences. See, for example, Fischer (1982).

32. See the recent volume by Lefcourt (1982) for a comprehensive survey of measurement and research on locus of control.

33. See also Rodin and Langer (1977) and Langer (1983) on the issue of whether perceived control is adaptive.

34. The absence of both environmental meaning and community seems to be involved in the genesis of alienation. See Schacht (1970) and Stokols (1975).

35. The literature on social networks is growing rapidly. For a recent overview see Gottlieb (1983).

36. The personality characteristics that appear to dampen the effectiveness of social network support resemble neuroticism, though they may simply reflect a general negativity and tendency to see existential bottles (and battles) as half-empty. For a discussion of this issue see Henderson and colleagues (1981).

37. The tendency to see solitude as a rather negative phenomenon can be balanced by examining the varieties of asceticism and voluntary isolation. See, for example, Harper (1965), who refers to this as metaphysical homelessness.

38. Again, the relationship between stress levels and well-being is likely to be moderated by personality variables. Some provocative work by Kobasa, Maddi, and colleagues, for example, has shown that psychological hardiness may be a key moderator of the relationship between stress and health status (Kobasa, 1979; Kobasa, Hilker, & Maddi, 1979; Kobasa, Maddi, & Kahn, 1982).

39. Many other examples of the impact of environmental variables on competence could be given. For example, Wicker (1969) reported a valuable study showing the association of undermanned settings with higher cognitive complexity for events within that domain.

40. Extensive research on this issue out of the Personality and Social Ecology Program at Illinois has been recently reported (see Diener, Larsen, & Emmons, 1984; Emmons, Diener, & Larsen, 1984).

41. Not only may individuals differ in the type of situations or setting to which they gravitate, but Snyder (1979) has argued convincingly that high self-monitors may be particularly sensitive to situational cues and will shift their social presentations to accommodate to the particular aspect of self most appropriate to the setting.

42. This has been referred to as dynamic interactionism (Overton & Reese, 1977; Magnusson, 1980) and organic interactionism (Buss, 1977).

43. Reproduced, with permission, from the *Annual Review of Psychology*, Volume 13, © 1982 by Annual Reviews Inc.

44. See Pervin (1983) for a discussion of the need for units that allow these kinds of questions to be asked.

45. Stern's (1970) Activity Checklist should also be cited as an early prototype of individual difference measures based on activity preference.

46. An annotated bibliography of studies using personal projects analysis is available from the Social Ecology Laboratory, Department of Psychology, Carleton University, Ottawa, Ontario, Canada, KIS 5B6.

REFERENCES

Abelson, R.P. (1981). Psychological status of the script concept. *American Psychologist, 36*, 715–729.

Alexander, C.A. (1967). The city as a mechanism for sustaining human contact. In W.R. Ewald, Jr. (Ed.), *Environment for man: The next 50 years*. Bloomington: Indiana University Press.

Alker, H.A. (1977). Beyond ANOVA psychology in the study of person-situation interactions. In D. Magnusson & N.S. Endler (Eds.), *Personality at the crossroads: Current issues in interactional psychology*. Hillsdale, NJ: Erlbaum.

Alston, W.P. (1971). Dispositions and occurrences. *Canadian Journal of Philosophy, 1*, 125–154.

Altman, I. (1975). *The environment and social behavior*. Monterey, CA: Brooks/Cole.

Anscombe, G.E.M. (1963). *Intention* (2nd ed.). Oxford: Blackwell.

Antonovsky, A. (1979). *Health, stress, and coping*. San Francisco: Jossey-Bass.

Argyle, M., & Little, B.R. (1972). Do personality traits apply to social behaviour? *Journal for the Theory of Social Behaviour, 2*, 1–35.

Atkinson, J.W., & Birch, D. (1970). *The dynamics of action*. New York: Wiley.

Bachelard, G. (1964). *The poetics of space*. New York: Orion.

Ballenger, J.C., Post, R.M., Jimerson, D.C., Lake, C.R., Murphy, D., Zuckerman, M., & Cronin, C. (1983). Biochemical correlates of personality traits in normals: An exploratory study. *Personality and Individual Differences, 4*(6), 615–625.

Bandura, A. (1982). The psychology of chance encounters and life paths. *American Psychologist, 37*, 747–755.

Barker, R.G. (1968). *Ecological psychology: Concepts and methods of studying the environment of human behavior*. Stanford, CA: Stanford University Press.

Bartz, W.R. (1970). While psychologists doze on. *American Psychologist, 25*, 500–503.

Bass, B. (1962). *Manual for the Orientation Inventory*. Palo Alto, CA: Consulting Psychologists Press.

Berry, J.W. (1977). An ecological approach to cross cultural psychology. *Man-Environment Systems, 4*, 365–383.

Bettelheim, B. (1959). Joey: A "mechanical boy." *Scientific American, 200*(3), 116–127.

Binkley, R., Bronaugh, R., & Marras, A. (Eds.). (1971). *Agent, action, and reason*. Toronto, Canada: University of Toronto Press.

Borden, R.J., & Francis, J.L. (1978). Who cares about ecology—Personality and sex-differences in environmental concern. *Journal of Personality, 46*(1), 190–203.

Bowers, K.S. (1973). Situationism in psychology: An analysis and a critique. *Psychological Review, 80*, 307–336.

Bronfenbrenner, U. (1979). *The ecology of human development*. Cambridge, MA: Harvard University Press.

Brunswik, E. (1943). Organismic achievement and environmental probability. *Psychological Review, 50*, 255–272.

Brunswik, E. (1956). *Perception and the representative design of experiments*. Berkeley: University of California Press.

Bryant, K.J. (1982). Personality correlates of sense of direction and geographical orientation. *Journal of Personality and Social Psychology, 43*(6), 1318–1324.

Burisch, M. (1984). Approaches to personality inventory construction. *American Psychologist, 39*, 214–227.

Burke, E.M. (1966). *Language as a symbolic action*. Berkeley: University of California Press.

Buss, A.R. (1977). The trait-situation controversy and the concept of interaction. *Personality and Social Psychology Bulletin, 3*, 196–201.

Buss, D.M., & Craik, K.H. (1980). The frequency concept of disposition: Dominance and prototypically dominant acts. *Journal of Personality, 48*(3), 379–392.

Buss, D.M., & Craik, K.H. (1983a). The act frequency approach to personality. *Psychological Review, 90,* 105–126.

Buss, D.M., & Craik, K.H. (1983b). Act prediction and the conceptual analysis of personality scales: Indices of act density, bipolarity, and extensity. *Journal of Personality and Social Psychology, 45,* 1081–1095.

Buss, D.M., & Craik, K.H. (1983c). Contemporary worldviews: Personal and policy implications. *Journal of Applied Social Psychology, 13*(3), 259–280.

Buss, D.M., & Craik, K.H. (1983d). The dispositional analysis of everyday conduct. *Journal of Personality, 51,* 393–412.

Buss, D.M., & Craik, K.H. (1984). Acts, dispositions, and personality. In B.A. Maher & W.B. Maher (Eds.), *Progress in experimental personality research: Normal personality processes* (Vol. 13). New York: Academic.

Butt, D.S. (1971). The psychological environment of the village: Obsolete or essential? In European Cultural Foundation (Ed.), *Citizen and city in the year 2000* (pp. 115–122). Deventer, The Netherlands: Kluwer.

Cameron, P., Stewart, L., Craig, L., & Eppelman, L. (1973). Things vs. self vs. other mental orientation across the life-span: A note. *British Journal of Psychology, 64*(2), 283–286.

Campbell, D.P. (1971). *Handbook for the strong vocational interest blank.* Stanford, CA: Stanford University Press.

Campbell, J.M. (1983). Ambient stressors. *Environment and Behavior, 15,* 355–380.

Canter, D.V., & Craik, K.H. (1981). Environmental psychology. *Journal of Environmental Psychology, 1,* 1–11.

Cantor, N., & Kihlstrom, J. (1983). *Social intelligence: The cognitive basis of personality* (Cognitive Science Tech. Rep. No. 60). Ann Arbor: University of Michigan.

Cantor, N., & Mischel, W. (1979). Prototypes in person perception. In L. Berkowitz (Ed.), *Advances in experimental social psychology* (Vol. 12). New York: Academic.

Cantor, N., Mischel, W., & Schwartz, J. (1982). A prototype analysis of psychological situations. *Cognitive Psychology, 14,* 45–77.

Carlson, R. (1971). Where is the person in personality research? *Psychological Bulletin, 75*(3), 203–219.

Cattell, R.B. (1979). *Personality and learning theory: Vol. 1. The structure of personality in its environment.* New York: Springer.

Chapin, F.S. (1968). Activity systems and urban structure: A working schema. *Journal of the American Institute of Planners, 34*(1), 11–18.

Chapin, F.S., & Hightower, H.C. (1966). *Household activity systems—A pilot investigation.* Chapel Hill, NC: Center for Urban and Regional Studies.

Charns, H. (1973). *Personality, preference and planning.* Unpublished master's thesis, University of California, Berkeley.

Christie, R. (1978). The person in the person × situation paradigm: Reflections on the (P)erson in Lewin's $B = f(P,E)$. In H. London (Ed.), *Personality.* New York: Wiley.

Cohen, S., Glass, D.C., & Singer, J.E. (1973). Apartment noise, auditory discrimination, and reading ability in children. *Journal of Experimental Social Psychology, 9,* 407–422.

Collins, J.B., & Hardwick, W. (1974). Unpublished data on environmental response inventory. Vancouver, Canada: University of British Columbia, Office of Academic Planning.

Condon, W.S., & Sander, L.W. (1974). Neonate movement is synchronized with adult speech: Interaction participation and language acquisition. *Science, 183,* 99–101.

Cooper, C. (1971). *The house as symbol of the self.* Berkeley: University of California, Institute of Urban and Regional Development.

Craik, K.H. (1966). The prospects for an environmental psychology. *IPAR Research Bulletin.* Berkeley: University of California.

Craik, K.H. (1968). The comprehension of the everyday physical environment. *Journal of the American Institute of Planners, 34*(1), 646–658.

Craik, K.H. (1970). Environmental psychology. In K.H. Craik, B. Kleinmuntz, R.L. Rosnow, R. Rosenthal, J.A. Cheyne, & R.H. Walters (Eds.), *New directions in psychology 4* (pp. 1–122). New York: Holt, Rinehart & Winston.

Craik, K.H. (1976). The personality research paradigm in environmental psychology. In S. Wapner, S. Cohen, & B. Kaplan (Eds.), *Experiencing the environment* (pp. 55–80). New York: Plenum.

Craik, K.H. (1983). The psychology of the large-scale environment. In N.R. Feimer & E.S. Geller (Eds.), *Environmental psychology.* New York: Praeger.

Cronbach, L.J. (1975). Beyond the two disciplines of scientific psychology. *American Psychologist, 30,* 116–127.

Csikszentmihalyi, M., & Rochberg-Halton, E. (1981). *The meaning of things: A study of domestic symbols and the self.* Cambridge, England: Cambridge University Press.

Diener, E., Larsen, R.J., & Emmons, R.A. (1984). Person × situation interactions: Choice of situations and congruence response models. *Journal of Personality and Social Psychology, 47,* 580–592.

Driver, B.L., & Knopf, R.C. (1977). Personality, outdoor recreation and expected consequences. *Environment and Behavior, 9,* 169–193.

Ekehammar, G. (1974). Interactionism in personality from a historical perspective. *Psychological Bulletin, 81,* 1026–1048.

Emmons, R.A., Diener, E., & Larsen, R.J. (1984). An affect-goal analysis of situational choice behavior. Paper presented at the 92nd annual convention of the American Psychological Association, Toronto, Canada.

Endler, N.S. (1982). Interactionism comes of age. In M.P. Zanna, E.T. Higgins, & C.P. Herman (Eds.), *Consistency in social behavior: The Ontario Symposium* (Vol. 2). Hillsdale, NJ: Erlbaum.

Endler, N.S., Hunt, J. McV., & Rosenstein, A.J. (1962). An S-R Inventory of Anxiousness. *Psychological Monographs, 76*(17), 133.

Endler, N.S., & Magnusson, D. (1976). *Interactional psychology and personality.* Washington, DC: Hemisphere.

Evans, G.W. (Ed.). (1982). *Environmental stress.* New York: Cambridge University Press.

Eysenck, H.J. (Ed.). (1981). *A model for personality.* Heidelburg, Germany: Springer.

Fischer, C.S. (1982). *To dwell among friends.* Chicago: University of Chicago Press.

Funder, D.C›, & Ozer, D.J. (1983). Behavior as a function of the situation. *Journal of Personality and Social Psychology, 44*, 107–112.

Furnham, A. (1984). Extraversion, sensation seeking, stimulus screening and Type-A behavior pattern: The relationship between various measures of arousal. *Personality and Individual Differences, 5*(2), 133–140.

Furnham, A., & Jaspars, J. (1983). The evidence for interactionism in psychology: A critical analysis of the situation-response inventories. *Personality and Individual Differences, 4*(6), 627–644.

Gans, H.J. (1962). *The urban villagers: Group and class in the life of Italian-Americans.* New York: Free Press.

Gauld, A., & Shotter, J. (1977). *Human action and its psychological investigation.* London: Routledge & Kegan Paul.

Gibson, J.J. (1960). The concept of the stimulus in psychology. *American Psychologist, 15*, 694–703.

Gifford, R. (1980). Environmental dispositions and the evaluation of architectural interiors. *Journal of Research in Personality, 14*, 386–399.

Gifford, R. (1981). Sociability: Traits, settings, and interactions. *Journal of Personality and Social Psychology, 41*, 340–347.

Glacken, C.J. (1967). *Traces on the Rhodian shore: Nature and culture in western thought from ancient times to the end of the eighteenth century.* Berkeley: University of California Press.

Glass, D., & Singer, J. (1972). *Urban stress.* New York: Academic.

Glass, D., & Singer, J. (1973). Responses to uncontrollable aversive events. *Representative Research in Social Psychology, 4*, 165–183.

Golding, S.L. (1975). Flies in the ointment: Methodological problems in the analysis of the percentage of variance due to persons and situations. *Psychological Bulletin, 82*, 278–288.

Gottlieb, B.H. (1983). Social support as a focus for integrative research in psychology. *American Psychologist, 38*, 278–287.

Gough, H.G. (1965). Conceptual analysis of psychological test scores and other diagnostic variables. *Journal of Abnormal Psychology, 70*, 294–302.

Gough, H.G. (1968). An interpreter's syllabus for the California Psychological Inventory. In P. McReynolds (Ed.), *Advances in psychological assessment* (Vol. 1). Palo Alto, CA: Science and Behavior Books.

Gough, H.G. (1972). *Manual for the Personal Values Abstract.* Palo Alto, CA: Consulting Psychologists Press.

Gough, H.G. (1975). *Manual for the California Psychological Inventory* (Rev. Ed.). Palo Alto, CA: Consulting Psychologists Press.

Gray, J.A. (1972). The psychophysiological nature of introversion-extraversion: A modification of Eysenck's theory. In V.D. Nebylitsyn & J.A. Gray (Eds.), *Biological bases of individual behavior* (pp. 182–205). New York: Academic.

Hampshire, S. (1953). Dispositions. *Analysis, 14*, 5–11.

Harper, R. (1965). *The seventh solitude: Metaphysical homelessness in Kierkegaard, Dostoevsky, and Nietzsche.* Baltimore, MD: Johns Hopkins Press.

Harré, R., & Secord, P.F. (1972). *The explanation of social behaviour.* Oxford: Blackwell.

Harrison, J., & Sarre, P. (1971). Personal construct theory in the measurement of environmental images: Problem and methods. *Environment and Behavior, 3*, 351–373.

Hart, R. (1977). Comparing the outdoor opportunities of girls and boys. In B. Sprung (Ed.), *Non-sexist curricula for pre-school children.* New York: Teachers College Press.

Hartmann, H. (1958). *Ego psychology and the problem of adaptation.* New York: International Universities Press.

Hase, H.D., & Goldberg, L.R. (1967). The comparative validity of different strategies of deriving personality scales. *Psychological Bulletin, 67*, 231–248.

Henderson, S., Byrne, D.G., & Duncan-Jones, P. (1981). *Neurosis and the social environment.* Sydney, Australia: Academic.

Herrmann, T. (1980). Die eigenschaftenkonzeption als-heterostereotyp: Kritik eines personlichkeitspsychologischen Geschichtsklischees. *Zeitschrift fur Differentielle und Diagnostische Psychologie, 1*, 7–16.

Hilgard, E.R. (1980). The trilogy of mind: Cognition, affection, and conation. *Journal of the History of the Behavioral Sciences, 16*, 107–117.

Hogan, R. (1982). A socioanalytic theory of personality. In M. Page & R. Dienstbier (Eds.), *Nebraska Symposium on Motivation* (pp. 55–89). Lincoln: University of Nebraska Press.

Hogan, R., & Cheek, J.M. (1983). Identity, authenticity, and maturity. In T.R. Sarbin & K.E. Schiebe (Eds.), *Studies in social identity.* New York: Praeger.

Hogan, R., Jones, W.H., & Cheek, J.M. (1985). Socioanalytic theory: An alternative to armadillo psychology. In B. Schlenker (Ed.), *The self and social life* (pp. 175–198). New York: McGraw-Hill.

Holland, J.L. (1966). *The psychology of vocational choice.* Waltham, MA: Blaisdell.

Hornsby, J. (1980). *Actions.* London: Routledge & Kegan Paul.

Hunt, D.E. (1975). Person-environment interaction: A challenge found wanting before it was tried. *Review of Educational Research, 45,* 209–230.

Hunter, M., Grinnell, R.M., Jr., & Blanchard, R. (1978). A test of a shorter Privacy Preference Scale. *The Journal of Psychology, 98,* 207–210.

Hurlburt, R.T. (1979). Random sampling of cognitions and behavior. *Journal of Research in Personality, 13,* 102–111.

Jackson, D.M. (1967). *Personality Research Form Manual.* Goshen, NY: Research Psychologists Press.

Jung, C.G. (1957). *Collected works* (Vol. 9). New York: Pantheon. (Original work published 1936.)

Kaplan, S. (1972). The challenge of environmental psychology: a proposal for a new functionalism. *American Psychologist, 27,* 140–143.

Kaplan, S. (1983). A model of person-environment compatibility. *Environment and Behavior, 15*(3), 311–332.

Kates, R.W. (1976). Experiencing the environment as hazard. In H.M. Proshansky, W.H. Ittelson, & L.G. Rivlin (Eds.), *Environmental psychology: People and their physical settings* (pp. 401–418). New York: Holt, Rinehart & Winston.

Kegel-Flom, P. (1976). Identifying the potential rural optometrist. *American Journal of Optometry and Physiological Optics, 53,* 479–482.

Kelly, G.A. (1955). *Psychology of personal constructs.* New York: Norton.

Klinger, E. (1975). Consequences of commitment to and disengagement from incentives. *Psychological Review, 82,* 1–22.

Klinger, E. (1977). *Meaning and void: Inner experience and the incentives in people's lives.* Minneapolis: University of Minnesota Press.

Klinger, E., Barta, S.G., & Maxeiner, M.E. (1980). Motivational correlates of thought content frequency and commitment. *Journal of Personality and Social Psychology, 39,* 1222–1237.

Kobasa, S.C. (1982). Commitment and coping in stress resistance among lawyers. *Journal of Personality and Social Psychology, 42*(4), 707–717.

Kobasa, S.C., Hilker, R.R.J., & Maddi, S.R. (1979). Who stays healthy under stress? *Journal of Occupational Medicine, 21,* 595–598.

Kobasa, S.C., Maddi, S.R., & Kahn, S. (1982). Hardiness and health: A prospective study. *Journal of Personality and Social Psychology, 42,* 168–177.

Langer, E.J. (1983). *The psychology of control.* Beverly Hills, CA: Sage.

Lefcourt, H.M. (Ed.). (1981). *Research with the locus of control construct* (Vol. 1). New York: Academic.

Leff, H.L. (1978). *Experience, environment, and human potentials.* New York: Oxford University Press.

Leff, H.L., & Gordon, L.R. (1980). Environmental cognitive sets. A longitudinal study. *Environment and Behavior, 12,* 291–328.

Lewin, K. (1936). *Principles of topological psychology.* New York: McGraw-Hill.

Little, B.R. (1968). Psychospecialization: Functions of differential interest in persons and things. *Bulletin of the British Psychological Society, 21,* 113 (Abstract).

Little, B.R. (1972a). *Person-thing orientation: A provisional manual for the T-P Scale.* Oxford, England: Oxford University, Department of Experimental Psychology.

Little, B.R. (1972b). Psychological man as scientist, humanist and specialist. *Journal of Experimental Research in Personality, 6,* 95–118.

Little, B.R. (1976a). *Personal systems and specialization.* Unpublished doctoral dissertation, University of California, Berkeley.

Little, B.R. (1976b). Specialization and the varieties of environmental experience: Empirical studies within the personality paradigm. In S. Wapner, S.B. Cohen, & B. Kaplan (Eds.), *Experiencing the environment* (pp. 81–116). New York: Plenum.

Little, B.R. (1983). Personal projects: A rationale and method for investigation. *Environment and Behavior, 15*(3), 273–309.

Little, B.R. (1982). Interactional assessment and human development. *A perspective on the Gaspé Conference.* Unpublished manuscript, Carleton University, Social Ecology Laboratory, Department of Psychology, Ottawa, Canada.

Little, B.R., & Ryan, T.J. (1978). *Children in context: The social ecology of human development.* Unpublished manuscript, Carleton University, Social Ecology Laboratory, Department of Psychology, Ottawa, Canada.

Little, B.R., & Ryan, T.J. (1979). A social ecological model of development. In K. Ishwaran (Ed.), *Childhood and adolescence in Canada* (pp. 273–301). Toronto: McGraw-Hill.

Loevinger, J. (1957). Objective tests as instruments of psychological theory. *Psychological Reports, 13,* 147–163.

Lynch, K. (1960). *The image of the city.* Cambridge, MA: MIT Press.

MacIntyre, A. (1981). *After virtue.* Notre Dame, IN: University of Notre Dame Press.

MacKinnon, D.W. (1963). The nature and nurture of creative talent. *American Psychologist, 17,* 484–495.

Magnusson, D. (1980). Personality in an interactional

paradigm of research. *Zeitschrift fur Differentialle und Diagnostiche Psychologie, 1,* 17–34.

Magnusson, D. (Ed.). (1981). *Toward a psychology of situations: An interactional perspective.* Hillsdale, NJ: Erlbaum.

Magnusson, D., & Endler, N.S. (Eds.). (1977). *Personality at the crossroads: Current issues in interactional psychology.* Hillsdale, NJ: Erlbaum.

Marshall, N. (1970). *Environmental components of orientations toward privacy.* Paper presented at the annual conference of the Environmental Design Research Association, Pittsburgh, PA.

Marshall, N. (1972). Privacy and environment. *Human Ecology, 1,* 93–110.

Martensson, S. (1977). Childhood interaction and temporal organization. *Economic Geography, 53*(2), 99–125.

Marx, L. (1967). *The machine in the garden.* New York: Oxford University Press.

McCarroll, J.E., Mitchell, K.M., Carpenter, R.J., & Anderson, J.P. (1967). Analysis of three stimulation-seeking scales. *Psychological Reports, 21,* 853–856.

McClelland, D.C. (1981). Is personality consistent? In A.I. Rabin, J. Aronoff, A.M. Barclay, & R.A. Zucker (Eds.), *Further explorations in personality* (pp. 87–113). New York: Wiley.

McKechnie, G.E. (1972). *A study of environmental life styles.* Unpublished doctoral dissertation, University of California, Berkeley.

McKechnie, G.E. (1974). *Manual for the Environmental Response Inventory.* Palo Alto, CA: Consulting Psychologists Press.

McKechnie, G.E. (1975). *Manual for the leisure activities blank.* Palo Alto, CA: Consulting Psychologists Press.

McKechnie, G.E. (1977). The Environmental Response Inventory in application. *Environment and Behavior, 9,* 255–276.

McKechnie, G.E. (1978). Environmental dispositions: Concepts and measures. In P. McReynolds (Ed.), *Advances in psychological assessment* (Vol. 4). San Francisco: Jossey-Bass.

McReynolds, P. (1975). Historical antecedents of personality assessment. In P. McReynolds (Ed.), *Advances in psychological assessment* (Vol. 3). San Francisco: Jossey-Bass.

Mehrabian, A. (1977). A questionnaire measure of individual differences in stimulus screening and associated differences in arousability. *Environmental Psychology and Nonverbal Behavior, 1*(2), 89–103.

Mehrabian, A., & Russell, J.A. (1973). A measure of arousal seeking tendency. *Environment and Behavior, 5,* 315–333.

Mehrabian, A., & Russell, J.A. (1974). *An approach to environmental psychology.* Cambridge, MA: MIT Press.

Milgram, S. (1970). The experience of living in cities. *Science, 167,* 1461–1468.

Mischel, W. (1968). *Personality and assessment.* New York: Academic.

Mischel, W., & Peake, P. (1982). In search of consistency: Measure for measure. In M.P. Zanna, E.T. Higgins, & C.P. Herman (Eds.), *Consistency in social behavior: The Ontario Symposium of personality and social psychology* (Vol. 2) (pp. 187–207). Hillsdale, NJ: Erlbaum.

Moos, R. (1974). *The Social Climate Scales: An overview.* Palo Alto, CA: Consulting Psychologists Press.

Moos, R. (1976). *The human context: Environmental determinants of behavior.* New York: Wiley.

Moos, R. (1979). *Evaluating educational environments: Procedures, measures, findings and policy implications.* San Francisco, CA: Jossey-Bass.

Moscowitz, D.S., & Schwarz, J.C. (1982). Validity comparison of behavior counts and ratings by knowledgeable informants. *Journal of Personality and Social Psychology, 42,* 518–528.

Murphy, G. (1947). *Personality.* New York: Basic Books.

Murphy, P.E. (1978). Preferences and perceptions of urban decision-making groups: Congruence or conflict. *Regional Studies, 12,* 749–759.

Murray, H.A. (1938). *Explorations in personality.* New York: Oxford University Press.

Nideffer, R.M. (1974). *Test of Attentional and Interpersonal Style Manual.* Rochester, NY: Behavioral Research Applications.

Olweus, D. (1977). A critical analysis of the "modern" interactionist position. In D. Magnusson & N.S. Endler (Eds.), *Personality at the crossroads: Current issues in interactional psychology* (pp. 221–233). Hillsdale, NJ: Erlbaum.

Osmond, H. (1957). Function as the basis of psychiatric ward design. *Mental Hospitals* (Architectural Suppl.), *8,* 23–29.

Overton, W.F., & Reese, H.W. (1977). General models for man-environment relations. In H. McGurk (Ed.), *Ecological factors in human development.* New York: North Holland.

Ozer, D.J. (1982). *Consistency, coherence, and convergence: A framework for the study of personality.* Unpublished doctoral dissertation, University of California, Berkeley.

Palys, T.S., & Little, B.R. (1983). Perceived life satisfaction and the organization of the personal project systems. *Journal of Personality and Social Psychology, 44,* 1221–1230.

Paulhus, D. (1983). Sphere-specific measures of perceived control. *Journal of Personality and Social Psychology, 44,* 1253–1265.

Pedersen, D.M., & Shears, L.M. (1973). A review of personal-space research in the framework of general system theory. *Psychological Bulletin, 80,* 367–388.

Perin, C. (1970). *With man in mind: An interdisciplinary prospectus for environmental design*. Cambridge, MA: MIT Press.

Pervin, L.A. (1978). Definitions, measurements, and classifications of stimuli, situations, and environments. *Human Ecology, 6*(1), 71–105.

Pervin, L.A. (1983). The stasis and flow of behavior: Toward a theory of goals. In M.M. Page (Ed.), *Nebraska symposium on motivation* (pp. 1–53). Lincoln: University of Nebraska Press.

Peterson, D.R. (1965). Scope and generality of verbally defined personality factors. *Psychological Review, 72*, 48–59.

Phillips, S.D. (1978). *Recreation and personality: A systems approach*. Unpublished master's thesis, University of Waterloo, Waterloo, Canada.

Proshansky, H.M., Fabian, A.K., & Kaminoff, R. (1983). Place-identity: Physical world socialization of the self. *Journal of Environmental Psychology, 3*, 57–83.

Rapley, A. (1983). *Thing-person orientation and personal projects: A test of act frequency versus act saliency models of trait assessment*. Unpublished master's thesis, Carleton University, Ottawa, Canada.

Reid, D.W., & Ware, E.E. (1974). Multidimensionality of internal versus external control: Addition of a third dimension and non-distinction of self versus others. *Canadian Journal of Behaviour Science, 6*(2), 131–142.

Richards, J.M., Jr. (1978). Review of Environmental Response Inventory. In O.K. Buros (Ed.), *The eighth mental measurements yearbook* (pp. 549–550). Highland Park, NJ: Gryphon.

Robbe-Grillet, A. (1965). *For a new novel: Essays on fiction*. (R. Howard, Trans.). New York: Grove.

Rodin, J., & Langer, E.J. (1977). Long-term effects of a control-relevant intervention with the institutionalized aged. *Journal of Personality and Social Psychology, 35*, 897–902.

Rogers-Warren, A., & Warren, S.F. (Eds.). (1977). *Ecological perspectives in behavior analysis*. Baltimore, MD: University Park Press.

Rosch, E. (1975). Cognitive reference points. *Cognitive Psychology, 7*, 532–547.

Rosch, E. (1978). Principles of categorization. In E. Rosch & B.B. Lloyd (Eds.), *Cognition and categorization* (pp. 27–48). Hillsdale, NJ: Erlbaum.

Rosch, E., Simpson, C., & Miller, R.S. (1976). Structural bases of typicality effects. *Journal of Experimental Psychology: Human Perception and Performance, 2*, 491–502.

Russell, J.A., & Ward, L.M. (1982). Environmental psychology. *Annual Review of Psychology, 33*, 651–688.

Ryle, G. (1949). *The concept of mind*. New York: Barnes & Noble.

Sampson, E.E. (1977). Psychology and the American ideal. *Journal of Personality and Social Psychology, 35*(11), 767–782.

Sarason, I.G., Smith, R.E., & Diener, W. (1975). Personality research: Components of variance attributable to the person and the situation. *Journal of Personality and Social Psychology, 32*, 199–204.

Sarbin, T.R. (1968). The transformation of social identity: A new metaphor for the helping professions. In L. Roberts, N. Greenfield, & M. Miller (Eds.), *Comprehensive mental health programs: The challenge of evaluation* (pp. 97–124). Madison: University of Wisconsin Press.

Sarbin, T.R. (1976). Contextualism: A world view for modern psychology. In M.M. Page (Ed.), *Nebraska symposium on motivation* (pp. 1–41). Lincoln: University of Nebraska Press.

Sarbin, T.R. (1983). Place identity as a component of self: An addendum. *Journal of Environmental Psychology, 3*, 337–342.

Schacht, R. (1970). *Alienation*. Garden City, NY: Doubleday.

Schachtel, E.G. (1959). *Metamorphosis: On the development of affect perception, attention and memory*. New York: Basic Books.

Schiff, M. (1971). *Psychological factors related to human adjustment to natural hazards in London, Ontario*. Presented at Association of American Geographers Meeting, Boston.

Schulz, R. (1976). The effects of control and predictability on the psychological and physical well-being of the institutionalized aged. *Journal of Personality and Social Psychology, 33*, 563–573.

Schulz, R., & Hanusa, B.H. (1978). Long-term effects of control and predictability-enhancing interventions: Findings and ethical issues. *Journal of Personality and Social Psychology, 36*, 1194–1201.

Searles, H.F. (1960). *The non-human environment: In normal development and in schizophrenia*. New York: International Universities Press.

Sechrest, L. (1976). Personality. *Annual Review of Psychology, 27*, 1–28.

Sewell, W.R.D., & Little, B.R. (1973). Specialists, laymen and the process of environmental appraisal. *Regional Studies, 7*, 161–171.

Shafer, E.L. (1969). Perception of natural environments. *Environment and Behavior, 1*, 71–82.

Sjoberg, L. (1981). Life situations and episodes as a basis for situational influence on action. In D. Magnusson (Ed.), *Toward a psychology of situations: An interactional perspective*. Hillsdale, NJ: Erlbaum.

Snyder, M. (1979). Self-monitoring processes. In L. Berkowitz (Ed.), *Advances in experimental social psychology* (Vol. 12) (pp. 85–128). New York: Academic.

Snyder, M., Gangestad, S., & Simpson, J.A. (1983). Choosing friends and activity partners: The role of self-monitoring. *Journal of Personality and Social Psychology, 45*, 1061–1072.

Sommer, R. (1969). *Personal space*. Englewood Cliffs, NJ: Prentice-Hall.

Sonnenfeld, J. (1969). Personality and behavior in environment. *Proceedings of the Association of American Geographers, 1*, 136–140.

Sprout, H., & Sprout, M. (1965). *The ecological perspective on human affairs* (pp. 236–294). Princeton, NJ: Princeton University Press.

Staub, E. (1980). Social and prosocial behavior: Personal and situational influences and their interactions. In E. Staub (Ed.), *Personality* (pp. 236–294). Englewood Cliffs, NJ: Prentice-Hall.

Stelmack, R.M. (1981). The psychophysiology of extraversion and neuroticism. In H.J. Eysenck (Ed.), *A model for personality* (pp. 38–64). Heidelburg, Germany: Springer-Verlag.

Stelmack, R.M., & Wilson, K.G. (1982). Extraversion and the effects of frequency and intensity on the auditory brain-stem evoked-response. *Personality and Individual Differences, 3*, 373–380.

Stern, G.G. (1958). *Preliminary manual: Activities Index— College Characteristics Index*. Syracuse, NY: Syracuse University, Psychological Research Center.

Stokols, D. (1975). Toward a psychological theory of alienation. *Psychological Review, 82*, 26–44.

Stokols, D. (1982). Environmental psychology: A coming of age. In A. Kraut (Ed.), *G. Stanley Hall Lecture Series* (Vol. 2, pp. 159–205). Washington, DC: American Psychological Association.

Stokols, D. (1983). Theoretical directions of environment and behavior research. *Environment and Behavior, 15*, 407–417.

Strawson, P.F. (1964). *Individuals: An essay in descriptive metaphysics*. London: Methuen.

Sundberg, N.D. (1977). *Assessment of persons*. Englewood Cliffs, NJ: Prentice-Hall.

Sundberg, N.D., Snowden, L.R., & Reynolds, W.M. (1978). Toward assessment of personal competence and incompetence in life situations. *Annual Review of Psychology, 29*, 179–221.

Szalai, A., Converse, P., Feldheim, P., Scheuch, E., & Stone, P. (Eds.). (1972). *The use of time*. The Hague, Netherlands: Mouton.

Taylor, S.M., & Konrad, V.A. (1980). Scaling dispositions toward the past. *Environment and Behavior, 12*, 283–307.

Toffler, A. (1980). *The third wave*. New York: Morrow.

Tolsdorf, C.C. (1976). Social networks, support and coping: An exploratory study. *Family Process, 15*, 407–417.

Tomlinson, P. (1981). *Understanding teaching*. New York: McGraw-Hill.

Trigg, L.J., Perlman, D., Perry, R.P., & Janisse, M.P. (1976). Antipollution behavior: A function of perceived outcome and locus of control. *Environment and Behavior, 8*, 307–313.

Tuan, Y.F. (1974). *Topophilia: A study of environmental perception, attitudes, and values*. Englewood Cliffs, NJ: Prentice-Hall.

Tversky, B., & Hemenway, K. (1983). Categories of environmental scenes. *Cognitive Psychology, 15*, 121–149.

van Dijk, T.A. (1976). Philosophy of action and theory of narrative. *Poetics, 5*, 287–338.

Wapner, S. (1981). Transactions of persons-in-environments: Some critical transitions. *Journal of Environmental Psychology, 1*, 223–239.

Wapner, S., Kaplan, B., & Ciottone, R. (1980). Self-world relationships in critical environment transitions: Childhood and beyond. In L. Liben, A. Patterson, & N. Newcombe (Eds.), *Spatial representation and behavior across the life span* (pp. 251–282). New York: Academic.

Werner, H. (1948). *Comparative psychology of mental development*. Chicago: Follet.

Westin, A.F. (1967). *Privacy and freedom*. New York: Atheneum.

White, L., Jr. (1967). The historical roots of our ecologic crisis. *Science, 155*, 1203–1207.

White, R.W. (1959). Motivation reconsidered: The concept of competence. *Psychological Review, 66*, 297–333.

Wicker, A.W. (1969). Cognitive complexity, school size and participation in school behavior settings: A test of the frequency of interaction hypothesis. *Journal of Educational Psychology, 60*, 200–203.

Wiggins, J.S. (1973). *Personality and prediction: Principles of personality assessment*. Reading, MA: Addison-Wesley.

Wiggins, J.S. (1974). *In defense of traits*. Invited address to the ninth annual symposium on Recent Developments in the Use of the MMPI, Los Angeles.

Wiggins, J.S. (1979). A psychological taxonomy of trait-descriptive terms: The interpersonal domain. *Journal of Personality and Social Psychology, 37*, 395–412.

Wiggins, J.S. (1982). Circumplex models of interpersonal behavior in clinical psychology. In P.C. Kendall & J.N. Butcher (Eds.), *Handbook of research methods in clinical psychology* (pp. 183–221). New York: Wiley.

Wilson, G. (1977). Introversion/extraversion. In T. Blass (Ed.), *Personality variables in social behavior* (pp. 179–217). Hillsdale, NJ: Erlbaum.

Windley, P.G. (1975). Environmental dispositions: A theoretical and methodological alternative. In P.G. Windley, T.O. Byerts, & F. G. Ernst (Eds.), *Theory development in environment and aging* (pp. 127–141). Washington, DC: Gerontological Society.

Winkel, G.H., Malek, R., & Thiel, P. (1969). The role of personality differences in judgments of roadside quality. *Environment and Behavior, 1*, 199–223.

Wirth, L. (1938). Urbanism as a way of life. *American Journal of Sociology, 44*, 1–24.

Witkin, H.A., Dyk, R.G., Faterson, H.F., Goodenough, D.R., & Karp, S.A. (1962). *Psychological differentiation*. New York: Wiley.

Wohlwill, J.F. (1973). The environment is not in the head. In W.F.E. Preiser (Ed.), *Environmental design research: Vol. 2. Symposia and workshops. Proceedings of the Fourth International Environmental Design Research Association Conference* (pp. 166–181). Stroudsburg, PA: Dowden, Hutchinson, & Ross.

Wolfram, J.R., & Wearing, A.J. (1982). Measuring the structure of privacy. *Melbourne Psychology Reports, 71* (pp. 1–27).

Wolk, S. (1976). Situational constraint as a moderator of the locus of control-adjustment relationship. *Journal of Consulting and Clinical Psychology, 44,* 420–427.

Wolk, S., & Kurtz, J. (1975). Positive adjustment and involvement during aging and expectancy for internal control. *Journal of Consulting and Clinical Psychology, 43,* 173–178.

Wolk, S., & Telleen, S. (1976). Psychological and social correlates of life satisfaction as a function of residential constraint. *Journal of Gerontology, 31*(1), 89–98.

Young, M., & Willmont, P. (1957). *Family and kinship in East London.* New York: Free Press.

Zuckerman, M. (1979). *Sensation seeking: Beyond the optimal level of arousal.* Hillsdale, NJ: Erlbaum.

Zuckerman, M. (1984). Sensation seeking: A comparative approach to a human trait. *The Behavioral and Brain Sciences, 7,* 413–471.

Zuckerman, M., Kolin, E.A., Price, L., & Zoob, I. (1964). Development of a Sensation-Seeking Scale. *Journal of Consulting Psychology, 28,* 477-482.

Chapter 8

EMOTION AND THE ENVIRONMENT

James A. Russell *and* **Jacalyn Snodgrass,** *Department of Psychology, University of British Columbia, Vancouver, British Columbia, Canada*

Environmental psychology is that branch of psychology concerned with providing a systematic account of the relationship between a person and the environment. Of course, psychologists in other branches of psychology are also concerned with the environment. But when they speak of an environment, they usually single out a sharply defined event or object. It is typically focal, potent, salient, and clearly delimited both in space and in time. For the subject in an experiment, it is the figure rather than the ground. The environment of concern to the environmental psychologist is more often the background. It consists of countless elements and is unbounded in space and time. The subject is unaware of much of it. Its influence is often subtle, or, rather, the influence of any one element may be subtle. Cumulatively, these elements make up an environment, which may be powerful but complex and difficult to understand.

A person's relationship to such a complicated entity as an environment is equally complex and difficult to understand. But we remain convinced that a key aspect of this relationship is emotional. Occasionally, emotional ties to a place are obvious. The names for some of the places in your life—home, motherland, church—may remind you of the powerful emotional bonds by which you are attached to them. But the more important fact about emotional links to places may be their pervasiveness. Before you go somewhere, you usually estimate how pleasant the experience will be. When you arrive there, you are likely struck by the place's affective quality: You notice how stressful, how depressing, how peaceful, or how delightful it is. Affective quality is the bottom line of an accounting of the many features in a place, and is, we believe, a guide for much of your subsequent relationship to that place—what to do there, how well it is done, how soon to leave, whether or not to return. Afterward, you often remember little more about a place than its affective quality. Affective quality may also be a key factor in accounting for the cumulative influence of the environment on mood, health, and subjective well-being. One reason the relationship between a person and environment is subtle might be that the relationship is indirect: Behavior may be influenced by the (estimated, perceived, or remembered) affective quality of an environment rather than by its objective properties directly.

In this chapter, we shall discuss the emotional relationship between person and environment. Unfortunately, writers on emotion have typically not viewed their field from the molar perspective of environmental psychology, nor have environmental psychologists focused on emotion. The relationship between emotion and environment thus remains largely uncharted. In the spirit of a new and changing discipline, this chapter does not present conclusions so much as raise questions. But one conclusion we did reach reviewing this topic is that it represents a rich source of opportunities for research and a potential vantage point for viewing the field of person–environment interactions.

We shall first discuss the nature of emotion, touching on conceptual and measurement issues. The word *emotion* refers to a heterogeneous class of different phenomena. The first problem encountered in a discussion of emotion is that any statement made about emotion may be true of one aspect or one type of emotion but not of another. The aspect of emotion studied by researchers interested in one environmental topic is often different from the aspect of emotion studied by those interested in another. Emotion can be defined narrowly to include only such prototypical episodes as falling in love or becoming enraged. Or emotion can be defined more broadly to include vague feelings of mood, attitudes, preferences, or just about anything that is not coldly rational. If we are to understand the emotional ties to the molar environment, we must first have a broad enough view of emotion to encompass diverse phenomena, but without confusing one thing for another. This first section proposes several needed distinctions and attempts to raise the sorts of conceptual issues about the nature of emotion that must be resolved before the emotional links involved in person–environment interactions can be understood.

The remaining sections concern a person's encounter with an environment. Environmental psychologists have found that understanding the relationship between a person and a complex, large-scale environment requires a new view of a person and behavior. For instance, a person's perception of the large-scale environment is an active process more like exploration than like a response. Ties to faraway places are mediated by memories of past encounters and plans about future encounters. Behavior is better understood at a molar level of personal projects (Little, 1983), often preplanned and carried out over a meaningful part of a person's life. In short, the large-scale, complex environment is less a "stimulus" to a "response" than a set of opportunities for large-scale, complex actions organized in space and time. We shall thus step backward in time from when a person enters a place, back to the time he or she first thinks of going there. We shall discuss the prototypical sequence involved in a molar action. A person plans an activity, selects an appropriate place to carry it out, travels there, and then completes the plan—or not, depending on circumstances. A focus on emotion sheds light on each step in this sequence as well as on its potential aftereffects.

8.1. EMOTION

Which phenomena are *emotional*? Everyone knows what emotion is—until asked to give a definition. Then, it seems, no one knows. Are emotions mental, behavioral, or physiological events? Does the term *emotion* include mood, motivation, preference, value, attachment? Everyone knows that anger, fear, and love are emotions, but are courage, pride, and serenity? The word *emotion* lacks a set of necessary and sufficient features that would allow us to answer such questions to everyone's satisfaction (Fehr & Russell, 1984). Rather, prototypical emotions fade gradually into nonprototypical emotions, which fade gradually into nonemotions, with no sharp boundaries to be found.

Terms such as *emotion, affect, mood,* or *feeling* are used more or less interchangeably in the psychological literature and are used by both psychologists and nonpsychologists to mean a variety of things. In the following section, we shall introduce and informally define four terms. We shall first distinguish relatively long-term emotional dispositions from short-term states. Needless to say, there is no sharp boundary to be found, but perhaps some confusion could be avoided. We next turn to short-term emotional events, of which we distinguish three: *affective appraisal, mood,* and *emotional episode.* There are no standard and accepted distinctions in the domain of emotion, and the terminology we are using should not be taken for anything other than convenience. We do not claim that these four exhaust the meaning of *emotion* nor that the words *emotion, affective appraisal,* and so on are used in everyday English, or by psychologists, in the way we describe. Nevertheless, some distinctions seem particularly important within environmental psychology.

By a long-term *emotional disposition* we mean a tendency to do or think or feel particular things when the right circumstances occur. For example, your love of your parents does not occur for just a few moments. It is a disposition because it is said to exist even during the times when you are not thinking or feeling anything about your parents, but it is manifested on certain occasions. By a *short-term state* or *event* we mean something that happens at a given moment or extends over at most a few days. By *affective appraisal* we mean an aspect of how someone interprets other persons, places, events, or things. It is a judgment of something as pleasant, attractive, valuable, likable, preferable, repulsive, and so on. By *mood* we mean the core emotion-tinged feelings of a person's subjective state at any given moment. To be in a certain mood is to feel calm, upset, depressed, excited, unhappy—or neutral. By our definition, a conscious person is always in some mood, and mood per se is not directed toward any particular object (i.e., it is not about anything in particular). By *emotional episode* we mean an emotional reaction to something, with the reaction typically involving coordinated and distinctive physiological, behavioral, and mental changes. Prototypical examples of emotional episodes are falling in love with someone, suffering grief at a death, getting angry at someone, and being frightened by a bear in the woods. Emotional episodes may be relatively rare, but they are the prototypical examples of what is meant by emotion (Fehr & Russell, 1984).

8.1.1. Emotional Dispositions

Emotional dispositions are largely outside the scope of this chapter, and we mention them primarily to point to an ambiguity: To speak of, for example, "an anxious person" is ambiguous because it could mean someone temporarily anxious or someone characteristically so. Consequently, measures of long-term conditions are sometimes confused with measures of temporary states: Questionnaires such as the Taylor (1953) Manifest Anxiety Scale, which were designed to assess long-term personality traits, are occasionally mistakenly used to measure the short-term emotional impact of an environmental variable. Because of this ambiguity in emotion-denoting terms, it is now common to distinguish *trait* levels from *state* levels, which correspond roughly to what we mean by long-term dispositions and short-term states, respectively.

Some persons are generally happy; others unhappy. Some are often aroused; others more phlegmatic. Indeed, for almost any emotion-denoting concept, it is possible to define a trait level of that emotion. Instruments have therefore been developed to assess characteristic levels of, for example, depression (Beck, 1967), well-being (Diener, 1984), and anxiety (Spielberger, Gorsuch, & Lushene, 1970; Taylor, 1953). Mehrabian and his associates (Mehrabian & O'Reilly, 1980; Mehrabian & Russell, 1974) argued that any such dimension can be defined in terms of three basic dimensions of temperament: trait-pleasure, trait-arousal, and trait-dominance. They found these three to be relatively independent of one another and to be constituents of many commonly studied personality traits. A related proposal was recently advanced by Watson and Clark (1984) based on an extensive meta-analysis of personality traits. To label long-term happiness a dimension of "temperament" seems to imply it is something inherited; to label it "well-being" seems to imply it is an outcome of life events. Neither implication has been established. The question to ask is how such individual differences come about: how inherited dispositions interact with the cumulative impact of environments.

Love of country, fondness for wilderness, attachment to the neighborhood, and concern over pollution are examples of another class of long-term emotional dispositions. These are usually thought of as attitudes: dispositions to think about, feel about, and act toward certain objects in certain ways. An interesting discussion of attitudes relevant to environmental psychology was recently published by Weigel (1983).

8.1.2. Mood

We shall use the word *mood* to refer to the core emotional feelings of a person's subjective state at any given moment. This is a much more restricted meaning than is commonly given the term. By our definition, although behavioral or physiological indicators of mood may someday be discovered, any candidate would have to be validated against a more direct measure of subjective experience. Although moods may persist, or change in cycles, or be relatively mild in intensity (as some writers have proposed), none of these statements is required to be true by our definition. Whether they are true remains unknown—they are the sorts of statements psychologists are more fond of making than testing. Similarly, although mood may be caused by external events, by our definition mood is not necessarily about anything. One can wake up feeling in a certain mood or drift into one for no apparent reason. (Thus the distinction we are drawing between mood and affective appraisal does not concern their cause; presumably both are caused.)

Today, mood is measured almost exclusively through verbal self-report. Research on mood questionnaires began with a series of factor-analytic studies by Nowlis and his colleagues (e.g., Nowlis & Nowlis, 1956). Nowlis anticipated that several large *bipolar* factors such as pleasure–displeasure and activation–deactivation would summarize the mood domain. Instead, his factor analyses indicated a larger number of independent *unipolar* factors. Subsequent research with similar methods yielded similar results (e.g., McNair & Lorr, 1964; Thayer, 1967), and most mood questionnaires used today provide scores on a list of purportedly independent unipolar factors (Izard, 1972; McNair, Lorr, & Droppleman, 1971; Nowlis, 1965; Thayer, 1967).

However, Nowlis's method capitalized on a series of artifacts and, in actual use, measures of the individual unipolar factors, rather than independent, were highly intercorrelated (Russell & Mehrabian, 1977; Russell & Steiger, 1982). For two items to be bipolar they must correlate -1.0; even random error works against such a result. Meddis (1972) showed that Nowlis's response format shifted the correlation toward the positive end of the scale. A more appropriate format resulted in evidence of a smaller number of bipolar dimensions, and further methodological refinements produced even stronger evidence for bipolarity (Russell, 1979; Svensson, 1978). Thayer (1978) and Lorr (Lorr & Shea, 1979), who provided some of the initial evidence for unipolar factors, report more recent evidence favoring bipolarity (see also Mackay, Cox, Burrows, & Lazzerini, 1978). Today the evidence favors one conclusion: A person's mood at a *given moment in time* is properly described in terms of bipolar dimensions.

A more conceptual resolution of conflicting intuitions about unipolar and bipolar dimensions of mood can be seen in Figure 8.1. In this circumplex model of mood, individual mood descriptors fall in a roughly circular order in a space defined by two underlying bipolar dimensions of feeling; the first having to do with pleasure–displeasure (or happiness–unhappiness) and the second with arousal–sleepiness. Thus each individual mood descriptor can be thought of as composed of a certain proportion of pleasure and arousal: Excitement consists of pleasure and high arousal, distress consists of displeasure and high arousal, depression consists of displeasure and low arousal, and relaxation consists of pleasure and low arousal. This way of thinking about mood applies not only to college undergraduates (Russell, 1980) but to grade school children (Russell & Ridgeway, 1983) and to speakers of languages other than English (Russell, 1983; Watson, Clark, & Tellegen, 1984). According to this model, the easiest way to measure mood is to measure the bipolar dimensions of pleasure–displeasure and arousal–sleepiness (Mehrabian & Russell, 1974). From scores on these two dimensions, values on specific "unipolar" scales such as degree of anxiety or degree of depression can be predicted with surprising accuracy (Russell & Mehrabian, 1977).

There is much controversy concerning the proper number of dimensions in the description of mood. Much of the controversy actually concerned bipolar versus unipolar dimensions, because many fewer

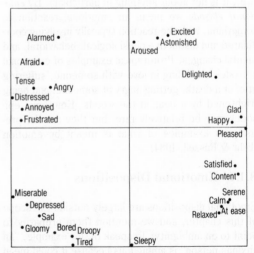

Figure 8.1. A circular ordering of mood descriptors. (*Source:* "A Circumplex Model of Affect" by J. A. Russell, 1980, *Journal of Personality and Social Psychology, 39.* Reprinted by permission.)

bipolar dimensions than unipolar ones are required. Beyond this question, how many dimensions are required may be a matter of convenience. If we restrict mood to *core* emotional feelings, the description of Figure 8.1 appears to be a good first approximation; two is the minimum number of dimensions. Many more terms could be added to Figure 8.1, "added" in the sense that their core emotional meaning could be defined in terms of pleasure and arousal. Dimensions orthogonal to these two can also be found, but they appear to refer to such factors as the causes and consequences of the mood (Russell, 1978) and to account for much less of the variance in descriptions of mood (Russell & Mehrabian, 1974, 1977) than the first two. We would therefore suggest emphasizing pleasure and arousal as key dimensions of mood.

8.1.3. Affective Appraisals

An affective appraisal is an attribution to some object, event, or place of an affective quality. Affective appraisal can be distinguished from mood, at least in principle, in that affective appraisal is thus always directed toward something. Subjectively, the appraisal refers to a quality of the object appraised: It is the object that appears pleasant or disgusting.

Failure to distinguish between affective appraisal and the mood change that may or may not accompany it can cause great confusion (Simon, 1982). One can acknowledge that an earthquake in, say, Tibet is a horrible event, much worse perhaps than anything personally experienced, but find that the mood change on hearing such news may be slight. Contrast this with admittedly less devastating events such as an editor's rejection of an article you have written. While mood and affective appraisal can obviously influence one another, they are independent enough to require a conceptual distinction. Or consider the case of a subject in a laboratory asked to state a preference between two polygons. There is little passion involved. The subject is simply *appraising* an affective quality of the polygons. While doing so, the subject could report something different: his or her own mood at that time. It is no contradiction for you to say that you like (or dislike) this polygon and, at the same time and independent of your preference, that you feel good (or bored, or sad, or whatever). By this definition, affective appraisal could occur with no inner emotional feelings. Thus to rate the pleasantness of a set of stimuli is not necessarily to ride an emotional roller coaster; in fact, the mood during such a chore might be steady boredom.

Affective appraisals seem to be what Mandler (1982, 1984) termed *evaluative cognitions* (and treats as cognitive events) and what Zajonc (1980) termed *affective reactions* (and suggests are at least partially independent of cognitive processes). We doubt that terms such as *emotion, cognition,* or *affect* are defined in a precise enough way to allow us to decide whether affective appraisals are really cognitions or really emotions. (See Russell & Woudzia, 1986.)

Mandler (1982, 1984) contends that the distinguishing feature of evaluative cognitions is that they are based on judgments about the *relations* among features of the object appraised. We would suggest an alternative characterization: Affective appraisals are those judgments concerning the capacity of the appraised object to alter mood. The English language provides hundreds of words such as *exciting, boring, disgusting, stressful,* and *relaxing* that people can use to describe the affective qualities of places. Our thesis is that any such word could be rendered excitement producing, boredom producing, disgust producing, and so on.

In spite of, or perhaps because of, the large array of affective descriptors available in English, environmental psychologists have focused their attention on only a few (such as *stressful*) and then only one at a time, implying pessimism over the possibility of including in their research or theorizing anything approaching a complete description and assessment of the affective qualities attributed to places. The model of Figure 8.1 suggests a very simple way to organize diverse descriptors of affective quality. Figure 8.2 shows 40 such descriptors, drawn systematically from a set of 105 adjectives (Russell, Ward, & Pratt, 1981) that are a relatively complete sample of commonly used terms highly saturated in affective meaning but with little or no reference to objective, perceptible properties of the place described. Various analyses converged on the two-dimensional representation shown in Figure 8.2. The axes are easily labeled: The horizontal axis ranges from unpleasant to pleasant, and the vertical axis ranges from soporific to arousing. Based on these analyses, scales of the affective quality attributed to places were developed (Russell & Pratt, 1980). An individual's rating of a place on these scales would constitute an operational definition of that individual's affective appraisal of the place. A group mean on these scales for a particular place would constitute an operational definition of the affective quality of the place.

A structural model such as Figure 8.2 represents the fact that people use these terms as if each one was connected to all the others. To illustrate this con-

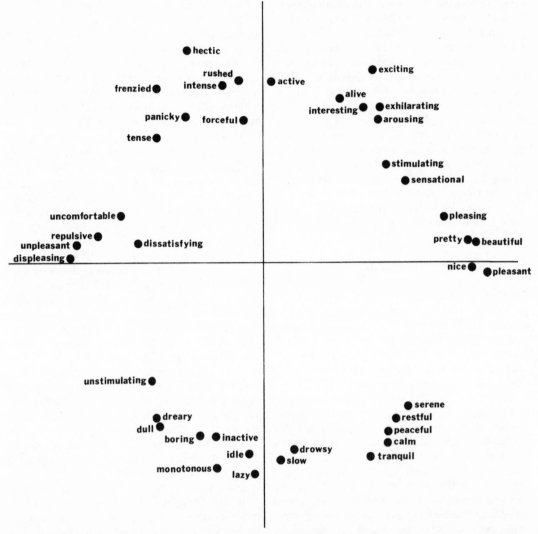

Figure 8.2. A circular ordering of descriptors of the affective qualities of places (*Source:* "Adaptation Level and the Affective Appraisal of Environments" by J. A. Russell and U. F. Lanius, 1984, *Journal of Environmental Psychology, 4.* Reprinted by permission.)

nectedness, Figure 8.3 shows how the 40 terms change in a coordinated fashion. Along the abscissa are the 40 terms in exactly the same order shown in Figure 8.2 (except that the two end points in Figure 8.3 must be thought of as adjacent). The ordinate represents the change in ratings on each term induced by a change in adaptation level (Russell & Lanius, 1984). Subjects were rating a single environmental scene after first seeing (or not, in the control group) an inducing scene. As shown in Figure 8.3, adjacent terms tended to rise or fall together. The scene was rated more lively, exciting, and the like; at

the same time it was rated less boring, dull, and the like. Our structural model predicted the sine wave curve found in Figure 8.3 such that a change in affective appraisal is manifested by a systematic change in all affective descriptors.

Research with the semantic differential had long ago produced a complementary result: two analogous factors, termed *evaluation* and *activity*, as well as a third factor, termed *potency* (Osgood, Suci, & Tannenbaum, 1957). The same three factors have been found in the more than 20 linguistic groups so far studied, indicating that they reflect universal aspects

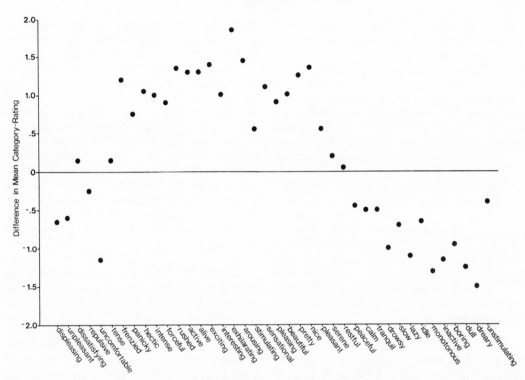

Figure 8.3. Difference in mean rating on 40 environmental descriptors. (*Source:* "Adaptation Level and the Affective Appraisal of Environments" by J. A. Russell and U. F. Lanius, 1984, *Journal of Environmental Psychology, 4.* Reprinted by permission.)

of the human perception of the external world (Osgood, May, & Miron, 1975). Although evaluation may be reasonably interpreted as pleasantness in some contexts, this may not be so in other contexts: In making aesthetic, moral, and rational judgments evaluation may mean something other than simply pleasantness. Similarly, activity apparently means arousing quality in some contexts, but not in others. Potency does not seem affective enough to fit within our definition of affective appraisal, and we have, somewhat arbitrarily, allocated it to the cognitive bin. In short, while we believe the evidence from the semantic differential is consistent with our proposed description of affective appraisal, we are reluctant to recommend the specific semantic differential verbal scales developed by Osgood and associates (1957) as the most appropriate measures of affective appraisal for environments (see also Craik, 1981).

8.1.4. Emotional Episodes

Emotional episodes cannot be distinguished sharply from either affective appraisals or moods. This is be-

cause an emotional episode typically *includes* both an affective appraisal and a mood change. Like affective appraisals, emotional episodes are about something in particular; they have objects. Like mood, emotional episodes involve core subjective feelings. In the prototypical case of an emotional episode, an external event is affectively appraised and causes a change in mood. Whether the affective appraisal or the mood change comes first appears to be a matter of debate (Lazarus, 1984; Zajonc, 1984). In the prototypical case of an emotional episode, there is also a change in physiology and a change in behavior; there has also been debate concerning which of these come first (James, 1890/1950; Schachter & Singer, 1962).

Emotional episodes are prototypical examples of what is ordinarily meant by an "emotion" and have therefore been the focus of psychological inquiry on emotion (Izard, 1977). The description of emotional episodes nevertheless remains a matter of controversy. Most emotion theorists do agree that emotional episodes consist of components (see, e.g., Izard, 1977; Lazarus, Kanner, & Folkman, 1980,

Schachter & Singer, 1962). Usually three are listed: behavioral, physiological, and mental. The behavioral component could be either expressive (such as frowns, smiles, weeping, gestures, or tone of voice) or instrumental (such as flight or aggression). The physiological component includes changes in, or activity clearly innervated by, the autonomic nervous system. Thus we attribute emotion to those who blush or tremble. But it also presumably includes more central processes, usually thought to occur in the limbic system.

The mental component of emotion is less well specified but includes at least three sorts of events: (1) You perceive external events or objects as threatening, pleasant, attractive, likable, preferable, disgusting, and so on—in our terms an *affective appraisal*. (2) You also feel aroused or depressed, happy or unhappy—in our terms *mood*. (3) You perceive your own emotional episode. Thus you are aware that you are afraid, or angry, or whatever. Let us refer to this as *emotional experience*.

Dividing emotional episodes into components raises a number of questions. At one time, psychologists debated which component *is* the emotion. Is emotion behavior (Watson, 1919), physiological activity (Wenger, 1950), or mental activity (James, 1890/1950)? There seems to be no empirical solution to this debate, and psychologists' favorite solution today is to say that all components are the emotion. One problem with such an answer, while reasonable in its own right, is that it may lead us to overestimate the extent to which the appropriate emotional behavior, physiological activation, and mental experience covary. It is too easy to say that in anger one frowns, behaves aggressively, shows physiological activation, perceives some event in the world as offensive, and feels angry. In the prototypical cases, yes. But the question is: What in general are the relationships among these components?

There are theoretical and empirical reasons to expect some degree of relationship among the components of an emotional episode. Indices of physiological arousal correlate positively (but moderately) with verbally reported subjective feelings of arousal (Thayer, 1967). Facial expressive behavior correlates with subjective feelings (Ekman, Freisen, & Ancoli, 1980). Nevertheless, there are also empirical and theoretical reasons to maintain that the components are at least somewhat separable. Such thinking lies behind the distinctions we proposed among mood, affective appraisal, and emotional episode. Behavioral, physiological, and verbal measures of, for example, anxiety are often only minimally correlated (Katkin,

1965; Martin, 1961). Individuals who respond to emotionally laden stimuli with more expressive facial patterns tend to show *smaller* psychophysiological responses than do less expressive individuals (Buck, 1976). Ekman (1972) introduced the concept of a display rule to account for occasions when there is a discrepancy between the outward display of emotion and the inward feeling. In a review of the clinical experience with fears, Rachman (1978) found that one component of fear often exists or changes in the absence of others. A patient may claim to experience fear of snakes but be willing to approach and even handle a snake. Another patient may lose his or her behavioral avoidance during the course of therapy but maintain physiological signs of fear. In clinical terminology, the various components of fear are discordant.

There is a methodological caution implied by discordances: No one measure suffices as an operational definition for the emotional episode as a whole. Thus the question of how to measure, say, fear is better replaced by a series of separate questions: How to measure fear behavior; how to measure physiological activation of fear; and so forth. A good measure of physiological activation might be galvanic skin response (GSR), but to use a person's GSR as a measure of fear is problematic: To do so implies that the person with a high GSR feels afraid, perceives something as threatening, and withdraws from the stimulus. Such inferences from one measure to another are at least questionable and often turn out to be wrong. It seems at this time safer to take GSR as a measure of physiological change and leave it as an open empirical question what, if any, affective appraisal, mood change, or behavior is occurring. The common approach has been to assume that the various components of emotion co-occur until proven otherwise; it may be time to assume them independent until proven otherwise.

Another implication of discordances concerns the relationship of emotional episodes to environment. An environmental variable need not relate to emotional behavior, physiological activation, affective appraisal, mood, and emotional experience in exactly the same way (although of course it might). Consider this question: Does noise cause anxiety? It is perhaps better replaced by a series of separate questions such as: Does noise cause behavioral withdrawal? Does noise cause physiological activation? Does noise cause subjective feelings of anxiety? We must not assume that all these questions have the same answer: Certain types of uncertainty and novelty may cause the emotional experience of anxiety but behavioral approach rather than withdrawal (consider horror movies). Certain social situations may elicit feelings of boredom but smiles and laughter (recall some cocktail parties). Physical sports may be experienced as exciting but not produce smiles (notice that skiers do not seem to smile). Of course, people may enjoy cocktail parties and not horror movies or skiing. But our analysis suggests that we need not conclude this. We cannot always infer inner experience from outer behavior. A given situation or a given environmental variable may influence different components of an emotional episode in different ways.

Is there a taxonomy of emotional episodes? In words such as *fear, guilt, envy, pride,*, and *anger,* the English language labels hundreds of types of emotional episodes. (Wallace & Carson, 1973, estimated that there are over 2000 emotion-denoting words in an unabridged English dictionary.) Some emotion theorists believe that any such type of emotion can be defined in terms of one or more basic emotions (Ekman, 1972; Izard, 1977; Plutchik, 1980; Tomkins, 1962, 1963). Ekman, for example, argues that there are at least six basic emotions: sadness, disgust, anger, fear, surprise, and happiness. To these, Izard (1977) adds shame and interest. Still, there is no agreement on the list of basic emotions or on the number of items on the list, nor is there agreement on how the remaining emotions can be defined in terms of the basic ones.

An alternative view is that emotional episodes can be defined in terms of their underlying mental, behavioral, and physiological components (James, 1890/1950, Mandler, 1984; Schachter & Singer, 1962). Pride in this view is not a blend of basic emotions such as happiness plus anger. Rather, pride is a combination of particular behavior, physiological changes, and mental experiences. This idea seems to be consistent with the layperson's view. Without special training, most of us know a *script* (Abelson, 1981) for each emotional episode. The script specifies the particular components of the emotional episode and the order in which they occur (Russell & Bullock, in press). Consider the script for the episode labeled *fear.* Typically fear is a very unpleasant state and involves high arousal: You feel yourself trembling, your heart pounding, and your palms sweating. But we know much more about fear. Typically, a dangerous situation occurs suddenly. You perceive the threat. Thoughts race through your mind as you plan how to escape. You turn and flee. At least this is the prototypical case of fear in which all the relevant components co-occur. Actual cases of fear

do not have to turn out exactly this way. You may stand rather than flee; you may inhibit the facial expression of fear. Actual episodes are said to be fear to the extent they resemble the prototypical sequence. And resemblance is a matter of degree rather than all or none.

To summarize, an emotional episode is a gestalt that consists of component events, including environmental, mental, physiological, and behavioral changes. At least since James's (1890/1950) thesis on emotion, the exact temporal and causal relationships among these component events have been debated. In doing so, most writers have, naturally enough, focused on the prototypical cases of emotion, even though prototypical cases are relatively rare in everyday life. Especially in a discussion of the emotional response to aspects of the physical environment, it is wise to keep in mind less prototypical cases, where components are discordant or occur alone. For that reason, we distinguished emotional episode from affective appraisal and mood. The domain of emotion is so complex that some divisions are required. We do not mean to suggest that each actual psychological event can be pigeonholed as a mood change, affective appraisal, and so on. The distinctions we propose are conceptual in nature, and we leave as empirical hypotheses the relations among them. It remains an empirical possibility that affective appraisal, in fact, always accompanies mood change and vice versa. Such a hypothesis could not be tested without a clear distinction between them in the first place. We suggest considering the possibility that mood change can occur alone (e.g., induced by drugs or diurnal rhythms) and that affective appraisal can occur alone (e.g., when appraising a set of polygons). When affective appraisal is coordinated with a mood change, we have the basic elements of an emotional episode.

8.2. STEP 1: BEFORE ENTERING THE ENVIRONMENT

Before entering a place, a person has typically planned to go there and planned what to do—however vague the plan might be. When an unplanned event occurs, it is often salient for just that reason. In turning now to a person's interaction with the molar physical environment, we shall therefore begin with a discussion of plans. Miller, Galanter, and Pribram (1960) proposed a theory of human action organized in time by means of plans. In their theory, a plan is an intended sequence of acts leading to a goal. A plan is hierarchically organized in the sense that each act in the sequence can be thought of as it-self composed of a sequence of subactions with a goal. Successive subdivision presumably leads ulti-mately to muscle actions and neuron firings. Moving in the other direction, we can usually think of a par-ticular plan as a unit within some higher-level plan. Writing an essay can be broken down into steps, or it can be seen as part of a larger plan for, for example, publishing a handbook.

We have found the concept of plan extremely use-ful in understanding how behavior is organized in space as well as time. The idea therefore led to the proposal that a sequence of steps might be a useful approach to environmental psychology (Russell & Ward, 1982). In the first step, a person, P, perceives a problem and plans how to do something about it. P plans a sequence of behaviors intended to accomplish a goal. P then chooses an appropriate place and travels there for execution of the plan. Finally, P ar-rives and carries out the plan—or not, as cir-cumstances allow.

The sequence of plan–travel–execute constitutes a unit that can vary in size. The unit sometimes will refer to a brief episode: At home, reading travel brochures, P feels that the room is uncomfortably warm and decides to go outdoors for fresh air (plan); P walks across the room (travel) and stands outside (execute). Other times, the unit will refer to a much longer episode: Noticing that job opportunities are dwindling, P considers the prospects in various re-gions of the world and eventually decides to migrate to Australia; P makes the arrangements, travels there, and settles down. In this example, the first episode could be one unit embedded within the sec-ond episode.

The framework proposed cannot be expected to apply to all cases, nor would it be useful to apply it too rigidly. But it does provide a broad perspective from which we can see how a person attempts to control his or her emotional state by choosing what to do and where to go. Emotional considerations are involved at each step of the way, from choosing where to go and what to do to the final step of leav-ing and experiencing the consequences. There are also emotional consequences to failures of the plan, disruptions, and unexpected events. The different steps thus highlight different aspects of emotion: Planning requires affective appraisal of the events planned. Encounter with a chosen place typically re-sults in a change in mood and an affective appraisal of the place. Failure of the plan may result in an emo-tional episode. Aftereffects may be mediated by mood change.

8.2.1. Planning

Imagine a person P choosing a course of action. Ra-tional choice requires that P pick the alternative with the greatest expected value. Expected value, in turn, depends on the probabilities of the various out-comes of those actions and the value of those out-comes. Psychological research has made much head-way in understanding judgments about probabilities (Kahneman, Slovic, & Tversky, 1982), but less in un-derstanding value and choice. The following discus-sion is thus necessarily speculative.

Value, Preference, and Choice

The account of value that is most compatible with our treatment of emotion is as follows: Value is the amount of pleasure or displeasure (happiness or un-happiness) produced by the outcome—in our terms, it is the improvement in the first dimension of mood. The value of a thing is the happiness it produces. *Ex-pected* value is thus the expected amount of pleasure of the outcome. In our terms, a judgment of the ex-pected value of the outcome is an affective appraisal of the outcome. Thus to *prefer* A over B is: to ap-praise A as more pleasure producing than B; to ap-praise A as more pleasant than B; and to expect A to produce more pleasure than B. We shall take these as different ways to say the same thing.

An account of choice that puts pleasure or happi-ness as an overriding human goal is not new: in the fifth century B.C. Democritus argued that cheerful-ness is the goal of life. Most psychologists would dis-courage any such hedonistic account of choice. Psychological hedonism has yet to be formulated into a precise and testable hypothesis within psychology. More important, people obviously do not always choose what brings happiness. On the other hand, we must acknowledge that, on at least some level of analysis, considerations of happiness play a role in the plans we make. After all, if you do something with the knowledge that its only consequence will be to make you happy, no one asks why you did it. If you do something with the knowledge that its only conse-quence will be to make you unhappy, an explanation is called for. And hard to imagine.

One reason that psychological hedonism may have been judged vacuous is the seemingly small step from saying that P acts to maximize happiness to saying that whatever P does is what makes him or her happy. This step is illegitimate, first, because it assumes P's own happiness is his or her goal and, second, because it ignores affective appraisal as a key part of the process. There is no reason to assume that P is a good judge of what will bring happiness. The processes whereby P goes about achieving happiness may make it elusive. P may be poor at anticipating what brings happiness, may not correctly judge the outcome of actions, or may not know how to calculate an optimal plan, or how to carry it out. Planning involves judgments about future outcomes and therefore involves the prediction of future happiness. P must somehow answer the question "Will I experience happiness at the time it happens?"

It was once assumed that a person possessed a stable set of values or preferences. (This assumption is implicit, e.g., in the concept of attitude.) Research indicates that people cannot consistently produce a set of well-ordered preferences (Kahneman & Tversky, 1984). For example, the preferred outcome often depends on how the choice is framed. One troubling example is the choice between treatment methods for an expected epidemic. In one version of the problem, the options were expressed in terms of probabilities of lives *saved*; in the other version, the identical options were expressed in probabilities of lives *lost*. The majority made opposite choices in the two cases (Kahneman & Tversky, 1982). The lack of well-ordered preferences presents a stumbling block for normative and descriptive models of choice. It would be relatively easy to construct a model that will identify the choice of maximum value—provided stable values have been identified. Looking at human values from the perspective of a designer of artificial value-driven decision systems, Pugh (1977) argued that evolution is more likely to have produced the kind of a disorganized and partially redundant value system that would be produced by a committee than the well-structured value system we seem to expect.

The lack of well-ordered preferences raises a number of questions. What is the process of affective appraisal by which we anticipate our own happiness? How well do we understand what brings about happiness? Or, what specifically does each person know and what biases and mistakes are made? When we are attempting to do something in the most pleasant way possible, do we have strategies, and how well do they work? To illustrate, one strategy might say: Given an unpleasant task, make it last as little time as possible. Another strategy might be the rule of thumb: "One for the road" makes the trip more pleasant. If we choose by simulating possible outcomes (Kahneman & Tversky, 1982), we may somehow imagine (or feel?) our degree of happiness as we imagine each option. The particular way we imagine the option would then influence the happiness we predict.

In a preliminary, unpublished study we asked whether subjects could predict the change in value of a stimulus that is known to occur with repeated exposure (Zajonc, 1968). We tested subjects' intuitions about the effect of repeated exposure on liking by showing them nonsense words and Chinese symbols similar to those used by Zajonc (1968) in his classic monograph on the exposure effect. Our subjects were asked to imagine they had seen each word either 0, 1, 2, 5, 10, or 25 times before, and to rate how much they thought they would like the word after seeing it that many times. On the average, subjects predicted some increase in liking with exposure, but not as much as actually occurred. There were also stable individual differences in ability to predict.

Mood as the Goal of the Plan

Saying that happiness is a goal of the plan fails to specify the desired mood sufficiently. Moods ranging from serenity to elation may be equally pleasurable. At different times, different specific moods will be sought. According to evidence already reviewed, the second major dimension of mood is arousal, and we can therefore ask about preference for different degrees of arousal. Psychological theory suggests that, in general, people prefer intermediate degrees of arousal (Berlyne, 1974)—this is the meaning of the inverted-U-shaped curve relating preference to arousal. Nevertheless, it would seem that the preferred level of arousal may vary from person to person and from time to time. For example, sensation seekers (arousal seekers) prefer higher levels of arousal than do sensation avoiders (Zuckerman, 1980); sensation seekers find high arousal more pleasant than do sensation avoiders (Ridgeway, Hare, Waters, & Russell, 1984). The preferred level of arousal also seems to vary with the accompanying degree of pleasure: Persons prefer an intermediate degree of arousal only when their mood is relatively neutral on pleasure–displeasure. When feeling happy, persons prefer higher arousal; when feeling unhappy, they prefer lower arousal (Russell & Mehrabian, 1977). The preferred level of arousal also varies with the task to be performed: Given a difficult or unpleasant task subjects preferred a less arousing environment; given a simple or pleasant task, subjects preferred a more arousing environment (Russell & Mehrabian, 1975, 1978).

Knowing the Affective Quality of Places

Most activities require a specific place or specific type of place: We shop in shops and garden in gardens. Consequently, one step in planning is the selection of a place where the plan is to be carried out. Sometimes there can be only one place; other times, there is a choice of places. An example of the former is a plan to go home; of the latter, a plan to eat in a restaurant.

Suppose P has decided to dine at a restaurant. In selecting which restaurant, many factors could play a role, but one factor is often the restaurant's affective quality. Will it be lively, relaxing, or exciting? This choice facing P raises a question: How does P appraise a place in its absence? How does P predict what the affective quality of the place will be? The restaurant example should not allow us to trivialize an important question. Affective appraisal is involved in such major decisions as deciding to migrate to a new country, to buy and sell real estate, to vote for or against issues and candidates, and to plan to develop regions and cities. Most such decisions must be made in the absence of the place or object being affectively appraised.

Several writers have proposed that a person possesses a mental atlas in which places are coded affectively. Gould and White (1975) used the term *mental map* and showed that residents of Britain could easily rate the preferability of British districts. Ley (1975) used the term *stress map* and showed that residents of Philadelphia could rate the desirability of specific blocks in their neighborhood, and that their plans for travel within the neighborhood took into account the information summarized in their stress map. Nasar (1979) used the term *evaluative image* and showed that both residents and tourists coded areas of Knoxville, Tennessee, as likable or dislikable. The concern so far has been limited to the pleasantness–unpleasantness of places, but a richer characterization of the mental atlas may be obtained by employing a fuller description of the affective qualities attributed to places such as that summarized in Figure 8.2. Still, evidence already mentioned on the instability of preferences suggests that the notion of an affective map may oversimplify how a person estimates affective quality.

One way in which affective appraisals about a place's affective quality may lack stability is that they rely on memory. This possibility raises several questions. For example, what exactly do we remember? Our mood the last time there? Our affective appraisal of the place the last time there? When the affective quality of a place is remembered, what exactly happens? Is the memory a reevocation of a feeling that occurred in the place, or is it a cold piece of information: That place is frightening? If the code is purely informational, is it verbal?

Alternatively, rather than remember the affective quality of a place, P may have to estimate it. If so, the question is how. What qualities of the place are taken into account and how are they integrated? Anything that influences our memory of the features of a place may influence its affective appraisal. How do we abstract an affective code for a place from the whole of our remembered experience there? When we have visited a place twice, how do we integrate information from the two occasions, and do we show recency or primacy effects? Numerous features of the environment will contribute to its actual affective quality—we might wonder which of these relationships people know about. Again, any factor that influences the judged features of the places would be expected to influence its affective appraisal.

We may not have to choose between the alternatives of recall and calculation. The most likely situation is that both processes are involved and that sometimes one dominates, sometimes the other. For a highly familiar place, presumably an affective code is available along with other attributes of the place. For unfamiliar places, presumably more calculation is required.

8.2.2. Individual Differences

Many personality traits have been described that predict individual differences in planning. For example, arousal-seeking tendency might be defined as follows: arousal seekers prefer and therefore seek high levels of stimulation; arousal avoiders prefer and seek low levels of stimulation. Various measures are available for this trait (McKechnie, 1974; Mehrabian & Russell, 1973; Zuckerman, 1980), and research with these measures illustrates an important point about personality: Personality plays a role both in the planning of activities and in the reaction to the actual environment. In one study, arousal seekers were found to anticipate that they would be happier in an arousing environment than in an unarousing environment; arousal avoiders anticipated just the reverse (Russell & Mehrabian, 1977). In another study, their prediction was borne out: Actual mood was measured during sessions of increasingly loud bursts of sound. Arousal avoiders were happier than arousal seekers during an initial period of quiet, but their positions were reversed by the time the loudest sounds were presented (Ridgeway et al., 1984).

Mehrabian (1977) proposed an orthogonal but conceptually related personality dimension: arousability versus stimulus screening. The arousable person reacts with greater arousal to novel stimuli, and the arousal habituates more slowly. Screeners, in contrast, disregard stimulation. Considering arousal-seeking tendency and arousability as orthogonal dimensions yields four types: arousable arousal seekers, screening arousal seekers, arousable arousal avoiders, and screening arousal avoiders. This typology has obvious value in understanding individual differences in planning for, and encounters with, physical environments.

Our original thought had been to review evidence concerning all personality traits relevant to the affective appraisal of places, but we soon realized that few traits could be left out. It is not difficult to define personality dimensions so as to highlight their relevance to affective appraisal of environments. For example, McKechnie's (1974) Environmental Response Inventory lists personality dimensions that can be directly defined in this way: Urbanism (enjoys city life), Environmental Trust (lacks fear of the physical environment), and Antiquarianism (enjoys the old). Kaplan's (1977) Environmental Preference Questionnaire includes a scale entitled Nature, which appears to measure the tendency to derive pleasure from natural settings. The scale entitled Romantic Escape seems to be the tendency to dislike manicured scenes such as parks and to prefer wild, untouched wilderness. Notice that, had the emotional reaction of the Romantic Escapers been specified more finely, we might discern two different types of romantic escapers: one type might find man-made scenes stressful and wilderness soothing; the other type might find man-made scenes boring and wilderness exciting. Even though both types prefer wilderness, their precise experiences and behaviors in the wilderness could differ considerably.

8.2.3. Travel

To carry out a plan, we often have to travel somewhere. It could be to another room, or to another continent. Our plans must therefore include a means for transporting ourselves and a travel route. This can be as simple as choosing which bus to take, or as complex as plotting a route through wilderness with a map and compass. Our transportation medium and the route we travel combine to form what we might call a travel environment.

A travel environment is not different in any special way from any other molar environment we might examine, and the interaction between plans and behavior is not unique to this context. Still, travel is an important issue in the province of environmental psychology and illustrates its central concerns. The

travel environment, as any place, may be appraised as pleasant or unpleasant, arousing or soothing. It may impede or facilitate our plans. Any of these dimensions may be the basis for our specific planning decisions. We may have little time and choose a means and route we expect to be fastest. We may feel sleepy and choose a route we expect to increase our arousal level. Or we may choose a travel environment on the basis of its expected pleasantness—as in taking a cruise—just as we may sometimes choose our destinations on this basis. Perhaps because travel is often associated with vacationing, it is easier to see the influence of the affective appraisal of an environment on plans in the context of travel than it is in contexts such as work where long-range goals may override preferences based on an appraisal of the place. Indeed, the affective quality of a travel environment is sometimes so salient that travel loses its incidental status and becomes itself the goal of a plan. Nearly half the estimated $120 billion spent by Americans each year for leisure activities is spent on travel (Mayo & Jarvis, 1981).

Much of the research related to travel environments is confined to studies of automobile drivers. Early research focused on measures of physiological activation. Stokols and Novaco (1981) reviewed much of this literature and reported that among the factors found to contribute to high arousal in automobile drivers are, not surprisingly, high traffic volume, complex interchanges, sharp curves, high temperatures, and high levels of noise.

Stokols and Novaco also examined dissatisfaction with transportation. They argued that the effects of transportation variables can only be understood within their larger context. In a field study of 100 Californians who drove to work each day, they looked at mood, physiological measures, dissatisfaction with travel, and intolerance for frustration on arrival at work. Their independent variables were time and distance traveled (which together is called *impedance*) plus aspects of the larger context: satisfaction with residence and personality type. They found that impedance was positively correlated with travel dissatisfaction: As time and distance increased, drivers became more dissatisfied. Impedance was also positively correlated with blood pressure and intolerance for frustration on arrival at work, although there was an interaction with personality type (A or B). Among high-impedance commuters, Type B's had higher blood pressure and less tolerance for frustration than Type A's, and among medium-impedance commuters these measures were reversed. In further support of the importance of contextual effects, measures of residential dissatisfaction helped predict travel dissatisfaction.

What effect does the affective quality of our travel experience have on our subsequent behavior? One effect has already been implied—the affective quality of the mode or route may be a factor in whether or not we use that mode or route again. In the case of the automobile, the rewards of driving per se may even outweigh other factors such as cost, leading to automobile addiction (Reser, 1980). On the other hand, in a survey of public transportation users, Taylor and Pocock (1974) found a positive correlation between the number of stages in the daily commute to work and the frequency of absence from work.

8.2.4. Moment Before Arrival

In the next section, P will arrive at the destination, but before discussing that, we would like to emphasize that a person does not enter a situation a blank slate. We have already mentioned the plan and individual personality and attitudinal characteristics. In this section, we mention several additional factors that influence a person's response to a place and that reside in the person prior to the encounter with the place.

Prior Mood
The best prediction of a person's mood in a particular place may be prior mood (Diener & Larsen, 1984; Epstein, 1979). The more important possibility about prior mood is that it may influence the affective appraisal of the present place. Gifford (1980) showed that persons in a more pleasant prior mood rated settings as more pleasant. Sherrod, Armstrong, Hewitt, Madonia, Speno, and Teruya (1977) showed that prior mood induced in one setting also influenced behavior observed in the next setting entered.

Adaptation Level
Responses to any aspect of the surrounding environment depend not on that environment alone, but on the person's history of encounters with other environments. Rather than fixed, the human standard of judgment is relative to the range and distribution of prior encounters (Helson, 1964; Parducci, 1968). Wohlwill (1974) has forcefully argued the relevance of the concept of adaptation level to the concerns of environmental psychologists. For example, Wohlwill and Kohn (1973) showed that persons' (affectively charged) judgments about their current city are relative to their background: Migrants from rural areas

judged their city as noisier and more polluted than did migrants from urban areas. Sonnenfeld (1969) similarly showed that the scenes people find beautiful depend on the sorts of scenes they typically encounter in their everyday life. According to a recent proposal (Russell & Lanius, 1984), it is possible to specify precisely how the affective quality of one place will influence the affective appraisal of the next place encountered: Combining the concept of adaptation level with the Russell-Pratt measure of affective appraisal predicts the amount and direction by which the affective appraisal of the next place will be shifted in the space of Figure 8.2.

Adaptation refers not to a single mechanism—the mechanisms underlying adaptation range from neurochemical depletion to cognitive reinterpretation—but to a function whereby the almost limitless variety of environmental inputs is processed in an efficient manner. As such, adaptation occurs for every aspect of the environment from chemicals we breathe to the aesthetic quality of the entire setting (Helson, 1964).

Expectations
Expectations also play a role in how elements of a place are affectively appraised. Indeed, expectations alter mood even before the expected event is encountered (Baum & Greenberg, 1975). You feel bad when expecting something bad to happen. Investigators have shown that expectations exert powerful effects on a person's reaction to a place (Langer & Saegert, 1977). Violation of expectation even provides a plausible alternative explanation for some of the standard findings in environmental psychology. For example, Klein and Harris (1979) showed that poor performance on a task apparently produced by crowding was actually due to the unexpectedness of the crowding. An unexpected event produces arousal (Berlyne, Craw, Salapatek, & Lewis, 1963), and it may be the arousal, rather than anything about the specific nature of the event that changes behavior.

Leff and Gordon (1980) have studied cognitive sets, which are organized plans to process environmental information in a certain way. A cognitive set involves certain expectations and has been shown to influence how a place is perceived, how much it is liked, and how it is responded to. Roles in society, functional orientation, higher-level plans, and personal attitudes probably create natural variation in the cognitive set with which different individuals approach the same place, but Leff and Gordon (1980) have shown that cognitive sets can also be taught.

8.3. STEP 2: EFFECTS OF THE ENVIRONMENT

We may be affected in an emotional way by almost any aspect of the physical environment—from chemicals we breathe to its symbolic meaning. The person affected may be aware of some of these influences but more often is not. Indeed, as will be seen, mood is influenced by aspects of the environment of which we are incapable of being aware. That emotion attaches to so many aspects of the environment may be helpful in explaining the complexity of our relationship to the environment, although it is anything but a help to the reviewer.

In this section, we seek to illustrate the types of relationships established between emotion and various features of environments. We have grouped together studies roughly according to the type of environmental variable involved. There is no agreed-on taxonomy of environments nor catalog of relevant environmental variables. And perhaps no simple description of environments is possible. Our grouping is therefore merely a temporary convenience to illustrate the sorts of research carried out.

8.3.1. The Imperceptible

In 1936, Winslow and Herrington exposed a group of workers to the odor of burnt dust. Anyone entering the work room in the middle of the experiment would have noticed the strong odor, but it was introduced gradually enough that the workers were never aware of its presence. The odor nonetheless resulted in a decline in the workers' appetite, as evidenced by a decline in the amount of food they ate. This incident is noteworthy for the possibility it raises of psychological change in the *absence* of conscious experience of its cause. There are other indications as well.

The world as described to us by physicists is full of events beyond our powers to detect. We now know that visible light is only a small part of the electromagnetic spectrum. There are gases and chemical compounds that have no properties directly perceptible to humans. There is no a priori reason to believe we must be aware of something for it to have an effect on our physiological or psychological state. For example, although radioactive substances can cause severe biological damage (Grosch & Hopwood, 1979), part of their danger lies in our inability to detect radioactivity without special instruments. Similarly, although in large enough doses carbon monoxide causes brain damage and death (Shepard,

1983), the human species never evolved the ability to detect carbon monoxide. It is perhaps not so well known that smaller doses of carbon monoxide result in feelings of exhaustion (Goldsmith, 1970) and "vague generalized weakness, fatigue, lassitude, and drowsiness" (Schulte, 1963, p. 524). Even for chemicals that are detectable, the mood-altering property may not be. For example, nitrous oxide has a distinctive odor, but its odor is not responsible for its common name "laughing gas" (Smith, 1982).

Exposure to various imperceptible chemicals may change mood. For example, the symptoms of mercury poisoning include clinical depression and lability of mood (Buckell, Hunter, Milton, & Perry, 1946; Gerstner & Huff, 1977). In a review of environmental pollutants, Anderson (1982) reported that other chemicals have effects on mood: Chemicals associated with unpleasant mood (reported nervousness, anxiety, depression, or irritability) include polybrominated biphenyls, lead, kepone, and carbon tetrachloride. Similarly, certain pesticides can alter mood (Gershon & Shaw, 1961; Levin, Rodnitzky, & Mick, 1976). For example, Levin and associates (1976) compared commercial pesticide sprayers and recently exposed farmers to a control group on the Taylor Manifest Anxiety Scale, the Beck Depression Inventory, and cholinesterase levels. They found that commercial sprayers, although not the exposed farmers, showed higher levels of anxiety and lower levels of cholinesterase. On the other hand, Rodnitzky, Levin, and Morgan (1978) fed volunteers small doses of insecticides for several days and found no changes in anxiety or depression on the same scales, perhaps because these scales were designed to measure long-term emotional dispositions. The research on the mood-altering effects of chemicals is not extensive, and conclusions are difficult to draw. The importance of the topic, however, suggests that the few clues we have should be followed up.

Infrasound (sound waves in frequencies below the normal range of human hearing) may also cause psychological change. For example, much of the sound energy produced by an automobile traveling a freeway is in the infrasonic region (Tempest & Bryan, 1972). When these levels of infrasonic stimulation (2 to 10 Hz at 130 to 146 dB) were reproduced in the laboratory for 60-sec periods, they were found to have both physiological and psychological effects (Evans & Tempest, 1972). Physiological measurements were on vertical eye movements, and psychological measurements included visual acuity and recognition reaction time. Eye movement measurements showed that the majority of subjects suffered vertical nystagmus, indicating that infrasound may affect balance. There were no effects of infrasound on visual acuity, but reaction time increased 30 to 40%. Subjects incidentally reported feeling lethargic and euphoric, something similar to being slightly drunk. (The reaction time changes were also similar to those produced by alcohol [Moskowitz, 1971; Evans, 1976].) On the other hand, Harris and Johnson (1978) found no effect of infrasound (7 Hz at up to 142 dB) on such cognitive tasks as serial search or counting.

Visible light is only a small part of the spectrum of electromagnetic radiation; most frequencies of radiation are not visible. Human beings can be exposed to increases in invisible radiation from, for example, fluorescent lighting fixtures or television, or to decreases through the blocking of part of the spectrum by windows or sunglasses. Is it possible that radiation outside the visible region of the spectrum such as ultraviolet or infrared radiation affects mood? Ott (1968, 1976) is convinced that it does. Ott suggested that such radiation affects the endocrine system and offers anecdotal evidence that it alters the activity level of children and caged animals. So the answer to the question is: Yes, it is *possible* that invisible radiation affects mood, although the idea has not been adequately tested.

Another imperceptible aspect of the environment that has been the subject of increasing, though controversial, research is the concentration of small ions (positively and negatively charged particles) in the air. Some believe that a high concentration of negative ions produces feelings of energy and pleasure (in our terms, excitement), whereas a high concentration of positive ions produces feelings of displeasure. Research is still inconclusive, with some evidence indicating that ions do have the predicted effect on self-reported mood (Charry & Hawkinshire, 1981; Hawkins, 1981; McGurk, 1959; Sigel, 1978; Sulman, 1980; Tom, Poole, Galla, & Berrier, 1981), but with other studies showing no measurable effect (Albrechtsen, Clausen, Christensen, Jensen, & Moeller, 1978; Chiles, Cleveland, & Fox, 1960). The problem may be in the way that mood is measured, because ion concentration is known to affect the level of serotonin in the bloodstream (Gilbert, 1973; Krueger, Andriese, & Kotaka, 1963, 1966, 1968; Krueger & Kotaka, 1969; Sulman, 1980) and serotonin is known to be involved in mood and emotion. A further problem is that ion concentration is often confounded with other physical or chemical components of the air (First, 1980).

In the research reviewed in this section, the dependent variable was almost always mood, and only occasionally another component of an emotional episode such as physiological activation or behavior. Cumulatively, the evidence indicates that a person's mood can be influenced by factors he or she cannot detect.

8.3.2. Sensory Experiences

Everyone knows that our sensory experiences are affectively charged. Everyone, that is, who has tasted good food, smelled a flower, heard a dissonant note, or lived through a hot, humid July day in New York. If evidence be required, Mehrabian and Russell (1974) summarized much of the research available to that time on pleasantness and arousing quality ratings of sound, temperature, color, or other single sensory dimensions. Sensory dimensions are consistently appraised as mood altering, although this does not necessarily guarantee that they are in fact mood altering. Slowly but steadily, evidence is accumulating on such topics as the actual comfortableness of different temperatures (Beshir & Ramsey, 1981; Hawkins, 1981; Rohles, 1981) and the actual mood-altering effects of noise (Standing & Stace, 1980; Tarnopolsky, Watkins, & Hand, 1980). But the exact relationship between appraised quality and actual mood-altering quality remains to be worked out. We shall illustrate research on sensory experiences by discussing the impact of light.

Cunningham (1979) offered evidence from several studies that sunlight improves mood, as indexed by willingness to help a stranger, the generosity of tips left a waitress, and self-ratings of mood. Thorington (1975) raised the possibility that artificial light, which differs from sunlight in its spectral distribution, may be a negative influence on mood. And, indeed, people prefer natural light to artificial light (Boyce, 1975). Hellman (1982) reported psychiatric cases in which lack of natural sunlight was thought to be a factor in depression, jet lag, and sleep disorders. Ott (1973) theorized that light affects the endocrine system (Wortman, Axelrod, & Fischer, 1964) and noted that amount and type of light appear to influence bird migration, egg production on poultry farms, and mating patterns and preference for alcohol in rodents. Ott (1973) helped to develop a flourescent bulb that closely approximates the distribution of wavelengths in natural sunlight, and Benfield (1973) reported that

Some remarkable testimonials have come from many industrial plants that have since installed this new lighting such as substantial reductions in absenteeism and accident rates and marked increases in production. (p. ix)

Further support for the notion that the spectral distribution of light has psychological impact can be seen in the evidence of a consistency in the affective appraisal of colors. People tend to prefer "cool" colors (blues and greens) over "warm" (reds and yellows) colors (McManus, Jones, & Cottrell, 1981). This preference was obtained cross-culturally (Adams & Osgood, 1973) and, using a behavioral measure of preference, in monkeys (Humphrey, 1972; Sahgal, Pratt, & Iverson, 1975) and pigeons (Sahgal & Iverson, 1975). Consistency has also been found in the rated arousing quality of different colors. People rate long-wavelength colors as more arousing than shorter-wavelength colors (Walters, Apter, & Sveback, 1982). These ratings may be correct in the sense that wavelength also correlates with magnitude of the galvanic skin response (GSR) to light: Both red (Wilson, 1966) and violet light (Nourse & Welch, 1971) produced greater GSR than did green.

Some people believe that a shade of hot pink can quell anger. A U.S. naval correctional center, the Santa Clara County jail, and the San Bernardino County youth center have painted their cells hot pink, and some clinicians have used pink to tranquilize their patients (Schauss, 1979). We could find no experimental evidence testing this idea, but it does raise an interesting issue: It we assume that hot pink would be appraised as arousing rather than calming, and if hot pink is actually calming, then the mood-altering effect of a color may differ from the way it is affectively appraised.

8.3.3. Collative Properties

Perhaps the only place you are likely to encounter a pure color or a pure tone is in a laboratory. Few would want to count the number of different sensory features in even the plainest of modern buildings. Moreover, our emotional response depends, at least in part, on how these features are mixed together and how they vary over time. In other words, it depends on such things as the novelty, complexity, incongruity, dissonance, surprisingness, and unpredictability of the particular combination of features. Berlyne (1974) introduced the term *collative properties* of a stimulus array to provide a systematic account of concepts such as these. Collative properties cannot be defined by a single sensory dimension nor by cognitive meaning (what Berlyne called *semantic content*). Instead, collative properties refer to com-

parisons: the relations among sensory features or changes over time in sensory features.

Berlyne believed that the essential quality of any collative variable could be described by the amount of information provided by the stimulus array. Many pieces of information are needed to represent a complex stimulus and just a few for a simple stimulus. A novel stimulus must be represented in its entirety, item by item. But once it becomes familiar, the stimulus can be represented simply by noting that it recurred. This idea led to the use of formal information theory (Attneave, 1959; Cherry, 1966; Garner, 1962) in the description of a stimulus array. Information theory allows us to subsume complexity, novelty, and the like within a single dimension. As Attneave (1959) summarizes:

Perhaps the most fundamental concept of information theory is that of a continuum extending from extreme lawfulness, or redundancy, or regularity on the one hand, to extreme disorder, or unpredictability, or uncertainty on the other. One end of this continuum is homogeneity, the other chaos. (p. 503)

One line of research generated by Berlyne's (1974) ideas attempted to create stimuli with precisely specified amounts of information—such as randomly generated polygons or sequences of tones. Two of the many experiments done may suffice to illustrate this approach. Berlyne (1974, chapter 5) constructed abstract visual patterns, or geometric designs, that varied systematically in amount of information. Subjects rated each display on a series of verbal scales. Factor analyses of these ratings yielded two factors: Hedonic Tone (with high loadings on displeasing–pleasing) and Uncertainty/Arousal (with high loadings on relaxed–tense). In the present terms, the dependent variable was affective appraisal; and pleasantness and arousing quality, respectively, were the principal factors found. Berlyne found that rated arousing quality was a direct linear function of the prespecified amount of information in the stimulus. Pleasantness, on the other hand, bore no simple relationship to amount of information. When pleasantness was plotted as a function of amount of information, the resulting curve was "multimodal," which means that it looked like the top of a mountain range. As a first approximation, however, the curve could be described as an inverted *U*.

Crozier's (1974) study of melody illustrates this same approach applied to temporal variation. Crozier (1974) constructed melodies that contained precisely defined amounts of information per unit of time by, for example, varying the number of alternative tone frequencies from which the melody was constructed. Responses followed Berlyne's predictions quite well. Rated arousing quality (e.g., "interesting") was largely determined by amount of information. Rated pleasing quality ("beauty" and "pleasing") followed a weaker, inverted-U-shaped curve.

Whether all collative properties can be handled in this way remains to be seen. Some such as complexity seem to lend themselves to objective specification, although this may be an illusion if different subjects code the same stimulus array differently. Others such as novelty are inherently relative to the observer. In one sense, most events are novel—any new tree or new person is literally novel. But some seem more novel than others. Not only are there degrees of novelty, there are types of novelty. Novelty of the individual thing or event, novelty of this type of thing, and novelty of an even more superordinate class—never encountered anything like this before. Subjective ratings may take such distinctions into account, but information theory, as so far proposed, does not. It is also uncertain whether or not all collative variables are related to emotional responses in the same way. Berlyne's attempt to subsume them within information theory assumes they are, but the correctness of the assumption remains to be demonstrated.

A second line of research is simpler and more directly relevant to environmental psychology: the attempt to assess the collative properties of actual places or preexisting stimulus arrays. In this approach, it is no longer possible to measure the amount of information precisely, but averaged verbal ratings of novelty or complexity or the like have proved a useful alternative (Mehrabian & Russell, 1974; Wohlwill, 1974).

Complexity

Wohlwill has carefully examined the literature relevant to the rated *complexity* of physical environments. Wohlwill (1976) concluded: "To sum up, it is apparent that complexity, however much it might be touted by aestheticians as well as designers, plays an uncertain role at best in the individual's aesthetic response to the environment" (p. 50). Our reading of the literature agrees with Wohlwill—provided the dependent variable is taken to be pleasantness. Pleasantness bears no strong, general, and reliable relationship to rated complexity. In several cases, a positive linear relationship was found for pleasantness (or preference) as a function of complexity (Kaplan, Kaplan, & Wendt, 1972; Wohlwill, 1976). More often, the re-

lationship is an inverted U: Pleasantness occurs at intermediate degrees of complexity; unpleasantness occurs at the extremes, high or low. There are many studies that support this hypothesis (Crozier, 1974; Wohlwill, 1968, 1975), but others do not. Moreover, even when it is obtained, the inverted-U-shaped curve is often only a rough approximation of the actual relationship. One example is a study by Wohlwill (1968).

Wohlwill (1968) attempted to replicate the inverted U between preference and complexity with photographs of real places. The result was the inverted U, but a highly irregular one. Moreover, Kaplan, Kaplan, and Wendt (1972) suggested that Wohlwill's result could be accounted for more simply as a preference for natural over man-made places. In reply, Wohlwill (1976) repeated the study separately for man-made and natural scenes. He found that the inverted-U function did obtain, although only among man-made scenes. Among natural scenes, liking increased approximately linearly with complexity.

When the dependent variable is judged arousing quality of the stimulus, a very different conclusion is warranted: Arousing quality bears a strong, linearly increasing relationship to rated complexity. This correlation was found repeatedly by Berlyne and replicated by others (e.g., Mehrabian & Russell, 1974). Berlyne further hypothesized that amount of time spent looking at a stimulus (an index of what he called *specific exploration*) is proportional to arousing quality and hence to complexity. This hypothesis was also supported in a number of studies (Wohlwill, 1968,1975). The arousal–complexity relationship has recieved less attention and emphasis than it merits, perhaps because it is not concerned with pleasantness.

Novelty–Familiarity

Temporal variation underlies such concepts as novelty, surprisingness, uniqueness, and familiarity. Wohlwill (1976) reviewed studies on ratings of such variables. Although Berlyne's theory predicts a pattern of results similar to that for complexity, actual results were highly idiosyncratic: "In light of the available data, one is impelled to withhold judgment about the actual role of the novelty variable in aesthetic evaluation of environments" (p. 52).

Specific English words rarely tap only one dimension of meaning. Thus the specific word used to rate the stimulus environment turns out to be important to the result. For example, *novel* seems to have a pleasant connotation (Mehrabian & Russell, 1974). At the same time, rated *familiarity*, which in an objective sense might be expected to be the opposite of novelty, also has positive connotation—thus familiar environments are also rated as more pleasant (Herzog, Kaplan, & Kaplan, 1976; Pedersen, 1978; Sonnenfeld, 1967). Ratings of *unique* showed a similar story in two studies, one a study of building exteriors (Canter, 1969) and the other a study of landscapes (Calvin, Dearinger, & Curtin, 1972). Uniqueness was highly correlated with positive evaluation, possibly because its opposite in both these studies was defined as *commonplace*, an unflattering descriptor.

Information Rate

Mehrabian and Russell (1974) attempted to combine the advantages of verbal ratings with the theoretical simplicity of information theory. They developed a verbal questionnaire of a single dimension, termed *information rate*, that subsumes novelty, complexity, and other collative properties of environments. In several studies, values on this scale were found to be uncorrelated with the rated pleasantness of environments but positively correlated with their arousing quality (Mehrabian & Russell, 1974; Ward & Russell, 1981).

Mere Exposure

The minimal case of temporal variation is simple repetition of a stimulus. Zajonc (1968) offered evidence that repeated exposure to a stimulus increases its pleasantness. If so, what has come to be called the *mere exposure effect*—the more you see something the more you like it—would be an important mechanism in determining the affective appraisal of places. For example, it provides a ready explanation for the preference for more familiar stimuli. Available evidence indicates that the mere exposure effect is a reliable phenomenon, but that its occurrence depends on many factors. The following review relies largely on Stang's (1974) analysis of the literature.

Occurrence of the mere exposure effect seems to depend on methodological details. There must be a delay between the exposures to the stimulus and the rating of liking (e.g., Harrison & Crandall, 1972). Without such a delay, the situation becomes more complicated, such that liking depends on the time between exposures: Distributed exposures produce no effect at all; and massed exposures produce an inverted-U-shaped curve (rather than the expected linear curve) of liking as a function of number of exposures.

More important, occurrence of the mere exposure effect seems to depend on the type of stimulus one is exposed to. Two important qualifications exist.

First, Brickman, Redfield, Harrison, and Crandall (1972) showed that, although exposure does enhance liking for initially pleasant or even neutral stimuli, exposure has the opposite effect on initially disliked stimuli: The more one is exposed to an unpleasant stimulus the *less* one likes it. (This result was replicated by Mandler & Shebo, 1981.) Second, the mere exposure effect may be more likely to occur for more complex and meaningful stimuli than for simple abstract patterns. For example, no mere exposure effect occurred in a study of geometric patterns (Cantor, 1968), whereas it did occur in studies of music (Heingartner & Hall, 1974) and of human faces (Mita, Dermer, & Knight, 1977). Hypothesizing that the main difference here was amount of complexity, Smith and Dorfman (1975) showed subjects visual patterns at one of three levels of complexity. As predicted, the mere exposure effect only occurred for the most complex patterns.

There is also a question whether the mere exposure effect constitutes a separate phenomenon or whether it can be explained as a special case of something else. Stang (1974) argued that the mere exposure effect could be an artifact resulting from subjects' guessing the experimental hypothesis. This explanation is unlikely in light of the extensive evidence that the mere exposure effect occurs with nonhuman subjects (Hill, 1978). Using choice or approach–avoidance as the dependent variable, researchers found increased preference for light after exposure to light with rats and monkeys, increased liking for a particular food among rats raised exclusively on that food, increased preference for saccharin with exposure to it, increased preference for double gravity in rats raised in a centrifuge, and increased preference for Mozart over other music in rats raised listening to Mozart.

Another explanation for the mere exposure effect points to some determining factor in the context. Suedfeld, Epstein, Buchanan, and Landon (1971) argued that the exposure effect depends on a favorable set induced by the experimental instructions. To demonstrate this point, they replicated one of Zajonc's studies, giving half the subjects Zajonc's original instructions to rate how *good* they found the stimuli. These subjects showed the mere exposure effect. The other half of the subjects were given an unfavorable set by being asked to rate how *bad* they found the stimuli. For these subjects, frequency of exposure enhanced liking only up to about 5 exposures; after that, liking declined with further exposures until the exposure effect disappeared at 25 exposures.

With a similar idea in mind, Burgess and Sales (1971) offered evidence that the enhancing effect of mere exposure is limited to those subjects who like the experimental context. For such subjects, exposure to a stimulus would therefore be a pairing of that stimulus with a positive stimulus (the liked context) and hence a classical conditioning effect. But Saegert, Swap, and Zajonc (1973) showed that the mere exposure effect can be replicated in the absence of a liked experimental context. A possibility on which no data are available is that the mere exposure effect is limited to subjects in a pleasant mood. On the assumption that in the typical experiment more subjects are in a positive than a negative mood, exposure would again be a pairing with a positive experience.

There is also reason to speculate that the mere exposure effect may be two different effects—one effect resulting from the first few exposures and another effect from subsequent exposures. Zajonc (1968) reports a linear increase in liking with the *log* of number of exposures. Put more simply, liking increases rapidly with the first few exposures and then builds more slowly thereafter. The first phase also seems to be the more reliable finding. Recall that Suedfeld and colleagues (1971) replicated the exposure effect up to five exposures even with subjects given a negative set. It was the second phase that was not replicated and, indeed, reversed when set was negative. Recall also that, if there is no delay between exposure and rating, massed exposures produce the same inverted-U-shaped curve—which is to say, the exposure effect again occurs only for the first several exposures but is then reversed.

Perhaps the first five exposures serve to consolidate a cognitive representation of the stimulus (which may be aided by a delay between exposure and rating and by massed as opposed to distributed exposures). Or the first five exposures may dissipate a sense of strangeness and wariness. In the typical study, the subject is confronted with a series of novel stimuli: The human faces are of strangers; the polygons are unfamiliar. After several exposures, the stimulus may come to be recognized as one seen before and may seem more familiar and less strange. Thus wariness with the strange and unfamiliar declines and then disappears. Further contact does not further dissipate wariness, but allows a variety of other psychological processes to take place. According to Suedfeld and colleagues (1971), during this second phase, if subjects look for pleasant aspects of the stimulus, the more exposures they have, the more pleasant aspects they find. If they look for unpleasant aspects,

again the more exposures, the more they find that is unpleasant. If so, it would not be surprising that complex stimuli allow a larger exposure effect.

8.3.4. Meaning

When we open our eyes on our physical world, we are typically not confronted with an assortment of sensations. What we see is not a spot of red surrounded by brown, but an apple on a table. Put another way, the places and objects of our physical world are meaningful. They are interpreted as a home, a tree, a street, and a cat (or rather a cat in the old tree in the Jones' home on my street) all located in a familiar three-dimensional world. Appleyard (1979) pointed out the key role played by meaning in a person's affective appraisal:

> A street in Barnsbury, London, was "improved": trees were planted, the sidewalks widened, benches installed, and traffic reduced. In subsequent interviews the residents maintained that conditions were worse than before. Why? They were working-class people in a neighborhood that was being "gentrified." Middle-class groups were moving in, and the older residents saw the improvements as symbols of the "Chelseaization" of Barnsbury. San Franciscans in like manner have fought the "Manhattanization" of San Francisco. However well they were designed, the new highrise buildings were labeled as symbolic imports from the outside. This is a recurrent theme in environmental conflicts.
>
> Social meaning also confounds research in environmental perception. Everyone knows that ocean waves breaking on a beach can have the same decibel count and even the same sound as heavy traffic, yet our perceptions of the ocean and the traffic are strikingly different because one is natural, the other man-caused. So it is that the noise, dirt, odors, buildings, signs, and traffic produced by "us" are viewed with far more tolerance than the same effects produced by "them." (p. 143)

Csikszentmihalyi and Rochberg-Halton (1981) carried out extensive and fascinating interviews with 351 residents of Chicago on "the meaning of things," the residents' own things in their own homes. The interviews revealed one recurring theme: Meaningful objects were tied to emotional feelings. We would like to recount several of the examples.

Objects that evoke memories evoke especially strong reactions. One interview is described in which a woman "broke down and started to cry" (p. 67) when asked what it would be like not to have a particular photograph of her brother. In another scene, a man was brought to tears by a 50-year-old snapshot of himself and his two brothers.

Rooms can be special. A 15-year-old girl was asked where in her home she felt "most at home." Her reply: "In my room. It has all the needs I want in there, except for food and I go to the kitchen for that. All the needs; if I'm scared or something, I go to my room and sit on my bed" (p. 135).

And of course the home itself is an object of emotion. Many residents express pride in their home and refer to it as comfortable, cozy, or relaxing. One 8-year-old is quoted: "It's big, roomy, comfortable, greenish brown on the outside. It has four floors, eleven rooms, lots of toys; it's beautiful and it has high ceilings. There's one cat, lots of posters, pictures, plants, and closets. It's happy and free" (p. 130).

Before we can have a general understanding of the link between emotion and meaning, we need to characterize meaning a little further. Part of an object's meaning is the category we place it in. According to Rosch's (1977) theory, the categories of everyday objects are arranged in a hierarchy of inclusion. There is a basic level that we label first and most easily: chair, truck, apple. Each object can also be categorized at a more general, inclusive, or "superordinate" level: furniture, vehicle, fruit. An object can often also be categorized at a more subordinate level: living room chair, postal delivery truck, and Jonathan apple.

In contrast to these three levels of classes of objects stands the level of the single object: my own living room chair, the postal delivery truck my neighbor drove home in last night, the apple I had in my lunch box. Let us refer to this last level as the level of *tokens*, and the first three as levels of *types*. We can think of these as four levels of a conceptual hierarchy such that the higher level includes all things at the lower level. To attribute meaning to a real world object then is to categorize it within this mental hierarchy. Categorization into the top three levels is called *categorization*; categorization into the bottom level is called *recognition*. *P*'s emotional response to an object depends on the level in the hierarchy in which he or she categorizes it. To love one's home is not the same as to love houses or buildings; and to love one's neighbor is not the same as to love the Joneses next door.

We seem to develop emotional feelings about specific places, the tokens. This was illustrated by the Csikszentmihalyi and Rochberg-Halton (1981) interviews. Fried (1963) found people strongly attached to their own neighborhood. Johnson and Burdge (1975) found that the economic value of one's own community was far short of its total value, suggesting that emotional ties play a role in decision making. Just how to characterize these ties, or their nature, remains unknown.

Jacobi and Stokols (1983) have further clarified the meaning of particular places by describing their *tradition*. Tradition summarizes three aspects of the historical association of a place. First, a place can be associated with historical events, traditional rituals, and meaningful actions. Second, a place can be associated with an identifiable group, culture, family, or organization. Third, a place may serve as a symbol for values, ideas, ideologies, beliefs, and so on. Tradition is not a physical property of a place but is rather in the mind of the beholder. Groups often share and pass on the traditions of a place. Still, tradition can be faked, as when artifacts are used to create the false impression of age. Tradition is strongly linked to emotion: The place evokes the feelings associated with the historical events, the reference group, or the idea symbolized by the place. Jacobi and Stokols (1983) give this example:

> The affective significance of the [Wailing Wall in the Old City of Jerusalem] is evident in the emotional reactions of visitors who often kiss and caringly touch the ancient stones. A vivid demonstration of the importance of the Wall occurred immediately after the June 1976 Six Day War when thousands of Israelis visited to Old City to commemorate the return of the Wailing Wall to Israeli sovereignty. (p. 164)

Do we have emotional ties at the more abstract levels, at the level of types? One concept is often found to be especially salient for categorizing physical scenes: man-made versus natural (Kaplan, Kaplan, & Wendt, 1972; Ward, 1977). In a series of studies, S. and R. Kaplan showed that people consistently prefer natural scenes over man-made scenes (e.g., R. Kaplan, 1982; Kaplan, Kaplan, & Wendt, 1972)—a result confirmed by others (Ulrich, 1983; Wohlwill, 1976). This preference, in turn, may be accounted for primarily by preference for two natural categories: water and trees. R. Kaplan (1982) found that the sight of trees, for example, improved residents' satisfaction with their entire neighborhood. She pointed out that indirect evidence supports this view:

> The encounter with the forest can serve a therapeutic need (Gibson, 1979); it is a source of emotional satisfaction. Gradually, an empirical literature is developing to substantiate the psychological benefits of the wilderness experience (S. Kaplan & Talbot, 1983) (p. 7).... The cognitive satisfaction the forest

provides is of major importance. It is difficult to fit into a rational analysis of human decisions. The often expressed frustration that the small woodlot owner is not economically oriented provides a persisting example. As Miller indicates, many of these people express little interest in the monetary gain they could reap from their land. (p. 11)

Another set of cognitive mechanisms are general dimensions along which objects (from many categories) may vary. Examples of such dimensions would be the frequently studied variables of perceived control and predictability. The degree of control we experience over the objects and places in our world may be a factor in how we appraise them. For example, the sensation arising from noise is not the only determinant of how we feel about the noise. Burger and Arkin (1980) showed that subjects became more depressed when exposed to blasts of 90-dB noise— but only when the noise was both uncontrollable and unpredictable. And Brown and Inouye (1978) showed that it is the belief in rather than the actual fact of control that is the critical variable.

8.3.5. Persons and Space

The physical presence of another person is a salient part of any environment. For example, the mere physical presence of another person increases arousal. This assertion stems from research on the social facilitation effect (Zajonc, 1965). In fact, the mere belief in the mere physical presence of another person increases arousal. When there is more than one other person, another increment in arousal may be obtained. Thus the number of others is positively correlated with arousal. As a possible consequence, the greater the population of a community, the greater the speed at which its citizens walk.

Moreover, the closer another person is, the more arousing he or she is (Middlemist, Knowles, & Matter, 1976). Closer interpersonal distances can stem from lack of space, a condition now called *spatial density*. Evans (1978) observed that the evidence on spatial density is consistent with the idea that greater spatial density is arousing, and that arousal can account for the observed behavioral effects attributed to spatial density. Worchel and Teddlee (1976) pointed out that in most studies, as well as in everyday life, spatial density is confounded with interpersonal distance. They separated the two variables by varying room size and the distance between chairs independently. Most behavioral effects obtained were due to distance between chairs rather than room size, a result suggesting that effects previously attri-

buted to spatial density may actually be attributable to interpersonal distance.

It should be obvious that variables such as presence of, number of, or physical distance to other persons cannot determine how pleasant an encounter with those other persons will be. This depends on who the other persons are. Consistent with this assertion is the finding that density and interpersonal closeness are neither positive nor negative per se, although they do serve to intensify either prosocial or antisocial behaviors already present (Baron, 1978; Freedman, 1975; Storms & Thomas, 1977). Nevertheless, much research has been devoted to the proposition that the presence of another person at a close distance is a personal disaster: the invasion of one's personal space. Without emphasizing the fact, research in this vein has typically employed as the invader someone who is a stranger and who is violating a social norm such as not asking permission before taking the adjacent seat. With such an unpleasant intruder, closeness is typically both arousing and unpleasant (which, according to Figure 8.1, constitute the key ingredients in stress, anger, fear, and similar states); the result is occasionally flight or, more rarely, fight. However, with the right person and the right circumstances, "invasion" of personal space might be pleasant.

Some investigators have turned from objectively definable conditions (such as density) to the person's perception of those conditions (termed *crowding* in the case of density). The distinction between social density (an increase in density produced by an increase in the number of persons) and spatial density (an increase in density produced by a decrement in available space) suggests a psychological counterpart: social crowding versus spatial crowding. The difference is whether the crowded person perceives the crowding as due to too many people or as due to too little space. We can anticipate subtly different emotional reactions in these two cases. Imagine two people at a crowded public park. One person believes there are too many people and becomes angry at the public, or at new arrivals. The other believes there is too little space and perhaps becomes sad at the loss of open space.

8.3.6. Blocking or Facilitating the Plan

From our point of view, the single most important thing that a person brings to an encounter with the environment is the plan. Presumably the place was chosen to maximize success of the plan, and presumably the place will be viewed positively if it does so.

If the place hinders the plan, it will be viewed negatively. Indeed, the single most important environmental variable affecting mood and affective appraisal may be the environment's ability to fulfill the goal.

The extensive research on crowding and density illustrates this idea. Despite experimenters' predictions of negative effects due to density, research demonstrated that smaller spaces did not necessarily lead to negative consequences (Freedman, 1975). The question then became: When does density matter? (Cohen & Sherrod, 1978). One answer was that density mattered when it interfered with a person's plans (Baum & Valins, 1979; Saegert, 1980), especially when the person lacked other resources with which to compensate. In our terms, whether a person finds a crowded environment pleasant or unpleasant depends on the plan with which he or she entered the environment.

The physical environment can hinder our plans in many ways, with results ranging from slight deviations in the sequence of activities to large-scale disasters. What are the emotional consequences of having to alter or give up a plan? Miller and colleagues (1960) observed that "the more or less sudden realization that an enduring plan must be changed at a strategic level is accompanied by a great deal of emotional excitation" (p. 116).

Mandler has further developed this idea. Mandler (1984) theorized that interruptions, be they of actions, thoughts, or plans, can create an emotional episode by altering our physiological arousal level. "Interruption is a sufficient and perhaps necessary condition for the occurrence of autonomic arousal" (p. 171). According to Mandler's theory, an emotional episode occurs when the arousal combines with an *evaluative cognition*. There are many sources of *evaluative cognition*, but the most important one is the ease of coping with the interruption. Interruptions do not necessarily cause negative emotional episodes. Many interruptions are negative, but not all: Increasing physiological arousal in the presence of a positive evaluative cognition can result in a more *positive* emotional episode than would have occurred had there been no interruption. For example, because there is a delay in onset of autonomic arousal, slight interruptions that are quickly accommodated are likely to result in a positive emotional episode. However, if the interruption is so severe as to preclude formation of an accommodating plan, one would expect a negative episode.

Widespread negative emotional episodes do often follow public disasters such as earthquakes, tornadoes, and fires (Dohrenwend, 1974). Contrary to popular opinion, however, the immediate response to disasters such as fire need not be panic. Sime (1980) analyzed the response to fires and observed that the behaviors exhibited were not irrational. The primary responses to the perception of a fire are attempts to flee, to fight the fire, and to warn others (Wood, 1980). If the environment allows a quick and simple plan for these goals, people's behavior will be orderly rather than panicky. Tragedy occurs when, for example, authorities delay information (supposedly to keep people from panicking) until there is not enough time left to evacuate the building, or when the building lacks clearly visible exit routes resulting in time-consuming extraneous movement. These observations are congruent with Mandler's theory that it is interruption of a plan that precipitates an emotional episode.

Which emotional episode will result from arousal change? Weiner and his associates (e.g., 1982) have explored how the particular type of emotional episode experienced depends on the meaning of the total situation. P will experience guilt when he or she attributes failure to something he or she is responsible for. P will experience anger when he or she attributes failure to something another person is responsible for.

Parenthetically, Mandler also employs the link between interruption and emotional episode to help explain emotional attachment. Earlier we mentioned Fried's observation that people become emotionally attached to places. Fried inferred this attachment from observing their grief on the destruction of their neighborhood. The explanation suggested by Mandler is that destruction of a place results in continual interruption of those plans that involved the destroyed place. The greater the role played by a particular place in one's habitual plans, the greater the interruption and therefore grief on loss of that place.

8.4. STEP 3: ACTIVITY IN THE ENVIRONMENT AND THE EFFECTS OF MOOD

The fundamental fact of the last section was that an environment alters mood, even if the person fails to understand how. We described how a person P arrived at a place and affectively appraised it. P attempted to carry out the plan and was aided or blocked by the environment. P's mood was thereby altered, and occasionally an emotional episode began. In this next section, we review evidence indicating that this change in mood and emotional state will influence all the rest of what P does and thinks in that place. For example, once a person is in a place, the mood created may affect the length of time spent there: An unpleasant odor in a room has been shown to decrease the time spent in the room (Rotton, Barry, Frey, & Soler, 1978). But more often, P cannot choose to leave. Often, in conducting the business of our daily lives, we must expose ourselves to unpleasantly loud levels of noise, noxious odors, or overly crowded conditions. How does the mood created by the environment influence behavior of those who stay in the place?

8.4.1. Behavior

Creating a pleasant mood appears to increase the positive or prosocial quality of behavior. An unpleasant mood increases antisocial behavior. Research on unpleasant odors (Rotton et al., 1978; Rotton, Frey, Barry, Milligan, & Fitzpatrick, 1979), the pleasantness of an entire room (Gifford, 1980), cigarette smoke (Jones & Bogat, 1978), and noise (Donnerstein & Wilson, 1976; Green & O'Neal, 1969; Konecni, 1975) supports this general conclusion. Similarly, pleasantness of mood is associated with a greater desire to be with other people (Bell, 1978; Gouax & Gouax, 1971; Mehrabian & Russell, 1974; Tomkins, 1962). A person in a pleasant mood also treats himself or herself more positively (Moore, Underwood, & Rosenhan, 1973).

Bell and Baron's (1976) research on temperature and aggression suggested a more complex relationship between mood and antisocial behavior. Previous research had shown that heat sometimes increases aggressive behavior (Baron & Bell, 1975; Baron & Lawton, 1972), but not linearly: While moderately high temperatures increased aggression, extremely high temperatures seemed to inhibit aggression (Baron, 1972). Bell and Baron hypothesized that heat induces an unpleasant mood (negative affective state) and that aggression is curvilinearly related to pleasure–displeasure with the highest levels of aggression occurring during moderately unpleasant mood. To support the hypothesis of mood as the mediating factor, they showed that aggression was curvilinearly related to mood regardless of whether the mood was induced by high temperature or by bogus personal evaluations. Nevertheless, the possible confounding effects of arousal were not entirely ruled out. It is conceivable that aggression does increase monotonically with displeasure, but that extremely high temperature reduces aggression because it lowers arousal.

Amato (1981) carried out a study suggesting that the laboratory findings relating mood to prosocial behavior can be generalized to actual environments. Amato observed the amount of help offered a stranger before and after construction of a pedestrian mall in an Australian city. Before construction began to convert a city street into a pedestrian mall, Amato unobtrusively counted the number of people who helped an experimenter pick up several pencils dropped "accidentally." The same procedure was repeated after completion of the new mall, with a significant increase in the proportion of people who stopped to help. While it is not possible to determine exactly what about the mall increased helping, slides of the mall were rated as more pleasant than slides of the street before construction.

8.4.2. Affective Appraisal: The Razran Effect

Affective appraisal of a specific object is affected by mood—a phenomenon first demonstrated by Razran (1938, 1940) but now replicated many times. Increasing the pleasantness of mood by, for example, providing a free gift, food, drink, or pleasant surroundings increases the rated liking for the present environment (Gifford, 1980), acceptability of sociopolitical slogans (Razran, 1940), liking of unpopular messages (Janis, Kaye, & Kirschner, 1965), pleasantness of photographs of strangers (Maslow & Mintz, 1956; Razran, 1938), and attractiveness of consumer products (Isen, Shalker, Clark, & Karp, 1978). What are now needed, rather than further replications of the Razran effect, are studies of the effects of the arousal dimension of mood on affective appraisal.

8.4.3. Cognition

Research by Bower and his associates illustrates an interest in the influence of mood on cognition (see, e.g., Gilligan & Bower, 1984). In a series of experiments, they used hypnosis to induce one of various moods and then examined its effect on subjects' performance on a variety of tasks. They have now reported an impressive and consistent range of results. Persons in a happy mood have superior recall for material learned in a happy mood; are more likely to recall pleasant incidents, or facts about a happy character in a story; give free associations, compose TAT stories, and write personality sketches of familiar people that are pleasant in tone; interpret their own behavior in a more positive way; and are more likely to recall personally happy events and to overestimate their pleasantness. Just the opposite occurs for sad mood (Bower, 1981; Laird, Wagener, Halal, & Szegda, 1982; Snyder & White, 1982, Teasdale & Fogarty, 1979; Teasdale & Taylor, 1981). In many of the comparisons reported, however, level of pleasure may have been confounded with level of arousal. That is, a happy mood (high pleasure, moderately high arousal) was compared with a sad mood (low pleasure, low arousal). Nevertheless, there seems little doubt that mood plays a central role in many cognitive processes.

If the preceding sentence is true, and if the physical environment can alter mood, then it follows that the physical environment can influence (although indirectly) many cognitive processes. Let us illustrate this role by suggesting one hypothesis. Evidence has long been available that previously learned material is recalled better in the place where it was learned than elsewhere. Students taking a final exam in a room other than their regular classroom perform more poorly than students tested in the regular classroom (Abernathy, 1940). Deep-sea divers were asked to learn word lists either on a boat or under water; subsequent recall was best when the divers were tested in the environment where the material was learned (Godden & Baddeley, 1975). Our hypothesis is that at least part of this effect may be due to the effects of mood induced by the environment. Returning to the same environment reinstates that same mood, and it is the similarity of mood that accounts for the improvement in memory.

Gilligan and Bower (1984) proposed a network theory that unites and explains these various findings. They treat each type of mood as a discrete node in memory, with memory thought of as a network. Learned information is thus linked to the mood felt during learning, and reinstatement of that mood activates that information. Although their concept of an emotion node accounts for their findings, it would seem unable to distinguish having an emotion from thinking about an emotion. And, indeed, their methodology tends to confound these two. Thus the use of hypnosis to induce mood leaves open the question of whether moods induced by less obtrusive means, or naturally occurring moods, would have similar effects. The problem we have in mind is not the demand characteristics of hypnotic command, but the fact that subjects are forced by these procedures to be highly *aware* of their own mood. The question then is how much the effects attributed to mood might be due to thinking about the mood.

Isen, Means, Patrick, and Nowicki (1982) suggested that mood influences not only what information comes to mind but how that information is processed. They offered evidence to support the claim that a person in a happy mood avoids cognitive work. He or she is more likely to settle for a simple but adequate solution than to search harder for the optimal solution, or, more likely, to rely on a simple (but sometimes erroneous) heuristic strategy than to find a more complex (but correct) algorithm.

8.4.4. Planning

There is reason to believe that *P*'s current mood or emotional episode might influence the plans *P* makes—and thus future actions. Suppose that *P* is in an emotional episode. Whether afraid, angry, or surprised, *P* may quickly formulate a plan and attempt to carry it out. There may be prototypical plans associated with these three emotional episodes—flight, fight, and search, respectively—to which *P* may be predisposed. Still, these may not be the only or even most typical plans. Faced with, say, a frightening event, *P* will likely at least try to formulate a plan to suit the particular circumstances. Afraid of a bear, *P* might flee. Afraid of a spider, *P* might kill it. Afraid of missing a train, *P* might run toward the train. Afraid of a nuclear holocaust, *P* might read about and discuss the issue.

More often the influence of the place would be smaller and *P*'s state better described as a mood. The typical case would be *P*'s formulating a plan—like going to work, doing the shopping, or spending Sunday at home—that is not directly or obviously linked to *P*'s current mood. The mood might nevertheless provide a vague impetus or hindrance to certain broad classes of action: *P* may feel like being lazy, or like doing some work. Or perhaps moods may predispose toward certain intensities of action: An excited mood might favor vigorous action; a calm mood might favor more contemplative action.

Another way mood might affect the plans that *P* makes—either what to do or where to go—could take the form of mood-specific preferences. Lyman (1982) asked people what foods they preferred during various moods and found distinct differences.

A person's present mood may also affect the plans he or she makes by limiting the information available from memory. As we just saw, what we are able to remember may depend on the mood we are in when we try to remember it—when we are happy it is easier to remember happy things, and when we are sad we remember sad things. If so, we may have a tendency to continue activities that are associated with our current mood. Feeling excited may make exciting activities and exciting places more available to memory. The places we think of going to may therefore tend to be similar in affective quality to the place we are in.

A third way in which mood could influence plans would be to influence judgments about the possible outcomes of those plans. Wright and Bower (1981) used hypnosis to induce either a happy or sad mood in subjects, who were then asked to judge, as objectively as possible, the probability of various good or bad events. The happy mood increased estimates of good events and lowered estimates of bad events; the opposite occurred with the sad mood. Subjects did not believe that their mood had influenced their judgments. Johnson and Tversky (1983) altered subjects' mood by asking them to read brief newspaper accounts of happy or sad events. The resulting change in mood was found to alter subjects' estimates of the risk of a range of events—irrespective of the event's similarity to the story used to induce the mood. Apparently, mood has a global effect that is independent of its source.

Comment

The causal power of mood has now been demonstrated in a sufficiently wide range of circumstances that we can turn our attention to its explanation. The evidence briefly reviewed here suggests a pattern: Positive mood makes positive information more available from memory, which influences choices and judgments in a positive direction, which influences behavior in a positive direction. Clark (1982) suggested a similar role for arousal. Clark also suggested that both these chained processes tend to occur automatically (i.e., unintentionally and without effort).

According to Clark (1982), mood can also trigger controlled (voluntary) processes that are often different from the automatic chain. For example, a mood of depression or fatigue (displeasure, low arousal), which automatically favors depressive thoughts and actions, might trigger a *conscious* effort to seek excitement. Presumably, conscious effort would involve planning—as demonstrated by several studies that run counter to the general rule seen in automatic processing. Positive mood decreased the willingness to help when helping entailed a bit of suffering (Isen & Levin, 1972); negative mood increased such positive behaviors as self-reward (Underwood, Moore, & Rosenhan, 1973). Presumably both behaviors result

from conscious attempts to preserve a good mood or improve a bad one.

8.5. AFTEREFFECTS

Leaving a place does not end its influence. The mood created by a place can continue to influence behavior even after leaving. In the preceding section we discussed several types of psychological processes that seem to be affected by mood. Here we would like to emphasize that the influence of mood may be independent of the cause of the mood. The event that alters mood may last only briefly, but the mood may persist. For example, in typical studies on the effects of mood on altruistic behavior, a positive experience in the experimental setting increases helping behavior *after* the subject has left the setting (Berkowitz & Connor, 1966; Isen, 1970; Isen, Horn, & Rosenhan, 1973; Isen & Levin, 1972; Moore, Underwood, & Rosenhan, 1973).

The behavioral effects of stress appear to be unique in that they seem to be *mainly* aftereffects (Glass & Singer, 1972)—although no one has shown this is not so for other moods. In a series of experiments, Glass and Singer could find no effects of such environmental stressors as unpredictable noise, electric shock, and bureaucratic red tape on performance of simple tasks—during exposure to the stressors. Yet all produced performance deficits and lowered tolerance for frustration after the exposure had ended. In our view, stress as typically assessed by environmental psychologists is a mood consisting of displeasure and high arousal, and the question can be raised whether both components contribute to the observed aftereffects or, if only one component, which one.

Zillman and his associates showed that one component— arousal—acquired in one context does affect behavior in another context. One common technique is to induce arousal through physical exercise and then to examine subsequent behavior. For example, provoked aggressive behavior was found to be greater if it followed physical exercise (Zillman, Katcher, & Milavsky, 1972). Similarly, subjects reported feeling more "sexually aroused" by an erotic film if viewing followed physical exercise (Cantor, Zillman, & Bryant, 1975). These subjects also rated the film more exciting and more enjoyable. In both the sex and the aggression studies, subjects reported being unaware of the residual arousal. An important factor in the "relabeling" of arousal may therefore be that the arousal is no longer noticeable, or at least no longer attributable to its initial cause. Arousal that is produced by the cumulative impact of the many elements that constitute an environment, especially if some of those elements are imperceptible, may therefore be particularly subject to relabeling.

Are such aftereffects specific to the arousal component of mood? Cantor, Bryant, and Zillman (1974) tried to manipulate arousal and pleasure independently by having subjects read stories varying in pleasantness and arousingness. Each subject read a story from one of four categories: unarousing pleasant, arousing pleasant, unarousing unpleasant, and arousing unpleasant. A manipulation check showed that subjects agreed with this classification. Subjects were then shown jokes and cartoons and asked to rate how funny they were. Prior arousal increased humor ratings, but there was no effect of the pleasantness of the story.

So far we have been discussing short-term aftereffects, but there is also evidence of long-term cumulative effects, again mainly from studies on stress (Rabkin & Streuning, 1976). Rahe (1979) found a positive correlation between the number of stressful experiences (operationalized as life changes) and incidence of illness. Is increased illness due only to the increased arousal associated with life change events, or is the pleasantness of the event also an important factor? Mehrabian and Ross (1979) used independent ratings of the pleasant and arousing qualities of life change events to determine the correlation with later illness of each dimension separately. The arousing quality of life changes was significantly correlated with illness, but pleasantness of the life changes was not. On the other hand, unpleasantness of life changes does correlate with such psychiatrically relevant symptoms as self-rated depression or hostile mood (Vinokur & Selzer, 1975).

Lowenthal and Prince (1976) emphasized the other side of the coin: The pleasure derived from encounters with a satisfying environment may help mitigate the impact of unfortunate events. Coles (1972), for example, argued that pleasant physical surroundings can help individuals cope with poverty. More recently, Ulrich (1984) compared hospital patients whose window looked onto a brick wall with those whose window looked onto a cluster of trees. The pleasant sight of trees was associated with shorter postoperative hospital stays, more positive evaluations in nurses' notes, and the decreased use of analgesics.

8.6. CONCLUDING REMARKS

Several writers have pointed to emotion as a key link between a person and the surrounding environment (Kaplan & Kaplan, 1984; Lowenthal & Prince, 1976; Mehrabian & Russell, 1974; Tuan, 1974; Ulrich, 1983; Wohlwill, 1976). We hope we have provided a convincing case that focusing on this link does indeed help us understand the relationship between person and environment. If that be granted, perhaps the reader will share our hope for progress on two fronts: (1) In studying environments, we need a better understanding of such basic psychological processes as affective appraisals, moods, and emotional episodes—knowing, for example, whether these distinctions are a useful way to carve up the domain of emotion. (2) In studying emotions, we need to grapple with problems raised by their occurrence in environments.

A greater interplay between basic research on emotion and applied research in environmental psychology would be mutually beneficial. For example, the power of mood to alter behavior and cognition is currently being documented in psychological laboratories. Presumably the value of this effort is that it tells us something about the consequences of naturally occurring moods. But do the relationships found in the laboratory hold when environmental variables are the causes of the mood? In the laboratory, mood is typically changed by something salient and obvious. Naturally occurring environmental variations are complex, subtle, and embedded in the context of the person's life. The person is unlikely to focus attention on the cause of mood change; the person may not even know the cause. Study of environmental variables provides the basic researcher with a nonobtrusive means to alter mood—and thus an important test case of the emerging theories of the effects of mood.

Environmental psychology is the current guardian of an ecological perspective on psychology. In studying emotions, environmental psychologists should ask the sorts of ecological questions raised so emphatically by Barker. Are emotional episodes as rare as we claimed? Where do they actually occur? There is no information available on such questions. Environmental psychologists might also ask about affective reactions to naturally occurring variations in physical parameters. For example, laboratory studies suggest that hot temperatures are unpleasant and lead to aggression. Does this statement hold true for tourists on a Caribbean beach? For a couple in a hot tub?

Understanding human interaction with the physical environment is hampered by not having a deeper understanding of basic psychological processes. For example, the best we could do in this chapter was to catalog some of the environmental variables that have been shown to influence mood. There remain the questions: Why do such factors as noise, chemicals, and collative variables influence mood? Why do they do so in the way they do? We offered no general principles about *how* something can influence mood, because the processes involved remain undiscovered. Knowledge of the mechanisms involved is required if we are to go beyond a catalog to an integration of the findings listed, to predictions about what mood will be created by future environments, and to a genuine understanding of mood and environment.

Similarly, we need a deeper understanding of affective appraisals. The available theories have not taken into account environmental psychology. For example, Mandler (1984) emphasized the degree of congruence between the object appraised and the mental representation of that object. Whether congruence plays more than a minor role in naturally occurring affective appraisals is a question environmental psychologists could contribute to. As another example, consider Zajonc's (1980) much discussed thesis that affective appraisal often precedes cognitive processing of the object appraised. When applied to person–environment interactions, this thesis can be seen in a broader perspective. Perhaps the most important affective appraisals occur during the planning stage—when memory for a particular place or knowledge about a class of places therefore must be relied on. At best, Zajonc's thesis is relevant to a subsample of cases of affective appraisal.

Informal everyday decision making and planning have evolved into such professional activities as regional planning and governmental regulation of technology. As a consequence, affective appraisal, planning, and processing of information have evolved into such professional activities as technology assessment, risk assessment, and environmental impact assessment. These three professional programs have in common the forecasting of costs and benefits and the use of these forecasts in decision making. Environmental impact assessment tends to focus on perceived environmental quality, scenic beauty, or more generally, the pleasant aspects of environments. Risk assessment, in contrast, tends to focus on the fear-arousing quality of environmental changes. Craik (1981) integrated these two technologies by means of the scheme seen here in Figure 8.2, which he described as a clock: Environmental impact assessment has been concerned with the zone from two to four o'clock, whereas risk assessment is associated with the zone from ten to eleven o'clock, of affective appraisals. Craik concludes: "A fuller application of concepts and methods from the psychological study of emotion offers a promising avenue to research linking risk perception to environmental perception more generally" (p. 18).

The subject matter of environmental psychology forces us to focus on time. Indeed, understanding how behavior is organized in time and space is central to environmental psychology (Russell & Ward, 1982). By characterizing person–environment interactions as a series of steps, we focused on time but necessarily oversimplified a continuously unfolding process. For example, mood shifts not just on success or failure of the plan but on progress or regress. Methodological and conceptual tools are required, both in the older areas of psychology and in environmental psychology, to study temporal change. To illustrate, consider the concept of attitude, which has been central to social psychology and frequently used by environmental psychologists (see, e.g., Weigel, 1983). The concept of attitude ignores time by assuming temporal stability. Here, we emphasized a more temporary phenomenon—affective appraisal—because it acknowledges that whether a person is pro-wilderness or anti-wilderness may vary from one time to the next depending on current plans, needs, and concerns.

In short, the study of environmental psychology promises to raise serious questions about some common research conclusions and to provide an important testing ground for theories of psychological processes. At the same time, a deeper understanding of basic psychological processes is needed to enrich our understanding of person–environment transactions.

REFERENCES

Abelson, R.P. (1981). Psychological status of the script concept. *American Psychologist, 36,* 715–729.

Abernathy, E.M. (1940). The effect of changed environmental conditions upon the results of college examinations. *Journal of Psychology, 10,* 293–301.

Adams, F.M., & Osgood, C.E. (1973). A cross-cultural study of the affective meaning of color. *Journal of Cross-Cultural Psychology, 4,* 135–156.

Albrechtsen, O., Clausen, V., Christensen, F.G., Jensen, J.G., & Moeller, T. (1978). The influence of small atmospheric ions on human well-being and mental performance. *International Journal of Biometeorology, 22,* 249–622

Amato, P.R. (1981). The impact of the built environment on prosocial and affiliative behavior: A field study of the Townsville city mall. *Australian Journal of Psychology, 33,* 297–303.

Anderson, A.C. (1982). Environmental factors and aggressive behavior. *Journal of Clinical Psychiatry, 43,* 280–283.

Appleyard, D. (1979). The environment as a social symbol. *Journal of the American Planning Association, 45,* 143–153.

Armstrong, S.L., Gleitman, H., & Gleitman, L.R. (1983). What some concepts might not be. *Cognition, 13,* 263–308.

Attneave, F. (1959). *Applications of information theory to psychology.* New York: Holt, Rinehart & Winston.

Baron, R.A. (1972). Aggression as a function of ambient temperature and prior anger arousal. *Journal of Personality and Social Psychology, 21,* 183–189.

Baron, R.A. (1978). Aggression and heat: The "long, hot summer" revisited. In A. Baum, S. Valins, & J. Singer (Eds.), *Advances in environmental research* (Vol. 1). Hillsdale, NJ: Erlbaum.

Baron, R.A., & Bell, P.A. (1975). Aggression and heat: Mediating effects of prior provocation and exposure to an aggressive model. *Journal of Personality and Social Psychology, 31,* 825–832.

Baron, R.A., & Lawton, S.F. (1972). Environmental influence on aggression: The facilitation of modeling effects by high ambient temperatures. *Psychonomic Science, 26,* 80–83.

Baum, A., & Greenberg, C.I. (1975). Waiting for a crowd: The behavioral and perceptual effects of anticipating crowding. *Journal of Personality and Social Psychology, 32,* 671–679.

Baum, A., & Valins, S. (1979). Architectural mediation of residential density and control: Crowding and the regulation of social contact. *Advances in Experimental Social Psychology, 12,* 131–175.

Beck, A.T. (1967). *Depression: Clinical, experimental and theoretical aspects.* New York: Harper & Row.

Bell, P. A. (1978). Affective state, attraction, and affiliation: Misery loves happy company, too. *Personality and Social Psychology Bulletin, 4,* 616–619.

Bell, P.A., & Baron, R.A. (1976). Aggression and heat: The mediating role of negative affect. *Journal of Applied Social Psychology, 6,* 18–30.

Benfield, J.W. (1973). Introduction. In J.N. Ott (Ed.), *Health and light.* Old Greenwich, CT: Devin-Adair.

Berkowitz, L., & Connor, W.H. (1966). Success, failure, and social responsibility. *Journal of Personality and Social Psychology, 4,* 644–669.

Berlyne, D.E. (Ed.). (1974). *Studies in the new experimental aesthetics: Steps toward an objective psychology of aesthetic appreciation.* New York: Wiley.

Berlyne, D.E., Craw, M.S., Salapatek, P.H., & Lewis, J.L. (1963). Novelty, complexity, incongruity, extrinsic motivation, and the GSR. *Journal of Experimental Psychology, 66,* 560–567.

Beshir, M.Y., & Ramsey, J.D. (1981). Comparison between male and female subjective estimates of thermal effects and sensations. *Applied Ergonomics, 12,* 29–33.

Bower, G.H. (1981). Mood and memory. *American Psychologist, 36,* 129–148.

Bower, G.H., Gilligan, S.G., & Monteiro, K.P. (1981). Selectivity learning caused by affective states. *Journal of Experimental Psychology: General, 110,* 451–473.

Boyce, P.R. (1975). The luminous environment. In D. Canter & P. Stringer (Eds.), *Environmental interaction.* London: Surrey University Press.

Brickman, P., Redfield, J., Harrison, A.A., & Crandall, R. (1972). Drive and predisposition as factors in the attitudinal effects of mere exposure. *Journal of Experimental Social Psychology, 8,* 31–44.

Brown, I., & Inouye, D.K. (1978). Learned helplessness through modeling: The role of perceived similarity in competence. *Journal of Personality and Social Psychology, 36,* 900–908.

Buck, R. (1976). *Human motivation and emotion.* New York: Wiley.

Buckell, M., Hunter, D., Milton, R., & Perry, K. (1946). Chronic mercury poisoning. *British Journal of Industrial Medicine, 3,* 55–63.

Burger, J.M., & Arkin, R.M. (1980). Prediction, control, and learned helplessness. *Journal of Personality and Social Psychology, 38,* 482–491.

Burgess, T.D.G., & Sales, S.M. (1971). Attitudinal effects of mere exposure: A re-evaluation. *Journal of Experimental Social Psychology, 7,* 461–472.

Calvin, J.S., Dearinger, J.A., & Curtin, M.E. (1972). An attempt at assessing preferences for natural landscapes. *Environment and Behavior, 4,* 447–470.

Canter, D. (1969). An intergroup comparison of connotative dimensions in architecture. *Environment and Behavior, 1,* 37–48.

Cantor, G.N. (1968). Children's "like-dislike" ratings of familiarized and nonfamiliarized visual stimuli. *Journal of Experimental Child Psychology, 6,* 651–657.

Cantor, J.R., Bryant, J., & Zillman, D. (1974). Enhancement of humor appreciation by transferred excitation. *Journal of Personality and Social Psychology, 30,* 812–821.

Cantor, J.R., Zillman, D., & Bryant, J. (1975). Enhancement of experienced sexual arousal in response to erotic stimuli through misattribution of unrelated residual excitation. *Journal of Personality and Social Psychology, 32,* 69–75.

Charry, J.M., & Hawkinshire, F.B.W., V. (1981). Effects of atmospheric electricity on some substrates of disordered social behavior. *Journal of Personality and Social Psychology, 41*, 185–197.

Cherry, C. (1966). *On human communication.* Cambridge, MA: MIT Press.

Chiles, W.D., Cleveland, J.M., & Fox, R.E. (1960). *A study of the effects of ionized air on behavior* (Tech. Rep. 60-598), Wright-Patterson Air Force Base, OH: U.S. Air Force, Wright Air Development Division, Air Research Development Command, U.S. Air Force.

Clark, M.S. (1982). A role for arousal in the link between feeling states, judgments, and behavior. In M.S. Clark & S.T. Fiske (Eds.), *Affect and cognition.* Hillsdale, NJ: Erlbaum.

Clark, M.S., & Isen, A.M. (1982). Toward understanding the relationship between feeling states and social behavior. In A.H. Hastorf & A.M. Isen (Eds.), *Cognitive social psychology.* Amsterdam, Netherlands: Elsevier/North Holland.

Cohen, S., & Sherrod, D.R. (1978). When density matters: Environmental control as a determinant of crowding effects in laboratory and residential settings. *Journal of Population, 1*, 189–202.

Coles, R. (1972). *Children of crisis, II: Migrants, sharecroppers, mountaineers.* Boston: Atlantic-Little, Brown.

Craik, K.H. (1981). Comments on "The psychological representation of molar physical environments" by Ward and Russell. *Journal of Experimental Psychology: General, 110*, 158–162.

Crozier, J.B. (1974). Verbal and exploratory responses to sound sequences varying in uncertainty level. In D.E. Berlyne (Ed.), *Studies in the new experimental aesthetics.* New York: Halsted.

Csikszentmihalyi, M., & Rochberg-Halton, E. (1981). *The meaning of things: Domestic symbols and the self.* Cambridge, England: Cambridge University Press.

Cunninghan, M.R. (1979). Weather, mood, and helping behavior. *Journal of Personality and Social Psychology, 37*, 1947–1956.

Diener, E. (1984). Subjective well-being. *Psychological Bulletin, 95*, 542–575.

Diener, E., & Larsen, R.J. (1984). Temporal stability and cross-situational consistency of affective, behavioral, and cognitive responses. *Journal of Personality and Social Psychology, 47*, 871–883.

Dohrenwend, B.S. (1974). Psychosomatic medicine in a changing society: Some current trends in theory and research. In P.M. Insel and R.H. Moos (Eds.), *Health and the social environment.* Lexington, MA: Heath.

Donnerstein, E., & Wilson, D.W. (1976). Effects of noise and perceived control on ongoing and subsequent aggressive behavior. *Journal of Personality and Social Psychology, 34*, 774–781.

Ekman, P. (1972). Universal and cultural differences in facial expression of emotion. In J.R. Cole (Ed.), *Nebraska Symposium on Motivation, 1971.* Lincoln, NE: University of Nebraska Press.

Ekman, P., Freisen, W.V., & Ancoli, S. (1980). Facial signs of emotional experience. *Journal of Personality and Social Psychology, 39*, 1125–1134.

Epstein, S. (1979). The stability of behavior: I. On predicting most of the people much of the time. *Journal of Personality and Social Psychology, 37*, 1097–1126.

Evans, G.W. (1978). Crowding and the developmental process. In A. Baum & Y.M. Epstein (Eds.), *Human response to crowding.* Hillsdale, NJ: Erlbaum.

Evans, M.J. (1976). Physiological and psychological effects of infrasound at moderate intensities. In W. Tempest (Ed.), *Infrasound and low frequency vibration.* London: Academic.

Evans, M.J., & Tempest, W. (1972). Some effects of infrasonic noise in transportation. *Journal of Sound and Vibration, 22*, 19–24.

Eysenck, H.J., & Eysenck, S.B.G. (1968). *Manual: Eysenck Personality Inventory.* San Diego, CA: Educational and Industrial Testing Service.

Fehr, B., & Russell, J.A. (1984). Concept of emotion viewed from a prototype perspective. *Journal of Experimental Psychology: General, 113*, 464–486.

First, M.W. (1980). Effects of air ions. *Science, 210*, 714–716.

Freedman, J.L. (1975). *Crowding and behavior.* San Francisco: Freeman.

Fried, M. (1963). Grieving for a lost home. In L.J. Duhl (Ed.), *The urban condition.* New York: Basic Books.

Garner, W.R. (1962). *Uncertainty and structure as psychological concepts.* New York: Wiley.

Gershon, S., & Shaw, F.H. (1961). Psychiatric sequelae of chronic exposure to organophosphorus insecticides. *Lancet, 1*, 1371–1374.

Gerstner, H.B., & Huff, J.E. (1977). Clinical toxicology of mercury. *Journal of Toxicology and Environmental Health, 2*, 491–526.

Gibson, P.M. (1979). Therapeutic aspects of wilderness programs: A comprehensive literature review. *Therapeutic Recreation Journal, 13*, 21–33.

Gifford, R. (1980). Environmental dispositions and the evaluation of architectural interiors. *Journal of Research in Personality, 14*, 386–399.

Gilbert, G.O. (1973). Effect of negative air ions upon emotionality and brain serotonin levels in isolated rats. *International Journal of Biometeorology, 17*, 267–275.

Gilligan, S.G., & Bower, G.H. (1984). Cognitive consequences of emotional arousal. In C.E. Izard, J. Kagan, & R.B. Zajonc (Eds.), *Emotions, cognition, and behavior.* Cambridge, England: Cambridge University Press.

Glass, D.C., & Singer, J.E. (1972). *Urban stress: Experiments on noise and social stressors.* New York: Academic.

Godden, D.R., & Baddeley, A.D. (1975). Context-dependent memory in two natural environments: On land and under water. *British Journal of Psychology, 66*, 325–331.

Goldsmith, J.R. (1970). Carbon monoxide research — Recent and remote. *Archives of Environmental Health, 21*, 118–120.

Gouaux, C., & Gouaux, S. (1971). The influence of induced affective status on the effectiveness of social and nonsocial reinforcers in an instrumental learning task. *Psychonomic Science, 22*, 341–343.

Gould, P., & White, R. (1975). *Mental maps.* Harmondsworth, England: Penguin.

Green, R.G., & O'Neal, E.C. (1969). Activation of cue-elicited aggression by general arousal. *Journal of Personality and Social Psychology, 11*, 289–292.

Grosch, D.S., & Hopwood, L.E. (1979). *Biological effects of radiations.* New York: Academic.

Harris, C.S., & Johnson, D.L. (1978). Effects of infrasound on cognitive performance. *Aviation and Space Environment, 49*, 582.

Harrison, A.A., & Crandall, R. (1972). Heterogeneity-homogeneity of exposure sequence and the attitudinal effects of exposure. *Journal of Personality and Social Psychology, 21*, 234–238.

Hawkins, L.H. (1981). The influence of air ions, temperature, and humidity on subjective well-being and comfort. *Journal of Environmental Psychology, 1*, 279–292.

Heingartner, A., & Hall, J.V. (1974). Affective consequences in adults and children of repeated exposure to auditory stimuli. *Journal of Personality and Social Psychology, 29*, 719–723.

Hellman, H. (1982). Guiding light. *Psychology Today, 10*, 22–28.

Helson, H. (1964). *Adaptation Level Theory.* New York: Harper & Row.

Herzog, T.R., Kaplan, S., & Kaplan, R. (1976). The prediction of preference for familiar urban places. *Environment and Behavior, 8*, 627–645.

Hill, W.F. (1978). Effects of mere exposure on preferences in nonhuman animals. *Psychological Bulletin, 85*, 1177–1198.

Humphrey, N.K. (1972). Interest and pleasure: Two determinants of a monkey's visual preferences. *Perception, 1*, 395–416.

Isen, A.M. (1970). Success, failure, attention, and reaction to others. *Journal of Personality and Social Psychology, 15*, 294–301.

Isen, A.M., Horn, N., & Rosenhan, D.L. (1973). Effects of success and failure on children's generosity. *Journal of Personality and Social Psychology, 27*, 239–247.

Isen, A.M., & Levin, P.F. (1972). Effects of feeling good on helping: Cookies and kindness. *Journal of Personality and Social Psychology, 21*, 384–388.

Isen, A.M., Means, B., Patrick, R., & Nowicki, G. (1982). Some factors influencing decision-making strategy and risk taking. In M.S. Clark & S.T. Fiske (Eds.), *Affect and cognition.* Hillsdale, NJ: Erlbaum.

Isen, A.M., Shalker, T.E., Clark, M.S., & Karp, L. (1978). Positive affect, accessibility of material in memory, and behavior: A cognitive loop. *Journal of Personality and Social Psychology, 36*, 1–12.,

Izard, C.E. (1972). *Patterns of emotions.* New York: Academic.

Izard, C.E. (1977). *Human emotions.* New York: Plenum.

Jacobi, M., & Stokols, D. (1983). The role of tradition in group-environment relations. In N.R. Feimer & E.S. Geller (Eds.), *Environmental psychology: Directions and perspectives.* New York: Praeger.

James, W. (1950). *Principles of psychology.* New York: Dover. (Original work published 1890.)

Janis, I.L., Kaye, D., & Kirschner, P. (1965). Facilitating effects of 'eating-while-reading' on responsiveness to persuasive communications. *Journal of Personality and Social Psychology, 1*, 181–186.

Johnson, E.J., & Tversky, A. (1983). Affect, generalization, and the perception of risk. *Journal of Personality and Social Psychology, 45*, 20–31.

Johnson, S., & Burdge, R.J. (1975). An analysis of community and individual reactions to forced migration due to reservoir construction. In D.R. Field, J.C. Barron, & B.F. Long (Eds.), *Water and community development.* Ann Arbor, MI: Ann Arbor Science.

Jones, J.W., & Bogat, G.A. (1978). Air pollution and human aggression. *Psychological Reports, 43*, 721–722.

Kahneman, D., Slovic, P., & Tversky, A. (1982). *Judgment under uncertainty: Heuristics and biases.* Cambridge, England: Cambridge University Press.

Kahneman, D., Tversky, A. (1982). The simulation heuristic. In D. Kahneman, P. Slovic, & A. Tversky (Eds.), *Judgment under uncertainty: Heuristics and biases.* Cambridge, England: Cambridge University Press.

Kahneman, D., & Tversky, A. (1984). Choices, values, and frames. *American Psychologist, 39*, 341–350.

Kaplan, R. (1977). Patterns of environmental preference. *Environment and Behavior, 9*, 195–216.

Kaplan, R. (1982, October). Human needs for renewable resources and supportive environments. Paper presented at Symposium on the Urban/Forest Interface, Seattle, WA.

Kaplan, S., & Kaplan, R. (1984). *Cognition and environment.* New York: Praeger.

Kaplan, S., Kaplan, R., & Wendt, J.S. (1972). Rated preference and complexity for natural and urban visual material. *Perception and Psychophysics, 12*, 354–356.

Kaplan, S., & Talbot, J.F. (1983). Psychological benefits of a wilderness experience. In I. Altman & J.F. Wohlwill (Eds.), *Human Behavior and environment: Vol. 6. Behavior and the natural environment.* New York: Plenum.

Katkin, E.S. (1965). Relationship between manifest anxiety and two indices of autonomic response to stress. *Journal of Personality and Social Psychology, 2*, 324–333.

Klein, K., & Harris, B. (1979). Disruptive effects of disconfirmed expectancies about crowding. *Journal of Personality and Social Psychology, 37*, 769–777.

Konecni, V. (1975). The mediation of aggressive behavior: Arousal level vs. anger and cognitive labeling. *Journal of Personality and Social Psychology, 32*, 706–712.

Krueger, A.P., Andriese, P.C., & Kotaka, S. (1963). The biological mechanism of air ion action: The effect of CO_2^+ in inhaled air on the blood level of 5-hydroxytryptamine in mice. *International Journal of Biometeorology, 7*, 3–16.

Krueger, A.P., Andriese, P.C., & Kotaka, S. (1966). The effects of inhaling nonionized or positively ionized air containing 2–4% CO_2 on the blood levels of 5-hydroxytryptamine in mice. *International Journal of Biometeorology, 10*, 17–28.

Krueger, A.P., Andriese, P.C., & Kotaka, S. (1968). Small air ions: Their effect on blood levels of serotonin in terms of modern physical theory. *International Journal of Biometeorology, 12*, 225–239.

Krueger, A.P., & Kotaka, S. (1969). The effects of air ions on brain levels of serotonin in mice. *International Journal of Biometeorology, 13*, 25–28.

Laird, J.D., Wagener, J.J., Halal, M., & Szegda, M. (1982). Remembering what you feel: Effects of emotion on memory. *Journal of Personality and Social Psychology, 42* ,646–657.

Langer, E.J., & Saegert, S. (1977). Crowding and cognitive control. *Journal of Personality and Social Psychology, 35*, 175–182.

Lazarus, R.S. (1984). On the primacy of cognition. *American Psychologist, 39*, 124–130.

Lazarus, R.S., Kanner, A.D., & Folkman, S. (1980). Emotions: A cognitive-phenomenological analysis. In R. Plutchik & H. Kellerman (Eds.), *Theories of emotion*. New York: Academic.

Leff, H.L., & Gordon, L.R. (1980). Environmental cognitive sets: A longitudinal study. *Environment and Behavior, 12*, 291–328.

Levin, H.S., Rodnitzky, R.L., & Mick, D.L. (1976). Anxiety associated with exposure to organophosphate compounds. *Archives of General Psychiatry, 33*, 225–228.

Ley, D. (1975). The street gang in its milieu. In G. Gappert & H. Rose (Eds.), *The social economy of cities*. Beverly Hills, CA: Sage.

Little, B.R. (1983). Personal projects: A rationale and method for investigation. *Environment and Behavior, 15*, 273–310.

Lorr, M., & Shea, T.M. (1979). Are mood states bipolar? *Journal of Personality Assessment, 43*, 468–472.

Lowenthal, D., & Prince, H.C. (1976). Transcendental experience. In S. Wapner, S.B. Cohen, & B. Kaplan (Eds.), *Experiencing the environment*. New York: Plenum.

Lyman, B. (1982). The nutritional values and food group characteristics of foods preferred during various emotions. *Journal of Psychology, 112*, 121–127.

Mackay, C., Cox, T., Burrows, G., & Lazzerini, T. (1978). An inventory for the measurement of self-reported stress and arousal. *British Journal of Social and Clinical Psychology, 17*, 283–284.

Mandler, G. (1982). The structure of value: Accounting for taste. In M.S. Clark & S.T. Fiske (Eds.), *Affect and cognition*. Hillsdale, NJ: Erlbaum.

Mandler, G. (1984). *Mind and body: Psychology of emotion and stress*. New York: Norton.

Mandler, G., & Shebo, B.J. (1983). Knowing and liking. *Motivation and Emotion, 7*, 125–144.

Martin, B. (1961). The assessment of anxiety by physiological behavioral measures. *Psychological Bulletin, 58*, 234–255.

Maslow, A.H., & Mintz, N.L. (1956). Effects of esthetic surroundings: I. Initial effect of three esthetic conditions upon perceiving 'energy' and 'well-being' in faces. *Journal of Psychology, 41*, 247–254.

Mayo, E.J., & Jarvis, L.R. (1981). *The psychology of leisure travel: Effective marketing and selling of travel services*. Boston: CBI Publishing.

McGurk, F. (1959). Psychological effects of artificially produced air ions. *American Journal of Physical Medicine, 38*, 36–37.

McKechnie, G.E. (1974). *Manual for the Environmental Response Inventory*. Palo Alto, CA: Consulting Psychologists Press.

McManus, I.C., Jones, A.L., & Cottrell, J. (1981). The aesthetics of color. *Perception, 10*, 651–666.

McNair, D.M., & Lorr, M. (1964). An analysis of mood in neurotics. *Journal of Abnormal and Social Psychology, 69*, 620–627.

McNair, D.M., Lorr, M., & Droppleman, L.F. (1971). *Manual: Profile of Mood States*. San Diego, CA: Educational and Industrial Testing Services.

Meddis, R. (1972). Bipolar factors in mood adjective checklists. *British Journal of Social and Clinical Psychology, 11*, 178–184.

Mehrabian, A. (1977). Individual differences in stimulus screening and arousability. *Journal of Personality, 45*, 237–250.

Mehrabian, A., & O'Reilly, E. (1980). Analysis of personality measures in terms of basic dimensions of temperament. *Journal of Personality and Social Psychology, 38*, 492–503.

Mehrabian, A., & Ross, M. (1979). Illnesses, accidents, and alcohol use as functions of the arousing quality and pleasantness of life changes. *Psychological Reports, 45*, 31–43.

Mehrabian, A., & Russell, J.A. (1973). A measure of arousal seeking tendency. *Environment and Behavior, 5,* 315–333.

Mehrabian, A., & Russell, J.A. (1974). A verbal measure of information rate for studies in environmental psychology. *Environment and Behavior, 6,* 233–252.

Mervis, C.B., & Rosch, E. (1981). Categorization of natural objects. *Annual Review of Psychology, 32,* 89–115.

Middlemist, R.D., Knowles, E.S., & Matter, C.F. (1976). Personal space invasions in the lavatory: Suggestive evidence for arousal. *Journal of Personality and Social Psychology, 33,* 541–546.

Miller, G.A., Galanter, E., & Pribram, K.H. (1960). *Plans and the structure of behavior.* New York: Holt, Rinehart & Winston.

Mita, T.H., Dermer, M., & Knight, J. (1977). Reversed facial images and the mere-exposure hypothesis. *Journal of Personality and Social Psychology, 33,* 597–601.

Moore, B., Underwood, B., & Rosenhan, D.L. (1973). Affect and altruism. *Developmental Psychology, 8,* 99–104.

Moskowitz, H. (1971). Crashes are caused by slowed up brain function. *New Scientists and Science Journal, 51,* 725.

Nasar, J.L. (1979). The evaluative image of a city. In A. Seidel & S. Danford (Eds.), *Environmental design: Research, theory, and application.* Proceedings of the Tenth Annual EDRA Conference. Buffalo, NY.

Nourse, J.C., & Welch, R.B. (1971). Emotional attributes of color: A comparison of violet and green. *Perceptual and Motor Skills, 32,* 403–406.

Nowlis, V. (1965). Research with the Mood Adjective Check List. In S.S. Tomkins & C.E. Izard (Eds.), *Affect, cognition, and personality.* New York: Springer.

Nowlis, V., & Nowlis, H.H. (1956). The description and analysis of mood. *Annals of the New York Academy of Sciences, 65,* 345–355.

Osgood, C.E., May, W.H., & Miron, M.S. (1975). *Cross-cultural universals of affective meaning.* Urbana: University of Illinois Press.

Osgood, C.E., Suci, G.J., & Tannenbaum, P.H. (1957). *The measurement of meaning.* Urbana: University of Illinois Press.

Ott, J.N. (1968a). Responses of psychological and physiological functions to environmental light—Part I. *Journal of Learning Disabilities, 1,* 18–20.

Ott, J.N. (1968b). Responses of psychological and physiological functions to environmental radiation stress—Part II. *Journal of Learning Disabilities, 1,* 6–12.

Ott, J.N. (1973). *Health and light.* Old Greenwich, CT: Devin-Adair.

Ott, J.N. (1976). Influence of fluorescent lights on hyperactivity and learning disabilities. *Journal of Learning Disabilities, 9,* 417–422.

Parducci, A. (1968). The relativity of absolute judgments. *Scientific American, 219,* 84–90.

Pedersen, D. (1978). Relationship between environmental familiarity and environmental preference. *Perceptual and Motor Skills, 47,* 739–743.

Plutchik, R. (1980). *Emotion: A psychoevolutionary synthesis.* New York: Harper & Row.

Pugh, G.E. (1977). *The biological origin of human values.* New York: Basic Books.

Rabkin, J.G., & Struening, E.L. (1976). Life events, stress, and illness. *Science, 194,* 1013–1020.

Rachman, S. (1978). *Fear and courage.* San Francisco: Freeman.

Rahe, R.H. (1979). Life change events and mental illness: An overview. *Journal of Human Stress, 5,* 2–10.

Razran, G.H.S. (1938). Conditioning away social bias by the luncheon technique. *Psychological Bulletin, 35,* 693.

Razran, G.H.S. (1940). Conditioning response changes in rating and appraising sociopolitical slogans. *Psychological Bulletin, 37,* 481.

Reser, J.P. (1980). Automobile addiction: Real or imagined? *Man-Environment Systems, 10,* 279–287.

Ridgeway, D., Hare, R.D., Waters, E., & Russell, J.A. (1984). Affect and sensation seeking. *Motivation and Emotion, 8,* 205–210.

Rodnitzky, R.L., Levin, H.S., & Morgan, D.P. (1978). Effects of ingested parathion on neurobehavioral functions. *Clinical Toxicology, 13,* 347–359.

Rohles, F.H. (1981). Thermal comfort and strategies for energy conservation. *Journal of Social Issues, 37,* 132–149.

Rorty, A.O. (1980). *Explaining emotions.* Berkeley: University of California Press.

Rosch, E. (1977). Human categorization. In N. Warred (Ed.), *Studies on cross-cultural psychology.* London: Academic.

Rotton, J., Barry, T., Frey, J., & Soler, E. (1978). Air pollution and interpersonal attraction. *Journal of Applied Social Psychology, 8,* 57–71.

Rotton, J., Frey, J., Barry, T., Milligan, M., & Fitzpatrick, M. (1979). The air pollution experience and physical aggression. *Journal of Applied Social Psychology, 9,* 397–412.

Russell, J.A. (1978). Evidence of convergent validity on the dimensions of affect. *Journal of Personality and Social Psychology, 36,* 1152–1168.

Russell, J.A. (1979). Affective space is bipolar. *Journal of Personality and Social Psychology, 37,* 345–356.

Russell, J.A. (1980). A circumplex model of affect. *Journal of Personality and Social Psychology, 39,* 1161–1178.

Russell, J.A. (1983). Pancultural aspects of the human conceptual organization of emotions. *Journal of Personality and Social Psychology, 45,* 1281–1288.

Russell, J.A., & Bullock, M. (in press). Fuzzy concepts and the perception of emotion in facial expressions. *Social Cognition.*

Russell, J.A., & Lanius, U.F. (1984). Adaptation level and the affective appraisal of environments. *Journal of Environmental Psychology, 4,* 119–135.

Russell, J.A., & Mehrabian, A. (1974). Distinguishing anger and anxiety in terms of emotional response factors. *Journal of Consulting and Clinical Psychology, 42,* 79–83.

Russell, J.A., & Mehrabian, A. (1975). Task, setting, and personality variables affecting the desire to work. *Journal of Applied Psychology, 60,* 518–520.

Russell, J.A., & Mehrabian, A. (1977). Evidence for a three-factor theory of emotions. *Journal of Research in Personality, 11,* 273–294.

Russell, J.A., & Mehrabian, A. (1978). Environmental, task, and temperamental effects on work performance. *Humanitas, 14,* 75–95.

Russell, J.A., & Pratt, G. (1980). A description of the affective quality attributed to environments. *Journal of Personality and Social Psychology, 38,* 311–322.

Russell, J.A., & Ridgeway, D. (1983). Dimensions underlying children's emotion concepts. *Developmental Psychology, 19,* 795–804.

Russell, J.A., & Steiger, J.H. (1982). The structure in persons' implicit taxonomy of emotions. *Journal of Research in Personality, 16,* 447–469.

Russell, J.A., & Ward, L.M. (1982). Environmental psychology. *Annual Review of Psychology, 33,* 259–288.

Russell, J.A., Ward, L.M., & Pratt, G. (1981). Affective quality attributed to environments: A factor analytic study. *Environment and Behavior, 13,* 259–288.

Russell, J.A., & Woudzia, L. (1986). Affective judgments, common sense, and Zajonc's thesis of independence. *Motivation and Emotion, 10,* 169–183.

Saegert, S. (1980). Crowding and cognitive limits. In J. Harvey (Ed.), *Cognition, social behavior and the environment.* Hillsdale, NJ: Erlbaum.

Saegert, S., Swap, W., & Zajonc, R.B. (1973). Exposure, context, and interpersonal attraction. *Journal of Personality and Social Psychology, 25,* 234–242.

Sahgal, A., & Iverson, S.D. (1975) Colour preferences in the pigeon: A behavioral and psychopharmacological study. *Psychopharmacologia, 43,* 175–179.

Sahgal, A., Pratt, S.R›, & Iverson, S.D. (1975). Response preferences of monkeys within wavelength and line-tilt dimensions. *Journal of the Experimental Analysis of Behavior, 24,* 377–381.

Schachter, S., & Singer, J.E. (1962). Cognitive, social, and physiological determinants of emotional state. *Psychological Review, 69,* 379–399.

Schauss, A.G. (1979). Tranquilizing effect of color reduces aggressive behavior and potential violence. *Journal of Orthomolecular Psychiatry, 8,* 218–221.

Schulte, J.H. (1963). Effect of mild carbon monoxide intoxication. *Archives of Environmental Health, 7,* 524–530.

Shepard, R.J. (1983). *Carbon monoxide: The silent killer.* Springfield, IL: Thomas.

Sherrod, D.R., Armstrong, D., Hewitt, J., Madonia, B., Speno, S., & Teruya, D. (1977). Environmental attention, affect, and altruism. *Journal of Applied Social Psychology, 7,* 359–371.

Sherrod, D.R., Hage, J.N., Halpern, P.L., & Moore, B.S. (1977). Effects of personal causation and perceived control responses to an aversive environment: The more control, the better. *Journal of Experimental Social Psychology, 13,* 14–27.

Sigel, S. (1978). *Bulletin of American Meteorology Society, 59,* 1522.

Sime, J.D. (1980). The concept of panic. In D. Canter (Ed.), *Fires and human behavior.* New York: Wiley.

Simon, H.A. (1982). Comments. In M.S. Clark & S.T. Fiske (Eds.), *Affect and cognition.* Hillsdale, NJ: Erlbaum.

Smith, G.F., & Dorfman, D.D. (1975). The effect of stimulus uncertainty on the relationship between frequency of exposure and liking. *Journal of Personality and Social Psychology, 31,* 150–155.

Smith, W.D.A. (1982). *Under the influence: A history of nitrous oxide and oxygen anaesthesia.* Old Woking, Surrey, England: Gresham.

Snyder, M., & White, P. (1982). Moods and memories: Elation, depression, and the remembering of the events of one's life. *Journal of Personality, 50,* 149–167.

Sonnenfeld, J. (1967). Environmental perception and adaptation level in the Arctic. In D. Lowenthal (Ed.), *Environmental perception and behavior* (pp. 42–49). Chicago: University of Chicago, Department of Geography.

Sonnenfeld, J. (1969). Equivalence and distortion of the perceptual environment. *Environment and Behavior, 1,* 83–100.

Spielberger, C.D., Gorsuch, R.L., & Lushene, R.E. (1970). *Manual for the State-Trait Anxiety Inventory.* Palo Alto: CA: Consulting Psychologists Press.

Standing, L., & Stace, G. (1980). The effects of environmental noise on anxiety level. *Journal of General Psychology, 103,* 263–272.

Stang, D.J. (1974). Methodological factors in mere exposure research. *Psychological Bulletin, 81,* 1014–1025.

Stokols, D., & Novaco, R.W. (1981). Transportation and well-being: An ecological perspective. In I. Altman, J.F. Wohlwill & P.B. Everett (Eds.), *Transportation and behavior.* New York: Plenum.

Storms, M.D., & Thomas, G.C. (1977). Reactions to physical closeness. *Journal of Personality and Social Psychology, 35,* 412–418.

Suedfeld, P., Epstein, Y.M., Buchanan, E., & Landon, P.B. (1971). Effects of set on the "effects of mere exposure." *Journal of Personality and Social Psychology, 17*, 121–123.

Sulman, F.G. (1980). *The effect of air ionization, electric fields, atmospherics and other electric phenomena on man and animal.* Springfield, IL: Thomas.

Svensson, E. (1978). Mood: Its structure and measurement. *Göteborg Psychological Reports, 8*, 1–19.

Tarnopolsky, A., Watkins, G., & Hand, D.J. (1980). Aircraft noise and mental health: I. Prevalence of individual symptoms. *Psychological Medicine, 10*, 683–698.

Taylor, J.A. (1953). A personality scale of manifest anxiety. *Journal of Abnormal and Social Psychology, 48*, 285–290.

Taylor, P.J., & Pocock, S.J. (1974). Commuter travel and sickness: Absence of London office workers. In P.M. Insel & R.H. Moos (Eds.), *Health and the social environment.* Lexington, MA: Heath.

Teasdale, J.D., & Fogarty, F.J. (1979). Differential effects of induced mood on retrieval of pleasant and unpleasant events from episodic memory. *Journal of Abnormal Psychology, 88*, 248–257.

Teasdale, J.D., & Taylor, R. (1981). Induced mood and accessibility of memories: An effect of mood state or of induction procedure. *British Journal of Clinical Psychology, 20*, 39–48.

Tempest, W., & Bryan, M.E. (1972). Low frequency sound measurement in vehicles. *Applied Acoustics, 5*, 133–139.

Thayer, R.E. (1967). Measurement of activation through self-report. *Psychological Reports, 20*, 663–678.

Thayer, R.E. (1978). Toward a psychological theory of multidimensional activation (arousal). *Motivation and Emotion, 2*, 1–34.

Thorington, L. (1975). Artifical lighting—What color and spectrum? *Lighting Design and Application, 16*, 16–21.

Tom, G., Poole, M.F., Galla, J., & Berrier, J. (1981). The influence of negative air ions on human performance and mood. *Human Factors, 23*, 633–636.

Tomkins, S.S. (1962-1963). *Affect, imagery, consciousness* (Vols. 1 & 2). New York: Springer.

Tuan, Y. (1974). *Topophilia: A study of environmental perception, attitudes, and values.* Englewood Cliffs, NJ: Prentice-Hall.

Ulrich, R.S. (1983). Aesthetic and affective response to natural environment. In I. Altman and J.F. Wohlwill (Eds.), *Human behavior and the natural environment.* New York: Plenum.

Ulrich, R.S. (1984). View through a window may influence recovery from surgery. *Science, 224*, 420–421.

Underwood, B., Moore, B.S., & Rosenhan, D.L. (1973). Affect and self-gratification. *Developmental Psychology, 8*, 209–214.

Vinokur, A., & Selzer, M.L. (1975). Desirable versus undesirable life events: Their relationship to stress and mental distress. *Journal of Personality and Social Psychology, 32*, 329–337.

Wallace, A.F.C., & Carson, M.T. (1973). Sharing and diversity in emotion terminology. *Ethos, 1*, 1–29.

Walters, J., Apter, M.J., & Svebak, S. (1982). Color preference, arousal, and the theory of psychological reversals. *Motivation and Emotion, 6*, 193–215.

Ward, L.M. (1977). Multidimensional scaling of the molar physical environment. *Multivariate Behavior Research, 12*, 23–42.

Ward, L.M., & Russell, J.A. (1981). The psychological representation of molar physical environments. *Journal of Experimental Psychology: General, 110*, 121–152.

Watson, D., & Clark, L.A. (1984). Negative affectivity: The disposition to experience aversive emotional states. *Psychological Bulletin, 96*, 465–490.

Watson, D., Clark, L.A., & Tellegen, A. (1984). Cross-cultural convergence in the structure of mood: A Japanese replication and a comparison with U.S. findings. *Journal of Personality and Social Psychology, 47*, 127–144.

Watson, J.B. (1919). *Psychology from the standpoint of a behaviorist.* Philadelphia: Lippincott.

Weigel, R.H. (1983). Environmental attitudes and the prediction of behavior. In N.R. Feimer & E.S. Geller (Eds.), *Environmental psychology: Directions and perspectives.* New York: Praeger.

Weiner, B. (1982). The emotional consequences of causal attributions. In M.S. Clark & S.T. Fiske (Eds.), *Affect and cognition.* Hillsdale, NJ: Erlbaum.

Wenger, M.A. (1950). Emotion as visceral action: An extension of Lange's theory. In M.L. Reymert (Ed.), *The second international symposium on feelings and emotions.* New York: McGraw-Hill.

Wilson, G.D. (1966). Arousal properties of red vs. green. *Perceptual and Motor Skills, 23*, 947–949.

Winslow, C.A., & Herrington, L.P. (1936). The influence of odor upon appetite. *American Journal of Hygiene, 23*, 143–156.

Wohlwill, J.F. (1968). Amount of stimulus exploration and preference as differential functions of stimulus complexity. *Perception and Psychophysics, 4*, 307–312.

Wohlwill, J.F. (1974). Human adaptation to levels of environmental stimulation. *Human Ecology, 2*, 127–147.

Wohlwill, J.F. (1975). Children's responses to meaningful pictures varying in diversity: Exploration time vs. preference. *Journal of Experimental Child Psychology, 20*, 341–351.

Wohlwill, J.F. (1976). Environmental aesthetics: The environment as a source of affect. In I. Altman & J.F. Wohlwill (Eds.), *Human behavior and environment.* New York: Plenum.

Wohlwill, J.F., & Kohn, I. (1973). The environment as experienced by the migrant: An adaptation-level view. *Representative Research in Social Psychology, 4*, 135–164.

Wohlwill, J.F., & Kohn, I. (1976). Dimensionalizing the environmental manifold. In S. Wapner, S.B. Cohen, & B. Kaplan (Eds.), *Experiencing the environment.* New York: Plenum.

Wood, P.G. (1980). A survey of behavior in fires. In D. Canter (Ed.), *Fires and human behavior.* New York: Wiley.

Worchel, S., & Teddlee, C. (1976). The experience of crowding: A two-factor theory. *Journal of Personality and Social Psychology, 34,* 30–40.

Wortman, R.J., Axelrod, J., & Fischer, J.E. (1964). Melatonin synthesis in the gland: Effect of light mediated by the sympathetic nervous system. *Science, 143,* 1328–1329.

Wright, W.F., & Bower, G.H. (1981). *Mood effects on subjective probability assessment.* Unpublished manuscript, Stanford University, Stanford, CA.

Zajonc, R.B. (1965). Social facilitation. *Science, 149,* 269–274.

Zajonc, R.B. (1968). Attitudinal effects of mere exposure [Monograph]. *Journal of Personality and Social Psychology, 8,* 1–29.

Zajonc, R.B. (1980). Feeling and thinking: Preferences need no inferences. *American Psychologist, 35,* 151–175.

Zajonc, R.B. (1984). On the primacy of affect. *American Psychologist, 39,* 117–123.

Zillman, D., Katcher, A.H., & Milavsky, B. (1972). Excitation transfer from physical exercise to subsequent aggressive behavior. *Journal of Experimental Social Psychology, 8,* 247–259.

Zuckerman, M. (1980). To risk or not to risk. In K.R. Blankstein, P. Pliner, & J. Polivy (Eds.), *Assessment and modification of emotional behavior.* New York: Plenum.

Chapter **9**

THE PHYSICAL ENVIRONMENT AND THE DEVELOPMENT OF THE CHILD

Joachim F. Wohlwill, *Department of Individual and Family Studies, Pennsylvania State University, University Park, Pennsylvania*

Harry Heft, *Department of Psychology, Denison University, Granville, Ohio*

The focus of this chapter is on the role of the stimulus environment in the psychological development of the child. That is, our emphasis will be on the significance of the physical or inanimate features of the environment considered from a developmental perspective. In order to delimit the range of problems to be examined, we will maintain a distinction between the physical and the social environment. At the same time, we will indicate how, in our view, the two domains are related. Alternative conceptions to our treatment of the environment as a source of physical stimuli, notably ecological perspectives, will also be considered. The chapter will begin with an examination of historical and theoretical views of the role of the physical environment in child development, as well as a consideration of the ways in which this issue has been approached by those in environmental psychology and environmental design. The presentation will then turn to a review of pertinent research by focusing on the home environment, institutional and school settings, outdoor environments such as playgrounds and the natural environment, and the variable of community size. In our concluding section we will try to reformulate certain conceptual issues in the field and point to possibilities for a synthesis between the environmental stimulation perspective and the ecological one. Finally, major research needs will also be pointed out.

9.1. THE ROLE OF THE ENVIRONMENT IN CHILD DEVELOPMENT

9.1.1. Historical Origins

The role of the environment has been considered to be of paramount importance since the earliest days of the establishment of child psychology and development as a major field of investigation, at least in American psychology. This environmental emphasis was in large part an outgrowth of the controversy over the issue of heredity versus environment that developed during the early years of this century, in reaction to the influence of Darwinian and neo-Darwinian notions and of McDougall's theory of instincts, as well as to the uncritical extrapolation from these views of behavior to major issues of social policy (cf. Cravens, 1978). Yet if this reaction turned into a virtual bias in favor of an environmental stance, it was frequently difficult to determine the meaning that child psychologists attached to the term *environment.*

This point, along with the changes in conceptions of the role of the environment in the development of the child, has been detailed in a recent publication (Wohlwill, 1983). Suffice it to point out here that when a theoretically grounded view of the role of environmental influences became prominent in child psychology, that is, in the 1940s and 1950s, these influences were considered primarily in interpersonal and sociocultural terms.

More recently, however, several major developments on the psychological scene have modified the previous one-sided emphasis on the social environment, and indeed the conception of the nature of the social environment itself. The first was the appearance of Hebb's (1949) formulation of the role of sensory stimulation in the organism's early experience. In part as a result of the effort made by Hunt (1961), in his influential volume *Intelligence and Experience,* to draw attention to Hebb's ideas and to the research they inspired, and also because this work received extensive treatment in Thompson and Grusec's (1970) review of early experience in the *Manual of*

Child Development, this conception was brought into the realm of developmental theorizing and research. One notable example is the interpretation of the effects of institutionalization as based on sensory rather than maternal deprivation propounded by Casler (1961, 1967).

While the influence of Hebb and his conception of the role of sensory stimulation appears to be on the wane, within psychology in general and within developmental psychology in particular, the concern for the impact of environmental stimulation on children in both a qualitative and a quantitative sense has by no means vanished; it is prominently represented on the current psychological scene in the work of Wachs in particular (Wachs, 1979; see also Wachs & Gruen, 1982), as will be shown in later sections of this chapter. At the same time we have been witnessing a major change in the conception of the social environment and the role it plays in development from an essentially unidirectional influence to an interactive system—a change that has allowed us to reformulate the distinction between physical and social influences in a new light, as will be seen presently.

A very different theoretical perspective on relations between the environment and child behavior, which in its original form likewise dates from the 1950s, is the ecological one. As originally developed by Barker, Wright, and the Kansas group (e.g., Barker, 1968), it represented an approach to the descriptive study of behavior in terms of behavior settings, which referred only incidentally to the behavior of children specifically, and even less consistently to their development. Yet perhaps in part because of its observational base it has continued to play a significant role in child psychology and in the analysis of situational and contextual factors in child behavior. In recent years, alternative ecological approaches in the study of children have sprung up from diverse sources, of which the system of Bronfenbrenner (1979) is probably the most influential. These various ecological perspectives differ among themselves in their definition and conception of ecological factors, but they share a concern for the role of the situational context in behavior. This concern sets them apart from the formulations of environmental influences that we find in the conceptions of Hebb and Hunt and other more recent ones that have focused on the role of stimuli and objects in the environment in the development of the child. Let us consider these theoretical perspectives more specifically, as they are encountered in contemporary research and theory.

9.1.2. Major Current Theoretical Approaches

The Environment as a Source of Stimulation

As mentioned, it was Hebb (1949) who in his volume *The Organization of Behavior* first presented a theoretical analysis of the role of the environment in the development of the individual that placed primary emphasis on the importance of environmental stimulation. Hebb's particular concern related to the role of patterned stimulus input, notably in the visual modality, as a basis for the laying down of fundamental neural pathways in the cortex. He thus regarded such input as the foundation for the development and maintenance of perceptual functioning as well as of higher forms of behavior such as problem solving, attention, and adaptive emotional and motivational response.

The significance of Hebb's contribution was in providing a new way of conceptualizing the effects of experience as an alternative to the standard conceptions of S–R learning. It stimulated interest in and experimental research on the role of variation in patterned stimulus input for normal development, which soon filtered into the awareness of child psychologists. Considerable discussion ensued in regard to the relevance of this conception to the condition of children growing up under seemingly unfavorable environmental circumstances, notably in institutions and in areas of poverty and cultural deprivation. This view did seem to fit the case of the institutionalized child rather well, since monotony and absence of information might well be said to characterize the perceptual ambience of a typical orphanage or similar institution for young children. However, the notion that surfaced briefly in the 1960s that the child of the inner-city slums or ghettos suffered from *stimulus* deprivation, was soon recognized as untenable. In fact, a surfeit of stimulation—and above all of high-intensity auditory background stimuli interfering with the child's attending to relevant verbal stimuli—appeared as a more plausible way of describing the quality of environmental stimulation to which these children were typically exposed (cf. Deutsch, 1964).

More current conceptions of environmental stimulation are best represented in the research and thinking of Wachs and his colleagues, to which we shall refer repeatedly throughout this chapter (e.g., Wachs, 1977). Two major differences from the original Hebbian view are to be noted. First, in contrast to the simplistic view of environmental stimulation as

categorizable along a dimension from deprivation to enrichment, which was implicit in Hebb's thinking and made explicit in the research of the Hebbians (e.g., Hymovitch, 1952), Wachs laid stress on the concept of an *optimal level* of stimulation, beyond which further stimulation, rather than serving an enriching role, acts to interfere with behavior and development. Second, a thorough review of both the animal and the human literature led Wachs to conclude that this optimal level is itself to be conceived of as relative to an organism's level of development. That is, the amount of stimulation that an individual can optimally assimilate is in part determined by the individual's prior history and present capacity for processing stimulus input, in accordance with Hunt's (1961) *hypothesis of the match.*

Finally, let us note an issue that must be faced with respect to the effects of environmental stimulation impinging on the individual. In Hebb's conception, these effects are produced by sheer exposure to the stimulation, independent of the individual's behavior in response to it. While the Hebb-Hunt-Wachs view of stimulation—in spite of the previously mentioned important differences among these writers—leaves the organism's response system out of account, there are good empirical as well as theoretical grounds for believing that the effects of sensory experience are mediated through the actions of the individual. The two approaches to be considered next illustrate two particular ways in which the individual's actions enter into a more complete account of the role of experience.

The Environment as a Source of Feedback to the Child's Behavior

A theoretical alternative to Hebb's sensory stimulation model is one that views perceptual learning as being mediated by motor responses. Environmental knowledge is seen to be essentially motor in nature, conceptualized typically as schemata, and the consequences of motor acts are to provide feedback as to the veridicality of these schemata. Thus an organism acts on the environment, and by perceiving the consequences of those responses it learns a particular correlation between motor acts and some stimulus pattern. In contrast to the Hebbian model, in which the organism is relatively passive in the process of perceptual learning (except for eye movements), the actions of the individual are critical in this approach: What are learned are particular motor–sensory correspondences, and these are calibrated through the individual's behavior. Representative accounts of this position can be found in Held (1965), Harris (1965), and Hein (1980).

It is important to examine the concept of feedback more closely. A child reaching for an object will receive feedback indicating whether contact is made; if it is not, subsequent adjustments and further feedback will eventually lead to accurate reaching. Similarly, the manipulation of an object will lead to feedback resulting in the gradual accommodation, for example, of the hand to its shape. The type of feedback arising from actions directed at physical features of the environment can be contrasted with that obtained from responses to the social environment. One of the signal features of the child's social environment is its *interactive* nature. From the smiles of the infant to the most complex forms of group behavior in adolescence, the individuals making up the child's social environment respond to the child's behavior and thus enter into a reciprocal, interactive relationship with the child. The child's interaction with the social environment has a more open-ended and generative quality than the closed response feedback loop characteristic of the child's relationship with the physical environment, where feedback is strictly contingent on the child's behavior. Accordingly, we may differentiate between physical and social aspects of the environment, or inanimate and animate aspects of the environment, in terms of the type of feedback relationship that obtains between the child and the environmental feature in question (cf. Wohlwill, 1983).

Whatever the validity of this proposed differentiation between the physical and the social environment, the importance of the feedback concept in contemporary analyses of environment–behavior relations in infancy and childhood is apparent from a perusal of much of the recent literature in the field (e.g., Ainsworth & Bell, 1974; Bell & Harper, 1974; Wachs & Gruen, 1982). Much of the interest in feedback relates to infants' and children's interactions with adults and peers; specifically, there has been a major shift in recent years from earlier formulations of the role of parents and other adults as socializing agents to an emphasis on the reciprocal relationship between parents' and children's behavior (Bell & Harper, 1974). At the same time, the role of feedback from physical objects in early development has become increasingly recognized (Wachs & Gruen, 1982; Yarrow, Rubenstein, & Pedersen, 1975).

Objects vary in terms of the variety and saliency of the feedback they provide. For example. the jack-in-the-box and variants of this toy offer a diversity of salient stimulation, for example, sudden movements and sounds, that are contingent on the actions of the child. In comparison, an object such as a block produces a much more limited kind of feedback when manipulated by a child. As we will see later, there is growing evidence for the positive relationship between the presence of highly responsive toys in the home and perceptual–cognitive development. It should also be noted that the notion of feedback is embodied in much of the work on response–contingent environments by psychologists working from an operant perspective (e.g., Krasner, 1980).

Our preceding analysis of the environment as a source of sensory stimulation as well as a source of feedback invites a comparison between two different modes of responsiveness to the environment. In the first mode, the organism acts as an essentially passive recipient of ambient stimulation impinging on it from its surroundings, and affecting its concurrent behavior and its development over time, without necessarily eliciting any specific overt response on the part of the individual. In the second, the organism is in active interaction with the environment. But rather than representing opposite philosophical or epistemological stances (cf. Reese & Overton, 1970) it is possible to consider these as complementary modes that operate in different situations, according to the developmental status of the organism on the one hand and the characteristics of the environment on the other (Wohlwill, 1983). Ambient stimulation (in the form of background levels of brightness and noise, or activity level) may be especially significant in the case of the immature organism whose capacities to control its exposure to stimulus conditions are limited. As the child becomes more behaviorally competent, the role of response feedback undoubtedly grows in significance. Furthermore, the relative preponderance of ambient stimulation and sources of feedback in the environment may vary across situations as well as temporary states of the organism.

Apart from pointing to very different but by no means mutually exclusive ways in which the individual may relate to his or her environment, the contrast just drawn between the ambient stimulation mode and the response feedback mode serves as a useful framework within which to consider further forms of the environment–behavior relationship. One alternative of particular significance for the developing child is a conceptualization of the environment as a set of affordances.

The Environment as a Set of Affordances

The affordance perspective offers a third view of environment–behavior relations relevant to development. Although this perspective has not as yet exerted a significant impact on developmental research, it presents new and exciting possibilities (cf. E.J. Gibson, 1982; Heft, 1984). The concept of affordances was developed by J.J. Gibson (1966, 1979) in the context of his theory of perception.

Simply stated, "the affordances of the environment are what it *offers* the animal, what it *provides* or *furnishes*, either for good or ill" (Gibson, 1979, p. 127). Affordances are features of the environment, considered at the terrestrial scale of everyday objects and places, which are identified because of their functional significance for an animal. For instance, in the case of human beings, a surface of support affords walking on, a knife affords cutting, a brink affords falling off, and a looming object affords imminent collision. The affordances of a setting can be thought of as its ecological resources from a functional point of view.

J.J. Gibson posits that actions of the perceiver play a fundamental role in the pickup of stimulus information. Rather than identifying visual perception solely with sensory functions, he stresses the significance of the perceiver's movements in facilitating the extraction of information in the ambient array of environmental stimulation. The collaboration of sensory functions and exploratory actions in perceiving is subsumed under the term *perceptual system* (J.J. Gibson, 1966). A species' perceptual systems are considered to have evolved in relation to the affordances comprising its ecological niche, and it is these functionally significant ecological features that the animal perceives and actively engages.

The concept of affordances expresses a *complementarity* between animal and environment. The animal's structural and functional characteristics are considered in relation to environmental affordances; conversely, an affordance can only be specified in relation to a specific animal.

Conceptually, affordances have an unusual status. Affordances are ecologically real; they are not mental representations of the environment. Affordances comprise the animal's ecological niche, and further, they are potentially specifiable in terms of invariants in the ambient array of stimulus information available to the individual. They are, in other words, "objective." At the same time, unlike most objective features, affordances are defined by their *meanings*, that is, their functional possibilities and biological consequences to the perceiver. Typically, meaning is considered to be a "subjective" quality that perceivers impose on sensory input. As features of the environment that are at once objective *and* meaningful, however, affordances cut across the traditional objective–subjective dichotomy in psychology and philosophy (cf. Heft, 1981). This concept thus extends a unique possibility to the environmentally minded psychologist: It provides a possibility for the formulation of an objectively specifiable *and* psychologically meaningful taxonomy of the environment.

Because affordances are specified in relation to an individual, they are readily incorporated into a developmental analysis of perception (see E.J. Gibson, 1982). As the individual's psychological and physical characteristics change developmentally, what action possibilities the environment affords changes in a reciprocal fashion. For example, those features of the environment that can serve as climbing-on places, getting-underneath places, getting-in-between places, graspable objects, and manipulatable objects all vary with development. Recognition of this fact indicates that there is a developmental dimension to the environment, just as there is for the individual.

It may be instructive to examine the affordance approach in relation to the two views considered earlier, namely, the sensory stimulation and response feedback models. It shares with the latter a view of perception as an active process, but emphasizes the role of the perceiver's actions as revealing stimulus information specifying environmental affordances, rather than establishing motor–sensory correlations. Like the sensory stimulation view, the affordance perspective focuses on environmental stimulus conditions, but these conditions are constructed in very different ways in each approach. Thus in the affordance view the perceiver actively engages the environment as sensory and motor processes collaborate in the pickup of environmental information (cf. J.J. Gibson, 1979).

The Differentiation Between the Inanimate and the Social Environment

Child psychologists have in the past viewed the environment primarily in interpersonal, social, and cultural terms. Perhaps implicitly and at times explicitly (cf. Provence & Lipton, 1962) it has been assumed that the physical side of the environment can exert an influence on children only as it is mediated through significant persons. The invalidity of such an assumption should be evident from a consideration of the animal literature alone (cf. Thompson & Grusec, 1970), in which attributes of the stimulus environment have been subjected to systematic manipulation, as well as from the growing evidence of significant and seemingly direct influences of such physical–environmental variables on child development (e.g., Wachs & Gruen, 1982). Relationships between the physical environment and child behavior have, furthermore, frequently been found to differ from relationships between interpersonal or social variables and behavior (e.g., Wachs & Gruen, 1982; Yarrow et al., 1975), in terms of both the specific aspects of behavior to which they relate and the ages at which relationships are found. An operationally viable differentiation between the two seems thus to represent an important desideratum in this area.

We propose to base such a differentiation on the distinction between animate and inanimate features of the environment. The former include people as well as animals—though it might be noted that the role of the latter, particularly in the form of household pets, has been sadly neglected by child and developmental psychologists. One characteristic that people and animals have in common is that they are responsive to the child's behavior; they thus have the potential for becoming parts of an interactive system with the child, involving reciprocal exchange between both parties. The features of the inanimate environment, on the other hand, include environmental objects that provide some feedback to the child, but, as noted earlier, this feedback is not the continuing, interactive type associated with the social environment. Rather, it is provided only as a direct and immediate product of the child's actions. Manipulation of an object may result in a change in the object's orientation and its location, rapping the object on a surface produces sounds, and so on.[1]

In general, we may distinguish animate from inanimate features of the environment on the basis that only the former seem to offer truly *interactive* feedback. Having said this, we should point out that there are certain exceptions to this distinction. At times, adults and peers can be nonresponsive, functioning in a noninteractive fashion with respect to a particular child. Conversely, there are highly responsive toys and mechanical devices, most notably computers, that approach an interactive relationship with the child. It may be that animate and inanimate features, considered with respect to feedback responsivity, are best differentiated along a continuum, rather than in terms of two discrete categories.

The Differentiation Between Focal and Background Stimulus Conditions

A second distinction that is important in conceptualizing the role of the stimulus environment involves the differentiation between focal and background conditions. Perhaps the most primitive aspect of perceptual experiences is the figure–ground distinction (Hebb, 1949). It is the nature of perception that objects are perceived not in isolation but in relation to a background. Research on problems such as object size constancy, induced motion, and achromatic and chromatic color constancy has demonstrated that the individual perceives both focal features and background, and that background information plays an essential role in perceiving (Hochberg, 1978). Further, as the phenomenologist Merleau-Ponty (1962) put it, "vision is an act with two facets," (p. 46) predicated on the necessity

> To put surroundings in abeyance the better to see the object, and to lose in background what one gains in focal figure, because to look at the object is to plunge oneself into it, and because objects form a system in which one cannot show itself without concealing others. (pp. 67–68)

Sensitivity to background information has *positive* consequences for perceiver–environment interaction to the extent that it contributes to veridical perception of environment features (e.g., as in the case of perceiving object size) as well as to the pickup of information in the surroundings concerning potentially critical stimuli or events. Functionally significant information may be anticipated by unexpected sights in the peripheral visual field such as a hole in the ground, by unexpected background sounds such as a loud street sound, or sudden occurrences of particular perceptual salience such as peripheral motion. Further, it appears that aesthetically pleasing surroundings can enhance ongoing activities in a setting, although the manner in which these particular background factors interact with focal tasks is not clear.

At the same time, however, responsiveness to background conditions may result in attention being drawn away from previously focal stimuli. Thus certain kinds of background information, for example, sudden movements, may distract the perceiver and thereby impede exploration of focal features. Further, background conditions may overwhelm focal aspects of perception, as in the case of loud background noises obtruding on perception of speech. In short, the nature of background conditions has important consequences for environmental perception, including that of affecting the opportunity for careful inspection of particular focal information. Because such opportunity significantly contributes to perceptual and cognitive development, background conditions in settings such as the home or the school deserve close scrutiny.

What is focal or background at any particular time is, however, dependent on the perceptual activities of the individual, rendering an independent assessment of focal and background conditions problematic. If we grant that this is the case, the results from factor analyses of two home environment inventories (Heft, 1979; Wachs, Francis, & McQuiston, 1979) still point to the viability of broad distinctions between those features that relate to focal information and those that are apt to serve as background for focal activities. Thus a recognition of the selective nature of perception and of the significance of background information in perceiving, as well as the results of empirical examinations of environmental conditions, reinforces the necessity for a conceptual distinction between focal and background stimulus conditions.

Ecological Perspectives on Development

A very different conception of the environment from that of stimulation, or that in terms of feedback or affordances, is provided by ecological psychology. In its strictest sense, this term refers to the naturalistic analysis of behavior as developed by Barker, Wright, and their associates and disciples at Kansas. This approach has consistently focused on children and adolescents as preferred subjects for much of their work (Barker & Gump, 1964; Schoggen & Barker, 1977; Wright, 1956), and in fact some of the major techniques employed in this approach, notably the analysis of the *stream of behavior* and the use of the *specimen record*, were developed via intensive study of individual children (e.g., Barker & Wright, 1951).

Yet it is only comparatively recently that this approach, with its stress on the primary role of the setting and the situation in behavior and its predominantly observational methodology, has started to exert an influence on the field of child development. Its central construct, that of the *behavior setting*, has come to be recognized as a potentially valuable focus for the study of children in schools, playgrounds, clubs, and the like. This construct, incidentally, cuts across the physical–social environment distinction. It has, furthermore, proved congenial to those who have wanted to place the study of environment–behavior relations in children (and across the life span) on an overtly behavioral footing so as to broaden such

study beyond the preoccupation with subjectivized perceptions, cognitions, and meanings that has characterized much of environmental psychology. And at the same time the perspective of ecological psychologists has broadened to provide fresh views of problems that developmental psychology has been concerned with all along such as the dynamic character of behavior–environment transactions (cf. Willems, 1973) and the role of the child in seeking out stimuli and exploring the environment (Schoggen & Schoggen, 1984).

There is, nevertheless, a strongly deterministic flavor to such behavior-setting analysis, which has been given explicit recognition by its proponents (e.g., Barker, 1963). This feature makes it difficult to relate the resulting findings to particular *processes* of behavioral development, but it is interesting to cite a finding by Schuster, Murrell, and Cook (1980) suggesting that, within the preschool period, this behavior-setting determinancy, that is, the degree of specificity of the relationships between setting and behavior, undergoes a significant increase.

Relevant in this connection is a distinction proposed by Gump (1975) concerning the application of the behavioral ecology framework to work with children, between a focus on behavior settings and a child-centered focus. The former, which appears to be more characteristic of behavioral ecology's stance in regard to the situational determination of human behavior, is illustrated in most of the classical studies of Midwest. Here the unit of reference is the behavior setting, rather than the individual child. That is, it entails observing the behaviors occurring in a given behavior setting on the part of whatever children happen to frequent it. (There is thus no independently defined *sample of subjects*.) This approach contrasts with one in which a given child or group of children is followed across diverse behavior settings, as Barker and Wright (1951) did in their pioneering study *One Boy's Day*.

A particular feature of the behavior-setting focus in the work of the Kansas group deserves mention since it has served to isolate their work from much of the work in environmental psychology. They tend to define such settings in molar terms, frequently in terms of the function served by the setting (e.g., church, school, etc.), without much attention to the specific physical characteristics of the setting. Yet such characteristics may not only provide important cues that serve to control or guide the behavior of the users (e.g., an open vs. a traditional classroom) but also in other ways influence behavior. For instance, Moore (1983a) reports that in day-care centers characterized by a high amount of spatial definition of their play areas more exploratory activity, interaction, and cooperation are observed than in settings that are less well defined spatially.

Let us note, further, that a considerable amount of work relating to children's use of environments exists that is not directly inspired by the works or concepts of ecological psychology, but is nevertheless closely compatible with that framework. In particular, research on children's territorial range (R. Moore & Young, 1978), which will be given considerable attention in the next section, is "ecological," at least in the sense of referring to children's use of the environment at large, and to a certain extent (e.g., Muchow & Muchow, 1935) even deals with an analysis in terms closely akin to that of behavior settings, that is, looking at children's activities in direct relationship to the characteristics of the environmental setting in which they take place.

But, as already mentioned, the perspective of the Kansas group is only one of a variety of "ecological" views of child behavior that have come into prominence in recent years. Several others should be mentioned, although we should note at the outset that for the most part these have limited themselves to the social environment in their ecological conceptions. This is particularly true of the recent work of Bronfenbrenner (1979), whose *Ecology of Human Development* focuses primarily on the role of the family, the school, and the culture at large, in child behavior, and in modulating the development of the child, with little explicit attention being given to the physical environment. The same is the case with such ecologically oriented work as that of Rogoff (1982), concerned with cultural determinants of cognitive performance in children, and of Oerter and others in Germany (cf. Walter & Oerter, 1979), concerned similarly with the role of the social environment, particularly in adolescent behavior. On the other hand, the work of Smith and Connolly (1980) on young children's behavior on the playground, though more descriptive than systematic–theoretical, represents a good illustration of an ecological stance that pays major attention to such variables as density and spatial organization of the environment, and to such physical attributes as resource availability.

Finally, mention should be made of certain recent trends in developmental psychology that focus on the interaction between developmental processes and factors relating to the environmental setting in which they take place (see Magnusson & Allen, 1983). One particular formulation worth citing here is that of Lerner (1983), which emphasizes the "fit" between the environment and the development of the child. Although originally conceived of to deal with mutual adaptations between parental behavior and that of the child, Lerner's work provides an interesting example of the concept of fit that refers to the physical environment, in terms of a match between the amount of space available to the child and forms of behavior that are attuned to the available space. Here we are indeed close to the ecological psychologists' concept of behavior-setting synomorphy, but in Lerner's treatments the concept of fit takes on a rather more dynamic, developmentally relevant form.

9.1.3. Environmental Psychology and Design in Relation to Child Development

The preceding treatment of recent trends in research and theory on relationships between the environment and the behavioral development of children has proceeded primarily from the perspective of developmental psychology. A rather different but no less significant influence on this field has come from the direction of environmental psychology, considered both as a basic discipline and as a field with more applied concerns. Much of this work has remained essentially divorced from that in developmental psychology proper; there are signs, however, of a definite convergence between these two perspectives (cf. Altman & Wohlwill, 1978).

This convergence has probably proceeded furthest in the realm of the study of spatial cognition and its development (cf. Liben, Patterson, & Newcombe, 1981). This topic, represented by work on cognitive maps, spatial orientation, and wayfinding, has from the start given a prominent place to developmental research, both from the side of geography and environmental psychology and from the developmental side. It is most profitably considered, however, in conjunction with the area of environmental cognition as such; Heft and Wohlwill, Chapter 6 of this volume, has been allocated to it, following upon the chapter by Golledge on environmental cognition.

A different emphasis within environmental psychology that has similarly contributed extensively to work with children is that provided by research on *proxemics*, that is, the study of the use of space in interpersonal behavior. It is represented in the proliferating research on effects of density and the problem of crowding. Although a considerable amount of this work has dealt with child behavior, for the most part it has not been carried out within a developmental framework (see Wohlwill & Van Vliet, 1984a, for a review of much of the relevant literature). The related topics of personal space and privacy (e.g.,

Aiello & Aiello, 1974; Wolfe, 1978) have similarly proved popular for work with children, as they have in environmental psychology more generally. Here, too, we are seeing some incipient signs of a rapprochement with developmental psychology, notably through the interest in problems of privacy and the effects of crowding in the home by some child psychologists such as Parke and Sawin (1979) and Wachs (Wachs & Gruen, 1982).

Yet a further influence emanating from the side of specialists in environment–behavior relations from a more applied direction has been the work concerned with the behavior of children in particular institutional environments, notably those of the school, the hospital, and the playground. This is, of course, the province of the architectural psychologist, or of the behaviorally oriented environmental designer. Because of the practical importance of these types of environments in the lives of children, a considerable amount of attention has been devoted to the features of designed environments considered to be conducive or inimical to optimal behavioral functioning (cf. Coates, 1974; Marcus & Moore, 1976; Moore, 1980a; Olds, 1982; Pollowy, 1977). Moore (in press) has provided a most useful review of the literature based on this approach (see Moore, Lane, & Lindberg, 1979, for a comprehensive bibliography).

On the whole, it seems fair to state that this work, more than that on the preceding topics, has remained largely divorced from the domain of child psychology per se, and from the study of development in particular. Its ties have been rather with the concerns of persons in early childhood education (Kritchevsky, Prescott, & Walling, 1969; cf. also Weinstein, 1979). Two exceptions to the preceding statement should, however, be noted. First, the school and the classroom as an institutional environment have been natural objects of interest to behavioral ecologists, and thus we have witnessed a fair degree of interaction among some representatives of that school—notably Gump (1978)—and persons in education on the one hand, and environmental design on the other. Second, Moore and associates (Moore, 1983b; in press) have been doing research on the effects of different types of environments for children's activities on their behavior, grounded in principles of cognitive development and child play. They have, furthermore, attempted to apply these principles to improve the design of facilities for children such as daycare centers, play environments, and institutions for the handicapped.

In the review of the literature to follow, we will give primary emphasis to two contrasting perspectives. The first is that considered in the first three subsections of Section 9.2.1, that is, relations between the stimulus environment and behavior, whether the former are considered as a source of stimulation, passively received, of affordances for particular forms of behavior or of feedback. The second perspective is that of ecological psychology, considered both from the standpoint of the behavioral ecologists of the Kansas school and in a broader sense.

It should be noted that much of this literature does not deal directly with the developmental aspects of our topic, though it is clearly relevant to developmental conceptions. We will try to preserve a developmental focus, however, as much as possible, through comments about the developmental implications at various points in our review, and more particularly in our concluding section.

As for material from the design areas, that will be considered primarily as it relates to the previously mentioned two perspectives; implications of the research to be reviewed for the design of environments for children will be brought out more specifically in our concluding section.

9.2. REVIEW OF THE RESEARCH LITERATURE

A truly comprehensive examination of the evidence on effects of environmental stimulation on development would ideally include coverage of the experimental research at the animal level, which has provided more clear-cut evidence on the role of specific environmental variables than the necessarily nonexperimental literature on human children. While there are always those who question or deny the relevance of findings on animals for the human level, the fact is that much of this research (notably that based on Hebbian views of development, and that carried out by Levine, Denenberg, and their associates on the role of early stress) does have important implications for human development. But limitations of space preclude consideration of this work in any detail. Interested readers are referred to the very comprehensive review of the early-experience literature by Thompson and Grusec (1970), as well as to the anthology covering this area edited by Newton and Levine (1967) (see particularly the chapters by Melzack, Denenberg, and Mason, Davenport, & Menzel). A shorter but more recent review of similar work is that of Henderson (1980).

Accordingly, our review is focused on work with children, starting out with studies that relate specifically to the home environment, and to alternative residential settings (e.g., institutions), as well as schools, concentrating in particular on aspects relevant to our concern for the stimulus environment. Our focus will be expanded beyond that particular concern to a consideration of the outdoor environment and of the role of environments considered at a macroscale (i.e., urban, rural).

Thus the review will be organized primarily on the basis of the *scale* at which the environment is considered, from that of individual rooms and spaces in the home to that of the city or the greater outdoors. But that scale turns out to be relevant to and partially isomorphic with the various conceptions of the environment–behavior relationship to which we alluded in the preceding section. Thus research on home environments brings out ideally the role of focal and background stimulation, as well as to some extent that of affordances and feedback. The last two are similarly relevant to research on children's activities on the playground, but at the same time we find a more ecological stance emerging in relation to these activities, which comes into its own in the work on territorial range and on children's behavior in environments at the scale of the neighborhood and the city. The topic of children's response to the natural environment, finally, prompts renewed attention to the role of environmental stimulation, if only because of the relatively undifferentiated character of that environment, and the lack, therefore, of specific behavior settings, or even of specific objects to which the child's response might be related.

9.2.1. The Home Environment

For the first years of life, the home is the primary environment for the developing child, although the increasing use of various types of day care indicates that for many young children the home is not the only significant setting for early development. Further, as the child grows older other places such as school environment and the neighborhood also become central in the child's everyday activities. However, even with these changes, the home remains the dominant setting throughout childhood (Barker & Wright, 1955).

Consistent with the theme of this chapter and with the conceptual distinctions drawn earlier, in the following discussion we shall focus on the inanimate features of the home environment, and in doing so we shall distinguish between focal and background conditions of stimulation present in the setting. Focal conditions will be differentiated into those relating to objects and those concerning temporal patterning of

events, and background conditions into noise and activity levels. In addition, opportunities for environmental exploration and needs for privacy will be considered more briefly.

Focal Objects

Although the nature of focal object conditions has been assessed in many different ways across various studies, it is possible to extract a set of stimulus dimensions that is common to most investigations. Drawing on the classification scheme suggested by Wachs and Gruen (1982), focal object conditions will be considered in terms of availability of objects, diversity and complexity of objects, and responsivity of objects.

AVAILABILITY OF OBJECTS

Availability refers to the presence and accessibility of objects of a given class such as toys. The availability of objects for the child has been found to be positively related to psychological development in a number of investigations. In a series of studies, Wachs and his colleagues have examined infant cognitive development as assessed by a Piagetian-based developmental index (Uzgiris & Hunt, 1975) in relation to home environment conditions. Access to magazines, books, and small, manipulatable objects and the presence of decorations in a child's room were positively correlated with developmental measures such as schema development and object permanence during the first 2 years of life (Wachs, 1976; Wachs, Uzgiris, & Hunt, 1971). It should be noted that typically these environmental variables were not related to a wide range of measures; rather, their effects seemed to be specific to one or two developmental indices. This pattern of findings suggests that the availability of particular types of environmental objects is most significant for certain aspects of development, rather than having a global impact—a relationship that Wachs and Gruen (1982) refer to as one of *environmental specificity*.

In the more recent studies in this series, Wachs (1978, 1979) has extended his analysis to longer-range effects of these environmental variables. For example, he found that the availability of newspapers, magazines, and books at 14 months was positively related to object permanence in males not only at 15 months, but at 24 months as well. Similarly, presence of decorations in the child's room, assessed at 14, 17, and 23 months, was positively correlated with intelligence (Binet scores) measured at 2½ years (Wachs, 1978). Such findings indicate that the effects of these environmental variables may be more than transitory.

Other studies have also reported a positive correlation between availability of objects and developmental measures. Ainsworth and Bell (1974) found that the presence of toys at 8 months and at 11 months was positively related to performance on the Griffiths Infant Scale at those times. Clarke-Stewart (1973) reported that the number of toys available in the home at 17 months was related to schema development and to overall infant competence, as assessed by a composite score on a variety of performance measures. At the same time, however, Clarke-Stewart did not find this environmental variable to be correlated with performance on standardized developmental indices such as the Bayley Scale and the Uzgiris-Hunt Scale.

In their view of the early-experience research, Wachs and Gruen (1982) point out that the relationship between availability of objects and development may be most apparent prior to 9 months of age. After this time the findings are less consistent, and they suggest that this is largely attributable to the onset of walking. Increased mobility after 9 months results in greater opportunities for exploration, and the child's activity is no longer limited to those objects that are immediately available.

DIVERSITY AND COMPLEXITY OF OBJECTS

A more qualitative aspect of focal object conditions concerns the diversity and complexity of the available objects, which can be considered to indicate the richness of stimulus information that the home environment affords.

Yarrow and colleagues (1975) assessed object variety and complexity in the home in relation to development for a sample of 5-month-olds. They defined variety as "the richness and nonrepetitive character of the inanimate environment" (p. 42), and this variable was operationalized as the number of different play objects immediately available to the infant. Object complexity was conceptualized in terms of "the amount of 'information' it provides the child through various sensory modalities" (p. 43). Complexity was assessed with respect to number of different colors, visual and tactile patterns, shape, size, and responsiveness of available toys. These investigators found that variety of toys was positively correlated with measures of infant mental and motor development (Bayley Scales), cognitive–motivational development (e.g., visually directed reaching and grasping, secondary circular reactions), and preference for novelty. Similarly, complexity of available

toys was positively related to cognitive–motivational development and preference for novelty. In contrast, Yarrow, Morgan, Jennings, Harmon, and Gaiter (1982) failed to uncover a relationship between variety of toys present in the home at 6 months and developmental assessment at 13 months of persistence and competence at tasks, and of cognitive and motor performance (Bayley Scales).

The diversity of object conditions also proved to be a significant variable in Wachs's research program. Specifically, variations in interior furnishings and in colors were both positively correlated with measures of infant cognitive development at different times during the first 2 years (Wachs et al., 1971). Similarly, the introduction of new toys into the home was positively related to the development of schemes and object permanence (Wachs, 1976). Further, measures of diversity among focal conditions were found to have relatively long-range effects. For example, introduction of new toys at 12 to 14 months and changes in decorations in the child's room at 15 to 17 months were positively correlated with two different measures of development at 24 months. These relationships differed, however, across gender—an interaction effect that Wachs and Gruen (1982) refer to as *organismic specificity*, as a counterpart to the environmental specificity described previously. Finally, the introduction of new toys in the home at 18 to 20 months was positively correlated with Binet performance at 31 months, for both genders (Wachs, 1978).

Additional evidence for possible long-range effects of diversity of focal object conditions can be found in the research of Caldwell and her colleagues, who employ the environmental inventory Home Observation for Measurement of the Environment (HOME; see Caldwell, Heider, & Kaplan, 1966; Elardo & Bradley, 1981). One dimension of this inventory assesses "provision of appropriate play materials" and contains nine items directed at availability of specific types of toys. (Only one out of four items comprising their "opportunities for variety in daily stimulation" dimension refers to focal objects.) Diversity in play materials assessed at 6 months was positively related to intelligence, as measured by the Binet (Elardo, Bradley, & Caldwell, 1975), and to language development (Elardo, Bradley, & Caldwell, 1977), both assessed at 3 years of age.

Finally, Clarke-Stewart (1973) assessed the variety and age appropriateness of toys (using a single item) and found that this variable was positively correlated with level or complexity of toy play by the child, length of involvement in toy play, and number and variety of objects played with, all examined during the period 12 to 17 months. Further, this environmental variable was positively related to performance on the Bayley Scale at 17½ months and to a composite measure of competence.

RESPONSIVITY OF OBJECTS

When children visually inspect an object by turning it in their hands or moving with respect to it, they discover its invariant properties and also their own capacity to create changes in the perceived environment. Interaction with objects thus has a dual function: It leads to identification of distinctive object properties, that is, its affordances, and it develops the individual's skills in interacting with the environment. Stimulated by White's (1959) formulation of the competence concept, researchers have come to recognize this latter type of learning as playing an important role in cognitive development (e.g., Harter, 1981; Yarrow et al., 1981; Yarrow, McQuiston, Mac-Turk, McCarthy, Klein, & Vietze, 1983).

Although all manipulatable objects provide some feedback to the individual manipulating them, some toys are particularly responsive to a child's actions on them, producing highly salient or novel effects. Rattles, tops, jack-in-the-boxes, and the more modern "busy boxes" are examples of such toys. Because of their capacity to provide response-contingent feedback, many investigators have supposed that such toys should have a facilitating effect on a variety of aspects of cognitive–motivational development. Thus far, the data have largely borne out this supposition.

A positive relationship between the presence of responsive toys in the home and infant cognitive development has been among the most consistent findings in Wachs's research. This environmental characteristic was found to be correlated with a variety of behavioral measures, both concurrently (Wachs, 1976; Wachs et al., 1971) and across longer time spans (Wachs, 1978, 1979). Similarly, Yarrow and colleagues (1975) have found that the presence of responsive toys is positively correlated with infant cognitive and motor development, as well as with exploration and novelty preference. Jennings, Harmon, Morgan, Gaiter, & Yarrow (1979) and Yarrow and colleagues (1982) also report that this variable is positively related to persistence in toy play and competence in task mastery. These findings suggest that feedback about one's capacity to effect change in the environment is an important contribution to cognitive–motor development.

Temporal Patterning of Focal Events

With reference to both the social and the physical environment, environmental predictability has generally been assumed to constitute an important determinant of the optimal development of a child. Accordingly, a considerable amount of research has dealt with the organization of the day in the home. An early suggestion of the possible significance of this variable came from Gray and Klaus's (1968) study of the homes of economically disadvantaged children. They noted that these home environments are often characterized by a lack of order and predictability in occurrences such as mealtimes. In a more precise analysis of daily events in the home, Wachs found that regularity of naptimes and mealtimes in infancy was positively correlated with cognitive development, both concurrently (Wachs, 1976, 1979) and at 2½ years (Wachs, 1978). Finally, Caldwell and her colleagues have found a positive relationship between the dimension "organization of physical and temporal environment" on the HOME Scale and cognitive developmental indices (Bradley & Caldwell, 1976; Elardo et al., 1975). This dimension is, however, rather more broadly defined, being made up of items that transcend the home (e.g., whether the child is regularly taken to a doctor) or relate to its spatial organization (e.g., whether there is a "special place" for the child's toys).

CONCLUDING COMMENT

Considering the work on focal stimulation more generally, one important shortcoming of all of these studies should be noted: They have been limited to the period of infancy, or at best extend up to very early childhood. This type of analysis will need to be expanded into later childhood and adolescence if we are to obtain a broader picture of the relevance of the relationships that have been demonstrated across the span of the development of the individual to maturity. More particularly, it would be important to determine whether specific environmental characteristics assume a dominant role at certain times in development. With regard to the latter point, Wohlwill (1983) has recently argued that the impact of different "environmental modes" (e.g., ambient vs. interactive) may change during the course of development. Further, it will be important to assess the possible long-range effects of particular focal conditions. Wachs (1978, 1979) has made an important initial step in this direction; however, studies with a more extensive time frame are needed. Some investigators (e.g., Clarke & Clarke, 1976; Kagan & Klein, 1973) have questioned the significance of *early* experience, although not environmental experience per se, and further stress the resiliency rather than the malleability of the developing individual. Longitudinal studies assessing the connections between early environmental experience and later development will help to resolve this controversy (cf. the discussion by Wachs & Gruen, 1982, pp. 2–7). Finally, a more complete uinderstanding of the selective effects of certain focal conditions will improve efforts to evalutate early envi romments and to determine the most appropriate environmental modifications in cases where such remediation is needed.

Background Conditions: Noise and Activity Level

As discussed earlier, a consideration of the environment in relation to psychological functioning must go beyond an analysis of focal objects and events. Background conditions may significantly affect the child's interactions with focal features, as we will see in the following discussion. Two aspects of background conditions may be distinguished: noise and activity level. Sources of background noise in the home include television, radio, stereo, appliances, family activities, and external sources such as surface and air traffic and neighborhood sounds. The general activity level in the home derives from such circumstances as the pace of family events and the rate of family interactions. This conceptual distinction between background noise and activity level has received some support from a factor-analytic study of the Purdue Home Stimulation Inventory in which measures of each of these environmental characteristics were found to load on distinct factors (Wachs et al., 1979).

The Concept of Noise and Its Measurement
Noise has been operationalized in different ways in the investigations directed at the effects of noise in the home and the school. The simplest methodological distinction to draw is between those studies utilizing physical measures versus those employing observer ratings. Most of the investigations to be considered employ decibel readings as physical estimates of sound intensity. Although in principle this approach promotes reliability as well as generalizability across different studies, the absence of a formal standardized procedure has kept these advantages from becoming fully realized to date.[2]

Observer ratings of sonic conditions are not as reliable measures as physical indices, but this is not to say that estimates of reasonably high reliability cannot be obtained with this approach (e.g., Heft, 1979; Wachs, 1982). Observer ratings have the advantage of permitting contextual and other psychological factors to be included in an evaluation, although the absence of a physical value makes it difficult to compare sonic conditions across different studies.

In short, each of these approaches has its advantages and disadvantages; since measures based on each appear to be poorly correlated with one another (Cohen & Weinstein, 1982), perhaps the safest approach would be to use them in combination, but that has rarely if ever been done, at least in research with children.

Apart from the measurement issue, it is important to recognize that noise is not a unitary dimension but can be separated into several different aspects, in functional terms. Thus noise may represent a source of distraction during attention to or exploration of a focal object (e.g., Turnure, 1970); it may serve to mask auditory messages—particularly for young children (Larson & Peterson, 1978), or it may create a state of nonspecific arousal that results in decreased sensitivity to both focal and nonfocal aspects of a situation or task (Cohen, 1978). Finally, noise may impair an individual's sense of control over his or her environment, especially in the case of children who generally lack the means to abate or avoid it, so as to develop behavioral manifestations of passivity or helplessness (e.g., Cohen, Evans, Krantz, & Stokols, 1980). This diversity of potential impacts of noise on children's behavior and functioning should be borne in mind in relation to the research literature to be reviewed (see Heft, 1982, for a more comprehensive treatment of this problem; also DeJoy, 1983, for a recent review of this literature).

Background Noise in the Home
Children's exposure to noise in the home, as well as in school and neighborhood settings, has recently been documented by Roche, Chumlea, and Siervogel (1982). In this research children between 6 and 18 years wore portable dosimeters for 24-hour periods and simultaneously kept a diary of their daily activities. With the data from these two sources the investigators could determine levels of noise exposure for particular settings and activities. Peak sound intensities from sources within the home (e.g., small appliances, radio, TV, conversations) were all within a comparable range, approximately $L_{eq} = 73$–77 dB. It is noteworthy that this range exceeds the safe intensity level for chronic noise exposure cited by EPA (U.S. Environmental Protection Agency, 1974). Ac-

cording to EPA, long-term daily exposure to intensities exceeding L_{eq} (24) = 70 dBA may lead to hearing loss. Further, Roche and colleagues (1982) report an inverse relationship between noise exposure and age; the younger children in the sample, and the boys in particular, were exposed to the highest sound levels. Whether this trend would continue with even younger children is an open question, but it is an important one since the developmental effects of noise exposure could be greatest during the early years, as suggested by results from animal research (Mills, 1975).

The effects of noise in the home on human infant development have been examined by Wachs in his comprehensive analysis of the early environment. In the initial study of this research series (Wachs et al., 1971), noise from the neighborhood, from the home, and from television sets in particular was found to be negatively correlated with infant cognitive development. In succeeding studies, Wachs developed a noise confusion index, which is an observer estimate of the intensity and duration of noise combined across all audible sources over the observational period. The number of sound sources audible in the home was also noted. The noise confusion measure was found to be negatively correlated with various measures of cognitive development, when measured both concurrently during the second year (Wachs, 1976) and across a 1-year time span (Wachs, 1978, 1979).

In a recent overview of this research, Wachs (1982) pointed out that sonic conditions in the home as assessed by his measures seem to have their greatest impact on language development. His data reveal consistent inverse relationships between both noise confusion and number of noise sources on the one hand and verbal imitation on the other. Further, unpublished data indicate that these noise measures obtained at 6 months were negatively correlated with a variety of language development indices at 24 months. It should be noted, however, that most of the negative correlations between noise and language development were limited to male infants—an instance of organismic specificity. In the same vein, Wachs and Gandour (1983) report an environment–temperament interaction: Specifically, noise confusion ratings were negatively correlated with several aspects of cognitive development at 6 months for temperamentally "difficult" infants, while this pattern of relationships did not obtain for temperamentally "easy" children. The researchers suggest that the latter group is more sensitive to social aspects of the home environment, whereas the "difficult" infants are especially susceptible to nonsocial aspects of the environment such as noise. In general, what emerges from this research is a complex picture of interrelationships between noise conditions and person characteristics. As Wachs (1982) suggests, the impact of noise might best be considered as an interaction effect rather than a main effect.

Heft (1979) examined the impact of sonic conditions in the home on the perceptual development of kindergarten-age children (mean age = 5 years, 8 months). Noise level in the home was assessed by combining ratings, from parent interviews concerning four sources of noise: family activities; television and radio or stereo; appliances; and exterior sources. Noise ratings were found to be correlated with two performance measures. Higher noise levels were inversely related to reaction time on a visual search task, as well as to sensitivity to incidental information on the same task. That is, children from the noisier homes were less efficient in perceiving either focal or peripheral aspects of the task. Children from the noisier homes were, however, less affected by an auditory distractor on a visual matching task than were their counterparts in the quieter homes; but, given their poorer performance on the visual search task overall, this lower degree of distractibility can be viewed, at best, as selective adaptation to sonic conditions. In other words, high noise levels in the home may have an adverse effect on the development of perceptual skills, in spite of adaptation to the distracting effects of noise onset on their task performance. These findings support Glass and Singer's (1972) contention that adaptation is selective rather than general (see also the discussion by Wohlwill, 1974).

The field investigation of the impact of noise on children by Cohen, Glass, and Singer (1973) differs from the studies just considered in that it focuses on noise sources outside the home. The site of their research was a high-rise apartment building located directly over an urban expressway. Taking advantage of the naturally occurring circumstance that sound levels from the traffic gradually diminish with building height, these investigators examined the relationship between floor location of an apartment and the auditory discrimination skills and reading achievement of its young occupants (grades 2 to 5). Both of these performance measures were found to be inversely related to floor level, even after demographic variables such as economic status and parents' educational level were partialed out. Thus those children living on the lower floors of the building and exposed to the higher levels of traffic noise were comparatively deficient in auditory discrimination skills and to a lesser extent in reading ability compared to their counterparts on the upper floors. The magnitude of the correlation between floor level and reading achievement was, however, reduced considerably when performance on the auditory discrimination test was partialed out, suggested that the primary impact of the sonic conditions was on auditory discrimination, which in turn probably plays a mediating role in the development of language and reading skills. It is further noteworthy that the correlations between floor level and both performance measures *increased* with the length of time the child had lived in the apartment, indicating a cumulative negative effect of chronic exposure to these noise conditions.

ACTIVITY LEVEL IN THE HOME

The background of activity level in the home, derived from family interactions and from various comings and goings during the day, may also serve to impede focal exploration. For example, sudden and unexpected movements in the peripheral visual field may distract the child from sustained interaction with focal features. Consequently, chronically high levels of background activity could have implications for perceptual learning and cognitive development. At the present time, attempts to assess this possible environment–development relationship have met with only partial success.

Wachs and colleagues (1971) found that observer ratings of activity level in the home assessed when the infant was 7 and 11 months of age were negatively correlated with a variety of cognitive developmental indices at those times. The home inventory used in Wachs's (1976, 1978, 1979) later research included items relating to activity level, number of people in the home during the observation period, and number of strangers in the home during that time. A factor-analytic study of the inventory revealed that these three items loaded on a common factor (Wachs et al., 1979). In the home studies employing the inventory, activity level ratings were related to a measure of cognitive development in females (understanding of causality), and significantly, ratings obtained at one time were correlated with performance at a later point (Wachs, 1979). Similarly, number of people and number of strangers in the home were both found to be inversely related to several measures of infant development, and in some instances there were long-term predictive relationships

(Wachs, 1978, 1979). In contrast to these findings, Heft (1979) failed to uncover a relationship between activity level in the home and psychological development, but in this study only a single rating of activity level was employed.

RESIDENTIAL DENSITY AS A MEASURE OF BACKGROUND STIMULATION

Measures of residential density may serve as indirect estimates of background conditions. Density measures, as such, are quantitative assessments of number of persons per spatial unit; in studies of the home, the measure most often employed is persons per room. It might be expected that as residential density increases experientially there is an increase in noise and crowding (Heft, 1984). For example, a relatively high level of density in the home may be associated with high noise levels generated from family activities in close proximity, as well as intersecting activity patterns with their attendant potentially distracting character. For this reason our examination of background conditions in the home will include a brief consideration of the relationship between residential density and development. It bears repeating that density is only an indirect estimate of background conditions; a statistical relationship between density and some developmental outcome may be attributable to numerous factors other than background conditions, many of which are probably related to socioeconomic factors. In most of the studies to be discussed, either socioeconomic status was statistically controlled, or the investigations focused on fairly circumscribed socioeconomic groups (see Baum & Paulus, Chapter 14, this volume, for a more extensive treatment of density and crowding issues).

Wachs (1976, 1978, 1979) found that higher levels of residential density were associated with lower performance scores on measures of infant cognitive development, including object permanence, development of schemes, and verbal imitation. Moreover, in the later studies of this series, density measures at one age (e.g., 12 to 14 months) were inversely related to performance at older ages (e.g., Binet scores at 31 months). Similarly, Heft (1979) reported that higher levels of residential density were negatively correlated with performance on a visual search task and, further, were associated with less susceptibility to auditory distraction, even after controlling for income level. As noted previously for the effects of noise, this pattern of findings points to adverse effects of environmental conditions, in spite of selective adaptation. In an examination of the reading achievement performance of second through sixth graders living in low-income public housing, Saegert (1980) found that the children living in those apartments with high densities had lower vocabulary scores when performance was examined in relation to both average scores for their grade level and average scores for their own class. Finally, Rodin (1976) has reported a relationship between level of residential density and the development of feelings of efficacy or control over environmental events. Specifically, she found that among children (6 to 9 years) of low-income families, those from high-density homes were less likely to attempt to control reward outcomes in a laboratory game situation and were more adversely affected by prior failures on a problem-solving task than their counterparts from lower-density homes.

CONCLUDING COMMENT

The preceding analyses of background conditions in the home have served as an important corrective to previous views about environment–development relations in addition to providing insight into the potential effects of the specific variables considered. As discussed earlier (Section 9.1.1), in the past an implicit assumption of researchers in the early experience area was that the relationship between environmental stimulation and development was a positive, monotonic one. This statement appears to represent a considerable oversimplification of the situation, however. While it may be warranted for focal stimulation, when we examine effects of background stimulation, the relationship with development is revealed as an *inverse* function. Further, certain environmental variables may selectively affect particular aspects of development (environmental specificity), and certain types of individuals may be especially sensitive to particular conditions (organismic specificity). Future research will likely apprise us of additional complexities of environment–development relationships, including, perhaps, some ways in which background conditions might positively contribute to ongoing focal activities and thus enhance behavioral development.

Note, finally, the practical relevance of the preceding analysis. The very conditions that have been shown to affect development adversely appear to be those that characterize the typical lower-class home according to Fein and Clarke-Stewart (1973, pp. 165–166): crowding, clutter, and high ambient noise levels from TV and radio; conversely, it is apt to be lacking in focal objects (toys and other educationally relevant materials). It does not seem implausible to see in

this set of conditions at least a potent contributor to the syndrome that has been designated as *cultural deprivation.*

Exploratory Activity in the Home Environment

Opportunities to explore the environment contribute directly to the child's psychological development. Knowledge about objects and environmental events (i.e., about their affordant properties), as well as awareness of one's own competencies in interacting with the environment, comes about through exploration. On their own, children spend much of their day exploring the world around them. One observational analysis estimated that children between the ages of 12 and 33 months devote 44% of their waking hours to such activities as seeking visual and auditory information, actively exploring their surroundings, and engaging in motor mastery actions (White, Kaban, Shapiro, & Attanucci, 1977). Given our focus in this chapter on the home environment, one important issue revolves around the question of whether the environment is supportive or restrictive of the child's explorations.

The supportive/restrictive character of the home environment depends primarily on the caretaker's orientation to child care. Exploration can be encouraged, and the child can be given the freedom to move about in the home, or such activities can be limited to varying degrees either through disciplinary restrictions or with physical restraints and barriers. Ainsworth and Bell (1974) report that floor freedom was positively correlated with infant development (Griffiths Scale) assessed at 8 and 11 months. Beckwith, Cohen, Kopp, Parmelee, and Marcy (1976) similarly found a positive relationship between floor freedom, including an absence of barriers, and development (Gesell Scale) at 8 months. Consistent with these findings, Jennings and colleagues (1979) reported a negative correlation between maternal prohibitions in the home and the child's production of effects during object play at one year.

The amount of floor freedom afforded the child during the second year was also found to be positively related to development. Specifically, Wachs (1976) reported a positive correlation between assessments of this variable and object permanence at 21 and 24 months. This variable was also found to be related to a different measure of development (foresight) among male infants during the second year (Wachs, 1979). Finally, Elardo and colleagues (1975) found that "avoidance of restriction and punishment," a factor on the HOME inventory, was positively related to measures of intellectual development at 3 years. However, only one of the eight items comprising this factor related to curtailing exploration as such.

With regard to the use of barriers or playpens specifically to limit exploration, Wachs (1976) found that the absence of such restraints was positively correlated with object permanence at 21 months. In addition, this same variable assessed at one point during the second year was associated with a variety of developmental measures later in infancy (Wachs, 1978, 1979). White and Watts (1973) presented further evidence for the long-range effects of physical restrictions on exploration. They found that those children evaluated by their preschool teachers as highly competent in the classroom spent considerably less time in playpens at home than those seen as less competent. Similarly, Tulkin and Covitz (1975) reported that time spent in a playpen at 10 months was negatively correlated with intelligence (Peabody Picture Vocabulary Test) at 6 years, although this relationship obtained for middle-class and not for lower-class children. In contrast to these findings, Jennings and colleagues (1979) found that use of barriers in the home was associated with a *greater* amount of exploration, when the latter was assessed in a laboratory setting.

In sum, the existing evidence indicates, for the most part, that opportunities to explore the home environment, including the absence of barriers as activity restraints, are positively associated with cognitive development.

Privacy and Territoriality in the Home: A Brief Note

Since the topics of privacy and territoriality are covered in Aiello, Chapter 12, this volume (including work with children), we will not deal with them extensively here. It is worth noting, however, that at the youngest age levels needs for privacy and territoriality may be closely related to what Wachs and colleagues (1971) have termed the role of a *stimulus shelter*, that is, the availability of a room into which the infant could retreat to escape the noise and the hustle and bustle of more central portions of the home. This factor turned out in fact to show highly consistent correlations with several measures of cognitive development in infancy, at ages 7, 11, 15, and 22 months; this relationship was confirmed in a later study (Wachs, 1979) that showed significant correlations between the availability of a stimulus shelter

early in the second year of life and several developmental measures obtained at the end of that year. (A shortcoming of Wachs's work, however, is that he failed to obtain direct measures of the extent of the infants' actual use of their rooms as a retreat.)

Of course this is not to suggest that privacy and territoriality serve this protection-from-overstimulation function exclusively; particularly in later years we need to consider privacy in relation to the emergence of the self-concept, presumably reflected in the finding that children at all age levels identified privacy with being *alone*, as reported by Wolfe and Laufer (1974) — a tendency that furthermore increased with age. Similarly, we may assume that sex-role socialization plays a part in behavior such as that of closing doors to bedrooms and bathrooms (cf. Parke & Sawin, 1976). The latter investigators document this relationship in the form of sex differences, indicating earlier onset of certain privacy-related behaviors in girls as compared to boys, consistent with the former's earlier maturation. At the same time they point to the important role of density within the home, somewhat independent of age, in determining such behaviors, in accord with Altman's (1975) concept of the regulation of rate of interaction with others as underlying privacy needs. It should be noted that Parke and Sawin report a curvilinear relationship between family density and the child's tendency to restrict access to the bathroom: The latter was least for intermediate density values. Such research, as well as the broader conceptualization of privacy provided both by Parke and Sawin and by Wolfe (1978), points to the value of a combined environmental and developmental attack on future research in this area.

9.2.2. Institutional Environments and Schools

Alternative Forms of Residential Environments for Children

While the single-family home, whether in the form of an apartment, a town house, or a freestanding house, is considered to be the norm for children in western societies as an environment to live and grow up in, there are of course alternative forms. These vary from communes and the closely related but rather larger and more tightly structured kibbutzim in Israel to institutional environments such as orphanages, homes for delinquent children, and institutions for the retarded. Few of these have been studied specifically with regard to their physical or spatial characteristics, however. Yet one presumes that the different physical space arrangements characterizing these environments, and the resulting alterations in privacy, noise, activity level, and the like, have significant impacts on the children living in them.

Institutional environments, notably orphanages, represent a partial exception to the general lack of evidence concerning alternative environments. The impact of institutional environments on children became of great concern in the 1940s, as reports started to accumulate of seemingly widespread cases of developmental deficit in the areas of physical, mental, and emotional growth. These reports led in fact to the postulation of a syndrome, coined hospitalism, to characterize the condition of institutionalized children (Spitz, 1945). Some of the evidence pointed, furthermore, to effects of such conditions of institutionalization in early life that persevered into later childhood and adolescence, even for children who had been placed into adoptive homes by the age of 3 (e.g., Goldfarb, 1943).

Although interpretations of the effects of institutionalization prevalently centered on the role of maternal deprivation (e.g., Bowlby, 1951), one significant alternative formulation of these effects made specific reference to absence of physical stimulation, and of variety of stimulation in particular, in the institutional environment. The major proponent of this view, Casler (1961, 1967), relied extensively on the previously mentioned theory of Hebb (1949)—the critical importance of a varied sensory input in early life for normal development—and referred to the experimental studies on animals carried out by Hebb's associates to buttress his position (see Thompson & Grusec, 1970, for an excellent review of the relevant evidence). This interpretation is not implausible on the face of it; indeed, there is more than a surface similarity between the highly diverse and generalized impairment of behavioral development found in research on the effects of isolation conditions in early life on the development of Scottish terriers by Thompson and his co-workers (see Thompson & Grusec, 1970) and similar across-the-board effects reported by Goldfarb (1943) for children institutionalized during their first 2 years of life. In both cases, furthermore, the deprivation effects proved rather long lasting. Yet evidence confirming the role of sensory impoverishment as the factor responsible for institutionalization effects has been difficult to come by; a study by White (1971) pointing to limited effects on development of an enrichment of the visual environment of an orphanage through provision of bright decorations as well as mobiles over the cribs represents a rare instance of such evidence.

Ultimately a much more potent kind of intervention focused on the ratio of infants to caretakers, which in many institutions had been distressingly unfavorable. Thus Paraskevopoulos and Hunt (1971) compared children in orphanages in Greece living under typical conditions (i.e., a 10:1 ratio of infants to caretakers) with those for whom that ratio had been radically improved (i.e., 3:1) and found marked beneficial effects from such a modification on their behavioral development. Apart from the more adequate interactive social stimulation from which the children benefited under the lower-ratio conditions, the latter permitted the caretakers to provide the infants under their care with much more opportunity for active motor exploration of their environment, which undoubtedly contributed to their improved development.

Partly as a result of such research and of the attention focused on the deficiencies of ordinary institutional environments, marked improvements appear to have occurred in more recent years in both the environmental supports and the care provided for children in institutional settings, and today it is probably no longer accurate to make any general statements about deprivation conditions operating in such institutions. That conclusion is strengthened by the findings of Tizard and her co-workers (Tizard, Cooperman, Joseph, & Tizard, 1972; Tizard & Rees, 1974), which indicate that under suitable conditions with regard to ratio of children to staff, as well as appropriate environmental stimulation through toys, books, outings, and the like, the severe effects of institutionalization observed earlier are at least considerably attenuated. In fact, Tizard and Hodges (1978) obtained evidence suggesting that favorable institutional conditions can make for an environment superior to that encountered by children raised in their homes under conditions of relative neglect or of inadequate stimulation or resources for play.

On the basis of such evidence, it would seem worthwhile to attempt some specifications of minimal standards for institutional environments and care, much as have been stipulated for day-care settings (e.g., American Academy of Pediatrics, 1973). To our knowledge, no such standards have as yet been promulgated, except in the areas of health and possibly nutrition. As for those relating to day-care centers, they tend to focus on amount of space, both in absolute terms and relative to numbers of children, and other aspects of space use—reflecting to a considerable extent the research carried out, which has tended to focus on problems of crowding and space use, as well as on availability of resources (see Smith & Connolly, 1980). Much of the work in this area is, however, significantly lacking in information on specific relations between features of the environment and the kind of behaviors that the children engage in, although one ecologically oriented study that does provide a descriptive beginning toward such a goal is worth noting in this connection (Shure, 1963).

As Moore (in press) points out, day-care environments provide the setting for an increasing number of children of preschool age in our society; more focused research on the role of particular aspects of those environments is thus clearly called for. One excellent example of such research is an investigation by Moore (1983b; see Moore, in press, for a detailed published account) comparing different spatial layouts of day-care settings. It points to the beneficial effects, for diverse aspects of the children's behavior, of a "modified open-plan facility" that combines the advantages of open-space arrangements with those of more highly structured spaces, the two being separated from one another in a flexible and readily interpenetrable fashion. For the most part, however, there is a dearth of systematic research available in this area; thus some may question the value of the numerous guides purporting to present empirically grounded recommendations for the design of day-care facilities, or of similar institutional environments for special groups of children such as the handicapped. This is true particularly for some of the earlier ones (e.g., Osmon, 1971; Prescott, Jones, & Kritchevsky, 1972) whose orientation is essentially pragmatic. Those by Moore and his associates, on the other hand (Moore, 1980b; Moore, Cohen, Oertel, & Van Ryzin, 1979; Moore, Lane, Hill, Cohen, & McGinty, 1979), as noted, are at least in part inspired by more general principles from the developmental psychology of cognition and play.[3]

The Stimulus Environment of the Classroom: Aesthetics and Noise

We will confine ourselves here to research that relates to our focus on physical background stimulation, first in the form of aesthetic aspects of the classroom environment, and second in regard to effects of noise. The reader is referred to Gump (Chapter 18, this volume) for a review of the growing literature on the physical environment of the school and the classroom as a factor in school learning and children's behavior more generally.

As regards the aesthetic factor, there is a paucity of research addressing effects of classroom decor and similar aspects of visual appearance. But we may call attention to two investigations designed specifically to address this topic, showing that colorful and aesthetically pleasing college classrooms with comfortable places to sit—that is, "soft rooms"—may affect level of participation (Sommer & Olson, 1980) as well as grades and student evaluations of the teacher (Wollin & Montagne, 1981). Similarly, Santrock (1976) found that the presence of "happy" pictures, that is, scenes with smiling children, in a testing room influenced the degree of persistence displayed by first and second graders on a motor task. Clearly, additional support for the relationship between the aesthetic character of the classroom and student performance is required, but corroboration of these findings would point to as yet unexploited possibilities for influencing educational processes.

Much of the research on effects of noise on children has focused on the school environment rather than on the home. Yet the relevance of this research is not limited to the educational sphere, for background noise conditions may not only impede formal learning activities in the classroom but also affect development more broadly construed, due to the fact that children spend so much of their time in this setting. Furthermore, noise from certain external sources may affect children in community settings as well as in the classroom. Consequently, the examination of noise effects in the school has implications beyond those directly related to education and educational settings.

Noise in the classroom may be attributable to occurrences within the setting such as classroom activities and conversation or to external sources, including hallway activity, street traffic, and other forms of transportation. Activities within the classroom have been found to contribute as much as 12 dB to the ambient sound level, although noise from such internal sources is typically controlled by the teacher (Lukas et al., 1981). A recent study of children's exposure to noise, monitored with portable dosimeters, revealed that peak sound levels during typical classroom activities were as high as $L_{eq} = 74.5$ for boys and $L_{eq} = 68.8$ for girls (Roche et al., 1982). It will be recalled that the EPA limit for safe sonic conditions is L_{eq} (24) = 70 dBA (U.S. Environmental Protection Agency, 1974). Substantially higher levels of noise have been reported in schools located in airport landing corridors (peak level = 95 dBA; Cohen et al., 1980) and schools adjacent to elevated train tracks (peak level = 89 dBA; Bronzaft & McCarthy, 1975). These assessments indicate that under typical conditions classrooms have fairly high sound levels, but in those circumstances where schools are located near significant noise sources, sonic conditions exceed federal guidelines by enough to warrant serious concern.

BACKGROUND NOISE IN THE CLASSROOM AND PERFORMANCE

The evidence for the *immediate* effects of background noise on classroom performance is somewhat mixed. Slater (1968) assessed seventh graders' reading achievement scores under three testing conditions: (1) a quiet classroom separated from potential noise sources such as busy hallways and bells (45 to 55 dBC), (2) a classroom with background noises from naturally occurring hallway traffic and activity in adjacent classes (55 to 70 dBC), and (3) a classroom in which the preceding conditions were supplemented by a lawn mower outside the window, loud recordings in the adjacent rooms, and high activity level in adjacent rooms (75 to 90 dBC). No significant performance differences were revealed across these three settings. Similarly, Weinstein and Weinstein (1979) found that naturally occurring classroom noise (mean = 60 dBA) did not affect reading performance when compared to measures obtained during quiet times in the room (mean = 47 dBA). In contrast to these studies, high sound levels in the classroom have been found to affect adversely aspects of student behavior other than reading such as performance on auditory discrimination, visual search, and visual–motor tasks (McCroskey & Devens, 1977) and participation and attention in class on the part of college students (Ward & Suedfeld, 1973).

Although additional research is required in order to evaluate more clearly the immediate effects of classroom noise, the evidence just presented appears to follow a pattern. Thus the failure to find immediate effects of noise on reading performance is consistent with past human factors research, which has usually shown that background noise has little effect on task performance (cf. Kryter, 1970). However, to the extent that noise conditions interfere with auditory discrimination and attentional processes, as in the studies of McCroskey and Devens (1977) and Ward and Suedfeld (1973), *chronic* exposure may lead to more clear-cut and wide-ranging effects.

Indeed, adverse effects of chronic exposure to noise in the classroom have been shown in studies undertaken in schools that are in close proximity to major sources of noise such as airports, train tracks,

and highways. Consequently, the children and teachers in these schools are confronted with high noise levels throughout the academic year, and in most instances over many years. In one such study, Cohen and associates (1980) assessed the impact of noise from airplane overflights on third and fourth grade children attending schools in the vicinity of the Los Angeles International Airport, using measures of health and performance. The number of flights over the selected schools averages one every 2½ minutes, and, as noted previously, the peak sound level in the classrooms at these times was 95 dBA. Both systolic blood pressure and diastolic blood pressure of the children from the noisy schools were higher than those of the children in a quiet-school control group matched with the former for age, socioeconomic status, and race, although the higher levels were not outside of the normal range for children of the age examined. In regard to psychological functioning, the noisy-school sample was more likely to fail a puzzle-solving task, and the length of time required for puzzle solution increased as a function of years in the school. Furthermore, among all children in both groups who failed in solution attempts, the children from the noisy-schools more often gave up on a subsequent puzzle. This latter result suggests that these samples can be characterized as showing passivity or helplessness in the face of environmental challenges; presumably this attribute is due to the chronic stressor conditions. There was, in addition, an interaction between exposure to noise and years of enrollment on a measure of auditory distractibility. Children who had attended the noisier school for less than 2 years were not as susceptible to auditory distraction as their quiet-school counterparts; however, after 4 years in their respective schools, this relationship was reversed, with the noisy-school sample demonstrating greater distractibility. When we apply this finding to our earlier discussion of the home environment, the apparently lower distractibility of children exposed to chronically high noise levels in the home (Heft, 1979) may in fact be a relatively short-term adaptation to these conditions.

In a follow-up study a year later, Cohen, Evans, Krantz, Stokols, and Kelly (1981) reported findings that are fairly consistent with the initial investigation, with a few exceptions. Differences in blood pressure across the schools did not reappear, although this seemed to be due more to sample attrition than to adaptation. Further, the earlier finding of a higher degree of distractibility among the noisy-school children was not replicated. Finally, while the children from the noisy schools were more likely to fail the puzzle task and had longer response latencies, the previous tendency for these children to give up on the task was not observed in the follow-up study. These differences aside, the significant result of this second investigation is that the children in the noisy-school settings did not adapt appreciably to continued exposure to high sound levels over this time period.

Two other recent studies have examined the effect of noise from air traffic on school children. Moch-Sibony (1981) compared children from schools near Orly Airport (Paris) with children from matched schools in the same vicinity that were soundproofed. Although there were no differences in reading achievement scores, the children from the noisy schools demonstrated poorer auditory discrimination and lower tolerance for frustration. Green, Pasternack, and Shore (1982) found an inverse relationship between reading achievement and noise exposure from aircraft, the latter estimated from Noise Exposure Forecast contours. The aggregate nature of these data and the accompanying lack of control, for example, for socioeconomic status and educational level of parents, limit the conclusiveness of this study (DeJoy, 1982), however.

Bronzaft and McCarthy (1975) examined the impact of noise from elevated trains on reading achievement among second and fourth graders. The target school was located adjacent to the train tracks, and a train passed by the school every 4½ minutes on the average. Those children whose classrooms were closest to the tracks had significantly lower reading scores than their counterparts located farther away from the noise. Hambrick-Dixon (1982) assessed effects of noise from this same source on children (5 to 6½ years old) in day-care centers located within 80 feet of elevated train tracks. In relation to comparison quiet schools, children in the former settings made fewer errors on a visual matching task if they had attended the centers for less than 2 years; however, children in these noisy centers made a higher number of errors than their counterparts after more than 2 years of exposure. These findings parallel Cohen and colleagues' (1981) report of initial lower distractibility of children exposed to aircraft noise followed by greater susceptibility over longer periods of time. In combination, these results suggest potential cumulative effects of noise exposure in the classroom.

The effects of traffic noise from roadways have been assessed in two investigations. Karsdorf and Klappach (1968) examined blood pressure readings, subjective complaints about noise, and the concentration of students in three secondary schools exposed to different levels of noise. They report that blood pressure levels and frequency of complaints were positively related to noise level, and that the time required to complete the concentration task as well as the number of errors committed increased with noise level in the classroom. In a more recent study, Lukas, DuPree, and Swing (1981) selected a number of schools near a freeway and a matched sample in quiet neighborhoods. They found that reading and mathematics achievement scores for third and sixth graders in the noisier schools were significantly lower than those of their counterparts in the quieter schools. In addition, correlations between noise level and performance indicated that the strongest relationship between these variables was for reading performance in the sixth grade. This latter finding is consistent with the outcome of Cohen and colleagues' (1973) investigation of the impact of traffic noise on sonic conditions in the home, which likewise found higher correlations associated with longer residence. In the case of the study of Lukas and associates (1981), however, the role of length of exposure to noise is inevitably confounded with that of age in the comparison of the sixth graders with the third graders.

Finally, let us note that high noise levels in the classroom may affect the teachers' behavior as well as the students', and in the process may adversely influence educational activities. Crook and Langdon (1974) report that noise from passing aircraft interrupted teachers' instruction, and Kyzar (1977) cites similar findings for road traffic noise (see Gump, Chapter 18, this volume, for a further discussion of effects of noise on classroom instruction).

The implications of the findings just reviewed are clear: Efforts are required to reduce excessive noise levels from external sources such as these. One approach to noise abatement in schools is improved sound insulation, particularly for those schools proximal to these noise sources. However, a recent evaluation of this approach in Los Angeles schools indicated that soundproofing was only minimally effective (Cohen et al., 1981). An alternative procedure, and one that has greater certainty of reducing ambient sound levels, is to control noise at its source.[4] Further, such an approach would have consequences beyond the classroom. After all, noise from these sources affects children not only while they are in school, but also while they are in other settings. As DeJoy (1982) has recently stated:

Consideration must be given to the total twenty-four hour noise exposure of the child. Noise abatement is a community-wide problem. Soundproofing (of schools) is not only costly, but it is of limited effectiveness, especially in situations where overall community noise levels remain high. (p. 12)

Assessment of the impact of noise on the school, though significant in itself, points to a broader set of environmental conditions that have implications for children in neighborhood settings and in the home as well (for further discussion of this issue see Heft, 1984; Wohlwill & Van Vliet, 1984b).

9.2.3. Child Behavior in the Outdoor Environment

From the standpoint of an analysis focused on the role of the stimulus environment, the distinction between indoor and outdoor environments might seem to be a somewhat artificial one. Undoubtedly, the problems of response to focal as well as background stimuli are relevant outside of the home as well as inside, as are the various environmental stimulation perspectives that we have considered (i.e., sensory stimulation, affordance, and response feedback). Yet there are some specific features of children's behavior in the outdoor environment that should be considered, having to do with the very considerable expansion of the environment potentially available to a child out of doors. First, there is greatly enhanced opportunity for free exploration of the outdoor environment (i.e., in comparison to the home); partly as a consequence, the environments frequented by the child tend to be self-selected to a much larger degree than is the case for indoor environments. A second attribute differentiating outdoor from indoor settings is their generally less structured character, in terms of the physical layout and arrangement of significant elements and the behavior appropriate to and supported by the settings. Finally, the extent to which outdoor settings are frequented and utilized seems to increase steadily with age (cf. Moore & Young, 1978), as reflected in the expanding territorial range of the child. Thus the spectrum of behaviors to be observed in the outdoor environment necessarily differs from that encountered indoors.

We will consider three aspects of children's behavior in the outdoor environment: (1) outdoor play, and the role of different types of playgrounds, both unstructured and structured, as well as of play equipment, (2) environmental exploration and territorial range, and (3) response to the natural environment.

Playground and Play Equipment
The literature on this topic is a varied one, emanating from diverse perspectives, including experimental

and environmental psychology, child psychology and education, and architecture and design. Much of it, however, is basically descriptive and unsystematic and by and large lacking in any explicit relationship to, let alone integration with, principles of child play and its development. That situation is not as anomalous as it may seem, for it is only recently that developmental psychologists have rediscovered the area of play and of such related topics as exploration and imaginative activity as a legitimate problem deserving of their attention (see Rubin, Fein, & Vandenberg, 1983, for a recent review). Apart from diverse material directed primarily at practitioners and professionals in early childhood education (e.g., Coates, 1974; Frost & Klein, 1979; Pollowy, 1977), there is a body of research pertaining to playground equipment and to use of structured playgrounds, as well as ecological studies of play in diverse settings, that merits more detailed consideration.

The work of Gramza (1973; Gramza, Corush, & Ellis, 1972; Gramza & Scholtz, 1974) is illustrative of the rather limited experimental literature on relationships between specific properties of outdoor play objects and the extent of their use by children. It is of interest in documenting the importance of "functional" as opposed to visual complexity, that is, the extent to which the object's shape and other properties provide for diverse forms of use (climbing, entering, tactual exploration, dramatic play), as opposed to complexity in a purely perceptual sense. This work thus suggests that the "collative" properties such as complexity, which Berlyne (1960) showed to be important in eliciting curiosity, are not necessarily relevant to an object's suitability for play—a conclusion in accord with views of play such as Hutt's (1966), which make a sharp differentiation between play and exploration.[5]

The preceding conclusion is only partly at variance with a finding from an unpublished study by Callecod cited by Moore (1985), who reports that the third-grade children observed by Callecod "overwhelmingly prefer and use playgrounds with high degrees of 'challenge,' 'novelty,' and 'complexity.'" Certainly challenge and novelty would in fact prove relevant to the play observed by Gramza as well, and it is possible that even the complexity variable being referred to by Callecod referred to something apart from the perceptual complexity of the play equipment, in Berlyne's sense. In any event, the work of Gramza and his colleagues and of Callecod, as well as that of others who have studied play on different types of playgrounds, especially on the part of children of school age (cf. Moore, 1985), lends some justification to the rather sharp criticism that has been leveled at traditional playgrounds by Ellis (1973), Frost and Klein (1979), and others. Yet we need to bear in mind the necessity in designing a playground to reconcile the needs of a large diversity of children, of different ages, sexes, and preferences for play.

An interesting study by Derman (1977, see Derman, 1974, for a preliminary report) provides additional confirmation of the sequence from exploration to play, in terms of children's response to large three-dimensional forms on a preschool playground over a period of 10 days. Derman further reports detailed analyses of relationships between diverse object characteristics such as surface area, complexity, openness versus closedness, and so on, and different types of child play, notably motor play and social play. His data point to rather specific relationships among these variables that are difficult to summarize but again indicate that play is a multidimensional variable and certainly cannot be predicted effectively on the basis of stimulus variables related to curiosity and exploration. A further noteworthy finding of Derman's research is shown in correlations obtained between ratings of the suitability of the diverse objects by adults (as judged from scale models) and measures of the extent of the children's use of them for different kinds of play: Adults turned out to be much more successful in their estimates for social than for motor play.

A number of investigators have undertaken comparative studies of children's behavior in play areas of different types. Hayward, Rothenberg, and Beasley (1974) report a comparison of activities observed on three different playgrounds in an (unspecified) urban environment, classified as traditional, contemporary, and adventure, on the part of groups of users varying from the preschool level to adults (though the latter were observed almost exclusively in a supervisory role). Interestingly, whereas preschool children were rarely encountered on the adventure playground, it proved the most popular for adolescents. Correlated with these differences in the predominant age groups of the users were age differences in the features of each setting that the children utilized, and corresponding differences in the *type* of activity that was observed on each. Because of the self-selection of these environments (particularly on the part of the older children), it is impossible to determine to what extent the differences in play reflect the differences in the features of each playground and to what extent they are accounted for by the different age group distribution encountered on each, or by socioeconomic and other differences associated with the different neighborhoods in which the playgrounds were situated. At a descriptive level, however, the study provides some useful information, notably as regards the use of adventure playgrounds, which those in the design field (Cooper, 1970; Frost & Klein, 1979) have championed for some time. Hayward and colleagues echo these sentiments, pointing out the value of the adventure type playground, by virtue of its openness and lack of fixed structure for creative and imaginative as opposed to purely physical play, and thus its suitability for children beyond the preschool level.

Some support for this view is to be found in Moore's (1983b) rather more fine-grained comparison of the play of children on adventure playgrounds with play in unstructured neighborhood settings (e.g., streets), which showed a heightening of constructive and fantasy play in the adventure playground, apparently at the expense of gross motor play. This difference apparently applied across the three gross age levels (preschool, elementary school, and teen) that Moore differentiated. (The age comparison is problematic, however, given the very different age distribution of the children using the two play environments, just as was the case in Hayward and colleagues' study.) Both Hayward and colleagues and Moore, however, fail to take into account preschool children's ability to turn motor play into more imaginative forms of role and dramatic play (e.g., on a jungle gym).

A dissertation by Ostro (1977) was directed at the role of a more specific feature of children's play environments, that of the availability of soft as opposed to hard playing surfaces, both in the child's general environment (e.g., around their homes) and in their preschools. Ostro compared children in three daycare programs. Two of these were located in inner-city areas; one provided for both soft and hard play surfaces, whereas the other was limited to only a hard play surface. The third program, like the first, contained both soft and hard surfaces, but it was located in a small town in a rural area. Ostro's interest centered on the extent to which these children engaged in *alterability* play, involving modification either of the environment or of the play object. He found that the children from the rural school were equivalent in the extent of this type of play to those from the urban school containing both hard and soft play surfaces; both showed higher amounts of such play than did the children in the other urban school that provided only a hard surface. In compensation, children limited to the hard-surface play environment engaged in significantly higher amounts of gross motor play. Thus the broader environmental context (urban vs. rural) of the child's activity, although it did influence the particular implements used in play and the themes of the children's play activity, did not seem to affect alterability play on the playground. The latter was determined rather by the child's access to soft play surfaces, through their experience on the school playground. To recast this conclusion in other terms, the affordances offered by the playing surfaces influenced the amount and type of play activities engaged in by the children.

Ostro's findings with respect to the role of the alterability of the play materials and of the play environments are consistent with the evidence from adventure playgrounds, much of whose seeming popularity appears to derive from the movability and modifiability of the play materials (e.g., Hayward, Rothenberg, & Beasley, 1974; Moore, 1985), as well as their manipulatability (Van Ryzin, 1979). The interpretation ascribed to the function that these playground features serve does not emerge clearly from this work, however. From the perspective of Gibson's theory of affordances, one may argue that manipulatability and movability provide occasions for the development of behavioral competencies corresponding to these particular environmental properties.

A study devised along broader ecological lines, by Berg and Medrich (1980), compared the play patterns of 11- to 12-year-old children from four contrasting neighborhoods of Oakland, California, utilizing home interviews of the children and their parents. The neighborhoods consisted of a low-density development in a relatively remote location, of well above average socioeconomic level and very predominantly white in its racial composition; a middle-class neighborhood, bounded by a freeway and several major thoroughfares, and over 50% black; and two high-density, inner-city neighborhoods that were predominantly black. (The child density ratios in the four areas, in terms of children per acre, are revealing: 1.56 and 1.04 in the first two; 7.04 and 6.69 in the last two.) Considerable differences among the four groups were found in the kinds of places in which children indicated they preferred to play, and their distances from their own homes. The findings point to a complex interplay of density, geographical isolation, problems of traffic, and personal safety as major determinants of the children's play patterns. Thus the remote location and low child density of the first neighborhood resulted in a high rate of play outside of their neighborhoods—typically with the parent driving the child to such locations—while children in the two inner-city neighborhoods were more likely to play in and around their homes. But children in the middle-class neighborhood likewise remained close to their homes, in spite of the very low density of children; problems of traffic, safety, and perhaps lesser opportunity for leaving the neighborhood served to confine them to an area near home. There were also some important but less readily interpretable differences between the two inner-city ghetto areas. The two major points that emerge from this study are the great importance of conditions of traffic, as well as of perceived safety, as determinants of choice of locations to play, and the relative lack of efficacy, in all neighborhoods, of planned and structured play areas in providing for the needs of these children, and their compensating preference for open or unplanned play sites.

This last point represents a common refrain in much of the writing on children's outdoor play, both that based on empirical research and that of a more impressionistic nature. That is, children, particularly of school age, and boys more so than girls, tend to prefer areas such as streets, empty lots, quarries, and undeveloped natural areas (such as woods, streams, and the like) for their play, as opposed to more structured, designed, and equipped playgrounds. This point has been amply confirmed in diverse recent work, apart from the above-mentioned study by Berg and Medrich (1980). Much of the evidence is contained in special reports that are difficult to access (for references see Marcus, 1974, p. 199; Berg & Medrich, 1980, p. 340; Moore, 1985), but Sanoff and Dickerson's (1971) study of children in a housing project is perhaps representative. It showed the street as the most popular play area, accounting for nearly one-quarter of the observations of play; back and front yards and public sidewalks were next in importance, accounting for nearly half of the observations between them, while the central playground contributed only 2%! Similarly, Marcus (1974) found only 15% of the play of children in a housing project taking place in the designated play areas, while 44% occurred in paved areas (exclusive of parking lots).

Moore and Young (1978) report a number of additional studies on the same topic carried out in various countries, though inevitably the categories used in each are not the same. Included is an unpublished study of Chicano children in Denver by Auslander and associates that showed results rather similar to those by Sanoff and Dickerson. A study by Dresel (1972) carried out in Germany, on the other hand, found that designated play areas contributed a large plurality (42%) of observations of play. Similarly, Coates and Sanoff (1972) found children in housing projects playing predominantly in areas intended for them (though not necessarily in designed playgrounds).

It should be noted that several of the studies of children in housing projects limited themselves to observations in the immediate vicinity of the project. Thus they could not detect instances of play in other unstructured (as well as structured) areas that older children undoubtedly frequent (cf. Berg & Medrich, 1980). By the same token, many of these studies underestimate the amount of play in more remote and less structured sites, because data from children of widely different ages (from 3 to 13 years, e.g., in the case of Sanoff & Dickerson and Coates & Sanoff) are aggregated. As we shall see presently in our discussion of children's territorial range, the older the child, the further away from the confines of the home and immediately surrounding neighborhood he or she is apt to travel for play and recreational activity.

A final point concerns the role of cultural factors in modulating the relationships between environmental features and characteristics and children's play activities reported in these studies. Clearly the differences among the various groups studied by Berg and Medrich (1980), drawn as these groups were from very different socioeconomic and racial populations, may well be at least in part a function of cultural factors that affect the amount of freedom for exploration and the like that parents allow their children, and the kinds of places they consider appropriate for them to frequent. The same point applies a fortiori to some of the international comparisons such as the differences between Dresel's (1972) findings in Germany and those of the other studies just cited concerning the incidence of play on structured and designated play areas. More generally, we clearly need to remain aware of the contribution of cultural variables to the relationships between the environment and child behavior considered in this chapter. If they have not been more explicitly acknowledged by us, it is in part because their role is difficult to disentangle from that of environmental variables, and in most of the studies it can be assumed to remain essentially constant.

Environmental Exploration and Territorial Range

In their comprehensive survey of children's behavior in outdoor settings, Moore and Young (1978) devote considerable attention to the concept of territorial range, as do Schoggen and Schoggen (1984), writing from the perspective of ecological psychology. The latter succeed, furthermore, in interrelating this concept with that of exploratory behavior, which represents a category of behavior of increasing concern to psychologists (Berlyne, 1960), and child psychologists in particular (Nunnally & Lemond, 1973; Rheingold & Eckerman, 1970).

Not surprisingly, most of the limited research that has been carried out on exploratory activity in children has been conducted in indoor settings such as the home or the nursery school or in special laboratory rooms, and in such public buildings as museums (e.g., Henderson, Charlesworth, & Gamradt, 1982). Exploration of the larger outdoor environment by children has rarely been subjected to systematic study, though speculations and impressionistic accounts on the theme of the urban environment as a basis for environmental learning through exploration abound (e.g., Carr & Lynch, 1968; Lynch, 1977; Southworth & Southworth, 1974). Zien (1974) goes beyond such accounts to describe in considerable detail a program designed to induce school-age children in Boston to become more fully acquainted with their city by using mass transit lines for exploration, familiarization, and fuller use of the city's resources. An interesting aspect of Zien's account of this project relates to the manifold fears, realistic and fanciful, that the children harbored concerning unknown features of the city and its transit system, which had to be overcome on the part of the participants in the project. It is unfortunate that no data were obtained evaluating the success of the program, the participant children's reactions to it, and the extent to which their subsequent forays into their larger urban environment were affected by it.

It might be noted parenthetically that the oft-reported preference of older children for undeveloped spaces, "wild" natural areas within their urban habitats, and similar areas for their play is undoubtedly attributable in large measure to the fact that such areas are so conducive to exploration, because of their relatively unstructured and frequently unfamiliar nature (cf. Lukashok & Lynch, 1956).

Related to the concept of exploration, but transcending it in its reference to environments both familiar and unfamiliar, is the work on children's home range, or territorial range—that is, the distance from home base to which a given child travels. Research on this issue suffers from some difficult methodological problems, partly relating to the measurement of such range. The measure originally proposed by Anderson and Tindall (1972), who were among the first to investigate this aspect of children's behavior, is that of total nonredundant path length, that is, the total distance covered by a child in traveling to various destinations away from home, counting overlapping portions of such itineraries only once. Resulting "Mean Home-Range" values are inevitably strongly affected by diverse factors whose influence it is difficult to control such as access to public transportation, spatial layout of the environment potentially within range of the child's travels, and the spatial distribution of relevant behavior settings. Workers in this area have further found it important to differentiate among different home ranges, for example, in terms of whether the child could travel to some destination (1) without parental permission, (2) with parental permission, and (3) only if accompanied by an adult (cf. Hart, 1979). Others have differentiated between habitual, frequented, and occasional ranges (e.g., Moore & Young, 1978).

Most of this work shows two consistent findings: large sex differences, that is, larger ranges for boys than for girls, as well as increases in range with age (see Moore & Young, 1978, for a summary of the relevant evidence; Saegert & Hart, 1978, for a valuable analysis of sex differences in environmental competence, including territorial range, constructive play, and spatial abilities; see also Webley, 1981). The sex differences are confirmed in a much earlier study by Muchow and Muchow (1935), but only for the area through which the children passed *occasionally*. The much smaller areas within which the children moved regularly (mostly to play) were equivalent in size for the two sexes. Parental restraints and environmental fears (relating to traffic problems above all) have generally been suggested as responsible for both the age and sex differences in territorial range; in any event, the sex differences appear to vanish by the time children reach adolescence, to judge by one recent study of urban teenagers (Van Vliet, 1983a). With regard to the age factor, however, the increasing permeability of a diversity of behavior settings to children as they grow older should also be taken into account (i.e., adolescents have more *reasons* for venturing further from home than do 7- or 8-year-olds—cf. Wright, 1956).

Moore and Young (1978) provide an interesting comparative analysis of the data on home range obtained by Anderson and Tindall (1972) with those from Hart's (1979) study; this analysis (cf. Table 3 of their chapter) not only confirms the expected sex as well as age differences but also allows one to compare urban and suburban children (from Anderson & Tindall's data) as well as either of these with children in a small-town rural area (from Hart's data). Taken at face value, this comparison reveals an interesting interaction between residential area and age: While the older children's ranges are roughly equivalent in all three groups, the younger rural children exhibit a very much curtailed range compared to both the urban and the suburban children of the same age. The results are not completely comparable, however,

as the exact age groups in the two studies differed somewhat, and the way in which mean home range was defined and measured differed likewise (see Moore & Young, 1978, for details).

It should be noted that the values obtained in these studies probably underestimate the true range—particularly for the older children—since the children were limited to citing places and paths on the aerial photo of their *neighborhoods*. It is interesting to note the vastly larger values obtained by Muchow and Muchow (1978), who asked their respondents (109 children ages 9 to 14) to indicate "streets and places that you know very well, in which you often play or through which you often pass, and that you can imagine to yourself if you close your eyes." The resulting mean home ranges were 8.9 km for boys and 8.2 km for girls; even the corresponding *minimal* values (2.5 km or about 1-1/2 miles for each sex) are well above the means obtained by Anderson and Tindall and by Hart, which do not exceed 2.2 km for any subgroup. One suspects the difference is based on the ready use by Muchow and Muchow's children, from the city of Hamburg, of public transportation (notably the subway); such use was excluded from the U.S. data just referred to, and would not, in any event, have been relevant for the rural children in Hart's study. It is apparent then that the restriction to the children's neighborhoods creates a misleading picture of the actual extent of their travel into their surrounding environment. Relevant to this point is the finding in Berg and Medrich's (1980) previously mentioned study of 11- to 12-year-old children residing in the Oakland (California) School District that a majority of the children (55%) were reported by their parents to go outside of their neighborhood on their own (or accompanied by friends) at least once a week.

Although not couched in territorial range terms, the work of the Kansas behavioral ecology group on the use of behavior settings by children is clearly pertinent in this context. Wright's (1956) "developmental" analysis of the number and type of behavior settings frequented by individuals at all periods of the life span, from infancy through old age (cf. Fig. 9.1), provides a good illustration of this type of study, documenting the dramatic changes with age in both type and number of settings occupied by the residents of Midwest, and above all the major shift from family to community settings occurring after preschool, which reaches a peak in adolescence and becomes reversed in adulthood and old age. A more functionally significant index concerns the degree of "penetration" into a setting, ranging from pure on-

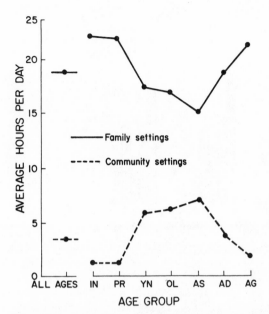

Figure 9.1. Average hours per day spent in farm and community behavior settings by different age groups of the town of Midwest. (*Source:* "Psychological Development in Midwest" by H.F. Wright, 1956, *Child Development, 27.* Reprinted by permission.)

looker behavior to the assumption of responsibilities as sole leaders in a given setting (see Fig. 9.2)

As Figure 9.2 shows, the younger school-age children (ages 6 to 9 years) fail to enter over a third of the settings at all and participate in another fourth of the settings only as onlookers; the picture is reversed for adults, who enter into the highest penetration zone for more than half of the settings that they frequent. It should be remembered that this study was carried out in the setting of a very small rural community; the "big school–small school" work (Barker & Gump, 1964) along with the comparisons carried out between communities of differing size (e.g., Gump & Adelberg, 1978) suggests that rather different results would have been obtained in larger communities, both as regards numbers of settings occupied at different ages and as regards setting penetrance. Specifically, the evidence suggests both that fewer settings are frequented and that penetration into any one setting is less deep in a larger institution, as well as in a larger community.

Data on children's territorial range can be made more meaningful by relating it to information on the goal or object of the child's travel. A noteworthy case in point is a most recent study by Van Vliet (1983a),

which provides data on the distance to which youngsters travel to engage in each of a diverse list of activities, reported comparatively for city and suburban residents from the metropolitan Toronto area. His data are not comparable to those mentioned earlier, as he confined himself to adolescents, ages 14 to 16 years; it is nevertheless of interest that the values differ widely according to the activity: Whereas city children travel on the average 0.8 km and 1.5 km for visiting a playground or engaging in an indoor sport, respectively, they travel 3.1 km to go shopping and as far as 4.9 km to attend a movie. Values for suburban children were uniformly higher, the ratios varying between 1.02 and 4.47. Van Vliet's results, and in particular a correlation of .45 between home range and the *diversity* of activities in which the youngster participated, led him to propose a functional interpretation of home range, stressing its relevance to the process of informal socialization and extension of the child's experience in the "fourth environment," that is, outside of the home, school, and formal play settings.

A more general comment concerning the work on territorial range may be in order. However valuable the basically descriptive information we have obtained to date, it seems that we are ready to move on to more of a process approach, one that would relate territorial range functionally to children's environmental cognition on the one hand and exploratory activity on the other and to their development in particular. As regards the first, correspondences between children's knowledge of their environment and the extent to which they venture forth into it have rarely been studied, at least on the per-individual basis that would allow the relationship between the two variables to emerge more sharply.[6] Obviously, even if a correlation were found, it would be a mistake to assume any simple causal relationship between them; the connection is more likely to be a reciprocal one, with exploration acting to change cognitive representation of an area, which may lead to further exploration. Furthermore, the relationship between these two variables is far from perfect, as suggested by Hart's (1979) finding that girls, though exhibiting much smaller territorial range, were equal to the boys in their spatial representation of the environment. Webley (1981) did find corresponding sex differences in both kinds of measures; differences in the methodology used to assess the child's cognitive representation as well as in the type of environment studied may account for this discrepancy.

The latter point suggests the value of adding a motivational component to conceptions of territorial

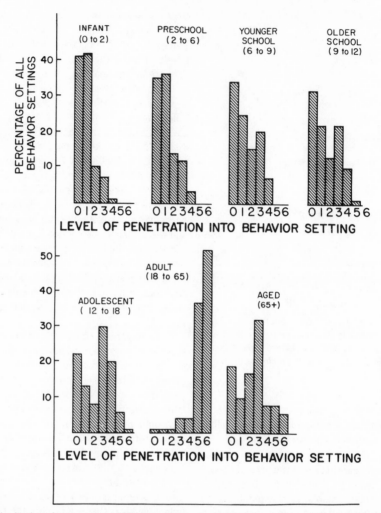

Figure 9.2.   Distribution of percentages of Midwest community settings entered by members of different age groups, by degree of penetration. (Penetration levels: 0 = no entrance into a given setting; 1 = onlooker; 2 = audience participant or invited guest; 3 = member or customer; 4 = performer or active functionary; 5 = joint leader; 6 = single leader.) (*Source:* "Psychological Development in Midwest" by H.F. Wright, 1956, *Child Development, 27.* Reprinted by permission.)

range, one that would link it up with a possible trait involving predisposition to explore the environment, as well as with curiosity more generally. Schoggen and Schoggen (1984) have recognized the relevance of exploration to this problem, although remaining within the framework of ecological psychology. What appears to be called for is an extension of the child psychologist's interest in environmental exploration (e.g., Henderson, Charlesworth, & Gamradt, 1982; Rheingold & Eckerman, 1970) to the larger outdoor environment at the scale of neighborhood, community, and beyond—much as has been taking place in the

domain of environmental cognition (see Heft and Wohlwill, Chapter 6, this volume).

Children's Response to the Natural Environment

An aspect of childhood outdoors—in Moore and Young's (1978) apt phrase—deserving of special consideration is represented by children's response to natural settings and environments. The natural environment is frequently assumed to occupy a rather special place in the affections of people generally, and a fair amount of research on outdoor recreation and on preference for and aesthetic response to natural scenes could be cited in support of this view (cf. Altman & Wohlwill, 1983).[7] Yet we know comparatively little about the origins and developmental history of the attraction of people to the realm of nature.

Impressionistic observations, to be sure, are not hard to find: Cobb (1959, p. 538) ascribes a "sense of ...profound community with natural processes" to the prepubertal child, who, in her view, experiences the natural world in a "highly evocative" way. A similar theme emerges from the recollections that Lukashok and Lynch (1956) have collected from students and other adults of their childhood and adolescence in urban areas, in which natural features (trees, parks, woods, lawns) figure prominently.

The picture becomes somewhat different when we look at the frequency with which natural elements are mentioned in children's representations of their environment, for example, through sketch maps. In a project described by Moore and Young (1978) (the CUULS project), single trees and lawns again showed up with some frequency as elements in maps drawn by 8- to 12-year-old children, but the frequencies for both are less than a third of the children, and their ranks among the elements listed as ninth and tenth, respectively. (The elements at the top of the list are, not very surprisingly, the child's own house, and through streets.) Rather similar results were obtained by Maurer and Baxter (1972). Aiello, Gordon, and Farrell (1974), furthermore, found natural settings to be decidedly subsidiary in importance among all settings in which children were observed to engage in some activity, making up only 5% of the total in the aggregate.[8] These authors point, however, to important individual differences among children from different families in this respect, which appear to reflect contrasting attitudes on the part of their parents towards natural areas, and their familiarity with them.

An interesting observation comes from Hart's (1979) study of rural Vermont children. Hart found that the children he studied made frequent mention of the woods in their interviews yet seemed hesitant to venture into them. This phenomenon of the natural environment as a source of fear (presumably based on a fear of novel stimuli) emerges even more sharply in reports of inner-city children transported into the countryside, who from some accounts (Kaplan, 1976; Riccio & Slocum, cited in Tuan, 1978) perceive the woods as a source of imminent dangers and experience a strong feeling of anxiety when taken into them. Apart from the element of unfamiliarity, there are probably other, more intrinsic features of

this kind of environment that may evoke fear such as its closed-in, relatively dark appearance, its unboundedness, the lack of clearly defined landmarks and other directional cues, and the sense of social isolation that it engenders.

Findings from a study of children's preferences for diverse types of topographical settings (represented through color slides) as places to visit may conceivably relate to this theme of the "fear of the unknown." Balling and Falk (1982) found that mean ratings (on a Likert scale) for jungle and desert areas declined steadily between 8 and 15 years, and in the case of the desert actually dipped below the neutral point of the scale at age 15 (the only such instance of a negative evaluation for any of the 24 combinations of four settings and six age groups reported). The most positive scores, on the other hand, were obtained for savanna scenes, perhaps because they conveyed a feeling of relative familiarity to the children.

The obvious relevance of these problems to the field of environmental education hardly needs belaboring. Yet a perusal of the major periodical for that field, the *Journal of Environmental Education*, suggests that workers in this field have not to date devoted much systematic effort, at either a theoretical or an empirical level, to the study of children's response to the natural environment. A notable exception is provided by Reseski's (1981) attempt to analyze children's conception and understanding of the realm of nature from a broader cognitive–developmental framework. A similar, more comprehensive effort has been undertaken by Hart and Chawla (1981); both of these contributions, however, deal primarily with the cognitive aspects of this problem and are thus more appropriately considered under the heading of environmental cognition in children (see Heft and Wohlwill, Chapter 6, this volume).

In the same vein, we may draw attention to a symposium entitled *Children, Nature, and the Urban Environment*, sponsored by the U.S. Forest Service (1977). It is noteworthy most of all for the paucity in the proceedings of facts or even ideas relevant to the topic of *children's* response to the domain of nature, in spite of the very impressive and sizable array of authorities assembled to consider it. One paper from this collection (More, 1977) may be singled out for particular mention, not so much because it represents an exception to the preceding statement, but because, dealing as it does with the place of wildlife in children's literature, it helps to alert us to the very central role that animals play in the lives as well as the imaginations of children. In a very real sense they represent a bridge between the inanimate and the personal or social world of the child, and any consideration of the role of nature in children's development that leaves the animal realm out of account clearly must remain very incomplete indeed. Yet as already noted earlier we know next to nothing about children's response to animals and their place in children's development.

9.2.4. The Role of Community Size and Density

If we consider the environment at a macroscale, it is apparent that a large metropolitan area provides a very different experience for the developing child than does a small rural town. This is the case regardless of whether that difference is considered in terms of (1) levels of stimulation and diversity of stimuli, (2) amount and frequency of social contact and interaction, (3) availability of behavior settings, or (4) opportunities for the development of specialized skills, interests, and the like—to mention only a few of the more obvious dimensions of difference between these contrasting types of human settlement. Yet our knowledge concerning actual differences in behavior and development that are directly attributable to large differences in population size and density remains most sketchy indeed.

This conclusion emerged clearly from a set of recently published papers (Wohlwill & Van Vliet, 1984a) prepared by a study group that was specifically convened to examine the role of residential density in the development of the child. The group's survey of the literature indicated that the available research that bears on these questions is very predominantly concentrated at the high end of the size and density scale, that is, dealing with urban environments, or with residential patterns such as large apartment buildings characteristic of such environments. Much less work has been carried out on the conditions of children living in very-low-density rural or otherwise relatively isolated settings, or on differences between children related to this dimension, studied through systematic comparative research (for a review of research on the verbal and intellectual development of children in rural areas, see Hollos, 1983).

In this section, then, we will consider, first and foremost, some of the work carried out on children living in urban or large metropolitan areas. Impacts of low-density or isolation conditions will be considered more briefly, and a final subsection will be devoted to an attempt to reexamine the urban–rural dimension itself, as a variable relevant to child behavior and development.

Children's Experience of Urban Environments

Environments at the urban scale are not very readily dealt with by behavioral scientists. They constitute a rather unwieldy entity for the purposes of analyzing the role of specific relevant factors in behavior. It is thus not surprising that with few exceptions (e.g., Milgram, 1970; Srole, 1972) psychologists have been willing to concede this territory to the sociologists and anthropologists.

This state of affairs is even more obvious when we turn to work on children's experience in urban settings. Apart from impressionistic accounts (e.g., Ward, 1978), probably the major work in this area is that emanating from the Child-in-the-City project at the University of Toronto, described by Michelson, Levine, and Spina (1979). Although it contains a few psychologically oriented chapters, the predominant focus of this volume is at an institutional and sociological level.

Before turning, though but briefly, to the approach of Michelson's group, and others from the direction of sociology, let us mention two individual-centered foci that might be—and in the case of one has in fact been—applied to this area. The first is the view of the urban environment as a source of high levels of stimulation, in the form of noise, social contact, motion, visual diversity, and complexity. This view has been frequently stated on the part of analysts of the urban scene, from Simmel (1950) to Milgram (1970) and others, but it has not proved readily testable or even useful as a source for programmatic study, even with adults, for at least two reasons. The first of these is the phenomenon of adaptation in adults, suggesting a progressive neutralization of response to whatever levels of stimulation may prevail, as a function of prolonged exposure to an environment. A second point is that adults are able within certain limits to escape or avoid stimulation experienced as noxious or undesirable, by choosing, altering, or creating the environments they frequent.

Both of these factors suggest the value of studying the impact of stimulation characterizing urban environments on children, who have had less opportunity to adapt to these conditions, and who have fewer opportunities to modify or avoid them. To date, such analyses have remained rare, however, and almost entirely confined to indoor environments, notably that of the home, and to a lesser extent the school. That work has been reviewed in the preceding discussion.

A second approach that likewise has seen only limited application to urban settings is that of behavioral ecology, notably that of the Kansas school, referred to earlier. Presumably their concentration in much of their earlier work on the very small rural town of Oskaloosa, Kansas, was based on its susceptibility to analysis in terms of behavior settings, which in the case of this village were relatively few in number. A notable advance in this regard, however, is represented by the work of Gump and Adelberg (1978) (see Adelberg, 1977, for a more complete account), who present an analysis of preadolescents in a neighborhood within a large city (Kansas City) in terms directly comparable to that employed for Oskaloosa (and for the intermediate-sized community of Lawrence, Kansas, as well). These researchers report, interestingly enough, that youngsters in the urban neighborhood are in some ways (e.g., penetrance of settings) more comparable to those in a small town (Oskaloosa) than those in the larger town of Lawrence. This finding presumably reflects the relative isolation and self-contained character of the ghettolike urban neighborhood studied by Gump and Adelberg. One suspects it would be less readily applicable to children living in a middle-class area toward the periphery of a city, and even less to children residing in a suburb (e.g., Van Vliet, 1981).

In the absence of more extensive research in urban settings carried out by the behavioral-ecology school itself, we may refer instead to a most interesting precursor of this approach, represented in the previously mentioned monograph by Muchow and Muchow (1978). This research provides a fascinating in-depth picture of the geographical life space of school-age children from a working-class district of the city of Hamburg, Germany, during the early 1930s.[9] We referred earlier to the quantitative data on territorial range and breadth of the children's cognitive maps, including comparisons between the sexes, reported by the Muchows, and confirmed by other researchers, indicating that boys' effective area of traversal is considerably broader than that of girls.

Perhaps more interesting than this quantitative aspect of their work are the observations made by the Muchows on the kinds of places in which the children from their chosen district congregate, and the uses made of them. Thus, consonant with frequent observations by others (see the earlier section on play environments), the children they observed made use of public spaces intended primarily for pedestrian and vehicular traffic — notably city streets — for their play, while avoiding areas specifically set aside for them such as developed parks. Similarly, they spontaneously selected undeveloped areas in a city block, adapting them for their play activities, while avoiding developed areas. Particularly intriguing is the authors' comparison of the contrasting use by adults and by children (primarily boys) of an area serving as a relatively little-used loading and unloading facility for canal ship traffic. This structure, which acts as a barrier for adult pedestrians walking along the edge of the canal, serves rather to attract children, who use it for diverse kinds of games and athletic activities exploiting the fences, dumps, and other features of the area. Of similar interest are the observations of children's exploration of a large department store, including the analysis of stratagems employed to trespass past the guard at the gate to gain access into it. This type of study, combining an ecological focus with a quasi-ethnographic approach, has been all too little applied in this area, with the notable exception of Hart's (1979) study of children in a small Vermont village.

It is important to recognize, however, that the ecological stance adopted by the Muchows does not extend to their theoretical framework, which reflects rather the influence of Stern and Werner in its phenomenological bent and its stress on the differences between a child's perception of a geographic locale and that of the adult. In this respect the work of the Muchows differs in important ways, not only from the behavioral ecological approach (e.g., Gump & Adelberg, 1978), but also from the body of research on territorial range reviewed previously, which provides an essentially descriptive account of children's "commerce" with and use of different locales and facilities in their urban surroundings.

Finally, we turn to work on children in urban environments emanating from the side of sociology, as represented in the Child-in-the-City project at the University of Toronto (Michelson, Levine, & Spina, 1979). This work focuses on the role in urban children's lives of community services, social supports for parenting, housing policy, and the like, along with the impact of the diversity of the urban population, as they affect the process of socialization and of developmental transitions, for example, from childhood to adolescence. A useful presentation of this approach is to be found in the chapter by Michelson and Roberts (1979), which focuses specifically on the physical environment. The chapter reveals, first of all, that a sociological analysis of relationships between the environment and child development is not as different from an environmental–psychological one as might have been expected. There is an emphasis on the phenomenon of home range, on the impact of social overload (with proper obeisance to Simmel, whose view of the city exerted a direct influence on Milgram's conception of this aspect of urban life), on effects of specific environmental variables such as pollution and noise, and on effects of crowding in the home, as well as outside. The chapter further conveys the impression that solid research evidence on these questions is as yet limited, with the partial exception of child behavior in playgrounds of different kinds, which was considered in a previous section.

Illustrative of relevant sociological work that has been carried out is a study by Gray and Brower (unpublished—see Michelson & Roberts, 1979) of the places in a child's neighborhood that children considered salient, as shown by their tendency to point them out to visitors to the neighborhood; these, in the case of a group of children in a downtown Baltimore neighborhood, included such features as stores and institutions not specifically designed or intended for use by children, which were frequented to almost the same degree as playgrounds and other similar facilities designed for children. As found in studies of play areas (see the preceding discussion), children frequently invent their own informal activity settings, in some cases in the form of "hidden spaces" where social gatherings, some of them with adults in the neighborhood, take place.

An issue of more specific relevance concerning the conditions of urban residential life on children is that of the effects of apartment living. It has received careful attention in reviews as well as empirical research by Van Vliet (1980, 1983b, 1984), working within the framework of the Child-in-the-City program at the University of Toronto. On the basis of a thorough review of the relevant literature, Van Vliet (1984) concludes that adverse effects on social adjustment, peer interaction, and the like, though frequently asserted and speculated about, are difficult to document. There is a suggestion, furthermore, that cultural factors may mediate whatever effect apartment living may have, as the results from studies carried out in different countries are discrepant. For instance, in Williamson's (1978) comparison of families living in high rises in Germany and in Italy, the parents of the German children felt that such living quarters acted to inhibit the formation of friendships, but this was not true for the Italian children—perhaps, as the author believes, because Italian children's ac-

tivities are centered more around their family and less around their peers.

Along with differences between apartment and single-family-home dwellings, a related issue that has been of particular concern to the Toronto group and has been specifically investigated by Van Vliet (1981) is the difference between urban and suburban environments as these affect children. He found that, correlated with the sheer difference in density of other children encountered by a given child in the two types of areas, the city child complained much less frequently about lack of others to play with and interact with, in comparison to suburban children. Similarly, city children were found to share more activities with friends, in comparison to those from suburban areas, who in compensation reported sharing more activities with other family members.

Impacts of Conditions of Isolation on Development

As noted earlier, the isolation end of the density continuum has been studied much less extensively than the crowding end, particularly in work with children. This is not surprising, since much of our knowledge about effects of isolation comes to begin with from the study of unusual or atypical conditions such as that of a space capsule, an underwater laboratory, or locales relatively inhospitable to man such as Antarctica (cf. Rasmussen, 1973). For both practical and ethical reasons, we are unlikely to expose children to such conditions. Thus what evidence we have on effects of isolation on children comes from studies of certain communities that are both small and relatively cut off from the outside world, as was true of the "hollows" of Appalachia some decades ago (and remains the case to a large extent even today—cf. Coles, 1971). Although a number of investigations have focused on children living in these areas (e.g., Sherman & Key, 1932; Wheeler, 1942; see Anastasi, 1958, for a review), that work is limited by the virtually exclusive concentration on intelligence test scores. These consistently disclosed significant gaps between children from such isolated areas and others living in nearby larger towns or small cities, and, more ominously, a strong pattern of cumulative deficit, indicating that this gap *increased* with age.

There is of course no way of isolating the factors responsible for these gaps; they presumably involve a complex of sociocultural differences, along with effects of social and geographic isolation per se, and above all differences in amount of education received by the children, which in the 1920s amounted to no more than 3 months per year, on the average, for children from the most isolated hollows. The situation today is probably different, as a result of the spread of television and other media into such areas, the improvement of roads providing access to them, the alleviation of the extreme economic disadvantage under which its inhabitants were living, and again, above all perhaps, the spread of schooling, on a more reliable basis, to the children in these hollows.

Direct information on this score is admittedly lacking, but in its absence it is instructive to compare these earlier findings from the Appalachian regions of the United States with rather similar conditions of marked geographic isolation in two European countries, Norway and Hungary. Children living on highly isolated farms in both of these countries have been studied by Hollos (Hollos, 1975; Hollos & Cowan, 1973; see also Hollos, 1974), and compared to others living in small villages, as well as in larger towns. On the basis of an array of measures of cognitive, verbal, and social role development administered to children between the ages of 7 and 10 in both countries, Hollos concludes that the rather substantial isolation, both geographic and social, experienced by these children resulted in selective effects on their development: Performance on basic cognitive tasks taken from Piaget's work were hardly affected at all (indeed, the farm children were *superior* to their age mates living in small villages); on measures of verbal ability and social role perception, on the other hand, the differences were consistent and substantial, showing an impairment of the children's development in these particular areas. Such a selective effect is understandable, given the lack of opportunity for social interaction, and for extensive linguistic interchange, which the farm children experienced. At the same time, in interpreting the much more positive picture obtained from the tests of general reasoning and concept development, the extent to which the children's isolation was attenuated through television and attendance in school (at least from the age of 8 years, and even earlier in the case of the Hungarian children) must be recognized.

A study rather similar to the one Hollos and Cowan carried out in Norway was undertaken in the same country by Haggard (1973);[10] it essentially confirmed as well as extended the former's findings. Haggard found selective effects of isolation not only on intellectual development, but on a variety of personality measures as well. For instance, the isolated children showed fewer instances of socialized expression of aggression, while displaying a very much higher ratio of personal as opposed to impersonal ref-

erences to parental figures. These group differences need not of course reflect the isolation conditions per se, but may in part relate to the sociocultural characteristics of the families residing in these different communities. Haggard's conclusion recognizes this ambiguity but is worth quoting in a more positive sense, for its stress on mechanisms of adaptation as underlying such selective effects: "Each subculture appears to foster the development of various adaptation patterns in its members which are appropriate to, and congruent with, the physical-cultural ecologies in which the members of each subculture live and function" (p. 137).

The Urban Versus Rural Distinction Revisited

Systematic comparisons between urban and rural environments in terms of the associated differences in children's cognitive, intellectual, or social development are much less common than they were decades ago (see Anastasi, 1958, for a review of earlier evidence). One reason for this seeming waning of interest in this issue might be the movement of the population over the course of this century from rural to urban areas, to the point that residents of rural areas made up less than 20% of the population by 1970. Yet there are signs of a reversal of that trend from the recent census (see Long & DeAre, 1982), and, for that matter, of a possible revival of interest in the psychosocial conditions characterizing rural life (Childs & Melton, 1983).

Nevertheless, a simple-minded comparison of urban with rural children is not likely to prove particularly informative or revealing, for a variety of reasons. First, there is clearly a complex of overlapping factors differentiating the two types of environments, including density of residential areas, conditions of under- versus overmanning of facilities, services, and so on (Wicker, 1979), opportunities for development of specialized skills and pursuit of specialized interests, along with a host of factors relating to the sociocultural, economic, and educational conditions prevailing in urban as compared to rural areas.

Furthermore, the differences in the experiences afforded to residents in different areas, particularly in the United States and the developed portions of the world, have become increasingly attenuated, due to the influence of the media and other technological advances (e.g., microcomputers) that have provided people, including children of all ages, with a core of shared stimulation and information virtually regardless of geographic locale. And finally the residential community has become less and less of a determinant of the range of experiences encountered by a child, as a result of the increasing access of individuals of virtually all ages to environments removed from their homes, by car, bus, or plane. One possibly direct manifestation of this leveling effect may be seen in the results of a study (Wohlwill & Sterns, 1974) that compared children living in three contrasting environments—an urban Pittsburgh neighborhood, a small mill town, and a very small rural Mennonite community—in terms of the children's preference for stimulus complexity. Over a series of five different sets of stimuli scaled for complexity, there were virtually no differences among these three groups at any age level between first grade and high school.

All of which is not to say that size and density of communities play no role in the child's experience. To the extent that these variables are translated into major differences in *opportunities*, for example, for participation in activities, development of skills, and the like, we may presume that there will be important differences in the children's behavioral repertoires, and perhaps in associated feelings of competence and of satisfaction. Similarly, by focusing on the variable of the *connectedness* of the child's environment to people and places in other locales (see Wohlwill, 1984), we may expect to obtain important differences in certain aspects of social and personality development, as well as possibly certain aspects of intellectual and linguistic development, just as Hollos and Haggard were able to demonstrate. But a much more incisive examination of the character of a given settlement, and of its resident children's experiences, beyond a simple characterization of them as urban or rural, will be required to determine the functional significance of such differential environmental experiences.

9.3. CONCLUSION: THE ENVIRONMENT AS CONTEXT FOR CHILD BEHAVIOR AND DEVELOPMENT

In this concluding section we will attempt to tie together the major strands of the literature just reviewed and point out some significant issues that remain to be resolved. We will do so first by examining both the stimulus environment and ecological approaches, with particular regard to issues that are in need of further attention within each orientation. We will proceed to a brief consideration of the complementarity of these approaches as well as the potential role that environmental psychology can play by bringing

about a synthesis with regard to them. Finally, we will draw attention to some important directions for future research on the relations between the stimulus environment and the development of the child and consider some implications for environmental design.

9.3.1. Appraisal of the Stimulus Environment Approach

In Section 9.2 we presented three approaches to conceptualizing the stimulus environment: namely, the sensory stimulation, the response feedback, and the affordance approaches. Although these perspectives differ in several ways, including the manner in which developmental processes are conceptualized, collectively they offer various possibilities for identifying environmental variables that are significant for development. During the course of the preceding literature review we have seen diverse instances of the relevance of these approaches to research findings. Several issues that emerged in the course of the preceding review are, however, in need of further attention and clarification. We will focus on three of these here.

Analysis of the Environment

A retrospective look at our review discloses that the view of the stimulus environment in terms of focal stimulus information and background stimulation appears to be most relevant and helpful for analyses of environment–development relations, particularly with regard to conditions in the home. At the same time, there appears to be a further differentiation necessary, one that partially overlaps ecologically with the focal–background one, although in a conceptual sense it is different, namely, that between intensive and structural aspects of environmental stimulation. By the former, we are referring to the arousal-producing character of environmental conditions, which is describable in terms of *levels* of stimulation. By the latter, we are referring to aspects of environmental stimulation that relate to its informational content, that is, to its structure. Not at all accidentally, it appears that intensive aspects of stimulation, such as noise and activity level, are pertinent primarily to background stimulation, whereas structural properties such as organization, predictability, and diversity are of greatest relevance to potential focal stimulus objects and events. For one thing, structure in the available stimulation is the target of focal activity, but to the extent that stimulation is too complex, it will lack structure for a young child and thus contribute mainly to the overall background conditions.

Having identified two potentially significant stimulus dimensions, the focal–background and the intensitive–structural, it is important to recognize that neither is without some ambiguities. First, with regard to the former dimension, it was noted previously that to a large degree what is focal or background depends on the individual's attentional focus at a particular moment, thus rendering a clear-cut distinction between the two problematic. Second, with regard to the intensitive–structural dimension, closer examination reveals that, rather than a single dimension, multidimensionality generally obtains. For instance, the structural properties of diversity and organization both appear to represent conditions favorable to development, though they represent in fact opposite poles of a single dimension, considered from an information-theoretic perspective. Further, predictability–unpredictability as applied to events that transpire over time constitutes an additional dimension within this structural category.

It is apparent that until or unless these types of dimensionality problems are effectively resolved the validity of the optimal level of stimulation hypothesis will necessarily remain moot. A fortiori, Hunt's (1961) *hypothesis of the match*, according to which the impact of a particular stimulus input depends on the degree to which it matches the individual's level of development, will remain difficult to verify, since it presupposes success in scaling both environments and individuals along some assumed dimension so as to allow one to determine the distance between them in some hypothesized person–environment space.

In contrast to the sensory stimulation approach, the response feedback and affordance models do not seem to admit of this kind of dimensional analysis of the environment. Instead, each points to potentially significant *qualities* of specific environmental features. Thus, for example, a setting such as a play area in the home may contain objects that provide response-contingent feedback. Similarly, a setting can be examined in terms of the availability of particular affordances, or put in another way, with respect to the opportunities that the available affordances provide for the individual. It may prove difficult to relate these environmental properties to developmental variables, in the manner of the hypothesis of the match. However, it may be possible to reconceptualize this hypothesis in order to specify the particular kinds of feedback or affordances that are especially appropriate at certain points in development. In other words, the effective range of these environmental properties might be specified in relation to developmental status, and envi-

ronments can be considered with respect to the fit between available ecological resources and certain emerging psychological functions, considered in a qualitative manner.

The Activity–Passivity Distinction

The preceding discussion has, in a sense, already made implicit reference to a second significant issue. This is the question whether the child should be regarded as a passive recipient of stimulation as opposed to an active assimilator, modulator, and modifier of stimulus information. Without minimizing the significant conceptual differences between these two views, it is possible that these alternatives are partially reconcilable when we take into account the types of environmental conditions that are under consideration as well as the level of development of the child and its consequent ability to select out information and to act on the environment.

Thus the ambient background conditions can probably be considered as impinging on an essentially passive perceiver, in part, because they function primarily in terms of their intensitive characteristics. With regard to focal conditions, on the contrary, the individual generally functions in an active mode, selectively responding to particular stimulus information, and it becomes important to consider the very different forms that such activity may take. As soon as the infant has developed the capacity to differentiate among stimulus objects and to manipulate them, its activities provide, as we have seen, for learning affordances, and for entering into interactive relationships with those aspects of the object and social environment that have the capacity for providing feedback for the child's behaviors. In addition, the developing child's increasing mobility in the environment allows him or her to select and seek out stimulus objects for active engagement, as well as to avoid or withdraw from other stimuli, so as to exercise a measure of control over the environment. That control is considerably expanded subsequently as the child's abilities and opportunities to explore the environment extend gradually to larger areas beyond the home.

This kind of exploratory activity, which serves increasingly to determine the character of a given child's interaction with the environment, creates a challenge for researchers to obtain a complete and valid picture of the environmental conditions actually encountered and confronted by a given child at successive ages. In other words, it vastly complicates the problem of environmental measurement, which we discussed in the preceding subsection.

The Specificity Issue

On the basis of his own research (Wachs, 1979) as well as a thorough review of the literature (Wachs & Gruen, 1982), Wachs has hypothesized that relations between environmental variables and the early development of the child, particularly in the cognitive area, are characterized by environmental, age, and organismic specificity (see Section 9.2.1). This hypothesis is not easy to evaluate on the basis of the available evidence. Not only would it be important to have Wachs's findings in this regard cross-validated, but refinements on the measurement front regarding both environmental and developmental variables are needed so that unreliability of measurement can be ruled out as an explanation for these effects and the robustness of the particular effects encountered can be assessed.

As regards environmental specificity, that is, the tendency for environment–behavior relationships to apply to rather specific environmental variables rather than in across-the-board fashion, it should be noted that this issue is intimately related to the preceding dimensionality issue. We need to do much more to determine the dimensionality of the environment as it relates to the development of the child, through application of factor-analytic techniques, canonic correlation, and similar multivariate approaches. While Wachs and his associates (Wachs, 1979; Wachs et al., 1979) have made an important start in this direction, the nine-factor solution revealed in their factor-analytic study seems suspect on the face of it and clearly needs cross-validation.

As regards age specificity, one would look for certain environmental variables to become relevant at particular ages. For instance, noise and activity level inside the home should become progressively less important with age, as the child becomes older, to the extent that children through their own actions can achieve increasing control over their immediate stimulus environment (by moving to a more quiet part of the house, turning off a blaring TV set, or eventually even going outside of the home). On the other hand, it would be much more difficult to achieve control over ambient sound levels emanating from outside of the home itself. And indeed there is some indication from Wachs's own data that this type of differential effect with age does indeed obtain (see Wohlwill, 1983). The child's increasing mobility with age and ability to explore and self-select environments should be expected to produce similar differential effects with age for other aspects of the environment relating to focal variables. This suggests the potential benefit from an expansion of ecological approaches to development in order to provide a more accurate indication of the range and distribution of environmental conditions that children at different ages confront, or expose themselves to.

Finally, investigation of organismic specificity, that is, the interaction between environmental stimulation and individual characteristics of the child, will require the identification of the relevant organismic variables. One variable that appears to be of this sort is temperament (Wachs & Gandour, 1983). Specification of other organismic dimensions that indicate this environment–individual interaction is indeed a challenge, but it will lead to a much richer view of the complex relations between environments and children. Analyses of differential psychological factors with reference to the child are a counterpart to approaches such as the ecological perspective that distinguish between differential effects of settings. Both environmental and organismic specificity remind us that monolithic views of the environment and the individual will result in only first-order generalizations. Just as environmental psychologists have recognized the differentiated nature of environments, so too will they need to acknowledge the differential characteristics of individuals and incorporate these factors into their models.

There is a further kind of specificity to be considered that transcends those that Wachs has dealt with and indeed cuts across the three we have just reviewed. It relates to the role of the environmental setting. For instance, effects of crowding, or the role of a stimulus shelter, may be in part a function of factors relating to the complex of physical, institutional, and sociocultural variables that define a particular setting. Thus relationships uncovered in the home may not apply to another setting such as the school, or to homes in a different culture. Of course this reflects in part our incomplete understanding of the total complex of factors that singly and in interaction codetermine the way in which a child responds to a given set of environmental circumstances. More positively, it points up the value and indeed the need of a complementary perspective, namely, the ecological one, to which we will now turn.

9.3.2. Appraisal of Ecological Models

The essence of any ecological view of child behavior is of course that it considers that behavior *in context*, in a much more explicit sense than is true of the environmental stimulation view. It does so in part by looking at the environmental situation in a unitary fashion, focusing on qualitative differences among settings. This has the undeniable advantage of allowing the situational determinancy of some given type of child behavior to emerge more clearly, and to afford, even if only at a descriptive level, a valuable picture of the range of behaviors exhibited by a given child. The price paid for this advantage, however, is that it fails to reveal the manner in which environmental or situational forces impinge on and interact with developmental processes.

The preceding statement represents a generalization that applies to different degrees to different ecological models that have in fact been used in the field of child development. As noted in Section 9.1, there are a variety of such models, and they differ in some important respects. For instance, Bronfenbrenner (1979) is much more concerned with processes operating within a given child and their development than are the behavioral ecologists of the Kansas group; correspondingly he is less emphatically deterministic in his conception of the role of the situation or environmental setting. His primary interest, however, is in the child's social environment, represented by family, school, and culture, and thus his conception is of uncertain relevance for our present purposes. On the other hand, as we pointed out in Section 9.1, the behavioral ecologists offer a deterministic view of the role of the behavior setting that is very difficult to integrate with developmental processes, even where they do exhibit an interest in age changes in the frequenting of and penetration into the behavioral settings of a community (e.g., Wright, 1956). Their attention to the "where" of behavior, and their concern for the *synomorphy* of a behavior setting, that is, the extent to which it is adapted to the behavior exhibited in it, represent nevertheless an important contribution to the work of the child psychologist, even if their conception of person–environment fit is a very different and perhaps less dynamic one than that espoused by developmentalists (e.g., Lerner, 1983).

9.3.3. Possibilities for Synthesis Between the Two Approaches

As Wohlwill noted previously (Wohlwill, 1981a, 1981b), the difference between developmental and ecological approaches to the study of relationships between the environment and child behavior can be formulated in the following terms. The former tend to focus on the role of particular dimensions abstracted from given environmental conditions (e.g., Hollos & Cowan, 1973), whereas the latter examine children either in a single community or comparatively in two different communities, considered in their totalities, as

in Barker and Schoggen's (1973) comparison between Midwest and Yoredale.

In spite of their evident differences, the two models can be used in conjunction with one another, if only in the sense of replicating a study on the role of particular environmental variables across different locations — just as Hollos (1975) did in replicating in Hungary her earlier Norwegian study of the effects of isolation. But that may be selling the ecological approach short. For the fact is that ecological factors may operate to modulate and even modify the expression and manifestation both of specific environmental conditions and of developmental processes. For instance, the role of residential density in the behavioral development of children may be a function of the broader ecological context in which they grow up, and more specifically of the "connectedness" of their environment (see Wohlwill, 1984), which determines the degree of access to other, different-sized settlements that the child enjoys, the degree of penetration by the media and other technological devices into the child's area of residence, and the like. Similarly, general manifestations of such phenomena as privacy and territoriality in a child of a given age are undoubtedly affected by the characteristics of a particular setting — for example, the child's home, as opposed to a summer camp.

Needless to say, the usefulness of the ecological approach need not to be judged in terms of its potential role in developmental analysis, which may appear rather too ancillary, as we have formulated it. But as long as it is construed as an autonomous, sui generis model for studying behavior, the ecological approach is apt to remain difficult to integrate with a functionally based developmental perspective on environment–behavior relationships.

9.3.4. Unresolved Issues and Directions for Future Research

At many points in our review, issues have been discussed that remain unresolved. Here we will limit ourselves to highlighting two such issues that appear to occupy a particularly central place in the subject matter under review.

The first concerns the role of the developing child's own behavior in regulating the stimulation impinging on it, and in selecting objects on which to focus attention and environmental settings in which to engage in diverse activities. This role has, however, been taken largely for granted in both our treatment of this subject and that of others who have emphasized the active nature of the child. What remain to be determined are the ways in which the child actually does achieve such relative control over its environment, through object manipulation and environmental exploration, and how these activities change over the course of development, both quantitatively and qualitatively. Developmental psychologists have, to be sure, made some important advances in this regard, in their work on exploration of objects in infancy and early childhood, but the process of selecting out and becoming acquainted with environments on a larger scale remains very little studied, let alone understood.

More specifically, we lack information on the functional characteristics of such activity. Just what do children learn about their environment, in terms of affordances, cognitive maps, or whatever, from their object manipulation, their inspection, and traversal of environments, whether it be a room in their home or the city in which they live? And secondly, what aspects of their environment, both physical and social, either promote or interfere with such activity? There is clearly a research program of major proportions implied in these questions.

The second issue relates to the child's adaptation to the environment. By and large our view of the child's response to the environment has remained static and lacking in a time dimension. It is clear that adaptation, along with other time-related processes, plays a major role in this area. But it is one that as yet we have very little information about, at least as it applies to children. There are a number of specific questions that warrant more intensive concern. For instance, at several points in our review evidence was cited pointing to an apparent discrepancy between short-range adaptation of children to noise and longer-range impairment of functioning. This is clearly an issue of both theoretical and practical interest, and it raises a number of further questions such as the generality of this phenomenon (is it limited to noise, or does it operate, e.g., with regard to activity level, and other similar variables?), the role of the child's development level in this regard, and other similar issues.

Speaking more generally, we are greatly in need of broadly conceived research on the child's response to environmental *change*, as one source of information on this question of adaptation, and on the related question of the resiliency as opposed to malleability of the child at different portions of development to maturity. Considering the ubiquity of change in our lives, and in those of our children, there is a singular gap here in our knowledge, which future researchers would do well to concern themselves with.

A beginning toward a systematic analysis of response to environmental change is being made by

Wapner and his colleagues at Clark University (e.g., Wapner, 1981; Wofsey, Rierdan, & Wapner, 1979; see also Wapner, Chapter 41, this volume). Although that work has been primarily conducted with college students, the theoretical framework in which it is placed is that of the organismic–developmental theory developed by Werner, Wapner, and their colleagues and students, and it should thus prove valuable for a thoroughgoing ontogenetic analysis of the manner in which the individual responds to a major alteration in the environment—whether through moves of the individual or through modification of the environment.

9.3.5. Implications for Design

According to an ideal image of the collaboration between psychology and design, environmental psychologists would provide environmental designers with clear-cut criteria for use in their creation of settings for children. Given the state of our knowledge of environment–development relations, environmental psychology is not yet prepared to make such a contribution, nor is it to be expected in the near future.[11] However, the preceding review indicates that the field can offer some broad guidelines and suggestions, as well as some conceptual tools, to aid the design professional. We will briefly point out several of these contributions in closing.

The accumulating evidence of a positive relationship between the diversity and responsivity of *focal* environmental features, on the one hand, and perceptual and cognitive development, on the other, points up the importance for designers to consider the informational quality of potential focal objects and displays. By approaching the design of these environmental features with the tools of psychologically toned concepts such as complexity, response feedback, and affordances, designers may be aided in their formulations. Thus environmental features and settings can be considered in terms of their potential for sensory stimulation (e.g., through variation in patterns, shapes, and colors), the distinctiveness of the feedback they can provide contingent on the child's actions, and the functional possibilities that they extend to the child.

At the same time, any straightforward view of the effects of focal features on development is immediately complicated by the possibility that environmental and organismic specificity are operative. That is, particular environmental features are apt to have selective rather than global effects, while environmental effects are mediated by characteristics of the individual, for instance, gender and temperament. Under these circumstances, the designer may need to recognize that specific environmental features are unlikely to have sweeping, across-the-board psychological effects. Consequently, in order to achieve a positive impact on a wide range of individuals, a diversity of features, rather than any single type, may be required. In short, effective environmental design will entail a congruence between setting characteristics and person variables, and this possibility will necessitate a more detailed understanding of person–environment relationships than we have at the present time.

There is one area, however, where research findings are sufficiently consistent to warrant the concern of designers, in order to mitigate adverse environmental conditions. As we have seen, intensive background stimulation can, for a variety of reasons, exert a negative impact on the developing child. This is true in particular of the effects of ambient noise in the child's environment. The need for efforts to deal with this problem is made the more acute in the light of the evidence that indicates that adaptation to noise and similar conditions of background stimulation is highly selective and ephemeral.

With regard to noise and activity from interior sources, careful attention to the layout of the interior space, focusing on the use functions of these areas, can yield significant results. For example, the separation of utility areas and other places that are likely sources of noise from play and study areas is an obvious desideratum. In the design of interiors, we will need to coordinate setting activities, aesthetics, and the psychological requirements of users of those spaces. Background noise can.be further reduced through acoustical insulation of interior walls, appropriate selection of sound-absorbing construction materials, and muffling of appliances and other equipment. Further, a concept stemming from the research literature that may be of particular significance in this context is the *stimulus shelter* (Wachs, 1976, 1978, 1979; Wachs et al., 1971). In this regard, the primary play or study areas in the home or school can be given special attention as far as location and acoustical insulation are concerned. More specifically, certain rooms or small enclosures that are removed from activity and noisy areas can be explicitly incorporated into interior design plans, and these places can be made available to the child to serve as buffers from environmental stimulation. Access to such places would enable the child to control exposure to background noise and activity levels to a degree.

Noise from exterior sources such as ground and air transportation may be reduced somewhat through construction modifications, for example, improved acoustical insulation, but it will be recalled that in one evaluation of the effectiveness of this procedure (Cohen et al., 1981) only modest improvements were found. As noted earlier, the best strategy may be to attempt to control such noise at its source, and this approach would entail political as well as technical intervention. However, considering the apparent psychological hazards that these conditions pose, psychologists and designers need to tackle this problem, as complicated as its solution may be.

In a broader vein, designers of environments for children may derive some general benefit from the affordance perspective. Unlike the traditional design emphasis on form in a geometric or abstract sense, an affordance perspective stresses the action possibilities that environmental features and environmental settings encourage or permit: "We modify the substances and surfaces of our environment for the sake of what they will afford, not for the sake of creating good forms as such" (Gibson, 1976, p. 5). Because of this functional orientation, the affordance framework may aid the designer in explicitly formulating design features with user characteristics in mind. In the case of designing environments for children, a sensitivity to the physical and psychological attributes of children at different periods of development can act as a guide in the creation of functionally appropriate environmental features. The value of the affordance concept specifically is that it extends psychological/functional considerations of the individual to an analysis of the environment. It suggests an approach to a psychologically meaningful description of the environment, and for this reason it should be of potential value to the design professional.

The affordance concept, along with the closely related view of environmental stimuli as sources of feedback for the child, considered in Section 9.1, would seem to have particular relevance for playground design. Both point to the value of providing for play surfaces and play objects that, by enhancing the child's action on and interaction with the environment, promote a sense of environmental competence and awareness. On these grounds, playgrounds that contain manipulatable and movable objects as well as softer, more pliant surfaces inviting contact with them should be beneficial for children's development.

There are a variety of other principles from child and developmental psychology as well as from the study of children and their play activities in different settings that merit closer attention by the designer. Moore and his associates (Moore, 1980b; Moore, Cohen, Oertel, & Van Ryzin, 1979; Moore, Lane, Hill, Cohen, & McGinty, 1979) have issued a number of design guides that attempt to apply such principles to the design of environmental spaces and facilities for special populations such as the handicapped, or services such as day care. Elsewhere, Moore (1985) has provided a useful set of recommendations for designers of play environments, similarly animated by an intensive immersion in children's play behavior. Thus Moore emphasizes the need to view play environments in a much broader sense than the delimited context of designated playgrounds and to provide for a combination of play areas of different types to serve the ends of children of different ages for a diversity of forms of play. In this regard, he notes the importance of considering not only physical and motor play, which represent the forms of play most typically provided for by playground designers, but other forms of a more cognitive and social nature. Through the efforts of Moore and his associates at the University of Wisconsin at Milwaukee, as well as others, we appear in fact to be witnessing a rare effort directly to translate principles concerning children's play behavior—and outdoor play behavior in particular—into considerations of design.

Finally, there is one potential contribution that designers and planners can undoubtedly make to stimulate the child's development. At various points in this chapter we have noted the important role that environmental exploration plays for the child, at all levels from that of the home to that of the realm of nature. Here designers have a clear opportunity to further development by facilitating such activities. This means, on the one hand, improving access to places and areas that a child might wish to visit and explore, and to do so in a safe manner, whether by providing traffic-free zones, pedestrian bridges, tunnels, and walkways to overcome barriers of major traffic arteries, and the like, or by making available safe, convenient, and efficient public transportation, which has generally tended to neglect the needs of both the young and the old in our society. The contrast between the environmental experience of some of Berg and Medrich's (1980) children in Oakland (California), hemmed in by heavy-traffic arteries and lack of suitable public transportation, and that of the youngsters studied by Muchow and Muchow (1978) in Hamburg (Germany) in the 1930s who appeared to roam through much of the city on their own, is instructive in this regard, as is the evidence of prevalent misinformation and fear on the part of American children in the face of an urban subway system (Zien, 1974).

But in addition to improving access, environmental designers might well give heed to the suggestion in so much of the literature that we have reviewed

that sites optimally conducive to exploration are frequently those that are unstructured and not specifically programmed for child use—such as vacant lots, river banks, and undeveloped woods or open fields. At the microlevel of the playground, this lesson has been recognized in the growth of adventure playgrounds, which are likewise built on the principle of minimizing structure, and fixity of environmental features. But at the broader scale of cities and towns, the solution indicated appears rather to inhibit the tendency to overdesign the environment, and, more positively, to provide a reasonable amount of open and undeveloped space for children. In many of our large cities this type of space has been virtually eliminated; imaginative efforts to recreate it would surely pay off, to the benefit of the development of children in our highly urbanized society.

Acknowledgments

Work in this chapter was supported in part through a Denison University Professional Development Award to Harry Heft. The authors wish to acknowledge with thanks the many helpful criticisms and suggestions made by Gary Moore, on the basis of a review of an earlier draft of the manuscript; for the section on noise effects and noise measurement, we also profited from extensive consultation and discussion with David DeJoy. Finally, we would like to express our grateful appreciation to Joy Barger for her invaluable assistance in the typing of the several drafts of this manuscript.

NOTES

1. Other aspects of the inanimate environment such as buildings and landscape features cannot be engaged in the ways that manipulatable objects can; movement of the child relative to such features does, however, produce changes in the visual field (i.e., in the information flow from the environment), and these changes serve as feedback for self-produced movements.

2. The choice of scale weighting (A, B, C, or D), time sampling criteria, monitoring equipment, and placement of the microphone all directly affect sound intensity readings (see Kryter, 1970, pp. 45–47). To the degree that these factors differ across investigations, interstudy comparisons can be problematic. In our discussion of noise research, physical estimates of sound intensity are reported as they were cited in the original source. In most of the studies, sound intensity was sampled over a limited period of time, and investigators report a single reading or a peak or mean decibel level. Alternatively, several recent studies have employed an L_{eq} meas-

ure that is an energy-averaged sound level assessed continuously over time for some specified duration (e.g., $L_{eq}(24)$). Further, in most studies the A-weighted scale is employed since it is judged to reflect the sensitivities of the human ear most accurately. However, some researchers (e.g., Lukas, DuPree, & Swing, 1981) suggest that other weightings are more appropriate at certain times of the day and under certain circumstances.

3. Weinstein and David (in press) have recently edited a volume dealing with diverse facets of relations between the built environment and child behavior, with particular reference to educational and institutional environments.

4. A recent direct attempt to modify noise produced by elevated trains has apparently resulted in a reduction of noise levels in adjacent classrooms (Bronzaft, 1980).

5. Note that such features of the playground— including equipment, sandboxes, and so forth—provide opportunities for learning of environmental affordances by children, as much as those encountered indoors. This point is nicely illustrated in a child negotiating a slide or seesaw, or learning the properties of sand as potential construction material.

6. The study by Van Vliet (1983a) represents a partial exception in this regard, in reporting information on the relationship between home range and the adolescent's knowledge about the use of and access to a variety of resources in Metropolitan Toronto. This is thus more a functional than a spatial measure of environmental cognition. The correlation between the two variables, though only .22, was highly significant statistically and represents, furthermore, a partial r with several demographic variables partialed out.

7. It is important to differentiate between response to the realm of nature as a whole, in its various manifestations, and response to wilderness. The latter, as many historical accounts have convincingly shown, has been frequently regarded as an object of mistrust and fear, and as something to be avoided, presumably in large part because of lack of familiarity with and knowledge about it on the part of most people throughout history, and probably even today. For a comprehensive account of people's response to natural recreation environments, see Knopf, Chapter 20, of this volume.

8. While an examination of the data for the natural elements used by children provides a somewhat different picture (see p. 194 of Aiello et al.'s report), even these amount to one-third of the number of man-made elements used.

9. An extended summary of the monograph by Muchow and Muchow in English is available (Wohlwill, 1985).

10. Note that Haggard's data are not entirely internally consistent. Thus Picture Arrangement showed the largest difference between the groups of any subtest; conversely, the Information and Similarities scales did not disclose any significant differences. Similarly, a particularly large difference was found on a measure of perceptual organization based on the Rorschach, while a set of linguistic measures based on a Picture Interpretation test showed no differences.

11. See Lutkus and Baird (1982) for a discussion of issues concerning the application of research findings from the field of environmental–developmental psychology by the design disciplines. These authors lay particular stress on the need to assess children's own reactions to and evaluations of the environments they use.

REFERENCES

Adelberg, B. (1977). *Activity ranges of children in urban and exurban communities*. Unpublished doctoral dissertation, University of Kansas, Lawrence, KS.

Aiello, J.F., Gordon, B., & Farrell, T.J. (1974). Description of children's outdoor activities in a suburban residential area: Preliminary findings. In R.C. Moore (Ed.), *Childhood city* (pp. 187–196). *EDRA 5: Proceedings of the Fifth Environmental Design Research Association Conference* (Pt. 12). Washington, DC: Environmental Design Research Association.

Aiello, J.R., & Aiello, T.D. (1974). The development of personal space: Proxemic behavior of children 6 through 16. *Human Ecology, 2*, 177–189.

Ainsworth, M.D.S., & Bell, S.M. (1974). Mother-infant interaction and the development of competence. In K.J. Connolly & J.S. Bruner (Eds.), *The growth of competence* (pp. 97–118). New York: Academic.

Altman, I. (1975). *The environment and social behavior*. Monterey, CA: Brooks/Cole.

Altman, I., & Wohlwill, J.F. (1978). *Human Behavior and Environment: Vol. 3. Children and the environment*. New York: Plenum.

Altman, I., & Wohlwill, J.F. (1983). *Human Behavior and Environment: Vol. 6. Behavior and the natural environment*. New York: Plenum.

American Academy of Pediatrics. (1973). *Recommendations for day care centers for infants and children*. Evanston, IL: Author.

Anastasi, A. (1958). *Differential psychology* (3rd ed.). New York: Macmillan.

Anderson, J., & Tindall, M. (1972). The concept of home range: New data for the study of territorial behavior. In W.J. Mitchell (Ed.), *Environmental design: Research and practice* (pp. 1.1.1–7). *Proceedings of the EDRA 3/ AR8 Conference*. Los Angeles: University of California.

Balling, J.D., & Falk, J.H. (1982). Development of visual preference for natural environments. *Environment and Behavior, 14*, 5–28.

Barker, R.G. (1963). On the nature of the environment. *Journal of Social Issues, 19*(4), 17–38.

Barker, R.G. (1968). *Ecological psychology: Concepts and methods for studying the environment of human behavior*. Stanford, CA: Stanford University Press.

Barker, R.G., & Gump, P.V. (1964). *Big school, small school*. Stanford, CA: Stanford University Press.

Barker, R.G., & Schoggen, P. (1973). *Qualities of community life: Methods of measuring environment and behavior applied to an American and an English town.* San Francisco: Jossey-Bass.

Barker, R.G., & Wright, H.F. (1951). *One boy's day.* New York: Harper & Row.

Barker, R.G., & Wright, H.F. (1955). *Midwest and its children.* New York: Harper & Row.

Beckwith, L., Cohen, S., Kopp, C., Parmelee, A., & Marcy, J. (1976). Caregiver-infant interaction and early cognitive development. *Child Development, 47,* 579–587.

Bell, R.Q., & Harper, L.V. (1974). *The effect of children on parents.* Hillsdale, NJ: Erlbaum.

Berg, M.A., & Medrich, E.A. (1980). Children in four neighborhoods: The physical environment and its effect on play and play patterns. *Environment and Behavior, 12,* 320–348.

Berlyne, D.E. (1960). *Conflict, arousal and curiosity.* New York: McGraw-Hill.

Bowlby, J. (1951). Maternal care and mental health. *Bulletin of the World Health Organization, 3,* 355–534.

Bradley, R.H., & Caldwell, B.M. (1976). Early home environment and changes in mental test performance in children from 6 to 36 months. *Developmental Psychology, 12,* 93–97.

Bronfenbrenner, U. (1979). *The ecology of human development: Experiments by nature and design.* Cambridge, MA: Harvard University Press.

Bronzaft, A.L. (1980, November). *The effect of elevated train noise on reading ability: Follow-up report.* Paper presented at the meeting of the Acoustical Society of America, Los Angeles.

Bronzaft, A.L., & McCarthy, D.P. (1975). The effect of elevated train noise on reading ability. *Environment and Behavior, 7,* 517–527.

Caldwell, B., Heider, J., & Kaplan, B. (1966, September). *Home observation for measurement of the environment.* Paper presented at the annual convention of the American Psychological Association, New York.

Carr, S., & Lynch, K. (1968). Where learning happens. *Daedalus, 97,* 1277–1291.

Casler, L. (1961). Maternal deprivation: A critical review of the literature. *Monographs of the Society for Research in Child Development, 26* (2, Serial No. 80).

Casler, L. (1967). Perceptual deprivation in institutional settings. In G. Newton & S. Levine (Eds.), *Early experience and behavior.* (pp. 573–626). Springfield, IL: Thomas.

Childs, A.W., & Melton, G.B. (1983). *Rural Psychology.* New York: Plenum.

Clarke, A., & Clarke, A. (1976). The formative years? In A. Clarke & A. Clarke (Eds.), *Early experience: Myth and evidence.* New York: Free Press.

Clarke-Stewart, K.A.(1973). Interactions between mothers and their young children: Characteristics and consequences. *Monographs of the Society for Research in Child Development, 38* (6–7, Serial No. 153).

Coates, G. (Ed.). (1974). *Alternative learning environments.* Stroudsburg, PA: Dowden, Hutchinson, & Ross.

Coates, G., & Sanoff, H. (1972). Behavior mapping: The ecology of child behavior in a planned residential setting. In W.J. Mitchell (Ed.), *Environmental design: Research and practice.* (pp. 13.2.1–11). *Proceedings of the EDRA 3/AR 8 Conference.* Los Angeles: University of California.

Cobb, E. (1959). The ecology of imagination in childhood. *Daedalus, 88,* 537–548.

Cohen, S. (1978). Environmental load and the allocation of attention. In A. Baum, J.E. Singer, & S. Valins (Ed.), *Advances in environmental psychology: Vol. 1. The urban environment* (pp. 1–30). Hillsdale, NJ: Erlbaum.

Cohen, S., Evans, G.W., Krantz, D.S., & Stokols, D. (1980). Physiological, motivational, and cognitive effects of aircraft noise on children: Moving from the laboratory to the field. *American Psychologist, 35,* 231–243.

Cohen, S., Evans, G.W., Krantz, D.S., Stokols, D., & Kelly, S. (1981). Aircraft noise and children: Longitudinal and cross-sectional evidence on adaptation to noise and the effectiveness of noise abatement. *Journal of Personality and Social Psychology, 40,* 331–345.

Cohen, S., Glass, D.C., & Singer, J.E. (1973). Apartment noise, auditory discrimination, and reading ability in children. *Journal of Experimental Child Psychology, 9,* 407–422.

Cohen, S., & Weinstein, N. (1982). Nonauditory effects of noise. In G.W. Evans (Ed.), *Environmental stress* (pp. 45–74). New York: Cambridge University Press.

Coles, R. (1971). *Children of crisis: Vol. 2. Migrants, sharecroppers, mountaineers.* Boston: Little, Brown.

Cooper, C.C. (1970). Adventure playgrounds. *Landscape Architecture, 61*(1), 18–29, 88–91.

Cravens, H. (1978). *The triumph of evolution: American scientists and the heredity-environment controversy, 1900–1941.* Philadelphia: University of Pennsylvania Press.

Crook, M.A., & Langdon, F.J. (1974). The effects of aircraft noise in schools around London airport. *Journal of Sound and Vibration, 34,* 221–232.

DeJoy, D.M. (1982, August). *Noise and children: Comments on recent progress in investigating this category of noise effects.* Paper presented at annual convention of the American Psychological Association, Washington, DC.

DeJoy, D.M. (1983). Environmental noise and children: Review of recent findings. *Journal of Auditory Research, 23,* 181–194.

Derman, A. (1974). Children's play: Design approaches and theoretical issues. In G. Coates (Ed.), *Alternative learning environments* (pp. 341–369). Stroudsburg, PA: Dowden, Hutchinson, & Ross.

Derman, A. (1977). *Pre-school children's responses to play-forms of varying complexity.* Unpublished doctoral dissertation, Pennsylvania State University, University Park.

Deutsch, C. (1964). Auditory discrimination and learning: Social factors. *Merrill-Palmer Quarterly, 10,* 277–296.

Dresel, P. (1972). Open space in new urban areas. In National Institute for Building Research, *Open space in housing areas.* Stockholm, Sweden: Author.

Elardo, R., & Bradley, R.H. (1981). The Home Observations for Measurement of the Environment (HOME) scale: A review of research. *Developmental Review, 1,* 113–145.

Elardo, R., Bradley, R.H., & Caldwell, B.M. (1975). The relation of infants' home environments to mental test performance from six to thirty-six months: A longitudinal analysis. *Child Development, 46,* 71–76.

Elardo, R., Bradley, R.H., & Caldwell, B.M. (1977). A longitudinal study of relation of infants' home environment to language development at age three. *Child Development, 48,* 595–603.

Ellis, M.J. (1973). *Why people play.* Englewood Cliffs, NJ: Prentice-Hall.

Fein, G., & Clarke-Stewart, A. (1973). *Day care in context.* New York: Wiley.

Frost, J.L., & Klein, B.L. (1979). *Children's play and playgrounds.* Boston: Allyn & Bacon.

Gibson, E.J. (1982). The concept of affordances: The renascence of functionalism. In W.A. Collins (Ed.), *The Minnesota symposia on child development: Vol. 15. The concept of development* (pp. 55–81). Hillsdale, NJ: Erlbaum.

Gibson, J.J. (1966). *The senses considered as perceptual systems.* Boston: Houghton Mifflin.

Gibson, J.J. (1976). *The theory of affordances and the design of the environment.* Paper presented at meeting of the American Society of Aesthetics, Toronto, Canada.

Gibson, J.J. (1979). *The ecological approach to visual perception.* Boston: Houghton Mifflin.

Glass, D.C., & Singer, J.E. (1972). *Urban stress: Experiments on noise and social stressors.* New York: Academic.

Goldfarb, W. (1943). The effects of early institutional care on adolescent personality. *Journal of Experimental Education, 12,* 106–129.

Gramza, A.F. (1974). Children's responses to visual complexity in a play setting. *Psychological Reports, 35,* 895–899.

Gramza, A.A., Corush, J., & Ellis, M.J. (1972). Children's play on trestles differing in complexity: A study of play equipment design. *Journal of Leisure Research, 4,* 303–312.

Gramza, A.F., & Scholtz, G.J.L. (1973). An analysis of stimulus dimensions which define children's encapsulating play objects. *Perceptual and Motor Skills, 37,* 495–501.

Gray, S.W., & Klaus, R.A. (1968). The early training project and its general rationale. In R.D. Hess & R.M. Bear (Eds.), *Early education: Current theory, research, and action* (pp. 63–70). Chicago: Aldine.

Green, K.B., Pasternack, B.S., & Shore, R.E. (1982, August). *Effects of aircraft noise on reading ability in elementary schools.* Paper presented at annual convention of the American Psychological Association, Washington, DC.

Gump, P.V. (1975). Ecological psychology and children. In E.M. Hetherington (Ed.), *Review of child development research* (Vol. 5) (pp. 75–126). Chicago: University of Chicago Press.

Gump, P.V. (1978). School environments. In I. Altman & J.F. Wohlwill (Eds.), *Human behavior and environment: Vol. 3. Children and the environment* (pp. 131–174). New York: Plenum.

Gump, P.V., & Adelberg, B. (1978). Urbanism from the perspective of ecological psychologists. *Environment and Behavior, 10,* 171–191.

Haggard, E.A. (1973). Some effects of geographic and social isolation in nature settings. In J. Rasmussen (Ed.), *Man in isolation and confinement* (pp. 99–144). Chicago: Aldine.

Hambrick-Dixon, P.J. (1982, August). *Subway noise and children's visual vigilance performance: A developmental perspective.* Paper presented at the annual convention of the American Psychological Association, Washington, DC.

Harris, C.S. (1965). Perceptual adaptation to inverted, reversed, and displaced vision. *Psychological Review, 72,* 419–444.

Hart, R. (1979). *Children's experience of place.* New York: Irvington.

Hart, R., & Chawla, L. (1981). The development of children's concern for the environment. *Zeitschrift für Umweltpolitik, 4,* 271–294.

Harter, S. (1981). A model of mastery motivation in children: Individual differences and developmental change. In W.A. Collins (Ed.), *The Minnesota symposia on child psychology: Vol. 14. Aspects of the development of competence* (pp. 215–255). Hillsdale, NJ: Erlbaum.

Hayward, D.G., Rothenberg, M., & Beasley, R.R. (1974). Children's play and urban playground environments: A comparison of traditional, contemporary and adventure playground types. *Environment and Behavior, 6,* 131–168.

Hebb, D.O. (1949). *The organization of behavior.* New York: Wiley.

Heft, H. (1979). Background and focal environmental conditions of the home and attention in young children. *Journal of Applied Social Psychology, 9,* 47–69.

Heft, H. (1981). An examination of constructivist and Gibsonian approaches to environmental psychology. *Population and Environment: Behavioral and Social Issues, 4,* 227–245.

Heft, H. (1982, August). *Noise and perceptual-cognitive development: A functional analysis.* Paper presented at the annual convention of the American Psychological Association, Washington, DC.

Heft, H. (1984). High residential density and perceptual-cognitive development: An examination of the effects of crowding and noise in the home. In J.F. Wohlwill & W. VanVliet- - (Eds.), *Habitats for children: Impacts of density* (pp. 39–76). Hillsdale, NJ: Erlbaum.

Hein, A. (1980). The development of visually guided behavior. In C.S. Harris (Ed.), *Visual coding and adaptability.* Hillsdale, NJ: Erlbaum.

Held, R. (1965). Plasticity in sensory-motor systems. *Scientific American, 213*(5), 84–94.

Henderson, B.B., Charlesworth, W.R., & Gamradt, J. (1982). Children's exploratory behavior in a novel field setting. *Ethology and Sociobiology, 3,* 93–99.

Henderson, N.D. (1980). Effects of early experience upon the behavior of animals: The second twenty-five years of research. In E.C. Simmel (Ed.), *Early experiences and early behavior* (pp. 45–78). New York: Academic.

Hochberg, J.E. (1978). *Perception* (2nd ed.). Englewood Cliffs, NJ: Prentice-Hall.

Hollos, M. (1974). *Growing up in flathill: Social environment and cognitive development.* Oslo: Norway: Universitetsforlaget.

Hollos, M. (1975). Logical operations and role-taking abilities in two cultures: Norway and Hungary. *Child Development, 46,* 638–649.

Hollos, M. (1983). Cross-cultural research in psychological development in rural communities. In A. Childs & G.B. Melton (Eds.), *Rural psychology* (pp. 45–73). New York: Plenum.

Hollos, M., & Cowan, F.A. (1973). Social isolation and cognitive development: Logical operations and role-taking abilities in three Norwegian social settings. *Child Development, 44,* 630–641.

Hunt, J.Mc.V. (1961). *Intelligence and experience.* New York: Ronald.

Hutt, C. (1966). Exploration and play in children. *Symposia of the Zoological Society, London* (No. 18) 61–81.

Hymovitch, B. (1952). The effects of experimental variations in early experience on problem solving in the rat. *Journal of Comparative and Physiological Psychology, 45,* 313–321.

Jennings, K.D., Harmon, R.J., Morgan, G.A., Gaiter, J.L., & Yarrow, L.J. (1979). Exploratory play as an index of mastery motivation: Relationships to persistence, cognitive functioning, and environmental measures. *Developmental Psychology, 15,* 386–394.

Kagan, J., & Klein, R. (1973). Cross-cultural perspectives on early development. *American Psychologist, 28,* 947–961.

Kaplan, R. (1976). Way finding in the natural environment. In G.T. Moore, & R.G. Golledge (Eds.), *Environmental*

knowing (pp. 46–57). Stroudsburg, PA: Dowden, Hutchinson, & Ross.

Karsdorf, G., & Klappach, H. (1968). The influence of traffic noise on the health and performance of secondary school students in a large city. *Zeitschrift für die gesamte Hygiene, 14,* 52–54.

Krasner, L. (1980). *Environmental design and human behavior.* New York: Pergamon.

Kritchevsky, S., Prescott, E., & Walling, L. (1969). *Planning environments for young children: Physical space* (2nd ed.). Washington, DC: National Association for the Education of Young Children.

Kryter, K.D. (1970). *The effects of noise on man.* New York: Academic.

Kyzar, B.L. (1977). Noise pollution and schools: How much is too much? *CEFP Journal* (Council of Educational Facility Planners), *4,* 10–11.

Larson, G., & Peterson, B. (1978). Does noise limit the learning of young listeners? *Elementary School Journal, 78,* 264–265.

Lerner, R.M. (1983). A "goodness of fit" model of person-context interaction. In D. Magnusson & V.P. Allen (Eds.), *Human development: An interactional perspective* (pp. 279–294). New York: Academic.

Liben, L., Patterson, A.H., & Newcombe, N. (Eds.). (1981). *Spatial representation and behavior across the life span: Theory and application.* New York: Academic.

Long, L., & DeAre, D. (1982). Repopulating the countryside: A 1980 census trend. *Science, 217,* 1111–1116.

Lukas, J.S., DuPree, R.B., & Swing, J.W. (1981). *Effects of noise on academic achievement and classroom behavior* (Report No. FHWA/CA/DOHS-81/01). Berkeley: California Department of Transportation.

Lukashok, A., & Lynch, K. (1956). Some childhood memories of the city. *American Institute of Planners Journal, 22,* 142–152.

Lutkus, A.D., & Baird, J.C. (1982). Advocacy, education and research. In J.C. Baird & A.D. Lutkus (Eds.), *Mind, Child, Architecture* (pp. 197–204). Hanover, NH: New England Universities Press.

Lynch, K. (1977). *Growing up in cities: Studies of the spatial environment of adolescence in Cracow, Melbourne, Mexico City, Salta, Toluca, and Warszawa.* Cambridge, MA: MIT Press.

Magnusson, D., & Allen, V.L. (1983). *Human development: An interactional perspective.* New York: Academic.

Marcus, C.C. (1974). Children's play behavior in a low-rise, inner-city housing development. In R.C. Moore (Ed.), *Childhood city* (pp. 197–211). *EDRA 5: Proceedings of the Fifth Environmental Design Research Association Conference* (Pt. 12). Washington, DC: Environmental Design Research Association.

Marcus, C.C., & Moore, R. (1976). Children and their environments: A review of research. *Journal of Architectural Education, 29*(4), 22–25.

Maurer, R., & Baxter, J.C. (1972). Images of the neighborhood and city among Black, Anglo- and Mexican-American children. *Environment and Behavior, 4*, 352–388.

McCroskey, R.L., & Devens, J.S. (1977). Effects of noise upon student performance in public school classrooms. *Proceedings of the Technical Program, National Noise and Vibration Control Conference*, Chicago.

Merleau-Ponty, M. (1962). *Phenomenology of perception.* London: Routledge & Kegan Paul.

Michelson, W., Levine, A.V., & Spina, A.R. (1979). *The child in the city: Changes and challenges.* Toronto, Canada: University of Toronto Press.

Michelson, W., & Roberts, E. (1979). Children in the urban physical environment. In W. Michelson, A.V. Levine, & A.R. Spina (Eds.), *The child in the city: Changes and challenges* (pp. 410–478). Toronto, Canada: University of Toronto Press.

Milgram, S. (1970). The experience of living in cities. *Science, 167*, 1461–1468.

Mills, J.H. (1975). Noise and children: A review of the literature. *Journal of the Acoustical Society of America, 58*, 767–779.

Moch-Sibony, A. (1981). Etude des effects du bruit à la suite d'une exposition prolongée des infants: comparison entre école insonorisée et non insonorisée. *Le Travail Humain, 44*, 169–178.

Moore, G.T. (1980a). The application of research to the design of therapeutic play environments for exceptional children. In W.M. Cruickshank (Ed.), *Approaches to learning.* Syracuse, NY: Syracuse University Press.

Moore, G.T. (1980b). Providing quality facilities for child care. In K.S. Perry (Ed.), *Employers and child care: Establishing services at the workplace.* Washington, DC: U.S. Government Printing Office, Department of Labor Women's Bureau.

Moore, G.T. (1983a, August). *Effects of definition of behavior settings on children's behavior.* Paper presented at the annual convention of the American Psychological Association, Anaheim.

Moore, G.T. (1983b). *Some effects of physical and social environmental variables on children's behavior: Two studies of children's outdoor play and child care environments.* Unpublished doctoral dissertation, Clark University, Worcester, MA.

Moore, G.T. (1985). State of the art in play environment research and applications. In J.L. Frost (Ed.), *When Children Play* (pp. 171–192). Wheaton, MD: Association for Childhood Education International.

Moore, G.T. (in press). The role of the socio-physical environment in cognitive development. In C.S. Weinstein & T.G. David (Eds.), *Spaces for children: The built environment and child development.* New York: Plenum.

Moore, G.T., Cohen, U., Oertel, J., & Van Ryzin, L. (1979). *Designing environments for handicapped children.* New York: Educational Facilities Laboratories.

Moore, G.T., Lane, C.G., Hill, A.W., Cohen, U., & McGinty, T. (1979). *Recommendations for child care centers.* Milwaukee: University of Wisconsin Center for Architecture and Urban Planning Research.

Moore, G.T., Lane, C.G., & Lindberg, L.A. (1979). *Bibliography on children and the physical environment.* Milwaukee: University of Wisconsin Center for Architecture and Urban Planning Research. (ERIC No. Document Reproduction Service ED 184-696 and NTIS No. AD AO88-589)

Moore, R., & Young, D. (1978). Childhood outdoors: Toward a social ecology of the landscape. In I. Altman & J.F. Wohlwill (Eds.), *Human Behavior and Environment: Vol. 3. Children and the environment.* (pp. 83–130). New York: Plenum.

More, T.A. (1977). An analysis of wildlife in children's stories. In U.S. Forest Service, *Children, nature and the urban environment: Proceedings of a symposium-fair* (General Tech. Rep. NE-30) (pp. 89–92). Upper Darby, PA: Author, Northeastern Forest Experiment Station.

Muchow, M., & Muchow, H. (1980). *Der Lebensraum des Grosstadtkindes.* Bensheim, Germany: päd. extra. (Original work published 1935.)

Newton, G., & Levine, S. (1967). *Early experience and behavior: The psychobiology of development.* Springfield, IL: Thomas.

Nunnally, J.C., & Lemond, C. (1973). Exploratory behavior and human development. *Advances in child development and behavior, 8*, 59–109.

Olds, A.R. (1982). Designing play environments for children under 3. *Topics in Early Childhood Special Education, 2*(3), 87–93.

Osmon, F.L. (1971). *Patterns for designing children's centers.* New York: Educational Facilities Laboratories.

Ostro, J. (1977). *An examination of the indoor and outdoor play patterns of urban and rural preschool children.* Unpublished doctoral dissertation, Pennsylvania State University, University Park.

Paraskevopoulos, J., & Hunt, J. McV. (1971). Object construction and imitation under differing conditions of rearing. *Journal of Genetic Psychology, 119*, 301–321.

Parke, R.D., & Sawin, D.B. (1979). Children's privacy in the home: Developmental, ecological, and child-rearing determinants. *Environment and Behavior, 11*, 87–104.

Pollowy, A.M. (1977). *The urban nest.* Stroudsburg, PA: Dowden, Hutchinson, & Ross.

Prescott, E., Jones, E., & Kritchevsky, S. (1972). *Daycare as a child-rearing environment.* Washington, DC: National Association for the Education of Young Children.

Provence, S., & Lipton, R.C. (1962). *Infants in institutions.* New York: International Universities Press.

Rasmussen, J. (Ed.). (1973). *Man in isolation and confinement.* Chicago: Aldine.

Reese, H.W., & Overton, W.F. (1970). Models of development and theories of development. In L.R. Goulet & P.B. Baltes (Eds.), *Life-span developmental psychology: Theory and research* (pp. 115–145). New York: Academic.

Reseski, D.J. (1981). Children look at nature: Environmental perception and education. *Journal of Environmental Education, 13*(4), 27–40.

Rheingold, H.L., & Eckerman, C.O. (1970). The infant separates himself from the mother. *Science, 168,* 78–83.

Roche, A.F., Chumlea, W.C., & Siervogel, R.M. (1982). *Longitudinal study of human hearing: Its relationship to noise and other factors III. Results from the first five years* (General Tech. Rep. 68-82). Dayton, OH: Wright-Patterson Air Force Base, Air Force Aerospace Medical Research Laboratory.

Rodin, J. (1976). Density, perceived choice and response to controllable and uncontrollable outcomes. *Journal of Experimental Social Psychology, 12,* 564–578.

Rogoff, B. (1982). Integrating context and cognitive development. In M.E. Lamb & A.L. Brown (Eds.), *Advances in developmental psychology* (Vol. 2). Hillsdale, NJ: Erlbaum.

Rubin, K.H., Fein, G.G., & Vandenberg, B. (1983). *Play.* In P.H. Mussen (Ed.), *Handbook of child psychology* (4th ed., Vol. 4). (pp. 693–774). New York: Wiley.

Saegert, S. (1980, September). *The effect of residential density on low income children.* Paper presented at the annual convention of the American Psychological Association, Montreal, Canada.

Saegert, S., & Hart, R. (1978). The development of environmental competence in girls and boys. In M.A. Salter (Ed.), *Play: Anthropological perspectives* (pp. 157–175). West Point, NY: Leisure Press.

Sanoff, H., & Dickerson, J. (1971). Mapping children's behavior in a residential setting. *Journal of Architectural Education, 25*(4), 98–103.

Santrock, J.W. (1976). Affect and facilitative self-control: Influence of ecological setting, cognition, and social agent. *Journal of Educational Psychology, 68,* 529–535.

Schoggen, P., & Barker, R.G. (1977). Ecological factors in development in an American and an English small town. In H. McGurk (Ed.), *Ecological factors in human development* (pp. 61–76). Amsterdam, Netherlands: North-Holland.

Schoggen, P., & Schoggen, M. (1984). Play, exploration, and density. In J.F. Wohlwill & W. Van Vliet (Eds.), *Habitats for children: Impacts of density.* (pp. 77–95) Hillsdale, NJ: Erlbaum.

Schuster, S.O., Murrell, S.A., & Cook, W.A. (1980). Person, setting and interaction contributions to nursery school social behavior patterns. *Journal of Personality, 48,* 24–37.

Sherman, M., & Key, C.B. (1932). Intelligence scores of isolated mountain children. *Child Development, 3,* 279–290.

Shure, M.B. (1963). Psychological ecology of a nursery school. *Child Development, 34,* 979–992.

Simmel, G. (1978/1950). *Die Grosstadt und das Geistesleben der Grosstadt.* Dresden: Zahn & Jaensch. In K.H. Wolff (Ed. & Trans.), *The sociology of George Simmel* (pp. 635–646). New York: Free Press. (Original work published 1903.)

Slater, B. (1968). Effects of noise on school performance. *Journal of Educational Psychology, 59,* 239–243.

Smith, P.K., & Connolly, K.J. (1980). *The ecology of preschool behavior.* Cambridge, England: Cambridge University Press.

Sommer, R., & Olsen, H. (1980). The soft classroom. *Environment and Behavior, 12,* 3–16.

Southworth, M., & Southworth, S. (1974). The educative city. In G. Coates (Ed.), *Alternative learning environments* (pp. 274–281). Stroudsburg, PA: Dowden, Hutchinson, & Ross.

Spitz, R.A. (1945). Hospitalism: An inquiry into the genesis of psychiatric conditions in early childhood. Part I. *Psychoanalytic Studies of the Child, 1,* 53–74.

Srole, L. (1972). Urbanization and mental health: Some reformulations. *American Scientist, 60,* 576–583.

Thompson, W.R., & Grusec, J. (1970). Studies of early experience. In P.H. Mussen (Ed.), *Carmichael's manual of child psychology* (3rd Ed.) (pp. 565–654). New York: Wiley.

Tizard, B., Cooperman, O., Joseph, A., & Tizard, J. (1972). Environmental effects on language development: A study of young children in long-stay residential nurseries. *Child Development, 43,* 337–358.

Tizard, B., & Hodges, J. (1978). The effect of early institutional rearing on the development of eight-year-old children. *Journal of Child Psychology and Psychiatry, 19,* 99–118.

Tizard, B., & Rees, J. (1974). A comparison of the effects of adoption, restoration to the natural mother, and continued institutionalization on the cognitive development of four-year-old children. *Child Development, 45,* 92–99.

Tuan, Y.F. (1978). Children and the natural environment. In I. Altman & J.F. Wohlwill (Eds.), *Human Behavior and Environment: Vol. 3. Children and the environment* (pp. 5–32). New York: Plenum.

Tulkin, S., & Covitz, F. (1975, April). *Mother-infant interaction and intellectual functioning at age 6.* Paper presented at the meeting of the Society for Research in Child Development, Denver, CO.

Turnure, J.E. (1970). Children's reactions to distractors in a learning situation. *Developmental Psychology, 2,* 115–122.

U.S. Environmental Protection Agency. (1974). *Information on levels of environmental noise requisite to protect public health and welfare with an adequate margin of safety* (EPA Rep. 550, 907400004). Washington, DC: U.S. Government Printing Office.

U.S. Forest Service. (1977). *Children, nature and the environment: Proceedings of a symposium-fair* (General Tech. Rep. NE-30). Upper Darby, PA: Author, Northeastern Forest Experiment Station.

Uzgiris, I.C., & Hunt, J. McV. (1975). *Assessment in infancy: Ordinal scales of psychological development.* Urbana: University of Illinois Press.

Van Ryzin, L. (1979). Environmental manipulability in children's play settings (Abstract). In A.D.D. Seidel & S. Danford (Eds.), *Environmental design: Research, theory, and applications. Proceedings of the 10th annual EDRA Conference, Buffalo, NY.* Washington, DC: Environmental Design Research Association.

Van Vliet, W. (1980). *Use, evaluation, and knowledge of city and suburban environments by children of employed and non-employed mothers.* Unpublished doctoral dissertation, University of Toronto, Toronto, Canada.

Van Vliet, W. (1981). Neighborhood evaluations by city and suburban children. *American Planning Association Journal, 47,* 458–467.

Van Vliet, W. (1983a). Exploring "the fourth environment"—An examination of the home range of city and suburban teenagers. *Environment and Behavior, 15,* 567–588.

Van Vliet, W. (1983b). Families in apartment buildings: Sad storeys for children? *Environment and Behavior, 14,* 211–234.

Van Vliet, W. (1984). The role of housing type, household density, and neighborhood density in peer interaction and social adjustment. In J.F. Wohlwill & W. Van Vliet (Eds.), *Habitats for children: Impacts of density* (pp. 165–200). Hillsdale, NJ: Erlbaum.

Wachs, T.D. (1976). Utilization of a Piagetian approach in the investigation of early experience effects: A research strategy and some illustrative data. *Merrill-Palmer Quarterly, 22,* 11–30.

Wachs, T.D. (1977). The optimal stimulation hypothesis and early development: Anybody got a match? In I.C. Uzgiris & F. Weizmann (Eds.), *The structuring of experience* (pp. 153–178). New York: Plenum.

Wachs, T.D. (1978). The relationship of infants' physical environment to their Binet performance at 2½ years. *International Journal of Behavioral Development, 1,* 51–65.

Wachs, T.D. (1979). Proximal experience and early cognitive-intellectual development: The physical environment. *Merrill-Palmer Quarterly, 25,* 3–41.

Wachs, T.D. (1982, August). *Relation of home noise-confusion to infant cognitive development.* Paper presented at the annual convention of the American Psychological Association, Washington, DC.

Wachs, T.D., Francis, J., & McQuiston, S. (1979). Psychological dimensions of the infant's physical environment. *Infant Behavior and Development, 2,* 155–161.

Wachs, T.D., & Gandour, M.J. (1983). Temperament, environment, and six-month cognitive-intellectual development. *International Journal of Behavioral Development, 6,* 135–152.

Wachs, T.D., & Gruen, G.E. (1982). *Early experience and human development.* New York: Plenum.

Wachs, T.D., Uzgiris, I.C., & Hunt, J. McV. (1971). Cognitive development in infants of different age levels and from different environmental backgrounds: An exploratory investigation. *Merrill-Palmer Quarterly, 17,* 283–317.

Walter, H., & Oerter, R. (Eds.). (1979). *Oekologie und Entwicklung.* Donauworth, Federal Republic of Germany: Auer.

Wapner, S. (1981). Transactions of persons-in-environments: Some critical transitions. *Journal of Environmental Psychology, 1,* 223–239.

Ward, C. (1978). *The child in the city.* New York: Pantheon.

Ward, L.M., & Suedfeld, P. (1973). Human responses to highway noise. *Environmental Research, 6,* 306–326.

Webley, P. (1981). Sex differences in home range and cognitive maps in eight-year-old children. *Journal of Environmental Psychology, 1,* 293–302.

Weinstein, C.S. (1979). The physical environment of the school: A review of the research. *Review of Educational Research, 49,* 577–610.

Weinstein, C.S., & David, T.G. (in press). *Spaces for children: The built environment and child development.* New York: Plenum.

Weinstein, C.S., & Weinstein, N.D. (1979). Noise and reading performance in an open space school. *Journal of Educational Research, 49,* 577–610.

Wheeler, L.R. (1942). A comparative study of the intelligence of East Tennessee Mountain children. *Journal of Educational Psychology, 33,* 321–334.

White, B.L. (1971). *Human infants: Experience and psychological development.* Englewood Cliffs, NJ: Prentice-Hall.

White, B.L., Kaban, B., Shapiro, B., & Attanucci, J. (1977). Competence and experience. In I.C. Uzgiris & F. Weizmann (Eds.), *The structuring of experience* (pp. 115–152). New York: Plenum.

White, B.L., & Watts, J. (1973). *Experience and environment.* Englewood Cliffs, NJ: Prentice-Hall.

White, R.H. (1959). Motivation reconsidered: The concept of competence. *Psychological Review, 66,* 297–333.

Wicker, A.W. (1979). *Ecological psychology.* Monterey, CA: Brooks/Cole.

Willems, E.P. (1973). Behavioral ecology and experimental analysis: Courtship is not enough. In J.R. Nesselroade & H.W. Reese (Eds.), *Life-span developmental psychology: Methodological issues* (pp. 197–218). New York: Academic.

Williamson, R.C. (1978). Socialization in the high-rise: A cross-national comparison. *Ekistics, 45*(268), 122–130.

Wofsey, E., Rierdan, J., & Wapner, S. (1979). Planning to

move: Effects on representing the currently inhabited environment. *Environment and Behavior, 11,* 3–32.

Wohlwill, J.F. (1974). Human adaptation to levels of environmental stimulation. *Human Ecology, 2,* 127–147.

Wohlwill, J.F. (1981a). *Ecological representativeness in developmental research: A critical view.* Paper presented at the meeting of the Society for Research in Child Development, Boston.

Wohlwill, J.F. (1981b). Umweltfragen in der Entwicklungspsychologie: Eine Kritische Betrachtung zu Repräsentanz und Validität. In H.J. Fietkau & D. Görlitz (Eds.), *Umwelt und Alltag in der Psychologie* (pp. 91–112). Weinheim, Federal Republic of Germany: Beltz.

Wohlwill, J.F. (1983). The physical and the social environment as factors in development. In D. Magnusson & V.P. Allen (Eds.), *Human development: An interactional perspective* (pp. 111–129). New York: Academic.

Wohlwill, J.F. (1984). Residential density as a variable in child development research. In J.F. Wohlwill & W. Van Vliet (Eds.), *Habitats for children:Impacts of density* (pp. 17–37). Hillsdale, NJ: Erlbaum.

Wohlwill, J.F. (1985). Martha Muchow and the life-space of the urban child. *Human Development, 28,* 200–209.

Wohlwill, J.F., & Sterns, H.L. (1974, April). *The development of response to stimulus complexity in rural and urban children.* Paper presented at the meeting of the Eastern Psychological Association, Philadelphia.

Wohlwill, J.F., & Van Vliet, W. (Eds.). (1984a). *Habitats for children: Impacts of density.* Hillsdale, NJ: Erlbaum.

Wohlwill, J.F., & Van Vliet, W. (1984b). Habitats for children: The state of the evidence. In J.F. Wohlwill & W. Van Vliet (Eds.), *Habitats for children: Impacts of density (pp. 201-229).* Hillsdale, NJ: Erlbaum.

Wolfe, M. (1978). Childhood and privacy. In I. Altman & J.F. Wohlwill (Eds.), *Human behavior and environment. Vol. 3, Children and the environment* (pp. 175–222). New York: Plenum.

Wolfe, M., & Laufer, R.S. (1974). The concept of privacy in childhood and adolescence. In S.T. Margulis (Ed.), *Privacy* (pp. 29–54). *EDRA 5: Proceedings of the Fifth Environmental Design Research Association Conference* (Pt. 6). Washington, DC: Environmental Design Research Association.

Wollin, D.D., & Montagne, M. (1981). College classroom environment: Effects of sterility versus amiability on student and teacher performance. *Environment and Behavior, 13,* 707–716.

Wright, H.F. (1956). Psychological development in Midwest. *Child Development, 27,* 265–286.

Yarrow, L.J., McQuiston, S., MacTurk, R.H., McCarthy, M.E., Klein, R. P., & Vietze, P.M. (1983). Assessment of mastery motivation during the first year of life: Contemporaneous and cross-age relationships. *Developmental Psychology, 19,* 159–171.

Yarrow, L.J., Morgan, G.A., Jennings, K.D., Harmon, R.J., & Gaiter, J.L. (1982). Infants' persistence at tasks: Relationships to cognitive functioning and early experience. *Infant Behavior and Development, 5,* 131–141.

Yarrow, L.J., Rubinstein, J.L., & Pedersen, F.A. (1975). *Infant and environment: Early cognitive and motivational development.* New York: Halsted.

Zien, J. (1974). Children in transit: The open city project. In G. Coates (Ed.), *Alternative learning environments* (pp. 256–273). Stroudsburg, PA: Dowden, Hutchinson, & Ross.

Chapter 10

ENVIRONMENT AND AGING

Frances M. Carp, *The Wright Institute, Berkeley, California*

10.1. INTRODUCTION

This chapter opens with an overview of the environment and aging field by putting it into the perspective of its links with environmental psychology and its differences from traditional gerontological research. A historical account is given of demographic and social conditions that have affected the environmental quality of elderly people in the United States and that led to changes in social policy as the federal government began to assume responsibility for the basic necessities of life for the poorest of its citizens, which include a disproportionate number of older persons. The most pressing need among the elderly poor was for housing. While older people had always been able to qualify for standard public housing, their plight was considered so serious that by the late 1950s legislation was enacted and moneys appropriated for construction of housing designed for and limited to the elderly.

Infusion of funds into communities across the country to provide these residential facilities introduced extralaboratory settings for aging and environment studies. Research funding agencies recognized the need for studies on the design and effects of these societal interventions. However, the first investigators to venture into this field were handicapped by the dearth of relevant studies, instruments, and theoretical formulations.

Agreement has not been reached about the most appropriate conceptual model. Two are presented that attempt to subsume most of the previous attempts at conceptualization, followed by descriptions of the work on which the two are based. Overviews of empirical trends associated with major content domains of aging and environment research and housing and the neighborhood follow. Then issues involved in relocation of the elderly are reviewed. Finally the discussion turns to issues for the future, and the chapter ends with a summary highlighting key themes and conclusions.

10.2. THE FIELD OF ENVIRONMENT AND AGING IN DISCIPLINARY CONTEXT

10.2.1. Relationship with Environmental Psychology

It need not have been surprising if a focus on the physical environment had emerged within psychology in the 1860s instead of the 1980s, as a straightforward extension of Fechner's psychophysics; nor if environmental psychology had never emerged as a distinct field, "since the analysis of stimulus and response, environment and behavior, setting and action pervades all of psychology" (Canter & Craik, 1981, p. 2). It would have been similarly unstartling if gerontological phenomena had been, from the start, an area of focal interest within psychology; since one of the events that helped to precipitate the field was the difference in recording times of stellar transit on the part of Maskelyne, an aging astronomer, and Kinnebrook, his young assistant who was dismissed on grounds of "error" that was later recognized as the "personal equation" (Boring, 1950).

Investigation of environment and aging, like that of other environment and person issues, is relatively new. Both came about in response to social changes: environmental psychology in response to issues such as crowding, noise, and air pollution; aging and environment to evaluate the total milieu of housing for the elderly. When psychologists became aware of the environment outside the laboratory as a new opportunity to test the ecological validity of their theories, a well-established body of knowledge was available to organize and implement investigations of many kinds, and this quickly led to development of a variety of research approaches, depending on each investigator's particular interest (Baum, Singer, & Valins, 1978). Psychologists interested in older adults and their environments found scarcer resources in the research literature than did those whose interests could be met with younger age groups. Because of ready access to students for data, theories of "adult behavior" tended largely to be based on material from college sophomores, and the validities of existing instruments for elderly respondents were questionable.

Therefore, to a considerable extent, research on environment–old person interactions has developed apart from environmental psychology in general. In early years this was accentuated by the nature of information about characteristics of old people. As late as the 1950s and 1960s, such psychological fields as cognition, learning, sensation–perception, and adaptation all presented bleak prospects for attempting environmental studies with the old. Rehousing was questioned on the grounds that old people cannot adapt and the resulting stress is deleterious. Separateness was fostered by the tendency of psychological journal editors to judge gerontological findings "not of general interest" and the consequent development of special publications that were read almost exclusively by gerontologists.

The past 20 years have seen dramatic changes, with the use of improved research designs, in our notions of the cognitive and other characteristics of old people, which document their competence to deal with environmental factors, and therefore the utility of old person–environment studies. Additionally, the wide range of individual differences in many traits observed among the old and their unusual sensitivity to some stimuli make them an unusually good age group for fine-grained investigations regarding certain behaviors. Psychology in general has not sufficiently capitalized on this information in research designs, probably because investigators outside gerontological channels remain unaware of it. There are hopeful signs that the gap is narrowing. It is now recognized that development does not end with adolescence, that studying old age in isolation is of limited value, and that life span investigations and conceptualizations are necessary to understand human behavior (e.g., Baltes, Reese, & Lipsitt, 1980). Reports of such investigations, as well as of gerontological studies, are appearing more frequently in psychological journals.

10.2.2. Relationship with Gerontology

One major focus of interest for gerontology is the question of which age changes are consequences of biological aging and which are environmentally induced, or the extent to which a given age-related phenomenon is biologically determined and the extent to which it can be influenced environmentally.

> Unfortunately there remains a strong bias, among many gerontological researchers, against anchoring their research in the social and ecological environments that may affect the variables being considered. There is a profound tendency...to view the number of years one has lived as an inexorable determinant of one's capacities and ways of behaving. There is an accompanying deemphasis on the influence of social structure and environmental factors on the behavior of older people. (Green, Parham, Kleff, & Pilisuk, 1980, p. 1)

However, from modest beginnings in the late 1950s, and stimulated by construction of special living environments for the elderly, there has been a rapid proliferation of research on environment and aging. It is now recognized as an important domain within gerontology that has its own roster of investigators, identified by their efforts to assess environmental effects.

10.2.3. Relationships with Other Disciplines

In introducing *The Journal of Environmental Psychology*, Canter and Craik define environmental psychol-

ogy as "that area of psychology which brings into conjunction and analyzes the transactions and inter-relationships of human experiences and actions with pertinent aspects of socio-physical surroundings" (1981, p. 2). They feel it important to emphasize that "the field of environmental psychology is clearly an area within psychology," though they recognize that "the multi-disciplinary nature of the problems studied inevitably requires that the concepts, methods and personnel involved in the field will be drawn from many parent disciplines" (1981, p. 2).

Environment and aging research has always been an explicitly and insistently multidisciplinary effort, including not only psychology but also such disciplines as sociology, anthropology, architecture, geography, economics, and medicine. Therefore the research and theory discussed in the chapter are not limited to the psychological. In the aging and environment domain, emphasis has been on team approaches in which psychologists, often in the majority or taking initial action, should not dominate in the conduct of studies.

10.3. THE IMPETUS FOR RESEARCH INTO ENVIRONMENT AND AGING

Research into environment and aging is of fairly recent origin in the United States. Other nations have longer and richer records of such investigations that unfortunately cannot be included because of space limitations. This chapter follows the historical development of research in this area in this country. The major impetus may be reasonably attributed to federal actions to relieve severe housing problems among the older population, with consequent construction of facilities in which investigations could be carried out regarding effects of this type of rehousing. The growth and direction of research have been strongly channeled by federal legislation and its implementation, and the interests of funding agencies. We turn now to changes in the population structure and other societal variables that led to these social policy innovations.

10.3.1. Changes in the Population Structure

Growth in the Older Segment
From 1900 to 1980, the percentage of Americans aged 65 and older almost tripled (from 4.1% in 1900 to 11.3%, or about one in every nine persons, in 1980), and their numbers increased more than eight times (from 3.1 million to 25.5 million). Over that

period the gain accelerated. For example, the number of older persons increased by 5.5 million or 28% from 1970 to 1980. Projections suggest even more dramatic increases. A conservative prediction is that by the year 2000 the population 65 and older will number almost 32 million and comprise about 12% of the population; and that by 2050 there will be over 55 million, representing 18% of the population (Vanhorenbeck, 1982). A different projection is that by the year 2000 there will be 35 million persons 65 and older, representing 13.1% of the population; and by the year 2030, 64.3 million persons comprising 21.1% of the population (American Association of Retired Persons, 1982). The most rapid increase is expected between the years 2010 and 2030 when the "baby boom" generation reaches 65. These changes in population structure result from three demographic factors: fertility, mortality, and immigration.

FERTILITY

High birth rates early in the twentieth century resulted in increases in the older portion of society now. The post-World War II "baby boom" is holding down that proportion today but will swell its ranks early in the twenty-first century. Recent declines in birthrate make it unlikely that, beyond the middle of the next century, the rate of growth and the proportions of older people will diminish. Evidence is not yet clear whether the late-1970s birthrate of 1.8 children per woman will increase as "baby boomers" approach a "biological deadline."

MORTALITY

The decrease in mortality rate has been primarily at younger ages, especially infancy. Increases in life expectancy have been modest. This may be because the major causes of death among older people (heart disease, cancer, and stroke) remain largely uncontrolled. However, it is not clear that their control would greatly increase longevity. Some biologists believe there is a natural limitation to humankind's life span. Special ways to prolong life have been suggested. One is nutritional. Many laboratory studies show that food restriction delays the occurrence of age-related disease in rats and extends their maximum life span (Masoro, 1981). It is not yet known whether the life-prolonging action of food restriction relates only to laboratory rodents. Even if it holds true for human beings, this approach is not likely to be widely accepted.

> On the assumption that undernourishment in humans would yield similar results, it is of interest to observe that in the forty years since this has been

known, no human has consciously chosen to do it, even the biologists who know that data best. (Hayflick, 1981, p. 39)

Slowing metabolism for extended periods (mimicking hibernation by use of drugs or cold) might add to the life span. However, "the potential societal dislocations resulting from such a scenario are awesome" (Hayflick, 1981, p. 41). He concludes that the role of mortality in changing the population structure will be modest in the near future.

IMMIGRATION

Prior to World War I most of the large number of immigrants were young and middle-aged. They are among the elderly today. After World War II immigration declined. However, continuing and accelerating immigration from Mexico and Central and South America and the recent influx from Southeast Asia complicate predictions regarding the population structure in terms of age, because of the differential fertility and mortality rates; and they make it difficult to describe even today's housing needs, because of cultural differences from those on whom research has been conducted.

Stages of Aging

Neugarten (1975) divides the elderly into *young-old* and *old-old* on the basis of age (55 to 75 vs. 75 and older). The young-old are mobile, active, ready to experiment with different types of experience, and often gregarious. The old-old are subject to severe health and activity restrictions. The increase in the older population is disproportionately large among the latter. Among those 65 and older in 1980, 15.6 million were between the ages of 65 and 74, 7.7 million were between the ages of 75 and 84, and 2.2 million were 85 or older. On July 1, 1982, there were more than 2.4 million people 85 or older, a 9.1% increase since the 1980 census; there were 32,000 people at least 100 years old, almost 24,000 of them women (American Association of Retired Persons, 1982).

If this rapidly increasing group of old-old is ill and inactive, the housing task will be one of humane warehousing. On the other hand there is evidence that individuals can maintain a high degree of wellness until close to death, and that this is reflected in the greater vitality of very old people today (Hayflick, 1981). Then a different environment is and increasingly will become appropriate for the latest years. Generalizations based on past studies using chronological age as the marker may fall wide of the mark in providing appropriate living environments.

The Sex Role Among Older People

Of those 65 and older in 1980, 15.2 million were women and 10.3 million were men, or 148 women to every 100 men. The ratio of women to men increases with age. It is 125 to 100 for the 65-to-69 group, but 229 to 100 for those 85 and older. In 1980 almost twice as many older men as older women were married (78% of men, 40% of women). Over half the older women were widows. There were over five times as many widows (7.0 million) as widowers (1.3 million). While less than 1.5 million men over 65 live alone, over 6 million women in the age group do (United States Bureau of the Census, 1982). In other words, about one in four elderly persons in the United States is a woman living alone. Men tend to marry younger women. The current trend for marriages to end in divorce indicates that the numbers of elderly women alone will continue to grow (Van Dusen & Sheldon, 1976; Weed, 1980).

Older women who live alone are especially vulnerable to conditions in their living environments. Their housing tends to be more dilapidated (Montgomery, Stubbs, & Day, 1980; Soldo, 1978) and they are less likely to make needed repairs (Haley & Wiseman, 1980). While only about 20% of all households spend more than one-quarter of their incomes for housing, 75% of single elderly women spend this much, and about 45% spend at least half their incomes (Yezer, 1978). This must be seen in the context that older women alone are the lowest income group (Brotman, 1980). There are other problems. Widowhood and living alone increase an older person's risk of institutionalization (Newman, 1976; Vicente, Wiley, & Carrington, 1979), and increase isolation (Morgan, 1976) and fear of criminal victimization (Campbell, Converse, & Rodgers, 1976; Lebowitz, 1975) — which are often consequences of environmental conditions.

There may be a positive cohort effect in that more women have entered the labor force (though the wage differential continues) and will retire with their own Social Security and other retirement benefits. Nevertheless, housing this large, growing, and vulnerable segment of the older population poses serious problems.

10.3.2. Other Societal Changes

As the population structure changed, the nation converted from an agrarian to an industrial and from a rural to an urban life-style, mobility increased, family size diminished, more women moved into the labor force, retirement came into fashion, and inflation rose. It became increasingly impractical for older people to live out their lives within the households of extended families. Family relationships did not weaken (Shanas, 1979). Society simply outgrew the extended-family household as a solution to housing the elderly. Old people are as desirous as are younger people of the new arrangement of independent living.

In the nineteenth century the typical pattern was to work until close to death. During the early twentieth century, few workers could look forward to retirement income benefits. The enactment of Social Security had revolutionary positive effects. Nevertheless, as the middle of the twentieth century approached, the savings of the elderly had been depleted by the Great Depression and their buying power shrank with inflation. Even today, with increases in Social Security coverage and benefits and the proliferation of other retirement programs, at retirement income is typically reduced by half. While some expenses (transportation and other work costs and reduced family size as children leave home) are lower, others (medical and pharmaceutical in particular) tend to rise with age.

10.3.3. Implications of These Population and Societal Factors

The increase in size of the older population during the first half of this century and the proportion of it with inadequate postwork incomes at mid–twentieth century confronted this (and other highly industrialized nations) with a situation novel in human experience, a social problem of dimensions seemingly incapable of individual solution. It became increasingly apparent that a significant proportion of the expanding older population was unable to afford adequate housing. The problem will not go away. While specific projections remain obscure, forecasters agree that older people will comprise an increasing proportion of the population. Without significant changes in retirement income programs, including coverage of women never (or not long enough) in the labor force, personal resources will be inadequate for many to obtain decent housing. The societal changes that accompanied the population changes seem irreversible and reduce the feasibility of family solutions.

10.3.4. The Federal Response

During the latter two-thirds of this century, the federal government has assumed increasing responsibility to provide a "floor" of basic necessities, including housing. In the 1937 Housing Act, Congress established a public housing program for low-income families and stated the national goal of "decent, safe and sanitary housing for every American family." The elderly numbered disproportionately among the low-income group, and their housing needs differed from those of other age groups. Legislation to permit construction of facilities designed for and limited to low-income elderly was enacted in 1956, and the first projects were under construction in 1959 and 1960. Table 10.1 shows the numbers of housing units built under this and other federal programs of the Department of Housing and Urban Development (HUD) and the Farmers Home Administration (FmHA) as of June 3, 1982. Under the Section 8 program for leased housing, assistance makes up the difference between established rent and occupants' required contribution to that rent, depending on income. Section 202 provides construction financing and low-term, low-interest loans to nonprofit and limited-dividend sponsors. Section 221(d)(3) was a mortgage insurance program for nonprofit, cooperative, and limited-dividend sponsors. Section 231 provided mortgage insurance for rental housing at least half of which must be occupied by elderly or handicapped persons. Farmers Home Administration programs for home repair loans and grants have benefited the elderly to a lesser degree.

10.4. THE IMPACT OF FEDERAL ACTIONS ON RESEARCH

Federal support of housing for the elderly resulted in the springing up of projects all across the country that provided opportunities to study the impacts of new environments on old people. Architects and planners turned to behavioral scientists for information to guide their work. What are the specific favorable features of a building for older tenants? How can one learn, by assessing effects of one facility, how to build better ones in the future? How is one to judge whether a facility is "successful"? The generation of investigators first asked such questions were not accustomed to dealing with "the environment" in such terms. Existing research did not provide the specific facts needed by architects and planners; relevant conceptual models did not exist to provide solid bases for research designs. Federal construction policy determined the types of environments that were studied, and policies of research-funding agencies influenced research designs and therefore theory development.

10.5. TWO CONCEPTUAL ORIENTATIONS TO ENVIRONMENT AND AGING

Consensus has not been reached regarding the most appropriate theoretical model. Two will be presented that are attempts to summarize the various positions. Subsequently, research and theorizing that seem to underlie various aspects of the two will be discussed.

10.5.1. A Model of Direct and Indirect Environmental Effects

In this model, the objective environment has direct effects as well as effects channeled through perception of and satisfaction with that environment (see

Table 10.1. Housing Units Provided for the Elderly Under Federal Housing Programs as of June 3, 1982

Program	Occupied Units	Elderly Units	Percentage of Total
HUD			
Public Housing	1,211,972	500,885	44.6
Section 8	1,211,211	630,111	52.0
Section 202	58,773	58,773	100.0
Section 236	386,754	71,800	19.0
Section 221(d)(3)	195,212	6,454	8.2
Section 231	44,088	44,088	100.0
Total	3,018,010	1,312,111	43.5
FmHA			
Section 502 (repair loans)	1,119,091	26,363	2.4
Section 504 (repair grants)	39,269	39,269	100.0

Source: Adapted from Vanhorenbeck (1982).

Figure 10.1). Environmental variables are aspects of the specific environment relevant to characteristics of its users. Person variables are traits relevant to the specified environment, including competence, needs, personality traits, past life-style, and age. Outcomes may be modified by: (1) other intrapersonal characteristics of users (sense of personal competence, coping style, and attitude toward one's health), (2) extrinsic situations (status resources/deprivations and social supports), and (3) recent life events. Intermediate outcomes are perception of and satisfaction with the environment and individual differences in behavior within it. Ultimate outcomes are survival, independence, and well-being.

10.5.2. A Complementary Congruence Model

This model is based on Murray's (1938) notion that adaptation depends on satisfaction of personal needs by the environment, and needs are organized accord-ing to Maslow's (1954) hierarchy. The Lewinian (1951) equation includes a complementary/congruence term: $B = f(P, E, PcE)$. The model has two parts, differentiated according to level of need and type of relationship between person and environment variables (see Figure 10.2). Part 1 is concerned with life-maintenance needs. Characteristics of person and of environment are those that facilitate/inhibit life-maintenance need satisfaction through performance of the activities of daily living requisite to continued (independent) living, that is, personal competence and environmental resources/barriers to performance of the basic activities of daily living. Here, congruence is the degree of *complementarity* between competence and environmental resources/barriers. Part 2 is concerned with other viscerogenic and psychogenic needs (e.g., harm avoidance, affiliation) and with characteristics of the environment that facilitate/inhibit their satisfaction. Here, the congruence concept is *similarity* between strength of need and quality of environmental resources for meeting it. Mod-

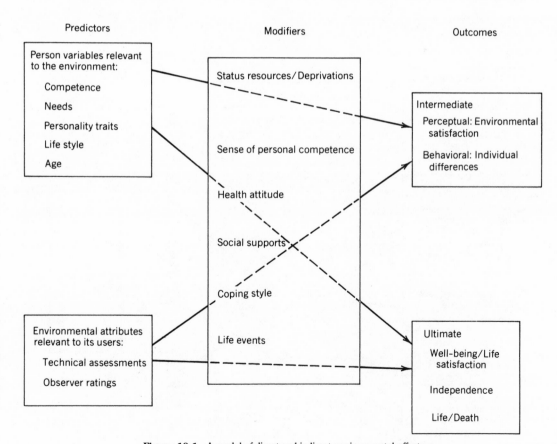

Figure 10.1. A model of direct and indirect environmental effects.

ifiers are the same as for the first model, as are intermediate and ultimate outcomes.

10.6. THE BACKGROUND FOR THE TWO MODELS

10.6.1. General Theories of Aging

Conceptualizations of the aging process are of limited value to investigators studying the impact of living environments on their elderly occupants. Successful aging has been conceived of in terms of accomplishment of developmentally appropriate tasks. For Erikson (1959) the major tasks of old age are acceptance of the life cycle and acceptance of significant people in it. Clark and Anderson (1967) set five tasks: (1) recognition of aging and definition of consequent limitations, (2) redefinition of physical and social life space, (3) substitution of alternative sources of need satisfaction, (4) reassessment of criteria for self-evaluation, and (5) reintegration of values and life goals. In de-

velopmental-task models, adaptation is assessed only in terms of accomplishment of allotted tasks. The only person variable is need to meet the task demand. Environmental influences are not specified.

Cumming and Henry (1961) saw normal aging as a process of disengagement in which person and environment undergo mutual withdrawal. Then the best milieu for the old is that which enables or fosters disengagement. However, while the phenomenon of disengagement is often observed, its attribution as an intrinsic aging process is questioned (Maddox, 1965). Disengagement brings low morale when it is involuntary (Lowenthal & Boler, 1965). It is not a unitary concept; individuals maintain contact selectively with aspects of their environments (Brown, 1974; Carp, 1968). Reengagement followed the move to a setting with enriched opportunities (Carp, 1978; Carp & Carp, 1980).

Other evidence points to positive relationships of activity to maintenance of function and life satisfaction (Havighurst, 1963; Havighurst, Neugarten, & Tobin, 1968). Following this view, environments

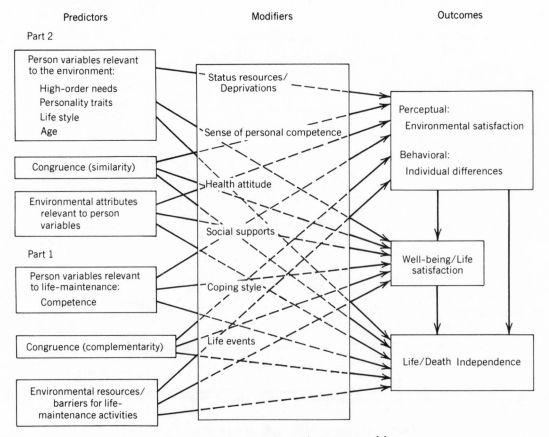

Figure 10.2. A complementary/congruence model.

should be judged according to the amount of activity they generate. It was quickly recognized that the aging process is not so simple as to be explained by either activity or disengagement, but that both are aspects of a more complex situation (Williams & Wirth, 1965).

According to another viewpoint, the trauma of growing old results from the discontinuities it entails (Rosow, 1963, 1973). Then rehousing the old will be deleterious and investigators should predict decrements among the rehoused. Another model (Berghorn, Schafer, Steere, & Wiseman, 1978) incorporates activity and disengagement as coping mechanisms and, between these extremes, the principle of continuity operates in the modification of earlier patterns to the exigencies of aging. This theory, which incorporates three previous ones, seems capable of explaining anything but provides tenuous footing for establishing testable hypotheses.

These formulations do not provide adequately for individual differences. Some persons, perhaps introverted all their lives, may disengage with relief and improved life satisfaction. Others may thrive throughout life on high rates of activity. Some elderly people seek and benefit from environmental discontinuity (Kahana & Kahana, 1983). Compared to other life stages, aging covers a long span of years. In studies of those 60 or 65 and older, groups include individuals young enough to be children of others. Perhaps the most beneficent milieu in which to grow old is the one that allows and provides resources for the widest possible expression of individual differences in behaviors.

10.6.2. Environmental Theories of Aging

Implicit in the provision of facilities for the elderly and in research on their impacts was the assumption that physical as well as interpersonal aspects of the environment affect outcomes. General theories of aging did not deal specifically with these issues. Some investigators developed models that directly address definition of personal and environmental components.

The Ecological Model

Lawton and his associates (Lawton, 1982; Lawton & Nahemow, 1973; Lawton & Simon, 1968; Nahemow & Lawton, 1973) define the terms in the Lewinian (1951) equation for relevance to the elderly and expand it by making explicit the interactional term: $B = f(P, E, P \times E)$. Person traits comprise competence and "competence is defined as the theoretical upper limit of capacity in the individual to function in

the areas of biological health, sensation-perception, motor behavior, and cognition" (Lawton, 1982, p. 38). Ego strength is deemed relevant but omitted due to measurement problems. The environment is conceptualized in terms of "demand" on competence, includes both social and physical, and should be measured at both Murray's (1938) alpha (real world) and beta press (perceived) levels. Excessive environmental demand in relation to competence leads to stress and negative outcomes; inadequate demand to loss of competence due to disuse. The ideal environment demands full use of residual competence ("the zone of maximum performance potential"). According to the docility hypothesis, the lower the level of competence, the greater the participation of environmental factors in accounting for behavior.

Congruence Models

THE VICTORIA PLAZA MODEL
The concept of congruence has influenced investigation of environment and aging since its early days. In one of the earliest studies of public housing for the elderly, the rationale was that individuals who had premove personality and behavior traits congruent with the physical, social, and managerial environment of that particular project would adapt best there, which proved true (Carp, 1966, 1974, 1985). In addition it was expected that persons whose traits before the move were incongruent with the specific new environment might be negatively affected by it. Those with premove seclusive life-styles and introverted personalities became, following relocation, even more seclusive and withdrawn than were members of the control group farthest toward this end of the scale (Carp & Carp, 1980). Similarly, those inactive and least desirous of additional activities in premove days became even less active than the most inactive members of the comparison group (Carp, 1978).

A SOCIOENVIRONMENTAL MODEL
Gubrium's (1972) model is concerned with congruence between persons' abilities and environmental demands for activity. The arena of action for the aged is assumed to be two-sided. One side is social and refers to the normative outcomes of social homogeneity, residential proximity, and local protectiveness. The second is individual and refers to activity resources such as health, solvency, and social support. "Persons feel most satisfied with themselves and their living conditions when there is congruency between what is expected of them by others of significance and what they may expect of themselves" (p. 283). Age composition of those in the environ-

ment is proposed to establish a social context with concomitant norms of appropriate activity. The relevant environmental variable, then, is its age composition.

THE MODEL OF KAHANA AND HER ASSOCIATES

Kahana (1975) and Kahana, Liang, and Felton (1980) based their model on one not specific to aging (French, Rogers, & Cobb, 1974) and proposed that the optimal environment is person specific and that its characteristics are defined by the degree to which it meets the individual's needs. To highlight the role of environmental variables, Kahana selected her study population on the basis of environmental vulnerability according to Lawton's docility hypothesis (relatively intact nursing home residents). She measured need in terms of resident preferences regarding aspects of nursing homes preselected as salient with regard to adjustment in such settings: Segregate, Congregate, Institutional Control, Affect Display, and Impulse Control; and environmental supply in terms of staff ratings of the nursing home on the same variables.

Congruence is measured by three variants of the person–environment difference score: one nondirectional (effects of oversupply and undersupply are assumed equal) and two one-directional terms measuring undersupply and oversupply. For statistical reasons involved with testing the significance of adding congruence to person and environment predictors in accounting for variance in outcome, the congruence terms are squared. Two personal variables and one environmental variable were significant predictors, accounting for 30% of variance in morale. When nondirectional congruence measures were added to the significant personal and environmental predictors, two made significant contributions, explaining an increment of 8% in outcome variance. Oversupply along two dimensions and undersupply along three dimensions explained an increment of 10% in outcome. Interestingly, *incongruence* (both nondirectional and one-directional) on the Congregate dimension was positively related to morale. The model was most efficient in the most institutional settings, and the study supports Lawton's docility hypothesis.

KIYAK'S MODEL

Kiyak (1978) studied the dimensions of Physical Privacy, Isolation, and Social Solitude, using nursing home resident preferences as person components and resident perceptions of the nursing home as environmental components. Dependent variables were satisfaction with the residence, the wish to remain there, and morale. For Physical Privacy and Isolation, congruence was a better predictor of outcomes than were personal and environmental predictors alone; while for Social Solitude, preference was the best predictor.

THE MODEL OF NEHRKE AND HIS ASSOCIATES

Nehrke, Turner, Cohen, Whitbourne, Morganti, & Hulicka (1981) found that Kahana's model did not apply to Veterans Administration domiciliaries and other care facilities they studied, using her instruments. Therefore they developed new instruments and 15 dimensions based on empirical clustering of items: Responsive Health Care, Excitement and Continuity, Staff Support for Personal Autonomy, Institutional Support for Religiosity, Personal Privacy, Tolerance for Restlessness, Freedom of Choice, Lack of Respect from Staff, Social Stimulation, Homogeneity, Physical Barriers to Mobility and Interaction, Discontinuity, Resident Interaction Level, Change versus Sameness, and Aloofness of Residents. Like Kiyak, they used resident perceptions as environmental indicators. Their results support the role of congruence in well-being, the docility hypothesis, and Kahana's finding that prediction is better in restricted or highly institutional milieus.

The Multiphasic Environmental Assessment Procedure (MEAP)

Though they have not presented a formal theory of environment and aging, a model is implicit in the development of MEAP (Moos & Lemke, 1980). It measures four environmental resource domains of sheltered-care facilities for the elderly: Physical and Architectural, Policy and Programs, Resident and Staff, and Perceived Social Climate. They analyzed data from 93 facilities for the elderly: skilled nursing, residential care, and apartment complexes. After controlling for type of facility, both environmental attributes (Policy Choice and Resident Control) and characteristics of the resident population (Social Resources, Functional Ability, and Proportion Female) explain significant variance in residents' perceptions of their facility's Social Climate and/or observer ratings of the Pleasantness of the facility. The interaction between the amount of Resident Control offered by the facility and Functional Ability of residents explains significant additional variance in three of the six scales of Perceived Social Climate and rated Pleasantness; and an interaction between degree of Policy Control allowed and Proportion of Female residents makes a significant contribution to rated Pleasantness. These findings support the proposition that personal and environmental variables, and interactions among them, are all predictive of outcomes.

The Windley and Scheidt Model

This path model posits three psychosocial variables adapted from Moos (Relationship—satisfaction with opportunities for social relations; Personal Development—satisfaction with community attributes that enhance personal growth and self-esteem; and Maintenance and Change—satisfaction with community resources for the survival of the town) as mediating the predictive relations of two Ecological/Architectural variables and three Personal variables with mental health among elderly residents of small towns. The two Ecological/Architectural variables are Dwelling Features (satisfaction with temperature, lighting, space, privacy, and housing and neighborhood quality) and Environmental Constriction (extent to which resident feels hindered by physical and social barriers). Personal Variables are Community Satisfaction (with town resources, personal development opportunities, and town relationships); Community Involvement (resident perceptions of how much town residents are involved in town affairs, how they see others as expecting them to participate, etc.); Involvement in Reciprocal Help with neighbors and friends in need; perception of the Community as Changing; and Isolation/Withdrawal (extent to which the town is perceived as individuals keeping to themselves, paying more attention to the young, and divided in opinion). A holdout sample confirmed the utility of the model, with Environmental Constriction, Dwelling Features, and Community Satisfaction as the best predictors of mental health (Windley & Scheidt, 1982).

10.7. PROBLEMS IN DEFINING TERMS IN THE MODELS

It is difficult to evaluate, compare, and integrate the foregoing models because of differences in investigators' conceptions of person and environment, use of control or moderator variables, and selection of outcomes.

10.7.1. Person Variables

The Ecological Model deals with the person in terms of competence to cope with environmental demands. Most older people are characterized not only by individual differences in competence but also by differences in needs, personality traits, and histories of life experience. The environment should not only minimize excess demand on competence in order to meet life-maintenance needs, but also provide physical and social resources to meet interpersonal, esteem, and self-actualization needs. Limitation of person descriptors to biological health, sensation-perception, motor behavior, and cognition seems restrictive when dealing with independently living people, which most elderly are. Within "adequate" ranges of competence and environmental demand, the effects of competence may be minimal, and other person traits may be more important to behavior and well-being.

When competence was augmented by social status and personality traits in predicting well-being, personality variables accounted for more criterion variance than did competence or status variables, and for criterion variance over and above that accounted for by competence and status variables combined (Carp, 1985). Similar to earlier experience with cognitive ability in educational research (e.g., Krech, Crutchfield, & Livson, 1969), competence may be effective in determining outcomes for elderly persons with competence below some threshold value, but of limited utility in predicting outcomes for those with competence above that limen. Therefore the person variables in the two summary models are expanded beyond competence.

Clearly the person dimensions of Kahana and her associates, Kiyak, Nehrke and his associates, and Moos and Lemke are inappropriate to the ordinary community-resident elderly. The fact that the Kahana and Nehrke models are most efficient in the most restricted or institutional nursing homes and domiciliaries suggests that these models will have little power in accounting for the behavior of the majority of the elderly.

There are measurement problems. Expressed preference may not be a satisfactory measure of psychological need. The problem is accentuated in situations such as Nehrke's and Kiyak's, where congruence is the difference between the same person's preference and his or her perception of the existing situation, due to this common source (McNemar, 1969). In such long-term care facilities as those in which these investigators work, expressed preference may reflect accommodation to institutional norms (which constitute Kahana's environmental measures), tendency to acquiescence, and time since admission (Firestone, Lichtman, & Evans, 1975; Kiyak, 1978; Lawton & Bader, 1970). Data on community resident elderly suggests that, while accommodation to negative circumstances is accompanied by increased satisfaction with the status quo, this is accomplished through lowering levels of aspiration and is accompanied by decreased happiness (Campbell et al., 1976).

10.7.2. Environmental Variables

Environment and aging studies have dealt from the first with complex, macrolevel, "real environment" issues. Several theoretical models include "objective environment." However, its definition and measurement have proved difficult. A central, continuing debate is over the locus of effective environmental stimuli. Early researchers in the field shared the common belief that Murray's (1938) beta press, the environment as perceived and reacted to, comprises the effective stimuli. They were not accustomed to being concerned with, let alone attempting to measure directly, aspects of the physical and social surround that might be relevant. It soon became apparent in multidisciplinary conferences, workshops, and publications that characterized development of the field that alpha press data were needed. For example, if the design of future facilities was to be better, the architects needed to know specifically which features of existing structures proved satisfactory and which did not. Residents were able to identify characteristics of the physical design and social milieu that they liked or disliked (Carp, 1976a). (Interestingly, many "special design" features were disliked.) However, characteristics favored or unfavored by residents may or may not be the same ones that most influence their well-being. Meanwhile, investigators into aging and environment saw the need to include the "real world out there" in order to avoid circularity in theory development (Ittelson, 1960; Wohlwill, 1974).

Recently there is increasing interest in the possibility that alpha press as well as beta press influences outcomes, and there is a corresponding cry for development of objective environmental measures and for inclusion of these variables in theoretical models. Such variables have two sources: observations by respondents or others, and technical-assessment data (e.g., distances, volumes, light readings).

For Kiyak and Nehrke, environmental measures are residents' perceptions, on the theory that staff views may not reflect reality for a resident. Kahana prefers staff ratings in order to maintain independence of source between person and environment components. For Moos, measures of the Physical and Architectural resource domains are observer rat-

ings, and those for Policy and Program, Resident and Staff, and Perceived Social Climate are questionnaires for staff and residents. Windley and Scheidt purport to use three types of environmental variables: Ecological/Architectural, Psychosocial, and Demographic. However, the Demographic variables relate to characteristics of the respondent (such as age and sex) rather than to demographic characteristics of the small town. The Ecological/Architectural variables, which might be expected to refer to objective attributes, consist instead of subjective perceptions, actually satisfactions, of respondents. Other investigators use satisfactions as outcomes.

In addition to the common-source problem noted by Kahana, especially in long-term care facilities, ratings by residents are as likely as their stated preferences to reflect accommodation to institutional norms, acquiescence, and time since admission. Insofar as this is true, such measures obscure the role of environmental reality. Regarding the elderly in general, "the dwelling assessments of old people may be as much a product of their perceived life situation as it is a product of a dwelling's observable, objective conditions" (Golant, 1982, p. 132). Therefore the two summary models do not include respondent evaluations among environmental predictors.

One of the great potentials of the Ecological Model is its insistence on inclusion of objective environmental variables. Lawton and his associates have not yet produced a standard set of variables and measures for the environmental component, as they have for the person component. However, they have attempted several strategies to measure the environment objectively. Lawton and Kleban (1971) collected data on various aspects of the environment that produced six factors: Central Location (near transportation, park, amenities), Distance from Shopping Facilities, Independent Household (own television, stove, toilet, refrigerator), Busy Block (traffic and people), Well-Kept Block and Buildings, and Non-Residential Block (commercial enterprises, vacant houses and lots).

In another study, four attributes of federally assisted housing projects explained 4% of housing satisfaction after controlling for tenant characteristics (Lawton, Nahemow, & Teaff, 1975). Using more extensive sets of objective predictor variables, 19 and 22% of the variance in housing satisfaction were explained (Lawton, 1978, 1980a). Findings were even more impressive for a community study (Lawton, Brody, & Turner-Massey, 1978). Five objective environmental items and four factor-based variables composed of observer ratings accounted for 47% of variance in housing satisfaction among applicants for an alternative housing plan.

Even these attempts to objectify measures of the environment involve data collected from residents and observers that may be affected by biases of various sorts. Measurement techniques are not always described, so that it is difficult to identify the source and evaluate the objectivity of the data. In addition, there is question whether some "objective housing" items belong under that rubric. Sponsorship (Lawton et al., 1975) may influence outcomes but is not a "physical" housing descriptor. Length of tenancy (Lawton, 1980a) seems less descriptive of housing than of the tenant's attachment to it; income is correlated with housing quality but is not an environmental descriptor; repairs in the last year may indicate good or bad present housing conditions; and the fact that rent or total housing costs exceed one-quarter of income is, again, related to outcomes but not descriptive of housing. Inclusion of items related to outcomes but not directly descriptive of housing can inflate the apparent contribution of the objective environment.

Technical Environmental Assessment Indices

Craik and Zube (1976) suggest that to create objective physical environment scales, technical environmental quality indices be used to identify areas with high and low scores and then a search be made for attributes that differentiate them. However, residents are not randomly assigned to living environments, nor are environments randomly applied to residents. Instead, environment and person are linked. Individuals who have options usually excercise them to maximize person–environment "fit." Lack of options for many of the elderly concentrates them in certain types of environments. These processes may so tie characteristics of environments to those of residents that objective environmental scales do not increase ability to account for variance in outcomes. Also, personal traits may affect outcomes such as longevity, satisfaction, and well-being.

In addition, it is of interest to know whether there is a meaningful structure underlying items of information directly descriptive of the physical and suprapersonal environment, and whether these data have their own inherent dimensions. Such dimensions would represent more abstract qualities of the objective environment that enable us to see the underlying structure of its vast array of concrete aspects.

Carp and Carp (1982a) used 19 physical environment items taken from U.S. Geological Survey maps to which other information was added. The maps included elevation relative to sea level and locations of railroads, highways, freeways, and arterials. Locations of rapid transit from Metropolitan Transportation Commission maps and land use from the U.S. census were coded into the maps, along with subjects' residences. Distances from home were measured, and the facilities within an area around the home were counted. The only observer data were type of unit (single family vs. other) and home construction (wood frame vs. other). Eight suprapersonal environment items were taken from census figures for the block on which the subject lived.

Nine principal components were obtained and cross-validated: (1) Housing Quality in Neighborhood (percentage of units in one-unit structures, percentage of units owner occupied, percentage of units in 10-plus unit structures, subject's housing single family or other, percentage of one-person households, number of transportation elements within a mile of home, ratio of population to dwelling units, and average dollar value of units); (2) Suprapersonal Environment of Neighborhood (percentage of units with one-plus persons per room, percentage of female household heads, percentage of population minority, and percentage of population under age 18); (3) Land Value in Neighborhood (elevation relative to sea level, distance to nearest railroad, type of nearest rapid-transit station, and type of nearest rapid-transit line); (4) Distance to Rapid Transit; (5) Buffering Against Rapid-Transit Impact (land barrier between home and nearest station, between home and nearest line); (6) Density of Land Use (vacant land within 14 mile of home, distance to arterial); (7) Variety of Land Uses (number of different land uses, open land, water, and industrial land use, all within 1/4 mile of home); (8) Distance to Freeway; and (9) Quality of Physical Housing (percentage of units in census block lacking some or all plumbing, and subject's home is wooden frame vs. other construction type).

In view of the nonindependence between residence and resident, the critical test of the utility of these technical-assessment indices is whether they add to the explanatory power of resident characteristics. Person items include status variables such as age, sex, income, rent/own, and length of residence, as well as general environmental orientations. This may provide advantage to the person component, but the purpose was a stringent test of the technical-assessment indices. The findings suggest that they complement resident characteristics. In accounting for variance in 15 outcome scales of environmental perception and well-being, the independent contributions of person components scales ranged from 2 to 18% and the independent contributions of environmental scales ranged from 2 to 18% for each sample; and together they accounted for from 8 to 38% of criterion variance for sample 1 and for from 12 to 37% for sample 2. Most criterion scales deal with specifics of the environment (e.g., esthetics). One probably measures overall well-being (Carp & Carp, 1983), suggesting that technical-assessment indices hold promise not only in regard to perceptions of specific environmental qualities but also in regard to psychological well-being.

A technical assessment approach was taken to environmental measures in a study of older women living alone in the community. Scales were developed to measure the objective resources of the living environment to meet life-maintenance needs through performance of the activities of daily living requisite to independent community living (food, sleep/rest, personal hygiene, housecleaning, laundry) and to meet other viscerogenic needs (harmavoidance, noxavoidance) and psychogenic needs (order, affiliation, privacy, person–suprapersonal environment similarity, esthetics) relevant to the person–environment transaction in everyday life. For some needs specific environmental issues were identified: Harmavoidance was subdivided into four areas of safety: crime, accident, fire, and health hazards; and noxavoidance was subdivided into noise level, air quality, and comfort/convenience. Separate scales were developed for the living unit and the neighborhood. Following the rationale that environmental scales should be developed independently of residents' perceptions, and since sample size did not allow factoring, scaling was based on internal consistency (Cronbach, 1951).

Intermediate outcomes were multiitem measures of satisfaction with housing and neighborhood; ultimate outcomes were two components derived from a battery of standard instruments in the domain of life satisfaction, morale, and psychological well-being. The environmental scales accounted for significant variance (28 and 26%) in intermediate outcomes (Carp & Christensen, 1986a) and ultimate outcomes (23 and 13%) (Carp & Christensen, 1986b) over and above the contributions of personal competence (cognitive, sensory/perceptual, motor, and health) and an 18-item index of socioeconomic resources, when R^2 was adjusted for sample size and the number of variables in the equation. Together the environmental scales, personal competence, and status resource/dep-

rivation accounted for 40% (adjusted $R^2 = .36$) of the variance in satisfaction with housing, 33% (adjusted $R^2 = .29$) of the variance in neighborhood satisfaction, and 29% (adjusted $R^2 = .25$) and 42% (adjusted $R^2 = .39$) of the variance in the two components of well-being.

In a second approach to the same data, measures of perceived qualities of the environment (e.g., residents' perceptions of the resources/barriers of the living unit for meal preparation) were criteria for selecting and weighting items for environmental scales. Control variables and intermediate outcomes were the same; ultimate outcomes were five of the standard instruments used in the component analysis in the first approach. Using unadjusted R^2 values, these environmental scales accounted for 41% and 27% of the variance in intermediate outcomes (Christensen & Carp, in press a) and for significant variance (6, 12, and 15%) in three of the five ultimate outcomes (Christensen & Carp, in press b). Together the environmental scales, personal competence, and status resource/deprivation accounted for 42% and 27% of the variance in intermediate outcomes and 36%, 23%, and 20% in three of the ultimate outcomes.

It is of interest to compare the predictive efficiency of the two sets of environmental scales, one based on internal consistency among objective environmental items and the other based on residents' perceptions of specifics of the environment. Using unadjusted R^2 values for comparability, the first set accounted for 32% and 30% of the variance in satisfaction with living unit and neighborhood, while the second set accounted for 41 and 27% of the variance. The results suggest that, at least for housing satisfaction, the second set of scales may be preferable. However, the second approach to scaling capitalizes more on chance factors within the data set and the common source of environmental scale criteria and outcomes. Intermediate outcomes were residents' perceptions of the two environmental domains, and items for predictor scales were selected and weighted on the same residents' perceptions of specific aspects of those domains. With regard to psychological well-being, the environmental scales based on internal consistency accounted for 27 and 17% of independent variance in the two well-being components while the second set accounted for significant independent variance in only three of the five criteria (6, 12, and 15%). Moreover, the three criteria used in the second approach are not independent; correlations among them are .51, .54, and .72. Only replication will assess the extent of shrinkage, which must be expected to be larger for the second set, and indicate which approach to scale construction produces more efficient predictors. The results with both strategies show promise for the utility of environmental scales at the technical-assessment level. Objective measures of the living environment were relevant not only to environmental satisfaction but also to psychological well-being.

Observer Ratings

The utility of technical-assessment scales does not negate use of reliable observer judgments. Observer-based measures may be influenced by characteristics of the panel (Canter, 1969; Craik & Zube, 1976; Gifford, 1980; Hershberger, 1970), which raises questions about their validity as descriptors of external reality. Observations by managers and planners of housing for the elderly do not agree with those of residents (Carp, 1976a; Carp & Carp, 1982b). However, some environmental characteristics may remain inaccessible except through human observation (Craik, 1981).

Implications

The appropriate course of action seems to be to develop both observer-based and technical-assessment-based indices, and to determine how best they can be used, separately and in combination. Therefore both are included as measures of the objective environment in both general models.

10.7.3. Moderator Variables

Investigators have varied widely in use of terms additional to personal and environmental variables that influence outcomes. The entries under the moderator category in both general models do not comprise an exhaustive list of influences that may modify relationships of personal and environmental components to outcomes. They are suggestive only.

Campbell and colleagues (1976) found that for younger adults objective conditions and evaluations of them were closely related, but for older adults there was a "loosening of bonds" between the two. They attribute this to age. However, their data show a similar relationship between objective and subjective indicators among the poor and those with little education, across age. This suggests the operation of other variables, situational and psychological.

A Status Deprivation Index based on factual situational information and a Sense of Personal Competence scale were more important in accounting for satisfaction with domains of life, including housing

and neighborhood, and in overall well-being than was age, for elderly Californians (Carp & Carp, 1981) and for Californians 25 and older (Carp, in press a). A similar Status Deprivation Index accounted for variance in 10 of the 15 indices of perceived environmental qualities and well-being when age was partialed out, for Bay Area residents 25 and older (Carp, in press b). These studies suggest that some response tendencies attributed to aging reflect, in part, situational resources/deprivations and psychological sense of one's ability to cope with the existing situation. This distinction is important to the extent that realistic deprivation is currently prevalent among the old, and that reduced sense of competence may be the result of negative circumstances from which one is unable to extricate oneself. Situational deprivation is the result of social processes, not intrinsic to aging though correlated with it at present. In order to understand environment and aging, it is necessary to separate intrinsic aging processes from current extrinsic concomitants.

Gerontological literature is replete with findings that subjective ratings of health are correlated with well-being (Bild & Havighurst, 1976; Edwards & Klemmack, 1973; Morgan, 1976; Palmore & Luikhart, 1972; Spreitzer & Snyder, 1974; Storandt, Wittels, & Botwinick, 1975; Tissue, 1972). Some studies report self-rated health correlating poorly with physician diagnoses (Linn, Linn, & Knopka, 1978), while others report consensus between objective and subjective health measures (Bultena & Oyler, 1971; Campbell et al., 1976; La Rue, Bank, Jarvik, & Hetland, 1979; Maddox & Douglass, 1973; Tissue, 1972). Therefore objective health is classified as a person predictor and perceived health as a moderator.

Social supports and networks are important in maintaining independent living and to well-being (Butler & Lewis, 1973; Cantor, 1980; Kastenbaum, 1983; Litwak, 1980; Pilisuk & Minkler, 1980; Reno, 1981; Sherwood, Greer, Morris, & Mor, 1981). The coping style of denying/suppressing the negative influenced environmental perceptions (Carp, in press c). The impact of recent life events on older people is recognized (e.g., National Heart & Lung Institute, 1974) and may modify effects of personal and environmental predictors.

10.7.4. Outcomes

There is wide variation also in selection of outcomes. Positive–negative perception of and satisfaction with the environment are common outcome variables. In the general models above it is treated as an intermediate outcome that may account for independent variance in ultimate outcomes. A basic definer of adaptation is life/death. Independent living is a national goal and is highly desired among the old. General well-being, morale, or life satisfaction seems highly desirable at any age.

10.8. HOUSING AND THE ELDERLY

This and the following section consider empirical findings in key topics of aging and environment research. This section deals with old people and their homes. The first topic is findings of research on those rehoused into special facilities for the elderly, the designs of those studies, and limitations of this set of knowledge in relation to the general issue of environment and aging. Then the situation of the majority living in ordinary houses and apartments is described and relevant studies cited. Next comes consideration of those living in institutions.

10.8.1. Studies in Housing for the Elderly

Early studies that showed psychological and social improvements following moves to low-cost elderly housing (Donahue, 1966) and to an affluent retirement community (Hamovitch, 1968) were inconclusive because of lack of control groups. Studies with comparison groups (Bultena & Wood, 1969; Lipman, 1968; Sherman, 1974) obtained positive results but were limited in causal attribution since comparisons were cross-sectional. A study using before-and-after design and a control group confirmed the beneficial effects of one of the first public housing facilities for the elderly, Victoria Plaza (Carp, 1966). The rehoused applicants made gains, relative to the nonrehoused, in satisfaction with housing, activity, sociability, self-evaluation of health, and life satisfaction.

Lawton and Cohen (1974) suggested that Victoria Plaza may be an unusually fine facility. To determine whether less exemplary projects have similar effects, they studied five projects chosen for diversity. Favorable effects were found on four of five criteria: perceived change for the future, housing satisfaction, involvement in activities, and satisfaction with the status quo. This consistency between the Carp and the Lawton and Cohen studies lends strong support to the idea that this type of housing for the elderly is beneficial to its tenants, since they used different settings, different instruments, and different tyes of comparison groups (Epstein, 1980). Carp controlled for the desire to move; Lawton and Cohen compared those

who wanted to move and were successful in doing so with those who did not want to move.

These before-and-after studies looked only at the first year of tenancy, which may not be definitive. However, a second follow-up at Victoria Plaza after an 8-1/2-year interval supported earlier conclusions (Carp, 1975a) and found an advantage to the rehoused in institutionalization and mortality rates (Carp, 1977).

The question remained whether random assignment of people would affect outcomes. Sherwood, Glassman, Sherwood, and Morris (1974) approached random assignment by a multivariate matching technique that chose comparison subjects from a waiting list for a long-term care unit so as to match each rehoused subject on background, social, psychological, and health characteristics. The rehoused showed advantage in perceived health, participation in activities, and satisfaction with housing and with social activity. Over a 5-year period the rehoused were less likely to be institutionalized and had a lower death rate, though they were more likely to have been hospitalized (perhaps because the residence is physically linked to a hospital).

The Sherwood and colleagues study is not comparable to the others in that the project included a wider range of services for long-term care and respondents were correspondingly more frail. In addition, while its matching technique speaks to one methodological problem, it raises another. The "waiting list phenomenon" is stressful (Tobin & Lieberman, 1976). Lawton and Yaffe (1970) studied three groups: (1) congregate-housing relocated, (2) congregate-housing nonrelocated, and (3) community nonrelocated matched on sex, age, and health. Mortality rates did not differ.

The perfect research design has not been implemented. However, results of the various studies generally show favorable impacts of housing designed for the elderly on persons who choose and are admitted to it. The only real disagreement is in respect to effects of rehousing on health: Lawton and Cohen found an unfavorable effect, Lawton and Yaffe found no effect, and both Carp and Sherwood and colleagues a favorable effect. Lawton (1980) suggests the difference between Carp's and Lawton and Cohen's results may be due to the superior quality of Victoria Plaza. The inconsistency may reflect research design differences. Comparison respondents for Carp were applicants who did not move in. Sherwood and colleagues compared people who obtained housing with people on the waiting list for it. Lawton and Cohen compared those who had chosen and were admitted to special housing with those who did not want such housing. As Schulz (1976) pointed out, Lawton and Yaffe also compared people who wanted to move with those who did not.

Limitations of These Studies

These studies were carried out in unusual environments and with selected residents. The facilities were high-rise housing restricted to the low- and moderate-income elderly and retirement communities. Results do not justify the conclusion that these types of situations would be beneficial for all older people. Residents were matched to environments by staff and self-selection. A large proportion of very inadequately housed applicants to one project decided not to move in, once they had seen it (Carp, 1976a). Person–environment "fit" is therefore maximized.

THE ROLE OF INDIVIDUAL DIFFERENCES
The generally benign effects for in-movers in general should not obscure the possibility that these environments have negative effects on some individuals. Prior to data collection, personality traits judged relevant to adjustment to the particular physical and social milieu of Victoria Plaza were selected. Data on these traits collected from applicants predicted adjustment (as defined by respondents, the resident group, and the staff) at the end of the first year of tenancy (Carp, 1966), and the regression equation held up remarkably well for outcome data 8-1/2 years later (Carp, 1974). The fact that this environment was predictably better for some tenants than for others raises the question of whether it might be detrimental for some older people.

NEGATIVE IMPACTS ON ACTIVITY AND SOCIABILITY FOR A MINORITY
Among tenants, group effects on activity and sociability in this active and sociable setting were positive However, applicants involved in the most activities and who desired the most additional activities showed greatest gains in activity following the move, while the activity-oriented milieu seemed to decrease activity on the part of those who as applicants were least active and least interested in additional activities (Carp, 1978). Similarly, persons most sociable and high in extraversion at baseline made greatest gains in social behaviors and satisfaction while, for a minority of originally unsociable and introverted people, the effects were reversed. The extreme introvert reacted by becoming more solitary and less satisfied with the interpersonal situation (Carp & Carp, 1980).

NONREPRESENTATIVENESS OF RESPONDENTS
The studies discussed in the previous paragraphs and others like them have looked at limited types of housing and unrepresentative samples of the older population. By mid-1982 federal funding programs provided about 1.3 million units occupied by the elderly, but the population aged 65 and over numbered about 25 million. While 44% of all federally assisted housing served the old, and there is legitimate question whether other population segments had had equitable consideration, it was estimated that over 3 million elderly persons remained in need of housing assistance (Vanhorenbeck, 1982).

10.8.2. The Majority in Ordinary Houses and Apartments

Among the noninstitutionalized in general, about 83% of older men and 57% of older women live in family settings. These proportions vary by age, being higher for the young-old. Nearly a third of these elderly live alone (41% of women and 15% of men). The remaining 2% (half a million) live with nonrelatives (Vanhorenbeck, 1982). Relatively little aging and environment research has been done on this majority of older Americans.

The median income of elderly headed families is only 61% of that for all families, and for every year since 1969 a larger proportion of persons 65 and older has been below the poverty level than is the case for all persons. A larger percentage of the elderly than of the nonelderly are home owners. A typical urban home-owning household spends 3.4% of its income on property taxes, while elderly home owners spend an average of 8.1% and in some cases exceed 20%. Homes owned by the elderly are generally older (built before 1939) and in need of repair. Lack of some or all plumbing is twice as frequent in units owned by the elderly as it is for all owned units. In view of the rising costs of other necessities such as utilities and food, home ownership can become a burden. Often the house is too large (54% of all one-person households in owned units are elderly), adding to the costs of repair and labor of maintenance (Vanhorenbeck, 1982).

The 30% of elderly households that rent are in no better conditions. Two-thirds of the rental units were built before 1939. The incidence of incomplete plumbing is greater than among elderly home owners (Vanhorenbeck, 1982). Objective assessments by various investigators show that the housing of many older people does not meet minimal standards (Montgomery, Stubbs, & Day, 1980; Struyk, 1977; United States Senate, 1977). About 10% of the community housing occupied by the elderly is inadequate; among the black and Hispanic old, only about one in five has adequate housing; and housing problems are much worse for the rural elderly (Brotman, 1980). Older people spend on an average a third or more of their incomes for housing; therefore it seems unlikely that they will be able to improve their situations without assistance (Vanhorenbeck, 1982).

The Frail Elderly in the Community

At least as many and perhaps twice as many sick and frail elderly persons live in communities as in nursing homes. Most live with or receive assistance from family members (Shanas, 1979). A recent review of studies on various samples of the frail elderly concludes that families are still the major source of long-term care for the impaired elderly in the home (Arling & McAuley, 1983). However, the strain on care givers and family relationships may be considerable (Cantor, 1983; Soldo & Myllyluoma, 1983). This is not only financial but also involves overcommitments of time and conflict in role relationships. According to Sager (1983) "there is evidence that publicly provided help bolstered and strengthened family care. Families' efforts were not displaced; they were sustained" (p. 15). There is an expanding literature on supportive services such as day care for the elderly (Weiler, 1978) to provide respite for family care givers.

With increase in the geographical separation between the elderly and their adult children, the needs of the elderly are increasingly being transferred from the family to public and voluntary organizations (Pilisuk & Minkler, 1980). A significant proportion of old people have no children, and children tend to be the family care givers (Brotman, 1980). Blum and Minkler (1980) trace the development of federal legislation to fund programs for community-based services to the elderly. Studies of demonstration and pilot projects document the effectiveness of such programs, but many communities, especially those most in need of such services, cannot provide continuing support. Gaps in service coverage and lack of interservice coordination are persistent problems (Kastenbaum, 1983).

One fundamental problem in delivery of services to the elderly is the "ageism" in American culture. As Pritchett (1979) pointed out, we have given them what we think is good for them and what will keep them away from the rest of us.

10.8.3. The Institutionalized Elderly

As part of the increase in the older population generally and especially in the old-old, there was a rise in numbers of dependent and infirm old people, many of whom lacked money to buy private care in their own homes or those of family members. The effect was to increase the nursing home industry enormously. "Even if the advocacy of vastly increased home-delivery service should result in early action, there will continue indefinitely to be hundreds of thousands of institutionalized old people" (Glasscote, 1976, p. 141).

Only 4 to 5% of the population 65 and older are in institutions at a given time, but many more live in such settings at some time, perhaps as many as 20% (Kastenbaum & Candy, 1973) or perhaps somewhat less (McConnell, 1983). The percentage institutionalized at any time is highly related to age, ranging from 1% for persons 65 to 74 to 7% for those 75 to 84 and to 22% for persons 85 and older (United States Bureau of the Census, 1982).

During recent years nursing homes have received wide public attention, mostly negative.

> There are...some excellent homes in which emphasis is on meeting needs in every possible way...but the remainder of homes run the gamut from filthy and unsafe to clean but cheerless and depressing. The worst of the homes are firetraps, with filthy living conditions and neglect of patient care. Other homes are stylized, motel-like, antiseptically clean horrors—patients sit in numb silence with dejected faces....Nutrition is often inadequate....Personal abuse on the part of staff to patients can occur because the older people are ill, vulnerable, and unable to defend themselves and the staff may be untrained, unmotivated, and improperly supervised. The majority of nursing home administrators have no specific training....There is a shortage of physician services, skilled nursing care, dental care, social services, and psychiatric care. Patients are often overmedicated and deprived of any decision-making. (Butler & Lewis, 1973, p. 216)

One reason for these conditions is the "scandalously low pay" (Glasscote, 1976, p. 142). This is especially true for aides, who have by far the most contact with patients. Glasscote found that nurses in nursing homes are often paid substantially less than nurses in acute medical facilities.

According to Kastenbaum (1983) the environment of the nursing home may lead to "existential despair" among residents. The usual staff response involves "neglect, social withdrawal, medication, and more neglect" (p. 12).

This pattern intensifies dependency, which increases the burden on staff and therefore staff turnover, which is both costly and inhibiting to development of human relationships. Kastenbaum believes this pattern can be altered by a systematic and encompassing network of positive expectations about patients. Instead of verbal and nonverbal statements to the effect that "you can't do that," positive suggestions should be made. This position is supported by studies in which alcoholic beverages were introduced into social settings (Mishara & Kastenbaum, 1980). "The situation spoke directly to the patients, telling them that they were acknowledged to be mature people capable of giving as well as receiving enjoyment on an adult level" (Kastenbaum, 1983, p. 13).

Giving nursing home residents control over when they would receive "friendly visitors" or simply giving them information about the schedule had beneficial effects on physical and psychological well-being, compared to receiving the visitors unexpectedly (Schulz, 1976). This and other evidence suggest that the physical and social milieus of many nursing homes lead to "learned helplessness," which often results in depression (Seligman, 1975). If staff could distinguish reactive depression from organic senility and programs were in place to strengthen residents' sense of their own competence, nursing homes might be more favorable settings for aging, and some residents might return to the community.

10.9. THE NEIGHBORHOOD AND THE ELDERLY

This section, like the preceding one on housing, considers empirical findings on a key topic of aging and environment research. After an introductory section on the importance of the neighborhood, and a description of where old people are located, studies of neighborhood qualities are presented.

10.9.1. The Importance of the Neighborhood to Older People

Galster and Hesser (1981) claim that "there are certain physical and social features of neighborhoods which people generally need or to which they aspire, and that people cannot adapt to the absence of these features" (p. 748). According to Marans (1976), "contemporary planners and designers have often suggested that improving the quality of the residential environment can profoundly affect the quality of people's lives" (p. 123). As people grow old and mobility is restricted, the influence of the neighborhood increases. It may become as important as the home (Carp, 1986).

10.9.2. Where Older People Live and How They Feel About It

The Geographical Distribution of Old People in the United States

Nearly half of those 65 and older live in seven states: California, New York, Florida, Illinois, Ohio, Pennsylvania, and Texas. Over 0.5 million moved to a different part of the country between 1975 and 1980, two-thirds of them from the northeast or north central regions to the south or west (compared to 49% of younger persons). Those 65 and older comprise 13% or more of the population in eight states: Florida, Arkansas, Rhode Island, Iowa, South Dakota, Missouri, Nebraska, and Kansas. In seven states the older population increased by more than 50% between 1970 and 1980: Nevada (113%), Arizona (91%), Hawaii (73%), Florida (71%), Alaska (71%), New Mexico (66%), and South Carolina (51%) (United States Bureau of the Census, 1982).

URBAN/SUBURBAN/RURAL RESIDENCE

URBAN. Like most people today, the elderly tend to live in urban settings. Studies in two large metropolitan areas (San Francisco and San Antonio) demonstrated that drawbacks such as noise, crime rate, and congestion are outweighed by advantages for older people. The degree of "urbanness" was positively related to active, autonomous, and satisfying use of time, space, and the social network by the elderly (Carp, 1979). However, for frail elderly at high risk of institutionalization in midsize towns, Chapman and Beaudet (1983) found the advantages of centrally located, convenient neighborhoods outweighed by negative features such as crime rate, noise, traffic, and transiency.

In a San Francisco study of effects of differences in traffic volume on residential streets, Appleyard (1977) expected old people to be an especially vulnerable group. "Older people, on the contrary, were the most content. This was a surprise ... not explained by traffic volumes" (p. 86).

Cantor (1979) asked elderly residents of the most deteriorated areas of New York City to evaluate their city as a place to live. Familiarity or "belongingness"; availability of facilities, services, and amenities; and the cosmopolitan atmosphere and vitality were important pluses. Personal safety, physical deterioration, dirt, noise, and the fast, impersonal tempo of life, living among people different from oneself, and the high cost of living were minuses. "The vitality of city life surging around them and its many possibilities for satisfying personal tastes, desires, and needs are as important to the old as to the young, even if sometimes enjoyed vicariously" (p. 60).

SUBURBAN. "The aging of the central city population is probably the most frequent observation made by social scientists and planners who report of the location of older people in the United States, but the shift to the suburbs, which has gone relatively unnoticed, has been far greater" (Golant, 1979, p. 39). For example, from 1970 to 1975, the growth rate of suburban elderly was 26.5% while that for the central city was only 7.8%. Since 1950 the suburban elderly population has grown more rapidly than the total suburban population. Some of this may be due to "aging in place," particularly in the older suburbs. However, the most prevalent destinations of the older movers Golant studied were the suburbs, followed by metropolitan areas, with central cities a distant third. As Rudzitis (1979) points out, these findings held only for whites; there was a net inmigration of older blacks to central cities. In the suburbs, the quality of housing and neighborhood tends to be better; however, facilities and services tend to be sparse or nonexistent within neighborhoods, and public transit does not meet the needs of older residents (Carp, 1971). As older residents stop driving, they are restricted in ability to meet their own needs (Carp, 1980).

RURAL. Recently there has been some reversal of the rural-to-urban migration that characterized the United States during most of the twentieth century (Zelinsky, 1976). This trend may be problematical, in view of distances to services and facilities, the reduced mobility that comes with age, and unfamiliarity with the rural milieu. However, the poorer objective conditions of rural residence are not necessarily associated with lower levels of well-being (Lee & Lassey, 1980). Other aspects of rural residence may compensate. Higher rates of social participation, lower rates of crime, a culture that allows a more gradual transition to an aged status, a slower pace of life, lower levels of cognitive complexity, more gradual change within the physical environment, and the smaller scale of rural life may make positive contributions to the quality of this milieu as one in which to grow old, for some persons.

Sofranko, Fliegel, and Glasgow (1982–1983) found a "decidedly higher" level of satisfaction among rural migrants. They seemed to be fulfilling a desire for rural residence, and so were more satisfied, more likely to perceive a net improvement over the former residence, and more attached to their residences than were town people. There may be confounding variables in this study: Rural migrants tended to be younger, and therefore probably more mobile for access to goods, services, and socializing; they were less likely to live alone, which would alleviate problems of loneliness common in rural areas (Harbert & Wilkinson, 1979); and they tended to be better off financially than comparison respondents. A selective factor may be involved: All the rural migrants had chosen rural living.

IMPLICATIONS. In this, as in other areas, satisfaction and well-being may be affected by the voluntary nature of location and the degree of person–environment "fit."

10.9.3. Studies of Neighborhood Qualities

What qualities of neighborhoods are important to old people? Bennett (1973), Lawton and Kleban (1971), and Schooler (1970) stress the effects of the physical appearance of the neighborhood on the morale of the elderly. Sundeen and Mathieu (1976) and Goldsmith and Tomas (1974) identify personal safety as of particular concern to the elderly. According to Rowles (1978), sociability and helpfulness of neighbors are particularly important because of constraints on mobility. Greater reliance on neighbors as friends was one reason Rosow (1967) gave for the advantageousness to older people of having many age peers nearby. Restrictions on mobility also inhibit access to retail and service resources, and influence neighborhood evaluations (Carp, 1976a; Lawton, 1980).

Californians 18 to 98 rated the importance of 15 neighborhood characteristics, if they were to consider moving (Carp & Carp, 1982b). One factor, Access to Services and Facilities, includes: school close, food store close, work close, restaurants and theaters close, freeway close, rapid-transit close, bus stop close, and good walking conditions. Another, Relationships with Others, includes: friends and relatives close, and friendly people in the area. The third, Esthetics, includes: generally attractive, clean and unlittered, minimal air pollution, quiet, and nicely landscaped.

For items in the first factor, age trends were observed with regard to work and schools; both were more important to young adults. Distance to a food store was "very important" for all age groups. A tendency for the young to attach more importance to proximity of restaurants and theaters did not cross-validate. In regard to items in the second factor, having friends and relatives close was "not at all important" to over a third, across age. Similarly, there was no age trend with regard to the importance of having friendly people in the area; two-thirds of all ages considered this "very important." Neither were there age differences for any of the Esthetic items. All were "very important" to the majority of respondents.

Generally the findings indicate that older people tend to have the same concept of desirable neighborhood qualities as do younger adults. The few differences seem consistent with life stages: Older people are less concerned with access to freeways and more concerned with bus stops, and they attach less importance to jobs and schools.

Investigators tend to ask for ratings of the importance of items, a response format that does not allow a respondent to express trade-offs between positive and negative concomitants. Regnier (in press) provided residents of housing for middle- and upper-income elderly with negative as well as positive preferences in regard to additional services. The negative preferences for some services reflected the greater weight of additional fees, relative to advantages of having the service. In community settings the trade-off may be between resource provision and negative impacts on neighborhood quality.

To get at this issue, old women living alone were asked for negative ("would *not* include") as well as positive ("would include") response options regarding an "ideal" neighborhood (Carp & Carp, 1982c). Because proximity is such a powerful influence on resource utilization (Lawton, 1980b), they were questioned separately about "within easy walking distance" and "within a block of home." To further clarify the meaning of responses, two additional response options were offered: "It wouldn't matter one way or the other" and "I have no opinion, don't know." Responses indicated that, ideally, an area within easy walking distance would be rich in facilities and services; but one's own block would include only residential buildings and a stop for the bus that takes you where you want to go.

The trade-off function was clear. Positive resource aspects of a facility were weighed against negative environmental quality implications, and the balance was influenced by proximity. Within walking distance, resource aspects can be utilized, and negative environmental impacts are not immediate. Within one's block, negative environmental connotations become dominant. For example, despite fear of crime among the elderly (e.g., Goldsmith & Goldsmith, 1976), nearly three-quarters of these elderly women living alone would not locate a police station within a block of home, while only 10% would. The noxious effects of noise, traffic, "dangerous people," and "unresidential appearance" make a police station undesirable within a block of home. Less than half would put one within walking distance.

Bohland and Davis (1983) found that the attributes of neighborliness, safety, and a pleasing appearance contribute to neighborhood satisfaction for adults of all ages. There were age differences in the relative significances of dimensions. Unexpectedly, major discrepancies were not between the elderly and the young, but between the elderly and the 55-to-64 group. Safety contributed most to neighborhood satisfaction among the latter group but was of "surprisingly" little significance to the former. Neighborliness was important for young and old, but not for those 55 to 64. It was strongest during childbearing years, diminished when children were less dependent on neighbors for social interaction, and became important again upon retirement.

Carp and Christensen (1986a) found that technical-assessment scales of resources for meeting needs of harmavoidance (safety from crime, fire, accident, health hazards), noxavoidance (noise level, air quality, convenience), and esthetic experience accounted for 32% (adjusted $R^2 = .26$) of the variance in neighborhood satisfaction, above and beyond the contributions of personal competence and socioeconomic status for elderly women living alone.

10.9.4. The Issue of an Old-Age Bias in Perceptions of Environmental Quality

The gerontological literature abounds with reports that older people give more favorable evaluations of their environments than seems warranted, and studies using full adult age ranges show that old people tend to evaluate conditions more favorably than do young adults (Campbell et al., 1976; Harris, 1975; Marans & Rodgers, 1975), supporting the idea that the tendency to favorable response is a characteristic of old age. However, many studies relied on expert judgment or a preconceived system to determine dimensions, and measures have not been demonstrably "age unbiased" in the psychometric sense (Cole, 1981; Peterson & Novick, 1976).

Carp and Carp (1982b) used items developed from open-end questions and factored them to be age unbiased. Most of the resulting indices reflect positive–negative perceptions of specific attributes: Esthetics, Safety, Air Quality, Privacy, City Maintenance, Maintenance by Neighbors, Neighbors' Characteristics, Noise from Neighbors and Equipment in Own Home, Noise from Traffic and Industry and Construction, Noise that Disturbs Activities Inside One's Home, Noise that Disturbs Outdoor Activities, and Access to Services and Facilities. Two are more general: General Quality Compared to Other Neighborhoods and Feelings about Living in This Neighborhood. The latter seems to reflect overall well-being, life satisfaction, or morale in that it correlates with traditional measures in this area as well as they correlate with each other (Carp & Carp, 1983).

Age trends are consistently linear for 12 age groups, the youngest group ranging in age from 18 to 20, and the oldest group 70 and older, indicating that the response tendency is not a gerontological phenomenon but one that increases regularly from early adult years. Women 18 to 20 and men 70 and older often had lower scores than did their age peers of the opposite sex. These differences may be realistic. Young women probably remain longer under the parental roof (with better environmental conditions) and receive more financial support from parents than do young men. Among the old, the inferior environmental status of women has been discussed.

10.10. RELOCATION ISSUES

Any relocation involves adaptation. Research on housing for the elderly, discussed in the previous section, involved people who moved voluntarily. The following section deals with relocation among the older population in general and among the institutionalized, highlighting the role of autonomy for the mover.

10.10.1. The Older Population in General

Older people are less likely to change their place of residence than are younger adults. From 1975 to 1980 only 21% of persons aged 65 and older moved, compared to 48% of those under 65. The majority of older movers remained within the same state. However, over half a million of them moved to a different part of the country, two-thirds of them from northeast or north central areas to the south or southwest (American Association of Retired Persons, 1982).

The relative infrequency of relocation on the part of older people would seem to document their greater satisfaction with existing situations. This is puzzling in view of the factual quality of their living environments. The extent to which nonmoving reflects genuine satisfaction, that is, the degree to which it is truly volun-

tary, remains moot. Many studies show that old people say they are happy with their present residences and do not move, while the housing does not meet minimal standards (Montgomery et al., 1980; Struyk, 1977; United States Senate, 1977). Similarly, many studies report favorable resident assessments of housing that investigators rated as poor (for reviews see Carp, 1976b; Lawton, 1977).

Attachment to home is relevant to the favorable evaluations of what seem unfavorable situations. O'Bryant and Wolf (1983) compared the efficiency in predicting residential satisfaction of: (1) personal and demographic characteristics (sex, race, and marital status); (2) physical characteristics (10 physical housing qualities as rated by residents); and (3) attachment to home (competence in a familiar environment, traditional family orientation, status value of home ownership, and cost vs. comfort trade-off). All three types of variables made useful contributions in explaining housing satisfaction of both older renters and home owners. Physical housing characteristics were better predictors for renters than for owners. Among the latter, attachment to home was a more powerful determinant and, at all levels of satisfaction, home owners showed greater attachment to home. The majority of older people are home owners. The findings of O'Bryant and Wolf must be qualified by the inequity of renters and owners in marital status, number of persons in the household, income, and education—all of which are related to housing satisfaction. Personal perception (Bem, 1970) may confound the results: Having purchased a home, one tends to justify one's decision.

"Satisfaction" may be, on the part of some, a psychologically defensive maneuver to sustain sense of competence or ego integrity. An instrument reliability check was carried out with applicants for public housing for the elderly, fortuitously, immediately after the first set of letters regarding admission were received. Ratings of housing were included. Responses were compared to those given by the same applicants a few weeks before, when no one knew who would be offered apartments, and it was clear that there were about twice as many applicants as apartments. Earlier, no respondent rated existing housing as worse than the center of a five-point scale, "Fair, OK." On the reliability check, those who had been offered admission (without seeing the facility) consistently changed their evaluations of the same housing to "Poor" or "Very Poor," while applicants who had received notice of nonadmission repeated their earlier ratings (Carp, 1975b). Nothing had changed between data collections except information about the reality of a housing option. Nothing more than information of access to a "better" situation altered verbal evaluation of present housing, suggesting that initial response was influenced by more than the housing. This calls into question the literature in which stated satisfaction has been the criterion and suggests that new approaches to this issue are needed to reduce the influences of personal perception, ego defense, resignation in the face of lack of real options, and similar effects on response. Some such strategies were mentioned in the Section 10.9.

Involuntary Moves

Some relocations of community-resident elderly are clearly involuntary. Kasteler, Gray, and Carruth (1968) compared elderly people forced to move because of highway construction with a matched sample of nonrelocated persons. The latter gave more favorable ratings on health, friends, work, economic security, religion, feelings of usefulness, and happiness. Brand and Smith (1974), in a similar study, found that the nonrelocated also scored higher in life satisfaction. They found that the least healthy were more susceptible to the stress of involuntary relocation. They also saw more adverse effects on women than on men, and on whites than on blacks.

The findings of Kral, Grad, and Berenson (1968) are in some ways contrary to those of Brand and Smith and in some ways in agreement with them. Kral and colleagues found that normal aged men suffered more from relocation than did normal aged women. For example, within 23 months the mortality rates were 42% for men and 20% for women. However, they also found that the physically or mentally ill did not adjust as well to the move as did the healthy.

SUMMARY

Most studies find negative consequences associated with forced relocation from one home to another. Persons with physical or mental health disabilities are more vulnerable to such a move. Conflicting evidence was reported regarding differences in effect on men and women. More information is needed on the ordinary community-resident elderly, who are the large majority. Still largely unknown are the extent to which their stated satisfaction is genuine or defensive, the readiness of their access to alternatives, and the specific positive and negative characteristics of their present and desired living environments.

10.10.2. The Institutionalized Elderly

Home-to-Institution Relocation

Institutionalization involves a spatial relocation but more importantly it requires an environmentally vul-

nerable person to develop a totally new "mode of being in space."

> Adjustment from a macro "outside environment" to a micro "inside" environment (sometimes no more than a single room) implies a radical reorientation of geographic experiences, defined here as "the individual's involvement within the spaces and places of his life." (Rowles, 1979, p. 81)

According to Butler (1975):

> Almost all older people view the move to a home for the aged or to a nursing home with fear and hostility. . . . All old people—without exception—believe that the move to an institution is a prelude to death. (p. 260)

Then, in disagreement with Pastalan (1983), these moves appear to be basically involuntary; though, as we shall see, the degree of unwillingness varies and affects outcomes.

Farrari (1963) compared two groups moving from home to an institution, one "voluntarily" and the other with no option. Ten weeks after relocation 94% (16 of 17) of the latter were dead, while only about 3% (1 of 38) of the former had died. The extreme results may reflect confounding effects of initial health status. Sherwood and colleagues (1974) divided persons who relocated from home to institution into those who had exercised more versus less control over the decision. Premove attitudinal measures showed that those who exercised less control were more dissatisfied with life; and postmove measures showed that life satisfaction improved for the more-control group.

Turner, Tobin, and Lieberman (1972) focused on the nature of the postrelocation environment. In institutions that stressed high levels of interaction, activity, and aggressiveness, a "vigorous if not combative" style on the part of a resident facilitated adaptation. Blenkner (1967) randomly assigned community residents to prerelocation service programs that provided minimal, moderate, or maximal care and information. Persons who received more intensive professional services were more likely to be placed in institutions. Those whose intellectual capacity, memory, and orientation to time, place, and person were seriously impaired had considerably lower chances of survival following relocation, regardless of the level of emotional or social adjustment.

Inter- and Intrainstitutional Relocation

Shulz and Aderman (1973) found that patients who came to one institution from another institution lived an average of 1 month longer than those who came to the second institution from home. The investigators conclude that people accustomed to exercising control in a home setting suffer more from feelings of helplessness on entering an institution than do those with previous institutional experience.

Results regarding relocation within and between institutions are conflicting. Miller and Lieberman (1965) and Markson and Cumming (1974) found no rise in mortality rate among older relocated mental hospital patients, the first study over an 18-week period and the second over an 11-week period. On the other hand, Aleksandrowicz (1961) found a 20% death rate among mental patients during the 3 months after transfer, compared to 7.5% during the 3 preceding months; and Killian (1970) found mortality rates to be from five to nine times greater for transferred compared to nontransferred patients. Aldrich and Mendkoff (1963) found the actual death rate of nursing home residents, following transfer, substantially higher than the rate anticipated on the basis of institutional history. During the first 3 months, the rate for relocatees was three times higher than expected, and for people 70 and older it was three and one-half times higher.

Differences in individuals affect outcomes. Relocated nursing home residents with physical impairment, brain syndrome, or motor impairment were more likely to experience negative consequences, including mortality rate (Goldfarb, Shahinian, & Burr, 1972). Individuals with either philosophical or angry responses to news of the transfer had a lower than average death rate, while those who reacted to the relocation news with the mechanism of denial had a higher than average mortality rate (Aldrich & Mendkoff, 1963).

Bourestom and Pastalan (1975) compared two relocated groups according to the extent of change. The radical-change group had to adjust to a new staff, a new program, a new physical plant, and a new patient population. The other group had to adjust only to change in the physical plant. Both groups had elevated mortality rates, but the elevation was greater for the radical-change group, 43% of whom died within 6 months preceding and 1 year following transfer.

Lieberman, Tobin, and Slover (1971) also found the nature of the postrelocation milieu to be the most important determinant of outcomes. Cold, dehumanizing settings tended to cause declines, while autonomy-fostering ones were likely to result in no change or even in improvement.

IMPLICATIONS

There is some disagreement about appropriate conclusions from the literature on inter- and intrainstitutional

relocation. Horowitz and Schulz (1983) conclude, from a review of studies and earlier reviews of them, that some investigators and reviewers risk making type II errors "for the purpose of discrediting what they believe to be the 'myth' of 'relocation trauma'" (p. 233) and suggest that, "due to the systematic bias in many relocation studies and to the fact that these studies are consulted for the purpose of making both private and public policy" (p. 233), researchers should endeavor to rule out type II rather than type I errors in order to be humane.

On the other hand, Borup (1983) cites 28 interinstitutional studies, 21 (75%) of which found no effect on mortality, 4 (14%) of which found increase, and 2 (7%) of which found both increase and decrease; and 3 intrainstitutional studies, of which 2 found no effect and 1 found an increase in mortality. In view of the evidence that relocation does not necessarily increase mortality, even among institutionalized and frail groups, he concludes that "research could better serve the elderly by focusing on environmental conditions that may intervene when relocation occurs" (p. 241). Borup argues that existing data should be interpreted to indicate not that such relocation is not stressful, but only that it does not consistently increase death rate. "We need now to direct our attention to possible adverse conditions that are causal to an individual's vulnerability" when relocating and derive guidelines for transfer of patients "with the greatest possible care and sensitivity" (p. 241).

The Importance of the Transfer Process

Several studies discussed in the previous section suggest the effect, on any type of institutional relocation, of the degree to which the person was willing to make the move. This suggests the potentially beneficial effect of preparation. Jasnau (1967) compared a group who were mass-moved with another group in which each person was given extensive individual preparation and no one was moved without his or her consent. The mass-move group had a mortality rate 35% greater than the rate for the institution during the year before the relocation. The group given special preparation and who had at least agreed to the move had a lower than expected mortality rate. Zweig and Csank (1975) studied the transfer of male veterans over age 64 suffering from a chronic incapacity that required constant attention, for whom a preparation program "to relieve pressure, allay anxiety, and build up realistic expectations" (p. 135) was provided. From the year before relocation to 1 year after, mortality rate decreased.

Gutman and Herbert (1976) studied extended-care male patients for whom a forced move was carefully planned to avoid confusion; furthermore, patients were assigned to rooms on the basis of friendships and compatibilities, and all personal belongings were transferred. Mortality during the first year was normal. There was no differential by age, length of hospitalization, or mental status. Pastalan (1976) carried out an extensive preparation for the involuntarily relocated. The postmove mortality rate was significantly lower than for the state's and nation's rates for nursing home patients. Advanced age, poor prognosis, and mental confusion were predictive of postmove mortality. The rate was 41% among those with a rejecting attitude but 14% among those who accepted the relocation.

10.10.3. General Implications Regarding Relocation

The literature seems to justify some generalizations. The degree of willingness to move or sense of participation in the decision is important. Adequate preparation can increase willingness and make necessary moves less traumatic. Personal characteristics are relevant. For some community residents (e.g., the unwell) relocation is more stressful. The frailty of candidates for institutionalization or institutional transfer makes them more vulnerable, though appropriate preparation can be ameliorative. For the competent community-resident elderly person, a move to a desired new living environment seems beneficial. Schulz and Brenner (1977) developed a "personal control model" on the basis of the relocation literature that highlights the role of autonomy.

In a recent review of the relocation literature Pastalan (1983) suggests that the reasons for some seemingly contradictory findings include five major factors: (1) the degree of choice in making the move, (2) the degree of environmental change, (3) the degree of health, (4) the degree of preparation, and (5) the study's methodolgy.

10.11. ISSUES FOR THE FUTURE

10.11.1. The Purposes of Research

There are three reasons for environment and aging research. First, from the viewpoint of theory development, old people are an ideal study population due to their sensitivity to environmental variation. This is documented, for example, by the various studies that support the environmental docility hypothesis. Second, person–environment relationships may not be constant across life stages, and there may be normative changes in old age. Third, changes in the population structure and other societal variables have given rise to concern about the living conditions of some elderly persons. The third reason, concerns of society, has provided the greatest impetus for research. Efforts to house low-income elderly and improve nursing homes resulted in the funding of evaluation studies. For better balance, attention should turn to the first and second reasons for the design of investigations.

10.11.2. The Need to Study the Full Range of the Elderly

One consequence of the focus on immediate societal concerns was to concentrate research on certain segments of the older population, unusual environments, and particular issues. Thus the matter of age segregation came to prominent attention (e.g., Lawton & Yaffe, 1979; Rosow, 1967; Sherman, 1971; Teaff, Lawton, Nahemow, & Carlson, 1978). In similar fashion, the issue of relocation effects came into prominence (e.g., Aldrich & Mendkoff, 1963; Borup, 1983; Bourestom & Pastalan, 1981; Carp, 1966; Tobin & Lieberman, 1976; Wittels & Botwinick, 1974). Because of both the social interventions and the research funding emphasis, and because institutionalized and segregated groups are easier to study, there has been relatively little learned about the vast majority of old people who live in ordinary communities.

In the absence of such information, there has been a tendency to generalize to "old people" what has been learned about nonrepresentative segments of the older population. Another result is that theories tended to be developed to account for the situations and behavior of the more frail elderly. There is need to recognize the limits on generalizing from much of the existing literature and to study the full range of older people (e.g., Carp, 1976b; Rowles & Ohta, 1983). More studies on competent community-resident elderly are appearing, and theorists are remodeling (e.g., Kahana & Kahana, 1983; Lawton, 1980c) or devising (e.g., Carp & Carp, 1984) formulations to cover the full range of older adults.

10.11.3. The Need to Study Aging in Life Span Perspective

Early aging and environment studies were limited to older respondents. One pitfall of studying only the elderly is the possibility of attributing to old age behaviors observed there that may also characterize younger adults. "Findings from these analyses leave unclear whether the…factors that significantly sustained or diminished the well-being of older persons would have the same effects on other population age groups" (Bohland & Davis, 1979, p. 95). Studies of full adult age ranges are becoming more common in such areas as projections of places of residence of old people (Lycan & Weiss, 1979) and environmental perceptions (Carp & Carp, 1982b) and their determinants (Carp & Carp, 1982a).

Baltes (1979) perceives influences on life span development to be of three types: (1) age graded, which exhibit strong correlations with age, (2) history graded, which occur in connection with biosocial change, for example, cohort effects, and which exhibit strong correlations with historical time, and (3) nonnormative, "which are significant in their effect on development but are not normative in the sense that they do not occur for all people through their life-course, or if they occur, not in easily discernible and invariant sequence or pattern" and their "major characteristic is that they do not show much normalization in onset, duration, and sequencing for different persons" (p. 11).

Today's elderly (but perhaps not, in the same ways, tomorrow's) seem vulnerable in the latter two categories. Such variables as education, which influences a wide variety of environmental and personal characteristics, are cohort related. Negative nonnormative influences such as poor health, low income, inadequate housing, and loss of social roles, while not restricted to the old, tend to occur with higher frequency among them and so to resemble Baltes's age-graded influences in exhibiting correlations with age. These conditions are fortuitously related to intrinsic aging processes in that they (1) do not similarly impinge upon all older persons and (2) may change with advances in medical research and practice and changes in social policy. The roles of such variables should be separated from those of age itself in research designs and models. Inclusion of deprivations that tend to be concentrated in the later years at present but that are not uniquely or necessarily associated with them seems to improve the power of models to account for behavior among the old and among other adults as well. So does inclusion of sense of personal competence and tendency to suppress/deny the unpleasant, which may turn out to be a consequence of status resources/deprivations or a personality trait related to the concept of ego strength.

10.11.4. The Importance of Individual Differences

Studies in housing for the elderly and in institutions have focused primarily on group effects, differences between the rehoused and others. Environment and aging researchers have been slow in heeding Kelly's (1955) statement that individual differences increase with age. Indeed, there has been an opposite tendency to lump "old people" together into homogeneous stereotypy. Increasingly, individual differences are being recognized. In regard to aging and the environment, they probably are of great importance. While special housing for the elderly seems generally beneficial in its effects on residents, these effects are not evenly distributed and, for a minority, are reversed (Carp, 1978; Carp & Carp, 1980). Differential rates of mortality have been observed in nursing home patients according to differences in frailty and in attitude (Aldrich & Mendkoff, 1963; Farrari, 1963; Goldfarb et al., 1972; Turner et al., 1972).

10.11.5. The Need to Avoid a Negative Stereotype

As Rowles and Ohta (1983) point out, while "the gerontological literature is permeated by an ethos of 'losses' or 'decrements' with advancing age" (p. 235), some studies suggest that older people are surprisingly competent and in control of their environments. Lawton (1980c) has broadened his attention to the old person as an initiator of environmental change as well as a responder to environmental demand. Ways in which older people actively mold their physical, psychological, and social environments should be more thoroughly explored in future studies.

10.12. SUMMARY

Environment and aging is a well-established domain of gerontological research. Though it is a multidisciplinary field, many of its investigators are psychologists; and increasing communication with general environmental psychology is beneficial. Conceptual models are under development. Empirical studies show that the external environment has direct effects on outcomes as well as indirect effects through environmental perceptions. Individual differences in many personal characteristics are important. Variables that moderate the effects of environment and person on outcomes have been identified. Person–environment interactions or congruences may account for additional outcome variance. Research has been strongly influenced by societal concerns for the elderly, so that much of it dealt with special older groups and environments. There is need to balance knowledge, correct unjustified generalizations, and reform theoretical models by studying the full range of older people and their environments, with attention to the wide ranges of differences in both, and to do so in a life span perspective.

REFERENCES

Aldrich, C., & Mendkoff, E. (1963). Relocation of the aged and disabled. *Journal of the American Geriatric Society, 11*, 185–194.

Aleksandrowicz, D. (1961). Fire and its aftermath on a geriatric ward. *Bulletin Menninger Clinic, 25*, 23–32.

American Association of Retired Persons. (1982). *A profile of older Americans.* Washington, DC: American Association of Retired Persons.

Appleyard, D. (1977). *Livable streets.* Berkeley, CA: University of California, Institute of Urban and Regional Development.

Arling, C., & McAuley, W.J. (1983). The feasibility of public payments for family caregiving. *Gerontologist, 23*, 300–306.

Baltes, P.B. (1979). Life-span developmental psychology. In P.B. Baltes & O.G. Brim (Eds.), *Life-span development and behavior* (Vol. 2). New York: Academic.

Baltes, P.B., Reese, H.W., & Lipsitt, L.P. (1980). Life-span developmental psychology. In M.R. Rosensweig & L.W. Porter (Eds.), *Annual review of psychology* (Vol. 31). Palo Alto, CA: Annual Reviews.

Baum, A., Singer, J.E., & Valins, S. (1978). *Advances in environmental psychology* (Vol. 1). New York: Wiley.

Bem, D.J. (1970). *Beliefs, attitudes and human affairs.* Belmont, CA: Brooks/Cole.

Bennett, R. (1973). Living conditions and everyday needs of the elderly with particular reference to social isolation. *Aging and Human Behavior, 4*, 179–198.

Berghorn, F.J., Schafer, D.E., Steere, G.H., & Wiseman, R.F. (1978). *The urban elderly.* Montclair, NJ: Allanheld Osmun.

Bild, B.R., & Havighurst, R.J. (1976). Senior citizens in great cities: The case of Chicago. *Gerontologist, 16*, 4–88, Part 2.

Blenkner, M. (1967). Environmental change and the aging individual. *Gerontologist, 7*, 101–105.

Blum, S.R., & Minkler, M. (1980). Toward a continuum of caring alternatives. *Journal of Social Issues, 36*, 133–152.

Bohland, J.R., & Davis, L. (1979). Sources of residential satisfaction among the elderly. In S.M. Golant (Ed.), *Location and environment of elderly population.* New York: Wiley.

Boring, E.G. (1960). *A history of experimental psychology.* New York: Appleton-Century-Crofts.

Borup, J.H. (1983). Relocation mortality research. *Gerontologist, 23*, 235–242.

Bourestom N., & Pastalan, L. (1975). *Forced relocation.* Ann Arbor, MI: University of Michigan, Institute of Gerontology.

Bourestom, N., & Pastalan, L.A., (1981). The effects of relocation on the elderly. *Gerontologist, 21*, 4–7.

Brand, F., & Smith, R. (1974). Life adjustment and relocation of the elderly. *Journal of Gerontology, 29*, 336–340.

Brotman, H.B. (1980). Every ninth American. *Developments in aging.* Washington, DC: U.S. Senate.

Brown, A.S. (1974). Satisfying relationships for the elderly and their patterns of disengagement. *Gerontologist, 14*, 258–262.

Bultena, G.L., & Oyler, R. (1971). Effects of health on disengagement and morale. *Aging and Human Development, 12*, 142–148.

Bultena, G.L., & Wood, V. (1969). The American retirement community. *Journal of Gerontology, 24*, 209–217.

Butler, R.N. (1975). *Why survive?* New York: Harper & Row.

Butler, R.N., & Lewis, M.I. (1973). *Aging and mental health.* St. Louis, MO: Mosby.

Campbell, A., Converse, P.E., & Rodgers, W.L. (1976). *The quality of American life.* New York: Russell Sage.

Canter, D.V. (1969). An intergroup comparison of connotative dimensions in architecture. *Environment and Behavior, 1*, 37–48.

Canter, D.V., & Craik, K.H. (1981). Environmental psychology. *Journal of Environmental Psychology, 1*, 1–11.

Cantor, M.H. (1979). Life space and social support. In T.O. Byerts, S.C. Howell, & L.A. Pastalan (Eds.), *Environmental context of aging.* New York: Garland.

Cantor, M.H. (1980). The informal support system. In E.F. Borgatta & N.G. McCluskey (Eds.), *Aging and society.* Beverly Hills, CA: Sage.

Cantor, M.H. (1983). Strain among caretakers. *Gerontologist, 23*, 597–604.

Carp, F.M. (1966). *A future for the aged.* Austin: University of Texas Press.

Carp, F.M. (1968). Some components of disengagement. *Journal of Gerontology, 23*, 382–386.

Carp, F.M. (1971). The mobility of retired people. In E. Cantilli & J. Shmelzer (Eds.), *Transportation and aging.* Washington, DC: U.S. Government Printing Office.

Carp, F.M. (1974). Short-term and long-term prediction of adjustment to a new environment. *Journal of Gerontology, 29*, 444–453.

Carp, F.M. (1975a). Impact of improved housing on morale and life satisfaction. *Gerontologist, 15*, 511–515.

Carp, F.M. (1975b). Ego defense and cognitive consistency in evaluations of living environments. *Journal of Gerontology, 30*, 707–711.

Carp, F.M. (1976a). User evaluation of housing for the elderly. *Gerontologist, 16*, 102–111.

Carp, F.M. (1976b). Housing and living environments of older people. In R. Binstock & E. Shanas (Eds.), *Handbook of aging and the social sciences*. New York: Van Nostrand Reinhold.

Carp, F.M. (1977). Impact of improved living environment on health and life expectancy. *Gerontologist, 17*, 242–249.

Carp, F.M. (1978). Effects of the living environment on activity and use of time. *Aging and Human Development, 9*, 75–91.

Carp, F.M. (1979). Life-style and location within the city. In T.O. Byerts, S.C. Howell, & L.A. Pastalan (Eds.), *Environmental context of aging*. New York: Garland.

Carp, F.M. (1980). Environmental effects upon the mobility of older people. *Environment and Behavior, 12*, 139–156.

Carp, F.M. (1985) Relevance of personality traits to adjustment in group living situations. *Journal of Gerontology, 40*, 544–551.

Carp, F.M. (1986). Neighborhood quality perception and measurement. In R.J. Newcomer, M.P. Lawton, & T.O. Byerts (Eds.), *Housing an Aging Society: Issues, Alternatives, and Policy*. New York: Van Nostrand Reinhold.

Carp, F.M. (in press a). Status deprivation and personal competence: Effects on domain satisfactions and well-being throughout adult life. *Research on Aging*.

Carp, F.M. (in press b). Age and status deprivation: Effects on environmental perceptions. *Environmental Psychology*.

Carp, F.M. (in press c). Status deprivation, coping style, and sense of personal competence: Effects on environmental perceptions and well-being. *Aging and Human Development*.

Carp, F.M., & Carp, A. (1980). Person-environment congruence and sociability. *Research on Aging, 2*, 395–415.

Carp, F.M., & Carp, A. (1981). Age, deprivation and personal competence: Effects on satisfaction. *Research on Aging, 3*, 279–298.

Carp, F.M., & Carp, A. (1982a). A role for technical assessment in perceptions of environmental quality and well-being. *Journal of Environmental Psychology, 2*, 171–191.

Carp, F.M. & Carp, A. (1982b). Perceived environmental quality assessment scales and their relation to age and gender. *Journal of Environmental Psychology, 2*, 295–312.

Carp, F.M., & Carp, A. (1982c). The ideal residential area. *Research on Aging, 4*, 411–439.

Carp, F.M., & Carp, A. (1983). Structural stability of well-being factors across age and gender, and development of scales of well-being unbiased for age and gender. *Journal of Gerontology, 38*, 572–581.

Carp, F.M., & Carp, A. (1984). A complementary/congruence model of well-being or mental health for the community elderly. In I. Altman, J. Wohlwill, & M.P. Lawton (Eds.), *Elderly people and the environment*. New York: Plenum.

Carp, F.M., & Christensen, D.L. (1986a). Technical environmental assessment predictors of residential satisfaction: A study of elderly women living alone. *Research on Aging, 8*, 269–287.

Carp, F.M., & Christensen, D.L. (1986b). Older women living alone: Technical environmental assessment predictors of psychological well-being. *Research on Aging, 8*.

Chapman, N.J., & Beaudet, M. (1983). Environmental predictors for at-risk older adults in a mid-sized city. *Journal of Gerontology, 38*, 237–244.

Christensen, D.L., & Carp, F.M. (in press a). Objective environmental predictors of the residential satisfaction of older women. *Journal of Environmental Psychology*.

Christensen, D.L., & Carp, F.M. (in press b). Objective environmental predictors of psychological well-being for older independent women. *Journal of Environmental Psychology*.

Clark, M., & Anderson, B. (1967). *Culture and aging*. Springfield, IL: Thomas.

Cole, N.S. (1981). Bias in testing. *American Psychologist, 36*, 1067–1077.

Craik, K.H. (1981). Environmental assessment and situational analysis. In D. Magnusson (Ed.), *Toward a psychology of situations*. Hillsdale, NJ: Erlbaum.

Craik, K.H., & Zube, E.H. (1976). The development of perceived environmental quality indices. In K.H. Craik & E.H. Zube (Eds.), *Perceiving environmental quality*. New York: Plenum.

Cronbach, L.J. (1951). Coefficient alpha and the internal structure of tests. *Psychometrika, 16*, 297–334.

Cumming, E., & Henry, W. (1961). *Growing old*. New York: Basic Books.

Donahue, W. (1966). Impact of living arrangements on ego development in the elderly. In F.M. Carp (Ed.), *Patterns of living and housing of middle-aged and older people*. Washington, DC: U.S. Government Printing Office.

Edwards, J.H., & Klemmack, D.L. (1973). Correlates of life satisfaction. *Journal of Gerontology, 28*, 497–502.

Epstein, S. (1980). The stability of behavior. *American Psychologist, 35*, 790–806.

Erikson, E.H. (1959). The problem of ego identity. *Psychological Issues, 1,* 101–164.

Farrari, N. (1963). Freedom of choice. *Social Work, 8,* 105–106.

Firestone, I., Lichtman, C., & Evans, J. (1975). *Determinants of privacy and sociability among institutionalized elderly.* Paper presented at the American Psychological Association Meeting, Chicago.

French, J., Rogers, W., & Cobb, F. (1974). Adjustment as person-environment fit. In D.A. Coelho, D.A. Hamburg, & J.E. Adams (Eds.), *Coping and adaptation.* New York: Basic Books.

Gifford, R.J. (1980). Judgment of the built environment as a function of individual differences and context. *Journal of Man-Environment Relations, 1,* 22–31.

Glasscote, R.M. (1976). *Old folks at homes.* Washington, DC: American Psychiatric Association.

Golant, S.M. (1979). Migration patterns of the elderly. In S.M. Golant (Ed.), *Location and environment of elderly population.* Washington, DC: Winston.

Golant, S.M. (1982). Individual differences underlying the dwelling satisfaction of the elderly. *Journal of Social Issues, 38,* 121–133.

Goldfarb, A.I., Shahinian, S.P., & Burr, H.T. (1972). Death rate of relocated nursing home residents. In D.P. Kent, R. Kastenbaum & S. Sherwood (Eds.), *Research planning and action for the elderly.* New York: Human Sciences Press.

Goldsmith, J., & Goldsmith, S.S. (1976). *Crime and the elderly.* Lexington, MA: Lexington.

Goldsmith, J., & Tomas, N. (1974, May–June). Crimes against the elderly. *Aging,* 10–13.

Green, B., Parham, I.A., Kleff, R., & Pilisuk, M. (1980). Introduction. *Journal of Social Issues, 36,* 1–7.

Gubrium, J.F., (1972). Toward a socio-environmental theory of aging. *Gerontologist, 12,* 281–284.

Gutman, G.M., & Herbert, C.P. (1976). Mortality rates among relocated extended care patients. *Journal of Gerontology, 31,* 352–357.

Haley, B.A., & Wiseman, R. (1980). *Repair responses of elders.* Paper presented at the 33rd annual meeting of the Gerontological Society of America, San Diego, CA.

Hamovitch, M.B. (1968). Social and psychological factors in adjustment in a retirement village. In F.M. Carp (Ed.), *The retirement process.* Washington, DC: U.S. Government Printing Office.

Harbert, A., & Wilkinson, C.W. (1979). Growing old in rural America. *Aging,* No. 291–292, 36–40.

Harris, L., & Associates. (1975). *The myth and reality of aging in America.* Washington, DC: National Council on the Aging.

Havighurst, R.J., Neugarten, B.L., & Tobin, S.S. (1968). Disengagement and patterns of aging. In B.L. Neugarten (Ed.), *Middle age and aging.* Chicago: University of Chicago Press.

Hayflick, L. (1981). Prospects for increasing human longevity. In P.W. Johnson, (Ed.), *Perspectives on aging.* Cambridge, MA: Ballinger.

Herschberger, R.G. (1970). A study of meaning in architecture. In H. Sanoff, & S. Cohn (Eds.), *EDRA 1: Proceedings of the First Annual Environmental Design Research Association Conference.* Stroudsburg, PA: Dowden, Hutchinson, & Ross.

Horowitz, M.J., & Schulz, R. (1983). The relocation controversy. *Gerontologist, 23,* 229–234.

Ittelson, W.H. (1960). *Visual space perception.* New York: Springer.

Jasnau, K. (1967). Individualized versus mass transfer of nonpsychotic geriatric patients from mental hospitals to nursing homes with special reference to death rate. *Journal of the American Geriatric Society, 15,* 280–284.

Kahana, E. (1975). A congruence model of person environment interaction. In P.G. Windley, T. Byerts, & E.G. Ernst (Eds.), *Theoretical development in environments and aging.* Washington, DC: Gerontological Society.

Kahana, E., & Kahana, B. (1983). Environmental continuity, futurity, and adaptation of the aged. In G.C. Rowles, & R.J. Ohta (Eds.), *Aging and milieu.* New York: Academic.

Kahana, E., Liang, J., & Felton, B.J. (1980). Alternative models of person-environment fit. *Journal of Gerontology, 35,* 584–595.

Kasteler, J., Gray, R., & Carruth, M. (1968). Involuntary relocation of the elderly. *Gerontologist, 8,* 276–279.

Kastenbaum, R. (1983). Can the clinic milieu be therapeutic? In G.D. Rowles & R.J. Ohta (Eds.), *Aging and milieu.* New York: Academic.

Kastenbaum, R., & Candy, S. (1973). The four percent fallacy. *Aging and Human Development, 4,* 15–21.

Kelly, L. (1955). Consistency of the adult personality. *American Psychologist, 10,* 659.

Killian, E. (1970). Effects of geriatric transfers on mortality rates. *Social Work, 15,* 19–26.

Kiyak, H.A. (1978). A multidimensional perspective on privacy preferences of institutionalized elderly. In W.E. Rogers & W.H. Ittelson (Eds.), *New directions in environmental design research.* Tucson: University of Arizona Press.

Kral, V., Grad, B., & Berenson, J. (1968). Stress reaction resulting from the relocation of an aged population. *Canadian Psychiatric Association Journal, 13,* 201–209.

Krech, D., Crutchfield, R., & Livson, N. (1969). *Elements of psychology.* New York: Knopf.

LaRue, A., Bank, L., Jarvik, K.L., & Hetland, M. (1979). Health in old age. *Journal of Gerontology, 34,* 687–691.

Lawton, M.P. (1977). The impact of the environment on aging and behavior. In J.E. Birren & W.K. Schaie (Eds.), *Handbook of the psychology of aging.* New York: Van Nostrand Reinhold.

Lawton, M.P. (1978). The housing problems of community-resident elderly. In R.P. Boynton (Ed.), *Occasional papers in housing and community affairs*. Washington, DC: U.S. Department of Housing and Urban Development.

Lawton, M.P. (1980a). Residential quality and residential satisfaction among the elderly. *Research on Aging, 2*, 309–328.

Lawton, M.P. (1980b). *Environment and aging*. Monterey, CA: Brooks/Cole.

Lawton, M.P. (1980c). Environmental change. In N. Datan & N. Lohmann (Eds.), *Transitions of aging*. New York: Academic.

Lawton, M.P. (1982). Competence, environmental press and adaptation. In M.P. Lawton, P.G. Windley, & T.O. Byerts (Eds.), *Aging and the environment*. New York: Springer.

Lawton, M.P., & Bader, J. (1970). Wish for privacy among young and old. *Journal of Gerontology, 25*, 48–54.

Lawton, M.P., Brody, E.M., & Turner-Massey, P. (1978). The relationships of environmental factors to changes in well-being. *Gerontologist, 18*, 133–137.

Lawton, M.P., & Cohen, J. (1974). The generality of housing impact on the well-being of older people. *Journal of Gerontology, 29*, 194–204.

Lawton, M.P., & Kleban, M. (1971). The aged resident of the inner city. *Gerontologist, 11*, 277–283.

Lawton, M.P. & Nahemow, L. (1973). Ecology and the aging process. In C. Eisdorfer & M.P. Lawton (Eds.), *Psychology of adult development and aging*. Washington, DC: American Psychological Association.

Lawton, M.P., Nahemow, L., & Teaff, J. (1975). Housing characteristics and the well-being of elderly tenants in federally assisted housing. *Journal of Gerontology, 30*, 601–607.

Lawton, M.P., & Simon, B. (1968). The ecology of social relationships in housing for the elderly. *Gerontologist, 8*, 108–115.

Lawton, M.P., & Yaffe, S. (1970). Mortality, morbidity and voluntary change of residence by older people. *Journal of the American Geriatric Society, 18*, 823–831.

Lebowitz, B. (1975). Age and fearfulness. *Journal of Gerontology, 30*, 696–700.

Lee, G.R., & Lassey, M.L. (1980). Rural-urban differences among the elderly. *Journal of Social Issues, 36*, 62–74.

Lewin, K. (1951). *Field theory in social science*. New York: Harper & Row.

Lieberman, M., Tobin, S., & Slover, D. (1971). *The effects of relocation on long-term geriatric patients*. Chicago: University of Chicago.

Linn, B.S., Linn, M.W., & Knopka, F. (1978). The very old patient in ambulatory care. *Medical Care, 16*, 604–610.

Lipman, A. (1968). Public housing and attitudinal adjustment in old age. *Journal of Geriatric Psychiatry, 2*, 88–101.

Litwak, E. (1980). Research patterns in the health of the elderly. In E.F. Borgatta & N.G. McCluskey (Eds.), *Aging and society*. Beverly Hills, CA: Sage.

Lowenthal, M., & Boler, D. (1965). Voluntary vs. involuntary social withdrawal. *Journal of Gerontology, 20*, 363–371.

Lycan, R., & Weiss, J. (1979). Age cohort projections of populations for metropolitan area census tracts. In S.M. Golant (Ed.), *Location and environment of elderly population*. Washington, DC: Winston.

Maddox, G.L. (1965). Fact and artifact. *Human Development, 3*, 117.

Maddox, G.L., & Douglass, E.B. (1973). Self-assessment of health. *Journal of Health and Social Behavior, 14*, 87–93.

Marans, R.W., & Rodgers, W. (1975). Toward an understanding of community satisfaction. In A. Hawley & V. Rock (Eds.), *Metropolitan America in contemporary perspective*. New York: Halstead.

Markson, E., & Cumming, J. (1974). A strategy of necessary mass transfer and its impact on patient mortality. *Journal of Gerontology, 29*, 315–321.

Maslow, A.H. (1954). *Motivation and personality*. New York: Harper.

Masoro, E.J. (1981). Nutritional intervention in the aging process. In P.W. Johnson (Ed.), *Perspectives on aging*. Cambridge, MA: Ballinger.

McConnel, C.E. (1983). A note on methodological fallacies in the "X% fallacy" literature. *Aging and Human Development, 17*, 57–69.

McNemar, Q. (1969). *Psychological statistics*. New York: Wiley.

Miller, D., & Lieberman, M. (1965). The relationship of affect state and adaptive capacity to reactions to stress. *Journal of Gerontology, 20*, 492–497.

Mishara, B.L., & Kastenbaum, R. (1980). *Alcohol and old age*. New York: Grune & Stratton.

Montgomery, J.E., Stubbs, A.C., & Day, S.S. (1980). The housing environment of the rural elderly. *Gerontologist, 20*, 444–451.

Moos, R.H., & Lemke, S. (1980). The multiphasic environmental assessment procedure. In A. Jegar & B. Slotnick (Eds.), *Community mental health*. New York: Plenum.

Morgan, L.A. (1976). A re-examination of widowhood and morale. *Journal of Gerontology, 31*, 687–695.

Murray, H.A. (1938). *Explorations in personality*. New York: Oxford University Press.

Nahemow, L., & Lawton, M.P. (1973). Toward an ecological theory of adaptation and aging. In W. Preiser (Ed.), *Environmental Design Research*: (Vol. 1). Stroudsburg, PA: Dowden, Hutchinson, & Ross.

National Heart and Lung Institute. (1974). *MRFIT (Multiple Risk Factor Intervention Trial) Inventory of Life Events*. Washington, DC: National Institutes of Health.

Nehrke, M.F., Turner, R.R., Cohen, S.H., Whitbourne, S.K., Morganti, J.B., & Hulicka, I.M. (1981). Toward a model of person-environment congruence. *Experimental Aging Research, 7,* 363–379.

Neugarten, B. (1975). The future and the young-old. *Gerontologist, 15,* 4–9.

Newman, S.J. (1976). Housing adjustments of the disabled elderly. *Gerontologist, 16,* 312–317.

O'Bryant, S.L., & Wolf, S.M. (1983). Explanations of housing satisfaction of older homeowners and renters. *Research on Aging, 5,* 217–233.

Palmore, E., & Luikart, C. (1972). Health and social factors related to life satisfaction. *Journal of Health and Social Behavior, 13,* 68–80.

Pastalan, L.A. (1976). *Report on Pennsylvania nursing home relocation program.* Ann Arbor: University of Michigan, Institute of Gerontology.

Pastalan, L.A. (1983). Environmental displacement. In G.D. Rowles & R.J. Ohta (Eds.), *Aging and milieu.* New York: Academic.

Peterson, N.S., & Novick, M.R. (1976). An evaluation of some models for culture-fair selection. *Journal of Educational Measurement, 13,* 3–29.

Pilisuk, M., & Minkler, M. (1980). Supportive networks. *Journal of Social Issues, 36,* 95–116.

Pritchett, V.S. (1979 June). Finite variety. *New York Review of Books,* pp. 7–8.

Regnier, V. (in press). Preferences of high income elderly for luxury housing. In V. Regnier & J. Pynoos (Eds.), *Housing for the elderly.* New York: Elsevier.

Reno, V.P. (1981). Family roles and social security. In R.W. Fogel, E. Hatfield, S.B. Kiesler, & E. Shanas (Eds.), *Aging: Stability and change in the family.* New York: Academic.

Rosow, I. (1963). Adjustment of the normal aged. In R. Williams, C. Tibbits, & W. Donahue (Eds.), *Processes of aging* (Vol. 2). New York: Atherton.

Rosow, I. (1967). *Social integration of the aged.* New York: Free Press.

Rosow, I. (1973). The social context of the aging self. *Gerontologist, 13,* 82–87.

Rowles, G.D. (1978). *Prisoners of space?* Boulder, CO: Westview.

Rowles, G.D. (1979). The last new home. In S.M. Golant (Ed.), *Location and environment of elderly population.* Washington, DC: Winston.

Rowles, G.D., & Ohta, R.J. (1983). Emergent themes and new directions. In G.D. Rowles & R.J. Ohta (Eds.), *Aging and milieu.* New York: Academic.

Rudzitis, G. (1979). Determinants of the central city migration patterns of older persons. In S.M. Golant (Ed.), *Location and environment of elderly populations.* Washington, DC: Winston.

Sager, A. (1983). A proposal for promoting more adequate long-term care for the elderly. *Gerontologist, 23,* 13–17.

Schooler, K. (1970). The relationship between social interaction and morale of the elderly as a function of environmental characteristics. *Gerontologist, 10,* 25–29.

Schulz, R. (1976). Effects of control and predictability on the physical and psychological well-being of the institutionalized aged. *Journal of Personality and Social Psychology, 33,* 563–573.

Schulz, R., & Aderman, D. (1973). Effect of residential change on the temporal distance to death of terminal cancer. *Omega, 4,* 157–162.

Schulz, R., & Brenner, G. (1977). Relocation of the aged. *Journal of Gerontology, 32,* 323–333.

Seligman, M.E.P. (1975). *Helplessness.* San Francisco, CA: Freeman.

Shanas, E. (1979). The family as a social support system in old age. *Gerontologist, 19,* 169–174.

Sherman, S.R. (1971). The choice of retirement housing among the well elderly. *Aging and Human Development, 2,* 118–138.

Sherman, S.R. (1974). Leisure activities in retirement housing. *Journal of Gerontology, 29,* 325–335.

Sherwood, S., Glassman, J., Sherwood, C., & Morris, J.N. (1974). Preinstitutional factors as predictors of adjustment to a long-term care unit. *Aging and Human Development, 5,* 95–105.

Sherwood, S., Greer, D.S., Morris, J.N., & Mor, V. (1981). *An alternative to institutionalization.* Cambridge, MA: Ballinger.

Sofranko, A.J., Fliegel, F.C., & Glasgow, N. (1982–1983). Older urban migrants in rural settings. *Aging and Human Development, 16,* 297–309.

Soldo, B.J. (1978). The housing characteristics of independent elderly. In R.P. Boynton (Ed.), *Occasional papers in housing and community affairs.* Washington, DC: U.S. Department of Housing and Urban Development.

Soldo, B.J., & Myllyluoma, J. (1983). Caregivers who live with dependent elderly. *Gerontologist, 23,* 605–611.

Spreitzer, E., & Snyder, E.E. (1974). Correlates of life satisfaction among the aged. *Journal of Gerontology, 29,* 544–548.

Storandt, M., Wittels, I., & Botwinick, J. (1975). Predictors of a dimension of well-being in the relocated healthy aged. *Journal of Gerontology, 30,* 97–102.

Struyk, R.J. (1977). The housing situation of elderly Americans. *Gerontologist, 17,* 130–139.

Sundeen, R., & Mathieu, J. (1976). The fear of crime and its consequences among the elderly in three urban communities. *Gerontologist, 16,* 211–219.

Teaff, J.D., Lawton, M.P., Nahemow, L., & Carlson, D. (1978). Impact of age integration on the well-being of elderly tenants in public housing. *Journal of Gerontology, 33,* 126–133.

Tissue, T. (1972). Another look at self-rated health among the elderly. *Journal of Gerontology, 27*, 91–94.

Tobin, S.S., & Lieberman, M.A. (1976). *Last home for the aged*. San Francisco, CA: Jossey-Bass.

Turner, B., Tobin, S., & Lieberman, M. (1972). Personality traits as predictors of institutional adaptation among the aged. *Journal of Gerontology, 27*, 61–68.

United States Bureau of the Census. (1982). *Marital status and living arrangements*. Washington, DC: U.S. Government Printing Office.

United States Senate, Special Committee on Aging. (1977). *Developments in aging*. Washington, DC: U.S. Government Printing Office.

Van Dusen, R.A., & Sheldon, E.B. (1976). The changing status of American women. *American Psychologist, 31*, 106–116.

Vanhorenbeck, S. (1982). *Housing programs affecting the elderly*. Washington, DC: U.S. Government Printing Office.

Vicente, L., Wiley, J.A., & Carrington, R.A. (1979). The risk of institutionalization before death. *Gerontologist, 19*, 361–367.

Weed, J.A. (1980). *National estimates of marriage dissolu-tion and survivorship*. Hyattsville, MD: National Center for Health Statistics.

Weiler, P.G., & Rathbone-McCuan, E. (1978). *Adult day care*. New York: Springer.

Williams, R., & Wirth, C. (1965). *Lives through the years*. New York: Atherton.

Windley, P.G., & Scheidt, R.J. (1982). An ecological model of mental health among small-town rural elderly. *Journal of Gerontology, 37*, 235–242.

Wittels, I., & Botwinick, J. (1974). Survival in relocation. *Journal of Gerontology, 29*, 440–443.

Wohlwill, J. (1974). The environment is not in the head! In W.F.E. Preiser (Ed.), *Environmental Design Research* (Vol. 2). Stroudsburg, PA: Dowden, Hutchinson, & Ross.

Yezer, A. (1978). *How well are we housed? 2. Female-headed households*. Washington, DC: U.S. Department of Housing and Urban Development.

Zelinsky, W. (1976). Nonmetropolitan Pennsylvania. *Rural Sociology, 45*, 1–4.

Zweig, J., & Csank, J.Z. (1975). Effects of relocation on chronically ill geriatric patients of a medical unit. *Journal of the American Geriatric Society, 23*, 132–136.

Chapter 11

APPLIED BEHAVIOR ANALYSIS AND ENVIRONMENTAL PSYCHOLOGY: FROM STRANGE BEDFELLOWS TO A PRODUCTIVE MARRIAGE

E. Scott Geller, *Department of Psychology, Virginia Polytechnic Institute and State University, Blacksburg, Virginia*

Perhaps no other discipline in psychology has emerged as rapidly and with as much breadth of content as environmental psychology. The chapter topics of this handbook attest to the variety of research areas and methodologies receiving attention by investigators claiming to be environmental psychologists. In his comprehensive review of environmental psychology, Stokols (1978) distinguished this field of scientific inquiry from other areas by referring to three basic characteristics of environmental psychology: (1) an interdisciplinary perspective; (2) an ecological emphasis; and (3) a focus on the solution of community/environmental problems. Similarly, Harold M. Proshansky, one of the founders of environmental psychology, recently typified this discipline as a "problem-focused, real-world approach [that] must necessarily also be interdisciplinary in its conceptual and methodological orientations" (Proshansky, 1983, p. 6).

There is one other discipline in psychology that claims as much (if not more) focus on real world problem solving—applied behavior analysis. Indeed, in the first issue of the *Journal of Applied Behavior Analysis (JABA)* this field was specifically identified as one that attends to socially significant problems. In particular, the essential criterion for significant research in applied behavior analysis is "its practical importance, specifically its power in altering behavior enough to be socially important" (Baer, Wolf, & Risley, 1968, p. 96). Consequently, researchers, practitioners, and students in applied behavior analysis are convinced that their subspecialty represents the "true" application arm of behavioral science—especially for problem solving among nonclinical populations (e.g., in homes, hospitals, schools, industries, prisons, and communities). At the same time, however, leaders in environmental psychology have tagged their field as "true" applied psychology, extending behavioral science beyond the one-on-one clinical setting to the everyday habitat of the general public, from residences to all other real life physical settings where person–environment problems occur (e.g., Baum, Aiello, Altman, Stokols, Willems, & Winkel, 1982; Proshansky, 1976; Stokols, Altman, Bechtel, Gutman, Howell, Moore, & Zeisel, 1982).

Given two disciplines within contemporary psychology with such similar basic goals, it is surprising that the bodies of literature within these fields can be so independent of each other. For example, most undergraduate textbooks in environmental psychology have given minimal or no attention to applied behavior analysis (e.g., Bell, Fisher, & Loomis, 1978; Holahan, 1982; Ittelson, Proshansky, Rivlin, & Winkel, 1974; Proshansky, Ittelson, & Rivlin, 1976). In fact, the most recent textbook in environmental psychology at the time of this writing (i.e., Holahan, 1982) covers practically every topic, methodology, and theory of contemporary psychology *except* applied behavior analysis. Moreover, a recent edited text entitled *Behavior and the Natural Environment* (Altman & Wohlwill, 1983) includes no reference to the large research domain that applied principles from behavior analysis to develop behavior change strategies for preserving the environment. This chapter offers potential reasons for this lack of interdisciplinary interaction, while explicating a rationale and approach for constructive collaboration between environmental psychology and applied behavior analysis. This author concluded years ago that these disciplines both possess unique qualities that can be combined to maximize the attainment of their common goal—the empirical-based solution of real world human–environment problems. This is indeed the premise of this chapter.

11.1. BASIC SIMILARITIES AND DIFFERENCES

Each of these disciplines, with a mutual focus on the practical application of behavioral science, has a relatively short history. Their first professional research journals started at approximately the same time (*JABA* in 1968, *Environment and Behavior* in 1969),

and the disciplines have flourished at equivalent high rates, spreading heuristic influence to numerous research endeavors and real world applications, developing additional discipline-specific journals with competitive review processes (e.g., *The Behavior Analyst*, *Behavior Modification*, *Journal of Environmental Systems*, *Journal of Environmental Psychology*, *Population and Environment*), and becoming the special focus of graduate training leading to a doctorate in psychology (e.g., University of California at Irvine, SUNY at Stony Brook, and Virginia Polytechnic Institute and State University for environmental psychology; University of Florida, Western Michigan University, and West Virginia University for applied behavior analysis). Both fields are behavior based and outcome oriented, founding their problem-solving strategies on laboratory and field observations of empirical relationships between individuals and their environment.

Most investigations of human–environment relationships address one of two questions: (1) How does the environment affect people? or (2) How do individuals influence the environment? And most research by environmental psychologists and behavior analysts can be interpreted with respect to one or both of these general questions. However, an examination of this research does suggest some basic differences between the disciplines.

Early reviews by Craik (1970) and Wohlwill (1970) and later ones by Cone and Hayes (1976; 1977), Pomeranz (1980), and Stokols (1978) showed that the vast majority of research in environmental psychology relates to the first question posed previously; that is, environmental variables have been studied most often for their effects on behavior rather than vice versa. Cone and Hayes (1980) referred to this research as *reactive* (as opposed to *active*) because it "examines reactions or responses *to* environmental problems rather than [examining] the problems themselves" (p. 12). It is noteworthy that recent work in environmental psychology has given increased emphasis to the dynamic interplay among active and reactive, as well as behavioral and cognitive/affective transactions between people and environments (e.g., see Saegert, Chapter 4, Heft & Wohlwill, Chapter 6, and Sanchez, Wisenfeld & Cronick, Chapter 38, of this volume).

The reactions (or dependent variables) studied by environmental psychologists have included attitudes, beliefs, and cognitions (usually inferred from questionnaires or interviews) as well as overt behaviors; most of the field investigations have been correlational in nature. In contrast, behavior analysts focus on overt behavior as their dependent variable (usually to the exclusion of all other indices), and their research is almost always "active" in the sense that the typical study in applied behavior analysis implements and evaluates an intervention to change behavior directly in specified directions. In other words, behavior analysts plan for cause and effect relationships, thus avoiding correlational statistics.

To the extent that solving human–environment problems requires behavior change, environmental psychologists are certainly concerned with affecting overt behavior. However, beliefs, attitudes, cognitions, and values have become the direct target of many environmental studies because of the assumption that changing these variables (or constructs) must precede behavior change (e.g., Stern & Oskamp, Chapter 29, this volume; Weigel, 1983). Herein lies a basic distinction between the theoretical perspective of most behavior analysts and that of environmental psychologists. Specifically, applied behavior analysis was founded on the assumption that solutions to human–environment problems require a direct attack on overt behaviors, either to increase the frequency of desired responses or to decrease the frequency of inappropriate responses. Some behavior analysts presume that changes in attitudes, values, even social norms may follow behavior change (Geller, Winett, & Everett, 1982), as predicted by cognitive dissonance theory (Festinger, 1957). This approach (often termed the *behavior model of abnormality*) contrasts sharply with the traditional medical model approach to clinical psychology, which presumes that insight (analogous to attitudes and values) should be developed or changed first, with behavior modification occurring as a consequence of insight development or attitude change. Thus the attitude-focused research in environmental psychology is more consistent with the medical model approach to clinical intervention than with the behavior model of applied behavior analysis.

Although there are clear and basic theoretical and methodological distinctions between mainstream environmental psychology and applied behavior analysis, these should not prevent mutual understanding and beneficial collaboration. Indeed, pursuing interdisciplinary, problem-oriented, and ecological goals (Craik, 1970; Stokols, 1978; Wohlwill, 1970) practically requires an appreciation of applied behavior analysis. Let's turn to a further delineation of the research approach followed by the applied behavior analyst.

11.2. FROM EXPERIMENTAL TO APPLIED BEHAVIOR ANALYSIS

Applied behavior analysis is founded on the approach to behavioral science expounded by B.F. Skinner (e.g., 1938, 1953, 1958). In his experimental analysis of behavior (or operant psychology), Skinner rejected inferred constructs such as drives, needs, motives, cognitions, and so on, while studying only overt behavior and its observable environmental, social, and physiological determinants. Furthermore, since the "natural datum in a science of behavior is the probability that a given bit of behavior will occur at a given time" (Skinner, 1966, p. 213), the dependent variable of an experimental analysis of behavior must be response rate. The independent variables in a science of behavior become environmental stimuli and contingencies, analyzed as determinants of response rate according to the natural event sequence of antecedent–behavior–consequence, sometimes referred to as the A–B–C model of behavior analysis (e.g., Geller et al., 1982).

Skinner's operant psychology further dictates a focus on individuals when studying relationships between dependent and independent variables. In other words, an experimental analysis of behavior should demonstrate the impact of antecedent or consequence conditions on the behavior of single organisms, and therefore, the classical statistical procedures that combine data from different individuals are considered superfluous. Instead, the behavior of a single organism is observed prior to an application of the independent variable(s) and until a stable rate of responding is indicated by a continuous recording of response frequency within successive time periods. This is referred to as the baseline phase of a behavior analysis, and it may continue over numerous daily sessions of response observation.

Following a reliable measurement of baseline response rate, an intervention is implemented, and this treatment phase is continued until a stable response rate occurs per observation session (perhaps over several weeks or months of daily observation). A comparison of stable response rates between the treatment and baseline periods demonstrates to some extent whether the intervention (i.e., antecedent or consequence manipulation) influenced the target behavior, but a true cause and effect relationship cannot be presumed unless response rate returns to the pretreatment baseline level after the treatment condition is removed. This third phase of an experimental behavior analysis is termed the withdrawal period, the three phases (baseline, treatment, and withdrawal) constituting the A–B–A reversal design (Hersen & Barlow, 1976). This design is the classic paradigm of operant psychology and is readily applied in laboratory settings, preferably within a chamber (termed a *Skinner box*) where environmental conditions and response consequences can be precisely controlled and the subject's rate of making a discrete target response (e.g., a lever press) can be automatically recorded.

11.2.1. A People's Science

The single-subject design of experimental behavior analysis can be traced to the classic research of Watson (Watson & Rayner, 1920) and Pavlov (1928). These investigators studied single organisms and obtained continuous response measures before and during treatment. Pavlov took behavioral recordings after his treatment condition (i.e., classical conditioning) and therefore demonstrated a reversal or return to baseline, termed *classical extinction*. Watson's subject (the famous 11-month-old infant "Little Albert") was taken from the hospital 5 days after a conditioned emotional response to a white rat was established (i.e., on the day that tests were given to demonstrate generalization of the conditioned fear), and therefore a reversal (or extinction) phase was not implemented. Four years later, Watson's student, Mary Cover Jones, completed an A–B–A reversal design with a number of children (including the famous "Little Peter") and thereby demonstrated the extinction of conditioned fear (Jones, 1924).

These classic case studies certainly show the wealth of instructive data available from single-subject experiments. The special advantages of the single-case experiment are discussed elsewhere (e.g., Chassan , 1967; Hersen & Barlow, 1976; Sidman, 1960) and include the following: (1) individual clinical outcome is not masked as it is with group averaging; (2) large numbers of subjects (matched on certain characteristics) are not necessary; (3) specific environment–behavior relationships of individual subjects can be generalized more readily to professional practice (e.g., clinical therapy) than can group averages; (4) within-subject variability or fluctuations in the course of a treatment condition can be traced (i.e., process research); (5) observation of individual subjects can be readily made in naturalistic, real world settings; and (6) the data displayed in an A–B–A reversal paradigm (without complex statistical transformations) can be readily understood and appreciated by the general public, thus providing for a

"people's science" (Hawkins & Fabry, 1979, p. 546). This final point becomes especially important for real world application of research findings.

The solution of societal problems related to human–environment relations often requires that "real people" (not behavioral scientists) become involved in the implementation of intervention strategies. This is especially the case when problem solutions require large-scale action in the attempts to attack such environmental problems as population explosion (Fawcett, 1969; Zifferblatt & Hendricks, 1974), energy conservation (Cook & Berrenberg, 1981; Edney, 1981; Shippee, 1981; Stern & Gardner, 1981a), hazardous waste (Fusco, Jula, & Musser, 1982; Price & Schmidt, 1979), air pollution (Committee on Environmental Improvement, 1978), waste reduction and resource recovery (Geller, 1980b, 1981), water conservation (Geller, Erickson, & Buttram, 1983; Winkler, 1982), energy-efficient travel (Everett, 1982; Reichel & Geller, 1981), transportation safety (Geller, 1982b, 1983a), and litter control (Geller, 1980a; Osborne & Powers, 1980). Therefore, the behavioral scientist who is concerned with real world problem solving must attend to the diffusion of intervention strategies to the community, commercial, and government sectors of society, with hopes of influencing large-scale modification of behavior, policy, and social norms.

Over the past decade or so the present author has had numerous occasions to discuss behavior change interventions and outcomes with groups of individuals whose actions could make a difference in a particular problem (e.g., community grass roots organizations concerned with environment preservation; government and industrial personnel targeting energy conservation, transportation safety, or health promotion; and institution administrators desiring improved management of human–environment interaction). For all of these occasions it was extremely advantageous to have clear, understandable displays of treatment outcome, including a dependent measure that was simple and straightforward (i.e., no data transformation more complex than a percentage) and a research design that was convincing and easy to explain.

11.2.2. Social Validity

In the first issue of *JABA*, three prominent leaders in the field (Baer, Wolf, & Risley, 1968) explored the meaning of several terms used by behavioral scientists. Three of their definitions distinguish *applied* behavior analysis from *experimental* behavior analysis and provide a framework for identifying the "social validity" of a research endeavor. These terms are *applied*, *effective*, and *generality*; each term identifies a critical characteristic of applied behavior analysis and refers to an aspect of social validity. The label *applied* means that particular environments, individuals, or target behaviors are studied "because of their importance to men and society, rather than their importance to theory" (Baer et al., 1968, p. 92). An *effective* intervention strategy is one that alters the behavior "enough to be socially important" (p. 96), and to determine what is "enough," it is necessary to answer the question, "how much did that behavior need to be changed?" (p. 96). Finally, an intervention that is effectively applied to a socially significant problem shows *generality* if it is "durable over time, if it appears in a wide variety of possible environments, or if it spreads to a wide variety of related behaviors" (p. 96).

It is noteworthy that determining the practical importance of a problem and assessing the impact of the behavioral intervention often require a survey of attitudes and opinions (i.e., verbal report) of relevant individuals. For example, Azrin (1977) reported use of a "happiness" index to assess therapeutic outcome, Baer and colleagues (1968) suggested that the opinions of those directly responsible for the targeted individual(s) be surveyed in order to estimate whether or not an intervention was "effective" (i.e., socially important), and Wolf (1978) advocated the use of subjective measures (i.e., rating scales or interviews) to determine the social validity of a treatment program at three levels: "1. The social significance of *goals*... 2. The social appropriateness of the *procedures*... [and] 3. The social importance of the effects" (p. 207).

Several behavior analysts have used verbal report to estimate the social validity of their interventions (e.g., Fawcett & Miller, 1975; Foxx & Azrin, 1972; Kent & O'Leary, 1976; Minkin et al., 1976). Furthermore, a number of behavior analysts have found it instructive to consider opinions of program participants or managers during the development of a treatment package (e.g., Azrin, 1977; Frederiksen, 1978; Geller, 1983a, Geller, Johnson, Hamlin, & Kennedy, 1977; Lovett, Bosmajian, Frederiksen, & Elder, 1983; Ollendick, Elliott, & Matson, 1980; Ollendick & Murphy, 1977), and several behavioral community psychologists have used self-report data to evaluate the impact of their behavior interventions (e.g., Bachman & Katzev, 1982; Geller, 1981; Hake & Zane, 1981; Winett, Hatcher, Fort, Leckliter, Love, Riley, & Fishback, 1982; Winett, Love, & Kidd,

1982–1983). And Van Houten (1979) introduced a variety of verbal report strategies for determining when and how much to change target behaviors.

The use of verbal descriptions of private events (or judgments) runs counter to an experimental behavioral analysis. Skinner (e.g., 1953, 1958) has argued forcefully against the use of introspective or subjective information, claiming that such data are unreliable, potentially distorted, and irrelevant for a functional analysis. However, this acceptance of introspective data by contemporary behavior analysts certainly increases compatibility between environmental psychology and applied behavior analysis.

11.2.3. Evaluation Issues

Extending the A–B–A reversal paradigm to field settings has resulted in substantial deviations from the classic laboratory procedures for the experimental analysis of behavior, but the basic concept of measuring the response rate of single organisms in a baseline–treatment–withdrawal format has clearly influenced the field research of behavior analysts. For example, a majority of the research that attempted to modify environment-related behavior in real world settings followed a basic A–B–A reversal design (see reviews by Cone & Hayes, 1980; Geller et al., 1982; Oskamp & Stern, 1984). That is, prior to implementing a particular strategy for increasing environment-protecting behaviors (e.g., litter disposals, newspaper recycling, residential weatherization, bus ridership, and ridesharing) or decreasing environment-destructive behaviors (e.g., littering, excessive driving, unnecessary electricity use, lawn trampling, and water wasting), baseline records were established. This recording of behaviors (or environment-relevant outcomes of behaviors) continued in the same field setting over several observation sessions during a treatment phase, and then after removing the intervention condition (i.e., during the withdrawal phase).

Although typically following an A–B–A reversal design, applications of behavioral analysis for environmental preservation have often deviated severely from experimental behavior analysis by observing the behaviors of several different individuals during baseline, treatment, and withdrawal phases without tracking the same individuals from one experimental condition to the next. Furthermore, the dependent variable in these studies has typically been not response rate but rather the percentage of individuals who emitted (or avoided) the target response during each observation session. In these studies the environmental setting could be viewed as the "single organism" subjected to an A–B–A reversal paradigm (as suggested earlier by Nietzel, Winett, MacDonald, & Davidson, 1977). To compensate for the inability to identify the same individuals across experimental phases in a community-based study, behavior analysts have applied standard statistical procedures (e.g., Geller, 1983b; Geller, Koltuniak, & Shilling, 1983; Mayer & Geller, 1982–1983; Winett et al., 1982), but as discussed later in this chapter the use of inferential statistics represents another deviation from experimental behavior analysis.

Since it is usually impossible to identify individuals for intrasubject comparisons in naturalistic settings (unless identification tags are naturally available such as vehicle license plates, e.g., Geller, 1983b), these deviations from experimental behavior analysis are probably necessary for many field studies. While some behavior analysts have demonstrated strong resistance to accepting such modifications of the single-subject A–B–A reversal design (e.g., Brownell, personal communication, 1981), others (Frederiksen, 1983; Winett, 1983) have suggested that observing random samples of multiple subjects during baseline, treatment, and withdrawal conditions may actually provide data that are more generalizable and useful than those obtained in the single-subject case study. At any rate, the application of a multiple-subject, A–B–A reversal design with statistical comparisons certainly narrows the methodology gap between applied behavior analysis and environmental psychology.

A–B–A Control Group Design

Adding a baseline control group to the A–B–A reversal design has permitted clear demonstrations of intervention effects in field settings where the response measures are variable (e.g., due to large numbers of subjects, limited experimental control, or prominent influences of extraneous factors). For example, when Everett, Hayward, and Meyers (1974) studied the effects of a positive reinforcement procedure to increase bus ridership, they applied an A–B–A reversal paradigm on one bus (the experimental bus) while measuring bus ridership throughout the study on a control bus that never received the incentive intervention. Similarly, Winett and his associates (e.g., Winett et al., 1982; Winett, Love, & Kidd, 1982–1983; Winett, Neale, & Grier, 1979) have typically employed this A–B–A control group design to demonstrate the impact of rebate, feedback, media, and/or self-monitoring strategies on residential electricity consumption while controlling for marked effects of weather changes (see Geller et al., 1982, for

more details on these extensions of the A–B–A reversal design).

Multiple-Baseline Designs

The multiple-baseline design (Baer et al., 1968) represents another deviation from experimental behavior analysis as conceptualized by Skinner and is a critical one for the naturalistic study of functional relationships between environments and behaviors. It seems paradoxical to design a treatment program for durability (i.e., to produce response maintenance) and then to apply the A–B–A reversal design, whereby intervention impact is demonstrated by a return to baseline levels of the dependent variable after the treatment is removed. Furthermore, it may be undesirable (perhaps unethical) to remove a treatment condition that has produced socially valid behavior change or benefited human–environment interaction. Indeed, program managers or participants might object strongly to such a reversal paradigm. These liabilities of the basic paradigm of experimental behavior analysis are handled by an alternative evaluation technique introduced by Baer and colleagues (1968) — the multiple-baseline design.

A multiple-baseline approach to evaluation does not include a withdrawal of treatment, but involves the systematic application of staggered A–B (baseline–treatment) phases across situations so that treatment is introduced in one situation while baseline measures continue in another situation. Considering that there are four variables that define a particular treatment situation (i.e., the target subject, the target response, the environmental setting, and the time of the intervention), there are four types of possible multiple-baseline designs, defined according to which situational variable is varied when the staggered treatment sessions are implemented.

An example of multiple baseline across subjects would result from an observation of the baseline levels of a particular response (e.g., driving speed) for two subjects in the *same* environmental situation (defined by vehicle, road, and time of day). Then an application of a motivational strategy would be applied to alter the driving speed of only one subject, while both subjects' target behavior would be systematically observed. Subsequently, the treatment intervention would be applied to the second subject. Note that for a valid assessment the driving behavior of the two subjects should be independent (i.e., a change in one subject's driving should not influence a change in the other's driving). Such independence is often difficult to achieve in real world settings, although the independence assumption is testable (e.g., by observing the amount of concomitant fluctuation during baseline recordings).

Geller and his associates (1982) introduced the notion of a multiple baseline across *time*, which requires systematic observations of the target behavior at two or more specified time periods while maintaining the environment, behavior, and subject constant. An example of such a paradigm would be the measurement of vehicular speeds on a particular highway at two different time periods (e.g., when the same drivers are traveling to work in the morning and driving home in the afternoon), with the initial application of an intervention technique (e.g., parking a police car at the side of the road) occurring at only one of these times.

Interventions: Component or Package

From the applied behavior analysis perspective, Geller (1980a) criticized the evaluation methodology followed by Keep America Beautiful, Inc. (KAB) in its nationwide effort to develop communitywide programs for the effective control of litter. Since 1977 KAB has been advocating a particular evaluation procedure in hundreds of U.S. cities that is contrary to one that a behavior analyst would support. The dependent variable of the KAB evaluation procedure is the *photometric index* (PI), which is derived from a systematic count and tabulation of the litter in photographs taken of various environmental settings (KAB, 1977). The fact that the PI is a measure of *outcome* (of responding from several individuals) rather than *process* (i.e., the response rate of a single individual) is certainly a serious liability from the perspective of experimental behavior analysis, although such a deviation has been typical in field applications of behavior analysis (Cone & Hayes, 1980; Geller et al., 1982).

Another weakness of the PI technique derives from the potential artifact of experimenter expectancy effects (Rosenthal, 1966) during actual photographing (Geller, 1980a). However, the most problematic deviation from experimental behavior analysis is the sampling procedure used for obtaining baseline, treatment, and follow-up PIs. Specifically, the instructions for obtaining a PI require that different settings should be photographed in each evaluation phase. "The validity of PI—one of the factors that makes it the only objective technique for measuring litter accumulation—rests in the random selection of sites each time measurements are taken" (KAB, 1977, p. 5). Thus from the perspective of behavior analysis the method of changing target sites results in minimal useful data (even if PI measure-

ments could be unbiased and objective). Indeed, the behavior analyst would advocate photographing the same exact areas of a particular milieu during baseline, treatment, and withdrawal phases.

The numerous communitywide programs following the KAB plan for litter control usually consist of a large variety of intervention strategies (e.g., litter control ordinances, educational programs, media campaigns, and special promotional events). As a result, a significant change in the PI is attributed to a treatment "package," any aspect of which could have been critical or inconsequential. To a certain extent this approach to evaluation is at variance with the tenets of scientific inquiry. The results of such an evaluation offer few data relevant to specific human–environment relations and little information useful for refining an intervention strategy for increased efficacy. It is noteworthy, however, that this is the basic evaluation approach used in numerous statewide litter control programs at exorbitant costs (e.g., Frounfelker & Belencan, 1981; Samtur, 1979; Syrek, 1975, 1977a, 1977b).

An experimental analysis of behavior requires an evaluation of precisely defined behavior change strategies. Therefore, the treatment condition should consist of a single environmental variable rather than a constellation of intervention strategies. Some behavior analysts have studied the independent impact of various behavior change techniques by linking together several A–B–A reversal designs in an A–B–A–C–A–D–A... format, whereby each treatment condition represents a different environmental manipulation (i.e., a behavioral antecedent or consequence). Hence the relative impact of each potential component of a proposed treatment package can be assessed, leading to a plan for the optimal mix of components or to guidelines for altering particular program components.

When working in real world settings with limited research funds and demands for immediate solutions, it is often necessary to implement an entire treatment package *at the start*. In fact, Azrin (1977), who has tackled numerous problems with applied behavior analysis (e.g., institutional management, toilet training, stuttering, marital counseling, enuresis, and job finding), recommended that a treatment package be developed and evaluated first with an A–B–A reversal or multiple-baseline design; once a successful treatment program is found, analytic study of treatment components can be undertaken to improve the package. This is one more deviation from experimental behavior analysis that has followed from the extension of Skinner's operant psychology to field settings.

Relevance to Environmental Psychology

The evaluation paradigms of the behavior analyst have been used almost exclusively with behavior change programs designed to influence environment preservation (Cone & Hayes, 1980; Geller et al., 1982). This was the case because all of this research was accomplished by behavior analysts. On the other hand, these evaluation strategies have rarely been used when environmental factors are manipulated as independent variables (as is the more frequent experiment in environmental psychology). There are perhaps a number of reasons for this, including: (1) difficulties in manipulating environmental conditions in an A–B–A fashion; (2) an emphasis on discrete, one-shot nonbehavioral measures of mediational processes (e.g., opinions, attitudes, perceptions, and cognitions) that are more conveniently taken once per individual in a between-subjects design than repeatedly for the same individual in a within-subjects paradigm; (3) the multifaceted nature of independent or dependent variables, which makes a complex statistical analysis necessary; and (4) a reliance on traditional statistical procedures due to the training of the investigator (e.g., personality, cognitive, or social psychology), the standards of the desired dissemination outlet (e.g., traditional journal format), or the biases of the investigators' peer reviewers (e.g., ior tenure and promotion).

It seems to this author that there have been numerous occasions when an A–B–A reversal or multiple-baseline design should have been (but wasn't) the chosen methodology for studying the impact of environment variables on human behavior. The treatment condition of an intrasubject, repeated-measures design could be the manipulation of such environmental factors as room size, social density, noise, temperature, lighting, furniture arrangements, recreational materials, privacy aids, territorial markers, and so forth. Actually, an A–B (pretest/posttest) control group design has been most popular for studying the impact of design modifications (e.g., see recent review by Wandersman, Andrews, Riddle, & Fancett, 1983). More specifically, these studies have usually included an initial sampling of behaviors or opinions among two independent groups of individuals (e.g., in different hospital wards or college dormitories), followed by environmental changes in one of the settings and a resampling of participant reaction in both settings (e.g., Baum & Davis, 1980; Holahan & Saegert, 1973; Knight, Zimring, Weitzer, & Wheeler, 1978). Such studies, however, would demonstrate more convincing environmental control if a reversal phase showed a return to pretreatment reactions (i.e., an A–B–A reversal design) or if the "control" group later received the environmental manipulation and reactions were observed that paralleled those that followed the earlier treatment given the experimental group (i.e., a multiple-baseline design across settings).

Another successive step toward applied behavior analysis would be continuous, systematic examination of single-subject behaviors across baseline and treatment conditions. Indeed, this is one useful approach to the study of individual differences—an underdeveloped area in environmental psychology (Wandersman et al., 1983) and one that has both conceptual (Craik, 1976; Wandersman & Florin, 1981) and empirical (Weinstein, 1978; Wohlwill & Kohn, 1973) significance for the study of human–environment relations.

Liabilities of a Nonstatistical Approach

The nonstatistical, single-case approach to behavioral research has been criticized on a number of accounts (e.g., Kiesler, 1971; Underwood, 1957), the issue of generality being raised most often. While the averaging procedures in the between-subjects, statistical approach present problems in generalizing from a heterogeneous group to an individual, the single-case, intrasubject procedures may offer minimal generality of findings to other individuals with varying characteristics. This problem may be alleviated with the replication of single-case experiments (Hersen & Barlow, 1976); and it is not so prevalent in the community-based applications of behavior analysis, because in these studies the behaviors of many individuals are typically recorded during baseline, treatment, and withdrawal conditions (e.g., Geller et al., 1982; Glenwick & Jason, 1980; Nietzel et al, 1977). Of course, the concern in community studies, as in all multiple-subject approaches, is whether the individuals sampled are representative of the population to which the generalization is made.

Perhaps the most obvious drawback of a nonstatistical approach to research is a lack of standard criteria for assessing the significance of findings. The "significance" or social importance of data in applied behavior analysis is typically determined by a visual inspection of repeated recordings of the dependent measure (Kazdin, 1975b, 1976). In other words, a particular treatment condition is presumed to have "significant" impact on the target behavior if observers of the data (which are typically graphed in a format that shows fluctuations between observation sessions within successive experimental conditions) agree that experimental control was demonstrated.

The critical observers are the journal reviewers who determine whether the research findings are scientifically sound and worthy of professional dissemination (Baer, 1977a). Problems occur, however, when reviewers disagree on the extent of experimental control shown in the graphic portrayal of such data; and research on this issue has indicated that such disagreement could be rather common (Jones, Weinrott, & Vaught, 1978; White, 1971), even among reviewers for *JABA* (DeProspero & Cohen, 1979).

In a comprehensive review of the problem of visual analysis, Yeaton (1982) concluded that this approach requires that effects be obvious (or "big") for visual argument that an experiment should be published. This could increase the likelihood of a Type II error, or a denial that a certain variable is functional when in fact it is. Baer (1977a) argued that this is as it should be for a technology of behavior; accepting a higher risk for a Type II error (than researchers following the traditional statistical approach to data analysis) will only mean that the behavior analyst will "learn about fewer variables, but these variables are typically more powerful, general, dependable, and— very important—sometimes actionable" (p. 171). Yeaton (1982) warned, however, that this "big effect" contingency could result in limiting the type of research that the behavior analyst will attempt. In other words, the behavior analyst might be controlled into choosing those experimental situations that maximize effect size rather than considering other factors that may be more pertinent to the solution of real world problems.

Yeaton (1982) suggested a number of dimensions that could be used to qualify the judgment of "big" when evaluating the outcome of an applied study, including: (1) cost of treatment; (2) nature of the problem; (3) special needs of the subjects; (4) the developmental stage of the intervention (e.g., demonstration vs. diffusion stage); (5) number of subjects treated; (6) number of independent variables manipulated (e.g., a treatment package vs. a single-component intervention); (7) duration of treatment effects or extent of response maintenance; (8) nature of the experimental situation (e.g., laboratory vs. field setting); (9) the training of the intervention personnel (e.g., skilled clinicians vs. paraprofessionals); (10) length of treatment session; (11) the behavioral conceptualization of the dependent variable (e.g., simple count of verbalizations vs. a reliable measurement of "fathering"); and (12) the number of target behaviors that are modified at once by the treatment condition. This listing is clearly not exhaustive, and many dimensions relate to the previous section on social va-

lidity. The point here is that these and other aspects of an experiment ought to enter into an evaluation of applied research.

Neither applied behavior analysis nor a statistical approach provides for a systematic consideration of numerous factors that determine the extent to which the results of an experiment can contribute to the solution of real world problems. It might be argued that a visual analysis of research outcome provides for more flexibility than inferential statistics; but without specific criteria (or factor weighings) the future of an experimental effect in applied behavior analysis is dependent on the subjective decisions of a group of behavior analysts (e.g., journal editors and reviewers) with varying concern and appreciation for unspecified dimensions that qualify the applied value of a behavior analysis.

11.2.4. Observer Reliability

Since the prime dependent variable in applied behavior analysis usually requires direct observation of the target response(s), demonstrating the accuracy of the behavioral recording methodology has been a paramount concern of the behavior analyst. Indeed, issues regarding the attainment and measurement of interobserver reliability have been the topic of numerous papers in the field of behavior analysis. For example, 7 articles on the reliability of measurement appeared in the spring 1977 issue of *JABA* (Volume 10, Number 1) and 9 of the 23 articles in a special issue of *JABA* on behavioral assessment (1979, Volume 12, Number 4) focused on the topic of interobserver reliability. These articles are sources of important information for researchers who rely on behavioral observations for their dependent variables, including environmental psychologists who approach problem investigation and solution from perspectives other than applied behavior analysis.

Although several techniques have been proposed for estimating interrater reliability (e.g., Birkimer & Brown, 1979a, 1979b; Hopkins & Herman, 1977; Yelton, Wildman, & Erickson, 1977), the most straightforward and easy-to-understand measure of observation reliability is the one that has been used most frequently by behavior analysts. This is a simple *percentage of agreement* score, calculated by dividing the total number of times that two independent observers agree on the categorization of a particular response (i.e., as occurring or not occurring, or being of a particular type) by the total number of response categorizations (i.e., agreements plus disagreements) and multiplying the result by 100. Generally, at least 80% agreement is considered a minimal acceptable standard (Kazdin, 1975a).

11.2.5. Unobtrusive Observation

The direct observation of behavior may result in a well-known artifact—a behavioral effect of the observers' presence (e.g., Kazdin, 1979; Kent & Foster, 1977; Orne, 1962). The impact of this observer biasing (often termed *reactivity*) is dependent on whether the subjects are aware of the assessment, which in turn is influenced by the obtrusiveness of the observation procedure. Several behavioral studies have demonstrated, per experimental design, significant behavioral impact of reactivity (i.e., obtrusive observers) on subject behaviors (e.g., Johnson, Christensen, & Bellamy, 1976; Mercatoris & Craighead, 1974; Surratt, Ulrich, & Hawkins, 1969; White, 1977); other experiments have even shown effects of reactivity (i.e., experimenter monitoring) on percentages of interobserver agreement (e.g., Kent, O'Leary, Diament, & Dietz, 1974; Romanczyk, Kent, Diament, & O'Leary, 1973).

The use of unobtrusive measures not only prevents reactivity bias, but also may provide information relevant to the generality of research results across settings, that is, whether behavior change is restricted to the treatment milieu. Kazdin (1979) classified the unobtrusive techniques used in applied behavior analysis as "direct observation" versus "product of behavior" (pp. 716–718). *Direct observation* refers to the recording of behavior without the subjects' knowledge and includes evaluations of videotapes and client reactions to phone calls. Often situations are contrived to provoke the target behavior, and then treatment effects are observed directly (e.g., through videotapes or observations of an accomplice).

Kazdin's *products of behavior* category represents the indirect, unobtrusive assessment of behavior by studying *archival records* (governmental and institutional records of such events as birth, crime, death, marital status, recidivism, school attendance, and grades) or *PUysical traces* (e.g., environmental litter, store items missing, curbside recyclables).

Much of the research designed to develop and evaluate behavior change strategies for environment preservation (e.g., as reviewed by Cone & Hayes, 1980; Geller et al., 1982; Oskamp & Stern, 1984) incorporated unobtrusive products of behavior measures to assess treatment outcome. For example, the impact of programs to reduce resource consumption was evaluated by reading electricity meters

(e.g., Becker & Seligman, 1978; Kohlenberg, Phillips, & Proctor, 1976; Walker, 1979), hygrothermographs (Winett et al., 1982), and thermostat settings of water heaters (Geller, 1981) and apartments (Walker, 1979); litter control programs have counted indigenous litter (e.g., Chapmen & Risley, 1974; Finnie, 1973; Hayes, Johnson, & Cone, 1975; NcNees, Schnelle, Gendrich, Thomas, & Beagle, 1979), planted litter (Clark, Burgess, & Hendee, 1972; LaHart & Bailey, 1975), handbill litter (Geller, 1973; Geller, Witmer, & Orebaugh, 1976; Krauss, Freedman, & Whitcup, 1978; Reich & Robertson, 1979), litter bags (Cope & Geller, 1984; Powers, Osborne, & Anderson, 1973); trash can disposals (Burgess, Clark, & Hendee, 1971; Geller, Witmer, & Tuso, 1977; O'Neill, Blanck, & Joyner, 1980), ashtray litter (Geller, Brasted, & Mann, 1979–1980), and traces of "clue spray" on subjects' hands from picking up marked litter (Bacon-Prue, Blount, Pickering, & Drabman, 1980); efforts to reduce transportation energy have included observations of odometers (Foxx & Hake, 1977; Hake & Zane, 1981; Reichel & Geller, 1980), readings of miles-per-gallon meters (Lauridsen, 1977; Runnion, Watson, & McWhorter, 1978), a measurement of communitywide gasoline consumption (Rothstein, 1980), counts of punches on bus transportation cards (Bachman & Katzev, 1982; Katzev & Bachman, 1982,) and counts of raffle tickets (Mayer & Geller, 1982–1983); and programs to encourage recycling have included observations of grocery store purchases (Geller, Wylie, & Farris, 1971; Geller, Farris, & Post, 1973), weighings of recyclable newspapers (e.g., Geller, Chaffee, & Ingram, 1975; Reid, Luyben, Rawers, & Bailey, 1979; Luyben & Bailey, 1979), counts of raffle coupons (Couch, Garber, & Karpus, 1979; Ingram & Geller, 1975; Witmer & Geller, 1976), observations of households with curbside recyclables (Jacobs & Bailey, 1982–1983; Nielsen & Ellington, 1983), and counts of drink containers deposited in collection boxes (Luyben, Warren, & Tallman, 1980). Many of these behavior change programs incorporated incentive strategies based on the products of behavior rather than on actual behaviors. Geller et al. (1982) referred to such programs as outcome-based reward contingencies, as opposed to response-based rewards where the *process* of making the desired behaviors is reinforced directly.

11.3. BEHAVIOR MODIFICATION

Behavior modification is often associated with applied behavior analysis, although the term has taken on numerous meanings over the past decade or so. For example, the media have termed *behavior modification* practically every method for therapeutic treatment, including chemotherapy, psychosurgery, brain stimulation, neuropharmacology, electroconvulsive therapy, hypnosis, psychoanalysis, behavioral instrumentation, genetic screening (Martin, 1974; Sage, 1974), and even group encounter sessions (Schwitzgebel, 1975). Psychologists usually reserve the term for intervention strategies that are directed at observable behaviors, but some therapy researchers have attached the *behavior modification* label to procedures for changing cognitions (e.g., Mahoney, 1974; Meichenbaum, 1974).

The type of intervention classified under the rubric of behavior modification has varied widely. Some writers have suggested that any technique that alters behavior should be considered behavior modification (e.g., Davison & Stuart, 1975; Geller et al., 1977), whereas other therapists and researchers have reserved the label for certain intervention procedures (e.g., Lazarus, 1971; Rimm & Masters, 1974). Geller et al. (1977) suggested that the term *behavior modification* be used not to identify a particular approach to therapeutic intervention, but rather to indicate the direct goal of the intervention. If the goal is behavior change then the term *behavior modification* is appropriate; hence intervention strategies that focus on attitude change would be called *attitude modification*.

Given the direct objective of an intervention (e.g., behavior or attitude change), the label attached to the particular intervention should reflect the conceptual system used (contingency management, implosive therapy, systematic desensitization, rational emotive therapy, transactional analysis, assertiveness training, psychoanalysis, etc). Thus the treatment phase of the behavior analyst's A–B–A reversal or multiple-baseline design might reflect any number of conceptual schemes, whether designed to modify behaviors or attitudes. To date, most of the behavioral scientists who attempted to change behaviors for environment preservation designed their interventions according to the antecedent–behavior–consequence (ABC) model defined earlier—a conceptualization that has been referred to as *behavioral engineering* (Ayllon & Michael, 1959; Homme, Baca, Cottingham, & Homme, 1968; Surratt et al., 1969).

Behavioral engineering is an approach toward behavior change that focuses on arranging the environment (i.e., behavioral antecedents or consequences) so as to increase the probability of desired behaviors and decrease the probability of undesired behaviors. In other words, behavioral engineering is actually the blending of two technologies: (1) the technology of *stimulus control* or antecedent manipulations for behavior change; and (2) the technology of *contingency management* or consequence manipulations for behavior change (Homme et al., 1968).

The study of functional relationships between behaviors and consequences (i.e., contingency management) has received substantially more attention from behavior analysts than has the study of antecedent–behavior relationships. This may be because laboratory settings (e.g., the Skinner Box) are more conducive to manipulating behavioral consequences than antecedents or because it is usually easier to control behavior effectively with contingency management than with stimulus control. Indeed, more behavior change strategies for environmental protection have been consequence-based than have been antecedent-based, and greater behavior modification was usually shown with contingency management than with stimulus control (see reviews by Cone & Hayes, 1980; Geller et al., 1982). We turn now to a discussion of consequence and antecedent strategies for increasing environment-preserving behaviors.

11.3.1. Contingency Management for Environment Preservation

Behavioral consequences can be pleasant or unpleasant. They can be distinct stimuli (e.g., a monetary rebate, a self-photograph, a speeding ticket, a verbal commendation or condemnation), or they can be opportunities to engage in certain behaviors (e.g., the privilege to use a preferred parking space, add one's name to an "Energy Efficient" honor roll, or attend a special litter control workshop). *Contingency management* refers to giving or taking away such stimulus events or response opportunities from an individual as a result of specific *behaviors* or *outcomes* of behaviors.

Punishment and negative reinforcement procedures to promote environment preservation usually take the form of laws or ordinances (e.g., fines for littering, illegal dumping, excessive water use, or polluting water or air) and usually require extensive enforcement and legal personnel to be effective. Technically, a behavior change procedure is only termed *punishment* when a particular target response decreases in frequency of occurrence after being followed by a particular consequence. In contrast, negative reinforcement occurs when individuals emit certain behaviors in order to escape or avoid a particular consequence. For both punishment and negative reinforcement, the aversive consequence that successfully modifies behavior as planned is termed a *negative reinforcer* (cf. Goldiamond, 1974).

Applied behavior analysts have shown a variety of reasons for preferring positive reinforcement over punishment and negative reinforcement, including observations that positive reinforcement is usually most acceptable and frequently easiest to administer, and it is often most cost-effective in the long run (Geller, 1982b; Geller et al., 1982). Therefore, when developing interventions for motivating response change, behavior analysts have avoided the use of punishment and negative reinforcement. However, it is true that governments and communities have applied positive reinforcement much less often than negative reinforcement and punishment. The "bottle bill" is one very effective, large-scale positive reinforcement procedure implemented by some state governments to protect the environment, whereby monetary remuneration is provided for the return of certain drink containers for recycling. Unfortunately, since the drink industry would be substantially inconvenienced (from packaging to sales) by an elimination of the throw away container, this single positive reinforcement contingency has probably caused more nationwide controversy than any of the numerous negative reinforcement and punishment procedures established by state or federal governments for environmental benefit (Geller, 1980a).

The positive reinforcement contingencies applied by behavior analysts for environment preservation have varied widely. Some rewards were given contingent on the occurrence of a particular response, whereas other consequence procedures did not specify a desired behavior but were based on reaching a particular *outcome* (e.g., specified reductions in environmental litter or electricity consumption).

A *response* consequence provides specific information regarding the appropriateness or inappropriateness of a particular behavior, but an *outcome* consequence (including consumption feedback) does not usually prescribe a specific response change. In other words, the pleasant consequence of a specific response serves to motivate the occurrence of a similar response, whereas an unpleasant response consequence may provoke the occurrence of alternative responses. However, outcome consequences are not necessarily associated with a particular behavior and consequently may not prompt specific behavior change. Therefore, outcome consequences should be less influential than response consequences, although the author is not aware of a field experiment that made this important comparison.

The following *response*-contingent consequences were successful in increasing the frequency of the target behavior significantly above baseline levels: (1) $5 payment in summer when room thermostat was set at 74° F. and all windows and doors were shut when air conditioner was running (Walker, 1979); (2) a raffle coupon awarded per trip to a particular location with recyclable paper (Geller et al., 1975); (3) 50% fare discounts (Katzev & Bachman, 1982) or a merchandise ticket redeemable for goods and services at local businesses (Deslauriers & Everett, 1977; Everett et al., 1974) for riding the bus; (4) a quarter (Powers, Osborne, & Anderson, 1973) or a raffle ticket (McNees, Schnelle, Gendrich, Thomas, & Beagle, 1979; Powers et al., 1973) for collecting a bag of litter; (5) a ticket redeemable for a soft drink following litter disposals in a trash receptacle (Kohlenberg & Phillips, 1973); (6) points exchangeable for family outings and special favors for reduced use of certain home appliances (Wodarski, 1976); and (7) McDonald's cookies (McNees et al., 1979), a quarter (Hayes et al., 1975) or a dollar and a self-photograph (Bacon-Prue et al., 1980) for collecting certain marked items of litter.

The following *outcome*-contingent consequences were applied successfully by behavior analysts for environment preservation: (1) a tour of a mental health facility (Foxx & Hake, 1977) or monetary payments (Hake & Foxx, 1978; Hake & Zane, 1981) for specified reductions in vehicular miles of travel; (2) a dime for cleaning a littered yard to criterion (Chapman & Risley, 1974); (3) raffle tickets (Couch et al., 1979; Ingram & Geller, 1975; Witmer & Geller, 1976) or monetary payments (Jacobs & Bailey, 1982–1983) for collecting specified amounts of recyclable newspapers; and (4) monetary rebates for particular reductions in electricity usage (e.g., Slavin & Wodarski, 1977; Slavin, Wodarski, & Blackburn, 1981; Winett & Nietzel, 1975).

Giving residents frequent and specific feedback regarding their energy consumption may also be considered an *outcome* consequence (e.g., see reviews in Cone & Hayes, 1980; Geller et al., 1982). Most of the feedback studies for energy conservation have targeted residential energy consumption, and for most of these studies the feedback was given individually to target residences.

Procedures for displaying energy consumption feedback have included: (1) the delivery of a special feedback card each month (Seaver & Patterson, 1976), each week (Kohlenberg, Phillips, & Proctor, 1976; Winett et al., 1979), or on a daily basis (e.g., Becker, 1978; Hayes & Cone, 1977; Palmer, Lloyd, & Lloyd, 1978; Seligman & Darley, 1977; Winett, Kaiser, & Haberkorn, 1977); (2) use of devices to display room temperature and humidity (Winett et

Table 11.1. Matrix Defining Four Types of Consequence Strategies for Promoting Energy-Efficient Travel[a]

		Nature of Consequence	
		Pleasant	Unpleasant
Action with Consequence	**Apply**	*Positive Reinforcement* A quarter for boarding the "Red Star" bus (response based) One raffle coupon per 5% reduction in weekly vmt (outcome based) (outcome based)	*Positive Punishment* Name of potential carpooler is listed on "Gas Waster" poster when observed driving to work alone (response based) Truckers call fellow employee a "gas guzzler" when his truck shows a decrease in mpg on feedback chart (outcome based)
	Remove	*Negative Punishment* Three-month suspension of license for driving 80 mph (response based) Worker loses preferential parking privilege after showing an increase in vmt (outcome based)	*Negative Reinforcement* Loss of company van avoided by finding sixth vanpooler (response based) Loss of gasoline credit card avoided by showing increase in mpg (outcome based)

[a]The first example in each cell is a response-based contingency, whereas the second contingency is based on a specified outcome. Adapted from Geller et al., 1982, Table 2.2.

al., 1982) or the peak periods of electricity use (Blakely, Lloyd, & Alferink, 1977; Kohlenberg et al., 1976); (3) installation of an electronic meter with digital display of electricity cost per hour (Becker & Seligman, 1978; McClelland & Cook, 1980); and (4) the application of training packages for teaching and motivating residents to read their own electric meters regularly and record kilowatt consumption (Winett, Neale, & Grier, 1979).

Some feedback studies have targeted transportation energy, demonstrating that vehicular miles of travel (vmt) can be reduced with public posting of vmt per individual (Reichel & Geller, 1980); and vehicular miles per gallon (mpg) can be increased through public posting of mpg (Runnion, Watson, & McWhorter, 1978) or the installation of a fuel flow meter that displays continuous mpg or gallons of gas used per hour (Lauridsen, 1977). In addition, a community-based litter control study by Schnelle, Gendrich, Beagle, Thomas, and McNees (1980) found a 35% average reduction in ground litter as a result of daily displays of litter counts on the front page of the local newspaper. Television is also being investigated as a way to provide community feedback and influence environment-related behavior (Rothstein, 1980; Winett, 1983).

Table 11.1, adapted from a previous display (Gel-ler et al., 1982), summarizes this discussion of consequence strategies for motivating behavior change. Four basic consequence strategies are defined, as determined by the *nature* of the consequence (pleasant or unpleasant) and the *action* with regard to the consequence (i.e., whether the consequence results in an *application* of a pleasant or unpleasant event, or whether the consequence is the *removal* of a pleasant or unpleasant event).

The examples given in the matrix of Table 11.1 depict the distinction between *response*-based and *outcome*-based contingencies. As illustrated, the application or removal of a pleasant or unpleasant event may occur after the contingency manager (the person in charge of administering the consequence) observes a particular behavior (i.e., response-based contingency) or a certain environmental outcome resulting from one or more prior behaviors (i.e., outcome-based contingency). Note that the positive versus negative distinction in the definition of the consequence strategies refers to whether the consequence is applied (positive) or removed (negative) in order to influence behaviors or outcomes, and is *not* concomitant with the distinction between pleasant and unpleasant consequences. Note also that negative punishment is the response-contingent or outcome-contingent removal of a desirable item (such as money) from the target individual's possession and should not be confused with the term *extinction*, which is not a response-based contingency but refers to the noncontingent termination of an existing reinforcement or punishment contingency.

Each example of Table 11.1 refers to a feasible contingency for motivating the conservation of transportation energy. More specifics regarding these and other techniques for conserving transportation energy can be found elsewhere (e.g., see reviews by Everett, 1980, 1982; Everett & Watson, chapter 26, this volume; Reichel & Geller, 1981), and additional examples relating to other areas of environment-preservation are given in Geller et al. (1982, Table 2.2).

Contingency Perceptions

Geller and colleagues (1982) suggested that the same contingency can be perceived as positive or negative, reinforcement or punishment. For example, a driver's reduction in vmt following receipt of an exorbitant gasoline credit card bill may be perceived as resulting from a decrease of energy-wasteful responses through *positive* punishment (e.g., the gasoline bill was an embarrassing, aversive stimulus, which indicated selfish consumption of environmental resources) or through *negative* punishment (e.g., the gasoline bill represented the loss or removal of money), or through a combination of both positive and negative punishment. On the other hand, the same driver may have increased energy-efficient travel (and reduced vmt) following a high gasoline bill in order to avoid receiving another similar bill (negative reinforcement). Thus a contingency manager may define a contingency in one way (e.g., "I'll apply positive reinforcement by offering special parking privileges to the work group that shows the greatest average reduction in mpg"), but the target population may perceive the contingency differently (e.g., "We'd better reduce our mpg in order to avoid losing parking privileges"— *negative* reinforcement). Furthermore, if the pleasant consequence in a positive reinforcement contingency is not earned, the subject(s) may actually perceive a punishment contingency that was not intended by the program administrators (e.g., "We lost our parking privileges because we used too much gasoline"—*negative* punishment). Determining one's perceptions of a particular consequence strategy would require the use of subjective indices—a radical deviation from experimental behavior analysis, but there may be important justification for making such assessments.

Geller and his colleagues (1982) entertained the notion that one's perception of a particular management contingency could influence the behavioral impact of that contingency. The authors referred to Skinner's (1971) important discussions of relationships between response–consequence contingencies and perceived freedom, whereby people are presumably more apt to feel controlled by extrinsic events when they are punished for certain behaviors or when they respond to avoid or escape aversive consequences (i.e., negative reinforcement) than when they emit behaviors to earn pleasant consequences (i.e., positive reinforcement). Therefore, positive reinforcement is presumably the consequence strategy that is most likely to preserve one's perceptions of personal freedom or control and least likely to promote contingency resistance or counteraction that might occur as a result of a perceived threat to personal control (Brehm, 1966, 1972).

Contingency resistance or counteraction would certainly decrease the intended beneficial impact of a behavior change program, and it could result in countercontrol measures whereby the target individuals actively attempt to undermine the program and exert control over the contingency administrator(s). Two summary points are relevant here: (1) A particular contingency may be perceived differently by program administrator(s) and program recipient(s), such that an *intended* positive reinforcement contingency might be perceived as negative reinforcement or punishment and elicit unexpected reactance; and (2) Measuring the contingency perceptions of the target population might not only be useful in predicting contingency resistance, but might also result in constructive data for the development of a more effective contingency management program. These hypotheses suggest a need for the behavior analyst to look beyond (or behind) overt behavior, a perspective radically deviant from experimental behavior analysis but congruent with the norm in environmental psychology.

Scheduling Contingencies

Experimental behavior analysis has given much research attention to the scheduling of response consequences. Operant research has shown clearly that the type of reinforcement or punishment schedule (e.g., whether the consequence occurs continuously or intermittently, in a fixed or random pattern) determines characteristic and predictable response patterns while the contingency is in effect and when the contingency is removed. Thus the long-term impact (or durability) of an intervention program (i.e., the maintenance of the target response) may often depend on the scheduling of contingencies during treatment. Unfortunately, most of the applications of behavior analysis for environment preservation have been short-term demonstration projects, designed to demonstrate marked behavioral effects of a particular intervention strategy without concern for program durability (Geller et al., 1982; Willems & McIntire, 1983). Therefore, the scheduling of response consequences has rarely been a topic of study in this research domain, except for some work that compared different ways of scheduling rewards for bus ridership (Deslauriers & Everett, 1977; Everett, Deslauriers, Newson, & Anderson, 1978; Katzev & Bachman, 1982).

One particular contingency schedule was introduced by behavior analysts researching behavioral solutions to environmental problems and has numerous applications in community settings when several individuals are observed during baseline and treatment conditions (i.e., the multiple-subject A–B–A design described earlier). Specifically, Hayes and Cone (1977) used the term *variable person ratio* (VPR) schedule for situations when positive reinforcers are delivered after the occurrence of a particular response among a variable number of persons making the target response. Whereas the *variable ratio* schedule of operant psychology refers to the delivery of a response consequence after a variable number of target responses by a single individual, the VPR schedule of applied behavior analysis represents a contingency schedule that is dependent on frequencies of different individuals making a particular response. For example, Kohlenberg and Phillips (1973) gave a drink coupon to an average of every tenth person who used a particular trash can, and Deslauriers and Everett (1977) gave a discount coupon for merchandise at local businesses to an average of every third person who boarded a special campus bus.

Although this author is only aware of applications of VPR schedules for increasing environment-improving behaviors, other "person schedules" are certainly possible (as extensions of the contingency schedules defined in the operant laboratory), and these need to be studied in naturalistic settings. Under a *fixed-person-ratio* (FPR) schedule a consequence would be offered after every fixed number of individuals emit the target response (e.g., for an FPR10 schedule every tenth person would be reinforced). For *variable-person-interval* (VPI) and *fixed-person-interval* (FPI) schedules, response consequences would be available after fixed or variable periods of time, and after a consequence is available it would be presented to the first individual who makes the target response (e.g., for an FPI 10-minute schedule the reinforcer would be available every 10 minutes and would be delivered to the first person who emitted the desired response after reinforcer availability).

11.3.2. Stimulus Control for Environment Preservation

Stimulus control procedures (often referred to as antecedent, prompting, or response-priming techniques) are environmental manipulations occurring before the target behavior in an attempt to increase the frequency of the target response if it is desirable or to decrease occurrences of the target response if it is undesirable. Antecedents for promoting environment preservation have been displayed through television commercials, pamphlets, films, verbal instructions, and demonstrations (e.g., from peers, parents, teachers, or public officials) and through environmental displays (such as speed limit signs, feedback meters, beautified trash receptacles, and "energy-saving" settings on appliance controls). Setting group or individual goals to conserve energy and pledging individual commitment to alter energy-wasteful responses are also varieties of antecedent strategies.

Geller and his colleagues (1982) introduced a scheme for categorizing stimulus control (or antecedent) strategies, based on the following dichotomies: (1) announcement of incentive or disincentive (e.g., $0.05 per returnable container, $100 fine for littering) versus no announcement of a response consequence; (2) discriminative stimulus (which signals when a pleasant or unpleasant consequence is available) versus a stimulus that is not discriminative; and (3) general exhortation with no specification of the target behavior (e.g., "Please don't litter!"; "Dispose of properly!") versus specific instructions that indicate the particular response to emit or avoid (e.g. "Turn off lights when leaving the room!"; "Don't trample the grass!"). This later dichotomy is usually only relevant for antecedent messages that neither announce nor signal a consequence strategy.

Table 11.2 summarizes this categorization scheme with examples referring to conservation of transportation energy. Details of the conservation programs from which these examples were taken are given elsewhere (e.g., Everett, 1980, 1982; Everett & Watson, Chapter 26, this volume; Reichel & Geller, 1981), and examples pertaining to other areas of environmental protection are given in Geller et al. (1982).

Note that the discriminative stimulus is the only type of stimulus control procedure studied in the operant laboratory, whereas stimulus control is much more complex in naturalistic settings. Some antecedents announce an incentive condition and also signal when the pleasant or unpleasant consequence is available, thus serving as a discriminative stimulus for the target response (such as a sign displayed in-

Table 11.2. Matrix Defining Four Types of Stimulus Control (or antecedent) Strategies for Promoting Energy-Conserving Travel

		Announce Consequence Strategy	
		Yes	No
Signal Avail- ability of Conse- quence	Yes	"Express lane open for cars with two or more passengers *when this sign is displayed*" "$100 gas tax when purchasing gas- *bearing this label*"	Presence of Red Star Bus Presence of police car
	No	"Discount coupon for riding buses with Red Star" "$50 fine for speeding 10 to 15 mph above 55"	"Please conserve gasoline" (general) "Accelerate slowly and maintain constant speeds to conserve gasoline" (specific)

Source: Adapted from Geller et al., 1982, Table 2.1.

termittently to indicate when reinforcement is available for a particular response). Other antecedent strategies do not specify a contingency but still serve as discriminative stimuli because they signal the occasion for a particular consequence if the response is emitted. In this latter case, it is presumed that the target population has become aware of the contingency. For example, a police car signals the availability of an unpleasant consequence if speeding occurs (without defining the particular contingency); and in the transportation conservation experiments by Everett and associates (e.g., Deslauriers & Everett, 1977; Everett, 1973; Everett, Hayward, & Meyers, 1974), the three large red stars on a special campus bus signaled the availability of a positive reinforcer (i.e., a quarter or discount coupon for boarding). The reinforcement contingencies for the studies by Everett and associates were described in the university newspaper that was itself a particular antecedent strategy— one that announced an incentive condition but did not serve as a discriminative stimulus for bus riding.

Stimulus control techniques without concomitant consequence contingencies are relatively cheap and easy to administer, but the impact of antecedent strategies for increasing environment-protecting behaviors or decreasing environment-destructive behaviors has been limited (e.g., Cone & Hayes, 1980; Geller et al., 1982; Stern & Oskamp, Chapter 28, this volume). In summary, antecedents that neither announced nor signaled a consequence were only successful in promoting substantial behavior change when they: (1) specified what behavior was desired (i.e., a *specific* appeal); (2) were administered in

close *proximity* to the opportunity to emit the requested response; (3) requested a response that was relatively *convenient* to emit; and (4) were given in *polite*, nondemanding language.

With regard to response convenience, stimulus control procedures alone have rarely been effective in influencing the occurrence of environmental protection responses that require more effort (or response cost) than flicking a light switch (Delprata, 1977; Winett, 1978), adjusting a room thermostat (Winett et al., 1982), purchasing drinks in one container over another (Geller et al., 1971, 1973), or dropping a handbill in a conveniently located trash receptacle (Geller, 1973, 1975; Geller et al., 1976, 1977).

As with certain contingencies, some verbal or written antecedents (e.g., demands rather than requests) may be perceived as threats to personal freedom (Brehm, 1966, 1972) and may motivate the occurrence of responses opposite to the desired behavior. This notion was supported in field research by Reich and Robertson (1979), who distributed antilitter fliers at a public swimming pool and found significantly more littering of fliers with the antilitter messages "Don't litter" and "Don't you *dare* litter" than of fliers with the messages "Help keep your pool clean" and "Keeping the pool clean depends on you." Similarly, this author and his students (detailed in Geller et al., 1982, Chapter 3) found significantly more patrons of a shopping center to comply with a specific, *polite* prompt at the bottom of distributed handbills (i.e., "Please dispose of in trash can in front of Woolco") than with a specific, *demand* prompt (i.e., "You must dispose of in trash can in front of Woolco").

Modeling

An additional stimulus control procedure for influencing behavior change is labeled *modeling* (cf. Bandura, 1977), which occurs when specific behaviors are demonstrated to the target individual(s). Modeling can occur through live demonstrations or via film, television, or videotape, and may actually imply a specific antecedent strategy with the announcement of a reinforcement contingency (as when the model receives a pleasant or unpleasant consequence following a specific response), or a specific antecedent with no specification of a reinforcement contingency (as when no response consequences are shown).

Energy studies and environmental protection programs have essentially ignored modeling strategies, yet modeling (through television or videocassette) has the potential of reaching and influencing millions of people at once. In fact, research by Winett and his students (Winett et al., 1982) showed that a videotape program (showing specific conservation practices and rewarding consequences) was instrumental in reducing the heating bills of 33 households an average of 27% and the cooling bills of 23 households an average of 33%. Much additional research is clearly needed in this area. For example, it would be instructive to test specific communication and diffusion principles (e.g., Darley, 1978; Darley & Beniger, 1981; Rice & Paisley, 1981; Rogers & Kincaid, 1981; Rogers and Shoemaker, 1971; Rosenberg, 1977) from the applied behavior analysis perspective discussed herein.

11.4. THE ECOLOGICAL PERSPECTIVE

The behavior analyst's approach to solving environmental problems has been criticized by many psychologists on the grounds that the research has been too reductionistic, too individualistic, too disciplinary, too insular, and critically negligent of an ecological or systems perspective (e.g., Hake, 1981; Stern & Gardner, 1981a, 1981b; Willems & McIntire, 1982). In other words, applied behavior analysis has not given enough attention to the fact that functional relationships between behaviors and environments are intertwined within a complex ecobehavioral system "of relationships that link person, behavior, social environment, and physical environment" (Willems, 1977, p. 42), and that a successful behavior change program does more than modify a single response of a single individual—it influences other behaviors and environments of targeted and nontargeted individuals in ways that may be quite unexpected and undesirable. Even behavior analysts who have targeted environmental problems have warned that applied behavior analysis alone "is at least insufficient and at times incorrect or misleading as a result of its failure to adopt a systemic (and economic) approach" (Winkler & Winett, 1982, p. 422).

This author's review of the literature has indicated that this criticism of applied behavior analysis is not particularly new (cf. Holland, 1978; Rogers-Warren & Warren, 1977a; Willems, 1965, 1974), nor is the problem relevant solely for the behavior analyst. Actually, this problem has been addressed by many behavior analysts and environmental psychologists—some referring to the need to adopt an ecological perspective (e.g., Gump, 1977; Willems, 1974, 1977), others placing most emphasis on the need to consider environmental contexts (e.g., Geller et al., 1983; Stokols, 1982; Winett, 1983), and still others focusing on the value of an interdisciplinary, systems-level approach (e.g., Geller et al., 1982; Geller & Winett, 1984; Wahler, Berland, Coe, & Leske, 1977; Winkler & Winett, 1982). Other scholars have introduced the term *ecobehavioral analysis* to reflect the problem in terms of the behavior change goals of the behavior analyst rather than the pure descriptive orientation of the ecologist (Rogers-Warren & Warren, 1977b; Willems, 1977).

From the various discussions of ecology and behavior analysis (e.g., Hake, 1981; Rogers-Warren & Warren, 1977a; Willems, 1965, 1974), the author gleaned the following 10 research directions as representative of an ecological/systems-level approach to the beneficial study and modification of environmental/conservation problems. Each of these recommendations implies a necessary collaboration between environmental psychology and applied behavior analysis.

1. Research should be interdisciplinary, featuring collaborations between the environmental, economic, and social sciences.
2. The target(s) of the behavioral intervention should be selected only after a careful study of the social, economical, and environmental ramifications of the therapeutic goals.
3. The environmental context(s), including social and physical factors, for the target individual(s), behavior(s), and treatment condition(s) should be studied before, during, and after intervention.
4. The evaluation should include assessments of therapeutic impact on people and environments that were not directly targeted by the

intervention but that could have been influenced by the behavioral or environmental changes.

5. Reciprocal relationships between behaviors and environments should be considered; that is, the impact of the target behavior(s) on the relevant environment(s) should be analyzed, as well as vice versa.

6. Treatment interventions should include naturally occurring contingencies in various environmental settings and involve indigenous delivery agents, from family members and peers to relevant others in the community at large.

7. Large-scale, systemwide applications and assessments of behavioral interventions should be attempted with both micro- and macroapproaches to data analysis.

8. Relevant policymakers should be consulted during the definition of target behaviors, the design of intervention techniques, and the planning of diffusion strategies.

9. Long-term intervention and withdrawal phases should be used, during which behavioral and environmental assessments should continue.

10. The design and evaluation of an intervention plan should include the development of communication networks between government, industry, and community sectors in order to ensure large-scale diffusion and implementation of cost-effective interventions.

Adhering to each of the research guidelines discussed would be a formidable undertaking, even given unlimited resources. Some writers (i.e., ecologists) seem to imply that behavioral intervention should not take place without following these ecology-based recommendations (e.g., Willems, 1974, 1977); others have applauded the heuristic value of the ecological perspective but have claimed that satisfying the requirements of this approach would be impossible for the behavior analyst (e.g., Baer, 1977c; Holman, 1977; Krantz, 1977). In fact, Holman (1977) asserted that "it seems economically impractical for behavior modifiers to become thoroughgoing ecologists and theoretically impossible for this field—or any field—to satisfy the ecological perspective" (p. 93). Furthermore, it is noteworthy to consider a critical interdisciplinary distinction— namely, that applied behavior analysis is concerned with intervening to help people with immediate prob-

lems, whereas the prime goal of ecological psychology is understanding through a "nonmanipulative examination of organism–environment interdependencies" (Holman, 1977, p. 69). Thus for the behavior analyst it may indeed be unethical to delay behavioral intervention for a complete ecological description. In other words, the cost of *not* modifying a problem behavior must be considered (Baer, 1974).

11.4.1. Side Effects

Some authors claim that behavior analysts have already adopted ecological orientations; they support their arguments with details of exemplary case studies that have incorporated ecological perspectives into an applied behavior analysis (e.g., Gump, 1977; Risley, 1977; Wahler et al., 1977). Perhaps the most widespread ecological perspective among behavior analysts is the consideration of "side effects" or behavioral reactions to an intervention that were unintended (or not targeted). For example, the first issue of *JABA* included an article by Risley (1968) entitled "The Effects and Side Effects of Punishing the Autistic Behaviors of a Deviant Child," which reported the results of continuous measurements on several nontargeted behaviors while punishment procedures were applied to one target. This research also studied direct and indirect side effects of the punishment intervention in two environments: the laboratory and the home.

Side-effect issues are especially important in community-based efforts to promote environment preservation. They have been emphasized in critical reviews of this research (Cone & Hayes, 1980; Geller et al., 1982) and have been approached in follow-up investigations. For example, the research by Everett and his colleagues on the design of community-based incentive programs to increase bus ridership has been criticized because the investigators did not show evidence that increased use of mass transit reduced vehicle miles traveled in personal cars (Reichel & Geller, 1981), and more recent research approached this issue by obtaining data on both riding the bus and driving personal cars (Katzev & Bachman, 1982). Others have written of the ecological ramifications of increasing bus ridership (Geller, 1982a; Geller et al., 1982; Zerega, 1981). For example, an overall increase in bus usage could cause special management problems, given the typical situation that there are only a few peak usage times per day, and meeting an increased demand at these times can result in an increase in nonproductive bus runs and idle bus drivers during the greatest proportion of the work day.

Additional evidence that potential side effects of behavioral intervention for environment preservation have been a prime concern of behavior analysts is indicated by the critical reviews of this research offered by the editors of *JABA*. For example, the litter control articles by Geller, Brasted, and Mann (1979–1980) and Jason and Figueroa (1980) were rejected from publication in *JABA* primarily because their litter reduction procedures may have been only "place specific," merely displacing litter from one situation to another. The paper recycling study by Luyben and Bailey (1979) was criticized by *JABA* reviewers because the authors' reinforcement contingency that successfully motivated children to collect recyclable newspapers may have resulted in undesirable side effects for adults (e.g., children littering newspapers in homes and stealing newspapers from neighbors). The extra gasoline consumption needed to deliver recyclable newspapers was identified by Geller (1980c, 1981) as a critical undesirable side effect of the effective school-based newspaper recycling programs developed and evaluated by Hamad, Bettinger, Cooper, and Semb (1979) and Hamad, Cooper, and Semb (1977). Furthermore, the research by Geller, Farris, and Post (1973) was criticized by *JABA* reviewers because the intervention of distributing fliers to prompt the purchase of drinks in returnable rather than throwaway containers could have resulted in the undesirable side effect of environmental litter. Indeed, this concern led to a series of studies that evaluated the impact of various stimulus control techniques for decreasing the littering of distributed handbills (Geller, 1973, 1975; Geller et al., 1976, 1977).

Contingency undermining (i.e., meeting contingency requirements in undesirable ways) has been a side effect of some community-based efforts to promote environment preservation. For example, ridesharing was increased with a program that offered commuters with two or more passengers reductions in monthly bridge tolls and the use of a faster priority lane on the San Francisco–Oakland Bay Bridge (MacCalden & Davis, 1972); but this contingency also motivated some drivers to undermine the program by placing mannequins in their cars to give the appearance of extra riders (Rice, 1975). Similarly, when priority lanes for carpoolers were implemented in Fairfax, Virginia, some drivers picked up additional riders at bus stops, thereby decreasing the cost-effectiveness of mass transit (Reichel & Geller, 1981).

Contingency undermining was reported in a recycling study by Geller et al. (1975) that rewarded college students with coupons for individual trips to a collection area with recyclable paper. Specifically, this reward contingency provoked some students to carry a stack of paper to the collection room entrance and then repeatedly deliver individual sheets of paper to the program manager inside the room, thereby receiving a raffle ticket for each delivery. Hence the reward contingency in revisions of this campus recycling program was based on amount of paper delivered (an outcome) rather than the response of making a delivery (Ingram & Geller, 1975; Witmer & Geller, 1976). That is, students were offered a lottery ticket for each pound of newspapers delivered to certain collection rooms. This program revision eliminated the unexpected problem, but a field test of the first version of the program was necessary in order to identify the problematic side effect. In a later campus program to motivate use of a bike path with a raffle contingency, the investigators (Mayer & Geller, 1982–1983) took special care to prevent the possibility of contingency undermining, recalling lessons learned from the earlier recycling program. The point here is that an ecological perspective cannot guarantee the avoidance of intervention mistakes, but it can certainly influence the application of evaluation procedures for identifying undesirable side effects and developing innovations for improving desirable program impact.

Thus attention to behavioral side effects, a critical component of an ecological perspective, is really not atypical in applied behavior analysis, although it is certainly true that more intervention-based research could (and should) consider side-effect issues. Also, the data systems of most behavior analysis research should be continued for much longer durations and be expanded to include observations of more subjects (target and nontarget), more response indices (especially nontarget behaviors), and more environmental settings.

11.4.2. Toward Communitywide Intervention

The application of behavior analysis for solving community-based problems has been termed *behavioral community psychology*. The initial textbooks in this subdiscipline of applied behavior analysis appeared only a few years ago (Glenwick & Jason, 1980; Martin & Osborne, 1980; Nietzel et al., 1977), and in each of these texts significant attention was given to the behavioral studies that targeted environment preservation (i.e., research on litter control, residential energy conservation, resource recovery, and transportation management). In fact, these environment-focused studies were among the first community-based, behavioral applications; most of the other research reported in these texts targeted problems in closed environments (e.g., schools, businesses, prisons, and mental health centers). A majority of these community-based studies were short-term demonstration projects, usually dealing with one environmental setting and a limited number of subjects. Thus the criticisms levied at the small-scale nature of this research and the lack of a true systems approach are justified (e.g., Stern & Gardner, 1981a, 1981b; Stern & Oskamp, Chapter 28, this volume; Willems & McIntire, 1982).

Initial approaches to the design and evaluation of behavior change strategies can be defended on grounds that innovations need to be tested and refined on a small scale (perhaps even in the laboratory) before real world field testing and subsequent large-scale application. However, after successful behavior change strategies are discovered, it is appropriate and desirable to attempt communitywide intervention. We have now reached this stage in the area of behavior modification for environment preservation.

Comprehensive plans have been developed for implementing communitywide behavior change programs for environment preservation (Geller, 1983c; Geller et al., 1982; Johnson & Geller, 1980; KAB, 1977), but constructive behavior-based evaluations of large-scale programs are rare in this area. There are a few exceptions, and these are worth noting, especially because each illustrates a systematic progression from small-scale demonstration experiments to communitywide intervention. For example, Bachman and Katzev (1982) evaluated community-level reward and commitment strategies for promoting bus ridership that were modeled after the earlier smaller-scale research by Everett and his colleagues at Penn State University (e.g., Everett, 1973; Everett et al., 1974); Hake and Zane (1981) tested a community-based gasoline conservation project that was an extension of prior reward-based campus programs designed to motivate reductions in use of personal vehicles (Foxx & Hake, 1977; Hake & Foxx, 1978; Reichel & Geller, 1980); McNees and colleagues (1979) implemented and tested a community litter control system for youth that incorporated many of the litter control strategies that had been demonstrated in a variety of smaller-scale experiments, including a technique for motivating the pickup of small litter items (Hayes et al., 1975; LaHart & Bailey, 1975) and the use of raffle contingencies to motivate the filling of litter bags (e.g., Powers et al., 1973); and Winett and col-

leagues (1982, 1982–1983) have shown how to implement communitywide the communication and feedback strategies for promoting residential energy conservation that developed from the case studies of a few residences (e.g., Hayes & Cone, 1977; Winett et al., 1979).

There are certainly more examples of behavior analysts working their way up from small-scale demonstration projects to community-level intervention, and the list is growing rapidly. A review of behavioral community psychology (Jason & Glenwick, 1983) displayed a remarkable growth in the quantity and quality of research in this subdiscipline, including an impressive expansion of the types of problems targeted. In fact, it is apparent that behavior analysts are much more likely to approach a new problem area and test the effectiveness of behavior change techniques on a small scale than to stick with one problem and work up to large-scale, long-term intervention. Obviously this occurs because of contingencies controlling the researchers (e.g., from environmental resources to professional competencies). The "publish or perish" pressures in academic settings certainly discourage the initiation of large-scale and long-term projects (cf. Holland, 1978); and the current lean reinforcement schedule for grant funding makes it risky to put aside the writing of a research article for the preparation of a grant proposal. Hence it is much easier to recommend an ecological perspective than it is to accomplish the research behaviors implied by such recommendation. It is clear, however, that the burgeoning field of behavioral community psychology is at a stage in its development when procedures and methodologies that successively approximate an ecological perspective are critically needed. This is especially the case for the research domain in behavioral community psychology, which has an impressive history of small-scale successes, that is, applications of behavior analysis for environment preservation.

It is noteworthy that obtaining large-scale adoption of successful interventions requires more than an ecological and systemic research approach. Indeed, Stolz (1981) pointed out that although "one of the defining characteristics of applied research is its focus on socially important problems,... technologies developed by applied behavior analysts have not been widely adopted by government at any level" (p. 491). Stolz described a few rare examples of large-scale adoption of technologies developed through behavioral research and then presented common characteristics of each successful case study as potentially critical variables for the adoption of research findings by policymakers. In particular, the target problems were all consistent with the continuing mission of the adopting agency; the proposed intervention programs were clearly effective, timely, and observable; and policymakers or potential program users were involved in problem identification, research implementation, and program dissemination. Although this was not identified by Stolz, the present discussion implies that the developers, adopters, and users of an innovation should consider an ecological perspective.

11.5. SUMMARY

This chapter introduced the reader to conceptual and methodological perspectives of applied behavior analysis, especially as they relate to the broader field of environmental psychology. Applied behavior analysis emerged from experimental behavior analysis, taking on an identity of its own in order to meet its prime goal—the solution of socially significant problems. One of the first community-based problems targeted by behavior analysts was the preservation of the natural environment, and this represented the point of convergence between applied behavior analysis and environmental psychology. That is, behavior change strategies, founded on principles of operant learning and an antecedent–behavior–consequence conceptualization, were applied to such environment-relevant problems as litter control, resource recovery, transportation management, and energy and water conservation.

The behavior analyst approaches a problem differently than the typical environmental psychologist does, and these differences were reviewed in this chapter. More importantly, however, there are basic commonalities between applied behavior analysis and environmental psychology, and clear advantages to mutual collaboration between these two disciplines. For example, the environmental psychologist could benefit greatly from an adoption of the rigorous evaluation methodologies of applied behavior analysis, while the behavior analyst needs to develop the necessary ecological perspective for producing behavior change that is not only socially valid but also readily noticeable in the community at large. Enough research and writing have been done to justify the existence of specialized approaches to studying human–environment relations; it is time to gather divergent philosophies and competencies together in mutual interdisciplinary efforts so as to attack real world problems in ways that will truly make a difference.

REFERENCES

Altman, I., & Wohlwill, J. (Eds.). (1983). *Human Behavior and Environment Series: Vol. 6. Behavior and the natural environment.* New York: Plenum.

Ayllon, T., & Michael, J. (1959). The psychiatric nurse as a behavioral engineer. *Journal of Experimental Analysis of Behavior, 2,* 323–334.

Azrin, N.H. (1977). A strategy for applied research: Learning based but outcome oriented. *American Psychologist, 32,* 140–149.

Bachman, W., & Katzev, R. (1982). The effects of non-contingent free bus tickets and personal commitment on urban bus ridership. *Transportation Research, 16A,* 103–108.

Bacon-Prue, A., Blount, R., Pickering, D., & Drabman, R. (1980). An evaluation of three litter control procedures—Trash receptacles, paid workers, and the marked item technique. *Journal of Applied Behavior Analysis, 13,* 165–170.

Baer, D.M. (1974). A note on the absence of a Santa Claus in any known ecosystem: A rejoinder to Willems. *Journal of Applied Behavior Analysis, 7,* 167–170.

Baer, D.M. (1977a). Perhaps it would be better not to know everything. *Journal of Applied Behavior Analysis, 10,* 167–172.

Baer, D.M. (1977b). Some comments on the structure of the intersection of ecology and applied behavior analysis. In A. Rogers-Warren & S.F. Warren (Eds.) *Ecological perspectives in behavior analysis.* Baltimore, MD: University Park Press.

Baer, D.M., Wolf, M.M., & Risley, T.R. (1968). Some current dimensions of applied behavior analysis. *Journal of Applied Behavior Analysis, 1,* 91–97.

Baltes, M.M., & Hayward, S.C. (1976). Application and evaluation of strategies to reduce pollution: Behavioral control of littering in a football stadium. *Journal of Applied Psychology, 61,* 501–506.

Bandura, A. (1977). *Social learning theory.* Englewood Cliffs, NJ: Prentice-Hall.

Baum, A., Aiello, J., Altman, I., Stokols, D., Willems, E., & Winkel, G. (1982, August). *Environmental psychology: Past, present, and future.* Symposium presentation at the 90th meeting of the American Psychological Association, Washington, DC.

Baum, A., & Davis, G.E. (1980). Reducing the stress of high density living: An architectural intervention. *Journal of Personality and Social Psychology, 38,* 471–481.

Becker, L.J. (1978). The joint effect of feedback and goal setting on performance: A field study of residential energy conservation. *Journal of Applied Psychology, 63,* 228–233.

Becker, L.J., & Seligman, C. (1978). Reducing air-conditioning waste by signalling it is cool outside. *Personality and Social Psychology Bulletin, 4,* 412–415.

Bell, P.A., Fisher, J.D., & Loomis, R.J. (1978). *Environmental psychology.* Philadelphia: Saunders.

Birkimer, J.C., & Brown, J.H. (1979a). A graphical judgmental aid which summarizes obtained and chance reliability data and helps across the believability of experimental effects. *Journal of Applied Behavior Analysis, 12,* 523–533.

Birkimer, J.D., & Brown, J.H. (1979b). Back to basics: Percentage agreement measures are adequate, but there are easier ways. *Journal of Applied Behavior Analysis, 12,* 535–543.

Blakely, E.Q., Lloyd, K.E., & Alferink, L.A. (1977). *The effects of feedback on residential electrical peaking and hourly kilowatt consumption.* Unpublished manuscript, Drake University, Des Moines, IA: Department of Psychology.

Brehm, J.W. (1966). *A theory of psychological reactance.* New York: Academic.

Brehm, J.W. (1972). *Responses to loss of freedom: A theory of psychological reactance.* New York: General Learning Press.

Brownell, K.D. (1981). Communication with the author.

Burgess, R.L., Clark, R.N., & Hendee, J.C. (1971). An experimental analysis of anti-littering procedures. *Journal of Applied Behavior Analysis, 4,* 71–75.

Chapman, C., & Risley, T.R. (1974). Anti-litter procedures in an urban high-density area. *Journal of Applied Behavior Analysis, 7,* 377–384.

Chassan, J.B. (1967). *Research design in clinical psychology and psychiatry.* New York: Appleton-Century-Crofts.

Clark, R.N., Burgess, R.L., & Hendee, J.C. (1972). The development of anti-litter behavior in a forest campground. *Journal of Applied Behavior Analysis, 5,* 1–5.

Committee on Environmental Improvement. (1978). *Cleaning our environment: A chemical perspective (2nd ed.).* Washington, DC: American Chemical Society.

Cone, J.D., & Hayes, S.C. (1976, September). *Environmental psychology: Conceptual and methodological issues.* Paper presented at the American Psychological Association Meeting, Washington, DC.

Cone, J.D., & Hayes, S.C. (1977). Applied behavior analysis and the solution of environmental problems. In J.F. Wohlwill & I. Altman (Eds.), *Human behavior and environment: Vol. 2, Advances in theory and research.* New York: Plenum.

Cone, J.D., & Hayes, S.C. (1980). *Environmental problems/Behavioral solutions.* Monterey, CA: Brooks/Cole.

Cook, S.W., & Berrenberg, J.L. (1981). Approaches to encouraging conservation behavior: A review and conceptual framework. *Journal of Social Issues, 37,* 73–107.

Cope, J.G., & Geller, E.S. (1984). Community-based intervention to increase the use of automobile litter bags. *Journal of Resource Management and Technology, 13,* 127–132.

Couch, J.V., Garber, T., & Karpus, L. (1979). Response maintenance and paper recycling. *Journal of Environmental Systems, 8,* 127–137.

Craik, K.H. (1970). Environmental psychology. In K.H. Craik, B. Kleinmutz, R.L. Rosnow, R. Rosenthal, J.A. Cheyne, & R.H. Walters (Eds.), *New directions in psychology* (Vol. 4). New York: Holt, Rinehart & Winston.

Craik, K.H. (1976). The personality research paradigm in environmental psychology. In S. Wapner, S.B. Cohen, & B. Kaplan (Eds.), *Experiencing the environment.* New York: Plenum.

Darley, J.M. (1978). Energy conservation techniques as innovations, and their diffusion. *Energy and Buildings, 1,* 339–343.

Darley, J.M., & Beniger, J.R. (1981). Diffusion of energy-conserving innovations. *Journal of Social Issues, 37,* 150–171.

Davison, G.C., & Stuart, R.B. (1975). Behavior therapy and civil liberties. *American Psychologist, 30,* 755–763.

Delprata, D.J. (1977). Prompting electrical energy conservation in commercial users. *Environment and Behavior, 9,* 433–440.

DeProspero, A., & Cohen, S. (1979). Inconsistent visual analysis of intrasubject data. *Journal of Applied Behavior Analysis, 12,* 573–579.

Deslauriers, B.C., & Everett, P.B. (1977). Effects of intermittent and continuous token reinforcement on bus ridership. *Journal of Applied Psychology, 62,* 369–375.

Edney, J.J. (1981). Paradoxes on the commons: Scarcity and the problems of equality. *Journal of Community Psychology, 9,* 3–34.

Everett, P.B. (1973). The use of the reinforcement procedure to increase bus ridership [Summary]. *Proceedings of the 81st Annual Convention of the American Psychological Association, 8*(2), 891–892.

Everett, P.B. (1980). A behavioral approach to transportation systems management. In D. Glenwick & L. Jason (Eds.), *Behavioral community psychology: Progress and prospects.* New York: Praeger.

Everett, P.B. (1982). Reinforcement theory strategies for modifying transit ridership. In I. Altman, J. Wohlwill, & P.B. Everett (Eds.), *Human behavior and the environment.* New York: Plenum.

Everett, P.B., Deslauriers, B.C., Newson, T., & Anderson, V.B. (1978). The differential effect of two free ride dissemination procedures on bus ridership. *Transportation Research, 12,* 1–6.

Everett, P.B., Hayward, S.C›, & Meyers, A.W. (1974). Effects of a token reinforcement procedure on bus ridership. *Journal of Applied Behavior Analysis, 7,* 1–9.

Everett, P.B., & Watson, B.G. (1987). Psychological contributions to transportation. In D. Stokols & I. Altman (Eds.), *Handbook of environmental psychology.* New York: Wiley.

Fawcett, J. (1969). *Psychology and population.* New York: Population Council.

Fawcett, S.B., & Miller, L.K. (1975). Training public-speaking behavior: An experimental analysis and social validation. *Journal of Applied Behavior Analysis, 8,* 125–136.

Festinger, L. (1957). *A theory of cognitive dissonance.* Evanston, IL: Row, Peterson.

Finnie, W.C. (1973). Field experiments in litter control. *Environment and Behavior, 5,* 123–144.

Foxx, R.M., & Azrin, N.A. (1972). Restitution: A method of eliminating aggressive-disruptive behavior of retarded and brain damaged patients. *Behaviour Research and Therapy, 10,* 15–27.

Foxx, R.M., & Hake, D.F. (1977). Gasoline conservation: A procedure for measuring and reducing the driving of college students. *Journal of Applied Behavior Analysis, 10,* 61–74.

Frederiksen, L.W. (1978). Behavioral reorganization of a professional service system. *Journal of Organizational Behavior Management, 2,* 1–9.

Frounfelker, R.E., & Belencan, H.L. (1981, November). *1981 Ohio statewide litter study: Executive summary.* Xenia, OH: Systech Corporation.

Fusco, R.A., Jula, R.J., & Musser, W.R. (1982). An approach to making hazardous waste economical. *1982 Hazardous Material Spills Conference Proceedings.* Washington, DC, 475–481.

Geller, E.S. (1973). Prompting anti-litter behaviors [Summary]. *Proceedings of the 81st Annual Convention of the American Psychological Association, 8,* 901–902.

Geller, E.S. (1975). Increasing desired waste disposals with instructions. *Man-Environment Systems, 5,* 125–128.

Geller, E.S. (1980a). Applications of behavioral analysis for litter control. In D. Glenwick & L. Jason (Eds.), *Behavioral community psychology: Progress and prospects.* New York: Praeger.

Geller, E.S. (1980b). Saving environmental resources through waste reduction and recycling: How the behavioral community psychologist can help. In G.L. Martin & J.G. Osborne (Eds.), *Helping in the community: Behavioral applications.* New York: Plenum.

Geller, E.S. (1981a). Evaluating energy conservation programs: Is verbal report enough? *Journal of Consumer Research, 8,* 331–334.

Geller, E.S. (1981b). Waste reduction and resource recovery: Strategies for energy conservation. In A. Baum & J.E. Singer (Eds.), *Advances in environmental psychology: Vol. 3. Energy conservation: Psychological perspectives.* Hillsdale, NJ: Erlbaum.

Geller, E.S. (1982a, February). *Applications of behavioral science to promote energy efficient travel: Reflections, directions, and speculations* (Tech. Rep. for Contract S3261-137). Road and Motor Vehicle Traffic Safety Branch, Transport Canada, Ottawa, Ontario, Canada.

Geller, E.S. (1982b). *Corporate incentives for promoting safety belt use: Rationale, guidelines, and examples.* Washington, DC: U.S. Department of Transportation.

Geller, E.S. (1983a). *Development of industry-based strategies for motivating seat belt usage* (Final Rep. for Contract DTRS5681-C-0032). Washington, DC: U.S. Department of Transportation.

Geller, E.S. (1983b). Rewarding safety belt usage at an industrial setting: Tests of treatment generality and response maintenance. *Journal of Applied Behavior Analysis, 16,* 43–56.

Geller, E.S. (1983c). The energy crisis and behavioral science: A conceptual framework for large-scale intervention. In A.W. Childs & G.B. Melton (Eds.), *Rural psychology.* New York: Plenum.

Geller, E.S., Brasted, W., & Mann, M. (1979–80). Waste receptacle designs as interventions for litter control. *Journal of Environmental Systems, 9,* 145–160.

Geller, E.S., Chaffee, J.L., & Ingram, R.E. (1975). Promoting paper-recycling on a university campus. *Journal of Environmental Systems, 5,* 39–57.

Geller, E.S., Erickson, J.B., & Buttram, B.A. (1983). Attempts to promote residential water conservation with educational, behavioral, and engineering strategies. *Population and Environment: Behavior and Social Issues, 6,* 96–112.

Geller, E.S., Farris, J.C., & Post, D.S. (1973). Prompting a consumer behavior for consumer control. *Journal of Applied Behavior Analysis, 6,* 367–376.

Geller, E.S., Johnson, D.F., Hamlin, P.H., & Kennedy, T.D. (1977). Behavior modification in a prison: Issues, problems, and compromises. *Criminal Justice and Behavior, 4,* 11–43.

Geller, E.S., Koltuniak, T.A., & Shilling, J.S. (1983). Response avoidance prompting: A cost-effective strategy for theft deterrence. *Behavioral Counseling and Community Interventions, 3,* 28–42.

Geller, E.S., & Winett, R.A. (1984). Reaction to Willems and McIntire's review of "Preserving the environment: New strategies for behavior change." *The Behavior Analyst, 7,* 71–72.

Geller, E.S., Winett, R.A., & Everett, P.B. (1982). *Preserving the environment: New strategies for behavior change.* Elmsford, NY: Pergamon.

Geller, E.S., Witmer, J.F., & Orebaugh, A.L. (1976). Instructions as a determinant of paper-disposal behaviors. *Environment and Behavior, 8,* 417–438.

Geller, E.S., Witmer, J.F., & Tuso, M.E. (1977). Environmental interventions for litter control. *Journal of Applied Psychology, 62,* 344–351.

Geller, E.S., Wylie, R.C., & Farris, J.C. (1971). An attempt at applying prompting and reinforcement toward pollution control [Summary]. *Proceedings of the 79th Annual Convention of the American Psychological Association, 6,* 701–702.

Glenwick, D., & Jason, L. (Eds.). (1980). *Behavioral community psychology: Progress and prospects.* New York: Praeger.

Goldiamond, I. (1974). Toward a constructional approach to social problems: Ethical and constitutional issues raised by applied behavior analysis. *Behaviorism, 2,* 1–85.

Gump, P.V. (1977). Ecological psychologists: Critics or contributors to behavior analysis. In A. Rogers-Warren & S.F. Warren (Eds.), *Ecological perspectives in behavior analysis.* Baltimore, MD: University Park Press.

Hake, D.F. (1981). Behavioral ecology: A social systems approach to environmental problems. In L. Michelson, M. Hersen, & S. Turner (Eds.), *Future perspectives in behavior therapy.* New York: Plenum.

Hake, D.F., & Foxx, R.M. (1978). Promoting gasoline conservation: The effects of reinforcement schedules, a leader and self-recording. *Behavior Modification, 2,* 339–369.

Hake, D.F., & Zane, T. (1981). A community-based gasoline conservation project: Practical and methodological considerations. *Behavior Modification, 5,* 435–458.

Hamad, C.D., Bettinger, R., Cooper, D., & Semb, G. (1979). *Using behavioral procedures to establish an elementary school paper recycling program.* Unpublished manuscript, University of Kansas, Department of Psychology, Lawrence, KS.

Hamad, C.D., Cooper, C., & Semb, G. (1977). *Resource recovery: The use of a group contingency to increase paper recycling in an elementary school.* Unpublished manuscript, University of Kansas, Department of Psychology, Lawrence, KS.

Hawkins, R.P., & Fabry, B.D. (1979). Applied behavior analysis and interobserver reliability: A commentary on two articles by Birkimer and Brown. *Journal of Applied Behavior Analysis, 12,* 545–552.

Hayes, S.C., & Cone, J.D. (1977). Reducing residential electrical use: Payments, information, and feedback. *Journal of Applied Behavior Analysis, 14,* 81–88.

Hayes, S.C., Johnson, V.S., & Cone, J.D. (1975). The marked item technique: A practical procedure for litter control. *Journal of Applied Behavior Analysis, 8,* 381–386.

Hersen, M., & Barlow, D.H. (1976). *Single case experimental designs: Strategies for studying behavior change.* New York: Pergamon.

Holahan, C.J. (1982). *Environmental psychology.* New York: Random House.

Holahan, C.J., & Saegert, S. (1973). Behavioral and attitudinal effects of large-scale variation in the physical environment of psychiatric wards. *Journal of Abnormal Psychology, 82,* 454–462.

Holland, J. (1978). Behaviorism: Part of the problem or part of the solution. *Journal of Applied Behavior Analysis, 11,* 163–174.

Holman, J. (1977). The moral risk and high cost of ecological concern in applied behavior analysis. In A. Rogers-Warren & S.F. Warren (Eds.), *Ecological perspectives in behavior analysis.* Baltimore, MD: University Park Press.

Homme, L., Baca, P., Cottingham, L., & Homme, A. (1968). What behavioral engineering is. *Psychological Record, 18,* 425–434.

Hopkins, B.L., & Hermann, J.A. (1977). Evaluating interobserver reliability of interval data. *Journal of Applied Behavior Analysis, 10,* 121–126.

Ingram, R.E., & Geller, E.S. (1975). A community-integrated, behavior modification approach to facilitating paper recycling (Manuscript No. 1097). *Journal Supplement Abstract Service Catalog of Selected Documents in Psychology, 5,* 327.

Ittelson, W.H., Proshansky, H.M., Rivlin, L.G., & Winkel, G. (1974). *An introduction to environmental psychology.* New York: Holt, Rinehart & Winston.

Jacobs, H.E., & Bailey, J (1982–83). Evaluating participation in a residential recycling program. *Journal of Environmental Systems, 12,* 141–152.

Jason, L.A., & Figueroa, Y. (1980, May). *Fences as a stimulus control strategy: Reducing dog litter in an urban area.* Paper presented at the meeting of the Association for Behavior Analysis, Dearborn, MI.

Jason, L.A., & Glenwick, D.S. (1983). Behavioral community psychology: A review of recent research and applications. In M. Hersen, R.M. Eisler, & P.M. Miller (Eds.), *Progress in behavior modification* (Vol. 17). New York: Academic.

Johnson, R.P., & Geller, E.S. (1980). Engineering technology and behavior analysis for interdisciplinary environmental protection. *Behavior Analyst, 3,* 23–29.

Johnson, S.M., Christensen, A., & Bellamy, G.T. (1976). Evaluation of family intervention through unobtrusive audio recordings: Experiences in "bugging" children. *Journal of Applied Behavior Analysis, 9,* 213–219.

Jones, M.C. (1924). The elimination of children's fears. *Journal of Experimental Psychology, 7,* 383–390.

Jones, R.R., Weinrott, M.R., & Vaught, R.S. (1978). Effects of serial dependency on the agreement between visual and statistical inferences. *Journal of Applied Behavior Analysis, 11,* 277–284.

Katzev, R., & Bachman, W. (1982). Effects of deferred payment and fare manipulations on urban bus ridership. *Journal of Applied Psychology, 67,* 83–88.

Kazdin, A.E. (1975a). *Behavior modification in applied settings.* Homewood, IL: Dorsey.

Kazdin, A.E. (1975b). Characteristics and trends in applied behavior analysis. *Journal of Applied Behavior Analysis, 8,* 332.

Kazdin, A.E. (1976). Statistical analysis for single case experimental designs. In M. Hersen & D.H. Barlow (Eds.), *Single case experimental designs: Strategies for studying behavior change.* New York: Pergamon.

Kazdin, A.E. (1979). Unobtrusive measures in behavioral assessment. *Journal of Applied Behavior Analysis, 12,* 713–724.

Keep America Beautiful, Inc. (1977). *Clean community system: Photometric index instructions.* Available from author, 99 Park Avenue, New York, NY 10016.

Kent, R.N., & Foster, S.L. (1977). Direct observational procedures: Methodological issues in naturalistic settings. In A.R. Ciminero, K.S. Calhoun, & H.E. Adams (Eds.), *Handbook of behavioral assessment.* New York: Wiley.

Kent, R.N., O'Leary, K.D., Diament, C., & Dietz, A. (1974). Expectation biases in observational evaluation of therapeutic change. *Journal of Consulting and Clinical Psychology, 42,* 774–780.

Kent, R.N., & O'Leary, K.D. (1976). A controlled evaluation of behavior modification with conduct problem children. *Journal of Consulting and Clinical Psychology, 44,* 586–596.

Kiesler, D.J. (1971). Experimental designs in psychotherapy research. In A.E. Bergin & S.L. Garfield (Eds.), *Handbook of psychotherapy and behavior change: An empirical analysis.* New York: Wiley.

Knight, R.C., Zimring, C.M., Weitzer, W.H., & Wheeler, H.C. (1978). Effects of the living environment on the mentally retarded. In A. Friedman, C. Zimring, & E. Zube (Eds.), *Environmental design evaluation.* New York: Plenum.

Kohlenberg, R.J., & Phillips, T. (1973). Reinforcement and rate of litter depositing. *Journal of Applied Behavior Analysis, 6,* 391–396.

Kohlenberg, R.J., Phillips, T., & Proctor, W. (1976). A behavioral analysis of parking in residential electricity energy consumption. *Journal of Applied Behavior Analysis, 9,* 13–18.

Krantz, D. (1977). Overview: On weddings. In A. Rogers-Warren & S.F. Warren (Eds.), *Ecological perspectives in behavior analysis.* Baltimore, MD: University Park Press.

Krauss, R.M., Freedman, J.L., & Whitcup, M. (1978). Field and laboratory studies of littering. *Journal of Experimental Social Psychology, 14,* 109–122.

LaHart, D., & Bailey, J.S. (1975). Reducing children's littering on a nature trail. *Journal of Environmental Education, 7,* 37–45.

Lauridsen, P.K. (1977, May). *Decreasing gasoline consumption in fleet-owned automobiles through feedback and feedback-plus-lottery.* Unpublished master's thesis, Drake University, Des Moines, IA.

Lazarus, A.A. (1971). *Behavior therapy and beyond.* New York: McGraw-Hill.

Lovett, S.B., Bosmajian, C.P., Frederiksen, L.W., & Elder, J.P. (1983). Monitoring professional service delivery: An organizational level intervention. *Behavior Therapy, 14,* 170–177.

Luyben, P.D., & Bailey, J.S. (1979). Newspaper recycling: The effects of rewards and proximity of containers. *Environment and Behavior, 11,* 539–557.

Luyben, P.D., Warren, S.B., & Tallman, T.A. (1980). Recycling beverage containers on a college campus. *Journal of Environmental Systems, 9,* 189–202.

MacCalden, M., & Davis, C. (1972). *Report on priority lane experiment on the San Francisco-Oakland Bay Bridge.* San Francisco, CA: Department of Public Works.

Mahoney, M.J. (1974). *Cognition and behavior modification.* Cambridge, MA: Ballinger.

Martin, G.L., & Osborne, J.G. (Eds.). (1980). *Helping the community: Behavioral applications.* New York: Plenum.

Martin. R. (1974). *Behavior modification: Human rights and legal responsibilities.* Champaign, IL: Research Press.

Mayer, J.A., & Geller, E.S. (1982–83). Motivating energy efficient travel: A community-based intervention for encouraging biking. *Journal of Environmental Systems, 12,* 99–112.

McClelland, L., & Cook, S.W. (1980). Energy conservation effects of continuous in-home feedback in all-electric homes. *Journal of Environmental Systems, 9,* 169–173.

McNees, M.P., Schnelle, J.F., Gendrich, J., Thomas, M.M., & Beagle, G.P. (1979). McDonald's litter hunt: A community litter control system for youth. *Environment and Behavior, 11,* 131–138.

Meichenbaum, D. (1974). *Cognitive behavior modification.* Morristown, NJ: General Learning Press.

Mercatoris, M., & Craighead, W.E. (1974). Effects of nonparticipant observation on teacher and pupil classroom behavior. *Journal of Educational Psychology, 66,* 512–519.

Minkin, N., Braukmann, C.J., Minkin, B.L., Timbers, G.D., Timbers, B.J., Fixsen, D.L., Phillips, E.L., & Wolf, M.M. (1976). The social validation and training of conversation skills. *Journal of Applied Behavior Analysis, 9,* 127–140.

Nielson, J.M., & Ellington, B.L. (1983). Social processes and resource conversation: A case study in low technology recycling. In N.R. Feimer & E.S. Geller (Eds.), *Environmental psychology: Directions and perspectives.* New York: Plenum.

Nietzel, M.T., Winett, R.A., MacDonald, M.L., & Davidson, W.S. (1977). *Behavioral approaches to community psychology.* New York: Pergamon.

Ollendick, T.H., Elliott, W., & Matson, J.L. (1980). Locus of control as related to effectiveness in a behavior modification program for juvenile delinquents. *Journal of Behavior Therapy and Experimental Psychiatry, 11,* 259–262.

Ollendick, T.H., & Murphy, M.S. (1977). Differential effectiveness of muscular and cognitive relaxation as a function of locus of control. *Journal of Behavior Therapy and Experimental Psychiatry, 8,* 223–228.

O'Neill, G.W., Blanck, L.S., & Joyner, M.A. (1980). The use of stimulus control over littering in a natural setting. *Journal of Applied Behavior Analysis, 13,* 379–381.

Orne, M.T. (1962). On the social psychology of the psychological experiment: With particular reference to demand characteristics and their implications. *American Psychologist, 17,* 776–783.

Osborne, J.G., & Powers, R.B. (1980). Controlling the litter problems. In G.L. Martin & J.G. Osborne (Eds.), *Helping in the community: Behavioral applications.* New York: Plenum.

Palmer, M.H., Lloyd, M.E., & Lloyd, K.E. (1978). An experimental analysis of electricity conservation procedures. *Journal of Applied Behavior Analysis, 10,* 665–672.

Pavlov, I.P. (1928). *Lectures on conditional reflexes* (W.H. Gantt, Trans.). New York: International.

Pomeranz, D. (1980). Environmental psychology. In L. Krasner (Ed.), *Environmental design and human behavior: A psychology of the individual in society.* Elmsford, NY: Pergamon.

Powers, R.B., Osborne, J.G., & Anderson, E.G. (1973). Positive reinforcement of litter removal in the natural environment. *Journal of Applied Behavior Analysis, 6,* 579–586.

Price, D.L., & Schmidt, J.W. (1979, May). Voluntary compliance: Effective prevention in hazardous materials transportation. *Professional Safety,* pp. 18–21.

Proshansky, H.M. (1976). Environmental psychology and the real world. *American Psychologist, 31,* 303–310.

Proshansky, H.M. (1983). Prospects and dilemmas of environmental psychology. In N.R. Feimer & E.S. Geller (Eds.), *Environmental psychology: Directions and perspectives.* New York: Plenum.

Proshansky, H.M., Ittelson, W.H., & Rivlin, L.G. (Eds.). (1976). *Environmental psychology: People and their physical settings* (2nd ed.). New York: Holt, Rinehart & Winston.

Reich, J.W., & Robertson, J.L. (1979). Reactance and norm appeal in antilittering messages. *Journal of Applied Social Psychology, 9,* 91–101.

Reichel, D.A., & Geller, E.S. (1980, March). *Group versus individual contingencies to conserve transportation energy.* Paper presented at the 26th annual meeting of the Southeastern Psychological Association, Washington, DC.

Reichel, D.A., & Geller, E.S. (1981). Attempts to modify transportation behavior for energy conservation: A critical review. In A. Baum & J.E. Singer (Eds.), *Advances in environmental psychology: Vol. 3. Energy conservation: Psychological perspectives.* Hillsdale, NJ: Erlbaum.

Reid, D.H., Luyben, P.D., Rawers, R.J., & Bailey, J.S. (1979). The effects of containers on newspapers recycling behavior. *Environment and Behavior, 8,* 471–483.

Rice, B. (1975). Fighting inflation with buttons and slogans. *Psychology Today, 7,* 49–52.

Rice, R.E., & Paisley, W.J. (Eds.). (1981). *Public communication campaigns.* Beverly Hills, CA: Sage.

Rimm, D.C., & Masters, J.C. (1974). *Behavior therapy: Techniques and empirical findings.* New York: Academic.

Risley, T.R. (1968). The effects and side effects of punishing the autistic behaviors of a deviant child. *Journal of Applied Behavior Analysis, 1,* 21–34.

Risley, T.R. (1977). The ecology of applied behavior analysis. In A. Rogers-Warren & S.F. Warren (Eds.) *Ecological perspectives in behavior analysis.* Baltimore, MD: University Park Press.

Rogers, E.M., & Kincaid, D.L. (1981). *Communication networks: A new paradigm for research.* New York: Free Press.

Rogers, E.M., & Shoemaker, F.F. (1971). *Communication of innovations.* New York: Free Press.

Rogers-Warren, A., & Warren, S.F. (Eds.). (1977a). *Ecological perspectives in behavior analysis.* Baltimore, MD: University Park Press.

Rogers-Warren, A., & Warren, S.F. (1977b). The developing ecobehavioral psychology. In A. Rogers-Warren & S.F. Warren (Eds.), *Ecological perspectives in behavior analysis.* Baltimore, MD: University Park Press.

Romanczyk, R.G., Kent, R.N., Diament, C., & O'Leary, K.D. (1973). Measuring the reliability of observational data: A reactive process. *Journal of Applied Behavior Analysis, 6,* 175–184.

Rosenberg, L.J. (1977). *Marketing.* Englewood Cliffs, NJ: Prentice-Hall.

Rosenthal, R. (1966). *Experimenter effects in behavioral research.* New York: Appleton-Century-Crofts.

Rothstein, R.N. (1980). Television feedback used to modify gasoline consumption. *Behavior Therapy, 11,* 683–688.

Runnion, A., Watson, J.D., & McWhorter, J. (1978). Energy savings in interstate transportation through feedback and reinforcement. *Journal of Organizational Behavior Management, 1,* 180–191.

Sage, W. (1974, September). Crime and the clockwork lemon. *Human Behavior,* pp. 16–25.

Samtur, H. (1979). *Litter control strategies: An analysis of litter, littering behavior, and litter control programs* (Tech. Rep.). U.S. Environmental Protection Agency, Office of Solid Waste Management Programs, Washington, DC.

Schnelle, J.G., Gendrich, J.G., Beagle, G.P., Thomas, M.M., & McNees, M.P. (1980). Mass media techniques for prompting behavior change in the community. *Environment and Behavior, 12,* 157–166.

Schwitzgebel, R.K. (1975). A contractual model for the protection of the rights of institutionalized mental patients. *American Psychologist, 30,* 815–820.

Seaver, W.B., & Patterson, A.H. (1976). Decreasing fuel oil consumption through feedback and social commendation. *Journal of Applied Behavior Analysis, 9,* 147–152.

Seligman, C., & Darley, J.M. (1977). Feedback as a means of decreasing residential energy consumption. *Journal of Applied Psychology, 62,* 363–368.

Shippee, G. (1981, March). Energy conservation and the role of the social services. *Energy Policy,* pp. 32–38.

Sidman, M. (1960). *Tactics of scientific research: Evaluating experimental data in psychology.* New York: Basic Books.

Skinner, B.F. (1938). *The behavior of organisms.* New York: Appleton-Century-Crofts.

Skinner, B.F. (1953). *Science and human behavior.* New York: Macmillan.

Skinner, B.F. (1958). *Science of human behavior.* New York: Macmillan.

Skinner, B.F. (1966). What is the experimental analysis of behavior? *Journal of Experimental Analysis of Behavior, 9,* 213–218.

Skinner, B.F. (1971). *Beyond freedom and dignity.* New York: Knopf.

Slavin, R.E., & Wodarski, J.S. (1977). *Using group contingencies to reduce natural gas consumption in master-metered apartments* (Tech. Rep. No. 232). Baltimore, MD: Johns Hopkins University, Center for Social Organization of Schools.

Slavin, R.E., Wodarski, J.S., & Blackburn, B.L. (1981). A group contingency for electricity conservation in master-metered apartments. *Journal of Applied Behavior Analysis, 14,* 357–363.

Stern, P.C., & Gardner, G.T. (1981a). Psychological research and energy policy. *American Psychologist, 36,* 329–342.

Stern, P.C., & Gardner, G.T. (1981b). The place of behavior change in the management of environmental problems. *Journal of Environmental Policy, 2,* 213–239.

Stern, P., & Oskamp, S. (1987). Managing scarce environmental resources. In D. Stokols & I. Altman (Eds.), *Handbook of environmental psychology.* New York: Wiley.

Stokols, D. (1978). Environmental psychology. *Annual Review of Psychology, 28,* 253–295.

Stokols, D. (1982). Environmental psychology: A coming of age. In A.G. Kraut (Ed.), *The G. Stanley Hall lecture series* (Vol. 2). Washington, DC: American Psychological Association.

Stokols, D., Altman, I., Bechtel, R.B., Gutman, R., Howell, S., Moore, G.T., & Zeisel, J. (1982, April). *Study on environmental design research directions for the 1980's: A panel discussion.* Symposium presentation at the 13th annual meeting of the Environmental Design Research Association, College Park, MD.

Stolz, S.B. (1981). Adoption of innovations from applied behavioral research: "Does anybody care?" *Journal of Applied Behavior Analysis, 14,* 491–505.

Surratt, P.R., Ulrich, R.E., & Hawkins, R.P. (1969). An elementary student as a behavioral engineer. *Journal of Applied Behavior Analysis, 2,* 85–92.

Syrek, D.B. (1975). *California litter—A comprehensive analysis and plan for abatement.* (Tech. Rep. prepared for the California State Assembly Committee on Resources and Land Use.) Sacramento, CA: Institute for Applied Research.

Syrek, D.B. (1977a). *Litter reduction effectiveness: Vol. 1. The clean community system in Tampa, Macon, and Charlotte* (Tech. Rep.). Sacramento, CA: Institute for Applied Research.

Syrek, D.B. (1977b). *Litter reduction effectiveness: Vol. 2. Washington's litter control program and Oregon's container deposit legislation* (Tech. Rep.). Sacramento, CA: Institute for Applied Research.

Underwood, B.J. (1957). *Psychological research.* New York: Appleton-Century-Crofts.

Van Houten, R. (1979). Social validation: The evolution of standards of competency for target behaviors. *Journal of Applied Behavior Analysis, 12,* 581–591.

Wahler, R.G., Berland, R.M., Coe, T.D., & Leske, G. (1977). Social systems analysis: Implementing an alternative behavioral model. In A. Rogers-Warren & S.F. Warren (Eds.), *Ecological perspectives in behavior analysis.* Baltimore, MD: University Park Press.

Walker, J.M. (1979). Energy demand behavior in a master-meter apartment complex: An experimental analysis. *Journal of Applied Psychology, 64,* 190–196.

Wandersman, A., Andrews, A., Riddle, D., & Fancett, C. (1983). Environmental psychology and prevention. In R. Felner, S. Farber, L. Jason, & J. Moritsugu (Eds.), *Prevention psychology: Theory, research and practice.* New York: Pergamon.

Wandersman, A., & Florin, P. (1981). A cognitive social learning approach to the crossroads of cognition, social behavior and the environment. In J. Harvey (Ed.), *Cognitive social behavior and the environment.* Hillsdale, NJ: Erlbaum.

Watson, J.B., & Rayner, R. (1920). Conditioned emotional reactions. *Journal of Experimental Psychology, 3,* 1–14.

Weigel, R.H. (1983). Environmental attitudes and the prediction of behavior. In N.R. Feimer & E.S. Geller (Eds.), *Environmental psychology: Directions and perspectives.* New York: Plenum.

Weinstein, N.D. (1978). Individual differences in reactions to noise: A longitudinal study in a college dormitory. *Journal of Applied Psychology, 63,* 458–466.

White, G.D. (1977). The effects of observer presence on the activity level of families. *Journal of Applied Behavior Analysis, 10,* 734.

White, O.R. (1971). *Pragmatic approaches to progress in the single case*. Doctoral dissertation, University of Oregon, Eugene, OR (University Microfilms, 72-8618, Ann Arbor, MI).

Willems, E.P. (1965). An ecological orientation in psychology. *Merrill-Palmer Quarterly, 11*, 317–343.

Willems, E.P. (1974). Behavioral technology and behavioral ecology. *Journal of Applied Behavior Analysis, 7*, 151–165.

Willems, E.P. (1977). Steps toward an ecobehavioral technology. In A. Rogers-Warren & S.F. Warren (Eds.), *Ecological perspectives in behavior analysis*. Baltimore, MD: University Park Press.

Willems, E.P., & McIntire, J.D. (1983). A review of "Preserving the environment: New strategies for behavior change," *Behavior Analyst, 5*, 191–197.

Winett, R.A. (1983). Cognitive perspectives: Dangers of neglecting the context. *Behavioral Counselling and Community Interventions, 3*, 7–11.

Winett, R.A. (1978). Prompting turning-out lights in unoccupied rooms. *Journal of Environmental Systems, 6*, 237–241.

Winett, R.A., Hatcher, J.W., Fort, T.R., Leckliter, I.N., Love, S.Q., Riley, A.W., & Fishback, J.F. (1982). The effects of videotape modeling and daily feedback on residential electricity conservation, home temperature and humidity, perceived comfort, and clothing worn: Winter and summer. *Journal of Applied Behavior Analysis, 15*, 381–402.

Winett, R.A., Kaiser, S., & Haberkorn, E. (1977). The effects of monetary rebates and daily feedback on electricity conservation. *Journal of Environmental Systems, 5*, 327–338.

Winett, R.A., Love, S.Q., & Kidd, C. (1982–1983). The effectiveness of an energy specialist and extension agents in promoting summer energy conservation by home visits. *Journal of Environmental Systems, 12*, 61–70.

Winett, R.A., Neale, M., & Grier, H.C. (1979). The effects of self-monitoring and feedback on residential electricity consumption. *Journal of Applied Behavior Analysis, 12*, 173–184.

Winett, R.A., & Nietzel, M. (1975). Behavioral ecology: Contingency management of residential use. *American Journal of Community Psychology, 3*, 123–133.

Winkler, R.C. (1982). Water conservation. In E.S. Geller, R.A. Winett, & P.B. Everett, *Preserving the environment: New strategies for behavior change*. Elmsford, NY: Pergamon.

Winkler, R.C., & Winett, R.A. (1982). Behavioral interventions in resource conservation: A systems approach based on behavioral economics. *American Psychologist, 37*, 421–435.

Witmer, J.F., & Geller, E.S. (1976). Facilitating paper recycling: Effects of prompts, raffles, and contests. *Journal of Applied Behavior Analysis, 9*, 315–322.

Wodarski, J.S. (1976). The reduction of electrical energy consumption: The application of behavior analysis. *Behavior Therapy, 8*, 347–353.

Wohlwill, J.F. (1970). The emerging discipline of environmental psychology. *American Psychologist, 25*, 303–312.

Wohlwill, J., & Kohn, I. (1973). The environments experienced by the migrant: An adaptation-level view. *Representative Research in Social Psychology, 4*, 131–164.

Wolf, M.M. (1978). Social validity: The cure for subjective measurement or how applied behavior analysis is finding its heart. *Journal of Applied Behavior Analysis, 11*, 203–214.

Yeaton, W.H. (1982). A critique of the effectiveness of applied behavior analysis research. *Advances in Behavior Research Theory, 4*, 75–96.

Yelton, A.R., Wildman, B.G., & Erickson, M.T. (1977). A probability-based formula for calculating observer agreement. *Journal of Applied Behavior Analysis, 10*, 127–131.

Zerega, A.M. (1981). Transportation energy conservation policy: Implications for social science research. *Journal of Social Issues, 37*, 31–50.

Zifferblatt, S.M., & Hendricks, C.G. (1974). Applied behavioral analysis of societal problems: Population change, a case in point. *American Psychologist, 29*, 750–761.

Chapter 12

HUMAN SPATIAL BEHAVIOR

John R. Aiello, *Department of Psychology, Rutgers-The State University, New Brunswick, New Jersey*

We treat space somewhat as we treat sex. It is there but we don't talk about it.
EDWARD T. HALL

Like the porcupine in Schopenhauer's fable, people like to be close enough to obtain warmth and comradeship but far enough away to avoid pricking one another.
ROBERT SOMMER

12.1. INTRODUCTION

Research into the area of human spatial behavior predates the 1960s, but it was during this decade that significant increases were made in the attention that social scientists paid to this topic. The appearance of two influential books, anthropologist Edward T. Hall's *The Hidden Dimension* in 1966 and psychologist Robert Sommers' *Personal Space: The Behavioral Basis of Design* in 1969, spurred considerable interest in this area and has led to the accumulation of a large number of research studies during the past two decades.

The purpose of this chapter will be to review this growing body of research (more than 700 studies as of this writing and recently averaging about 50 per year) and the methods and theoretical frameworks associated with it. Following a brief historical overview of early human spatial behavior research, several definitional problems with the most commonly used label (*personal space*) in this area are discussed. *Proxemic behavior* or *interaction* (or *interpersonal*) *distance* are alternative terms that are suggested as more appropriate concepts for human spatial behavior.

Prior to a rather comprehensive review of the relevant findings of this research literature, the theoretical frameworks and measurement procedures that have evolved in this area are considered. It will be argued that because of various methodological problems (including questionable external validity of numerous measures) *more than half* of the findings of this research literature, those obtained using projective (e.g., paper and pencil) or quasi-projective (e.g., stop-distance) techniques, have to be interpreted with *extreme caution*. The review then builds from a consideration of how spatial behavior *develops* from infancy through adulthood to an integration of established findings in six substantive areas. (Throughout the chapter are a like number of comprehensive summary tables.)

The study of human spatial behavior actually derives from a number of disciplines. The earliest work in this area was based primarily on the work of ethologists (e.g., Calhoun, 1962; Lorenz, 1955; Tinbergen, 1952) and ornithologists (e.g., Bain, 1949; Howard, 1920), who focused on the territorial behavior and distance regulation of animals and birds. Zurich's Henri Hediger, an animal psychologist, probably had the greatest influence on the early work focusing on human spatial behavior. In his 1950 book *Wild Animals in Captivity* Hediger identified and described a number of distances used by most animals. Four of these distances, flight distance, critical distance, personal distance, and social distance, were the building blocks of Hall's (1966) spatial distance zones. Hediger's contributions influenced Sommer (1969) and many other researchers interested in human spatial behavior as well.

While Hall and Sommer were influenced by the ethologists' research on animal spatial behavior, they also maintained a broad view of the use of space that included the environments in which we live. For example, Hall (1963) coined the term *proxemics* to refer to "the study of how man unconsciously structures microspace—the distance between men in the conduct of daily transactions, the organization of space in his houses and buildings, and ultimately, the layout of his towns" (p. 1003). He (1966) further dif-

ferentiated among three types of spatial organization. Fixed-feature space is associated with the arrangement of environments like cities, towns, buildings, houses, and rooms. Semifixed-feature space encompasses movable furniture like tables and chairs. Informal space refers to the distances maintained in encounters with others and will be the primary focus of attention in the present chapter. Sommer's (1969) book *Personal Space* is aptly subtitled *The Behavioral Basis of Design*. His treatment of a number of specific environmental settings is the focus of the majority of his book and is a reflection of his strong interest in environmental engineering. Therefore, the area of human spatial behavior is rooted solidly in the field of environmental psychology.

A parallel development was also beginning in the 1960s for another set of researchers interested in human spatial behavior. This development modified somewhat the integral link between human spatial behavior research and environmental psychology but reinforced the need expressed by Hall (1959) and others that space be but one of many variables used by people to establish a desired involvement level for interaction. Psychologist Michael Argyle and his colleagues at Oxford included interaction distance or proximity as one of a *number* of components of a more general intimacy regulation process. Argyle and Dean (1965) stimulated a great deal of research primarily among social psychologists, who examined spatial behavior in a much less central way, relegating it to the role of one of a series of variables rather than *the* single variable of interest. Rosenfeld (1965, 1966) and Mehrabian (cf. 1969) were also including distance as a variable of interest in their early role-playing studies of approval seeking and attitude inference about this time.

Investigators from disciplines other than psychology and anthropology were beginning to conduct research in human spatial behavior as well. The work of sociologists, ecologists, geographers, psychiatrists, and architects (to name but a few) added an interdisciplinary richness and diversity to this budding research domain.

12.2. DEFINITIONS AND CONCEPTUAL UNDERPINNINGS

The diversity of the disciplines represented by researchers in the area of human spatial behavior has led to an abundance of terms (e.g., *personal space, interpersonal distance, interpersonal spatial proximity*) and operationalizations of the spatial behavior concept (e.g., proxemics). The term *personal space* was first used by Katz (1937). Subsequently, it was Hediger (1950) who initially suggested the notion that each animal is surrounded by a series of "bubbles or balloons" that allow proper spacing between it and other animals. Both Hall (1966) and Sommer (1959, 1969) adopted this operational definition of the spatial mechanism for humans.

Hall (1966) begins his book: "The central theme of this book is social and personal space and man's perception of it" (p.1) and refers to "personal distance" as "a small protective sphere or bubble that an organism maintains between itself and others" (p. 119). *Personal distance* is but one of four spatial "envelopes" or distance zones for Hall. Little (1965) proposed the term *personal distance* to refer to "the area immediately surrounding the individual in which the majority of his interactions with others take place" (p. 237).

Sommer (1969) defines the term *personal space* as "an area with invisible boundaries surrounding a person's body into which intruders may not come" (p. 26). Earlier, he (1959) had distinguished personal space from territoriality by describing the former as portablé, having invisible boundaries, and having the person's body at its center (p. 248). The term *personal space* continues to be the label most often used to refer to human spatial behavior (e.g., Hayduk, 1983). The choice of this term is *not* without its problems, however.

Unfortunately, the term *personal space* as it has been defined by Sommer and others stresses the *protection* component of spatial behavior but not the more active component that is linked to the *communication* function of spatial behavior. It is a dichotomous concept. As Knowles (1980a) has noted, "one is either in or out of your personal space" (p. 132). Patterson (1975) has argued that it is time to "burst" the personal space "bubble" and that the personal space concept is "unnecessary and probably misleading" (p. 67). He arrived at this conclusion because the personal space concept implies stability when actually it has been shown to change considerably based on setting, relationship, and environmental conditions. Furthermore, he noted that personal space is more interpersonal than "personal" and that it places too heavy an emphasis on distance alone rather than on other interaction behaviors (e.g., eye contact).

I agree that the *personal space* concept *has been* misleading, and I would prefer that it not be used as the *primary* term for human spatial behavior. The use of Hall's *proxemic* concept or, under more specific cir-

cumstances, the term *interpersonal distance* would seem more fitting since what we are primarily interested in is the spatial context or more specifically *the distance between people*. Distance is really after all a milieu within which a variety of behaviors and phenomena occur. This particularly would be the case for the distance between individuals engaged in what Goffman (1963) refers to as *focused interaction*; under these engagement conditions, either *proxemic behavior* or the term *interaction distance* would be especially preferable to the *personal space* label. However, I believe that the *personal space* concept is too well established in the human spatial behavior literature and that it has been broadened sufficiently beyond the serious limitations of the rather constraining "protection" function restriction of its original definition and in its research applications simply to be abandoned. The bubble analogy, on the other hand, is both misleading *and* unnecessary, as it does not capture the meaning or substance of human spatial behavior at all (e.g., "bursting bubbles"), and I would strongly recommend abandoning it.

12.3. THEORETICAL FRAMEWORKS

12.3.1. Hall's Proxemic Framework

Perhaps the most important milestone for the development of human spatial behavior research was Hall's proxemic framework (1963, 1966). In addition to the definition noted earlier, Hall used the term *proxemics* to refer to:

> the interrelated observations and theories of man's use of space as a specialized elaboration of culture. (1966, p. 1)

> the study of man's transactions as he perceives and uses intimate, personal, social and public space in various settings while following out-of-awareness dictates of cultural paradigms. (1974, p. 2)

Hall's comprehensive and insightful approach to our use of space clearly emphasizes how people make active use of and manipulate it and the physical environment in order to achieve preferred degrees of closeness and attain desired levels of involvement during interaction. His four distance zones reflect the four principal categories of relationships (intimate, personal, social, and public) and the types of activities and spaces corresponding to them. Each of these zones (which contain a near and far phase) provides a different level of sensory information and reflects the different relationship between the interactants. Altman and Vinsel (1977), who provided a thorough review of the first 10 years of research findings relating to Hall's hypotheses pertaining to these spatial zones (see Figure 12.1), concluded that "human spatial distancing is reasonably consistent and not overly discrepant from Hall's qualitative ideas" (p. 200).

Intimate distance ranges from 0 to 18 inches and is characterized by strong and intense sensory inputs. The voice is normally held at a very low level or even at a whisper. Sight is a bit distorted, heat and smell from another is inescapable and involvement is unmistakable.

Personal distance ranges from 1.5 to 4 feet and another is within "arm's length." The voice level is moderate, vision is no longer distorted, and body heat and olfaction are either no longer or minimally perceptible. This distance is more likely to be used by friends and aquaintances.

Social distance extends from 4 to 12 feet. Nobody touches or expects to touch another person. Voice level is louder and transactions are more formal and businesslike.

Public distance extends beyond 12 feet. This distance is more characteristic of speakers and their audience or interactions with public figures. The voice and everything else must be exaggerated or amplified.

Hall's focus on the types of sensory information available to interactants at different distances ad-

vances us well beyond a simple dichotomous concept like personal space but is still lacking in an important regard. In my review of the human spatial behavior literature I find no evidence that it is *at* the zonal transition points that marked differences in the experiences of interactants occur. Rather, these different experiences occur *more gradually* as sensory inputs change from one distance zone to another. An almost endless number of characteristics of the interactants and their environments would therefore make *any set distances* for the four zones proposed by Hall very approximate at best. Although this is virtually never cited in the literature, Hall (1966) himself has noted that "the measured distances vary somewhat with differences in personality and environmental factors" (p. 116). While a category system of four distance zones is appealing for the purpose of illustration, I agree with Knowles (1980a), who argued that the use of *any* category system (whether it is a dichotomous classification like personal space or a quadripartite classification like Hall's) makes the questionable assumption that reactions to distance are *not continuous*. Again, the concept of interpersonal distance would appear better to characterize human spatial behavior.

While Hall's proxemic framework is by far the most well developed of the theories of human spatial behavior, a number of other theories or models have been derived or (more typically) adopted by researchers in this area. Theory testing and development have for the most part been sparse. Since human spatial behavior research developed from animal spatial

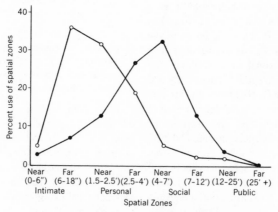

Distribution of use of near and far phases of spatial zones.o—o= standing relationships (*n* = 59),●—●= seated relationships (*n* = 30).

Figure 12.1. Distribution of use of near and far phases of [Hall's] spatial zones. (*Source:* From "Analysis of Hall's Proxemic Framework" by I. Altman and A.M. Vinsel, in *Human Behavior and the Environment, Vol. 2: Advances in Theory and Research,* (p. 199), by I. Altman and J.F. Wohlwill (Eds.) 1977, New York: Plenum. Copyright 1977 by Plenum. Reprinted by permission.)

behavior research with a strong ethological tradition, it is not surprising that the emphasis was on the *protective* function of space (e.g., Dosey & Meisels, 1969).

Evans and Howard (1973) in the first major review of this burgeoning area of research described the manner in which personal space functions at a cognitive level and how this function has been selected out of an evolutionary process to control intraspecies aggression and reduce stress. Similar examples of a primary focus on the protective function of space from spatial invasion and early crowding research (involving high spatial density conditions) are numerous.

A number of other theoretical approaches to human spatial behavior have been adapted from the more general theories of environmental psychology (for more complete discussions of these perspectives see Fisher, Bell, & Baum, 1984; Gifford, 1985; Holahan, 1982). Most of these theoretical frameworks overlap considerably and relate to the consequences of inappropriately close spacing. Overstimulation models of stress, arousal, and overload suggest that an individual maintains a preferred interaction distance from others in order to avoid excessive arousal, stimulation, and a variety of stressors associated with proximity that is too close. Behavioral constraint models maintain that adequate personal space prevents our behavioral freedom from being threatened. Again, it is the *protective* function of human spacing that remains as the common thread among these frameworks.

Once it is acknowledged that humans all have a "spatial mechanism" built in which is behavioral and rooted in our biological past, the acquisition of specific personal space norms and behaviors is almost invariably explained within the context of cultural experience and with reference to a theory of social learning. That is, through the processes of imitation and reinforcement, children learn the accepted cultural patterns of appropriate proxemic behavior (e.g., Aiello & Aiello, 1974; Duke & Nowicki, 1972).

This brings us to the second primary function of spatial behavior, which is *communication*. Hall (1966) conceptualizes the use of space as a medium through which communication occurs. It is fitting that in *The Silent Language* (1959) Hall titles his only spatial behavior chapter "Space Speaks." For Hall the distance at which one chooses to interact with others is fully entwined with all other sensory modalities and determines the quality and quantity of stimuli exchanged. As noted, close proximity allows considerably higher levels of sensory input (e.g., sound, smell, touch) and communicates information about the type of relationship between interactants (i.e., desire for great-

er involvement). Similar communications approaches are taken by Pedersen and Shears (1973) and Kaplan (1977). Pedersen and Shears (1973) have used a general systems framework to examine spatial behavior as a vehicle for the communication of attitudes, feelings, and facts between interactants. Kaplan (1977) adapted Smith, Lasswell, and Casey's (1946) nine-component verbal communication paradigm to study messages conveyed over the nonverbal spatial medium. *Who* says *what* to *whom*, in what place (*where*), at what time (*when*), and for what reason (*why*) are the situational and interactant factors that combine to form a standard value (expectancy) of intimacy. The difference between it and the observed value (actual intimacy level) determines the behaviors in the interaction. If the difference is great (intimacy is too great or too low), the interactants withdraw. If the difference is small or nonexistent, they approach.

Because he is a cultural anthropologist, it is probably not surprising that most of Hall's attention is focused on how various cultures display different norms for spatial usage. For Hall as for the present author, individual differences in the use of space are primarily a reflection of the different types of learning experiences we have within our effective cultures (e.g., country, gender, socioeconomic class).

Consistent with Hall's perspective a number of other theorists have developed models to explain the relationships among spatial behavior and verbal and other nonverbal variables (e.g., gaze, topic intimacy, body orientation). For purposes of comparison the models have been grouped into three categories: conflict or intimacy equilibrium models, arousal or attribution models, and expectancy or discrepancy models. *Conflict* or *intimacy equilibrium models* are those in which the opposition of approach and avoidance forces is considered critical to the establishment of desired levels of intimacy in an interaction. *Arousal* or *attribution models* are those in which the positive or negative arousal caused by the approach of another is crucial in establishing intimacy. Finally, those models in which the discrepancy between the interactants' expectancies and the actual approach of another is said to be the main factor in an interaction will be referred to as *expectancy* or *discrepancy models*.

12.3.2. Conflict or Intimacy Equilibrium Models

The most widely known of the conflict models is Argyle and Dean's (1965) affiliative-conflict theory (later modified by Argyle & Cook, 1976, and referred to as the *intimacy equilibrium model*). This approach is adapted from the S–R psychology approach of Miller (1944), who theorized that in an organism, approach forces and avoidance forces are in conflict with each other. At some point between the goal and the organism, these forces are in equilibrium. Closer to the goal, the avoidance forces are stronger than the approach forces. Past the equilibrium point, the approach forces are stronger than the avoidance forces. Thus there is a stable equilibrium point.

Argyle and Dean postulated that this is how it is for humans engaged in interaction. According to this compensatory model, approach and avoidance forces are present in every interpersonal encounter. Individuals develop an *equilibrium point* for intimacy, which is a joint function of several immediacy behaviors (e.g., interpersonal distance, eye contact, amount of smiling). If one of these components changes resulting in more or less intimacy than is desired, a reciprocal change occurs in one or more of the other behaviors in order to restore the desired level of intimacy. When successful compensation is not possible, however, discomfort results. Even though compensatory behaviors can be used consciously and strategically, under most circumstances they are employed *outside* of the realm of consciousness. This process usually occurs quickly and automatically, although often incompletely. Changes in the overall intimacy level of a relationship, however, typically occur very gradually over time.

This theory has proven popular for a number of reasons. First of all, it is simple and makes intuitive sense. Furthermore, it has received empirical support from a fair number of studies for stable interpersonal relationships (see Table 12.1). The affiliative conflict model has several limitations, though. Stephenson and Rutter (1970), Aiello (1972), Knight, Langmeyer, and Lundgren (1973), and Stephenson, Rutter, and Dore (1973) identified several methodological problems for a number of the early studies supportive of the model. Other studies have found no relation between either distance and gaze (Schneider & Hansvick, 1977) or between distance and verbal productivity (Rogers, Rearden, & Hillner, 1981). More important, however, is the sizable number of studies that have discovered instances of nonverbal matching (i.e., reciprocity), particularly in relationships that have not yet stabilized (e.g., developing relationships). For example, Hall (1966) found that an increase in topic intimacy brought interactants closer together and Breed (1972) found that increased intimacy resulted in more forward leans and greater eye contact. Further, Kendon (1967) found that confederates' gazes were reciprocated by subjects and similarly Sodikoff, Firestone and Kaplan (1974) found that gaze avoidance by confederates resulted in more backward lean by their subjects.

Despite these seemingly contradictory results, Argyle and Dean's theory is not really refuted, which points out another limitation in the model. Since it is a multifactor model with the behaviors rather vaguely defined (e.g., it includes an all-encompassing "etc."), it could not reasonably be disproved unless one were to control an almost infinite number of behaviors. The model also suffers from an absence of explanatory mechanisms for *how* and *why* equilibrium levels are modified. Argyle and Dean's affiliative conflict model remains the bellwether, however, for the many subsequent models to which I will now turn.

12.3.3. Modifications of Conflict/Intimacy Equilibrium Models

Because of the experimental results that Argyle and Dean's affiliative conflict model does not explain very well, several investigators (Firestone, 1977; Kaplan, 1977; Knowles, 1980a; Marcus-Kaplan & Kaplan, 1984) have developed conflict models that purport to explain situations that proceed in directions contrary to those described by an equilibrium model. Kaplan's model, for example, is an adaptation of later work by Miller (1959) and Kelman (1962), which was apparently not considered by Argyle and his colleagues. Implicit in their model is that the avoidance gradient is steeper than the approach gradient in an interaction, as is the case in stable equilibrium described by Miller (1944). In his later writings, however, Miller (1959) allowed that the opposite situation, in which the approach gradient is steeper than the avoidance gradient, could be possible.

Kaplan has applied such a match to human interaction. His model attempts to explain why equilibrium levels change. It posits that attraction mediates an individual's likelihood of reciprocating or compensating. If attitudinal outcomes of initial interaction are positive, a shift in equilibrium toward greater approach toward the other results. That is, approach accelerates between the goal and the intersection of the gradients. Past that point, avoidance accelerates as a function of negative initial interaction (unattractive) outcomes and the preferred equilibrium level shifts accordingly. This can explain how in certain situations one person reciprocates the approach of another rather than compensating for it.

Like Argyle and Dean's model, Kaplan's approach has limitations. First of all, these approach and avoidance gradients are internal and most likely cannot be

Table 12.1. Distance and Intimacy Equilibrium

Study		Methodology	Results
Aiello (1972)		Subjects observed while seated 2 ft, 6 ft, 10 ft from confederate with 0, 90° orientation.	Females' gaze was greater at 6 ft than 2 ft or 10 ft. Males increased gaze progressively as distance increased. Glances were longer when subjects were face-to-face with confederates.
Aiello (1977a)		Five highly related visual behaviors of male and female subjects were observed during seated interaction distance of 2.5 ft, 6.5 ft, or 10.5 ft. Confederate engaged in 85% then 15% gaze or 15% then 85% gaze at face-to-face orientation.	Females engaged in most looking at intermediate distance of 6.5 ft. Males increased gaze steadily with distance.
Aiello (1977b)		Subjects observed during seated interaction at 7 ft, 9.5 ft, 12 ft, 14.5 ft. Confederates gazed 75% while listening and 50% while speaking.	While speaking, females looked *less* with increasing distance, males looked *more* with increasing distance. While listening, males looked more with increasing distance, females looked most at 9.5 ft.
Aiello & Thompson (1980a)		Subjects were seated at intermediate (5 ft) or far (11 ft) distance. Subjects' stress-related arousal, state anxiety, mood, other feelings, locus of control, and nonverbal behavior assessed.	While both sexes were more uncomfortable and more anxious at the farther distance, females were most stressed and reacted more negatively than males at the large interaction distance.
Aiello & Thompson (1984)		Subjects' verbal and (nine) visual behaviors were observed while seated at 2 ft or 5 ft from (one of eight) black or white, male or female interviewers.	Interviewees looked more at the intermediate distance (5 ft), regardless of the sex or race of the interviewer. White interviewers looked more than black interviewers.
Argyle & Dean (1965)	I.	Subjects took standing position near: photo of man's face; man seated eyes open; man seated eyes closed.	Children and adults stood farthest from man with eyes open.
	II.	Subjects observed in seated interaction at 90°: 2 ft; 6 ft; or 10 ft.	Eye contact increased progressively with distance for both sexes.
Argyle & Ingham (1972)	I.	Subjects observed while seated 2 ft or 10 ft from each other at 90° angle.	Subjects looked more at greater distance.
	II.	Subjects observed while seated 3 ft or 6 ft from each other at 90° angle.	Subjects looked more at greater distance.
Argyle, Lalljee, & Cook (1968)		Subjects observed while seated at 4 ft and 10 ft. Visibility varied by one member of dyad: (1) normal vision; (2) dark glasses; (3) mask; (4) one-way screen; (5) no vision.	At 4 ft subjects more comfortable. When concealed at 10 ft both sexes more comfortable observed by males than females. At 10 ft females like to observe neither sex. Opposite sex pairs less comfortable at 10 ft.
Aronow, Reznikoff, & Tryon (1975)		Measure of seating distance.	More direct angle associated with greater distance.
Baker & Shaw (1980)		Subjects stood at three distances (1 ft, 2 ft, 5.5 ft) and discussed topics of three intimacy levels. Questionnaire evaluation of discussion.	Both friends and strangers showed a tendency to rate 2-ft distance more favorably than 1 ft or 5.5 ft.
Batton, Squires, & Lund (1982)		Subjects given verbal conditioning in four different positions: near eye-to-eye; far side-by-side; near side-by-side; and far eye-to-eye.	Orientation did not affect verbal conditioning of nonschizophrenic subjects. Indirect as opposed to eye-to-eye orientation facilitated verbal conditioning in schizophrenics.

Table 12.1. *(Continued)*

Study	Methodology	Results
Baxter & Rozelle (1975)	Subjects were videotaped with confederate in police interview simulation. Confederate shifted distance every 2 min: Experimental– 4 ft, 2 ft, 8 in., 2 ft; Control–4 ft, 2 ft, 2 ft, 2 ft.	Subjects in the experimental group showed reactions to 8-in. distance: (1) speech disruption; (2) gaze aversion; (3) increased defensive arm positions; (4) increased arm movement; (5) decreased foot movement; (6) increased trunk rotation.
Breed (1972)	Confederates behaved three ways: (1) 100% gaze, forward lean, 0° orientation; (2) "intermittent" gaze, erect, 0° orientation; (3) gazed twice, backward lean, 45° orientation. Measured gaze, lean, angle of subjects.	Subjects gazed more, leaned forward more in the *high*-intimacy condition.
Burgoon (1978)	In a standardized interview subjects were given positive or negative feedback. Interview conducted at one of four distances: (1) normative distance: Interaction norms were set through pilot test for interacting dyads: (interviewer listed first) MM-40 in.; FM & FF-38 in.; and MF-34 in.; (2) threat condition; less than 6 in.; (3) close: for both 6 in. closer than normative distance; (4) far: 6 ft.	Curvilinear relationships found for evaluations of interviewer. Punishing interviewer evaluated most negatively at near and far distances. Rewarding interviewers rated most positively at near distances.
Burgoon & Aho (1982)	Confederates established three distances from subject: (1) norm–allowed subject to establish distance; (2) close–norm distance halved after 1 min; (3) far–norm distance doubled after 1 min. High or low reward condition (how much confederate indicated would spend).	Verbosity was lowest in the norm condition. In low reward condition, females more likely to comply with request for help than in the norm condition.
Carr & Dabbs (1974)	Subject and experimenter in discussion of intimate topic. Distance (1.5 ft, 8 ft) and lighting (bright or dim) were varied. Compared behaviors (gaze, verbal output) to those in baseline interview ("neutral" distance, lighting and intimacy).	Distance had no effect on gaze. Expressed preference for mean distance in intimate discussion. Distance failed to affect verbal behavior.
Chapman (1975)	7-year-olds listened to humorous tapes on headphones. Subjects seated face-to-face 2.7 ft or 5.5 ft. Observers recorded eye contact, smiling, and laughing.	Eye contact, laughter, and smiling were greater in the near condition. Laughter hypothesized to reduce social arousal.
Coutts & Ledden (1977)	Subjects interviewed twice by same-sex interviewer. Baseline rates of gaze, smiling, orientation, and lean gathered in session 1. In session 2, interviewer increased seated distance (2.17 m), decreased distance (0.83 m), or kept same distance with subject.	When the interviewer sat farther away, subjects' gaze and smiling increased. Subjects' orientation and body lean were also more direct. When the interviewer moved closer, subjects' gaze and smile decreased.
Coutts & Schneider (1975)	Observation of seated interactions: 2 ft; 7 ft.	Visual behavior decreased over time, also decreased with increased proximity.
Coutts & Schneider (1976)	Subjects observed in seated interaction measured: (1) distance; (2) orientation; (3) body lean; (4) smiling; (5) mutual gaze; (6) individual gaze. Confederate reduced gaze over time.	Reduced gaze did not result in compensatory reactions on other behaviors.

Table 12.1. *(Continued)*

Study		Methodology	Results
Dabbs, Johns & Powell (1976)	I.	Observed in seated interaction at two distances: 5 ft; knees almost touching. Observed eye contact.	At close distance, both sexes maintained greater eye contact with female partner than with male partner. Eye contact decreased with crowding.
	II.	Observed with mixed-sex pair of confederates seated at 1.5 ft or 6 ft.	Eye contact decreased at close distance. Subjects shifted from equal gaze toward confederates to more gaze toward females at close distance.
Dinges & Oetting (1972)		Subjects shown photographs of models seated at same distances used by Haase (1970). Rated anxiety associated with each.	Subjects rate near (30 in.) and far (88 in.) distances as associated with most anxiety.
Dietch & Hense (1975)		Distance varied (5 ft, 2.5 ft), judges rated subjects' self-disclosure. Eye contact observed and discomfort questionnaire administered. Tested with experimenter.	Less self-disclosure at near distance. No effect of distance or disclosure on eye contact. No effects of any kind for discomfort.
Eberts & Lepper (1975)		Approach toward experimenter. Increasing levels of gaze.	Increased gaze associated with increase in distance.
Efran & Cheyne (1974)		Subjects observed while forced to intrude or not on a conversation.	Greatest number of agonistic facial expressions & increased heart rate in violation condition.
Felipe & Sommer (1966)	I.	Male experimenter invaded male subjects at distance of 6 in. while seated. Observed compensatory behaviors and latency of flight. Subjects were patients at a mental hospital.	Latency of flight shorter when invaded than for controls (not invaded but within sight). More compensatory blocking behaviors and leaning away also noted.
	II.	Female experimenter invaded female subjects. College students in library were subjects.	Closer approaches led to quicker flight and more compensatory behaviors.
Ford, Cramer, & Owens (1977)		Unobtrusive photographs.	Voice amplitude directly related to distance. No effect of eye contact on distance.
Ford, Knight, & Cramer (1977)		Subject asked to approach inanimate object to simulate distance she had been approached by confederate.	When confederate approached at close distance (30.5 cm), subjects underestimated the distance they had stood apart.
Fromme & Beam (1974)		Stop approach of experimenter.	During high levels of gaze by experimenter, dominant subjects approached closer.
Gale, Spratt, Chapman, & Smallbone (1975)		EEG measured at 2, 4, 8, 16, 32 ft. Subjects seated, exposed to direct or averted gaze.	For all distances, direct gaze resulted in higher EEG than averted gaze. EEG highest at 2 ft, direct gaze.
Goldberg, Kiesler, & Collins (1969)		"Impression" questionnaires measured cumulative time looking at experimenter. Seated either 2.5 or 6 ft.	Less gaze at closer distance. Most favorable impressions on questionnaire accompanied higher gaze.

Table 12.1. *(Continued)*

Study	Methodology	Results
Goldberg & Wellens (1979)	Subject sat 3 ft from television monitor or interviewer. Varied intimacy of questions within each condition.	Subjects spent more time gazing with the low intimacy questions. More time spent looking with the interactive television.
Greenbuam & Rosenfeld (1978)	Observed drivers at intersection. Confederate stood 0 to 3.66 m; Confederate stared or did not stare.	Staring and closer proximity decreased latency of exit. Verbalizations from drivers increased by stare and closer proximity.
Greenberg & Firestone (1977)	Intrusion: (1) interviewer sat touching subject's legs; (2) 100% gaze; (3) forward lean. No intrusion: (1) interviewers sat 1.22 m (a bit less than 4 ft); (2) looked at subject twice per question; (3) backward lean. Compensatory behaviors and verbal output recorded.	Subjects gazed less in intrusion condition. Subjects disclosed less in the intrusion condition.
Haase (1970)	Subjects were asked to rate attitudes toward models engaged in an interaction. Models presented on slides were shown at 30, 39, 50, 66, 88 in. apart.	Distances of 30 to 50 in. rated more highly than distances of 66 & 88 in.
Hansen & Schuldt (1982)	Subjects' self-disclosure (in intimacy of topic and time spent speaking) were measured. Subject and interviewer sat at right angle and at 3 or 6 ft.	Subjects disclosed more at "culturally appropriate" distance than at "culturally inappropriate" distance.
Hardee (1976)	Observation of seating distance from confederate.	Subjects sat closer to "blind" targets who wore sunglasses than to controls.
Hendrick, Geisen, & Coy (1974)	Observed placement of seating cushions in relation to moderator. Confederate placed own cushion first (close or far from moderator).	Regardless of where confederate put cushion, other two subjects managed to place cushions so that group configuration was similar in both conditions.
Hughes & Goldman (1978)	Observation of intrusion behavior in elevator.	Females more often invaded space of experimenter engaging in high levels of eye contact and smiling. Opposite effect for males.
Janik, Goldberg, & Wellens (1983)	Measured heart rate and pulse amplitude in relation to changes in apparent distance and eye contact from confederate. Images appeared on interactive television (distance manipulated by altering image size).	Heart rate decreased from baseline as apparent distance increased. Pulse amplitude increased during the experimental period.
Johnson & Dabbs (1976)	Subjects discussed topics of three intimacy levels at different distances (18, 36, 54 in.).	Subjects disclosed more (in seconds) on the high–intimacy topics at the greater distances.
Johnson, Pick, Siegel, Cicciarelli, & Garber (1981)	Subjects (one adult, one child) stood 6, 12, 24 ft, apart. Measured vocal intensity.	All groups increased vocal intensity with distance.
Kleck (1970)	Observation of videotapes of interaction. Seated, face-to-face 4, 10 ft distances.	Head nodding was greater at the closer distance. Self-manipulations were greater in close condition. No effect of distance on smiling.

398

Table 12.1. *(Continued)*

Study	Methodology	Results
Kleinke, Staneski, & Pipp (1975)	Subjects observed in seated interaction with female confederate. Confederate either moved to 68 or 29 in. from original distance of 45 in. 90%, 10% gaze from confederate.	Confederate's attractiveness had effect on liking of confederate. No effect for distance or gaze.
Klukken (1971)	Interpersonal Distance Questionnaire.	No difference in distance for high and low disclosers.
Knight, Langmeyer, & Lundgren (1973)	Observation of confederate interaction. 2, 5, 8 ft, normal or continuous gaze by confederate.	Subjects' gaze increased with increasing distance.
Lassen (1973)	Videotaped interview: (1) patient speech disturbances (anxiety measure); (2) rater-judged overt anxiety; (3) rater-judged content anxiety; (4) post-interview questionnaire at 3, 6, 9 ft.	(1) Patient speech disturbances increased with increased distance; (2) patients did not feel they expressed themselves clearly at 9 ft; (3) patients talked more, rated selves more open at intermediate (6 ft) distance; and (4) all therapists expressed preference for the intermediate (6 ft) distance.
Mahoney (1974)	Observed compensatory behaviors when confederates invaded subjects in library. Same procedure as Patterson et al. (1971). Questionnaires evaluated affective state.	Two and three seats adjacent not reported by subjects as invasion. Invasion across and adjacent did not increase compensation from baseline (no invasion) in females, across invasion *decreased* blocking responses.
McBride, King, & James (1965)	Measured GSR as experimenter sat at different distances (1, 3, 9 ft) to present flash cards.	Greater arousal (lower skin resistance) with closer approaches, with frontal rather than side approaches, and with opposite-sex experimenters.
McDowell (1973)	Subjects interacted with confederate. Confederate instructed to maintain 0.97 m or 0.48 m distance; 80%, 20%, or "normal" gaze. Observers recorded subjects' gaze, speech output.	Distance manipulation had no effect on speech output or gaze.
Mehrabian & Diamond (1971a)	I. & II. Subjects under "waiting room" conditions placed at one of four distances (3, 4.5, 6, 9 ft) and sat at one of three orientations (0, 90, 180°). Observed nonverbal relaxation & affiliative behavior & questionnaire measures of affiliative tendency & sensitivity to rejection included.	Subjects relaxed more as distance increased. Affiliative behavior decreased with indirectness of orientation, particularly for those with more of an affiliative tendency.
	III. Subjects sat at 4.5 ft apart and at 90° orientation. Exposed to prop condition (abstract sculpture & puzzle poster) or not. Dependent measures same as above.	Attention to puzzle decreased affiliative behavior. Attention to sculpture by subjects "sensitive to rejection" facilitated interaction.
Patterson (1973)	Observation of: Approach distance to experimenter; approach orientation; amount of interviewer-directed gaze.	Compensatory relationship between distance and orientation.

Table 12.1. *(Continued)*

Study		Methodology	Results
Patterson (1977)	I.	Subjects observed in interview in each of three positions: (1) First, subject was instructed to place chair at comfortable distance, then (2) place chair back where he or she began to feel uncomfortable, then (3) place chair forward where he or she began to feel uncomfortable.	Eye contact increased with larger distances, less direct orientations were associated with smaller distances.
	II.	Observed in field settings in standing interaction.	Larger angles adopted with smaller interaction distances.
Patterson, Mullens, & Romano (1971)		Experimenter invaded subjects seated at tables in college library. Measured latency of flight and observed compensatory behaviors (blocking, leaning, cross glances). Experimenter seated one seat across, two, three seats from subject.	Invasion did not evoke flight. Compensatory reactions did increase with immediacy of invasion. Both sexes responded negatively to invasion but males displayed greater discomfort.
Patterson & Sechrest (1970)		Subjects seated 2, 4, 6, 8 ft from interviewer. Rated impressions of interviewer.	Interviewing at closest distance seen as less socially active (explained as a compensation for close physical distance).
Pedersen & Sabin (1982)		Students approached by survey taker at near (6 to 18 in.) or far distance.	More movement recorded in near condition.
Pellegrini & Empey (1970)		Measured angle and distance subject placed own chair from that of a same-sex confederate.	Angles were less direct for those who placed their chairs closer to confederate.
Rodgers, Rearden, & Hillner (1981)		Subject interviewed by two female confederates at three distances about personal, social, and academic topics.	Anxiety was least at intermediate (5 ft) distance. A moderate correlation between anxiety and verbal productivity was reported.
Russo (1975)		Measure of gaze; pairs of subjects.	Percentage of time subject engaged in eye contact increased with increasing distance. Higher for females than males. Did not differ with degree of friendship. Mean length of eye contact did not change with distance. Higher for females and higher for friends.
Savitsky & Watson (1975)		Hall's notation system.	No effects for sex or age. Distance was negatively correlated with gaze and axis and positively correlated with touch.
Scherer & Schiff (1973)		Rate intimacy of seating positions depicted in slides. Distances (3, 4.5, 6 ft) and angles (0, 30, 45, 60, 90°) were varied.	Distance was salient to ratings of intimacy. 3 ft rated more intimate than 4.5 or 6 ft. Eye contact and corner seats are perceived as more intimate. Head orientation not a salient determinant of intimacy.
Schneider & Hansvick (1977)		Observation in lab. Two patterns of confederate gaze—at, then away, then at.	Subjects' distance unaffected by gaze pattern. Reciprocated confederate's gaze.
Schulz & Barefoot (1974)		Unobtrusive recording of nonverbal behaviors at 3 and 5.5 ft for low- and high-intimacy topics.	Looking while listening greater at larger interaction distances. Smiling increased at increased distances. Looking while talking greater at low levels of intimacy.

Table 12.1. *(Continued)*

Study	Methodology	Results
Scott (1984)	I. Subjects shown photograph of room with seats at 2.0, 4.5, 6.75, 9.25 ft. Asked to choose seat for discussion of several topics.	Both males and females chose closer seats for more intimate topics with each target person (boy, girlfriend, roommate, classmate, lawyer).
	II. Ratings of comfort at each of above distances while discussing topics of ranging intimacy.	Subjects rated closer seats more comfortable for discussing intimate topics.
Skotko & Langmeyer (1977)	2-, 4-, and 10-ft interaction distance for each dyad (seats at table). Ratings of self-disclosure from audiotape.	Males increased self-disclosure as distance increased. Opposite effect for females.
Sommer (1962)	Observed seating preferences for discussion. Compared side-by-side to direct orientation.	When distances were set to be equal, or direct orientation closer, subjects preferred a direct orientation.
Sommer (1968)	Subjects were observed in their choice of seat for a one-on-one discussion.	Nonschizophrenic patients prefer an intermediate level of immediacy (close distance, indirect angle) to great (close distance, direct angle) and low immediacy (close distance, very indirect angle; or very great distance).
Stephenson & Rutter (1970)	Observation of dyads.	Recorded eye contact increased with increase in distance, but as a function of observer, not participant performance.
Stephenson, Rutter, & Dore (1973)	Videotaped each subject. Combined images on split-screen. Subjects seated at 2 or 6 ft.	Mean duration of look was greater at greater distance. Total duration and number of looks not affected by distance.
Stewart & Patterson (1973)	Subjects measured for comfort (by amount of responses per trial on TAT). Seated 3 or 6 ft from female experimenter. Experimenter varied body lean and gaze.	Subjects more comfortable in the high gaze–far distance condition than high gaze–near distance. Control condition was intermediate. Body lean did not affect comfort.
Stone & Morden (1976)	Subjects were seated 2, 5, 9 ft from interviewer of same sex. Topics discussed were personal, social, or academic.	For personal topics only, subjects talked more at the *intermediate* distance than the near or far distance. For academic topic, verbal productivity decreased with distance. No differences for social topics.
Storms & Thomas (1977)	I. Subjects seated 12 or 30 in. from male confederate. Confederate gave autobiographical speech that was similar or dissimilar to subject's.	In condition where subject had no choice of distance, ratings were highest for similar other at close distance. Least high ratings were for dissimilar at close distance.
	II. Same except positive and negative cues were friendly or unfriendly words from confederate.	Liking for confederate was highest in close, friendly condition. Least liking in the close, unfriendly condition.
Sundstrom (1978)	Pairs of subjects seated at two distances (2 ft 2 in., 4 ft 2 in.). Pairs were friends or strangers. Measured gaze, speech, compensatory behavior. Intimate and nonintimate discussion topics.	Strangers and friends shared compensatory reactions to intimate topics. Distance produced no effects.

Table 12.1. *(Continued)*

Study	Methodology	Results
Thompson, Aiello, & Epstein (1979)	Subjects were asked to rate comfortableness, appropriateness, & preference for videotaped presentations of two- and four-person groups. Models were seated at 0, 2, 4, 6, 8, & 10 ft.	Subjects rated intermediate (4, 6, 8 ft) distances as most appropriate, comfortable, and preferable.
Tobiasen & Allen (1983)	Subjects interacted with confederates. During first session, confederate gazed at subject 0, 50, 100%. Observed seating distance from confederate in second session.	In a subsequent interaction subjects sat farther from confederate who had continuously gazed at them in their first interaction.

measured. Therefore, one cannot predict behavior from this model. It can serve only for post hoc explanation. Furthermore, this model cannot explain situations where experimenters have found a curvilinear relationship between distance and eye contact (e.g., Aiello 1972; Aiello, 1977a; 1977b) and distance and topic intimacy (e.g., Baker & Shaw, 1980). Apparently the relationship between distance and other variables is linear only up to a certain distance, past which it becomes uncomfortable regardless of attempts at compensation.

It has been suggested that this compensatory change process might not be observable when only small variations occur in immediacy behaviors (e.g., Patterson, 1973). When this area of relatively minor variations during interaction is exceeded, however, compensation processes would be expected to occur. The curvilinear "comfort" models of acceptable range (Aiello, Epstein, & Karlin, 1974), privacy regulation (Altman, 1975), optimal distance (Sundstrom & Altman, 1976), personal space violation (Burgoon, 1978; Burgoon & Jones, 1976), and affiliative conflict (Knowles, 1980a), as well as a modified equilibrium model (Aiello, 1977a, 1977b; Aiello & Thompson, 1980a), are all consistent with this viewpoint.

These models maintain that there is an optimal range of distance preferred by interacting individuals and that deviations from this range, whether too large or too small, result in discomfort. When the optimal range of interpersonal distance is exceeded, compensatory reactions are used to restore the desired level of intimacy. In addition, these homeostatic models posit that the degree of comfort or discomfort experienced varies not only as a function of interpersonal distance but also as a function of the nature of the interaction situation, the relationship between interactants, and the individual characteristics of the participants. These models anticipate the more comprehensive and quite promising expectancy–discrepancy models described later in this section.

An example of the comfort models is the model we have suggested (Aiello & Thompson, 1980a), which represents an extension of Argyle and Dean's (1965) intimacy equilibrium theory. This extension (see Figure 12.2) posits that beyond a critical discomfort level compensatory processes can no longer be easily employed to reestablish a desired level of involvement. Consequently, approach forces cease to be aroused and avoidance forces predominate, resulting in an individual's subsequent withdrawal from the interaction.

As Figure 12.2 illustrates, it is hypothesized that often somewhat different equilibrium points of physical proximity exist for different groups (in this example males and females), with females in this case preferring somewhat closer distances than males. Prior research has demonstrated that females (after about age 10) actually do prefer closer interaction distances than males (e.g., Aiello & Aiello, 1974; Tennis & Dabbs, 1975). Moreover, it has also been suggested that females are more comfortable at closer interaction distances than males because they are more oriented toward affectionate and inclusive relationships (e.g., Exline, Gray, & Schuette, 1965; Kagan, 1964). However, as can be seen in this example, the areas of minor variation around the male and female equilibrium points overlap to some extent so that certain seated interaction distances (e.g., 5 ft) are similarly judged as comfortable and preferable by both males and females (e.g., Aiello, 1977b; Patterson, 1977; Sommer, 1962). Within the area of minor variation, only relatively minor deviations from the equilibrium point occur, and these are adapted to fairly easily.

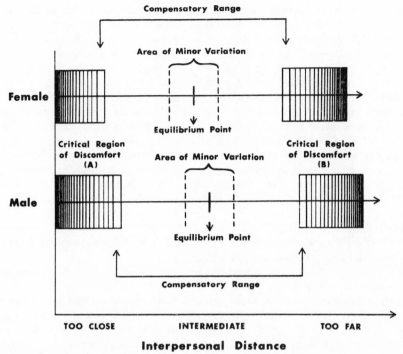

Figure 12.2. Extending the equilibrium model of social intimacy. (*Source:* From "When Compensation Fails: Mediating Effects on Sex and Locus of Control at Extended Interaction Distances" by J.R. Aiello and D.E. Thompson, 1980, *Basic and Applied Psychology, 1* (1), p. 67. Copyright 1981 by Lawrence Erlbaum Associates. Reprinted by permission.)

Outside of this area is a compensatory range of physical proximity that overlaps substantially for males and females. This area is similar to the optimal range of interpersonal interaction distance proposed by several of the curvilinear comfort models. Variations in distance that fall within the compensatory range but outside of the area of minor variation produce considerable discomfort. Typically, a series of compensatory mechanisms are set in motion to adjust interpersonal distance and other immediacy behaviors (e.g., eye contact, body orientation, and smiling) in order to restore the desired level of involvement (for a review of the literature examining the process of compensation, see Patterson, 1973). These compensatory adjustments become increasingly ineffective in reducing discomfort at distances further away from the equilibrium point and the compensatory range. Because of their interpersonal distance preferences, males in this example would be expected to show somewhat greater discomfort at distances in Area A of the compensatory range of physical proximity, whereas females would be expected to show somewhat greater discomfort at distances in Area B.

The areas falling outside of the compensatory range in Figure 12.2 represent the critical regions of discomfort, wherein it becomes increasingly difficult, if not impossible, to employ any compensatory processes to reduce the discomfort experienced and to reestablish the desired involvement level. At the present time, there is some behavioral evidence that clearly indicates that at extended distances people do attempt to use compensatory behaviors (e.g., leaning forward and increasing eye contact) but that these behaviors are not very effective regulators of the level of intimacy that is desired (Aiello, 1972, 1977a, 1977b; Aiello & Thompson, 1980a). What is being hypothesized, therefore, is that approach forces will continue to predominate during interaction only as long as there is some possibility of relieving some of the discomfort. Once the deviations from the desired level of involvement become too great, avoidance forces are much more likely to predominate, and as a result individuals will be more likely to withdraw from the interaction.

Investigations focusing on the reactions of people that occur at inappropriately close interaction distances have demonstrated that individuals who cannot adjust this distance experience physiological arousal and anxiety and display signs of discomfort (e.g., Aiello, DeRisi, Epstein, & Karlin, 1977; McBride, King, & James, 1965; Stokols, Rall, Pinner, & Schopler, 1973). In addition, individuals have been found to display nonverbal behavioral indications of discomfort at these distances. Both gaze and directness of body orientation have been found to decrease at very close distances (e.g., Aiello, 1972; Aiello & Jones, 1971; Goldberg, Kiesler, & Collins, 1969). Moreover, although both sexes respond negatively when someone invades their "personal space" by standing or sitting *too close*, males display more discomfort than females (e.g., Garfinkel, 1964; Patterson, Mullens, & Romano, 1971).

Few studies have examined the reactions that occur as a result of interaction distances that are *too far*. It is equally probable that these excessively large distances will be experienced as uncomfortable as well. Two studies (Dinges & Oetting, 1972; Haase, 1970) that showed pictures of interactants at various distances to subjects yielded ratings of the largest distances as most uncomfortable. Similarly, in a videotape study of interactants at varying seated distances, subjects characterized a distance of 10 ft as inappropriate and even less comfortable and less preferable than those of 1 to 2 ft; they reported greatest comfort for moderate distances (Thompson, Aiello, & Epstein, 1979). There is also some behavioral evidence indicating that males and females will respond differentially at inappropriately far distances. Studies of visual behavior during social interaction at extended distances (Aiello, 1972, 1977a, 1977b) have found that although males looked more as distance increased females looked less after an intermediate distance of 6.5 ft. We have suggested that this decrease in eye contact is representative of withdrawal due to the discomfort experienced at greater distance. These findings on the differential effects of distance on male and female visual behavior lend only partial support for Argyle and Dean's linear equilibrium model, which posits that, for both males and females, the greater the interaction distance, the greater the resulting looking behavior. These data do support the proposed extension of the equilibrium model, which specifies that very uncomfortable interaction distances, whether too small or too large, may lead to decreases in the involvement level desired by an individual (which may then be reflected in these studies by a decrease in eye contact).

Taken together the preceding evidence and the results of Aiello and Thompson (1980a) suggest that, although both males and females may experience discomfort at inappropriate interaction distances, males appear less able to employ effective coping strategies at inappropriately close distances, and females appear less able to employ effective coping strategies at inappropriately far distances. Therefore, males would be expected to withdraw more at close distances and females would be more likely to withdraw at far distances. Parallel predictions could be made for individuals from "noncontact"–"contact" cultures, adults–children, black–white Americans, acquaintances–friends, extroverts–introverts, peers–individuals differing in status, and many other categories of people who have *divergent interpersonal distance preferences and expectations* (as will be delineated in the following section).

12.3.4. Arousal or Attribution Models

The limitations of Argyle and Dean's (1965) intimacy equilibrium model are particularly highlighted by those studies that have found reciprocity or matching of intimacy responses, rather than compensation, when an existing intimacy level is disturbed. Argyle has had to acknowledge that, unlike the predictions from the theory:

> both reciprocity and equilibrium maintenance have been found to operate under different conditions in the case of proximity (Breed, 1972). The equilibrium effect would be expected to operate most clearly (i) in a well-established relationship, and (ii) where changes in an intimacy signal are seen as externally caused. (Argyle & Cook, 1976, pp. 66–67)

These last two qualifications for the application of the model significantly narrow its focus.

Patterson (1976) developed an arousal model of intimacy exchange to overcome several of the limitations of the Argyle and Dean model, particularly those related to situations involving incidences of nonverbal reciprocation. This approach proceeds from that of Schachter and Singer (1962), whose arousal-labeling research demonstrated that we cognitively label physiological arousal as either positive or negative and then behave accordingly.

Patterson's arousal attribution perspective postulates that any interaction involves arousal. An approach (increase in immediacy) by one of the interactants will often produce a change in the physiological arousal (if it is sufficiently strong) in the other. The other then labels this shift in arousal as either positive or negative; existing evaluations (or cognitive sets) are therefore *intensified*. If he or she has labeled it positive, the interactant will reciprocate the approach. If it has been labeled as negative, he or she will compensate by withdrawing.

While a number of studies have provided at least some support for Patterson's arousal model of intimacy (e.g., Foot, Chapman, & Smith, 1977; Schiffenbauer & Schiavo, 1976; Smith & Knowles, 1978), Patterson (1982) has concluded that "a substantially different framework may be needed" (p. 232). Most damaging for the arousal model are critiques by Ellsworth (1977) and Knowles (1977). Ellsworth suggested that Patterson's cognitive self-focus in the model may be overstated, given our tendency to make attributions about others much more frequently than we do about ourselves. Knowles (1977) argued that there is considerable ambiguity regarding the temporal ordering of arousal and labeling (the model of course calls for noticed arousal to be *followed* by labeling); cognitions may be primary and arousal secondary rather than the reverse as Patterson suggests. Further, because the model provides for both approach and avoidance throughout the interaction, this model purported to explain the full range of adjustments in nonverbal intimacy. As Hayduk (1983) notes, the model does not take baseline emotional states into account, does not specify what causes positive or negative evaluation to occur, and is prone to getting caught up in endless feedback loops. With little to guide one in determining how the interactants will label the arousal, only post hoc explanations can be devised (as with Kaplan's conflict model). We can only explain the process through an observation of the resulting behaviors.

Lastly, other theorists (Cappella & Greene, 1982) have criticized the arousal models more generally for another reason. They argue that the cognitive labeling of arousal postulates an unnecessary step that is too complex to explain behavior that occurs without conscious effort on the part of the interactants. Further, they claim that this process is too complex to explain the behavior of infants in whom these processes have also been observed.

A recent extension of the arousal attribution approach is offered by Andersen (Andersen, 1984; Andersen & Andersen, 1984), who adds an important feature to this type of model. He suggests that perceiving a change in your partner's immediacy is a necessary stage in producing behavioral adjustments. Arousal changes that are very *high or low* can initiate behavioral adjustments without conscious efforts, when they are *subsequent* to a perceived change in immediacy. While this recent model is still vulnerable to many of the criticisms discussed, empirical tests should prove informative.

12.3.5. Expectancy and Discrepancy Models

Several theorists have attempted to devise models that comprise all of the possible outside variables that can affect the interactants' behavior. These models include norms and situational factors as well as interactants' personalities, experiences, and relationship. These factors all combine to form an expectancy. The deviation from this expectancy that occurs in the interaction determines the behavior of the interactants. As with the comfort models described previously, if intimacy is too much greater or too much less than the expected level, the person withdraws. If it is close to the expected level, there is reciprocation. These models would seem to explain any of the experimental results already discussed (i.e., compensation, reciprocation, or both).

Patterson (1982) and Cappella and Greene (1982) have proposed the two major expectancy-discrepancy models of interaction. Cappella and Greene and Patterson add to situational and individual characteristics a consideration of the norms of interaction and the interactants' experiences in past interaction, which also affect the interactants' expectancies. Furthermore, the emphasis in these two theories is *interpersonal*; that is, the exchange is affected by mutual feedback. Cappella and Greene do allow, however, that self-feedback is more important than feedback from the other. Both of the models nevertheless stress the importance of *arousal* and *affect* in influencing the behavior of the interactants and suggest that "arousal may be the result of cognitive activity and not the trigger for that activity" (Patterson, 1984, p. 354).

While these recent models are similar, they differ in important respects. Cappella and Greene's discrepancy-arousal model differs in that: (1) it takes into account the fact that the interactants' expectancies may be different; (2) it has less of a ("top heavy") cognitive emphasis (the arousal level resulting from the discrepancy between expected and actual involvement level of partner is said to *cause* both affect and behavioral changes); and (3) it considers (realistically) the rapid reaction times necessary for the coordination of reciprocity and compensation processes in ongoing interactions. Patterson's sequential functional model, while not as specific or testable as the discrepancy-arousal model, is more comprehensive and incorporates multiple functions for nonverbal components of involvement, like interpersonal distance, and posits that arousal is *not* a necessary cause of subsequent behavioral adjustments (see Figures 12.3 and 12.4).

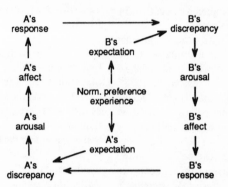

Figure 12.3. A schematic representation of the linkages among variables for the discrepancy-arousal model. (*Source:* From "A Discrepancy-Arousal Explanation of Mutual Influence in Expressive Behavior in Adult and Infant–Adult Interaction" by J.N. Cappella and J.O. Greene, 1982, *Communication Monographs, 49,* p. 97. Copyright 1972 by Speech Communications Assn. Reprinted by permission.)

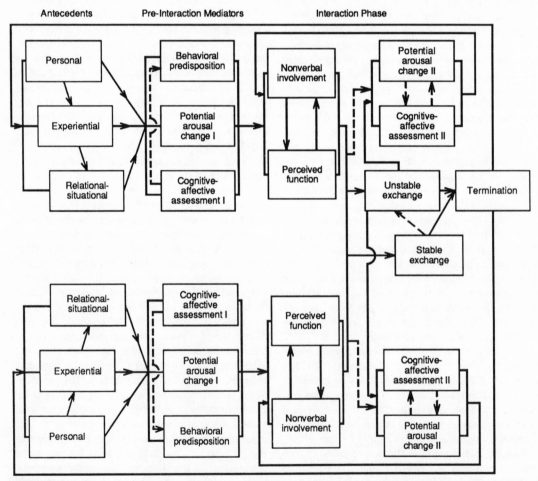

Figure 12.4. A sequential functional model of nonverbal exchange. (*Source:* From "A Sequential Functional Model of Nonverbal Exchange" by M.L. Patterson, 1982, *Psychological Review, 89,* p. 238. Copyright 1982 by American Psychological Assocation. Reprinted by permission.)

The expectancy-discrepancy models, while not ideal, would seem to have the best potential for explaining the process of nonverbal exchange (including of course the role of interpersonal distance) that occurs throughout the full range of human interactions. Both the sequential functional model and the discrepancy-arousal models make an important contribution by pointing out that the level of nonverbal involvement in an interaction is not necessarily synonomous with the interactants' level of intimacy. Patterson indicates that the level of involvement may reflect nothing or very little about a social relationship. High nonverbal involvement (including a close interaction distance), for example, may be associated not at all with high intimacy but instead with the managed and purposive function of *social control* (e.g., an attempt to persuade; a desire to create a favorable impression or sell a product) or the impersonal function of *service or task* (e.g., a physician examining a patient; two co-workers at a meeting reading from the same document). Further, this class of models can explain not only the positive relationships found between nonverbal variables (reciprocation) and the negative relationships (compensation) but also the nonlinear relationships. Stable exchanges occur when discrepancies between expectations and interactions are small, and unstable exchanges occur when those discrepancies are great.

The primary limitation of this set of models is similar to that of the arousal models: The expectancy-discrepancy models take into account a number of individual characteristics that are internal and hence difficult to measure. Therefore, since one can only measure some of the factors affecting expectancies (e.g., situational variables), one cannot always accurately *predict* behavior with these models. Further, it is unclear whether these models, as currently structured, are fully testable (i.e., able to be disconfirmed). However, they represent an important and significant improvement over early models for treating the complexities of interpersonal interactions.

12.4. MEASUREMENT OF SPATIAL BEHAVIOR: CONSIDERATIONS AND CONCERNS

As illustrated in the previous section, interpersonal distance has been treated primarily as an independent variable in studies examining the relationship between spatial behavior and other interaction behaviors. Distances have typically been manipulated in

order to observe the effects produced (e.g., compensation, reciprocation). For example, in a test of Argyle and Dean's intimacy equilibrium model or later variations two or more distances have been established (manipulated) in order to observe associated patterns of other immediacy behaviors (e.g., visual behavior). Some studies have used a within-subjects design (e.g., a confederate moves from one distance to another within the same interaction) and other investigations have used a between-subjects research design (e.g., different sets of subjects, who have been placed and remain at a single, constant distance, are compared). Occasionally, both of these designs (i.e., within- and between-subjects) have been incorporated in the same study (e.g., Rosenfeld, Breck, Smith, & Kehoe, 1984). The only other research areas that have tended to treat proximity as an independent variable are studies focusing on the effects of spatial invasion or intrusion and those investigating the consequences associated with crowded conditions involving high spatial density. An example of the former type of investigation is Sommer's (1959) classic study of reactions (e.g., time of departure) by patients of a mental hospital to his deliberate invasion of their personal space (i.e., Sommer sat at a distance of 6 in.). An example of the latter class of studies is one that we (Aiello, et al., 1977) performed to determine whether an individual's interpersonal distance preference (operationalized as the chair placement distance the subject assumed with a confederate with whom she was "to get acquainted") would predict physiological, behavioral, and subjective reactions during a short-term crowding experience (i.e., under very close proximity conditions with others) and their cognitive task performance following this experience. The current review indicates that about 25% of the 700 or so studies in the spatial behavior literature have focused on distance as an independent variable.

Hall's (1959, 1963, 1966, 1974) approach to spatial behavior is different. He views it as a product of cultural conditioning. His insightful treatments of human spatial behavior, which he called our hidden dimension, were based almost exclusively on his naturalistic observations of individuals' actual use of space. These were for the most part qualitative and nonexperimental. He did suggest however, that researchers adopt a perspective about distance that includes a focus on the communication and behavioral possibilities associated with his distance zones. Toward this end, Hall (1963) developed a system for the notation of proxemic behavior. This measurement system, which was later (1974) expanded to 19 variables, included: postural identification (e.g., standing, sitting); body angle or axis (sociopedal—sociofugal orientation); voice loudness, visual interaction and touching; thermal and olfactory codes; and, most important for our consideration in this chapter, distance or the potential for touch (which he labeled the kinesthetic code). As Hall (1963) notes:

> The kinesthetic code and notational system is based on what people can do with their arms, legs, and bodies....Another person is perceived as close ...not only because one may be able in some instances to even feel the heat radiating from him, but also because there is the potential for holding, caressing, or being struck....The *measured* distance depends largely on the size and shape of the individuals involved. (p. 1010)

This latter point is extremely important and has influenced much of my own work, particularly when investigating the *development* of personal space. Translating one figure of speech to literal terms, keeping an interaction partner "at arm's length" means an absolute distance of more than 2 ft for 16-year-olds but only about 1½ ft for 6-year-olds. As will be reported in a later section, adolescents and adults do interact at a standing distance of just under an arm's length (measured at their larger body size) or about 2 ft but younger school age children (i.e., 6- to 8-year-olds) interact at less than a forearm's length (measured at their smaller size) or about 1 ft of distance (cf. Aiello & Aiello, 1974; Aiello & Cooper, 1978; Pagán & Aiello, 1982).

The recommended use of this system is consistent with Hall's view that space is a medium through which communication occurs and each of our senses plays a role in this process. Unfortunately, his notation system or others like it (e.g., Ciolek's 1978 taxonomy) have rarely been used for the measurement of human spatial behavior.

Those techniques that have been employed by researchers in this area can be divided into three separate categories: projective or simulation methods, quasi-projective or laboratory methods, and interactional or field/naturalistic methods. *Projective or simulation* studies are the most numerous among the three categories, accounting for about 40% of the investigations. These methods require subjects to imagine some interaction situation and to project into that situation how they *think they would* behave. They include such techniques as asking subjects to represent their spatial behavior in hypothetical situations by the manipulation of dolls or miniature figures, the placement of marks on a prepared form to indicate preferred distances from others, and the

choice of sitting or standing positions represented in a photograph. For example, Meisels and Guardo (1969) had children place self-referent figures with silhouettes of numerous depictions in a multilithed test booklet. Duke and Nowick (1972), using their Comfortable Interpersonal Distance Scale (a paper and pencil measure with a representation of the self in the center of a prepared form and eight lines or radii extending in different directions from the center), asked subjects to place marks on the form at the distance (that would begin to produce discomfort) that they would stop someone's approach along each of the eight radiating lines. The ease of administration is most clearly the primary benefit of this type of method.

Quasi-projective or *laboratory* methods involve subjects using their own bodies in relation to a real or imagined other under laboratory conditions to distance themselves *as if* a real interaction were occurring. No *interaction* actually takes place. The most common of these techniques is the stop-distance procedure, which has been used in just under 100 studies. Subjects are asked to approach or be approached by another person (often an experimenter or confederate) and to stop the approach at the point where the subject begins to feel uncomfortable (cf. Horowitz, Duff, & Stratton, 1964). Different angles of approach have been included in some studies (e.g., Hayduk, 1981), but most have measured the distance of the two participants facing each other directly. Another technique asks subjects to imagine themselves with another person, represented by a coatrack, a manikin, or some other object, and to position themselves as they would sit or stand if they were involved in interaction (e.g., Mehrabian, 1968). While there is no scaling required of subjects using this type of technique, the distance dimension is very much in evidence.

Interactional or *field/naturalistic* measures are those that involve the direct (and usually unobtrusive) observation of people involved in actual interaction. Subjects may be observed in naturalistic settings (which we refer to as *unstructured interactive measures*) or may be asked to engage in social interaction in a laboratory or "laboratorylike" setting (which we refer to as *structured interactive measures*). The structured approach allows researchers to overcome all of these problems; people can be informed that they are participating in a study, researchers can identify (or control) factors such as relationships (e.g., only pairs of friends or strangers are observed) or the content of the interaction (e.g., "We are doing a survey and we'd like you to talk about your favorite

TV programs"), and greater accuracy of measurement is usually obtainable (cf. Gifford, in press). Obviously, if the setting is not one that participants in the research are used to experiencing (e.g., you bring subjects into your university laboratory rather than "bring your lab out to the children's school"), there is always the risk of limited generalizability (the price paid at times for greater control over extraneous variables, e.g., high level of noise).

The ideal circumstance for generalizing the results of human spatial behavior research would seem to be to work from studies using *valid and unobtrusive observations of distances maintained between identifiable interacting (or copresent) individuals in their naturalistic settings* (i.e., those of their own choosing). Unfortunately, only a very small proportion of the research finding from the more than 700 studies conducted in this area to date meet these ideal circumstances.

In fact almost one-half of the studies in this area have employed methods requiring subjects to imagine and reconstruct from memory how they *would* use space in a scaled-down representation of themselves and others. These projective or simulation techniques make the distance dimension very salient. Since we usually go about the process of establishing distances from others without much conscious awareness, another serious potential problem for the use of these measures would appear to be self-evident. As Hall (1963) has argued:

> Proxemic patterns, once learned, are maintained largely out of conscious awareness and thus have to be investigated without resort to probing the conscious minds of one's subjects....Indeed, the very absence of conscious distortion is one of the principal reasons for investigating behavior on this level. (p. 1003)

Regretfully, this problem would appear to be shared by the large number of studies using quasi-projective or laboratory (e.g., stop-distance) procedures. Asking a subject to stop an approaching confederate (who is often avoiding eye contact by gazing in the direction of his or her chin) at the distance that begins to make the subject "feel somewhat uncomfortable about the approacher's presence" or to approach another person until the subject is at a distance where he or she "begins to feel uncomfortable," transforms an "out of awareness" process into one in which subjects are made very conscious of their distancing behavior (i.e., precluding it from its role as a "hidden dimension" and rendering it vulnerable to a host of experimentally produced artifacts).

It is imperative therefore that before continuing with this review of the current state of our knowledge about spatial behavior we pause to examine the nature of the relationship between the projective (simulation) and quasi-projective (laboratory) methods on the one hand and the interactional (field/naturalistic) interpersonal distance measurements on the other hand and also to consider carefully the degree of correspondence among the findings obtained by studies using these three types of methods. Given the concerns expressed previously, we need to ask whether the projective and laboratory methods are *valid* measures of *actual* spatial behavior.

Hayduk (1983) in a recent review of the personal space literature argues that "an overwhelming accumulation of evidence weighs against the use of projective measurement strategies" (p. 293) and further that "the projective techniques are inferior and unacceptable measures of personal space" (p. 296). While test–retest reliabilities (across more than 20 studies) were fairly adequate (averaging about .72), the average correlation (across more than 30 studies) between projective measures and a combination of laboratory and interactional methods (called real-life measures by Hayduk) is only .39—very poor indeed! He further analyzes the pattern of results obtained using these different methods and concludes that the projective measures "provide markedly different results from real-life measures" (p. 295) and that "the scaled distances [from the smaller projective figure size to the larger human size] implied by the projective measures often fail to correspond closely [varying from 30% to 200%] to real-life distances" (p. 296). My review leads me to similar conclusions: Correlations between projective and other personal space measures are objectionably low; scaled projective distances do not parallel "life-size" distances; and results from studies using projective measures do not match well with those not requiring people to simulate the distance process.

My disagreement with Hayduk (1976, 1983) is that he does not go far enough—he "stops" his analysis prematurely and does not go the "distance"! When turning to a consideration of how the quasi-projective or laboratory measures (e.g., the stop-distance procedure) correlate with the unobtrusive interactional or field/naturalistic measures, Hayduk (1983) indicates:

> The reports of only modest correlations between the stop-distance and unobtrusive procedures (cf. Slane, Petruska, & Cheyfitz, 1981) cannot be as easily dismissed as the low correlations between the projective and real-life measures. If modest correlations

continue to appear after demonstration that similar stopping criteria are used, it would become an analytical and theoretical problem to explain why people should routinely and unknowingly stand at distances bearing little relationship to the distances at which they consciously decide they become uncomfortable about another's approach. (p. 296)

While only Slane and colleagues (1981) were noted as reporting low or "modest" correlations between the stop-distance and interactional measures, many more examples can be cited. The Slane and colleagues' study is noteworthy though because the stop-distance procedures were administered to subjects *immediately following* having their interaction distance measured; the authors record:

Subjects were unaware until that moment that distancing was being assessed. The distance between the confederate and the subject was measured with a tape rule. The subject was then thoroughly debriefed as to the real purpose of the experiment— "to compare various methods of personal space assessment." (p. 148)

Despite seeing their measured distances and hearing the purpose of the experiment, the correlations of the subjects' interaction distances with the two commonly used stop-distance procedures (i.e., stopping an approaching confederate at "the point where the subject began to feel uncomfortable" and approaching the confederate until the subject "began to feel uncomfortable") were only .38 and .44 (see also Aiello & Thompson, 1980b; Knowles & Johnsen, 1974; Pedersen, 1973).

Results from a half dozen studies from my own program of research in this area (e.g., Aiello, 1976; Aiello & Cooper, 1978; Aiello, Epstein, & Karlin, 1975a; Jones & Aiello, 1979; Love & Aiello, 1980) suggest that even the low correlations of Slane and colleagues (1981) may be *inflated* somewhat. Beginning in 1971 for comparison purposes I included projective and laboratory (i.e., stop-distance) measures along with my primary interactional measures in what has now accumulated to more than a dozen studies comparing multiple measures of interpersonal distance. As indicated, projective measures and the findings obtained using these measures did not relate very well at all to interactional measures and results obtained with them. More important for our present discussion, however, is the fact that *neither did the laboratory measures* (i.e., stop-distance), nor did their results relate very well to the unobtrusively observed interactional distances!

Two types of correlations involving stop-distance measures were computed: those that were based on average stop-distances for the pairs of subjects (a purposeful confound), and those using individual stop-distances of the pairs. In addition, two types of stop-distance instructional procedures were employed; the first asked subjects to approach or be approached to distances where they "began to feel uncomfortable" and the second asked for approaches to distances where they "felt comfortable." While researchers using the stop-distance procedure have not typically made mention of it, we should expect that instructions requesting that subjects proceed to (or stop an approaching confederate who has proceeded to) a distance where the subjects "begin to feel *uncomfortable*" would yield *smaller* distances than the other instructional set (that has been used, cf. Haase & Markey, 1973), which requests that subjects stop at (or stop an approaching confederate at) a distance *"comfortable* for a conversation." Both of these were in turn performed (in separate studies) with and without the maintenance of eye contact between pair members (Hayduk, e.g., recommends avoidance of eye contact by having the confederate stare at a subject's chin). Average correlations between stop-distance measures and actual interactional distances *never* exceeded .2 for any of these variations in these half dozen studies (see also Knowles & Johnsen, 1974, who report $r = .14$ for a similar comparison) and mean distances differed considerably when stop-distances were compared with interactional distances. In fact in one study (Love & Aiello, 1980) we asked subjects whose interpersonal distance had just been recorded during discussions on a prearranged topic simply to *replicate* their previous distance behavior using the stop-distance procedure and two simulation tasks (i.e., felt figure board placement and doll placement). People were *unable* to do so and correlations ranged from −.23 to +.15.

Should we therefore discard all those results obtained using projective (simulation) and quasi-projective (laboratory) measures and recommend that researchers refrain from using these techniques in future studies? My answer to this question is a *qualified no*.

First, there are some differences among factors associated with spatial behavior (i.e., social affect and degree of acquaintance) that have been reliably identified by all three types of measures. People typically place representational figures closer together, walk up closer, and allow closer approaches under stop-distance instructions, and actually sit or stand nearer (during interaction) to an "other" who is liked than one who is not liked. I suspect this is a result however of an interesting and rather infrequent intersection of *psychological closeness* and *physical dis-*

tance mechanisms. It will remain for future research to discover for which other factors associated with spatial behavior (e.g., similarity) this overlapping of mechanisms exists. The ease of administration advantage of the projective (simulation) measures would make their use under these circumstances particularly attractive. We would not necessarily learn a great deal about individuals' spatial behavior but we would likely learn a considerable amount about how they think of themselves in relation to others (cf. Gifford & Price, 1979, for a discussion of the subjective experience of beta personal space).

Second, to examine the protective function of personal space a procedure like the stop-distance technique affords the researcher the opportunity systematically to establish "working" boundary conditions under a variety of circumstances for the size and shape, as well as for the flexibility and permeability, of personal space (cf. Hayduk, 1981a, 1981b, 1983). Recently, Hayduk (1985) provided us with a good example of this productive use of laboratory measurement techniques. Using maximum likelihood estimation of structural equation models (LISREL), he supplied additional evidence that the stop-distance procedure measurements are reliable but, more important, showed that the stop-distance measurements do not gauge a single underlying personal space dimension as many personal space "bubble" theorists have maintained. He instead suggests from these new data that (the stop-distance measurement of) personal space consists of a "*momentary* spatial preference" (p. 148) that is dynamic and "continually open to modification" (p. 140). This description of personal space closely parallels one that could be offered for interpersonal distance. Should these results be replicated with interactional (field/naturalistic) measures, a very constructive linkage could be forged between personal space researchers from the (primarily "protection" function, e.g., Dosey & Meisels, 1969; Sommer, 1969) ethological and environmental psychology traditions and the interpersonal distance researchers from the (primarily "communication" function, e.g., Argyle & Dean, 1965; Hall, 1966; Patterson, 1982) social psychology and anthropology traditions.

It would be virtually impossible to study this domain of spatial behavior using interactional (field/naturalistic) measures of interpersonal distance exclusively. Great caution in generalizing results from studies using laboratory measures is urged even here however since reported correlations with interaction distance have been low to moderate, mean distances using interactional and laboratory measures have frequently differed, and research findings (while often in the "same direction") have not adequately corresponded with those employing interactional measures.

In sum, projective (simulation) and quasi-projective (laboratory) measures of personal space (by themselves) are both found to be lacking as adequate assessment devices for human spatial behavior and at this point have to be regarded as having questionable external validity. Both of these measurement strategies make the usually "out of awareness" distancing process *very* salient. The projective measures in particular, because they require subjects to *imagine* and *reconstruct* from *memory* how they *would* use space (almost invariably) in a *scaled-down* representation of themselves and others, lack face validity as well. Findings from studies using these measures do *not* parallel those employing interactional measures, correlations with interaction measures are *low,* and scaled projective distances are *not* at all comparable to "life-size" interactional distances. The projective (simulation) measures appear to be adequate for measuring "psychological distance" under *certain* circumstances but *not* for measuring human spatial behavior.

Quasi-projective (laboratory) measures, on the other hand, even though they do not consist of actual *interactions* between study participants, do at least involve some of the proprioceptive cues available to people engaged in "real" interaction. Since correlations between the quasi-projective and interactional measures of interpersonal distance are rather low, obtained mean distances using these two types of measures have been found to differ, findings have often not been parallel, and, more important, subjects could not even replicate the interaction distance they had maintained moments before (using the stop-distance method), we must be very cautious about generalizing the results obtained using the quasi-projective (laboratory) measures.

Findings from these studies can therefore most profitably be regarded as working hypotheses until interactional distance results become available. Given the utility of experimental controls available to researchers through the laboratory procedures (e.g., employing multiple approaches, varying angles of approach, manipulating characteristics and postures of confederate), some very creative uses of quasi-projective measures can be made (e.g., Hayduk, 1985). So there is at least the potential for valuable contributions to our understanding of human spatial behavior from these techniques — *if* these measures are used not just for the convenience of the researcher (i.e., to take the place of the often more time-consuming interactional measures), but rather to investigate questions not as easily tackled using interactional (field/naturalistic) measures.

12.5. SPATIAL BEHAVIOR: A REVIEW

This section will examine and summarize the existing spatial behavior research literature with a particular emphasis on the factors that influence the way people use space and the consequences that result from inappropriate spacing patterns.

I will begin this review with a discussion of the factors that center on the individual (i.e., the individual's age, gender, culture and subculture, and personality). People develop normative patterns of spatial behavior within the context of their effective culture and as a result of their particular socialization experiences, which are strongly tempered by an individual's stage of development, gender, and personality.

However, individuals interact and encounter others not in a vacuum but rather in specific social, situational, and environmental settings. These contextual factors exert their own (additional) influence on the preferred spatial behavior patterns of the participating individuals. For example, the nature of the mutual attraction and liking between interactants, what they happen to be talking about or doing, and whether the activity takes place in one type of environment or another can substantially affect interpersonal spacing.

I will conclude the present treatment of spatial behavior with a review of research investigating the consequences of spatial invasion/intrusion. Most of this research has focused on the reactions of unsuspecting victims who are approached at an overly close distance in libraries, cafeterias, and even bathrooms! Other research on this topic, however, has concentrated on the behavior of individuals forced by conditions in the environment to invade the space of others in settings like elevators, shopping malls, and city streets. These results are analyzed within the context of the **theoretical frameworks** presented earlier in the chapter.

12.5.1. Development of Spatial Behavior

Research examining the *development* of human spatial behavior between the age of 5 and middle adulthood has proven consistent. Spatial behavior develops gradually and systematically. As school-age children mature through adolescence, *larger and larger* inter-

personal distances are used during interaction and then these interaction distances remain fairly constant from adolescence through middle age. Conflicting evidence has been reported, however, for children prior to age 5 and for older adults.

Prior to age 5 reports of any developmental trend have been *unreliable*, with some studies showing decreases in interpersonal distances through age 5 (e.g., Burgess & McMurphy, 1982; Sarafino & Helmuth, 1981) and others demonstrating increases in distance during these early years (e.g., Lomranz, Shapira, Choresh, & Gilat, 1975; Smetana, Bridgeman, & Bridgeman, 1978). These mixed results are consistent with the analysis of children's abilities at this age level to *evaluate* distances by Sauvy and Sauvy (1972/1974), who in their introduction to topology (i.e., the study of the general properties of space, including nearness, connection, and continuity) concluded that "children of less than six years can in general distinguish near from far but, through lack of ability to measure distances are obliged to limit themselves to approximate comparisons" (p. 26). My observation, based on the small number of studies done with very young children and my own research, is that preschoolers and particularly toddlers typically display considerably greater *variability* in spacing behavior than older children, sometimes playing or interacting at distances so close that there is bodily contact and at other times at distances so far that the children have to raise their voices to hear each other. During this period children are first becoming aware of the cultural norms for spatial behavior—yet adults are providing mixed messages about what is expected of them. Often young children are told to "stop acting like a baby" when they want to be held after getting scared or scraping a knee, and yet are also often told to "give Aunt Mary a hug" or to "come over here and sit on my lap." Adults also provide different reinforcement for very young children. In one study (Fry & Willis, 1971) adults waiting in line for a movie were approached as closely as possible (without touching) by 5-, 8-, and 10-year-old children. Whereas 5-year-olds elicited positive reactions from the adults (smiling, pats on the head, etc.), 8-year-olds were ignored and 10-year-olds received negative reactions (see also Dean, Willis, & LaRocco, 1976, for similar results). Clearly, children are expected to have learned proper spacing norms by age 10 but are still considered "cute" when they have not by age 5.

From age 5 through middle adulthood, however, the development process is well documented. Interaction distance increases with age through adolescence. While adultlike spatial norms are discernible by about age 12, development continues (distance increases) through the teens. In one such study from my own program of research in this area (Aiello & Cooper, 1979) we examined interpersonal distances maintained by mutually positive and mutually negative same-sex pairs of children ages 7 to 17 using an adaptation of Hall's distance scale (which takes children's body size into account in the distance measurement). As can be seen in Fig. 12.5, interaction distance increases with age (even when body size is accounted for!). While 7-year-olds stand less than 1 ft apart while conversing, 17-year-olds typically stand more than 2 ft apart. Similar findings have been reported for other of our developmental studies (e.g., Aiello & Aiello, 1974; Jones & Aiello, 1973; Pagàn & Aiello, 1982; Thompson & Aiello, 1981) and those of other investigators who have also studied actual interaction distances (e.g., Baxter, 1970; Burgess, 1981; Ford & Graves, 1977; Tennis & Dabbs, 1975; Willis, Carlson, & Reeves, 1979).

It is important for us to point out here the *potential danger of generalizing from investigations using projective and quasi-projective methods*. Unlike the studies previously discussed, which directly observed interaction distance and found the clear pattern of increasing distance with age, studies using these indirect methods, which do *not* involve observing individuals actually engaging in interaction, have not found any consistent developmental pattern from childhood through young adulthood, with some studies finding decreases in projected distances with age (e.g., Meisels & Guardo, 1969; Petri & Huggins, 1975; Severy, Forsyth, & Wagner, 1979; Whalen, Flowers, Fuller & Jernigan, 1975), others finding increases in projected distances with age (e.g., Bass & Weinstein, 1971; Lerner, 1973; Melson, 1977), others finding no differences in approach (stop-distance) as a function of age (e.g., Hayduk & Mainprize, 1980; Terry & Lower, 1979), and still others finding a curvilinear relationship between projected distance and age (e.g., Duke & Nowicki, 1972; Pedersen, 1973a). Again, as we argued earlier in the methodology section, studies using projective measures may be useful (and expedient) when psychological "closeness" is being examined, but they are virtually useless (and often misleading) to us when we are interested in learning about actual interpersonal distance behavior—here, the *development* of spatial behavior.

Unfortunately, very few investigations have included older adults in the examination of the developmental use of space, and the findings obtained from these few studies are contradictory. Three studies (each studying females) have reported that older adults used larger distances (Gioiella, 1977; Leibman, 1970; Winogrond, 1981), two studies indicated that their elderly subjects adopted smaller distances (DeLong, 1970; Heshka & Nelson, 1972), one investigation found no correlation between subjects' age and their approach distance (Hayduk & Mainprize, 1980), and two studies demonstrated that close physical proximity (crowded) conditions were responded to more positively by older than by younger adults and actually enhanced their performance on a task (Aiello et al., 1978; Smith, Reinheimer, & Gabbard-Alley, 1981).

Given these mixed results and the fact that two of these eight studies used institutionalized, mentally impaired (DeLong, 1970) or visually impaired (Hayduk & Mainprize, 1980) subjects, no conclusions can be reached at this point about any changes in spatial behavior that might occur later in life. This brings to mind, however, Goffman's (1963) observation that in American society the very young and the very old have "special license" with respect to involvement levels, such that there are fewer restrictions applied to these age groups. This would seem to pertain here in our analysis of "appropriate" distance norms for those under 6 and over 60.

12.5.2. Gender Differences in Spatial Behavior

The result reported most often in the spatial behavior literature is that males and females differ in their use of interpersonal distance. But exceptions abound! Often these differences, when they exist, are a function not only of the sex of the subject but also of the sex of the other interactant, the situational context, and the age of and relationship between the interactants. All of these factors combine to affect the observed spatial behavior; once they are considered along with gender, the pattern of seemingly inconsistent results becomes considerably clearer (see Table 12.2).

The predominant finding in this area is that males use more interaction space than females (see the discussion of our modified equilibrium theory). This finding is obtained most frequently and consistently when the interactants are of the same sex, at least age 10, and involved in what Goffman (1963) has referred to as focused interaction. This holds true for unobtrusive observation of subjects engaged in actual interaction (e.g., Aiello & Aiello, 1974; Baxter, 1970; Rosegrant & McCroskey, 1975; Sussman & Rosen-

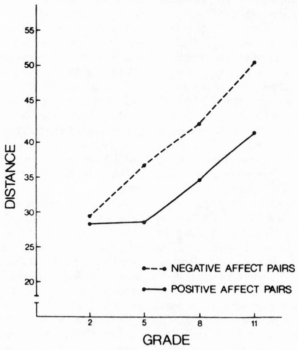

Figure 12.5. Interaction distances of reciprocated, positive and negative affect pairs at four grade levels. (*Source:* Aiello & Cooper, 1979.)

feld, 1982; Willis, 1966; Wittig & Skolnick, 1978) and even for reports from (some but not most) studies using projective tasks, where the subjects are asked to place figures of persons interacting (e.g., Ashton & Shaw, 1980; Duke & Nowicki, 1972; Gifford & Price, 1979; Pedersen, 1973a).

When the relationship between the interactants is considered, we find that the results are not as clear. Willis (1966) had a fairly large number of "experimenters" approach subjects to converse with them. The subjects were either close friends, friends, acquaintances, or persons unknown to the experimenters. Willis found that for women but not for men degree of acquaintance affected the distance they allowed. Women stood closer to close friends than to acquaintances or friends. Similar results were obtained in a photographic study of walking pairs by Heshka and Nelson (1972), who reported that while females walked closer to male or female friends than to "strangers" male spacing did not differ. Aiello and Cooper (1972, 1979), on the other hand, reported that same-sex pairs of males *and* females who liked one another interacted at much closer distances than those who did not like one another.

Another seemingly confusing pattern of results

that may be importantly affected by the relationship of the interactants is the distance used by mixed-sex pairs. In laboratory studies of interactions, mixed-sex pairs typically use an *intermediate* amount of space, more than female pairs but less than male pairs (e.g., Brady & Walker, 1978; Rosegrant & McCroskey, 1975). Field studies, however, have often found that mixed-sex pairs (who are usually spouses or lovers) use the *least* amount of space (e.g., Baxter, 1970). Apparently, mixed-sex dyads who have a *close* relationship use the least amount of space of any of the types of dyads. In one field study that specifically focused on interpersonal distance of pairs of acquaintances, Rohner and Aiello (1976) found that female pairs stood closer than male pairs but mixed-sex pairs stood at approximately the same distance as male pairs.

When one looks at the studies investigating unfocused interactions, including observations of people in waiting rooms, on lines, in spatial invasion studies and stop-distance studies, the results would appear to be far less clear. In his recent review of the personal space literature Hayduk (1983) contended that there are "sterile mountains of conflicting reports" (p. 323) relating to sex effects and argues:

Table 12.2. Influence of Gender and Age

Study	Subjects	Methodology	Results
Adler & Iverson (1974)	216 male and female college students.	Measure chair placement distance from confederate.	In same-sex dyads, subjects sat farther from a low-status other who gave "false" praise. Praise had no effect for high-status other. Males kept greater distance than females in same-sex dyads.
Ahmed (1979)	120 males, 120 females.	Latency of departure when invaded.	Females departed sooner when invaded than males. Both sexes left more quickly if intruder was male than if intruder was female.
Aiello & Aiello (1974)	424 white children age 6 to 16 in same-sex pairs.	Unobtrusive observation in field (modified classroom) using adaptation of Hall's (1963) proxemic scales.	Males stood farther apart than females at all but youngest ages tested. Interaction distance gradually increased from ages 6 through 12.
Aiello & Cooper (1979)	128 reciprocated positive or negative same-sex pairs at grades 2, 5, 8, & 11.	Unobtrusive observation in field (modified classroom) using adaptation of Hall's (1963) scales.	Positive affect pairs interacted closer distances at all but youngest age. Children regardless of affect stood at larger distances as they grew older.
Aiello, Heady, & Thompson (1978)	36 females, 20 males, 60 to 90 years old, same-sex groups of four.	Groups "waited" in small (4 ft × 4 ft) or moderate-sized (8 ft × 8 ft) room. Skin conductance data; group cohesion task (Tajfel, 1970); member's perception of environment, others in group, and subjective indications of discomfort during short-term crowding involving close proximity gathered.	Elderly men and women were more affected physiologically by the close physical proximity condition and reported feeling more crowded but did *not* find the experience aversive (as younger adults do) and were *not* the least bit bothered by bodily contact. Instead, they responded more positively to the members of their crowded group and labeled the environment "cozy." Elderly males were somewhat more uncomfortable due to crowding but overall there was a considerable narrowing of the sex difference found for younger adults.
Aiello & Jones (1971)	35 white males, 35 white females, 35 black males, 35 black females, 35 Puerto Rican males, 35 Puerto Rican females, same-sex pairs 6 to 8 years old.	Unobtrusive observation in field (schoolyard) using adaptation of Hall's (1963) proxemic scales.	For white children, girls stood closer than boys but for black and Puerto Rican children, no sex differences were found.

Table 12.2. *(Continued)*

Study	Subjects	Methodology	Results
Aiello & Jones (1979)	35 white lower-class, 26 white middle-class, 18 black lower-class, 27 black middle-class, approximately half each male and female same-sex adolescent pairs.	Unobtrusive observation in field (modified classroom) using adaptation of Hall's (1963) proxemic scales.	Adolescent boys stood farther apart and maintained more indirect head orientation than girls.
Aiello & Thompson (1980)	41 male, 46 female college students.	Subjects were seated at intermediate (5 ft) or far (11 ft) distance. Subjects' related arousal, state anxiety, mood, other feelings, locus of control, and nonverbal behavior assessed.	While both sexes were more uncomfortable and anxious at the farther distance, females reacted more negatively than males at the large interaction distance.
Allgeier & Byrne (1973)	10 male, 10 female college students tested singly.	Choice of seat in relation to interviewer in lab.	Both males and females sat closer to interviewers who were liked.
Argyle & Dean (1965)	3 male, 3 female adults; 3 male, 3 female children.	Subjects approached Argyle (eyes open or closed) or his picture.	Children stood closer than adults in each of the three conditions. Adults approached Argyle closer when his eyes were shut than when they were open.
Ashton & Shaw (1980)	40 male, 40 female college student targets.	Paper and pencil approach from different targets.	Females preferred less distance than men.
Ashton, Shaw, & Worsham (1980)	20 male, 20 female college students, opposite-sex pairs.	Subjects' ratings of actual interpersonal distances between themselves and a friend or stranger.	Both males and females preferred to keep strangers at greater distances.
Bailey, Hartnett, & Gibson (1972)	40 male, 40 female college students.	Stop approach of and toward experimenter.	Closest distances were with female experimenter and by male subjects. Female experimenter allowed to approach and was approached closer than male experimenter. Male-male was greatest distance. No correlation between male anxiety and distance. Positive correlation for females between anxiety and distance from male experimenter. Inverse relationships for males between distance and degree of heterosexuality.
Baily, Hartnett & Glover (1973)	102 males & females, grades 5 & 6.	Subject approaches and approached by 41-year-old female. Model-11.9-year-old boy approaches close (2.5 ft) or far (14.5 ft).	Boys approach closer and allow closer approach than girls. Close model resulted in distance shorter than no-model and far model resulted in greater than no-model.

Table 12.2. *(Continued)*

Study	Subjects	Methodology	Results
Barnard & Bell (1982)	I. 59 male, 71 female college student dyads.	Interactions unobtrusively measured by interpersonal distance MAT(IDM) with switches to measure location.	Female dyads did not interact more closely than males.
	II. 19 male, 22 female college students	Approach toward confederate using IDM	Females approached closer than males. Females approached a female closer than they approached a male.
Barrios & Giesen (1977)	22 male, 22 female college students.	Subjects given expectations of hostile or friendly discussion. Observers recorded distance subject sat from male moderator and other subject.	Females sat closer to other subjects and moderator. More favorable expectations resulted in less subject-subject distance and no change in subject-moderator distance.
Bass & Weinstein (1971)	59 males, 54 females, kindergarten to third grade.	Placement of paper silhouettes.	Children used more space in higher grade levels. Authors recommended using other techniques with children because many of the younger children placed the figures inappropriately.
Batchelor & Goethals (1972)	80 male, 80 female high school students in groups of eight.	Observers estimated seating distances among group members.	When instructed to solve a problem individually, distances were greater than when instructed to solve problems as a group. Females and males did not differ in distance. Subjects more likely to sit next to same-sex other.
Bauer (1973)	15 white male, 15 white female, 15 black male, 15 black female college students.	Approach toward black or white experimenter.	Black females approached closest, followed by black males, white females, and white males.
Baxter (1970)	859 dyads, Anglo, black, & Chicano male & female children, adolescents, & adults.	Unobtrusive observation of pairs in field (zoo).	For all groups, interpersonal distance increased with age. Male pairs were most distant, female pairs were intermediate, and male-female pairs stood closest.
Beach & Sokoloff (1974)	8 male, 6 female 4- to 5-year olds, groups of three.	Choice of seat in relation to interviewer (interaction in lab).	Both males and females sat closer to interviewers who were liked.
Beck & Ollendick (1976)	28 nondelinquent males, 28 delinquent males.	Stop apporach of male & female experimenter.	Both groups allowed female to approach closer than male.
Blede & Blede (1978)	54 males, 54 females, 18 to 45 years, tested singly	Stop approach of experimenter in field.	For both sexes, greater approach of female experimenter was tolerated before fleeing.

417

Table 12.2 *(Continued)*

Study	Subjects	Methodology	Results
Breuer & Lindeuer (1977)	16 male, 16 female college students.	Distance from entrance of "museum" that subjects placed enlarged photos of statues.	Males place photos of nude statues (both male and female) farther than did females.
Brody & Stoneman (1980)	18 2-year-olds and parents; 18 3-year-olds and parents.	Adaptation of Hall's notation system. Interactions were: mother-child, father-child and mother and father-child.	Larger distances used in triadic context. Mothers and children used less space than fathers and children. Parents and daughters used less space than parents and sons.
Buchanan, Juhnke, & Goldman (1976)	122 males, 122 females.	Observed likelihood of invading the space of a confederate standing by control panel in elevator.	81% of subjects chose panel with no one in front rather than invade. 72% of males, 62% of females chose to invade space of female over male.
Buchanan, Juhnke, & Goldman (1977)	I. 86 males, 61 females.	Recorded selection preference for right or left control panel in elevator. Confederate standing in front of one panel making eye contact with subject.	Male confederate: 70% of males avoided intrusion; 60% of females avoided intrusion. Female confederate: 33% of males avoided intrusion; 32% of females avoided intrusion.
	II. 68 males, 44 females.	Same as study I, except no eye contact (back turned reading), confederate added.	Male confederate: 71% of males invaded confederate with back turned; 77% of females invaded confederate with back turned. Female confederate: 78% of males invaded confederate with back turned; 72% of females invaded confederate with back turned.
	III. 28 males, 18 females.	Same as studies I & II, except one male confederate and one female confederate so that subjects would have to intrude on one or other of the confederates.	Males invaded male confederate 57% and female 43%; Females invaded male confederate 17% and invaded female confederate 83%.
Burgess (1981)	Mentally retarded children: grades 1 to 3, 10 male, 15 female; grades 4 to 6, 13 male, 12 female, 48 nonretarded.	Distances estimated by observers during outdoor free play.	Younger children use less distance than older children. retarded use less distance than nonretarded.
Burgess & McMurphy (1982)	6 to 18 months: 6 male, 5 female; 19 to 27 months: 4 male, 6 female; 30 to 60 months: 5 male, 4 female.	Distances from first to fifth nearest caretakers and first to fifth nearest playmates estimated from photographs taken at 60-sec intervals.	Distance to surrounding adults increased with age. Distances to playmates and spatial variability decreased with age. Only infants (6 to 18 months) stayed closer to caretakers.

Table 12.2. *(Continued)*

Study	Subjects	Methodology	Results
Burgoon (1978)	79 male & female college students.	In a standardized interview or negative or nonverbal feedback. Interview conducted at one of four distances. (1) Normative distance: Interaction norms were set through pilot test for interacting dyads: (interviewer listed first) MM-40 in.; MF-34 in.; FM and FF-38 in.; (2) Threat condition: less than 6 in.; (3) Close: for both 6 in. closer than normative distance; (4) Far: 6 ft.	In the "pilot test" to establish normative distances, males maintained largest distances.
Byrne, Baskett, & Hodges (1971)	50 male, 50 female, college students paired with confederate.	Seating distance, relative seating position.	For females, less distance used for similar other. Males chose to sit across from similar other.
Cade (1972)	48 Hawaiian Oriental, 24 Hawaiian Caucasian.	Kuethe's Felt Figure Placement Task.	Woman and child figures placed closer than man and child figures.
Caudill & Aiello (1979)	20 males, 20 females, paired with same-sex confederate.	Unobtrusive observation in lab of subjects' chosen seated distance (as in Aiello et al., 1977) and self-disclosure.	Females chose closer interpersonal distances and disclosed more than males.
Crowe (1975)	67 male, 90 female undergraduates.	Approach by confederate.	Females allow same-sex other to approach closer than males. Males also allow females to approach closer than males.
Dabbs & Stokes (1975)	Males & females.	Observed distance deviated in path from confederates on sidewalk.	Subjects gave males more distance than females, two people more than one, and an attractive female more than an unattractive female.
Dabbs & Wheeler (1976)	40 male, 40 female college students.	Unobtrusive observation in field.	Males' approach to female experimenter was greater than females'.
Dean, Willis, & LaRocco (1976)	48 white male, 48 white female, 48 black male, 48 black female adults tested singly.	Unobtrusive observation.	Avoidance behavior elicited by 10-year-old invaders; five-year-olds reinforced for invasion; 8-year-olds were ignored.
DeJulio & Duffy (1977)	50 male, 43 female college students.	Choice of seat (3, 6, 9 ft) from male and female confederates. Neurosis scale.	Persons with neurotic tendencies prefer larger distances. Both males and females sat closer to female confederate. No effect for sex of subject.
Dennis & Powell (1972)	200 dyads, 7- to 14-year-olds, black, white, other groups.	Unobtrusive observation. Dennis Infracommunication Analysis Device (field).	Black males interacted with white partner closer than did black females.

Table 12.2. *(Continued)*

Study	Subjects	Methodology	Results
Dosey & Meisels (1969)	91 male, 95 female college students.	Approach toward same-and opposite-sex target. Rorschach administered to assess anxiety and body boundaries. Stress and no-stress conditions.	Females approached another female closer than another male; males approached females and other males about the same distance.
Duke & Nowicki (1972)	23 male, 21 female college students, 61 male, 41 female high school students, elementary school students tested singly.	Comfortable Interpersonal Distance (CID) scale in lab.	Pattern of IPD—college students: MM>MF = FF; high school students: MM>MF>FF; elementary school students: MM>MF = FF. For same-sex pairs; E.S.<H.S.>C. Opposite-sex pairs: E.S.>H.S.<C.
Duncan (1978)	24 white male, 24 white female, 24 black male, 24 black female dyads, grades K, 2, 4.	Unobtrusive observation in field (schoolyard) using adaptation of Hall's (1963) proxemic scales.	Blacks stood closer than whites in kindergarten and grade 2. This difference nearly disappeared by grade 4. Black females stood closest. Blacks faced one another less directly than whites, this effect strengthened as children grew older. Males of both races stood less directly than females.
Edney, Walker, & Jordan (1976)	80 male, 80 female dyads.	Same-sex pairs assigned to different interaction distances (3, 7, 15, 30 ft). Ratings of distance.	Males claimed more space than females.
Fisher & Byrne (1975)	62 males, 62 females tested singly.	Evaluation of confederates, environment in field (library).	Females reacted more negatively to invasion from side; males reacted more negatively to invasion from across.
Ford, Cramer, & Owens (1977)	40 males, 40 females tested singly.	Unobtrusively photographed in lab.	Voice amplitude directly related IPD in females; no effect of eye contact on IPD.
Ford & Graves (1977)	20 white males, 20 white females, 20 chicano males, grades 2 & 8.	Stop approach toward a confederate of same age, gender ethnic background (in lab).	Chicano children stand closer than whites in grade 2. No difference in grade 8. Younger children approached more closely than older children. Females approached closer than males.
Fry & Willis (1971)	60 male, 60 female adults.	Adults in line for a movie were invaded by 5-, 8-, 10-year-old children. Invaders instructed to move as close as possible without touching and initiate no conversation. Compensatory reactions were observed.	Positive reactions (smiling, speaking, turning toward) more likely to be elicited by 5-year-olds. 8-year-olds received little reaction. Negative reactions (moving away, leaning, non-task behaviors) more likely to be elicited by 10-year-olds.

Table 12.2. *(Continued)*

Study	Subjects	Methodology	Results
Fromme & Beam (1974)	24 male, 24 female college students in pairs.	Stop approach of experimenter in lab.	During high levels of eye-contact by experimenter, dominant subjects of both sexes approached closer; males approached closer than females.
Gifford & Price (1979)	18 male, 16 female 3½- to 5½-year-olds.	Placement of paper figures in relation to stationary figures in lab.	Male-male pairs used more distance than female-female pairs in all settings.
Gioiella (1977)	100 female 55 to 88-year-olds.	Preferred Personal Space Questionnaire.	Preferred personal space increased with age.
Greenbaum & Rosenfeld (1980)	152 male & female dyads.	Unobtrusive observation in field.	Sex makeup of dyad made no difference in rate of touching during greetings; male-male pairs most frequently engaged in handshaking; dyads containing females engaged in more embracing, mutual lip-kissing.
Giesen & McClanten (1976)	48 male, 48 female college students. Same-sex groups of three.	Distance subjects sat from moderator was freely chosen or fixed at 24 in. Subjects completed rating scales of impressions.	Females sat closer to moderator than males (in free choice). Both sexes sat closer to female moderator. Female moderator was rated more highly than male.
Griffitt, May, & Veitch (1974)	27 male, 25 female college students.	Observation of distance from videotape.	Those subjects who were negative toward a sexually arousing stimulus sat farther from opposite sex other and closer to same-sex other.
Hai, Khairullah, & Coulmas (1982)	I. 852 passengers in mixed-sex dyads.	Observed which member of the pair used an armrest during flight.	Males (even when size of body considered) used armrest three times as often as women.
	II. 56 males, 45 females.	Questionnaire concerning distance seating.	Men more likely to be annoyed if neighbor used armrest.
Hartnett, Bailey, & Gibson (1970)	32 male, 32 female college students.	Stop approach of experimenter and subject in lab.	Female subjects allowed greater approach by experimenters of both sexes; both sexes allowed experimenter to approach closer than they approached experimenter; men high in heterosexuality allowed female experimenter to approach closer.
Hartnett, Bailey, & Harley (1974)	41 male, 43 female college students.	Subjects approach a tall (6 ft 3 in.) or short (5 ft 4 in.) object or person (male) while he is seated and standing.	Females approached short person closer than males do, but males approached the tall object closer. Both sexes approached seated object closer than tall object.

Table 12.2. *(Continued)*

Study	Subjects	Methodology	Results
Hayduk & Mainprize (1980)	Institutionalized blind: 12 male; 13 female. Noninstitutionalized blind: 13 male, 12 female. Sighted: 4 male, 24 female.	Stop approach of experimenter, from eight directions. (Steps counted aloud for blind subjects.)	No differences for blind vs. sighted, sex or age.
Heckel & Hiers (1977)	36 male, 26 female college students.	Seating choice.	No differences between sexes on seating distance from confederate.
Hendrick, Giesen & Coy (1974)	72 males, 72 females, divided into same- and mixed-sex triads.	Observed placement of seating cushions from discussion moderator.	No differences between sexes on placement of cushions.
Hendricks & Bootzin (1976)	80 white females.	Three measures were used: (1) initial seating choice from black and white confederates, (2) reported level of discomfort at various approach distances, (3) closest position to which subject was willing to advance.	White subjects maintained greater seating distance from black confederates than white confederates. Female subjects approaching male confederates reported greater discomfort than those approaching female confederates. No significant effects were found on the measure of overt approach.
Heshke & Nelson (1972)	57 dyads, males and females, 19 to 76 years old.	Estimation of interaction distance from photographs (nose-to-nose).	Curvilinear relationship between age and distance. Male-female and female-female pairs of friends stood closer than pairs of strangers but male-male pairs stood at similar IPD.
Hollender, Duke, & Nowicki (1973)	21 males, 34 females, grades 3 & 4; 20 male, 19 female college students.	Comfortable Interpersonal Distance, Parental Contact Questionnaires.	Negative correlation between IPD and maternal contact for males only. For females number of older brothers correlated positively with distance.
Horowitz, Duff, & Stratton	19 normal male, 10 normal female, 19 male & female schizophrenics.	Approach toward target.	Schizophrenics use more space whether target is male, female, or inanimate object.
Hughes & Goldman (1978)	90 males, 86 females tested singly.	Unobtrusive observation in field (public elevator).	Females more often invaded space of experimenter engaging in high eye-contact and smiling; opposite effect found for males.
Ickes & Barnes (1977)	60 males, 60 female college students, same-sex pairs.	Observations from videotaped interaction in lab.	No significant difference in IPD between sexes if distance is measured shoulder to shoulder. Females face each other more directly than males.
Jones (1971)	100 black, 75 Puerto Rican, 51 Italian, 86 Chinese adult pairs.	Unobtrusive observation in field (city streets) using adaptation of Hall's notation system.	Male-male axis less direct than female-female axis.

422

Table 12.2. *(Continued)*

Study	Subjects	Methodology	Results
Jones & Aiello (1973)	48 black, 48 white pairs from grades 1, 3, 5.	Unobtrusive observation in field (modified classroom) using adaptation of Hall's (1963) proxemic scales.	Males faced less directly than females. Blacks stood closer in grade 1 but this difference diminishes in grade 3 and is reversed in grade 5.
Kassover (1967)	200 males, 200 females.	Approach toward experimenter. closer than male. Males	Both sexes approached female approached closer to female and farther from male than did females.
Katz, Katz, & Cohen (1976)	80 white children 5- & 6-year-olds, 9- & 10-year-olds.	Measure seating distance from experimenter.	Children sat closer to white than black experimenter. This effect increased with age for boys, decreased with age for girls. Children sat closer to nonhandicapped white experimenter than handicapped white experimenter. For younger children, this was reversed if experimenter was black.
Kleck (1967)	20 male college students.	Silhouette placement.	Subjects placed "themselves" closer to female than male targets.
Kline & Bell (1983)	83 male, 78 female college students.	Distance sat from confederate on bench was measured. Privacy Preference Scale.	For females high-preference-for-privacy subjects sat closer to confederate.
Klukken (1971)	28 male, 28 female college students.	Interpersonal Distance Questionnaire.	Males are similar on distance in all settings. Degree of acquaintance an important determinant for females.
Knowles & Brickner (1981)	24 male, 24 female college students.	Informed subjects that they were similar or dissimilar to confederate. Observed if subject protected group space with confederate from invasion.	Males protected group space more in the similar condition. Females protected group space in both conditions.
Krail & Leventhal (1976)	36 male, 36 female college students.	Confederate of same sex invaded subject seated at library conditions: (1) across; (2) seated next to; (3) seated next to, reading subjects' book. Measured latency of response (blocking, leaning or verbal response).	Latency of response decreases with immediacy of intrusion. Same-sex dyads showed shorter latency of response. For mixed-sex dyads, females responded more quickly to male invader than vice versa.
Kuethe (1962)	100 male college students.	Felt figure placement.	Woman and child placed closer than man and child.
Latta (1978)	780 male, 48 female college students tested singly.	Seating distance in lab.	Subjects seated themselves at a distance directly related to age of confederate. Female subjects sat closer than males to a peer, but farther from younger target.

Table 12.2. *(Continued)*

Study	Subjects	Methodology	Results
Leffler, Gillespie, & Conaty (1972)	28 male, 28 female college students, each assigned a role (student or teacher) in the interaction.	Observed amount of vertical (towards other) or horizontal (side-to-side) space each used across table in a seated interaction.	Males used only more horizontal space than females.
Leibman (1970)	98 white female, 18 black female adults.	Observations of subjects seated distance from white female confederate, white male confederate, black female confederate, or black male confederate on a 6-ft bench in a waiting area. In a second set of four conditions, subjects were given the choice between intrusive seats with white vs. black females, male vs. female whites, and male vs. female blacks. In the third set of conditions, subjects were given a choice between an empty bench and a bench occupied by a white female confederate.	For both subcultural groups, interpersonal distance was not affected by the race of the confederate. Larger distances tended to be used when interacting with a male confederate than with a female confederate. When given a choice, subjects chose an empty bench over one that was occupied. Race of the confederates was not found to influence the subjects' choice of intrusive seats.
Lerea & Ward (1966)	10 male, 10 female children with speech defects (and a comparable group) tested singly.	Felt figure placement in lab.	Clinical group used more IPD than control group. Sex was not a significant factor.
Lerner (1973)	44 males, 42 females, grades K to 3.	Felt figure placement.	Distance increased with age. Children placed self farther from endomorph figure than ectomorph and mesomorph figures.
Lerner, Iwakaki, & Chihara (1976)	184 males, 184 females, Japanese grades K to 3.	Felt figure placement.	Opposite-sex pairs given more space than same-sex pairs.
Lerner, Karabenick, & Meisels (1975)	26 male, 19 female kindergarteners; 26 males, 27 females, grade 1; 32 males, 25 females, grade 2; 22 males, 25 females, grade 3.	Placement of silhouettes of average, ectomorph, endomorph, mesomorph builds. Male and female figures.	Place mesomorph closest followed by ectomorph and endomorph. Greater space for female targets. Space increased with grade level.
Lerner, Kenning, & Knapp (1975)	38 fourth graders, 36 fifth graders, 33 sixth graders.	Same as above.	No effect for grade level on distance. Females used more space toward males, males used more space toward females. Greater space placed with endomorphs.
Leventhal, Lipshultz, & Chiodo (1978a)	60 males, 60 females.	Stop approach of invader in lab.	Both sexes required more space if invader was male.

Table 12.2. *(Continued)*

Study	Subjects	Methodology	Results
Leventhal, Lipshultz, & Chiodo (1978b)	176 male and female pairs seated at table.	Observed seating arrangements in social (cafeteria or restaurant) or nonsocial (library or quiet lounge) settings.	In social situations, same-sex pairs prefer across seating, mixed pairs prefer side to side. In nonsocial settings all pairs prefer side-to-side seats.
Leventhal, Matturro, & Schanerman (1978)	60 white male, 60 white female college students.	Projective measure of distance kept from liked, disliked, or stranger. Stop approach by confederate showing positive, negative, or no affect.	Males allow females to approach closer than males. Males allow liked closest, next stranger, than disliked. Females allowed liked females closer than disliked and strangers; allowed liked males closer than disliked males and disliked males closer than strangers. For the stop-distance measure: males keep positive and negative at greater distance than neutral. Females keep negative farthest followed by positive and neutral.
Lewitt & Joy (1967)	Male and female college students.	Kuethe's felt figure placement.	Male–female figure pairs placed closer than male–female figure pairs.
Little (1968)	53 American male, 53 American female, 42 Swedish male, 43 Swedish female, 50 Scottish male, 50 Scottish female, 35 Greek male, 35 Greek female, 36 Italian male, 35 Italian female college students.	Doll placement in lab.	No overall differences between sexes in doll placement. Women saw interactions of women with authority figures taking place at a greater distance than men.
Lockard, McVittie, & Isaac (1977a)	88 males and females 19 to 60 years old.	Divided elevator into squares recorded where people stood relative to confederate.	People chose to stand in three farthest squares.
Lockard, McVittie, & Isaac (1977b)	454 female, 346 male college students.	Same as above; confederate either smiled or kept neutral face.	Subjects, particularly females, stood closer if confederate smiled.
Lomranz, Shapiro, Choresh, & Gilat (1975)	34 male, 40 female 3- to 7-year-olds.	Measurement of seating distance (subject invades upon a target).	3-year-olds used less distance than 5- and 7-year-olds.
Long (1984)	40 males, 40 females, 18 to 26 years.	Subjects asked to complete CID in different natural settings. Settings were designated high or low tension.	No effect for sex of subject.

Table 12.2. *(Continued)*

Study	Subjects	Methodology	Results
Long, Selby, & Calhoun (1980)	65 male, 52 female college students tested singly.	Subjects choice of "seat" in a drawing.	Males preferred to sit closer to females than to other males. Females preferred to sit closer to other females than to males.
Loo & Kennelly (1979)	36 males, 36 females, 5 years old.	Children were placed in groups of different density. Each child's personal space was measured by a stop-distance approach technique (child approached by female adult experimenter). Observers recorded children's behavior.	Child's personal space had no effect on children's reports of crowding. More distress and nonplay in the crowded condition. More positive interactions in the uncrowded condition. For males, crowding produced more activity, aggression, and anger.
Lott & Sommer (1967)	224 male and female college students.	Questionnaire of seating preference; actual seating choice with confederate. Status of other varied (high, low, equal).	Subjects give most distance to higher-status other. More likely to choose side by side with equal-status other.
Mallenby (1974a)	20 males, 20 females, mentally retarded, 7 to 14 years.	Figure placement self and "normal" reference person (same-sex). Approach toward female experimenter.	Males placed figure closer to self than they stood next to female experimenter. Opposite result for females.
Marshall & Heslin (1975)	142 male, 142 female college students.	Subjects solved problems in small or large room, under crowded or uncrowded conditions.	Males in particular, preferred mixed-sex groups to same-sex groups. Females preferred mixed-sex groups if room was large or crowded.
McBride, King, & James (1965)	20 male, 20 female college students.	Measured GSR as experimenter sat at different distances (1, 3, 9 ft) to present flash cards.	Greater arousal (lower skin resistance) with closer approaches, with frontal rather than side approaches, and with opposite-sex experimenters.
Meisels & Guardo (1969)	235 males, 196 females, grade 3 to 10.	Silhouette placement in field.	Inverse relationship between liking and distance. Females used more distance than males in neutral or negative affect situations. Males used more in positive affect situation. Except for same sex, children use less space in positive affect situations as they grow older.
Mehrabian & Diamond (1971)	124 male, 124 female, groups of four, same sex.	Observers recorded seating distances and orientations among four subjects. Questionnaire measures of affiliative tendency and sensitivity to rejection.	Females and more affiliative persons had tendency to choose closer positions. No effect for affiliative tendency on orientation.

Table 12.2. *(Continued)*

Study	Subjects	Methodology	Results
Melson (1977)	36 males, 44 females, in pairs, 3- to 5-year-olds.	Placement of felt figure pairs.	4- and 5-year-olds use more space than 3- to 4-year-olds. Both sexes gave more distance to opposite-sex pairs.
Morris & Smith (1980)	2 males, 2 females, approximately 3 years old.	Observed in interaction with two adults. Established baseline distances. Observed subjects in interaction with the adult from whom they originally interacted farthest.	Children's distances decreased when adult showed affectionate nonverbal behavior (eye contact, smiles) and positive verbal reinforcement.
Naus & Eckenrode (1974)	47 male, 7 female college students.	Silhouette placement.	Young–young pairs placed closer than young–old pairs. No effect for acquaintance.
Norum, Russo, & Sommer (1978)	16 pairs of children.	Observation of seating arrangement in field.	Side-by-side seating observed to be more intimate than corner or opposite seating. Girls sat side by side more often than boys. A second study failed to find a sex effect.
Pagán & Aiello (1982)	138 male, 146 female children & adolescents; Puerto Ricans from New York and San Juan.	Unobtrusive observation in field (modified classroom) using adaptation of Hall's (1963) proxemic scales.	Distance increased with age in both groups.
Patterson & Holmes (1966)	Males & females (no. not specified).	Choice of seating distance from male interviewer.	For females only, a significant correlation between MMPI Introversion–Extraversion and distance.
Patterson, Roth, & Schenk (1979)	72 six-person groups, female, male, mixed.	Asked for ratings of room and other participants. Arrangement of chairs was circular or *L*-shape.	Females preferred circular shape, males had no preference, and mixed groups preferred *L*-shaped arrangement. Circular arrangement seen as more crowded, but participants in circular arrangement seen as more friendly.
Patterson & Schaeffer (1977)	270 groups of 4, 6, 8 persons, all male, all all female, mixed.	Observation of seating distance.	Closer distances in all-female groups.
Pedersen (1973a)	66 males, 66 females, grades 1 to 6, tested singly.	Profile placement in lab.	Females used less space than males. Curvilinear function between age and distance.

Table 12.2. *(Continued)*

Study	Subjects	Methodology	Results
Pedersen (1973b)	20 male, 20 female college students.	Pedersen Behavioral Personal Space Measure; Pedersen Personal Space; Sensation Seeking Scale.	Males and females responded similarly to approaches from males and females. For males, simulated and behavioral personal space measures were related. Those measures were unrelated for females.
Pedersen & Heaston (1972)	20 male, 20 female college students.	Pedersen Behavioral Personal Space Measure; Pedersen Personal Space; Sensation Seeking Scale.	Subjects allowed females to approach closer, allowed males and females to approach more closely on sides than front. No difference between males and females on either measure.
Pedersen & Sabin (1982)	20 male, 20 female college students.	Students approached in several field settings. Experimenter approached at 6 to 18 in. or 4 to 6 ft to ask question for survey. Approach and avoidance movements recorded.	No differences for interactions. Female experimenter more likely to be approached; more movement in near condition.
Pellegrini & Empey (1970)	30 male, 30 female college students.	Chair placement in relation to seated confederates.	Females sat closer to female confederate than males sat to a male confederate. Males sat more directly.
Petri, Huggins, Mills, & Barry (1974)	38 males, 62 females.	Comfortable Interpersonal Distance.	Both sexes kept males farther, females under 20 years kept strangers at equal distance in front & rear, females over 20 kept strangers farther to rear, males allowed females closer approach than males from rear.
Rice & Belnap (1975)	8 male (hearing), 6 female, 8 male (deaf), 6 female college students.	Approach toward male and female confederate.	No difference between males and females. Deaf students approached closer.
Rohner & Aiello (1976)	208 high school juniors & seniors in same-sex and mixed-sex pairs.	Unobtrusive observation in field (modified classroom) using adaptation of Hall's (1963) proxemic scales.	Female–female pairs stood closer and more directly than male–male pairs; mixed-sex pairs adopted intermediate orientation.
Rosegrant & McCroskey (1975)	60 white males, 60 white females, 60 black males, 60 black females.	Measured distance subjects chose from empty chair (choice made before interviewer entered).	Males' space greater from males than females' space from males, and females' from females.
Russo (1970)	12 male dyads, 12 female dyads, grades K, 3, 6.	Seating distance.	No change in distance with age. Difference between males and females (males greater) became significant with age.

Table 12.2. *(Continued)*

Study	Subjects	Methodology	Results
Sanders (1978)	84 female college students.	Stop approach toward male experimenter.	Personal space was larger during menstrous flow than during middle of cycle.
Sarafino & Helmuth (1981)	Male and female preschoolers, 14 ages 25 to 42 months, 87 ages 43 to 63 months.	Seating distance; choice of seat on bench occupied by another child (modified classroom).	Females used less space than males. 25- to 42-month-olds chose larger seating distance than 43- to 63-month-olds.
Savinar (1975)	30 male, 30 female college students.	Stop approach of experimenter.	No effect of ceiling height (6 ft, 9 ft) for females. Males used more space with 6 ft ceiling. Males allowed females to approach closer.
Savitsky & Watson (1975)	22 males, 20 females, 41 to 57 months; 20 males, 18 females, 58 to 66 months.	Hall's (1963) notation system.	No effects for sex or age. Distance was negatively correlated with gaze and axis. It was positively correlated with touch.
Schmidt & Hore (1970)	15 high-SES, 15 low-SES Canadian 5-year-old–mother pairs.	Observation of videotaped interaction between mother–child pairs.	More body contact between low SES mother/child than between high SES mother/child but no distance differences.
Schwarzwald, Kavish, Shoham, & Waysman (1977)	40 male, 40 female Israeli college students.	Distance estimated between subject and same- or opposite-sex confederate. Conditions were fear or no fear of impending shock.	Both sexes stood closer to same-sex other in fear condition. In no-fear condition both sexes stood closer to opposite-sex other.
Scott (1974)	10 male, 10 female kindergartners; 8 males, 8 females, grade 1; 10 males, 10 females, grade 2; 11 males, 9 females, grade 3.	Subjects shown photographs of male, female, mixed pairs at 1 ft, 3 ft, 8 ft, 25 ft. Asked to identify picture as: telling a secret, discussion of dinner, direction to a store, calling for dinner.	Kindergartners correctly identified only at chance level. Numbers of correct answers increased with grade level. Public distance identified earliest, intimate distance next, with intermediate distances identified last.
Severy, Forsyth, & Wagner (1979)	36 white male, 36 white female, 36 black male, 36 black female, 7-, 11-, 15-year-olds.	Approach from and toward same-race target; seat placement; CID felt figure placement.	Overall, distance decreased with age, mixed-sex dyads used more space than same-sex. Blacks used less space at age 7. Methods appear to interact with variables of sex, race, and age, however.
Skotko, & Langmeyer (1977)	138 male and female college students, same-sex dyads.	2, 4, 10-ft interaction distance for each dyad (seats at table). Ratings of self-disclosure from audiotapes.	Males increased self-disclosure as distance increased. Opposite effect for females.

Table 12.2. *(Continued)*

Study	Subjects	Methodology	Results
Smetana, Bridgeman, & Bridgeman (1978)	113 pairs of 2- to 5½- year-olds.	Observation of videotapes in lab.	Slight increase in personal space with age.
Sobel & Lillith (1975)	53% male, 27% black.	Observed amount of space given to a confederate who walked toward subjects on a collision path.	Males given less frontal space than females. 42% of encounters ended in physical contact.
Stephenson, Rutter, & Dore (1973)	27 pairs of college students.	Videotaped each subject. Combined images on split-screen. Subjects seated at 2 or 6 ft.	Mean duration of look was greater at greater distance. Total duration and number of looks not affected by distance.
Stratton, Tikippe, & Flick (1973)	19 male, 14 female college students.	Subjects completed Tennessee Self-Concept Test. Distance measures were: silhouette placement, approach male student, approach clothed, headless female sewing dummy.	High self-concept males and females approached object and person closest. Approach distances varied more for females as a function of self-concept. Low self-concept placed *figures* closest.
Sundstrom (1978)	65 female college students.	Pairs of subjects seated at two distances (2 ft, 2 in., 4 ft, 2 in.). Pairs were friends or strangers. Measured gaze, speech, compensatory behavior. Intimate and nonintimate discussion topics.	Strangers and friends showed compensatory reactions to intimate topics. Distance produced no effects.
Sundstrom & Sundstrom (1977)	24 males, 16 females, tested singly.	Observation of compensation reactions in field.	Males fled more quickly if invader did *not* ask permission. Opposite results found for females.
Sussman & Rosenfeld (1982)	College students. Japanese: 18 male, 16 female; Venezuelan: 16 male, 15 female; American: 19 male, 20 female.	Unobtrusive observation of chair placement in relation to a same-sex, same-nationality confederate.	Females sat closer than males.
Tennis & Dabbs (1975)	20 male, 20 female in each of the following: grades 1, 5, 9, 12, college sophomores.	Stop approach of same-sex confederate.	Males use more space at all ages except grade 1. Differences between sexes increase with age. Subjects use more space in corner than in center of room.
Terry & Lower (1979)	16 males, 16 females, grades 7 & 10.	Subjects invaded by experimenter seated 20 in. or adjacent; measured amount of movement in task.	Subjects in invasion condition avoided contact with experimenter by moving less. No effect for age or sex.

Table 12.2. *(Continued)*

Study	Subjects	Methodology	Results
Thompson & Aiello (1981)	264 same-sex, same-race pairs of nonretarded and retarded students 5 to 19 years old.	Unobtrusive observation in field (modified classroom) using adaptation of Hall's (1963) proxemic scales and 10 other nonverbal behaviors.	Interpersonal distance increased with age for all groups. A consistent developmental pattern occurred for movements toward partner, as the number of such moves decreased with age. Body orientation became more direct by age 11. Females stood more directly than males and moved away from their partners less frequently.
Tolor & LeBlanc (1974)	72 male, 35 female college students.	Approach toward experimenter. Chair placement distance from confederate.	Males' approach distance (toward male) greater than females'. Males sat farther from female confederate than did females.
Walker & Borden (1976a)	466 males, 234 females, college campus.	Observed how many subjects intruded on interacting dyads.	Males and females just as likely to intrude. Mixed-sex dyads were more likely to be intruded upon than same sex dyads.
Walker & Borden (1976b)	497 males, 245 females.	Same as above.	Same as above.
Walker & Borden (1976c)	632 males, 340 females.	Same as above except status of confederate varied.	Subjects invaded low-status dyad more often than high-status. Same pattern as above for low-status groups. For high-status dyads, MM least likely to be intruded upon, followed by MF and FF.
Weinstein (1965)	54 males, 8 to 12 years old.	Felt figure placement.	Child figure placed closer to female figure than male figure.
Wellens & Goldberg (1978)	120 male, 120 female college students.	Evaluation of positions of silhouettes.	Negative attributions made more often for same-sex pairs. Females more lenient in evaluations of female–female pairs.
Whalen, Flowers, Fuller, & Jernigan (1975)	38 male, 47 female, grades 6 to 8, tested singly.	Stop approach of experimenter and subject in lab.	Older children used less space than younger children. Younger children of both sexes used more space in opposite-sex than same-sex pairs. Older children used less space in opposite-sex than in same-sex pairs.

Table 12.2. *(Continued)*

Study	Subjects	Methodology	Results
Willis (1966)	755 males and females tested individually.	Initial distance from a large number of male and female experimenters in field (homes, businesses, and in halls of a university).	Women approached closer than men. Women stand closer to close friends than to acquaintances or friends. Peers approach each other more closely than older individuals.
Willis, Carlson, & Reeves (1979)	408 white males, 383 white females, 143 black males, 113 black females, grades K to 6, in groups.	Unobtrusive observation in field (cafeteria lines).	In all-white and integrated schools, IPD increased with age; in all-black schools, no increase with age. In all schools, grade-school children stand farther from opposite sex, in all-white schools, this increased with age.
Winogrond (1981)	18 females, 19 to 24 years old, white; 18 females, 63 to 85 years old, white; 18 females, 53 to 86 years old, black.	Measured distance approached toward a friend.	Young whites approached closer than elderly blacks and whites. White and black elderly women interacted at the same distance.
Wittig & Skolnick (1978)	40 male, 40 female college students.	Unobtrusive observation of distance from experimenter.	Males given more space than females. For both sexes, high-status other given more space. For males but not females, high-sociability other given less space than low-sociability other.

The MM > MF > FF pattern is also seemingly at odds with the "space as a buffer against threat" perspective proposed some time ago by Dosey and Meisels (1969). Since physical/biological sex differences are most imbalanced for male-female interactions, these contacts should produce the largest distances. (p. 308)

I believe that this view illustrates the problems that result from the *overemphasis of the protection function* of interpersonal distance (as I argued earlier, in Section 12.4) by researchers primarily or exclusively using quasi-projective (i.e., laboratory) techniques. *An integration of the protection and communication functions* would allow for both the MM > MF > FF pattern and the often-found MM > FF > MF pattern described in the preceding paragraph—under certain identifiable circumstances.

A careful examination of Table 12.2 indicates that a complex pattern *can* be discerned. While women

are approached much more closely than men and *allow* closer (nonthreatening) approaches, they are *less* likely than males to intrude on another person's space—unless it appears that the other is "accepting" and relatively harmless (cf. Hartnett, Bailey, & Gibson, 1970). The former results of *closer* female distances are consistent with the most frequently proposed rationale for male–female differences in nonverbal behavior, that females adopt closer distances because they are more affiliative, friendly, and positive toward others than men are (e.g., Mehrabian, 1972). The latter result, that females sometimes stop their approach toward another at *larger* distances than males, needs another explanation.

LaFrance and Mayo (1978) interpret these results using Bakan's (1966) *duality* analysis, which argues that there are two forces operating in all living forms: *agency* (linked to proactivity and self-protection and self-assertion) and *communion* (linked to reactivity and interpersonal sensitivity and support). They propose that these modalities "have become arbitrarily linked with gender: males demonstrate agency, and females communion" (p. 157). So when another approaches, women display the dominant *reactive* dimension by being more "giving" (and allowing the *closer* approach), but "when the *proactive* dimension is being emphasized, women react differently" (LaFrance & Mayo, 1978, p. 164) and "give" the other person *more* space by using an approach that is not as close under these unfocused interaction conditions that are necessarily more ambiguous.

Consistent with the finding that women are generally approached more closely than men (cf. Kassover, 1967; Long, Selby, & Calhoun, 1980) is the observation that male intruders receive more negative evaluations and create more distress and flight responses (e.g., Ahmed, 1979; Bleda & Bleda, 1978; Krail & Leventhal, 1976; Murphy-Berman & Berman, 1978). In ambiguous settings, since men are somewhat larger and often more proactive, they may be perceived as more threatening. In less ambiguous settings (e.g., a beach, pub), however, a male invasion (toward a female) may be responded to with considerably less surprise and greater favor (cf. Skolnick et al., 1977). It is also not surprising that males tend to react more negatively and strongly than females to an invader and to having "their" space invaded (e.g., Garfinkel, 1964; Patterson, Mullens, & Romano, 1971). As was noted in Figure 12.2, males have a lower tolerance than females for distances that are perceived to be *too close*.

Situational factors that help to clarify ambiguities of an unfocused interaction context also moderate sex differences in spatial behavior. Hughes and Goldman (1978), for example, in a study conducted in a public elevator, found that females chose to invade on another's space if he or she was smiling and engaging them in eye contact. On the other hand, males chose to invade on someone engaging in low levels of eye contact and not smiling (see also Lockard, McVittie, & Isaac, 1977). For women the look and smile apparently serve to dilute some of the threat potential of the situation and additionally make an intrusion more acceptable. In another study that used obtrusively high levels of experimenter eye contact without an accompanying smile, women were more reticent about their (stop-distance) approach and males approached the experimenter more closely. Males may have been proactively meeting a potentially threatening challenge with a closer distance.

In other unfocused situations, however, females will use less space than men, especially if the presence of the other is not made salient. In a relatively safe waiting room, for example, females have been observed to sit closer together (Mehrabian & Diamond, 1971), while in other situations of intrusion females were more likely to leave (flee) when the intruder made his or her presence salient by speaking to the subject (Polit & LaFrance, 1977; Sundstrom & Sundstrom, 1977).

Several studies have found that various situational factors will also affect how males and females react both to being invaded and to invading the space of others. Patterson and colleagues (1971) had suggested that males and females react differently to invasions from the side and front. Fisher and Byrne (1975) found that invading males and females seated at tables in a library from the side or front did in fact affect the subject's feeling toward the invader. Consistent with their own preferred seating choices (e.g., Sommer, 1959), females reacted much more negatively to side invasions, whereas males reacted more negatively to frontal invasions.

Recent field research has examined two other types of unfocused interaction (subtle intrusion situations that reflect our expectations that women will "take up" less space through more restrictive postures, and that men will "take up" more space through more expansive postures, (cf. Mehrabian, 1972). Hai, Kairullah, and Coulmas (1982) studied mixed-sex pairings of airline passengers during flights and found that males (even when body size was considered) used the common armrest (i.e., located between them) three times as often as females. They further report (from a follow-up questionnaire study) that men would be much more likely to get annoyed if their neighbor used the armrest. Two studies of pedestrians on sidewalks further illustrate this difference—both observed that male pedestrians are given more space than female pedestrians (Dabbs & Stokes, 1975; Silveira, 1972). Whereas in same-sex encounters the two approaching pedestrians got out of each other's way about the same number of times, in mixed-sex encounters women got out of the man's way *four times as often* as men got out of the woman's way (Silveira, 1972)!

The results of these studies show that, in addition to the age, sex, and relationship of interactants, a consideration of the situation is necessary to predict how males and females will use space. Situations that involve affiliation such as focused interaction involving people in a close relationship, or situations involving someone behaving in an affiliative manner (high eye contact, smiling), lead women to interact at closer distances than men. In contrast, situations that imply threat such as approach by another, invading someone who is not affiliative (not smiling, no eye contact), or being invaded by a threatening other who makes his or her presence very salient, all seem to elicit greater distances and earlier flight from females.

In sum, except for young children, there are sex differences in spatial behavior and reactions to spatial invasion that are consistent, systematic, and predictable—if the other's sex and his or her relationship with the person are known and enough information about the situation and interaction context is available. I agree with LaFrance and Mayo (1978), however, who noted: "The display of gender-linked nonverbal behavior is neither permanent nor immutable....But gender is itself a context for other nonverbal behaviors" (p. 170).

12.5.3. Influence of Culture and Subculture

Research in the area of cultural differences in spatial behavior proceeds from the work of the anthropologist Edward T. Hall (1966), who observed that people in different cultures utilize space differently from one another. He proposed that people in "*contact*" cultures such as Southern Europeans, Latin Americans, and Arabs, maintain closer interaction distances and exhibit a higher amount of involvement with each other when interacting. This greater level of involvement includes not only closer proximity, but also larger amounts of touching and eye contact, and more direct body orientation. Those who are members of *noncontact* cultures (North Americans, Northern Europeans) are less involved with each other when interacting. We have discussed elsewhere (Aiello & Thompson, 1980b) Hall's qualitative observations and descriptive accounts of these cultures. Here I will focus on relevant empirical research.

It is unfortunate that the majority of cultural studies have been performed with participants who were in residence in a country outside of their own at the time of the investigation. Generalizing from data gathered with subjects of this category must, of course, be done with a good deal of caution. These subjects may not be representative of their respective countries, since they are usually better educated and have traveled more extensively than the majority of their fellow countrymen. The spatial behavior of these subjects has probably also been influenced at least to some degree by the proxemic patterns of the culture in which they have been residing.

Although research investigating the differences among cultures in personal space is relatively sparse, trends do appear that support the hypotheses put forth by Hall (see Table 12.3). Watson and Graves (1966), for example, found that Arab college students did sit closer, at a more direct angle, engaged in more eye contact, spoke louder, and touched each other more than American students when observed in interaction. In a similar but more extensive investigation Watson (1970) observed the proxemic behavior of male foreign students from a number of contact cultures (Arabs, Latin Americans, Southern Europeans) and noncontact cultures (North Americans, Northern Europeans, Asians). The observational method was similar to that employed in his earlier study. Subjects were also interviewed and completed a background questionnaire concerned with basic demographic and experiential information. The data from the American male subjects from the preceding investigation (Watson & Graves, 1966) were also included in this study. Foreign students from contact cultures generally faced each other more directly, touched more, and spent more time looking into each other's eyes than students from noncontact cultures. Of greatest importance to us here is the finding that Arab students sat closest together while Northern European students sat farthest apart. Also of interest were the questionnaire data that indicated that individuals from different cultures did not attach the *same meaning* to the same components of proxemic behavior. Similarly, Vaksman and Ellyson (1979) reported that male American students (noncontact culture) sat farther apart and looked less than male foreign students from a variety of contact cultures (i.e., Argentina, Guatemala, Honduras, Iran, Libya, Saudi Arabia, and Venezuela).

In a doll placement task, Little (1968) found that Greeks placed figures closest, followed by Italians and Americans, with Swedes and Scots placing the figures farthest apart. In several studies, Noesjirwan (1977, 1978) found that Indonesians used less space than Australians and were also more likely to seek out companionship (e.g., start a conversation with a stranger) than Australians. While it does appear that Indonesians seek greater involvement with others, Noesjirwan (1978) did find that they regarded each other less directly and used less gaze. Apparently the sensory modes with which one involves oneself with another differ from culture to culture.

While several studies have found support for Hall's observations, several others have found no differences between cultures in interaction distances where differences would be expected according to Hall. Forston and Larson (1968) found no differences

Table 12.3. Influence of Culture and Subculture

Study	Subjects	Methodology	Results
Aiello & Jones (1971)	210 dyads, equal numbers of black males & females, white males & females, Puerto Rican males & females, 6 to 8 years old.	Unobtrusive observation in field (schoolyard) using adaptation of Hall's (1963) proxemic scales.	Middle-class white children stood farther apart than lower-class black and Puerto Rican children when interacting. Black children stood less directly than white children.
Aiello & Jones (1979)	White: 35 lower-class, 26 middle-class; black: 18 lower-class, 27 middle-class. Approximately half each male and female same-sex adolescent pairs.	Unobtrusive observation in field (modified classroom) using adaptation of Hall's (1963) proxemic scales.	Black adolescents stood farther apart and maintained a more indirect head orientation than white adolescents. Lower-class adolescents interacted at larger distances than middle-class adolescents.
Banks (1973)	Blacks & whites.	Preferred Distance Questionnaire.	Blacks preferred more distance than whites.
Bauer (1973)	College students, 15 white males, 15 white females, 15 black males, 15 black females.	Approach toward black or white experimenter.	Black females approached closest, followed by black males, white females, and white males.
Baxter (1970)	859 dyads, Anglo, black, Chicano; male & female; children, adolescents, adults.	Unobtrusive observation of pairs in field (zoo).	Mexican-Americans stood closest, followed by whites, then blacks. Blacks stood closer in indoor setting; Chicanos stood closer outdoors.
Baxter & Rozelle (1975)	29 male white college students.	Subjects were videotaped with confederate in police interview simulation. Confederate shifted distance every 2 min: Experimental-4 ft, 2 ft, 8 in., 2 ft; Control-4 ft, 2 ft, 2 ft, 2 ft.	Subjects in the experimental group showed following reactions to 8-in. distance: (1) speech disruption; (2) gaze aversion; (3) increased defensive arm positions; (4) increased arm movement; (5) decreased foot movement; and (6) increased trunk rotation.
Booraem Flowers, Bodner, & Satterfield (1977)	60 male black & white delinquent youths.	Approach by confederate male (European-American) confederate (eight axes).	Those who committed crimes against property allowed greater approach than those who committed crimes against persons. European-Americans allowed closer approach than African- and Mexican-Americans.
Brown (1981)	263 white females, 213 white males, 20 black females, 12 black males.	Observation of likelihood of subjects to invade upon conversation in a shopping mall.	Subjects more likely to pass through all-black dyad than white or mixed dyad.

Table 12.3. *(Continued)*

Study	Subjects	Methodology	Results
Cade (1972)	I. 48 Hawaiian Oriental, 24 Hawaiian Caucasian.	Kuethe's Felt Figure Placement Task.	No difference between subcultures in distances they placed family members from each other.
	II. 21 American, 18 Filipino, 26 Japanese.	Kuethe's Felt Figure Placement Task.	No difference between subcultures in distances they placed family members from each other.
Collett (1971)	10 Arab male, 50 English male college students.	Rating of liking for other subject.	Arab subjects gave more favorable ratings to Englishmen instructed in Arab-like (greater immediacy) behaviors than those who were not.
Connolly (1974)	24 black, 24 midwestern children (38 males, 10 females).	Four sets of photographs showing teacher–student dyads in spacings ranging from 12 to 84 in. were presented to subjects. Subjects made three judgments choosing those that represented: (1) the most appropriate spacing; (2) enough forward movement to change the interaction; and (3) enough backward movement to change the interaction. Measurements of proxemic behavior were also correlated with their choices.	Black subjects placed less space between interactants than white subjects for all three choice conditions. They also appeared to use more spatial manipulation to mark different changes in content and context during a conversation. All subjects agreed that a negative meaning was conveyed when the interactants were moved far enough apart. There was no agreement on the meaning of a close distance.
Dean, Willis, & LaRocco (1976)	48 white male, 48 white female, 48 black male, 48 black female adults, tested singly.	Unobtrusive observation.	Avoidance behavior elicited by 10-year-old invaders; 5-year-olds reinforced for invasion; 8-year-olds were ignored.
Dennis & Powell (1972)	200 dyads, black, white, other groups, 7 to 14 years old.	Unobtrusive observation, using the Dennis Infracommunication Analysis Device in field.	Space between black–white dyads increased with age. Black males interacted closer than black females with white partner.
Duke & Nowicki (1972)	120 black, 363 white, elementary through college students.	Comfortable Interpersonal Distance Scale.	Subjects projected smaller distances for stimulus persons of the same race than for those of a different race.

Table 12.3. *(Continued)*

Study	Subjects	Methodology	Results
Duncan (1978)	96 dyads, equal numbers of same-sex (male or female), same-race (black or white) pairs in grades K, 2, 4.	Unobtrusive observation in field (schoolyard) using adaptation of Hall's proxemic scales.	Blacks interacted at closer distances than whites in earlier grades but difference disappeared by fourth grade. Black females stood closest. Black faced one another less directly than whites; this effect strengthened as children grew older. Males of both races stood less directly than females.
Edwards (1973)	South African males: 30 white students, 30 Xhosa students, 30 rural Xhosa, 30 urban Xhosa, tested singly.	Doll placement in lab.	All groups placed friends closest, followed by acquaintances, then strangers, except urban Xhosa, who placed strangers closer than acquaintances. Rural and urban Xhosa placed acquaintances at greatest angle. Xhosa placed men more directly in M–F pairs. No difference for white students.
Engelbretson (1972)	Sanse Japanese: 26 male, 24 female; American Caucasians: 24 male, 25 female; mainland Japanese: 32 male, 24 female, college students.	Kuethe's Felt Figure Task in lab.	Cultural differences do not correspond to placement distance.
Engelbretson & Fullmer (1970)	Native Japanese: 32 male, 24 female; Hawaii Japanese: 26 male, 24 female; American Caucasian: 24 male, 25 female.	Adaptation of Kuethe's Felt Figure Technique. Six different interaction scenes that varied as a function of interactants and conversational contents.	No difference between Hawaii Japanese and American Caucasian placement distances but native Japanese had significantly larger placements. Across all groups, students with friend placements were closer than student with father or professor.
Ford & Graves (1977)	20 white males, 20 white females, 20 Chicano males, grades 2 & 8.	Stop approach toward a confederate of same age, gender, ethnic background (in lab).	Chicano children stand closer than whites in grade 2. No difference in grade 8. Younger children approached more closely than older children. Females approached closer than males.
Forston & Larson (1968)	32 pairs, Latin American, North American.	Unobtrusive observation in lab of seated interaction.	No physical contact between members of either group. No differences between groups in either axis or seating distance.

Table 12.3. *(Continued)*

Study	Subjects	Methodology	Results
Frankel & Barrett (1971)	40 male, Caucasian, native-born Americans.	Approach technique in which subjects were approached by white or black confederates in a counterbalanced order.	High-authoritarian and low-self-esteem white subjects allowed closer approach distances for white than for black approacher.
Gilmour & Walkey (1981)	73 male New Zealand prison inmates, 22% Polynesian.	Distances estimated from videotapes.	Violent prisoners used more distance than non-violent. No difference between Europeans and Polynesians.
Graubert & Adler (1977)	77 Australian, 96 South American, 94 Great Britain, 113 American, males & females, 18 to to 20 years old.	Figure Placement Task.	Male students from all four groups appear similar on both neutral and mental-patient-related stimuli, as well as in importance of attractiveness of opposite sex other. Females were similar only on neutral items. All groups kept "mental hospital" and "mental patient" at greatest distance.
Hendricks & Bootzin (1976)	80 white females.	Three measures were used: (1) initial seating choice from black and white confederates; (2) reported level of discomfort at various approach distances; and (3) closest position to which subject was willing to advance.	White subjects maintained greater seating distance from black confederates than white confederates. Female subjects approaching male confederates reported greater discomfort than those approaching female confederates. No significant effects were found on the measure of overt approach.
Hore (1970)	15 high-SES, 15 low-SES children.	Videotaped interactions between mother and child.	Low-SES mothers showed more physical closeness on a practical task. No difference on verbal task.
Jones (1971)	I. 22 black, 35 Puerto Rican, 19 Italian dyads.	Observation of photographs in field (city streets) adaptation of Hall's notation system.	The subcultural groups did not differ in distance or axis.
	II. 100 black, 75 Puerto Rican, 51 Italian, 86 Chinese, MM, MF, & FF dyads.	Unobtrusive observation in field (city streets) adaptation of Hall's notation system.	For all groups, male–male axis less direct than female–female axis. No differences among the subcultural groups in distance.

Table 12.3. *(Continued)*

Study	Subjects	Methodology	Results
Jones & Aiello (1973)	48 black, 48 white pairs, grades 1, 3, 5 equal number of MM, FF pairs.	Unobtrusive observation in field (modified classroom) using adaptation of Hall's (1963) scales.	Blacks stood closer than whites in grade 1, same in grade 3, and farther in grade 5. Blacks faced each other less directly than whites. Males of both groups faced less directly than females.
Katz, Katz, & Cohen (1976)	80 white children, 5 & 6 years old, 9 & 10 years old.	Measures seating distance from experimenter.	Children sat closer to white than black experimenter. This effect increased with age for boys, decreased with age for girls. Children sat closer to nonhandicapped white experimenter than handicapped white experimenter. For younger children, this was reversed if experimenter was black.
Keating & Keating (1980)	40 male Kenyans.	Estimated distance from photographs of pairs seated on public benches.	Acquainted pairs sat closer than unacquainted pairs.
Leibman (1970)	98 white, 18 black female adults.	Observations of subject's seated distance from white female confederate, white male confederate, or black male confederate on a 6-ft bench in a waiting area. In a second set of four conditions, subjects were given the choice between intrusive seats with white vs. black females, white vs. black males, male vs. female whites, and male vs. female blacks. In the third set of conditions, subjects were given a choice between an empty bench and a bench occupied by a white female confederate.	For both subcultural groups, interpersonal distance was not affected by the race of the confederate. Larger distances tended to be used when interacting with a male confederate than with a female confederate. When given a choice, subjects chose an empty bench over one that was occupied. Race of the confederates was not found to influence the subjects' choice of intrusive seats.
Lerner, Iwawaki, & Chihara (1976)	Male & female Japanese, grades K to 3 (number not specified).	Felt figure placement.	Space increased with age, opposite-sex pairs given more space than same-sex pairs.
Little (1968)	College students, 53 American males, 53 American females, 42 Swedish males, 43 Swedish females, 50 Scottish males, 50 Scottish females, 35 Greek males, 35 Greek females, 36 Italian males, 35 Italian females.	Doll placement in lab.	No significant differences between males and females in IPD. Pattern found for IPD was Greek<Italian-American<Swedish<Scottish.

Table 12.3. *(Continued)*

Study	Subjects	Methodology	Results
Lomranz (1976)	15 Argentinian, 15 Iraqui, 15 Russian males.	Doll placement in lab.	Overall mean interaction distances were greatest for Argentinians, followed by Russians, then Iraquis. Iraquis, however, used least IPD for good friends.
Lothstein	Adolescent prisoners: 16 male high-assault white & black, 16 male low-assault white & black. High school students: 16 black males, 16 white males.	Approach by experimenter.	High-assaultive use more personal space. Blacks use more space than whites.
Mazur (1977)	38 American male, 25 Moroccan male, 26 Spanish male, unacquainted pairs.	Observation from photographs in field (on park benches).	No cross-cultural differences in seating distances.
Noesjirwan (1977)	139 Australians (68% female), 147 Indonesians (74% female), patients in a waiting room.	Unobtrusive observation of seating distance.	Indonesians were more likely to enter with a companion, sit closer to a stranger, and talk to a stranger.
Noesjirwan (1978)	32 Australian dyads, 22 Indonesian dyads.	Unobtrusive observation using adaptation of Hall's notation system.	Indonesians interact at closer distances than Australians, but with less direct gaze and body orientation.
Pagán & Aiello (1982)	148 male, 146 female children and adolescents; Puerto Rican, from New York and San Juan.	Unobtrusive observation in field (modified classroom) using adaptation of Hall's (1963) proxemic scales.	Personal space increased with age in both groups. This increase came later in the San Juan group.
Roger & Mjoli (1976)	16 acculturated (ACC) male, 16 nonacculturated (N-ACC) male Xhosa.	Doll placement.	ACC group placed themselves farther from chief than peer figure. N-ACC group placed themselves closer to chief figure than boy figure.
Rosegrant & McCrosky (1975)	60 white male, 60 white female, 60 black male, 60 black female college students.	Measure of seating distance.	Whites space themselves farther from blacks than whites, farther than blacks from whites, and blacks from blacks. Female blacks used least distance.
Scherer (1974)	I. 15 black dyads, 20 white dyads, grades 1 to 4, male & female lower-class SES.	Children in schoolyard were unobtrusively photographed, distances estimated from photos.	No effect for race on interaction distance (although white children tended to stand farther apart than black children).

Table 12.3. *(Continued)*

Study	Subjects	Methodology	Results
	II. 17 lower-class black pairs, 14 middle-class black pairs, 20 lower-class white pairs, 17 middle-class white pairs, same-sex pairs (number and age of each not specified).	Observation sites were middle-class school playground and lower-class district playground.	Middle-class whites stood farther apart than lower-class whites. No difference existed between middle- and lower-class blacks although trend was the same as for whites.
Schofield & Sagar (1977)	109 black, 138 white seventh & eighth graders, male & female (numbers of each not specified).	Observations of side-by-side and face-to-face seating patterns using gender and racial aggregation indices in an integrated school's cafeteria containing 32 rectangular (16-seat) tables.	Race was found to be extremely important grouping criterion (even for students choosing to attend a desegregated school). Sex was found to be an even more important grouping criterion. Racial aggregation decreased over time in one grade (7) but increased in the other.
Severy, Forsyth, & Wagner (1979)	36 white male, 36 white female, 36 black male, 36 black female 7-, 11-, 15-year-olds.	Approach from and toward same-race target seat placement, CID. Felt figure placement.	Blacks used less space than whites at age 7 but this effect appears to reverse as children age. Method and race, sex, & age appear to interact, however.
Schmidt & Hore (1970)	15 high-SES, 15 low-SES Canadian 5-year-old–mother pairs.	Observation of videotaped interaction between mother–child pairs.	More body contact between low-SES mother and child than between high-SES mother and child but no distance difference.
Shuter (1976)	137 Costa Rican, 124 Panamanian, 132 Colombian male and female dyads.	Unobtrusive observation in field using modification of Hall's notation system.	Costa Ricans use least space, engage in more touching followed by Panamanians, then Colombians. Same pattern found for directness of axis.
Sobel & Lillith (1975)	116 pedestrians, 27% black, 53% male.	Observed amount of space given to a confederate who walked toward subjects on a collision path.	Males given less frontal space than females. 42% of encounters ended in physical contact. Male confederate was brushed more often than female confederate.
Sommer (1968)	90 American, 112 Swedish, 131 English, 98 Scottish, 93 Pakistani college students.	Ratings of intimacy of seating positions in lab.	Americans, Swedes, and English rate seating similarly, with across seating seen as more intimate. Dutch subjects rate corner seats less intimate. Pakistanis rate side-by-side seating as most intimate.

Table 12.3. *(Continued)*

Study	Subjects	Methodology	Results
Sussman & Rosenfeld (1982)	Bilingual Japanese: 18 male, 16 female; Bilingual Venezuelan: 19 male, 15 female; American: 19 male, 20 female.	Unobtrusive observation of chair placement distance in relation to same-sex, same-nationality confederate.	When speaking in native language: Japanese> American-Venezuelan. When speaking English all groups approximated American pattern of distance.
Tennis & Dabbs (1976)	28 black female, 28 white female adults.	Stop approach (own and experimenter) of same-race other in lab.	Whites allowed closer approach than blacks. Both races preferred more space in corner than in center of room.
Thayer & Alban (1972)	44 males 25 to 55 years old.	Distance allowed experimenter (male, wearing a flag or peace button) to approach in field.	In Little Italy, politically similar experimenter allowed to approach closer. In Greenwich Village, no difference in approach allowed for similar and dissimilar experimenter.
Thompson & Aiello (1981)	262 same-sex, same-race pairs of nonretarded and educable mentally retarded students 5 to 19 years old.	Unobtrusive observations in field (modified classroom) using adaptation of Hall's (1963) proxemic scales and 10 other nonverbal behaviors.	Blacks stood farther apart and less directly.
Thompson & Baxter (1973)	10 pairs of each: white–black, white–Mexican Americans, black–Mexican Americans, males & females.	Observed compensatory reactions (movement forward and away during interaction) in real life (e.g., high school, hospital).	Whites move away from Mexican-Americans; blacks retreat from both whites and Mexican-Americans; whites move forward with blacks (to decrease distance).
Tolor (1968)	Emotionally disturbed: 9 black, 11 white. Nondisturbed: 26 white, 31 male, 15 female.	An adaptation of Kuethe's Felt Figure Technique was used. There were four non-social stimuli (shapes) and four social stimuli (homogeneous and heterogeneous pairings of black and white boys and girls).	Interracial and male–female reconstructions were found to be made at greater distances than male–female pairings of the same ethnic background. No differences in replacement distance were obtained for emotionally disturbed children.
Tolor & Orange (1969)	10 male & 10 female nondisadvantaged; 10 male & 10 female disadvantaged (75% black).	Felt figure placement. Maps task.	Disadvantaged children used more space in both tasks.
Vaksman & Ellyson (1979)	College students, 15 American male, 15 foreigner male, from Argentina, Guatemala, Honduras, Iran, Libya, Saudi Arabia, Venezuela.	Unobtrusive observation of chair placement.	Foreign students used less distance and gaze than Americans.

Table 12.3. *(Continued)*

Study	Subjects	Methodology	Results
Watson (1970)	Contact cultures: 20 Arab, 20 Latin American, 10 South European. Noncontact cultures: 12 Asian, 12 Indian–Pakistanis, 32 North European. All male.	Unobtrusive observation in lab (seated interaction). A demographic questionnaire and proxemics research interview were also included.	Subjects from contact cultures faced each other more directly, touched more, and looked into each other's eyes more than subjects from noncontact cultures. Arabs sat the closest together, significantly differing from all groups except the Southern Europeans and Indian–Pakistanis. Northern Europeans sat farther apart than all other groups except Asians. South Europeans sat closer than North Europeans but did not differ from other groups. Asians sat farther apart than Indian-Pakistanis but did not differ from other groups. No significant differences were found among cultures within the two contact/noncontact categories.
Watson & Graves (1966)	16 American males, 16 Arab males, pairs.	Unobtrusive observation in lab (seated interaction).	Arabs sat closer, more directly, touched more, engaged in more eye contact, and talked louder than Americans.
Willis (1966)	I. 30 black pairs, 30 white pairs.	Initial speaking distance when approached by experimenter.	Whites tended to stand closer than blacks.
	II. 9 black–white pairs, 9 white–white pairs.	Initial speaking distance when approached by experimenter.	Black–white pairs stood farther apart than white–white pairs.
Willis, Carlson, & Reeves (1979)	408 white males, 383 white females, 143 black males, 113 black females, grades K to 6, in groups.	Unobtrusive observation in field (cafeteria lines).	In all-white and integrated schools, IPD increased with age, except for male–male pairs. In all-black schools, no increase with age. In all schools, grade school children stand farther from opposite sex, and in all-white schools, this increases with age.
Winogrond (1981)	18 white females, 19 to 24 years old; 18 white females, 63 to 85 years old; 18 black females, 53 to 86 years old.	Measured distance subject approached toward a friend.	Young whites approached closer than elderly blacks and whites. White and black elderly women interacted at same distance.

Table 12.3. *(Continued)*

Study	Subjects	Methodology	Results
Word, Zanna, & Cooper (1974)	15 white college students.	Judges behind one-way mirrors observed distance, forward lean, eye contact, shoulder orientation during interviews. Confederate "applicants" were 2 black male, 3 white male high school students.	White interviewers engaged black applicants with less immediacy than white applicants.
Zimmerman & Brody (1975)	38 black males, 40 white males, grades 5 & 6; unacquainted dyads.	Unobtrusive observation while playing (in lab). Biracial dyads then watched a televised warm or cold biracial interaction and were observed again.	Pairs of black youngsters interacted at greater distances, faced each other less directly than all-white dyads. Black–white pairs were intermediate in distance, axis, and talk. Watching models on TV in a warm (compared to a cold) interaction decreased IPD for both groups. White dyads played closer than blacks.

between Latin American college students and North American students in seating distance (when discussing a political topic) but did report that the interaction distances of the Latin Americans were much more variable than those of the North Americans. A number of methodological concerns regarding this study should be noted, however. First, obtrusive measures of distance were used. The floor of the experimental room was marked off in 2-ft intervals. Moreover, the experimenter remained in the experimental room, noting the proxemic patterns and distances of the subjects. The participants were photographed twice during the interaction, as well. Second, and perhaps more important, the intimacy of the conversation topic, the timing of the distance measures, and the sex of the members of each dyad were not controlled in this investigation. Mazar (1977) and Keating and Keating (1980) found no difference in the seated distances between unacquainted males on public benches in business districts of America, Spain, Morocco, and Kenya. The lack of differences, however, may be attributable to the varied sizes and shapes of the benches in the different countries and the presence of numerous international businessmen.

Several researches have sought to study the similarities in personal space among Americans and other cultures. I consider the research process of uncovering *common* spatial behavior patterns to be *just as important* (as identifying disparate patterns) to our fuller understanding of the factors that may eventually make intergroup communication more effective, rather than potentially laden with misunderstandings, misattributions, and miscommunications. Unfortunately, most of the studies in this area do not use real-life measures, making their validity suspect. Graubert and Adler (1977) found that American, Australian, British, and South African young adults placed figures representing mental patients at approximately the same distances. Similarly, Sommer (1968) found that American, British, Scottish, Swedish, and Pakistani subjects all rated different seating distances similarly for intimacy level. Cade (1973) found no differences in the figure placements that reflected various nuclear family relationships of American, Filipino, and Japanese subjects. In a series of two investigations, which also used a felt figure technique, Engelbretson (Engelbretson, 1972; Engelbretson & Fullmer, 1970) reported that native Japanese subjects had significantly larger interfigure distance placements than Hawaiian Japanese and American caucasian subjects.

However, no differences between the interfigure distance placements of the two latter cultural groups were found.

While most studies have examined the more global distinction between contact and noncontact cultures, few have systematically examined Hall's hypotheses concerning spatial usage by the people in a number of the specific countries (e.g., Japan, Germany) toward which Hall has directed his attention. In fact, most of the comparisons involved American subjects and other cultural groups. There were actually very few comparisons made between members of *different* cultural groups. It is also important to note here that even cultures that are assumed to be similar may actually have different spatial practices. For example, in a replication of Sommer's (1965) questionnaire study, Cook (1970) found that his English subjects chose to sit at greater distances than Sommer's American subjects for projected interactions involving cooperation and conversation. Similarly, Shuter (1976) reported that Costa Ricans were observed to use less space, orient more directly, and engage in more touching than Panamanians, who were themselves more involved during interaction than Colombians.

So even *within* the contact and noncontact categories, differences in spatial behavior have been found. Much more research along these lines is needed.

Another fertile area for research is suggested by a recent study by Sussman and Rosenfeld (1982). They found that when their bilingual Japanese subjects spoke in their own native language, they sat farther from a same-sex, same-nationality confederate than either Americans or bilingual Venezuelans. But when all subjects spoke English during their interactions the three groups approximated the American seated interaction distance pattern. Future studies might profitably explore the generality of this finding and also the process by which a change in the language spoken is accompanied by a change in proxemic behavior. Does the particular language spoken act as a releasor for the more general normative interaction pattern that includes the interpersonal distance adopted?

Very badly needed are studies of interactions between members of cultures differing in spatial behavior patterns. While the fact that people of different cultures use space differently does not necessarily mean that miscommunication is inevitable, it may be that misinterpretations and misattributions about another's intentions would be more likely, given this divergence in an area usually outside of our conscious awareness (Hall's "hidden dimension").

Virtually no evidence was available until very recently as to whether the developmental trend of increasing distance with age occurs in other cultures. One of my graduate students and I (Pagàn & Aiello, 1982) extended the study of proxemic interaction patterns to Puerto Rican children at three grade levels (first, sixth, and eleventh) in San Juan, Puerto Rico, and in New York City, using a methodology identical to that of Aiello and Aiello (1974). Puerto Rican children in both countries showed very similar proxemic patterns (i.e., did not differ), and displayed increasing interaction distances and more direct body orientations as they increased in age.

Only three other such investigations have been conducted in other countries. Two of these studies (one in Canada: Bass & Weinstein, 1971; one in Japan: Lerner, Iwawacki, & Chira, 1976) used a projective, felt board technique and found that for very young children (both studied 5- to 8-year-olds) less space was placed between figures by the youngest children tested. In the other investigation, Lomranz and colleagues (1975) found this same age trend for their Israeli subjects (ages 3 to 7), whose seating approach distance toward a same-sex, same-age mate was measured.

While the small numbers of cross-cultural studies generally support Hall's notion of contact and noncontact cultures, the studies conducted with different *subcultural* groups have yielded results that are far more complex. These studies have been undertaken primarily in the United States (over 90%) with Anglo, black, and Hispanic groups. Hall (1966) stated that differences in spatial behavior patterns are *basic* not only to cultural groups but to subcultural groups as well, and extended his distinction between contact and noncontact cultures to subcultural groups, particularly in the United States. Accordingly, he used the term *American* to refer to the dominant noncontact group of Americans of Northern European ancestry. Hall (1966) posited that lower-income black and Spanish subcultures were more highly involved than white middle-class Americans and therefore would use closer interaction distances. Moreover, he posited that black and Spanish subcultures may be particularly open to discomfort from misunderstandings, since these subcultures occupy different "sensory worlds" from that of the dominant North American (western) culture. The growing body of research examining these contentions is actually much larger than the research investigating cultural similarities and differences in spatial behavior. In a recent review of this area (Aiello & Thompson, 1980b), we concluded that:

while twice as many subcultural as cultural studies have been conducted, our knowledge in this area is still quite meager. Fairly consistent evidence has been obtained to support Hall's observation that Hispanic-Americans are more spatially involved than Anglo-Americans, but his contention that [blacks] "have a much higher involvement ratio" (Hall, 1966, p. 172) has not been supported, except with young children. In fact, available evidence runs contrary to this position. (p. 155)

It appears that Hispanics do use less space than Anglos when interacting both as children (Aiello & Jones, 1971; Baxter, 1970; Pagàn & Aiello, 1982) and as adults (Baxter, 1970; Thompson & Baxter, 1979). In the only quasi-projective study Ford and Graves (1977) found that Mexican-American children approached more closely than Anglos in grade 2 (but this difference diminished in grade 8). One study (Jones, 1971) did find no difference among several ethnic groups, including Hispanics, in observations of interactions of the streets of New York. It has been proposed, however, that the high level of environmental stimulation (e.g., noise) in such settings may overcome any of the cultural predispositions for differential usage of space.

When one looks at the reported differences between the American black and Anglo subcultures, however, one finds that it is absolutely necessary to consider the *age* of the participants of the applicable research investigations. While the developmental process is similar for these groups (i.e., larger interpersonal distances as children grow older), comparisons of young black and white children have shown differences that are precisely *the reverse* of patterns found for adults. Apparently, it is the *slopes* of these developmental curves for black and white children that differ, with the slope of the former much steeper than the slope of the latter. Research investigating interpersonal distances maintained by black and white children at the youngest ages (i.e., 5 to 7) has consistently reported that very young black children stand *closer* together than very young white children (cf. Aiello & Jones, 1971; Jones & Aiello, 1973; Severy et al., 1979). By ages 8 or 9, studies have reported *no differences* between these two groups (cf. Jones & Aiello, 1973; Duncan, 1978; Scherer, 1974). Investigations of spacing patterns maintained by adults and children age 12 and older have reported that blacks stand *farther* apart than whites (cf. Aiello & Jones, 1979; Baxter, 1970; Tennis & Dabbs, 1976; Thompson & Baxter, 1973; Willis, 1966). Clearly, the age of research participants *must* be considered to understand and to generalize this complex pattern of results.

As noted, Hall's contention was that *lower-income* blacks (and Hispanics) were "more highly involved" than *middle-class* whites. It was *that* hypothesis that we tested (and for which we found evidence) in our first study examining the proxemic behavior of very young children (Aiello & Jones, 1971). In our second study we examined this obtained difference across three age levels to investigate the stability of this finding given the divergent (i.e., opposite) results reported for adults (cf. Willis, 1966), controlled for the topic of conversation and size of the interaction area, and *narrowed* the *purposeful* confounding of race with social class (adopted to test Hall's hypothesis) by including upper lower-class black children and middle-class white children. In addition to replicating the results (i.e., black children stand closer together than whites) of our first study (Aiello & Jones, 1971) at the earliest and common age level (age 6), under these conditions, we found the pattern described at ages 8 and 10 (i.e., the absence of differences at age 8 and the beginnings of a reversal of this difference at age 10).

Only two studies have examined the role of socioeconomic status (SES) as another factor potentially contributing to the black/white differences in spatial behavior (Aiello & Jones, 1979; Scherer, 1974). Scherer (1974) conducted two field studies in schoolyards. Still photographs were taken of standing, interacting pairs of same-sex, same-race dyads of black and white children in grade 1 through 4. In the first study, lower-class white children were found to stand farther apart than lower-class black children; but this difference was not statistically significant. In the second study, the spatial behaviors of black and white middle- and lower-class children were compared. Middle-class children were found to stand farther apart than lower-class children; this difference was only significant for the white children, however. No differences were found between white and black middle-class children, or between white and black lower-class children. Scherer suggested that the previously reported findings indicating differences between black and white proxemic behavior patterns may have been due to socioeconomic factors, and not subcultural background. However, the generalizability of these findings is somewhat limited, in that Scherer unfortunately confounded in his analyses the sex composition of the dyads he photographed and had no way of assessing whether his groups differed in the topic of conversation they had chosen. More important, the failure to replicate the racial differences in proxemic behavior found by Aiello and Jones (1971) may be accounted for by the larger age range selected by Scherer. As noted, the development of personal space by blacks and whites appears to be somewhat different, and while very young black children stand closer together than white children the difference between these groups has been found to diminish at about age 8 or 9 (half of Scherer's sample) and actually reverses by about age 10. This study does, however, provide an important contribution, as it was the first study to uncover socioeconomic class differences in the use of space during interaction.

Aiello and Jones (1979) further investigated social class and race differences in spatial behavior to resolve the apparent discrepancies in the existing proxemic literature by focusing on the interaction patterns of black and white, lower- and middle-class, male and female pairs of adolescents. Adolescents were selected to provide the "next step" in the developmental sequence. These observations were made under conditions that allowed for a similar environmental context (i.e., the same-sized interaction area, a partitioned classroom in their high schools) and for discussion to focus on the same topic of conversation (i.e., their favorite television programs). The procedure was the same as that used in our previous investigations (Aiello & Aiello, 1974; Aiello & Cooper, 1972; Jones & Aiello, 1973).

The results of this study indicated that blacks of this age group stood farther apart (27 in.) than did their white counterparts (22 in.), suggesting that the reversal trend for 10-year-olds found in Jones and Aiello (1973) had become pronounced by the midteens. There was in addition an effect for socioeconomic class. As was not the case with the results obtained for younger children in Scherer's (1974) study, lower-class children tended to stand *farther* apart while conversing (26 in.) than middle-class children (22 in.). There was no significant interaction between these variables for distance or the other two dependent measures of this study. Consistent with the results of virtually all of the studies cited including our previous studies, blacks faced each other less directly and looked in the direction of their partners less than did white adolescents. Also, consistent with previous results, females stood closer together and looked in the direction of their partners more than did their male counterparts.

With only two studies having investigated social class differences in spatial behavior, it is, of course, not possible to generalize a pattern of results—particularly since these two studies found results in direct opposition to one another! It will be important for future research to examine whether age is once again a moderating factor. Might it be that just as blacks stand closer than whites at a very early age

(cf. Aiello & Jones, 1971) and yet farther than whites as adolescents and adults (cf. Aiello & Jones, 1979), lower-SES children stand closer together than middle-SES children (cf. Scherer, 1974) but lower-SES adolescents and adults stand farther apart than middle-SES adolescents and adults (cf. Aiello & Jones, 1979)? Again, it is to be hoped that future research will answer this and related questions.

From this investigation and the studies described, it can be concluded that by adolescence (and all through adulthood):

> Blacks have adopted an interaction style that places them farther apart than whites, a result that is consistent with the adult findings of previous investigators (e.g., Baxter, 1970; Willis, 1966). Since blacks also were found to be more indirect in their body and head orientations than whites, Hall's (1966, 1974) speculation that blacks have a "much higher involvement ratio" than whites does not receive support, and, at least for these variables, just the opposite appears to be the case.[1] His concern about blacks' and whites' "misreading" each other is, however, well taken, since differences between these groups appear early in life, and, after disappearing during pubescence, reappear (albeit in a reversed form) in adolescent and adult years. (Aiello & Thompson, 1980b, p. 153)

A number of studies have also investigated the spatial behavior of *interracial* interactions. Of these 10 studies, 2 found similar (Leibman, 1970) or intermediate (Zimmerman & Brody, 1975) distances for interracial compared to same-race interactions but, all of the others found interracial distances to be *larger* than same-race distances (cf. Booraem, Flowers, Bodner, & Satterfield, 1977; Hendricks & Bootzin, 1976; Rosegrant & McCroskey, 1975; Willis, 1966). Further, Dennis and Powell (1972) report that this difference in spacing (for interracial dyads) grows larger as children grow older (from 7 to 14).

Recently, Garratt and colleagues (1981) trained white police officers to use spatial patterning typical of either blacks (somewhat larger distance) or whites (somewhat smaller distance) in an interview of black citizens, who participated in two such interviews (one of each type). Black citizens expressed a strong preference for the white officer displaying the "black" spacing behavior and judged him more personally, socially, and professionally competent. These results are suggestive. They are similar to those of Collett (1971), who used spacing norms obtained for Arab students by Watson and Graves (1966) to train English students to interact with Arab students adopting distances reflecting either Arab distance norms (i.e., closer) or English distance norms (i.e., farther). He found that Arab students were much more positive about English students when they displayed the closer, "Arab" distance behavior.

The lesson from these two investigations would seem to be that knowledge about cross-subcultural differences in spatial behavior may provide a crucial ingredient for smoother, more effective communication with individuals outside one's own (sub-)culture and could decrease the likelihood of people "misreading" each other. More research in this area of (what I will label) *communication intervention* is obviously needed, particularly now that we have at least some of the underpinnings of the normative spacing patterns for a number of cultures and subcultures. The spatial behavior patterns of many cultures and subcultures have yet to be investigated, however.

12.5.4. Influence of Personality and Psychological Disorders

Many researchers have attempted to relate different personality types or traits to the use of space. As can be seen in Table 12.4, the results in this area have been mixed, with some studies showing clear trends between a personality variable and interpersonal distance and others showing no consistent pattern. Interestingly, observation of actual interactions has not been used very extensively. Stop-distance measures and paper and pencil or figure placement tasks have dominated this area of research. It is possible that the low correlations between these measures and actual spatial behavior in interactions (cf.

Love & Aiello, 1980) are part of the reason for the lack of consistent patterns of results.

The trends that have been demonstrated, however, seem to show that, as noted by Altman and Vinsel (1977)), interpersonal distance seems to be affected by how confident or "in control" a person perceives himself or herself to be. One could perhaps also extend this dimension to include a consideration of how competent one is in interpersonal exchanges (e.g., degree of schizophrenic or neurotic tendencies). The results of research in these areas seem to show that locus of control, self-esteem, and degree of mental disorder are good indicators of how much space people require.

For example, Horowitz (Horowitz, 1965; Horowitz et al., 1964) examined rather extensively the relationship between schizophrenia and personal space. Asking subjects to approach human and inanimate targets, Horowitz found that schizophrenics used significantly more space and were considerably more variable in their use of space than normals. Similar results have been found in other studies (cf. Blumenthal & Meltzoff, 1967; Sommer, 1959; Ziller & Grossman, 1967; Ziller, Megas, & DiConcio, 1964). Some convincing evidence for the illness itself causing this increase in space is that the same groups, after treatment, show reductions in their personal space (Booraem & Flowers, 1972; Horowitz, 1968).

Such an increase in space appears not only in schizophrenics but also in those with neurotic tendencies. DeJulio and Duffy (1977) tested college students for neurotic tendencies and found that those

Table 12.4. Influence of Personality

Study	Subjects	Methodology	Results
Aiello & Thompson (1980a)	41 male, 46 female college students.	Subjects seated at intermediate (5 ft) or far (11 ft) distance. Subjects' stress-related arousal, state anxiety, mood, other feelings, locus of control, and nonverbal behavior assessed.	Internals had greater negative reactions to the "inappropriate" far interaction distance.
Aronow, Reznikoff, & Tryon (1975)	Process schizophrenics: 61 males; Reactive schizophrenics: 43 males; Normal hospital employees: 30 males, 18 to 55 years old.	(1) Seating distance; (2) Kuethe Felt Figure; (3) MAPS test; (4) Psychological Distance Scale.	No differences between groups on any measure.

Table 12.4. *(Continued)*

Study	Subjects	Methodology	Results
Bailey, Hartnett, & Gibson (1972)	40 male, 40 female college students.	Stop approach of and toward experimenter.	Closest distances were with female experimenter and by male subjects. Female experimenter allowed to approach and was approached closer than male experimenter. Male–male was greatest distance. No correlation between male anxiety and distance. Positive correlation for females between anxiety and distance from male experimenter. Inverse relationships for males between distance and degree of hetero-sexuality.
Bartels (1976)	24 female friends, 24 female strangers.	Unobtrusive observation administered Rotter's (1972) I-E Scale.	No support for hypothesis that I-E score would be a determinant of distance for strangers.
Beck & Ollendick (1976)	28 normal males, 28 delinquent males.	Stop approach of experi-menter from four angles. Measured locus of control.	No difference between normals and delinquents. No difference for I-E. All had greater space to rear, all allowed female to approach closer.
Booraem & Flowers (1972)	14 male hospitalized psychotics.	Stop approach of experi-menter.	Assertiveness training resulted in decreased personal space. No reduc-tion for control group.
Booraem, Flowers, Bodner, & Satterfield (1977)	60 black & white male delinquent youths.	Approach by male (European-American) confederate (eight axes).	Those who committed crimes against property allowed greater approach than those who com-mitted crimes against persons. European-Americans allowed closer approach than African- and Mexican-Americans.
Burgess (1981)	Mentally retarded chil-dren, grades 1 to 3: 10 male, 15 female; grades 4 to 6: 13 male, 12 female. 48 nonretarded.	Distances estimated by observers during outdoor free play.	Younger children use less distance than older children. Retarded use less distance than nonretarded.
Cavallin (1976)	100 male college students.	Approach from and toward confederate.	High in aggression used more distance than those low in aggression.

Table 12.4. *(Continued)*

Study	Subjects	Methodology	Results
Cavallin & Houston (1980)	100 college students.	Approach from and toward experimenter. Pretests for: aggression, maladjustment, body boundary, and body size estimates.	Positive correlations found between: aggressiveness and frontal approach by experimenter; maladjustment and frontal approach by experimenter; and body boundaries and frontal approach toward experimenter. Negative correlation between body estimates and distance.
Cook (1970)	University students.	Subjects were asked to pick a seat at a table in diagram. Subjects completed a personality inventory measuring introversion–extraversion.	Extraverts chose to sit opposite or next to another (closer) and *not* to sit at an angle (farther).
Cozby (1973)	72 female college students.	Measured subjects' "personal space" by approach from and toward two persons. Evaluated model room. Completed personality and background questionnaire.	Closer approach distances (somewhat) related to higher self-esteem, lower social avoidance, and higher need for dominance.
Daves & Swaffer (1971)	13 male, 24 female college students.	Approach from experimenter measured unobtrusively.	No effect for Rotter I-E or California F-scale; dogmatism had slight effect (positively correlated).
DeJulio & Duffy (1977)	50 male, 43 female college students.	Choice of seating distance observed. Tested for neurotic predispositions.	Neurotics selected seats farther from experimenter.
Dosey & Meisels (1969)	91 male, 95 female college students.	Approach toward same- and opposite-sex target. Rorschach administered to assess anxiety and body boundaries. Stress and no-stress conditions.	No effect for personality type. Stressed subjects kept more distance from target. Females approached another female closer than another male; males approached females and other males at about the same distance.
Duke & Marshall (1973)	20 schizophrenic, 20 affective disorder, 20 normals, all females.	CID, Rotter's I-E Scale.	Schizophrenics used more space than other patients and normals. Schizophrenics classified as externals used most space.

Table 12.4. *(Continued)*

Study	Subjects	Methodology	Results
Duke & Nowicki (1972)	107 males, 110 females, CID scores and locus of control; 16 male, 39 female, "friend/stranger"; 20 male, 20 female "authority figure."	CID, Adult Nowicki-Strickland Locus of Control Scale.	Generally, the more external the subject the larger the projected distance, but female externals projected less distance. Correlations reported are significant but very low. Internals projected smaller distances than externals for interactions with strangers and authority figures. No difference between these groups for friends.
Dunn (1971)	80 males.	Personal Distance Questionnaire.	No relationship between stress and distance. Persons possessing similar personality variables possess similar distance characteristics.
Eberts (1972)	100 male college students.	Initial approach to experimenter.	Subjects who lived alone and subjects who rated friends as politically conservative approached less closely. Self-acceptance negatively related to distance.
Edmonson & Han (1983)	19 mentally retarded females, 19 to 32 years old, institutionalized.	Distance estimated from videotapes. Subjects engaged in placebo or socialization game prior to IPD measurement.	Members displayed closer IPD after socialization game than placebo. IPD was less in morning than afternoon for experimentals. Opposite effect for controls.
Fromme & Beam (1974)	24 male, 24 female college students, in pairs.	Stop approach of experimenter in lab.	During high levels of eye-contact by experimenter, dominant subjects of both sexes approached closer; males approached closer than females.
Fromme & Schmidt (1972)	16 male college students.	Approach male confederate under "fear," "anger," "sorrow," and "neutral" instructions. Administered anxiety scale and Social Introversion scale.	No effect for personality measures. Approached closest in anger condition, farthest in fear condition, with neutral and sorrow intermediate.

451

Table 12.4. *(Continued)*

Study	Subjects	Methodology	Results
Frankel & Barrett (1971)	40 white males, 17 to 20 years old.	Stop approach of white and black confederate. Administered F-Scale and Self-Esteem questionnaire.	Low-self-esteem and high-authoritarian subjects allowed closer approach distances for white than for black approacher.
Gifford (1982)	22 male, 20 female college students.	Placement of chairs in a scale model of an interview room. Subjects were given different social situations to simulate.	Aspects of the social interaction (cooperation–competition, amount of liking, status of other) were dominant. Liking and cooperation resulted in closer chair placement. High-status subjects chose larger distances in competitive situations.
Greenberg, Aronow, & Rauchway (1977)	41 female, 24 male college students.	CID, stop approach toward experimenter, ink blot.	Positive correlations between CID and approach distance and anxiety and hostility. Negative correlations between CID and human content and barrier scores.
Greene (1983)	41 mental health students.	"Boundary Fusion Test" to assess self-boundaries. Distances estimated from videotapes of group (8 to 9 person) interactions.	High-boundary subjects used more space than low-boundary subjects.
Grossman (1977)	60 male high school students.	Approach toward experimenter.	High-dominance subjects approached closer than low-dominance subjects. Distance increased with status of experimenter. Interaction of status and dominance.
Hayduk & Mainprize (1980)	Institutionalized blind: 12 male, 13 female; noninstitutionalized blind: 13 male, 12 female; sighted: 4 male, 24 female.	Stop approach of experimenter, from eight directions (steps counted aloud for blind subjects).	No differences for blind vs. sighted, sex or age.
Hayes & Siders (1977)	60 mildly retarded, 60 nonretarded 14- to 16-year-olds.	Figure placement.	Both groups placed figures designated with positive affect closest, followed by neutral and then negative. Both groups placed self figure closer to figure labeled "smart" than to figure labeled "not smart." Retarded children exhibited less distance with teacher figure.

Table 12.4. *(Continued)*

Study	Subjects	Methodology	Results
Heckel & Hiers (1977)	36 male, 26 female college students.	Seating choice observed, administered Locus of Control Scale.	Internals sat closer to confederate. No difference for sex.
Hetherington (1972)	24 females, 13 to 17 years old, daughters of divorced mothers, widowed mothers, or intact families.	Choice of seating distance from male and female interviewers.	Daughters of divorced women sought closer proximity to male interviewers. Daughters of widowed mothers showed withdrawal from males. This effect more pronounced for girls separated from father earlier in life.
Hildreth, Derogatis, & McCusker (1971)	14 aggressive, 22 non-aggressive male inmates.	Stop approach of experimenter.	Aggressive prisoners use more space than non-aggressive prisoners.
Holahan (1972)	120 male psychiatric patients.	Room arrangements: (1) sociofugal— chairs against walls; (2) sociopetal— chairs around tables; (3) mixed; (4) fire–chairs stacked by walls.	Social behaviors (conversations, games) occurred most in sociopetal arrangements, least in sociofugal.
Horowitz (1968)	30 female schizophrenics before and after treatment.	Approach toward target.	Subjects used less space after treatment.
Horowitz, Duff, & Stratton (1964)	19 normal male, 10 normal female, 19 male & female schizophrenics.	Approach toward target.	Schizophrenics use more space whether target is male, female, or inanimate object.
Ickes & Barnes (1977)	60 male, 64 female college students.	Distance estimated from videotape. Administered Snyder's Self-Monitoring Scale.	No relation between S–M and distance.
Iwata (1978)	132 female college students.	Questionnaire concerning crowding. Pedersen personal space measure. Approach of and toward experimenter.	Familiarity, ethnicity, sex, age, and social status influence reactions to crowding. No relationship between personal space and crowding.
Karabenick & Meisels (1972)	99 male college students.	Stop approach from and toward confederate. Administered TAT to measure nACH and test anxiety questionnaire. Positive and negative feedback conditions.	Test anxious and negative feedback. Subjects kept greater distance. No interaction.
Kinzel (1970)	15 violent male, 14 non-violent male inmates.	Stop approach by experimenter.	Violent inmates used more space and, opposite of nonviolent prisoners, used more space to the rear.

Table 12.4. *(Continued)*

Study	Subjects	Methodology	Results
Kleck, Buck, Goller, London,	I. 78 male college students.	Felt figure placement. Attitudes toward disabled.	Subjects placed liked others and "normal" others closer than disabled or disliked others.
Pfeiffer, & Vukcevic (1968)	II. 25 male college students.	Observed seating distance maintained from confederate. Either confederate said to have epilepsy or no mention given of physical problem.	Subjects sat farther from "epileptic" confederate.
Kline & Bell (1983)	83 male, 78 female college students.	Distance subject sat from confederate on bench was measured. Privacy Preference Scale.	For females, high preference for privacy. Subjects sat closer to confederate.
Klukken (1971)	28 male, 28 female college students.	Interpersonal Distance Questionnaire.	No difference in distance for high disclosers and low disclosers.
Lex (1978)	14 high dogmatic, 14 low dogmatic.	Hall's (1963) notation system.	No difference in distance for high and low dogmatics.
Lothstein (1972)	Adolescent prisoners: 16 male high-assault, white and black; 16 male low-assault, white and black. High school students: 16 black male, 16 white male.	Approach by experimenter.	High-assaultive subjects use more personal space. Blacks use more space than whites.
Mallenby (1974a)	20 male, 20 female mentally retarded, 7 to 14 years old.	Figure placement of self and "normal" reference person (same-sex). Approach toward female experimenter.	Males placed figure closer to self than they stood next to experimenter. Opposite result for females.
Mallenby (1974b)	(1) Institutionalized hearing-impaired children; (2) hearing-impaired children transferred to a public school; (3) normal public school children.	Observation of interaction distance with a "normal" student.	Hearing-impaired children use more space than normal when interacting with a normal child. Hearing-impaired students at the public school, however, more closely approximate spacing patterns of normal children.
McGurk, Davis, & Grehan (1981)	20 aggressive, 20 non-aggressive male inmates.	Stop approach from experimenter.	No difference between groups for distance.

Table 12.4. *(Continued)*

Study	Subjects	Methodology	Results
Mehrabian & Diamond (1971a)	I. 144 male, 144 female pairs.	Subjects under "waiting room" conditions placed at one of four distances (3, 4.5, 6, 9 ft) and sat at one of three orientations (0, 90, 180°). Observed nonverbal relaxation & affiliative behavior and questionnaire measures of affiliative tendencies and sensitivity to rejection.	Subjects relaxed more as distance increased. Affiliative behavior decreased with indirectness of orientation, particularly for those with more of an affiliative tendency.
	II. 88 males, 88 females.	Subjects sat at 4.5 ft apart and at 90° orientation. Exposed to prop condition (abstract sculpture & puzzle poster) or not. Dependent measures same as above.	Attention to puzzle decreased affiliative behavior. Attention to sculpture by subjects "sensitive to rejection" facilitated interaction.
Mehrabian & Diamond (1971b)	124 male, 124 female groups of four, same sex.	Observers recorded seating distances and orientations among four subjects. Questionnaire measures of affiliative tendency and sensitivity to rejection.	Females and more affiliative persons tended to choose closer positions. No effect for sex or affiliative tendency on orientation.
Meisels & Cantor (1970)	I. 52 female college students.	Choice of seating distance observed. Introversion–extraversion measured.	No effect of introversion–extraversion.
	II. 96 female college students.	Choice of seating distance observed. Introversion–extraversion measured. MMPI used to measure deviancy.	No relation between deviancy and distance.
Meisels & Dosey (1971)	80 male, 80 female college students.	Stop approach to experimenter. Administered TAT to measure defense against expression of anger. Angered and not angered conditions.	Angered subjects approached closer. Angered subjects low in defense against expression of anger approached closest.
Newman & Pollack (1973)	30 male deviants, 30 male controls.	Stop approach from experimenter.	Deviants used more space than controls. Both groups used more space to rear than front.
Patterson (1973)	I. 36 males, 36 females.	Unobtrusive observation in lab. Approach distance and orientation; personality scales.	More anxious subjects kept greater distance from experimenter.
	II. 13 males, 13 females.	Unobtrusive observation in lab. Approach distance and orientation.	Subjects who assumed greater distances rated themselves as "less at ease."

Table 12.4. *(Continued)*

Study	Subjects	Methodology	Results
Patterson & Holmes (1966)	Females and males (number not specified).	Choice of seating distance.	With a male interviewer, for females only, a significant correlation between MMPI Introversion–Extraversion score and seat choice.
Pedersen (1973a)	170 males.	Approach of subject (both naive subjects) in lab. Guilford-Zimmerman Aptitude Survey, verbal comprehension test, Maudsley Personality Inventory, biographical items.	Subjects who used less distance: (1) scored higher on verbal comprehension; (2) more extroverted; (3) oldest or youngest child; (4) from larger community; and (5) less physically active—neuroticism unrelated.
Pedersen (1973b)	170 male undergraduate paid volunteers.	Stranger approach subject, Figure placement, Pedersen Personal Space, Rawls Personal Space, in lab.	Body-accessibility toward mother, father, and male friend interrelated, body accessibility toward best female friend unrelated.
Pedersen (1973c)	20 male, 20 female college students.	Pedersen Behavioral Personal Space, Pedersen Personal Space, Sensation-Seeking Scale.	Female high sensation-seeking had greater simulated personal space. Males who liked new and interesting experiences had greater side and diagonal simulated personal space. Females high on same scale had closer behavioral personal space from males except on sides.
Pittavino (1976)	146 college students.	CID, Locus of Control Scale.	Locus of control significantly related to distance preference.
Rice & Belnap (1975)	8 male & 8 female hearing, 6 male & 6 female deaf college students.	Subjects approach male and female confederate.	No differences for subjects' sex. Deaf students approach closer than hearing students.
Rierdon & Wiener (1977)	Schizophrenic: 16 male, 16 female; nonschizophrenic: 16 male, 16 female.	Seating choice relative to experimenter (near vis-à-vis, far vis-à-vis, near juxtaposed, far juxtaposed).	No differences between groups. Closer, more direct seats were preferred.
Roger & Schalekamp (1976)	15 violent, 15 nonviolent male prisoners, South African, black.	Stop approach from experimenter.	Violent prisoners used more space. Front and rear zones were equal.
Rogers (1972)	50 male, 50 female college students.	Subject's approach toward experimenter.	No difference in distance for high, low sociability subjects. For all subjects, distance was greater in morning than afternoon.

Table 12.4. *(Continued)*

Study	Subjects	Methodology	Results
Sanders (1976)	34 male, 43 female college students.	CID, inkblot measure of body boundary.	Positive correlation between barrier score and distance preference.
Sewell & Heisler (1973)	35 male college students.	Seating distance.	"Exhibition" and "impulsivity" scores negatively correlated with distance. Twenty other correlations were nonsignificant.
Slane, Dragan, Crandall, & Payne (1980)	36 males, 36 females.	Observation of distance (seated).	Sensitizers use more distance than repressors regardless of stress level.
Sommer (1959)	26 schizophrenic pairs, 11 nonschizophrenic pairs, male and female.	Observed choice of seating distance at table.	Nonschizophrenics chose the closer seats (opposite corner, side) exclusively. Schizophrenics showed no consistent pattern of choice, choosing even the most distant seat 40% of the time.
Stratton, Tekippe, & Flick (1973)	19 male, 14 female college students.	Subjects completed Tennessee Self-Concept Test. Distance measures were: silhouette placement; approach male student; approach headless female sewing dummy.	High self-concept males and females approached object and person closest. Approach distances varied more for females as a function of self-concept. Low self-concepts placed *figures* closest.
Thompson & Aiello (1981)	264 same-sex, same-race pairs of nonretarded educable mentally retarded students 5 to 19 years old.	Unobtrusive observations in field (modified classroom) using adaptation of Hall's (1963) proxemic scales and 10 other nonverbal behaviors.	Mentally retarded students stood less directly and looked less at their partners than their nonretarded peers but interacted at similar distances.
Williams (1971)	20 male introverts, 20 male extroverts.	Chair placement, questionnaire of preferred distances and experimenter approach.	No difference for chair placement but extroverts did state on questionnaire that they would use less space and allowed closer distance in experimenter approach.
Wormith (1984)	49 male prison inmates, 16 to 40 years old.	Stop distance of experimenter. Psychological test battery. Measurements taken at two intervals.	Increasing psychological stability related to lessened personal space.

with greater neurotic tendencies had chosen seats farther from the experimenter while completing the test.

Another factor that affects spatial behavior appears to be self-esteem. Those subjects who have been evaluated negatively (Karabenick & Meisels, 1972) or who have tested lower on self-esteem (Frankel & Barrett, 1971) or self-concept (Stratton, Tekippe, & Flick, 1973) have been shown to use a greater amount of space on approach measures. Such results appear to be consistent with the explanation that persons who feel more confident about themselves seem more inclined both to approach others closer and to allow others to approach them closer.

Altman and Vinsel (1977) also stated that those who feel that they are in control of a situation will allow others to approach them closer or will approach others closer. This has been demonstrated in a number of studies relating personal space to locus of control. Using both observations of actual interactions (Aiello & Thompson, 1980a; Heckel & Hiers, 1977) and paper and pencil techniques (Duke & Nowicki, 1972), it has been found that subjects with an internal locus of control use less space and react more negatively to inappropriately far distances. Similarly, Fromme & Beam (1974) found that both males and females who tested high in dominance approached a confederate at closer distances. Consistent with these results, Patterson (1972, 1977) reported that individuals higher in social anxiety remained more distant, and Mehrabian and Diamond (1971b) found that those higher in affiliation sat closer to others. Meisels and Dosey (1971) also found that subjects low in the ability to control anger approached closer to the confederate who had insulted them. This would suggest an intermediate "appropriate" approach distance. Those high in control would not surpass this range either too close or too far.

Another variable related to perceived control would be the assaultiveness of the subject. It has been found consistently that subjects who have assaultive or violent tendencies use more space than normals (as much as three times the space of normals), particularly from the rear (Hildreth, Derogatis, & McCusker, 1971; Kinzel, 1970; Lothstein, 1972; Roger & Schalekamp, 1976). Recently, Wormith (1984) reported that for male prison inmates increases in psychological stability were associated with smaller approach distances. Apparently, those with a history of violent behavior are more aware of threat from others, particularly if they cannot be monitored. As a result, they feel more comfortable if the approaching person keeps a greater distance.

When it comes to personality variables that do not imply control or confidence, there seem to be virtually none that have been shown to be consistently related to spatial behavior. Introversion–extraversion is the exception. It has been shown to be related to personal space (i.e., extraverts adopted closer seated distances) in some studies (Cook, 1970; Liepold, 1963; Patterson & Holmes, 1966; Patterson & Sechrest, 1970) but not in others (Meisels & Canter, 1970; Porter, Argyle, & Salter, 1970; Williams, 1971). Williams (1971) did find, however, that extraverts were more likely than introverts to respond that they *would* interact at distances closer than those reported by introverts.

The large majority of other variables studied in this area have shown no relationship between personality variables and personal space. These include self-monitoring (Ickes & Barnes, 1977), delinquency (Beck & Ollendick, 1976), anxiety (Dosey & Meisels, 1969), and body boundary (Dosey & Meisels, 1969).

Patterson (1974, 1978) has suggested that studying clusters of personality traits may yield better explanations of spatial behavior than studying individual traits. It also seems logical, as has been suggested by Karabenick and Meisels (1972), that situations and personality traits interact to affect the use of space. For example, in their study need for achievement, test anxiety, and negative evaluation were shown to increase interpersonal distance. Similarly, Frankel and Barrett (1971) found that high-authoritarian, low-self-esteem white subjects kept the greatest distance from a black confederate. Therefore, it seems that many personality variables may not be meaningful in predicting spatial behavior unless they are *salient* in a given situation.

Future research would do well to heed the advice that personality traits be studied in *clusters* (e.g., dominance, social anxiety, affiliative tendency, introversion–extraversion) rather than individually and that these clusters be studied in *situations* where the personality dimension would be expected to be *salient* rather than in ambiguous or neutral contexts. This latter suggestion further strengthens our earlier argument that much of human spatial behavior is situation and relationship specific and only through the use of interactional (field/naturalistic) measures of interpersonal distance in contexts that are unambiguous can we better understand this domain. I now turn to a sampling of relationship and situational factors that have been studied.

12.5.5. Influence of Relationship, Situation, and Environment

One carries the previously discussed individual characteristics, which an individual has acquired largely through the socialization experiences of his or her effective culture, from situation to situation. Once one is in a particular situation with a particular other or set of others, however, another class of forces come into play that is a product of the *relationship* one has with another or others and the response one has to the characteristics of the *situation* and the *environment*.

An examination of the broad area of research focusing on interpersonal relations and spatial behavior (see Table 12.5) indicates that overall, except for very young children, people use least space with friends and others they like than with acquaintances and others about whom they feel slightly positive to neutral, and they use less space with individuals in this intermediate affect category than with strangers and others they dislike (cf. Aiello & Cooper, 1972, 1979; Burgess, 1983; Willis, 1966). Further, situations in which perceived threat is low incline people, especially females, to interact at closer distances than situations in which threat is high; such situations affect the amount of control a person feels he or she has in an interaction. It will be recalled that, while the focus on interpersonal relations derives more from the *communication* function of spatial behavior, the focus on the degree of threat in situations relates more to the *protection* function of spatial behavior.

Additional space is required when people are insulted, angered, stressed, made more tense, or placed in a competitive or formal setting (e.g., O'Neal, Brunault, Marguis, & Carifio, 1979; Ugwuegbu & Anusiem, 1982). Studies have also shown that greater distance is maintained with individuals who are hostile, threatening, physically impaired, "stigmatized," disfigured, or smoking (e.g., Kunzendorf & Denney, 1982; Rumsey, Bull & Gahagan, 1982; Worthington, 1974). People clearly wish to distance themselves from others who make them uncomfortable, anxious, or annoyed.

On the other hand, research (e.g., Byrne, Ervin, & Lamberth, 1970; Gifford, 1982; Tedesco & Fromme, 1974) has demonstrated that closer distances are selected with individuals who are attractive, cooperative, positively reinforcing, "warm or friendly," cooperative, or similar (in age, political orientation, race, sexual preference, status, etc.). Studies observing actual (rather than projected) distance have *not* shown a relationship between spatial

behavior and attitude similarity, however (cf. Byrne et al., 1970). People apparently wish to "get closer" to others whom they like, who are like them, to whom they are attracted, and who generally make them feel better about themselves. One further interesting aspect of the relationship between liking and interpersonal distance is that a decrease in interaction distance not only *indicates* a greater degree of liking, but in some circumstances can *result* in more liking of an other (Goldring, 1967; Haase & Pepper, 1972; Kelly, 1972; Mehrabian, 1968a).

Environmental factors have also been demonstrated to affect interpersonal spacing (e.g., Cochran, Hale, & Hissam, 1984; Dabbs et al., 1973; Tennis & Dabbs, 1975). In general people maintain closer distances when in the center (rather than the corner) of a room; in rooms with higher (rather than lower) ceilings; in narrow (rather than square) rooms; in larger (rather than smaller) rooms; and outside (rather than inside). So as individuals move from larger, more open spaces (e.g., outside) to smaller, more confining spaces (e.g., corner of room, narrow space, etc.) they apparently adapt to these environmental constraints by increasing their interpersonal distance.

12.5.6. Consequences of Inappropriate Distances: Effects of Spatial Invasion/Intrusion

Of all the topics studied under the rubric of human spatial behavior, the one area that has probably produced the most straightforward results is spatial invasions. Research on this topic has been very productive and relatively autonomous (of other spatial behavior research) during the past two decades or so in uncovering many of the consequences of spatial invasion and in identifying a number of factors associated with the intensification or abatement of these effects (see Table 12.6). To be understood best however, these results should be viewed within the more general context of outcomes associated with *inappropriate* distances (i.e., those deviating from distances typically chosen, both *close* and *far*). When these inappropriate distances are extreme (as is the case for spatial invasion/intrusion), they fall into the category we (Aiello & Thompson, 1980a) have called the *critical region of discomfort* (see Figure 12.2). Attempts to employ compensatory processes to reduce the discomfort frequently fail, resulting in a predominance of "avoidance forces" and a greater proclivity to withdraw.

It can be stated with a great deal of confidence that people will become uncomfortable if they are ap-

Table 12.5. Influence of Relationship and Situation

Study	Subjects	Methodology	Results
Adler & Iverson (1974)	I. 216 male and female college students.	Measure chair placement distance from confederate.	In same-sex dyads, subjects sat farther from a low-status other who gave "false" praise. Praise had no effect for high-status other. Males kept greater distance than females in same-sex dyads.
	II. 36 male college students.	Measure chair placement distance from confederate.	Status and praise produced no significant results.
Aiello & Cooper (1972)	112 eighth graders, same-sex, reciprocated positive & negative affect pairs.	Unobtrusive observation in field (modified classroom) using adaptation of Hall's (1963) proxemic scales.	Positive affect pairs interacted at closer distances. Negative affect pairs faced each other less and less directly as interaction progressed.
Aiello & Cooper (1979)	128 reciprocated positive or negative same-sex pairs in grades 2, 5, 8, & 11.	Unobtrusive observation in field (modified classroom) using adaptation of Hall's (1963) proxemic scales.	Positive affect pairs interacted at closer distances at all but youngest age. All children regardless of affect stood at larger distances as they grew older.
Aiello, DeRisi, Epstein, & Karlin (1977)	32 female college students, median split of distance preference used to determine "far" and "close" IPD preferences.	Interpersonal distance preference unobtrusively assessed (chair placement distance) as subjects were "getting acquainted" with confederate. Physiological, behavioral, & subjective indications of discomfort during short-term crowding involving close proximity and cognitive performance (creativity) following crowding were obtained.	Subjects with far distance preference experienced greater physiological, stress-related arousal (higher skin conductance level) and more self-reported somatic stress. Crowded subjects experienced more stress during the session and performed more poorly after the session.
Albert & Dabbs (1970)	90 male college students.	Perceived distance questionnaire (subjects placed 1 to 2 ft, 4 to 5 ft, 14 to 15 ft from confederate).	Attitude change decreased linearly with distance, becoming negative for close speaker.
Allgeier & Byrne (1973)	10 male, 10 female college students.	Seating distance, score of liking (in lab).	Both males and females sat closer to liked experimenter.
Ashton & Shaw (1980)	I. 40 male, 40 female college students.	Approach toward another.	No effect for degree of friendship. Front>side>back approach.
	II. 32 college students.	Approach from another.	No effect for degree of friendship. Front>side>back approach.
Ashton, Shaw, & Worsham (1980)	20 male, 20 female college students.	Subjects' ratings of actual IPD (in lab).	Both males and females kept strangers at greater distances.

Table 12.5. *(Continued)*

Study	Subjects	Methodology	Results
Baker & Shaw (1980)	45 mixed-sex pairs of strangers, 45 mixed-sex pairs of friends, college students.	Subjects stood at three distances (1, 2, 5.5 ft) and discussed topics of three intimacy levels. Questionnaire evaluation of discussion.	Both friends and strangers showed a tendency to rate the 2-ft distance more favorably than 1 ft or 5.5 ft.
Barrios & Giesen (1977)	22 male, 22 female college students.	Subjects given expectations of hostile or friendly discussion. Observers recorded distance subjects sat from male moderator and other subject.	Females sat closer to other subjects and moderator. More favorable expectations resulted in less subject–subject distance and no change in subject–moderator distance.
Bartels (1976)	24 female friends, 24 female strangers.	Unobtrusive observation of interaction.	Friends were not more immediate in distance, body orientation, and gaze.
Batchelor & Goethals (1972)	80 male, 80 female high school students in groups of 8.	Observers estimated seating distances among group members.	When instructed to solve a problem individually, distances were greater than when instructed to solve problem as a group. Females and males did not differ in distance. Subjects more likely to sit next to same-sex other.
Blumenthal & Meltzoff (1967)	30 male schizophrenics, 30 male-control, tested singly.	Reproduce distance between cardboard figures (in field).	For both groups, relationship of figures had no effect.
Brady & Walker (1978)	I. 32 male, 32 female college students.	Seated distance measured (nose to nose).	Subjects in evaluation anxiety condition used more space than those in no-anxiety condition.
	II. 24 male, 24 female college students.	Seated distance measured (nose to nose).	Subjects in evaluation anxiety condition used more space than those in no-anxiety condition.
Breuer & Lindauer (1977)	16 male, 16 female college students.	Distance from "entrance" subjects placed enlarged photos of statues.	Males placed photos of nude statues (both males and females) farther than did females.
Brody & Stoneman (1980)	18 2-year-olds and parents, 18 3-year-olds and parents.	Adaptation of Hall's notation system. Interactions were: mother–child, father–child, and mother and father–child.	Larger distances used in triadic context. Mothers and children used less space than fathers and children. Parents and daughters used less space than parents and sons.

Table 12.5. *(Continued)*

Study	Subjects	Methodology	Results
Brooks & Wilson (1978)	School children classified by teachers as "accepted," "concerned," "indifferent," "rejected."	Teacher behavior coded using Hall's notation system.	Teachers kept greatest distance from "rejected" child and least from "concerned" child, with "accepted" and "indifferent" in the middle.
Burgess (1983)	I. 2014 males & females.	Subjects were photographed as they walked through a shopping mall.	Distances from strangers were random.
	II. 117 males & females.	Subjects were observed while they sat on benches in a shopping mall.	Subjects sat closer to companions than strangers.
Byrne, Baskett, & Hodges (1971)	50 male, 50 female college students tested with confederate.	Seating distance, relative seating position (in lab).	For females only, subjects sat closer to similar other. Males chose to sit across from similar other.
Byrne, Ervin, & Lamberth (1970)	44 male–female pairs, college students.	Unobtrusive observation of distance pairs stood from each other (in lab).	Attractiveness predicted closer IPD between subjects. Similarity had no effect.
Cade (1972)	48 Hawaiian Orientals, 24 Hawaiian Caucasians.	Kuethe's Felt Figure Placement Task.	For both groups parent and child peer distances were less than mother–child distances, which were less than father–child.
Castell (1970)	23 male, 17 female 15- to 36-month-old pairs.	Unobtrusive observation in field (homes).	Child stays closer to mother in partially unfamiliar social and physical environment (another's living room) than in a partially unfamiliar social but familiar physical environment (own living room). Child–child interaction distances averaged about 3.5 ft.
Cochran, Hale, & Hissam (1984)	96 males & females.	Each subject was approached by male and female confederates who were acquainted, but not friends with subject. Subject stops approach of confederate.	The subjects allowed closer approach outdoors than indoors.
Cochran & Urbanczyk (1982)	24 male, 24 female college students.	Studied effect of ceiling height on approach by stranger allowed.	Subjects allowed closer approach with 10-ft ceiling than 7-ft ceiling. No effect for sex of subject.

Table 12.5. *(Continued)*

Study	Subjects	Methodology	Results
Comer & Piliavin (1972)	30 males, physically disabled, 23 to 54 years old.	Subjects were observed in an interview with an apparently disabled or normal confederate. Measured distance, gaze, comfort (from questionnaire).	Subjects gazed more and felt more comfortable with disabled confederate. Kept greater distance from disabled confederate.
Coutts & Schneider (1976)	80 female college students, in pairs.	Unobtrusive observation of seated interactions (in lab).	Level of nonverbal intimacy greater in strangers. No difference in IPD.
Cozby (1973)	72 female college students.	Measures subject's "personal space" by approach from and toward two different persons. Evaluated model room (clothespins represented people). Completed personality and background questionnaires.	Close and far "personal space" subjects responded differently only when social activities are specified (as situation depicted in model).
Crane & Griffin (1983)	24 married couples.	Subjects stop approach of other member of couple. Marital status inventory, Marital Adjustment Test, chair placement.	Both chair placement and stop distances were smaller, the higher the adjustment.
Dabbs (1971)	112 male college students, in pairs.	Placed subjects in a small room (chairs 2 ft apart) or a large room (chairs 6 ft apart).	Subjects' evaluations of the situation were more negative in the small room.
Dabbs, Fuller, & Carr (1973)	30 male, 30 female college students, 60 prison inmates.	Stop approach of, and toward, experimenter.	Students and prisoners both gave more room and used more room in corner than in center of room. Prisoners approached closer than they allowed another to approach.
Daniell & Lewis (1972)	18 male, 18 female college students.	Unobtrusive observation of seating distance from interviewer. Three interviews with same or different interviewer.	Eye contact and distance remain very stable across interviews. No difference for same or different interviewers.
Daves & Swaffer (1971)	13 male, 24 female college students.	Approach from experimenter measured unobtrusively.	Room size was inversely related to approach distance.
Dean, Willis, & Hewitt (1975)	562 male U.S. Navy personnel.	Unobtrusive observation of initial interaction distance of dyads in field (military settings).	Interactions initiated with superiors (in rank) were characterized by greater distance. When interactions initiated with subordinates, interaction distance was unrelated to rank.

Table 12.5. *(Continued)*

Study	Subjects	Methodology	Results
Dosey & Meisels (1969)	91 male, 95 female college students, groups of 5 to 6.	Stop approach from and toward another, silhouette placement, seating distance, questionnaires (in lab).	Stress did not increase IPS in anxious subjects.
Edwards (1973)	30 male college students.	Doll placement in different situations.	Distances were greater in "asymmetrical" interactions (only one member of the pair was described as distressed).
Engelbretson & Fullmer (1970)	Native Japanese: 32 male, 24 female; Hawaiian Japanese: 26 male, 24 female; American Caucasian: 24 male, 25 female.	Adaptation of Kuethe's Felt Figure Technique. Six different interaction scenes that varied as a function of interactants and conversational contents.	No difference between Hawaiian Japanese and American Caucasian placement distances but native Japanese had significantly larger placements. Across all groups, students with friend placements were closer than student with father or professor.
Ettin (1976)	119 college students.	CID.	Subjects exposed to near or far models were significantly different in CID score, with scores differing in direction of models' behavior.
Ford, Knight, & Cramer (1977)	64 female college students.	Subject asked to approach inanimate object to simulate distance she had been approached by confederate.	When confederate approached at close distance (30.5 cm), subjects underestimated the distance they had stood apart.
Fromme & Schmidt (1972)	16 male college students.	Approach male confederate under "fear," "anger," "sorrow," and "neutral" instructions. Administered Anxiety scale and Social Introversion scale.	No effect for personality measures. Approached closest in anger condition, farthest in fear condition, with neutral and sorrow intermediate.
Gardin, Kaplan, Firestone, & Cowan (1973)	80 male college students.	Varied seating arrangement and possibility for eye contact. Side by side or across, with or without barrier.	Most cooperation in PD game if across with no barrier. Least in across barrier. Same results for attitude and approach–avoidance questionnaire. Most positive in across no barrier, least in the across barrier condition.

Table 12.5. *(Continued)*

Study	Subjects	Methodology	Results
Gifford (1982)	22 male, 20 female college students.	Placement of chairs in a scale model of an interview room. Subjects were given different social situations to simulate.	Aspects of the social situation (cooperation–competition, amount of liking, status of other) were dominant. Liking and cooperation resulted in closer chair placement. High-status subjects chose larger distances in competitive situations.
Gifford & Price (1979)	18 male, 16 female same-sex pairs, ages 3½ to 5½.	Figure placement (in field).	Inverse relationship between IPD and acquaintance.
Goldring (1967)	75 female college students, tested singly.	Evaluation of the relationship between figures (in lab).	Closer distance rated more positively.
Griffitt, May, & Veitch (1974)	27 male, 25 female college students, tested singly.	Observation of videotape (in lab).	No effect of sexual arousal on IPD or looking at opposite-sex other. Those who felt negatively toward stimulus sat farther from opposite-sex other and closer to same-sex other.
Griffitt & Veitch (1971)	121 male & female college students, tested singly.	Ratings of feelings and attitudes toward stranger (in lab).	Under high temperature and high population density, ratings of other were more negative than under comfortable conditions.
Guardo (1969)	30 males, 30 females, grade 6.	Subjects placed silhouettes that were designated to be the same sex as subject.	Subjects placed "acquainted" or "liked" pairs closer than "unliked" or "unacquainted." Placed "friends" closer to "self" than strangers or feared peer.
Guardo (1976)	25 males, 25 females, grade 6.	Silhouette placement (same sex).	Both boys and girls placed silhouettes described attractively (outgoing, happy-go-lucky, intelligent, etc.) closer than those described unattractively (shy, apprehensive, expedient, etc.). Sex differences depended on individual characteristics.
Haase & DiMattia (1976)	54 male college students.	Interviewer seated from subject: (1) face to face, no desk; (2) across corner of desk; (3) face to face, desk between.	No effect of seating in self-referent statements.

465

Table 12.5. *(Continued)*

Study	Subjects	Methodology	Results
Hardee (1976)	Males & females (number not specified).	Observation of seating distance from confederate.	Subjects sat closer to "blind" targets and targets wearing sunglasses than controls.
Heshka & Nelson (1972)	57 dyads, male & female, 19 to 76 years old.	Distance estimated from photographs.	For females, not males, acquaintances, good friends, and relatives interacted more closely than strangers.
Hill, Blackham, & Crane (1982)	37 married couples, white, 20 to 54 years old.	(1) Pedersen Awareness Personal Space Measure; (2) Figure placement: (H—husband, W—wife, F—female confederate, M—male confederate) (a) HW; (b) HF; (c) HM; (d) WF; (e) WM.	HW dyads required least space in both tests. HW dyads required least space on both tests in presence of other dyads. WF dyads were second closest. Other dyads required more space.
Holahan (1972)	120 male psychiatric patients.	Room arrangements: (1) sociofugal—chairs against walls; (2) sociopetal— chairs around tables; (3) mixed; (4) fire—chairs stacked by walls. Observed interactions.	Social behaviors (conversations, games) occurred most in sociopetal arrangements, least in sociofugal.
Hollender, Duke, & Nowicki (1973)	21 males, 34 females, grades 3 & 4; 20 male, 19 female college students.	CID, Parental Contact Questionnaire.	Distance positively correlated with number of older brothers for females. For males only, maternal affection correlated negatively with distance.
Hunt (1974)	Number not specified.	Approach from and toward confederate.	When subjects had face-to-face contact with confederate, maintained greater distance when approached than when approaching. Opposite for those who had no prior contact.
Ickes, Patterson, Rajecki & Yanford (1982)	98 male college students in dyads.	Observation of distance subjects sat from each other. Varied expectancies of one subject: (1) expected unfriendly partner; (2) expected friendly partner; (3) no expectations.	Subjects sat closest to "friendly" partner, farthest from "no expectancy" partner.
Imada & Hakel (1977)	72 female college students.	Interviewers instructed to maintain immediate (small distance, greater eye contact, smiling, attentive posture, direct orientation) or nonimmediate behaviors.	Immediate interviewers were rated as more competent, motivated, likable, successful by "applicant."

Table 12.5. *(Continued)*

Study	Subjects	Methodology	Results
Jorgensen (1975)	88 pairs of equivalent status, 33 pairs of discrepant status, white males.	Unobtrusive observation in courtyard at lunch using Hall's notation system.	Groups were not different in distance. Equivalent-status groups faced more directly than discrepant-status.
Kahn & McGaughey (1977)	44 male, 44 female college students.	Observation of interaction ratings of confederate.	Less distance with greater attraction only in cross-sex pairs.
Karabenick & Meisels (1972)	171 male college students tested with 3 confederates.	Stop approach toward, and from experimenter (in lab).	IPD is affected by performance evaluation. Failure feedback increases IPD, success feedback decreases it.
Katz, Katz, & Cohen (1976)	80 white children, 5 & 6 years old, 9 & 10 years old.	Measured seating distance from experimenter.	Children sat closer to white than black experimenter. This effect increased with age for boys, decreased with age for girls. Sat closer to nonhandicapped white experimenter than handicapped white experimenter. For younger children, this was reversed if experimenter was black.
Keating & Keating (1980)	40 male Kenyans.	Distance from photographs of pairs seated on public benches.	Acquainted pairs sat closer than unacquainted pairs.
Kelly (1972)	60 males, clinical group, control group, tested singly.	Ratings of liking of therapist (in lab).	Closer interaction distance resulted in greater liking.
Kiesler & Goldberg (1968)	160 males, 13 to 18 years old, tested singly.	Ratings of interpersonal attraction (including preferred seating distance) (in lab).	Blunder by a competent other decreased ratings in social–emotional category (including IPD).
King (1966)	6 male triads, 6 female triads, children 3 to 5 years old.	Unobtrusive observation of approach distance.	Distance was positively related to aggressive acts from one subject to another. Introducing a liked toy decreased distance.
Kleck (1967)	20 male college students, tested singly.	Approach toward experimenter.	Distance between self and unknown female was less than distance between self and liked male, which was less than between self and disliked male.

Table 12.5. *(Continued)*

Study	Subjects	Methodology	Results
Kleck, Buck, Goller, London, Pfeiffer, & Vukcevic (1968)	I. 78 male college students. II. 25 male college students.	Figure placement. Initial chair placement.	"Stigmatized" figures placed farther from self figures than affectively positive figures. Ascription of epilepsy to confederate resulted in greater seating distance.
Kmiecik, Mausar, & Banziger (1979)	120 male and female pedestrians.	Attractive or unattractive female confederate intruded or did not intrude on subjects at intersection (15 cm). Measured latency of flight.	Unattractive confederate produced shorter latency than baseline (no intrusion). Attractive confederate resulted in longer latency.
Knowles & Brickner (1981)	24 male, 24 female college students.	Informed subjects that they were similar or dissimiliar to confederates. Observed whether subject protected group space with confederate from invasion.	Males protected group space more in the similar condition. Females protected group space in both conditions.
Kuethe (1962)	100 male college students, tested singly.	Felt figure placement and replacement (in lab).	Woman and child placed closer than man and child. Man and woman replaced closer together than geometric figures.
Kunzendorf & Denney (1982)	47 college students.	Stop approach of experimenter. Seated experimenter either holding cigarette or not holding cigarette.	Subjects required more space if experimenter had cigarette. Nonsmoking subjects allowed closer approach than smokers.
Lee & Roberts (1981)	Squash players: 15 male, 15 female; badminton players: 15 male, 15 female.	Modified Comfortable Interpersonal Distance Scale administered.	Squash players projected a closer approach tolerance than badminton players. Females projected tolerance for closer distances than males.
Leffler, Gillespie, & Conaty (1982)	28 male, 28 female college students, each assigned a role (student or teacher) in the interaction.	Observed amount of vertical (toward other person) or horizontal (side-to-side) space each used across table in a seated interaction.	High-status ("teacher") used more space during interaction than low-status ("student") subjects.
Lerner, Karabenick, & Meisels (1975)	Kindergarten: 26 male, 19 female; Grade 1: 26 male, 27 female; Grade 2: 32 male, 25 female; Grade 3: 22 male, 25 female.	Placement of silhouettes. Average build and each of ectomorph, endomorph, mesomorph. Figures were male and female of each type.	Place mesomorph closest followed by ectomorph and endomorph. Greater space for female targets. Space increased with grade level.
Leventhal, Lipshultz, & Chiodo (1978)	176 male and female pairs seated at tables.	Observed seating arrangements in social (cafeteria restaurant) or nonsocial (library or quiet lounge) settings.	In social situations, same-sex pairs prefer across seating, mixed pairs prefer side seats. In nonsocial settings, all pairs prefer side seats.

Table 12.5. (*Continued*)

Study	Subjects	Methodology	Results
Leventhal, Matturro, & Schanerman (1978)	60 white male, 60 white female college students.	Projective measure of distance kept from liked, disliked, or stranger. Stop approach by confederate showing positive, negative, or no affect.	Males allow females to approach closer than males. Males allow liked closest, next stranger then disliked. Females allow closer approach than males. Females allowed liked females closer than disliked and strangers. Allowed liked males closer than disliked males closer than strangers. For the stop-distance measure: Males keep positive and negative at greater distance than neutral. Females keep negative farthest followed by positive followed by neutral.
Little, Ulehla, & Henderson (1968)	48 male college students, tested singly.	Figure placement (in lab).	People placed figures according to similarity in attitudes toward Johnson and Goldwater. GG pairs were placed closer than GJ pairs, but JJ pairs were not.
Long (1984)	40 males, 40 females, 18 to 26 years old.	Subjects asked to complete CID while in natural settings. Settings were classified as high or low tension.	Subjects in high-tension settings required more distance than those in low-tension setting.
Loo & Kennelly (1979)	36 male, 36 female 5-year-olds.	Children were placed in groups of different density. Each child's personal space was measured by a stop-distance approach technique (child approached by female adult experimenter). Observers recorded children's behavior.	Child's personal space had no effect on children's reports of crowding. More distress and nonplay in the crowded condition. More positive interactions in the uncrowded condition. For males, crowding produced more activity–aggression–anger.
Lott & Sommer (1967)	224 male & female college students.	Questionnaire of seating preference, actual seating choice with confederate. Status of other varied (high, low, equal).	Subjects give most distance to higher status other. More likely to choose side-by-side seat with equal-status other.
Matthews, Paulus, & Baron (1979)	80 male college students.	Groups of 4 (2 confederates) in large (3.9 m × 3.4 m) or small (2.0 m × 1.7 m) room, involved in cooperative or competitive task. Given immediate or 30-min delayed chance to aggress toward confederate (using Buss machine).	Only in immediate condition, subjects in crowded, competitive situation showed less aggression.

Table 12.5. *(Continued)*

Study	Subjects	Methodology	Results
McGrew (1970)	11 females, 9 males, 3 to 5 years old.	Observed interactions of children in playroom. Children were allowed access to 100% of room or 80% of room. Social density conditions were 16 to 20 students or 8 to 10 students.	Children maintained closer proximity in the smaller group condition. Close proximity was significantly higher when density was increased by spatial manipulations but not by social manipulations.
McGrew & McGrew (1975)	3 males, 2 females, 55 to 59 months old, nursery experienced; 4 males, 4 females, 39 to 49 months old, nursery inexperienced.	Observed amount of peer and adult contact by children.	Children experienced (familiar) with nursery spent more time in close proximity to peers than inexperienced children. Inexperienced children spent more time alone.
McKenzie & Strongman (1981)	84 adults.	Doll placements for simulated high-, low-, & peer-status and leader, nonleader, & ordinary group member interactions.	Subjects made more distant doll placements for simulated higher-status interactions than simulated peer- or low-status interactions.
Mehrabian (1968a)	30 males, 30 females, tested singly.	Ratings of liking of self by person in picture (in lab).	Smaller IPD signals liking.
Mehrabian (1968b)	25 male, 25 female college students, tested singly.	Unobtrusive observation of seating position (in lab).	IPD decreases with liking.
Mehrabian & Diamond (1971a)	I. 144 male, 144 female pairs.	Subjects under "waiting room" conditions placed at one of four distances (3, 4.5, 6, 9 ft) and sat at one of three orientations (0, 90, 180°). Observed nonverbal relaxation & affiliative behavior; questionnaire measures of affiliative tendencies and sensitivity to rejection included.	Subjects relaxed more as distance increased. Affiliative behavior decreased with indirectness of orientation, particularly for those with more of an affiliative tendency.
	II. 88 males, 88 females.	Subjects sat at 4.5 ft apart and at 90° orientation. Exposed to prop condition (abstract sculpture & puzzle poster) or not. Dependent measures same as above.	Attention to puzzle decreased affiliative behavior. Attention to sculpture by subjects "sensitive to rejection" facilitated interaction.
Mehrabian & Friar (1969)	24 male, 24 female college students.	Observed subject from behind mirror while subject sat alone and assumed position relative to a liked–disliked, low–high status, male–female "other."	Positive attitudes were signaled by closer distances.
Mehrabian & Williams (1969)	I. 36 male, 36 female college students.	Observers judged persuasiveness of subject and also estimated distance.	Those rated higher on persuasiveness also used less distance.

Table 12.5. *(Continued)*

Study	Subjects	Methodology	Results
	II. 114 male, 113 female college students.	Rate persuasiveness of confederate on TV 4 ft or 12 ft away.	Closer distance resulted in more persuasiveness.
Meisels & Dosey (1971)	80 male, 80 female college students.	Stop approach toward another, TAT (in lab).	Those who had stronger defenses against expression of anger employed greater IPD when angered. Opposite result for those low in defense against expression of anger.
Melson (1977)	24 males, 24 females, 3 to 6 years old.	Figure placement and judgments (attributed sex & affect).	Subjects 4 to 6 years old but not 3 years old used distance to communicate affect difference.
Minton, Steger, & Smrtic (1968)	64 male college students, groups of 4 subjects and 2 confederates.	Observed attitude change in discussion where participants were equidistant (circular) or unequally distant (rectangular).	No difference between arrangement for attitude change. A significant attitude shift occurred for both.
Morris & Smith (1980)	2 males, 2 females, approximately 3 years old.	Observed in interaction with two adults. Established baseline distances. Observed in interaction with adult from whom they had originally interacted farthest.	Children's distances decreased when adult showed affectionate nonverbal behavior (eye contact, smiles) and positive verbal reinforcement.
Naus & Eckenrode (1974)	47 male, 7 female college students.	Silhouette placement.	Young–young pairs placed closer than young–old pairs. No effect for acquaintance.
O'Neal, Brunault, Marquis, & Carifio (1979)	32 male college students.	Stop approach from six axes (in lab).	Angered subjects used more IPD than nonangered subjects, especially from front.
O'Neal, Brunault, Carifio, Troutwine, & Epstein (1980)	60 male college students, tested singly.	Stop approach from four axes (in lab).	Those who were insulted required greater personal space, regardless of whether or not approacher had insulted them.
Patterson, Kelley, Kondracki, & Wolf (1979)	32 4-person groups (same sex).	Groups sat in L configuration or circle. Close (1.03 m) or far (1.98 m).	No effects for sex on distance or satisfaction or behaviors. Non-facing (L-shaped) group resulted in more pauses and manipulative behavior than the facing (circle) orientation.

Table 12.5. *(Continued)*

Study	Subjects	Methodology	Results
Patterson, Roth, & Schenk (1979)	72 6-person groups (female, male, mixed).	Asked for ratings of room and other participants. Arrangement of chairs was circular or *L*-shaped.	Females preferred circular shape, males had no preference, and mixed groups preferred *L*-shaped arrangement. Circular arrangement seen as more crowded, but participants in circular arrangement seen as more friendly.
Pedersen & Shears (1974)	170 male college students.	Stop-distance toward and from another subject, unobtrusive observation (seating choice), projective task (Rawls Personal Space Measure).	Largest decrease in personal space after crowding and game interaction as compared to separation.
Porter, Argyle, & Salter (1970)	54 males, 15 to 17 years old interacted with 21-year-old male.	Subjects held interview or conversation at 2, 4, 8 ft (seated). Completed rating scales concerning confederate.	Distance did not affect evaluations of the confederates.
Rierdon & Wiener (1977)	Schizophrenic: 16 male, 16 female; nonschizophrenic: 16 male, 16 female.	Seating choice relative to experimenter (near vis-à-vis, far vis-à-vis, near juxtaposed, far juxtaposed).	No differences between groups. Closer, more direct seats were preferred.
Roger (1982)	128 male British Marine recruits.	Doll placement (self and peer) as a function of self-esteem (performance on tests) manipulation.	No effect for self-esteem. Leaders showed preference for less distance.
Roger (1983)	91 male U.S. Army recruits.	Same as Roger (1982) (figures were self & peer and self & higher-status other).	No effect for self esteem. Subjects placed higher-status other farther than peer.
Roger & Reid (1978)	128 male Marines.	Distance between chairs. Doll placement.	Ordinary members sat closer to leaders than nonleaders. Doll placement positively correlated with seating distance.
Rogers, Rearden, & Hillner (1981)	36 college students.	Interviewed by 2 female confederates at three distances about personal, social, and academic topics.	Anxiety was least at intermediate (5 ft) distance. A moderate correlation between anxiety and verbal productivity was reported.
Rosenfeld (1965)	18 female college students tested with confederate.	Pedersen chair placement distance (in lab).	Subjects assigned to approval-seeking condition sat closer to target than those assigned to avoidance-seeking condition.

Table 12.5. *(Continued)*

Study	Subjects	Methodology	Results
Rumsey, Bull, & Gahagan (1982)	450 pedestrians.	Confederate made up to simulate "disfigurement" below right eye: (1) "strawberry" birthmark; (2) trauma bruising and scarring; (3) control-no disfigurement. Confederate made no eye contact as she passed pedestrians. Observed distance pedestrians crossing street kept from her.	Pedestrians kept greater distance from "disfigured" confederate than control. Pedestrians walked more often to the confederate's left, or nondisfigured side, than they did if confederate was not disfigured.
Ryen & Kahn (1975)	123 male triads.	Observation of seating choice.	No feedback group members sat closer to own group than outgroup. Winning feedback group sat closer to losing group than did no feedback group.
Savinar (1975)	30 male, 30 female college students.	Stop approach of experimenter.	No effect of ceiling height (6 ft, 9 ft) for females. Males used more space with 6-ft ceiling. Males allowed females to approach closer.
Schiavo, Schiffenbauer, & Roberts (1977)	32 female college students.	Studies effect of room size on stop distance.	No effect for room size. Subjects approached closer than they allowed other to approach.
Schiffenbauer & Schiavo (1976)	76 female college students.	Subject and confederate sat (2 ft or 5 ft) across from subject while solving a puzzle. Asked for ratings of liking for confederate.	Close distance amplified feelings toward confederate. After insulting feedback, confederate was rated more negatively at the close distance. After complimentary feedback, confederate was rated more positively at the close distance.
Schwarzwald, Kavish, Shoham, & Waysman (1977)	40 male, 40 female Israeli college students.	Distance estimated between subject and same- or opposite-sex confederate. Conditions were fear or no fear of impending shock.	Both sexes stood closer to same-sex other in fear condition. In no-fear condition both sexes stood closer to opposite-sex other.
Silverstein & Stang (1976)	201 naturally occurring triads at tables at college (males & females).	Observed talkativeness of triads at table.	Found that person seated across from two others talked the most. Hypothesized it is due to visual and physical centrality.

Table 12.5. *(Continued)*

Study	Subjects	Methodology	Results
Snyder & Andelman (1979)	45 male, 45 female psychology students.	Subjects received bogus feedback (low, moderate or high similarity to object–person). Measured chair placement toward empty chair where other "subject" would sit.	Distances were greatest in the slightly similar condition and least in the moderately similar condition.
Storms & Thomas (1977)	I. 159 male college students.	Subjects seated 12 or 30 in. from male confederate. Confederate gave autobiographical speech that was similar or dissimilar to subject's.	In condition where subject had no choice of distance, ratings were highest for similar other at close distance. Least high ratings were for dissimilar at close distance.
	II. 120 male college students.	Same as I. except positive and negative cues were friendly or unfriendly words from confederate.	Liking for confederate was highest in close, friendly condition. Least liking in the close unfriendly condition.
Sundstrom (1975)	96 male college students, groups of 3 subjects and 3 confederates.	Discussions were in 36-sq-ft room or 228-sq-ft room. Confederate intruded or did not intrude on subject.	Subjects reported being less comfortable in the small room. Nonverbal behaviors (manipulation) also increased in small room. Intrusion also increased stress.
Sykes, Larntz, & Fox (1976)	60 male Naval boot camp recruits.	Observed proximity of bunks. Observers recorded frequencies of interactions among recruits. Compared for similarity on demographic variables.	Bunkmates interact more than those in adjacent bunks. The fewer similar persons in an area, the more subjects sought a nonproximate person with whom to interact.
Tedesco & Fromme (1974)	18 male college students.	Forced seating choice.	Subjects sat closer to confederate after a cooperative prisoner's dilemma game with the confederate than after a neutral or competitive PD game.
Tennis & Dabbs (1975)	20 males, 20 females, in each of the following: grades 1, 5, 9, 12, college sophomores.	Stop approach of same-sex subject.	Males use more space at all ages except grade 1. Differences between sexes increase with age. Subjects use more space as they age & in corner than in center of room.
Tesch, Huston, & Indenbaum (1973)	116 female college students.	Measured subjects' placement of chair relative to female confederate. Recorded distance and orientation. Questionnaires measured perceived similarity and liking.	Distance was unrelated to both liking and perceived similarity.

Table 12.5. *(Continued)*

Study	Subjects	Methodology	Results
Thompson & Aiello (1984)	67 female college students assigned to interviewee role with a same-sex, "cold" or "warm" nonverbal communication style manager.	Communication style operationalized by eight nonverbal variables, including large (8 ft) distance ("cold" condition) and smaller (4 ft) distance ("warm" condition). Unobtrusive observations during interview in lab (simulated office) of nine subject nonverbal behaviors. Following interview anxiety measure and self-reported feelings, perceptions, attributions, and behavioral intentions of subjects obtained.	Subjects interacting with warm (nonverbal) managers displayed greater involvement (e.g., gazed more, oriented more directly) and less nervousness/defensiveness (e.g., object & automanipulation, arms-folded posture). They also experienced less anxiety, were more positive about the manager, and indicated intentions to work harder for the warm manager.
Tipton, Bailey, & Obenchain (1975)	72 female college students.	Approach toward male and female confederates. Attitude Toward Woman Scale score used to classify subjects as feminists or traditionals.	Traditionals and feminists did not differ in approach distance to another female, but traditionals stopped at a larger distance from male confederate than did feminists.
Ugwuegbu & Anusiem (1982)	16 male, 16 female Nigerian secondary school students.	Observed seating distance from experimenter.	Stressed subjects sat farther from experimenter than nonstressed subjects. Under stress females sat farther than males, opposite under no stress.
Vautier & Aiello (1982)	48 female college students, each assigned to interact with higher-, equal-, or lower-status partner.	Observed interaction distance, body orientation, and eight other nonverbal behaviors.	Subjects interacted with equal-status (peer) partner at closer distance and more direct body orientation than higher status peer.
Walden & Forsyth (1981)	48 male, 48 female college students.	Same-sex groups of 6 sat at chairs 40 cm apart or touching. Expected stressful or nonstressful event.	Distance only, not stress affected perceived crowding. Crowded conditions enhanced feelings of stress in the stressful condition.
Walker & Borden (1976)	I. 466 males, 234 females on college campus.	Observed how many subjects intruded on interacting dyad.	Males and females just as likely to intrude. Mixed-sex dyads were most likely to be intruded upon than either same-sex dyad.
	II. 497 males, 245 females.	Same as study I.	Same as study I.

Table 12.5. *(Continued)*

Study	Subjects	Methodology	Results
	III. 632 males, 340 females.	Same as study I, except status of confederate varied.	Subjects invaded low-status dyad more often than high status. Same pattern as described above in studies I & II for low-status groups. For high status dyads, male–male least likely to be intruded upon, followed by male–female and female–female.
Weinstein (1965)	54 males, 8 to 12 years old, tested singly; emotionally disturbed control group.	Felt figure placement and replacement (in field).	Controls placed child closer to female than male. Reverse true for clinical group. They replaced humans farther apart than geometric figures.
Weinstein (1967)	153 males, grades 2 to 6, tested singly.	Reconstruction of figure distance (in field).	Underestimation of distance positively related to both peer and parental acceptance. Peer and parental acceptance not correlated with each other.
Willis (1966)	755 males & females. Sample obtained in homes, places of business, and in the halls of the university.	Unobtrusive observation of initial distance from confederate (in field).	Strangers stand farthest. Friends stand closer than strangers. Males stand closer than females to friends. Close friends stand closest. All groups stand closer to females than males. Peers stand closer than older subjects.
White (1975)	40 male, 40 female college freshmen.	Unobtrusive observation.	Personal space inversely related to room size. No effect for sex, status of interactants.
Wolfgang & Wolfgang (1971)	I. 30 male college students.	Distance from stick figure representing self. Subjects placed following figures: normal, police, drug addict, and obese.	Subjects placed self farther from drug addict and obese than police and normal.
	II. 40 male military personnel.	Same as above except figures were: normal, marijuana user, heart disease patient, homosexual.	Subjects placed selves closer to normal and heart disease patient than marijuana user and homosexual.
Worchel & Teddlie (1976)	315 male college students, groups of 7 to 8.	Rating of experiment.	More negative evaluations of experience in crowded conditions. Personal space invasion not necessarily related to conditions of high density.

Table 12.5. *(Continued)*

Study	Subjects	Methodology	Results
Worthington (1974)	16 males, 13 females, people walking through airport.	Observers estimated distance to which subject approached experimenter who asked for directions.	Subjects approached closer to a control than a person who appeared to be physically impaired (tube inserted in nostril and terminated under jacket).

Table 12.6. Consequences of Spatial Invasion/Intrusion

Study	Subjects	Methodology	Results
Aiello, Headly, & Thompson (1978)	36 females, 20 males, 60 to 90 years old, same-sex groups of 4.	Groups "waited" in small (4-ft × 4-ft) or moderate sized (8-ft × 8-ft) room. Skin conductance data; group cohesion task (Tajfel, 1970); members' perception of environment, others in group, and subjective indications of discomfort during short-term crowding involving close proximity gathered.	Elderly men and women were more affected physiologically by the close physical proximity condition and reported feeling more crowded but did *not* find the experience aversive (as younger adults do) and were *not* the least bit bothered by bodily contact. Instead, they responded more positively to the members of their crowded group and labeled the environment "cozy."
Barash (1973)	Males, females.	Measured latency of departure after invasion.	Close approach in faculty attire produced quickest departure, followed by close approach in student attire, medium approach faculty attire, and control.
Barefoot, Hoople, & McClay (1972)	Male college students.	Observed percentage of passersby who drank at water fountain and duration of drinking.	Subjects were less likely to drink if confederate was seated 1 ft from fountain compared to 5 ft and 10 ft.
Baron (1978)	42 male, 40 female college students.	Male and female confederates invaded at 12 to 18 in. or 36 to 48 in. (face-to-face) while subject was seated at cafeteria table. Confederate asked for favor of low or high apparent need. Questionnaire measured affective reactions.	Only interaction between need and distance had significant effect on helping. For high need, close invasion increased helping. Opposite result for low need. For affective responses, subject reported more positive reactions for near–high need condition than far–high need condition. For low need, far distance elicited more positive responses.

Table 12.6. *(Continued)*

Study	Subjects	Methodology	Results
Baron & Bell (1972)	Males, females.	Confederates stood 38 to 54 in. apart at entrance to store in shopping mall.	Presence of confederate reduced number of persons walking through the area. Mixed dyads prevented more invasions, male dyads the least.
Baron & Bell (1976)	80 male, 80 female college students.	Male and female confederates invaded at 12 to 18 in. or 36 to 48 in. (face-to-face) while subject was seated at cafeteria table. Confederate asked for favor of low or high apparent need. Questionnaire measured affective reactions.	Female subjects offered more assistance than males. Both sexes more likely to help in near condition. Subjects reported being more calm in the near condition.
Baum, Reiss, & O'Hara (1974)	310 males and females.	Observed likelihood of passerby stopping to use drinking fountain and duration of drinking.	Screened fountain led to subjects drinking longer when confederate was near (1 ft or 5 ft). People less likely to drink if confederate was present.
Becker & Mayo (1971)	Males & females.	Observed whether or not subjects defended spaces they had marked at cafeteria tables.	Virtually no subjects defended territory, concluded markers were used to designate personal space, not territoriality. Extreme invasion was related to flight, however.
Bleda & Bleda (1978)	54 male, 54 female shoppers, 18 to 45 years old.	Confederates of both sexes invaded subjects sitting on benches in shopping mall. Distances were 6, 18, 30 in. Measured latency of flight.	Only in the 6-in. condition, males elicited sooner flight than females. Females departed sooner than males.
Bouska & Beatty (1978)	231 males, 569 females.	Observed likelihood of subjects to intrude upon the confederates' conversation.	Subjects were less likely to intrude if confederates were dressed formally (businessman, priest) than if they dressed casually.
Brown (1981)	263 white females, 213 white males, 20 black females, 12 black males.	Observation of likelihood of subjects to invade upon conversation in a shopping mall.	Subjects more likely to pass through all-black dyad than white or mixed dyad.
Buchanan, Juhnke, & Goldman (1976)	122 males, 122 females.	Observed likelihood of subjects invading the space of a confederate standing by control panel in elevator.	81% of subjects chose panel with no one in front rather than invade. 72% of males, 62% of females chose to invade space of female over male when invasion unavoidable.

Table 12.6. *(Continued)*

Study	Subjects	Methodology	Results
Buchanan, Juhnke, & Goldman (1977)	I. 86 males, 61 females.	Recorded selection preference for right or left control panel in elevator. Confederate standing in front of one panel making eye contact with subject.	Male confederate: 70% males avoided intrusion; 60% females avoided intrusion. Female confederate: 33% males avoided intrusion; 32% females avoided intrusion.
	II. 68 males, 44 females.	Same as study I, except no eye contact (back turned reading), confederate added.	Male confederate: 71% males invaded confederate with back turned; 77% females invaded confederate with back turned. Female confederate: 78% males invaded confederate with back turned; 72% females invaded confederate with back turned.
Caplan & Goldman (1981)	182 male & female adults.	Commuters in a train station corridor given option of invading space of a tall or short male confederate or a tall or short female confederate.	Commuters, especially female commuters, intruded into the space of both the short male and short female confederate more frequently.
Cheyne & Efran (1972)	60 male & female college students.	Measured number of subjects who invaded conversation of same- and mixed-sex dyads. Stood in corridor 41 in. apart leaving 33-in. distance to wall. Controls were: (1) confederates standing at same distance not facing each other; (2) waste baskets placed in hallway.	Fewer people walked through confederates than control objects. People avoided invading interacting pairs (males and mixed-sex more than twice as much; females more than ten times as much). Interacting males more likely to be invaded than other interacting dyads.
Coss, Jacobs, & Allerton (1975)	I. 10 male, 10 female college students.	Male confederate intruded upon subject seated at student union. Measured stereotypic (auto & object manipulation, hand or leg movement) and nonstereotypic (grooming, object adjustment, change of position) reactions under crowded and noncrowded conditions.	Only females increased movement following intrusion at 1 ft side by side.
	II. 6 male, 6 female college students.	Same as study I, confederates of both sexes.	In all groups, invasion increased overall motor activity.

Table 12.6. *(Continued)*

Study	Subjects	Methodology	Results
Dabbs (1972)	321 males, 322 females.	Measured amount of movement after invasion by confederate.	Male invaders elicited more movement at bus stop (long-duration setting). Female subjects moved more at traffic light (short-duration setting).
Dabbs & Stokes (1975)	Males & females.	Observed distance subject deviated in path from confederates on sidewalk.	Subjects gave males more distance than females, two people more than one, and an attractive female more than an unattractive female.
Davis & Lennon (1983)	40 males, 40 females in shopping mall.	Observed number of shoppers who walked through conversation of two females. In one condition neither was pregnant. In other one women made up to appear pregnant.	When one woman appeared pregnant, less people intruded on conversation than when neither appeared pregnant.
Efran & Cheyne (1973)	People walking through halls of a building on a college campus. Confederates were same-sex pairs (male and female).	Observed number of people who walked between the interacting pair.	As distance increased between the pair, more people walked through their shared space.
Efran & Cheyne (1974)	39 male college students.	Subjects observed while forced to intrude on a conversation.	Greatest number of agonistic facial expressions in violation condition also significant increase in heart rate.
Felipe & Sommer (1966)	I. Male mental hospital patients sitting alone.	Male experimenter invaded subject at distance of 6 in. while seated. Observed latency of flight and compensatory behaviors.	Within 2 min, one-third invaded subjects but less than 2% of noninvaded subjects fled. Within 19 min two-thirds invaded subjects but less than one-third control subjects fled. More compensatory behaviors (blocking and leaning) also noted for invaded subjects.
	II. Female college students.	Female experimenter sat on chair 3 in., 15 in., 2.5 ft, 5 ft, or across from subject. Latency of flight and compensatory behaviors again noted.	Closer approaches led to quicker flight and more compensatory behaviors.
Fisher & Byrne (1975)	62 male, 63 female college students.	Male and female confederate invaded subjects at library table. Invader sat adjacent, one seat away, or across. Questionnaire evaluated affective responses.	Females rated more negatively the adjacent intruder. Males rated intruder from across more negatively.

480

Table 12.6. *(Continued)*

Study	Subjects	Methodology	Results
Fortenberry, MacLean, Morris, & O'Connell (1978)	120 males and females.	Observed likelihood that passerby would invade upon conversation.	Subjects were less likely to intrude if interactants were dressed formally than if they were dressed casually.
Fry & Willis (1971)	60 male, 60 female adults.	Adults in line for a movie were invaded by 5-, 8-, 10-year-old children. Invaders instructed to move as close as possible without touching and initiate no conversation. Compensatory reactions were observed.	Positive reactions (smiling, speaking, turning toward) more likely to be elicited by 5-year-olds. 8-year-olds received little reaction. Negative reactions (moving away, leaning, non-task behaviors) more likely to be elicited by 10-year-olds.
Greenberg & Firestone (1977)	128 male college students.	Intrusion: (1) Interviewer sat knees touching subject's legs; (2) 100% gaze; (3) Forward lean. No intrusion: (1) Interviewer sat 1.22 m (a bit less than 4 ft); (2) Looked at subject twice per question; (3) backward lean. Compensatory behaviors and verbal output recorded.	Subjects gazed less in intrusion condition. Subjects disclosed less in the intrusion condition.
Hansvick (1976)	35 male, 35 female college students.	Subjects invaded (6 in.) or not invaded (2.5 ft) by male confederate in preexperiment meeting. Distance subject stood from seated confederate during experiment was estimated.	Subjects modeled confederates and stood closer in the invasion condition. Female subject stood closer to confederate than male.
Hughes & Goldman (1978)	86 female, 90 male adults.	Observation of seating distance from confederate.	Subjects sat closer to "blind" targets who wore sunglasses than to controls.
Hosch & Himelstein (1982)	1553 persons passing bottom of stairs or escalator, 149 controls.	Recorded number of subjects who passed through photographer and subject in 1-min intervals. Varied distance between camera and presence or absence of human subject and apparent skill of photographer.	Closer distance, higher status of photographer and presence of human subject decreased violations.
Knowles (1972)	72 same- and mixed-sex dyads.	Observed whether dyads shifted together or separately when an invader walked between them.	Total: 61% shifted together; male–female: 83% shifted together; female–female: 62% shifted together; male–male: 32% shifted together.

Table 12.6. *(Continued)*

Study	Subjects	Methodology	Results
Knowles (1973)	429 males and females.	Measured likelihood of passersby intruding on conversation of a mixed-sex group.	Larger groups (4 members vs. 2 members) and higher-status groups (formal vs. casual dress) less likely to be invaded.
Knowles & Bassett (1976)	1003 males and females.	Videotaped people as they walked by group of people standing in front of library. Varied size and activity of group, and similarity.	Crowd activity (staring at top of building) caused more deflection from passersby than discussion activity. Size and similarity did not affect distance.
Knowles & Brickner (1981)	24 male, 24 female college students.	Informed subjects that they were similar or dissimilar to confederates. Observed whether subjects protected group space with confederate from invasion.	Males protected group space more in the similar condition. Females protected group space in both conditions.
Knowles, Kreuser, Haas, Hyde, & Schuchart (1976)	437 students, staff, & faculty.	Observed hallway pedestrians' distances from an empty bench, one, two, three, or four person(s) in alcove or hallway.	Pedestrians walked farther away from groups than individuals and farther from individuals than from empty bench.
Konecni, Libuser, Morton, & Ebbesen (1975)	60 males, 60 females.	Measured speed of crossing street after being invaded, and willingness to help invader.	Closer invasions (1 ft, 2 ft) resulted in faster walking than farther distance (5 ft, 10 ft). No difference in helping unless invader continued to invade subjects' space.
Leibman (1970)	98 white female, 18 black female adults.	Observed distances at which subjects invaded different target-persons (black or white, male or female confederate).	White females sat at same distance from whites and blacks, males and females. Preferred to invade female than male if forced to choose. No difference for race of confederate.
Lockard, McVittie, & Isaac (1977)	I. 88 males and females, 19 to 60 years old. II. 454 (F), 346 (M) college students.	Observed distance subjects stood from confederate in an elevator. Same as study I. Confederate either (1) smiled or (2) did not smile.	Subjects distanced themselves as far as they could from confederate. Subjects (particularly with female confederates) stood closer if confederate smiled.

Table 12.6. *(Continued)*

Study	Subjects	Methodology	Results
Mahoney (1974)	10 male, 10 female college students.	Same procedure as Patterson et al. (1971).	Two and three seats adjacent not seen as invasion. Across and adjacent did not increase compensatory responses. In females, across invasion decreased blocking responses.
McBride, King, & James (1965)	20 male, 20 female college students.	Measured GSR as experimenter sat at different distances (1, 3, 9 ft) to present flash cards.	Greater arousal (lower skin resistance) with frontal rather than side approaches, and with opposite-sex experimenter.
Middlemist, Knowles, & Matter (1976)	60 male college students.	Unobtrusive observation in three-urinal lavatory. Confederate adjacent to subject, one urinal removed, or absent.	Closer invasions increased delay in micturation and decreased duration of micturation.
Murphy-Berman & Berman (1978)	24 male, 24 female college students.	Subjects asked to evaluate invader who either had choice of seat or was seated by experimenter.	Evaluations were more negative if invader had apparent choice and if invader was male.
Nesbitt & Steven (1974)	Males & females.	Observed distance subjects kept from confederate while standing in line.	For both male and female target, subjects kept greater distance from loudly dressed or heavily perfumed confederate.
Patterson, Mullens, & Romano (1971)	College students.	Experimenter invaded subjects seated at tables in library. Measured latency of flight and compensatory behaviors (blocking, leaning, cross glances). Experimenter seated one, two, three seats away or across.	Invasion did not produce flight. Compensatory (discomfort) reactions increased with immediacy of invasion.
Polit & LaFrance (1977)	60 male, 60 female college students.	Measured latency of fleeing from a library table. Compared asking permission to invade to *not* asking permission.	Females fled more quickly than males, especially when they were asked permission.
Reid & Novak (1975)	263 males, students and faculty.	Observed distance subjects kept from confederate in lavatory.	Subjects preferred to use urinal farthest from confederate.

Table 12.6. *(Continued)*

Study	Subjects	Methodology	Results
Schiffenbauer & Schiavo (1976)	76 female college students.	Confederate sat (2 ft or 5 ft) across from subject while solving a puzzle. Asked for ratings of liking for confederate.	Close distance amplified feelings toward confederate. After insulting feedback, confederate was rated more negatively in the close distance. After complementary feedback, confederate was rated more positively in the close distance.
Smith & Knowles (1978)	18 males, 15 females.	Measured speed of subjects crossing street.	Subjects who were invaded crossed street faster.
Smith & Knowles (1979)	64 males, 64 females.	Observed whether or not subjects helped an invader who was either sketching or not sketching on an artist's pad.	Subjects were more likely to pick up pen dropped by artist than nonartist. Affective ratings also more negative for nonartist.
Sobel & Lillith (1975)	116 pedestrians, 27% black, 53% male.	Observed amount of space given to a confederate who walked toward subjects on a collision path.	Males given less frontal space than females. 42% of encounters ended in physical contact.
Soper & Karasik (1977)	Adults walking through halls on college campus.	Observed number of subjects who walked between pair of interacting male confederate in hallways (180, 117, 95, 72 in.) of varying widths.	Greater distances were more often invaded. This distance was greatest in widest halls. Consistent ratio of space between confederate when 100% of subjects invade dyad.
Sundstrom (1975)	96 male college students.	Discussions were in 36-sq-ft or 228-sq-ft room. Confederate intruded or did not intrude on subject.	Subjects reported being less comfortable in the small room. Nonverbal behaviors (manipulation) also increased in small room. Intrusion also increased stress.
Sundstrom & Sundstrom (1977)	24 male, 16 female college students.	Confederate of same sex approached subjects seated outdoors on college campus at 9 in. or 18 in. Observed compensatory reactions and latency of flight. Confederate asked or did not ask permission to invade.	Males fled more quickly if confederate did not ask permission. Opposite for females. Females showed more compensation (when they stayed) in the "no-ask" condition. Males (when they stayed) showed more compensation in the "ask" condition.
Terry & Lower (1979)	16 males, 16 females, grades 7 & 10.	Subjects invaded by experimenter seated 20 in. or next to subject. Measured amount of movement in task.	Subjects in invasion condition avoided contact with experimenter by moving less. No effect for age or sex.

484

Table 12.6. *(Continued)*

Study	Subjects	Methodology	Results
Thalhofer (1980)	1200 males and females.	Observed number of passersby who drank at water fountain with female confederate absent or present in high/low social density.	No difference for presence of confederate under high social density. Fewer subjects drank with confederate present under low social density.
Thayer & Alban (1972)	44 males, 25 to 55 years old.	Observed distance subject allowed experimenter to approach when asking for help. Manipulated political similarity-dissimilarity by nature of lapel pin.	In little Italy, politically similar confederate allowed to approach closer than dissimilar. No difference for subjects in Greenwich Village.

proached at a distance that is judged to be too close (typically defined experimentally as 18 in. or less). Experimenters in the United States generally use a distance of about 18 in. as the boundary for an inappropriate approach because Hall (1966) defined this distance as the outer edge of the intimate zone into which adults generally do not allow strangers without sufficient reason (e.g., standing in a crowded subway car).

The settings used by researchers in these studies have primarily been in the *field* (e.g., cafeterias, elevators, libraries, pathways, shopping malls). Related research has also been conducted, however, in a number of laboratory investigations. Principally, studies using modifications of the stop-distance procedure have tested the "permeability" of one's personal space by measuring levels of discomfort associated with closer and closer approaches by a confederate (e.g., Hayduk, 1981a) and other studies have examined the effects of short-term crowding involving close interpersonal proximity (i.e., a number of individuals under high spatial density conditions). The salient factor in these latter studies is *not* the number of others (e.g., 4, 12, or 30), but the physical spacing between individuals. These studies of crowding involving close physical proximity are treated in a later chapter of this *Handbook* so I will not detail them here.

The withdrawal, flight, and compensatory reactions observed when subjects are invaded can be explained by any of the models of spatial behavior described in Section 12.3. The "invasion" is an approach at too great a level of intimacy and, according to the conflict/intimacy equilibrium models and discrepancy models, the behaviors that have been observed would be expected to occur, barring any situational or environmental constraints. In cases of spatial invasion, however, the conflict/intimacy equilibrium models and their modifications provide an adequate and parsimonious explanation for the behaviors that occur. Simply stated, the invasion necessitates a compensatory reaction (flight, reduction in eye contact, blocking, etc.) in order to keep the invader at an acceptable level of involvement.

The explanation of "why" leads to a consideration of "what actually occurs" when a person has his or her space invaded by another. During the invasion or intrusion, an individual experiences a considerable accretion of stress-related (physiological) arousal (e.g., increased heart rate, elevated levels of skin conductance, etc.). While the presence of others is in and of itself arousing, the *very close* presence of others is so much more so. The greater the immediacy of the invasion/intrusion, the more discomfort or arousal is experienced by the person. This increase in arousal then in turn normally generates a pattern of withdrawal or avoidance.

It should be recalled, of course, that closer distances increase the possibility of positive as well as negative forms of intimacy (cf. Cappella, 1981). Schiffenbauer and Schiavo (1976) reported that close distances amplified an individual's feelings toward another. At a close distance their subjects rated a confederate who gave insulting feedback more negatively and a confederate who gave complementary feedback more positively. Similarly, Freedman, Heshka, and Levy (1975) found that crowded (i.e., high spatial density) conditions intensified the positive experience for some subjects who received only positive responses to their speeches and intensified as well the negative experience of other subjects who received only negative comments about their speeches.

Reactions typical of those invaded have been observed by Felipe and Sommer (1966) and Patterson and colleagues (1971). The subjects in the Felipe and Sommer study, mental patients, were observed to flee the setting when a confederate sat next to them at 6 in. Other behaviors observed when subjects were invaded included shifting of postures and auto-manipulative behaviors. In the investigation by Patterson and colleagues college students were invaded while they sat at tables in a library. The students were observed to flee the area more quickly, the closer the invasion. Prior to flight, behaviors such as blocking or turning away from the invader were observed.

Overall, studies find that, unless the situation is unique in some way (e.g., a beach, singles bar, etc.) or the confederate behaves in a mannner that makes the invasion/intrusion more acceptable, people have a *shorter latency of flight* when invaded. Exceptions include: if the invader is a *young child* (Fry & Willis, 1971); if the invader *asks permission*, females flee more quickly, while males do not (Polit & LaFrance, 1977; Sundstrom & Sundstrom, 1977); if the confederate appears to be (an artist) at work (Smith & Knowles, 1979); if the invader is very *well dressed*, is very *involved in an activity* (like reading), or *has a very good and obvious reason* for the invasion, like an extremely crowded subway platform (Schiavo, Schiffenbauer, & Roberts, 1977); or if the invader seems to have *no choice* but to invade (Murphy-Berman & Berman, 1978). Studies have also found other variables that will intensify the effect of an invasion such as if the person *prefers and normally adopts farther distances* (i.e., has a larger "personal space") for interaction (Aiello et al., 1977; Dooley, 1978; Hayduk, 1981a); if the invader is of a *higher status* than the person invaded (Barash, 1973); if the invader is *male* (Bleda & Bleda, 1978; Murphy-Berman & Berman, 1978); if the subject *expects to be unable to flee the situation* immediately, as when waiting for a bus (Dabbs, 1972); or if the invader *pleads great need for help* as he or she invades (Baron, 1978).

While the effects of spatial invasion appear rather consistent and easily explained by the conflict/intimacy equilibrium models and their modifications, the effects of forcing someone to intrude on the space of others seem to be more dependent on external factors and thus not as easily explained by these models. When one intrudes upon others, it would seem that the discrepancy models, which take into account situational factors and the characteristics of the other person, would better explain the behaviors that are observed in these experiments. In these experiments subjects are put into a situation within which,

if they are to proceed on their way in the direction and path they have been traveling, they will be forced to intrude on the interaction space of the confederates.

Typically, it is observed that subjects prefer to go out of their way to avoid intruding on the interaction of others. The choice of whether or not the subject invades, however, includes considerations of how much room there is to go around the interactants or other environmental constraints (e.g., social density; Thalhofer, 1980) or characteristics of the interactants. The latter include the status of the interactants (Knowles, 1973), their appearance (Bouska & Beatty, 1978), their political similarity (Thayer & Alban, 1972), and their race (Brown, 1981). Apparently, the more the interactants are like the subject, the greater the likelihood that the subject's intruding on them is seen as inappropriate.

Similarly, investigations of whether or not a person will invade the space of another individual (in situations such as standing in a line or walking on a sidewalk) have shown that external factors such as the characteristics of the other(s), are critical. Variables like the flamboyance of the person's clothes or perfume (Nesbitt & Steven, 1974); their height (Caplan & Goldman, 1981); an individual's sex (Buchanan, Goldman, & Juhnke, 1977; Buchanan, Juhnke, & Goldman, 1976; Dabbs & Stokes, 1975; Leibman, 1970); the degree to which they are perceived as attractive (Dabbs & Stokes, 1975); the formality of their dress (Fortenberry, MacLean, Morris, & O'Connell, 1978); whether a woman is pregnant (Davis & Lennon, 1983); the size of the group (Knowles, 1973; Knowles, Kreuser, Haas, Hyde, & Schuchart, 1976); the activity of the group (Knowles & Bassett, 1976); or the sex composition of the group (Baron & Bell, 1972; Cheyne & Efran, 1972) can make a difference in how much space the person is allowed to another or others by the subject.

Regarding the last variable, for example, Cheyne and Efran (1972) found that people were five times *less* likely to walk through (rather than around) an interacting pair of females than an interacting pair of males or a mixed-sex pair. Males' joint interaction spaces are *most* likely to be invaded (cf. Baron & Bell, 1972), despite the fact that individual males are "given" more space than individual females (cf. Dabbs & Stokes, 1975) and that males react more negatively to invaders (cf. Hai et al., 1982). Related to these findings, Knowles (1972) reported that, while only about one-third of the male pairs he observed "shifted together" when an invader walked toward them, two-thirds of the female pairs and almost

85% of the male–female pairs "shifted together" as the invader approached. Further, Knowles and Brickner (1981) found that group cohesiveness was the critical determinant of its members protecting the "group space," but that women were more likely than men to defend this shared space from the impending invasion. Therefore, one can hypothesize that a process similar to that described by the discrepancy models is taking place when a person is forced to invade upon another.

Lastly, it should be noted that, just as people experience distress as a result of distances that are inappropriately close, so too do they experience discomfort and anxiety and react much more negatively as a consequence of distances that are inappropriately far (cf. Aiello & Thompson, 1980a). Females in particular have been found to experience considerably greater stress-related arousal at inappropriately large distances and find it more difficult (see Figure 12.2) to employ effective coping strategies at larger distances (just as males experience similarly greater difficulties at an inappropriately close distance). Also of concern is the finding that individuals (and particularly females) *misattributed* the source of their discomfort at the inappropriately large distance to their interaction partners (Aiello & Thompson, 1980a).

Of interest in future research would be an exploration of these attributional processes that lead people to a generalization of negative feelings engendered by an environmental source to other (innocent) people. Also of value would be an investigation of which other groups might experience an exacerbation of the discomfort at the larger distances that has been reported for females (e.g., contact cultures, children, friends, etc). Clearly, more research is required for an understanding of the consequences of inappropriately far distances. While much is known about the effects of spatial invasion, we know very little about responses to "spatial extrusion."

12.6. SUMMARY, CONCLUSIONS, AND FUTURE DIRECTIONS

This chapter has briefly reviewed the origins and conceptual underpinnings of human spatial behavior research. I argued that the term *personal space*, with its primary focus on the protection component of spatial behavior and its link to a "bubble" analogy, is rather limited and somewhat misleading and that we would be better served by a term like *interpersonal* or *interaction distance*, or even Hall's *proxemic* behavior concept.

Next, the chapter provided an analysis of the major theoretical frameworks in this area: beginning with Hall's proxemic framework, continuing with Argyle and Dean's intimacy equilibrium model and its modifications, and concluding with two recent expectancy/discrepancy models (Cappella & Greene, 1982; Patterson, 1982) that are touted as having considerable potential for integrating future research. Since it is suggested that *interpersonal distance is best viewed as one of a number of variables used by individuals with particular socialization experiences and from specific effective cultures to establish the desired level of interpersonal involvement*, these frameworks would appear to be especially appropriate. Research testing these new integrative "high-potential" models and the role of spatial behavior should be one of our top priorities.

The chapter then turned to the crucial issue of the validity of the various methods used in spatial behavior research. My analysis of this area led me to conclude that both projective (i.e., simulation) and quasi-projective (i.e., laboratory and stop-distance) measures of spatial behavior (by themselves) are *inadequate* assessment techniques, given their questionable external validity. Results and obtained mean distances (scaled when projective) from studies using these measures do *not* parallel those employing interactional measures (although those using quasi-projective methods are at least in the same direction). Correlations with interactional measures are low for projective measures and rather low for quasi-projective measures and, surprisingly, people cannot even replicate the interaction distance they have maintained moments before using either method. Furthermore, while the stop-distance measure allows for some of the proprioceptive cues available to people engaged in actual interaction, neither the projective nor the quasi-projective measures involve any "real" *interaction* between subjects.

My appraisal is that under some *very limited* circumstances projective measures can provide adequate assessment of "psychological distance," but they should *not* be used to gauge spatial behavior. On the other hand, although the reader is strongly advised to interpret results with caution, studies might creatively and productively use quasi-projective measures (particularly the stop-distance procedure) to establish working hypotheses for later testing with interaction measures.

The chapter's concluding section was a synthesis of human spatial behavior research, given these methodological considerations and constraints. Spatial behavior is found to *develop* gradually and systematically as children grow older; interaction spaces get larger and less variable from childhood through adolescence and then stabilize to middle adulthood. This developmental pattern has been extensively documented in the United States and replicated in a few other cultures, but future research is needed to determine whether the pattern is as *universal* as it now seems. Research is badly needed on the spatial patterns of very young children and older adults; conflicting findings have been reported by the small number of studies focusing on these age groups.

The effects associated with age are introduced first because conflicting patterns of results involving other effects (e.g., gender, subculture, relationship) can *only* be unraveled when age is taken into account. This is certainly the case for the influence of gender. While females are most typically found to interact at closer distances and generally to take up less space than males, the influence of gender is considerably more complex than that. First, these differences are *not reliable* for *young* children. Second, in situations involving *affiliation* (e.g., focused interaction between friends) women are likely to interact more closely than men, but in situations implying *threat* (e.g., being invaded by an unknown, potentially menacing other) just the reverse is found and women are also likely to leave the scene sooner than men. Third, the spacing pattern for mixed-sex interactions is age related, as it is not consistent at various age levels: For very young children differences are minimal (although there is a *tendency* for same-sex children to interact closer); for prepubescent children male–female interactions usually occur at greater distances than same-sex interactions; and for adolescents and adults these patterns based on situational factors are most common, with interactions involving females typically found to be closer.

It is unfortunate that so few studies have heeded Hall's suggestion that distance be measured in terms of "body potential" (a relative unit) rather than a fixed scale (e.g., feet, meters). Particularly in studies involving children (of differing ages and sizes) and to a lesser extent gender (males are on the average somewhat larger), a relative scale would seem far more meaningful.

Altman (Altman, 1975; Altman & Vinsel, 1977) and others have appropriately described the "secondary" role played by gender in spatial behavior research. Future research focusing a more primary emphasis on this variable to determine, for example, the relative contributions of biological sex and socialization experiences is much needed: Cross-cultural studies including populations with very different socialization practices from those studies (i.e., modern western); investigations of the role played (if any) by hormones and hormone levels (particularly estrogen and testosterone) in human spatial behavior; and research examining sex role identification (in addition to gender) and spatial behavior would be especially welcomed.

Together with one of my graduate students, I very recently completed an experiment (Bernstein & Aiello, 1985) in the last suggested area that systematically varied the interaction context (affiliative, competitive, ambiguous) for males and females representing three different sex role orientations (masculine, feminine, androgynous). Nonverbal behaviors observed during the interaction indicated that masculine males and feminine females exhibited the greatest involvement in the traditionally sex-typed interaction context (i.e., competitive, affiliative) but strongest effects were found for gender. Might sex role orientation simply intensify more potent differences between the sexes? I suspect the relationship is far more complex.

Most studies examining the influence of culture on spatial behavior have concentrated on Hall's hypothesis that contact cultures have higher involvement levels and hence maintain closer distances during interaction than noncontact cultures. Empirical research has been surprisingly sparse, but existing studies are generally supportive of Hall's observations. Research investigating Hall's predictions about spatial usage in a number of specific countries (e.g., Japan, Germany) is virtually nonexistent, however. Accordingly, are patterns of systematic differences identified in American studies (e.g., age, gender, responses to spatial invasion) the same in other cultures where socialization practices differ? Needed also are studies examining spatial behavior differences *within* the more global contact and noncontact categories; these would contribute to our information base of specific countries and, more important, help us decide whether Hall's contact–noncontact distinction is adequate.

Most needed, however, are investigations focusing on interactions between members of cultures *differing* in spatial behavior. Particularly useful would be studies tapping the attribution processes of these dissimilar interactants. Such information should enhance our understanding of the circumstances surrounding miscommunications that occur between people of different cultures.

Subcultural investigations of spatial behavior have been more numerous but are, for the most part, similarly derived from Hall's (1966) contact–noncontact distinction. He extended this distinction to propose that lower-income black and Hispanic subcultures in the United States are "more highly involved" and hence adopt smaller interaction spaces than (the dominant) white middle-class Americans of northern European ancestry. Research evidence strongly supports the contention that Hispanics do use less space than Anglo-Americans, but Hall's prediction that blacks use less space than whites has received little support.

In order to unravel the complex pattern of reported differences between blacks and whites in spatial behavior, it is essential to consider the age level of research study participants. When we do this, we find that Hall's contention that lower-SES blacks use less space than middle-class whites holds *only for very young children*. By age 8 or 9, studies report no differences between blacks and whites; thereafter, black adolescents and adults are *more* distant than whites — the reverse of Hall's prediction.

Only two studies have examined the influence of social class. While both found SES effects independent from race, one studied *young* children and found that middle-class children stood farther apart than lower-class children and the other studied *adolescents* and found the reverse, that lower-class adolescents stood farther apart than middle-class children. Future research with adult blacks and whites of varying SES levels should provide additional information about the moderating role of age.

Of the 10 studies of interracial interactions, 8 reported larger distances for these mixed-race dyads than for same-race dyadic interactions. One study actually traced the increase in this difference as children grew older. Future research that would focus on ameliorative strategies for interactions involving individuals of dissimilar proxemic patterns is greatly needed. The two studies of this type (i.e., cross-cultural) have shown how effective minimal amounts of training can be in facilitating these heterogeneous interactions.

Research studies assessing the influence of personality and psychological disorders were more abundant in the early years of the spatial behavior literature than currently. A number of "dead ends" and a surprising (and unfortunate) linkage to projective and quasi-projective methodology strategies led many investigators to abandon this area as not very productive.

My treatment of this area follows others (e.g., Altman, Patterson) who have recently recommended that personality traits need to be studied in *clusters* (e.g., dominance, social anxiety, affiliative tendency,

introversion–extraversion) rather than individually and further that these clusters should be studied in *situations* where the particular personality dimension(s) would be expected to be *salient* rather than in situations that are ambiguous or neutral. Only through the use of *interactional* methods and contexts (i.e., field or creative laboratory simulation procedures), which involve people actually interacting, would we expect there to be more opportunities for significant contributions to this area of spatial behavior research.

The relationship between individuals has a strong effect on their spatial behavior. Generally, interactions with friends and others who are liked are most proximate. Transactions with acquaintances and others of a more neutral affective tone tend to occur at an intermediate distance and encounters with strangers and disliked others (when "protection" and confrontation are not necessary) most often take place at larger distances.

When threat is high or there is the potential for threat in a situation, distances tend to be larger, especially for females. The greater the control one feels, the greater the proclivity toward closer spacings. Research has demonstrated that we distance ourselves from others who make us feel uncomfortable, anxious, and annoyed and move closer to those whom we like and who are like us, those to whom we are attracted, who are a source of comfort or strength, and who make us feel better about ourselves.

Environmental factors also play an important role in how space is used. Smaller, more confining spaces serve to increase interaction distances; larger or more "overstimulating" environments prompt people to adopt distances that are smaller.

Section 12.5.6, returns us to the pattern of linkages described in Section 12.3. We find that, as the compensatory models (e.g., affiliative conflict theory) would predict, spatial invasions/intrusions (i.e., distances that are inappropriately close) are most typically associated with increased levels of physiological arousal (usually taking the form of discomfort or stress) and often lead to flight, withdrawal, avoidance, and compensatory reactions (e.g., blocking, turning away, reduced eye contact) meant to decrease (or eliminate) the excessively high involvement level produced. Importantly, what makes any *particular* distance "inappropriately close" is determined by *all* of the individual, relationship, situational, and environmental factors discussed above.

While most of the research reported in this chapter is generally supportive of the compensatory models discussed in Section 12.3, enough examples to the contrary are clearly available to necessitate our adoption of the more comprehensive expectancy (discrepancy) models described in that section. Under various circumstances people do not compensate for spatial intrusions but rather reciprocate by moving still closer or remain unaffected by the spatial behavior of others and make no adjustments whatsoever. The expectancy/discrepancy models allow for all of these varied effects.

Some variables have been shown to make spatial invasions/intrusions less aversive or even acceptable (e.g., if the invader is a young child, has an obviously good reason, or does not have a choice but to invade). Other variables intensify the discomfort of a spatial invasion/intrusion (e.g., if the invader is perceived as more threatening—often strangers, high-status others, or even males fall into this category; or if the subject believes he or she would be unable to flee the situation promptly).

Future research could profitably identify other variables and, more importantly, develop a conceptual framework for classifying these variables. I suggest that we start with three dimensions: (1) the perceived threat potential of the invader, (2) the perceived control of the subject, and (3) the reason for and circumstances surrounding the invasion/intrusion.

People will go to great lengths to avoid invading the interaction space of others and are quite uncomfortable when they cannot help but intrude. How likely a person will be to invade another's space has been found to depend on environmental factors (e.g., the amount of room available to go around the interactants; social density level) and characteristics of the interactants (e.g., the sex composition of the group; status of the interactants; their similarity to the subject). Further developments in the expectancy/discrepancy models (described previously) should facilitate our understanding of the external factors associated with when particular types of individuals would be likely to invade the interaction space of various others under particular environmental conditions.

Finally, the chapter briefly considers the consequences of inappropriately far distances, within the context of intimacy equilibrium processes. While reactions of people under these understimulating conditions are less severe than those of individuals exposed to excessively close distances, individuals (particularly females) who cannot adjust the inappropriately large interaction space experience considerable discomfort and distress and (in some cases) withdraw prematurely from the interaction. A great deal more research is obviously needed on this topic.

NOTE

1. Hall (1974) did find some support for his contention that blacks have a "much higher involvement ratio" in a photographic study that he did with working-class blacks and Hispanic-Americans interacting on the streets of Chicago, and with whites at an educators' convention. But, as Altman and Vinsel (1977) have indicated, "There were a number of results unique to different raters, making it difficult to draw firm conclusions. While Hall's monograph provides a comprehensive description of a methodology for proxemics analysis, his data are primarily illustrative and only in a pilot form, and it is difficult to draw conclusions about the spatial behavior of the various groups" (p. 247).

Acknowledgments

I am grateful to Donna E. Thompson and Mark Loughney for their generous assistance toward my preparation of this chapter.

REFERENCES

Adler, L.L., & Iverson, M.A. (1974). Interpersonal distance as a function of task difficulty, praise, status orientation, and sex of partner. *Perceptual and Motor Skills, 39*, 683–692.

Ahmed, S.M.S. (1979). Invasion of personal space: A study of departure time as affected by sex of the intruder and saliency condition. *Perceptual and Motor Skills, 49*, 85–86.

Aiello, J.R. (1972). A test of equilibrium theory: Visual interaction in relation to orientation, distance, and sex of interactants. *Psychonomic Science, 27*(6), 335–336.

Aiello, J.R. (1976). *Development of spatial behavior.* Paper prepared for presentation at the American Association for the Advancement of Science, Boston.

Aiello, J.R. (1977a). A further look at equilibrium theory: Visual interaction as a function of interpersonal distance. *Environmental Psychology and Nonverbal Behavior, 1*(2), 122–140.

Aiello, J.R. (1977b). Visual interaction at extended distances. *Personality and Social Psychology Bulletin, 3*(1), 83–86.

Aiello, J.R., & Aiello, T.D. (1974). The development of personal space: Proxemic behavior of children 6 through 16. *Human Ecology, 2*(3), 177–189.

Aiello, J.R., & Cooper, R.E. (1972). Use of personal space as a function of social affect. *Proceedings of the 80th Annual Convention of the American Psychological Association, 7*, 207–208.

Aiello, J.R., & Cooper, R.E. (1979). *Personal space and social affect: A developmental study.* Paper presented at the Meeting of the Society for Research in Child Development, San Francisco.

Aiello, J.R., DeRisi, D.T., Epstein, Y.M., & Karlin, R.A. (1977). Crowding and the role of interpersonal distance preference. *Sociometry, 40*(3), 271–282.

Aiello, J.R., Epstein, Y.M., & Karlin, R.A. (1974). *Methodological and conceptual issues in crowding.* Paper presented at the Western Psychological Association Convention, San Francisco.

Aiello, J.R., Epstein, Y.M., & Karlin, R.A. (1975a). *Field experimental research on human crowding.* Paper presented at the Eastern Psychological Association Convention, New York.

Aiello, J.R., Epstein, Y.M., & Karlin, R.A. (1975b). Effects of crowding on electrodermal activity. *Sociological Symposium, 14*, 42–57.

Aiello, J.R., Headly, L., & Thompson, D.E. (1978). Effects of crowding on the elderly: A preliminary investigation. *Journal of Population, 1*(4), 288–297.

Aiello, J.R., & Jones, S.E. (1971). Field study of the proxemic behavior of young school children in three subcultural groups. *Journal of Personality and Social Psychology, 19*(3), 351–356.

Aiello, J.R., & Jones, S.E. (1979). *Proxemic behavior of black and white adolescents of two socioeconomic class levels.* Paper presented at the meeting of the Society for Research in Child Development, San Francisco.

Aiello, J.R., Nicosia, G.J., & Thompson, D.E. (1979). Physiological, social, and behavioral consequences of crowding on children and adolescents. *Child Development, 50*(1), 195–202.

Aiello, J.R., & Thompson, D.E. (1980a). When compensation fails: Mediating effects on sex and locus of control at extended interaction distances. *Basic and Applied Social Psychology, 1*(1), 65–82.

Aiello, J.R., & Thompson, D.E. (1980b). Personal space, crowding, and spatial behavior in a cultural context. In I. Altman, A. Rapoport, & J.F. Wohlwill (Eds.), *Human behavior and environment: Advances in theory and research: Vol. 4 Environment and culture.* New York: Plenum.

Aiello, J.R., & Thompson, D.E. (1984). *Effects of interviewer's race, sex, and distance on visual and verbal interaction.* Paper presented at the American Psychological Association Convention, Toronto, Canada.

Albert, S., & Dabbs, J.M., Jr. (1970). Physical distance and persuasion. *Journal of Personality and Social Psychology, 15*, 265–270.

Allgeier, A.R., & Byrne, D. (1973). Attraction toward the opposite sex as a determinant of physical proximity. *Journal of Social Psychology, 90*, 213–219.

Altman, I. (1975). *The environment and social behavior: Privacy, personal space, territory, crowding.* Monterey, CA: Brooks/Cole.

Altman, I. & Vinsel, A.M. (1977). Personal space: An analysis of E.T. Hall's proxemics framework. In I. Altman & J.F. Wohlwill (Eds.), *Human behavior and the environment: Vol. 2. Advances in theory and research.* New York: Plenum.

Andersen, P.A. (1984). *An arousal-valence model of nonverbal immediacy exchange.* Paper presented at the Central States Speech Association Convention, Chicago.

Andersen, P.A., & Andersen, J.F. (1984). The exchange of nonverbal intimacy: A critical review of dyadic models. *Journal of Nonverbal Behavior, 8*(4), 327–349.

Argyle, M., & Cook, M. (1976). *Gaze and mutual gaze.* Cambridge, England: Cambridge University Press.

Argyle, M., & Dean, J. (1965). Eye-contact, distance, and affiliation. *Sociometry, 28*, 289–304.

Argyle, M., & Ingham, R. (1972). Gaze, mutual gaze, and proximity. *Semiotica, 6*, 32–49.

Argyle, M., Lalljee, M., & Cook, M. (1968). The effects of visibility on interaction in a dyad. *Human Relations, 21* 3–17.

Aronow, R., Reznikoff, M., & Tryon, W. (1975). The interpersonal distance of process and reactive schizophrenics. *Journal of Consulting and Clinical Psychology, 43*(1), 94.

Aronow, E., Reznikoff, M., Tyron, W., & Rauchway, A. (1977). On construct validity of the concept of interpersonal distance. *Perceptual and Motor Skills, 45*, 550.

Ashton, N.L., & Shaw, M.E. (1980). Empirical investigations of a reconceptualized personal space. *Bulletin of the Psychonomic Society, 15*, 309–312.

Ashton, N.L., Shaw, M.E., & Worsham, A.P. (1980). Affective reactions to interpersonal distances by friends and strangers. *Bulletin of the Psychonomic Society, 15*, 306–308.

Bailey, K.G., Harnett, J.J., & Gibson, F.W., Jr. (1972). Implied threat and the territorial factor in personal space. *Psychological Reports, 30*, 263–270.

Bailey, K.G., Hartnett, J.J., & Glover, H.W. (1973). Modeling and personal space behavior in children. *Journal of Psychology, 85*, 143–150.

Bain, A.D. (1949). Dominance in the Great Tit, Parus Major. *Scottish Naturalist, 61*, 369–472.

Bakan, D. (1966). *The duality of human existence.* Chicago: Rand McNally.

Baker, E., & Shaw, M.E. (1980). Reaction to interpersonal distance and topic intimacy: A comparison of strangers and friends. *Journal of Nonverbal Behavior, 5*(2), 80–91.

Barash, D.P. (1973). Human ethology: Personal space reiterated. *Environment and Behavior, 5*, 67–73.

Barefoot, J.C., Hoople, H., & McClay, D. (1972). Avoidance of an act which would violate personal space. *Psychonomic Science, 28*, 205–206.

Barnard, W.A., & Bell, P.A. (1982). An unobtrusive apparatus for measuring interpersonal distance. *Journal of General Psychology, 107*, 85–90.

Baron, R.A. (1978). Invasions of personal space and helping: Mediating effects of invader's apparent need. *Journal of Experimental Social Psychology, 14*, 304–312.

Baron, R.A., & Bell, P.A. (1976). Physical distance and helping: Some unexpected benefits of "crowding in" others. *Journal of Applied Social Psychology, 6*, 95–104.

Barrios, B., & Giesen, M. (1977). Getting what you expect: Effects of expectation on intragroup attraction and interpersonal distance. *Personality and Social Psychology Bulletin, 3*, 87–90.

Bartels, B.D. (1977). Nonverbal immediacy in dyads as a function of degree of acquaintance and locus of control. (Doctoral dissertation, University of North Dakota, 1976). *Dissertation Abstracts International, 38*, 387B.

Bass, H.M., & Weinstein, M.S. (1971). Early development of interpersonal distance in children. *Canadian Journal of Behavioural Science, 3*, 368–376.

Batchelor, J.P., & Goethals, G.R. (1972). Spatial arrangements in freely formed groups. *Sociometry, 35*, 270–279.

Batton, D., Squyres, V., Lund, N., & Puente, A.E. (1982). Effects of reinforcement, proximity, and orientation on verbal behavior of female schizophrenics. *Journal of Clinical Psychology, 38*(4), 718–722.

Bauer, E.A. (1973). Personal space: A study of blacks and whites. *Sociometry, 36*(3), 402–408.

Baum, A., Reiss, M., & O'Hara, J. (1974). Architectural variants of reaction to spatial invasion. *Environment and Behavior, 6*, 91–100.

Baxter, J.C. (1970). Interpersonal spacing in natural settings. *Sociometry, 33*, 444–456.

Baxter, J.C., & Rozelle, R.M. (1975). Nonverbal expression as a function of crowding during a simulated police-citizen encounter. *Journal of Personality and Social Psychology, 32*, 40–44.

Beach, D.R., & Sokoloff, M.J. (1974). Spatially dominated nonverbal communication of children: A methodological study. *Perceptual and Motor Skills, 38*, 1303–1310.

Beck, S., & Ollendick T.H. (1976). Personal space, sex of experimenter, and locus of control in normal and delinquent adolescents. *Psychological Reports, 38*, 383–387.

Becker, F.D., & Mayo, C. (1971). Delineating personal space and territoriality. *Environment and Behavior, 3*, 375–381.

Bernstein, M.D., & Aiello, J.R. (1985). *Influences on nonverbal behavior: Gender, sex-role, and interaction context*. Paper presented at the annual meeting of the American Psychological Association, Los Angeles.

Bleda, P., & Bleda, S. (1978). Effects of sex and smoking on reaction to spatial invasion at a shopping mall. *Journal of Social Psychology, 104*, 311–312.

Blumenthal, R., & Meltzoff, J. (1967). Social schemas and perceptual accuracy in schizophrenia. *British Journal of Social and Clinical Psychology, 6*, 119–128.

Booraem, C.D., & Flowers, J.V. (1972). Reduction of anxiety and personal space as a function of assertion training with severely disturbed neuropsychiatric inpatients. *Psychological Reports, 30*, 923–929.

Booraem, C., Flowers, J., Bodner, G., & Satterfield, D. (1977). Personal space variations as a function of criminal behavior. *Psychological Reports, 41*, 1115–1121.

Bouska, M., & Beatty, P. (1978). Clothing as a symbol of status: Its effect on control of interaction territory. *Bulletin of the Psychonomic Society, 11*, 235–238.

Brady, A.T., & Walker, M.B. (1978). Interpersonal distance as a function of situationally induced anxiety. *British Journal of Social and Clinical Psychology, 17*, 127–133.

Breed, G. (1972). The effect of intimacy: Reciprocity or retreat? *British Journal of Social and Clinical Psychology, 11*, 135–142.

Breuer, L.F., & Lindauer, M.S. (1977). Distancing behavior in relation to status in a simulated museum setting. *Perceptual and Motor Skills, 45*(2), 377–378.

Brody, G.H., & Stoneman, Z. (1981). Parental nonverbal behavior within the family context. *Family Relations, 30*, 187–190.

Brooks, D.M., & Wilson, B.J. (1978). Teacher verbal and nonverbal behavioral expression toward selected pupils. *Journal of Educational Psychology, 70*, 147–153.

Brown, C.E. (1981). Shared space invasion and race. *Personality and Social Psychology Bulletin, 7*(1), 103–108.

Buchanan, D.R., Goldman, M., & Juhnke, R. (1977). Eye contact, sex and the violation of personal space. *Journal of Social Psychology, 103*, 19–25.

Buchanan, D.R., Juhnke, R., & Goldman, M. (1976). Violations of personal space as a function of sex. *Journal of Social Psychology, 99*, 187–192.

Burgess, J.W. (1981). Development of social spacing in normal and mentally retarded children. *Journal of Nonverbal Behavior, 6*, 89–95.

Burgess, J.W. (1983). Interpersonal spacing behavior between surrounding nearest neighbors reflects both familiarity and environmental density. *Ethology and Sociobiology, 4*(1), 11–17.

Burgess, J.W., & McMurphy, D. (1982). The development of proxemic spacing behavior: Children's distances to surrounding playmates and adults change between 6 months and 15 years of age. *Developmental Psychobiology, 15*(6), 557–567.

Burgoon, J.K. (1978). A communication model of personal space violations: Explication and an initial test. *Human Communication Research, 4*, 129–142.

Burgoon, J.K., & Aho, L. (1982). Three field experiments on the effects of violations of conversation distance. *Communication Monographs, 49*(2), 71–88.

Burgoon, J.K., & Jones, S.B. (1976). Toward a theory of personal space expectations and their violation. *Human Communication Research, 2*, 131–146.

Byrne, D., Baskett, G.D., & Hodges, L. (1971). Behavioral indicators of interpersonal attraction. *Journal of Applied Social Psychology, 1*(2), 137–149.

Byrne, D., Ervin, C.R., & Lamberth, J. (1970). Continuity between the experimental study of attraction and real-life computer dating. *Journal of Personality and Social Psychology, 16,* 157–165.

Cade, T.M. (1973). A cross-cultural study of personal space in the family. *Dissertation Abstracts International, 33,* 2759A. (University Microfilms No. 72-31, 051)

Calhoun, J.B. (1962). Population density and social pathology. *Scientific American, 206*(2), 139–148.

Caplan, M.E., & Goldman, M. (1981). Personal space violations as a function of height. *Journal of Social Psychology, 114,* 161–171.

Cappella, J.N., & Greene, J.O. (1982). A discrepancy-arousal explanation of mutual influence in expressive behavior in adult and infant-adult interaction. *Communication Monographs, 49,* 89–114.

Carr, S.J., & Dabbs, J.M., Jr. (1974). The effects of lighting, distance, and intimacy of topic on verbal and visual behavior. *Sociometry, 37,* 592–600.

Castell, R. (1970). Effect of familiar and unfamiliar environments on proximity behavior of young children. *Journal of Experimental Child Psychology, 9,* 342–347.

Caudill, B.D., & Aiello, J.R. (1979). *Interpersonal equilibrium: A study of convergent and predictive validity.* Paper presented at the Eastern Psychological Association Convention, Philadelphia.

Cavallin, B.J. (1976). The relationship between aggression, body image and the use of personal space. *Dissertation Abstracts International, 38,* 889B. (University Microfilms No. 77-16, 265).

Cavallin, B.J., & Houston, B.K. (1980). Aggressiveness, maladjustment, body experience, and the protective function of personal space. *Journal of Clinical Psychology, 36,* 170–176.

Chapman, A.J. (1975). Eye contact, physical proximity and laughter: A reexamination of the equilibrium model of social intimacy. *Social Behavior and Personality, 3,* 143–155.

Cheyne, J.A., & Efran, M.G. (1972). The effect of spatial and interpersonal variables on the invasion of group controlled territories. *Sociometry, 35,* 477–489.

Ciolek, M.T. (1978). Spatial arrangements in social encounters: An attempt at a taxonomy. *Man-Environment Systems, 8,* 52–59.

Cochran, C.D., Hale, W.D., & Hissam, C.P. (1984). Personal space requirements in indoor versus outdoor locations. *Journal of Personality, 117*(1), 121–123.

Cochran, C.D., & Urbanczyk, S. (1982). The effect of availability of vertical space on personal space. *Journal of Psychology, 111,* 137–140.

Collett, P. (1971). Training Englishmen in the non-verbal behaviour of Arabs. *International Journal of Psychology, 6*(3), 209–215.

Comer, R.J., & Piliavin, J.A. (1972). The effects of physical deviance upon face to face interaction: The other side. *Journal of Personality and Social Psychology, 23,* 33–39.

Cook, M. (1970). Experiments on orientation and proxemics. *Human Relations, 23,* 61–76.

Connolly, P.R. (1974). An investigation of the perception of personal space and its meaning among Black and White Americans. (Doctoral dissertation, University of Iowa, 1973). *Dissertation Abstracts International, 34,* 4689B.

Coutts, L.M., & Ledden, M. (1977). Nonverbal compensatory reactions to changes in interpersonal proximity. *Journal of Social Psychology, 102,* 283–290.

Coutts, L.M., & Schneider, F.W. (1975). Visual behavior in an unfocused interaction as a function of sex differences. *Journal of Experimental Social Psychology, 11,* 64–77.

Coutts, L.M., & Schneider, F.W. (1976). Affiliative conflict theory: An investigation of the intimacy equilibrium and compensation hypotheses. *Journal of Personality and Social Psychology, 34,* 1135–1142.

Cozby, P.C. (1973). Effects of density, activity, and personality on environmental preferences. *Journal of Research in Personality, 7,* 45–60.

Crane, D.R., & Griffen, W. (1983). Personal space: An objective measure of marital quality. *Journal of Marital and Family Therapy, 9*(3). 325–327.

Crowe, W. (1977). The relationship between self-disclosure, locus of control, personal space, social risk-taking, desire-for-novelty, novelty-experiencing and biographical variables: Multivariate approach. (Doctoral dissertation, York University, 1975). *Dissertation Abstracts International, 37,* 4642B.

Dabbs, J.M., Jr. (1971). Physical closeness and negative feelings. *Psychonomic Science, 23,* 141–143.

Dabbs, J.M., Jr. (1972). Sex, setting, and reactions to crowding on sidewalks. *Proceedings of the 80th Annual Convention of the American Psychological Association, 7,* 205–206.

Dabbs, J.M., Jr., Fuller, P.H., & Carr, T.S. (1973). Personal space when "cornered." College students and prison inmates. *Proceedings of the 81st Annual Convention of the American Psychological Association, 8,* 213–214.

Dabbs, J.M., Jr., & Stokes, N.A., III. (1975). Beauty is power: The use of space on the sidewalk. *Sociometry, 38*(4), 551–557.

Dabbs, J.M., Jr., & Wheeler, P.A. (1976). Gravitation toward walls among human subjects. *Social Behavior and Personality, 4,* 121–125.

Daniell, R.J., & Lewis, P. (1972). Stability of eye contact and physical distance across a series of structural interviews. *Journal of Consulting and Clinical Psychology, 39,* 172.

Daves, W.F., & Swaffer, P.W. (1971). Effect of room size on critical interpersonal distance. *Perceptual and Motor Skills, 33,* 926.

Davis, L.L., & Lennon, S.J. (1983). Social stigma of pregnancy: Further evidence. *Psychological Reports, 53*(3), 997–998.

Dean, L.M., Willis, F.N., & Hewitt, J. (1975). Initial interaction distance among individuals equal and unequal in military rank. *Journal of Personality and Social Psychology, 32*, 294–299.

Dean, L.M., Willis, F.N., & LaRocco, J.M. (1976). Invasion of personal space as a function of age, sex, and race. *Psychological Reports, 38*, 959–965.

DeJulio, L., & Duffy, K. (1977). Neuroticism and proxemic behavior. *Perceptual and Motor Skills, 45*, 51–55.

DeLong, A.J. (1970). The micro-spatial structure of the older person: Some implications of planning the social and spatial environment. In L.A. Pastalan & D.H. Carson (Eds.). *Spatial behavior of older people.* Ann Arbor: University of Michigan Press.

Dennis, V.C., & Powell, E.R. (1972). Nonverbal communication in across-race dyads. *Proceedings, 80th Annual Convention of the American Psychological Association, 7*, 557–558.

Dietch, J., & Hense, J. (1975). Affiliative conflict and differences in self-disclosure. *Representative Research in Social Psychology, 6*, 69–75.

Dinges, N.G., & Oetting, E.R. (1972). Interaction distance anxiety in the counseling dyad. *Journal of Counseling Psychology, 19*(2), 146–149.

Dooley, B.B. (1978). Effects of social density on men with "close" or "far" personal space. *Journal of Population, 1*(3), 251–265.

Dosey, M.A., & Meisels, M. (1969). Personal space and self-protection. *Journal of Personality and Social Psychology, 11*(2), 93–97.

Duke, M.P., & Nowicki, S. (1972). A new measure and social-learning model for interpersonal distance. *Journal of Experimental Research in Personality, 6*, 119–132.

Duncan, B.L. (1978). The development of spatial behavior norms in black and white primary school children. *Journal of Black Psychology, 5*, 33–41.

Dunn, B.A. (1972). Stress and personal distance: An analysis of stress and personal distance as related to personality and recreational preferences. *Dissertation Abstracts International, 32*, 4181B. (University Microfilms No. 72-2474, 113).

Eberts, E. (1972). Social and personality correlates of personal space. In W.J. Mitchell (Ed.), *Environmental design: Research and practice. Proceedings of the EDRA II/AR VIII Conference.* Los Angeles: University of California Press.

Eberts, E., & Lepper, M. (1975). Individual consistency in the proxemic behavior of preschool children. *Journal of Personality and Social Psychology, 32*, 841–849.

Edinger, A.J., & Patterson, M.L. (1983). Nonverbal involvement and social control. *Psychological Bulletin, 93*, 30–35.

Edmonson, B., & Han, S.S. (1983). Effects of socialization games on proximity and prosocial behavior of aggressive mentally retarded institutionalized women. *American Journal of Mental Deficiency, 87*(4), 435–440.

Edney, J.J., Walker, C.A., & Jordan, N.L. (1976). Is there reactance in personal space? *Journal of Social Psychology, 100*, 207–217.

Edwards, D.J.A. (1973). A cross-cultural study of social orientation and distance schematic by the method of doll placement. *Journal of Social Psychology, 89*, 165–173.

Efran, M.G., & Cheyne, J.A. (1973). Shared space: The cooperative control of spatial areas by two interacting individuals. *Canadian Journal of Behavioral Science, 5*, 201–210.

Efran, M.G., & Cheyne, J.A. (1974). Affective concomitants of the invasion of shared space: Behavioral, psychological, and verbal indicators. *Journal of Personality and Social Psychology, 29*, 219–226.

Ellsworth, P.C. (1977). *Some questions about the role of arousal in the interpretation of direct gaze.* Paper presented at the American Psychological Association Convention, San Francisco.

Engelbretson, D.E. (1972). Some experiments of instrumental modification of autonomic responses. *Psychologia, 15*, 101–109.

Engelbretson, D.E., & Fullmer, D. (1970). Cross-cultural differences in territoriality: Interaction distances of native Japanese, Hawaii Japanese, and American Caucasians. *Journal of Cross-Cultural Psychology, 1*, 261–269.

Esser, A.H. (Ed.). (1971). *Behavior and environment: The use of space by animals and men.* New York: Plenum.

Ettin, M. (1977). The effect of modeling on personal space (Doctoral dissertation, University of Wyoming). *Dissertation Abstracts International, 37*, 4137B. (University Microfilms No. 77-3256, 1064).

Evans, G.W., & Howard, R.B. (1973). Personal space. *Psychological Bulletin, 80*, 334–344.

Exline, R.V., Gary, D., & Schuette, D. (1965). Visual behavior in a dyad as affected by interview content and sex of respondent. *Journal of Personality and Social Psychology, 1*, 201–209.

Felipe, N.J., & Sommer, R. (1966). Invasions of personal space. *Social Problems, 14*, 206–214.

Firestone, I.J. (1977). Reconciling verbal and nonverbal models of dyadic communication. *Environmental Psychology and Nonverbal Behavior, 2*, 30–44.

Fisher, J.D., Bell, P.A., & Baum, A. (1984). *Environmental Psychology (2nd ed.).* New York: Holt, Rinehart & Winston.

Fisher, J.D., & Byrne, D. (1975). Too close for comfort: Sex differences in response to invasions of personal space. *Journal of Personality and Social Psychology, 32*, 15–21.

Foot, H.C., Chapman, A.J., & Smith, J.R. (1977). Friendship and social responsiveness in boys and girls. *Journal of Personality and Social Psychology, 35,* 401–411.

Ford, J.G., Cramer, R., & Owens, G. (1977). A paralinguistic consideration of proxemic behavior. *Perceptual and Motor Skills, 45,* 487–493.

Ford, J.G., & Graves, J.R. (1977). Differences between Mexican–American and white children in interpersonal distance and social touching. *Perceptual and Motor Skills, 45,* 779–785.

Ford, J.G., Knight, M., & Cramer, R. (1977). The phenomenological experience of interpersonal spacing. *Sociometry, 4,* 387–396.

Forston, R.F., & Larson, C.U. (1968). The dynamics of space: An experimental study in proxemic behavior among Latin American and North Americans. *Journal of Communication, 18,* 109–116.

Fortenberry, J., MacLean, J., Morris, P., & O'Connell, M. (1978). Mode of dress as a perceptual cue to deference. *Journal of Social Psychology, 104,* 139–140.

Frankel, A.S., & Barrett, J. (1971). Variations in personal space as a function of authoritarianism, self-esteem, and racial characteristics of a stimulus situation. *Journal of Counseling and Clinical Psychology, 37*(1), 95–98.

Freedman, J.L., Heshka, S., & Levy, A. (1975). Population density and pathology: Is there a relationship? *Journal of Experimental Social Psychology, 11,* 539–552.

Fromme, D.K., & Beam, D.C. (1974). Dominance and sex differences in nonverbal responses to differential eye contact. *Journal of Research in Personality, 8,* 76–87.

Fromme, D.K., & Schmidt, C.K. (1972). Affective role enactment and expressive behavior. *Journal of Personality and Social Psychology, 24,* 413–419.

Fry, A.M., & Willis, F.N. (1971). Invasion of personal space as a function of age of the invader. *Psychological Record, 21,* 385–389.

Gale, A., Spratt, G., Chapman, A., & Smallbone, A. (1975). EEG correlates of eye contact and interpersonal distance. *Biological Psychology, 3,* 237–245.

Gardin, H., Kaplan, K.J., Firestone, I.J., & Cowan, G.A. (1973). Proxemic effects on cooperation, attitude and approach avoidance in a prisoner's dilemma game. *Journal of Personality and Social Psychology, 27,* 13–18.

Garfinkel, H. (1964). Studies of the routine grounds of everyday activities. *Social Problems, 11,* 225–250.

Garrett, G.A., Baxter, J.C., & Rozelle, R.M. (1981). Training university police in black-American nonverbal behavior. *Journal of Social Psychology, 113,* 217–229.

Giesen, M. & McClarten, H.A. (1976). Discussion, distance, and sex: Changes in impressions and attractions during small group interaction. *Sociometry, 39,* 60–70.

Gifford, R. (1982). Projected interpersonal distance and orientation choices: Personality, sex, and social situation. *Social Psychology Quarterly, 45,* 145–152.

Gifford, R. (in press). *Environmental Psychology.* Newton, MA: Allyn & Bacon.

Gifford, R., & Price, J. (1979). Personal space in nursery school children. *Canadian Journal of Behavioral Science, 11,* 318–326.

Gilmour, D.R., & Walkey, F.H. (1981). Identifying violent offenders using a video measure of interpersonal distance. *Journal of Consulting and Clinical Psychology, 49,* 287–291.

Gioiella, E.C. (1977). The relationships between slowness of response, state anxiety, social isolation and self-esteem and preferred personal space in the elderly. *Dissertation Abstracts International, 38,* 1651B–1652B. (University Microfilms No. 77–20, 743).

Goffman, E. (1963). *Behavior in public places.* New York: Free Press.

Goldberg, G.N., Kiesler, C.A., & Collins, B.E. (1969). Visual behavior and face-to-face distance during interaction. *Sociometry, 32,* 43–53.

Goldberg, M.L., & Wellens, A.R. (1979). A comparison of nonverbal compensatory behaviors within direct face-to-face and television mediated interviewers. *Journal of Applied Social Psychology, 9,* 250–260.

Goldring, P. (1967). Role of distance and posture in the evaluation of interactions. *Proceedings of the 75th Annual Convention of the American Psychological Association, 2,* 343–344.

Graubert, J.G., & Adler, L.L. (1977). Cross-national comparisons of projected social distance from mental patient-related stimuli. *Perceptual and Motor Skills, 44,* 881–882.

Greenbaum, P., & Rosenfeld, H.M. (1978). Patterns of avoidance in response to interpersonal staring and proximity: Effects of bystanders on drivers at a traffic intersection. *Journal of Personality and Social Psychology, 36,* 575–587.

Greenberg, C., & Firestone, I. (1977). Compensatory responses to crowding: Effects of personal space intrusion and privacy reduction. *Journal of Personality and Social Psychology, 35,* 637–644.

Greenberg, E., Aronow, E., & Rauchway, A. (1977). Inkblot content and interpersonal distance. *Journal of Clinical Psychology, 33,* 882–887.

Greene, L.R. (1983). On fusion and individuation processes in small groups. *International Journal of Group Psychotherapy, 33*(1), 3–19.

Griffitt, W., May, J., Veitch, R. (1974). Sexual stimulation and interpersonal behavior: Heterosexual evaluative responses, visual behavior, and physical proximity. *Journal of Personality and Social Psychology, 30,* 367–377.

Griffitt, W., & Veitch, R. (1971). Hot and Crowded: Influences of population density and temperature on interpersonal affective behavior. *Journal of Personality and Social Psychology, 17,* 92–98.

Grossman, S. (1977). Interdistancing behavior in dyadic encounter: The effect of status on high and low dominance people (Doctoral dissertation, Long Island University, Brooklyn, NY, 1977). *Dissertation Abstracts International, 37*, 4140B.

Guardo, C.J. (1969). Personal space in children. *Child Development, 40*, 143–151.

Guardo, C.J. (1976). Personal space, sex differences, and interpersonal attraction. *Journal of Psychology, 92*, 9–14.

Guardo, C.J., & Meisels, M. (1971). Child-parent spatial patterns under praise and reproof. *Developmental Psychology, 5*, 365.

Haase, R.F. (1970). The relationship of sex and instructional set to the regulation of interpersonal interaction distance in a counseling analogue. *Journal of Counseling Psychology, 17*(3), 233–236.

Haase, R.F., & DiMattia, D.J. (1976). Spatial environments and verbal conditioning in a quasi-counseling interview. *Journal of Counseling Psychology, 23*, 414–421.

Haase, R.F., & Markey, M.J. (1973). A methodological note on the study of personal space. *Journal of Consulting and Clinical Psychology, 40*, 122–125.

Haase, R.F., & Pepper, D.T. (1972). Nonverbal components of empathic communication. *Journal of Counseling Psychology, 19*, 417–424.

Hai, D.M., Khairullah, Z.Y., & Coulmas, N. (1982). Sex and the single armrest: Use of personal space during air travel. *Psychological Reports, 51*(3), 743–749.

Hall, E.T. (1959). *The silent language.* New York: Doubleday.

Hall, E.T. (1963). A system for the notation of proxemic behavior. *American Anthropologist, 65*, 1003–1026.

Hall, E.T. (1966). *The hidden dimension.* New York: Doubleday.

Hall, E.T. (1974). *Handbook of proxemics research.* Washington, DC: Society for the Anthropology of Visual Communication.

Hansen, J.E., & Schuldt, W.J. (1982). Physical distance, sex, and intimacy in self-disclosure. *Psychological Reports, 51*(1), 3–6.

Hardee, B.B. (1976). Interpersonal distance, eye contact, and stigmatization: A test of the equilibrium model. *Dissertation Abstracts International, 37*, 1970B–1971B. (University Microfilms No. 76–22, 290).

Harper, R.G., Wiens, A.N., & Matarazzo, J.D. (1978). *Nonverbal communication: The state of the art.* New York: Wiley.

Hartnett, J.J., Bailey, K.G., & Gibson, F.W., Jr. (1970). Personal space as influenced by sex and type of movement. *Journal of Psychology, 76*, 139–144.

Hartnett, J.J., Bailey, K.G., & Hartley, C.S. (1974). Body height, position, and sex as determinants of personal space. *Journal of Psychology, 87*, 129–136.

Hayduk, L.A. (1981a). The permeability of personal space. *Canadian Journal of Behavioural Science, 13*, 274–287.

Hayduk, L.A. (1981b). The shape of personal space: An experimental investigation. *Canadian Journal of Behavioural Science, 123*, 87–93.

Hayduk, L.A. (1983). Personal space: Where we now stand. *Psychological Bulletin, 94*, 293–335.

Hayduk, L.A. (1985). Personal space: The conceptual and measurement implications of structural equation models. *Canadian Journal of Behavioural Science, 17*(2), 140–149.

Hayduk, L.A., & Mainprize, S. (1980). Personal space of the blind. *Social Psychology Quarterly, 43*, 216–223.

Hayes, C.S., & Siders, C. (1977). Projective assessment of personal space among retarded and nonretarded children. *American Journal of Mental Deficiency, 82*(1), 72–78.

Heckel, R.V., & Hiers, J.M. (1977). Social distance and locus of control. *Journal of Clinical Psychology, 33*(2), 469–471.

Hediger, H. (1950). *Wild animals in captivity.* London: Butterworth.

Hendrick, C., Giesen, M., & Coy, S. (1974). The social ecology of free seating arrangements in a small group interaction context. *Sociometry, 37*, 262–274.

Hendricks, M., & Bootzin, R. (1976). Race and sex as stimuli for negative affect and physical avoidance. *Journal of Social Psychology, 98*, 111–120.

Heshka, S., & Nelson, Y. (1972). Interpersonal speaking distance as a function of age, sex, and relationship. *Sociometry, 35*(4), 491–498.

Hetherington, E.M. (1972). Effects of father absence on personality development in adolescent daughters. *Developmental Psychology, 7*, 313–326.

Hildreth, A.M., Derogatis, L.R., & McCusker, K. (1971). Body buffer zone and violence: A reassessment and confirmation. *American Journal of Psychiatry, 127*, 1641–1645.

Hill, R.D., Blackham, R.E., & Crane, D.R. (1982). The effect of the marital relationship on personal space orientation in married couples. *Journal of Social Psychology, 118*, 23–28.

Holahan, C.J. (1972). Seating patterns and patient behavior in an experimental dayroom. *Journal of Abnormal Psychology, 80*, 115–124.

Holahan, C.J. (1982). *Environmental Psychology.* New York: Random House.

Hollender, J.W., Duke, M.P. & Nowicki, S. (1973). Interpersonal distance: Sibling structure and parental affection antecedents. *Journal of Genetic Psychology, 123*, 35–45.

Hore, T. (1970). Social class differences in some aspects of the nonverbal communication between mother and preschool child. *Australian Journal of Psychology, 22*, 21–27.

Horowitz, M.J. (1968). Spatial behavior and psychopathology. *Journal of Nervous and Mental Disease, 146*, 24–35.

Horowitz, M.J., Duff, D.F., & Stratton, L.O. (1964). Body-buffer zone: Exploration of personal space. *Archives of General Psychiatry, 11*, 651–656.

Hosch, H.M., & Himelstein, P. (1982). Factors influencing the violation of space between a photographer and subject. *Journal of Psychology, 111*(2), 277–283.

Howard, E. (1920). *Territory in bird life*. London: Murray.

Hughes, J., & Goldman, M. (1978). Eye contact, facial expression, sex, and the violation of personal space. *Perceptual and Motor Skills, 46*, 579–584.

Hunt, S.L. (1974). Factors affecting comfortable interpersonal distance. *Dissertation Abstracts International, 34*. (University Microfilms No. 74–24, 188).

Ickes, W., & Barnes, R.D. (1977). The role of sex and self-monitoring in unstructured settings. *Journal of Personality and Social Psychology, 35*, 315–330.

Ickes, W., Patterson, M.I., Rajecki, D.W., & Yanford, S. (1982). Behavioral and cognitive consequences of reciprocal versus compensatory responses to preinteraction expectancies. *Social Cognition, 1*, 160–190.

Imada, A.S., & Hakel, M.D. (1977). Influence of nonverbal communication and rater proximity on impressions in simulated employment interviews. *Journal of Applied Psychology, 62*, 295–300.

Iwata, O. (1978). Some personal attributes and spatial factors in the perception of crowding. *Japanese Psychological Research, 20*, 1–6.

Janik, S.J., Goldberg, M.L., & Wellens, A.R. (1983). Cardiovascular responses to television-mediated nonverbal approach. *Journal of Applied Social Psychology, 13*(1), 17–30.

Johnson, C.F., & Dabbs, J.M., Jr. (1976). Self-disclosure in dyads as a function of distance and the subject-experimenter relationship. *Sociometry, 39*, 257–263.

Johnson, C.J., Pick, H.L., Siegel, G.M., Cicciarelli, A.W., & Garber, S.R. (1981). Effects of interpersonal distance on children's vocal density. *Child Development, 52*, 721–723.

Jones, S.E. (1971). A comparative proxemics analysis of dyadic interaction in selected subcultures of New York City. *Journal of Social Psychology, 84*, 35–44.

Jones, S.E., & Aiello, J.R. (1973). Proxemic behavior of black and white first, third, and fifth-grade children. *Journal of Personality and Social Psychology, 25*(1), 21–27.

Jones, S.E., & Aiello, J.R. (1979). A test of the validity of projective and quasi-projective measures of interpersonal distance. *Western Journal of Speech Communication, 43*(2), 143–152.

Jorgenson, D.O. (1975). Field study of the relationship between status discrepancy and proxemic behavior. *Journal of Social Psychology, 97*, 173–179.

Kagan, J. (1964). Acquisition and significance of sex-typing and sex-role identity. In M.L. Hoffman & L.W. Hoffman (Eds.) *Review of Child Development Research (Vol. 1)*. New York: Russell Sage Foundation.

Kahn, A., & McGaughey, T.A. (1977). Distance and liking: When moving closer produces increased liking. *Sociometry, 40*(2), 138–144.

Kaplan, K.J. (1977). Structure and process in interpersonal "distancing." *Environmental Psychology and Nonverbal Behavior. 1*(2), 104–121.

Karabenick, S.A., & Meisels, M. (1972). Effects of performance evaluation on interpersonal distance. *Journal of Personality, 40*, 275–286.

Kassover, C.J. (1972). Self-disclosure, sex, and the use of personal distance. *Dissertation Abstracts International, 32*, 442B. (University Microfilms No. 72-19, 618).

Katz, D. (1937). *Animals and men*. New York: Longmans, Green.

Katz, P.A., Katz, I., & Cohen, S. (1976). White children's attitudes toward blacks and the physically handicapped: A developmental study. *Journal of Educational Psychology, 68*, 20–24.

Keating, C.F., & Keating, E.G. (1980). Distance between pairs of aquaintances and strangers on public benches in Nairobi, Kenya. *Journal of Social Psychology, 110*, 285–286.

Kelly, F.D. (1972). Communication significance of therapist proxemic cues. *Journal of Consulting and Clinical Psychology, 39*(2), 345.

Kendon, A. (1967). Some functions of gaze-direction in social interaction. *Acta Psychologica, 26*, 22–63.

King, M.G. (1966). Interpersonal relations in preschool children and average approach distance. *Journal of Genetic Psychology, 109*, 109–116.

Kinzel, A.F. (1970). Body-buffer zone in violent prisoners. *American Journal of Psychiatry, 127*(1), 99–104.

Kleck, R. (1967). The effects of interpersonal affect on errors made when reconstructing a stimulus display. *Psychonomic Science, 9*(8), 449–450.

Kleck, R. (1970). Interaction distance and nonverbal agreeing responses. *British Journal of Social and Clinical Psychology, 9*, 180–182.

Kleck, R., Buck, P.L., Goller, W.L., London, R.S., Pfeiffer, J.R., & Vukcevic, D.P. (1968). Effect of stigmatizing conditions on the use of personal space. *Psychological Reports, 23*, 111–118.

Kleinke, C.L., Staneski, R.A., & Pipp, S.L. (1975). Effects of gaze, distance, and attractiveness on males' first impressions of females. *Representative Research in Social Psychology, 6*, 7–12.

Kline, L.M., & Bell, P.A. (1983). Privacy preference and interpersonal distancing. *Psychological Reports, 53*(3), 1214.

Klukken, P.G. (1972). Personality and interpersonal distance. *Dissertation Abstracts International, 32*, 6033B. (University Microfilms No. 72-12, 484).

Kmiecik, C., Mausar, P., & Banziger, G. (1979). Attractiveness and interpersonal space. *Journal of Social Psychology, 108*, 227–278.

Knight, D.M., Langmeyer, D., & Lundgren, D.C. (1973).

Eye-contact, distance, and affiliation: The role of observer bias. *Sociometry, 36,* 390–391.

Knowles, E.S. (1972). Boundaries around social space: Dyadic responses to an invader. *Environment and Behavior, 4,* 437–446.

Knowles, E.S. (1973). Boundaries around group interaction: The effect of group size and member status on boundary permeability. *Journal of Personality and Social Psychology, 26,* 327–331.

Knowles, E.S. (1977). *Affective and cognitive mediators of spatial behavior.* Paper presented at the American Psychological Association Convention, San Francisco.

Knowles, E.S. (1980a). An affiliative conflict theory of personal and group spatial behavior. In P.B. Paulus (Ed.), *Psychology of group influence.* Hillsdale, NJ: Erlbaum.

Knowles, E. (1980b). Convergent validity of personal space measures: Consistent results with low correlations. *Journal of Nonverbal Behavior, 4,* 240–248.

Knowles, E.S., & Bassett, R.I. (1976). Groups and crowds as social entities: Effects of activity, size, and member similarity on nonmembers. *Journal of Personality and Social Psychology, 34,* 837–845.

Knowles, E.S., & Brickner, M.A. (1981). Social cohesion effects on spatial cohesion. *Personality and Social Psychology Bulletin, 7,* 309–313.

Knowles, E.S., & Johnsen, P.K. (1974). Intrapersonal consistency in interpersonal distance. *JSAS Catalog of Selected Documents in Psychology, 4,* 124 (MS. No. 768).

Knowles, E.S., Kreuser, D., Haas, S., Hyde, M., & Schuchart, G.E. (1976). Group size and the extension of social space boundaries. *Journal of Personality and Social Psychology, 33*(5), 647–654.

Konecni, V.J., Libuser, L., Morton, H., & Ebbesen, E.B. (1975). Effects of a violation of personal space on escape and helping responses. *Journal of Experimental Social Psychology, 11,* 288–299.

Krail, K., & Leventhal, G. (1976). The sex variable in the intrusion of personal space. *Sociometry, 39,* 170–173.

Kuethe, J.L. (1962). Social schemas. *Journal of Abnormal and Social Psychology, 64*(1), 31–38.

Kunzendorf, R.G., & Denney, J. (1982). Definitions of personal space: Smokers versus nonsmokers. *Psychological Reports, 50*(3), 818.

LaFrance, M., & Mayo, C. (1978). *Moving bodies: Nonverbal communication in social relationships.* Monterey, CA: Brooks/Cole.

Lassen, C.L. (1973). Effects of proximity on anxiety and communication in the initial psychiatric interview. *Journal of Abnormal Psychology, 81,* 226–231.

Latta, R.M. (1978). Relation of status incongruence to personal space. *Personality and Social Psychology Bulletin, 4,* 143–146.

Lee, M.J., & Roberts, H. (1981). Personal distances of squash and badminton players: A preliminary study. *Journal of Sport Psychology, 3*(3), 239–243.

Leffler, A., Gillespie, D.L., & Conaty, J.C. (1982). The effects of status differentiation on nonverbal behavior. *Social Psychology Quarterly, 45*(3), 153–161.

Leibman, M. (1970). The effects of sex and race norms on personal space. *Environment and Behavior, 2,* 208–246.

Lerea, L., & Ward, B. (1966). The social schema of normal and speech-defective children. *Journal of Social Psychology, 69,* 87–94.

Lerner, R.M. (1973). The development of personal space schemata toward body build. *Journal of Psychology, 84,* 229–235.

Lerner, R.M., Iwawaki, S., & Chihara, T. (1976). Development of personal space schemata among Japanese children. *Developmental Psychology, 12,* 466–467.

Lerner, R.M., Karabenick, S.A., & Meisels, M. (1975). Effects of age and sex on the development of personal space schemata towards body build. *Journal of Genetic Psychology, 127,* 91–101.

Lerner, R.M., Venning, J., & Knapp, J.R. (1975). Age and sex effects on personal space schemata toward body build in late childhood. *Developmental Psychology, 11,* 855–856.

Leventhal, G., Lipshultz, M., Chiodo, A. (1978). Sex and setting effects on seating arrangement. *Journal of Psychology, 100,* 21–26.

Leventhal, G., Matturro, M., & Schanerman, J. (1978). Effects of attitude, sex, and approach on nonverbal, verbal and projective measures of personal space. *Perceptual and Motor Skills, 47,* 107–118.

Lewit, D.W., & Joy, V. (1967). Kinetic versus social schemas in figure grouping. *Journal of Personality and Social Psychology, 7,* 63–72.

Lex, A. (1979). An investigation of the relationship between dogmatism and proxemic behavior (Doctoral dissertation, University of Pittsburgh, 1978). *Dissertation Abstracts International, 39,* 1342A.

Liepold, W.E. (1963). Psychological distance in dyadic interview. Unpublished doctoral dissertation. University of North Dakota.

Little, K.B. (1965). Personal space. *Journal of Experimental Social Psychology, 1,* 237–247.

Little, K.B. (1968). Cultural variations in social schemata. *Journal of Personality and Social Psychology, 10*(1), 1–7.

Little, K.B., Ulehla, Z.J., & Henderson, C. (1968). Value congruence and interaction distances. *Journal of Social Psychology, 75,* 249–253.

Lockard, J.S., McVittie, R.I., & Isaac, L.M. (1977). Functional significance of the affiliative smile. *Bulletin of the Psychonomic Society, 9*(5), 367–370.

Lomranz, J. (1976). Cultural variations in personal space. *Journal of Social Psychology, 99,* 21–27.

Lomranz, J., Shapira, A., Choresh, N., & Gilat, Y. (1975). Children's personal space as a function of age and sex. *Developmental Psychology, 11*(5), 541–545.

Long, G.T. (1984). Psychological tension and closeness to others: Stress and interpersonal distance preference. *Journal of Psychology, 117*(1), 143–146.

Long, G.T., Selby, J.W., & Calhoun, L.G. (1980). Effects of situational stress and sex on interpersonal distance preference. *Journal of Psychology, 105*, 231–237.

Loo, C., & Kennelly, D. (1979). Social density: Its effect on behaviors and perceptions of preschoolers. *Environmental Psychology and Nonverbal Behavior, 3*, 131–146.

Lorenz, K. (1955). *Man meets dog.* Cambridge, MA: Riverside.

Lothstein, L.M. (1973). Personal space in assault-prone male adolescent prisoners (Doctoral dissertation, Duke University, 1972). *Dissertation Abstracts International, 33*, 1271B.

Lott, B.S., & Sommer, R. (1967). Seating arrangements and status. *Journal of Personality and Social Psychology, 7*, 90–95.

Love, K.D., & Aiello, J.R. (1980). Using projective techniques to measure interaction distance: A methodological note. *Personality and Social Psychology Bulletin, 6*, 102–104.

Mahoney, E.R. (1974). Compensatory reactions to spatial immediacy. *Sociometry, 37*, 423–431.

Mallenby, T.W. (1974a). Personal space: Projective and direct measures with institutionalized mentally retarded children. *Journal of Personality Assessment, 38*, 28–31.

Mallenby, T.W. (1974b). Personal space: Direct measurement techniques with hard-of-hearing children. *Environment and Behavior, 6*, 117–122.

Markus-Kaplan, M., & Kaplan, K.J. (1984). A bidimensional view of distancing: Reciprocity versus compensation, intimacy versus social control. *Journal of Nonverbal Behavior, 8*(4), 315–326.

Marshall, J.E., & Heslin, R. (1975). Boys and girls together: Sexual composition and the effect of density and group size on cohesiveness. *Journal of Personality and Social Psychology, 31*, 952–961.

Matthews, R.W., Paulus, P.B., & Baron, R.A. (1979). Physical aggression after being crowded. *Journal of Nonverbal Behavior, 4*, 5–17.

Mazur, A. (1977). Interpersonal spacing on public benches in "contact" vs. "noncontact" cultures. *Journal of Social Psychology, 101*, 53–58.

McBride, G., King, M.G., & James, J.W. (1965). Social proximity effects on galvanic skin response in adult humans. *Journal of Psychology, 61*, 153–157.

McDowell, K.V. (1973). Accommodations of verbal and nonverbal behaviors as a function of the manipulation of interaction distance and eye contact. *Proceedings of the 81st Annual Convention of the American Psychological Association, 8*, 207–208.

McGrew, P.L. (1970). Social and spatial density effects on spacing behavior in preschool children. *Journal of Child Psychiatry, 11*, 197–205.

McGrew, P.L., & McGrew, W.C. (1975). Interpersonal spacing behavior of preschool children during group formation. *Man-Environment Systems, 5*, 43–48.

McGurk, B.J., Davis, J.D., & Grehan, J. (1981). Assaultive behavior personality and personal space. *Aggressive Behavior, 7*, 317–324.

McKenzie, I.K., & Strongman, K.T. (1981). Rank (status) and interaction distance. *European Journal of Social Psychology, 11*, 227–230.

Mehrabian, A. (1968a). Relationship of attitude to seated posture, orientation, and distance. *Journal of Personality and Social Psychology, 10*, 26–30.

Mehrabian, A. (1968b). Inference of attitudes from the posture, orientation, and distance of a communicator. *Journal of Consulting and Clinical Psychology, 323*, 296–308.

Mehrabian, A. (1969). Significance of posture and position in the communication of attitude and status relationships. *Psychological Bulletin, 71*, 359–372.

Mehrabian, A. (1972). *Nonverbal communication.* Chicago: Aldine-Atherton.

Mehrabian, A., & Diamond, S.G. (1971a). Effects of furniture arrangement, props, and personality on social interaction. *Journal of Personality and Social Psychology, 20*(1), 18–30.

Mehrabian, A., & Diamond, S.G. (1971b). Seating arrangement and conversation. *Sociometry, 34*, 281–289.

Mehrabian, A., & Friar, J.T. (1969). Encoding of attitude by a seated communicator via posture and position cues. *Journal of Consulting and Clinical Psychology, 33*, 330–336.

Mehrabian, A., & Williams, M. (1969). Nonverbal concomitants of perceived and intended persuasiveness. *Journal of Personality and Social Psychology, 13*, 37–58.

Meisels, M., & Canter, F.M. (1970). Personal space and personality characteristics: A nonconfirmation. *Psychological Reports, 27*, 287–290.

Meisels, M., & Dosey, M.A. (1971). Personal space, anger-arousal, and psychological defense. *Journal of Personality, 39*, 333–344.

Meisels, M., & Guardo, C.J. (1969). Development of personal space schemata. *Child Development, 49*, 1167–1178.

Melson, G.F. (1976). Determinants of personal space in young children: Perception of distance cues. *Perceptual and Motor Skills, 43*, 107–114.

Melson, G.F. (1977a). Sex differences in proxemic behavior and personal space schemata in young children. *Sex Roles, 3*, 81–89.

Melson, G.F. (1977b). Sex differences in use of indoor space by preschool children. *Perceptual and Motor Skills, 44*, 207–213.

Middlemist, R.D., Knowles, E.S., & Matter, C.F. (1976). Personal space invasions in the lavatory: Suggestive evidence for arousal. *Journal of Personality and Social Psychology, 33,* 541–546.

Miller, N. (1944). Experimental studies in conflict. In J. McV. Hunt (Ed.), *Personality and the behavior disorders (Vol. 1).* New York: Ronald.

Miller, N. (1959). Liberalization and basic S-R concepts: Extension of conflict behavior, motivation, and social learning. In S. Koch (Ed.), *Psychology: A study of a science (Vol.2).* New York: McGraw-Hill.

Minton, H.L., Steger, J.A., & Smrtic, G.R. (1968). Group opinion change as a function of circular vs. rectangular seating arrangement. *Psychonomic Science, 12,* 357–358.

Morris, E.K., & Smith, G.L. (1980). A functional analysis of adult affection and children's interpersonal distance. *Psychological Record, 30,* 155–163.

Murphy-Berman, V., & Berman, J. (1978). The importance of choice and sex in invasions of interpersonal space. *Personality and Social Psychology Bulletin, 4,* 424–428.

Naus, P.J., & Eckenrode, J.J. (1974). Age differences and degree of acquaintance as determinants of interpersonal distance. *Journal of Social Psychology, 93,* 133–134.

Nesbitt, P.D., & Steven, G. (1974). Personal space and stimulus intensity at a southern California amusement park. *Sociometry, 37*(1), 105–115.

Newman, R.C. II, & Pollack, D. (1973). Proxemics in deviant adolescents. *Journal of Consulting and Clinical Psychology, 40*(1), 6–8.

Nicosia, G.J., Hyman, D., Karlin, R., Epstein, Y.M., & Aiello, J.R. (1979). Effects of bodily contact on reactions to crowding. *Journal of Applied Social Psychology, 9,* 508–523.

Noesjirwan, J. (1977). Contrasting cultural patterns of interpersonal closeness in doctors' waiting rooms in Sydney and Jakarta. *Journal of Cross-Cultural Psychology, 8*(3), 357–368.

Noesjirwan, J. (1978). A laboratory study of proxemic patterns of Indonesians and Australians. *British Journal of Social and Clinical Psychology, 17,* 333–334.

Norum, G.A., Russo, N.G., & Sommer, R. (1967). Seating patterns and group tasks. *Psychology in the Schools, 4,* 276–280.

O'Neal, E.C., Brunault, M.A., Carifio, M.S., Tronturne, R., & Epstein, J. (1980). Effect of insult upon personal space preferences. *Journal of Nonverbal Behavior, 5,* 56–62.

O'Neal, E.C., Brunault, M.A., Marquis, J., & Carifio, M.S. (1979). Anger and the body-buffer zone. *Journal of Social Psychology, 108,* 135–136.

Pagàn, G., & Aiello, J.R. (1982). Development of personal space among Puerto Ricans. *Journal of Nonverbal Behavior, 7*(2), 59–68.

Patterson, M.L. (1973). Compensation in nonverbal immediacy behaviors: A review. *Sociometry, 36,* 237–252.

Patterson, M.L. (1975a). Eye contact and distance: A reexamination of measurement problems. *Personality and Social Psychology Bulletin, 1,* 600–603.

Patterson, M.L. (1975b). Personal space: Time to burst the bubble? *Man-Environment Systems, 5*(2), 67.

Patterson, M.L. (1976). An arousal model of interpersonal intimacy. *Psychological Review, 83,* 235–245.

Patterson, M.L. (1977). Interpersonal distance, affect, and equilibrium theory. *Journal of Social Psychology, 101,* 205–214.

Patterson, M.L. (1982). A sequential functional model of nonverbal exchange. *Psychological Review, 89,* 231–249.

Patterson, M.L. (1984). Nonverbal exchange: Past, present, and future. *Journal of Nonverbal Behavior, 8*(4), 350–359.

Patterson, M.L., & Holmes, D.S. (1966). Social interaction correlates of the MMPI extroversion-introversion scale. *American Psychologist, 21,* 724–725.

Patterson, M.L., Kelley, C.E., Kondracki, B.A., & Wulf, L.J. (1979). Effects of seating arrangement on small-group behavior. *Social Psychology Quarterly, 42,* 180–185.

Patterson, M.L., Mullens, S., & Romano, J. (1971). Compensatory reactions to spatial intrusion. *Sociometry, 34*(1), 114–121.

Patterson, M.L., Reidhead, S.M., Gooch, M.V., & Stopka, S.J. (1984). A content-classified bibliography of research on the immediacy behaviors: 1965–82. *Journal of Nonverbal Behavior, 8*(4), 360–393.

Patterson, M.L., Roth, C.P., & Schenk, C. (1979). Seating arrangement, activity, and sex differences in small group crowding. *Personality and Social Psychology Bulletin, 5,* 100–103.

Patterson, M.L., & Schaeffer, R. (1977). Effects of size and sex composition on interaction distance, participation, and satisfaction in small groups. *Small Group Behavior, 8,* 433–442.

Patterson, M.L., & Sechrest, L.B. (1970). Interpersonal distance and impression formation. *Journal of Personality, 38,* 161–166.

Pedersen, D.M. (1973a). Developmental trends in personal space. *Journal of Psychology, 83,* 3–9.

Pedersen, D.M. (1973b). Prediction of behavioral personal space from simulated personal space. *Perceptual and Motor Skills, 37,* 803–813.

Pedersen, D.M. (1973c). Relations among sensation seeking and simulated an behavioral personal space. *Journal of Psychology, 83,* 79–88.

Pedersen, D.M., & Heaston, A.B. (1972). The effects of sex of subject, sex of approaching person, and angle of approach on personal space. *Journal of Psychology, 82,* 227–286.

Pedersen, D.M., & Sabin, L. (1982). Personal space invasion. Six differentials for near and far proximities. *Perceptual and Motor Skills, 55*(3), 1060–1062.

Pedersen, D.M., & Shears, L.M. (1974). A review of personal space research in the framework of general system theory. *Psychological Bulletin, 80*(5), 367–388.

Pellegrini, R.J., & Empey, J. (1970). Interpersonal spatial orientation in dyads. *Journal of Psychology, 76,* 67–70.

Petri, H.L., & Huggins, R.G. (1975). *Some developmental characteristics of personal space.* Paper presented at the Eastern Psychological Association Convention, New York.

Petri, H.L., Huggins, R.G., Mills, C.J., & Barry, L.S. (1974). Variables influencing the shape of personal space. *Personality and Social Psychology Bulletin, 1,* 360–361.

Pittavino, S.L. (1977). Interpersonal space, locus of control and tolerance for ambiguity, (Doctoral dissertation, University of Wyoming, 1976.) *Dissertation Abstracts International, 38,* 375B.

Polit, D., & LaFrance, M. (1977). Sex differences in reaction to spatial invasion. *Journal of Social Psychology, 102,* 59–60.

Porter, E., Argyle, M., & Salter, V. (1970). What is signalled by proximity? *Perceptual and Motor Skills, 30,* 39–42.

Reid, E., & Novak, P. (1975). Personal space: An unobtrusive measures study. *Bulletin of the Psychonomic Society, 5,* 265–266.

Rice, C.A., & Belnap, S. (1975). Personal space in the deaf. Paper presented at the Eastern Psychological Association Convention, New York.

Rierdon, J., & Wiener, M. (1977). Spatial behavior of schizophrenic and non-schizophrenic psychiatric patients. *Perceptual and Motor Skills, 45,* 1295–1301.

Roger, D.B. (1982). Body-image, personal space and self-esteem: Preliminary evidence for "focusing" effects. *Journal of Personality Assessment, 46*(5), 468–476.

Roger, D.B. (1983). Body-image, personal space, and self-esteem: A field study. *Journal of Personality Assessment, 47*(3), 288–293.

Roger, D.B., & Mjoli, Q.T. (1976). Personal space and acculturation. *Journal of Social Psychology, 100,* 3–10.

Roger, D.B., & Reid, R.L. (1978). Small group ecology revisited: Personal space and role differentiation. *British Journal of Social and Clinical Psychology, 17,* 43–46.

Roger, D.B., & Schalekamp, E.E. (1976). Body-buffer zone and violence: A cross-cultural study. *Journal of Social Psychology, 98,* 153–158.

Rogers, J.A. (1972). Relationship between sociability and personal space at two different times of day. *Perceptual and Motor Skills, 35,* 519–526.

Rogers, P., Rearden, J.J., & Hillner, W. (1981). Effects of distance from interviewer and intimacy of topic on verbal productivity and anxiety. *Psychological Reports, 49,* 303–307.

Rohner, S.J., & Aiello, J.R. (1976). *The relationship between sex of interactants and their nonverbal behaviors.* Paper presented at the Eastern Psychological Association Convention, New York.

Rosegrant, T.J., & McCroskey, J.C. (1975). The effects of race and sex on proxemic behavior in an interview setting. *Southern Speech Communication Journal, 40,* Summer, 408–420.

Rosenfeld, H.M. (1965). Effects of an approval-seeking induction on interpersonal proximity. *Psychological Reports, 17,* 120–122.

Rosenfeld, H.M. (1966). Approval-seeking and approval-inducing functions of verbal and nonverbal responses in the dyad. *Journal of Personality and Social Psychology, 4,* 597–605.

Rosenfeld, H.M., Breck, R.E., Smith, S.E., & Kehoe, S. (1984). Intimacy-mediators of the proximity-gaze compensation effect: Movement, controversial role, acquaintance, and gender. *Journal of Nonverbal Behavior, 8*(4), 235–249.

Rozelle, R.M., & Baxter, J.C. (1978). The interpretation of nonverbal behavior in a role-defined interaction sequence: The police-citizen encounter. *Environmental Psychology and Nonverbal Behavior, 2,* 167–180.

Rumsey, N., Bull, R., & Gahagan, D. (1982). The effects of facial disfigurement on the proxemic behavior of the general public. *Journal of Applied Social Psychology, 12,* 137–150.

Russo, N.F. (1975). Eye contact, interpersonal distance, and the equilibrium theory. *Journal of Personality and Social Psychology, 31,* 497–502.

Ryen, A.H., & Kahn, A. (1975). Effects of intergroup orientation on group attitudes and proxemic behavior. *Journal of Personality and Social Psychology, 32,* 302–310.

Sanders, J. (1976). Relationship of personal space to body-image boundary definiteness. *Journal of Research in Personality, 10,* 478–481.

Sanders, J. (1978). Relation of personal space to the human menstrual cycle. *Journal of Psychology, 100,* 275–278.

Sarafino, E.P., & Helmuth, H. (1981). Development of personal space in preschool children as a function of age and day-care experience. *Journal of Social Psychology, 115,* 59–63.

Sauvy, J., & Sauvy, S. (1974). *The child's discovery of space. From hopscotch to mazes: An introduction to intuitive topology* (P. Wells, Trans.). Baltimore, MD: Penguin. (Original work published 1972.)

Savinar, J. (1975). The effect of ceiling height on personal space. *Man-Environment Systems, 5*(5), 321–324.

Savitsky, J.C., & Watson, M.J. (1975). Patterns of proxemic behavior among preschool children. *Representative Research in Social Psychology, 6,* 109–113.

Schachter, S., & Singer, J.E. (1962). Cognitive, social and

physiological determinants of emotional state. *Psychological Review, 69*, 379–399.

Scherer, S.E. (1974). Proxemic behavior of primary school children as a function of their socioeconomic class and subculture. *Journal of Personality and Social Psychology, 29*(6), 800–805.

Scherer, S.E., & Schiff, M.G. (1973). Perceived intimacy, physical distance and eye contact. *Perceptual and Motor Skills, 36*, 835–841.

Schiavo, R.S., Schiffenbauer, A., & Roberts, J. (1977). Methodological factors affecting interpersonal distance in dyads. *Perceptual and Motor Skills, 44*, 903–906.

Schiffenbauer, A., & Schiavo, R.S. (1976). Physical distance and attraction: An intensification effect. *Journal of Experimental Social Psychology, 12*, 274–282.

Schmidt, W., & Hore, T. (1970). Some nonverbal aspects of communication between mother and preschool child. *Child Development, 41*, 889–896.

Schneider, F.W., & Hansvick, C.L. (1977). Gaze and distance as a function of changes in interpersonal gaze. *Social Behavior and Personality, 5*(1), 49–53.

Schofield, J.S., & Sagar, H.A. (1977). Peer interaction patterns in an integrated middle school. *Sociometry, 40*, 130–138.

Schulz, R., & Barefoot, J. (1974). Non-verbal responses and affiliative conflict theory. *British Journal of Social and Clinical Psychology, 13*, 237–243.

Schwartzwald, J., Kavish, N., Shoham, M., & Waysman, M. (1977). Fear and sex-similarity as determinants of personal space. *Journal of Psychology, 96*, 55–61.

Scott, J.A. (1984). Comfort and seating distance in living rooms: The relationship of interactants and topic of conversation. *Environment and Behavior, 16*(1), 35–54.

Scott, J.S. (1974). Awareness of informal space: A longitudinal analysis. *Perceptual and Motor Skills, 39*, 735–738.

Severy, L., Forsyth, D., & Wagner, P.J. (1979). A multimethod assessment of personal space development in female and male, black and white children. *Journal of Nonverbal Behavior, 4*, 68–86.

Sewell, A.G., & Heisler, J.T. (1973). Personality correlates of proximity preferences. *Journal of Psychology, 85*, 151–155.

Shuter, R. (1976). Proxemics and tactility in Latin America. *Journal of Communication, 26*, 46–52.

Silveira, J. (1972). Thoughts on the politics of touch. *Women's Press, 1*, 13.

Silverstein, C.H., & Stong, D.J. (1976). Seating position and interaction in triads: A field study. *Sociometry, 39*, 166–170.

Skolnick, P., Frasier, L., & Hadar, I. (1977). Do you speak to strangers? A study of invasions of personal space. *European Journal of Social Psychology, 7*, 375–381.

Skotko, V.P., & Langmeyer, D. (1977). The effects of interaction distance and gender on self-disclosure. *Sociometry, 40*, 178–182.

Slane, S., Dragan, W., Crandall, C.J., & Payne, P. (1980). Stress effects on the nonverbal behavior of repressors and sensitizers. *Journal of Psychology, 106*, 101–109.

Slane, S., Petruska, R., & Cheyfitz, S. (1981). Personal space measurement: A validational comparison. *Psychological Record, 31*, 145–151.

Smetana, J., Bridgeman, D.L., & Bridgeman, B. (1978). A field of study of interpersonal distance in early childhood. *Personality and Social Psychology Bulletin, 4*, 309–313.

Smith, B.L., Lasswell, H.D., & Casey, R.D. (1946). *Propaganda, communication and public opinion.* Princeton, NJ: Princeton University Press.

Smith, M.J., Reinheimer, R.E., & Gabbard-Alley, A. (1981). Crowding, task performance, and communicative interaction in youth and old age. *Human Communication Research, 7*(3), 259–272.

Smith, R.J., & Knowles, E.S. (1978). Attributional consequences of personal space invasions. *Personality and Social Psychology Bulletin, 4*, 429–433.

Smith, R.J., & Knowles, E.S. (1979). Affective and cognitive mediators to reactions to spatial invasions. *Journal of Experimental Social Psychology, 15*, 437–452.

Snyder, C.R., & Andelman, J.R. (1979). Effects of degree of interpersonal similarity on physical distance and self-reported attraction: A comparison of uniqueness and reinforcement theory predictions. *Journal of Personality, 47*, 492–505.

Sobel, R.S., & Lillith, N. (1975). Determinants of nonstationary personal space invasion. *Journal of Social Psychology, 97*, 39–45.

Sodikoff, C.L., Firestone, I.J., & Kaplan, K.J. (1974). Subject self-disclosure and attitude change as a function of interviewer self-disclosure and eye contact. *Personality and Social Psychology Bulletin, 1*, 243–246.

Sommer, R. (1959). Studies in personal space. *Sociometry, 22*, 247–260.

Sommer, R. (1962). The distance for comfortable conversation: A further study. *Sociometry, 25*, 111–116.

Sommer, R. (1968). Intimacy ratings in five countries. *International Journal of Psychology, 3*(2), 109–114.

Sommer, R. (1969). *Personal space: The behavioral basis of design.* Englewood Cliffs, NJ: Prentice-Hall.

Soper, W.B., & Karasik, R. (1977). Use of spatial cues with regard to the invasion of group space. *Psychological Reports, 40*, 1175–1178.

Stephenson, G.M., & Rutter, D.R. (1970). Eye-contact, distance and affiliation: A re-evaluation. *British Journal of Psychology, 61*(3), 385–393.

Stephenson, G.M., Rutter, D.R., & Dore, S.R. (1973). Visual interaction and distance. *British Journal of Psychology, 64*, 251–257.

Stern, W. (1938). *General Psychology*, (H.D. Spoerl, Trans.). New York: Macmillan.

Stewart, D.J., & Patterson, M.L. (1973). Eliciting effects of verbal and nonverbal cues on projective test responses. *Journal of Consulting and Clinical Psychology, 41*, 74–77.

Stokols, D., Rall, M., Pinner, B., & Schopler, J. (1973). Physical, social and personal determinants of the perception of crowding. *Environment and Behavior, 5*, 87–115.

Stone, G.L., & Morden, C.J. (1976). Effect of distance on verbal productivity. *Journal of Counseling Psychology, 23*, 486–488.

Storms, M.D., & Thomas, G.C. (1977). Reactions to physical closeness. *Journal of Personality and Social Psychology, 35*, 412–418.

Stratton, L.O., Tekippe, D.J., & Flick, G.L. (1973). Personal space and self-concept. *Sociometry, 36*(3), 424–429.

Sundstrom, E. (1975). An experimental study of crowding: Effects of room size, intrusion, and goal-blocking on nonverbal behavior, self-disclosure and self-reported stress. *Journal of Personality and Social Psychology, 32*, 645–654.

Sundstrom, E. (1978). A test of equilibrium theory: Effects of topic intimacy and proximity on verbal and nonverbal behavior in pairs of friends and strangers. *Environmental Psychology and Nonverbal Behavior, 3*, 3–16.

Sundstrom, E., & Altman, I. (1976). Interpersonal relationships and personal space: Research review and theoretical model. *Human Ecology, 4*(1), 47–67.

Sundstrom, E., & Sundstrom, M.G. (1977). Personal space: What happens when the invader asks permission? *Environmental Psychology and Nonverbal Behavior, 2*, 76–82.

Sussman, N.M., & Rosenfeld, H.M. (1982). Touch, justification, and sex: Influences on the aversiveness of spatial violations. *Journal of Social Psychology, 106*, 215–225.

Sykes, R.E., Larntz, K., & Fox, J.C. (1976). Proximity and similarity effects on frequency of interaction on a class of naval recruits. *Sociometry, 39*, 263–269.

Tedesco, J.F., & Fromme, D.K. (1974). Cooperation, competition and personal space. *Sociometry, 37*(1), 116–121.

Tennis, G.H., & Dabbs, J.M., Jr. (1975). Sex, setting and personal space: First grade through college. *Sociometry, 38*(2), 385–394.

Tennis, G.H., & Dabbs, J.M., Jr. (1976). Race, setting, and actor-target differences in personal space. *Social Behavior and Personality, 4*, 49–55.

Terry, R.L., & Lower, M. (1979). Perceptual withdrawal from an invasion of personal space: A methodological note. *Personality and Social Psychology Bulletin, 5*, 396–397.

Tesch, F.E., Huston, T.L., & Indenbaum, E.A. (1973). Attitude similarity, attraction and physical proximity in a dynamic space. *Journal of Applied Social Psychology, 3*, 63–72.

Thalhofer, N.N. (1980). Violation of a spacing norm in high social density. *Journal of Applied Social Psychology, 10*, 175–183.

Thayer, S., & Alban, L. (1972). A field experiment on the effect of political and cultural factors on the use of personal space. *Journal of Social Psychology, 88*, 267–272.

Thomas, D.R. (1973). Interaction distances in same-sex and mixed-sex groups. *Perceptual and Motor Skills, 36*, 15–18.

Thompson, D.E., & Aiello, J.R. (1981a). *Nonverbal behavior: Development in mentally retarded and nonretarded children and adolescents.* Paper presented at the meeting of the Society for Research in Child Development, Boston.

Thompson, D.E., & Aiello, J.R. (1981b). *Women and management: Communication style and managerial effectiveness.* Paper presented at the American Psychological Association Convention, Toronto, Canada.

Thompson, D.E., & Aiello, J.R. (1982). *Manager's nonverbal communication style: Its effects on motivation and behavior.* Paper presented at the Eastern Psychological Association Convention, Baltimore, MD.

Thompson, D.E., Aiello, J.R., & Epstein, Y.M. (1979). Interpersonal distance preferences. *Journal of Nonverbal Behavior, 4*, 113–118.

Thompson, D.J., & Baxter, J.C. (1973). Interpersonal spacing in two-person cross-cultural interactions. *Man-Environment Systems, 3*, 115–117.

Tinbergen, N. (1952). The curious behavior of the stickleback. *Scientific American, 187*(6), 22–26.

Tipton, R.M., Bailey, K.G., & Obenchain, J.P. (1975). Invasion of males' personal space by feminists and non-feminists. *Psychological Reports, 37*, 99–102.

Tobiasen, J.M., & Allen, A.A. (1983). Influence of gaze and physical closeness: A delayed effect. *Perceptual and Motor Skills, 57*(2), 491–495.

Tolor, A. (1968). Psychological distance in disturbed and normal children. *Psychological Reports, 23*, 695–701.

Tolor, A., & LeBlanc, R.F. (1974). An attempted clarification of the psychological distance construct. *Journal of Social Psychology, 92*, 259–267.

Tolor, A., & Orange, S. (1969). An attempt to measure psychological distance in advantaged and disadvantaged children. *Child Development, 40*(2), 407–420.

Ugwuegbu, D.C., & Anusiem, A.U. (1982). Effects of stress on interpersonal distance in a simulated interview situation. *Journal of Social Psychology, 116*, 3–7.

Vaksman, E., & Ellyson, S.L. (1979). Visual and spatial behavior among U.S. and foreign males: A cross-cultural test of equilibrium theory. Paper presented at the Eastern Psychological Association Convention, Philadelphia, PA.

Vautier, J.S., & Aiello, J.R. (1982). *Nonverbal communication within and across status levels*. Paper presented at the Eastern Psychological Association Convention, Baltimore, MD.

Walden, T.A., & Forsyth, D.R. (1981). Close encounters of the stressful kind: Affective, physiological, and behavioral reactions to the experience of crowding. *Journal of Nonverbal Behavior, 6*, 46–64.

Walker, J.W., & Borden, R. (1976). Sex, status, and the invasion of shared space. *Representative Research in Social Psychology, 7*, 28–34.

Watson, O.M. (1970). *Proxemic Behavior: A cross-cultural study*. The Hague, Netherlands: Mouton.

Watson, O.M., & Graves, T.D. (1966). Quantitative research in proxemic behavior. *American Anthropologist, 68*, 971–985.

Weinstein, L. (1965). Social schemata of emotionally disturbed boys. *Journal of Abnormal Psychology, 70*(6), 457–461.

Weinstein, L. (1967). Social experience and social schemata. *Journal of Personality and Social Psychology, 6*(4), 429–434.

Wellens, A.R., & Goldberg, M.L. (1978). The effects of interpersonal distance and orientation upon the perception of social relationships. *Journal of Psychology, 99*, 39–47.

Whalen, C.K., Flowers, J.V., Fuller, M.J., & Jernigan, T. (1975). Behavioral studies of personal space during early adolescence. *Man-Environment Systems, 5*, 289–297.

White, M.J. (1975). Interpersonal distance as affected by room size, status, and sex. *Journal of Social Psychology, 95*, 241–249.

Williams, J.L. (1971). Personal space and its relation to extroversion-introversion. *Canadian Journal of Behavioral Sciences, 3*, 155–160.

Willis, F.N., Jr. (1966). Initial speaking distance as a function of the speakers' relationship. *Psychonomic Science, 5*, 221–222.

Willis, F.N., Carlson, R., & Reeves, D. (1979). The development of personal space in primary school children. *Environmental Psychology and Nonverbal Behavior, 3*, 195–204.

Winogrond, I.R. (1981). A comparison of interpersonal distancing behavior in young and elderly adults. *International Journal of Aging and Human Development, 13*, 53–60.

Wittig, M.A., & Skolnick, P. (1978). Status versus warmth as determinants of sex differences in personal space. *Sex Roles, 4*(4), 493–503.

Wolfgang, J., & Wolfgang, A. (1971). Explanation of attitudes via physical interpersonal distance toward the obese, drug users, homosexuals, police, and other marginal figures. *Journal of Clinical Psychology, 27*, 510–512.

Worchel, S., & Teddlie, C. (1976). The experience of crowding: A two-factor theory. *Journal of Personality and Social Psychology, 34*(1), 30–40.

Word, C.O., Zanna, M.P., & Cooper, J. (1974). The nonverbal mediation of self-fulfilling prophecies in interracial interaction. *Journal of Experimental Social Psychology, 10*, 109–120.

Wormith, J.S. (1984). Personal space of incarcerated offenders. *Journal of Clinical Psychology, 40*(3), 815–827.

Worthington, M.E. (1974). Personal space as a function of the stigma effect. *Environment and Behavior, 6*, 289–294.

Ziller, R.C., & Grossman, S.A. (1967). A developmental study of the self-social constructs of normals and the neurotic personality. *Journal of Clinical Psychology, 23*, 15–21.

Ziller, R.C., Megas, J., & DiCencio, D. (1964). Self-social constructs of normal and acute neuropsychiatric patients. *Journal of Consulting Psychology, 28*, 59–63.

Zimmerman, B., & Brody, G. (1975). Race and modeling influences on the interpersonal play patterns of boys. *Journal of Educational Psychology, 67*, 591–598.

Chapter 13

TERRITORIALITY

Barbara B. Brown, *Department of Psychology, Texas Christian University, Fort Worth, Texas*

13.1. INTRODUCTION

A student at work in a library carrel leaves briefly to find another reference. The student is dismayed to find an interloper seated at the carrel 10 minutes later and asks for the seat back.

Two navy recruits enter an isolation chamber for a 10-day isolation experiment. The two men immediately divide the small room in half. Although the division reduces the amount of space available for each, the men respect the invisible boundary line. A new college student is decorating her dormitory room. She tapes up her collection of family photos and displays her consuming passion for ballet by hanging up 17 ballet posters, ticket stubs from recent performances, and a well-worn pair of practice shoes.

Despite the variety of the examples, they all illustrate the operation of territoriality. The first example is perhaps the most prototypical in that it focuses on the demarcation and defense of space, a reflection of the biological roots of the concept of territoriality. Biologists first employed the concept to describe the behavior of nonhuman populations. Popularized applications of these concepts suggested that humans were similarly predisposed to be aggressive defenders of turf. Ironically, although many social scientists still link biological determinism with territoriality, many biologists no longer do so. Nevertheless, the biological heritage has made a lasting imprint on the field. This imprint is evident in definitions of territoriality, in anthropological investigations of its human origins, and in demonstrations of the resource control functions. In tracing these influences, it becomes clear that a strict biological interpretation of territoriality, while useful, is inadequate.

The newer and more social perspective on territoriality is apparent in the final two examples. Although the biological approach demonstrated that territoriality can regulate host–intruder encounters, territoriality can also be involved in the regulation of more sustained social interactions. In the example of the isolated recruits, territoriality helps to maintain the viability of the dyad under stressful conditions. Finally, the college student's dormitory personalizations demonstrate that territoriality can be a vehicle for the display of identity.

Unlike the biological approach, the social approach to territoriality really cannot claim a unified intellectual heritage. Instead, its proponents come from the fields of biology, anthropology, humanistic and behavioral geography, and environmental and social psychology. Some of these proponents have grown dissatisfied with the limitations of their biological approach, while others do not even consider their work to be within the scope of territoriality. Yet they all focus on the ways in which places and things are inherently a part of social processes and human identity.

Major reviews of the field of environmental psychology reveal the emergence of the second, more social perspective. Craik accurately labeled the field's bias by assigning territorial research in 1973 to the *human spatial behavior* approach and in 1977 to the *functional adaptation* paradigm. But by 1978

Stokols noted that "recent analyses have emphasized the cognitive and social–organizational functions of human territoriality rather than its biological (reproductive and survival-related) aspects" (p. 271). Finally, in 1982 Russell and Ward continued the trend by claiming that cognitive and affective aspects of territoriality were becoming popular.

Yet on closer examination the studies that represented this new direction in 1978 still restrict their attention to the abilities of territory holders to resist intrusions or influence attempts. Although these studies provide novel applications of the concept of territoriality to the topics of gang conflict, crime, and home-owner defensiveness, territorial functions still appear quite utilitarian. By 1982, half of the six cited studies continued to deal with territorial intrusion.

Thus although it is clear that research in territoriality is broadening it is also clear that the bulk of empirical support reflects active behavioral components of territoriality. Studies of territorial marking and intrusion are common; studies of cognitive and affective psychological ties to territory are rare. This bias in research distorts the picture of human territorial functioning by suggesting that territories become important only when they are violated or threatened. Their potential for contributing to identity expression and social system functioning has not been realized.

The interplay of the two major perspectives on territoriality will be addressed in the present chapter. The biological perspective will be shown to emphasize the control of resources via the demarcation and defense of space. The social perspective will show how a territory can enter into social processes and reveal itself in dominance patterns or as a promoter of system viability. The social perspective also reveals how territories engage cognitive and affective ties and serve to support the possessor's identity.

The basis for the two perspectives appears in the shades of difference among various definitions of territoriality. Although the biological perspective on demarcation and defense is still prevalent, a review of both the biological and the anthropological literature reveals the limitations of such a focus and the shift toward a more social perspective on territoriality. The unique qualities of human territoriality are taken into account in an outline of the structural variations among human territories. Finally, empirical support for the role of territoriality in resource control, system viability, and identity is presented and research directions designed to strengthen the social approach to territoriality are discussed.

13.1.1. Definitions of Territoriality

In Table 13.1 two clusters of definitions of territoriality are offered. The clusters differ not so much in terms of major concerns as in subtle shifting of attention to one or more of the common themes of territoriality. The first cluster, characteristic of the biological approach, directs attention to the demarcation, control, and defense of space; the owner's feelings about or valuation of the space receives little attention.

The second set of definitions attend more to the organizational benefits of territoriality. Here we get some notion of why a territory might be useful.

Table 13.1. Definitions of Territoriality

Definitions that Emphasize Occupation and Defense

Altman & Haythorn (1967), Altman, Taylor, and Wheeler (1971), and Sundstrom and Altman (1974): "Territoriality involves the mutually exclusive use of areas and objects by persons and groups" (Altman, 1975, p. 106).

Ardrey (1966): "A territory is an area of space—water, earth, or air—that an animal or group defends as an exclusive preserve primarily against members of their own species" (p. 3).

Eibl-Eibesfeldt (1970): "I propose that any space-associated intolerance be called territoriality, where a 'territory owner' is that animal before which another conspecific must retreat" (p. 309).

Davies (1978): "Whenever individual animals or groups are spaced out more than would be expected from a random occupation of suitable habitats" (p. 317).

Dyson-Hudson & Smith (1978): "We define a territory as an area occupied more or less exclusively by an individual or group by means of repulsion through overt defense or some form of communication" (p. 22).

Goffman (1963): "Territories are areas controlled on the basis of ownership and exclusiveness of use."

Hall (1959): "The act of laying claim to and defending a territory is called territoriality" (p. 146).

Sommer (1969), Sommer & Becker (1969), Becker (1973), and Becker and Mayo (1971): "Territories are geographical areas that are personalized or marked in some way and that are defended from encroachment."

Van den Berghe (1974): "*Territoriality* means the defense of a relatively fixed space against occupation and/or use by co-specifics."

Definitions that Emphasize Organizational or Attachment Functions

Altman (1975): "Territorial behavior is a self–other boundary regulation mechanism that involves personalization of or marking of a place or object and communication that it is 'owned' by a person or group. Personalization and ownership are designed to regulate social interaction and to help satisfy various social and physical motives. Defense responses may sometimes occur when territorial boundaries are violated" (p. 107).

Austin & Bates (1974): "Possession of valued objects and of space" (p. 448).

Bakker & Bakker-Rabdau (1973): "Territoriality . . . will indicate *the inclination toward ownership*. . . . Territory will refer to *the object of ownership*, be it a stretch of land, a particular object, an idea, or anything else that holds an individual's fancy to such a degree that he seeks to own it" (p. 3).

Brower (1980): "The relationship between an individual or group and a particular setting, that is characterized by a feeling of possessiveness, and by attempts to control the appearance and use of the space" (p. 180).

Edney (1976): "Territoriality in humans is largely a passive affair. . . defined by the criterion of continuous association of person or persons with specific place. . . . (It) is an important organizer in human life and behavior" (p. 33).

Malmberg (1980): "Human behavioural territoriality is primarily a phenomenon of ethological ecology with an instinctive nucleus, manifested as more or less exclusive spaces, to which individuals or groups of human beings are bound emotionally and which, for the possible avoidance of others, are distinguished by means of limits, marks, or other kinds of structuring with adherent display, movements, or aggressiveness (pp. 10–11).

Pastalan (1970): "A territory is a delimited space that a person or group uses and defends as an exclusive preserve. It involves psychological identification with a place, symbolized by attitudes of possessiveness and arrangements of objects in the area."

Sack (1983): "By human territoriality I mean the attempt to affect, influence, or control actions and interactions (of people, things, and relationships) by asserting and attempting to enforce control over a geographic area" (p. 55).

These definitions do not contradict the first set; they just bring to mind the fact that territories endure over time and their owners are not perpetually involved in demarcation and defense. These definitions also focus on the idea of psychological identification with spaces. Territories are not only organizational devices; they may be important and valued in their own right due to their symbolic value. These definitions shift attention to the feelings and thoughts of the owners and the symbolic value of the personalizations, not just their mere presence.

Given the preponderance of definitions of the first type, one might question whether a broader definition of territoriality that incorporates social system functioning and identity issues is useful. In order to answer that question the next two sections will review animal territoriality and the anthropological debate on the historical origins of human territoriality. Surely, if territorial occupation and defense for the purposes of resource control provide a sufficient framework for the study of territoriality, then such will be the case in anthropological and biological studies where the biological definitions first emerged.

13.1.2. Animal Territoriality

Earlier summaries (Edney, 1975a; Sundstrom & Altman, 1974) of human and nonhuman territoriality (hereafter called *animal* territoriality) identified the following eight differences. In animals, uses of space are stereotyped, suggesting a biologically based mechanism; human uses of space are variable, suggesting a learned mechanism. In animal territories, there is a link between aggressive defense and territoriality; this link does not hold for humans. Animal territories are intact; human territories are geographically dispersed. Animals claim exclusive ownership of territories; humans have both exclusive and time-shared ownership. Total invasion by another group is uncommon for animals; it is common for humans. Animals must invade the territory in an intrusion; humans can use weapons to invade territories without trespass. Animals exclude all other co-specifics from their territories; humans entertain co-specific visitors.

Thus it appeared that a biological basis for territoriality could only be applied to animals. Since the time of that conclusion, growth in the field of sociobiology and an increase in experimental studies of animal territories (in, e.g., the *Journal of Animal Ecology*) led to a more complex view of territoriality. Now, even biologists question whether the original

biological framework is appropriate for animal populations and early human societies. Currently, although some still claim a biological origin for animal territoriality, the notion of a territorial instinct that was unresponsive to learning and driven to expression is less accepted. The major change instigated by this research was to focus on territoriality as an adaptive mechanism that is responsive to different ecological demands.

The learned component of animal territoriality received support from studies that demonstrate that animals are less stereotyped in their use of territories and exhibit a greater variety of territorial signals than previously believed. For example, some animals alternate between territorial systems and dominance systems in a way that allows them to adapt to fluctuating ecological conditions (Freedman, 1979). Some species have been observed to maintain geographically dispersed territories, for instance, birds who use different trees for nut storage. Time-sharing of territories among animals has also been noted. Squirrels that have different peak activity times will share a territory; nocturnal and diurnal lizards share the same space (Ferguson, Hughes, & Brown, 1983). Animals also have the ability to intrude on other territories without entering them; their birdcalls or colorful throat displays serve as vocal and visual "weapons."

Even the link between territoriality and aggressive defense is not clear. Some researchers have emphasized that the possession of territory actually decreases the likelihood of aggression, at least when territorial claims are clear. Others note that territories may be claimed with nonaggressive means such as chemical smell secretions or visual displays that defend the territory by preventing intrusion.

In sum, animal territorial behaviors are flexible and can often vary across the life span of the animal and across different types of resources.

13.1.3. Early Human Territoriality

Further drawbacks to a strict biological interpretation of territoriality are found in anthropological literature. A biological interpretation of human territoriality could be appealing if early human societies possessed territories. Consequently, anthropologists search for the presence of territoriality in hunter–gatherer societies, the forerunners to contemporary settled agricultural or industrial societies. To the extent that present-day hunter–gatherer groups mirror earlier ones, demonstration of territoriality among current hunter–gatherers may argue for historical continuity of and possible biological basis of human territoriality.

One problem with this approach is that many anthropologists looked to kinship rather than territoriality to provide social organization (Gold, 1982). Furthermore, anthropologists may limit their search to the resource control functions of territoriality; other functions might be ignored.

These problems have created some confusion in the literature. Lee (1968), for example, argued that territoriality is neither universal nor biologically impelled because he could find no evidence of it among the !Kung bushmen. In contrast, Eibl-Eibesfeldt (1974) found several sources of evidence that support the existence of territoriality among the !Kung. Such contradictions may stem from differences among researchers in their definitions of territoriality— whether it exists at the individual or group level (Godelier, 1979), whether it is defined by active defense or by regular use (Altman & Chemers, 1980), or whether it changes with fluctuations in resource availability (Trigham, 1972).

However, the same trend away from biological determinism that was observed in biologists' accounts of animal territoriality can be seen in anthropologists' investigations of the parameters of human territoriality. Dyson-Hudson and Smith (1978) argued that territorial systems would be present only when benefits outweighed costs and that ecological conditions influence the balance of benefits and costs. Benefits may include more efficient harvesting of resources (Cass & Edney, 1978) and greater familiarity with and access to territorial resources. Costs include the time, energy, and risks associated with territorial defense, and the spatial limitations imposed. Conditions of resource availability and abundance are the two ecological conditions that they propose will affect cost–benefit ratios and the social forms in a culture. They argued on the basis of anthropological accounts that a territorial group will be chosen over dispersed–isolated groups, dispersed information-sharing groups, or home-ranging groups when the resources are predictable (temporally and spatially) and abundant (in patches or over the entire territory). The other three exploitation systems were found to develop under other combinations of resource predictability and abundance.

Even though Dyson-Hudson and Smith's theory appeared to deviate from strict biological interpretations of territoriality, it was criticized by Cashdan (1983) for remaining too firmly rooted in the animal model. She argues that the "cognitive and cultural capacities of our species alter the ways in which territories can be defended" (p. 47). Animals' costs of territorial defense increase with increases in the size of the territories because the larger the territory, the more time and energy spent in patrolling and defending territorial boundaries. In contrast, humans have sophisticated communication and memory systems that allow potential intruders to teach their children or others to avoid the rival group's claim to territory. Thus potential confrontations may be less frequent among humans than among animals because humans have more ways of learning to avoid territorial intrusions.

Cashdan also proposed that social boundary defense is a second, uniquely human form of territorial defense whereby a group perimeter is defended instead of a geographic one. Social boundary territories, characteristic of some Australian and Eskimo groups, arise when territories are very large due to sparse or unpredictable resources. These groups adapt by cultivating social and political ties with other dispersed groups so that information concerning the location of food resources may be exchanged. A group that desires to forage in another group's territory can attain foraging rights by enacting a series of greeting rituals. The costs of territorial access across the social boundaries involve the time and energy devoted to greeting rituals themselves and the long-term cultivation of reciprocal social and political ties.

Other anthropological accounts of territoriality have also deviated from the biological focus in emphasizing the social, cultural, or religious meanings that become intertwined with territories. For example, the Tiv "viewed their land as an extension of their geneology [sic]" (Gold, 1982, p. 51) and had a complex system of shifting territories that maintained their juxtapositions to other lineage groups' territories. The Australian aborigines maintained "dreaming space" territories that were symbolically connected to the ancestors (Tuan, 1977). In fact, one researcher views territory as "a set of ideas" and studies the ways in which these "cognitive models are expressed on the ground" (Blundell, 1983, p. 58). Clearly, even nomadic groups who do not accumulate property view their territories as more than devices to protect resources such as food.

Although the debate concerning hunter–gatherer territoriality still continues, it demonstrates some trends evident in more recent treatments of territoriality. First, there is less adherence to the view that territoriality is a biologically determined drive or impulse among humans. Some deviate from the biological position by concluding that human ancestors were not territorial (Suttles, 1972) while others are content to point out the variability in the form and expression of territoriality (Wilson, 1975). Without denying that territories serve biological needs, the new approach is to consider the situations in which territoriality provides flexible adaptation to certain ecological conditions. And, finally, there is recognition that territoriality serves cultural purposes in providing tangible symbols to reinforce a common cultural heritage.

But despite this growth and diversity in the field, the term *territoriality* still conjures up images of aggressive, instinctual defense systems. For example, in a comment on Cashdan's work, Ehrenreich (1983) states:

> I have only one misgiving about the work. It seems regrettable that the analysis is framed in reference to the issue of "territoriality." No matter how carefully or broadly this concept is defined, it conjures up a biological imperative. Like the idea of the "naked ape," territoriality is a concept "we could live without." (pp. 58–59)

Because Cashdan had explicitly opposed a wholesale application of animal models to human territoriality, the stigma attached to the word can be strong indeed.

13.1.4. Unique Qualities of Human Territoriality

The research reviewed previously offers two conclusions. First, the original biological approach has been modified by biologists themselves. They observed that an exclusive emphasis on demarcation and defense was inappropriate. The revised biological perspective points out that human and animal uses of territory are much more flexible, much less biologically impelled than first believed.

Although the research advances show that human and animal uses of territory differ quantitatively rather than qualitatively, the boundaries between the two types of territory are not completely blurred. Social and cultural concerns are more prominent in human territoriality than in animal territoriality. Consequently, humans exhibit more territorial behavior toward significant objects, for example, than do animals. A pet dog's territorial claim to a toy does not compare with a human attachment to a family heirloom. Human attachments to objects are much

more frequent and appear to be based on an object's symbolic evocations of cultural, family, and individual histories (Csikzentmihalyi & Rochberg-Halton, 1981).

This ability to confer cultural meanings onto objects is only one example of the larger role that culture plays in the regulation of territoriality (Cashdan, 1983). For example, human cultures have laws that maintain over time the abstract rights to possession of territory. Consequently, human territorial defense does not depend on the occupant's physical strength or cunning in defeating potential claimants to the territory. Instead, the culture provides laws that become proxy defenders of territory.

Perhaps the most general difference between human and animal territories is that human territories serve different needs. "Whereas animal territoriality is rooted in physiological needs connected with survival, human territoriality may also embrace 'higher' needs for, say, status, recognition by others, and achievement or self-image" (Gold, 1982, p. 48). Territories also facilitate the achievement of certain human psychological processes including needs for privacy, intimacy, and solitude (Altman, 1975; Taylor & Ferguson, 1980; Westin, 1970). In contrast, the principal function of territoriality in animal populations is to provide clear and predictable ways of regulating access to resources, thereby clarifying the animal's exchanges with the environment and decreasing moment-to-moment conflicts over the use of space. Thus one difference between human and animal territoriality is that human territories project identities to visitors.

Another difference is that animals rarely engage in social visits across territorial borders. Some species will habituate to the presence of (Wilson, 1975) or even synchronize breeding schedules with their neighbors (termed the Fraser Darling effect). These conditions of social stimulation clearly do not approach the sociability that humans have with visitors.

Humans, in contrast, often use their territories to entertain legitimate visitors. Although visitors are not allowed the same use of space as owners, they are allowed access to otherwise well-protected territories such as living rooms. The existence of territorial visits among humans underscores the role of territoriality as a social system regulator and conveyer of symbols of identity. Yet these more central functions of identity are not equally supported in all types of territories. The following review suggests how structural differences among territories may correlate with their functions.

13.2. STRUCTURAL CHARACTERISTICS OF TERRITORIES

13.2.1. Occupancy and Centrality

Altman (1975) proposed that three different types of territory exist that differ along dimensions of the duration of occupancy and psychological centrality. Primary territories such as homes or bedrooms are typically occupied for long periods and are central to the lives of their owners. Secondary territories are somewhat more accessible to a greater range of users, but regular occupants exert some control over who may enter the territory and what range of behaviors may take place. Although there may be regular users such as bar "regulars" or members of a country club, the time spent within a secondary territory is usually somewhat more limited than the time spent in a primary territory. The limits of occupancy are determined not solely by the users, but by collective owners of secondary territories. Furthermore, secondary territories, while important, are generally not as central to the lives of their occupants as are primary territories. Public territories such as seats on a bus or at a library table are usually occupied for short stretches of time and are not very central to the lives of their occupants. Occupancy of public territories is open to almost everyone and is usually determined on a "first come, first served" basis.

Because the type of territory is not defined strictly by any physical feature, conflicts may arise over the ownership of a space. For example, a graduate student may come to define a certain regularly used library table as a secondary territory. An infrequent user of the library may not recognize this claim and may become puzzled when the graduate student overreacts on finding the seat taken. Or a student who has been used to living in a single-room primary territory may resent the college roommate who invites strangers into the room. Home owners who have joined a Neighborhood Watch anticrime group may come to define the residential block as a secondary territory and react defensively to strangers who use the block as a public territory.

Despite these potentials for misperception on the part of competing users, Taylor and Stough (1978) found, via a repertory grid methodology, that individuals can distinguish between territories on the basis of psychological centrality and duration of use. The differences parallel the sociological distinctions between primary and secondary groups. Primary groups involve face-to-face interactions and affective relations while secondary group relations may be more distant or segmental (Litwak & Szelenyi, 1969). In keeping with these distinctions, Taylor and Stough's respondents perceived that greater comfort, control, privacy, and familiarity with others are available in more primary territories. Consequently, additional dimensions, beyond duration and centrality, draw attention to the more social qualities of the distinctions among primary, secondary, and public territories.

13.2.2. Marking, Markers, and Intrusion

These additional distinctions serve to reinforce a more social perspective on territoriality, whereby territories promote identity display and social system regulation. A third distinction, described in Table 13.2, concerns the motivations underlying territorial marking. A resident of a home may intend a nameplate to be a decorative self-expression; yet the nameplate may have the effect of conveying a primary territorial claim (Brown & Altman, 1981, 1983). The act of personalization is more of a conscious claim for space in other territories; users of public or secondary territories are much more aware of the need to defend their turf by conspicuous placement of books or other markers. Consequently, the functions of territorial markers may be more self-expressive for primary territories and more utilitarian for secondary or public territories.

A fourth dimension depicted in Table 13.2 concerns the range, type, and mix of markers that are used in various territories. Marker characteristics may reveal the owners' marking intentions as well as the territory's durability and psychological centrality. For example, primary territories, because of their centrality and durability, often contain markers reflecting personal characteristics of their occupants. The markers themselves may appear to reflect more central values, may be more durable, and may portray highly personal qualities of the owners. For example, primary territory markers can include permanent nameplates, artworks, and furnishings. Because such territories are long term, the markers need not be portable and can vary in size, permanency, and attachment to the territory itself.

In secondary territories, markers may be valuable, yet they may be specially protected when the regular users are absent. For example, the trophy case in a country club may be kept locked due to the vulnerability of the territory when it is not occupied by the regulars. Other markers may be more explicit statements of territorial boundaries such as "members only" or "keep out" signs.

Table 13.2. Dimensional Variations Between Public, Secondary, and Primary Territories

Dimension	Public	Secondary	Primary
Duration	Short	Short, but regular usage common	Long
Centrality	Not central	Somewhat central	Very central
Marking intentions	Intentionally claiming territory	Often claiming territory	Usually personalizing or decorating
Marking range	Few physical markers or barriers; much bodily and verbal marking	Some reliance on physical markers; bodily and verbal marking common	Heavy reliance on a wide range of markers and barriers; bodily and verbal marking usually not necessary
Responses to invasion	Can relocate or use immediate bodily and verbal markers	Can often relocate, use immediate bodily and verbal markers, as well as some re-emphasis of physical markers	Cannot relocate easily, can use legal recourse, reestablishment of physical markers and barriers, as well as bodily and verbal markers

Source: "Territoriality and Residential Crime: A Conceptual Framework" by B. Brown and I. Altman, 1981, in *Environmental Criminology* by P. J. Brantingham and P. L. Brantingham, Beverly Hills: Sage Publications. Copyright 1981 by Sage Publications. Reprinted by permission.

Public territories are almost always defended with occupancy and/or minimal physical or nonverbal markers. Physical markers are often limited to items that are convenient and available such as books or umbrellas. In recognition of the ephemeral nature of these territories, owners do not risk using valuable markers such as purses to protect the territory.

A fifth dimension along which territories vary involves reactions to territorial intrusion. In general, both the strength of territorial defenses and the impact of territorial intrusions increase from public to secondary to primary territories. Intrusions of primary territories appear intentional, because the intruder has had to ignore salient markers or boundaries such as closed doors. Owners have a wide range of territorial defenses available in such cases, including legal defenses and physical retaliation. The owners may react strongly to an intrusion for a number of reasons: The place symbolizes the personal identity of the owner; valuable territorial markings may be ruined or taken by intruders; the owners may have no territory to retreat to after the most central territory has been intruded on (Brown, 1983). Thus for economic, physical, and psychological reasons intrusions into primary territories are serious matters.

Secondary territories, with their mix of public and private use, lesser importance to owners, and less clear-cut evidence of marking and personalization, may be more susceptible to intrusion. The motives for invasions may be variable, ranging from a deliberate attempt at intrusion to an accidental invasion. Similarly, the reactions to invasion may vary considerably, depending on the extent to which the occupants feel that the territory is central and that they have adequately marked it. Reactions to an invasion will also be affected by the motives that owners attribute to the intruders.

When a public territory is invaded, the owner has some but only minimal "rights" to the territory. Because such territories assume the least importance to owners, owners or invaders are likely to respond by retreating. If a user wants to reclaim an invaded territory, verbal request or nonverbal signals may be the only recourse.

13.2.3. Structural–Functional Relationship

With respect to all five dimensions, it is apparent that different types of territories are used for different functions. The primary territory is the most multifunctional. It allows for a great deal of order, organization, predictability, and control. But it also allows for the expression of a sense of identity. It is likely that these two functions are related. Control can promote a sense of efficacy that becomes incorporated into the self-identity. Similarly, a certain amount of control might be a prerequisite to the development of deep psychological investments in a place. One would not develop a sense of identification with something that cannot be relied on to express the self.

The type of control available will also be likely to influence the type of identity displayed in a territory. Primary territories are often controlled by an individual who can choose to display unique aspects of personal identity. Secondary territories are often associated with groups such as neighbors, co-workers, the regulars at the bar, or members of a street gang, and they are therefore more likely to be controlled by a group than an individual. The type of identity displayed may be a group identity and thus may emphasize only one role within the repertoire of its owners.

In public territories, where control is fleeting, displays of identity are typically restricted to the occupants' immediate appearance and belongings. Any sense of control the users have may derive from the predictability of behavior in the setting rather than the ability to create and enforce one's choice of rules. For example, occupants may not be able to erect a "no smoking" sign, but they can predict that others present will obey the rules for the use of the territory.

One exception to the association between identity functions and primary territories occurs in what Stokols and Jacobi (1984) call *commemorative environments* such as the Statue of Liberty, a mosque, or the Lincoln Memorial. Although these places may have the same limitations on demarcation and occupancy as most public territories do, they also support aspects of individual or group identity the way primary territories do. While such religious, ethnic, or historical attachments are important, they are not derived in the same manner as territorial attachments. That is, territorial attachments are usually forged through a combination of activities (such as occupying, personalizing, and defending space) and psychological transformations (such as developing feelings of territorial attachment, ownership, and identification) that emerge from experience with a place. Attachments to commemorative environments do not qualify as territorial attachments because they can be created independently of actual experience with a place.

A second form of person–place relationship that is not considered territorial is one that involves exclusive ownership. For example, legal ownership of a piece of investment property does not constitute territorial ownership if the territorial cognitions and feelings do not accompany the ownership. That is, unless the owner develops a feeling of ownership, attachment, or identification, mere legal ownership does not constitute a territorial relationship. Similarly, an absence of legal ownership does not imply an absence of territoriality. A child can become territorial about his or her toys without legally owning them.

The present conceptualization and the bulk of the empirical work focus on territories where attachments are forged through actual use, not vicariously. Activities such as occupancy, defense, and personalization and psychological ties such as feelings of ownership, attachment, or identification are assumed to be necessary to constitute a territorial relationship. Admittedly, the bulk of the research in public territories has assumed the presence of territoriality simply by demonstrating behavioral components of territorial demarcation and defense. Nonetheless, it is assumed that such behaviors indicate a psychological claim to the space as well.

Furthermore, it is argued that primary territories allow for the greatest degree of control and the greatest potential for individualistic identity displays. Secondary territories have a moderate degree of control; identity may be that of a role within a group. Finally, public territories emphasize order, organization, and control; identity displays are more limited, deriving from the appearance of the owner or objects carried by the owner.

13.3. TERRITORIAL DEMARCATION AND DEFENSE OF SPACE

13.3.1. Physical Territorial Markers

Most studies of territoriality emphasize the demarcation and defense of public territories. Public territories are often self-consciously marked to reserve space; owners realize that their claims to space are tenuous. Consequently, public territorial marking is especially geared toward preventing intrusions rather than providing cues that facilitate interactions or express identity.

Limiting conditions for the effectiveness of public territorial markers in settings such as libraries include the duration of absence of the owner, the availability of alternative spaces, and the desirability of the territory. All markers appear to prevent intrusions when the other users of the library have plenty of alternative spaces available. However, as population density increases and alternative spaces decrease, a marker will lose its effectiveness (Sommer & Becker, 1969).

Although it has been claimed that personal markers provide better protection than impersonal ones (Sommer & Becker, 1969), the impersonal quality of the marker is likely to be confounded with its functional ambiguity. A marker is particularly susceptible to intrusion if it can be mistaken for litter such as racing forms in racetrack seats (Arenson, 1977), school newspapers on snack bar tables, and scattered journals on library tables (Sommer & Becker, 1969). Markers such as notebooks and jackets are typically not abandoned permanently, so that could account for their greater effectiveness. The functional ambiguity of certain markers may explain their limited effectiveness better than their personal or impersonal nature does.

In line with this interpretation, it was found that a half-empty beer mug is a more effective deterrent to intrusion of a table at a bar than a more personal marker such as a sports jacket (Hoppe, Greene, & Kenny, 1972). The authors reasoned that prospective customers realize that patrons may forget their jackets when leaving the bar but that they (or the bartenders) seldom leave half-empty beer mugs. Prospective customers assume that the bartender expects the patron to return. Similarly, it is possible to think of situations in which not only would personal markers provide less protection than impersonal markers, but they themselves would be at risk in the setting. For example, in bus stations or airports where thievery is frequent, individuals avoid using their luggage or jackets as objects to defend a territory in their absence. Thus rather than concluding that personal markers are superior to impersonal ones it is appropriate to take into account the local norms and customs that govern the use and protection of territory.

13.3.2. Social Defenders of Territory

Perhaps because of the limited effectiveness of public territorial markers, users sometimes enlist the aid of neighbors to save seats at a game or movie theater when temporarily vacating the seat. Sommer and Becker (1969) observed that neighbors were more likely to defend an adjacent space when the user had been absent a relatively short time (e.g., 15 min vs. 60 min). Likelihood of defense was unrelated to the user's prior duration of occupancy (5 vs. 20 min), or degree of personalized contact with the neighbor (no contact vs. asking for the time vs. chatting informally, all for 5 min). However, when neighbors are explicitly asked to defend a territory, a large proportion (71%) will do so, and many will put their own territorial markers on the claimed space (Hoppe et al., 1972).

13.3.3 Nonverbal Territorial Markers

In public territories, there are instances in which the shape and extent of the territory are not marked or bounded by physical markers. For example, Goffman (1963) contends that museum visitors claim the space encompassed by their apparent path of gaze toward an art object. Less anecdotal evidence has supported the use of nonverbal markers in public territories. For example, restaurant diners appear to touch their plates of food in two ways (Truscott, Parmelee, & Werner, 1977). They reposition the plate of food to achieve better placement of the food or they touch the plates without moving them. This second, nonutilitarian form of plate touching appeared to serve territorial functions because it was more likely to occur when the diner had more need to establish a territorial claim. That is, the touching was more likely to occur after service by a waiter or waitress than by the self and when the plate was served with food rather than empty.

The validity of the role of touch as a territorial marker was extended by examination of the phenomenon in another locale—the pinball parlor. In this study (Werner, Brown, & Damron, 1981), the roles of two other nonverbal behaviors—body orientation and closeness—were examined for their ability to protect a territory from intrusion. In the game arcade, as was not the case in Goffman's museum example, merely gazing at a pinball machine did not protect it. (However, Lindskold, Albert, Baer, & Moore, 1976, demonstrated that gazing at a store window does deter passersby from intervening.) But standing close to or touching the machine did deter intrusion. Similarly, individuals who were engaging in play would touch the machine more frequently when approached by a stranger than when playing in isolation. Thus touch is an easy, dynamic marker used to establish a public territory and to protect it from an impending intrusion.

Interactional or *portable territories* arise when territorial claims are made to protect an ongoing interaction rather than the space itself. Goffman (1963) has described these as "line of talk" territories. These spaces are not bubble shaped like personal spaces but are elongated to encompass the space that connects two or more interactants. These territories are also protected by nonverbal signals. For example, they are defended better when the interactants are relatively close together (Efran & Cheyne, 1973), are interacting (Cheyne & Efran, 1972), are in large groups (four vs. two individuals) or are high status (e.g., older vs. younger; Knowles, 1973), or are mixed-sex dyads (63% vs. 49% for same-sex dyads, Cheyne & Efran, 1972). Thus a variety of both static and dynamic nonverbal signals protect interactional territories.

13.3.4. Characteristics of Territorial Occupants

Investigators have examined the effect of group size, culture, and gender on territorial occupancy, intrusion, and defense. As occupancy time increases, same-sex groups claim larger spaces and mixed-sex groups use more markers. It was suggested that the mixed-sex groups used markers to keep territorial boundaries intact while same-sex groups on these beach territories kept boundaries unmarked in order to socialize across boundaries. Generally, as group size increases, the average space per person decreases (Edney & Jordan-Edney, 1974), although this may be true only for groups of friends, not strangers (Edney & Grundmann, 1979).

A cross-cultural study of beach territories, while failing to replicate effects of group size for either French or German samples, found a greater clarity of territorial boundaries for Germans than for French (Smith, 1983). A comparison of American and Greek reactions to territorial contaminations also yielded more differences than similarities. While both groups were quick to remove a garbage sack from their lawns, Greeks were not as quick to remove one from the sidewalk or street in front of their house (Worchel & Lollis, 1982). These two samples of cross-cultural territories suggest that culture plays a role in the way in which territorial spaces are claimed and regulated.

Sex differences have appeared in some studies but not in others. French and German males use fewer markers on beach territories than females (Smith, 1983), while U.S. males claim larger beach (Edney & Jordan-Edney, 1974) and dormitory room territories (Mercer & Benjamin, 1980). A comparison of female and male markers in a bar showed that male markers are intruded on on fewer trials and, when intruded on, protect the territory for a longer amount of time. Male territories were never invaded by a lone intruder (Shaffer & Sadowski, 1975). As if to underscore this point, Haber (1980) instructed

confederates to intrude on male and female students' classroom desk territories. She had to abort her plans when her confederates could not bring themselves to complete all the planned invasions; however, they completed twice as many invasions for females.

The reluctance to intrude on male territories is well founded; when fraternity and sorority tables in a cafeteria were invaded the males were more likely to say unfriendly things to the intruders (Calsyn, 1976). Other studies show that males and females who find their library seats taken are equally likely to withdraw (McAndrew, Ryckman, Horr, & Solomon, 1978), or to ask the intruder to leave (Taylor & Brooks, 1980). Thus anticipated negative reactions by intruded-on males may only materialize when their rights to space are established via occupancy rather than marking. These findings stand in contrast to observations of interactional territories. These territories are best defended from interlopers by mixed-sex dyads rather than male (or female) dyads. Thus the perceived intimacy or strength of the bond between territorial owners may provide more deterrence than does fear of male retaliation.

13.3.5. Styles of Territorial Occupancy and Intrusion

Despite the fact that public territories appear to be easily violated, many intruders do not invade these spaces lightly. For example, if intruders must sit at occupied tables, they tend to choose the most distant seat possible and they leave earlier than control subjects who seat themselves at unmarked tables (Becker, 1973).

Some intruders appear more comfortable with their role than others. Consistent findings suggest that there are both deferential and offensive styles of intrusion. Sommer labeled the styles he observed *avoidant* and *offensive* (1967). When students wanted to establish a territory that would allow them to avoid distractions by others, they chose end chairs at six-person tables (Sommer, 1967) or spaces near the wall or facing away from the door (Sommer & Becker, 1969). Offensive claimants, ones who desire a territory by themselves, tended to select the middle seats of a six-person table (Sommer, 1967) or seats facing the door and center or aisle seats (Sommer & Becker, 1969).

Sommer and Becker (1969) observed the effects of three different styles of intrusion by a confederate—verbal requests, nonverbal requests, and nonverbal aggressiveness. Only the direct verbal query led to frequent defense by the neighbor; both nonverbal approaches—barging into the territory or hesitantly approaching the seat—decreased the neighbor's defense of space. In the game arcade naive intruders also adopted deferential or assertive styles of claiming a video game that was guarded but not used by a confederate (Werner, et al., 1981). Other studies have noted that intruders apologize, avert their eyes, purse their lips, or stare at the intruded-on individuals; again this supports the existence of intrusive and apologetic styles of intrusion (Efran & Cheyne, 1974). Why intruders select a particular style is not yet known; however, Lavin (1978) found that apologetic or deferential styles are more frequent when intruders can see the territory holder and are not blocked by physical barriers protecting the territory. Thus relative openness of the current occupant may elicit a more deferential approach.

If occupants of public territories are intruded on, their most frequent reaction is to abandon the territory. All individuals who found their marked seats invaded on returning from a cafeteria line retreated and most individuals retreated when an invader had taken the adjacent seat (Becker & Mayo, 1971) or when the owner's markers had been brushed aside and replaced with a different set of markers (McAndrew et al., 1978). When occupants do try to reclaim their territories, acts of surprise or intimidation may precede the request. For example, invaded owners of carrel spaces in the library walk past the intruder before returning to demand their space (Taylor & Brooks, 1980). Intruded-upon owners of classroom seats stop and stare at the intruder before requesting their space (Haber, 1980).

13.3.6. Architectural Features and Territorial Claims

Certain architectural features appear to encourage the development of territoriality in public spaces. Students are more likely to make territorial claims for library tables that are close to a wall, facing away from the distractions of the main entrance, and toward the rear of the room (Sommer & Becker, 1969). Passersby are more likely to drink from a water fountain if it is shielded from the spatial proximity of others by a physical barrier (Baum, Reiss, & O'Hara, 1974).

Territorial claims are clearer for well-demarcated carrel sites in a library than for unbounded tables (Taylor & Brooks, 1980). The private nature of the carrels was confirmed by descriptions of carrel intruders. They were more likely to be seen as more

pushy and rude (65%) than table intruders (22%). In an experimental test, a female confederate invaded a marked but recently vacated table or carrel space. All of the carrel owners asked for their spaces back while half of the table owners did so, suggesting that the salient boundary line of the carrels enhanced the legitimacy of the user's claim.

In sum, strength of territorial ownership and defense has been shown to vary according to characteristics of the setting such as territorial markers, architectural features, and social defenders and characteristics of the occupants such as their gender, cultural background, or group size. The implications these variations have for other ongoing social processes are not apparent; the emphasis to this point has been on the ways in which territories create "keep out" messages. The following section reviews ways in which territories involve group processes such as dominance displays, communication of status, and social system maintenance.

13.4. TERRITORIALITY AND SYSTEM VIABILITY

13.4.1. Dominance and Territoriality

Among animals, dominance hierarchies and territorial systems interact in complicated ways. Dominance hierarchies may substitute for or exist within territorial systems. When they coexist, the individual on home turf may actually be able to dominate others who are higher in the hierarchy (Wilson, 1975). Or the dominance rankings can overrule individual territorial claims. For example, an overlord male lizard may have free access to female lizard territories although the females defend their borders against encroachment by other females.

In human populations, dominance and territoriality are related in complex ways, and empirical studies often yield inconsistent results. Altman (1975) suggests that the inconsistency of results may be due to variations in measures of dominance, to the social dynamics within the sample, and to characteristics of the samples studied.

Dominance is sometimes measured as the amount of social contact and other times as powerful or directive behaviors. When the first definition is used, highly dominant individuals in mental hospitals act as overlords who claim territories that encompass the territorial borders of lower-status members of the group (Esser, 1968; Esser, Chamberlain, Chapple, & Kline, 1965; lack of confirmation was provided by Esser, 1973). When dominance is defined in terms of behaviors such as name-calling, issuing orders, and physical attack, then more dominant individuals occupy the more desirable territories (Austin & Bates, 1974; Sossin, Esser, & Deutsch, 1978).

The influence of social dynamics on the relation between dominance and territoriality was illustrated in a study of 17 boys in a rehabilitation center (Sundstrom & Altman, 1974). According to the boys' own judgments of dominance ranks and desirable territories, the most dominant boys early on had the most desirable spaces such as those near the television. But when two highly dominant boys were replaced by two newcomers, the group renegotiated the division of territories through fights and disturbances, a process often observed in animal territories (Wilson, 1975). For 3 weeks the number of fights and disturbances increased and the boys showed no fixed territories. In the third phase, the low- and medium-dominant boys began to carve out individual territories, while the high-dominant ones were struggling with the other boys. This study along with others (cf. DeLong, 1970, 1973) demonstrates that a relationship between dominance and territoriality may or may not exist depending on fluctuations in group structure and process.

13.4.2. Territoriality and Status Relations

Studies of settings other than residential treatment facilities illustrate the more diverse and subtle connections between territoriality and influence. These situations differ from previous studies of dominance in that individuals are not aiming for rights to exclusive use of space. Visitors are accepted into the territories, yet the owners still draw on their territorial resources to shape and guide interactions within those territories.

In sports encounters, the opposing team is allowed access to the home turf, yet the hosts attempt to dominate the game. In these encounters, the home team has the "home court advantage" (Altman, 1975; Schwartz & Barsky, 1977). A home team advantage may be partially due to greater familiarity with idiosyncratic court conditions or the absence of travel fatigue. Schwartz and Barsky (1977) reasoned that the noisy support by home crowd fans was an advantage because the effect is stronger for indoor games such as basketball than for outdoor games such as football.

Other studies examine the ability of territory owners to dominate visitors when the domination does

not involve physical superiority. It has been found that individuals believe they have more control in the more central primary territories than in secondary or public territories (Taylor & Stough, 1978) and they actually are more likely to influence decisions made there (Taylor & Lanni, 1981). Several studies have examined the advantages that college students have over visitors to their dormitory room. Hosts have the advantage in negotiation tasks (Martindale, 1971) and can dominate a cooperative task when visitors are dissimilar to the residents (Conroy & Sundstrom, 1977).

In that last study it was revealed that territories could facilitate pleasurable exchanges as well as contentious ones. The territorial dominance effect reversed itself when the visitor had similar opinions to the host. Thus territories can also facilitate prosocial encounters when conditions favor good treatment of visitors. In addition, hosts may have greater psychological comfort on their home turf. Edney (1975) found that dormitory residents evaluated their room more positively and appeared more relaxed and secure than visitors.

In many settings status rankings also correlate with territoriality in work environments. Offices comprising the more desirable territories are expected to be assigned to those who have greater status or power within the organization. Indications of high status in an office include low accessibility, large floor space, high-quality furnishings (i.e., wood is higher status than metal, carpeting is higher status than bare floor). A study of 529 office workers indicated that, especially for high-status individuals, the presence of high-status markers correlated positively with employees' beliefs that the work space accurately reflected their rank within the organization (Konar, Sundstrom, Brady, Mandel, & Rice, 1982). This study did not examine whether status markers were related to dominant behaviors, but it does suggest that the visitors to the offices could gauge the statuses of the officeholders via their territorial cues and adjust strategies of interaction accordingly.

The role of territorial claims in ongoing interactions was pinpointed more precisely in a symbolic interactionist's investigations of role-played negotiations between a boss and an employee (Katovich, 1986). The conversations took place in either the employee's or the boss's office. Territorial claims entered into the conversation in quite subtle ways. For example, the officeholder rather than the visitor assumed the right to initiate a handshake. But the power to designate visitor space within the office depended upon rank. In the boss's office, the boss appeared to direct the person to a visitor's space (e.g., "Have a seat") or to question his or her right to space ("What can I do for you?"). When the boss entered the employee's space, the boss sat without invitation, presuming the power to claim visiting space without permission. In this case, according to Katovich, the "turf master" is relegated to the role of "turf guardian." The subtle ways in which an employer's status and territorial ownership become entwined in the interaction with an employee illustrate that territories can enhance system viability by clarifying interactions and making them predictable. Territories also can enhance the functioning of systems in ways that have nothing to do with dominance or power.

13.4.3. System Maintenance

At the level of the primary territory, studies of living environments demonstrate that the long-term stability of the residential environment system is related to the establishment of territoriality. For example, U.S. Navy volunteers who are isolated in pairs inside one room for extended lengths of time are more likely to maintain their compatibility with each other and elect to complete the isolation experiment if they quickly develop and maintain individual territories (Altman & Haythorn, 1967; Altman, Taylor, & Wheeler, 1971). Although the volunteers were in temporary quarters and had little ability to personalize the room, the territorial provision of control appeared to help them withstand the isolation. Even in less stressful environments, married couples (Rosenblatt & Budd, 1975) and families (Altman, Nelson, & Lett, 1972) develop territorial systems that promote smooth functioning within the social units.

In secondary territories, Suttles (1968) investigated the division of territorial groupings among Chicago gangs and found that they enhanced both the members' sense of group identity and their ability to control entry into certain areas at certain times. Separate gangs existed for ethnicity (black, Italian, Mexican-American, and Puerto Rican) and, within those groups, for age gradations. A more recent study of ethnic gangs in Los Angeles (Moore, Vigil, & Garcia, 1983) corroborates these findings and further demonstrates that cohesive gangs may even import members who do not live in the area to take a proprietary interest in and identify with a neighborhood. Less formally defined neighborhood groups may also feel a high degree of security and community, may experience fewer incidents of residential burglary (Brown, 1983), and may more effectively

fight proposed zoning changes in the neighborhood (Smith, 1975). A more extensive treatment of the relationship between territoriality and the functioning of social systems, especially with reference to residential settings and crime, is found in Taylor, Chapter 25, this volume.

13.4.4. Personalization and Social Interaction

The very act of personalizing may enhance system viability by facilitating certain interactions. For example, some researchers have noted that gardening, yard work, or other upkeep tasks are ways of personalizing territory that create opportunities for neighbors to become acquainted with one another. The social ties may increase the owners' commitments to the individual territory as well as the neighborhood territory (Beck & Teasdale, 1978; Bush-Brown, 1969; Lewis, 1979; Newman, 1972). Backyard gardeners have also reported better ability to distinguish between neighbors and strangers as well as fewer problems with intruders on the street (Taylor, Gottfredson, & Brower, 1981).

The effects of environmental personalizations on actual interactions between strangers have also been demonstrated. Visitors to a waiting room have been shown to affiliate more when there are easily understood conversation pieces decorating the room (Mehrabian & Diamond, 1971). Thus the mere presence of certain environmental personalizations may enter into social processes even when the interactants have no role in the personalization process itself.

Personalization may enhance system viability partially by clarifying the personal qualities of the territory owners, as illustrated in a study of personalizations in dormitory rooms (Vinsel, Brown, Altman & Foss, 1980). It was found that the students' choice of personalizations in the freshman year related to the students' likelihood of remaining in school. Two themes distinguished between those who dropped out (for reasons other than academic failure) and those who chose to remain. First, the diversity of interests displayed via the decorations was much narrower in scope for the future dropouts. Whereas a "stay-in" might display interests in sports, abstract art, statements of values, personal relationships, and theater, a dropout would display fewer of such decorative categories. A second difference was found in the pattern of commitments displayed. Stay-ins appeared to be committing themselves to the university environment by displaying such things as university club or Greek insignia, maps of the campus and local area, and mementos of local events such as concerts. The dropouts appeared to have maintained their commitments to hometown people and places. Their decorations included items such as letters from younger siblings, dried prom flowers, and posters of hometown attractions. Thus the type of identity conveyed through the decorations was quite different for the two groups. It is possible that the decorative differences actually contributed to and shaped the students' interactions in the room and the impressions received by others. Certain types of identity messages may prove dysfunctional in the students' attempts to adjust to the new living environment. This study illustrates how processes involved in maintaining a viable system may involve the presentation of certain types of identity displays, a theme elaborated below.

13.5. TERRITORIALITY AND IDENTITY

The space-claiming and system viability functions of territoriality are relatively easy to observe in concrete behaviors involving occupancy, dominance, demarcation, or defense of space. The provision of identity is more difficult to study because it is manifested more in cognitions and affective ties to places or things. Nonetheless, the substance of self-identity may be studied through owners' choices of personalizations. Furthermore, the very act of personalizing or caring for one's territory may create strong bonds of attachment to the territory. Finally, identity functions can be revealed through the psychological states that accompany occupancy, demarcation, or personalization of space. Although claiming and identifying with space are two different activities, they are actually intertwined. That is, activities that control space also provide feedback relevant to the individual's sense of identity, as illustrated in the following section.

13.5.1. The Development of Control and Identity Functions

The best research available on the beginnings of territorial behavior is found in cross-cultural studies of the acquisition of concepts of possessiveness, typically involving objects. Furby (1974, 1978, 1980, 1982) argues that among humans objects play a complex role in social coordination and identity display.

When a child learns cultural rules governing possessions, the child begins to develop a sense of self and a sense of competence in the world. In all societies children acquire a sense of control and competence partially by manipulating objects around them. When adults interfere with the child's attempts to touch and play with certain objects, children learn boundary conditions for ownership. Thus the child's early identity development involves experiences with feeling competent and in control with regard to objects. Consequently, the first encounters with objects appear to establish a link between ownership, identity, and competence.

In a later stage of development, the manipulation of objects becomes important for social interaction. For example, possessing a toy draws the attention of other age mates. Or simultaneous play can lead to social interchanges when two toddlers are attracted to the same toy. Furby notes that peers respond to each other more when showing, giving, or taking an object than when interacting without an object. Consequently, concepts of ownership are immediately linked to social interaction experiences. This connection is maintained through adulthood. Furby's older respondents reported not only that ownership implies social power and status, but that ownership helps to define individuality when possessions can be viewed as extensions of the self, as discussed in the following section.

13.5.2. Personalizations and Identity Messages

Illustrations of the identity functions of territoriality rarely come from territory researchers themselves. Although definitions of territoriality from the social approach (Table 13.1) referred to feelings of attachment or valuations of space, the bulk of research comes from other disciplines. Researchers who study various facets of attachments to places may be from Table 13.3 summarizes some of the ways these researchers describe the identity aspects of the possession of things. Although territory researchers refer to the actual territory only incidentally as a space that is staked out and defended, place attachment researchers emphasize the symbolic contents that make the territories worth defending.

Personalizations may enter into territorial functioning in several ways that have little to do with an intentional claim to or defense of territory. First, onlookers may form impressions of occupants based upon the personalizations. Second, territorial per-

Table 13.3. Identity Functions of Places and Objects

Tuan (1980): "Likewise with our houses, streets, and buildings: the constraints that they put on us focus our energies and intentions; the clear images that the structures present to us sharpen our sense of self" (p. 465). "[Artifacts] stabilize experience, support our sense of a perdurable self, and confirm our belief in a comprehensible universe. The house in many societies is a microcosm that encapsulates with clear and graspable detail what the larger world is like and how we should behave in that world. The house imparts lessons implicitly, without demands on conscious thought" (p. 471). "Our fragile sense of self needs support, and this we get by having and possessing things because, to a large degree, we are what we have and possess" (p. 472).

Hayward (1977): "What people call 'home' serves as a symbol of how they see themselves and how they want to be seen by others" (p. 3).

Kimber (1973): "Gardens . . . represent social territories in which persons define their own places and express their self-images" (p. 7).

Dovey (in press): "To accuse someone, their possessions or 'home' of being inauthentic implies a strong moral judgment and arouses righteous indignation" (p. 1).

Sadalla, Burroughs, & Quaid (1981): "The design of a house may be construed as a symbol or a set of symbols which communicate something of the owner's identity and social status" (p. 201).

Csikszentmihalyi & Rochberg-Halton (1981): "A home is much more than a shelter; it is a world in which a person can create a material environment that embodies what he or she considers significant. In this sense the home becomes the most powerful sign of the self of the inhabitant who dwells within" (p. 123).

sonalizations allow the territory owner to foster certain impressions that may or may not be accurate reflections of the owner. Third, the very act of personalizing may create or intensify bonds of attachment between owner and territory.

A number of studies have revealed links between personalizations of a place and perceived characteristics of the occupants. Maslow and Mintz (1956) had judges rate pictures of individuals when seated in beautiful or ugly rooms. The judges in beautiful rooms rated the pictures higher on dimensions of energy and well-being than judges in ugly rooms. In a follow-up study, Mintz (1956) found that experimenters who conducted interviews in both types of rooms actually stayed longer in and reported more positive mood states in the beautiful rooms. Another study revealed that the judged levels of formality and friendliness of rooms were also believed to characterize their occupants (Canter, West, & Wools, 1974). Judges have also been shown to agree on inferences of residents' personality, occupational type, and occupational prestige from pictures of residents' houses (Cherulnik, 1982).

Finally, several studies demonstrate that the choice of personalizations creates impressions of social, not just personal, identity. For example, the styles of gardening surrounding Puerto Rican households have been described as representing "social territories in which persons define their own places and express their self-images" (Kimber, 1973, p. 7).

Six distinct styles were identified that represent the degree of allegiance the resident showed to two contrasting traditions: the vernacular and high style. Gardens in the vernacular tradition were treated as a utilitarian source of work space, food source, and waste receptacle. High-style gardens were used to "create artificial landscapes, to decorate the dwelling, and to express the esthetic taste of the owner or of the local landscape architect" (p. 23).

Personalizations do not always create positive images of occupants. Personalizing may also be considered a form of deviance by the larger society, as in the case of vandalism or graffiti. Use of vandalism or graffiti can symbolize individual identity (Ley & Cybriwsky, 1974), group identity, or dominance over another's territory (Pablant & Baxter, 1975). Graffiti wars may take place where territorial boundary lines are disputed. Vandalism may be a symbolic form of personalization that restores the vandal's feelings of control over the space (Allen & Greenberger, 1980).

13.5.3. Personalizations and Actual Identity

Many researchers assume that personalizations are accurate reflections of some aspects of the owners' identity. For example, Cooper (1972), using Jungian theory, suggested that houses are sacred symbols of the self. Rapoport (1969) emphasizes that house form may demonstrate the owner's tie to cultural identity. Altman and colleagues (Altman & Chemers, 1980; Altman & Gauvain, 1981; Gauvain, Altman, & Fahim, 1983) noted that houses may reflect an individual's need simultaneously to establish individuality from and communality with the culture.

In more traditionally empirical studies, it has been demonstrated that personalizations do reflect individual or family characteristics. Artifacts found in living rooms correlate with the owner's social status (Laumann & House, 1972). Similarly, the decorative complexity of housing interiors correlates with materialistic values espoused by the owners (Weisner & Weibel, 1981). Using the concept of front region from Goffman (1959), one study examined whether living rooms served as front regions by conveying desirable images of the occupants. Naive judges could accurately infer the residents' idealized self-images by scrutinizing the living room (Sadalla, Burrough, & Quaid, 1981).

Social group memberships are also reflected in personalizations. Duncan (1973) found that two distinct social clusters in one village were identifiable by personalization styles. One group preferred the "English upper-class style of studied seediness," (p. 343) complete with colonial houses and bucolic landscapes. The second group preferred a prosperous neighborly style evoked by newer colonial reproduction houses personalized with Americana symbols and unfenced yards. The environmental differences reflected social differences with the first group belonging to different churches and clubs and preferring less contact with neighbors than the second. Similar group identities were revealed by Pratt (1982), who focused on house interior personalizations. In his study, one social group decorated to convey uniqueness while the other strove to follow decorative standards of the group.

Ethnic identities may also be reflected in choices of territorial personalization. Mexican-American houses in Tucson are much more likely to have chain link fences than Anglo houses in the same area (Arreola, 1981). Slavic-American houses in Kansas City are personalized differently from the houses of their non-Slavic neighbors (Greenbaum & Greenbaum, 1981). The Slavic households had more potted plants, better sidewalk and house maintenance, more extensive landscaping, and more attractive yards. Interviews revealed the Slavs to be more involved in neighborhood sociability, suggesting that they had formed a secondary neighborhood territory.

Home interiors contain a wide variety of objects that hold special meanings for identity. Interviews with 315 members of 82 lower- and upper-middle-class families revealed that 1694 objects were cited as special or meaningful (Csikszentmihalyi & Rochberg-Halton, 1981). The objects could be grouped into 17 categories to reflect the object's use, meaning, personal significance, or mode of acquisition. Some objects were meaningful because they invoked the past such as family reunions or travels; others were symbols of ethnic or religious identities. Emotional qualities such as feelings of enjoyment or accomplishment were also conveyed through objects. Thus objects served to embody a wide range of emotional meanings, social ties, or other aspects of authentic identity.

The role of exterior personalization in reflecting ties to the local community has been corroborated in other studies. In a neighborhood that generally encouraged neighborliness, neighborly behaviors and attitudes were related to the likelihood and value of home improvements made by the residents (Galster & Hesser, 1982). Within a middle-class neighborhood the presence of temporary personalizations in the form of Halloween decorations was associated with both reports of neighborhood cohesiveness and cul-de-sac street designs (Brown & Werner, 1985). Thus territorial personalizations can symbolize a wide range of affect-laden identity commitments.

13.5.4. Place Attachments

Conceptual work on attachment to place has rarely been the focus of traditionally trained psychologists. While the feeling of being "at home" may be commonly experienced, is difficult to capture the essence of this feeling in concrete instances of behavior. Even when psychologists consider the verbal responses to interviews or questionnaires as legitimate data, they tend to concentrate their efforts on measuring beliefs or reports of behavior. Affective concerns may be tapped in attitude questionnaires, but it is typical to conceive of affective states very globally in terms of a general evaluative dimension whereby something is judged to be good or bad (Fishbein & Ajzen, 1975).

Because traditionally trained psychologists are not very fluent when assessing the experiential components of emotional or affective bonds (De Rivera, 1984), various phenomenological and philosophical works prove more informative when examining place attachment (cf. Buttimer & Seamon, 1980; Relph, 1976; Rowles, 1978, Seamon, 1979). The special feeling of attachment to place was described by Eliade (1957) as an attitude toward the "sacred" as contrasted with the "profane." Heidegger (1971) formulated the concept of *dwelling* that describes an active, caring process by which individuals transform a house into a home. This work has been continued by European scholars who examine the *appropriation* of space, whereby places become meaningful due to the activities, work, and attachments embedded within them (Barbey, 1982; Korosec-Serfaty, 1985). Bachelard (1964) argues that the house serves as a place to study attachments, but that "all really inhabited space bears the essence of the notion of the home" (p. 5). Along with an emphasis on activities that make the house meaningful, Bachelard argues that the "house is one of the greatest powers of integration for the thoughts, memories, and dreams of mankind" (p. 6). Finally, Tuan (1974) discusses *topophilia*, an affective bond between people and place that may vary in strength from ephemeral sensory delight to deeply rooted attachment. Thus conceptual approaches from outside of psychology emphasize that sensory experiences, memories, cognitive integration, affective concern, and activities all contribute to the bonds between people and place.

More traditionally empirical researchers have recently been attracted to these conceptions of affective bonds between people and places. Rather than using concepts such as dwelling or appropriation that appear to evolve experientially, Stokols and colleagues (Stokols, 1981; Stokols & Shumaker, 1981) describe the state of *place dependence*, a perceived association between persons and the environment. Dependence results when the occupants perceive that an available space meets their needs better than alternative spaces. The dependence is greater when a greater variety of needs or more basic needs are met. A subset of place dependence experiences could be related to territoriality. In many cases, a high degree of place dependence corresponds to primary territorial ties. An exception to this linkage would exist when a place is very dissatisfying, yet no satisfactory alternatives exist (Stokols, Shumaker, & Martinez, 1983). In this example, the occupants are place dependent but unlikely to establish the identification with and concern for the place that are necessary for primary territorial attachments. The emotional and cognitive experiences might involve alienation, helplessness, or destructive impulses that are inconsistent with primary territorial ties.

Another conceptualization that could involve territoriality is the construct of *place identity*, a substructure of self-identity. It contains "memories, ideas, feelings, attitudes, values, preferences, meanings, and conceptions of behavior and experience which relate to the variety and complexity of physical settings that define the day-to-day existence of every human

being" (Proshansky, Fabian, & Kaminoff, 1983, p. 59). This conceptualization emphasizes the role of places in organizing memory as well as providing expressive opportunities. Territorial attitudes and cognitions can serve similar functions of displaying identity. Because territories also play a role in system maintenance, it is likely that they promote the organization of memory, too, although this possibility has yet to be investigated. In sum, concepts such as dwelling, topophilia, and place identity may point to areas of territorial functioning that have yet to be articulated.

Empirical work on the more elusive qualities of place attachment is limited. Some research considers the positive emotional states that accompany territoriality among home owners. For example, home personalizations made by residents of low- to moderate-income housing developments made the home feel "comfortable and home-like" (Becker & Coniglio, 1975). Furthermore, "the emotional connotations of objects were very important to their owners—objects used to personalize an interior carried emotional meaning to their owners beyond their territorial marking function" (p. 62). However, if one defines territory more broadly than a defended turf, it is clear that these personalizations, more than the geographical area of the territory, help to create the feeling of territorial ownership and the blending of personal and environmental identities.

Results of interviews with home owners have helped to illuminate the psychological processes involved in creating primary territorial ties. Respondents reported that transforming a house into a "home" involves more than just liking a place or admiring its beauty: "A variety of places may have emotional and aesthetic significance to a person, yet no place feels like home" (Horwitz & Tognoli, 1982, p. 337). One way respondents turned a house into a home was through active personalization or shaping of the environment. These results corroborate the traditional territory literature in that qualities of the physical environment per se do not determine the possession of territory. Some type of cognitive and affective transformation process is a prerequisite to a place becoming a territory. Empirical research on home owners suggests that females and the elderly may forge stronger territorial attachments than others.

13.5.5. Sex Differences in Attachment to Territory

Sex differences in affective ties to territories appear to be most prominent in primary territories such as the home. Although males are often home owners in a financial sense, women are often the ones to decide on home personalization style, to care for daily upkeep, and to spend more time there. In terms of territorial feelings and attitudes, women appear to have more intimate associations with the home environment. Men are more frequently mentioned as intruders and defenders of territories and they appear to occupy larger territories.

A study of middle-class Israeli apartment owners illustrates the differing territorial investments of men and women (Sebba & Churchman, 1983). An interview of 90 residents revealed that, while few (20%) of the women felt that the entire apartment "belonged" to them, a majority (53%) felt that it "represented" them. In contrast, the men felt they owned the home more frequently than they felt represented by it (31% vs. 17%). These territorial feelings of identity appeared to be engendered by the activities of personalization and upkeep, duties more likely to be performed by women. Similarly, Tognoli (1980) found in intensive interviews of 10 adults that women were more likely to feel that their first abode after leaving the family home was truly their own "home." He speculated that the greater homemaking experiences for females allowed them to convert a new house into a home more easily.

Saegert and Winkel (1980) note this blend of home activities and self-identity for females. "The home is both a physical space where certain activities are performed and a value-laden symbol. Both meanings of the word are closely linked to definitions of the female sex role in our culture" (p. 41). In fact, a content analysis of the meanings of home reveals that women more often reported the home to be a source of affection, a secure family place, and a personalized place (Hayward, 1977). There was a trend for men to report that *home* meant an impersonal structure of their own childhood home. Yet even the one personal association to home by males was not confirmed in a later study (Holahan, 1978). In that study, women reported more personal and social associations for both their present and childhood homes.

Even when females are not performing roles such as homemaker and mother, they personalize their environments in a more intimate manner. Women students chose to personalize their college dormitory walls, for example, with more numerous symbols of personal relationships such as photos of or letters from friends and family (Vinsel et al., 1980). Males were more likely to personalize with sports themes, or with entertainment equipment such as stereo speakers.

13.5.6. Age Differences in Attachment to Territory

Rowles (1980) contends that one's attachment to home territories intensifies with age. He has examined elders' attachment to place through a phenomenological perspective. From interviews of elders in an Appalachian community he proposed that attachment to home engenders the feeling of physical, social, and autobiographical *insideness* based on contemporary and historical levels of involvement. A *physical* insideness is generated from the "immediacy of everyday activity" (1980, p. 158) and the rhythmical or routine patterns of travels around the community. A *social* insideness involves a continuing role in various social networks.

The deepest level of place attachment is reflected in an *autobiographical* insideness, a condition in which the elders make a "heavy historical investment in this place. Each has created an environment richly differentiated as an array of places laden with personal meaning in relation to a life history. Over the years, each one of them has become more a part of the place to the point where it becomes an autobiography—literally an extension of the self" (1980, p. 162). When one is returning from a long sojourn, the sense of autobiographical insideness must be reestablished by reacquainting oneself with the environmental cues that serve as symbols for the incident memories. Rowles contends that feeling "inside" a place can actually help individuals cope with the stresses of growing old. But, because a past relationship with a place is needed in order to create insideness at a deep level, relocation of the elderly can deny them this source of participation in a place (p. 165).

13.6. RESEARCH DIRECTIONS

13.6.1. Territorial Cognitions and Affect

In order to develop a complete explanation of the identity functions of territoriality, it will be necessary to give further attention to the ways in which humans are affectively and cognitively bonded to territories. These bonds are implicit in the concept of centrality that distinguishes among public, secondary, and primary territories (Altman, 1975). Seamon (1979) noted that "research in territoriality has defined attachment to place and space largely in terms of fear, protection, exclusiveness, and preservation" (p. 70). He calls for greater attention to qualities of "at-homeness" that allow for warmth, "at-easeness,' roots, regeneration, and appropriation.

One possible reason for the absence of work on territorial attachments and cognitions, beyond the methodological difficulties, is a cultural reluctance to admit to the importance of owning places and things. Although psychologists' discussions of territoriality often focus on the benefits of possessing a territory, scholars from other fields view the existence of ownership and possessiveness as a pessimistic comment on basic human nature. For example, within the Judeo-Christian heritage, Belk (1982) has noted that four of the seven deadly sins (greed, pride, gluttony, and envy) counsel against indulging in possessiveness. Within sociological thought, both Marx and Veblen condemned those who seek happiness, power, or prestige through the possession of objects (Belk, 1982). Others (Malthus, 1836; Schumacher, 1973) contend that humans' insatiable appetites for possessions drain the planet of limited resources. Despite these criticisms, humans continue to value and identify with certain possessions. The cultural heritage of derogatory comment on possessiveness may explain the relative absence of research on the topic.

Current attempts to assess place attachments via traditional questionnaire formats have shifted from simple, unidimensional assessments toward more complex and multidimensional ones (Brown & Werner, 1985; Fischer, Jackson, Stueve, Gerson, Jones, & Baldassare, 1977; Kasarda & Janowitz, 1974; Riger & Lavrakas, 1981). Nevertheless, these measurements are limited to variables such as home ownership, duration of residence, evaluations of space, and reports of social activities. They do not tap the richness of concepts such as topophilia or dwelling that are more apt measures of the ways in which environments support memories, cognitive integrations, and affective ties.

13.6.2. Impression Formation

Despite the lack of good operational measures of place attachment, the experiential provisions of attachments to place may underlie the more "visible" indications of territoriality such as personalization and defense. Although the phenomenological approach is counter to some researchers' conceptions of acceptable scientific practice, the place attachment interpretation of territoriality is not inherently phenomenological. To illustrate, there are several research possibilities intrinsic to conceptions of place attachment that can be pursued via a more traditional methodology.

The expressive function of place attachment (Proshansky, Fabian, & Kaminoff, 1983) can easily mesh with other impression formation research, for example. Borrowing from attribution theorists, it has been established that firm attributions concerning personal qualities of an individual depend especially on nonnormative or unexpected behaviors (Jones & Davis, 1965). Similarly, visitors to a territory may gain firmer (though not necessarily more accurate) impressions of inhabitants from the expressive qualities of their environments than from their required attributes. These impressions may then shape and guide interactions between owners and visitors.

13.6.3. Dysfunctional Territorial Stability

An emphasis on the social and identity aspects of territories suggests that future research can examine territorial dysfunctions in this light. Possible angles of approach involve the temporal qualities of territories and the evaluative meaning of territories that fail to support the owners' territorial needs. Some temporal features of territories are flexible, in that window shades may be pulled and doors opened and closed or books placed on library tables to indicate desires for openness and closedness. But many more features of the territory are less changeable — housing styles are difficult and costly to alter, neighborhood traffic flows are stable, and walls are a constant thickness.

The stability of the territory may create dysfunctions when the owner undergoes a major change in identity but the territory remains stable. For example, a recently divorced couple is presented with a problem due to the inflexible nature of their territorial stability. Both members of the couple may desire to shed their old, intertwined identities but the house continues to reinforce their old identities as marriage partners. Changing the old territory or finding a new one will require tremendous amounts of time and effort. Similarly, individuals who relocate may regret having to relinquish their old territorial ties. Along these lines, it has been found that individuals who have clear plans for relocation also exhibit themes of *preparatory detachment* in cognitive maps of their current environment (Wolfsey, Rierdan, & Wapner, 1979). Thus future research needs to examine both the personal problems and the coping mechanisms that evolve when territorial contexts fail to change in synchrony with personal aspects of identity.

The stability of territories may also create problems at the societal level. The old allocation of territories may not accurately reflect new societal values, for example. New laws and social values may support equal opportunity while existing land use patterns conform more to old racist values. Or the spatial dimensions of the single-family home may be poorly adapted to many families' needs for space (cf. Hayden, 1981). The time required for the environment to catch up with changing social values may adversely affect certain groups in their attempts to control or identify with their territories.

13.6.4. Dysfunctional Territorial Identity

Territories may become dysfunctional when they communicate damaging information about the personal identity of the owner. Goffman (1963) noted that places can communicate stigmas, morally reprehensible aspects of identities. For example, a mental patient cannot hide the identity of the building in which he or she lives. Visitors cannot be prevented from acquiring this aspect of the individual's identity. Newman (1972) had the same observation of the design of most public housing projects. He noted that the typical institutional design of a public housing project makes its identity unmistakable. This has the effect of injuring the residents' pride and self-esteem and also communicates openness to criminal activity. Territories then may be dysfunctional when the owner cannot disguise damaging information about his or her financial circumstances or other undesired characteristics.

Territoriality theory can also help to illuminate some of these reasons why true identities may not be displayed in a territory. First, the individual may not feel enough security in a place to risk revealing to others important elements of the self. It is known that feelings of security increase from more public to more primary territories (Taylor & Stough, 1978). Given greater control and protections afforded by primary territories, it is likely that the most personally revealing expressions of the self will be created in settings where the owner has secure knowledge of who will be admitted and how they will behave.

In some circumstances, territories give off undesirable information even when the territory owner has complete control and choice over territorial appearances. For example, new college students may decorate their dormitory rooms in keeping with the style used back home. However, in a new environment with new potential friends, the decor may appear unsophisticated or unattractive. The students may come to realize that aspects of their identity may require change in order to fit in at college; meanwhile, the territory only serves to reinforce their lack of fit. These undesirable meanings may be communicated through territories either wittingly or unwit-

tingly. In Goffman's terms, impressions may be given or they may be given off, pointing to the role that a lack of awareness may play in territorial personalization.

13.6.5. Dysfunctional Territorial Commitments

Trade-offs among one's territories may create dysfunctions that affect one's time commitments or even one's identity. Some (Edney & Uhlig, 1977; Mithun, 1973) note that commitments must sometimes follow a hydraulic model whereby the time put into one territorial commitment lessens the time available for others. Thus limited time and energy can be invested in primary territories when the secondary ties in the neighborhood are very demanding. Edney and Uhlig (1977) suggested that the particular problem of investing in both group and individual territories is due to more than just scarce time resources. They speculated that a territorial investment in a group territory might lead to "a forfeiture of identity for the sake of group unity" (p. 458).

On the other hand, different territorial commitments may solidify attachments to a range of territories. For example Rivlin (1982) describes how the secondary territorial commitments within a Lubavitcher Jewish neighborhood complemented and strengthened the individual identities of members of the community. The identities supported in the primary territory of the home may grow stronger when supported by a congruent neighborhood identity. Thus commitments to different types of territories may have a synergetic effect when the demands across territories are congruent; different territorial commitments may become stressful when the demands across territories are incongruent.

13.6.6. Social Interactions and Territoriality

Finally, greater emphasis on the role of social functions is likely to highlight the implications territoriality holds for social interaction—including interactions between co-owners of a territory. Sharing a territory has been found to help foster a sense of security and identity and to be associated with lower risk of territorial intrusion for block territories (Brown, 1983). Yet researchers have not examined the processes involved in sharing territories. Of course, group members may solve the problem of sharing by carving out individual territories within the group territory. This territorial division has been found to take place within families (Laufer & Wolfe, 1977; Sebba &

Churchman, 1983) and between individuals who share rooms (Altman & Haythorn, 1975; Rosenblatt & Budd, 1975). However, the physical separations (walls, room dividers, etc.) that can be provided by territorial boundaries may not be available in the group setting. In those territorial groups, some other form of interaction regulation must evolve. Altman's privacy regulation theory would point to norms, rules, and personal spacing as likely sources of management within a territory. Other mechanisms would include dominance hierarchies, turn-taking norms, scheduling (Rapoport, 1975), or developing an interpersonally reserved style (Westin, 1970).

A second domain where research is needed involves the way in which territorial contexts shape social interactions with visitors themselves. Katovich (1986) found that territorial claims enter into role-played conversations between bosses and employees. Similarly, in the study of student dormitory territories it was suggested that personalizations might help to encourage certain types of social encounters and discourage others (Vinsel et al., 1980). However, it is not clear what general processes underlie the ways in which territorial claims facilitate or constrain interactions with co-owners, visitors, or intruders to the territory and how these interactions would differ if they took place in other territorial contexts.

Concepts of territoriality offered by sociologists Lyman and Scott (1967) may prove helpful in this area. Their definitions of territories, intrusions, and defenses are often referenced, but rarely used, within the psychological literature. They emphasize the ways in which social roles and statuses of territory owners affect the management of a territory. Consequently, Lyman and Scott's territorial encroachments involve disruptions of the social roles or statuses of the owners rather than the violation of spatial boundaries.

Similarly, their typology of territorial defenses downplays physically aggressive defenses in favor of defending social interactions and meanings. For example, *insulation*—the erection of a barrier to indicate that interaction is unwelcomed—might include wearing uniforms or sunglasses to convey inpenetrability symbolically. In the *linguistic collusion* defense the territory owners flaunt their territorial identities so clearly that any outsider will be made to feel unable to take over the territorial program. For example, professors may escalate their use of academic jargon to keep undergraduates at bay and blacks may play "the dozens" to communicate inaccessibility to whites. While these examples of interactional defenses of territories may enhance group identity and aid territorial organization, they have not received recognition within psychology as legitimate territorial regulators.

13.6.7. Identity Management

A uniquely human aspect of territoriality that deserves more attention is what biologists term *intraspecific deceit* (Dawkins & Krebs, 1978). Deceitful territorial displays are common interspecifically, for example, when insects elude predators by taking on the appearance of twigs. But intraspecific examples of deceit are rare because fake territorial signals must be indistinguishable from true territorial signals to be effective. Fake signals are often difficult to produce because many territorial signals correspond to the animal's true ability to protect a territorial claim. For example, deer may use roaring contests as signals of their intent to claim territories. Because their vocal pitch corresponds to their size, it is likely that the winners of a roaring contest are larger than the losers. Thus there is a veridical basis for the territorial signals.

In contrast, the notion of intraspecific deceit could have wide applicability to human territoriality, although it too is a neglected area of research. The concept of deceitful places has been described but not fully researched by the sociologist Goffman. He describes a *back region* as "a place, relative to a performance, where the impression fostered by the performance is knowingly contradicted as a matter of course" (1959, p. 112). Social psychologists also study a variety of ways in which individuals make strategic use of social behaviors such as impression management (Schlenker, 1980), ingratiation (Jones, 1964), self-monitoring (Snyder, 1979), and script-enactment (Zanna & Pack, 1975) to gain social goals. All of these processes may be used strategically with little or no correspondence between the actor's true feelings and identity. However, social psychologists typically study these processes without reference to the strategic use of the environment to develop or maintain certain impressions. Research within territoriality needs to be attuned to territorial sociability and impression management for a well-rounded understanding of human territoriality.

In sum, this chapter has argued that territoriality should expand past its biological origins. The behaviors that are involved in claiming spaces have received more attention than other important aspects of territoriality. Territoriality is more than just claiming and defending space; even biologists and anthropologists have started to abandon the original emphasis on demarcation and defense. Now the attention needs to shift to the positive benefits of territoriality for the psychological and social life, including its role in social interaction and identity maintenance.

In particular, future research needs to articulate the more "hidden" cognitive, affective, and social interactional features of territoriality. Primary territories afford the best opportunity to study the ways in which places become central to individuals and groups. It has been suggested that these territories serve cognitive functions by supporting memories and integrating cognitions. Expressive functions are served by territorial personalizations—important symbols that may strategically or actually communicate aspects of individual and group identities. Researchers should strive for more sophisticated assessments of the ways in which territories and their personalizations serve social and affective concerns. Similarly, concepts such as appropriation need to be investigated to discover how activities can cultivate affective and cognitive bonds. Finally, the ways in which territories enter into and guide social interactions deserve investigation.

REFERENCES

Allen, V.L., & Greenberger, D.B. (1980). Destruction and perceived control. In A. Baum & J.E. Singer (Eds.), *Advances in environmental psychology: Vol. 2. Applications of personal control* (pp. 85–109). Hillsdale, NJ: Erlbaum.

Altman, I. (1975). *Environment and social behavior: Privacy, personal space, territory and crowding.* Monterey, CA: Brooks/Cole.

Altman, I., & Chemers, M.M. (1980). *Culture and environment.* Monterey, CA: Brooks/Cole.

Altman, I. & Gauvain, M. (1981). A cross-cultural and dialectic analysis of homes. In L. Liben, A. Patterson, & N. Newcomb (Eds.), *Spatial representation and behavior across the life span: Theory and application.* New York: Academic.

Altman, I., & Haythorn, W.W. (1967). The ecology of isolated groups. *Behavioral Science, 12,* 168–182.

Altman, I., Nelson, P.A., & Lett, E.E. (1972). The ecology of home environments. *Catalog of Selected Documents in Psychology.* Washington, D.C.: American Psychological Association.

Altman, I., Taylor, D.A., & Wheeler, L. (1971). Ecological aspects of group behavior in social isolation. *Journal of Applied Social Psychology, 1,* 76–100.

Ardrey, R. (1966). *The territorial imperative.* New York: Atheneum.

Arenson, J. (1977). Reactions to invasions of marked seats at a racetrack. *Social Behavior and Personality, 5,* 225–228.

Arreola, D.D. (1981). Fences as landscape taste: Tucson's barrios. *Journal of Cultural Geography, 2,* 96–105.

Austin, W.T., & Bates, F.L. (1974). Ethological indicators of dominance and territory in a human captive population. *Social Forces, 52,* 447–455.

Bachelard, G. (1964). *The poetics of space.* New York: Orion.

Bakker, C.B., & Bakker-Rabdau, M.K. (1973). *No trespassing! Explorations in human territoriality.* San Francisco: Chandler and Sharp.

Barbey, G. (1982). The appropriation of home space. In P. Korosec-Serfaty (Ed.), *Appropriation of space* (pp. 215–217). Strasbourg, France: Louis Pasteur University.

Baum, A., Reiss, M., & O'Hara, J. (1974). Architectural variants of reaction to spatial invasion. *Environment and Behavior, 6,* 91–100.

Beck, R.J., & Teasdale, P. (1978). Dimensions of social lifestyle in multiple dwelling housing. In A. Esser & B.B. Greenbie (Eds.), *Design for communality and privacy* (Based on a workshop convened at the Sixth Annual Conference of the Environment Design Research Association, Lawrence, Kansas). New York: Plenum.

Becker, F.D. (1973). Study of spatial markers. *Journal of Personality and Social Psychology, 26,* 439–445.

Becker, F.D., & Coniglio, C. (1975). Environmental messages: Personalization and territory. *Humanitias, 11,* 55–74.

Becker, F.D., & Mayo, C. (1971). Delineating personal space and territoriality. *Environment and Behavior, 3,* 375–381.

Belk, R.W. (1982). *Acquisitiveness and possessiveness: Criticisms and issues.* Paper presented at the meeting of the Association for Consumer Research, San Francisco.

Blundell, V. (1983). Comments. *Current Anthropology, 24,* 58.

Brower, S. (1980). Territory in urban settings. In I. Altman, A. Rapoport, & J. Wohlwill (Eds.), *Human behavior and environment.* New York: Plenum.

Brown, B.B. (1983). *Territoriality, street form, and residential burglary: Social and environmental analyses.* Unpublished doctoral dissertation, University of Utah.

Brown, B.B., & Altman, I. (1981). Territoriality and residential crime: A conceptual framework. In P.J. Brantingham & P.L. Brantingham (Eds.), *Environmental criminology* (pp. 55–76). Beverly Hills, CA: Sage.

Brown, B.B., & Altman, I. (1983). Territoriality, street form, and residential burglary: An environmental analysis. *Journal of Environmental Psychology, 3,* 203–220.

Brown, B.B., & Werner, C.M. (1985). *Social cohesiveness, territoriality, and holiday decorations: The influence of cul-de-sacs. Environment and Behavior, 17,* 539–565.

Bush-Brown, L. (1969). *Garden blocks for urban America*. New York: Scribners.

Buttimer, A., & Seamon, D. (1980). *The human experience of space and place*. London: Croom Helm.

Calsyn, R. (1976). Group responses to territorial intrusion. *Journal of Social Psychology, 40*, 51–58.

Canter, D., West, S., & Wools, R. (1974). Judgements of people and their rooms. *British Journal of Social and Clinical Psychology, 13*, 113–118.

Cashdan, E. (1983). Territoriality among human foragers: Ecological models and an application to four bushman groups. *Current Anthropology, 24*, 47–66.

Cass, R., & Edney, J.J. (1978). The commons dilemma: A simulation testing the effects of resource visibility and territorial division. *Human Ecology, 6*, 371–386.

Cherulnik, P.D. (1982). Impressions of neighborhoods and their residents. *Proceedings of the 13th International Conference of the Environmental Design Research Associates, 13*, 416–423.

Cheyne, J.A., & Efran, M.G. (1972). The effect of spatial and interpersonal variables on the invasion of group controlled territories. *Sociometry, 35*, 477–489.

Conroy, J., & Sundstrom, E. (1977). Territorial dominance in a dyadic conversation as a function of similarity of opinion. *Journal of Personality and Social Psychology, 35*, 570–576.

Cooper, C. (1972). The house as a symbol of self. In J. Lang, C. Burnette, W. Moleski, & D. Vachon (Eds.), *Designing for human behavior: Architecture and the behavioral sciences*. Stroudsberg, PA: Dowden, Hutchinson, & Ross.

Craik, K. (1973). Environmental psychology. *Annual review of psychology, 24*, 403–422.

Craik, K. (1977). Multiple scientific paradigms in environmental psychology. *International Journal of Psychology, 12*, 147–157.

Csikszentmihalyi, M., & Rochberg-Halton, E. (1981). *The meaning of things*. New York: Cambridge University Press.

Davies, N.B. (1978). Ecological questions about territorial behavior. In J.R. Krebs & N.B. Davies (Eds.), *Behavioral ecology: An evolutionary approach*. Sunderland, MA: Sinauer.

Dawkins, R., & Krebs, J.R. (1978). Animal signals: Information on manipulation. In J.R. Krebs & N.B. Davies (Eds.), *Behavioral ecology*. (pp. 282–309). Sunderland, MA: Sinauer.

De Rivera, J. (1984). Emotional experience and qualitative methodology. *American Behavioral Scientist, 27*, 677–688.

Delong, A.J. (1970). Dominance-territorial relations in a small group. *Environment and Behavior, 2*, 190–191.

Delong, A.J. (1973). Territorial stability and hierarchical formation. *Small Group Behavior, 4*, 56–63.

Deutsch, R.D., Esser, A.H., & Sossin, K.M. (1978). Dominance, aggression, and the functional use of space in institutionalized female adolescents. *Aggressive Behavior, 4(4)*, 313–329.

Dovey, K. (in press). The quest for authenticity and the replication of environmental meaning. In D. Seamon & R. Mugerauer (Eds.), *Dwelling, place and environment.*. The Hague, Netherlands: Martinus Nijhof.

Duncan, J.S. (1973). Landscape taste as a symbol of group identity. *Geographical Review, 63*, 334–355.

Dyson-Hudson, R., & Smith, E.A. (1978). Human territoriality: An ecological reassessment. *American Anthropologist, 80*, 21–41.

Edney, J.J. (1974). Human territoriality. *Psychological Bulletin, 81*, 959–975.

Edney, J.J. (1975). Territoriality and control: A field experiment. *Journal of Personality and Social Psychology, 31*, 1108–1115.

Edney, J.J. (1976). Human territories: Comment on functional properties. *Environment and Behavior, 8*, 31–47.

Edney, J.J., & Buda, M.A. (1976). Distinguishing territoriality and privacy: Two studies. *Human Ecology, 4*, 283–295.

Edney, J.J., & Grundmann, M.J. (1979). Friendship, group size, and boundary size: Small group spaces. *Small Group Behavior, 10*, 124–135.

Edney, J.J., & Jordan-Edney, N.L. (1974). Territorial spacing on the beach. *Sociometry, 37*, 92–104.

Edney, J.J., & Uhlig, S.R. (1977). Individual and small group territories. *Small Group Behavior, 8*, 457–478.

Efran, M.G., & Cheyne, J.A. (1973). Shared space: The cooperative control of spatial areas by two interacting individuals. *Canadian Journal of Behavioral Science, 5*, 201–210.

Efran, M.G., & Cheyne, J.A. (1974). Affective concomitants of the invasion of shared space: Behavioral, physiological, and verbal indicators. *Journal of Personality and Social Psychology, 29*, 219–226.

Ehrenreich, J. (1983). Comments. *Current Anthropology, 24(1)*, 58–59.

Eibl-Eibesfeldt, I. (1970). *Ethology: The biology of behavior*. New York: Holt, Rinehart & Winston.

Eibl-Eibesfeldt, I. (1974). The myth of the aggression-free hunter and gatherer society. In R.L. Holloway (Ed.), *Primate aggression, territoriality, and xenophobia* (pp. 435–458). New York: Academic.

Esser, A.H. (1968). Dominance hierarchy and clinical course of psychiatrically hospitalized boys. *Child Development, 39*, 147–157.

Esser, A.H. (1973). Cottage fourteen. *Small Group Behavior, 4*, 131–146.

Esser, A.H., Chamberlain, A.S., Chapple, F.D., & Kline, N.S. (1965). Territoriality of patients on a research ward. In J. Wortis (Ed.), *Recent advances in behavioral psychiatry, 7*, 36–44.

Ferguson, G.W., Hughes, J.A., Brown, K.A. (1983). Food availability and territorial establishment of juvenile sceloporus undulatus. In R.B. Huey, E.R. Pianka, & T.W. Schroener (Eds.), *Lizard ecology: studies of a model organism* (pp. 134–148). Cambridge, MA: Harvard University Press.

Fischer, C.S., Jackson, R.M., Stueve, C.A., Gerson, K., Jones, L.M., & Baldassare, M. (1977). *Networks and places: Social relations in the urban setting.* New York: Free Press.

Fishbein, M., & Ajzen, I. (1975). *Belief, attitude, intention, and behavior: An introduction to theory and research.* Reading, MA: Addison-Wesley.

Freedman, D.G. (1979). *Human sociobiology.* New York: Free Press.

Furby, L. (1974). Socialization practices with respect to possession and ownership: A study using the Human Relations Area Files. *·Oregon Research Institute Research Bulletin, 14,* 20.

Furby, L. (1978). Possessions: Toward a theory of their meaning and function throughout the life cycle. In P.B. Baltes (Ed.), *Life span development and behavior* (Vol. 1, pp. 297–336). New York: Academic.

Furby, L. (1980). The origins and early development of possessive behavior. *Political Psychology, 2,* 30–42.

Furby, L. (1982). *Some aspects of possessive behavior during the second year of life.* Paper presented at the meeting of the Association for Consumer Research, San Francisco.

Galster, G.C., & Hesser, G.W. (1982). The social neighborhood: An unspecified factor in homeowner maintenance? *Urban Affairs Quarterly, 18,* 235–254.

Gauvain, M., Altman, I., & Fahim, H. (1983). Homes and social change: A cross-cultural analysis. In N.R. Feimer & E.S. Geller (Eds.), *Environmental psychology: Directions and perspectives.* New York: Praeger.

Godelier, M. (1979). Territory and property in primitive society. In M. von Cranach, K. Foppa, W. Lepenies, & D. Ploog (Eds.), *Human ethology.* Cambridge, England: Cambridge University Press.

Goffman, E. (1959). *The presentation of self in everyday life.* New York: Doubleday.

Goffman, E. (1963a). *Behavior in public places.* New York: Free Press.

Goffman, E. (1963b). *Stigma.* Englewood Cliffs, NJ: Prentice-Hall

Gold, J.R. (1982). Territoriality and human spatial behavior. *Progress in human geography, 6,* 44–67.

Greenbaum, P.E., & Greenbaum, S.D. (1981). Territorial personalization: Group identity and social interaction in a Slavic-American neighborhood. *Environment and Behavior, 13,* 574–589.

Haber, G.M. (1980). Territorial invasion in the classroom: Invadee response. *Environment and Behavior, 12,* 17–31.

Hall, E.T. (1959). *The silent language.* New York: Doubleday.

Harrington, M. (1965). Resettlement and self-image. *Human Relations, 18,* 115–137.

Hart, R. (1978). *Children's experience of place.* New York: Halstead.

Hayden, D. (1981). *The grand domestic revolution: A history of feminist designs for American homes.* Cambridge, MA: MIT Press.

Hayward, D.G. (1977, April). An overview of psychological concepts of "home." *Proceedings of the Meeting of the Environmental Design Research Association, 8,* 418–419.

Heidegger, M. (1971). *Poetry, language, and thought.* (Albert Hofstadter, Trans.). New York: Harper & Row.

Holahan, C. (1978). *Environment and behavior: A dynamic perspective.* New York: Plenum.

Hoppe, R.A., Greene, M.S., & Kenny, J.W. (1972). Territorial markers: Additional findings. *Journal of Social Psychology, 88,* 305–306.

Horwitz, J., & Tognoli, J. (1982). Role of home environment in adult women: Women and men living alone describe their residential histories. *Family Relations, 31,* 335–341.

Jones, E.E. (1964). *Ingratiation.* New York: Appleton-Century-Crofts.

Jones, E.E., & Davis, K. (1965). From acts to dispositions: The attribution process in person perception. In L. Berkowitz (Ed.), *Advances in experimental social psychology* (Vol. 2). New York: Academic.

Kasarda, J., & Janowitz, M. (1974). Community attachment in mass society. *American Sociological Review, 39,* 328–339.

Katovich, M. (1986). Ceremonial openings in bureaucratic encounters: From shuffling feet to shuffling papers. In N.K. Denzin (Ed.), *Studies in symbolic interaction* (Vol. 6). Greenwich, CT: JAI Press.

Kimber, C.T. (1973). Spatial patterning in the door yard gardens of Puerto Rico. *Geographical Review, 63,* 6–26.

Knowles, E.S. (1973). Boundaries around group interaction: The effect of group and member status on boundary permeability. *Journal of Personality and Social Psychology, 26,* 327–331.

Konar, E., Sundstrom, E., Brady, C., Mandel, D., & Rice, R.W. (1982). Status demarcation in the office. *Environment and Behavior, 14,* 561–580.

Korosec-Serfaty, P. (1985). Experiences and uses of the dwelling. In I. Altman & C.M. Werner (Eds.), *Home environments.* New York: Plenum.

Laufer, R.S., & Wolfe, M. (1977). Privacy as a concept and as a social issue: A multidimensional developmental theory. *Journal of Social Issues, 33,* 22–42.

Laumann, E.O., & House, J.S. (1972). Living room styles and social attributes: The patterning of material artifacts in a modern urban community. In E.O. Laumann, P.M. Sigel, & R.W. Hodges (Eds.), *The logic of social hierarchies* (pp. 189–203). Chicago: Markham.

Lavin, M.W. (1978, August). *Cognitive and nonverbal responses to boundaries of territorially controlled spaces.* Paper presented at the 86th annual meeting of the American Psychological Association, Toronto, Canada.

Lee, R.B. (1968). What hunters do for a living, or how to make out on scarce resources. In R.B. Lee & I. DeVore (Eds.), *Man the hunter* (pp. 30–48). Chicago: Aldine.

Lewis, C.A. (1979). Comment: Healing in the urban environment. *Journal of the American Institute of Planners, 45,* 330–338.

Ley, D., & Cybriwsky, R. (1974). The spatial ecology of stripped cars. *Environment and Behavior, 6,* 53–68.

Lindskold, S., Albert, K.P., Baer, R., & Moore, W.C. (1976). Territorial boundaries of interacting groups and passive audiences. *Sociometry, 39,* 71–76.

Litwak, E., & Szelenyi, I. (1969). Primary group structures and their functions: Kin, neighbors, and friends. *American Sociological Review, 34,* 465–481.

Lyman, S.M., & Scott, M.B. (1967). Territoriality: A neglected sociological dimension. *Social Problems, 15,* 236–249.

Malmberg, T. (1980). *Human territoriality.* New York: Mouton.

Malthus, T.R. (1836). *Principles of political economy.* London: Kelley.

Martindale, D.A. (1971). Territorial dominance behavior in dyadic verbal interaction. *Proceedings of the 79th Annual Convention of the American Psychological Association, 6,* 306.

Maslow, A., & Mintz, M. (1956). Effects of aesthetic surroundings: I. Initial effects of three aesthetic conditions upon perceiving "energy" and "well being" in faces. *Journal of Psychology, 41,* 247–254.

McAndrew, F.T., Ryckman, R.M., Horr, W., & Solomon, R. (1978). The effects of invader placement of spatial markers on territorial behavior in a college population. *Journal of Social Psychology, 104,* 149–150.

Mehrabian, A., & Diamond, S.G. (1971). Effects of furniture arrangement, props, and personality on social interaction. *Journal of Personality and Social Psychology, 20,* 18–30.

Mercer, G.W., & Benjamin, M.L. (1980). Spatial behavior of university undergraduates in double-occupancy residence rooms: An inventory of effects. *Journal of Applied Social Psychology, 10,* 32–44.

Mintz, H. (1956). Effects of aesthetic surroundings: II. Prolonged and repeated experience in a "beautiful" and an "ugly" room. *Journal of Psychology, 41,* 459–466.

Mithun, J.S. (1973). Cooperation and solidarity as survival necessities in a black urban community. *Urban Anthropology, 2,* 247–259.

Moore, J., Vigil, D., & Garcia, R. (1983). Residence and territoriality in Chicano gangs. *Social Problems, 31,* 182–194.

Newman, O. (1972). *Defensible space: Crime prevention through urban design.* New York: Macmillan.

Pablant, P., & Baxter, J.C. (1975). Environmental correlates of school vandalism. *Journal of the American Institute of Planners, 41,* 270–279.

Pastalan, L.A. (1970). Privacy as an expression of human territoriality. In L.A. Pastalan & D.H. Carson (Eds.), *Spatial behavior of older people.* Ann Arbor: University of Michigan.

Pratt, G. (1982). The house as expression of social worlds. In J.S. Duncan (Ed.), *Housing and identity: Cross-cultural perspectives.* New York: Holmes & Meier.

Proshansky, H.M., Fabian, A.K., & Kaminoff, R. (1983). Place identity: Physical world socialization of the self. *Journal of Environmental Psychology, 3,* 57–83.

Rapoport, A. (1969). *House form and culture.* Englewood Cliffs, NJ: Prentice-Hall.

Rapoport, A. (1975). Towards a redefinition of density. *Environment and Behavior, 7,* 133–158.

Relph, E. (1976). *Place and placelessness.* London: Pion.

Riger, S., & Lavrakas, P. (1981). Community ties: Patterns of attachment and social interaction in urban neighborhoods. *American Journal of Community Psychology, 9,* 55–66.

Rivlin, L.G. (1982). Group membership and place meanings in an urban neighborhood. *Journal of Social Issues, 38,* 75–93.

Rosenblatt, P.C., & Budd, L.G. (1975). Territoriality and privacy in married and unmarried cohabiting couples. *Journal of Social Psychology, 97,* 67–76.

Rowles, G. (1978). *Prisoners of space?* Boulder, CO: Westview.

Rowles, G.D. (1980). Growing old "inside": Aging and attachment to place in an Appalachian community. In N. Datan & N. Lohmann (Eds.), *Transition of aging* (pp. 153–172). New York: Academic.

Russell, J.A., & Ward, L.M. (1982). Environmental psychology. *Annual Review of Psychology, 33,* 651–688.

Sack, R.D. (1983). Human territoriality: A theory. *Annals of the Association of American Geographers, 73,* 55–74.

Sadalla, E.K., Burroughs, J., & Quaid, M. (1980). House form and social identity. In R. Stough (Ed.), *Proceedings of the 11th International Meeting of the Environmental Design Research Association, 11,* 201–206.

Saegert, S., & Winkel, G. (1980). The home: A critical problem for changing sex roles. In G. Wekerle, R. Peterson, & D. Morley (Eds.), *New space for women.* Boulder, CO: Westview.

Schlenker, B.R. (1980). *Impression management: The self-concept, social identity, and interpersonal relations.* Monterey, CA: Brooks/Cole.

Schumacher, E.F. (1973). *Small is beautiful: Economics as if people mattered.* New York: Harper & Row.

Schwartz, B., & Barsky, S.F. (1977). The home court advantage. *Social Forces, 55,* 641–661.

Seamon, D. (1979). *A geography of the lifeworld.* London: Croom Helm.

Sebba, R., & Churchman, A. (1983). Territories and territoriality in the home. *Environment and Behavior, 15,* 191–210.

Shaffer, D.R., & Sadowski, C. (1975). This table is mine: Respect for marked barroom tables as a function of gender of spatial marker and desirability of locale. *Sociometry, 38,* 408–419.

Smith, H.W. (1983). Estimated crowding capacity, time, and territorial markers: A cross-national test. *Sociological Inquiry, 53,* 95–99.

Smith, R.A. (1975). Measuring neighborhood cohesion: A review and some suggestions. *Human Ecology, 3,* 143–160.

Snyder, M. (1979). Self-monitoring processes. In L. Berkowitz (Ed.), *Advances in experimental social psychology* (Vol. 12, pp. 85–128). New York: Academic.

Sommer, R. (1967). Sociofugal space. *American Journal of Sociology, 72,* 654–659.

Sommer, R., & Becker, F.D. (1969). Territorial defense and the good neighbor. *Journal of Personality and Social Psychology, 11,* 85–92.

Sossin, K.M., Esser, A., & Duetsch, R.D. (1978). Ethological studies of spatial and dominance behavior of female adolescents in residence. *Man-Environment Systems, 8,* 43–48.

Stokols, D. (1978). Environmental psychology. *Annual Review of Psychology, 29,* 253–295.

Stokols, D. (1981). Group × place transactions: Some neglected issues in psychological research on settings. In D. Magnusson (Ed.), *Toward a psychology of situations: An interactional perspective* (pp. 393–415). Hillsdale, NJ: Erlbaum.

Stokols, D., & Jacobi, M. (1984). Traditional, present oriented, and futuristic modes of group-environment relations. In K. Gergen & M.M. Gergen (Eds.), *Historical social psychology.* Hillsdale, NJ: Erlbaum.

Stokols, D., & Shumaker, S.A. (1981). People in places: A transactional view of settings. In J. Harvey (Ed.), *Cognition, social behavior, and the environment* (pp. 441–488). Hillsdale, NJ: Erlbaum.

Stokols, D., Shumaker, S.A., & Martinez, J. (1983). Residential mobility and personal well-being. *Journal of Environmental Psychology, 3,* 5–19.

Sundstrom, E., & Altman, I. (1974) Field study of territorial behavior and dominance. *Journal of Personality and Social Psychology, 30,* 115–124.

Suttles, G.D. (1968). *The social order of the slum: Ethnicity and territory in the inner city.* Chicago: University of Chicago Press.

Suttles, G.D. (1972). *The social construction of communities.* Chicago: University of Chicago Press.

Taylor, R.B., & Ferguson, G. (1980). Solitude and intimacy: Linking territoriality and privacy experiences. *Journal of Nonverbal Behavior, 4,* 227–239.

Taylor, R.B., & Brooks, D.K. (1980). Temporary territories?: Responses to intrusions in a public setting. *Population and Environment, 3,* 135–143.

Taylor, R.B., Gottfredson, S.D., & Brower, S. (1981). Territorial cognitions and social climate in urban neighborhoods. *Basic and Applied Social Psychology, 2,* 289–303.

Taylor, R.B., & Lanni, J.C. (1981). Territorial dominance: The influence of the resident advantage in triadic decision making. *Journal of Personality and Social Psychology, 41,* 909–915.

Taylor, R.B., & Stough, R. (1978). Territorial cognition: Assessing Altman's typology. *Journal of Personality and Social Psychology, 36,* 418–423.

Tognoli, J. (1980). Differences in women's and men's responses to domestic space. *Sex Roles, 6,* 833–842.

Trigham, R. (1972). Territorial demarcation of prehistoric settlements. In P.J. Ucko (Ed.), *Man, settlement, and urbanism* (pp. 463–475). London: Duckworth.

Truscott, J.C., Parmelee, P., & Werner, C. (1977). Plate touching in restaurants: Preliminary observations of a food-related marking behavior in humans. *Personality and Social Psychology Bulletin, 3,* 425–428.

Tuan, I.F. (1974). *Topophilia.* Englewood Cliffs, NJ: Prentice-Hall.

Tuan, Y. (1980). The significance of artifact. *Geographical Review, 70,* 462–472.

Van Den Berghe, P.L. (1974). Bringing beasts back in: Toward a biosocial theory of aggression. *American Sociological Review, 39,* 777–788.

Vinsel, A., Brown, B.B., Altman, I., & Foss, C. (1980). Privacy regulation, territorial displays, and effectiveness of individual functioning. *Journal of Personality and Social Psychology, 39,* 1104–1115.

Weisner, T.S., & Weibel, J.C. (1981). Home environment and lifestyles in California. *Environment and Behavior, 13,* 417–460.

Werner, C.M., Brown, B.B., & Damron, G. (1981). Territorial marking in the game arcade. *Journal of Personality and Social Psychology, 41,* 1094–1104.

Westin, A. (1970). *Privacy and freedom.* New York: Atheneum.

Wilson, E.O. (1975). *Sociobiology.* Cambridge, MA: Harvard University Press.

Wolfsey, E., Rierdan, J., & Wapner, S. (1979). Planning to move: Effects on representing the currently inhabited environment. *Environment and Behavior, 11,* 3–32.

Worchel, S., & Lollis, M. (1982). Reactions to territorial contamination as a function of culture. *Personality and Social Psychology Bulletin, 8,* 370–375.

Zanna, M.P., & Pack, S.J. (1975). On the self-fulfilling nature of apparent sex differences in behavior. *Journal of Experimental Social Psychology, 11,* 583–591.

Chapter 14

CROWDING

Andrew Baum, *Department of Psychology, Uniformed Services University of the Health Sciences, Bethesda, Maryland*

Paul B. Paulus, *Department of Psychology, University of Texas at Arlington, Arlington, Texas*

Although we have only recently become sensitized to a broad range of environmental problems such as pollution, toxic waste, and noise, concern about overpopulation and crowding has been part of the general public awareness for a relatively long time. Most of us are familiar with Malthus's warning about the danger of overpopulation in terms of natural resources or food supply. In more contemporary times, a number of scientists have expressed concern for the dangers of overpopulation and crowding (e.g., Calhoun, 1970; Ehrlich & Ehrlich, 1970; Zlutnick & Altman, 1972). Physical density and crowding-related phenomena have been implicated in the development of a variety of societal ills such as deteriorating quality of life in cities, crime, and the breakdown of families (cf. Zlutnick & Altman, 1972). Despite this, by the late 1960s and early 1970s, only a few attempts had been made systematically to examine the

physical, psychological, and social impact of crowding, and the differences between density and crowding were only vaguely recognized. Since then, however, there has been an explosion of research and
theorizing on this topic, and our understanding has
expanded dramatically. We will not attempt to review
all of this work since fairly extensive reviews already
exist (cf. Stockdale, 1978; Sundstrom, 1978). Instead we will attempt to sift through this literature
for empirical and theoretical consistencies in order to
provide the reader with a clear understanding of the
nature of crowding phenomena.

Modern research on crowding can be classified
into three genres. The first is concerned with animal
behavior, examining the effects of increasing population density on groups of animals. In these studies,
physical conditions of density and experiential aspects of crowding were equated, and explanations for
effects were necessarily inferences about observed
behaviors and their causes. As interest shifted to
relationships between crowding and human behavior,
a number of correlational studies of urban density
and social pathology appeared. Again, the terms *density* and *crowding* were used interchangeably, and
method-based limitations on causal inferences created problems in interpreting findings. Interest in
psychological processes underlying crowding led to a
third approach, emphasizing experimental control and
manipulation of relevant variables. *Density* and *crowding* meant different things, but because much of this
work was done in laboratories, findings were interpreted cautiously.

There is a rough historical progression to these
developments, as research on animals generally preceded work with humans, and so on. However, the
chronology of this progression is not absolute;
studies of human response to high-density cities
were conducted before systematic work with animals
had begun (e.g., Park, Burgess, & McKenzie,
1925), and animal research continues today. However, as a description of changes in the central focus
of research activity, this progression is fairly accurate
and allows one to evaluate individual studies in the
context of the prevailing research ethos of the
period. Most research reported since 1970, for example, was conducted in controlled settings (usually
laboratories) with human subjects and included
examination of various mediating variables (e.g., gender, social conditions). Much of the research reported prior to 1970, on the other hand, was based
either on animal studies or on archival or survey-
based analysis of census data and indicators of
pathology.

14.1. BASIC ISSUES

Marking the transition between these stages of
crowding research and a third approach that emphasized experimental manipulation of crowding and
density were Stokols's thoughtful analyses of crowding in the early 1970s (e.g., Stokols, 1972). He distinguished between the physical condition of density
(the number of people in a given space) and the subjective experience of crowding. Density was described as a necessary but not sufficient condition for
the experience of crowding, and a variety of situational and psychological factors that could affect this
relationship were identified. Where early research
was primarily concerned with demonstration of the
potential pathological consequences of crowding, the
research that followed focused on the importance of
mediating variables such as social structure, architectural properties of the setting, group composition,
privacy, and so on. By studying human response to
controlled variations in density and by examining subjective as well as physical aspects of these variations,
more confident causal conclusions were drawn.

In this chapter, then, *density* refers to physical
conditions associated with numbers of people in
given amounts of space. *Crowding*, on the other
hand, refers to an experience—the outcome of appraisal of physical conditions, situational variables,
personal characteristics, and coping assets. Under
some conditions and for some people, a given level of
density in a setting will lead to crowding, while in
other conditions or for other people, it may not. In
much the same way as people evaluate and interpret
stressors (Lazarus, 1966), crowding is an outcome of
evaluation of *settings*. Density is only one of several
aspects of settings that appear to determine the outcomes of these appraisals. In Figure 14.1, we have
depicted density as a discrete input into appraisal because of its central role in crowding judgments. As
Stokols (1972) suggested, density is probably necessary but insufficient by itself to elicit the experience
of crowding.

Elaborations on the concept of density followed
Stokols's distinction, and, despite the unitary nature
of density (the ratio of people to space), several
types of density have been identified. The most basic
of these typologies referred to the different ways of
increasing density. One can increase the number of
people without changing the amount of space they
occupy, shrink the space that a constant-sized group
uses, or both. Varying group size with the amount of
space held constant is called *social density*, while
changing space while holding group size constant is

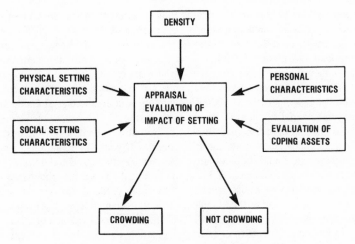

Figure 14.1. Crowding as an appraisal of density.

referred to as *spatial density* (Loo, 1972; McGrew, 1970; Zlutnick & Altman, 1972). These differences were initially used to distinguish between procedural aspects of studies on crowding and, as we will see later, have come to reflect the prominent aspects of the experience of crowding.

In addition to making this basic distinction between social and spatial density, researchers have confirmed the importance of the context in which density occurs. For example, Galle, Gove, and McPherson (1972) examined the relationships between physical density and various pathologies but broke density down into location-based categories reflecting density on an individual apartment level (e.g., people per room) and on a larger scale (e.g., structures per acre). This kind of distinction between locally occurring density and more remote "overall" density allowed Galle and colleagues to obtain a more fine-grained view of the dynamics that they were studying. A similar distinction was made between density in primary and density in secondary environments (Stokols, 1976; Zlutnick & Altman, 1972). For example, Zlutnick and Altman define *inside density* as the density in one's primary area of functioning (e.g., home or classroom). *Outside density* is defined as the density in secondary areas such as the community, school, or shopping center. Stokols (1976) suggests that crowding in primary environments may have more significant effects on the individual than crowding in secondary ones, possibly because it is more difficult to avoid.

These treatments of the density construct are not inconsistent with our earlier discussion of appraisal of setting characteristics. Inherent in both the nature of density and the nature of settings are a number of possible outcomes.

The degree to which any one of these outcomes is appraised as real or likely depends on the interaction of setting characteristics. The differences between primary and secondary environments interact with density to produce outcomes; if this interaction leads to the decision that negative outcomes are likely, crowding will probably be experienced.

Several other issues could be discussed here, but they are best examined after consideration of the crowding literature. At times throughout the remainder of the chapter we will refer to distinctions between density and crowding, but at this point we will turn our attention away from conceptual issues. We will summarize research findings for both humans and animals, following the organization suggested by the phases of research described at the outset. First, we will consider work with animal populations, including the uses and limitations of these studies. Next, we will turn to those studies reporting correlations between human density and pathology, again noting strengths and weaknesses. Experimental and quasi-experimental research will be discussed in the third and fourth sections, and the importance of this work will be considered in the context of methodological limitations of the approach. Finally, emerging theoretical perspectives will be reviewed and evaluated.

14.2. POPULATION DENSITY AND ANIMAL BEHAVIOR

As is the case with many topics, the modern study of crowding began with investigations of animal behavior. Among the many reasons for this are the relative ease of housing animals in large numbers for long periods of time, and the ability to select animal subjects to minimize genetic or background differences. However, there are a number of limitations to this approach as well. One can never know how animals feel in a given situation, but can only infer this from their behavior. For this reason, animal studies are best thought of as studies of the effects of density rather than of an experience as is indicated by crowding. It is also difficult to determine the implications of animal research when considering humans. While physiological response patterns may be similar across species, the intensity of response and of the stimuli required to evoke it often vary. Nevertheless, research on animals can allow investigators to answer questions not readily addressed within the bounds of ethical human research. Results of studies of animals can provide a useful empirical and theoretical context for evaluating studies of human response to crowding.

14.2.1. Social Stress Among Animals

Christian's (1963) research has suggested that density acts as a stressor in animals and that its effects are mediated by endocrine response. Animals exposed to high physical densities were observed to suffer from several different physiological syndromes, including kidney damage, sterility, reproductive dysfunction, and reduced resistance to infectious disease. These kinds of effects have been associated with stress and the endocrine system's activity during stress (e.g., Baum, Singer, & Baum, 1981).

In one study, Christian (1963) described the growth of a herd of deer on an island in the Chesapeake Bay. The island, cut off from the mainland, provided a limited amount of space and a finite resource base for expansion of the herd. It also prevented unlimited growth and division of the herd; eventually, deer could not leave a dense area and start a new group in a less dense place. The herd grew steadily, but suffered a massive die-off. Autopsies on the deer that died revealed that their adrenal glands were greatly enlarged. The adrenals are primary organs in the endocrine system's role in stress, and hypertrophy (enlargement) of the adrenals is a common result of prolonged stress (e.g., Selye, 1976).

Christian and Davis (1964) explained these findings in terms of social pressure—the stress caused by the presence of too many animals. This stress stimulated secretion of corticosteroids—hormones released by the adrenal cortex. The elevation of these hormones in the bloodstream was believed to be a cause of the physiological breakdown that was observed. These breakdowns, in turn, contributed to the death of many of the deer, and the rapid decrease in herd size relieved the social pressures causing stress. Thus after the death of a sufficient number of deer, the die-off ended and the herd size stabilized.

This severe kind of response to crowding is not common to human populations. Some would have it that war, pestilence, and the like are forms of population control—when the population of the earth becomes too great, a war or great blight helps to reduce the population (e.g., Booth & Welch, 1973). There is no good evidence of this as a mechanism of population control, but it is clear that these pressures play some role. Why do animal populations appear to be more susceptible to this kind of die-off than are human populations?

To some extent this may be due to the relatively limited adaptive abilities of nonhuman subjects or to the more concentrated densities to which animals may be exposed. What is more important, reasons for the dysfunction observed in high-density animal populations could be considered. While reproductive problems, overactive adrenal glands, cannibalism, homosexuality, withdrawal, or massive die-offs may appear pathological at the individual level, they could be adaptive at the group or species level. Population crashes, retardation of maturational processes, and social abnormalities, for example, may reflect regulatory mechanisms that serve as a check on population size or density. When density is in an optimal range for a given species, the concentration of animals is ideal for survival of the group. When it is too low, increased reproductivity may reflect a way of readjusting density upward toward the optimal level. Death and precipitous drops in reproduction may readjust density downward and facilitate survival of the remaining animals when population density climbs above the optimum.

14.2.2. Crowding and the Social Use of Space

A somewhat more elaborate description of high-density animal populations has been provided by Calhoun's classic series of studies of crowded rodent populations (e.g., Calhoun, 1957, 1962, 1970, 1973; Marsden, 1972). In an initial study, Calhoun observed a group of wild rats housed in an outdoor 1/4-acre enclosure. The "colony" was protected from predators and disease, and abundant food, water, nesting materials, and other necessities were provided. As a result, the rats should have been able to multiply and increase their number to about 5000. Instead, the population leveled off after 2-1/2 years at about 150 animals. The reason that the population size never reached its potential, according to Calhoun (1962), was an extremely high rate of infant mortality. As Calhoun concludes, "Even with only 150 adults in the enclosure, stress from social interaction led to such disruption of maternal behavior that few young survived" (p. 147). In other words, the projected capacity of the enclosure was never reached because the problems associated with too many animals led to death of young rats, maintaining a relatively stable group size.

This observation led Calhoun to attempt a series of experimental studies. The basic design for the initial studies was straightforward: Healthy rats, just past weaning, were placed into specially designed enclosures and were observed. Each group was equally male and female, and the rats were again allowed to multiply and increase their number. This time, however, Calhoun artificially suppressed maximum population size—by removing infants that had survived weaning, he kept the population in the enclosures at 80 adult animals.

The enclosures were designed to have four separate areas within them. Each of the four pens created by the internal partitions was a complete living unit. The total number that would normally live comfortably in each quadrant was 12 adult animals, and at the stabilized population of 80 animals we would expect to see 20 in each pen. The design of the pens, however, was intended to prevent homogeneous densities. The two lower pens were connected to other pens on both sides, while the upper pens had only a single entrance. By isolating the upper pens from one another (there was no way to go from one to the other), Calhoun created two end pens and two middle pens. In order to go from one upper pen to another, animals had to make a complete circuit through the four quadrants of the enclosure.

In most of the studies, the rats congregated in the center pens, leaving the end pens relatively empty. One reason for this was dominance struggles among male rats. When male rats reach the age of about 6 months, they begin fighting. This combat, which rarely ends in death or serious injury, eventually determines each male's position in the hierarchy of the group. And, although these fights were observed in all four quadrants of the enclosure, Calhoun observed that it was possible for a single male rat to control or dominate an end pen and claim it for his territory. This was due largely to the single ramp providing access to and from each end pen. By preventing other males from entering or returning to the end pens, a dominant male rat was able to defend each and selectively allow females to use it. The result was a sparsely populated pen (the male and his "harem"). As Calhoun noted, the defense of this space became very important:

> Once a male had established his dominion over an end pen and the harem it contained, he was usually able to maintain it. Although he slept a good deal of the time, he made his sleeping quarters at the base of the ramp. He was, therefore, on perpetual guard. (1962, p. 7)

This situation forced a large number of male rats into the two middle pens. While one group in an end pen might consist of 1 male and 7 females, a group in a middle pen was likely to consist of 20 males and 10 females. Population density varied across pens, and Calhoun began to note the development of pathology in the crowded middle pens. Among males, behavior disturbances ranged from sexual deviation to cannibalism, from hyperactivity to withdrawal. Yet these problems were not as pronounced as were those among females.

The problems experienced by these females focused on reproduction and maternal behavior. Many were unable to carry pregnancy to delivery of the young, and many infants did not survive birth. Most common, however, was a failure of normal maternal behavior—care of the newborn rats. The pregnancy rates for middle-pen females were comparable to those for rats in the end pens, but a smaller percentage of middle-pen pregnancies resulted in live births. In addition, fewer young rats survived past weaning in the middle pens. In two studies, Calhoun reported that 80 to 90% of the animals born in the middle pens died before weaning.

Calhoun believed that much of the disturbance generated in the middle pens was related to the development of *behavioral sinks*. He defined these sinks as a congregation of unusually large numbers of animals. He considered this nonuniform distribution of animals to be pathological: "The unhealthy connotations of the term [*behavioral sink*] are not accidental: A behavioral sink does get to aggravate all forms of pathology that can be found within a group" (1962, p. 7).

The basis for the severe effects in these sinks, according to Calhoun, was the social interaction required by such an arrangement. As the number of animals in any pen increased, the frequency of interaction among them also increased. As we shall see, excessive or unwanted interaction is related to stress, and Calhoun argued that these problems were at the root of the pathology that he observed. As Calhoun concluded, "Regardless of which pen a rat slept in, it would go to one particular middle pen several times a day to eat. Therefore it was compelled daily to make some sort of adjustment to virtually every other rat in the experimental population" (1962, p. 7).

Optimal Group Size

By 1970, Calhoun had elaborated on these observations, postulating that stress resulted from the growth of a group beyond its ideal or most healthy size. He believed that there was a certain number of daily interactions that ensured a balance between social gratification and frustration. If the number of interactions exceeded this number, the balance was upset and the social experience of each animal became more frustrating and unsuccessful. When this persisted over long periods of time, physiological and psychological aberrations occurred.

Under normal conditions, groups of animals increase in size until the number of adults exceeds the optimum—that point at which frustrating and gratifying social contacts are balanced. At this point, the group splits and one new group leaves and finds a different place in which to live. In the enclosures that Calhoun observed, this quickly became impossible, since there was no empty place for new groups to go. The result, he argued, was the extreme pathology that he reported.

In a more recent study of mice, Calhoun (1973) demonstrated the catastrophic effects of unchecked population growth. In this study a large enclosure was built for a colony of mice. Adequate resources (e.g., food, water, nesting material) were provided, and there was protection from predators, extreme weather, and disease. Based on expectations of mice and their needs, there was sufficient food for 9500 animals, sufficient water for 6144, and sufficient nesting areas for almost 4000. These levels were never reached; at the colony's peak size, nearly 20% of the nesting areas were unused.

The population of mice in this study was allowed to grow unchecked. Originally, four pairs of mice were placed in the enclosure. By day 315 of the study, there were 620 mice. By day 500, the population had reached 2200. This proved to be its peak: after this, the population size began to decrease. Once again, successful reproduction slowed and pathology emerged. Some animals became withdrawn while others became aggressive. The latter was evident primarily among females in nesting areas and was often inappropriate. In some cases, females attacked their young, forcing them to leave the nest before weaning. Other aspects of normal maternal behavior also broke down and infant mortality increased greatly. Gradually the population declined. By day 811, there were 1871 mice, by day 965, there were 1650, and on or about day 1660, the last surviving mouse died. The colony could not reverse itself—the last successful birth was recorded around day 600, and the failure to reproduce persisted until the very end.

Calhoun and his associates witnessed the extinction of a once viable group of animals. And it was not caused by predation, climatic shift, or the like. It was caused, he believed, by crowding.

14.2.3. Additional Findings

Calhoun's work has been central to the continued study of the effects of high density in animal populations. Few, however, have attempted studies of the scale that Calhoun accomplished. The severe pathologies that Calhoun reported have similarly not been the focus of these investigations. For example, Southwick (1967) found an increase in aggression among monkeys exposed to increasingly high density. Other studies have found density-related withdrawal among monkeys (e.g., Anderson, Erwin, Flynn, Lewis, & Erwin, 1977), and Calhoun's findings of reproductive failure have been supported (Chapman, Masterpasqua, & Lore, 1976; Dahlof, Hard, & Larsson, 1977). There is also some evidence that density affects animals' ability to learn. Goeckner, Greenough, and Maier (1974) reported that rats raised under crowded conditions showed poorer performance on complex tasks than did rats raised alone or in small groups. Bell, Miller, Ordy, and Rolsten (1971) found decreased exploratory behavior among animals housed in large groups relative to those living in smaller groups.

A great deal of research has been directed at health consequences to animals in high-density settings. Dubos (1965) suggests that high-density facilitates the transfer of infection by increasing the probability of contact with animals who have contagious illness and by moderating response to these pathogens when they are encountered. Crowding is associated with increased corticosteroid secretion (recall Christian's [1963] discussion of this) that can suppress immunological functioning and reduce resistance to infection. He reported evidence of this from a study of mice infected with Trichinella. Mice caged together developed more intestinal worms than mice kept in isolation. Since all animals were exposed to the same risk, these results suggested that being caged together reduced resistance to the disease. While it is possible that isolation strengthened immune response rather than the other way around, Dubos concluded that the effect of crowding on tissue response accounted for the decrease in resistance to infection.

Dubos's logic is consistent with studies of the effects of high density on animals' susceptibility to infection or parasitic invasion (e.g., Brayton & Brain, 1974). One study found differences in antibody response between very large and small groups of animals (Edwards & Dean, 1977). Dubos's contentions are limited, however, by results of another study that he reports, in which isolated mice were less resistant than were grouped mice to gastrointestinal disturbances caused by antimicrobial drugs. Thus while Dubos placed greater emphasis on reporting that crowding may affect diverse physiological systems, he also concluded that isolation of laboratory animals can arouse fear and decrease ability to adapt to problems such as cold stressors and food restriction or selection. These findings are not necessarily contradictory, however. They may reflect the fact that there is an ideal range of density, and that deviations above or below this range may lead to illness. This is consistent with depictions of crowding and isolation in human populations (e.g., Altman, 1976).

Additional research suggests that high density is associated with organ damage among animals (Myers, Hale, Mykytowycz, & Hughes, 1971). Several studies conducted by Henry and his associates (e.g., Henry, Meehan, & Stephens, 1967; Henry, Stephens, Axelrod, & Mueller, 1971) indicate that density may cause increases in blood pressure among animals. In one study, Henry and his associates (1967) manipulated density, group composition, and a number of other variables to study the development of hypertension in mice. Stable social organization was associated with lower blood pressure. Mixing of groups in limited space led to aggressive behavior and a sharp elevation in blood pressure. Aggression and increased blood pressure were associated with the pairing of adult male mice under conditions of high spatial density.

In this study, density may have indirectly caused blood pressure change. For example, spatial density may have caused aggressive response, which may in turn have been related to blood pressure. Another study (Henry & Stephens, 1977) compared densely housed mice with mice caged with approximately three times as much space and reported blood pressure differences approaching 20 mm Hg. However, low-density groups were composed of siblings while high-density groups were not, limiting any conclusions about density and blood pressure.

14.2.4. Relevance of Animal Research

Despite the usefulness of research on animal populations for its "own sake," an inevitable question is the extent to which findings with animals will generalize to human populations. As will become apparent, the effects of density on humans have not been nearly as severe as those observed among animals. There are a number of possible explanations of this. The most frequently invoked explanation is that humans are far better at coping than are most animals (Baron & Needel, 1980; Freedman, 1979).

A number of animal species, with humans among them, are able to modify their environment directly by hoarding food, building shelters, and so on. The ability of humans to modify their environment would suggest that many of the species-wide biological triggers common among animals are of less value in humans and may have been selected out of the gene pool. Changes in food and water availability do not appear to necessitate population crashes among humans as long as storage of food and water and agricultural exchange flourish. During increases in population density, our intellectual skills allow us to restructure our environments and to reduce the number of interactions or the press of other people (e.g., Calhoun, 1970). Symbolic thought processes and learning play a predominant role in regulating the extent to which stress reactions occur in humans (Lazarus, 1966). Cognitive processes combine with physiological response to determine the intensity and quality of emotional response and directly regulate the extent of subsequent changes accompanying the stress response (Lazarus, 1977; Mason, 1975).

Evidence that appraisal of threat by cognitive processes is involved in the initiation of the body's stress response is reported by Symington, Currie, Curran, and Davidson (1955). Their research indicated that the adrenal glands of patients dying of cancer who remained conscious during the terminal phase of their illness showed marked adrenal pathologies, while those of patients who remained in a coma during the terminal phase of their illness showed normal functioning. Thus the stress response appeared to be at least partly controlled by cognitive functioning.

The results of animal studies are not simply and directly applicable to human research. One might expect to see greater similarities in physiological changes between animals and those members of human populations whose ability to cope with environmental stressors breaks down and becomes ineffective. As a stressor, high density should have some effects on behavior, health, and well-being. But the extent and strength of these effects will be limited by the rather advanced adaptive abilities that most people possess.

On a more positive note it should be mentioned that there exist many similarities among the findings of humans and those of animals (cf. Freedman, 1979). For example, the deleterious effects of exposure to high numbers of interactions are evident from both types of research (cf. Baum & Valins, 1979; Calhoun, 1962). Similarly social structure seems to affect response to high density in both animals (cf. Lobb & McCain, 1978) and humans (e.g., Reddy, Baum, Fleming, & Aiello, 1981; Schopler & Walton, 1974). Thus while the impact of crowding on humans will be influenced by the unique adaptive abilities of humans, some of the variables causing or mediating crowding may be similar for both humans and animals. As we will note later, a number of conceptual analyses of animal response to high density have been incorporated in models of human behavior under high-density conditions.

14.3. DENSITY AND CORRELATIONS WITH SOCIAL PATHOLOGY

A second line of research, characterized by an epidemiological approach to studying crowding, the effects of high density, represented the first step in relating animal findings to human populations. The severity of conditions generated by high density among animals led to a great deal of interest in possible density-related pathology among people. As a result, several correlational studies focusing on relationships between urban density and social or physical pathology were conducted. The presumption motivating most of these studies was that high levels of density in urban environments would be associated with increased pathology. This pathology could be seen as a direct result of exposure to the urban stressors associated with living in high-density housing and/or in overpopulated cities. Yet the exact mechanisms underlying the anticipated results were not usually considered, and when they were, discussions of them were limited.

The general design of these studies required a measure of density such as people per census tract, people per acre, or people per building, and a mea-

sure of pathology such as hospital admissions rates, arrests for juvenile delinquency, and so on. Correlations were computed between density and pathology measures and, in some studies, the effects of socioeconomic factors were controlled. The fact that the data being correlated were aggregate values meant that a good deal of specificity was being lost, but the results of these studies were often interpreted as supporting or conflicting with those based on animal populations. The archival nature of the research also limited the ability of researchers to determine the existence of psychological and social mediators of observed effects.

Some of these studies have suggested that density is related to a number of pathologies or social problems. Schmitt (1966), for example, reported relationships between density and death rate, incidence of tuberculosis and venereal disease, mental hospital admissions, juvenile delinquency, and imprisonment. Similarly, Booth and Welch (1973) reported that density was related to the rates of a number of different crimes, including assault, rape, robbery, burglary, auto theft, and larceny. Both of these studies controlled for income and education and both used census data for their analyses.

Booth and Welch (1974) also reported that many of these relationships were observed in a number of cultures. Their data, drawn from 65 countries, revealed relationships between density and homicide, civil strife, life expectancy, and infant mortality. Galle and colleagues (1972) reported relationships between density and mortality, fertility, mental hospital admissions, and juvenile delinquency in Chicago, while Levy and Herzog (1974) found evidence of density-related health problems (mortality rates, heart disease, hospital admissions, etc.) in the Netherlands. A study in Germany also provided evidence of a relationship between density and mortality (Manton & Myers, 1977).

These studies suggest that urban density is an important factor and that it can be associated with pathologies ranging from disease and mortality to crime and delinquency. There are a number of cautions, however, that must be considered. For example, these all claim to examine urban density, but they do so in different ways. Booth and Welch (1973) used three different indices of density based on the number of people per room (housing), the number of dwellings per square mile, and the product of the two. Their later study (Booth & Welch, 1974) used similar measures of density.

Galle and colleagues (1972) also considered several measures of density including people per room, rooms per dwelling, dwellings per structure, and structures per acre. Levy and Herzog (1974) used measures of people per room and people per economic district. In some cases, outside measures of density (e.g., dwellings per acre, people per census tract) were related to pathology, and in some, household density measures (e.g., persons per room) were more important. Galle et al. (1972) found that these indices of density were related to crime and health variables while outside density was not. Similarly, household density appeared to be related to more indicators of pathology than did outside density in Booth and Welch's (1974) multinational study.

Because the data that are analyzed in these studies are aggregate data, variations within measures cannot be considered. Measures of population per census tract, for example, ignore the great variation in density within a census district. Apartment buildings and single-family homes may be located within a block or two of one another and will be averaged together in any measure more general than the distance between them. This presents a problem that may actually moderate the strength of the findings of these studies and suggests why smaller measures of density may be more useful than larger ones.

Another reason for caution in interpreting these effects is that they are inconsistent, appearing in some studies but not in others. Winsborough (1965), in a study of Chicago communities, found that infant mortality was positively related to density (person per acre) but that deaths, incidence of tuberculosis, and public assistance were negatively related to density. Freedman, Heshka, and Levy (1975) found that density was not related to crimes, hospital admissions, or any of a number of other variables. Only termination of psychiatric treatment was associated with density. Levy and Herzog (1974) also reported some negative relationships between density and hospital admissions, crime, and delinquency, and Cholden and Roneck (1975) found no relationships between density and mortality or crime. Housing density did have a low positive correlation with violent crime. Mitchell (1971) found some evidence of a relationship between square feet per person and self-reported psychological stress among low-income Hong Kong families, but not among high-income families. However, density was not related to self-reports of psychosomatic symptoms and withdrawal from family and work roles.

Thus the overall pattern of results is rather mixed and provides only weak evidence of a relationship between urban density and pathology. Furthermore, several studies find some evidence that living alone is positively related to increased use of stress-reducing drugs, to suicides, and to admissions to mental hospitals (Collette & Webb, 1975; Galle et al., 1972; Levy & Herzog, 1974).

The limitations of the correlational approach and corresponding statistical techniques have been reviewed elsewhere (e.g., Epstein & Baum, 1978; Fischer, Baldassare, & Ofshe, 1975; Ward, 1975). All of the obvious socioeconomic factors may be controlled for, but one can still point to a host of other variables that could differentiate populations living in low- and high-density areas or conditions. Self-selection of individuals into areas or housing presents a major interpretational problem. Individuals with physical or mental health problems or antisocial tendencies may gravitate toward dense urban areas, or may be forced to live there by economic or social pressure. Other features of highly dense areas such as noise and pollution may also be important, and their effects cannot be separated from measures of density. The higher crime rates in dense urban areas, which may be in large part due to nonresidents, may be a significant source of stress. Furthermore, aggregate measures of density may not accurately reflect the actual experience of crowding of residents. Such experience may be affected by familiarity with residents, traffic flow, and the arrangement of both the internal and external spaces. Finally, aggregate data may mask relationships that exist at the individual level. These and other criticisms (e.g., Fischer et al., 1975; Kermeyer, 1978; Sundstrom, 1978) suggest that other approaches such as field studies are to be preferred to correlational studies of aggregate data. These correlational studies, however, do provide information about the potential generality of results from field studies.

14.4. EXPERIMENTAL INVESTIGATION OF HIGH DENSITY AND CROWDING

The third stage of research following the implementation of large archival studies was characterized by its experimental approach. Although it was primarily limited to the laboratory, some studies were conducted in field settings as well. Most of these studies were also relatively brief; few considered the effects of crowding lasting beyond 4 or 5 hours. Despite the many limitations of this approach, however, a number of consistent findings have been reported. Initially, these studies were concerned with determining whether crowding had any effects and, as a result, much of this work can be grouped on the basis of the type of effect considered. We will review these findings and return to methodological limitations of this approach at the end of this section.

Much of what we know about human response to high density is derived from this research. Usually, it involved manipulation of density and attempts to control all other setting and personal characteristics. Crowding was also measured in most studies, allowing examination of relationships between density variations and experiential changes. In addition, setting or personal variables were manipulated one or two at a time and crossed with density levels, allowing examination of complex determination of both crowding and its related effects. The focus of this research was on individual response, and its approach allowed a finer level of detail in its observation of response to high-density settings.

The results of this research indicate that there are a number of physiological, social, and psychological effects associated with crowding and high density. Interestingly, they are all consistent with research on other stressors such as noise, disaster, commuting, and so on. As one would expect from this perspective, exposure to high density and consequent crowding are associated with physiological changes linked to arousal of the sympathetic nervous system and pituitary–adrenocortical system. In addition, there is limited evidence of a connection between density and illness, and changes in task performance and other psychological correlates of crowding are also consistent with research on stress. Finally, social responses to high density are predictable from examination of research on coping with other threats and pressures. Density and crowding appear to be associated with physiological changes that may potentiate illness, arousal that affects performance and emotional tone, coping that alters one's social posture, and so on.

14.4.1. Physiological Effects of Crowding

Most studies that have examined physiological response to high density have considered measures of peripheral response typically associated with arousal and stress. For the most part, these studies suggest that even brief encounters with high density can affect physiological response. Skin conductance, reflecting among other things perspiration, has been shown to increase under high-density conditions (Aiello, Epstein, & Karlin, 1975). Saegert (1974) found similar evidence of arousal based on palmar sweating. Subjects in the Aiello et al. (1975) study were exposed to high density for only 30 minutes, while those in Saegert's (1974) study remained in the setting for 75 minutes. Other studies have examined physiological response over longer periods of time. Evans (1979), for example, measured blood pressure and heart rate after 3 hours in settings of varying

density and found that higher density was associated with increases over precrowding levels.

Quasi-experimental studies in field settings have provided evidence of endocrine response as well (e.g., Lundberg, 1976; Singer, Frankenhaeuser, & Lundberg, 1978). These studies considered passengers of a Swedish commuter train, comparing response to trips made under varying levels of density. Despite the fact that even under the most dense conditions there were seats available for everyone, perceived crowding increased as more people rode the train. Further, urine samples were collected and analysis of them showed higher levels of epinephrine among subjects after crowded trips than after less crowded ones. Epinephrine, involved in sympathetic arousal, is associated with the other measures of response that have been used (e.g., blood pressure, heart rate, skin conductance) and is frequently used to measure stress (cf. Baum, Grunberg, & Singer, 1982).

A second finding, however, suggested that a specific aspect of crowding in this situation may have caused this effect. Regardless of level of density, riders boarding at the first stop experienced less distress and exhibited lower levels of epinephrine than did those boarding halfway to the city. Their ride was considerably longer and they were exposed to the same densities as later boarders, but those boarding at the first stop entered an empty train and were able to choose where and with whom they sat. The control afforded those boarding first may have reduced the effects of increasing numbers of riders along the way, and/or the lack of control associated with boarding an already crowded train exacerbated these effects (Lundberg, 1976; Singer et al., 1978).

A related focus of research has attempted to identify links between crowding and illness. For example, McCain, Cox, and Paulus (1976) reported that prison inmates living under low-density conditions made fewer illness complaints than did those who lived in higher densities and reported more perceived crowding. Further study indicated that density was related to blood pressure increases and to death rates (Paulus, McCain, & Cox, 1978). D'Atri (1975) and D'Atri and Ostfeld (1975) also found that increases in density were associated with rising blood pressure, and Stokols and Ohlig (1975) found a relationship between reported crowding in college dormitories and visits to the student health center. Dean, Pugh, and Gunderson (1975, 1979) have also reported associations between crowding and illness complaints.

Available evidence, then, suggests that density and crowding are associated with physiological arousal. In much the same way as other stressors have been, density has been linked with increased skin conductance, cardiovascular response, and endocrine activity. There is also some evidence that density and crowding are associated with illness or symptoms of illness, but much of this is based on research in specialized settings or on self-reported measures of illness. The evidence thus suggests that humans as well as animals experience stress-related physiological effects under high-density conditions. The extent of arousal and physiological change, as well as the mechanisms underlying response and the degree of correspondence between animal and human response, remains to be clarified.

Crowding and Task Performance

Another frequent topic of research has been task performance and how density and crowding impair or interfere with it. This is so for a number of reasons, among them the important implications such findings would have for workplaces and the fact that arousal appears to have specific effects on performance. Yet it was here that early disagreements and inconsistent findings were reported. Before 1975, a number of studies examining high density in laboratory settings had failed to find any effects on task performance (e.g., Bergman, 1971; Freedman, Klevansky, & Ehrlich, 1971; Freedman, Levy, Buchanan, & Price, 1972; Rawls, Trego, McGaffey, & Rawls, 1972; Ross, Layton, Erickson, & Schopler, 1973; Stokols, Rall, Pinner, & Schopler, 1973). Other studies had reported performance decrements as a result of crowding (e.g., Dooley, 1974; Saegert, 1974).

Research evidence since 1975, however, has more strongly suggested that crowding can impair performance, especially when tasks are complex rather than simple ones (e.g., Aiello et al., 1975; Evans, 1979; Klein & Harris, 1979; Paulus, Annis, Seta, Schkade, & Matthews, 1976; Saegert, Mackintosh, & West, 1975). Most of the tasks used involved problem solving, discriminations, concentration, and/or persistence, suggesting that crowding effects on task performance are more likely to be observed on difficult tasks. Furthermore, certain features of the task situation, such as degree of perceived control and the use of multiple tasks, seem to influence the degree to which crowding effects are observed (Paulus & Matthews, 1980).

It is also of interest that crowding, like noise and other stressors, is associated with aftereffects (cf. Glass & Singer, 1972). Aftereffects may reflect emotional residue from exposure to stress or some cost of coping, and they include decreases in persistence, success at solving challenging tasks, and concentration (e.g., Cohen, 1980). Research has indicated that

postexposure effects of crowding impair task performance, primarily by reducing persistence and tolerance for frustration (Dooley, 1974; Evans, 1979; Sherrod, 1974).

Social Response to Crowding

Crowding is essentially a social phenomenon. Regardless of how dense—how little space is available and how *cramped*—a room may be, it is not crowded unless other people are present. As a result, one would expect that one of the primary foci of response to crowding would be social. Not unexpectedly, research has identified a number of coping responses and effects of exposure to crowding that involve interpersonal behavior.

Two basic forms of social response have been identified. Withdrawal or avoidance of social contact has been found primarily in settings where many people are present and reported crowding is related to frequency or quality of social contact. Aggressive response has been observed in situations characterized by fewer people but very small spaces where reported crowding has more to do with spatial restriction or inappropriate proximity of others. It is possible that the specific use of these coping strategies in different kinds of situations reflects their relative success in past encounters or that the environmental demands posed by different settings determine the specific mode of response. The relative importance of mediating variables in determining response is also important.

Withdrawal has been viewed as an active coping response to residential settings characterized by frequent contact with a large number of people (Baum & Valins, 1977). Students confronted with frequent unwanted interaction with their neighbors reported experiencing crowding and avoided contact with strangers in a laboratory and in their residential environments. They also appeared to withdraw from their immediate residential setting, exhibiting withdrawal from friends, but this tended to be less marked than when acquaintances or strangers were involved. The expectation of being in a room with a large number of people also elicits withdrawal, including reduced levels of eye contact, increased interindividual distances, and head movements away from others (Baum & Greenberg, 1975; Baum & Koman, 1976). Withdrawal is also evident in naturalistic observation of high-density urban areas. Low-priority social contacts (i.e., strangers, acquaintances) may be disregarded in favor of more important contacts (friends, relatives), and the streamlining of interactions and legitimization of norms of ignoring people appear to be ways of coping with the large number of potential social contacts in urban centers (Milgram, 1970). McCauley and Taylor (1976) reported evidence of this by comparing areas in a field study. They found that city residents reported fewer conversations per day, suggesting either that city residents were not exposed to excessive contact or that they have dealt with overload by greatly reducing social contact.

A second study (McCauley & Newman, 1977) measured eye contact between strangers in urban and nonurban areas. Eye contact is an initiator of social interaction, and looking away from people suggests an unwillingness to interact. Willingness to interact with strangers was greater in small-town or suburban settings than in urban areas. City residents apparently try to reduce excessive interaction or regulate it by withdrawing from potential interaction. A third study (McCauley, Coleman, & DeFusco, 1978) provided further evidence that withdrawal is an active attempt to cope with some high-density situations.

Evidence of withdrawal may also be found in studies examining the effects of crowding on helping. The expectation is that people are less likely to help one another when they feel crowded, and this has been the general finding of a number of studies (e.g., Bickman, Teger, Gabriele, McLaughlin, Berger, & Sunaday, 1973; Jorgenson & Dukes, 1976; Korte, 1978). Situational variables are important in determining these effects; studies may, for example, confound density with building type (high- vs. low-rise) or with setting (urban vs. rural). Thus high-rise, high-density housing may be associated with less helping than a low-rise, low-density building. Regardless, research seems to indicate a line, and one explanation of this effect suggests that it represents the desire to avoid social involvement and therefore is part of an overall attempt to cope with frequent interaction. At present, however, research is not sufficient to conclude that reduced helpfulness reflects withdrawal.

Although most studies reporting withdrawal are field studies, some evidence for withdrawal reactions to crowding has been noted in laboratory studies. Interestingly, these studies indicate that response is affected by the sexual composition of the group. For example, Ross and colleagues (1973) found that females in all-female groups spent relatively more time in mutual gazing under crowded conditions, while the opposite effect was obtained for males. Thus males showed withdrawal tendencies under crowded conditions while females showed affiliative tendencies. These findings can be interpreted as reflecting either differential coping styles or differential sensitivity to personal space invasions (cf. Paulus, 1980).

Just as withdrawal seems a logical response to excessive social interaction, aggressive behavior may be a realistic approach when space is limited. Aggressive or dominant behavior may cause others to move away, ceding some of "their space" to the aggressive individual. This in turn would reduce many of the constraints associated with spatial density. As one would expect, then, several studies have reported evidence of increased aggression among people exposed to crowding in small spaces (e.g., Aiello, Nicosia, & Thompson, 1979; Ginsburg, Pollman, Wanson, & Hope, 1977; Hutt & Vaizey, 1966). However, other studies have not reported this effect (e.g., Loo, 1972).

The nature of aggressive response to crowding has been clarified by consideration of several intervening conditions. First, it appears that resources must be sufficiently scarce to make less aggressive coping ineffective. Rohe and Patterson (1974) suggested that competition for scarce resources, including space, may be a major determinant of aggressiveness during exposure to high density. Their research with children supported this contention, and subsequent research also identified resource scarcity as important (Smith & Connolly, 1977).

Another important qualification of a crowding–aggression link is the fact that men exhibit more aggressive responses to crowding characterized by spatial restriction than do women (e.g., Freedman et al., 1972; Stokols et al., 1973). Schettino and Borden (1976) found evidence of gender differences among large groups of people as well.

Baum and Koman (1976) found evidence of sex differences only when groups were small, but also reported evidence of aggressive "posturing" as a preparatory coping response when expecting crowding in a small room. Men anticipating interaction with four other men in a very small room assumed more aggressive seat positions and interaction styles than did men anticipating a session with the same size group in a larger room. Women did not exhibit aggressive responses, and when larger groups were expected, withdrawal rather than aggressiveness was observed in both large and small rooms and by both genders. Other studies also indicate that low levels of density can lead to heightened aggression and that high density can actually reduce aggression (Loo, 1978; Matthews, Paulus, & Baron, 1979).

Evidence of aggressive responses is not strong, primarily because of difficulties in studying it. Most investigations of aggressive response have been conducted in the laboratory, and the kinds of measures of aggression available in such a situation are limited. Instead of "real world" aggression that cannot adequately be studied in the laboratory, studies have examined responses to bargaining games, jury simulations, and other approximations of real world aggression. This is a serious limitation to any conclusions about crowding and aggression and is only partly resolved by correlational studies that show tenuous relationships between high density and various indicators of crime (e.g., Galle et al., 1972). One study reported evidence that high density is more strongly associated with fear of crime than with actual victimization (Gifford & Peacock, 1977).

The extent to which withdrawal and aggression are effects of density and crowding or are active modes of coping with them is yet to be determined. The evidence presently available suggests an intentionality underlying this kind of response. People appear to prepare for and cope with excessive social contact by withdrawing from involvement with others. Further, men appear to cope with spatial restriction by becoming more aggressive. Other evidence of changes in mood and regard for others may also reflect this coping process, or they may be determined by exposure alone (Evans, 1978; Saegert et al., 1975). The answers to these and other issues await further research.

14.4.2. Mediating Variables and Response to Crowding

Crowding appears to be mediated by a number of intervening variables that affect the severity or intensity of density-related conditions or the degree to which one can cope with them. This is consistent with research that suggests that stress is influenced by a number of psychosocial variables (Baum, Singer, & Baum, 1981) and with Stokols's (1972) distinction between density and crowding. Recall that in Figure 14.1 we depicted crowding as the outcome of evaluation of density in the context of setting and personal variables. The physical conditions associated with density can have a number of different effects, and the extent to which they have any or all of them depends on the situation and the people involved.

Social and Spatial Density
One of the most important of these conditions is reflected in the kind of density that is present. Throughout this chapter we have made reference to crowding characterized by large numbers of others and crowding characterized by small amounts of space. These two conditions are reflected in the ratio defining density: number of people to amount of space. For density to increase, one needs to increase the number of people, decrease the amount of availa-

ble space, or both. Depending on how this occurs, one can expect different responses by the setting inhabitants.

Traditionally, increases in group size have been referred to as increases in *social* density, while decreases in spatial availability with group size held constant are referred to as increases in *spatial* density (Loo, 1972). Laboratory studies have considered both; some examine different-sized groups in constant spaces, while others observe same-sized groups in large and small spaces. Until recently, these manipulations of density were used almost interchangeably. However, it now appears that the two reflect different conditions. Research in field settings has suggested that social and spatial density translate into different experiences and consequences (Baum & Valins, 1979), and a consistent pattern of findings in laboratory settings has suggested different responses under the two manipulations (e.g., McClelland & Auslander, 1975; Paulus, 1980).

Perhaps the best way to consider the differences between social and spatial density is to examine the kinds of problems that may be salient in each. Increasing numbers of people may cause reductions in the amount of space available to each (if space remains constant), but such increases are also associated with more interaction, a greater need for social structure, more social interference, and greater threats to control over social experience (e.g., Baron & Rodin, 1978). Decreases in space available, when the number of people is constant, are associated with physical disruption, loss of intimacy regulation, spatial invasion, physical constraint, and so on (e.g., Baum & Valins, 1979; Patterson, 1976; Stokols, 1972; Sundstrom, 1975). Clearly, the kind of experience one has as density increases will depend on how it increases.

Research suggests that responses to social and spatial density are different. For example, Baum & Koman (1976) manipulated expectations of group size and room size on 2:1 ratios in a laboratory study. As a result of this, two conditions (10 people, large room; 5 people, small room) reflected identical physical densities but differed on whether social or spatial density was salient. When group size was large, subjects were more concerned with social problems, withdrawn, and less aggressive than when room and group size were small. Social structure mediated response by subjects expecting large groups but did not when smaller groups were expected. Conversely, gender differences in response were evident when small groups were expected in the small room but not when larger groups were expected in the large room. This and other studies suggest that social concerns reflected by numbers of people may be more salient than spatial concerns and that response to spatial limitation emerges when social problems are less relevant. Research indicates that social density is a more prominent concern for people in natural settings (Paulus, 1980) and that people can differentiate between social and spatial density (Switzer & Taylor, 1983).

Social and Physical Mediators

A number of different conditions have been found to affect the way in which crowding is experienced. When group size is large, providing social structure or the anticipation of such structure can reduce distress (Baum & Koman, 1976; Schopler & Walton, 1974). Interpersonal relationships are also important — depending on the relationship among those in the setting, density may or may not lead to the experience of crowding (Aiello, Baum, & Gormley, 1981; Baron, Mandel, Adams, & Griffen, 1976; Baum, Shapiro, Murray, & Wideman, 1979; Reddy, Baum, Fleming, & Aiello, 1981; Stokols, 1972, 1978).

Stokols (1976, 1978) has noted the effects of primacy of setting (primary or secondary) and of source of thwarting (negative experience caused by the environment or by other people). High density will be experienced more negatively in primary settings and when others are seen as responsible for inconveniences or distress. We will return to this later, but for now it suggests that characteristics of the social environment are important in determining the effects of density and crowding.

Some physical variables also appear to affect the way in which density is experienced. Architectural designs that differed in the ways in which shared spaces were arranged mediated the experience of comparable physical densities in college dormitories (Baum & Valins, 1977). One design, requiring large numbers of residents to share spaces, was associated with reported crowding, negative affect, and withdrawal. Another design, grouping people around shared space in smaller numbers, was not associated with this syndrome of stress. Further, architectural changes in the former design appeared to prevent the experience of crowding and related distress (Baum & Davis, 1980).

For the most part, physical and social mediators function in the same way. Variables that make density more intrusive, apparent, or disruptive will increase the likelihood that crowding will be experienced, while variables that minimize these problems will decrease this likelihood. Thus features of a setting that make it look larger or that reduce the apparent number of people present reduce judgments of crowding, and features that make it look smaller or that increase the prominence of other people increase judgments of crowding (e.g., Baum & Davis, 1976; Desor, 1972; Worchel & Teddlie, 1976).

Individual Differences

Differences in the approaches and assets that people bring with them in a given setting are also important determinants of response. Gender differences in response to spatial density may reflect differences in interpretation of the situation or adjustment to it or in requirements for comfortable interaction. Thus decreasing amounts of space may be more aversive to men because they are more likely to appraise spatial restriction as threatening, because their style of coping with it is more aggressive, or because they simply require more personal space. Research has suggested that different appraisal orientations, such as perceived locus of control, mediate the experience of crowding (e.g., Matthews, 1979; Schopler, McCullum, & Rusbult, 1978; Schopler & Walton, 1974). It is also apparent that different coping styles affect the likelihood that crowding is experienced (Baum, Calesnick, Davis, & Gatchel, 1982; Miller, Rossbach, & Munson, 1980). Thus withdrawal from social contact, aggressive ordering of a situation, prioritization of social contacts, or narrowing of attention may be useful in some situations, and may, therefore, reduce distress or block the experience of crowding by facilitating a nonthreatening appraisal. Finally, people with preferences for larger interpersonal distances appear to be more negatively affected by increasing spatial density than are those with more modest spatial preferences (Aiello, DeRisi, Epstein, & Karlin, 1977).

14.4.3. The Nature of Human Crowding Phenomena

The implications of these findings are important for a number of reasons. They reinforce the notion that density must be regarded as a physical condition that may or may not be associated with crowding. They also underscore the complex interaction between salient aspects of density and intervening physical and psychosocial factors. Consistent with modern treatments of stress (e.g., Baum, Singer, & Baum, 1981; Lazarus, 1966; Lazarus & Launier, 1978; Mason, 1975), factors that influence the appraisal of density also influence the crowding responses we have discussed. The kinds of interpretations and coping mechanisms that are central to this process vary from theory to theory and will be considered in a later section. Despite these differences, however, they all share the basic assumptions just outlined.

14.5. STUDIES OF CHRONIC EXPOSURE TO CROWDING

Approaches to research on density and crowding have gradually changed over the years. They have evolved from studies of animal populations and correlational examinations of human urban density and pathology to experimental research in the laboratory. Each approach has strengths and weaknesses. Animal studies may provide the researcher with more control over genetic and extraneous environmental variables, but they do not appear adequately to reflect human coping abilities and therefore may overestimate the severity of different effects. Correlational studies are relatively insensitive to variations of density within a geographical area and cannot provide causal information, but they provide information about possible consequences of urban density. Both of these types of studies have also provided basic data for theory building, and both will undoubtedly continue to be important as researchers return to them for additional information.

Experimental research has provided a wealth of data reflecting various effects and mediators of crowding. These studies have also provided important theory-relevant information. However, they sacrifice realism when conducted in the laboratory and do not address the important issue of long-term consequences of crowding in highly dense settings. Because of ethical considerations and the time constraints associated with laboratory studies, they have been used primarily to examine acute episodes of crowding. Quasi-experimental studies, conducted over longer periods of time, have addressed these concerns and eliminated some of the methodological limitations of previous research. As with many innovations, however, this approach has introduced new problems as well.

Research on chronic problems associated with prolonged exposure to high density has typically been done in specialized residential settings. The most common site, for many reasons, is the college dormitory (e.g., Aiello et al., 1975; Baum & Valins, 1977; Bickman et al., 1973; Schopler & Stockdale, 1977). Other settings, ranging from naval vessels and oildrilling platforms at sea to prisons and hospitals, have also been considered (Cox, Paulus, McCain, & Schkade, 1979; D'Atri & Ostfeld, 1975; Dean et al., 1975; Wolfe, 1975). In this section, however, we will focus on two research programs with which we have

been associated in order to demonstrate the findings of this type of research.

14.5.1. Crowding in Prison Settings

Prisons are a useful site for studying the effects of long-term exposure to crowding for a variety of reasons. First, they provide a wide variety of housing conditions. Some of these are spacious and private, while others are extremely dense and may severely limit space and house large numbers together. The broad range of housing in prison settings also allows assessment of the impact of much higher density levels than can typically be examined in studies of other environments. Laboratory studies are typically brief, and one of the most crowded chronic conditions that has been studied involved up to 9 people living in a one-bedroom apartment (Rodin, 1976). In contrast, researchers study prison conditions in which up to 70 inmates are confined in open dormitories with less than 20 sq ft per person. A 1000-sq-ft apartment would have to house 50 people in order to reach this level of spatial density alone, and social density in prison settings was also considerably higher than has been typically examined. These high levels of density should be sufficient to produce indications of pathology if indeed density is associated with such consequences (Paulus, McCain, & Cox, 1981).

In the prison studies, social density of housing units varied from singles to open dormitories with 70 inmates and spatial density ranged from levels allowing 260 sq ft of space per inmate to those allowing only 19 sq ft per inmate (cf., McCain, Cox, Paulus, & Karlovac, 1981; Paulus & McCain, in press). Although the more socially dense units also tended to be more spatially dense, there was enough variability to allow for an assessment of their relative importance. Moreover, the wide variety of housing and design of prisons allowed an evaluation of a number of rather specific questions about various features of prison housing. For example, comparisons of single and double cells provided information about the importance of privacy at relatively low density (Altman, 1976; Baron & Rodin, 1978), while comparisons of large, open dormitories with similar dormitories housing inmates in partitioned cubicles provided information about the importance of privacy at higher densities.

The prison research was carried out on about 1500 inmates in six federal prisons, two state prisons, and three county jails (Paulus et al., 1981; Paulus & McCain, in press). Archival data on prison size and overall prison crowding were obtained for three state prison systems. During research visits, detailed questionnaire information was obtained about each inmate's background, present psychological reactions to the environment, and activities in the prison. Blood pressures and various measures of crowding tolerance were also collected. Additional background information and data about use of the medical clinic were derived from prison records.

These studies showed that increased social density led to increased negative reactions and in some cases increased illness complaints (McCain et al., 1980). For example, in one medium-security prison, ratings of doubles were more negative than were ratings of singles, and these two-prisoner units produced higher nonaggressive disciplinary infraction rates and elevated illness complaint rates (McCain et al., 1980). Double cells provided less privacy, suggesting that this mechanism was important. However, doubles also involved double bunking, allowed half the space of singles, and were different from singles in other ways as well. Thus it was difficult to determine the specific factor responsible for these negative findings. However, a comparison of doubles with open dormitories housing 28 or more inmates suggested that social factors were the important ones. These dormitories also had double bunks and similar or more spacious accommodations than doubles, but the dormitories produced more negative reactions to the housing, more negative mood states, and higher illness complaint rates than either doubles or singles. This suggested that the number of people one has to deal with in one's housing rather than space and double bunking was primarily responsible for negative effects of dense prison housing. Similar patterns of findings were obtained at three other prisons (McCain et al., 1980).

Additional evidence of the importance of "number" in housing was obtained in studies of the Atlanta Federal Penitentiary. Inmates there were housed in singles or in large cells with 3, 4, 5, or 6 residents. Increased number of residents per cell was associated with increased negative reactions and illness complaints. Social issues were underscored; the triples were similar in space to the singles but produced more negative reactions.

If social density or having to interact with a large number of others is the most important factor in prison housing, certain features that reduce or help regulate interaction may reduce the impact of this factor. In two prisons it was possible to study the extent to which privacy cubicles in dormitories ameliorated the negative effects of dormitory living. Inmate evaluations of two institutions indicated that inmates

found cubicles (areas surrounded by high partitions and containing desk and storage space) as desirable as rooms or cells. Since these cubicles were found in large dormitories, it appeared that they moderated the effects of high social density. A recent study examined dormitories in which about half of the inmates were provided cubicles (McGuire & Gaes, 1982). Inmates in the open areas had more negative reactions to their environment and had higher noncontagious illness complaint rates than those in cubicles. These data provided evidence that the cubicles reduced crowding stress associated with the high social density in open dormitories.

Another way in which dormitory living may be made more tolerable is by dividing it into smaller subunits. At Texarkana Federal Correctional Institution, dormitories consisted of either one large open area containing 29 to 39 inmates or a dormitory containing 41 to 50 inmates that was divided into three segments by a central lounge area. The segments contained 10 to 20 inmates. The segmented dormitory was rated more positively and had lower illness complaint rates than the conventional dormitories.

In Texas, where almost all of the prisons are maximum security prisons, large prisons (pop. 1400, $\bar{X} = 1700$) were found to have 10 times higher suicide rates, 78% higher psychiatric commitment rates, and three times higher death rates than small prisons (pop. 1100, $\bar{X} = 830$) (Paulus et al., 1981). In three state systems it was possible to examine the impact of increased population while the housing facilities remained relatively constant. In all three prison systems increased crowding was associated with increased death rates. In one system, data on disciplinary infractions and suicides were also available, and increased levels of these variables were associated with increased crowding (cf. Paulus et al., 1981). As discussed earlier, archival data are replete with potential interpretive problems. However, when the influences of age and racial and ethnic groups were examined, it was found these did not account for the effects. In the Texas data it was also possible to demonstrate that the inmate–security personnel ratio did not relate to the various measures of pathology.

14.5.2. Social Density and Crowding in Dormitories

Another program of research that has provided evidence of the negative effects of crowding and the importance of social density over prolonged exposure is the work by Baum and Valins (1977, 1979). This research considered responses to college dormitories using a conceptual framework drawn directly from Calhoun's (1962, 1970) work with animals. Like the prison researchers, Baum and Valins were concerned with the effects of density and the nature of crowding in naturalistic housing environments. Students in the settings that were studied were exposed for long periods of time to different types of dormitory housing. Studies examined the effects of these different types of housing on a number of psychological and behavioral dimensions and sought to determine some of the factors that mediated these effects.

In all, this research examined three dormitory types that differed in the ways in which their design structured interior, residential space. One type was a traditional corridor design with 17 to 22 double-occupancy bedrooms and common bathroom and lounge facilities arranged along a central double-loaded corridor. Another was also a corridor design dormitory, with only about 10 double-occupancy rooms. A third design housed students in small 4- to 6-person suites, with self-contained bath and lounge facilities. All three designs housed 32 to 44 residents per floor and all had comparable spatial densities. However, they differed in the ways in which space was arranged and in the number of residents required to share common areas. The research focused on new freshmen who either had chosen or were arbitrarily or randomly assigned to their housing.

It was initially predicted that the long-corridor design would produce crowding stress and related reactions relative to the other two dormitory designs. Baum and Valins focused on the relationship between social density and problems dormitory residents experienced when they tried to regulate social interaction. Long-corridor designs did not provide intermediate group sizes—residents shared their bedroom with a single other person, and the hallway, bathroom, and lounge with 33 others. In contrast, short-corridor residents shared their room with a single other and the remaining amenities with only 18 or 19 others. Suite residents also shared the bedroom with a single other but shared their lounge and bath with 3 or 5 others and only the hallway with 33 neighbors. These differences in functional social density meant that the number of people routinely encountered in the dormitory was highest for residents of housing of long-corridor design.

Crowding and social experience varied along these proposed dimensions. Buildings of long-corridor design were associated with reports of excessive social stimulation and unwanted contact. Residents reported a larger number of unpredictable and unwanted encounters with acquaintances and strangers in the common areas of their floors, making it difficult for them to regulate or control interactions with others. Overall, they reported problems regulating when, where, and with whom they might interact, and this was seen as leading to crowding stress. The residents of the suite dorms or the short-corridor settings, on the other hand, seemed better able to develop mechanisms for regulating social interactions because the effective group size was smaller. The smaller group appeared to allow for formation of norms and other ways of regulating social interaction in shared areas. Residents also became familiar with the other members of their group, and this seemed to reduce unpredictability. Further, since bathroom and lounge areas were provided within the suites, there was less need to use the hallways, which further limited exposure to unpredictable encounters. Short-corridor dorms had similar advantages primarily because of the small number of residents sharing areas and likely to be in the hallway at any given time. Although these residents had to share a common bath and lounge area, the small number of total residents allowed for group formation and more effective regulation of interaction. In some senses the small-corridor dorm may function as one large suite with little "outside" encounter.

Extensive self-report and behavioral data were obtained from residents over the academic year. The behavioral data consisted of observations of behavior in the dormitory and in laboratory settings. Long-corridor residents evidenced elevated feelings of crowding, complained about the number of neighbors and the degree of unwanted interaction, and expressed a desire to avoid interactions. Behavioral observations indicated that long-corridor residents spent relatively more time isolated in their bedrooms than the residents of the other two dormitory types. This avoidance tendency on the part of the long-corridor residents was evident in settings outside of the dormitory. For example, when brought to the laboratory to participate in studies of social bargaining, long-corridor residents sat further away from another person in a waiting room while waiting to begin the study, avoided looking at this person, and expressed more discomfort than did suite residents (Baum & Valins, 1977).

Another feature of the dormitory research was its analysis of changes over time. This allowed examination of adaptation and coping in the different environments. Several findings suggested that residents of long-corridor dorms did not effectively adapt to their environment in the sense of becoming more tolerant of it. For example, the avoidance reactions demonstrated in the laboratory were maintained at a similar level throughout the course of the year. Similarly, the degree to which long-corridor residents isolated themselves in their bedrooms increased over the course of the semester (Baum & Davis, 1980). Long-corridor residents initially reacted to loss of control over social experience by trying to reassert control over their interactions (Baum, Aiello, & Calesnick, 1978; Baum & Gatchel, 1981). After 5 or more weeks, failure to achieve control appeared to diminish controlling behavior and allow the emergence of withdrawal reactions. This pattern is consistent with Wortman and Brehm's (1975) conceptualization of the impact of loss of control, and prolonged exposure to the long corridor produced symptoms associated with learned helplessness (Seligman, 1975).

These studies provided information about the dynamics of coping with conditions of high social density. The evidence indicates that problems of controlling unwanted and unpredictable interactions with others play a central role in crowding stress. Residents may react initially with strong negative feelings and attempts to regain control, but the apparent futility of attaining control in high-density settings leads to a helplessnesslike state of social withdrawal, passivity, and lowered feelings of control over the environment.

14.5.3. Convergence of Prison and Dormitory Findings

There are a number of ways in which the dormitory and prison studies support and complement each other. Both programs have found that social density is an important factor in crowding stress. In both prisons and college dormitories it is the number of people one has to interact with in one's immediate environment that appears crucial in producing crowding stress. The dormitory research further indicates that the uncontrollability and unpredictability of these unwanted interactions are what mediate this impact of social density. To the extent that there is an increase in structure of the interaction, crowding stress may be reduced. For example, two other field studies have found that in "crowded" tripled rooms, coalitions often form between two residents, leaving one of the residents isolated (Aiello, 1981; Baum et al., 1979). This isolate appears to experience the brunt of the crowding stress. Rooms with four residents are less likely to produce isolates and thus present fewer control-related problems and produce less crowding because of the structure provided by the coalitions between two or among four residents (Reddy et al.,

1981). This structure can facilitate regulation of the interaction. Similarly, McCain and associates (1981) found that degree of turnover in prison units led to increased inmate complaints.

Architectural features that reduce exposure to unwanted interactions or facilitate attempts at regulation of these interactions have been shown to reduce crowding effects in both settings. Baum and Davis (1980) found that dividing a long-corridor floor into two short corridors reduced the negative effects of long-corridor living. In prisons, dividing a large dormitory into three segments or providing privacy cubicles helped mitigate crowding stress (McCain, Cox, & Paulus, 1980).

Another common point between the prison and dorm research is the fact that it is difficult for residents to cope or adapt to high-density living. In prisons, increased length of residence in dormitories does not significantly reduce the negative reaction to them or the rate of illness complaints (McCain et al., 1980). In fact, increased length of residence in crowded housing was associated with reduced tolerance for crowded living conditions (Cox, McCain, & Chandler, 1979; Paulus, 1975). The college dormitory studies have also provided evidence that individuals have difficulty coping with dense living conditions over time and appear to give up or reduce efforts to structure or regulate their interactions (Baum & Valins, 1979). In fact, many affective reactions toward dormitory living become more negative over time (Baum & Aiello, 1978; Baum & Gatchel, 1981; Calesnick, 1978).

The college and prison studies have thus provided converging evidence on a number of issues related to high-density living. They have demonstrated that the effects and dynamics of crowding are similar in two highly discrepant environments and populations. A number of other investigations of naturalistic manipulations of density have also yielded important findings. One that is particularly important in the context of discussion of prison and dormitory studies is the work by Saegert (1982) focusing on the effects of residential density on low-income children.

In Saegert's studies, density was determined by two separate indices. The highest-density settings housed large numbers of people per room in individual apartments (up to 2.6 people per room) and were in the largest (i.e., 14-story) buildings. The lowest-density settings housed fewer people in an apartment (i.e., less than a single person per room) and were in smaller (i.e., 3-story) buildings. Analyses considered 257 schoolchildren and data were collected through interviews with the children, teachers' ratings of children's behavior, and reading achievement scores collected independently by school systems.

The results of this research provided further evidence of the negative impact of high density and revealed additional evidence of cross-situational effects. Density was associated with behavior problems as rated by teachers; overall, children living in higher-density housing were rated more negatively and they also exhibited more evidence of anxiety and hyperactive distractibility than did children in lower-density housing. Interview data suggested that children showed little awareness of apartment crowding, but that higher densities were associated with more frequent interaction and conflict. Reading scores were also affected; children living in higher-density apartments exhibited lower vocabulary scores and reading comprehension. Though these effects were related to other factors as well, evidence suggested that density was at least partly responsible for departure of reading skills from class averages.

Other important investigations, such as Rodin's (1976) examination of apartment density and conditioning of helplessness and Loo's (1978) research on children's responses to density, also suggest a powerful influence of naturalistic variations of density. Space does not allow for detailed discussion here, and several of these studies are discussed elsewhere. It is sufficient to note at this juncture that these studies have provided important confirmation of findings and hypotheses suggested by animal work, correlational studies, and laboratory experiments and have suggested a number of things not previously considered. Many of these issues are of particular relevance in considering the emergence of theories of density and crowding-related phenomena.

14.6. EMERGING MODELS OF CROWDING

A number of different theories have been proposed to account for crowding phenomena. These theories range from relatively brief statements or hypotheses to more elaborate and involved models. Since many of the theories have elements similar to those of others, we will not attempt to detail all of the theoretical statements. Instead, we will focus on the seminal statements and the most complete elaborations of these approaches to facilitate evaluation of the different approaches.

Theoretical approaches to crowding can be categorized in a number of ways. Some focus primarily on the stimulus aspects of density and crowding while others emphasize response factors. Some are concerned mainly with spatial factors of crowded settings while others emphasize social elements. Some focus primarily on psychological reactions while others deal with a wide variety of psychological and behavioral outcomes. These differential emphases result in theories that vary widely in their scope. Some see crowding as primarily the study of spatial restriction (e.g., Freedman, 1975): Crowding occurs when available space is limited. This spatial factor differentiates the study of crowding from that of personal space, territoriality, and group size. Other researchers have emphasized different elements such as frequency of social contact, control, and interference, and have attempted to link these different factors together. From this perspective crowding involves too many people in too little space (Baum & Valins, 1979; Paulus, 1980; Saegert, 1978). This condition can be characterized by large numbers of people, paucity of space, lack of privacy or territoriality, and lack of personal space. A comprehensive theory of crowding may need to incorporate all of these elements (e.g., Baron & Rodin, 1978; Paulus, 1980) and their consequences.

Before we discuss the theoretical approaches, a few points should be reiterated. As we noted at the beginning of this chapter, Stokols (1972) proposed that one must distinguish between crowding (perceived inadequacy of space) and objective physical density. This proposal was intended to account for findings in many studies of little if any effects of density. Stokols argued that only if there is a perceived inadequacy of space will significant impacts of crowding be observed. Not all research has accepted this notion (e.g., Freedman, 1975) and negative effects have been observed without subjects evidencing subjective experience of crowding. Stokols (1977) has responded that the psychological perspective is essentially an emphasis on the use of intervening constructs in explaining crowding-related effects but does not ignore the impact of situational factors. In fact, the most fruitful approach is one that considers the confluence of both situational and psychological factors as noted in Figure 14.1. We consider each theoretical approach from this perspective.

14.6.1. Overload

One perspective that has deep roots and that saw extensive early use in interpreting effects of crowding is the overload model. This perspective focuses on one social consequence of density. Since each individual in a setting represents a potential social contact, high levels of density are a potential source of excessive stimulation resulting in a possible state of stimulus or social overload. Notions of overload were initially developed to account for the impact of urban life. Wirth (1938) and Simmel (1950) argued that the size, density, and heterogeneity of urban environments can be sources of excessive levels of physical and social stimulation, and Simmel (1950) also proposed that this excessive social stimulation leads urban residents to be involved in fewer and more superficial interactions in order to conserve psychic energy. Milgram (1970) elaborated on this perspective and proposed the use of the term *overload* from systems analysis. The overloaded individual withdraws from social involvement with less important people as social demands increase, and the resulting situation is typified by the aloof and unfriendly demeanor of many city residents.

The concept of overload or overstimulation has been incorporated into several treatments of crowding. Desor (1972) proposed that feelings of crowding result from the experience of excessive stimulation, and studies suggested that this stimulation could come from social and nonsocial sources (e.g., Worchel, 1978). Esser (1972) noted that crowding involves stimulus overload from exposure to unfamiliar or inappropriate social contacts. Baum and Valins (1977) conceptualized crowding in terms of having to deal with too many uncontrolled and unwanted interactions. Saegert (1973, 1978) proposed that high-density conditions tax one's attentional capacity when the numbers of actual or potential interactions reach high levels. This overload comes about in part because of demands of having to regulate the involuntary and unpredictable interactions in such settings.

Overload may be a source of stress or arousal and may result in attempts to reduce it—one may cope by routinizing behavior, avoiding novel situations, withdrawing from unfamiliar others, and behaving in stereotypical ways. One may also make decisions on the basis of less information and analysis and, hence, be more responsive to salient social cues such as gender or race. Saegert's model goes beyond a simple concern with the level of social stimulation induced by high density and focuses on the demands made on the individual in highly dense settings. Any feature that increases such demands (such as absence of resources, lack of familiarity, or turnover) should contribute to this overload.

Cohen (1978) has also developed a model using overload notions. Relying heavily on Kahneman's

(1973) model of attention, he proposed that people have only a limited attentional capacity to allocate to the environment. When this capacity becomes strained or overloaded, the individual will focus on the most relevant aspects of his or her environment and ignore less relevant aspects. The individual presumably monitors and evaluates actual or potential environmental stimuli to determine their significance and the coping responses required. Effort involved in such a process increases with the uncertainty and intensity of the stimuli, and prolonged exposure to such demanding stimulation depletes attentional capacity. The end result is cognitive fatigue and withdrawal. Specific predictions made by this model have gained support in regard to task performance. Generally, exposure to intense, unpredictable, and uncontrollable stressors is associated with poorer performance on secondary or subsidiary tasks and increased focusing on the most task-relevant cues to the detriment of less relevant ones (e.g., Cohen & Lezak, 1977). In social situations, evidence also exists for a lowered likelihood of helping others under conditions of attentional overload (e.g., Korte, Ypma, & Toppen, 1975). Decreased helping is seen as being caused by lessened attentiveness and cognitive fatigue present under conditions of environmental stress.

Rapoport (1975) has also emphasized perceptual responses to environmental stimulation in analyzing the effects of crowding. Perceived density is a function of the amount and rate of information that one has to process in an environment and of environmental cues of high levels of potential interactions. However, actual feelings of crowding depend on perception of the level of stimulation as unwanted or exceeding some appropriate level. Rapoport emphasizes that there is a wide variety of cultural and individual differences in tolerance and desire for an ability to cope with various levels of interactions. As do Cohen and Saegert, he suggests that uncertainty and uncontrollability are important factors in the experience of overload.

One assumption made by Rapoport is that there exists some optimal level of social stimulation. Individuals seek to avoid both being overloaded and not having sufficient social stimulation (isolation). This feature has been developed extensively in Altman's (1975) privacy regulation model of crowding. He proposed that individuals have a certain desired level of social stimulation that depends on personal characteristics and situational factors. If the individual does not attain the desired level of stimulation, attempts will be made to adjust the level of stimulation by various behavioral, psychological, or cultural coping mechanisms. Overstimulation (crowding) would lead to attempts to reduce stimulation by means of withdrawal, aloofness, and so on. Understimulation (isolation) would lead to seeking additional social stimulation by seeking opportunities for interaction, being friendly, and so on.

Although the various overload theories have unique characteristics, there is a clear common thread among them. All emphasize the cognitive demands of functioning in highly dense environments. When these demands exceed the individual's capacity to handle them, overload is experienced and various adaptive mechanisms ensue to reduce the overload. Implicit in these theories is the assumption that the number of people and interactions one has to deal with is a more important factor in overload than limited space. These actual or potential interactions are especially problematic if they are unpredictable or uncontrollable.

Figure 14.1 is a simple description of the crowding process. Physical density is depicted as a unitary condition whose potential effects are mediated by situational and psychological variables. These mediators determine whether density yields an appraisal of threat or harm—the degree to which potential consequences of high density are seen as real and aversive. If the judged impact of density is sufficient, crowding will be experienced. Overload theory is an elaboration of this basic scheme, focusing on a specific source of stress inherent in high-density settings.

Density, among other things, involves numbers of people and therefore numbers of social contacts. When density increases, there are more potential contacts and therefore more potential social stimulation. Appraisal of such conditions would involve the factors previously discussed. Physical properties such as the presence or absence of walls or barriers will affect whether excessive contact is actually experienced. Similarly, social relationships such as friendships or group structures influence the frequency and nature of social stimulation.

Different coping styles may also affect appraisal of social experience under high-density conditions, and personal goals and experience will also affect whether the potential for social overload is high or low. When these variables increase the likelihood that overload will occur, appraisal of crowding ensues. When some combination of these variables reduces the impact of increased social activity, high density is less likely to result in crowding.

By elaborating on the sources of stress inherent

in high-density settings, overload theory allows prediction of specific responses to or effects of crowding. Withdrawal from social contact, narrowing of attention, and decreased sensitivity to social stimuli are all possible given the conditions that are reflected in appraisal of overload. There is empirical support for the basic propositions of overload theory, and its application to crowding has proven to be useful (e.g., Baum & Valins, 1977; Cohen, 1978; Saegert, 1978). Attentional allocation effects have been observed in task performance situations (Cohen, 1978), and social withdrawal has been observed under crowded conditions (Baum & Valins, 1977; McCauley & Taylor, 1978; Paulus, 1980). Yet a number of important questions remain. What is the relative importance of different environmental and social elements (e.g., space, distance, number, unpredictability, etc.)? How can one differentiate overload from the helplessness concept central to control theories of crowding that make similar predictions? And how does an individual cope with chronic overload? If it is temporarily overcome and overload is no longer experienced, will the use of adaptive mechanisms be relaxed? Or will they be maintained even more strongly because of the rewards they have provided, even if they are no longer adaptive?

14.6.2. Arousal Theory

Arousal is given a central role in several models of crowding (Evans, 1978; Paulus, 1980). These models propose that dense conditions increase arousal and, in turn, affect task performance and social behavior. Evans (1978) focuses on the arousing effects of spatial confinement and interpersonal distance. He argues that overarousal will lead to decrements on complex tasks and attempts by individuals to minimize the arousal by minimizing visual contact. Paulus (1980) proposed that fear of potential negative consequences in crowded settings leads to enhanced arousal and subsequent decrements on complex tasks and facilitation on simple ones (cf. Zajonc, 1965). As noted earlier, studies of task performance and physiological arousal provide support for an arousal model of crowding, but ambiguities exist about the measurement and interpretation of measures of arousal (Evans, 1978). Many of these measures restrict movement, which can amplify the effects of limited space or make these effects more likely in adequate space. Further, these measures almost always address acute experiences, but do not address the cumulative impact of chronic or episodic crowding.

Unlike overload theory, where the emphasis was on identifying a source of crowding within the density construct and then specifying responses and relevant conditions, arousal theory seeks primarily to identify mediators of the effects of crowding and density. Density still must be appraised, but here the appraisal either may directly yield arousal or may suggest several consequences, of which arousal is one. The arousal that is generated then causes the effects that make up the crowding syndrome.

Arousal is also an important element in a number of attributional theories of crowding. These positions are derived from Schachter and Singer's (1962) theory of emotions. They propose that, while the experience of emotion requires a state of arousal, the particular emotion experienced depends on the interpretation or label that the individual assigns to the arousal state. This interpretation can be affected by various situational or cognitive cues that could feasibly be related to this arousal level (e.g., another's expressed emotions, environmental cues). Worchel and Teddlie (1976) contended that violations of personal space experienced in crowded settings are a source of arousal. Individuals in such situations will be motivated to seek an explanation of this arousal, and the experience of crowding will result if the individual attributes the arousal to others being too close. If arousal is attributed to some other factor, or if the attribution process is inhibited or interrupted, the experience of crowding can be reduced (Aiello, Thompson, & Brodzinsky, 1983).

Keating and his colleagues have also emphasized this attributional approach. Their concern has been primarily with the *scapegoating* phenomenon in which people may attribute arousal induced by various stressors (e.g., disconfirmed expectations or unfulfilled goals) to crowding when density is a salient factor (Gochman & Keating, 1980; Kalb & Keating, 1980). Schmidt and Keating (1980) view crowding as an attributional label for arousal that occurs when social factors produce behavioral and perceptual interference (lack of control) and density is a salient environmental stimulus.

The attributional model derives support from a number of studies in which the attribution process has been manipulated. For example, the presence of pictures or the anticipation of "subliminal" noise can reduce the impact of density variables (Worchel & Teddlie, 1976; Worchel & Yohai, 1979), presumably because density-produced arousal was attributed to these salient nondensity stimuli. However, if density is the most prominent contextual factor, stress in-

duced by other less salient factors (e.g., unfulfilled goals or disconfirmed expectations) may be attributed to crowding (Gochman & Keating, 1979; Kalb & Keating, 1979).

Patterson (1976, 1979) has elaborated on the arousal model and has described a perspective that takes more account of behavioral, physiological, and psychological factors. According to this intimacy arousal theory, high-density situations increase the intensity and probability of nonverbal intimacy behavior (e.g., inappropriate closeness, eye contact, touching, etc.). This increased intimacy can be a source of arousal, and this arousal can be labeled either positively or negatively, depending on context.

Patterson's model fits more directly with the other perspectives we have discussed or will discuss than do other theoretical portrayals of arousal or crowding. As with Evans (1978), causal conditions that derive from the level of density present are appraised in situational and personal contexts. As part of this appraisal, the impact (and arousal) of the situation is judged, arousal is generated, and crowding ensues.

One remaining problem, however, is that the attributional process in dense situations is likely to be more involved than specified by these models. Baron and Rodin (1978) point out that attributing the source of arousal to density would have different implications depending on whether the attribution is made to social or spatial factors. This type of attribution could influence not only the initial responses to crowding but also coping (e.g., Baum & Koman, 1976). Furthermore, several studies have shown that providing a subject with prior information that arousal experienced in a dense environment may be due to crowding reduces the negative impact of crowding (Langer & Saegert, 1977; Paulus & Matthews, 1980). Possibly such information serves to enhance feelings of control or facilitates selection of appropriate strategies. Other studies have found that both the type and the amount of information are important in determining its impact (Baum, Fisher, & Solomon, 1981). Fisher and Baum (1980) found that information about emotional responses reduced ratings of crowdedness but was associated with greater discomfort than information that focused attention on characteristics of the crowded situations.

14.6.3. The Density–Intensity Hypothesis

Another model that focuses on density as a source of stimulation, although it is not concerned with overload, arousal, or attributions, is Freedman's (1975) density–intensity hypothesis. According to this notion, crowding is not inherently good or bad. Instead, crowding serves to intensify a person's typical reactions to situations. If the situation is a normally pleasant one, density should increase the pleasure experience. If, on the other hand, the situation is basically unpleasant, density will make it more unpleasant. This intensification occurs because high density increases the importance of people or characteristics of the setting and hence intensifies the typical reactions to them.

Evidence for the density–intensity theory comes from a number of studies by Freedman and his colleagues (Freedman, 1975) in which individuals were exposed to positive and negative situations under varying conditions of density. He also interprets some findings of sex differences related to crowding as support for this model. A number of studies have shown that increased spatial density may elicit positive reactions for all-female groups but negative ones for all-male groups (cf. Sundstrom, 1978). These findings may reflect intensification of females' positive feelings and negative ones for males. Yet the data in crowded conditions do not indicate such initial baseline differences (cf. Paulus, 1980). Other studies have failed to support Freedman's predictions (Sundstrom, 1978).

Freedman's model differs from the others in several ways. Appraisal is not typically specified but could clearly be included. Instead of a focus on one or another source of stress, appraisal would involve a more quantitative judgment about the overall impact of the setting. Crowding is not necessarily associated with either a positive or negative judgment, but responses to the setting are determined by judgments about the intensity of social and spatial conditions and by one's typical responses to the setting. Appraisal mediates the intensity of response rather than whether crowding is experienced.

Some aspects of this model are appealing. That density can increase the intensity of response is undoubtedly true, and there are many instances in which this model accurately predicts response. However, it does not account for the fact that crowding affects the quality of experience and that some conditions associated with density are almost always negative experiences for many people. Loss of control, for example, may be a consequence of high-density settings, and research has indicated that not having control is associated with negative outcomes (e.g., Cohen, 1980; Davidson, Baum, & Collins, 1982; Glass & Singer, 1972; Seligman, 1975; Wortman & Brehm, 1975).

14.6.4. Behavioral Constraint

Probably the most popular theoretical perspective focuses on limitations of freedom to choose among a number of behavioral options in dense environments. Limitations and restrictions of behavior are the source of crowding stress and related behavioral and psychological reactions. Proshansky, Ittelson, and Rivlin (1970) emphasized the importance of freedom of choice in residential settings and used this idea to organize the concepts of territoriality, personal space, and crowding. Feelings of crowding are induced by violations of normative expectations about the use of space and frustration of goals by the physical presence of others. These factors are seen as threats to one's freedom of choice (cf. Brehm, 1966). Altman (1975) has developed a similar but more elaborate model that was briefly discussed earlier. He proposed that individuals are motivated to regulate their level of privacy or degree of social stimulation so as to attain preferred levels. If a preferred level is not achieved, various verbal, nonverbal, and physical coping responses are engaged to adjust the level of privacy. High density levels may inhibit the ability of individuals to use these coping mechanisms successfully to attain desired levels of privacy.

Goal interference and constraint were also major elements of Stokols's theorizing (Stokols, 1972, 1976). He focuses on the problem of control and interference that is experienced when the individual's need for space is not met in a particular environment. The important factor in the experience of crowding is one's feelings that the inability to obtain desired or needed space will lead to unpleasant consequences. That is, one will not be able to attain certain goals or complete desired activities. As a result, the individual makes various behavioral and psychological adjustments to increase the space. Feelings of crowding are expected to be greatest when failure to attain space requirements represents a potential personal threat to one's security.

Stokols (1976) also suggested some dimensions that are important in determining the severity of reactions to crowding. Goal interference or thwarting may take a neutral or unintentional form, or a personal or intentional form. Crowding can occur in environments that play a central role in one's life (primary — such as home and work) or in environments where one's dealings with others are temporary and relatively unimportant (secondary—such as public places). He predicted different consequences for the various combinations of primary and secondary environments with personal and neutral thwarting. Generally, the most severe and long-term effects are expected for personal crowding in primary environments, with the weakest effects anticipated for neutral crowding in secondary environments.

There are a number of other investigators who have emphasized behavioral constraint. Saegert (1973, 1978) describes spatial constraint induced by limited space as restricting freedom of movement, increasing coordination demands, and increasing social overload. This results in feelings of loss of control and frustration. Schopler and Stockdale (1977) have emphasized that others may be a source of interference in crowded settings because they may prevent or hinder goal attainment. The degree of interference determines the level of crowding stress experienced. A number of studies have shown the impact of goal interference (e.g., Sundstrom, 1975; Wicker, Kirmeyer, Hanson, & Alexander, 1976) and physical interference (Heller, Groff, & Solomon, 1977; Schopler & Stockdale, 1977).

Another perspective that focuses on goal interference is the ecological approach described by Wicker (1973, 1979). This approach is derived from earlier work by Barker and his colleagues (cf. Barker, 1968) on the effects of understaffing in settings in which there are not sufficient people available to fill necessary roles, jobs, or positions (as in small schools or churches). Wicker (1973) proposed that crowded environments can be seen as the opposite state, in that the number of people may exceed the number of opportunities available. This should lead to lowered feelings of involvement and of being needed. Thus the presence of many others inhibits one's attainment of certain desired resources or goals. Supposedly, if sufficient resources or opportunities exist in highly dense settings, there should be very little negative impact.

14.6.5. Control

A major underlying theme in many of the theoretical perspectives of crowding has been the degree to which crowding affects actual or perceived control of the individual over the environment (e.g., Baron & Rodin, 1978; Rodin & Baum, 1978; Schmidt & Keating, 1980; Sherrod & Cohen, 1979). Uncertainty and unpredictability are viewed as contributing to social overload (Cohen, 1978; Saegert, 1978), and behavioral constraint models are concerned with the

restriction in one's behavioral freedoms or goal interference. Baron and Rodin (1978) presented an extensive model in which they attempted to account for the broad range of crowding phenomena by means of the concept of personal control. Personal control is defined as "the ability to establish correspondence between intentions and environmental consequences of one's actions" (p. 146), and a number of forms of control were considered. *Decision control* referred to the extent to which one could select one's goals, *outcome control* referred to the degree to which one's actions influenced one's outcomes, *onset control* referred to the extent to which one could choose and moderate exposure to crowded situations, and *offset control* referred to the ability to leave or terminate the crowding exposure. These different dimensions contribute to the complexity and uncertainty of high-density conditions and require intense attentional monitoring. Crowding stress is experienced if control is impaired or threatened. One should be able to adapt rather easily if only overload or attention-induced arousal occurs. Additional loss of control, however, can lead to more serious long-term consequences. Crowding stress in such a case would be associated with negative mood states, stress, and disruption of task performance and social behavior.

Crowding is associated with a range of anticipatory and corrective coping responses designed to reassert cognitive or behavioral control. If such coping is unsuccessful or very intense, the individual will evidence various residual costs. Baron and Rodin's theoretical development is unusual in its detailed and thoughtful analysis of a wide variety of these issues. One strength is the separate analyses of the impact of different aspects of highly dense environments—diminished space, social stimulation in dyadic situations, and increased number of people. These different elements can instigate crampedness stress, privacy stress, and numerosity stress, each with its unique intervening control processes and coping mechanisms. Initial reactions to these crowding stressors may involve reactance or aggression. However, failure of these and other coping mechanisms will result in apathy or learned helplessness (Seligman, 1975). Although Baron and Rodin (1978) recognize three different sources of stress, they propose that the numerosity-based one is more likely to be a source of negative consequences because of the greater control-related problems with larger groups in confined spaces.

There are a number of studies that have provided explicit evidence for the impact of control factors in crowding. Rodin, Solomon, and Metcalf (1978) found that individuals who had control over activities in a crowded environment (onset control) felt less crowded. In a study by Sherrod (1974), subjects who had the option to leave a crowded situation (offset control) showed a reduction in negative aftereffects. Langer and Saegert (1977) and Paulus and Matthews (1980) demonstrated that increasing informational control by providing subjects in a crowded situation with expectations about the potential effects of this condition reduced the negative effects of crowding. These studies demonstrate that increased feelings of control can mitigate the effects of crowding. Other studies have reported evidence of links between exposure to high-density conditions and behaviors indicative of helplessness (cf. Rodin & Baum, 1978). Rodin (1976) found that students who lived in high-density, three-room apartments were relatively less likely to exercise options in an experimental setting. These students also showed a diminished ability to solve a solvable puzzle after an initial experience with an unsolvable puzzle. Baum and Valins (1977) found increased feelings of helplessness and passivity among residents of long-corridor dormitories compared to residents of short-corridor dorms.

Although the control perspective seems to be able to integrate a wide variety of findings and has considerable research support, it does have several shortcomings. These shortcomings are characteristic of any approach based on control. Loss of control can have a variety of effects besides passivity, helplessness, and impairment of cognitive functioning. Initial exposure to learned helplessness can lead to resistance or attempts to regain control (Wortman & Brehm, 1975). Only after these attempts have been unsuccessful or expectations for control have waned will helplessness ensue. Baum and colleagues (1978) and Baum and Gatchel (1981) have found evidence for this in studies of dormitory crowding. It seems, therefore, that helplessness is less likely to be manifested in short-term laboratory situations but more likely to appear in studies of longer-term, high-density living conditions. Baron and Rodin account for this by arguing that lack of control produces initial crowding stress and that this stress is responsible for short-term effects.

Although the control perspective is attractive for its inclusiveness and apparent simplicity, the model developed by Rodin and Baron (1978) is rather complex and provides few definitively testable predictions that allow one to differentiate it clearly from other models. For example, a combined overload and behavioral constraint model (Saegert, 1978; Stokols, 1976) can also account well for the present range of data. Combined predictions and assumptions about underlying processes are similar to the control perspective, and it may be difficult to demonstrate clearly the superiority of one over the other. Of course, one could argue that the overload and behavioral constraint model can be subsumed under the control model. Regardless, the degree to which the control notion can account for other factors suggests that elements of control are important determinants of crowding stress.

The important question, however, remains: Is it really lack of control that is the important factor, or is it simply the exposure to aversive events such as overstimulation, threats, and goal frustration? Just demonstrating that having some sense of control over such aversive events mitigates crowding effects does not prove that control is the crucial mediator. In highly dense naturalistic situations it is difficult to disentangle the potential contributions of overload, constraint, fear, and control. Only precisely controlled experimental studies are likely to achieve this goal, but they would likely do so in settings where ambient stimuli have been reduced to artificial levels. It is of interest in this light that most theoretically relevant crowding studies were designed to demonstrate the importance of a particular theoretical element. Very few studies have attempted tests of competing theories (e.g., Paulus & Matthews, 1980). This is in part the result of the focus of these theories on different domains (e.g., task performance vs. social behavior) but also may reflect the difficulty in making definitive differential predictions because of the similarities of the various theories.

14.6.6. Integrating Competing Perspectives

In some ways, these theoretical approaches are essentially complementary, and a complete perspective of crowding may require inclusion of the major elements of these differing approaches (cf. Bell, Fisher, & Baum, 1978; Paulus, 1980; Stokols, 1976). A descriptive integration of these perspectives would suggest that density is potentially associated with a number of psychologically relevant conditions, and the degree to which any of them cause crowding is mediated by appraisal.

We have summarized the major elements of the various perspectives in Table 14.1. Except for density–intensity, all of the models focus both on spatial and social density factors. However, as indicated earlier, the overload and personal control models emphasize the impact of number, while the behavioral

Table 14.1. Comparison of Models of Crowding

Model	Environmental Focus	Mediating Variables	Response Focus
Overload	Number of people Number of interactions Spatial construction Environmental demands	Intensity of stimuli Uncertainty of stimuli Unpredictability Unfamiliarity Complexity Novelty Unwanted stimulation	Attentional allocation Attentional capacity Cognitive fatigue Withdrawal
Arousal	Number of people Space Interpersonal distance	Attributions Uncertainty Fear stimuli	Arousal state Quality of task performance Crowding label
Density–intensity	Space	Context (positive/negative)	Affect
Behavioral constraint	Spatial constraint Number	Restriction of freedom Lack of control Inability to regulate interaction or stimulation Coordination of problems Interference Limited resources Goal blocking Violations of normative expectations Primary versus secondary environment Intentionality of constraint	Psychological and behavioral adjustments Feelings of crowding
Personal control	Number Space Privacy	Degree of perceived control Uncontrollability Decision control Onset control Offset control Cognitive control	Mood Stress Task performance Social behavior Helplessness/passivity

constraint model emphasizes space. Interpersonal distance (or personal space) is given primacy only in several arousal models. The response focus of the models is also quite discrepant. While the personal control model focuses on a broad range of responses, the other models have a more limited focus. A broad range of mediating variables has been posited, especially by the overload and constraint models. Although it may be possible to subsume the mediators of these two models under the construct of *personal control*, some important distinction could be lost. The mediators of the overload model are essentially control/predictability-related aspects of environmental stimulation. The mediating variables of the behavioral constraint approach focus on control-related aspects of behaviors and behavioral options in dense settings. Thus one focuses on the stimulus aspects of density while the other focuses on the behavioral problems.

This may be an important distinction to maintain. That is, while explaining crowding effects by a singular construct may be parsimonious, a focus on specific aspects of control and crowding may be more likely to lead to increased understanding of the dynamics of crowding phenomena. Furthermore, by using a concept that has been used to explain the effects of a wide variety of stressors, crowding may be relegated to the position of "just another stressor." As a result, the unique issues of the crowding area may be lost. The perspectives discussed earlier, by focusing on stimulus aspects, mechanisms, and behavioral problems in dense environments, help maintain the uniqueness of the crowding issue. This is particularly true of such models as Altman's description of privacy regulation. This model focuses specifically on need for social stimulation, variables that hinder attainment of desired levels of this stimulation, and the various ways individuals attempt to reach and maintain their optimum level of stimulation.

There is, however, redundancy in the mediating variables listed, and a smaller number of conceptual variables can probably represent most of them. Cox, Paulus, McCain, and Karlovac (1982) have recently proposed a model that subsumes the mediating variables of the behavioral constraint, overload, and control perspectives under the concepts of uncertainty, goal interference, and cognitive load (see Figure 14.2). Uncertainty is meant to capture the lack of control, uncertainty, and unpredictability aspects of the constraint, control, overload, and arousal positions. Goal interference refers to the goal blocking and interference emphasized by the constraint model. Cognitive load refers to the cognitive effort required in dealing with stimulation and social interaction. Uncertainty, goal interference, and cognitive load are presumed to lead to specific consequences of fear (stress), frustration, and cognitive strain respectively. Uncertainty and goal interference also contribute to cognitive strain.

Although the utility of the above model remains to be determined, there are advantages in such an approach. Focusing on a subset of basic process variables may stimulate process-oriented research and eventually lead to a clearer specification of crowding-related processes.

Another theoretical approach to crowding that has some integrative potential is one that schematizes the process by depicting various sequential and interrelated processes. For example, as shown in Figure 14.3, Altman suggests that individuals have a particular level of desired privacy at any point in time and will engage various behavioral control mechanisms if the desired level is not attained (either too low or too high). Level of stress is determined by degree of mismatch between desired and achieved privacy. Various personal, interpersonal, and situational factors are seen as influencing the efficacy of the coping process, because of goal blocking and social interference, and so on. Stress is directly related to negative outcomes or costs.

Sundstrom (1978) extended this model and incorporated some of Stokols's (1972) ideas. This model has several notable features. Instead of focusing primarily on achievement of desired privacy, this model focuses on modifying variables (e.g., degree of exposure, type of activity). The extent to which density and related physical and social conditions are a source of stress depends on these modifying factors. A similar emphasis is found in the multidensity model of Paulus (1980). Another unique feature of the Sundstrom model is its acknowledgment of the adaptation or decreased responsiveness effect, though no definitive suggestions for the nature of this effect are made.

Another eclectic model that incorporates some features of the preceding ones and is an extension of a broader stress model is presented by Fisher, Bell, and Baum (1984). High-density conditions and pertinent social, situational, and personal factors combine to determine whether or not one perceives the environment as crowded. The perception of crowding is seen as the cause of stress and will lead to various coping responses. This model has a number of im-

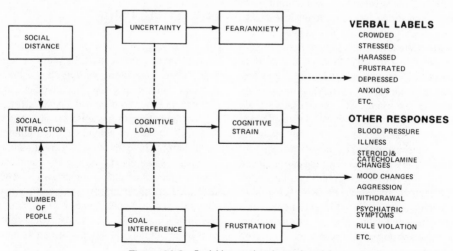

Figure 14.2. Social interaction-demand model.

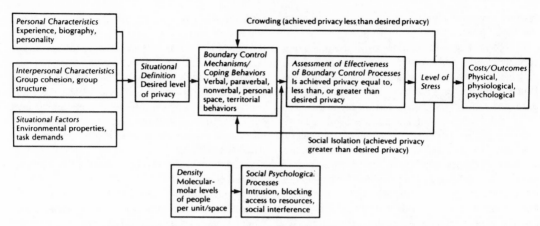

Figure 14.3. Schematic process depicting sequential and interrelated processes.

portant characteristics. It recognizes the influence of situational, social, and personal factors, it assumes the existence of an optimal range of stimulation, and it considers the consequences of both successful and unsuccessful coping.

Each of these schematic frameworks is a potentially useful representation of crowding-related problems. Yet these models have the same difficulty with imprecision as do the other models we have discussed. They do not tell us the relative importance of the various situational, physical, and social variables, though they suggest that these may change. Further, these models are not specific as to the nature of the coping adaptation and habituation processes that are likely. However, these models do make a number of specific predictions that are amenable to empirical test. Both the Altman (1976) and Fisher and colleagues (1984) models refer to an optimum level of privacy or stimulation. Studies should investigate whether individuals make such determinations and the factors that influence such judgments. Altman's theory suggests that density functions primarily to hinder the efficacy of coping or adaptive behaviors. Such coping behaviors and their relation to crowding conditions should be examined. That is, studies could determine whether variables have their influence primarily by influencing the efficacy of coping responses. The Fisher and colleagues model, as well as previously discussed theories, suggests that the perception of crowding is important in producing effects. The extent to which negative effects of crowded conditions are mediated by such perceptions should be more definitively assessed. The sequential nature of the crowding-related processes depicted also should be examined. It is possible that many of

the depicted processes occur in parallel fashion rather than in sequence (see Fig. 14.4).

It appears likely to us that further progress in the crowding area will require lively competition among several rather than specific heuristic theoretical models. Researchers should focus on the precise processes underlying the impact of density rather than glossing over theoretical differences in a premature attempt at integrative simplicity. Such progress would be greatly aided by more specific model development to allow finer distinctions and more precise tests. Further, these models should address the interesting but difficult issues of tolerance/adaptation and the coping process. We will suggest some specific directions along these lines in the next section.

14.7. CONCLUSION

Our knowledge of crowding phenomena has increased greatly in the past 15 years. There is evidence that, consistent with earlier expectations, crowding can have physical, psychological, and social consequences for humans and animals. However, the severity and range of these effects appear to depend on a wide variety of individual, environmental, and social factors. In spite of the apparent complexity of crowding-related effects, our review has pinpointed a large number of empirical consistencies. These consistencies are most gratifying since they have been observed across a wide range of research paradigms and environments. In some cases, consistent results have been obtained in studies of human and nonhuman populations.

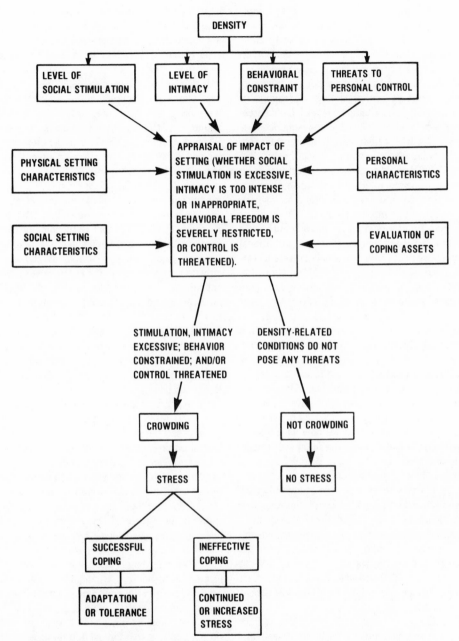

Figure 14.4. Summary model of crowding stress: Density gives rise to a number of potential consequences that are mediated by appraisal and pose various demands.

There also appears to be considerable theoretical convergence. Most of the theoretical models reviewed have emphasized the importance of uncertainty, unpredictability, or lack of control in dense environments. There is considerable support for this perspective. However, at present, it is not possible to point to one theory as reflecting most accurately all of the processes underlying the broad range of crowding-related phenomena we have considered. Certainly, one important concern of future research on crowding should be theoretical refinement. Studies should examine more precisely the processes underlying the effects of density in order to allow more adequate theory building and assessment. In particular, there is a large gap in our understanding of the interrelationship of various responses to crowding. How important are psychological feelings of crowding or different attributional labels? Do differential perceptions lead to differential consequences, or is the particular label or perception unimportant, except for its being either negative or positive (cf. Patterson, 1977)? How does previous experience with crowding affect one's tolerance for subsequent experience? How do different behavioral responses to density influence the impact of dense environments? Are observed behaviors simply relatively automatic reactions to density or do they represent intentional coping responses with definitive ameliorative effects?

Also, there is still much to be learned about the interrelationship of psychological, behavioral, and physiological reactions to crowding, particularly over relatively long periods of exposure to crowding. It is unfortunate that work on crowding slowed at the point where significant theoretical breakthroughs became feasible because of the solid groundwork laid by prior research. In some ways, the reduced research activity on crowding is quite sensible. Many of the goals of researchers on crowding have been accomplished. Convincing evidence for its negative effects has been marshaled, and we now have a fairly good understanding of some of the processes underlying these effects. Yet the "pathology" focus may have blinded many to the fact that research on crowding has, to a large extent, been the study of human response to social stressors. Although the response to crowding shares many similarities with responses to nonsocial stressors such as noise, research has unearthed a number of unique factors involved in human response to and coping with the stress of dealing with people in crowded settings. Crowding research thus represents an important contribution to human stress research.

While there are a number of issues that remain unsettled and several directions for future research to take, we will consider only a few in any detail. Clearly, continued investigation along a number of dimensions is needed fully to understand both crowding and our ability to deal with it.

14.7.1. Tolerance

Many studies and several theories have addressed the issue of tolerance for crowding. While this is a central issue in some of the earlier efforts in the field (e.g., Desor, 1972), it has generally been treated as a sidelight in later studies. Tolerance for crowding in a particular setting may be related to exposure to crowded conditions or may be brought with the individual from prior experiences. While it is plausible that increased tolerance to crowding is associated with increased exposure, only a small number of studies have found such a relationship (Eoyang, 1974; Wohlwill & Kahn, 1973). The studies report that individuals from a large urban area or a large family reacted relatively more favorably to crowded conditions. Yet studies in prisons indicate that inmates from urban areas respond more *negatively* to crowded conditions than those from rural areas (Paulus, 1984). Further complicating this is the finding that those who lived in crowded homes seem to respond more *positively* to prison crowding than did those from less crowded ones (Paulus, 1984). However, Baron and colleagues (1976) also found that individuals from crowded home environments reacted more negatively to crowded college dormitories than those from less crowded homes. Further, a number of studies have found that repeated or continual exposure to crowded conditions is associated with increasingly negative reactions (e.g., Aiello et al., 1975; Baum & Valins, 1977).

It appears evident from previous research that past exposure to crowding does not inevitably result in increased tolerance, but that such experiences can lead to either increased or decreased tolerance. This issue is obviously fertile ground for theoretical and empirical work. We will suggest some directions that future researchers may wish to follow. Prediction of the direction of the effects requires clearer specifications of the nature of the experience and the behaviors being assessed. Several hypotheses are plausible. First, it is possible that development of tolerance for crowding is specific to setting type. Living in a crowded home may prepare one to function in crowded residential conditions, but not for crowded urban environments. Living in crowded areas (e.g., cities) may lead to enhanced tolerance of such conditions, but not to increased tolerance of crowded "home" environments.

Another possibility is that tolerance development will depend on individuals' ability to develop successful coping responses and/or whether they have generally positive experiences. When successful coping responses do not develop and/or negative experiences dominate, tolerance will, in fact, decrease. Tolerance and preference for various environmental conditions will be consistent when coping responses are associated with positive experiences. Thus individuals who learn to function effectively in large cities and take advantage of their many unique opportunities should show both high tolerance of and preference for large cities. Other individuals who may cope effectively with city living but whose experience is limited to negative aspects of city living (e.g., noise, pollution, and litter) may demonstrate tolerance of but not preference for city life. Tolerance and preference are thus inconsistent under these conditions. A similar analysis could be made of responses to living in crowded homes. The converse of this would suggest that crowded conditions in which coping responses are not successful and/or negative experiences dominate will result in reduced tolerance for crowding and enhanced desire for uncrowded conditions.

Finally, it is possible that, if one functions successfully under crowded conditions and/or has mostly positive experiences, increased desire for exposure to such conditions may ensue. One basis for this hypothesis is the research showing that stress reduction is related to positive interpersonal feelings (e.g., Epley, 1974; Kenrick & Cialdini, 1977). Need or preference for stimulation and arousal research provide another basis for this hypothesis (Zuckerman, 1983). Some research suggests that urban residents have a higher need for stimulation (Sales, Guydosh, & Iacano, 1974). Both the need for stimulation and stress reduction perspectives suggest that highly dense settings may become "addictive."

14.7.2. Coping

Certainly one of the central issues in crowding research is the coping process—how people deal with crowding stress. By coping we mean an explicit attempt by an individual to deal with stressful conditions either by changing the situation or by dealing with his or her distress. Research on stress has long focused on the coping process (e.g., Lazarus, 1966), and considerable evidence exists for the efficacy of various coping responses. Several models of crowding give detailed consideration to the coping process (e.g., Altman, 1975; Baron & Rodin, 1978), yet very few studies have examined this process, and many interesting issues remain to be addressed.

One possibility is that coping is specific to the conditions that are responsible for crowding. Different sources of crowding stress may be associated with different coping responses (Baron & Rodin, 1978). Of course, perception of the situation is central here as well. This seems to be a reasonable hypothesis, but only limited evidence for it exists.

For example, it has been found that conditions of high social density lead to withdrawal or avoidance reactions, while spatially dense conditions may lead to attempts to structure or control the interactions (e.g., Baum & Koman, 1976). However, this is a general finding and only suggests that coping is specific to the conditions responsible for stress.

Whether avoidance, attempts at control, or psychological reevaluation occurs in response to crowding should depend on the perceived efficacy of the various approaches and the extent to which the individual has choices about exposure. If one has a high degree of choice about exposure to crowded conditions, avoidance should be the most likely response since this would be the least involved and most effective way to reduce crowding stress. This coping response is most evident in the college dormitory studies, with students attempting to avoid interactions in common areas and other settings (e.g., Baum & Valins, 1977). Attempts at control should be used in situations where exposure to crowding stress is inevitable (e.g., one has to work in the city or has to share a cell with an inmate). Attempts at control can involve, among others, territorial mechanisms and group formation or structuring. If neither avoidance nor control is feasible or successful, cognitive reevaluation of the stress or palliative coping may be the primary coping option left. If one evaluates the situations in less threatening or more positive ways, the inevitable exposure to them may be less aversive.

Another interesting question about coping with crowding is tied to issues concerning general and situation-specific coping strategies. People may have generally preferred coping styles based on past experiences of success with these styles. For example, males appear more likely to use avoidance coping responses than females (Aiello et al., 1977). One might also expect high sensation seekers to be more prone to the control and cognitive coping styles than low sensation seekers. It could be predicted that individuals who are forced to use a nonpreferred coping style experience more stress than those allowed their preferred style.

This discussion suggests that a broad series of studies is needed to assess how various experiences in dense environments are related to the emergence of coping responses and how these coping styles influence reactivity to other environments. The relationship of coping styles to the differential development of tolerance of and preference for density and crowding levels would also be of interest. A clear assessment of the various hypotheses would require a series of longitudinal studies in conjunction with some laboratory studies or assessment.

14.7.3. Other Issues

Coping and tolerance are both related to outcomes— when tolerance for crowding is high and/or when coping is successful, the effects of crowding should be more mild than when tolerance is low or when coping fails. However, research on other stressors suggests that even when coping is successful and negative outcomes are minimized there may be problems. This suggests a number of possibilities.

Costs of Coping

Several models suggest that people pay a price for coping even if the coping is successful (Baron & Rodin, 1978; Selye, 1976). Yet clear demonstrations of such a price do not exist in the crowding area. For example, one could compare individuals whose coping involves great effort with those whose coping involves little effort. Those whose coping involves great effort should demonstrate greater deficits after cessation of the crowding experience. Active and passive coping (e.g., Obrist, 1981) should also be considered. The mechanisms by which coping itself, independent of outcome, has costs for an organism experiencing crowding should be examined.

Aftereffects

Studies of various stressors such as noise have shown that exposure to uncontrollable stressors may lead to deficits in task performance after cessation of the stressor (e.g., Cohen, 1980; Glass & Singer, 1972). This occurs even if no deficits appear during actual exposure to the stressor. Crowding studies have shown similar results, but task deficits represent only one of many types of potential aftereffects of crowding. Social interaction styles, sensation seeking, and capacity to deal with complexity or uncertainty are just some of the response domains that may be influenced by past crowding experiences. It would be of interest to demonstrate positive consequences of exposure to crowding as well. It is conceivable that individuals who have had to deal with the complexity and uncertainty of highly dense environments develop their cognitive and social skills to a greater extent than those who are exposed only to low-density environments.

Combination with Other Stressors

Crowding may often be accompanied by other stressors such as noise, pollution, and heat. Is the impact of crowding enhanced or reduced when other stressors are present? The presence of one or more other stressors may increase one's sensitivity to crowding stress. Yet attributional theories would seem to imply that the presence of multiple stressors increases ambiguity about the sources of stress and may then reduce actual sensitivity to crowding stress (Paulus & Matthews, 1980).

A related question addresses the outcomes of situations in which one is sequentially exposed to various stressors including crowding. Do the types of strategies or coping styles used with one stressor generalize to the next one? If one copes successfully with one stressor, is one likely to do so with another? Does prior exposure to one stressor make one more tolerant of the next stressor or does one become more sensitized to the aversive properties of subsequent stressors?

14.7.4. Applications

Research on crowding has also not realized its full "engineering" potential. Although evidence exists for crowding effects in a broad range of environments, much remains to be learned about the impact of density on different types of populations (e.g., the aged) and in different environments (e.g., schools). We now know that crowding can be an influential factor, but we don't know enough about the generalizability of our findings. In particular, it would seem important to know what levels of density are required to produce negative effects in schools, prisons, homes for the aged, offices, and homes.

Finally, a great deal of research must be done in order to learn how to prevent crowding stress or reduce its negative effects. Some theoretically derived interventions have been successful in preventing the conditions responsible for distress (e.g., Baum & Davis, 1980; Baum et al., 1981; Langer & Saegert, 1977). Research has also considered ways of reducing distress once it has occurred. However, tests of these interventions have been limited, and much remains to be done.

In short, it is our feeling that important work remains to be done at both the practical and the theoretical level. The crowding literature probably represents one of the most extensive empirical and theoretical literatures in environmental psychology. Furthermore, it has implications for a wide range of other environmental issues (e.g., personal space, architecture, urban design). The fruits of the labors of the crowding researchers are just now ready for the picking, but much of the potential fruit is still to be realized.

REFERENCES

Aiello, J.R., Baum, A., & Gormley, F. (1981). Social determinants of residential crowding stress. *Personality and Social Psychology Bulletin, 7,* 643–649.

Aiello, J.R., DeRisi, D., Epstein, Y.M., & Karlin, R.A. (1977). Crowding and the role of interpersonal distance preference. *Sociometry, 40,* 271–282.

Aiello, J.R., Epstein, Y., & Karlin, R. (1975). Effects of crowding on electrodermal activity. *Sociological Symposium, 14,* 42–57.

Aiello, J.R., Nicosia, G., & Thompson, D.E. (1979). Physiological, social, and behavioral consequences of crowding on children and adolescents. *Child Development, 50,* 195–202.

Aiello, J.R., Thompson, D.E., Brodzinsky, D.M. (1983). How funny is crowding anyway? Effects of room size, group size, and the introduction of humor. *Basic and Applied Social Psychology, 4*(2), 193–207.

Altman, I. (1976). *The environment and social behavior.* Monterey, CA: Brooks/Cole.

Anderson, B., Erwin, N., Flynn, D., Lewis, L., & Erwin, J. (1977). Effects of short-term crowding on aggression in captive groups of pigtail monkeys. *Aggressive Behavior, 3,* 33–46.

Barker, R.G. (1968). *Ecological psychology: Concepts and methods for studying the environment of human behavior.* Stanford, CA: Stanford University Press.

Baron, R.M., Mandel, D.R., Adams, C.A., & Griffen, L.M. (1976). Effects of social density in university residential environments. *Journal of Personality and Social Psychology, 34,* 434–446.

Baron, R.M., & Needel, S.P. (1980). Toward an understanding of the differences in the responses of humans and other animals to density. *Psychological Review, 87,* 320–328.

Baron, R., & Rodin, J. (1978). Personal control as a mediator of crowding. In A. Baum, J.E. Singer, & S. Valins (Eds.), *Advances in environmental psychology.* Hillsdale, NJ: Erlbaum.

Baum, A., Aiello, J., & Calesnick, L.E. (1978). Crowding and personal control: Social density and the development of learned helplessness. *Journal of Personality and Social Psychology, 36,* 1000–1011.

Baum, A., Calesnick, L.E., David, G.E., & Gatchel, R.J. (1982). Individual differences in coping with crowding: Stimulus screening and social overload. *Journal of Personality and Social Psychology, 43,* 821–830.

Baum, A., & Davis, G. (1976). Spatial and social aspects of crowding perception. *Environment and Behavior, 8,* 527–544.

Baum, A., & Davis, G. (1980). Reducing the stress of high-density living: An architectural intervention. *Journal of Personality and Social Psychology, 38,* 471–481.

Baum, A., Fisher, J.D., & Solomon, S. (1981). Type of information, familiarity, and the reduction of crowding stress. *Journal of Personality and Social Psychology, 40,* 11–23.

Baum, A., & Gatchel, R.J. (1981). Cognitive determinants of reaction to uncontrollable events: Development of reactance and learned helplessness. *Journal of Personality and Social Psychology, 40,* 1078–1089.

Baum, A., & Greenberg, C.I. (1975). Waiting for a crowd: The behavioral and perceptual effects of anticipated crowding. *Journal of Personality and Social Psychology, 32,* 671–679.

Baum, A., Grunberg, N.E., & Singer, J.E. (1982). The use of psychological and neuroendocrinological measurements in the study of stress. *Health Psychology, 1*(3), 217–236.

Baum, A., & Koman, S. (1976). Differential response to anticipated crowding: Psychological effects of social and spatial density. *Journal of Personality and Social Psychology, 34,* 526–536.

Baum, A., Shapiro, A., Murray, D., & Wideman, M. (1979). Interpersonal mediation of perceived crowding and control in residential dyads and triads. *Journal of Applied Social Psychology, 9,* 491–507.

Baum, A., Singer, J.E., & Baum, C.S. (1981). Stress and the environment. *Journal of Social Issues, 37,* 4–35.

Baum, A., & Valins, S. (1977). *Architecture and social behavior: Psychological studies of social density.* Hillsdale, NJ: Erlbaum.

Baum, A., & Valins, S. (1979). Architectural mediation of residential density and control: Crowding and the regulation of social contact. In L. Berkowitz (Ed.), *Advances in experimental social psychology* (Vol. 12). New York: Academic.

Bell, P.A., Fisher, J.D., & Loomis, R.J. (1978). *Environmental psychology.* Philadelphia: Saunders.

Bell, R.W., Miller, C.E., Ordy, J.M., & Rolsten, C. (1971). Effects of population density and living space upon neuroanatomy, neurochemistry and behavior in the C57B1/10 mouse. *Journal of Comparative Physiological Psychology, 75,* 258–263.

Bergman, B.A. (1971). *The effects of group size, personal space, and success-failure on physiological arousal, test performance, and questionnaire response.* Unpublished doctoral dissertation, Temple University, Phildelphia.

Bickman, L., Teger, A., Gabriele, T., McLaughlin, C., Berger, M., & Sunaday, E. (1973). Dormitory density and helping behavior. *Environment and Behavior, 5,* 464–491.

Booth, A., & Welch, S. (1973). *The effects of crowding: A cross-national study.* Unpublished manuscript, Ministry of State for Urban Affairs, Ottawa, Canada.

Booth, A., & Welch, S. (1974). *Crowding and urban crime rates.* Paper presented at the annual meeting of the Midwest Sociological Association, Omaha, NE.

Brayton, A.R., & Brain, P.F. (1974). Studies of the effects of differential housing on some measures of disease resistance in male and female laboratory mice. *Journal of Endocrinology, 61,* 48–49.

Brehm, J.W. (1966). *A theory of psychological reactance*. New York: Academic.

Calhoun, J.B. (1957). Social welfare as a variable in population dynamics. *Journal of Mammalogy, 33*, 139–159.

Calhoun, J.B. (1962). Population density and social pathology. *Scientific American, 206*, 139–148.

Calhoun, J.B. (1970). Space and the strategy of life. *Ekistics, 29*, 425–437.

Calhoun, J.B. (1973). Death squared: The explosive growth and demise of a mouse population. *Proceedings of the Royal Society of Medicine, 66*, 80–88.

Chapman, R., Masterpasqua, F., & Lore, R. (1976). The effects of crowding during pregnancy on offspring emotional and sexual behavior in rats. *Bulletin of the Psychonomic Society, 7*, 475–477.

Cholden, H., & Roneck, D. (1975, April). *Density and pathology: The issue expanded*. Paper presented at the meeting of the Population Association of America, Seattle, WA.

Christian, J.J. (1963). The pathology of overpopulation. *Military Medicine, 128*, 571–603.

Christian, J.J., & Davis, D.E. (1964). Endocrines, behavior and population. *Science, 146*, 1550–1560.

Cohen, S.A. (1978). Environmental load and the allocation of attention. In A. Baum, J.E. Singer, & S. Valins (Eds.), *Advances in environmental psychology* (Vol. 1). Hillsdale, NJ: Erlbaum.

Cohen, S.A. (1980). Aftereffects of stress on human performance and social behavior: A review of research and theory. *Psychological Bulletin, 88*, 82–108.

Cohen, S.A., & Lezak, A. (1977). Noise and inattentiveness to social cues. *Environment and Behavior, 9*, 559–572.

Collette, J., & Webb, S.D. (1975). *Urban density, crowding, and stress reactions*. Unpublished manuscript, University of Utah, Salt Lake City.

Cox, V.C., Paulus, P.B., McCain, G., & Karlovac, M. (1982). The relationship between crowding and health. In A. Baum & J.E. Singer (Eds.), *Advances in environmental psychology* (Vol. 4). Hillsdale, NJ: Erlbaum.

Dahlof, L., Hard, E., & Larsson, K. (1975). Influence of maternal stress on offspring sexual behavior. *Animal Behavior, 7*, 237–251.

D'Atri, D.A. (1975). Psychophysiological responses to crowding. *Environment and Behavior, 7*, 237–252.

D'Atri, D.A., & Ostfeld, A.M. (1975). Crowding: Its effects on the elevation of blood pressure in a prison setting. *Preventive Medicine, 4*, 550–566.

Davidson, L.M., Baum, A., & Collins, D.L. (1982). Stress and control-related problems at Three Mile Island. *Journal of Applied Social Psychology, 12*, 349–359.

Dean, L.M., Pugh, W.M., & Gunderson, E.K. (1975). Spatial and perceptual components of crowding: Effects on health and satisfaction. *Environment and Behavior, 7*, 225–236.

Dean, L.M., Pugh, W., & Gunderson, E. (1978). The behavioral effects of crowding. *Environment and Behavior, 10*, 419–431.

Dean, L., Pugh, W., & Gunderson, E. (1979). The behavioral effects of crowding in humans. *Journal of Applied Social Psychology, 9*, 27–46.

Desor, J.A. (1972). Toward a psychological theory of crowding. *Journal of Personality and Social Psychology, 21*, 79–83.

Dooley, B. (1974). *Crowding stress: The effects of social density on men with close or far personal space*. Unpublished doctoral dissertation, University of California, Los Angeles.

Dubos, R. (1965). *Man adapting*. New Haven, CT: Yale University Press.

Edwards, E.A., & Dean, L.M. (1977). Effects of crowding of mice on humoral antibody formation and protection to lethal antigenic challenge. *Psychosomatic Medicine, 39*, 19–24.

Ehrlich, P., & Ehrlich, A. (1970). *Population resources and environment*. San Francisco: Freeman.

Eoyang, C.K. (1974). Effects of group size and privacy in residential crowding. *Journal of Personality and Social Psychology, 30*, 389–392.

Epley, S. (1974). Reduction of behavioral effects of aversive stimulation by the presence of companions. *Psychological Bulletin, 81*, 271–283.

Epstein, Y.M., & Baum, A. (1978). Crowding: Methods of study. In A. Baum & Y.M. Epstein (Eds.), *Human response to crowding*. Hillsdale, NJ: Erlbaum.

Esser, A.H. (1972). A biosocial perspective on crowding. In J. Wohlwill & D. Carson (Eds.), *Environment and the social sciences: Perspectives and applications*. Washington, DC: American Psychological Association.

Evans, G.W. (1978). Crowding and the developmental process. In A. Baum & Y. Epstein (Eds.), *Human response to crowding*. Hillsdale, NJ: Erlbaum.

Evans, G.W., (1978). Design implications of spatial research. In J. Aiello (Ed.), *Residential crowding*. New York: Plenum.

Evans, G.W. (1978). Human spatial behavior: The arousal model. In A. Baum & Y. Epstein (Eds.), *Human response to crowding*. Hillsdale, NJ: Erlbaum.

Evans, G.W. (1979). Crowding and human performance. *Journal of Applied Social Psychology, 9*, 27–46.

Fischer, C., Baldassare, M., & Ofshe, R. (1975, November). Crowding studies and urban life: A critical review. *Journal of the American Institute of Planning*, 400–418.

Fisher, J.D., & Baum, A. (1980). Situational and arousal-based messages and the reduction of crowding stress. *Journal of Applied Social Psychology, 10*, 191–201.

Fisher, J.D., Bell, P.A., & Baum, A. (1984). *Environmental psychology* (2nd ed.). New York: Holt, Rinehart, & Winston.

Freedman, J.L. (1975). *Crowding and behavior.* San Francisco: Freeman.

Freedman, J.L. (1979). Reconciling apparent differences between the responses of humans and other animals to crowding. *Psychological Review, 86,* 80–85.

Freedman, J.L., Heshka, S., & Levy, A. (1975). Population density and pathology in metropolitan areas. In J.L. Freedman (Ed.), *Crowding and behavior.* San Francisco: Freeman.

Freedman, J.L, Klevansky, S., & Ehrlich, P.I. (1971). The effect of crowding on human task performance. *Journal of Applied Social Psychology, 1,* 7–26.

Freedman, J., Levy, A., Buchanan, R., & Price, J. (1972). Crowding and human aggressiveness. *Journal of Experimental Social Psychology, 8,* 528–548.

Galle, O.R., Gove, W.R., & McPherson, J.M. (1972). Population density and pathology: What are the relations for man? *Science, 176,* 23–30.

Gifford, R., & Peacock, J. (1979). Crowding: More fearsome than crime-provoking? *Psychologia, 22,* 79–83.

Ginsburg, H.J., Pollman, V.A., Wanson, M.S., & Hope, M.L. (1977). Variation of aggressive interaction among male elementary school children as a function of changes in spatial density. *Environmental Psychology and Nonverbal Behavior, 2,* 67–75.

Glass, D.C., & Singer, J.E. (1972). *Urban stress: Experiments on noise and social stressors.* New York: Academic.

Goeckner, D., Greenough, W., & Maier, S. (1974). Escape learning deficit after overcrowded rearing in rats: Test of a helplessness hypothesis. *Bulletin of the Psychonomic Society, 3,* 54–57.

Heller, J., Groff, B., & Solomon, S. (1977). Toward an understanding of crowding: The role of physical interaction. *Journal of Personality and Social Psychology, 35,* 183–190.

Henry, J.P., Meehan, J.P., & Stephens, P.M. (1967). The use of psychosocial stimuli to induce prolonged systolic hypertension in mice. *Psychosomatic Medicine, 29,* 408–432.

Henry, J.P., & Stephens, P.M. (1977). *Stress, health, and the social environment.* New York: Springer-Verlag.

Henry, J.P., Stephens, P.M., Axelrod, J., & Mueller, R.A. (1971). Effect of psychosocial stimulation on the enzymes involved in the biosynthesis and metabolism of noradrenaline and adrenaline. *Psychosomatic Medicine, 33,* 227–237.

Hutt, C., & Vaizey, M.J. (1966). Differential effects of group density on social behavior. *Nature, 209,* 1371–1372.

Jorgenson, D.O., & Dukes, F.O. (1976). Deindividuation as a function of density and group membership. *Journal of Personality and Social Psychology, 34,* 24–39.

Kahneman, D. (1973). *Attention and effort.* Englewood Cliffs, NJ: Prentice-Hall.

Kalb, L.S., & Keating, J.P. (1980). Nonspatial factors affecting crowding attributions in a dense field setting. In I.G. Sarason & C.D. Spielberger (Eds.), *Stress and anxiety* (Vol. 7). New York: Halstead.

Kenrick, D.T., & Cialdini, R.B. (1977). Romantic attraction: Misattraction versus reinforcement explanations. *Journal of Personality and Social Psychology, 35,* 381–391.

Kirmeyer, S. (1978). Urban density and pathology. *Environment and Behavior, 10,* 247–270.

Klein, R., & Harris, B. (1979). Disruptive effects of disconfirmed expectancies about crowding. *Journal of Personality and Social Psychology, 37,* 769–777.

Korte, C. (1979). Helpfulness in the urban environment. In A. Baum, J.E. Singer, & S. Valins (Eds.), *Advances in environmental psychology: The urban environment* (Vol. 1). Hillsdale, NJ: Erlbaum.

Korte, C., Ypma, I., & Toppen, A. (1975). Helpfulness in Dutch society as a function of urbanization and environmental input level. *Journal of Personality and Social Psychology, 32,* 996–1003.

Langer, E.U., & Saegert, S. (1977). Crowding and cognitive control. *Journal of Personality and Social Psychology, 35,* 175–182.

Lazarus, R.S. (1966). *Psychological stress and the coping process.* New York: McGraw-Hill.

Lazarus, R.S. (1977). Cognitive and coping processes in emotions. In A. Monat & R.S. Lazarus (Eds.), *Stress and coping.* New York: Columbia University Press.

Lazarus, R.S., & Launier, R. (1978). Stress-related transactions between person and environment. In L.A. Pervin & M. Lewis (Eds.), *Internal and external determinants of behavior.* New York: Plenum.

Levy, L., & Herzog, A.N. (1974). Effects of population density and crowding on health and social adaptation in the Netherlands. *Journal of Health and Social Behavior, 15,* 228–240.

Lobb, M., & McCain, G. (1978). Population density and nonaggressive competition. *Animal Learning and Behavior, 6,* 98–105.

Loo, C. (1972). The effects of spatial density on the social behavior of children. *Journal of Applied Social Psychology, 4,* 372–381.

Loo, C. (1978). Density, crowding, and preschool children. In A. Baum & Y. Epstein (Eds.), *Human response to crowding.* Hillsdale, NJ: Erlbaum.

Lundberg, U. (1976). Urban commuting: Crowdedness and catecholamine excretion. *Journal of Human Stress, 2,* 26–32.

Malthus, R.T. (1969). An essay on the principle of population. In G. Hardin (Ed.), *Population evolution and birth control.* San Francisco: Freeman.

Manton, K.G., & Myers, G.C. (1977). The structure of urban mortality: A methodological study of Hanover, Germany (Pt. 2). *International Journal of Epidemiology, 6,* 213–223.

Marsden, H.M. (1972). Crowding and animal behavior. In J.F. Wohlwill & D.H. Carson (Eds.), *Environment and the social sciences: Perspectives and applications.* Washington, DC: American Psychological Association.

Mason, J.W. (1975). Emotion as reflected in patterns of endocrine integration. In L. Levi (Ed.), *Emotions: Their parameters and measurement.* New York: Raven.

Matthews, R.W. (1979). *Coping with crowding: Reappraisal versus avoidance.* Unpublished doctoral dissertation, University of Texas, Arlington.

Matthews, R.W., Paulus, P.B., & Baron, R.A. (1979). Physical aggression after being crowded. *Journal of Nonverbal Behavior, 4,* 15–17.

McCain, G., Cox, V.C., & Paulus, P.B. (1976). The relationship between illness complaints and degree of crowding in a prison environment. *Environment and Behavior, 8,* 283–290.

McCain, G., Cox, V.C., & Paulus, P.B. (1980). *The effect of prison crowding on inmate behavior.* Washington, DC: National Institute of Justice.

McCain, G., Cox, V.C., Paulus, P.B., & Karlovac, M. (1981, April 30). *Social disorganization as a factor in "crowding."* Paper presented at the Midwestern Psychological Association.

McCauley, C., Coleman, G., & DeFusco, P. (1977). *Commuters' eye contact with strangers in city and suburban train stations: Evidence of short-term adaptation to interpersonal overload in the city.* Unpublished manuscript, Bryn Mawr College, Bryn Mawr, PA.

McCauley, C., & Neuman, J. (1977). Eye contact with strangers in the city, suburb, and small town. *Environment and Behavior, 9,* 547–558.

McCauley, C., & Taylor, J. (1976). Is there overload of acquaintances in the city? *Environmental Psychology and Nonverbal Behavior, 1,* 41–55.

McClelland, L., & Auslander, N. (1975). *Determinants of perceived crowding and pleasantness in public settings.* Unpublished manuscript, University of Colorado, Boulder.

McGrew, P.L. (1970). Social and spatial density effects on spacing behavior in preschool children. *Journal of Child Psychology and Psychiatry, 11,* 197–205.

McGuire, W.J., & Gaes, G.G. (1982). *The effects of crowding versus age composition in aggregate prison assault rates.* Unpublished manuscript, Office of Research, Federal Prison System, Washington, DC.

Milgram, S. (1970). The experience of living in cities. *Science, 167,* 1461–1468.

Miller, S., Rossbach, J.C., & Munson, R. (1980, April). *Person–environment fit in university residence environments.* Paper presented at the meeting of the Eastern Psychological Association, Hartford, CT.

Mitchell, R. (1971). Some social implications of high density housing. *American Sociological Review, 36,* 18–29.

Myers, K., Hale, C.S., Mykytowycz, R., & Hughes, R.L. (1971). Density, space, sociality and health. In A.H. Esser (Ed.), *Behavior and environment.* New York: Plenum.

Obrist, P.A. (1981). Cardiovascular psychophysiology: A perspective. New York: Plenum.

Park, R.E., Burgess, E.W., & McKenzie, R.D. (Eds.). (1925). *The city.* Chicago: University of Chicago Press.

Patterson, A.H. (1977). Methodological developments in environment-behavioral research. In D. Stokols (Ed.), *Perspectives on environment and behavior.* New York: Plenum.

Patterson, M.C. (1976). An arousal model of interpersonal intimacy. *Psychological Review, 83,* 235–245.

Paulus, P.B. (1980). Crowding. In P.B. Paulus (Ed.), *Psychology of group influence.* Hillsdale, NJ: Erlbaum.

Paulus, P.B., Annis, A.B., Seta, J.J., Schkade, J.K., & Matthews, R.W. (1976). Crowding does affect task performance. *Journal of Personality and Social Psychology, 34,* 248–253.

Paulus, P.B., Cox, V., McCain, G., & Chandler, J. (1975). Some effects of crowding in a prison environment. *Journal of Applied Social Psychology, 5,* 86–91.

Paulus, P.B., & Matthews, R. (1980). Crowding attribution, and task performance. *Basic and Applied Social Psychology, 1,* 3–14.

Paulus, P.B., & McCain, G. (in press). Crowding in jails. *Basic and Applied Social Psychology.*

Paulus, P.B., McCain, G., & Cox, V.C. (1978). Death rates, psychiatric commitments, blood pressure, and perceived crowding as a function of institutional crowding. *Environmental Psychology and Nonverbal Behavior, 3,* 107–116.

Paulus, P.B., McCain, G., & Cox, V. (1981). Prison standards: Some pertinent data on crowding. *Federal Probation, 15,* 48–54.

Proshansky, H.M., Ittelson, W.H., & Rivlin, L.G. (1970). Freedom of choice and behavior in a physical setting. In H.M. Proshansky, W.H. Ittelson, & L.G. Rivlin (Eds.), *Environmental psychology.* New York: Holt, Rinehart & Winston.

Rapoport, A. (1975). Toward a redefinition of density. *Environment and Behavior, 7,* 133–158.

Rawls, J.R., Trego, R.E., McGaffey, C.N., & Rawls, D.J. (1972). Personal space as a predictor of performance under close working conditions. *Journal of Social Psychology, 86,* 261–267.

Reddy, D.M., Baum, A., Fleming, R., & Aiello, J.R. (1981). Mediation of social density by coalition formation. *Journal of Applied Social Psychology, 11,* 529–537.

Rodin, J. (1976). Crowding, perceived choice and response to controllable and uncontrollable outcomes. *Journal of Experimental and Social Psychology, 12,* 564–578.

Rodin, J., & Baum, A. (1978) Crowding and helplessness: Potential consequences of density and loss of control. In A. Baum & Y.M. Epstein (Eds.), *Human response to crowding.* Hillsdale, NJ: Erlbaum.

Rodin, J., Solomon, S., & Metcalf, J. (1978). Role of control in mediating perceptions of density. *Journal of Personality and Social Psychology, 36,* 988–999.

Rohe, W., & Patterson, A.H. (1974). *The effects of varied levels of resources and density on behavior in a day care center.* Paper presented by the Environmental Design Research Association, Milwaukee, WI.

Ross, M., Layton, B., Erickson, B., & Schopler, J. (1973). Affect, facial regard, and reactions to crowding. *Journal of Personality and Social Psychology, 28,* 69–76.

Saegert, S. (1973). Crowding: Cognitive overload and behavioral constraint. In W. Preiser (Ed.), *Environmental design research. Proceedings of EDRA IV.* Stroudsburg, PA: Dowden, Hutchinson, & Ross.

Saegert, S.C. (1974). *Effects of spatial and social density on arousal, mood, and orientation.* Unpublished doctoral dissertation, University of Michigan, Ann Arbor.

Saegert, S. (1978). High-density environments: Their personal and social consequences. In A. Baum & Y.M. Epstein (Eds.), *Human Response to Crowding.* Hillsdale, NJ: Erlbaum.

Saegert, S. (1982). Environment and children's mental health: Residential density and low income children. In A. Baum & J.E. Singer (Eds.), *Handbook of psychology and health* (Vol. 2). Hillsdale, NJ: Erlbaum.

Saegert, S.C., Mackintosh, E., & West, S. (1975). Two studies of crowding in urban public spaces. *Environment and Behavior, 7,* 159–184.

Sales, S.M., Guydosh, R.M., & Iacano, W. (1974). Relationship between "strength of the nervous system" and the need for stimulation. *Journal of Personality and Social Psychology, 29,* 16–22.

Schachter, S., & Singer, J.E. (1962). Cognitive, social and physiological determinants of emotional state. *Psychological Review, 69,* 379–399.

Schettino, A.P., & Borden, R.J. (1976). Group size versus group density: Where is the affect? *Personality and Social Psychology Bulletin, 2,* 67–70.

Schmidt, D.E., & Keating, J.P. (1979). Human crowding and personal control: An integration of the research. *Psychological Bulletin, 86,* 680–700.

Schmitt, R.C. (1966). Density, health, and social disorganization. *American Institute of Planners Journal, 32,* 38–40.

Schopler, J., McCullum, R., & Rusbult, C. (1978). *Behavioral interference and internality-externality as determinants of subjects' crowding.* Unpublished manuscript, University of North Carolina, Chapel Hill.

Schopler, J., & Stockdale, J. (1977). An interference analysis of crowding. *Environmental Psychology and Nonverbal Behavior, 1,* 81–88.

Schopler, J., & Walton, M. (1974). *The effects of structure, expected enjoyment and participant's internality-externality upon feelings of being crowded.* Unpublished manuscript, University of North Carolina, Chapel Hill.

Selye, H. (1976). *The stress of life.* New York: McGraw-Hill.

Sherrod, D.R. (1974). Crowding, perceived control and behavioral aftereffects. *Journal of Applied Social Psychology, 4,* 171–186.

Sherrod, D.R., & Cohen, S. (1979). Density, personal control, and design. In A. Baum & J.R. Aiello (Eds.), *Residential crowding and design.* New York: Plenum.

Simmel, G. (1950). The metropolis and mental life. In G. Simmel (Ed.), *The sociology of George Simmel.* Glencoe, IL: Free Press.

Singer, J.E., Lundberg, U., & Frankenhaeuser, M. (1978). Stress on the train: A study of urban commuting. In A. Baum., J.E. Singer, & S. Valins (Eds.), *Advances in environmental psychology* (Vol. 1). Hillsdale, NJ: Erlbaum.

Smith, P.K., & Connolly, K.J. (1973). Toys, space and children. *Bulletin of the British Psychological Society, 26,* 167.

Smith, P.K., & Connolly, K.J. (1977). Social and aggressive behavior in preschool children as a function of crowding. *Social Science Information, 16,* 601–620.

Southwick, C.H. (1967). An experimental study of intragroup antagonistic behavior in Rhesus monkeys. *Behavior, 28,* 182–209.

Stockdale, J.E. (1978). Crowding: Determinants and effects. In L. Berkowitz (Ed.), *Advances in experimental social psychology* (Vol. 11). New York: Academic.

Stokols, D. (1972). On the distinction between density and crowding: Some implications for future research. *Psychological Review, 79,* 275–277.

Stokols, D. (1976). The experience of crowding in primary and secondary environments. *Environment and Behavior, 8,* 49–86.

Stokols, D. (1978). A typology of crowding experiences. In A. Baum & Y. Epstein (Eds.), *Human response to crowding.* Hillsdale, NJ: Erlbaum.

Stokols, D., Novoco, R., Stokols, J., & Campbell, J. (1977, August). *Traffic congestion, type A behavior, and stress.* Paper presented at the meeting of the American Psychological Association, San Francisco.

Stokols, D., & Ohlig, W. (1975). *The experience of crowding under different social climates.* Paper presented at the meeting of the American Psychological Association, Chicago.

Stokols, D., Rall, M., Pinner, B., & Schopler, J. (1973). Physical, social, and personal determinants of the perception of crowding. *Environment and Behavior, 5,* 87–115.

Sundstrom, E. (1975). An experimental study of crowding: Effects of room size, intrusion, and goal-blocking on nonverbal behaviors, self-disclosure, and self-reported stress. *Journal of Personality and Social Psychology, 32,* 645–654.

Sundstrom, E. (1978). Crowding as a sequential process: Review of research on the effects of population density on humans. In A. Baum & Y.M. Epstein (Eds.), *Human response to crowding.* Hillsdale, NJ: Erlbaum.

Switzer, R., & Taylor, R.B. (1983). Sociability versus privacy of residential choice: Impacts of personality and local social ties. *Basic and Applied Social Psychology, 4,* 123–136.

Symington, T., Currie, A.R., Curran, R.S., & Davidson, J.N. (1955). The reaction of the adrenal cortex in conditions of stress. In *Ciba Foundations Colloquia on Endocrinology: Vol. 8. The human adrenal cortex* (pp. 70–91). Boston: Little, Brown.

Ward, S.K. (1975). Methodological considerations in the study of population density and social pathology. *Human Ecology, 3,* 275–286.

Wicker, A.W. (1973). Undermanning theory and research: Implications for the study of psychological and behavioral effects of excess human populations. *Representative Research in Social Psychology, 4,* 185–206.

Wicker, A.W. (1979). *An introduction to ecological psychology.* Monterey, CA: Brooks/Cole.

Wicker, A.W., Kirmeyer, S., Hanson, L., & Alexander, D. (1976). Effects of manning levels on subjective experiences, performance and verbal interaction in groups. *Organizational Behavior and Human Performance, 17,* 251–274.

Winsborough, H. (1965). The social consequences of high population density. *Law and Contemporary Problems, 30,* 120–126.

Wirth, L. (1938). Urbanism as a way of life. *American Journal of Sociology, 44,* 1–24.

Wohlwill, J., & Kohn, I. (1973). The environment as experienced by the migrant: An adaptation level view. *Representative Research in Social Psychology, 4,* 135–164.

Wolfe, M. (1975). Room size, group size, and density: Behavior patterns in a children's psychiatric facility. *Environment and Behavior, 7,* 199–224.

Worchel, S. (1978). The experience of crowding: An attributional analysis. In A. Baum & Y. Epstein (Eds.), *Human response to crowding.* Hillsdale, NJ: Erlbaum.

Worchel, S., & Teddlie, C. (1976). The experience of crowding: A two-factor theory. *Journal of Personality and Social Psychology, 34,* 30–40.

Worchel, S., & Yohai, S. (1979). The role of attribution in the experience of crowding. *Journal of Experimental Social Psychology, 15,* 91–104.

Wortman, C.B., & Brehm, J.W. (1975). Responses to uncontrollable outcomes: An integration of reactance theory and the learned helplessness model. In L. Berkowitz (Ed.), *Advances in experimental social psychology* (Vol. 8). New York: Academic.

Zajonc, R. (1965). Social facilitation. *Science, 149,* 269–274.

Zlutnick, S., & Altman, I. (1972). Crowding and human behavior. In J.F. Wohlwill & D.H. Carson (Eds.), *Environment and the social sciences: Perspectives and applications.* Washington, DC: American Psychological Association.

Zuckerman, M. (1983). *Biological bases of sensation seeking, impulsivity, and anxiety.* Hillsdale, NJ: Erlbaum.

Chapter 15

ENVIRONMENTAL STRESS

Gary W. Evans, *Program in Social Ecology, University of California, Irvine, California*

Sheldon Cohen, *Carnegie-Mellon University, Pittsburgh, Pennsylvania*

15.1. INTRODUCTION

One way to understand the relationship between the environment and human behavior is to analyze environmental conditions that are capable of interfering with optimal human functioning. In this chapter we examine how the concept of stress has been used to specify environmental characteristics that may lead to physiological or psychological discomfort and, in some cases, ill health.

Individual appraisals of the potential threat or harm of an environmental array plus the extent of available, efficacious coping resources largely determine how environmental conditions affect human health and well-being. This chapter can be distinguished from most other writings on stress in that our focus is on the physical characteristics of settings that are likely to evoke the stress and coping process. We contend that this aspect of the transactional process between environment and human behavior has largely been overshadowed by psychological and sociological investigations of personal, organizational, and societal factors that influence the stress and coping process.

Physical environments have enduring characteristics that can influence whether or not stress is produced. All biological systems must self-regulate in the context of changing environmental demands. To understand our responses to such demands, we require knowledge of both individual processes and environmental features of the ecological niches we inhabit (Sells, 1963, 1969). Situations are the source of many stress-provoking stimuli that influence both psychological and physiological responses as we learn cognitive coping strategies. Stress emanates from individual appraisals of and reactions to actual environmental conditions (Baum, Singer, & Baum, 1982; Magnusson, 1982). The conditions of the physical environment weigh significantly in the stress and coping process. Certain environmental conditions are more

capable than others of straining the adaptive resources of human beings. A strict focus on individual
differences in people's reactions to environmental
conditions overlooks the fact that human beings, as
all other organisms, have some general requirements. We can examine whether settings support or
hinder some of these requirements (S. Kaplan,
1983). We also know that individual differences in
reactivity to some stressors can be systematically
comprehended when certain features of settings are
held constant rather than allowed to vary. Better understanding of some of the situational variation as it
interacts with individual vulnerability to stressors
may provide more insight into the stress and coping
process (Forsman, 1983; Magnusson, 1982).

To emphasize a point made throughout this chapter, we are not claiming that stress is inevitably or
even predominantly a function of variation in environmental quality. Stress is inevitably a person-based
concept. Nevertheless, many stress researchers have
overlooked properties of physical situations most
likely to place greater adaptive demands on human
coping resources.

15.2. FOCUS AND ORGANIZATION

In this chapter we restrict our view to environmental
conditions typically experienced in daily life. Furthermore, we will focus on physical characteristics of environments. Thus our review focuses on crowding,
noise, heat, and air pollution. Water pollution is not
discussed because of the paucity of behavioral research on this topic (Coughlin, 1976). Housing and
other aspects of the influence of special settings on
human satisfaction and health are covered in Chapters 17, 22, 24, and 25 of this volume.

Environmental stressors are typically aversive,
primarily uncontrollable, and of variable duration and
periodicity and require low to moderate adjustments.
One of the unfortunate consequences of the neglect
of physical characteristics of stressors in the study of
stress and coping has been the relative absence of
theoretical or empirical work on how such characteristics as duration, intensity, and so forth affect
human health and functioning. A related consequence
of the emphasis on interpersonal coping processes
and psychosocial mediating variables between stressors and outcome has been the lack of research on
single and multiple stressor interactions. It is instructive to reread early books on stress and note the high
value placed on systematic evaluation of varying

stressor intensity across a large range as well as
measuring multiple stressor effects (cf. Appley &
Trumbull, 1967; McGrath, 1970b).

The chapter is organized into four major sections
following a brief introduction. The first section describes the focus and organization of the chapter.
Section 15.2 gives an overview of the stress
paradigm including definitions of stress, characteristics of stressors, and general theoretical perspectives
in the stress field as well as hypothetical mechanisms
for the actions of environmental stressors and a brief
summary of the effects of stressors on human health
and behavior. The next section summarizes the effects of the four major environmental stressors reviewed in this chapter: noise, crowding, heat, and air
pollution. The stress paradigm is then evaluated as
an explanatory heuristic for these four stressors. The
last major section of the chapter discusses several
theoretical and methodological problems with the
stress paradigm and its application to noise, crowding, heat, and air pollution.

15.3. OVERVIEW OF THE STRESS PARADIGM

15.3.1. Definitions of Stress

Stress is a difficult concept to define. Early definitions varied in the extent to which they emphasized
the responses of the individual, or the situations that
caused disruptions of ongoing behavior and functioning. Appley and Trumbull (1967), McGrath (1970a),
and Mason (1975) have summarized several objec-
tions to each of these approaches to defining stress.
Response-based definitions are often insensitive to
critical temporal parameters in stress. The duration
and periodicity of stressors have important influences
on human health and well-being. Furthermore, a
focus on outcomes ignores the fact that highly variable situations (e.g., negative, positive, ambiguous)
can lead to similar response outcomes. For example,
exercise as well as threat of personal injury heightens
blood pressure. Other factors apart from the individual also have an impact on responses and may be
obscured by a strict focus on response outcomes.
Other sources of stress, cultural norms, or the resources provided by other people may all mediate responses to stressors (H.B. Kaplan, 1983; Levine &
Scotch, 1970; Mechanic, 1978; Pearlin, 1982). Finally, there is a noteworthy lack of correspondence
among measures of stress. It has proven difficult to

isolate a set of responses that invariably occur when adaptive resources are taxed. (Lacey, 1967; Mason, 1975).

Situation-based definitions of stress have been criticized because of large variations in individual responses to the same situation. Past history, threat appraisal, and coping styles vary across persons. Furthermore, with the exception of very extreme stimuli, no stimulus is a stressor to all persons or the same person across all different times or situations. It has also proven difficult to scale situations in terms of the degree of stress they evoke. Finally, the importance of the consequences of behavioral or physiological disruption is not adequately conceptualized by situation-based models of stress.

These problems have led most stress researchers both inside and outside environmental psychology to adopt more relational, interactive definitions of stress. According to this perspective, stress is a process that occurs when there is an imbalance between environmental demands and response capabilities of the organism (Lazarus, 1966; Lazarus & Launier, 1978, McGrath, 1970a).

A specific aspect of this relational perspective on stress emphasized by Lazarus and his co-workers is that for stress to occur the individual must evaluate this imbalance. Thus stress occurs when one decides that environmental stimuli are likely to tax or exceed one's personal coping capacities. In general, environmental psychologists have accepted the interaction perspective. Recent books and major reviews of environmental stress all emphasize that stress is fundamentally a relational concept signifying an imbalance between environmental opportunities and individuals' goals, and capabilities to cope with that imbalance (Baum, Singer, & Baum, 1982; Caplan, 1982; Carson & Driver, 1970; Evans, 1982; French, Rodgers, & Cobb, 1974; Lazarus & Cohen, 1977; McGrath, 1976; Stokols, 1979). We favor this perspective because it encompasses both major components of the organism–environment interface. Nevertheless, the task of developing criteria that indicate when adaptive resources are critically strained remains formidable. There are several important unresolved theoretical and methodological issues with respect to the stress construct. Some of the more salient issues are discussed later in the chapter.

Several concerns have been raised about interactive approaches to defining stress. One concern is that reliance on measures of perceived stressors eliminates the study of objective correlates of stressors (Dohrenwend, Krasnoff, Askenasy, & Dohren-

wend, 1978). Moreover, if denial or other intrapsychic coping strategies are functioning, individual reports of perceived stress may obscure the severity of environmental conditions. Measures of perceived stress may also be inaccurate because they reflect the degree to which stress is attributed to a particular situation. Errors in explaining sources of stress have been shown in studies of emotions (Schachter & Singer, 1962) as well as for crowding (Keating, 1979; Worchel & Teddlie, 1976).

A second concern raised about the interactive approach to defining stress is that other variables such as individual psychological status (e.g., neuroticism, sick role behavior) may influence the relationship between reports of perceived stress, objective situational conditions, and outcome measures. Some dispositional tendencies may influence personal views of both health and levels of stress experienced (Mechanic, 1974, 1978; Schroeder & Costa, 1984).

Another problem in relying on measures of perceived stress emanates from ambiguity about direction of causality. It is often difficult to determine whether stress has produced greater negative mental health outcomes or whether the direction of causality is the reverse (Dohrenwend & Dohrenwend, 1974, 1981; Moss, 1973; Rutter, 1983).

Finally, controversy exists over whether the degree of association between perceived measures of stress and psychological or physical health outcomes is inflated because of overlap between items contained in the two sets of measures (Dohrenwend, Dohrenwend, Dodson, & Shrout, 1984; Lazarus, DeLongis, Folkman, & Gruen, 1985). This problem is exacerbated by an overreliance on self-report measures of both perceived stress and perceived health.

Lazarus (Lazarus et al., 1985), McGrath (1970a), Stokols (1979), and others have argued that stress, like most psychological constructs, is inherently relational and cannot be reduced into separate personal and environmental components (cf. Magnusson, 1981). Stress is best considered, according to this view, as a complex rubric reflecting a dynamic, recursive relationship between environmental demands, individual and social resources to cope with those demands, and the individual's appraisal of that relationship.

Nevertheless, a major source of information about stressors and various coping opportunities lies within the configuration of the physical environment. We are not arguing that stimulus characteristics are more important than other factors influencing the dynamic, mediational process of person–environment transactions. Our goal is simply to draw greater attention to many aspects of the physical settings in which we work and live that are likely to cause stress. Because of the psychologists' interest in human behavior, there has been a tendency to focus attention in stress research on individual and social resources that affect coping abilities plus personal appraisals of threat. Insufficient attention has been paid to qualities of physical environments that may be more likely to place adaptive demands on the organism (Dubos, 1965; Evans, 1982).

15.3.2. Characteristics of Stressors

Four general types of environmental stressors have been identified: cataclysmic events, stressful life events, daily hassles, and ambient stressors (Baum, Singer, & Baum, 1982; Campbell, 1983; Lazarus & Cohen, 1977). Cataclysmic events are sudden catastrophes that demand major adaptive responses from all individuals directly affected by the event. Usually cataclysmic events affect whole communities of people. Fischhoff, Svenson, and Slovic, Chapter 29, this volume, reviews several examples of natural and technological disasters that fall within this category of stressful environmental events. Floods, earthquakes, volcanic eruptions, major storms, nuclear power plant accidents, and discoveries of toxic waste dumps are examples of cataclysmic events. Two other types of cataclysmic events not discussed in this volume are war and imprisonment (cf. Monat & Lazarus, 1977).

Stressful life events are major incidents in the lives of people that typically require personal or social adaptive responses. Life events typically have clearly delineated time referents. Life events include such things as major change in family status (e.g., divorce, marriage, birth, death), or major changes in economic conditions (e.g., gain or loss of job, change in job position, change in educational status). Events that are uncontrollable, undesirable, or unscheduled in the life cycle are more likely to cause harmful outcomes (Dohrenwend & Dohrenwend, 1974; Pearlin, 1982; Rabkin & Struening, 1976; Thoits, 1983; Wheaton, 1983).

Daily hassles are the typical events of ordinary life that may cause frustration, tension, or irritation. Environmental events (e.g., noisy party, crowded elevator), work issues (e.g., argument with coworker, deadline), or interpersonal problems (e.g., argument with friend or family member) constitute the majority of daily hassles (DeLongis, Coyne,

Dakof, Folkman, & Lazarus, 1982; Kanner, Coyne, Schaefer, & Lazarus, 1981). Daily hassles are more common and short-lived than most life events.

The term *ambient stressors* has been developed to distinguish more continuous, relatively stable, and intractable conditions of the physical environment (Campbell, 1983). Many ambient stressors are background conditions, passing largely unnoticed unless they interfere with some important goal or directly threaten health. Individuals living with chronic air pollution, for example, are likely to habituate to these environmental conditions. More active, instrumental coping responses to air pollution are infeasible or come at a higher perceived cost (e.g., relocating) than accommodating to the suboptimal living conditions (see also Wohlwill, 1974).

Sociologists have drawn a similar distinction between life events and chronic sources of stress. Chronic strains are the persistent, difficult, and demanding experiences of daily life. Unlike life events, chronic strains are continuous with largely unnoticeable peaks or discrete impact periods (Pearlin, 1982; Wheaton, 1983). Examples of chronic strains include work overload, rapid social change, poverty, and family conflicts. Many chronic strains emanate from conflicts between individual or social resources and values, beliefs, and aspirations (H.B. Kaplan, 1983; Mechanic, 1978; Pearlin, 1982).

The various types of environmental stressors can be categorized along eight dimensions. One dimension is the degree to which a stressor is *perceptually salient* or easily identifiable or noticeable (Baum, Singer, & Baum, 1982; Campbell, 1983; Stokols, 1979; Wohlwill, 1974). Many physical sources of stress, particularly if chronic, of low-moderate intensity, and uncontrollable, rapidly become background stimuli. Habituation in response sensitivity and general awareness is a by-product of chronic exposure to many low-level ambient stimuli (Glass & Singer, 1972; Sonnenfeld, 1967; Wohlwill, 1974).

A second dimension for characterizing sources of environmental stress is the *type of adjustment required* by the environmental condition. Environmental conditions that are very intense or uncontrollable are likely to lead to accommodation and emotion-focused coping rather than efforts to deal with the stressor directly (Kiretz & Moos, 1974; Lazarus & Cohen, 1977). These coping and adaptation processes may in turn influence the health consequences of exposure to that stressor.

The *value or valence of events*, whether one gains or loses, may also bear important consequences for reactions to the stressor. Some environmental sources of stress, while demanding major adaptive resources, may be positively valued. This dimension for characterizing stressors highlights one of the major differences between the physiological and psychological approaches to stress. The physiological perspective emphasizes the disruption of equilibrium and consequential adaptive efforts to restore homeostasis. The psychological perspective, while acknowledging the importance of adaptive demands, asserts that the negative value of the threat to equilibrium is also crucial.

Degree of controllability over an environmental stressor is the fourth dimension in distinguishing different kinds of stress. Control can function as a psychological (appraisal) process that is influenced primarily by individual disposition (e.g., locus of control) or personal coping resources. Here control is viewed as an intrapersonal moderator of stress. Control also can refer to instrumental opportunities to exercise influence over the occurrence or duration of an environmental event. In this sense control refers to characteristics of a situational variable. Uncontrollable stressors are typically appraised as more threatening, at least initially, and are frequently associated with negative effects on health and behavior (Baum, Singer, & Baum, 1982; Cohen, 1980; Glass & Singer, 1972).

Yet somewhat paradoxically if a stressor remains uncontrollable and is chronic, it is probably more likely to become an unnoticed, background characteristic due to habituation (Campbell, 1983). Accommodation to stressors impervious to change through instrumental efforts has been noted in research on coping with various interpersonal sources of strain (Kiretz & Moos, 1974). When an aversive situation cannot be modified or eliminated, one has few options available other than some form of denial or reappraisal of the stressor (Folkman & Lazarus, 1980; Pearlin & Schooler, 1978; White, 1974).

Related to controllability is the *predictability* of stressors. Some environmental stressors may be more predictable than others, which can have consequences for both the way they influence our health and the manner in which we may choose to cope with them. For example, habituation to continuous noise (e.g., highway traffic) is probably more readily accomplished than habituation to airport noise, which is intermittent and less predictable.

A sixth dimension is the *necessity and importance* of the source of a stressor. Environmental stressors that are seen as necessary and/or important (e.g., military aircraft vs. pleasure flying) cause different kinds of reactions. Related to importance of source is whether the source of the stressor is *tied to human behavior*. As we shall see, air pollution and heat do not fit the same pattern of stress effects that crowding and noise do. Most citizens view air pollution and heat as either natural phenomena or caused by other societal entities (e.g., industry) rather than caused by the behaviors of individuals. Personal responsibility cannot be easily affixed for pollution and heat. This may have consequences for the way in which these environmental conditions are appraised and coped with.

Finally, the *duration and periodicity* of environmental stressors are important characteristics of stimuli. Duration has two dimensions—the extent of previous personal history with the stressor and the length of current exposure to the condition. The term *periodicity* refers to the regularity or predictability of the stressor as well as its continuity. Some stressors are more discrete (e.g., stressful life event), whereas others are more continuous (e.g., air pollution). Adaptation processes may be strongly affected by both duration and periodicity.

15.3.3. General Theoretical Perspectives on Stress

One way of viewing research in environmental stress is to classify work as falling within one of two research traditions: the physiological tradition or the psychological tradition. These theoretical paradigms are not necessarily contradictory, but rather focus on somewhat different dimensions of the stress process. In order to provide an overview of theoretical approaches to environmental stress, we will describe these broader traditional approaches first, and then we will discuss several less encompassing models that elaborate on the linkages between environmental stressors and a range of very specific outcomes.

Physiological Perspective

Two of the pioneer researchers on stress, Walter Cannon and Hans Selye, developed physiological models of stress that centered on the sympathetic nervous system and the pituitary–adrenocortical axis, respectively. Each of these models emphasized the physiological responses of the body to noxious stimuli. In addition, each model concentrated on homeostatic processes wherein the body responds to aversive conditions that disrupt some internal equilibrium. Responses to these aversive agents, termed *stressors*, are focused on reequilibration to achieve homeostatic balance.

SYMPATHETIC NERVOUS SYSTEM

Cannon (1932) argued that the body has an autonomic, emergency response system allowing the organism to fight or flee from any serious, aversive, or challenging situation. Stress is a direct strain on the homeostatic mechanisms of the body. Homeostasis reflects the necessity of maintaining the internal composition of the body within some limits despite the fluctuations of the external environment. The sympathetic nervous system acts directly on the adrenal medulla to secrete catecholamines including epinephrine. These substances in turn heighten response readiness for dealing with the emergency at hand. This response readiness includes increased metabolism of carbohydrates to produce more glucose and the release of fatty acids for greater energy, higher heart rate and oxygen consumption, and constriction of blood flow to peripheral areas of the body with greater blood supply to the skeletal muscles, kidneys, and brain. While the adaptive value of this array of physiological readiness for response to aversive circumstances is evident, Cannon was also mindful of some of the potential deleterious consequences of this emergency response syndrome. In particular Cannon was concerned about continual triggering of the response syndrome as well as what happens if this physiological readiness is activated but the individual is unable to "fight" or "take flight." If some somatic discharge is unavailable because of physical or social restraints, are there damaging consequences due to continual activation of this body mobilization system?

Many scholars since Cannon have raised the interesting dilemma of whether the stress and strain of modern, urbanized civilization are particularly harmful because of their distinctiveness from the type of environmental settings under which we evolved as a species (Boyden, 1970; Dubos, 1965; Esser, 1974; Kaplan & Kaplan, 1982). Social norms, complexity of organizational roles, and physical construction of the settings where we work and live have dramatically altered the quality of the environmental sources of stimulation and demands that modern human beings must cope with in comparison to the types of stimulation and stressors that challenged our forebears.

While the importance of modernization on stress and health is difficult to assess, we do know that chronically increased levels of circulating catecholamines have direct links to cardiovascular diseases causing fibrin formation in arterial walls, platelet aggregation, hemodynamic effects like increased blood pressure, ventricular arrhythmia, and uptake in oxygen requirements of the heart (Krantz & Manuck, 1984; Steptoe, 1981).

PITUITARY–ADRENAL AXIS

A complementary, physiological model of stress has been developed by Selye (1956, 1975). According to Selye, various psychological and physiological insults elicit both specific effects and nonspecific physiological reactions. These nonspecific effects, which Selye called the general adaptation syndrome, include three stages: alarm, resistance, and exhaustion. During the alarm phase, the pituitary gland secretes various chemicals, including ACTH, which stimulates the adrenal cortex to produce various substances including a group of anti-inflammatory hormones called corticosteroids. In the resistance phase of the general adaptation syndrome, increase in these steroids sets up a feedback loop stimulating adrenal medulla activity and subsequent release of catecholamines. Exhaustion, the third phase of the syndrome, occurs if the stressor is sufficiently severe or prolonged to deplete somatic defenses. During exhaustion, the adrenal glands are unresponsive to environmental demands, with various susceptible organs suffering breakdown or damage.

Three specific implications of the physiological stress model need to be emphasized:

1. Various environmental pathogens and social–psychological strains will cause nonspecific responses characterized by the nonspecific, tripartite response syndrome, the general adaptation syndrome. This in turn implies that stress may be additive. Responses to a specific stressor will be influenced by both the severity of the specific event and the severity and recency of other threatening events (Fleming, Baum, & Singer, 1984).

2. Some costs or pathological effects can occur from the adaptation processes themselves. In addition to the effects of catecholamines on the cardiovascular system, there is emerging evidence for enhanced susceptibility to infectious diseases due to interference with the immune system by corticosteroids (Ader, 1981; Jemmott & Locke, 1984; Krantz, Grunberg, & Baum, 1985; Moss, 1973).

3. The body has a finite amount of adaptive energy. When this capacity has been exceeded, deleterious effects occur (Cohen,

Evans, Stokols, & Krantz, 1986; Glass & Singer, 1972).

One of the most problematic aspects of Selye's model of stress has been understanding the mechanism(s) that triggers the general adaptation syndrome. There is some evidence that the initial stimulation of the pituitary is from the hypothalamus, but how it becomes directly involved is less clear. Related to this issue is recent evidence that the pituitary–adrenal sequence is triggered only when the person perceives threat or psychological harm (Mason, 1975; Mason et al., 1976). Whether cognitive appraisal of threat or harm is necessary to precipitate a stress response is a point of major controversy both in the stress literature itself (cf. Mason, 1975; Selye, 1975) and in research on emotion more generally (cf. Lazarus, 1984; Zajonc, 1984).

Mason and others have also challenged claims that the stress response syndrome is largely nonspecific. Mason's work suggests that particular types of stressors cause unique patterns of physiological responses in terms of both the types and the amounts of different psychendocrine responses (Mason, 1975; Mason et al., 1976). There is also increasing evidence that the kinds of coping processes engaged in can also influence physiological responses to stress. Efforts to maintain optimum task performance during stress cause a physiological profile distinct from stressor exposure where little or no coping efforts are made to maintain performance (Frankenhaeuser, 1980; Lundberg, 1978; Manuck, Harvey, Lechleiter, & Neal, 1978; Obrist et al., 1978). Lacey's research indicates as well that the kinds of cognitive tasks one is engaged in during stressor exposure can influence physiological outcomes (Lacey, 1967).

Psychological Perspective

Psychological stress focuses on the individual's interpretation of the meaning of environmental events plus an appraisal of personal coping resources (Lazarus, 1966). *Primary appraisal* is the term used to describe the process of evaluation of the stressor. Stressors are evaluated for potential threat–anticipated harm, harm/loss–damage that has already occurred, or challenge–threat that can be dealt with.

Primary appraisal of stressors depends on personal and situational variables. Personal factors influencing primary appraisal include general beliefs about self-efficacy or mastery, the centrality of goals/needs threatened by the stressor, and various dispositional factors. Situational variables that may influence primary appraisal include the imminence of harm, the magnitude of the stressor, the ambiguity of the stressor, the duration of the stressor, and the potential controllability of the stressor.

If the individual makes an appraisal of threat, harm, or challenge, then secondary appraisal processes come into play. During these processes, one evaluates his or her coping resources to deal with the stressor. Coping processes can generally be partitioned into problem-focusing coping or emotion-focused coping. Problem-focused coping strategies involve changes in the situation to reduce aversive impact whereas emotion-focused coping strategies alter individual responses to the negative situation. Either of these coping styles can assume various forms such as information seeking, direct action, or palliative activity (see Lazarus, 1966; Lazarus & Launier, 1978, for more details).

In terms of the psychological perspective, stress occurs when a situation has been appraised as demanding with the potential of exceeding coping resources. Three important implications of the psychological stress perspective are:

1. The individual's perception of environmental demands and personal coping resources is the critical variable in determining the nature of the stress response. The objective conditions of the environment are important only to the extent that they influence these processes of primary and secondary appraisal.

2. Stressful situations are not uniformly aversive. Important personal and social mediators can ameliorate or enhance the effects of stressors. This mediation can occur by influencing either one or both of the appraisal processes. Thus for example perceived control over a stressor may make the stressor seem less threatening (primary appraisal) and/or enable the individual to feel that he or she will have more options available to cope with the stressor (secondary appraisal).

3. Stressors will affect the individual in a host of ways in addition to the physiological impacts emphasized by Cannon and Selye. These impacts will include self-reports of stress and related symptoms (e.g., nervousness, tension, anxiety), negative affect and interpersonal behaviors, and deficits in task performance (for

further discussion and comparison of the psychological and physiological models of stress see Baum, Singer, & Baum, 1982; Cohen et al., 1986; Fleming et al., 1984).

15.3.4. Models of Environmental Stressors

In addition to the traditional models of the stress process described in the previous section, there have been several less encompassing models that significantly influenced environmental stress research. These models primarily derive from the psychological stress tradition, although some influence of the physiological tradition is also found. Each elaborates on the nature of properties of the environment and individual that lead to a stress response, and/or the linkage between environmental stressors and a specific type of outcome. In the following section, we describe five such models: stimulation level, adaptation and coping, control, predictability, and systems models.

Stimulation Levels

The most common explanation of the effects of environmental stressors has been the stimulus or information load model. The stimulus-level hypothesis posits an inverted-U-shaped function between physical stimulation levels and human affect, performance, and health. Either too much (overload) or too little stimulation (sensory deprivation) in the environment is said to produce stress. Physical variables related to stimulation load include the intensity of stimulation, the complexity or variety of stimulation, novelty, ambiguity, conflict or inconsistent sources of information, and, finally, instability or change (Berlyne, 1960, 1971; Fiske & Maddi, 1961; Mehrabian & Russell, 1974; Wohlwill, 1974). In addition to single-stimulus properties like complexity or incongruity, patterns of environmental stimulation may influence stimulation levels as experienced by the individual. Patterns of stimulation as influenced by multiple features that are repetitive or express some underlying theme or symbolic meaning may contribute to an overall sense of coherence and thus reduce information levels (Kaplan & Kaplan, 1982; Lynch, 1960). Scott and Howard (1970) have emphasized that not only do physical factors influence the characteristic activity levels of people, but sociocultural variables (e.g., multiple roles, work demands) can also produce stimulation overload.

Crowding and noise can readily be incorporated into the stimulation load models since each stressor increases the amount of physical stimulation in an ambient environment (Hall, 1966; Kaminoff & Proshansky, 1982; Saegert, 1976; Wohlwill, 1974). Two principal mechanisms, arousal and information overload, have been suggested as the underlying mechanisms of the inverted-U-shaped function between crowding or noise with human responses.

Arousal is a behavioral continuum ranging from sleep to high excitement that has a physiological basis in the reticular activating system of the brain. Persons usually perform optimally under and prefer moderate levels of alertness. Low arousal levels render one sluggish and inattentive whereas too much arousal makes it difficult to concentrate and control one's activities well. Evidence of increases in arousal include elevated catecholamines, skin conductance, and blood pressure, as well as self-reports of restlessness, nervousness, tension, and anxiety. Furthermore, observational indices of overarousal consist of more frequent automanipulative behaviors and behavioral sterotypies (Evans, 1978b).

One of the more complicated and interesting links between stimulus levels and environmental stressors has been in the area of task performance. Considerable research indicates that human performance under higher stress levels produces a particular pattern of deficits. Little or no effects of short-term stressors are noted for simple tasks but decrements are apparent on complex performance tasks (Broadbent, 1971; Hockey, 1979; Kahneman, 1973; Keele, 1973). Although the effects of underarousal on task performance can readily be explained, why too much arousal is debilitating, particularly for more complex tasks, has been the center of considerable discussion. One position holds that under stress overarousal produces a narrowing of attention to more dominant or central task cues. Since complex tasks have greater numbers of cues per unit time that must be attended to (e.g., multiple-signal tasks, rapid frequency signal), this narrowing of attention causes errors because some relevant cues are missed. Simple tasks on the other hand have fewer task-relevant cues per unit of time and thus are less affected by attention narrowing (Easterbrook, 1959; Hockey, 1979; Kahneman, 1973). Some tasks, like the Stroop effect (e.g., word *red* written in green ink), may actually be improved under stress because of attention narrowing and the subsequent enhanced filtering of task-irrelevant distraction cues (see Cohen, 1978, Evans, 1978b, for more details on the meaning of task complexity).

Alternatively, stimulus overload may be understood in terms of demands on information-processing capacity. The demands to monitor a stressor, particularly if unpredictable and uncontrollable, plus the cognitive demands of a task itself may exceed the limits of an individual's information-processing capacity. Capacity will be exceeded more easily when performance demands are high, that is, for more complex tasks (Cohen, 1978). Furthermore, when there are prolonged, extremely high demands from a stressor and/or a difficult task, information-processing capacity may shrink because of fatigue. When overload does occur, available resources will be directed toward the most relevant aspects of the task. Simmel (1950) and Milgram (1970) in their analyses of urban residents' adaptations to the high stimulation of the city setting argued similarly that people deal with overload by either eliminating or filtering low-priority inputs.

Changes in interpersonal behaviors such as altruism during stress can be explained by attention focusing from hyperarousal or overload demands on cognitive capacity. Several studies reveal that persons under stress from noise, for example, do not perceive subtle social cues for distress (e.g., an arm cast, Matthews & Cannon, 1975) or cues in photographs indicating people in need of assistance (e.g., person falling off a bicycle, Cohen & Lezak, 1977). Because of attention focusing under stress, peripheral cues including information about the needs of other persons for help may not be perceived.

Two advantages of the information overload model in comparison to the arousal model of environmental stressors are: (1) The overload model more readily explains why uncontrollable or unpredictable stressors produce greater stress; and (2) the overload model can more readily account for aftereffects of stressors. Stressors that are uncontrollable or unpredictable are more difficult to monitor and thus place greater demands on information capacity. An important distinction should be made between ambient stimulus levels and information; while the latter demands some cognitive response from the receiver, the former does not (Saegert, 1973, 1978, 1981; Suedfeld, 1979, 1980; Wohlwill, 1974). Saegert notes for example that crowding is aversive not so much because of heightened stimulus intensity and variety but rather because of high information loads produced by involuntary and unpredictable social interaction. The relative salience of social and physical, nonsocial cues is an important, largely unresearched question. Aftereffects are a residue of cognitive fatigue, reflecting some of the costs of trying to operate at or above maximum cognitive capacity.

An advantage of the arousal-based models of environmental stressors is that they more readily explain the physiological changes accompanying reactions to environmental stressors. Arousal models also explain more straightforwardly how combinations of some stressors (e.g., noise plus sleep deprivation) cancel out one another's aversive effects in comparison to exposure to either stressor alone (Broadbent, 1971; see McGrath, 1970b, Moss, 1973, Wohlwill, 1974, for more discussion of these two models of environmental stressors).

Adaptation and Coping

Another perspective that has proven useful for understanding environmental stressors is provided through models of adaptation and coping. These models of environmental stress emphasize psychological aspects of human adaptive capabilities. Human beings have a broad and flexible repertoire of coping resources that allows them to maintain equilibrium or near equilibrium in the face of a broad array of environmental conditions. People are able to withstand, at least for short periods of time, substantial environmental demands. Of particular interest to the adaptation and coping perspective on environmental stress is the question: Are there costs associated with human adaptation to environmental demands? This question can be addressed on at least two levels. For the human species in general, we can wonder what the long-term costs are of accommodating to physical surroundings that are drastically different from the types of environments that human beings first evolved in (Boyden, 1970; Dubos, 1965; Iltis, Loucks, & Andrews, 1970; Kaplan & Kaplan, 1982).

Adaptation-level theory may be a psychological expression of these concerns at the individual level. According to adaptation-level theory, human standards of judgment to dimensions of physical stimuli (e.g., brightness) change in proportion to both current and previous, chronic experiences with that dimension. Specifically, adaptation-level theory predicts that either immediate or previous exposure to a high intensity of some dimension will cause a habituation process wherein current judgments of the intensity of that dimension will be lowered relative to judgments by others without exposure to that dimension (Helson, 1964; Wohlwill, 1974). In applying this perspective to air pollution, for example, Wohlwill and Kohn (1976) and Evans, Jacobs, and Frager (1982) have shown that individuals who have resided in areas of the United States with poor visual air quality (e.g., smog) habituate to poorer visibility. However, one's history of environmental demands is probably not the key to understanding how an individual will react to such demands. Instead individual experiences in developing and utilizing coping resources to meet environmental challenges are most likely the crucial factors in predicting how one will respond to a current stressful context (Moss, 1973). The adaptation-level perspective is particularly valuable in focusing our attention on some of the potentially positive effects of dealing with stressors. It is unfortunate that nearly all stress research has focused on the negative consequences of coping with adaptive demands of environmental challenges.

Dubos and others have also raised the interesting issue of how the increasing power of human beings to alter the environment to fit human needs is creating settings that are less diverse and challenging than prehistoric environments (see also Parr, 1966). The selective advantage of the ability to adapt to a variety of ecological niches may slowly become less salient in human evolution. The adaptive advantage of adaptability may no longer be as powerful. The long-term implications of this trend are potentially important, especially given the increasingly poor conditions of the global ecosphere.

Looking at the issue of adaptation at a more individual level, Glass and Singer (1972) and Cohen (1978, 1980) have suggested that a cumulative cost of adapting to stress may be cognitive fatigue. Coping with stressors, particularly uncontrollable ones, requires effort. Negative aftereffects in frustration tolerance or cognitive performance following exposure to crowding, noise, or air pollution are examples of the cumulative effects of effort expended to cope with environmental stressors. Cumulative fatigue may also reduce the capacity to cope with subsequent environmental demands. Frankenhauser and Lundberg (1977) found that immediately prior exposure to loud noise produced poorer performance during a second noise session. Subjects had worked on the same task (mental arithmetic) in an initial session under one of three levels of uncontrollable, continuous white noise. In session two, subjects were all exposed to the same level of moderate noise. Evans, Jacobs, Dooley, and Catalano (in press), looking at a chronic stressor, found that individuals in the greater Los Angeles area who had recently experienced one or more stressful life events suffered psychological symptoms from exposure to higher smog levels.

Levels of smog had no main effects on individuals' psychological symptoms.

Another result of coping with stressors may be overgeneralization, where a strategy that has been adopted to cope with a stressor becomes a characteristic operating mode for the individual even when the stressor is no longer present. Milgram (1970), for instance, argued that urban residents become characteristically different than rural people because of adaptations urbanites make to cope with the high level of information associated with city living. People's coping processes of blocking or filtering low-priority information are said to generalize and become part of one's urban personality, as manifested, for example, by the alleged defensive and brusque urban character as well as inattentiveness to those in need of assistance (e.g., the bums and beggars working the streets, crime victims). This view of urban character development as an overgeneralized manifestation of coping with overload has not gone unchallenged, however (cf. Fischer, 1976; Korte, 1978).

A more specific example of overgeneralization to environmental stress that has been empirically validated is tuning out noise. Evidence from several studies (Cohen, Evans, Krantz, & Stokols, 1980) shows that one way individuals learn to cope with noisy settings is to tune out auditory stimuli. Unfortunately, however, this tuning-out process becomes indiscriminate and includes both speech-irrelevant and speech-relevant sounds. As a consequence persons with normal auditory thresholds tested under quiet conditions who have resided in noisy areas develop poorer auditory discrimination abilities. Decrements in measures of auditory discrimination ability from chronic noise exposure have included the perception of similar-sounding words or subjects' ability to distinguish optimum auditory-signal-to-noise ratios. Poorer auditory discrimination in turn has been associated with difficulties in the acquisition of reading skills (Cohen, 1980; Cohen & Weinstein, 1982). Other evidence for tuning out includes data indicating that children from noisier residential settings are less susceptible to auditory distractors while performing tasks (Cohen et al., 1980; Cohen, Evans, Krantz, Stokols, & Kelly, 1981; Heft, 1979). Overgeneralization of responses to crowding has also been documented, with prior experiences of crowding causing greater social withdrawal from strangers in uncrowded, interactive laboratory tasks (cf. Baum & Paulus, Chapter 14, this volume; Epstein & Karlin, 1975).

Finally, coping responses themselves may have direct physiological effects. Smoking or drug consumption may function to relieve stress, but each has clear health costs of its own. When effort is expended to maintain task performance during stress or to assert control over an aversive event (e.g., reactance), cardiovascular activity greatly increases. Furthermore, if control efforts do not yield direct, relevant feedback to the organism about the efficacy of the coping attempts, even more physiological activity results. Moreover, if these activities are prolonged, they can lead to ulcers and other evidence of direct damage (see Cohen et al., 1986, for more details). Chronic adaptive efforts may lead to disease, either directly, as in the case of greater cardiovascular activity, or more indirectly, as by reduced immunological defenses to infectious diseases. More research is sorely needed both on the precise mechanisms of these two general types of stress–disease links and on the physical, social, and psychological characteristics of situations that are more or less likely to support coping activities that are successful (Cohen et al., 1986).

Control

There is considerable evidence that human beings have a strong need for environmental mastery and a sense of self-efficacy (Averill, 1973; White, 1959). Negative consequences associated with lack of control include negative affect, cognitive deficits, and reduced motivation to behave instrumentally when the option is available (Seligman, 1975). Actual or perceived control over a stressor generally leads to fewer negative consequences than exposure to stressors that are uncontrollable (Averill, 1973). This is particularly true if the individual believes that control has the potential to modify his or her experience of the stressor.

Research consistently shows that environmental stressors that are uncontrollable or unpredictable cause greater stress in human beings. Studies on crowding (Baum & Paulus, Chapter 14, this volume; Epstein, 1982), noise (Cohen & Weinstein, 1982), air pollution (Evans & Jacobs, 1982), and heat (Bell & Greene, 1982) have found complete or partial amelioration of many negative impacts of exposures to these environmental stressors with the provision of instrumental control over the stressor. Thus control may function as a powerful situational mediator of the stress process.

Furthermore, research on crowding suggests that, when control is further restricted, for example, by blocking of goals or interfering with physical movement, greater negative outcomes occur. This has led some researchers to suggest that crowding is aversive precisely because it reduces freedom by constraining certain behavioral options (Proshansky, Ittelson, & Rivlin, 1970; Stokols, 1972). Moreover, crowding, noise, and other stressors are viewed as especially aversive when they occur in residential settings or other places where people expect to have reasonable control over the conditions of their surroundings (Stokols, 1976). In addition, people rate settings as more crowded when they attribute behavioral constraints to the close presence of other people or to insufficient space (Baron & Rodin, 1978; Schmidt & Keating, 1979).

Chronic exposure to environmental stressors that are uncontrollable may also produce greater susceptibility to learned helplessness. If one cannot predict or assert control over an environmental source of stress, one may learn that he or she has little ability to influence environmental outcomes by his or her own behaviors. Thus if coping efforts fail to modify an environmental source of stress it is possible that an individual may experience some helplessness. Several recent studies provide suggestive evidence that persons who reside in crowded or noisy settings may be more susceptible to learned helplessness. Rodin (1976), for example, found that children from more crowded residences suffered helplessness more frequently in a laboratory experiment where they were confronted with a series of failure experiences. Saegert (1981), however, did not find any effects of residential density on learned helplessness among children. Baum and his colleagues (Baum & Paulus, Chapter 14, this volume) have found greater withdrawal and giving up in competitive game situations by college students who live in dormitories that are perceived as more crowded and with greater unwanted social interactions. Finally, Cohen and his colleagues (Cohen et al., 1980; Cohen et al., 1981; Cohen et al., 1986) have found children who attend noisy schools giving up more often on challenging puzzles than quiet school counterparts. Rodin (1976) and Cohen et al. (1986) have also found evidence that children chronically exposed to environmental stressors more readily abrogate choice over positive reinforcements or opportunities to experimenters.

Data on aftereffects from noise, crowding, and air pollution suggest some evidence of helplessness as well. Persons previously exposed to uncontrollable sources of environmental stress often are less persistent on cognitive tasks that require frustration tolerance (Cohen, 1980). Furthermore, these negative aftereffects are essentially eliminated by providing perceived control over the stressor during the administration period. Sherrod (1974), for example, found that the negative aftereffects from exposure to high density in a laboratory setting were virtually eliminated by informing crowded subjects that they could leave the room if they needed to.

Recent revision of learned helplessness theory suggests that learned helplessness in human beings is a more complex phenomenon than first developed with animal operant-learning paradigms. In particular, the attributions individuals make about the causes of their inability to control a stressor bear directly on whether or not helplessness is likely to occur or generalize to other situations (cf. Abramson, Garber, & Seligman, 1980). Furthermore, under some circumstances (e.g., important goal blocked) lack of control, at least temporarily, may lead to reactance and greater efforts to establish mastery. Recently Baum and his colleagues have applied the revised model of human helplessness to students' reactions to living in crowded college dormitories. They find, for example, that changes over the first semester in attributions about the causes of unwanted social interactions in the residential living environment accompany shifts in susceptibility to learned helplessness in game-playing situations conducted in the laboratory (see Baum & Paulus, Chapter 14, this volume, for more details).

Another effect of coping with chronic exposure to aversive, uncontrollable stressors may be a shift in coping strategies from problem-focused to emotion-focused coping. Reappraisal of threat may occur, for example, whereupon an aversive condition (e.g., smog) that was initially critically viewed becomes reappraised as a minor problem or threat. Denial of harmful effects or other rationalizations may also occur as continual experience with an uncontrollable ambient stressor occurs (Campbell, 1983).

Evans and colleagues (1982), for example, compared two groups of persons who had recently migrated to a residential location with high levels of smog. One group had little or no previous residential experience with air pollution, whereas the other had chronically been exposed to poor air quality. The newly exposed group were much more likely to rate smog as a serious community problem, sought out information about smog, complained about it, and believed more strongly that smog could be reduced if people would use mass transportation. Furthermore, recent migrants who were more internal in locus of control, in comparison to recent migrants more external in locus of control and in comparison to all residents with previous exposure to poor air quality, reduced outdoor activities during smog episodes. Persons with a previous residential history of smog exposure, however, showed few if any of these behaviors, instead engaging in more emotion-focused coping. For example, persons chronically exposed to smog were less aware of visual air pollution in photographic scenes, exaggerated their own relative imperviousness to negative health effects from air pollution, and overestimated the extent of their own personal knowledge about the causes and effects of smog.

In sum, there is considerable evidence that chronic exposure to environmental stressors can cause negative reactions because of restrictions in individual control. Furthermore, provision of actual or perceived control over stressors frequently ameliorates or at least partially reduces the negative effects of environmental stressors on human health and behavior. Nevertheless, there is an emerging body of literature suggesting that control over stressors is not uniformly positive (cf. Folkman, 1984). An interesting area of further work in environmental stress research is the examination of situational characteristics that can influence the efficacy of control over stressors. More research is also needed to understand the interrelationships among variable environmental opportunities to exercise control over stressors and psychological appraisal processes of control.

Predictability

A number of scholars have noted the tendency of environmental stressors like noise to disrupt or interfere with ongoing behaviors. Unpredictable stressors are more distracting and make concentration on tasks more difficult. Poulton (1977, 1978) has emphasized that distraction is the principal mechanism of task decrements noted in noise (see Broadbent, 1978, for an alternative view). Distraction has physiological consequences as well, related to the orienting reflex, which triggers a state of mental alertness and vigilance (Berlyne, 1960). Predictability is also related to patterns of environmental stimulation. Settings that are unfamiliar or highly ambiguous or difficult to interpret may be stressful. When one cannot discern the meaning or function of an object or a setting, confusion as well as stress may occur (Archea, 1978; Gibson, 1979).

Predictability has also been linked to control and stress. Aversive events that are unpredictable are more difficult to control and prepare for. Mechanic's (1962, 1978) work has emphasized the role of preparation inadequacy as a cause of stress. A person's ability to master difficult situations is often highly dependent on individual preparation for problem solving. Unpredictable stressors may also be more aversive because individuals are left without any cues indicating when the aversive event is not present; that is, one cannot estimate when it is safe (Seligman, 1975). When confronted with an aversive stimulus condition that is predictable, one can at least relax momentarily and thus achieve some recovery during safe periods.

Prediction also relates to the concept of interruption. Changes in response sequences that have previously been organized produce stress. This stress is caused by the blocking of actions that were judged by the initiator of the response sequence as most appropriate for that situation (Mandler, 1975). People plan many activities before executing them. Activities are mentally rehearsed, alternatives are assessed, and reasonably fixed decisions are made prior to engaging in behavioral sequences (Hebb, 1972; Miller, Galanter, & Pribram, 1960). With interruption come cognitive disorganization and accompanying emotional arousal, followed closely by attempts to persevere in the originally planned response sequence. Physiological data indicate strong arousal activation by incongruity between novel experiences and personal memories and expectancies, which Pribram has termed *neural plans* (Pribram & McGuinness, 1975).

Systems Models

The psychological perspective on stress, as discussed earlier, emphasizes the dynamic balance between environmental demands and the organism's ability to cope with those demands. Congruence or the extent of fit between person and environment has been used to explain stress. Stress occurs when environmental opportunities are insufficient in affording important personal or group needs and goals. Stress is an outcome of incongruence between person and environment (Caplan, 1982; Michelson, 1970; Stokols, 1979).

This approach to environmental stress has been applied primarily to human spatial behavior by several authors. Argyle and Dean (1965) as well as Patterson (1976) state that the regulation of interpersonal intimacy is the underlying dynamic that explains most proxemic behavior. Thus persons tolerate closer interpersonal distance without eye contact or accompanied by more defensive body postures because of the compensatory relationships among these different nonverbal behaviors in maintaining interpersonal intimacy. Analogously, individual needs for privacy may help regulate proxemic behaviors. Crowding can be viewed as a state of the person when achieved privacy levels are less than desired privacy levels. Personal space and other spatially related behaviors can be understood in part as boundary control mechanisms that help maintain or modify desired levels of privacy. When perceived and achieved privacy levels match, congruence is achieved and satisfaction results (Altman, 1975). When a discrepancy occurs between desired and achieved privacy, tension to reequilibrate the system occurs. If this tension cannot be resolved, stress results.

Ecological models of spatial behavior also adopt a systems view by emphasizing the relationship between the number of people in a setting and the number of roles needed adequately to maintain that setting. When overstaffing occurs, crowding results because of less personal involvement and feelings of not being needed by the organization. These feelings in turn cause alienations, negative affect, and possibly more negative interpersonal interactions (Wicker, 1979, Chapter 16, this volume).

It is interesting to note that, while the various models of congruence and stress are essentially psychological theories of stress, they rely on a key component of the original psychologically based models of stress. The body has a natural tendency to maintain homeostasis, and stress is seen as a response to environmental conditions that create strong pressures to disequilibrate the system.

Zimring (1982) has applied the concept of misfit or incongruence as a source of stress to poorly designed and planned architectural settings. He suggests that design features can produce stress by interfering with the achievement of personal goals in designed environments or by limiting coping strategies available to reduce incongruence. Certain psychosocial needs may be facilitated by environments that provide spatial hierarchies ranging from opportunities for public social interaction (e.g., social contact and networking) to very private spaces (e.g., solitude, intimacy). Environments that do not provide ready access to spatial hierarchies may interfere with variable personal needs for social interaction. Stress may result from these unmet needs.

Another systems perspective on stress has been described by Magnusson (1982, 1984). Stress reactions are considered a joint function of individual vulnerability that can be psychological or somatic and the extent of environmental demands. In an important series of studies, Magnusson has shown that individual differences in reaction to stressors cannot be adequately explained without careful specification of the situation in which the individuals are stressed. Consistent gender, age, and cultural differences, for example, have been found in situation-specific contexts. When the situation is similar, good stability in rank order of individual behavioral and physiological reactions to various stressors is demonstrated. Over discontinuous situations, however, marked shifts in relative individual standings in degree of stress reactivity are noted.

15.3.5. Effects of Stressors

In this subsection we briefly review the range of stressor effects noted in previous studies. This overview of stressor impacts will provide a template for us to match the influences of various environmental stressors. This is one way in which we will be able to evaluate the utility of the stress paradigm for understanding how various components of the environment affect human health and well-being. Five specific areas of stressor impacts have been identified.

Physiological Effects

As suggested by both physiological models of stress, various endocrinological responses have been used to measure stress in human beings. There is a good deal of evidence that a wide variety of aversive stimuli cause increased catecholamine and corticosteroid output that is detectable either in blood or in urine (Baum, Grunberg, & Singer, 1982; Frankenhauser, 1971; Mason, 1968). These circulating hormones, epinephrine in particular, produce secondary changes in various target organs related to activation of sympathetic arousal. Thus numerous investigations of a wide array of noxious stimuli have recorded psychophysiological indices of stress including increased blood pressure, skin conductance, respiration rates, muscle tension, and cardiac output (e.g., heart rate) (Baum, Grunberg, & Singer, 1982; Lazarus, 1966; McGrath, 1970b). Heart rate measurement, however, has proven to be more problematic because of the influences of cognitive activity on heart function (Jennings, in press; Lacey, 1967). For example, tasks that require attention to external information sources cause cardiac deacceleration, thus offsetting the effects of sympathetic arousal.

Task Performance

The influence of stressors on human task performance continues to be extremely difficult to characterize. The reason for this is probably that, at least for short periods of time, most people can effectively overcome the aversive effects of a stressor by coping devices such as increased effort or concentration. Nevertheless, there are certain patterns of task deficits that occur under stress. Stressors interfere with tasks that require rapid detection, sustained attention, or attention to multiple sources of input. Rapid-detection tasks typically require individuals to respond to information appearing at a very rapid rate. A serial reaction time task, for example, requires subjects to respond as rapidly as possible to a signal. As soon as a response is made, another signal appears and the sequence repeats. Sustained attention to uncertain, low-frequency signals is also interfered with by stressors. Vigilance tasks, for example, require persons to detect the presence of infrequent target signals. Stress may also interfere with multiple-cue tasks where more than one target cue must be attended to. In this procedure the subject must monitor two different signals. It is of particular interest that stressors interfere only with the secondary signal and usually do not affect the primary signal. *Primary* and *secondary* refer to the relative importance of the two signals as specified to the subject by the experimenter.

Two principal memory deficits have also been noted under stressors. Memory for incidental or secondary information in a task is poorer under stressor conditions. An example of an incidental memory measure would be to ask a person to recall the style of typeface words were printed in. Stressors also cause faster processing of information in working memory but apparently at the expense of total capacity. Working memory is defined as a temporary storage where operations are carried out prior to storage in long-term memory (Hockey, 1979). The memory span in working memory may be shorter under stress. There is also evidence of poorer comprehension of complex information such as context or thematic structure that is believed to occur because of reduced working memory capacity (Broadbent, 1971; Cohen et al., 1986; Hockey, 1979).

Affect and Interpersonal Behavior

Both self-reports of affect and interpersonal behaviors like aggression are influenced by stressors. Many studies have demonstrated greater anxiety, tension, and nervousness plus greater ratings of stress under aversive conditions (Lazarus, 1966; McGrath, 1970a). As noted by Baum and colleagues (Baum, Singer, & Baum, 1982), self-reports of stress can generally be classified into reports of experiences believed to be associated with stress (e.g., stressful life events), the emotional or somatic expression of symptoms (e.g., anxiety, tension), or ratings of the aversiveness of the stressor itself (e.g., stress, threat, harm). Two important issues need to be considered with respect to self-reports of stress. First, to what extent can individuals validly report the degree of stress they are experiencing? Second, according to the psychological perspective on stress, perceived stress rather than some objective indicator (e.g., temperature) should be the driving force behind response outcomes to an aversive situation.

Some research has found more negative social interpersonal behavior under stress, including less altruism and cooperation and greater competitiveness, hostility, and aggression. Aggressive behaviors are typically elicited in game situations or mock learning experiments where participants believe they are delivering punishment (e.g., shocks) to fellow subjects. Furthermore, these behaviors are more pronounced when subjects have been previously angered or exposed to aggressive modeling behaviors (Cohen & Spacapan, 1984; Rule & Nesdale, 1976). There is some evidence that hostility and aggression have a curvilinear, inverted-U-shaped relationship to stress. The reason for this is believed to be that under extreme stress (e.g., very high temperature) individuals become so debilitated that their primary motivation becomes escape or avoidance of the noxious conditions (Baron, 1978). Helping behavior has also been directly measured by observing persons' reactions to a person in distress or by monitoring cooperation to requests for aid. In general, helping is found to decrease under stress (Cohen, 1980; Evans, 1982).

Another aspect of interpersonal behavior influenced by stress is decision making. Studies suggest that stress causes premature closure wherein decisions are made before all pertinent data have been considered (Janis, 1982; Janis & Mann, 1977). Related deficits in decision making under stress include fixation on one or two dominant aspects of a task with little regard for other components. Stereotyped thinking also may result in oversimplified classification and decision categories. Reversion to dominant, traditional thinking patterns is common under stress. Novel information or tasks requiring different approaches are more apt to be redefined in terms of preexisting schemata (Holsti, 1978; Staw, Sandelands, & Dutton, 1981).

Observation

Both verbal and nonverbal categories of stress measurement have been developed. Verbal indicators include speech faults (e.g., repetition, sentence change, tongue slips), filled pauses (e.g., *ah, um*), accelerated rate under certain conditions, and in-creased pitch. Words or phrases that reveal tension or anxiety about the problem at hand (e.g., *hopeless, worried*) may also occur (Siegman, 1982; Spence, 1982). Nonverbal indicators of stress include more defensive body posturing (e.g., leaning away, crossing arm/leg), reduced eye contact or facial regard, greater automanipulative behaviors (e.g., itching, touching hair, fidgeting with clothes), and stereotyped object play (e.g., tapping pencil, manipulating small objects such as beads) (Ekman & Friesen, 1974; Hutt & Hutt, 1970; McGrath, 1970a; Webb, Campbell, Schwartz, Sechrest, & Grove, 1981).

Adaptation

If people are able to adapt to stressors through various coping mechanisms, cumulative costs associated with the adaptive processes may manifest themselves after stressor exposure. While these adaptive behaviors may reduce the immediate stress response in the form of habituation, the process itself may take its toll. These negative aftereffects of coping may include less ability to cope with subsequent stressors, lower motivation, socioemotional adjustment problems, and greater susceptibility to infectious diseases (Cohen, 1980; Dubos, 1965; Glass & Singer, 1972).

There are three general clusters of adaptive effects. The first group of effects is habituation or decrements in response sensitivity with repeated exposure to a stressor (Glass & Singer, 1972; Wilkinson, 1969). Another aspect of habituation is characterized by adaptation-level theory (Helson, 1964; Wohlwill, 1974). According to adaptation-level theory, judgments of stressor intensity are a function of both immediate background conditions and chronic history with the stressor. Adaptation level is an acquired reference point or baseline one uses to make comparative judgments. Previous experience or current background conditions of loud noise, for example, will raise one's comparison level for evaluating a specific noisy stimulus. Persons with little previous noise experience and/or low-noise background conditions would judge a given loudness as noisier than persons previously experiencing loud noise and/or under current noisy background conditions.

Adaptation effects in the second group are related to the cumulative or residual costs of coping with stressors. Cohen (1980) has identified several types of aftereffects following exposure to acute stressors, including decrements in tasks requiring moderate or high motivation, decreased altruism and sensitivity to the needs of others, increased aggression, and increased susceptibility to learned helplessness. Another type of residual coping behavior is overgeneralized coping responses. An example of over-generalization is learning to cope with loud noise by tuning or filtering out auditory stimulation. Evidence indicates that tuning out becomes a routine part of the cognitive repertoire of persons chronically exposed to noise even when they are in quiet conditions (cf. Cohen et al., 1980).

The final group of aftereffects from chronic exposure to stressors includes physiological and psychological disorders. Immediately following exposure to acute, uncontrollable noise, catecholamine levels drop (Frankenhauser & Lundberg, 1974; Lundberg, 1978). Similar patterns have been identified after helplessness induction using inescapable electric shock (Seligman, 1975). Furthermore, as suggested by Selye and Dubos, when adaptive resources are continually summoned over long time periods, some deleterious health effects are likely to occur. Three general types of physiological effects associated with coping with chronic stressors are cardiovascular disorders, gastrointestinal problems, and lowered immunological resistance to infectious diseases (Dubos, 1965; Elliott & Eisdorfer, 1982; Moss, 1973). It should be noted that, while some progress has been made in identifying the mechanisms of these effects, this area of research is just beginning. Chronic exposure to stressors has also been linked to psychological disorders including symptomatology, case openings, and hospitalization (Dohrenwend & Dohrenwend, 1974; Neufeld, 1982; Rabkin & Struening 1976; Thoits, 1983). A more specific syndrome, posttraumatic stress disorder, has been identified following exposures to extremely stressful, traumatic events. This syndrome is characterized by sleep disturbance, diminished interest in significant activities, feelings of social estrangement, and emotional detachment and numbness (e.g., work on Vietnam combat veterans, Roberts et al., 1982).

Summary
Table 15.1 is a summary of the effects of stressors on human health and functioning. Three points about measures of stress should be reiterated here. These measures generally do not correlate highly with one another. There are large individual differences in both the magnitude and the profile of responses to stressors. Several major factors can moderate reactions to a stressor. We will return to these issues in a later section of this chapter.

15.4. ENVIRONMENTAL STRESSORS

In this section of the chapter we discuss the effects of noise, crowding, heat, and air pollution on human health and behavior. Additional research on crowding as well as information on proxemic variables (personal space, territoriality) can be found in Chapters 12, 13, and 14 of this volume. Following an overview of the effects of environmental stressors, the utility of the stress paradigm for understanding these four environmental problems is examined.

15.4.1. Effects of Environmental Stressors

One of the greatest contributions of applying the stress perspective to environmental problems is the broadened scope of analysis that is provided. This point is perhaps best illustrated by noise research. Until the 1960s, the major focus of noise research was on auditory impacts (cf. Kryter, 1970). Yet we know that there are several very important nonauditory effects of noise. These nonauditory effects are generally understood within the perspective of stress.

Another major contribution of applying the stress perspective to environmental problems has been to sensitize biological and physical scientists to the importance of moderating factors. There is strong impetus within the fields of medicine, public health, and engineering to document dose–response curves for environment–health relationships. The concept of psychological stress provides an alternative framework that highlights the importance of individual differences in response sensitivity.

In this part of the chapter we review the stress effects of noise, crowding, heat, and air pollution. Overviews and summaries are provided because of space limitations in this volume plus the availability of several good reviews on these areas (Baum & Epstein, 1978; Baum & Singer, 1982; Baum, Singer, & Valins, 1978; Carson & Driver, 1970; Cohen et al., 1986; Cohen, Glass, & Phillips, 1979; Evans, 1982; Glass & Singer, 1972). An additional purpose of this part of the chapter is to map out what is and what is not known about the stress effects of these four environmental stressors. This will be done by comparing research on each environmental stressor to the array of stress effects outlined in Table 15.1.

Noise
Noise is defined as unwanted sound. Noise is typically characterized by intensity (e.g., dBA), frequency (e.g., pitch), periodicity (continuous or intermittent), and duration (acute or chronic). Other important characteristics include predictability of noise bursts (random or fixed interval) and degree of personal control over noise. Although the importance

Table 15.1. Effects of Stressors

Physiological	Task Performance	Affect and Interpersonal Behavior	Observation	Adaptation
Elevated catecholamines	Deficits in rapid detection	Greater self-report of negative affect	Increased speech faults and filled pauses	Habituation in response sensitivity
Elevated corticosteroids	Deficits in sustained attention	Reduced altruism and other forms of social cooperation	Accelerated speech rate	Negative performance aftereffects
Elevated blood pressure	Deficits in multiple signal tasks[b]	Greater aggression and hostility[c]	Higher vocal pitch	Reduced altruism and interpersonal sensitivity aftereffects
Elevated skin conductance	Deficits in incidental memory	Overly focused and stereotyped decision making	Lexical leakage	Greater susceptibility to learned helplessness
Elevated respiration rate	Increased processing speed in working memory with reduction in capacity		More defensive body postures	Reduced immunological resistance following chronic exposure
Elevated muscle tension			Reduced eye contact	Higher rates of cardiovascular disorders from chronic exposure
Elevated cardiac output[a]			Greater automanipulative behaviors Greater stereotyped object play	Higher rates of psychological symptoms from chronic exposure

[a]Deceleration is possible under some tasks—see text for details.
[b]Deficits occur primarily in secondary tasks—see text for details.
[c]The relationship between aggression and stress may be curvilinear—see text for details.

of these various characteristics of noise has been widely acknowledged, in most research programs noise has been treated simply as high sound levels. Common sources of noise include occupational exposures, transportation sources, and activities of nearby residences.

There is strong evidence that loud (usually > 90 dBA), unpredictable noise exposure increases catecholamines, elevates blood pressure, and increases heart rate and skin conductance (Cohen & Weinstein, 1982; Glass & Singer, 1972; McLean & Tarnopolsky, 1977). As noted earlier there are emerging data suggesting that these psychophysiological indices are elevated when individuals expend effort to cope with a stressor during task

performance conditions. Research on noise, for example, shows that, when subjects are instructed to allow performance to drop off, cognitive efforts diminish along with epinephrine levels and heart rate (Lundberg & Frenkenhaeuser, 1978). There are few data on noise and corticosteroids, respiration, or muscle tension.

Noise levels of 90 dBA and above also interfere with some types of tasks. Several studies have found decrements in secondary tasks in dual-task paradigms under noise. Noise also interferes with tasks requiring rapid detection and response to continuous signals (e.g., serial reaction time tasks). Finally, there is evidence that noise interferes with detection of infrequent signals during sustained vigilance

(Broadbent, 1971; Cohen & Weinstein, 1982; Hockey, 1979).

Tasks that require gating or filtering of competing stimuli are sometimes enhanced by noise. For example, performance on the Stroop task may be better under noisy than under quiet conditions. In the Stroop task one is required to name the color of the print that color words are written in, ignoring the word itself (e.g., the word *red* written in green ink) (Kahneman, 1973). Most studies of noise and task performance have employed simple tasks requiring little to moderate information-processing capacity. As we shall see, stress has little or no effects on concurrent task performance unless the task places considerable demands on processing capacity of the individual.

Noise may also influence memory in complex ways, producing both decrements on some tasks and enhanced performance on others. Noise appears to speed up processing in working memory but with concomitant reductions in memory capacity. For example, if subjects in a memory experiment are suddenly stopped in the middle of a string of words and then asked to recall as many words as possible, recall of recent items is the same or better under noise conditions. However, the span or length of items back into the list is shorter for noise subjects. Some data also suggest that the speeded processing of information in working memory may be responsible for poorer comprehension of complex meaning and thematic/abstract knowledge. Verbatim memory of words, names, and so on as well as the order in which they occurred in a prose passage is better under noise. This also may occur because of the speeded processing of information in working memory (Hamilton, Hockey, & Rejman, 1977; Hockey, 1979).

Memory for incidental information is poorer under noise conditions. For example, if individuals are asked to memorize a list of words written on cards and then probed about what color or typeface the words are printed in or in which corner of each card they were located, noise will interfere with incidental recall. Noise typically will not interfere with the verbal recall of the list (Cohen et al., 1986; Hockey, 1979).

Affect and interpersonal behaviors are also influenced by exposure to noise. Many community studies have documented annoyance with loud sources of noise (e.g., housing adjacent to airports). It is instructive to note, however, that the intensity of noise levels is only a modest predictor of the degree of annoyance. Other situational and personal factors contribute significantly to the prediction of annoyance. For example, fear of airplane crashes, whether the noise is viewed as necessary and important, perceived control over the noise, and the types of activities interfered with (e.g., sleeping children) are all strong predictors of annoyance with airport noise (Cohen & Weinstein, 1982). Some persons may be more sensitive to noise. Self-report measures of general noise sensitivity have been associated with more negative physical and psychological health reactions to high community noise levels (Tarnopolsky, Barker, Wiggins, & McLean, 1978; Weinstein, 1978). Preliminary work suggests that noise-sensitive individuals may have less developed interpersonal coping skills (Weinstein, 1978) and be emotionally less stable and more anxious in general (Iwata, 1984). Acute exposure to noise under laboratory conditions also causes self-reports of stress, tension, and annoyance.

There is abundant evidence that altruistic behavior and sensitivity to others diminish in noise (Cohen & Spacapan, 1984; Cohen & Weinstein, 1982). The effects of noise on aggression and hostility are more complex. Some studies have found greater aggression and hostility under noise, particularly if subjects have had prior anger provocation or exposure to aggressive models (Cohen & Spacapan, 1984; Rule & Nesdale, 1976). As we shall see later, for other stressors there appears to be a curvilinear relationship between the level of stress and aggression, with less aggression under extremely noxious levels of heat or air pollution, for example. This possibility has not been adequately evaluated with noise since most studies have used moderate levels of noise. The evidence for effects of noise on attraction and interpersonal judgments is equivocal, with some studies finding no effects and others suggesting less positive evaluation of others under noise (Cohen & Spacapan, 1984).

A few data on noise and decision making are potentially interesting. Noise may produce more extreme and premature judgments (Siegel & Steele, 1979) and seems to interfere with the individual's ability to differentiate characteristics of people occupying different roles (e.g., self or best friend) (Rotton, Olszewski, Charleston, & Soler, 1978).

There are insufficient data on verbal and nonverbal indices of stress during noise. However, several studies have examined adaptation to both acute and chronic noise. Glass and Singer (1972), for example, reviewed evidence of physiological habituation to acute noise. Loud noise that is unpredictable or uncontrollable often leads to negative performance aftereffects (Cohen, 1980) and in some cases aftereffects of reduced altruism or increased aggression (Cohen, 1980). Evidence for habituation in response sensitivity to chronic noise is decidedly mixed (Cohen & Weinstein, 1982). There is also some suggestive evidence that chronic exposure to noise leads to greater susceptibility to learned helplessness (Cohen et al., 1980; Cohen et al., 1981).

Reviews of occupational noise exposure generally conclude that there is moderate to strong evidence linking noise to cardiovascular disorders in workers (Welch, 1979). Several community studies have also associated residential noise exposure to heart disease (Cohen & Weinstein, 1982). The effects of chronic noise exposure on gastrointestinal disorders as well as on resistance to infectious diseases are inconclusive.

Many studies have noted associations between chronic noise exposure and psychological symptoms, psychiatric admissions, and use of tranquilizers. Because of the serious methodological weakness of these studies as well as the existence of a sufficient number of inconclusive studies, the data on noise and mental health must be regarded as contradictory or insufficient at this time (Cohen & Weinstein, 1982).

In comparing noise results with Table 15.1, it is clear that there are many partially or completely unanswered questions about noise and stress. Of the seven physiological indices of stress, high-intensity noise has been clearly linked to four; increased catecholamines, blood pressure, heart rate, and skin conductance. Insufficient data exist on noise and corticosteroids, respiration, and muscle tension. Of the five human performance impacts of stress, noise has yielded somewhat consistent data on all but one of the measures, speeded processing in working memory. There is also good evidence linking noise with negative affect and interpersonal behaviors, with decision making the only inconclusive category. There are little data on observations of verbal or nonverbal behaviors during noise and a noteworthy mix of evidence on adaptation results. The data on long-term adaptation to noise are contradictory, as are studies linking noise exposure to psychological symptoms.

Crowding

Crowding has been distinguished from density, which is a physical measure of the number of persons per unit of space (e.g., room, acre, square mile). Crowding is a psychological state that occurs when needs for space exceed the available supply (Stokols, 1972). While most environmental psychologists recognize

the value of distinguishing between crowding and density, there have been some criticisms of this approach (Freedman, 1975). Different measures of crowding have been discussed in the literature. Crowding has been associated with measures of inside or outside density (Galle, Gove, & McPherson, 1972; Zlutnick & Altman, 1972). *Inside density* refers to the number of people per living or interior spatial unit (e.g., number of persons per room, or per square feet of interior space). *Outside density* refers to measures of a real extent outside of the residential unit (e.g., people per square mile, buildings per acre). Several researchers have noted limitations of external density measures. Galle and colleagues (1972) and Zlutnick & Altman (1972), for example, argue that external density measures do not adequately capture the individual's daily experience of cramped living space, lack of privacy, interference from others, and so forth. Furthermore, descriptive measures of external density are frequently misleading because of the unequal distribution of people over geographic space. Thus to speak of the mean number of people per square mile in the United States as one country combines density measures of major cities that are quite high with extremely sparsely populated areas like New Mexico (Day & Day, 1973).

Crowding can also be defined in terms of changes in the number of people per unit of space (social density) or changes in the amount of area provided for a given number of people (spatial density) (Loo, 1972; McGrew, 1970). As in the case of noise, most researchers have not paid careful attention to these various characteristics of crowding. For example, few if any studies have used crowding as an independent variable in experimental designs, relying on density manipulations instead. This issue and other problems with ignoring defining characteristics of the various stressors are discussed further in the last section of this chapter.

Only a few studies have measured endocrine levels under varying density conditions. Elevated catecholamines were noted in crowded commuter trains in Sweden (Lundberg, 1976; Singer, Lundberg, & Frankenhaeuser, 1978), as well as elevated cortisol levels among crowded shoppers (Heshka & Pylypuk, 1975). Aiello, Epstein, and Karlin (1975), however, failed to find increases in cortisol levels in crowded dormitory residences. Many studies have found significant density-related increases in blood pressure, heart rate, and skin conductance (Baum & Paulus, Chapter 14, this volume; Evans, 1978b). No data are available on respiration rate or muscle tension.

Research on density and task performance has found deficits for information-processing tasks with multiple signals, tasks requiring sustained attention (Baum & Paulus, Chapter 14, this volume; Evans, 1978b), tasks requiring rapid responses to sequential stimuli (Evans, 1978b), and decrements in incidental memory (Saegert, MacKintosh, & West, 1975). Few or no other data exist for density and other memory tasks. Much as has been the case with noise research, many crowding studies have found no effects of high density on simple task performance (Evans, 1978b; Freedman, 1975).

Crowding is frequently accompanied by negative affect, including reports of tension, anxiety, and stress (Baum & Paulus, Chapter 14, this volume; Sundstrom, 1978). Preliminary evidence indicates that certain individuals are more sensitive to the effects of high density. Males tend to be more negatively affected, particularly under competitive conditions (Epstein, 1982; Sundstrom, 1978). Moreover, persons with external locus of control respond more negatively, at least to acute high-density exposures (see Baum & Paulus, Chapter 14, this volume), along with persons who have larger personal space zones (Dooley, 1978; Evans & Eichelman, 1976). Finally, there is some evidence suggesting that younger children are more susceptible to residential density than are young adults (Evans, 1978a; Saegert, 1981).

A few studies have noted reduced helping behavior under high-density conditions, but a more consistent finding has been greater social withdrawal. Social withdrawal has been shown by several indices during high-density encounters, including: less eye contact, greater interpersonal distancing, and less initiation of conversation (Baum & Paulus, Chapter 14, this volume; Sundstrom, 1978). The potential link between greater social withdrawal and less sensitivity to others' needs has not been investigated in any systematic manner.

Research on density and aggression is very complex. Studies with children, for example, have found evidence for both increased and decreased aggression under very dense conditions (Loo, 1978; Sundstrom, 1978). Less aggression may be caused by the greater social withdrawal behaviors as noted previously. It is possible that a curvilinear relationship might exist between degree of crowding and aggression. When density levels are sufficient to produce extreme discomfort and crowding, motivation to withdraw from other people may predominate over aggressive or hostile feelings. As in the case of noise, insufficient attention has been given to manipulating a wide range of densities within an experiment. Extremely few studies have compared more than two levels of density. There is also some evidence that the ratio of the number of people to the number of resources influences aggression under crowded conditions (Wicker, 1979). Children are more aggressive, for example, when there are fewer toys than when a sufficient number of toys is available. There is also evidence of gender differences in aggressive reactions to crowded environments. Negative interpersonal behaviors are much more common among crowded males than among crowded females (Baum & Paulus, Chapter 14, this volume; Epstein, 1982).

In addition to the nonverbal indices of social withdrawal, a few density studies have found evidence of greater automanipulative and behavioral stereotype behaviors (Evans, 1978b). There are insufficient data on crowding and decision making to draw any firm conclusions. A few studies have found suggestive evidence of interference in group cooperation tasks under high density (Evans, 1979a).

Several investigations of density have examined evidence for adaptation. Most studies have found that short-term exposures to high density do *not* lead to decreased response sensitivity. Chronic exposure to high-density environments, however, does seem to lead to greater tolerance for crowding (Sundstrom, 1978). Negative aftereffects in performance have also been noted in several studies of density, particularly when subjects have no control over the crowding (Cohen, 1980; Sherrod, 1974). Insufficient data exist on altruism aftereffects from exposure to density. A few studies have linked high residential densities with greater susceptibility to learned helplessness (Baum, Aiello, & Calesnick, 1978; Rodin, 1976).

There are a large number of crowding studies in the animal literature that have linked high-density living environments with heightened susceptibility to infectious diseases as well as directly to cardiovascular disease (Christian, 1961; Dubos, 1965; Thiessen, 1964). Human high-density studies on cardiovascular data are too few in number to draw any conclusions, but several studies have found associations with poorer physical health (Baum & Paulus, Chapter 14, this volume; Cox, Paulus, McCain, & Karlovac, 1978; Sundstrom, 1978). Many of these studies are static, correlational designs using aggregate levels of analysis and thus suffer from serious methodological limitations. Nevertheless, there are evident trends in the literature to suggest some link between residential density and poor physical health. The data on high density and psychological health are very contradictory and emanate primarily from seriously flawed field studies (Esser, 1974; Sundstrom, 1978).

The degree of overlap between the stress effects matrix and research on crowding is also reasonably good, although not as complete as in the case of noise. There is strong evidence that high density causes elevated blood pressure, heart rate, and skin conductance, weaker data on catecholamines, and contradictory findings on corticosteroids. As in the case of noise, there are insufficient data on density and respiration rate and muscle tension. The evidence on human task performance and high density is generally weak, with the only clear trend showing more errors in multiple-signal tasks during crowding. The data on density and self-reports of negative affect as well as interpersonal behavior are mixed. There are weak or insufficient data linking density with changes in altruistic behavior or decision making, and contradictory results on aggression. There are, however, reasonably consistent data showing that crowding increases ratings of negative affect. The data on high density and aggression are potentially understandable in terms of an inverted-U-shaped function wherein increases in density up to some moderate point cause increasing aggression but then lead to withdrawal as higher levels are approached. There is some evidence linking high density and nonverbal indices of stress but contradictory findings on crowding and adaptation. Several short-term exposure studies have found exacerbation of reactions over time, whereas long-term studies have found some evidence for habituation to high-density settings. There are contradictory data on density and psychological health but reasonably consistent data showing that high density is linked to greater ill health in animals and possibly in humans as well. Finally, several studies have found negative aftereffects following exposure to uncontrollable high-density conditions.

Heat

The perception of temperature is due primarily to the relationship between the temperature of the external environment and the core temperature of the body. Thermoregulation by the human body maintains core temperature within a restricted range around 37°C. If the core exceeds this temperature, serious disorders of heat stroke and heat exhaustion may occur that can lead to death (Bell & Greene, 1982). Other factors that affect the exchange of heat between the body and the atmosphere also influence the effects of ambient temperature on human health and well-being. Among the more important factors af-

fecting heat exchange are relative humidity, clothing, and acclimatization.

The physiological effects of heat center around the thermoregulatory mechanism, which is controlled by the hypothalamus. It is believed that changes in ambient temperature are monitored by thermosensitive cells in the skin that feed back to the cortex, which in turn innervates the hypothalamus. Elevations in temperatures produce an initial increase in blood pressure that is quickly followed by peripheral vasodilation (to allow heat escape). The peripheral vasodilation causes a subsequent drop in blood pressure. If the body is unable to restore core temperature within a safe range, blood pressure will rise again. This is actually a sign of imminent danger that if not dealt with may rapidly lead to heat exhaustion and a marked dropping off of blood pressure and other vital signs. If core temperature is not quickly restored, serious consequences including death may arise. Both heart rate and skin conductance increase as ambient temperature rises. Excessive demands on the thermoregulatory system may lead to heart attack. During prolonged heat wave conditions there are marked increases in cardiac arrests, particularly among the elderly (see Bell & Greene, 1982, for more details on physiological reactions to heat).

While some of these physiological reactions to heat are similar to stress responses (e.g., heightened heart rate and skin conductance), in general it is probably fair to say that there is little direct physiological evidence linking heat to the stress response pattern outlined in Table 15.1. Nearly all of the physiological responses to heat are centered on improving heat exchange between the body and the environment. Skin conductance, for example, elevates because of increased sweating, which is a cooling mechanism. There are few data on endocrine responses to heat stress. This is unfortunate since they are less directly influenced by thermoregulation mechanisms and thus might show more unambiguously whether heat is a psychological stressor for some individuals.

Mason and his co-workers (1976) have used heat as one type of stressor to study the importance of psychosocial factors in endocrine responses to noxious environmental conditions. As noted earlier, Mason's work suggests that perception of threat or harm may be necessary to provoke the array of physiological responses suggested by Selye (1956). Human subjects were exposed to very gradual temperature changes (ranging from 74 to 105°F at relative humidity of 50%). Core temperature and urinary corticosteroids were monitored. No evidence of psychoendocrine responsiveness was found even under the hottest conditions where core temperature increased by 1.6°. There are insufficient data on heat and muscle tension or respiration rate.

The effects of heat on task performance are extremely complex and not well understood from any one theoretical perspective. Generally, heat is more likely to produce performance decrements in unacclimatized subjects exposed to heat (approximately 32°C) over a long period of time. Tasks with multiple signals are adversely affected by heat. Studies have shown vigilance tasks improved, unaffected, and worsened by performance during heat exposure. For rapid signal detection and response tasks, heat exposure seems to improve initial performance, which then tapers off and eventually declines under heat conditions (Bell & Greene, 1982; Poulton, 1970).

Research on heat and task performance is particularly difficult to characterize because there are several important methodological variables that vary markedly across studies. Levels of heat and whether it is measured at core body temperature or at ambient levels, relative humidity, duration of exposure, and use of acclimatized or unacclimatized subjects all bear importantly on the relationship between heat and human performance. To our knowledge there is no research on heat and memory.

Self-report measures of heat focus on thermal comfort ratings. Thermal comfort is strongly related to ambient temperature, humidity, and clothing insulation properties (Griffiths, 1975). For moderate clothing and 45% relative humidity, the range of comfort for most persons is 24 to 27°C. When temperatures are higher than this, people typically report discomfort, irritability, and, if exposure is prolonged, fatigue. Measures of perceived tension, nervousness, anxiety, or stress have not been monitored systematically in heat research (Bell & Greene, 1982). There are mixed data on heat and interpersonal attraction, with some suggestive evidence that heat reduces interpersonal attraction only for persons who are not also suffering from the same uncomfortable conditions (i.e., no shared distress) and when there are no strong preexisting attitudes about the target person(s) (Bell & Greene, 1982). Heat has little or no effects on altruistic behaviors (Bell & Greene, 1982). There are also insufficient data on heat and decision-making behaviors.

As noted in the above sections on noise and crowding, the relationship between environmental stressors and aggression may be curvilinear. This theory comes primarily from research on heat and negative affect. As ambient temperature rises there is a linear increase in negative affect that is accompanied by greater hostility and aggression. However, at some point (approximately 35°C) the hot setting becomes so negative or noxious that, instead of aggression, behaviors to withdraw or escape from the hot environment predominate. Thus at some moderately high temperature aggressive behaviors actually drop off (Baron, 1978).

The evidence for this model of negative effect, heat, and aggression is pretty consistent. As heat increases beyond a certain point, whereas negative affect continues to mount, aggression decreases. Self-reports are also consistent, with subjects indicating that their primary needs as temperature continues to climb are to escape from the situation (see Baron, 1978, for a good review of the evidence). Furthermore, manipulations that hold temperature constant but reduce negative affect (e.g., giving someone a cool glass of water) show a drop in negative affect and a continuing increase in aggression at high temperatures. Field studies of collective violence tend to show the same curvilinear effect, with rioting increasing as temperatures rise up to some point (around 32°C) and then dropping off with increasing temperature (Baron, 1978; Bell & Greene, 1982).

There are few or no data on verbal and nonverbal indicators of stress during heat but some interesting research on heat and adaptation. While there are few data on heat and aftereffects, susceptibility to infectious diseases, or changes in vulnerability to helplessness, there are consistent findings showing increased risk of cardiovascular disease during periods of increased temperature. Yet if people live in a hotter climate there is no evidence of increased cardiovascular disease. These two sets of data suggest that it is a change in temperature rather than higher temperature per se that challenges the cardiovascular system. Acclimatization to heat is a well-documented phenomenon that occurs typically after 4 to 7 days of exposure to a hotter environment. Acclimatization is caused by increased sweating efficiency and is accompanied by lower discomfort, less physiological reactivity, lower core temperature, and better task performance during hotter temperatures. There is also a large but contradictory body of work on genetic differences in heat acclimatization (Frisancho, 1979).

While there are enough trends in both the noise and the crowding literature to suggest that the stress model has some support, the situation is markedly hazier for heat. There are insufficient data for most of the physiological indices of stress and heat, with most physiological changes accompanying heat probably due to thermoregulatory activities. Research on heat and task performance is very mixed, and insufficient data exist for altruism and decision making. The inverted-U-shaped function between heat and aggression is strongly supported. There are also many studies showing habituation with heat exposure. Data on heat and observational indices as well as various measures of psychological adaptation processes are largely absent.

Air Pollution

It is immediately apparent when examining the air pollution literature that there is considerably less research on air pollution and human behavior than there is on the other three environmental stressors we have considered thus far. Furthermore, especially in the case of air pollution and perhaps for heat as well, few researchers have explicitly examined whether these environmental conditions are stressors.

Air pollution is a ubiquitous problem, affecting the majority of the population of the United States, and costing upwards of $250 million per year in direct health costs alone (Evans & Jacobs, 1982). Air pollution is actually a collection of several toxic agents that include photochemical oxidants or smog (chiefly ozone as the toxin), sulfur oxides, nitrogen oxides, carbon monoxide, and particulates. There are two other categories of air pollutants that are not as thoroughly documented as the list of ambient pollutants. The first of these, indoor air pollutants, is only now gaining the serious attention it deserves in the health community (National Academy of Science, 1981). Indoor gas heating and cooking exhausts, insulation and other construction materials, and occupationally related toxin exposures are the most prominent sources of indoor air pollution exposure. The most common harmful compounds found in indoor air pollution include nitrogen dioxide, carbon monoxide, formaldehyde, asbestos, and various solvents.

The second category of air pollutants that have not been as extensively analyzed as the ambient pollutants includes heavy metals such as lead, mercury, cadmium, and other compounds. These chemicals find their way into the human body via particulant settlement from the air, ground water supplies, and plant absorption (Waldbott, 1978).

Unfortunately, to date, even fewer behavioral scientists have been involved in studying indoor air pollution or heavy metal toxins than the already paltry numbers looking at ambient air quality and human behavior. This is particularly unfortunate because

many of the effects of the toxic compounds found indoors (e.g., formaldehyde) or in heavy metals (e.g., lead) include neurosensory dysfunction (Weiss, 1983). There is also evidence for critical developmental periods for childhood exposure to some of these compounds. Many of these chemicals may not have obvious direct negative outcomes until years after childhood exposure. The emerging field of teratology is examining such issues (Fein, Schwartz, Jacobson, & Jacobson, 1983).

As one might expect, the overwhelming majority of air pollution and human studies have focused on respiratory-related outcomes. Since this research has been extensively reviewed (Coffin & Stokinger, 1977; Goldsmith & Friberg, 1977), we will focus our attention here on the few behavioral studies of air pollution. As will be apparent from reading the next few paragraphs, this research is at a very early stage.

With the exception of cardiovascular measures, no research to our knowledge has examined physiological indices of stress from exposure to air pollution. There is evidence that exposure to carbon monoxide increases heart rate because of demands for more oxygen. There is a good deal of evidence that carbon monoxide interferes with tasks requiring sustained attention and may also disrupt multiple-attention tasks (Evans & Jacobs, 1982). There are conflicting data on rapid signal detection tasks. For example, some studies have found slowing of reaction times during exposure to carbon monoxide, whereas other studies have found either no effects or the same pattern of decrements, but only for those individuals with preexisting respiratory impairments. There are insufficient data on air pollution and memory, but there is some suggestive evidence that carbon monoxide may slow down working memory. Note that this is in direct opposition to what noise and other stressors do to working memory. There are very few data on other pollutants and human task performance. Nearly all of this work has focused on carbon monoxide (Evans & Jacobs, 1982; Gliner, Raven, Horvath, Drinkwater, & Sutton, 1975). It is difficult to know whether any of the task deficits associated with pollutant exposures are due to stress. At least in the case of carbon monoxide, it is probably more parsimonious to attribute task deficits to oxygen deprivation to the brain.

There is a moderate amount of survey research measuring citizens' attitudes and awareness of air pollution. Individuals are annoyed by air pollution and will indicate that it is a serious community problem when directly queried (Evans & Jacobs, 1982). However, when individuals are simply asked to rank order community problems, air pollution is not very salient in comparison to other community issues (Barker, 1976). Much of the survey research has focused on other variables that influence people's reactions to air pollution. Consistent data suggest for example that concern and awareness are greater for those with more education, for women, and for individuals with greater internal locus of control. Individuals who have resided under poor ambient air quality for a long period of time or those economically dependent on a major pollution source are less likely to be bothered by air pollution (Barker, 1976; Evans & Jacobs, 1982). The significance of these and other moderating factors for environmental stress is discussed in more detail in a later section of this chapter.

Interpersonal relationships have been examined in a few studies of air pollution. Both malodors and cigarette smoke cause annoyance and more negative evaluations of the immediate environment. Interpersonal attraction appears to diminish under poor air quality so long as the target individual is not viewed as also suffering from exposure to similarly noxious conditions. When subject and target are both exposed to poor air quality (e.g., malodor), a sense of shared distress seems to create empathy for the other person (Rotton, Barry, Frey, & Soler, 1978). Note the similarity of this trend with earlier data on heat and interpersonal attraction. Furthermore, some research indicates less altruism under poor air quality conditions and increased aggression up to a point with increasing air pollution (Evans & Jacobs, 1982). Rotton, Frey, Barry, Milligan, and Fitzpatrick (1979), however, found a curvilinear relationship, as in the heat studies, between air pollution levels and aggression. Once again subjects' behaviors and self-reports suggested that, when environmental conditions became sufficiently noxious, efforts to withdraw from the situation were more salient than hostility or aggression. There are no data to our knowledge on decision making under air pollution nor observations of verbal or nonverbal indices of stress.

Some recent research, however, has begun to examine possible evidence of adaptation to air pollution. Rotton (1983) found performance aftereffects following exposure to uncontrollable, malodorous pollution. This finding and several survey studies suggest some feelings of helplessness in the face of exposure to chronic air pollution. Few people feel any personal means are available for reducing air pollution, and for some this leads to feelings of hopelessness about the problem (Evans & Jacobs, 1982). For example, Rankin (1969) found that very

few people felt like complaining about air pollution even when they were annoyed by it. About half of those who were annoyed did not complain because they felt it would not do any good. Air pollution may become an accepted, largely unnoticed background characteristic of the everyday environment because nothing can be done about it (Campbell, 1983; Wohlwill, 1974). Both physiological (Dubos, 1965) and psychological evidence exists for habituation in response sensitivity with chronic exposure to air pollution. Evans and colleagues (1982) found that persons who had previously lived in high air pollution zones were less aware and less affected by poor quality in their current residence in a high pollution area that they had recently migrated to than new migrants who had previously lived in low pollution areas. There is also some evidence of short-term habituation in respiratory sensitivity to air pollutants plus inhibited immunological response with chronic air pollution exposure as well as greater incidence of cardiovascular disease (Goldsmith & Friberg, 1977). The latter effects are probably due to direct effects of greater oxygen demand. Some pollutants like carbon monoxide also accelerate atherosclerosis.

Finally, there are a few studies linking air pollution levels with poorer mental health. Simple correlations without extensive controls for other factors have been found between pollution levels and psychiatric admission rates (Briere, Downes, & Spensley, 1983; Strahelivitz, Strahelivitz, & Miller, 1979). Several other studies have reported no such associations, however. Two recent studies with more thorough controls and better research designs have found evidence for poorer psychological health as measured on a standardized scale (Evans et al., in press) and 911 emergency calls for psychiatric-related problems (Rotton & Frey, 1984). In the study by Evans and associates, however, only persons who had recently experienced a stressful life event were vulnerable to the negative psychological impacts of air pollution. This finding is interesting in light of earlier discussions about adaptation to stressors. Exposure to a stressor that is either major or prolonged may interfere with subsequent ability to cope with other environmental sources of stress.

The overall picture is incomplete for characterizing air pollution as an environmental stressor. The only consistent evidence linking air pollution to stress is from negative affect data. There is also some support for task performance data, although these findings are limited to carbon monoxide. Furthermore, as noted in the text, these performance deficits may be due to hypoxia and not stress. There is also moderate support, showing habituation in response sensitivity with chronic exposure to air pollution. While the data on rapid signal detection tasks are contradictory, the remaining stress-related effects are either weak or for the most part insufficient to draw any firm conclusions about the status of air pollution as an environmental stressor.

15.4.2. Evaluating the Stress Paradigm

A central question addressed by this chapter is whether the four environmental problems of noise, crowding, heat, and air pollution can be understood, at least in part, as psychological stressors. We suggest that the answer is yes for noise and crowding and possibly yes, pending further investigation, for heat and air pollution. Both noise and crowding have effects on human health and behavior that can be characterized as stress effects. Heat and air pollution may or may not function as stressors with too few data available to warrant any conclusions at this time. When one examines the various matrices of stress effects and environmental stressor data, several research questions are immediately apparent. The important conceptual issue of whether perceived threat is a prerequisite to experiencing psychological stress is a central issue for work on environmental stressors as well. While theoretical distinctions have been made between physical measures of the environment, density and sound levels, and corresponding perceived measures, crowding and noise, these same distinctions have not been developed and evaluated for heat or air pollution. Furthermore, for all of these four stressors, we really do not know to what extent each of them is perceived as threatening to health or well-being, nor do we know what the relative, empirical relationships are between perceived versus actual measures of environmental conditions and human health and behavioral outcomes (Cohen et al., 1986).

Heat and air pollution are typically low-level, chronic aversive conditions that may not be salient to most people. Perhaps among more vulnerable subgroups of the population (e.g., heat and cardiac patients or air pollution and those with respiratory impairments), these stressors may be threatening and initiate a wider array of symptoms resembling psychological stress. Heat and air pollution may also be viewed as more "natural" stressors that are harder to attribute directly to the behavior of other individuals. This may produce less annoyance and an attitude of acceptance that such conditions are part of everyday life and not readily modifiable.

Considerably more work is needed on environ-

mental stressors and task performance. This type of research, however, will continue to be plagued by weak and inconsistent findings until a better conceptual understanding of stress and cognition is developed. More basic research is needed on how cognitive mechanisms are affected by stress. In addition, the roie of individuals' attitudes toward the stressor may prove to be a critical parameter in performance research on stress. We already know, for example, that cognitive effort for at least short periods of time can strongly influence the effects of stressors on performance (Cohen et al., 1986).

In the area of affect and interpersonal behavior, two prospective research areas stand out. First, there is a noticeable dearth of studies on environmental stressors and decision making. The effects of psychological stressors on decision making are sufficiently validated that they warrant examination under aversive environmental conditions. More work is also called for on aggression and environmental stressors. We know from heat research that high levels of temperature appear to depress aggressive behaviors in the face of rising negative affect. There are some similar findings in the air pollution literature as well. We also know that under high-density levels, a frequent social behavior is withdrawal. While these patterns of data may fit the inverted-U-shaped function between aggression and negative affect posited by Byrne (1971), an alternative explanation of the data may be learned helplessness, which also is associated with retarded aggression responses. Perhaps under very averse environmental conditions individual feelings of helplessness cause withdrawal and less aggression.

Another large research gap in environmental stressors is observation indices of stress. With the exception of a few crowding studies (Evans, 1978b), there has been essentially no work on verbal or nonverbal indices of stress during exposure to environmental stressors. Research on adaptive processes and environmental stressors has focused primarily on habituation, performance aftereffects, and indices of health status. Both heat and air pollution could be studied with aftereffect paradigms, as has been done more extensively with noise and crowding. Another type of aftereffect that warrants further research in all four of the environmental conditions reviewed here is susceptibility to other stressors. One of the costs associated with coping with stressors may be reduced capacity to respond to other environmental challenges. There is markedly little research on how coping with one stressor affects our ability to deal with another source of environmental demand (see

Cohen, 1980; Cohen et al., 1986, for some preliminary ideas on the effects of coping with environmental stressors).

More work is also needed to understand the physical and social conditions that predispose some individuals at certain times to habituate to chronic stressors as opposed to increasing their reactance with experience. Some research suggests that the extent of threats to health and/or the importance of goals interfered with by the stressor may influence the ways in which people cope with chronic environmental stressors (Campbell, 1983; Stokols, 1979). The relationship between exposure and learned helplessness also warrants further exploration. While there is some noise and crowding research on helplessness, we do not understand what aspects of the environment produce these effects, nor do we know much about the circumstances that are more likely to augment them. Of particular interest in this regard and more generally is the question: What are the environmental conditions that are most likely to cause one to perceive a general sense of loss of environmental mastery?

A final question emanating from our comparison of the overall stress matrix with the various results on environmental stressors is: To what extent are physical and mental health influenced by chronic exposure to suboptimal environmental conditions? Basic research is rapidly emerging on the physiological mechanisms that link stress to cardiovascular diseases as well as infectious diseases. Environmental stress research on physical health needs to take advantage of this emerging knowledge.

15.5. THEORETICAL AND METHODOLOGICAL ISSUES

15.5.1. Cognitive Mediation of Environmental Stressors

A critical limitation in focusing only on physical sources of stress in situations is the fact that people vary greatly in their reactions to the same configuration of physical demands. The role that cognitive analyses of stress have played in the development of the noise or crowding literature, for example, is apparent in the lexicon of both of these literatures. The distinctions between sound and noise or between density and crowding point to the importance of individual evaluations of environmental demands. Cognitive appraisals of a stimulus configuration as threatening or harmful are a core component of

stress (Lazarus, 1966; Lazarus & Launier, 1978). Stress occurs when environmental demands are perceived as taxing or exceeding the organism's ability to cope with those demands. Thus the meaning of a physical configuration of an environment has powerful influences on whether those physical conditions will elicit stress.

It is interesting to note that, while most environmental psychologists accept this position on the central, mediating process of appraisal, there is markedly little research comparing, for example, density to crowding measurements or sound to noise measurements in their respective explanatory power to predict human health on behavioral outcomes. Cohen and his colleagues (1986) have recently compared actual sound levels and perceived noise ratings on several measures of children's health and behavior. These analyses suggest that children's perceptions of noise accounted for significant proportions of variation in some outcome measures (e.g., blood pressure) when controlling for actual noise levels. Teachers' perceptions of noise-related classroom interference also predicted children's performance on attentional tasks, after controlling for objective noise levels. The latter finding is particularly interesting because it suggests possible links between children's and adults' reactions to shared stress. Research on crowding also suggests that subjective feelings of crowding may be associated with negative outcomes after controlling for physical density measures (Baldassare, 1979). On the other hand, Saegert (1981) has found that, while apartment density was significantly related to classroom behaviors and school performance among elementary school children, perceived crowding did not mediate the effects of density. Moreover, Evans and his colleagues (in press) found that ozone levels, but not visibility, in conjunction with recent stressful life events, were related to psychological health symptoms.

The stressful life events literature has examined the issue of objective versus perceived stress levels in some detail. This issue has some important conceptual roots going back to the physiological and psychological perspectives on stress discussed at the beginning of this chapter. The early stressful life event literature derived primarily from Selye and Cannon's emphases on stress as symptomatic of bodily reactions to reestablish homeostasis in the face of adaptive challenges from the environment. Stressful life events were thus originally conceived of in terms of the amount of change or disruption the events produced, that is, the amount of disequilibrium (Dohrenwend & Dohrenwend, 1974, 1981;

Holmes & Rahe, 1967). Subsequent research has suggested, however, that the perceived severity of a stress life event is a better predictor of health outcomes than is the amount of environmental change or disruption per se (Cohen, 1981; Cohen, Kamarck, & Mermelstein, 1983; Evans, Palsane, & D'Souza, 1983; Thoits, 1983).

Some important tasks for persons interested in the issue of perceived versus objective measures of environmental stressors are: (1) to develop some conceptual framework to explain how and when perceived stressors will predict some outcomes better or worse than objective measures of environmental stressors; (2) to construct outcome measures that are not overly confounded with the perceived stress measures in terms of both actual content (e.g., use of illness symptoms as stressors) and the method used (measures using the same method typically share some method-based error, e.g., linking self-reports of perceived stress to self-reports of anxiety or health); and (3) to determine what characteristics of physical and social environments are most likely to cause different patterns of perceived stress. Some preliminary progress has been made on some of these issues. Data suggest that subjective measures predict better than objective ones under low or moderate levels of stressors. Under very aversive conditions such as extremely high noise impact zones, decibel levels are more highly associated with outcome measures (Neus, Ruddel, & Schulte, 1983). Research in the environmental assessment field has also examined the interrelationships among objective and subjective indices of environmental quality (cf. Carp & Carp, 1982; Craik & Zube, 1976).

The most investigated mediating construct between environmental stressors and human outcome measures has been perceived control (Averill, 1973; Glass & Singer, 1972). Control has been implicated as a principal mechanism for the aversive effects of several environmental stressors (see Section 15.3.4). Research on crowding, noise, and to some extent air pollution has shown that, generally, when these stressors are uncontrollable, they produce more negative effects on human functioning. Furthermore, the provision of actual or perceived control over environmental stressors significantly reduces their aversive impacts (Cohen, 1980; Cohen et al., 1986; Glass & Singer, 1972). Chronic exposure to uncontrollable environmental sources of stress has also been implicated in learned helplessness.

Several aspects of further research on control and environmental stressors are apparent. More work on control and heat and air pollution is warranted. There is suggestive evidence that prolonged exposure to either or both of these conditions may lead to feelings of hopelessness (Bell & Greene, 1982; Evans & Jacobs, 1982). Moreover, at least one study has shown that perceived control over air pollution dramatically reduces some of its aversive effects (Rotton, 1983).

The manner in which people adapt to chronic exposure to environmental stressors may vary as a function of the intractability of the stressor. People may be more likely to seek instrumental coping strategies when the negative environmental costs are viewed as malleable (Campbell, 1983; Evans et al., 1982). Control may also influence both the perceived severity of a stressor and the relative predictive power of objective and perceived measures of environmental stress.

Finally, there are forms of control in addition to behavioral control, such as cognitive control, which may prove to be potent mediators of environmental impacts. For example, Mechanic's research on students preparing for exams found that mastery was achieved primarily through cognitive preparation and social comparisons prior to the exams (Mechanic, 1962). Similarly, research on medical procedures shows that preparatory information, particularly if coupled with suggestions for pain reduction, strongly influences patient recovery and well-being (Janis, 1983). Saegert and her colleagues have applied this type of cognitive control intervention with some success in crowded settings. When individuals are forewarned about impending crowding conditions in retail stores, their task performance is less severely affected by crowding and they feel less stress (Langer & Saegert, 1977; Love & Saegert, 1978; Saegert, Mackintosh, & West, 1975). Baum and his colleagues have also shown differences in behavioral reactions to high-density settings utilizing different cognitive control manipulations (see Baum & Paulus, Chapter 14, this volume). Furthermore, as noted earlier, while greater control is generally efficacious, some situational and personal factors may lead to no effects or possibly negative effects from instrumental control over a stressor. More research is needed on this topic.

The attitude of the individual toward environmental stressors is another important cognitive mediator. For example, as noted earlier, many studies of annoyance with environmental sources of stress like noise indicate that attitudes about sound levels are consistently better predictors of citizens' annoyance than are physical measures of sound. Fear of crashes, perceptions of whether the noise source is necessary and important, and whether any attempts are being made to modify the noise have all been found to be potent mediators of the sound level–perceived annoyance relationship (Cohen & Weinstein, 1982).

The mediating role of expectancies is dramatically illustrated by research on crowding and noise showing that anticipation of these environmental stressors causes reactive symptoms strikingly similar to actual exposure to stressors (Baum & Paulus, Chapter 14, this volume; Spacapan & Cohen, 1983). These anticipated stressor effects include performance aftereffects, physiological arousal, coping behaviors, and negative affect.

The social climate of a setting may also moderate individual reactions to specific environmental stressors. Three basic dimensions characterize the social environments of most organizations. The relationship dimension describes how involved individuals are in a setting as well as the extent of social support offered by that setting. The personal development dimension deals with opportunities in a setting for personal growth and self-enhancement. The system maintenance dimension reflects the degree of order, control, and clarity in a setting (Insel & Moos, 1974; Kiretz & Moos, 1974; Moos, 1973). Unfortunately, research on various environmental stressors has generally ignored the potent interplay of organizational factors like social climate, work pressure, and role structures with various physical stressors (McGrath, 1976; Zimring, 1982). Hospital settings illustrate the importance of organizational factors as well in understanding influences of the designed environment on behavior. The large and often sterile physical form of hospital settings (e.g., bright lighting, tile floors and walls) plus organizational policies (e.g., patient management strategies, physician status) may interact to augment feelings of helplessness and vulnerability among patients (Shumaker & Reizenstein, 1982). Finally, Ahrentzen and her colleagues have indicated that the interactions of social climate variables with physical (e.g., noise) and architectural setting (e.g., open plan) variables are better predictors of student behavior than either of these factors alone (Ahrentzen, Jue, Skorpanich, & Evans, 1982).

The critical role of mediators in the environmental stressor–human reaction process reiterates the importance of measuring and explaining human variation in response to aversive physical conditions. An important task for environmental psychologists is to uncover how the physical setting itself contributes to these mediating processes.

15.5.2. Coping with Environmental Stressors

It is clear that human beings are not passive respondents to environmental conditions. We maintain a dynamic transaction with our physical and social surroundings that typically includes instrumental attempts to achieve mastery as well as cognitive and emotional equilibrations that enable us to accommodate changing environmental conditions that are more difficult to control instrumentally (White, 1974). Environmental stress researchers need to integrate coping and adaptation concepts more fully into their research and theory. We know, for example, that cognitive efforts can mask, for at least short periods of time, many of the negative effects of environmental stressors like noise on task performance. It is only when we carefully monitor tasks that demand considerable cognitive capacity (Cohen, 1978; Evans, 1978b) or use aftereffects paradigms (Cohen, 1980; Glass & Singer, 1972) that some of these short-term aversive effects are manifested.

An intriguing question that the previously discussed pattern of results and others like them suggest is: What are the direct effects of stressors on human health and well-being, and what are the effects of coping with environmental stressors? The gains and losses associated with coping with chronic stressors are an important issue that is just beginning to be looked at in the environmental stress field. As noted earlier, some of the suspected effects of coping with chronic environmental stressors include cumulative fatigue (e.g., aftereffects), overgeneralization of learned coping responses (e.g., tuning out noise), and physiological activation due to efforts to maintain control or optimum functioning (e.g., reactance behaviors or catecholamine activity). Personal failures to cope with stressors adequately may cause some persons to become susceptible to other control-related situations such as learned helplessness. Continual exposure to environmental sources of stress that are not responsive to instrumental efforts may also lead to greater emotion-focused coping such as denial, rationalization, or various defensive reactions (Cohen et al., 1986).

Social support consists of the resources provided by one's interpersonal relationships. Current research on social support generally considers support to consist of several dimensions, including the availability of material aid (tangible support), the availability of someone to discuss problems with (appraisal support), the availability of others to compare oneself to (self-esteem support), and the opportunity to engage in social interactions with other people (belonging support) (Cohen & Syme, 1985; Gottlieb, 1978; House, 1981). While social support as a possible stress buffering agent has been examined in occupational and medical settings as well as interpersonal conflicts, to our knowledge the potential mediating role of social support in environmental sources of stress has only been examined in one study. Fleming, Baum, Gisriel, and Gatchel (1982) found that persons living near the Three Mile Island nuclear plant reported fewer psychological symptoms when they had persons available to talk to about problems than when they did not. Support was relatively unimportant for persons in nonstressed control areas. The role of support processes in protecting persons from stress may be especially interesting in relation to crowding, noise, and temperature because of their interplay with social relations. Crowding in particular raises some intriguing questions for social support research since members of a primary social support system may also function under certain physical circumstances as a source of stress (Epstein, 1982; Evans et al., 1983). Noise might interact with the close availability of others to provide support by interfering with interpersonal communication. Heat and air pollution can increase interpersonal attraction and create empathy for others when they too are perceived as suffering from stress (cf. Rotton, Barry, Frey, & Soler, 1978).

15.5.3. Methodological Issues

In addition to the theoretical questions raised about environmental stressors, there are several remaining areas of concern in the environmental stress literature. We discuss several important methodological issues in the following sections, which include individual differences, temporal parameters, multiple levels and types of stressors, setting, measurement, and theoretical concerns.

Individual Differences

The search for mediators of the stressor–stress reaction process was initiated early on by Lazarus and others primarily because of individual differences in response to similar aversive conditions. Social scientists often view individual differences as nuisances because they make theoretical work considerably more difficult and contribute to the impression that theories of human behavior are not scientific. Social scientists may be relieved to learn that a similar situation exists for our biological colleagues interested in environmental problems. The fact is that large individual differences, some explainable, most not, are the rule rather than the exception when examining the relationship between health effects and exposures to environmental toxins (Weiss, 1983). The question of central concern is explaining individual differences that are systematic. One issue in particular that warrants further research is the concept of vulnerability to stressors. Some individuals may have lower or higher resistance to stressors in general, whereas for others variable resistance may be stressor specific (Magnusson, 1982; McGrath, 1982). For example, Kobasa argues that the individual characteristics of hardiness inoculates some high-risk individuals (e.g., business executives) from stress-related disorders (Kobasa, 1979). Hardiness consists of feelings of commitment, the tendency to appraise demands as challenging, and a sense of self-efficacy. Children, the poor, the elderly, and institutionalized persons may on the whole be more susceptible to aversive effects of environmental stressors because they have less control over stressors and may have fewer coping resources to draw upon to deal with them (Cohen et al., 1986; Evans, 1978a; Sherrod & Cohen, 1979).

Children, for example, appear to be more vulnerable than adults to negative consequences from exposure to residential crowding in measures of both psychological and physical status (Evans, 1978a; Saegert, 1981). Children are also more reactive to respiratory effects of air pollution (Evans et al., 1982). The effects of early physical environments on the development of social and cognitive competence are receiving increasing attention in the developmental community (cf. Wachs & Gruen, 1982). This recent work continues a long tradition of research on critical periods of development, which has focused on issues like the effects of insufficient physical stimulation or social isolation during various restricted periods of development on maturation processes (cf. Denenberg, 1972; Wohlwill & Heft, Chapter 9, this volume).

Research with elderly people also suggests greater sensitivity to physical surroundings (Lawton, 1980), particularly among institutionalized individuals. Orientation and way finding, building quality, spaces for social interactions, privacy opportunities, and security from crime have been identified as important dimensions of housing for senior citizens (Rowles & Ohta, 1983; Schooler, 1982).

More specific stressor-related susceptibility may

prove valuable for gaining some understanding of the processes by which stressors influence people in different ways. Weinstein's (1978) and Iwata's (1984) research on noise-sensitive individuals is an example of this approach. Other variables worth exploring are control-related phenomena like locus of control and Type A behavior; stimulus seeking and screening (cf. Mehrabian & Russell, 1974); quantity as well as variability of individual coping resources; previous experience and other variables related to learning and expectations about a specific stressor; and developmental, gender, and cultural factors.

Measurement

There are some important measurement implications for research on environmental stress that follow from the previous discussion of individual differences. Scaling of self-reports of stress is an area that has received very little attention in the stress literature in general. Paper and pencil measures of perceived stress, threat, annoyance, and so on implicitly assume various underlying measurement models. Before we can adequately understand what variables predict annoyance or how perceived stress interrelates with objective measures of the physical environment to affect human health and behavior, more psychometric work is needed to develop self-report scales that are reliable and valid.

As an example of this work, the Berglunds and their colleagues have documented that survey measures of community annoyance to noise or malodor can be dramatically improved by calibration procedures. When response criteria are established to a common reference point when judging how annoying a particular situation is, dose–response relationships between the physical configuration (e.g., sound level) and annoyance are dramatically better than are the dose–response curves when the typical scaling approach is followed (e.g., "Please rate how annoyed you are where 1 = extremely little annoyance and 7 = extremely annoyed.") (Berglund, Berglund, & Lindvall, 1975). These data suggest that earlier research indicating low correlations between noise levels and annoyance (Cohen & Weinstein, 1982) or air pollution content and annoyance (Barker, 1976; Evans & Jacobs, 1982) may reflect both the absence of meaningful conceptual components of the relationship and poor measurement properties of the annoyance scales themselves.

Another reason that some measures of stress have not been as sensitive as they may be is the problem of range adjustment. Both the initial resting value and the maximum possible value for a scale

have strong influences on how one's reactions to a given physical or psychological demand are scaled (Borg, 1978; Wilder, 1968). For example, initial resting levels of various physiological indices correlate in the .4 to .6 range, with difference scores between the resting, control condition and reactions during stress (Pittner, Houston, & Spiridigliozzi, 1983). Failure to make statistical adjustments for initial values and range of effects renders many research designs in stress work very inefficient for detecting effects. This may also contribute to the generally low intercorrelations found among various measures of stress. This problem is particularly serious in between-subjects designs.

Measurement issues also occur on the independent variable side. Nearly all studies of the four environmental stressors discussed herein have used two levels of the independent variable, consisting of a control condition with little or no stressor present (e.g., background noise levels or silence) and either a moderate or a high level of the experimental conditions (e.g., 75 dBA or 90 dBA). There are several very important limitations of this state of affairs. First, given the suggestive evidence of some nonlinear functions between stressor intensity and human reactions such as found in heat and aggression, it is very important at a minimum to expose individuals in experiments to low, moderate, and high levels of the environmental stressor. Second, the concept of threshold, which predominates in epidemiological research on environmental health effects, suggests the presence of some minimum level or range of a pollutant that is necessary for any health effects to occur. Low-level exposure to an environmental stressor, particularly for short time periods, may yield incorrect assumptions of no effects. It is important to establish some sense of the threshold range of the various environmental stressors in order to present properly various levels of stressors in experiments.

Temporal Issues

There are several temporal issues in stress research generally that apply strongly to environmental work (see McGrath, 1970a, 1982, for an excellent discussion of temporal issues). The pioneering work of Glass and Singer (1972) on stress aftereffects has sensitized many researchers to the importance of temporal factors in assessing stress reactions. Measurements of reactions in anticipation of, during, and after the presence of a stressor are clearly warranted, and can yield important insights into the stress process. Looking at temporal issues from a more macro perspective, it is important to examine environmental stressors under both acute and chronic conditions. People who have to live with aversive environmental conditions undoubtedly develop various coping strategies. Laboratory research on short-term reactions to stressors can provide us models of the effects of stressors that then need to be examined under field conditions (Cohen et al., 1980). We also need to bring people experienced with various stressors into the laboratory to see how they respond to controlled presentations of various sources of stress. Research on adaptation to air pollution, for example, has shown that people chronically exposed to smog react in some systematically different ways to laboratory tasks (e.g., visual detection of smog in pictorial scenes) than do residents recently exposed to ambient air pollution (Evans et al., 1982). The issue of long-term adaptation to environmental stressors has only been touched on by environmental psychologists. We know very little about the physical, social, or interpersonal processes that predispose individuals to become more or less sensitive to environmental pollutants over time (Campbell, 1983; Wohlwill, 1974). We do not know what it is that people do to cope successfully or unsuccessfully with environmental stressors.

Temporal parameters also influence measurement. Various dependent measures of stress have differential sensitivity over time to stressors. Urinary catecholamine measures are responsive to cumulative secretions of psychoendocrine hormones over relatively long periods of time whereas plasma catecholamine measures reflect momentary reactions to stress. Moreover, physiological measurements are often monitored continuously, whereas self-report variables are usually summary reports (Mechanic, 1978). Because different measures of stress have different temporal characteristics, convergence among multiple measures of stress may be low when taken at one point in time.

Multiple Stressor Levels

A major question about multiple stressors concerns the issue of examining the additive and multiplicative effects of environmental stressors. From a conceptual perspective, the concepts of convergent and divergent validity are very applicable here. If two or more environmental stressors operate through some similar mechanism (e.g., arousal levels or interference with control), then there should be some measurement convergence reflected by either parallel results between two different stressors or some additive effects when the two stressors are combined.

Broadbent (1971), for example, reasoned that, if the effects of noise were due to overarousal, experimental treatments that reduced arousal (e.g., sleep deprivation, pharmaceuticals) should interact with noise at least partially to cancel out its effects on task performance. While Broadbent's data were generally consistent with his hypothesis, others have been less successful in finding additive effects when combining stressors that should each increase arousal (Finkelman, Zeitlin, Romoff, Friend, & Brown, 1979). At a more general level, the issue raised earlier about the degree of specificity (cf. Mason, 1975) or nonspecificity (cf. Selye, 1975) inherent in the stress concept is embedded in this issue as well. The degree to which individuals are vulnerable to stressors in general versus manifest stressor—specific vulnerabilities can also be examined by the analysis of individual and multiple stressor effects.

Both from a conceptual and a policy perspective, research on multiple stressors is important because of ecological covariation. Most sources of environmental stress covary in the natural environment. Crowding and noise, for example, or heat and air pollution frequently fluctuate together in the natural environment. From a policy standpoint we need to know whether and how much stressors interact to influence human health and well-being. Conceptually speaking, important theoretical questions are raised by suppression or amplification effects of interacting variables (cf. Winkel, Chapter 3, this volume). For example, biologists have developed explanations about the mechanisms of particle transport from the observation that sulfur dioxide effects are amplified by high humidity or the presence of ozone, a toxic component of photochemical smog.

Setting

Much has been written about the relative strengths and weaknesses of laboratory and field research settings (cf. Cohen et al., 1980; Patterson, 1977; Stokols, Chapter 2, this volume; Winkel, Chapter 3, this volume). Some of the concerns about settings are very salient for work on environmental stressors. The issue of realism is one very critical concern. If threat is an important component of stress, then participants' feelings about the validity of threat present in an experimental setting are critical (Cohen, 1981; McGrath, 1982). Most laboratory contexts minimize threat because of the implied if not explicit contract between the experimenter and the subject that no serious harm will befall him or her. Furthermore, experimental periods are usually of short duration and subjects are told that they can exit from the situation at any time without penalty if they so choose. Thus most laboratory experiments provide subjects choice and some degree of control over aversive events (Gardner, 1978). On the other hand, some aspects of laboratory settings such as physiological recording equipment may also artificially increase threat or aversiveness of the setting.

The problem of realism is also affected by task variables. It is often difficult to simulate meaningful tasks that may be affected by sources of stress. Furthermore, as noted earlier, we typically have little knowledge of the cognitive processes involved in specific performance measures. This has prohibited the development of a performance-based taxonomy of tasks that would in turn allow us to assess, except at the grossest level (e.g., whether memory is involved), how particular tasks are related to one another. Reactivity may result from responses to tasks that are viewed as trivial or unrelated to the individual's concerns at work or in other realistic performance contexts.

Field settings are not a panacea for all of the problems associated with doing research on stress in laboratory environments. In the field one frequently has a problem of mutual selection, wherein those who could not cope well with a particular stressor have left, whereas those remaining have developed good coping resources to deal with the stressor (Cohen et al., 1981; McGrath, 1982). For instance, Cohen and his colleagues found in a longitudinal study of airport noise that individuals with the highest blood pressures at time 1 were more likely to be absent from the longitudinal sample, measured a year later. The myriad of potential methodological problems in the field should not be ignored, either. Self-selection of subjects into the setting as well as attrition can raise serious questions about causality. Adequate control groups can also be very difficult to construct.

Thus the issue is not one of the laboratory versus the field situation, but rather one of determining what factor(s) in each situation is important in influencing the stress and coping process. Stress researchers can ask questions such as: Are differences in length of exposure, perceived control (escape), feelings of importance about the setting, and so on likely to differ between the laboratory and the setting in which a particular environmental stressor is present? Probably the best methodological strategy is to examine the effects of environmental stressors in both field and laboratory situations. Reliable effects of stressors can be carefully charted in the laboratory and then validated under more natural conditions. Field research can suggest certain dimensions

of the stressor that appear to be important, and laboratory work can rule out plausible rival hypotheses that exist in the field (Cohen et al., 1980).

Because individuals will vary in their sensitivity to various environmental demands, in the ways in which they appraise them, and in personal coping resources, stress will not invariably result when one or more aversive physical characteristics are present. Nonetheless, since stress is a function of environmental demands and individual coping resources, it behooves us to develop a more thorough description and analysis of the physical and social components of everyday situations that are likely to evoke the stress and coping process.

Acknowledgments

We thank Irwin Altman, Andrew Baum, and Daniel Stokols for critical feedback on earlier drafts. Preparation of this chapter was partially supported by the California Air Resources Board, AI-087-32, and a University of California Faculty Research Fellowship.

REFERENCES

Abramson, L., Garber, J., & Seligman, M. (1980). Learned helplessness in humans: An attributional analysis. In J. Garber & M. Seligman (Eds.), *Human helplessness* (pp. 3–34). New York: Academic.

Ader, R. (Ed.). (1981). *Psychoneuroimmunology.* New York: Academic.

Ahrentzen, S., Jue, G., Skorpanich, M.A., & Evans, G.W. (1982). School environments and stress. In G.W. Evans (Ed.), *Environmental stress* (pp. 224–255). New York: Cambridge University Press.

Aiello, J., Epstein, Y., & Karlin, R. (1975). *Field experimental research on human crowding.* Sacramento, CA: Western Psychological Association.

Altman, I. (1975). *The environment and social behavior: Privacy, territoriality, crowding and personal space.* Monterey, CA: Brooks/Cole.

Appley, M., & Trumbull, R. (Eds.). (1967). *Psychological stress.* New York: Appleton-Century-Crofts.

Archea, J. (1978). The place of architectural factors in behavioral theories of privacy. *Journal of Social Issues, 3,* 116–137.

Argyle, M., & Dean, J. (1965). Eye contact, distance and affiliation. *Sociometry, 28,* 289–304.

Averill, J.R. (1973). Personal control over aversive stimuli and its relationship to stress. *Psychological Bulletin, 80,* 286–303.

Baldassare, M. (1979). *Residential crowding in urban America.* Berkeley: University of California Press.

Barker, M. (1976). Planning for environmental indices: Observer appraisals of air quality. In K. Craik & E. Zube (Eds.), *Perceiving environmental quality* (pp. 175–204). New York: Plenum.

Baron, R. (1978). Aggression and heat: The "long hot summer" revisited. In A. Baum, J. Singer, & S. Valins (Eds.), *Advances in environmental psychology* (Vol. 1, pp. 57–84). Hillsdale, NJ: Erlbaum.

Baron, R.M., & Rodin, J. (1978). Personal control as a mediator of crowding. In A. Baum, J. Singer, & S. Valins (Eds.), *Advances in environmental psychology* (Vol. 1, pp. 145–190). Hillsdale, NJ: Erlbaum.

Baum, A., Aiello, J., & Calesnick, L. (1978). Crowding and personal control: Social density and the development of learned helplessness. *Journal of Personality and Social Psychology, 36,* 1000–1011.

Baum, A., & Epstein, Y. (Eds.). (1978). *Human response to crowding.* Hillsdale, NJ: Erlbaum.

Baum, A., Brunberg, N., & Singer, J.E. (1982). The use of psychological and neuroendocrinological measurements in the study of stress. *Health Psychology, 1,* 217–236.

Baum, A., & Paulus, P. (1987). Crowding. In D. Stokols & I. Altman (Eds.), *Handbook of environmental psychology.* New York: Wiley.

Baum, A., & Singer, J.E. (Eds.). (1982). *Advances in environmental psychology* (Vol. 4). Hillsdale, NJ: Erlbaum.

Baum, A., Singer, J.E., & Baum, C. (1982). Stress and the environment. In G.W. Evans (Ed.), *Environmental stress* (pp. 15–44). New York: Cambridge University Press.

Baum, A., Singer, J.E., & Valins, S. (Eds.), (1978). *Advances in environmental psychology* (Vol. 1). Hillsdale, NJ: Erlbaum.

Bell, P., & Greene, T. (1982). Thermal stress: Physiological comfort, performance, and social effects of hot and cold environments. In G.W. Evans (Ed.), *Environmental stress* (pp. 75–104). New York: Cambridge University Press.

Berglund, B., Berglund, U., & Lindvall, Y. (1975). Scaling of annoyance in epidemiological studies. *Proceedings of the International Symposium on Recent Advances in the Assessment of the Health Effects of Environmental Pollution* (Vol. 1, pp. 119–137). Luxembourg: Commission of the European Communities.

Berlyne, D.E. (1960). *Conflict, curiosity and arousal.* New York: McGraw-Hill.

Berlyne, D.E. (1971). *Aesthetics and psychobiology.* New York: Appleton-Century-Crofts.

Borg, G. (1978). Subjective effort in relation to physical performance and work capacity. In H.L. Pick, Jr., H.W. Leibowitz, J.E. Singer, A. Steinschneider, & H. Stevenson (Eds.), *Psychology from research to practice* (pp. 333–361). New York: Plenum.

Boyden, S.V. (Ed.). (1970). *The impact of civilization on the biology of man.* Toronto, Canada: University of Toronto Press.

Briere, J., Downes, A., & Spensley, J. (1983). Summer in the city: Urban weather conditions and psychiatric-emergency room visits. *Journal of Abnormal Psychology, 92,* 77–80.

Broadbent, D. (1971). *Decision and stress.* New York: Academic.

Broadbent, D. (1978). The current state of noise research: A reply to Poulton. *Psychological Bulletin, 85,* 1052–1067.

Byrne, D. (1971). *The attraction paradigm.* New York: Academic.

Campbell, J. (1983). Ambient stressors. *Environment and Behavior, 15,* 355–380.

Cannon, W.B. (1932). *The wisdom of the body.* New York: Norton.

Caplan, R. (1982). Person-environment fit: Past, present, and future. In C. Cooper (Ed.), *Stress research: Where do we go from here?* (pp. 37–78). Chichester, England: Wiley.

Carp, F.M., & Carp, A. (1982). A role for technical environmental assessment in perceptions of environmental quality and well being. *Journal of Environmental Psychology, 2,* 171–192.

Carson, D.H., & Driver, B. (1970). *An environmental approach to human stress and well being: With implications for planning* (Preprint No. 94). Ann Arbor: University of Michigan, Mental Health Research Institute.

Christian, J. (1961). Phenomena associated with population density. *Proceedings of the National Academy of Science, 47,* 428–449.

Coffin, D., & Stokinger, H. (1977). Biological effects of air pollutants. In A.C. Stern (Ed.), *Air pollution* (3rd ed. Vol. 3, pp. 231–360). New York: Academic.

Cohen, S. (1978). Environmental load and the allocation of attention. In A. Baum, J. Singer, & S. Valins (Eds.), *Advances in environmental psychology* (Vol. 1, pp. 1–29). Hillsdale, NJ: Erlbaum.

Cohen, S. (1980). Aftereffects of stress on human performance and social behavior: A review of research and theory. *Psychological Bulletin, 88,* 82–108.

Cohen, S. (1981). Cognitive processes as determinants of environmental stress. In I. Sarason & C. Speilberger (Eds.), *Stress and anxiety* (Vol. 7, pp. 171–183). New York: Hemisphere.

Cohen, S., Evans, G.W., Krantz, D.S., & Stokols, D. (1980). Physiological, motivational, and cognitive effects of aircraft noise on children: Moving from the laboratory to the field. *American Psychologist, 35,* 231–243.

Cohen, S., Evans, G.W., Krantz, D.S., Stokols, D., & Kelly, S. (1981). Aircraft noise and children: Longitudinal and cross sectional evidence on adaptation to noise and the effectiveness of noise abatement. *Journal of Personality and Social Psychology, 40,* 331–345.

Cohen, S., Evans, G.W., Stokols, D., & Krantz, D.S. (1986). *Behavior, health and environmental stress.* New York: Plenum.

Cohen, S., Glass, D., & Phillips, S. (1979). Environment and health. In H.E. Freeman, S. Levine, & L.G. Reeder (Eds.), *Handbook of medical sociology* (pp. 134–149). Englewood Cliffs, NJ: Prentice-Hall.

Cohen, S., Glass, D., & Singer, J.E. (1973). Apartment noise, auditory discrimination and reading ability in children. *Journal of Experimental Social Psychology, 9,* 407–422.

Cohen, S., Kamarck, T., & Mermelstein, R. (1983). A global measure of perceived stress. *Journal of Health and Social Behavior, 24,* 385–396.

Cohen, S., & Lezak, A. (1977). Noise and inattentiveness to social cues. *Environment and Behavior, 9,* 559–572.

Cohen, S., & Spacapan, S. (1984). The social psychology of noise. In D.M. Jones & A.J. Chapman (Eds.), *Noise and society* (pp. 221–245). New York: Wiley.

Cohen, S., & Syme, L. (Eds.). (1985). *Social support and health.* New York: Academic.

Cohen, S., & Weinstein, N. (1982). Nonauditory effects of noise on behavior and health. In G.W. Evans (Ed.), *Environmental stress* (pp. 45–74). New York: Cambridge University Press.

Coughlin, R. (1976). The perception and evaluation of water quality: A review of research method and findings. In K. Craik & E. Zube (Eds.), *Perceiving environmental quality* (pp. 205–228). New York: Plenum.

Cox, V., Paulus, P., McCain, G., & Karlovac, M. (1978). The relationship between crowding and health. In A. Baum & J.E. Singer (Eds.), *Advances in environmental psychology* (Vol. 4, pp. 271–294). Hillsdale, NJ: Erlbaum.

Craik, K., & Zube, E. (1976). *Perceiving environmental quality.* New York: Plenum.

Day, A., & Day, L. (1973). Cross-national comparisons of population density. *Science, 181,* 1016–1023.

DeLongis, A., Coyne, J., Dakof, G., Folkman, S., & Lazarus, R.S. (1982). Relationship of daily hassles, uplifts, and major life events to health status. *Health Psychology, 1,* 119–136.

Denenberg, W.H. (1972). *The development of behavior.* Stamford, CT: Sinauer.

Dohrenwend, B.S., & Dohrenwend, B.P. (Eds.). (1974). *Stressful life events: Their nature and effects.* New York: Wiley.

Dohrenwend, B.S., & Dohrenwend, B.P. (Eds.). (1981). *Life stress and illness.* New York: Watson.

Dohrenwend, B.S., Dohrenwend, B.P., Dodson, M., & Shrout, P. (1984). Symptoms, hassles, social supports, and life events: Problem of confounded measures. *Journal of Abnormal Psychology, 93,* 222–230.

Dohrenwend, B.S., Krasnoff, L., Askenasy, S., & Dohrenwend, B.P. (1978). Exemplification of a method for scaling life events: The PERI life events scale. *Journal of Health and Social Behavior, 19,* 205–229.

Dooley, B.B. (1978). Effects of social density on men with "close" or "far" personal space. *Journal of Population, 1,* 251–265.

Dubos, R. (1965). *Man adapting.* New Haven, CT: Yale University Press.

Dubos, R. (1970). The biology of civilisation—With emphasis on perinatal influences. In S.V. Boyden (Ed.), *The impact of civilisation on the biology of man* (pp. 219–230). Toronto, Canada: University of Toronto Press.

Easterbrook, J.A. (1959). The effect of emotion on cue utilization and the organization of behavior. *Psychological Review, 66,* 183–201.

Ekman, P., & Friesen, W.V. (1974). Nonverbal behavior and psychopathology. In R. Friedman & M. Katz (Eds.), *The psychology of depression: Contemporary theory and research* (pp. 203–232). Washington, DC: Winston.

Elliott, G., & Eisdorfer, C. (Eds.). (1982). *Stress and human health.* New York: Springer.

Epstein, Y. (1982). Crowding stress and human behavior. In G.W. Evans (Ed.), *Environmental stress* (pp. 133–148). New York: Cambridge University Press.

Epstein, Y., & Karlin, R. (1975). Effects of acute experimental crowding. *Journal of Applied Social Psychology, 5,* 34–53.

Esser, A.H. (1974). Environment and mental health. *Science, Medicine and Man, 1,* 181–193.

Evans, G.W. (1978a). Crowding and the developmental process. In A. Baum & Y. Epstein (Eds.), *Human response to crowding* (pp. 117–140). Hillsdale, NJ: Erlbaum.

Evans, G.W. (1978b). Human spatial behavior: The arousal model. In A. Baum & Y. Epstein (Eds.), *Human response to crowding* (pp. 283–303). Hillsdale, NJ: Erlbaum.

Evans, G.W. (1979a). Behavioral and physiological consequences of crowding in humans. *Journal of Applied Science Psychology, 9,* 27–46.

Evans, G.W. (1979b). Design implications of spatial research. In J. Aiello & A. Baum (Eds.), *Residential crowding and density* (pp. 197–216). New York: Plenum.

Evans, G.W. (1980). Environmental cognition. *Psychological Bulletin, 88,* 259–287.

Evans, G.W. (Ed.). (1982). *Environmental stress.* New York: Cambridge University Press.

Evans, G.W., & Campbell, J.M. (1983). Psychological perspectives on air pollution and health. *Basic and Applied Social Psychology, 4,* 137–169.

Evans, G.W., & Eichelman, W. (1976). Preliminary models of conceptual linkages among some proxemic variables. *Environment and Behavior, 8,* 87–116.

Evans, G.W., & Jacobs, S.V. (1982). Air pollution and human behavior. In G.W. Evans (Ed.), *Environmental stress* (pp. 105–132). New York: Cambridge University Press.

Evans, G.W., Jacobs, S.V., Dooley, D., & Catalano, R. (in press). The interaction of stressful life events and chronic strain. *American Journal of Community Psychology.*

Evans, G.W., Jacobs, S.V., & Frager, N.B. (1982). Behavioral responses to air pollution. In A. Baum & J. Singer (Eds.), *Advances in environmental psychology* (Vol. 4, pp. 237–270). Hillsdale, NJ: Erlbaum.

Evans, G.W., Palsane, M.N., & D'Souza, R. (1983). Life stress and health in India. *Indian Psychologist, 2,* 62–78.

Eysenck, H.J. (1983). Stress, disease, and personality: The 'inoculation effect'. In C. Cooper (Ed.), *Stress research* (pp. 121–146). New York: Wiley.

Fein, G., Schwartz, P., Jacobson, S., & Jacobson, J. (1983). Environmental toxins and behavioral development. *American Psychologist, 38,* 1188–1197.

Finkelman, J., Zeitlin, L., Romoff, R., Friend, M., & Brown, L. (1979). Conjoint effect of physical stress and noise stress on information processing performance and cardiac response. *Human Factors, 21,* 1–6.

Fischer, C.S. (1976). *The urban experience.* New York: Harcourt Brace Jovanich.

Fiske, D., & Maddi, S. (Eds.). (1961). *Functions of varied experience.* Homewood, IL: Dorsey.

Fleming, R., Baum, A, Gisriel, M., & Gatchel, R. (1982). Mediating influences of social support on stress at Three Mile Island. *Journal of Human Stress, 7,* 14–22.

Fleming, R., Baum, A., & Singer, J.E. (1984). Toward an integrative approach to the study of stress. *Journal of Personality and Social Psychology, 46,* 939–949.

Folkman, S. (1984). Personal control and stress and coping processes: A theoretical analysis. *Journal of Personality and Social Psychology, 46,* 839–852.

Folkman, S., & Lazarus, R.S. (1980). An analysis of coping in a middle-aged community sample. *Journal of Health and Social Behavior, 21,* 219–239.

Forsman, L. (1983). *Individual and group differences in psychophysiological responses to stress.* Unpublished doctoral dissertation, University of Stockholm, Stockholm, Sweden.

Frankenhaeuser, M. (1971). Behavior and circulating catecholamines. *Brain Research, 31,* 241–262.

Frankenhaeuser, M. (1980). Psychoneuroendocrine approaches to the study of stressful person-environment transactions. In H. Selye (Ed.), *Selye's guide to stress research* (Vol. 1, pp. 46–70). New York: Van Nostrand.

Frankenhaeuser, M., & Lundberg, U. (1974). Immediate and delayed effects of noise on performance and arousal. *Biological Psychology, 2,* 127–133.

Frankenhaeuser, M., & Lundberg, U. (1977). The influence of cognitive set on performance and arousal under different noise loads. *Motivation and Emotion, 1,* 139–149.

Freedman, J. (1975). *Crowding and behavior.* San Francisco: Freeman.

French, J., Rodgers, W., & Cobb, S. (1974). Adjustment as person–environment fit. In G. Coelho, D. Hamburg, & J. Adams (Eds.), *Coping and adaptation* (pp. 316–333). New York: Basic.

Frisancho, A. (1979). *Human adaptation.* St. Louis: Mosby.

Galle, O., Gove, W., & McPherson, J. (1972). Population density and pathology: What are the relationships for man? *Science, 176,* 23–30.

Gardner, G. (1978). Effects of federal human subjects regulations on data obtained in environmental stressor research. *Journal of Personality and Social Psychology, 36,* 628–634.

Gibson, J.J. (1979). *The ecological approach to visual perception.* New York: Houghton Mifflin.

Glass, D., & Singer, J. (1972). *Urban stress.* New York: Academic.

Gliner, J., Raven, P., Horvath, S., Drinkwater, B., & Sutton, J. (1975). Man's physiological response to long term work during thermal and pollutant stress. *Journal of Applied Physiology, 39,* 628–632.

Goldsmith, J., & Friberg, L. (1977). Effects of air pollution on human health. In A.C. Stern (Ed.), *Air pollution* (3rd ed., Vol. 3, pp. 458–610). New York: Academic.

Gottlieb, B. (1978). The development and classification scheme of informal helping behaviors. *Canadian Journal of Science, 10,* 105–115.

Griffiths, I.D. (1975). The thermal environment. In D. Canter & P. Stringer (Eds.), *Environmental interaction* (pp. 21–54). New York: International Universities Press.

Hall, E.T. (1966). *The hidden dimension.* New York: Doubleday.

Hamilton, R., Hockey, R., & Rejman, M. (1977). The place of the concept of activation in human information processing theory. In S. Dornic (Ed.), *Attention and performance* (Vol. 6, pp. 463–486). New York: Academic.

Hebb, D.O. (1972). *Textbook of psychology* (3rd ed.). Philadelphia: Saunders.

Heft, H. (1979). Background and focal environmental conditions of the home and attention in young children. *Journal of Applied Social Psychology, 9,* 47–69.

Helson, H. (1964). *Adaptation-level theory: An experimental and systematic approach to behavior.* New York: Harper.

Heshka, S., & Pylypuk, A. (1975, June). *Human crowding and adrenocortical activity.* Quebec, Canada: Canadian Psychological Association.

Hockey, R. (1979). Stress and the cognitive components of skilled performance. In V. Hamilton & D. Warburton (Eds.), *Human stress and cognition* (pp. 141–177). New York: Wiley.

Holmes, T., & Rahe, R. (1967). The social readjustment scale. *Journal of Psychosomatic Research, 4,* 189–194.

Holsti, O. (1978). Limitations of cognitive abilities in the face of crisis. In C.F. Smart & W.T. Stanbury (Eds.), *Studies on crisis management* (pp. 35–55). Toronto, Canada: Butterworth.

House, J.S. (1981). *Work stress and social support.* Reading, MA: Addison-Wesley.

Hutt, S., & Hutt, C. (1970). *Behavior studies in psychiatry.* London: Pergammon.

Insel, P., & Moos, R.H. (1974). Psychological environments: Expanding the range of human ecology. *American Psychologist, 29,* 179–188.

Iltis, H., Loucks, W., & Andrews, P. (1970). Criteria for an optimum human environment. *Bulletin of the Atomic Scientists, 26,* 2–6.

Iwata, O. (1984). The relationship of noise sensitivity to health and personality. *Japanese Psychological Research, 26,* 75–81.

Janis, I. (1982). Decisionmaking under stress. In L. Goldberger & S. Breznitz (Eds.), *Handbook of stress* (pp. 69–87). New York: Free Press.

Janis, I. (1983). Stress inoculation in health care. In D. Meichenbaum & M. Jaremko (Eds.), *Stress reduction and prevention* (pp. 67–100). New York: Plenum.

Janis, I., & Mann, L. (1977). *Decision making.* New York: Free Press.

Jemmott, J., & Locke, S. (1984). Psychosocial factors, immunological mediation and human susceptibility to infectious diseases: How much do we know? *Psychological Bulletin, 95,* 78–108.

Jennings, J.R. (in press). Bodily changes during attention. In M. Coles, E. Donchin, & S. Porges (Eds.), *Psychophysiology: Systems, processes and application.* New York: Guilford.

Kahneman, D. (1973). *Attention and effort.* Englewood Cliffs, NJ: Prentice-Hall.

Kaminoff, R., & Proshansky, H.M. (1982). Stress as a consequence of the urban physical environment. In L. Goldberger & S. Breznitz (Eds.), *Handbook of stress* (pp. 380–409). New York: Free Press.

Kanner, A., Coyne, J., Schaefer, C., & Lazarus, R.S. (1981). Comparison of two modes of stress measurement: Daily hassles and uplifts versus major life events. *Journal of Behavioral Medicine, 4,* 1–39.

Kaplan, H.B. (1983). Psychological distress in sociological context: Toward a general theory of psychosocial stress. In H.B. Kaplan (Ed.), *Psychosocial stress* (pp. 195–266). New York: Academic.

Kaplan, S. (1983). A model of person-environment compatability. *Environment and Behavior, 15,* 311–332.

Kaplan, S., & Kaplan, R. (1982). *Cognition and environment.* New York: Praeger.

Keating, J. (1979). Environmental stressors: Misplaced emphasis. In I. Sarason & C. Spielberger (Eds.), *Stress and anxiety* (Vol. 6, pp. 55–66). Washington, DC: Hemisphere.

Keele, S. (1973). *Attention and human performance.* Pacific Palisades, CA: Goodyear.

Kiretz, S., & Moos, R.H. (1974). Physiological effects of social environments. *Psychosomatic Medicine, 36,* 96–114.

Kobasa, S. (1979). Stressful life events, personality, and health: An inquiry into hardiness. *Journal of Personality and Social Psychology, 37,* 1–11.

Korte, C. (1978). Helpfulness in the urban environment. In A. Baum, J.E. Singer, & S. Valins (Eds.), *Advances in environmental psychology* (Vol. 1, pp. 85–110). Hillsdale, NJ: Erlbaum.

Krantz, D., Grunberg, N., & Baum, A. (1985). Health psychology. *Annual Review of Psychology, 36,* 349–383.

Krantz, D., & Manuck, S. (1984). Acute psychophysiologic reactivity and risk of cardiovascular disease: A review and methodologic critique. *Psychological Bulletin, 96,* 435–464.

Kryter, K.D. (1970). *The effects of noise on man.* New York: Academic.

Lacey, J.I. (1967). Somatic response patterning and stress: Some revisions of activation theory. In M.H. Appley & R. Trumbull (Eds.), *Psychological stress* (pp. 14–37). New York: Appleton-Century-Crofts.

Langer, E.J., & Saegert, S. (1977). Crowding and cognitive control. *Journal of Personality and Social Psychology, 35,* 175–182.

Lawton, M.P. (1980). *Environment and aging.* Monterey, CA: Brooks/Cole.

Lazarus, R.S. (1966). *Psychological stress and the coping process.* New York: McGraw-Hill.

Lazarus, R.S. (1984). On the primacy of cognition. *American Psychologist, 39,* 124–129.

Lazarus, R.S., & Cohen, J. (1977). Environmental stress. In J. Wohlwill & I. Altman (Eds.), *Human behavior and environment* (pp. 90–127). New York: Plenum.

Lazarus, R.S., DeLongis, A., Folkman, S., & Gruen, R. (1985). Stress and adaptational outcomes: The problem of confounded measures. *American Psychologist, 40,* 770–779.

Lazarus, R.S., & Launier, R. (1978). Stress-related transactions between person and environment. In L. Pervin & M. Lewis (Eds.), *Perspectives in interactional psychology* (pp. 1–67). New York: Plenum.

Levine, S., & Scotch, N. (Eds.). (1970). *Social stress.* Chicago: Aldine.

Loo, C. (1972). The effects of spatial density on the social behavior of children. *Journal of Applied Social Psychology, 2,* 372–381.

Loo, C. (1978). Issues of crowding research: Vulnerable participants, assessing perceptions, and developmental differences. *Journal of Population, 1,* 336–348.

Love, K., & Saegert, S. (1978). *Crowding and cognitive limits: Capacity or strategy?* Toronto, Canada: Meeting of the American Psychological Association.

Lundberg, U. (1976). Urban commuting: Crowdedness and catecholamine excretion. *Journal of Human Stress, 2,* 26–34.

Lundberg, U. (1978). Psychophysiological aspects of performance and adjustment to stress. In H. Krohne & L. Laux (Eds.), *Achievement, stress and anxiety* (pp. 75–91). Washington, DC: Hemisphere.

Lundberg, U., & Frankenhaeuser, M. (1978). Psychophysiological reactions to noise as modified by personal control over noise intensity. *Biological Psychology, 6,* 51–60.

Lynch, K. (1960). *The image of the city.* Cambridge, MA: MIT Press.

Magnusson, D. (1981). Wanted: A psychology of situations. In D. Magnusson (Ed.), *Toward a psychology of situations* (pp. 9–36). Hillsdale, NJ: Erlbaum.

Magnusson, D. (1982). Situational determinants of stress: An interactional perspective. In L. Goldberger & S. Breznitz (Eds.), *Handbook of stress* (pp. 231–253). New York: Free Press.

Magnusson, D. (1984). On the situation context in psychological research. In K. Lagerspetz & P. Niemi (Eds.), *Psychology in the 1990's* (pp. 95–105). Amsterdam, Netherlands: Elsevier.

Mandler, G. (1975). *Mind and emotion.* New York: Wiley.

Manuck, S., Harvey, A., Lechleiter, S., & Neal, K. (1978). Effects of coping on blood pressure responses to threat of aversive stimulation. *Psychophysiology, 15,* 544–549.

Mason, J.W. (1968). A review of psychoendocrine research on the pituitary-adrenal cortical system. *Psychosomatic Medicine, 30,* 576–607.

Mason, J.W. (1975). A historical review of the stress field (Pts. 1 & 2). *Journal of Human Stress, 1,* 6–12, 22–36.

Mason, J.W., Maher, J., Hartley, L., Moughey, E., Perlow, M., & Jones, L. (1976). Selectivity of corticosteroid and catecholamine responses to various natural stimuli. In G. Serban (Ed.), *Psychopathology of human adaptation* (pp. 147–171). New York: Plenum.

Matthews, K.E., & Canon, L. (1975). Environmental noise level as a determinant of helping behavior. *Journal of Personality and Social Psychology, 32,* 571–577.

McGrath, J. (1970a). Major methodological issues. In J. McGrath (Ed.), *Social and psychological factors in stress* (pp. 41–57). New York: Holt.

McGrath, J. (Ed.). (1970b). *Social and psychological factors in stress.* New York: Holt.

McGrath, J. (1976). Stress and behavior in organizations. In M.D. Dunnette (Ed.), *Handbook of industrial and organizational psychology* (pp. 1351–1395). Chicago: Rand McNally.

McGrath, J. (1982). Methodological problems in research on stress. In H. Krohne & L. Laux (Eds.), *Achievement, stress, and anxiety* (pp. 19–48). Washington, DC: Hemisphere.

McGrew, P. (1970). Social and spatial density effects on spacing behavior in preschool children. *Journal of Child Psychology and Psychiatry, 11,* 197–205.

McLean, E.K., & Tarnopolsky, A. (1977). Noise, discomfort, and mental health: A review of the socio-medical implications of disturbances by noise. *Psychological Medicine, 7,* 19–62.

Mechanic, D. (1962). *Students under stress.* New York: Free Press.

Mechanic, D. (1974). Discussion of research programs on relations between stressful life events and episodes of physical illness. In B.S. Dohrenwend & B.P. Dohrenwend (Eds.), *Stressful life events* (pp. 87–98). New York: Wiley.

Mechanic, D. (1978). *Medical sociology.* New York: Free Press.

Mehrabian, A., & Russell, J. (1974). *An approach to environmental psychology.* Cambridge, MA: MIT Press.

Michelson, W. (1970). *Man and his urban environment.* Reading, MA: Addison-Wesley.

Milgram, S. (1970). The experience of living in cities. *Science, 167,* 1461–1468.

Miller, G., Galanter, E., & Pribram, K. (1960). *Plans and the structure of behavior.* New York: Holt, Rinehart & Winston.

Monat, S., & Lazarus, R. (Eds.). (1977). *Stress and coping.* New York: Columbia University Press.

Moos, R.H. (1973). Conceptualizations of human environments. *American Psychologist, 28,* 652–665.

Moss, G.E. (1973). *Illness, immunity, and social interaction.* New York: Wiley.

National Academy of Sciences, Committee on Indoor Air Pollutants. (1981). *Indoor pollutants.* Washington, DC: National Academy Press.

Neufeld, R. (Ed.). (1982). *Psychological stress and psychopathology.* New York: McGraw-Hill.

Neus, H., Ruddell, H., & Schulte, W. (1983). Traffic noise and hypertension: An epidemiological study on the role of subjective reactions. *International Archives of Occupational and Environmental Health, 51,* 223–229.

Obrist, P., Gaebelein, C.J., Teller, E., Langer, A., Girignolo, A., Light, K., & McCubbin, J. (1978). The relationship among heart rate, carotid dP/dt and blood pressure in humans as a function of the type of stress. *Psychophysiology, 15,* 102–115.

Parr, A.E. (1966). Psychological aspects of urbanology. *Journal of Social Issues, 4*, 39–45.

Patterson, A.H. (1977). Methodological developments in environment-behavior research. In D. Stokols (Ed.), *Perspectives on environment and behavior* (pp. 325–344). New York: Plenum.

Patterson, M.L. (1976). An arousal model of interpersonal intimacy. *Psychological Review, 83*, 235–245.

Pearlin, L. (1982). The social contexts of stress. In L. Goldberger & S. Breznitz (Eds.), *Handbook of stress* (pp. 367–379). New York: Free Press.

Pearlin, L., & Schooler, C. (1978). The structure of coping. *Journal of Health and Social Behavior, 19*, 2–21.

Pittner, M., Houston, B.K., & Spiridigliozzi, G. (1983). Control over stress, Type A behavior pattern, and response to stress. *Journal of Personality and Social Psychology, 44*, 627–637.

Poulton, E. (1970). *Environment and human efficiency.* Springfield, IL: Thomas.

Poulton, E. (1977). Continuous intense noise masks auditory feedback and inner speech. *Psychological Bulletin, 84*, 977–1001.

Poulton, E. (1978). A new look at the effects of noise: A rejoinder. *Psychological Bulletin, 85*, 1068–1079.

Pribram, K.H., & McGuinness, D. (1975). Arousal, activation, and effort in the control of attention. *Psychological Review, 82*, 116–149.

Proshansky, H., Ittelson, W., & Rivlin, L. (1970). Freedom of choice and behavior in a physical setting. In H. Proshansky, W. Ittelson, & L. Rivlin (Eds.), *Environmental psychology: Man and his physical setting* (pp. 173–182). New York: Holt, Rinehart & Winston.

Proshansky, H.M., Nelson-Shulman, Y., & Kaminoff, R. (1979). The role of physical settings in life-crisis experiences. In I. Sarason & C.D. Spielberger (Eds.), *Stress and anxiety* (Vol. 6, pp. 3–26). Washington, DC: Hemisphere.

Rabkin, J., & Streuning E. (1976). Life events, stress, and illness. *Science, 194*, 1013–1020.

Rankin, R. (1969). Air pollution control and public apathy. *Journal of the Air Pollution Control Association, 19*, 565–569.

Roberts, W., Penk, W., Gearing, M., Robinowitz, R., Dolan, M., & Patterson, E. (1982). Interpersonal problems of Vietnam combat veterans with symptoms of posttraumatic stress disorder. *Journal of Abnormal Psychology, 91*, 444–450.

Rodin, J. (1976). Density, perceived choice and response to controllable and uncontrollable outcomes. *Journal of Experimental Social Psychology, 12*, 564–578.

Rotton, J. (1983). Affective and cognitive consequences of malodorous pollution. *Basic and Applied Social Psychology, 4*, 171–191.

Rotton, J., Barry, T., Frey, J., & Soler, E. (1978). Air pollution and interpersonal attraction. *Journal of Applied Social Psychology, 8*, 57–71.

Rotton, J., & Frey, J. (1984). Psychological costs of air pollution: Atmospheric conditions, seasonal trends, and psychiatric emergencies. *Population and Environment, 1*, 3–6.

Rotton, J., & Frey, J. (1985). Air pollution, weather, and violent crimes: Concomittant time-series analysis of archival data. *Journal of Personality and Social Psychology, 49*, 1207–1220.

Rotton, J., Frey, J., Barry, T., Milligan, M., & Fitzpatrick, M. (1979). The air pollution experience and physical aggression. *Journal of Applied Social Psychology, 9*, 397–412.

Rotton, J., Olszewski, D., Charleston, M., & Soler, E. (1978). Loud speech, conglomerate noise and behavioral aftereffects. *Journal of Applied Psychology, 63*, 360–365.

Rowles, G.D., & Ohta, R.J. (Eds.). (1983). *Aging and milieu.* New York: Academic.

Rule, B.G., & Nesdale, A.R. (1976). Environmental stressors, emotional arousal, and aggression. In I.G. Sarason & C.D. Spielberger (Eds.), *Stress and anxiety* (Vol. 3, pp. 87–103). Washington, DC: Hemisphere.

Rutter, M. (1983). Stress, coping, and development. In N. Garmezy & M. Rutter (Eds.), *Stress, coping, and development in children* (pp. 1–42). New York: McGraw-Hill.

Saegert, S. (1973). Crowding: Cognitive overload and behavioral constraint. In W. Preiser (Ed.), *Environmental design research* (Vol. 2, pp. 254–261). Stroudsberg, PA: Dowden, Hutchinson, & Ross.

Saegert, S. (1976). Stress-inducing and stress-reducing qualities of environment. In H.M. Proshansky, W.H. Ittelson, & L. Rivlin (Eds.), *Environmental psychology* (2nd ed., pp. 218–223). New York: Holt.

Saegert, S. (1978). High density environments: Their personal and social consequences. In A. Baum & Y. Epstein (Eds.), *Human response to crowding* (pp. 259–282). Hillsdale, NJ: Erlbaum.

Saegert, S. (1980). Crowding and cognitive limits. In J Harvey (Ed.), *Cognition, social behavior, and the environment* (pp. 373–391). Hillsdale, NJ: Erlbaum.

Saegert, S. (1981). Environment and children's mental health: Residential density and low income children. In A. Baum & J.E. Singer (Eds.), *Handbook of psychology and health* (Vol. 2, pp. 247–271). Hillsdale, NJ: Erlbaum.

Saegert, S., MacKintosh, E., & West, S. (1975). Two studies of crowding in urban public spaces. *Environment and Behavior, 7*, 159–184.

Schachter, S., & Singer, J. (1962). Cognitive, social, and physiological determinants of emotional states. *Psychological Review, 69*, 379–399.

Schmidt, D.E., & Keating, J.P. (1979). Human crowding and person control: An integration of the research. *Psychological Bulletin, 86*, 680–700.

Schooler, K. (1982). Response of the elderly to environment: A stress theoretical perspective. In M.P. Lawton, P. Windley, & T.O. Byerts (Eds.), *Aging and the environment* (pp. 80–96). New York: Springer.

Schroeder, D., & Costa, P. (1984). Influence of life events on physical illness: Substantive effects or methodological flaws? *Journal of Personality and Social Psychology, 46*, 853–863.

Scott, R., & Howard, A. (1970). Models of stress. In S. Levine & N. Scotch (Eds.), *Social stress* (pp. 259–278). Chicago: Aldine.

Seligman, M.E.P. (1975). *Helplessness.* San Francisco: Freeman.

Sells, S.B. (1963). Dimensions of stimulus situations which account for behavior variance. In S.B. Sells (Ed.), *Stimulus determinants of behavior* (pp. 3–15). New York: Ronald.

Sells, S.B. (1969). Ecology and the science of psychology. In E. Willems & H. Rausch (Eds.), *Naturalistic viewpoints in psychological research* (pp. 15–30). New York: Holt.

Selye, H. (1956). *The stress of life.* New York: McGraw-Hill.

Selye, H. (1975). Confusion and controversy in the stress field. *Journal of Human Stress, 1*, 37–44.

Sherrod, D. (1974). Crowding, perceived control and behavioral aftereffects. *Journal of Applied Social Psychology, 4*, 171–186.

Sherrod, D., & Cohen, S. (1979). Density, personal control, and design. In J. Aiello & A. Baum (Eds.), *Residential crowding and design* (pp. 217–228). New York: Plenum.

Shumaker, S.A., & Reizenstein, J. (1982). Environmental factors affecting inpatient stress in acute care hospitals. In G.W. Evans (Ed.), *Environmental stress* (pp. 179–223). New York: Cambridge University Press.

Siegel, J., & Steele, C. (1979). Noise level and social discrimination. *Personality and Social Psychology Bulletin, 5*, 95–99.

Siegman, A.W. (1982). Nonverbal correlates of anxiety and stress. In L. Goldberger & S. Breznitz (Eds.), *Handbook of stress* (pp. 306–319). New York: Free Press.

Simmel, G. (1950). The metropolis and mental life. In G. Simmel, *The sociology of George Simmel.* Glencoe, IL: Free Press. (Original work published 1903)

Singer, J., Lundberg, U., & Frankenhauser, M. (1978). Stress on the train: A study of urban commuting. In A. Baum, J. Singer, & S. Valins (Eds.), *Advances in environmental psychology* (Vol. 1, pp. 41–56). Hillsdale, NJ: Erlbaum.

Sonnenfeld, J. (1967). Environmental perception and adaptation level in the Arctic. In D. Lowenthal (Ed.), *Environmental perception and behavior* (pp. 42–59). Chicago: University of Chicago.

Spacapan, S., & Cohen, S. (1983). Effect and aftereffects of stressor expectations. *Journal of Personality and Social Psychology, 45*, 1243–1254.

Spence, D. (1982). Verbal indicators of stress. In L. Goldberger & S. Breznitz (Eds.), *Handbook of stress* (pp. 295–305). New York: Free Press.

Staw, B., Sandelands, L., & Dutton, J. (1981). Threat-rigidity effects in organizational behavior: A multilevel analysis. *Administrative Science Quarterly, 26*, 501–524.

Steptoe, S. (1981). *Psychological factors in cardiovascular disorders.* New York: Academic.

Stokols, D. (1972). On the distinction between density and crowding. *Psychological Review, 79*, 275–277.

Stokols, D. (1976). The experience of crowding in primary and secondary environments. *Environment and Behavior, 8*, 49–86.

Stokols, D. (1979). A congruence analysis of stress. In I. Sarason & C. Spielberger (Eds.), *Stress and anxiety* (Vol. 6, pp. 27–53). New York: Hemisphere.

Stokols, D. (1987). Conceptual strategies of environmental psychology. In D. Stokols & I. Altman (Eds.), *Handbook of environmental psychology.* New York: Wiley.

Strahelivitz, M., Shrahelivitz, A., & Miller, J. (1979). Air pollution and the admission rate of psychiatric patients. *American Journal of Psychiatry, 136*, 205–207.

Suedfeld, P. (1979). Stressful levels of environmental stimulation. In I. Sarason & C. Spielberger (Eds.), *Stress and anxiety* (Vol. 6, pp. 109–130). Washington, DC: Hemisphere.

Suedfeld, P. (1980). *Restricted environmental stimulation.* New York: Wiley.

Sundstrom, E. (1978). Crowding as a sequential process: Review of research on the effects of population density on humans. In A. Baum & Y. Epstein (Eds.), *Human response to crowding* (pp. 32–116). Hillsdale, NJ: Erlbaum.

Tarnopolsky, A., Barker, S., Wiggins, R., & McLean, E. (1978). The effect of aircraft noise on the mental health of a community sample: A pilot study. *Psychological Medicine, 8*, 219–233.

Thiessen, D. (1964). Population density and behavior: A review of theoretical and psychological contributions. *Texas Reports on Biology and Medicine, 22*, 266–314.

Thoits, P.A. (1983). Dimensions of life events that influence psychological stress: An evaluation and synthesis of the literature. In H.B. Kaplan (Ed.), *Psychosocial stress* (pp. 33–104). New York: Academic.

Thompson, W., & Grusec, J. (1970). Studies of early experience. In P.H. Mussen (Ed.), *Carmichael's manual of child psychology* (3rd ed., pp. 565–654). New York: Wiley.

Wachs, T., & Gruen, G. (1982). *Early experience and human development.* New York: Plenum.

Waldbott, G. (1978). *Health effects of environmental pollutants* (2nd ed.). St Louis, MO: Mosby.

Webb, E.J., Campbell, D.T., Schwartz, R.D., Sechrest, L., & Grove, J.B. (1981). *Nonreactive measures in the social sciences* (2nd ed.). Boston: Houghton Mifflin.

Weinstein, N. (1978). Individual differences in reactions to noise: A longitudinal study in a college dormitory. *Journal of Applied Psychology, 63*, 458–466.

Weiss, B. (1983). Behavioral toxicology and environmental health science. *American Psychologist, 38*, 1174–1187.

Welch, B.L. (1979). *Extra-auditory effects of industrial noise: Surveys of foreign literature.* Aerospace Medical Research Laboratory, Aerospace Medical Division, Air Force Systems Command, Wright-Patterson.

Wheaton, B. (1983). Stress, personal coping resources, and psychiatric symptoms: An investigation of interactive models. *Journal of Health and Social Behavior, 24*, 208–229.

White, R.W. (1959). Motivation reconsidered: The concept of competence. *Psychological Review, 66*, 297–333.

White, R.W. (1974). Strategies of adaptation: An attempt at systematic description. In G.V. Coehlo, D.A. Hamburg, & J.E. Adams (Eds.), *Coping and adaptation* (pp. 47–68). New York: Basic Books.

Wicker, A. (1979). *An introduction to ecological psychology.* Monterey, CA: Brooks/Cole.

Wicker, A. (1987). Behavior settings reconsidered: Temporal stages, resources, internal dynamics, context. In D. Stokols & I. Altman (Eds.), *Handbook of environmental psychology.* New York: Wiley.

Wilder, J. (1968). *Stimulus and response: The law of initial values.* Baltimore, MD: Williams & Wilkens.

Wilkinson, R. (1969). Some factors influencing the effects of environmental stressors upon performance. *Psychological Bulletin, 72*, 260–272.

Winkel, G.H. (1987). The implications of environmental content for validity assessments. In D. Stokols & I. Altman (Eds.), *Handbook of environmental psychology.* New York: Wiley.

Wohlwill, J.F. (1974). Human response to levels of environmental stimulation. *Human Ecology, 2*, 127–147.

Wohlwill, J.F., & Heft, H. (1987). The physical environment and the development of the child. In D. Stokols & I. Altman (Eds.), *Handbook of environmental psychology.* New York: Wiley.

Wohlwill, J., & Kohn, I. (1976). Dimensionalizing the environmental manifold. In S. Wapner, S. Cohen, & B. Kaplan (Eds.), *Experiencing the environment* (pp. 19–54). New York: Plenum.

Worchel, S., & Teddlie, C. (1976). The experience of crowding: A two-factor theory. *Journal of Personality and Social Psychology, 34*, 30–40.

Zajonc, R. (1984). On the primacy of affect. *American Psychologist, 39*, 117–123.

Zimring, C. (1982). The built environment as a source of psychological stress: Impacts of buildings and cities on satisfaction and behavior. In G.W. Evans (Ed.), *Environmental stress* (pp. 151–178). New York: Cambridge University Press.

Zlutnick, S., & Altman, I. (1972). Crowding and human behavior. In J.F. Wohlwill & D.H. Carson (Eds.), *Environment and the social sciences* (pp. 44–60). Washington, DC: American Psychological Association.

PART 3

LEVELS OF ENVIRONMENTAL ANALYSIS: SITUATIONS, SETTINGS, AND PLACES

BEHAVIOR SETTINGS RECONSIDERED: TEMPORAL STAGES, RESOURCES, INTERNAL DYNAMICS, CONTEXT

Allan W. Wicker, *Department of Psychology, The Claremont Graduate School, Claremont, California*

16.1. INTRODUCTION

16.1.1. Chapter Overview

This chapter presents an elaboration and extension of the behavior-setting concept developed by Roger Barker and his associates (e.g., Barker, 1968; Barker & Schoggen, 1973). (In the chapter, the terms *behavior setting* and *setting* are used interchangeably.)

To set the stage for the discussion, in this section I review briefly some of the early work on settings and describe the essential features of the concept. (Readers familiar with behavior settings may wish to skip Section 16.1.2. Those who would like a more complete introduction are referred to Barker's chapter in this volume, and to Barker, 1978, and Wicker, 1979/1983). I then note the key assumptions and emphases of the traditional work that contrast with those developed in present chapter. Subsequently I clarify the types of settings considered in the present analysis and discuss distinctions among the concepts of *organization*, *behavior setting*, and *small group*. I present in Section 16.2 an overview of the revised conceptual framework for behavior settings. In the following three sections (16.3, 16.4, 16.5) I discuss in more detail the key facets of settings. In Section 16.6. I outline a strategy for further developing behavior-setting theory and note several promising directions for future research.

16.1.2. Background and Main Features of Behavior Settings

In the earliest conception, behavior settings were not much more than convenient units from which to sample children's everyday behavior. Barker and Wright initially called the endeavor they founded in the late 1940s *psychological ecology*. The primary concern of this field was to discover and describe the behavior and psychological habitat of particular children. Included in the psychological habitat were "all of the things and events with *meaning* for the child that go to make up *his* environment" (Barker & Wright, 1950, p. 12).

After collecting and analyzing narrative records of the entire days of individual children, Barker concluded that the immediate environments of children were more important determinants of their behavior than were personal characteristics. Thereafter he focused on the events and conditions that surrounded the behavior of adults as well as children. For more than 25 years, he and his associates studied the pub-

licly available places and activities—the behavior settings—of small towns in Kansas and Yorkshire, England. Much of the research effort was devoted to identifying and quantitatively describing hundreds of behavior settings such as grocery stores, court sessions, high school basketball games, and Rotary Club meetings (e.g., Barker & Schoggen, 1973).

During the period that he was cataloging and describing the numerous events that occurred in the towns, Barker also clarified and refined his view of behavior settings (cf. Barker, 1960, 1963, 1968, Chapter 40, this volume; Barker, et al., 1978; Barker & Schoggen, 1973; Barker & Wright, 1949). Settings took on a more stable, more deterministic quality. To convey the shift in emphasis away from individual persons, and toward their environments, Barker now calls the study of behavior settings *eco-behavioral science* (Barker, 1978, p. 191).

Barker views behavior settings as small-scale social systems whose components include people and inanimate objects. Within the temporal and spatial boundaries of the system, the various components interact in an orderly, established fashion to carry out the setting's essential functions. To illustrate, in a gift shop, the temporal and spatial boundaries would be the hours the shop is open and the walls of the rooms it occupies. The shop's components include its employees and customers as well as inanimate objects such as goods for sale, display shelves, cash registers, money, and gift-wrapping materials. The orderly interaction of these components results in merchandise being displayed, bought, wrapped, and removed.

The fit between the actions of people and the features and arrangements of physical objects within a setting is called behavior–environment *synomorphy*. An example is the fit between (1) the design of the cash register and its location on a counter and (2) the behaviors of customers and shop clerks when a purchase is made. Customers approach the counter with goods they wish to buy. Clerks behind the counter face the customer and are within easy reach of the register's keys. The cash register displays the entered cost of each item and the amount due so they can be read by both customer and clerk. Virtually any behavior setting has many such instances of synomorphy.

The *program* of a behavior setting is a time-ordered sequence of person–environment interactions that leads to the orderly enactment of essential setting functions. In the gift store the program includes the owner's ordering merchandise, keeping records, and overseeing the activities of the clerks, whose duties include receiving, pricing, and shelving merchandise, waiting on customers, ringing up sales, and wrapping purchased gifts.

Another important aspect of Barker's concept is lack of dependence on particular persons. Although human components are a necessary feature of behavior settings, the jobs they perform can be carried out by any qualified individual. From the perspective of the setting, people are interchangeable. For example, one clerk can be replaced by another without the operation of the gift shop being seriously impaired.

Barker also views behavior settings as capable of dealing with threats to their programs. In his words, settings "are superordinate, self-regulating, dynamic entities which manipulate the behavior of their human components toward an equilibrium state *for the setting*" (Barker, Chapter 40, this volume). For example, if an essential component—whether a person or an object—is absent, setting occupants will seek it out and bring it in. For example, if there are not enough one-dollar bills in the cash register to make change, a clerk will take a larger bill to the bank to obtain some. And if a component interferes with the setting program, the staff will attempt to correct or remove it. A clerk who repeatedly puts incorrect prices on merchandise may be fired, and a malfunctioning cash register may be repaired.

16.1.3. Applications of the Behavior-Setting Concept

This conception of behavior settings has been employed in numerous investigations. In addition to the studies of entire communities mentioned previously, Barker and his associates have conducted research on behavior settings in schools (e.g., Barker & Gump, 1964), churches (e.g., Wicker, 1969b), hospitals (e.g., LeCompte, 1972), a National Park (Wicker, 1979/1983), and offices of a state policy agency (Kirmeyer, 1983) (for more complete reviews of the literature on behavior settings, see Barker, 1978; Schoggen, 1983; and Wicker, 1979b; a review in German has been published by Saup, 1983).

The usefulness of the behavior setting concept also has been noted by numerous scholars outside the Barker group. They have suggested, for example, that the concept is appropriate for a wide range of scientific purposes:

To provide a link between social and environmental psychology (Kaminski, 1981)

To contribute to a metatheory of group interaction processes (McGrath, 1984, chapter 1)

To develop a taxonomy of everyday situations (Price & Blashfield, 1975)

To furnish community psychologists with an alternative to the clinical/personality model (Sarason, 1976)

To provide a basic unit suitable for converging the interests of several social science disciplines (Fox, 1983)

To contribute to the development of a comprehensive social accounting scheme (Fox & Ghosh, 1980)

16.1.4. Contrasting Assumptions About Behavior Settings

Of course, the work on behavior settings also has had its critics, most of whom have been sympathetic with the main thrust of the work (e.g., Devereux, 1977; Kaminski, 1982; Moos, 1983; Smith, 1974). Some reviewers of the behavior-setting literature have found fault with the tedious methods of surveying settings, with the generation of a large volume of data without explicit theoretical underpinnings, and with one or another aspect of the substantive theory (cf. Wicker, 1979, 1979/1983).

This chapter is an attempt to address what I believe are the most serious conceptual limitations of the traditional framework. Readers should be advised, however, that the chapter does not present a formally stated theory, or even any propositions or hypotheses ready to test. Rather, some new directions are suggested for a more comprehensive and more adequate theory of behavior settings.

My present view of behavior settings contrasts in numerous ways with the traditional view. Some of the issues I discuss are ones that Barker also has recognized, but has not developed; others he has not directly addressed in print. In some instances, he has dealt with the same issues differently than I have. Throughout the chapter I try to make clear how the present framework relates to Barker's work. Some of the main contrasts are summarized in the following paragraphs.

Behavior settings have traditionally been viewed as "givens"—as intact, mature, fully functional systems that can be found in any organization or community. In the present framework, I take a more expanded temporal perspective that considers the creation, growth, differentiation, decline, and termination of settings, as well as conditions that existed before they were created.

According to the traditional view, behavior settings have a preexisting reality; that is, they are part of a natural order that is independent of any person's awareness of them. They are empirical entities like magnets or meteorites; concepts and theories dealing with settings must be compatible with their essential characteristics (cf. Barker, 1983, p. 173). In the present perspective, behavior settings are, at least to a considerable extent, social constructions—the result of sense-making and interactive behaviors of participants.

A closely related contrast has to do with the stability of settings. In the traditional perspective, behavior settings are homeostatically controlled by maintenance mechanisms that correct deviations from a quasi-stationary level (Barker, 1960). In the present chapter, more attention is given to the actual operations of settings—how the program is initially organized and carried out over time. And I do not assume that over its life course a setting will generally return to a preset level of functioning. Rather, settings are continually constructed and reconstructed as new personnel and equipment are added or exchanged for exiting components. Behavior settings can and do grow, shrink, and change their operating levels.

I noted previously that in eco-behavioral science the role of particular individuals in behavior-setting functioning is deemphasized. When personnel changes are made, settings operate much as before. In this view, the most significant aspects of people are their program-related actions. Slight recognition is given to people's motives and almost no attention is paid to their cognitions, which unlike overt actions cannot be readily monitored and corrected. My framework gives considerably more recognition to the role of particular individuals, noting that the fate of settings—especially newly created ones—may depend upon key persons; substitutions in such instances may not be feasible. I also place greater emphasis on the motives and cognitive schemata that founders and staff members have regarding setting operations.

A basic assumption of the traditional view, and of the present view as well, is that human behavior cannot be adequately understood without examining the context in which it occurs. It seems likely that a parallel principle applies to behavior settings and *their* contexts. Like people, behavior settings exist in a larger social/physical environment that affects their "behavior." The traditional view, however, pays little attention to conditions beyond the boundaries of settings. Some observers have thus formed the impression that settings are rather closed and isolated systems. In the present framework, greater recognition

has been given to the role of such contextual factors as cultural and economic conditions, setting history, and the links that exist among settings.

Behavior settings have traditionally been studied in one of two ways: as units in descriptive surveys of the environments of towns and organizations, or as sites for research on behavioral and experiential consequences of understaffing. The former type of research is largely atheoretical; settings are quantitatively described in terms such as numbers of occupants, their duties, the amount of time they spend in the setting, and the extent to which certain behaviors occur in the setting program. The other type of research is based on staffing theory and typically uses questionnaires (cf. Barker, 1960; Wicker, 1979/1983). In the present chapter I advocate another approach to research: theory development through intensive, wide-angle observations of a relatively small number of contrasting settings. This is the *grounded theory* approach of Glaser and Strauss (1967).

Most behavior-setting researchers have had a scientific purpose—they have sought to understand human behavior and its immediate context. The problems they posed were not immediately practical ones. However, the knowledge they have generated on events of everyday life often can be used in beneficial ways. Barker has not participated in technological applications of behavior-setting research, but he applauds such efforts (e.g., Barker, 1979b). In this chapter I endorse the practical application of concepts, methods, and findings that may arise from research relevant to the present framework. Such applications are likely to include the creation of new settings and interventions in setting programs by outside specialists in behavior-setting technology.

16.1.5. Types of Behavior Settings Considered

In this chapter I am primarily concerned with behavior settings that have the following characteristics: (1) an indefinite life expectancy; (2) exclusive use of the space where the program is enacted; and (3) a staff of entrepreneurs and/or paid workers. This domain excludes some settings that would be found in a community survey, including those planned to occur a limited number of times and those staffed by volunteers. Much of the discussion in the chapter is, however, also applicable to such settings.

Perusal of Barker and Schoggen's (1973) data on all of the public behavior settings in two small towns suggests that the present criteria do not unduly restrict the population of settings to be considered. For example, settings in which programs were carried out by paid staff accounted for two-thirds of the community habitats[1], and for nearly 90% of the time that people spent in the town's settings. Other data indicate that the settings meeting the criteria are quite diverse, and that they include settings controlled by businesses (in Barker and Schoggen's research, about 60% of the towns' habitats), schools (20%), and government agencies (10%). Among the types of settings included are drugstores, dentists' offices, automobile repair shops, restaurants, elementary school classes, and county assessors' offices.

16.1.6. Distinguishing Among Organizations, Behavior Settings, and Small Groups

In preparing this chapter I have drawn on theoretical statements from several areas of psychology, particularly organizational and social psychology, and from other social sciences, particularly sociology. In general, the theories that proved most useful were ones that examine social systems at the group or organizational level. I have attempted to apply portions of these theories to behavior settings. At this point it may therefore be helpful to distinguish among three related concepts: organizations, behavior settings, and small groups. I will provide not categorical and arbitrary boundaries, but rather some fuzzy distinctions (cf. McGrath, 1984, chapter 1).

All three concepts refer to social aggregations that exist over time, have some reason for being, have patterned behavioral routines, and have actual or potential links among their members. Small groups and behavior settings also share the characteristics of being relatively small-scale social systems whose members engage in coordinated, face-to-face interactions.

According to the working definitions I have followed, the three concepts are not mutually exclusive, but neither do they overlap completely. For present purposes, the distinguishing features of an organization include a formally or legally recognized status (evidenced by, e.g., a charter or a business license), a paid work force, and the absence of a single higher centralized authority that governs most of its activities; that is, it is relatively autonomous. A behavior setting that meets these criteria also would be an organization. Examples would include an independently owned and operated gas station and a neighborhood grocery store. Most organizations encompass more than one behavior setting, however. They also tend to have administrative structures with several or perhaps many levels of decision making, and

they tend to be differentiated into hierarchical social structures that include relatively specialized subunits. Most behavior settings are subunits of larger parent organizations. Examples would be the machine shop of a small manufacturing firm and the medical records office in a clinic.

Behavior settings are distinctive because they are tied to places and to inanimate objects. The patterned activities of settings take place within specifiable spatial boundaries, and they mesh with the arrangement and design of physical objects (synomorphy).

The kinds of behavior settings we are concerned with here almost always envelop small groups of the kind McGrath (1984) calls *standing crews*. Such groups are naturally occurring groups that carry out a limited set of activities and have an indefinite life expectancy. They are distinguished from natural groups having very broad ranges of activities such as families and expeditions—these groups transcend particular settings. Standing crews also differ from concocted groups, such as participants in laboratory experiments and simulations—these groups typically exist for a limited time. Standing crews engage in "patterned behavior...within a behavior setting, in relation to [their] task/situation and environment" (McGrath, 1984, p. 13). Examples would be the staff of a retail bakery and the work crew of an automobile inspection station. The behavior setting incorporates, but is more than, such acting groups. It provides the "time–place–thing–person complex" that is the site for the group's behavior (McGrath, 1984, p. 16).

16.2. OVERVIEW OF THE CONCEPTUAL FRAMEWORK

The conceptual framework for the expanded view of behavior settings is represented in Table 16.1. There are two major aspects of the framework: setting facets and their elements (represented in the left-hand column) and temporal stages of behavior settings (represented at the top of the table). In this section these major aspects are briefly introduced and illustrated. In subsequent sections, each setting facet is discussed in more detail and its elements are traced over the temporal stages of settings.

16.2.1. Setting Facets over the Temporal Stages

I will continue to use the example of a gift shop to illustrate the features of a behavior setting that are represented in Table 16.1. The *resources* of such a setting in-

Table 16.1. Main Features of the Present Framework

Setting Facets and Elements	Temporal Stages of Behavior Settings			
	Preconvergence	Convergence ⟶	Continued Existence ⟶	Divergence
Resources				
People	Prior	Assembling	Adding,	Uncoupling
Behavior objects	placement	and	modifying,	and
Space	of	configuring	discharging	dispersing
Information	resources	required	resources	resources
Reserves		resources		
Internal dynamics				
Personal cognitions and motives				
Functional	Prior	Founding;	Adapting;	Dissolving;
activities	experience	initiation	continuation	cessation
Social processes	and training	of	of	of
Growth and	of staff	organizing,	organizing,	organizing,
differentiation		negotiating	negotiating	negotiating
Stability and flexibility				
Decline				
Interventions				
Context				
General environmental factors, e.g., culture, legal system, economy	General and specific conditions in the social world	Emerging	Finding and preserving a niche	Disappearing
Setting history				
Setting networks				

clude its staff, equipment and merchandise, usable space, information on potential markets and suppliers, and money or credit available for future use.

In the present framework the resources and other setting facets are considered at four temporal stages. Before the gift shop is established, that is, during the *preconvergence* stage, most or all of its (future) resources exist, but in a number of other locations, and perhaps in different form. At *convergence*, the stage during which the setting begins to function, the resources are assembled and arranged.[2] Space is located, equipment installed, clerks recruited, and merchandise ordered, received, and shelved. The *continued existence* stage is the mature period of a setting that has been the focus of Barker's work. During this stage, resources are added, modified, and discharged in piecemeal fashion as described earlier. At *divergence*, or the demise of the setting, resources are released to other settings. Merchandise is liquidated, equipment sold, clerks terminated, and space vacated. (The fact that some new settings succumb before achieving a quasi-stable state is represented in Table 16.1 by the arrow directly linking convergence to divergence.)

Internal dynamics are the arrangements worked out in the setting to enact its program and to meet, at least at some minimal level, the personal needs of setting occupants. In the gift shop, these arrangements would be affected by the owner's and staff's cognitive schemes for the shop, and their motives for working there. Other aspects of the shop's internal dynamics include the way tasks are divided up and assigned and interactions among staff and customers. How the gift shop operates will be conditioned as well by its periods of growth and decline, and by the degree of stability and flexibility in its procedures. Interventions by outside agents, such as a representative of a local retail clerks' union or a small business consultant, also may significantly alter the shop's internal dynamics.

Prior to the convergence of the gift shop, the (future) owner and staff members have transactions in other settings that bear on the shop's subsequent operation. These experiences may include formal or on-the-job training as well as a broader range of activities that affect their motives, interests, and knowledge.

Throughout the life of a behavior setting, its occupants continually identify aspects of their environments with which to interact, take actions, make interpretations, and remember portions of what they have concluded. These cycles typically include interactions with other people (cf. Strauss, 1978; Weick, 1979b). The content of these organizing and negotiating processes varies somewhat with the stage of the setting. At convergence, the focus is on issues relating to the founding of the setting, for example, developing a working relationship among the clerks and owner and establishing procedures for dealing with recurrent events such as checking in newly arrived goods. During the continued existence of the setting, numerous adjustments are made to events within and beyond the setting boundaries. Adaptations may have to be made to the sudden departure of a clerk or to a complaint made through a consumers' organization. At the divergence stage, the issues may concern how to achieve an orderly dismantling of the setting. Organizing and negotiating continue until the staff departs.

The third facet of a setting is its *context*, which is represented here by three elements. One is the larger social world that includes these and other forces: cultural, political, legal, economic, technological, demographic, and geographic. A gift shop is affected, for example, by gift-giving practices in the culture, as well as by economic trends. Every setting also has a history—a particular set of events that precedes its establishment and shapes its subsequent development. For the gift shop, such events as the owner's receiving an inheritance, the availability of a desirable location, and her prior sales experience bear on that setting's founding and subsequent course. The third element of context is the network of other settings with which a particular setting is tied by resource or social influence linkages. Our gift shop is linked to its suppliers for merchandise, to its customers for merchandise disposal, to its attorney for legal advice, and to its regulators by tax and other obligations.

In considering setting context across temporal stages, we may find it useful to draw upon a metaphor. The preconvergence conditions of a setting can be likened to a stream—a flow of events and conditions in a larger social world that includes the aspects mentioned above. Behavior settings coalesce out of this stream and, at a particular time/place juncture, become identifiable entities distinguishable from their surroundings (convergence). During their continued existence, settings must find and preserve a niche in this environment, or they will disappear (divergence). A new gift shop must find a relatively secure place in the complex social world from which it emerged. It needs to be part of a supportive network of settings and—at least to some degree—to be in harmony with the larger social world.

It should be obvious that the setting facets and elements identified here are highly interrelated. For example, resources become usable through the internal dynamics of settings, and they are often drawn from the broader social world through other settings. For purposes of discussion, however, we will consider these facets in sequence as they appear in Table 16.1. This sequence follows a part-to-whole, inside-to-outside, simpler-to-more-complex logic.

16.2.2. Related Work on Temporal Stages of Settings and Other Social Systems

Before we consider the present framework in more detail, note should be made of previous research that has considered the temporal development of behavior settings. Until recently, this issue has not been dealt with by environmental or ecological psychologists. The only conceptual treatments to date are a symposium presentation by Wicker (1980) and portions of a chapter by Stokols and Shumaker (1981). The present chapter supersedes Wicker's (1980) presentation.

Relative to the present formulation, Stokols and Shumaker (1981) place greater emphasis on these factors: physical spaces and their symbolic meaning to individuals and groups; social conflicts associated with territorial domains; and degree of congruence between the actual and desired conditions in settings. Stokols and Shumaker also propose more stages (eight in all) in the life cycle of settings. Among the similarities between the two approaches is greater attention than in the past to changes within settings. Both assign to occupants a more active role in structuring and restructuring their proximal environments.

Life cycles of larger social systems, most notably organizations, have been discussed recently by a number of writers. The references most relevant to behavior-setting development are cited in later sections of this chapter. One contribution deserves comment here, however. Community psychologist Seymour Sarason has written a rich narrative based on his experiences as a founder of and consultant to new community social service agencies (Sarason, 1972; see also Sarason, Zitnay, & Grossman, 1971). He has also drawn on first-hand accounts of other founders. Sarason thoughtfully analyzes a number of aspects of new social service organizations, including their "prehistory," facilities where they are housed, organizing activities and personal experiences of founders, and symptoms of organizational decline.

While there are numerous similarities between Sarason's work and the present chapter, there are also differences. In spite of the fact that Sarason also uses the term *setting*, he focuses on a larger unit of analysis than the behavior setting. My approach is also more theoretical and systematic in that I develop a framework that draws upon relatively few concepts from the social science literature. Another distinction is that the present analysis gives more attention to the day-to-day activities of all staff members, and less attention to the strategies and perspectives of agency heads and other designated leaders.

16.3. BEHAVIOR-SETTING RESOURCES

16.3.1. Necessary Resources

We have noted that behavior settings have human and nonhuman components, and that they occur within bounded spaces. These features make up three of the five necessary setting resources recognized in the present framework: people, behavior objects, and space. The others are information and reserves. Another kind of resource often needed by a setting is the expertise of off-site technicians or professionals, such as plumbers, electricians, attorneys, and accountants (cf. Smith, 1982, pp.83–92). In the present scheme, contributions from these "on-call" personnel are considered inputs from other settings, and are discussed in the section on context.

Before discussing each of these resources, I should note that, in order for anything actually to serve as a resource in a setting, it must have the potential to contribute to the setting, and this potential must be recognized by those who would use it. Thus if it is to be a setting resource, an item must be operable, compatible with other setting components, and

seen as appropriate to and usable in the setting. A dental chair, for example, must work properly and be configured compatibly with the other equipment used by a dentist. Other equipment such as headphones that allow patients to listen to music while being treated, may or may not be considered appropriate. Judgments about which resources are appropriate in a setting are likely to vary with setting occupants: One dentist may find an old but usable dental chair unacceptable yet another dentist may not; one may see no need for a dental assistant but the other may. (More details on the cognitive schemata of setting occupants are considered in a later section.)

Behavior settings require human resources. More specifically, staff members must have a basic working knowledge of their assigned jobs, as well as the motivation and time necessary to carry out those duties. A working knowledge of one's job includes the ability to handle routine procedures, as well as some understanding of the materials or documents handled, equipment used, and usual patterns of behavior of co-workers and also of clients, if they are present (Kusterer, 1978). Settings that provide services or supply products also require clients or customers whose patronage directly or indirectly supports the setting.

Several types of behavior objects may be necessary to the program of a setting: equipment or tools, supplies, and raw materials or finished goods. Specific needs depend on the program of the setting, but most settings require two or more of these types of objects. To illustrate, an attorney's office would require equipment and tools such as desks, chairs, typewriters, and a legal library, and supplies such as paper and pens, but perhaps no raw materials or merchandise. The latter kinds of objects would be required by settings that manufacture products or that sell goods.

The space occupied by a setting must be sufficiently large to accommodate the setting program. Its boundaries should clearly demarcate the limits of the setting. Other built or natural features also need to be configured in a way that is compatible with the routine behaviors that occur there (cf. Gump & Ross, 1977). The ambient conditions such as temperature, light, air quality, and the like have to be within the range of tolerance of the people and behavior objects within the setting. And the space must be located such that essential components can enter or be brought into the setting (cf. Becker, 1981).

The next two resource categories, information and reserves, are not considered in the traditional view of settings. The importance of these resources is most evident when one considers the development of settings over time, as we will see in the following section.

Information, as a setting resource, is specific or general knowledge that bears on any aspect of the setting's operation. Such information would include data on the current status of a setting, records of previous activities and their outcomes, timely data or intelligence on settings to which a setting is linked, descriptions of products or procedures that can be used to improve (according to any of several criteria) the enactment of the setting program. Each of these types of information needs to be accurate, readily accessible, and in a form that is usable by staff members.

Reserves are money and other resources not committed to current operations but available for future use. The clearest example of financial reserves is uncommitted cash on hand. Another example is an allocated but unspent budgetary item. A somewhat broader conception of reserves that may include money or credit but is not limited to them is the notion of slack resources (cf. Cyert & March, 1963). A behavior setting that has the capacity to increase its output without requiring additional resources would have such slack (cf. Katz & Kahn, 1978). Any of the resources discussed could contribute to slack: unused space, underused equipment, stores of supplies, overstaffing, and workable plans for increasing setting efficiency.

16.3.2. Resources and the Temporal Stages of Behavior Settings

In order for a behavior setting to come into being, its requisite resources must be located, assembled at one place and time, and configured into the intricate set of routines that constitutes the setting program (cf. Barker, 1979a, p. 86). Subsequently, resources are treated in a more piecemeal fashion. This sequence is represented in the Resources row of Table 16-1.

The preconvergence conditions of the needed resources are among the realities with which the founders and staff members of a new setting must cope: These resources may not currently exist in a usable form, they may currently exist but be inactive, or they may be in service at other locations. Specific resource components such as buildings and office suites, bench saws and counters, lathe operators and typists must be selected. The task of converging resources may vary depending on whether the new setting is an autonomous organizational unit, a franchise

operation, or part of a larger organization. In the last two cases many decisions about resources may be dictated by higher authorities.

At the convergence of a behavior setting, founders must attend to many resource components in a short time span. Spaces may have to be remodeled and redecorated, equipment may need to be arranged, tested, and adjusted, and staff members may require training. Some of the direction for shaping of resources may come from the working knowledge of setting founders and staff. However, the assistance of outside professionals such as interior designers, engineers, and other technical specialists may also be enlisted. Trial and error is also likely to play a role in assembling and configuring resources in any new setting.

The functioning of a setting in the convergence phase may be further complicated due to insufficient resources. The staff may be spread too thinly to perform their tasks, raw materials or merchandise may not be available in the quantities needed, or information on how to make setting components function more smoothly may be lacking. Such deficiencies may have consequences of varying degrees of seriousness, depending on how central they are to the setting program. For example, a photocopy service cannot operate without copy paper, but it need not have a full range of weights and colors.

There is more stability in settings that survive the convergence stage; adjustments in resources are generally not so comprehensive. Components are often modified or replaced in piecemeal fashion: New merchandise is ordered, work areas are rearranged, equipment is traded in for a newer model. Major reorganizations can occur, of course, and in these instances outside consultants or change agents may be brought in to suggest the acquisition, modification, or removal of setting components.

Information and reserves are likely to be important considerations at the very beginning of the convergence stage, as founders assess whether they have or can acquire the knowledge, financing, and other resources needed to establish a new setting. When it appears that the information and reserves are adequate to launch the setting, these resources may become less of a concern than the particular components that have to be assembled and set in operation. Once the setting has stabilized, that is, when routines have been established and relatively few nonrecurring decisions have to be made, greater emphasis may again be placed on informational resources. Procedures may be developed for keeping better records and systematically summarizing data related to the setting's operations. Steps may also be taken to keep track of events and conditions in other settings with which the new setting is linked. Settings that have survived the convergence stage may begin to accumulate reserves for such longer-term purposes as growth, planning, improved facilities, and upgrading of staff (cf. Smith, 1982).

Among the conditions that guarantee the demise of a behavior setting are the loss and nonreplacement of essential resources. The most widely publicized lack is financial resources—money, credit, budget allocation. Inadequate finances can mean that other resources are lost: Buildings have to be vacated because mortgages cannot be paid, equipment is removed because lease payments are delinquent, staff members leave when payroll checks cannot be issued (in some cases, inadequate funding may not be fatal to a setting, but instead may lead to other types of exchanges; see Lyon, 1974).

Settings may also enter the divergence phase for reasons that are not directly or obviously financial: A building may be condemned with no suitable alternative space for sale or rent, raw materials may no longer be in sufficient supply due to depletion or embargo, all applicants for staff positions may lack required technical knowledge.

When a setting does cease to operate, for whatever reason, its components typically disperse. The components may continue to exist, and in some cases continue to function much as before, but their configuration is different. The close interdependence of components that characterizes a behavior setting is gone—the components have assumed different alignments. Staff members take positions elsewhere, spaces house other settings, equipment and other behavior objects are stored, used in other locations, or junked.

Several references have been made in this section to the need for behavior-setting resources to be configured in such a way that the setting's program is carried out. The organizing process by which setting programs occur is considered in the following section.

16.4. INTERNAL DYNAMICS OF BEHAVIOR SETTINGS

The traditional view of the internal workings of settings is given in Barker's theory of behavior settings, which subsumes the more specialized theory of manning (here called staffing theory) (Barker, 1968, chapters 6 & 7). This section begins with a summary and critique of the traditional theory. It is followed by a new, elaborated view of the internal dynamics of settings. Key features of the expanded view are shown in the middle section of Table 16.1. The present view places greater importance on the role of particular persons and examines in greater detail the group interaction processes associated with establishing and carrying out setting programs. Developmental processes in settings, including growth and differentiation, stability and flexibility, decline and divergence, are then considered. The section concludes with a discussion of interventions in settings.

16.4.1. Summary and Critique of Behavior-Setting Theory

Barker has been impressed by the fact that behavior settings continue their functions over long periods of time, even in the face of changing internal and external conditions. For example, even though this year's fourth grade elementary class has a new teacher and a new set of student occupants, it will function largely as did last year's class. The stability of this and other behavior settings is, in Barker's view, attributable to certain internal self-regulating processes (circuits) that link the components of a setting (e.g., teacher, students, desks, classroom).

These circuits are of two types: *operating circuits* carry out the setting program and provide satisfactions to occupants, while *maintenance circuits* preserve settings in a homeostatic state by dealing with threats to the setting program. Most of the time, in most settings, operating circuits occur—the usual routines are carried out. Maintenance circuits are enacted only when it appears that some event or condition may disrupt the program. Frequently these maintenance circuits act on people in the setting, because they are typically the most versatile and malleable components—they can hurry, crowd into smaller spaces, shift attention to immediate problems, and so on.

Barker's theory of behavior settings is essentially a theory of maintenance circuits: A balanced or homeostatic state is restored to a setting by correcting (deviation-countering) or removing (vetoing) troublesome components. For example, workers whose careless actions threaten to disrupt a setting can be trained or exhorted to improve, or they can be fired.

The most specific theoretical statements on maintenance circuits are a set of propositions indicating how behavior settings adapt to understaffing, and the consequences of this condition for setting occupants. The theory states, for example, that, when setting programs are threatened by staff shortages, the staff members who are present will engage in more frequent, more vigorous, and more varied actions to carry out the program and to deal with the threats. Staff members who are not performing adequately are more likely to have their behavior shaped by others than to be ejected from the setting. Participants are likely to perform tasks that are more responsible, more difficult, and more varied than normal. They tend to feel more involved and important, and to be more task oriented than when staffing is optimal (Barker, 1968).

Subsequent extensions of staffing theory, which deal with overstaffing (Wicker, McGrath, & Armstrong, 1972) and with staff reactions to overload in work settings (Wicker & Kirmeyer, 1976), have continued to emphasize the self-regulating processes of settings. Staffing theory and its extensions have stimulated most of the recent research on behavior settings (for a review of this research see Wicker, 1979/1983; work published since that review is cited in a later section of this chapter).

This brief review illustrates several contributions of behavior setting theory: It has provided a framework for representing important processes within settings, and it has stimulated research and further theoretical development. The theory and its extensions also have a number of limitations; several of them are considered in the following paragraphs.

Although the maintenance circuits considered in behavior-setting theory are presumed to be applicable to any condition or event that threatens a setting program, the only threats that have been considered in detail are personnel deficiencies and surpluses. The ways that settings cope with nonoptimal amounts of other resources such as spaces, equipment, supplies, information, and reserves remain to be dealt with theoretically. The theory also needs to consider in more detail how settings deal with threats of other kinds, for example, lack of synomorphy or interpersonal conflict.

Behavior-setting theory explains setting stability exclusively in terms of intrasetting events. It does not consider the conditions and events outside settings that contribute to stability and inhibit change. For example, among the factors that contribute to similarities in successive years' fourth grade classes are state curriculum requirements, school system policies, the teacher labor pool, and elementary principals' oversight. We will consider such factors in the discussion of setting context.

There is no satisfactory way in the traditional theory to account for changes in the level of functioning of a setting, or for setting growth or decline. Virtually all of the internal dynamics recognized by the theory are devoted to keeping setting operations within a narrow range. In a later section of this chapter a more fluid view of setting operations is proposed.

Finally, although the theory identifies operating circuits, it does not provide any details of how programs are organized and carried out, or how personal inputs affect these processes. This is a notable omission, because operating circuits are the reason settings exist—they are the primary processes that maintenance circuits protect and restore.

The theoretical neglect of operating circuits may follow from taking behavior settings as "givens." If one begins with an image of settings as mature, stable entities, then that stability needs to be explained. If, on the other hand, one regards settings as social constructions that are continually being built and rebuilt through the deliberate actions of individuals, then explanations are needed for the organizing and operating processes (cf. Berger & Luckmann, 1967; Weick, 1979b). My development of this view begins in the next section with a discussion of the contribution of particular individuals to behavior-setting programs.

16.4.2. The Role of Human Components

According to Barker, "of all the attributes of settings, people are the *sine qua non*" (Barker, 1960, p. 21). People produce the behavior that settings surround, and people are often agents and recipients of operating and maintenance circuits. Barker further states that, "although essential, people are anonymous; they are equipotential; their individuality is irrelevant to behavior settings. People in this respect are not different from other behavior objects in the setting" (Barker, 1960, p. 21). Barker's argument here is based on the common observation that in many settings people can and do substitute for others, with the setting programs continuing much as before.

A number of scholars sympathetic with Barker's general approach have criticized his assumption that setting occupants are interchangeable; they find it too "coarse" for an adequate analysis of setting dynamics (e.g., McGrath, 1984, chapter 1; Moos, 1983, pp. 179–180). I agree with the substance of these criticisms. On the one hand, newcomers do have to conform to the broad outlines of the setting program as Barker suggests. But close inspection will reveal that such personnel changes do not leave settings and their programs unaffected. Newcomers bring with them individual characteristics—traits, habits, beliefs, and the like. These factors and the pattern of their interactions with other occupants lead newcomers to construct their own meanings and develop their own styles of carrying out setting operations (cf. Kusterer, 1978; Van Maanen, 1977). The degree to which setting programs are affected by personnel changes is likely to vary with each of the factors mentioned: the nature of the program, the characteristics of the newcomer, and the interaction styles of the continuing occupants.

The presumed indifference of behavior settings to particular individuals seems especially inappropriate at the convergence stage. Founders or other staff members may be indispensible to newly established settings because they have knowledge, skills, or energy that no one else can duplicate. In such instances, the fate of the new setting will hinge on their continued participation.

It seems likely that in many settings the strongest personal influence on setting programs comes from the founders. This influence can sometimes be traced to the preconvergence period, when founders anticipate the requirements for converging a setting and analyze the feasibility of their being able to meet those requirements. Analyses of this kind reflect the psychological processes of one or a few individuals. Yet their significance for behavior settings can be great: Decisions are made whether to try to establish a setting, and if so, how it should be structured. In the next section we consider in more detail some ways that the cognitions of founders and others affect the internal dynamics of settings.

16.4.3. Cognitions of Setting Occupants

The theory of behavior settings pays very little attention to the cognitions of setting occupants. Although the theory states that maintenance circuits are enacted only when setting events are judged to be incompatible with the setting program, neither the nature of the template for the setting program nor the process of evaluation is specified.[3]

The concern here is people's representations of behavior settings, particularly of setting programs. Nearly everyone can identify many different behavior settings and can describe—in varying degrees of detail—many setting programs. They can, for example, indicate at least some of the routine actions that occur in the settings where they work, shop, dine, and worship. In general, the more experienced a person is with settings of a particular type, the more elaborated the person's cognitions of such settings (Wicker, 1969a).

I noted previously that the cognitions of founders

can significantly affect the development of settings. Founders may, for example, have images of the settings they hope to establish. Depending on their experience, they also may envision in some detail the steps necessary to create the settings. Similarly, staff members may bring to settings well-defined notions of how tasks are carried out and what are appropriate ways to interact with co-workers and clients.

The planning of a new setting is not, however, equivalent to the creation of a new form or structure. As Barker has noted, "people establish new settings according to designs they carry with them from previous settings" (Barker, 1979b, p. 2155). Even if several persons participate in the planning process, the range of alternatives examined is likely to be considerably narrower than what is logically possible or feasible. Channelized thinking by the founder or members of the planning group may inhibit creative ways of organizing (cf. Weick, 1979b).

An example of the restricted consideration of alternatives is provided by Sarason (1972, chapter 8), who notes that planners of residential care for children almost invariably assume that there must be a newly constructed central facility that will house the children and a variety of professional and nonprofessional staff members. Such possibilities as occupying existing community buildings close to the families of the children, and placing small housing units near high schools to facilitate staff training and to have a ready source of volunteers and facilities for recreational activities, are rarely considered. Similarly, duties of staff members are frequently considered only in terms of traditional staff roles.

The absence of clear images or plans for new behavior settings also has implications for the internal dynamics of settings. If none of the participants has a detailed understanding of how the setting could or should operate, familiar but inappropriate routines may be tried. Many of the early activities in such a setting will be devoted to trial-and-error exploration.

Several constructs in the psychological and sociological literature resemble what are called here *cognitions of setting programs*. The two that come the closest are the *script* (Schank & Abelson, 1977) and *social episode* (Forgas, 1979, 1982) concepts.[4] In some ways, the script appears to be a rediscovery of behavior-setting programs from a quite different approach than Barker's:

> A script is a [cognitive] structure that describes appropriate sequences of events in a particular context. A script is made up of slots and requirements about what can fill those slots. The structure is an

interconnected whole....Scripts handle stylized everyday situations....There are scripts for eating in a restaurant, riding a bus, watching and playing a football game, participating in a birthday party, and so on. (Schank & Abelson, 1977, p. 41)

More recently, Abelson (1981) has elaborated on the concept to consider the "action rules" that people follow when they enact or "enter" a script. Other statements by Schank and Abelson (1977) call to mind Barker's genotypes ("tracks," p. 40) and maintenance circuits ("interferences and distractions," pp. 51–57).

In contrast to Schank and Abelson, Forgas (1979) acknowledges the relevance of the behavior-setting concept to his work. He finds that, conceptually, social episodes and behavior-setting programs are "remarkably similar. Both refer to stereotypical, culture-specific sequences of behavior with a consensually understood rule-structure" (p. 149).

Several differences that Forgas (1979) notes between social episodes and behavior-setting programs (or their representations) also apply to scripts. Social episodes and scripts are more diffuse; both incorporate events that are not anchored to specified times and places, and both incorporate subjective interpretations and affective responses as well as behaviors in support of setting programs. In addition, purely cognitive operations, such as how people fill gaps in event sequences to yield a comprehensible composite, are not a major concern in the present framework as they are in Schank and Abelson's model.

Perhaps the most significant difference between social cognition concepts and the present notion of representations of behavior-setting programs is the person focus of the former. Scripts and social episodes represent events and actions from the perspective of a single person. They are limited to transactions of the focal person, and do not necessarily incorporate the entire set of transactions that make up the program of a setting.

Despite these differences, the three concepts are sufficiently similar that further cross-fertilization of ideas is possible. Research on scripts and social episodes may take directions that will shed light on ways that setting occupants, particularly staff members, construe setting programs. And research on the latter could be used to refine and extend the social cognition concepts (cf. Forgas, 1979; Kruse, 1986). A particularly important topic for future research is the process by which participants' cognitions are formed and shaped through their transactions in settings. Weick's (1979b) description of the

processes by which cause maps are formed is one promising approach to this problem.

Occupants' conceptions of behavior-setting programs are, of course, only a starting point for analyzing operating circuits. Functioning behavior settings entail considerably more than images in the minds of participants; actions must be undertaken and their effects assessed. Some insight into the actions taken in settings can be derived from considering the personal motives of participants, the next topic.

16.4.4. Motives of Setting Occupants

According to Barker, behavior settings will exist only as long as they continue to provide *satisfactions* to occupants. He does not specify the types of satisfactions that settings provide, but he notes that even in the same setting different people achieve different goals, depending on "their own unique natures" (Barker, 1960, p. 25). The various satisfactions that people gain from settings are products of the orderly enactment of setting programs: in a baseball game, for example, "the pitcher may achieve satisfactions by striking out batters, the umpire by earning $25, the concessionaire by selling many hot dogs, and the hometown fans by cheering the team to victory" (Barker, 1968, p. 167).

The various satisfactions that bind people to settings could be classified in numerous ways. According to one scheme, people may become integrated into social systems such as behavior settings on the basis of: (1) meaningful work roles (functional basis); (2) supportive relations with their fellow members (socioemotional); (3) shared expectations and evaluations of behavior (normative); and (4) shared generalized values (ideological) (Katz & Golomb, 1974, pp. 286–287).

Because of such benefits, setting occupants are motivated to maintain settings; they initiate—and tolerate—maintenance circuits in order to protect the satisfactions they receive. Certain secondary motives may develop out of maintenance actions: For example, as noted earlier, shortages in personnel may lead occupants to work harder, and to take on tasks that are more important and more difficult than their usual duties (Barker, 1968).

This view of the motives of setting occupants is compatible with Allport's (1962) more general explanation for individuals' participation in group activities: "Collective structuring...[is] the result of the heightened probability of satisfactions through integrated or articulated behaviors, a probability that is afforded by the presence and potential interactions of others" (p. 15). Allport further suggests that people have

> a deep-seated tendency so to act as to establish some sort of give-and-take, *structural*, relation with one's fellows—to be 'not left adrift' but included as a part of a present collectivity; or to help create, if necessary, such a structural relationship so that one *can* be a part of it. (p. 14)

The notion that behavior settings provide satisfactions to all occupants seems problematic for at least some settings. An alternative view that is consistent with much of the work on behavior settings has been suggested by Dubin (1979). In Dubin's framework, people's actions in organizational settings—their *behavioral investments*—may or may not be accompanied by *affective investments*, or attachment of positive feelings. (Dubin does not consider the attachment of negative feelings.) The areas of a person's life in which major affective investments are attached to behavioral investments constitute the person's central life interest.

In the present terms, a person's zone of central life interest includes the settings where the person carries out situationally appropriate behaviors and displays a relatively high level of concern about and involvement in the setting program. According to this view, settings may differ in the degree of total satisfaction they provide to occupants, and occupants in any given setting may differ in the degree of satisfaction they receive from the setting. Settings that represent a person's central life interest are typically described by the person in such terms as *desirable*, *worthy*, *challenging*, and *demanding* (Dubin, 1979, p. 41). Occupants who evaluate a setting in these terms would, according to the present view, be more likely than others to undertake setting maintenance actions. There is evidence to support this expectation: Workers who reported more involvement with their jobs also reported taking more actions to deal with problems they noticed at work, even when the problems were not their responsibility (Mentes, 1982).

Dubin also suggests that affective investments are attached only to voluntary behavior. Although such behavior may occur in settings that we generally regard as required, for example, work sites and high school academic classes, it is probably more prevalent in voluntary settings. Thus the assumption that all occupants derive satisfaction from the settings they occupy may be less true in the kind of settings we are considering here (ones in which the staff is paid) than in voluntary settings.

Although Dubin does not deal with the issue of how people develop central life interests, it seems certain that experiences in behavior settings play a major role. Within settings people can explore their abilities and interests. On the basis of such experiences, they choose to enter some settings and not others. In the settings they enter—whether voluntarily or not—participants' experiences affect the extent to which they attach affective investments to their actions. For example, people who serve in responsible positions in voluntary settings tend to report greater involvement than other participants (Wicker, 1968).

While the motives that people bring to a setting (such as a desire for certain satisfactions) may affect setting operations, it is the interaction of personal desires with setting conditions and processes that is most promising for analyzing setting dynamics (cf. Secord, 1977, p. 46). Generalized personality dispositions such as industriousness or need for stimulation are less useful for understanding operating circuits than are the interactions of such dispositions with events that occur in the setting such as deliberations on how the setting program is to be divided into discrete jobs.

Among the personal characteristics of staff members that seem worthy of investigation are their task preferences, commitment to the setting, attachments to people in and beyond the setting, and vested interests. The fit of staff members' self- or professional images with their roles in the setting may also be important. For founders, these characteristics may be significant: energy levels, and strength of their desire for self-expression, achievement, independence, competition, power, legitimacy, and wealth (Stinchcombe, 1965, pp. 146–148).

16.4.5. Functional Activities in Settings

Although personal characteristics of setting occupants may significantly influence the development of behavior settings, they are not sufficient to explain behavior-setting dynamics. Setting programs are collective endeavors. To understand them we need to consider the means by which people, behavior objects, spaces, and other setting resources are organized into a social system.

Some of the actions needed to initiate and sustain a behavior setting can be characterized as primarily functional: assembling resources, identifying tasks and grouping them into jobs, matching staff members with jobs, arranging and configuring behavior objects, performing tasks that are part of operations and maintenance circuits. Activities of these kinds are recognized in behavior-setting theory. The theory does not, however, recognize the finer-grained social interactions such as interpersonal negotiations and organizing activities, that produce such actions. These social processes are assigned a major role in the present framework. Before I consider them in more detail, however, I will make an additional point regarding functional activities.

Although the operation of a behavior-setting program is considered here under the rubric of internal dynamics, it is important to note that the functional activities we are considering are often constrained by events and conditions beyond the setting boundaries—a fact not emphasized in the traditional view of behavior settings. For example, the division of labor in a setting may depend upon outside authorities. From Steiner's (1972) discussion of how groups organize to perform divisible tasks, we can identify three different levels of autonomy in determining division of labor: (1) Both the jobs to be performed and the persons assigned to them are specified by authorities outside the setting. An example would be a setting formed by dividing up a larger, existing setting. (2) Outside authorities parcel out tasks into specific jobs, but the persons to perform the jobs—except perhaps the manager—are selected by setting occupants. Certain franchise operations, such as fast-food restaurants, are examples. (3) The ways jobs are set up and who performs them are not constrained by outsiders. A stationery store would be an example.

Other functional activities may involve establishing channels of inputs and outputs with other settings: securing reliable sources of supplies and raw materials, recruiting clients, and arranging for product and waste disposal. Further examples of externally imposed constraints are health and safety regulations, land use and development codes, and contractual arrangements with labor unions. These factors will be considered in more detail in Section 16.5, on setting context.

16.4.6. Social Processes in Settings

Functional activities such as identifying tasks and assigning people to work on them do not just happen. Often they are worked out in a series of exchanges among the participants in the setting. The present analysis of these social processes draws on negotiated order theory (Strauss, 1978; see also Day & Day, 1977) and on the organizing model (Weick, 1979b). Both perspectives share with behavior-setting theory the assumption that stability in a social

system derives from patterned behaviors of interacting individuals. (Behavior setting theory, in fact, provides a more inclusive notion of social structure than the other two models; it explicitly links the patterned behavior to behavior objects, and to particular places and times.)

Both perspectives also challenge and complement the thinking of ecological psychologists regarding the social dynamics of behavior settings. Rather than focusing on stability and maintenance, for example, these theories emphasize the fluidity of social systems, and both consider the role of psychological variables in system dynamics. In the next few paragraphs, some essential features of the theories are summarized. I will then consider their implications for understanding social processes in behavior settings.

Negotiated Order Theory

This theory grew out of studies of social interactions among hospital staff members. More recently the theory has been applied to a much wider range of organizations (Strauss, 1978). Negotiated order theory assigns to individuals "an active, self-conscious role" in shaping organizations, largely through daily interactions that may include tacit, unofficial agreements and arrangements (Day & Day, 1977, p. 134). Individuals are seen as guided primarily by their vested (personal or professional) interests. The social order in an organization is at least partially due to such negotiations. The orderly arrangements are not permanent, however; they must eventually be "reviewed, reevaluated, revised, revoked, or renewed" (Strauss, 1978, p. 4). (It should be clear that the negotiations considered here are not formal interactions such as working out a labor contract, but are more subtle and informal arrangements.)

Events that affect the negotiated order, such as the introduction of new equipment or personnel, call for renegotiation (cf. Hall & Spencer-Hall, 1982). Organizations are thus seen as "highly fragile social constructions of reality" whose features are continuously emerging (Day & Day, 1977, p. 134). Negotiated order theorists acknowledge that there are limits to the negotiation process—clearly everything is not "up for grabs" at all times. Rather, "smaller-scale negotiations are continuously taking place in very large numbers *within* the context of the larger-scale arrangements which are changing more slowly and less visibly to participants" (Gerson, 1976, p. 796). This perspective, incidentally, is not as foreign to Barker's present views as one might think. He notes in this volume that "behavior settings and their human components continually change and some of the changes become permanent with settings, persons, or both being permanently modified."

The Organizing Model

From the organizing perspective we would expect the content of negotiations in a group to change over time. In a group's formative stages negotiations are likely to focus on certain specific functional behaviors (*operating circuits*, to use Barker's terminology) that members are to enact: "Individuals come together because each wants to perform *some* act and needs the other person[s] to do certain things to make the performance possible" (Weick, 1979b, p. 91). The fact that these individuals typically have different interests and abilities is not significant:

> All they ask of one another at these initial stages is the contribution of their action....Partners in a collective structure share space, time, and energy, but they need not share visions, aspirations, or intentions. That sharing comes much later, if at all. (Weick, 1979b, p. 91)

Weick suggests that the earliest shared goal of most groups is to preserve the collective structure that helps individuals get what they want. A topic for negotiation at this point would be individuals' responsibilities for monitoring and correcting threats to the structure, or what Barker calls *maintenance circuits*.

Later in the development of some groups, members' interests may shift from the common goal of preserving the structure to more idiosyncratic, personal goals. As a result of division of labor, persons having specialized tasks may become more concerned with their particular domains than with the overall group effort. Also, members may seek to reassert their uniqueness by emphasizing their dissimilarity from others with whom they are behaviorally linked (Weick, 1979b, pp. 93–94). In these instances, negotiations may deal with more refined operational and maintenance issues.

The organizing model also stresses the fluidity of social systems: "organizations keep falling apart... they require chronic rebuilding" (Weick, 1979b, p. 44). The processes by which organizations are socially constructed are the substance of the organizing model. A three-step cycle occurs: Members of interacting groups (1) act on portions of the environment, (2) interpret the results, and (3) then retain some causal explanation (a *cause map*) of the events. People's cause maps constrain their subsequent actions — the maps help determine what aspects of the environment will be attended to and acted upon in

the future. These processes help members develop a sense of understanding about organizational events, and they contribute to the formation of routines for handling new inputs. Stated differently, the processes produce recipes for reducing uncertainty, which according to Weick is the central goal of all organizations (Weick, 1979b).

This cycle can also be dysfunctional. People's cause maps may, over time, lead them to respond to environmental events more in terms of what they expect to find than in terms of what is really there. Even inputs that are novel or worthy of more examination may be treated routinely. Reduced sensitivity to surrounding events, coupled with fixed procedures and narrow interpretations, can lead to the demise of an organization. Such a result would occur if the organization is unable to register and respond appropriately to new environmental realities. In order to maintain flexibility yet still deal effectively with present conditions, members of organizations need both to doubt and to trust their memories (cause maps).

Application of the Negotiated Order and Organizing Models to Behavior Settings

From these models, we would expect functional activities in behavior settings to be subject to continual negotiation by setting occupants (empirical evidence consistent with this expectation has been reported by McNeil, 1980; Morgan, 1975; Schatzman & Bucher, 1964). The latitude of negotiation — the number of negotiable issues and the range of potential resolutions — will vary with a number of factors.

One way of thinking about negotiation latitude is in terms of the ratio of constructed to preexisting realities in a setting (Weick, personal communication, August 29, 1983). Constructed realities are meanings and procedures worked out by setting occupants; preexisting realities are generally recognized as "givens." This ratio will vary from one setting to another depending on a number of factors. For example, in a converging setting that is not modeled on an established setting elsewhere, the ratio of constructed to preexisting realities would be high, and the latitude of negotiation great. This ratio may vary considerably in mature settings depending upon such factors as the nature of the program, the demographics of the staff, the strength of the ties to other settings, and whether a "crisis" is pronounced. A higher ratio of constructed to preexisting reality — and a wider latitude of negotiation — would be expected in newspaper offices than in local social security offices, in settings staffed mostly by newcomers, in settings that are not tightly coupled to other settings or to a parent organization, and in settings where there is a recognized crisis.

The content of negotiations in a setting undoubtedly changes over its temporal stages. At convergence, negotiations are likely to focus on functional activities. Relatively many alternatives are possible if routines have not been established and the staff and behavior objects have not yet been selected. In the early life of a setting, maintenance actions will occur—indeed there may be numerous serious threats to the setting—but routine maintenance actions may not be established until the setting has achieved a degree of stability and members are achieving satisfactions from it. Then maintenance duties may become a significant subject of negotiation. Early negotiations on this subject are likely to be conditioned by the maintenance responsibilities that various staff members had previously assumed in the setting.

Negotiations regarding the functional activities in settings, like other negotiations in organizations, are affected by the cognitive and motivational characteristics of setting occupants. For example, founders with detailed cognitions of behavior-setting programs may be less willing to negotiate on how the setting will be structured. Staff members with exclusive or extensive working knowledge of aspects of the program will be more influential than less-informed staff. The nature and strength of staff motivations also will affect what is negotiated and the nature of the resolutions. For example, the way tasks are divided up into jobs and the way staff are assigned to jobs may be of major concern to staff members with strong preferences and aversions to certain tasks. Such concerns may arise from perceived fit between the task requirements and one's self- or professional image. Other factors such as commitment to the setting and dependency on it for meeting social and expressive needs may influence negotiations (cf. Weick, 1979b, p. 96).

Fitting together the diverse components of behavior settings to create a smoothly operating setting program requires many cycles of acting, interpreting, and remembering. Through a series of interactions, including small- and large-scale negotiations, staff members will adjust their individual interpretations, actions, and working knowledge (recollections) to be more congruent with those of their co-workers and clients. They will come to some agreement as to what aspects of the environment are appropriate to act upon, and which actions various persons will take to reduce uncertainty in these inputs. Tasks may also become differentiated into *Realwork*—duties that are the central responsibility of staff members—and other duties that interfere with these main activities (Van Maanen, 1977, p. 26–27).

The number of cycles that must occur before a setting program is operating smoothly depends on both personal and extrapersonal factors. Different types of settings have different behavioral requirements, and, as vocational testing efforts have shown, personal abilities and interests are related to success in performing setting tasks. Compatibility of interacting staff members on relevant personal characteristics also can be critical (cf. Steiner, 1972). Among the extrapersonal factors that lead to large numbers of cycles during the convergence stage of settings are intricate setting programs, large staffs, and diverse cause maps held by staff members.

Once the program of a new setting is working smoothly, the next important transition may be when new staff members replace or join the founding staff. All members of the founding staff are aware of alternative procedures that were considered or tested before routines were established. They recognize that many aspects of the current program could be changed or even eliminated. And they are likely to see nothing mysterious about a program they helped to develop. New staff members, in contrast, may learn only the practices that survived. They may thus regard their tasks as less changeable, particularly if they do not understand other aspects of the program. In the interests of efficiency, founding staff members may reinforce these conceptions. For the newcomers, then, the ratio of constructed to preexisting realities may be low.

Over time and generations of staff members—particularly if newcomers are always in the minority—how setting practices are regarded may evolve from "a way" to "our way" to "the way" to "the only possible way" (cf. Berger & Luckmann, 1967, pp. 53–67). In other words, preexisting realities become regarded as objective realities, and negotiation latitudes constrict accordingly. Of course, not all settings become so rigid. Whether they do depends on a variety of factors including those discussed earlier.

16.4.7. Growth and Differentiation of Settings

The functional activities in settings, and the social processes that produce them, are typically adjusted as a setting grows and matures. In this section I consider maturational changes in behavior settings.

Some insights into these changes can be derived from discussions of developmental processes of living systems at other levels, specifically, persons and organizations. The theoretical perspectives drawn on here are the Lewinian model of human development (Barker, Dembo, & Lewin, 1941) and on Katz and Kahn's open systems analysis of organizational growth (Katz & Kahn, 1978).

Theories of Human Development and Organizational Growth

Lewin stressed the increased differentiation over time of children's behaviors and cognitions. Behavior, he said, becomes more varied, more hierarchically organized, and more interdependent. Greater variety is seen in the types of activity, emotions, needs, interests and goals, and knowledge that children show over time. Greater organization of behavior is revealed in the development of hierarchically ordered sequences of actions: Children learn to pursue subgoals in order to achieve their primary goals, for example. Increased interdependence of behavior is the result of two opposing processes:

> Development seems to increase the number of relatively independent subparts of the person, and their degree of independence, thus decreasing the degree of unity of the individual. On the other hand, development involves integration which increases the unity of the person. (Barker, Dembo, & Lewin, 1941, p. 20)

Very similar processes are identified by Katz and Kahn at the organizational level: Organizations tend to become more differentiated by increases in the division of labor and number of hierarchical levels. Accompanying these developments are "processes that bring the system together for unified functioning" (Katz & Kahn, 1978, p. 29), that is, coordination and integration processes. Katz and Kahn add the observation that both specialization and coordination can be extended beyond the point of maximum return to the organization, a matter to which I will return shortly.

According to the Lewinian analysis, as children develop, their psychological environments or life spaces expands in several ways: in area, in the temporal dimension, and in degree of realism. More aspects of the environment are attended to. There is also a greater awareness of prior events and a greater concern for the extended future. Perceptions become more adjusted to realities (Barker, Dembo, & Lewin, 1941).

Katz and Kahn's (1978) presentation of growth stages in organizational structures is compatible with the Lewinian analysis and is somewhat more elaborated. They suggest that a converging organization is initially concerned with coordinating the tasks necessary for production (Stage 1). Once a primitive production structure has been established, managerial and maintenance subsystems are set up (Stage 2) to oversee production and to ensure that "people will stay within the system and will carry out their roles in a reliable fashion" (p. 72). At Stage 2, informal structures develop to meet the social and emotional needs of members—needs that are not met by the formal structures. In a statement reminiscent of Strauss's (1978) view of negotiation processes, Katz and Kahn note that members "interact, make decisions of their own, cooperate among themselves" (p. 73).

Greater concern with environmental conditions and events characterizes the third and final stage discussed by Katz and Kahn. Elaborated boundary subsystems develop for procuring materials and personnel, for disposing of products, and for creating and maintaining a favorable image of the organization in the larger community. Longer-term transactions with the environment are the focus of adaptive subsystems, which are devoted to assessing and promoting the ability of the organization to meet future environmental contingencies.

Application of the Theories to Behavior Settings

The developmental patterns that occur in particular settings or types of settings have not been empirically studied. It is likely, however, that these patterns will reflect not only internal maturational influences but also forces outside settings such as directives from authorities and growth of the parent organization (S. Kirmeyer, personal communication, December 1, 1982). Some possible developmental events suggested by the two theories reviewed above are considered in the next paragraphs.

After they have converged, behavior settings may become more differentiated in a number of ways. The variety of their functional activities and sense-making cycles can increase, and wider ranges of satisfactions may become available to setting occupants. The elaborations of functional activities may be more specialized and more hierarchically organized: Tasks may be grouped into subprograms that become the province of one or several staff members, whose interests and activities become more narrowly focused. Boundaries between the work domains of staff members may become clearer and firmer. Often such arrangements are coupled with a more hierarchical ordering of staff positions with respect to influence on the setting and responsibility for its functioning.

With these developments, the founder's influence on day-to-day operations is likely to erode. Responsibilities may be delegated and more formal procedures established. As they cope with the realities of enacting a setting program, founders may also have to revise their dreams and expectations for the setting (cf. Adizes, 1979; Kimberly, 1980; Sarason, 1972).

Routines develop in settings to meet the social and emotional needs of occupants. Such routines often are not directly supportive of the functional activities, but may contribute indirectly through increased group cohesion or personal dependencies. In some instances, "side programs"—regular routines serving functions that are secondary to, but compatible with, the main program—may appear (cf. Wicker, 1981). Examples would be good-natured banter and horseplay during work breaks in a machine shop (Roy, 1959), or informal exchanges of information around the office coffeepot before work begins.

Concern with conditions beyond the setting is an early preoccupation of founders who must assemble the resources needed to converge a setting. Once the essential components are in place, attention is likely to shift to events and objects within the setting, particularly as they bear on establishing the setting program. Both the range and reality of such stimuli are explored. One consequence of such actions is an increased awareness of past events. In Weick's (1979b) terms, the staff's cause maps become more elaborated through interactions within the setting.

One way that settings differentiate is by elaborating their maintenance circuits. Different types of threats to the program become the province of different staff members. Generally, the range of threats with which a staff member must deal roughly corresponds with his or her hierarchical position in the setting. The manager of a restaurant, for example, will be concerned with more kinds of threats to that setting than will the cook.

When a setting is first getting organized, staff members are likely to take a narrowed time and space perspective: "When the realities of today require solution in order for tomorrow to go smoothly, it is not easy to keep in mind and deal with the crucial past and what appears to be a distant future"

(Sarason, 1972, p. 87). Pressing events within the setting seem more important than the past or future or what is happening outside the setting.

Once a setting's program is functioning smoothly and procedures have been established for dealing with internal threats, adaptive mechanisms concerned with the future and with environmental events may become increasingly prominent. Contemplation of the future may lead to more refined procedures for ensuring continued supply of needed resources, for continued disposal of setting products, and for demonstrating the setting's legitimacy to the parent organization or to the larger community.

More attention may also be devoted to events outside the setting as staff members realize that the setting's long-range survival depends on future developments beyond its boundaries, and on how the setting responds to these changes. Procedures for obtaining systematic data on current setting activities and on relevant environmental trends may be established. These concerns typically would be in the domain of the person in charge of the setting.

Physical growth may accompany many of the changes in settings described above. Settings may become physically larger by increases in space, equipment, staff, clients, and volume of inputs and outputs processed. Such growth may temporarily disturb the normal synomorphy (fit between behaviors and physical features) of settings, but it will generally be restored. For example, addition of more specialized equipment or staff may require more space, or new floor arrangements. Temporal expansion, that is, extending hours of operation, is another type of setting growth. Even successful settings do not grow indefinitely, however; they may become too large and unwieldy. Rather they are likely to subdivide, either by duplicating themselves or by subdividing along functional lines to produce additional, more specialized settings (cf. Katz & Kahn, 1978).

An example of the creation of a new setting by differentiation has been provided by Roger Barker (personal communication, October 18, 1983):

When we first went to Yoredale there was a two-man barber shop which, in addition to barbering, sold toiletries and a few antiques and collectibles in which the proprietor was interested. As demand for the articles increased, the shop was redesigned with one whole side of shelves devoted to objects for sale. Still the proprietor and his son barbered and sold, but later the neighboring room, separated by a thick, stone wall and with a display window, was rented for the sales goods and a shop assistant installed. So a gift shop was born as a separate setting. This development covered a period of, maybe, ten years.

16.4.8. Balancing Stability and Flexibility

Growth and differentiation generally characterize the convergence stage of settings, and may also be present during the continued existence stage. For mature settings, however, another dynamic may be more important: the need to maintain stability while preserving flexibility.

The Organizing Perspective

Organizations need to deal effectively with current conditions and to retain the capacity to adapt to new conditions that may exist in the future. As Weick's organizing model recognizes, too much attention to the current situation may lead to excessive stability—the establishment of many intricate behavioral routines or "standard operating procedures" carried out by specialists and coordinated by several layers of management (cf. Sarason, 1972, p. 143). Under such conditions, adaptations to new contingencies are hard to accomplish. Excessive flexibility can also be a threat, particularly to current activities. Without orderly procedures, organizations may not be able to process inputs or regulate their internal functioning—they may lose their identity, and fail in the short term (cf. Katz & Kahn, 1978, Weick, 1979b).

Weick's prescription for this dilemma is simultaneously to preserve both stability and flexibility in different parts of the system. More specifically, he suggests that organizations treat their retained wisdom as valid for some purposes and as invalid for others. For example, in their actions, staff members might presume their cause maps are accurate and deal with events in the usual fashion, but when interpreting the results of their actions, they might employ new assumptions. Or actions might be guided by new assumptions, and interpretations by old ones. The result of such "split usage of retained content" is to enable the organization "to fit into a particular environment, generate immediate activities, and still detect the necessity for altered actions to improve that fit" (Weick, 1979b, p. 219).

Weick notes the difficulty of putting this prescription into practice: "routines, standard operating procedures, and grooved thinking (Steinbruner, 1974) work against the organization being able to discredit its past knowledge" (Weick, 1979b, p. 225). Yet organizations that are able to doubt their wisdom will

have more timely environmental knowledge and a greater ability to discover and respond appropriately to complex environmental conditions.

Application of the Organizing Perspective to Behavior Settings

Behavior settings also need to maintain a balance between stability and flexibility. However, settings are somewhat simpler than large, multiple-setting organizations and thus are more limited in the degree to which they can change and still maintain their identities. As noted, setting stability is emphasized in behavior-setting theory. But excessive stability or rigidity can limit a setting's ability to adapt. For example, if jobs or task assignments in a setting are rigidly specified, the setting can be incapacitated by the absence of a key worker.

Flexibility in settings might be preserved by deliberately introducing procedures that follow Weick's admonition to discredit retained wisdom. For example, even if necessity does not require it, the grouping of tasks into jobs and the job assignments of staff members might be periodically juggled. The order of processing inputs could be changed. Different (perhaps older or newer) technologies might be introduced into the setting program. The priorities assigned to various setting inputs might be shifted, and familiar inputs might be treated in unfamiliar ways.

16.4.9. Decline and Divergence

Thus far I have considered the upside of behavior-setting development. Settings, we have noted, grow and differentiate, and they cope with the present and prepare for the future. There is also a downside, to which I now turn. Settings also may wane and eventually fail.

Unfortunately there is relatively little research on the decline and termination of social systems at the level of groups or organizations. The extant literature consists mostly of case studies of the failure of large corporations, and prescriptions for managing retrenchment in social service agencies and educational institutions. This literature is of limited use in formulating a general analysis of the decline and divergence of behavior settings.

I will consider behavior-setting decline to exist whenever a setting program suffers from relatively long-term interference or deficiencies, or when changes necessary for setting survival are not implemented into its program. In general, the longer a setting program is hindered and the longer the delay in adjusting to it, the more serious the decline that the setting will suffer. A setting has diverged when its program ceases to be carried out within specifiable time and place boundaries, and its configuration of components has been dismantled.

Even if there were detailed theories on the decline of organizations, their applicability to behavior settings still might be problematic. As I note in a later section, higher-level social systems generally are more differentiated (i.e., they have more and more varied components) than are lower-level systems. One implication is that during periods of decline multisetting organizations have more ways of changing than do single settings. For example, an electronics firm whose product line of home computers is selling poorly could set up a larger sales and distribution system, increase its advertising budget for the computers, or eliminate all of the settings that make and distribute the product. In a setting where the computers are assembled, there are fewer options. The changes that are made cannot radically change the behavior-setting program, or the setting will no longer exist. It cannot, for example, become a research laboratory and be the same setting. A different setting using some of the same components, perhaps the space or personnel, could be created, of course.

A different factor limits the usefulness of theories at levels of analysis below behavior settings. Life expectancy of organisms tends to be negatively related to age: The older an organism is, the shorter its life expectancy. But in social systems, including behavior settings, essential components can often be replaced and, in general, life expectancy is higher, the older the system (Miller, 1972, p. 142). Thus theories that stress the degenerative nature of aging have limited applicability to settings.

In spite of these limitations, it is possible to extract from the present conceptual framework and a few other sources some preliminary observations about the waning and demise of behavior settings.

Sources of Setting Decline and Divergence

The following paragraphs describe some factors that can contribute to the failure of a behavior setting. It is generally easier to name possible causes of setting divergence, as we do here, than to identify the particular reasons that a given setting diverged. Explanations for why a setting failed may, for example, depend on such factors as whether the analysts are staff members of the defunct setting or outsiders, or whether they come from the public or private sector. One reviewer of the literature on organizational decline has noted that in private enterprise reduced profits are usually attributed to internal factors such as poor management rather than to environmental conditions such as a depressed economy. In contrast, in the public sector, declining resources are often attributed to an unfavorable environment rather than to internal performance (Whetten, 1980, pp. 372–373).

The sources of decline and divergence I will consider are categories of events and conditions such as resource deficiencies and intersetting links derived from the present conceptual framework. Although these sources are mentioned sequentially, they are in many cases highly interdependent: A setting resource may be lacking because a link with another setting was severed. Longer lists of specific shortages and constraints within these categories could be generated, but that seems unnecessary. Most, if not all, of the measures of decline that one might think of — such as volume of business, staff morale and involvement, quality of decision making, and condition of equipment — would fall within categories to be discussed. Of course, in any empirical study of setting decline, more specific indicators appropriate to particular settings would have to be developed.

Prolonged absence of any essential setting resource will lead to setting divergence. I considered several kinds of deficiencies in Section 16.3.2, including shortages of knowledgeable staff, raw materials, and space. For example, early departure of a setting's founder or of key founding staff members may lead to the immediate decline or demise of a setting (Sarason, 1972, chapter 7). Settings may also suffer from a lack of timely information about conditions within or beyond their boundaries such as depressed sales or unfavorable market conditions. Catastrophic events such as epidemics, floods, earthquakes, fires, and bombings can also temporarily or permanently terminate behavior settings by removing some or all essential resources (cf. Miller, 1971a, 1972).

Settings are impaired and may even fail when their operating, maintenance, or adaptive circuits falter or break down. Most behavior-setting programs are intricate — if their operating circuits are to function, the required resources not only must be present, they must be appropriately configured and work properly. Thus absenteeism, employee burnout, poorly designed workshops, untrained workers, and defective equipment may be symptomatic of setting decline.

Maintenance circuits normally counteract threats to or deficiencies in operating circuits. If corrective actions are not taken, the internal coherence that characterizes a setting program may disappear and the setting may fail. For example, if the disruptive students in a high school English class are not dealt with, the teacher may lose control and no instruction will take place. If maintenance circuits are weak or absent, settings may not survive due to excessive flexibility. An example would be a failing auto repair shop whose management tolerates mechanics who do not keep regular hours, who answer the telephone or return calls only when they have nothing else to do, who forget to itemize parts they install, and who freely loan out the shop's tools.

A setting also can suffer if its adaptive circuits fail to sense significant environmental changes, or to implement internal changes necessary to cope with the environmental events. For example, a retail store may be jeopardized when its owner, unaware that the town's major employer is about to shut down, places a large order for merchandise. Excessive stability can also be a source of decline: The manager of an independent bank may find that the bank's staff and facilities lack the flexibility required to deal with the many complexities resulting from banking deregulation.

Unfavorable conditions and events outside the setting constitute another class of events that can cause setting decline and divergence. Some environmental influences are general conditions in the larger social and physical world that affect many settings. For example, cultural practices and laws may restrict or prohibit privately owned shops, worship services of particular faiths, or liquor stores. Other environmental influences are more immediate and direct such as events affecting the links among settings. Suppliers may fail to provide needed goods; superiors in the organization may cut budgets or even summarily terminate a setting. (I will further consider environmental influences in a later section.)

Responses to Setting Decline or Threat of Divergence

Most managers and staff members would probably assign high priority to preserving the settings they occupy. However, the way they respond to decline will vary depending on their understanding of how the current state of affairs came about and what can be done about it.

When a resource deficiency appears to be responsible for the decline, managers and staff members will, if it seems feasible, try to locate and bring in the needed resource. Such efforts may lead to new links with other settings. For example, a federally funded legal services agency whose budget has been reduced may seek financial support from corporate sponsors or local government, and it may approach successful law firms to solicit volunteer work (cf. Gilmore, 1983).

If a needed resource is not restored, staff members may temporarily attempt to get by with what they have. As we have noted, people in understaffed settings may work harder or put in longer hours (Barker, 1968). The positive outcomes that we have identified with understaffing such as increased feelings of challenge and involvement may not continue if the understaffing condition is severe or long lasting. Workers may come to feel exploited, cynical, and alienated. Temporary shortages of other resources may lead setting managers to stockpile and ration their existing supplies, and to undertake a search for any slack resources that can be drawn on (Levine, 1978).

Chronic resource deficiencies almost invariably force changes in the internal operations of a setting. For example, reduced budget allocations or declining sales volume may lead managers and staff members to review the setting program in search of inefficient, unprofitable, or nonessential activities that can be corrected or eliminated. A social service agency may reduce the number of hours that a receptionist is available to schedule appointments, or an academic department may decide that its secretaries can no longer type research reports for faculty members. Setting programs may also be reorganized in ways that make better use of limited resources such as reducing job specialization, increasing the autonomy of staff members, replacing more responsibility on clients or customers, introducing new monitoring procedures, and automating (cf. Hirschhorn & Andrews, 1983; Sarason, 1972, chapter 6). In some cases, reorganization of setting programs is tied to changes in other settings. This would be the case when two field offices of a mental health agency are consolidated, or when a photocopy service relocates in a bookstore (cf. Gilmore & Snow, 1983).

Setting decline associated with faulty operating, maintenance, or adaptive circuits may also lead to reorganization of settings. When production lags, when errors are not caught and corrected, or when significant environmental changes are not noticed or responded to appropriately, those in charge may redesign the setting program.

16.4.10. Interventions in Settings

A somewhat broader perspective on the reconstruction of social systems is provided by Benson's dialectical view of organizations (Benson, 1977). This perspective links the previous discussions of the fluidity of settings and setting decline with the present topic of setting interventions, and with the following section on the context of behavior settings.

The Dialectical Model

According to the dialectical view:

> social arrangements [such as organizations and behavior settings] are created from the basically concrete, mundane tasks confronting people in their everyday life. Relationships are formed, roles are constructed, institutions are built from the encounters and confrontations of people in their daily round of life. (Benson, 1977, p. 3)

The social systems that result from such interactions may seem "fixed and permanent" but are in reality only "temporary, arbitrary patterns" properly regarded as "one of many possibilities" (p. 3). Present arrangements not only can, but should, be transformed to develop their "latent possibilities." Social scientists have an ethical obligation to contribute to the reconstruction of social systems—their aim should be to develop new arrangements that "liberate human potential" (p. 6).

One condition that may lead to the reconstruction of existing social structures is *contradictions*. The concept is not well defined, but apparently it refers to potentially disruptive inconsistencies and inequities in existing social arrangements. Procedures that lead to the exploitation of one group of participants by another (e.g., of captive clients by service providers) would indicate a contradiction. Some contradictions within organizations appear to have internal origins such as conflicts among people charged with different responsibilities, such as sales and production. However, the most significant contradictions can be traced to conditions beyond the organization—to larger institutional and societal arrangements. Examples include organizations charged with multiple, incompatible functions, such as a prison charged with rehabilitating and controlling inmates or an organization whose structure reflects fundamental conflicts in the social order, for example, racial inequities (Benson, 1977).

The dialectical model's emphasis on conditions beyond the focal social system—on historical factors, on multiple, interconnected links of organizations, and on the importance of underlying social structures—is congruent with the present view of behavior-setting context, which will be presented shortly. In the following section I consider briefly two kinds of interventions: those that create new settings and those that alter the internal workings of existing settings.

Application of the Dialectical Model to Behavior Settings

Like other social scientists, ecological psychologists have a responsibility to draw on their knowledge to improve conditions and opportunities of participants in the social systems they study. They should participate in "the free and creative reconstruction of social arrangements on the basis of a reasoned analysis of both the limits and the potentials of present social forms" (Benson, 1977, p. 5).

This admonition by Benson is congruent with the emphasis in community and health psychology on *preventive interventions*—programs of various kinds that are introduced into a community or organization to help people adjust to new events or avoid serious problems in their lives. The need for new behavior settings often becomes evident in the course of research on social systems. For example, Kelly's (1979) ecological study of two high schools in the Detroit area yielded several proposals: Discussion groups should be formed for adolescents during their first year of high school. These groups would provide opportunities for students to develop their interpersonal skills, voice complaints about school matters and search for constructive solutions, and interact with a school adult on a regular basis (Newman, 1979, p. 148). The number of school activity settings should be increased to the point that nonparticipating students are drawn in (Todd, 1979, pp. 184–185).

A positive example of researchers' intervention in a social system is Chavis, Stucky, and Wandersman's (1983) assistance to block organizations in a Nashville neighborhood; these organizations are intended to deal with residents' common concerns, such as street safety and quality of sanitation services. After a series of investigations of these groups, the researchers carefully organized a new setting—a workshop in which they communicated their findings and assisted groups in formulating action plans. They continued to consult with the groups after the workshop was held.

Epidemiological research suggests that participation in community settings is associated with lower mortality rates, even when variables such as initial health status and socioeconomic status are controlled (Berkman & Syme, 1979). These findings have led community and health psychologists to propose the formation of a variety of settings that foster social support. Two types of such settings are those that provide training to nonprofessionals (e.g., bartenders and hairdressers, who are frequently asked for advice in their work settings), and those that provide contacts with peers who are facing similar problems. Groups may be established to promote adjustments to heart attacks, divorce, remarriage, parenthood, widowhood, and other significant life events (Gottlieb, 1981).

Interventions also can be made in existing settings. One specific proposal is the development of a technology aimed at improving setting functioning and increasing the satisfaction and well-being of setting occupants. This technology could draw on the concepts, methods, and findings of ecological psychology. Such a development is clearly within Barker's vision of the field: He reports being pleased with his colleagues' success in applying his work to practical problems (Barker, 1979b, p. 2157). And more recently he has stated that "an important task for psychology [is] to provide expertise for persons desiring to create, alter, and choose behavior settings and for persons who are subordinate setting components" (Barker, Chapter 40, this volume). Before innovations are introduced, the setting's operations and context must be analyzed, ideally by persons who are not regular occupants. Some steps in this assessment stage have previously been described:

> Behavior-setting technologists would observe the setting...during its busy, normal, and slack periods; obtain the perspectives of both staff and clients on the setting—its functions, any dysfunctions they see, and the satisfactions and dissatisfactions the setting provides; and where possible, spend some time actually participating in the various staff and client roles....The technologists would also scrutinize the required behaviors, physical facilities and their arrangements, standard operating procedures, and workers' abilities to identify any instances of poor fit among these aspects of the setting. (Wicker, 1979, p. 763)

The context (history, present links with other settings, and general social conditions) would also be studied—how the setting came into being, the expectations of its founders, significant conflicts in its past, how the functions it currently serves were met prior to its convergence, its traditional and current connections with other settings, changes in relevant qualities of its environment.

In the assessment phase, the technologists should discover significant aspects of the setting and its environment that are not attended to by setting occupants. The outsiders will have different retention systems, including grounded concepts and hypotheses regarding how behavior settings function and change (cf. Weick, 1979b, p. 177). They will also be "outside the power fields of the settings to be changed" (Barker, Chapter 40, this volume).

From their initial assessments, behavior-setting technologists would identify facets of the focal setting where modifications are feasible. They would design and propose intervention packages, and would modify them on the basis of local feedback. Intervention

plans should be flexible, and they should include procedures for evaluation and options for further change after the technologists have left. The revised plans would then be enacted and their effects continuously monitored. The elements of intervention plans that obviously do not work would be dropped after a reasonable trial period. Those that seem to be successful would be analyzed carefully and interpreted in light of existing concepts and hypotheses.

Whether a technology of behavior settings actually develops and what forms it will take remain to be seen. One promising development is the *evolutionary experimentation/social learning paradigm* (Dunn, 1971; Studer, 1978, 1980). In Studer's adaptation of the paradigm, setting events are observed, analyzed, and compared with explicit objectives. Modifications are systematically introduced into settings and their effects are assessed. A distinctive feature of the paradigm is its recognition that environmental goals are expressions of values worked out in social interactions. Drawing on critical theory (Habermas, 1971; Bernstein, 1976), Studer (1980) suggests the development of a *reflective–dialectical methodology* that fosters broad participation in environmental decision making and planning. The goal of the methodology is to improve people's environments—and thereby their lives—through self-conscious reflection on current social and political conditions.

16.5. THE CONTEXT OF BEHAVIOR SETTINGS

Several times in the preceding discussions of setting resources and internal dynamics, I have referred to the larger context in which settings exist. I noted, for example, that essential resources are drawn into settings from the outside, that images for new settings depends on founders' past experiences in other settings, and that adaptive mechanisms require an analysis of events beyond a setting's boundaries.

The influence of external forces on behavior settings has been acknowledged but not emphasized in the traditional work (cf. Barker, 1960, pp. 18–21; Barker & Schoggen, 1973, pp. 67–79; Barker & Wright, 1950, pp. 14–16, 72–73; Barker & Wright, 1955/1971, pp. 50–53). In both theory and method, most attention has been paid to the internal features of settings. For example, only two of the numerous standard descriptors of settings represent extrasetting links: One reflects the degree of local autonomy in decisions affecting the setting, and the other is a classification of the type of authority—such as government, private enterprise, or voluntary associations—that primarily influences the setting program (cf. Barker, 1968). The lack of emphasis on setting contexts has led some observers to infer that settings are rather closed systems.

By contrast, the present framework recognizes the open-system nature of settings—they depend on events, conditions, and entities beyond their boundaries. In this section I consider three aspects of setting context: general environmental factors such as cultural and economic forces; setting history; and setting networks (see the last row in Table 16.1). I begin by listing some general forces that operate in human social life, and by illustrating their influence on behavior settings. The presentation draws on discussions of organizational environments by Hall (1977), Stinchcombe (1965), and Katz and Kahn (1978).

According to the view presented here, external factors are not merely sources of change of behavior settings—they are also sources of stability. Contextual supports often provide continuity and conditions that help preserve settings just as internal regulation mechanisms do.

16.5.1. General Contextual Factors

The following are among the contextual factors that significantly influence the creation and life course of behavior settings:

1. Value patterns and other cultural conditions
2. Political and legal conditions
3. Economic conditions
4. Technological and informational conditions
5. Demographic and geographic conditions

These factors are, of course, interdependent, and they fluctuate over time. Each has broad (e.g., international, national) as well as more local (regional, community, organizational) aspects. The broader influences are emphasized here.

The Factors Considered

Prevailing social values affect whether certain types of settings are conceived of, planned, and established, and whether they survive. Community values may, for example, determine the fate of planned libraries, birth control clinics, trash recycling centers, and exercise classes. Also, the norms shared by most members of a society or culture contribute to the stability of settings. Prior cultural knowledge about matters such as accepting orders from designated authorities and assuming and sharing responsibility facilitates the transactions within settings.

Political and legal conditions can preserve or disrupt existing settings and can influence the creation of new settings. For example, regulations may govern the serving of liquor in restaurants and the prescription of drugs in clinics. After elections and revolutions, behavior settings may be affected by new mandates or ideologies; for example, health service systems may be changed in ways that influence numerous settings.

Virtually all settings are affected by economic conditions. In hard times, small businesses that lack reserves may have to close their doors and large corporations may cut back certain operations. More fundamentally, a stable money-based economic system makes possible many behavior settings that otherwise could not exist without such a convenient medium of exchange (Stinchcombe, 1965, p. 152).

New technological information—whether it deals with physical or social developments—often leads to the creation of new types of settings and the modification of existing ones. Examples of recent forms based on new knowledge include video game arcades, retail computer stores, behavior modification clinics, and personnel assessment centers. The programs of many settings in organizations such as banks, police departments, health clinics, and manufacturing plants also have changed with technological advances. From a global and historical perspective, the most fundamental technological/informational influence on organizations and settings is probably the level of literacy in a population (Stinchcombe, 1965, p. 151).

The characteristics of the people living in an area and the area's climate, physical features, and natural resources are important factors in the emergence and continued existence of behavior settings. For example, age distributions affect the number of academic classes and nursing homes that are found in a community. Historically, urbanization has contributed to the founding of new organizational forms: When knowledge and experience are relatively concentrated, there is a greater chance that new kinds of settings will be imagined, created, and sustained (Stinchcombe, 1965, pp. 151–152). The types of settings that are supported in a region or community are also affected by natural and artificial geographic features, such as annual snowfall, grasslands, and lakes (cf. Harloff, Gump, & Campbell, 1981).

Context Issues

It may be somewhat misleading to state, as I did previously, that general contextual factors "influence" behavior settings. This could be taken to mean that we are dealing with relatively distinct entities, one of which acts on the other. A more accurate image is of a social fabric that includes behavior settings as well as the kinds of forces I have considered. Behavior settings as we know them depend on numerous conditions that we often take for granted such as widespread literacy and relative political and economic stability. Yet at the same time, settings may contribute to these conditions—they may serve to advance literacy, and to sustain political and economic practices. Settings have their own internal dynamics and to a degree serve their own purposes, yet they are simultaneously part of the interplay of events and forces that make up the larger social world. Exploration of intersystem relationships is a promising area for further inquiry (cf. Benson, 1977; Sampson, 1981).

Another issue deserves comment here: Should we define the context of a setting in terms of objective events (as disinterested observers would interpret them) or in terms of participants' perceptions? If a setting is to respond to the environmental forces described previously, those forces or their consequences must be sensed by people who are in the setting, or in the case of converging settings, by setting planners. These individuals do not—and could not—attend to all relevant environmental events, or even the most significant ones. The past knowledge and sensitivities of the participants direct their attention and actions toward certain events and away from others. To some extent, then, the environments responded to are constructions or interpretations—and not "real" environments (Starbuck, 1976; Weick, 1979b).

In the long run, however, the interpretations of at least some environmental events must correspond rather closely to how they are regarded in the larger social world or the setting will not survive. A small business with no reserves and a substantial debt cannot, for example, continue to operate if its proprietor ignores or misconstrues a negative cash flow. Some settings may require more accurate readings than others, however, and the particular events that must be accurately perceived and interpreted also vary for different settings.

16.5.2. Setting History

Any given behavior setting occupies a particular niche in a continually changing world. This niche is partially defined by the general conditions just discussed, but it can be more fully specified by considering the setting's history and how the setting is linked with other settings. The historical dimensions of behavior settings have not been considered by ecologi-

cal psychologists.[5] Here I merely suggest the importance of this topic and sketch one or two factors that might be considered. Setting history is a promising area for future research.

A historical analysis of a setting should consider (1) events and other settings that contributed to the setting's establishment and maintenance, and (2) antecedent settings that previously served—and may still serve—the same or similar functions now provided by the focal setting. Many of the events in such an analysis will have occurred before the setting's convergence.

To give a brief example, the relevant history of a community swimming pool might include these facts: Children formerly swam in a nearby lake whose waters were polluted and where no lifeguard was present; except for the town's tavern, there were few other recreational facilities available to the town's youth; and the state provided matching funds to local communities for construction of public pools. The analysis might also consider the role of other settings such as public meetings of citizens to promote the building of a pool, a bond election authorizing it, and organizing meetings of a pool authority to oversee its operation.

Settings that are created as a result of the growth of a parent organization would have rather different histories. Growth sometimes occurs by duplicating existing settings: A successful restaurant might be copied in another part of town, or in certain franchises nationwide. Sometimes new settings are formed when antecedent settings are split, making the new entities more specialized. An example would be the division of a personnel office into separate offices for salaried and hourly employees. Reorganizations of parent organizations, such as often occur during organizational mergers, can result in new setting programs that combine activities in different ways (Katz & Kahn, 1978, pp. 78–80).

Additional considerations in the emergence of settings have been noted by Sarason (1972, chapter 2): When new settings are created within a parent organization, participants in existing settings may regard the new unit as a competitor for organizational resources. And if the new setting takes over activities formerly served by other settings, it may be resented by the staff whose functions have been taken over. Moreover, the creation of a new setting may be taken as an indication that existing settings are in some way inadequate. Different sectors within the organization may support and oppose the founding of the new setting, depending on how it is perceived to affect their interests.

When a new setting is not part of a larger organizational structure, its emergence may also stimulate mixed reactions for reasons similar to those above. The new setting may be seen as a threat to settings of the same type, either because it can draw off customers and clients, or because its emergence may seem to signal shortcomings in the services of existing settings. On the other hand, if a new setting provides visibility and attracts people to an area, it may be regarded favorably by staff of neighboring settings that are not competitors. Similarly, settings that provide needed services to areas that have previously been poorly served also may meet with approval.

16.5.3. Setting Linkages

To some organizational theorists, the most important and salient aspects of an organization's environment are the other organizations with which it has direct transactions (cf. Perrow, 1970, p. 121; Pfeffer & Salancik, 1978). A parallel statement could be made for behavior settings, whose links with other settings were alluded to in the preceding sections. In the following paragraphs I consider three facets of this topic: the structural arrangements by which settings are related to one another and to larger social systems; the qualitatively different kinds of relationships that connect settings; and practical issues in analyzing setting networks.

Nested Hierarchical Systems

The question of how behavior settings are linked to larger social systems is complicated by the fact that, although many settings are components of a larger parent organization, some are not. Those attached to parent organizations are easier to deal with conceptually; they fit the description of nested hierarchical systems, in which each higher level is composed of systems of lower levels. A progression of living systems would include cells, tissues, organs, persons, behavior settings (or small groups), organizations, societies, and supranational systems (Miller, 1971b).

In this progression, the higher of two adjacent levels is the proximal environment of the lower level. Barker (1960, 1968, Chapter 40, this volume) has stated that, although any two such adjacent systems are highly interdependent, they operate according to different principles or laws. For example, he asserts that, even though behavior settings are dependent upon people, and people's behaviors are shaped by settings, an adequate explanation for the dynamics of behavior settings cannot be derived solely from psychological principles. Similarly, setting dynamics are insufficient to explain all human experience and behavior. To understand settings or persons—or any other system level—one must seek principles that apply to that particular level.[6]

Applying Barker's reasoning one step up in the system progression—to settings and organizations—produces this view: Behavior settings and their parent organizations mutually constrain and are constrained by one another. The principles that explain dynamics at one level can provide only limited information about the other. Knowledge of behavior settings is helpful in understanding some aspects of organizational functioning, but insufficient to explain other aspects. Similarly, principles of organizational functioning may provide some insights into how settings work, but they leave other events unexplained. For example, the level of staffing of the various settings in a manufacturing plant may help explain its overall productivity, but it does not explain decisions to drop or add product lines. And knowledge of how an agency retrenchment plan was drawn up might explain some events in the agency's settings, such as which persons are relieved of duty, but not other events, such as the ways settings cope with understaffing. A fuller understanding of settings, and of organizations, is possible when each is considered on its own terms, and not in terms of the other level.

Incidentally, these extrapolations of Barker's analysis of hierarchical systems seem most appropriate when organizations and settings differ considerably in scale. That is, the argument that different laws apply to settings and organizations seems more valid when the organizations are relatively large firms of agencies having (1) multiple lines of authority and (2) so many behavior settings that some members of the organization rarely interact personally with other members.

Statements about adjacent systems do not fit the case of free-standing settings that are themselves organizations, for example, independent retail sales and service operations such as hair styling salons, and stationery stores. There seems to be no obviously appropriate proximal unit for single-setting organizations. Miller's (1971b) next higher level, societies, seems too large a step. Nor does the literature on organizational environments provide a solution—it deals almost exclusively with qualities of the environment, such as turbulence, munificence, and heterogeneity, rather than with its structure (cf. Aldrich, 1979, chapter 3; Katz & Kahn, 1978, chapter 5). One possible way to deal with this issue is to consider as the meaningful environment of a single-setting organization other settings with which it has direct transactions. Such groupings are discussed later in the chapter.

Nearly Decomposable Systems

Relationships between adjacent systems may not be as symmetrical as the preceding discussion implies. Lower-level systems tend to have less varied components and programs (Barker, 1960, p. 23) and to be more internally coherent than their suprasystems. In hierarchic systems, the interactions within subsystems are typically stronger and more frequent than interactions between subsystems. Such systems are nearly decomposable in the short run—their subsystems are relatively independent of one another. And, in the long run, the subsystems have only an aggregate dependence on one another (Simon, 1962).

Compared to multisetting organizations, behavior settings have fewer and less varied components, narrower repertoires, and stronger internal ties. Settings are relatively autonomous, self-regulated entities. Their unity derives from highly interdependent relationships among human and nonhuman components within the setting, and relative independence of events outside the setting (Barker, 1968, pp. 16–17).

This configuration of hierarchic systems helps explain the stability of living systems including organizations. In a system whose parts are semiautonomous and loosely connected, subsystems can respond directly and quickly to local environmental forces. The impact of such forces need not reverberate through the entire system. Systemwide responses to environmental change are less likely to occur than subsystem responses, and they are likely to be slower since they depend upon the reaction times of several subsystems (Glassman, 1973). A caveat should be issued: Although subsystems often have a wide latitude in their adaptive responses to environmental events, they are nonetheless constrained in their responses by other subsystems to which they are linked. These constraints may be sufficient to give the casual observer an impression that the overall system is responding with a "unity of purpose" (Aldrich & Whetten, 1981, p. 388).

Behavior settings serve to stabilize an organization by absorbing environmental forces that affect them. These forces include contextual events originating in other settings of the organization, as well as events outside the organization. Events that cannot be adequately dealt with by a given setting may spill over or be relayed to other settings without necessarily affecting the entire organization. If the entire organization is involved, responses will be slowed by the need for different settings to coordinate their actions.

To illustrate, decreased sales in the sporting goods department of a large retail store might lead the staff to sell more aggressively. Or the department might enlist the help of the store's advertising office to promote sporting goods. Decreased sales in many departments might lead to a storewide promotion, which would require more coordination than a promotion for a single department. If sales continued to be disappointing, a storewide program to cut costs might be instituted, forcing all departments to reduce expenditures. Cost cutting in every department might indicate a directed organizationwide effort, but the degree to which it was implemented and the particular actions taken could still be localized.

Behavior Setting Couplings

Loose coupling is a term often used to describe the links between semiautonomous subsystems. A somewhat more suitable term—one that allows for stronger as well as weaker links—is *strength of coupling*. There are two facets to coupling strength: (1) the number of qualitatively different linkages between subsystems; and (2) the strength of those linkages (Glassman, 1973). I consider below some of the qualitatively different ways that behavior settings are linked. I will continue the discussion of hierarchic systems, looking specifically at three implications of the strength of coupling imagery for understanding behavior settings and their context.

Perhaps the most significant implication is that relatively small units such as behavior settings are appropriate for understanding many important workings of organizations. Behavior settings are tightly coupled internally. They are stable and capable of being assembled into organizations that are so complex no single person can understand them. Small units of analysis reveal and perpetuate a wide variety of organizational phenomena (paraphrased from Weick, 1979b, p. 236; Weick, however, prefers an even smaller unit called the *double interact*). However, from Barker's analysis of hierarchies it also seems likely that other important facets of organizations can be known only by looking at organizations as units.

A second implication is that loosely coupled behavior settings, as they respond to local environmental events, also serve important sensing and testing functions for the parent organization. Collectively, such settings interpret, respond to, and store knowledge about a wide range of external conditions. During times of rapid environmental change, successful

Table 16.2. Examples of Links Between Behavior Settings

Resource inputs:
   A retail store that depends on drop-in customers is tied to the pedestrian trafficway just outside its door.
   An insurance agency relies on an employment agency to recruit and screen its clerical personnel.
   Behavior settings maintain links with suppliers of equipment, parts, supplies, raw materials, and sale goods, as well as
      with the settings that provide transportation for them.
   A setting's need for more space requires dealing with the corporation's facilities management office.
   Budget allocations are made to various city deparments by the budget office.
   Stock brokerage offices maintain nearly instantaneous informational links with stock exchanges.

Social influence:
   In bureaucratic agencies, offices are linked to superordinate and subordinate offices by the directives they receive and
      send.
   Restaurants are regulated by health inspectors, fire departments, sales tax revenue offices, and in some cases, immigra
      tion authorities.
   Work practices in a shipyard are guided by agreements with several trade unions.
   Settings whose programs are in conflict with neighborhood or community values may be eliminated or changed through
      public hearings, special elections, or close police department scrutiny.

Product outputs:
   A wholesale distributor transfers automobile tires to retail businesses.
   Assembly line workshops that complete part of a product are closely tied to the setting where the product goes next.
   In a high school, the French I class serves as a "feeder" for the French II class.
   Waste products of a manufacturing process are transferred to another area of the plant for storage.

adaptations of individual settings can be used as models or as sources of ideas for other settings—provided there are intersetting communication links. Localized failures to adapt can occur without the entire organization being jeopardized (Weick, 1976, pp. 6–8).

Third, while there are potentially many links between behavior settings, an adequate description may be obtained by attending to relatively few of them. As Simon (1962, pp. 476–477) notes, in most systems there are practical constraints that preclude simultaneous interactions among large numbers of subsystems. Only part of any setting program involves connections outside the setting's boundaries, and the number of different linkages is similarly limited by the program.

Types of Intersetting Links

I have just noted that at any given time there may be only a few critical links between any pair of settings. But over a diverse group of settings, as would be found in any complex organization, many different kinds of links may be significant. It would probably not be worthwhile to attempt a comprehensive, atheoretical listing of the numerous ways behavior settings are interrelated. I can, however, illustrate the breadth of setting linkages that may be important in particular instances.

Three categories of links can be derived from open-systems theory (cf. Duncan, 1972; Katz & Kahn, 1978; Miller, 1971a, 1972). One type of link is *resource inputs*, the transfer of essential resources—people, behavior objects, space, reserves, and information—into a setting. Settings may also be connected by *social influence* channels such as hierarchical or line authority, legal regulation, bargaining coalitions, and expressions of public opinion or preference. The third type of link, *product outputs*, is defined by the channels that transfer products from one setting to another. (Of course, the same link can be both an input and an output link—how it is regarded depends on whether the setting is a contributor or a recipient.) Several examples of these intersetting links are given in Table 16.2.

Setting Networks

Thus far, I have spoken of links between settings as if only two settings were involved. But any given setting may have links with some or perhaps many other settings. Exploration of these links can provide further information on the open-system qualities of settings—on their inputs, influence channels, and outputs—and on the niches they occupy in the larger social world. For example, we would have a clearer understanding of a machine shop and of its place in a community or organization if we knew its ties with major suppliers, regulators, competitors, and customers.

There is another reason for examining setting links: If, as was suggested earlier, behavior settings are fundamental units (subsystems, subroutines) of larger social systems such as organizations and communities, then examination of setting networks should yield insights into the structure and dynamics of these larger systems. For example, a map of the kinds, numbers, and strengths of links among the various behavior settings in a high school would be quite useful for understanding that system (cf. Gump, 1979, pp. 240–241). If we were also to examine the ties that the settings had outside the school, we would obtain a more complete picture. A still more comprehensive view could be obtained by analyzing how these connections change over time. Such a mapping would provide a more dynamic view of the school than a traditional survey of its settings.

Next I consider some practical issues in representing such complex connections among settings. Chapters on interorganizational relations by Aldrich (1979, chapter 11) and Aldrich and Whetten (1981) are the primary sources for this discussion.[7] Wellman (1981) presents an equally useful discussion of networks at the interpersonal level.

Any attempt to represent intersetting links empirically involves a number of decision points. First, will the inquiry examine only the direct ties of a single focal setting to other settings, or will relations among a bounded population of settings be examined? We might, for example, be interested in learning about the ties between the main terminal room of a university computer facility and other settings on campus. In this case settings without direct ties to the terminal room would not be included in the analysis. Or we might wish to determine the relationships that exist among all of the settings under the direct control of the campus computing center, including the main terminal room, classes offered by the center's staff, the director's office, and so on.

Second, how many different kinds of links, and which particular ones, will be considered in the analysis? In the simplest case, only one kind of link, such as flow of information among settings, would be examined. A more complex investigation might consider several types of links, including transfers of personnel, products, and information.

Third, precisely how is each type of link to be measured? A number of decisions will be required to devise appropriate operational definitions for the types of links to be examined. For example, informational flows might be measured in a variety of ways,

including written communications or telephone or face-to-face conversations. Data might be obtained by observation, interview, or survey. Procedures for sampling times of observation, events, or personnel would have to be determined. A considerable amount of qualitative knowledge of the settings under study will be needed for investigators to make appropriate decisions about the measurement of intersetting links.

Fourth, will the network be examined on a single occasion or on multiple occasions? Relationships among settings may change significantly over time. Changes such as the processes of coupling and decoupling, or changes in strength of coupling, are best studied longitudinally. In these cases, the timing of observations is critical. Successive measures must be taken at intervals appropriate to the rate of the processes observed. And in cross-sectional studies, decisions must be made about the appropriate times for measurement.

If intersetting links are described directionally, that is, from each setting to every other setting in a population, the data can be presented in a directed graph or matrix. From such representations, a number of potentially useful quantitative descriptors can be derived. For example, the degree of interconnectedness of a network, or its density, can be operationalized as the ratio of existing links to logically possible links, or as a matrix representing the number of steps needed to connect each setting with every other setting. Related procedures can be used to identify the degree of centrality of any given setting, and the existence of subgroups (sets of highly interconnected settings) within the larger network (Aldrich & Whetten, 1981).

16.6. ADVANCING BEHAVIOR-SETTING THEORY AND RESEARCH

Research on setting networks is only one of numerous potentially fruitful approaches for further developing the present conceptual framework. Ideally, the framework outlined here will stimulate the formulation of a more comprehensive and more broadly acceptable theory of behavior settings. One approach that seems particularly appropriate for this goal is presented below. Other alternatives based on recent work are then briefly suggested.

Further conceptual developments, if they are to be of lasting value, should adhere to ecological psychology's tradition of grounding its concepts and theories in observations. However, these developments need not—indeed, should not—simply follow the procedures that ecological psychologists have used in the past. Greater gains can be achieved by using methods that diverge from tradition (McGrath, Martin, & Kulka, 1981). The present is a good time to begin another period of discovery research on behavior settings (cf. Barker, Chapter 40, this volume). Researchers should consider a greater diversity of setting-relevant events than has been considered in the past. Qualitative data need to be generated and intensively examined; this need was noted by Barker and Wright in their first discussion of ecological research methods (1950, p. 72).

Quantitative descriptions of settings on standardized scales should be deemphasized for the present. A more dynamic, interactive relationship is needed between conceptual/theoretical issues and data. For example, rather than simply measuring settings on a previously defined set of scales, researchers should begin their study of settings using an explicit but tentative conceptual framework that is continually refined on the basis of their observations. In the process of refining the framework, researchers should self-consciously construe, interpret, distill, and sharpen the concepts they are working with. More of the complexities and subtleties of setting events should be grasped, and to a degree preserved (cf. Kaminski, 1983). In such an intensive analysis, relatively few cases may be examined. Illustrations of this approach are given below.

Once further conceptual development has occurred and new concepts, hypotheses, and theories have been thoughtfully advanced, it will be appropriate to resume the more common research activities of hypothesis testing on large samples, and providing baseline data for numerous settings. In the meantime, methods that have not been extensively employed by ecological psychologists—such as intensive interviewing, archival analyses, and organizational diagnostic procedures—may become prominent (cf. Wicker, 1979, 1981).

16.6.1. Developing Grounded Theories of Behavior Settings

The task at hand can be stated in a deceptively simple way: Researchers should

use multiple data sources
and multiple measurement procedures
to examine in some detail

a variety of behavior settings
that fall within a specified domain
in order to refine existing concepts and generate new ones
that can be related in hypotheses and more inclusive theory.

This prescription is largely derived from Glaser and Strauss's (1967; Glaser, 1978) guidelines for discovering grounded theory, and from a perspective on research methods advanced by McGrath and his colleagues (McGrath, 1964, 1968, 1981; McGrath & Brinberg, 1983; McGrath, Martin, & Kulka, 1981; Runkel & McGrath, 1972). Additional helpful suggestions, particularly regarding criteria for determining the scope and specificity of contextual research, are provided by Stokols (1982).

Theories do not spring full-blown from observations. Intermediate steps are evaluating existing concepts and generating new ones on the basis of what is observed. The concepts should be abstractions or generalizations that refer to characteristics of events, but not to the events themselves. They also should have the quality of sensitizing others to conditions that can be grasped as meaningful. Through the interplay of conceptualizing and observing, concept meanings can be sharpened, and apparent relationships among concepts can be noted and examined. Relationships that are consistently observed can lead to statements of hypotheses, which may be tied together into broader, more integrated theoretical networks (Glaser & Strauss, 1967, pp. 35–43). Useful guidelines for systematically classifying concepts are found in McGrath (1968).

Although Glaser and Strauss (1967; Glaser, 1978) do not stress the point, researchers who adopt the grounded approach to theorizing need to keep clearly in mind the boundaries of the domain they are exploring. Otherwise they can quickly become lost pursuing this or that interesting lead without having a sense of the territory they are covering. Any conceptual inquiry regarding behavior settings should have clearly specified spatial, temporal, and categorical boundaries. Obviously the most general would be all kinds of settings that ever existed anywhere. Parenthetically, such generality seems to be assumed in much psychological theorizing, even when the empirical base for such an assumption is limited to a single type of setting (e.g., laboratory experiments in colleges).

Here are some examples of narrower boundaries that researchers might specify:

Behavior settings where paid employees provide service to clients in face-to-face interaction

Currently operating hospital emergency facilities in the United States

Los Angeles restaurants that were started between January 1 and June 30 of last year

Psychology classes taught at Claremont Graduate School during the past spring semester

Initial attempts at grounded theory may best be limited to a single substantive area such as emergency medical service facilities or computerized offices (cf. Glaser, 1978; Glaser & Strauss, 1967, pp. 32–35; Stokols, 1982).

Boundaries are also needed for the range of setting events or aspects that is to be considered. The breadth of these boundaries can vary a great deal. For example, a researcher might be interested in any identifiable factors relating to the founding of the settings, scripts of setting founders, supply and equipment links among settings, changes in behavior-setting programs due to a 10% reduction in departmental budgets, physician–patient interactions, or ways of creating resource slack. There is a trade-off in boundary setting that researchers should keep in mind. Broadly framed approaches—those that encompass many times, places, and events—are likely to sacrifice parsimony and testability for comprehensiveness. Simple or relatively reductionistic approaches may be readily testable, but accurate within narrow limits (cf. Stokols, 1982; Weick, 1979b).

A crucial feature of the grounded theory approach as outlined by Glaser and Strauss (1967; Glaser, 1978) is the use of comparison groups (or comparison behavior settings) in formulating and refining concepts and hypotheses. Glaser and Strauss advocate the sequential selection of groups that promise to increase informational yield or to permit further theoretical refinements. A developing framework also can suggest the particular groups that are worthy of examination. To illustrate, Glaser and Strauss's developing framework for analyzing the awareness of dying among hospitalized patients included the factors of expectancy of death and speed of death. These factors became the basis for their selection of particular settings for observation, as the following research memo shows:

> I wished first to look at services that minimized patient awareness (and so first looked at a premature baby service and then at a neurosurgical service where patients were frequently comatose). I wished next to look at dying in a situation where expectancy of staff and often of patients was great and

dying was quick, so I observed on an Intensive Care Unit. Then I wished to observe on a service where staff expectations of terminality were great but where the patient's might or might not be, and where dying tended to be slow. So I looked next at a cancer service. I wished then to look at conditions where death was unexpected and rapid, and so looked at an emergency service. (Glaser & Strauss, 1967, p. 59).

If researchers are at an early stage in their theorizing, the settings initially selected for observation may be convenience samples; much can be learned when little is known. Subsequent selections should reflect the potential of settings for providing information on the most significant issue at hand. In general, it is desirable to include a fairly diverse group of settings that are within the specified domain to assess the generality of the emerging concepts and hypotheses. If consistencies are not found, the domain may need to be narrowed. Or very similar settings might be chosen to verify the usefulness of a concept or test the reliability of an apparent relationship between concepts (Glaser, 1978, chapter 3; Glaser & Strauss, 1967, pp. 45–60).

It should be clear from the foregoing discussion that both the boundaries of the domain and the framework used to select similar and dissimilar settings are themselves subject to reinterpretation as research is conducted. What seems similar from one perspective or framework may seem quite dissimilar when a conceptual structure is refined. And settings that were outside the domain as originally defined may subsequently seem sufficiently relevant to be brought in, and the domain extended. Or close examination of settings may reveal less consistency than anticipated, leading researchers to narrow the domain.

Also, it should be clear that this approach to sampling is quite different from that followed in most psychological research. Although the domain of settings may be (tentatively) specified in advance, the complete sample cannot be. Moreover, settings may be chosen because they differ from those already examined—not because they represent another like case. Sample sizes in this approach are also likely to be considerably smaller than in conventional research.

Different kinds of data provide researchers with different vantage points on events. And research methods differ in their strengths and weaknesses. Glaser and Strauss (1967) advocate the "multifaceted investigation, in which there are no limits to the techniques of data collection, the way they are used, or the types of data acquired" (p. 65). McGrath (1981) is more blunt: "No strategy, design or method *used alone* is worth a damn. Multiple approaches are *required...*" (p. 209). Essentially, the researcher needs to learn whatever is relevant to the issue at hand. Often this means obtaining a fairly detailed set of data, particularly on the settings studied initially. It is likely that some methods cannot be applied to every setting due to setting differences that limit various methods. Absence of privacy may inhibit intensive interviewing, and a setting's record-keeping practices will determine whether archival analyses are feasible, for example.

For researchers who develop grounded theories, there may be no clear answer to the question of when to stop and communicate the theory to others. Very likely there will always be other comparison groups that one will wish to examine. But if such theories are to stimulate research and profit from the critical examination of others, they must be formulated and presented in formats acceptable to other scholars.

A particularly appealing aspect of this approach to theorizing is its direct confrontation of the generality issue (cf. McGrath & Brinberg, 1983). Theories developed in this way would have demonstrated—not merely presumed—relevance to a specified group of settings. Given the labor-intensive nature of grounded theorizing, it seems likely that the first applications of the method to behavior settings will be in relatively limited substantive areas such as converging community mental health centers or launching small retail businesses. These theories may subsequently be drawn upon to formulate theories about behavior settings in general. It is possible, of course, to begin with the goal of formulating a general theory, but given the need to examine diverse settings in some detail, such an undertaking would surely require considerably more time and effort.

16.6.2. Illustrative Directions for Grounded Research on Behavior Settings

However broad the researcher's theoretical goals, the concepts dealt with in this chapter may serve as useful starting points. Given the rather general and abstract nature of these concepts, many topics might be explored. Some directions such as analyses of setting history and setting networks have already been mentioned.

Two other illustrations, including one from the published literature, may be helpful.[8] In keeping with the grounded theory approach, only early steps in research are suggested. Later steps would be determined from the initial findings.

Lyon's (1974) investigation of a voluntary theatrical group incorporates a number of features of the proposed grounded approach to studying behavior settings. She observed the group over several months while serving as a rehearsal assistant and prompter for a play; she also interviewed a number of group members.

Lyon's report provides qualitative information on a number of topics considered previously, including the following: the role of the founder in assimilating such setting resources as actors, a place to perform, and scripts; members' different images of how the group should evolve; the collective working out of the "messages" of plays and how the plays should be interpreted; negotiations between members and the director regarding task assignments and rehearsals; and affiliative and enjoyment needs served by the group.

Lyon also notes that one consequence of the lack of stage technicians—a form of understaffing—was that actors shared responsibilities for cleaning the stage and reorganizing props and costumes. Lyon gives particular attention to ways that the group was constrained by lack of financial resources. Without money the group was limited in the plays it could perform, the places it could rehearse, and the costumes available, for example.

Important contextual influences on the group included an external grant it succeeded in getting; the distance the group maintained from another, but more conventional, theatrical group; the legal restriction that only persons over 21 could be admitted to the bar where the group performed; and the clientele that could be attracted to performances in the poor industrial neighborhood where the bar was located.

Particularly noteworthy is Lyon's description of consequences that followed from a change in one resource—a place to perform. (The group arranged to give outdoor performances in the sculpture court of a museum.) The events illustrate the interdependence of setting facets, and the complications of reconverging a behavior setting: In anticipation of a new and different audience, a new play with a larger cast was selected. In hopes that the performance would further promote the group, more money than usual was spent in constructing the stage, advertising, and preparing costumes. Given this special situation, the usual collective interpretation of the play was foregone, and decisions were left to the director. Conflict developed between the director and the actors, resulting in low morale among the players.

Lyon's research is a case study, without comparison groups as recommended by Glaser and Strauss. The investigation did result in a number of conceptual distinctions that could profitably be explored in other theatrical settings: (1) implications for organizing when financial resources are scarce and when they are plentiful (a well-heeled voluntary theatrical group might next be studied); (2) personal needs that must be met in voluntary settings, but not in settings where staff members are paid (comparisons with a professional acting group would be in order); and (3) the roles and relative power of actors and the director when plays are performed by persons assembled for a single production rather than by people who continue to work together (one-shot productions could be studied). If subsequent observations confirmed the utility of these or other distinctions, they could be further explored in other settings, including other types of performing arts groups and social service agencies (Lyon, 1974).

The other illustration is hypothetical.[9] A researcher interested in ways that retail stores are founded might first set these boundaries: Settings to be studied will be drawn from the retail stores that began operation in the city of Claremont, California, during the last 6 months. The conceptual domain will be preconvergence and convergence factors derived from the framework of the present chapter. The framework would be reviewed to identify questions and issues on which information is to be sought. For each question or issue, thought would be given to the best methods for obtaining data, for example, direct observation, records of the establishments studied, city and state business codes, interviews of founders and staff members. Research on new businesses would be examined (e.g., Cooper & Dunkelberg, 1981). Books on how to start a new business (e.g., Burstiner, 1981; Siegel, 1977; Smith, 1982) and publications from the U.S. government's Small Business Administration would be obtained and perused. An initial sample of settings would be selected and the owners or managers contacted.

In such an investigation, interviews are likely to provide the widest range of information. For example, questions of the following sorts would bear on factors in the current framework:

Who decided what items of equipment (sales goods, supplies) were needed? What factors were considered in these decisions? Were the following factors considered, and if so how: skills of staff, available space, traffic flows of clients, costs?

How did you go about securing the present space? What remodeling or redecorating was done? How was this space used before you occupied it?

(to the founder) Why did you want to set up this business? Where did you get the idea for it? What was your initial image of how it would be set up? How has your image been changed? Have you been influenced by your employees' ideas of how this business should operate? What seem to be the needs and motives of your employees relative to this business? How dedicated are they to preserving the setting?

Describe the various activities of this business. How are tasks divided up among the people working here? How does the current way of operating compare with the arrangements when the business opened? What were the reasons for the changes?

What do you see as the most important outside factors influencing this business? (Probe for social, demographic, technical, economic, and other influences.)

With what other organizations does this business have important connections? What is the nature of these connections? (Probe for resource input, social influence, and product output links.)

From the information initially collected, the existing concepts would be refined, tentative relationships and hypotheses formulated, and other settings selected and studied. With considerably more work, the elements of a grounded theory on converging of retail sales operations should emerge.

Grounded theories of behavior settings should serve all of the functions that we generally expect of theory. They should provide explanations of events, allow us to make predictions, provide an explicit perspective on phenomena and a sense of understanding of them, furnish a framework for assimilating already existing knowledge, stimulate and guide future research, and be useful in practical applications.

The last function deserves additional comment. Because of the way grounded theories are generated, we can expect them to "fit and work"—their concepts and propositions should be readily applicable to the settings being examined and should provide powerful explanations of significant, meaningful events in those settings. Grounded theories of behavior settings should make sense to workers in the domains studied, and this understanding should make them more willing to draw on the theories in practical ways. The theories may help the workers to be more sensitive to problems they face and to see ways of making changes. Because grounded theories emerge from a diversity of settings, they should be broadly applicable within the domain specified (Glaser & Strauss, 1967, pp. 237–250).

16.6.3. Other Promising Research Directions

There are, of course, numerous other promising directions for future research on behavior settings. Many of them are based on recent theoretical and/or empirical work. I will suggest a few directions here.

One prospective research area bridges the present framework with Stokols and Shumaker's (1981) recent work on place dependence, the degree to which setting occupants see themselves as identified with or dependent upon particular physical locations. These authors have advanced a number of hypotheses linking place dependence with reactions to such setting conditions as disruptive events, understaffing and overstaffing, and setting termination (Stokols & Shumaker, 1981, pp. 473–478).

Recent research on staffing theory suggests a number of topics worth further investigation. More work is needed, for example, to develop broadly applicable and reliable measures of staffing levels in settings and in larger social units. Promising beginnings include Mentes's (1982) preliminary work on a self-report measure of staffing/workload, Vecchio and Sussman's (1981) use of supervisors' reports of staffing levels, and Dean, Harvey, Pugh, and Gunderson's (1979) archival and self-report indices of manning and manpower utilization.

The degree to which staffing levels can account for differential levels of member participation in large and small organizations or organizational subunits is another issue worth further effort. Morgan and Alwin (1980) recently suggested that staffing effects depend on setting centrality (importance placed on a setting by the parent organization and its constituents) and elasticity (degree to which a setting can accommodate variable numbers of active participants). Staffing theory has guided research on size differences in participation in branch banks (Oxley & Barrera, 1984) and college academic departments (Goldstein & Baranowskyj, 1983).

Several researchers have suggested additional factors that should be considered when examining the effects of staffing levels on occupants' experiences and behavior. Among the factors are the degree to which performance is evaluated in terms of individual or group tasks (Goldstein & Baranowskyj, 1983); structure of tasks, including job design and redesign

(Greenberg, 1979; Greenberg, Wang, & Dossett, 1982; Perkins, 1982; Vecchio & Sussman, 1981; Wicker, 1979); composition of work groups (Perkins, 1982; Wicker, 1979); social support from supervisors and co-workers (Oxley & Barrera, 1984); arousal levels (McGrath, 1976); and participants' interest in the task (Wicker, Kirmeyer, Hanson, & Alexander, 1976). Mentes's (1982) research suggests that workers' feelings of involvement are more closely related to their undertaking setting maintenance actions than to the level of their program-supportive actions.

The organizational development literature is another source of ideas for refining staffing theory, particularly as it relates to work sites. To illustrate, Hirschhorn (1983, p. 112) suggests that workers in understaffed settings tend to keep long-term rather than short-term accounts in evaluating their work-related outcomes. They trust that although there may be temporary inequities their co-workers will not permit them to be exploited over longer periods. And Hirschhorn and Militello (1983) have described a department where overstaffing was accompanied by overspecialized task assignments, a superfluous control hierarchy, and passive acceptance of reductions in work force.

Implications of staffing levels for worker stress and health have been discussed and studied by several investigators (e.g., Dean, et al., 1979; Kirmeyer, 1978, 1983). Two theoretical statements that are particularly relevant to staffing of behavior settings are McGrath's (1976) model of social psychological stress and Altman's (1975) model of crowding (see Wicker, 1979/1983, chapter 9).

Willems and his associates (e.g., Willems & Halstead, 1978) have conducted important research demonstrating that behaviors of patients in a rehabilitation hospital are significantly linked with the particular hospital settings they enter. Besides providing findings bearing on rehabilitation practices, this research serves as a model for studying interactions between the daily behaviors of individuals and the organizational settings they occupy.

Other promising work has employed behavior settings to study organizational structure. Pigg (1983) has grouped behavior settings of four industrial organizations according to authority (line/staff) and technological (process/nonprocess) classifications. He has suggested refinements for the scales used to measure setting interdependence.

Behavior-setting surveys have been employed by Bechtel and his associates to evaluate a number of built environments, including housing projects and entire communities (e.g., Bechtel, 1982). Particularly interesting is Bechtel's identification of behavior settings that serve as *behavioral focal points* — central meeting places where members of an organization or community can informally meet and interact (Bechtel, 1977).

The behavior-setting concept has been suggested by Kaminski (1981) as the basic building block for a new paradigm in social psychology. Everyday human interactions would be analyzed in their natural context, resulting in a more complex — and more accurate — view of social life than is evident in current social psychological theories. In this new paradigm, the behavior-setting concept might be reframed somewhat to take on a more person-centered meaning. Kaminski (1982) has suggested, for example, conceiving of the behavior setting as an *orientating context* by which individuals cope with claims from their environment. Even though this development is only in its earliest stages, it holds considerable promise.

In a broader application, economist Fox and his colleagues have used the behavior-setting concept and Barker's descriptive data from Midwest to develop a comprehensive social accounting system. This scheme models people's allocations of time to various behavior settings within specified political/geographical/economic areas such as cities, regions, and nations. An accounting scheme based on how much time people spend in various activities is superior to one based on gainful employment because the former is more comprehensive. Only about 15% of adults' waking time flows through the labor market. The remaining 85% of time is left out of accounts based on money transactions (Fox & Ghosh, 1980, p. 34). Thus behavior settings provide a vehicle for assessing and estimating time allocations. Fox and his associates have probed Barker's data for new insights and have linked their findings with other information sources such as the *Dictionary of Occupational Titles* and the Standard Industrial Classification code (Fox, 1980, 1983; Fox & Ghosh, 1980; Prescott, 1983). This work could have an enormous impact on both social research and the practical world.

16.6.4. Concluding Comment

Whatever direction future research may take, I think it is essential that traditional work in ecological psychology be regarded as a sound beginning, but not as discovered truth to be proclaimed. If behavior-setting theory and research are to advance, researchers must think new thoughts, be open to ideas from other fields, and pursue a variety of research strategies and methods. The framework I have developed is a step in the continuing evolution of behavior-set-

ting theory. Barker anticipated that the theory would be refined and extended. He concluded his best-known work by stating that his "present knowledge of behavior settings relates to only a few of their many facets, so the theory [I] have fashioned on the basis of this knowledge is necessarily incomplete. Hopefully, it is a first approximation to, or a component of, the theory or theories that an eco-behavioral science will finally have" (Barker, 1968, p. 205). The statement applies to my framework as well.

Acknowledgments

This chapter is dedicated to Roger G. Barker, whose behavior-setting concept is the foundation for the ideas presented here. I am indebted to Roger for his gracious, nondirective encouragement of my attempt to refine and expand the concept to which he has devoted much of his professional career.

A number of the ideas in this chapter originated in discussions that Sandra Kirmeyer and I had in 1981 and 1982. At that time we intended to produce a jointly authored paper along the lines of this one. Although she was unable to continue on the project, I benefited from her early participation, and her comments on two earlier versions of this chapter.

It has been a pleasure again to work with editors Daniel Stokols and Irwin Altman. They have helped to shape the chapter in important ways. The following colleagues also provided helpful comments on the manuscript: Edward Devereux, Joseph McGrath, and Karl Weick. Jeanne King made valuable editorial suggestions on the penultimate draft.

NOTES

1. The habitat measure employed — the *urb* — takes into account not only number of settings, but also how frequently they occur and the number of hours they are in operation (Barker & Schoggen, 1973).

2. In this chapter, *convergence* refers to the creation or establishment of any new setting, whether it represents a new or a familiar form. In future work, it may be useful to distinguish among several categories of new settings: those that are similar to existing settings in function and structure (e.g., an additional branch of a bank), those that have innovative functions but familiar forms (e.g., college lecture classes on unorthodox topics), those that have familiar functions but innovative forms (e.g., dental offices for children where the staff are in costume and treatments are part of a make-believe scenario), and those whose function and form are both innovative (an informal medical school class where herbal cures are presented and experimented with) (these distinctions were suggested by S. Kirmeyer, personal communication, December 1, 1982).

3. Cognitive representations of setting programs are also mentioned in Barker's procedures for determining whether two or more settings should be classified in the same functional category or *genotype* (Barker, 1968, pp. 80–89). Programs are said to be *encoded* in the minds of the central functionaries of settings, for example, an attorney in an attorney's office, a bank manager. When persons in charge of two settings can change places and still carry out the settings' programs without delay or with a minimum of retraining, the settings are of the same genotype. The nature of the information (in the encoded programs) that permits such exchanges is not considered, however.

4. Other related concepts are *social maps* (Van Maanen, 1977, p. 22), *cause maps* (Weick, 1979b), *schemata* (see Weick, 1979a, pp. 48–53), *plans* (Miller, Galanter, & Pribram, 1960), and *frames* (Goffman, 1974).

5. Community and environmental psychologists have given some attention to historical factors. For example, Sarason (1972) has devoted a chapter to organizational history; Gauvain, Altman, and Fahim (1983) have considered changes in residences over time; and Stokols and his associates have discussed the temporal depth and environmental symbolism of settings (Stokols & Jacobi, 1983, 1984; Stokols & Shumaker, 1981).

6. Barker's view that adjacent levels are not commensurate contrasts with Miller's general systems theory, which emphasizes the similarities in processes across levels. Miller does, however, recognize that higher-level systems may have some characteristics (*emergents*) not present at lower levels (Miller, 1971b, pp. 285–287).

7. Intersetting linkages have previously been considered in ecological research. Barker and Wright (1955/1971) described a data-based method for determining whether two closely related events should be considered as distinct settings, or whether they should be merged and designated as a single setting (the K-21 procedure). Raters using this procedure indicate the degree of interdependence of the two potential settings on seven different dimensions or scales, including overlap in populations and in leadership, and behavioral continuity across the two potential settings (Barker, 1968, pp. 40–46). This index has also been used to represent the degree to which each of 584 settings in the town of Midwest were interdependent with a *core behavior setting*, Clifford's Drug Stores (Barker & Wright, 1955/1971). Also, Bronfenbrenner (1979) has suggested studying interrelations among the various settings that directly or indirectly influence a given *developing person*.

8. Another example is Kusterer's (1978) analysis of the working knowledge of *unskilled* workers.

9. Work along the lines suggested here has proceeded since the writing of this chapter (see Wicker & King, in press).

REFERENCES

Abelson, R.P. (1981). Psychological status of the script concept. *American Psychologist, 36,* 715–729.

Adizes, I. (1979). Organizational passages: Diagnosing and treating lifecycle problems of organizations. *Organizational Dynamics, 8*(1), 2–25.

Aldrich, H.E. (1979). *Organizations and environments.* Englewood Cliffs, NJ: Prentice-Hall.

Aldrich, H.E., & Whetten, D.A. (1981). Organization-sets, action-sets, and networks: Making the most of simplicity. In P.C. Nystrom & W.H. Starbuck (Eds.), *Handbook of organizational design: Vol. 1. Adapting organizations to their environments* (pp. 385–408). New York: Oxford University Press.

Allport, F.H. (1962). A structuronomic conception of behavior: Individual and collective. *Journal of Abnormal and Social Psychology, 64,* 3–30.

Altman, I. (1975). *The environment and social behavior.* Monterey, CA: Brooks/Cole.

Barker, R.G. (1960). Ecology and motivation. In M.R. Jones (Ed.), *Nebraska Symposium on Motivation* (Vol. 8, pp. 1–49). Lincoln: University of Nebraska Press.

Barker, R.G. (1963). On the nature of the environment. *Journal of Social Issues, 19*(4), 17–38.

Barker, R.G. (1968). *Ecological psychology: Concepts and methods for studying the environment of human behavior.* Stanford, CA: Stanford University Press.

Barker, R.G. (1979a). The influence of frontier environments on behavior. In J.O. Steffen (Ed.), *The American West: New perspectives, new dimensions* (pp. 61–93). Norman: University of Oklahoma Press.

Barker, R.G. (1979b). Settings of a professional lifetime. *Journal of Personality and Social Psychology, 37,* 2137–2157.

Barker, R.G. (1983). Discussion of 'The enigma of ecological psychology' by G. Kaminski. *Journal of Environmental Psychology, 3,* 173–174.

Barker, R.G. (Ed.). (1978). *Habitats, environments, and human behavior: Studies in ecological psychology and eco-behavioral science from the Midwest Psychological Field Station, 1947–1972.* San Francisco: Jossey-Bass.

Barker, R.G., Dembo, T., & Lewin, K. (1941). Frustration and regression: An experiment with young children. *University of Iowa Studies in Child Welfare, 18*(1), 1–314.

Barker, R.G., & Gump, P.V. (1964). *Big school, small school: High school size and student behavior.* Stanford, CA: Stanford University Press.

Barker, R.G., & Schoggen, P. (1973). *Qualities of community life: Methods of measuring environment and behavior applied to an American and an English town.* San Francisco: Jossey-Bass.

Barker, R.G., & Wright, H.F. (1949). Psychological ecology and the problem of psychosocial development. *Child Development, 20,* 131–143.

Barker, R.G., & Wright, H.F. (1950). *Methods in psychological ecology: A progress report.* Topeka, KS: Ray's Printing Service.

Barker, R.G., & Wright, H.F. (1971). *Midwest and its chil-*

dren: The psychological ecology of an American town. Hamden, CT: Archon. (Original work published 1955)

Bechtel, R.B. (1977). *Enclosing behavior.* Stroudsburg, PA: Dowden, Hutchinson, & Ross.

Bechtel, R.B. (1982). Contributions of ecological psychology to the evaluation of environments. *International Review of Applied Psychology, 31,* 153–166.

Becker, F.D. (1981). *Workspace: Creating environments in organizations.* New York: Praeger.

Benson, J.K. (1977). Organizations: A dialectical view. *Administrative Science Quarterly, 22,* 1–21.

Berger, P.L., & Luckmann, T. (1967). *The social construction of reality.* Garden City, NJ: Anchor.

Berkman, L.F., & Syme, S.L. (1979). Social networks, host resistance, and mortality: A nine-year followup study of Alameda County residents. *American Journal of Epidemiology, 109,* 186–204.

Bernstein, R.J. (1976). *The restructuring of social and political theory.* New York: Harcourt Brace Jovanovich.

Bronfenbrenner, U. (1979). *The ecology of human development.* Cambridge, MA: Harvard University Press.

Burstiner, I. (1981). *Run your own store.* Englewood Cliffs, NJ: Prentice-Hall.

Chavis, D.M., Stucky, P.E., & Wandersman, A. (1983). Returning basic research to the community: A relationship between scientist and citizen. *American Psychologist, 38,* 424–434.

Cooper, A.C., & Dunkelberg, W.C. (1981, August). *Influences upon entrepreneurship—A large scale study.* Paper presented at the meeting of the Academy of Management, San Diego, CA.

Cyert, R.M., & March, J.G. (1963). *A behavioral theory of the firm.* Englewood Cliffs, NJ: Prentice-Hall.

Day, R., & Day, J.V. (1977). A review of the current state of negotiated order theory: An appreciation and a critique. In J.K. Benson (Ed.), *Organizational analysis: Critique and innovation* (pp. 128–144). Beverly Hills, CA: Sage.

Dean, L.M., Harvey, R.A., Pugh, W.M., & Gunderson, E.K.E. (1979). Manning levels, organizational effectiveness, and health. *Human Relations, 32,* 237–246.

Devereux, E.C. (1977). *Psychological ecology: A critical analysis and appraisal.* Unpublished manuscript, Cornell University, Department of Human Development and Family Studies, Ithaca, NY.

Dubin, R. (1979). Central life interests: Self-integrity in a complex world. *Pacific Sociological Review, 22,* 405–426.

Duncan, R.B. (1972). Characteristics of organizational environments and perceived environmental uncertainty. *Administrative Science Quarterly, 17,* 313–327.

Dunn, E.S. (1971). *Economic and social development.* Baltimore, MD: Johns Hopkins Press.

Forgas, J.P. (1979). *Social episodes: The study of interaction routines.* New York: Academic.

Forgas, J.P. (1982). Episode cognition: Internal representations of interaction routines. In L. Berkowitz (Ed.), *Advances in experimental social psychology* (Vol. 15, pp. 59–101). New York: Academic.

Fox, K.A. (1980). Philosophical implications of a system of social accounts based on Roger Barker's ecological psychology and a scalar measure of total income. *Philosophica, 25,* 33–54.

Fox, K.A. (1983). The eco–behavioural view of human societies and its implications for systems science. *International Journal of Systems Science, 14,* 895–914.

Fox, K.A., & Ghosh, S.K. (1980). Social accounts for urban–centered regions. *International Regional Science Review, 5,* 33–50.

Gauvain, M., Altman, I., & Fahim, H. (1983). Homes and social change: A cross-cultural analysis. In N. Feimer & S. Geller (Eds.), *Environmental psychology: Directions and perspectives* (pp. 180–218). New York: Praeger.

Gerson, E.M. (1976). On "Quality of Life." *American Sociological Review, 41,* 793–806.

Gilmore, T.N. (1983). Overcoming crisis and uncertainty: The search conference. In L. Hirschhorn (Ed.), *Cutting back: Retrenchment and redevelopment in human and community services* (pp. 70–90). San Francisco: Jossey-Bass.

Gilmore, T.N., & Snow, R.M. (1983). Consolidating offices within an organization. In L. Hirschhorn (Ed.), *Cutting back: Retrenchment and redevelopment in human and community services* (pp. 181–198). San Francisco: Jossey-Bass.

Glaser, B.G. (1978). *Theoretical sensitivity: Advances in the methodology of grounded theory.* Mill Valley, CA: Sociology Press.

Glaser, B.G., & Strauss, A.L. (1967). *The discovery of grounded theory: Strategies for qualitative research.* New York: Aldine.

Glassman, R.B. (1973). Persistence and loose couplings in living systems. *Behavioral Science, 18,* 83–98.

Goffman, E. (1974). *Frame analysis.* New York: Harper & Row.

Goldstein, M.B., & Baranowskyj, A. (1983, August). *Undermanning and academic behavior: An exploratory study.* Paper presented at the meeting of the American Psychological Association, Anaheim, CA.

Gottlieb, B.H. (1981). Preventive interventions involving social networks and social support. In B.H. Gottlieb (Ed.), *Social networks and social support.* Beverly Hills, CA: Sage.

Greenberg, C.I. (1979). Toward an integration of ecological psychology and industrial psychology: Undermanning theory, organization size and job enrichment. *Environmental Psychology and Nonverbal Behavior, 3,* 228–245.

Greenberg, G., Wang, Y., & Dossett, D.L.T. (1982). Effects of work group size and task size on observers' job characteristics ratings. *Basic and Applied Social Psychology, 3*, 53–66.

Gump, P.V. (1979). Reflections on a multi-method investigation of high schools and their inhabitants. In J.G. Kelly (Ed.), *Adolescent boys in high school: A psychological study of coping and adaptation* (pp. 231–243). Hillsdale, NJ: Erlbaum.

Gump, P.V., & Ross, R. (1977). The fit of milieu and programme in school environments. In H. McGurk (Ed.), *Ecological factors in human development.* New York: North-Holland.

Habermas, J. (1971). *Theorie and Praxis* [Theory and praxis]. Frankfurt am Main, Germany: Suhrkamp Verlag.

Hall, P.H., & Spencer-Hall, D.A. (1982). The social conditions of negotiated order. *Urban Life, 11*, 328–349.

Hall, R.H. (1977). *Organizations: Structure and process* (2nd. ed.). Englewood Cliffs, NJ: Prentice-Hall.

Harloff, H.J., Gump, P.V., & Campbell, D.E. (1981). The public life of communities: Environmental change as a result of the intrusion of a flood control, conservation, and recreational reservoir. *Environment and Behavior, 13*, 685–706.

Hirschhorn, L. (1983). Professional teamwork, the autonomous professional, and organizational survival. In L. Hirschhorn (Ed.), *Cutting back: Retrenchment and redevelopment in human and community services* (pp. 109–120). San Francisco: Jossey-Bass.

Hirschhorn, L., & Andrews, C.B. (1983). Analyzing productivity improvement programs. In L. Hirschhorn (Ed.), *Cutting back: Retrenchment and redevelopment in human and community services* (pp. 229–239). San Francisco: Jossey-Bass.

Hirschhorn, L., & Militello, J. (1983). Retrenchment in an overstaffed setting: Layoffs at a freight shipping company. In L. Hirschhorn (Ed.), *Cutting back: Retrenchment and redevelopment in human and community services* (pp. 320–336). San Francisco: Jossey-Bass.

Kaminski, G. (1981, June). *The behavior setting as a middle-sized meeting ground.* Paper presented at a conference, Toward a Social Psychology of the Environment, Paris.

Kaminski, G. (1982, April). *What follows from looking at behavior settings in a naturalistic way.* Paper presented at the second annual Symposium on Environmental Psychology, University of California, Irvine.

Kaminski, G. (1983). The enigma of ecological psychology. *Journal of Environmental Psychology, 3*, 85–94.

Katz, D., & Golomb, N. (1974). Integration, effectiveness, and adaptation in social systems. *Administration and Society, 6*, 283–315.

Katz, D., & Kahn, R.L. (1978). *The social psychology of organizations* (2nd ed.). New York: Wiley.

Kelly, J.G. (Ed.). (1979). *Adolescent boys in high school: A*

psychological study of coping and adaptation. Hillsdale, NJ: Erlbaum.

Kimberly, J.R. (1980). Initiation, innovation, and institutionalization in the creation process. In J.R. Kimberly & R.H. Miles (Eds.), *The organizational life cycle: Issues in the creation, transformation, and decline of organizations* (pp. 18–43). San Francisco: Jossey-Bass.

Kirmeyer, S.L. (1978). Effects of overload and understaffing on rangers in Yosemite National Park. *Dissertation Abstracts International, 39*, 1543B. (University Microfilms No. 78-14, 841).

Kirmeyer, S.L. (1983, August). *Stress in police dispatchers: An observational analysis of work demands.* Paper presented at the meeting of the American Psychological Association, Anaheim, CA.

Kruse, L. (1986). Drehbücher für Verhaltensschauplätze oder: Scripts für Settings. In G. Kaminski (Ed.), *Ordnung und Variabilität im Alltagsgeschehen: Das Behavior Setting-Konzept in den Verhaltens- und Sozialwissenschaften* [Order and variability in everyday happenings: The behavior setting concept in behavior and social sciences]. Gottingen, Germany: Hogrefe.

Kusterer, K.C. (1978). *Know-how on the job: The important working knowledge of "unskilled" workers.* Boulder, CO: Westview.

LeCompte, W.F. (1972). The taxonomy of a treatment environment. *Archives of Physical Medicine and Rehabilitation, 53*, 109–114.

Levine, C.H. (1978). Organizational decline and cutback management. *Public Administration Review, 38*, 316–325.

Lyon, E. (1974). Work and play: Resource constraints in a small theater. *Urban Life and Culture, 3*, 71–97.

McGrath, J.E. (1964). Toward a "theory of method" for research on organizations. In W. Cooper, H. Leavitt, & M. Shelly II (Eds.), *New perspectives in organization research* (pp. 533–556). New York: Wiley.

McGrath, J.E. (1968). A multi-facet approach to classification of individual, group, and organizational concepts. In B. Indik & K. Berrien (Eds.), *People, groups, and organizations: An effective integration* (pp. 191–215). New York: Teachers College Press.

McGrath, J.E. (1976). Stress and behavior in organizations. In M.D. Dunnette (Ed.), *Handbook of industrial and organizational psychology* (pp. 1351–1395). Chicago: Rand-McNally.

McGrath, J.E. (1981). Dilemmatics. *American Behavioral Scientist, 25*, 179–210.

McGrath, J.E. (1984). *Groups: Interaction and performance.* Englewood Cliffs, NJ: Prentice-Hall.

McGrath, J.E., & Brinberg, D. (1983). External validity and the research process. *Journal of Consumer Research, 10*, 115–124.

McGrath, J.E., Martin, J., & Kulka, R.A. (1981). Some

quasi-rules for making judgment calls in research. *American Behavioral Scientist, 25,* 211–224.

McNeil, L.M. (1980, April). *Knowledge forms and knowledge content.* Paper presented at the meeting of the American Educational Research Association, Boston.

Mentes, Z.D. (1982). *Development of a self-report measure of staffing level.* Unpublished master's thesis, Claremont Graduate School, Claremont, CA.

Miller, G.A., Galanter, E., & Pribram, K.H. (1960). *Plans and the structure of behavior.* New York: Holt, Rinehart & Winston.

Miller, J.G. (1971a). Living systems: The group. *Behavioral Science, 16,* 302–398.

Miller, J.G. (1971b). The nature of living systems. *Behavioral Science, 16,* 277–301.

Miller, J.G. (1972). Living systems: The organization. *Behavioral Science, 17,* 1–182.

Moos, R.H. (1983). Discussion of 'The enigma of ecological psychology' by G. Kaminski. *Journal of Environmental Psychology, 3,* 178–180.

Morgan, D.H.J. (1975). Autonomy and negotiation in an industrial setting. *Sociology of Work and Occupations, 2,* 203–226.

Morgan, D.L., & Alvin, D.F. (1980). When less is more: School size and student social participation. *Social Psychology Quarterly, 43,* 241–252.

Newman, B.J. (1979). Interpersonal behavior and preferences for exploration in adolescent boys: A small group study. In J.G. Kelly (Ed.), *Adolescent boys in high school: A psychological study of coping and adaptation* (pp. 133–150). Hillsdale, NJ: Erlbaum.

Oxley, D., & Barrera, M. (1984). Undermanning theory and the workplace: Implications of setting size for job satisfaction and social support. *Environment and Behavior, 16,* 211–234.

Perkins, D.V. (1982). Individual differences and task structure in the performance of a behavior setting: An experimental evaluation of Barker's manning theory. *American Journal of Community Psychology, 10,* 617–634.

Perrow, C. (1970). *Organizational analysis: A sociological view.* Monterey, CA: Brooks/Cole.

Pfeffer, J., & Salancik, G.R. (1978). *The external control of organizations: A resource dependence perspective.* New York: Harper & Row.

Pigg, G.L. (1983). *Describing organizations: An assessment of shape, environment and technology.* Unpublished master's thesis, University of Kansas, Lawrence.

Prescott, J.R. (1983). *Behavior settings as a spatial basis for a system of social accounts.* Unpublished manuscript, Iowa State University, Department of Economics, Ames.

Price, R.H., & Blashfield, R.K. (1975). Explorations in the taxonomy of behavior settings: Analysis of dimensions and classifications of settings. *American Journal of Community Psychology, 3,* 335–351.

Roy, D.F. (1959). "Banana time": Job satisfaction and informal interaction. *Human Organization, 18,* 158–168.

Runkel, P.J., & McGrath, J.E. (1972). *Research on human behavior: A systematic guide to method.* New York: Holt, Rinehart & Winston.

Sampson, E.E. (1981). Cognitive psychology as ideology. *American Psychologist, 36,* 730–743.

Sarason, S.B. (1972). *The creation of settings and the future societies.* San Francisco: Jossey-Bass.

Sarason, S.B. (1976). Community psychology, networks, and Mr. Everyman. *American Psychologist, 31,* 317–328.

Sarason, S.B., Zitnay, G., & Grossman, F.K. (1971). *The creation of a community setting.* Syracuse, NY: Syracuse University, Division of Special Education and Rehabilitation and the Center on Human Policy.

Saup, W. (1983). Barkers Behavior Setting-Konzept und seine Weiterentwicklung [Barker's behavior setting concept and its further development]. *Psychologische Rundschau, 34,* 134–146.

Schank, R.C., & Abelson, R.P. (1977). *Scripts, plans, goals, and understanding.* Hillsdale, NJ: Erlbaum.

Schatzman, L., & Bucher, R. (1964). Negotiating a division of labor among professionals in the state mental hospital. *Psychiatry, 27,* 266–277.

Schoggen, P. (1983). Behavior settings and the quality of life. *Journal of Community Psychology, 11,* 144–157.

Secord, P.F. (1977). Social psychology in search of a paradigm. *Personality and Social Psychology Bulletin, 3,* 41–50.

Siegel, W.L. (1977). *How to run a successful restaurant.* New York: Wiley.

Simon, H.A. (1962). The architecture of complexity. *Proceedings of the American Philosophical Society, 106,* 467–482.

Smith, I. (1982). *Diary of a small business.* New York: Scribner.

Smith, M.B. (1974). Psychology in two small towns (Review of Qualities of Community Life by R.G. Barker and P. Schoggen). *Science, 184,* 671–673.

Starbuck, W.H. (1976). Organizations and their environments. In M.D. Dunnette (Ed.), *Handbook of industrial and organizational psychology* (pp. 1069–1123). Chicago: Rand-McNally.

Steinbruner, J.D. (1974). *The cybernetic theory of decision.* Princeton, NJ: Princeton University Press.

Steiner, I.D. (1972). *Group process and productivity.* New York: Academic.

Stinchcombe, A.L. (1965). Social structure and organizations. In J.G. March (Ed.), *Handbook of Organizations* (pp. 142–193). Chicago: Rand-McNally.

Stokols, D. (1982). Environmental psychology: A coming of age. In A. Kraut (Ed.), *G. Stanley Hall lecture series* (Vol. 2, pp. 155–205). Washington, DC: American Psychological Association.

Stokols, D., & Jacobi, M. (1983). The role of tradition in group-environment relations. In N. Feimer & S. Geller (Eds.), *Environmental psychology: Directions and perspectives* (pp. 157–179). New York: Praeger.

Stokols, D., & Jacobi, M. (1984). Traditional, present oriented, and futuristic modes of group-environment relations. In K. Gergen & M. Gergen (Eds.), *Historical social psychology* (pp. 303–324). Hillsdale, NJ: Erlbaum.

Stokols, D., & Shumaker, S.A. (1981). People in places: A transactional view of settings. In J.H. Harvey (Ed.), *Cognition, social behavior, and the environment* (pp. 441–488). Hillsdale, NJ: Erlbaum.

Strauss, A. (1978). *Negotiations: Varieties, contexts, processes, and social order.* San Francisco: Jossey-Bass.

Studer, R.G. (1978). The design and management of environment-behavior systems. In H. Hanloff (Ed.), *Bedingungen des Lebens in des Zukunft und dic Folgen für die Erziehung* [Conditions of life in the future and the consequences for education] (pp. 312–343). Berlin: Technische Universität Berlin.

Studer, R.G. (1980). Environmental design and management as evolutionary experimentation. *Journal of Design Studies, 1*, 365–371.

Todd, D.M. (1979). Contrasting adaptations to the social environment of a high school: Implications of a case study of helping behavior in two adolescent subcultures. In J.G. Kelly (Ed.), *Adolescent boys in high school: A psychological study of coping and adaptation* (pp. 177–186). Hillsdale, NJ: Erlbaum.

Van Maanen, J. (1977). Experiencing organization: Notes on the meaning of careers and socialization. In J. Van Maanen (Ed.), *Organizational careers: Some new perspectives* (pp. 15–45). New York: Wiley.

Vecchio, R.P., & Sussman, M. (1981). Staffing sufficiency and job enrichment: Support for an optimal level theory. *Journal of Occupational Behavior, 2*, 177–187.

Weick, K.E. (1976). Educational organizations as loosely coupled systems. *Administrative Science Quarterly, 21*, 1–19.

Weick, K.E. (1979a). Cognitive processes in organizations. In B.M. Staw (Ed.), *Research in Organizational Behavior* (Vol. 1, pp. 41–74). Greenwich, CT: Jai Press.

Weick, K.E. (1979b). *The social psychology of organizing* (2nd ed.). Reading, MA: Addison-Wesley.

Wellman, B. (1981). Applying network analysis to the study of support. In B.H. Gottlieb (Ed.), *Social networks and social support.* Beverly Hills, CA: Sage.

Whetten, D.A. (1980). Sources, responses, and effects of organizational decline. In J.R. Kimberly & R.H. Miles (Eds.), *The organizational life cycle: Issues in the creation, transformation, and decline of organizations* (pp. 342–374). San Francisco: Jossey-Bass.

Wicker, A.W. (1968). Undermanning, performances, and students' subjective experiences in behavior settings of large and small high schools. *Journal of Personality and Social Psychology, 10*, 255–261.

Wicker, A.W. (1969a). Cognitive complexity, school size, and participation in school behavior settings: A test of the frequency of interaction hypothesis. *Journal of Educational Psychology, 60*, 200–203.

Wicker, A.W. (1969b). Size of church membership and members' support of church behavior settings. *Journal of Personality and Social Psychology, 13*, 278–288.

Wicker, A.W. (1979). Ecological psychology: Some recent and prospective developments. *American Psychologist, 34*, 755–765.

Wicker, A.W. (1980, March). *The organizational contexts and life cycles of behavior settings.* Paper presented at the meeting of the Environmental Design Research Association, Charleston, SC.

Wicker, A.W. (1981). Nature and assessment of behavior settings: Recent contributions from the ecological perspective. In P. McReynolds (Ed.), *Advances in psychological assessment* (Vol. 5, pp. 22–61). San Francisco: Jossey-Bass.

Wicker, A.W. (1983). *An introduction to ecological psychology.* New York: Cambridge University Press. (Original work published 1979).

Wicker, A.W., & King, J.C. (in press). Life cycles of behavior settings. In J.E. McGrath (Ed.), *Research toward a social psychology of time.* Beverly Hills, CA: Sage.

Wicker, A.W., & Kirmeyer, S.L. (1976). From church to laboratory to national park: A program of research on excess and insufficient populations in behavior settings. In S. Wapner, S.B. Cohen, & B. Kaplan (Eds.), *Experiencing the environment* (pp. 157–185). New York: Plenum.

Wicker, A.W., Kirmeyer, S.L., Hanson, L., & Alexander, D. (1976). Effects of manning levels on subjective experiences, performance, and verbal interaction in groups. *Organizational Behavior and Human Performance, 17*, 251–274.

Wicker, A.W., McGrath, J.E., & Armstrong, G.E. (1972). Organization size and behavior setting capacity as determinants of member participation. *Behavioral Science, 17*, 499–513.

Willems, E.P., & Halstead, L.S. (1978). An eco-behavioral approach to health status and health care. In R.G. Barker (Ed.), *Habitats, environments, and human behavior: Studies in ecological psychology and eco-behavioral science from the Midwest Psychological Field Station, 1947–1972* (pp. 169–189). San Francisco: Jossey-Bass.

Chapter 17

RESIDENTIAL ENVIRONMENTS

Jerome Tognoli, *Department of Psychology, C.W. Post Campus, Long Island University, Greenvale, New York*

17.1. INTRODUCTION

Residential environment is used here as a neutral term to represent both home and housing, neighborhood and community. This chapter will examine this concept in three ways: by providing a critical overview of work centering on residential environments, a theoretical framework and organizational context for viewing such work, and some fruitful directions that work in the field must pursue.

Psychology, sociology, geography, anthropology, architecture, and planning all contribute to the multidisciplinary and interdisciplinary study of residential environments. Research in the field has proliferated over the last 20 years, focusing during this time on postoccupancy evaluation, mobility, cross-cultural observations, housing and the elderly, household roles, residential crowding, and the perception and meaning of housing and home. No theoretical approach appears to describe these disparate issues beyond a general interest in residential environments and the more specific concerns of each researcher, such as aging, perception, or sex roles. However, two basic organizing principles do emerge in the research literature: (1) emphasizing the differences between housing and home and (2) delineating a theory of residential adaptation, adjustment, and optimization.

As the constructs of *home* and *housing* are explored here, aspects of adaptation theory will be interwoven as they apply to various residential situations. In many cases, adaptation theory will have actually been used as a basis of particular research work, whereas in other cases, a reinterpretation of research findings is suggested according to adaptation theory.

17.1.1. Home and Housing

Research on home is concerned with that private and personal place that is highly idiosyncratic, whose shape changes fairly frequently, and whose image can be both multifaceted and also highly ephemeral. Home is both a physical place and a cognitive concept. The actual physical features of the dwelling, however, account for only a small portion of the definition of home. In fact, research on home shows a deemphasis on the physical and spatial, and a reliance on social, cognitive, cultural, and behavioral issues that emphasize home as security, comfort, and as a symbol of a place of departure and return. Humanistic geographers, psychologists, anthropologists, and architects interested in theory from a psychological perspective are concerned with the home. Their methodologies include armchair speculation, in-depth analysis of a few select individuals, a concentration on smaller units of behavior/action analysis, or more comprehensive statements of behavior sequences expressed in everyday language. Their data may be phenomenological, emphasizing intact and lengthy descriptions of cognitions and actions, or clinical and psychoanalytic case studies and interpretations emphasizing unconscious processes.

Housing is a term that defines the public rather than the private sphere. It emphasizes an ultimately knowable set of physical and spatial parameters rather than the behavior of only one individual in one house. Housing research is often large scale, emphasizing social concerns—the ultimate welfare and general satisfaction of the inhabitants. Sociologists, environmental psychologists, geographers, and planners are the foremost researchers on housing. Their methodology frequently involves large-scale surveys intended to yield universal statements regarding residents' behaviors, cognitions, and patterns of social activity. Although studies have compared changes over a long time span, housing research presents more often a static view of residents' lives. Thus once an evaluation of individuals in a housing project has been conducted, little interest is shown in residents' attitudes and behaviors. Housing research is often applied, representing a concern to address a particular problem or question concerning social groups—such as ways to reduce crime in neighborhoods or to increase feelings of security among elderly residents.

17.1.2. Adaptation, Adjustment, and Optimization

In outlining his theory of human adaptation to the environment, Wohlwill (1974) recommended that instead of describing settings in terms of particular places or attributes, one should characterize settings in terms of their stimulus dimensions, drawing on work in perception and motivation. He regarded potential environmental stressors in terms of both sensory deprivation and overstimulation and utilized dimensions of intensity, diversity, and patterning. Wohlwill draws on Helson's (1964) adaptation-level theory in defining adaptation as a "quantitative shift in the distribution of judgmental or affective responses along a stimulus continuum, as a function of continued exposure to a stimulus" (p. 134). Although insisting that adaptation was not a passive process, he also understood the need for including the process of adjustment—based on Sonnenfield (1966)—as a "change in the behavior which has the effect of mod-

ifying the stimulus conditions to which the individual is exposed" (p.135). Thus the system emphasizes individuals changing either by conforming to pressures from environmental stimuli (adaptation) or by affecting changes on the environment causing it to conform to their needs (adjustment). The basic aim is to neutralize the negative aspects of the affect state. One would expect some combination of adaptation and adjustment to occur in order to optimize the affect state. Stokols's (1978) concept of optimization is a further necessary extension to adaptation theory because it stresses a cyclical and feedback model incorporating cognitive and behavioral elements in which individuals attempt to fulfill needs by establishing goals and plans. Adaptation and optimization are expressed by individuals with respect to residential environments in a variety of ways. These include establishing forms of place attachment, affective bond, identification, expressions of satisfaction, preferences for particular residential settings, and engaging in mobility or in social interaction centering around family, household, and neighborhood relations.

In most cases, individuals live in a residence to which they are expected to adjust, adapt, or with which they are expected to cope. The relationship to residential setting is an evolving one best described as ongoing rather than based on a static attitude or fixed set of responses. The resident is viewed over time as someone who is affected by, and who changes, those places described as housing and home. The extensive literature on mobility emphasizes the part played by planning and goal attainment to satisfy housing needs. Unfortunately, not all expectations that residents have are met. In fact, Brickman and Campbell (1971) suggest that because of the unstable nature of adaptation levels, permanent satisfaction with one's environment is impossible to achieve. Nevertheless, individuals are constantly in a state of movement, shifting their attitudes, emotional responses, and behaviors in order to optimize personal satisfaction or happiness and a sense of congruence between self and place of residence.

Place dislocation can be viewed as a motivational basis of adaptation. When individuals experience or perceive a negative, disturbing, or disruptive state in terms of their relationship with their place of residence, a motivation to seek harmony or at least to stop the negative state from continuing should occur. This concept is aligned with theories of dissonance, cognitive congruence, balance, and social comparison, and it assumes that individuals will attempt to achieve the most harmonious relationship between themselves and their residence, when evaluation of the person–residence fit indicates a negative state. Virtually no research has been concerned with this intervening motivational state in connection with place of residence, but it is obvious from the structure of a great many studies that a state of disruption in relation to dwelling is a commonplace phenomenon. In the residential environment literature, negative states are manifested as feelings of isolation, alienation, dislocation, desire to move home, stress and strain, and a variety of residence-related pathologies including general ill health, depression, grief, and mental illness. In some cases, an emotional or motivational response to a setting provides a positive desire to achieve change. Those persons whose place of residence arouses feelings of alienation or isolation might engage in a variety of behaviors or changes in cognitive evaluation to allow themselves to feel more of a sense of harmony with their home. These might include redecorating or personalizing aspects of the home, changing social relationships within it such as opening up territorial boundaries or tightening them up to achieve greater privacy, or they might include a general reassessment or reemphasis of aspects of the home in order to alter the perception of it more positively.

In the majority of cases cited in the literature, negative reactions to home or residence are not treated as the basis of drive states or motivational forces leading to further behavioral or attitudinal change. The negative reactions are most often viewed as end states caused by antecedent conditions such as architectural style, social or physical density, economic deprivation, or the establishment of a particular set of domestic roles. Up to now, such a causal model has not proved to be useful for generating a theoretical approach to the study of residential environments—spaces that, of necessity, are defined as continuous, ongoing, enduring, historical, and future oriented, and imbued with vast and often contradictory meaning. On the other hand, a cyclical and temporal, though not necessarily linear and one-way, system more accurately describes the interaction process that individuals experience toward the residential environment. The continual input from such stimuli as the antecedent conditions cited before will probably continue to impinge on the person, and yet a state of complete adaptation or optimization will possibly never be achieved. In fact, there is always the probability that conditions that are initially viewed as satisfactory no longer provide pleasure and that boredom and a need for further stimulation will arise.

A final section of this chapter will be devoted to examining the way that new directions in research on home and housing are indicated. Changing social roles, a sensitivity to the needs of various social groups, a softening of the lines of definition between housing and home, and an understanding of the psychohistorical aspects of residence are all part of this changing landscape.

17.2. HOME AND HOUSING

17.2.1. Home

Six aspects of home to be explored in this section include (a) centrality, rootedness, and place attachment; (b) continuity, unity, and order; (c) privacy, refuge, security, and ownership; (d) self-identity and gender differences; (e) social and family relationships; and (f) sociocultural context. These components relate to an ideal concept of home that emerges as the product of adjustment and optimization of goals through the satisfaction of certain needs. Additionally, circumstances of alienation and homelessness, forced relocation, crowding, and domestic stress all indicate the presence of an underlying motivational force that most likely gives rise to adaptive responses or optimizing behaviors designed to return one to a less negative state. Although it is possible to describe individuals who have overcompensated—who are too centered or attached and overly concerned with continuity, privacy, self-identity, and social and family relations and therefore would need to reduce these in order to achieve a more harmonious domestic experience—little, if any, research has been aimed in this direction. This section will explore situations that indicate underrepresentation or underachievement of the ideal state, such as feelings of alienation or diffusedness regarding personal and cultural identity, detachment, social deprivation, low social or high spatial density, discontinuity with the past, overconcern with the public sphere, overemphasis of mobility and relocation, and a lack of unity. Attention will likewise be given to those occasions where adaptation and adjustment follow.

Centrality, Rootedness, and Place Attachment

Home is seen as rootedness and the central place of human existence and is discussed by a variety of writers (Bachelard, 1969; Dovey, 1978; Jung, 1963; Marc, 1977; Norberg-Schulz, 1971; Relph, 1976; and

Tuan, 1977). *Home* refers to a pivotal point around which human activity revolves. This concept of centeredness also implied rootedness, territoriality, attachment to place, and seeing the home as a place from which to reach out and to which to return. It is also a base of activity and a place where significant experiences occur. It represents an ideal toward which individuals will gravitate, especially when disruptions to the physical or social system occur producing alienation or diffusion or an overly centered existence. The profound and central nature of dwelling is addressed in Jung's (1963) autobiography, *Memories, Dreams and Reflections*, in which he discusses the construction and dwelling experience of his own towerlike home as an archetypal form whose meaning resonated with his own psyche. Jung's work had a strong influence on Bachelard (1969) who also recognized the central importance of home as a psychological concept. In fact, Bachelard felt that the physical structure that individuals experienced as their childhood home had a strong bearing on all other life experiences. These ideas have been put to empirical test in the work of Korosec-Serfaty (1979) who observed that home did have a persistent and continuous influence over time on her respondents. Researchers have only begun to comprehend, phenomenologically, what houses mean to children—how they perceive them and conceptualize them. A Piagetian model of children's development of dwelling space is offered by Thornberg (1973) in which four stages emerge from children's explanations of constructions made from play materials. Whereas the youngest age group maintained a ritualized sense of space, later stages reflected functional identity and fixed roles, a concrete concept of place accompanied by deep change in structure, and lastly the enclosing of forms to signify social function.

A similar set of stages was suggested in the work of Filipovitch, Juliar, and Ross (1981) who asked children from the fourth, seventh, and twelfth grades in the United States to draw a picture of where they lived. The youngest drew stereotyped houses (equivalent, perhaps, to Thornberg's ritualized space), the middle group indicated interest in exploring beyond the boundaries of the house (suggestive of Thornberg's deep change in structure), and the older group centered on the dwelling as an individualized and personalized place (somewhat evocative of Thornberg's social function). These perceptual features appear to range between intimate and public and correspond roughly to the distinctions between home and housing. Closely related, then, to the issue of centrality is the one concerning continuity and memory that will be addressed in the next section.

Other work on dwelling as a Jungian archetype and core concept of human consciousness includes Rykwert's (1972) exploration of the hut as a basic house form and as being representative of the mother's womb and Marc's (1977) study of children's drawings as an expression of rudimentary aspects of dwelling. Although the ideas espoused by these authors may have important consequences, they still require empirical verification. Similarly, the works of Norberg-Schulz (1971), Bochner (1975), Relph (1976), Tuan (1977), Dovey (1978), and Seamon (1982) discuss the strong centering quality that home has in people's lives, but again empirical research is lacking. In this work, rootedness is stressed as an essential feature of home, and it is implied that individuals, once rooted, feel freer to venture outside home boundaries to explore their environments, knowing that there is the security of a place to which to return. Hart (1978), Newson and Newson (1976), and Whiting and Edwards (1973) discuss home range in terms of important distinctions that develop between parents and children. Girls acquire a much more restricted sense of distances traveled from home when accompanied by parents. Parents are more likely to meet their young daughters after school and escort them home, whereas sons will be allowed more freedom to travel home on their own—especially at an earlier age. Thus adjustment and adaptation have different meanings for different social groups.

The psychoanalytic notions of "separation anxiety" and "refueling" as outlined by Winnecott (1971) and Mahler (1968) seem most relevant here if one is willing to equate home with parent. Object relations theory describes a situation where the child makes gradual attempts to separate out successfully from the parents (and the home) into a strange and sometimes fearful world. It likewise becomes critical to return to the parents (and to the home) for a boost of confidence, security, rootedness, or a sense of centeredness. Empirical research here will be useful to explore the possible connections object relations theory poses for environmental psychology and residential environments in particular.

Those individuals possessing high degrees of place attachment will be more firmly rooted, less motivated to seek change, and more satisfied with their place of residence. Closely allied with place attachment is the concept of territoriality that argues that individuals are predisposed to be attached to place. Presumably, if territoriality is disturbed through invasion of privacy or forced relocation, equilibratory moves should occur to reclaim territory as quickly as possible or to adjust one's cognitive state with respect to territorial claims so that the invasion is no longer perceived as threatening.

As an aspect of place attachment, the concept of defensible space essentially represents an attempt to maintain a state of equilibrium plus the degree of privacy, territoriality, and personal space sufficient to achieve satisfaction, comfort, and security in one's dwelling space. Disruption, invasion, or deprivation of access to one's home can give rise to a motivational state to recover that space. Opportunity for control over one's home space appears to be an essential aspect of defensible space. Similarly, research using the concept of appropriation suggests that there is a basic human need to occupy and claim space to achieve some sense of belonging and identification and usually some degree of personalization of dwelling space. There appears to be a recognition that unless appropriation claims are allowed to be fulfilled, residents will experience tension because optimization did not obtain.

Continuity, Unity, and Order

The concept of temporal continuity of home will be explored first, followed by the related issues of order, ritual, and unity. Home as continuity (explored by Allott & Ladd, 1976; Anthony, 1984a; Bachelard, 1969; Cooper, 1974; Dovey, 1978; Hayward, 1975, 1977; Helphand, 1978; Hester, 1979; Hollerorth, 1974; Horwitz, Klein, Paxton, & Rivlin, 1978; Horwitz & Tognoli, 1982; Korosec-Serfaty, 1979; Ladd, 1977; Seamon, 1979; Lawrence, 1983b; Tognoli & Horwitz, 1982; Tuan, 1977) includes aspects of heritage, rootedness, life and death, time, generational life span, connections with one's origins, memory of childhood home, and connection with one's past. Although there is strong evidence for a direct line of continuity connecting present with past, it is also possible that memories of past homes are distorted to fit the current conception of one's present abode. Evidence of discontinuity and a desire by children to break from the constraints of the parents' home suggests that direct continuity is not always the case. There are also those individuals who might be described as overconnecting with the past so as to fail to establish a firm self–residence link. In these cases, however, the establishing of connections is a form of adjustment. Presumably, when disconnection

occurs, this serves as a motivating state to goad the individual into an adjustment mode allowing reconnection with home.

Continuity is explored in research work in a variety of ways (Allott & Ladd, 1976; Helphand, 1978; Hester, 1979; Horwitz, et al., 1978; Horwitz & Tognoli, 1982; Tognoli & Horwitz, 1982). These studies use memories of childhood home to tap into rich associations that place memory provides. In other cases (Dovey, 1978; Hayward, 1977; Korosec-Serfaty, 1979; Relph, 1976; Seamon, 1979; Tuan, 1977), the interest is in the home itself—how a sense of it evolves and what are its antecedents. Anthony (1984a) examined memories of favorite homes among a population who had moved away and later returned to visit them and noted a very high degree of emphasis on meaningful experiences rather than on the physical features of these places. This adaptive response helps affirm the proposed distinction surrounding home and housing. Other work, primarily of a psychoanalytic persuasion (Bachelard, 1969; Cooper, 1974; Hollerorth, 1974; Jung, 1963) is concerned to show how home represents an archetypal image whose memory evokes powerful sexual and social associations that allow a person to comprehend a more complete and complex sense of self, both in conjunction with home and also outside it.

Although the psychoanalytic notions are hardest to submit to empirical test, all the previously mentioned aspects are potentially researchable and in need of further investigation. There is a surprisingly large amount of anecdotal, literary, and fictional material published on reminiscences about childhood and early home experiences (Hollerorth, 1974), much of which indicates what an emotionally charged and important topic it is. Environmental psychologists can help create an interface with the work of literary critics in order to develop a viable and energetic area of research.

Home has been viewed as a symbol of unity, order, ritual and sacredness by the following authors: Raglan (1964), Bachelard (1969), Sommer (1972), Pynoos, Schafer, and Hartman (1973), Gardiner (1974), Cooper (1974), Tagg (1974), Lugassy (1976), Barbey (1976), Marc (1977), Dovey (1978), Tuan (1977, 1979), Seamon (1979), Saile (1977, 1986), Csikszentmihalvi and Rochberg-Halton (1981), Heidmets (1983), and Korosec-Serfaty (1984b). There is much overlap here with the concept of home as continuity as illustrated in the work of Lord Raglan (1964). He asserted that the sacred quality of dwelling was traceable, first, to the idea that gods and kings inhabited temples whose architectural features were later imitated by the general population and second, that this notion of filtering or influence always occurred from the top down and never the other way around. Although a loosely organized cultural lag theory does seem to support the thesis, it leaves much more to be explained because the majority of researchers seem to prefer a more complex and multifaceted definition of home. Even if house structure and domestic design features did have their origins in sacred and royal contexts, it is extremely unlikely that the meaning of such features has survived in any recognizable form to influence current inhabitants. It seems more likely that symbolic qualities of home evolve into new forms as they are culturally communicated from one generation to the next.

Home itself is represented as an ideal of unity and order, and many individuals are motivated to seek these qualities in order to achieve an optimal relation with home. But it could happen that this ideal raises too much conflict in individuals because their own homes are too disordered, which thereby creates a constant source of tension. It would be important to examine the expectations about home life held by individuals who are divorced, separated, or engaged in severe marital discord. It is possible that these groups feel they cannot reconcile their nonordered domestic lives with an idealized concept of home as expressed through the concept of unity. Nevertheless, there are others who maintain a strong belief in the unifying powers of home even though these are discrepant with actual behaviors. One aspect that needs to be explored further is the conditions under which the idealized concept of unity manages to be tolerated as opposed to being a source of tension.

Privacy, Refuge, Security, and Ownership

Home is a place where one feels comfortable and at ease, which feels familiar and warm, and which one loves and which can serve as a retreat from the more public world of work. It is also a place that can provide an opportunity for restoration, energy, and regeneration. Writers on this aspect of home include Pynoos, Schafer, and Hartman (1973), Norberg-Schulz (1971, 1980a,b), Relph (1976), Barbey (1976), Hayward (1977), Tuan (1977), Dovey (1978), Wolfe (1978), Parke (1978), Seamon (1979), Vinsel, Brown, Altman, and Foss (1980), Korosec-Serfaty (1979), Altman and Gauvain (1981), Anthony (1984b), and Sanford (1984).

Home is often established as a dialectic polarity in which nonhome and the outside world are juxtaposed with privacy and retreat. Here, home dwellers are depicted as preparing for the onslaught and ravages of the world outside by obtaining strength, often of a spiritual nature. In the nineteenth-century works of Harriet Beecher Stowe and her sister Katherine Beecher, discussed by the social critic architects Hayden (1980) and Wright (1981), it was assumed to be the woman's responsibility to provide a secure, warm, and restorative domestic environment so that men would not be led too far astray by worldly temptations. If the home were spiritually and physically clean, then men would be drawn back to its female bosom, thus affirming its harmonious quality. However, as women enter the labor market in increasingly greater numbers today, both men and women will be in competition for those qualities of home that will provide this refuge and a place of comfort.

It is assumed that the home is where privacy is most needed. Carlisle (1982) examines privacy markers in French upper-middle-class homes and notes how the more intimate areas of the house are often located behind a number of barriers such as doors, windows, hallways, grillwork, and curtains. This adaptive response of residents to possible outside threats has evolved culturally over a long period of time. Although it might appear difficult for researchers to conceptualize research designs to study adaptation and adjustment in such a long-term context, they should rise to meet this challenge with imaginative projects. One possible way is suggested by Anthony (1984b) who discusses the role of the physical environment of home in regulating family conflicts over issues such as privacy. Her study illustrates a way in which therapists could learn to monitor clients' responses to the physical setting over a period of time in order to document adaptive and adjustment changes.

With regard to children, privacy in the home appears to be less available to boys than girls. Possibly this is because girls are expected to be at home more than boys, and therefore some compensation must be made for the girls. Parke (1978) has noted that more rigid and restrictive household rules arise concerning girls than boys. For example, parents tend to be more respectful of rules for knocking on bedroom doors before entering for daughters than for sons. Also, fathers were restricted from entering bathrooms by daughters when the girls reached the ages of 10 to 13. This restrictiveness was not exercised until the ages of 14 to 17 for most sons. Adaptations to reductions in privacy may prove difficult for many boys, thus leading to social withdrawal and subsequent alienation from other individuals outside the family. On the other hand, access to privacy for children was generally found to be connected with self-esteem (Aloia, 1973; Golan, 1978), the production of positive social behavior (Golan, 1978; Murray, 1974), and allowing the child to separate from others in order to individuate and become more self-reliant (Wolfe, 1978). All of these findings serve as examples of adaptive behavior designed to optimize one's relationship with the home and, subsequently, with the world outside.

Home ownership is tangentially connected with privacy in that ownership signifies less permeable and inviolable boundaries than renting. Much of what appears in this section would apply equally well to housing, thus indicating some of the overlap that exists regarding the definitions of housing and home. Writers concerned with the issues of ownership include Pynoos, Schafer, and Hartman (1973), Hayward (1975, 1977), Relph (1976), Barilleau and Lombardo (1976), Burns (1975), Agnew (1982), Altman and Gauvain (1981), Korosec-Serfaty (1979, 1984a), Lawrence (1981, 1982b), Gans (1962, 1967, 1968), Seeley, Sim, and Loosley (1963), Couper and Brindley (1975), Werthman (1968), and Perin (1977).

Those who rent are more likely to be perceived by homeowners as those who lack a commitment to stay put. But this will depend on the community itself. It has been suggested by Perin (1977) that when individuals rent, they are disenfranchised from many aspects of community life such as the social networking among social and business groups in a particular setting. This may apply particularly to individuals who rent houses in a suburban community. On the other hand, in more urban contexts where renting is the norm, individuals who live in close social groupings will have an opportunity for social networking based on physical proximity and shared social values.

In some cases, individuals will be motivated to own, simply as investment, irrespective of feelings of attachment to place. It has been suggested that a sort of possessive individualism results (Agnew, 1982), thus predisposing residents toward a reduced sense of social consciousness and lack of community involvement. Exchange value and the concept of home as a source of status are important here, as are issues surrounding home as investment and the protection of equity.

In light of adaptation theory, one can visualize how the physical structure can be adapted in order to maximize satisfaction. Owner and renter options might include choosing housing to suit one's needs or making changes in the housing or decor to create a more comfortable setting, each under differing degrees of perceived control.

Self-Identity and Gender Differences

Home as self-identification incorporates the following aspects: personalization, individualism, appropriation, social and gender identification with home, identification as belonging, feeling in control, feeling habituated or adapted, and feeling that one has the freedom to do as one chooses. The following authors have written on these subjects: Lauman and House (1970), Norberg-Schulz (1971, 1980), Pynoos, Schafer, and Hartman (1973), Cooper (1974), Vershure, Magel, and Sadalla (1976), Barilleau and Lombardo (1976), Barbey (1976), Relph (1976), Allott and Ladd (1976), Hayward (1977), Ladd (1977), Helphand (1978), Horwitz et al. (1978), Dovey (1978), Hester (1979), Korosec-Serfaty (1979, 1984a), Ofrias and Tognoli (1979), Altman and Gauvain (1981), Seamon (1979), Vershure (1980), Sadalla, Burroughs, and Quaid (1980), Altman and Gauvain (1981), N. Duncan (1982), Csikszentmihalyi and Rochberg-Halton (1982), Horwitz and Tognoli (1982), Loyd (1982), Tognoli and Horwitz (1982), Cowan (1983), and Kron (1983). In the majority of cases, self-identification means that there is a necessary connection with place—a person–home connection—in which the boundaries between person and home become enmeshed and in which home becomes an expression of its occupants. There have been a number of popular treatments of home and furnishings as personality indicators of their owners. Kron's (1983) *Home-Psych* suggests ways in which empirical research on person–home identification can be undertaken. Findings already exist that show that individuals do invest a portion of their personalities into home decoration. For example, Hansen and Altman (1976) studied dormitory room personalization in terms of whether students remained or left university after their first year. Other work on home personalization attests to its importance for a variety of subject groups (Altman & Chemers, 1980; Altman, Nelson, & Lett, 1972; Sommer, 1969; Vinsel, et al., 1980).

One attempt to explore the connection between self and place (home) is in Cooper's (1974) often-quoted article on the symbol of home as a concept of the self. Cooper isolates features of the home setting and shows how they serve as concrete manifestations of an individual's personality. Here, identification of self with home provides a sense of harmony and equilibrium as an ideal. But, as with many cases of anecdotal reports, stronger empirical verification is needed.

The one area where empirical verification of home/self-identification has been vigorously explored is with respect to work on sex roles and the home. Because more women are taking on the demanding dual roles of wife/mother and worker outside the home, demands to adapt to role pressures may occur rather than allowing for the possibility of adjustment or alteration of the conditions. This may result simply because the latter are more difficult to achieve. Men, on the other hand, even when forced to contend with increasing demands to participate in household management, may not experience the same pressures to adapt to the press of these domestic and work conditions. Men often find it easier to adjust the stimulus conditions to lessen the negative impact. More means are at men's disposal as a function of being a part of an advantaged group.

A dichotimization of domestic sex role identity is documented for both Western and non-Western cultures. Basically, women spend a greater amount of time inside the home compared to men (Saegert & Hart, 1976; Saegert & Winkel, 1980), and more women than men tend to regard the home in terms of self-identity, according to Hayward (1977). Women tend to do a proportionally greater amount of housework compared to men (Berk, 1980; Mackintosh, Olsen, & Wentworth, 1977; Pleck, 1975, 1979; Pleck & Rustad, 1980; Walker & Woods, 1976), even when the women are employed at full-time occupations outside the home. Also, household activities have been shown to be differentially conceptualized by male and female occupants (Tognoli, 1980). That men spend less time in the home than women, especially when divorced or when socializing with friends, has been noted by Hetherington, Cox, and Cox (1976), and Watson and Kivett (1976) report low father involvement with their families as a constant finding across the life span.

Content analyses of television programming and commercials have shown a consistent trend depicting female characters in demeaned domestic settings and male characters in varied and more prestigious settings outside the home (Belson, 1959, 1967; Cantor, 1978; Hennessee & Nicholson, 1972; Hoffman, 1972; Thorne & Henley, 1975; Tognoli & Storch, 1980; Women on Words and Images, 1975). Tibbetts (1975) showed a similar trend with respect to characters in children's books and textbooks. These conditions in the media are felt to be causal agents in shaping domestic sex role attitudes and behaviors, and some empirical evidence now exists to support this contention (Tognoli & Hornberger, 1984).

Whereas the dichotomy in United States and Western cultures exists primarily through role differentiation, there is cross-cultural work among non-Western cultures showing that physical areas of the house are designated or identified as female or male (Cunningham, 1973; Littlejohn, 1967; Morgan, 1965) or that women and men and girls and boys actually occupy separate houses (Fraser, 1968, 1974; LeVine, 1962; Rapoport, 1969) or have access to separate spheres of influence (J. Duncan, 1982a). Stea and Prussin (1978), in fact, argue that as Western cultures impinge on more traditional cultures, such as with the trend toward sedentarization among nomadic groups, considerable strain to adapt or adjust to new sex roles arises.

Some research indicates an aroused affect state when changes result in family role stimulus conditions (Burke & Weir, 1976; Cohen, 1979; Howell, 1976; Keith & Schafer, 1980; Voydanoff, 1980). Men who reach middle age or older and whose roles are most traditional and least flexible often find themselves in conflict with family life experiences that demand change and perhaps some adjustment of stimulus conditions. Instances of marital discord, depression, or poor mental health were reported among these men. As pressures for men to engage in the sharing of family work increase so that the opportunity for adjustment of the stimulus conditions becomes less possible, those men who are least flexible in their outlook are likely to report the greatest difficulty adapting or achieving a satisfactory level of family involvement.

Middle-class women in dual-career families report role strain and depression, according to Keith and Schafer (1980) and Pleck (1979), and much of that seems to be the result of stress induced by household labor and role overload. In the Mackintosh et al. (1977) study of urban families who had moved to the suburbs where fewer jobs for women were available, the women generally disliked the move and claimed that they felt isolated and that they had become boring to their husbands and families. On the other hand, greater satisfaction with suburban locations was indicated by husbands than by their wives. In these situations, there is often little that can be done by the wife to alleviate the conditions through direct adjustment of role pressures if the husband is unwilling to cooperate. Therefore, she is left to adapt to the role demands.

There is a body of work on children's play that affirms the domestic sex role dichotomy just described for adults. Maccoby and Jacklin (1974) summarize data that indicate that by the age of 3 to 4, a sex role identity is established showing girls devoting more time to household-oriented toys such as doll houses, clothes, and cooking equipment, and boys devoting more time to play that is suggestive of an outdoor orientation involving carpenter tools, wheeled toys, and blocks. Hart (1978) observed outdoor play among young children and found that boys preferred to construct miniature landscapes of large-scale, nondomestic environments such as highways, airports, towns, or racetracks, whereas girls would only engage in these settings if they were with the boys. Otherwise, the girls preferred to construct houses and decorate their interiors.

Evidence suggests that domestic sex role attitudes among children are acquired early on—probably through a socialization process involving modeling, social reinforcement, and identification. One might expect that when children in play situations do not show "sufficient" development along "appropriate" sex role lines, they will be goaded into adapting. It is also perhaps in these early years that boys learn that adjustment of stimulus conditions is more within their realm of possibility than it is for girls.

Home as a Context of Social and Family Relations

This definition of home refers to household or domestic life. It would more than double the number of citations of the research literature to include all the available studies dealing with family life, family and marital relations, and children because most of these situations do occur within a home context. Yet, it is often serendipitous as to whether the physical context of home is actually mentioned. Therefore, unless the concept of home specifically prefigures in research studies, they will not be included here. Those writers concerned with the concept of home as a set of social relationships include Pynoos, Schafer, and Hartman (1973), Cooper (1974), Hollerorth (1974), Allott and Ladd (1976), Lugassy (1976), Relph (1976), Hayward (1977), Ladd (1977), Helphand (1978), Horwitz et al. (1978), Hester (1979), Seamon (1979), Csikszentmihalyi and Rochberg-Halton (1981), Altman and Gauvin (1981), N. Duncan (1982), Horwitz and Tognoli (1982), Lawrence

(1982a, 1983a), Tognoli and Horwitz (1982), and Staines and Pleck (1983).

Within this category of social relations comes work on sex role differences already discussed. Also, much of the work on home as continuity is based on the idea that past relations with family and friends have helped shape the current concept of home. Additionally, social relations include aspects of privacy, refuge, and crowding. When one thinks of home, one often construes it as a set of interactions illustrated by examples such as "at home my parents often have drinks together before dinner," "dinner time is the only time we ever get together and talk as a family," "my parents never entertain anyone at home except relatives," "I like to bring my friends over to my house to play," or "my wife and I share equally in childcare activities about the house." By serving as a context of social interaction, often of an intense and highly personal or intimate nature, the home acquires an idiosyncratic definition that might be useful for understanding family relations in a therapeutic context. Anthony (1984b) suggests something similar when she recommends that therapists attend to the meaning of the home setting when dealing with family conflict.

In this social context, adjustment and adaptation and optimization are commonplace activities. There are homes in which children must adapt to regimented life-styles of their parents, and these might include having precise mealtimes with a high standard of table manners and expectations of involved conversations. On the other hand, there are families where the parents have adapted to their children's erratic life-styles, which might mean the children are not even present at the table because they are with friends or at meetings or perhaps are eating or watching television in their bedrooms.

Parke and Sawin (1979) have noted the way in which television has come to occupy a central position in the home environment for parents and children alike. The implications of this are pointed out in terms of the shortage of time then left for other activities. Again, this appears to be an instance of adaptation to a changing environment rather than one in which an optimal relationship with the home is purposely sought. The influence of television on children and on family life has been documented by Maccoby (1951), Belson (1959), Lyle (1971), and Parke (1978). Although families with television spend more time at home, less of it is spent in joint family activity not involving television. Parke (1978), in fact, felt that the negative impact of high amounts of television watching in children could be manifested years later as social isolatedness.

Home as a Sociocultural Context

Acting as a transition between the two sections on home and housing is work that emphasizes the dwelling in its cultural context. Anthropological studies often refer to the terms *house* or *dwelling* rather than *home*, thus connoting a definition that is less personal and introspective and more sociobehavioral and rooted in physical surroundings. It is the work of Rapoport that will concern us here—primarily because he has written so extensively on dwelling in the sociocultural context and because his theoretical positions regarding congruence mesh so well with adaptation theory.

Whereas culture, generally, was viewed as having a direct influence on house form (as advocated in the work of Lord Raglan [1964] and Deffontaines [1948]), Rapoport's (1969) now classic *House Form and Culture* claimed that because of the complex nature of various forces, one must speak of coincidences, or as Altman and Chemers (1980) call it, the "interplay" of environmental and cultural factors. Physical features such as climate, construction methods, and availability of materials are designated as secondary factors, whereas the primary sociocultural factors would include way of life, societal ordering, attendance to basic needs, family structure, position of women and men, privacy, territoriality, and social organization and social relations. This chapter views these factors as dependent measures, as manifestations of adaptation and also as part of a person–residence interaction where specification of cause and effect is impossible to sort out.

In Rapoport's (1980b) work on cross-cultural definitions of housing, he cites a variety of different conceptual approaches to the study of meaning and the nature of dwelling and housing. These include housing as product, process, function, place, behavior setting, territory, privacy, and as a multidimensional entity. Rapoport makes us aware that housing cannot be viewed according to conventional Western standards primarily because it is conceptualized so differently by the vast majority of people who live outside Western and U.S. cultures. In fact, even within U.S. culture, Rapoport argues that no single a priori definition is suitable. Instead, one must really examine the house–settlement complex especially in relation to activities which occur there. Rapoport describes eight criteria that he feels can be used to provide a profile or a more culturally valid definition of housing.

These aspects include 1) the symbolic and physical characteristics of those places that are used; 2) who uses these places; 3) where the user groups locate themselves; 4) when the settings are used; 5) the amount of time spent in various places; 6) the rules accompanying each place; 7) the overall activity systems and their latent aspects; and 8) the spatial and temporal relationships among the various settings. In conjunction with notions of adaptation, it would follow that the flexibility of the preceding list would allow residents to locate a set of behaviors and to name a variety of settings that would provide for them optimal person–environment relationships, given the constraints of the culture.

In a later statement written for Duncan's (1982b) *Housing and Identity*, Rapoport (1982) argued that the dwelling was subsidiary to the culture in which it is located and also was ultimately inseparable from the cultural core. Also, he felt that communication within the culture was facilitated when environment and identity were congruent. When such circumstances occur, life becomes more simplified, and routine substitutes for chaos or disruption. The dwelling and the activities surrounding it, as a function of the coded meaning communicated (or reflected), circumscribes a limited set of responses that residents will then be induced to emit. Thus the dwelling acts to control or limit behavior, and it serves the role of ordering the world.

Rapoport (1982) felt that sociocultural identity was partly expressed in terms of the distinction of dwelling according to various orderings—such as front–back, male–female, sacred–profane, and good–bad. Lawrence's (1981, 1982b) set of bipolar concepts—clean–dirty, front–back, and public–private—on the other hand, presented binary classification as a way of understanding how activities were coordinated with home space. Achieving a successful sense of sociocultural identity and the coordination of behavior with home space are two ways of describing adaptation or adjustment, thus providing an alternative approach for examining cross-cultural work.

In an elaborate statement on cross-cultural aspects of environmental design, Rapoport (1980a) delineated a cognitive congruence model in which environments (in this case dwellings or settlements) are considered to be approximations of the cognitive schemata held by residents of a particular culture. Culture is defined as either cognitive and symbolic meanings or as life-style. A third aspect, dealing with the process of cultural adaptation is not considered because cultures themselves are meant to be fairly resistant to change. Inhabitants, on the other hand, are perceived as having control over their setting (a form of adjustment), and this can be expressed through habitat selection and behaviors connected with relocation. If these behaviors are blocked, they can create a major crisis for individuals, presumably because of the failure to achieve congruence between life-style and dwelling/settlement. Elements important in maintaining this congruence include the nature of the group, communication and privacy needs, symbols of status, the nature of activity systems, and the social organization.

The introduction of Western aspects of dwelling into traditional settings is discussed by Rapoport (1980a) in terms of the disruptions and subsequent adaptations that might result. For example, Jaulin (1971) and Hamilton (1972) stressed the positive significance of darkness inside the homes of the Motilone Indians and the Australian aborigines, respectively, and both these settings were shown to be negatively affected by the introduction of lighting and increased ventilation. Saile (1976) actually advised architects from developing countries to employ design methods that had meanings for local communities, that could be afforded, that responded to climate and geography, and that contributed to a local sense of home or place. One approach was to look for solutions that were rooted in the local community.

A particular type of adaptation, referred to as "defensive structuring," is cited by Rapoport (1980a) as providing social identity and helping to create solidarity. Through the concept of perceived homogeneity of neighborhoods, for example, a variety of positive adaptive outcomes are achieved, including increased predictability, reduced stress, relaxation, reduction in perceived density, temporal organization, agreement over environmental quality and reduced conflicts over standards, mutual support during times of stress and cultural change, increases in perceived control, and increased personalization that in turn leads to coherent character, urban complexity (but not chaos), and a social identity.

In the sections on neighborhood, mobility, and crowding, further cross-cultural work is cited as it applies to housing research in conjunction with adaptation theory. By definition, cross-cultural studies often place themselves outside the province of home by insisting, as Rapoport has, that dwelling can be best understood by knowing about the settlement in which it is located. In essence, housing research emphasizes a macroscopic, socially based conception of residence as the basic unit of analysis, but like the research work on home, it, too, emphasizes both the personal and the psychological as well as the public and the social.

17.2.2. Housing

Whereas home appears to be a concept as well as a physical entity, the definition of housing is more rooted in the concrete world. The areas of research dealing with residential environments that give rise to a definition of housing include methodology, perception and preference of housing, and behavioral observations of individuals in a variety of residential settings. More specifically, six categories seem to account for and name the concerns of housing research: (1) cognitive evaluation: perception, preference, satisfaction, and place attachment; (2) neighborhood; (3) mobility and relocation; (4) crowding; (5) group identification among special populations: the elderly, children, and the developmentally disabled; and (6) housing and social issues.

Housing research is concerned with objective measurement and description. Also, many housing research studies demonstrate that a certain degree of adaptation, adjustment, or optimization to new (or even old) stimulus conditions has taken place. Words like *adaptation, adjustment*, and *coping* appear frequently in the research literature, but they are often used casually, with no real empirical proof that such processes have actually occurred. The intention in the following sections is to show the potential that exists for utilizing adaptation theory as a unifying principle in discussing this large body of research. Certain areas lend themselves readily to this theoretical mode — especially those dealing with housing for the elderly, cognitive evaluation, and residential mobility and relocation. In fact, it is when there has been a change in the stimulus conditions of housing that residents must begin to make sense of their dwelling both behaviorally and cognitively and to recreate a situation where emotional arousal is no longer a dominant negative force.

Much of the literature dealing with housing as structure concentrates on the description of physical parameters. Research studies center on forms that include single-family detached dwellings, low-level massing, high-rise housing, mobile homes, duplex and row houses, garden apartments, temporary shelters, irregular housing form, and unusual dwellings like underground housing (Dillman & Dillman, 1981; Egolf & Herrenkohl, 1975; Faletti, 1979; Laudadio, 1977; Marans, 1976; Robinson, 1980; Snyder-

McKenna & Morris, 1981; Volkman, 1981; Wallis, 1982; Weber, 1981).

Cognitive Evaluation: Perception, Preference, Satisfaction, and Attachment

HOUSING PERCEPTION

Housing perception research (see Marans's 1976 review) represents a rudimentary aspect of cognitive evaluation by providing some objective descriptions of the parameters of dwelling. A wide range of parameters exists, and these include variation, umbrageousness and openness (Garling, 1972), length of residence, age of individual and size of residential area (Taylor & Townsend, 1976), diversity, clarity, and decreasing building prominence (Nasar, 1979), housing as symbol, art, and social status (Tobey, 1982), contrast, complexity, naturalness, and visible development as predictors of appropriateness of residential structures (Gobster, 1983), the influence of attention and activity on defining the focal point of a room (Canter, Gilchrist, Miller, & Roberts, 1974), and cleanliness, silence, privacy, energy efficiency, concern about window views, and possible lowered socioeconomic class associations among residents of underground housing (Volkman, 1981).

An unexplored aspect of research on housing perception concerns its connection with adaptation theory. The cognitive shifting of one's perception to accommodate changes in stimulus conditions means that individuals are able to make adjustment and coping responses concerning residence in order to achieve a more harmonious sense of it. For example, the list of qualities cited at the beginning of this section acknowledges that housing is multifaceted and therefore that residents should be able to shift their attention to a variety of different aspects in order to achieve a satisfactory relationship with the dwelling. How that process of attention occurs should be the focus of attention in future research.

HOUSING PREFERENCE

Housing preference forms a second area of concentration related to cognitive evaluation. According to a number of reports—both anecdotal and empirical—the preferred form of housing is the detached single-family variety. Authors who have written on this subject include Cramer (1960), Cowburn (1966), Lansing (1966), Michelson (1970a, 1977), Foote, Abu-Lughod, Foley, & Winnick (1970), Hinshaw & Allott (1972), Cooper (1974), Ward (1976), Kaplan (1977), Marc (1977), Mulvihill & McHugh (1977), Robinson

(1980), Thorne, Hall, & Munro-Clark (1982), and Marmot (1982). Irregular forms of housing and those with the lowest levels of massing are also preferred according to Faletti (1979), and in some cases reference is specifically made to the nonpreference for multifamily housing, because such dwellings signify lack of control and lack of self-expression (Robinson, 1980). In addition, Conway and Adams (1977) point out that parents with young children indicate a dislike of high-rise housing. In fact, Hancock (1980) has discussed how the concept of the apartment in the United States has acquired a negative image since the early twentieth century, particularly because it was thought to be a carrier of disease. Even as late as 1929, apartments were not perceived as homes—perhaps serving to justify our twofold classification system of home and housing.

A variety of studies on housing obtains ratings concerning which forms are most preferred, and an unusual assortment of contingencies appear to qualify people's decisions. For example, in a study of residential migration among affluent British families by Bateman, Burtenshaw, and Duffett (1974), the actual physical nature of the choice of housing stock hardly affected the search process, whereas factors like the commuting distance from work, comparison with working class housing and developments, and being nearby to shops and a small village but yet remaining on the outskirts of the town were of greater importance. Other studies of decision making involving housing preference have been described by Hobson and Kohn (1973) using a utility model and by Manning (1981) using a simulation game to understand housing choice and housing adjustment. Research on house styles by Klein (1976) showed that preferences for modern and more traditional styles were linked with personality type. Sanoff (1973), examining housing preferences among teenagers in conjunction with the types of houses in which they actually lived, noted significant factor loadings for modernism, humanism, stimulus-seeking/exploratory behavior, and territoriality. In studies of preference for housing type, adaptation and adjustment are not used as a theoretical base, although they could be, especially where preferences must be realigned to fit changes in family and work status, age status, and financial condition.

HOUSING SATISFACTION

Three common approaches in the research literature are devoted to housing satisfaction: relationships with management (Ahlbrandt & Brophy, 1976; Anderson & Weidemann, 1979; Cooper, 1972; Francescato,

Weidemann, Anderson, & Chenoweth, 1974; Newman, 1972; Saile, Borodah, & Williams, 1972) and some aspect of comparison (Anderson & Weidemann, 1979; Campbell, Converse, & Rogers, 1976; Hollingshead & Rogler, 1963; Michelson, 1977; Onibokun, 1973; Saegert, 1980; Yancey, 1972). The following authors have dealt with a third approach—characteristics of the physical setting: Lansing, Marans, and Zehner (1970), Kaiser, Weiss, Burby, and Donnelly (1970), Cooper (1971), Francescato et al. (1974), Schafer (1974), Ahlbrandt and Brophy (1976), Beaux (1976), Anderson and Weidemann (1979), Hanna and Lindamood (1981), Morrissey and Handal (1981), and Mackintosh (1982). Each of these approaches appears to bear on achieving satisfactory adaptation or adjustment to housing.

References to satisfactory management–tenant concerns appear frequently in the research literature. For example, it is possible that residents might adapt to an established routine of neglect by building management as housing conditions worsen, as heating becomes unreliable, and as repair work takes so long that residents stop making demands. But in a more positive light, on the other hand, adjustments might be made to the system through tenant associations, thereby achieving successful management–tenant relations through group effort.

Comparison with some alternative residence also appears to be an important issue for establishing satisfaction. If, for example, the comparison dwelling is perceived to be equal to or better than the current dwelling, residents will probably adapt to their circumstances and indicate satisfaction. On the other hand, if comparisons show the current dwelling to be inferior, then it is likely that residents will experience dissatisfaction and—if sufficiently motivated and if behavioral alternatives for adjustment and optimization are possible—will make significant changes in their evaluation of the setting and what they do to it.

A consideration of characteristics of the physical setting could refer to availability of storage space, room arrangement, and type of furniture used in various rooms. Over time, residents might adapt to the novelty of certain furniture arrangements or the abundance of storage space and in some cases actually feel they need more storage space because the original amount had been filled to capacity. Clearing of attics, garages, and cellars—a frequently occurring occupation in many Western homes—may serve the function of adjusting to inflexible residential design, especially when a decision such as to build an extra room onto a house might prove to be too expensive to actually carry out.

Research has explored the relation between residential satisfaction and adaptive responses among a variety of groups including high-rise residents (Michelson, 1977; Mackintosh, 1982), occupants of earth-sheltered housing (Volkman, 1981; Weber, 1981), and different social classes (Fried, 1982). Some of these studies have specified those conditions that were responsible for satisfaction. For example, Michelson (1977) has shown that recreation facilities are important for newly arrived high-rise residents but that adaptation will eventually set in and such facilities become less important the longer the residents stay. Mackintosh (1982), in her study of New York City middle-class high-rise residents, found that those individuals who were most satisfied lived in the newest development that contained the newest design features such as interior play spaces, duplexes, and large apartments. Female family members who worked outside the home and those persons who had grown up in apartments were the two groups who predictably registered the highest satisfaction. Among U.K. residents living in "rough" versus "respectable" housing estates, those in the respectable areas indicated more of a sense of belonging, more social contacts, and a larger space that was defined as "home ground" (Lipman & Russell-Lacey, 1974). Gillis (1977) found a negative correlation among male residents of Canadian high-rise housing between vertical location and psychological strain—with the opposite occurring for women. Among those individuals with a higher social class standing, there was a greater satisfaction with the particular place of residence as well as with the overall community (Fried, 1982).

The research literature has also yielded a rather idiosyncratic array of features that residents described as problematic and causing dissatisfaction. These include inadequate storage space, room size, soundproofing and poor management among high-rise dwellers, having to travel great distances to work, and having no easy access to recreation areas and shopping for suburban residents, especially housewives (Michelson, 1977); having some or all children under the age of 5 and living in high-rise dwellings (Conway & Adams, 1977); and living on the upper stories for Canadian women high-rise residents (Gillis, 1977). Schafer (1974) actually found that suburban apartment dwellers rated items like playgrounds, swimming pools, and social directors as negative features. Among nonstandard dwellings, such as the earth-sheltered housing studied by Weber (1981), factors that related to the greatest resident dissatisfaction included spatial design, lighting, and ventilation. When attempts were made to distinguish between housing and neighborhood, only ratings for housing dissatisfaction proved to be predictive of a desire to move house.

A necessary element often not included in the studies that describe negative evaluations of housing concerns the sort of actions or cognitive adjustments or adaptive responses individuals engage in, in order to optimize their affective state. Few studies, in fact, do attempt this, and yet follow-up approaches of this sort would seem essential if a dynamic model involving adaptation or optimization is to have any viability. One approach might include a study of in-depth decision making within a few respondents. This then might provide some test of how cognitions change and how negative evaluations are dealt with in a constructive (optimal) way.

PLACE ATTACHMENT

Although the following concepts are treated in other sections—rootedness and territoriality home, as central place in human existence, home as continuity and unity, and home as self-identity—much has been made of these concepts as they apply to housing—namely in the form of work on place attachment. Relevant research in this area has been done by Taylor, Gottfredson, Brower, and O'Brien (1981) and Taylor, Gottfredson, and Brower (1981). Also, there is related work by Gerson, Stueve, and Fischer (1977) on individual commitment to neighbors and neighborhood, by Stokols and Shumaker (1982) on place dependence, by Proshansky (1978) on place identity, and by Peachey (1981) on residential area bond. In a series of studies by Dockett, Brower, and Taylor (1981) and Brower, Dockett, and Taylor (1983), residents' creations of various adaptive mechanisms to increase territorial functioning and to keep out intruders appeared to be effective. Real barriers like fences and plantings were perceived as deterrents to intrusion, whereas low curbing and ornamentation were not perceived as adequate deterrents. The research indicated that the process involved behavioral action in conjunction with motivational state and a cognitive assessment of the situation.

Carson (1972) studied the connection between territoriality and residents' perceptions of threats in middle-class residential areas of Philadelphia. The need to adapt or adjust appeared to arise when the stimulus conditions aroused a negative affect state within the residents. In general, when evaluative responses are under consideration, place attachment, rather than satisfaction, ought to be emphasized. The latter appear to offer a more general evaluative

statement, whereas the former names a much more specific type of connection.

Housing as Neighborhood

It is common to view housing within a context of neighborhood and culture, where physical features and social relationships assume prominence for the resident. For example, Sadalla, Snyder, and Stea (1976) found that the concept of settlement was more central to people's lives than the concept of home was, but Ohnuku-Tierney (1972), studying the Ainu of Japan, found that residence is most significantly represented by the landscape, the settlement, and the dwelling.

Housing, by definition, is a pluralistic concept, and through physical proximity, residents of one house will undoubtedly be forced to acknowledge and interact with those living in nearby houses. The concept of neighborhood and community, although treated separately in Chapters 20 and 21 must be mentioned here as an integral and yet separate part of the definition of housing. For example, Rent and Rent (1978) found only moderate connection between satisfaction ratings for the housing unit and the neighborhood. This provides justification for employing the two separate measures and concurs with Crull's (1981) findings that use of a single index of housing and neighborhood should be avoided. Along similar lines, Kaiser et al. (1970) found that planners' evaluations of neighborhood physical characteristics bore no resemblance to characteristics of social compatibility and neighborhood as valued by residents. In Danahy's (1984) study of Toronto neighborhood streetscapes, little resemblance was noted between the fundamental adaptive physical and behavioral characteristics of typical residential neighborhoods and designers' intentions in an ongoing housing project involving the creation of a complete neighborhood. In Rivlin's (1982) study of the Lubavitch religious sect in Brooklyn, the definition of residence encompassed an extended sense of community involving physical, interpersonal, and religious aspects, which is similar also to Rapoport's (1980b) definition of dwelling as including the settlement.

Neighboring—a concept studied by Festinger, Schachter, and Back (1950), Fried and Gleicher (1961), Jacobs (1961), Gans (1962), Suttles (1968), Michelson (1970b), Heuman (1979), and Argyle and Henderson (1984)—emphasizes social interaction that derives from community. Neighbors must adjust and adapt to the social and physical components of their community in order to optimize outcomes. Goodey (1970) and Francis and Stone (1981), for example, discuss the importance of community-based planning in which residents concerned with neighborhood conditions participate in decisions that can affect change. In a negative sense, Perin (1977) describes how influential members of a community—such as bankers, developers, planners, and civic and neighborhood leaders—might act to keep apartment housing clustered and separate from single-family dwellings in order to maintain neighborhood stability. This might activate community members into making adjustments in the stimulus conditions, thus dramatically altering the sense of community, sometimes for better and sometimes for worse.

Mobility and Relocation

One of the prime concerns with mobility research has been with the conditions under which moves have caused disruption (either cognitive or behavioral) and then how individuals have managed to adjust or adapt or have failed to do so, as demonstrated by studies of satisfaction and well-being.

For Rossi (1955), moving involves a decision process incorporating three stages: the decision to leave the former home, the search for a new place, and a choice among alternatives. The function of mobility is to provide a family with a mechanism for bringing its housing into adjustment with its housing needs. He saw these needs as changing over the life cycle of the family, with the most dramatic level being reached by young families with children. Rossi (1980) emphasized the need to explore the social, political, and economic bases that determine the meaning that various locations have in influencing the distribution of housing and populations. For example, single-parent women prefer central city locations because such locations offer affordable housing, mass transportation, and opportunities for child care, thereby optimizing conditions surrounding the move.

The disruption accompanying the experience of moving has been described as involving a lack of social integration (Rossi, 1955), feelings of alienation (Butler, McAlister, & Kaiser, 1973; McKain, 1972), negative effects on women's careers (Long, 1974), and a decrease in neighborhood participation after a move (Tropman, 1974). In cases of forced relocation, male-headed families experienced crowding and increased housing costs, whereas female-headed families were more likely to be forced onto welfare (Newman & Owen, 1982). Although frequent relocation has been cited to be connected with illness-related symptoms (Lazarus, 1966; Rahe, 1969; Selye, 1956; Stokols & Shumaker, 1982, Stokols, Shumaker, & Martinez, 1983), it has been pointed

out by Fischer and Stueve (1977) and Byrne, Henderson, Duncan-Jones, Adcock, Scott, and Steele (1979) that there were no adverse consequences to the health of the populations they studied.

Shumaker and Conti (1986) stress the importance of adaptation theory for move-related issues that include attachment to the residence, negative effects, demographic factors, theory, community concerns, causal considerations, choice, congruence, social support, value, prepared relocation (such as among the elderly), and relocation of entire communities. Family adjustment to moves can be seen in the large number of studies that follow. Barrett (1972) and Wagenheim (1974) identify times of the year in which moves have the least disruption for school-age children and the role of particular objects or ordinary possessions in minimizing the stress felt by being uprooted. According to Jones (1972), successful adjustment to a move included the arrival of furniture and familiar objects, the return to a normal schedule, the recognition of familiar chain stores and restaurants, and the viewing of favorite family television programs. In a study by McAlister, Butler, and Kaiser (1972), women showed adjustment by integrating into the community through social contacts facilitated by their school-aged children. In Stewart's (1972) study of 761 middle-income families relocating in Toronto, dichotomized sex roles helped women and men cope with household issues and also helped men deal with financial matters, commuting, and recreation concerns. Tropman (1974) examined a variety of adjustments of moving for men and found that mental illness was lower among movers than among those who did not move and that occupational achievement was generally positive. Wekerle (1975) studied adjustment among a group of upper-middle-class single young adults who moved to a central city high-rise development and found a general level of satisfaction due to age segregation and the facilitation of meeting recreational activities that enabled residents to meet one another socially.

Blauw (1982) examined adjustments to the move from old neighborhoods to new town developments in Holland and noted that suburbanites, for example, were found to be more active in formal participation in various associations. Similar results were obtained by Tomeh (1964), Tallman and Morgner (1970), and Fischer and Jackson (1976). Stokols et al. (1983) found that mobility rate was actually mediated by three psychological factors, each of which relates to aspects of adaptation and adjustment: tendencies for individuals to engage in environmental exploration, individual levels of residential choice and congruence, and quality of residence, in conjunction with expectation of availability of residential options. Stokols and Shumaker (1982) also examined health consequences of mobility. In a number of situations, intention to relocate was examined as positive adjustment to negative circumstances (Clark & Cadwallader, 1973; Clark & Moore, 1982; Hesser & Moline, 1982; Morris, Crull, & Winter, 1976).

Much of the theory surrounding work on the elderly is concerned with adaptation—successful and unsuccessful—in response to some move. For example, Carp (1966) felt that individuals over the age of 50 have the capacity to adjust to the stresses of relocation when particular factors like the following are present: intelligence, physical and mental health, living with one's spouse, sociability, activity, self-esteem, optimism, and maintaining socioeconomic status of earlier years. Steinfeld (1982), on the other hand, saw successful adaptation of the elderly in a new residential setting as giving rise to self-esteem rather than adaptation being dependent on self-esteem. He further argued that some of the motivation to adapt is brought about by a desire to achieve a strong sense of self-identity. When such housing is not respectable, this can undermine a positive sense of identity for the aged.

A variety of approaches has been used in studying adaptation among the elderly, including an emphasis on a congruence model of person–environment fit (Kahana, 1975), individual competence in relation to environmental press (Lawton, 1975), and disengagement (Simpson, Woods, & Britton, 1981).

Miller and Lieberman (1965) claimed that adaptation resulting from stress caused by a move to a new location would require that the individual would need to adopt a new set of roles and behaviors, but, according to Golant (1982), stress was greater for older persons because of a reduced ability to handle the additional stimulation brought about through experience with a new residence and its concomitant roles.

Lieberman (1961) pointed out the negative effects of mobility on longevity of the elderly. He stressed that some reason for this was because the elderly were ill more often and their moves were not always voluntary. Also, involuntary moves seem to have their greatest impact when individuals are most firmly attached to their former residences, according to Kasteler, Gray, and Caruth (1968) and Fried (1963). Alternatively, positively adaptive responses appeared to occur when moves were voluntary as shown in the findings of high satisfaction among residents of the Victoria Plaza housing project in San Antonio, Texas (Carp, 1966; Carp & Carp, 1982). High satisfaction continued even after an 8-year period, but it should also be remembered that this new housing represented a marked improvement over the former residence. Lawton and Cohen (1974) and Hasselkus (1977) report similar findings.

When mobility and relocation are examined in terms of cross-cultural work, adaptation is often discussed as a behavioral consequence. For example, in Gauvain, Altman, and Fahim's (1983) study on relocation of Nubian people from the Nile Valley, a redefinition of dwelling had to be established in terms of the design aspects that were to be incorporated into the new residences. Krissdottir (1982) noted that Icelandic immigrants to North America incorporated few if any aspects of their native sod houses, even though climatic conditions were similar. But there was a strong reliance on cultural values such as wood carving, spinning and weaving, and reading aloud in the evenings as a communal activity. In Beckman's (1976) comparison of bush and urban dwellers from Liberia all of whom originally grew up in the bush, there was a tendency for the bush dwellers to devalue their traditional housing forms, suggesting a lack of congruence or fit between their residence and their evaluation of it. Lack of fit is also an issue among the Australian aborigines who experienced considerable disruption as a function of having to adapt to Western residential designs that replaced their original housing (Savarton & George, 1971).

Although some researchers like Pastalan (1973) have concentrated on adaptive measures to moving such as health, well-being, and mortality, the general trend among researchers has been to deemphasize these in favor of measures of well-being that include cognitive and psychomotor functioning (Storandt, Wittels, & Botwinick, 1975), personal attributes and characteristics (Carp, 1974), independence, self-reliance, and an increase in home range (Blum & Minkler, 1980; Osterberg, 1981; Tucker, Combs, & Woolrich, 1975), exercising mastery and control over one's housing (Golant, 1982), and demonstrating the importance of household possessions (Kalymun, 1983). In virtually all the preceding cases, relocation is seen as a negative experience, even if it is chosen by the resident, because it means leaving the familiar places and routines and entering into new settings— a process that might require more energy than elderly residents have access to.

Stokols and Shumaker's (1982) criticism of the general model of mobility as being insufficient on three levels relates to issues of adaptation. First, they point out that mobility cannot be assumed to be available for all members of a culture, and second they stress that the models tend to ignore forced relocation and often assume that choice adjustment and optimization were true options. Third, they argue that moves are not solely an individual decision process but rather are part of a more complex set of social forces whose interplay would require a more interdisciplinary analysis. Disadvantaged groups, because of a relative lack of power, will have to adapt or cope rather than to bring about adjustments in the stimulus conditions.

Crowding

The majority of research studies on crowding concerns housing settings and individuals' abilities to adjust or adapt to negative conditions surrounding high social and low spatial density. In home settings, crowded conditions seemed to be strongly related to pathologies in mental and physical health, social relationships and child care, thus indicating a tendency toward maladaptive responses (Gove, Hughes, & Galle, 1979). Although Hwang (1979) found similar results among an urban Taiwanese population, it appears that those most affected negatively espoused individualistic values rather than embraced the traditional cultural norms of interpersonal cooperation.

A variety of cross-cultural studies cited by Aiello and Thompson (1980) confirms that crowding is pervasive and negatively experienced in a variety of residential contexts, including Peruvian low-income housing (Alexander, 1969), one-bedroom windowless apartments in Mexico City (Lewis, 1961), Puerto Rican homes (Zeisel, 1973), and the wall-less encampments of the !Kung bush dwellers (Draper, 1973). Additionally, cross-cultural research shows adaptation of residents to constraints of social and spatial density in Chinese homes (Anderson, 1972), in Japanese homes (Canter & Canter, 1971; Michelson, 1970b), and among Indian families from Bombay (Choldin, 1976).

Being crowded also means being out of control—control is a value that is esteemed by many residents. Privacy also signifies control and regulation of interpersonal contact (Goffman, 1959) and conflict (Inman & Graff, 1982). By appropriating space (marking it, furnishing it, arranging it, and maintaining it), one achieves a sense of identity and privacy and also an avoidance of alienation and crowding, according to Graff (1976), Haumont (1976), Bayazit, Yonder, and Ozsoy (1976), and Greenbaum and Greenbaum (1981). In those situations involving forms of residential crowding, research can easily be focused on adaptive and adjustment-type mechanisms for achieving a reduction in crowding. Whereas student dormitory settings might be easier to study, they represent an unusual situation. How residents cope in low-income dwellings of high social or low spatial density is in need of close examination—especially in terms of whether residents feel they have recourse to adjustment as opposed to adaptive responses.

In examining research on housing for students, we find strong expectations that adaptive responses will occur to what are implicitly understood to be negative conditions. In student dormitory housing, there is frequently high social density and inadequate provision of privacy. Under these negative circumstances, one would expect problems to arise such as social incompatibility, feelings of crowdedness, inability to work, and a general sense of physical and mental malaise. To the extent that adaptation occurs, such responses would become less intense. Often research studies are not designed to measure responses over time, and therefore such studies only summarize residents' reactions to their surroundings. Concurrent with adaptive responses would be a variety of adjustments that could conceivably be made to the stimulus conditions. In the case of dormitory life, these might include changing rooms, moving to off-campus housing, utilizing facilities outside the dormitory (such as the library or the student union) for expanded study space, and generally avoiding social interaction with roommates. Of course, the amount of liking that roommates show for one another will then influence how well they are able to adapt to the restricted living conditions.

In general, the research on student dormitory life centers around satisfaction ratings and conditions of crowding, often involving comparison of high-rise and corridor buildings with suites. Among college students living in socially dense dormitory settings, Baum and Valins (1973) and Valins and Baum (1973) found a general tendency for students to avoid their roommates, and Baum, Harpin, and Valins (1975) found that there was a tendency for students to participate less in social residential groups. In comparisons of students in two- and three-person rooms, those in the denser settings experienced more crowding, social tension, and negative affect (Aiello, Baum, & Gormley, 1981). Baron, Mandel, Adams, and Griffen (1976) compared students in double and triple rooms and found that triple-room residents felt more crowded, less in control, and had more negative attitudes toward others and also perceived the room ambience negatively. The authors actually interpreted the more positive responses by the double room students to be a function of adaptation brought about by a reorganization of space according to a variety of conceptual areas.

The ability to make changes in dormitory settings over a period of time or to adapt to what might be perceived as initially negative conditions of crowding appears to be a recurring, but not overt, theme in the research literature. For example, in a study by Null (1979), 10 students crowded into suites planned for 8 showed a consistent shift from negative to positive perceptions of the social and academic climate over the course of a year. In other words, adaptation to adverse conditions seemed to be in evidence through shifts in cognitive evaluations of the housing. Other studies suggest that the stimulus conditions are initially negatively arousing for highrise as compared with low-rise settings (Bickman, Teger, Gabriele, McLaughlin, Berger, & Sunaday, 1973; Davis, 1978; Holahan, 1976; Holahan & Wilcox, 1978; Valins & Baum, 1973). These researchers were not concerned to follow possible adaptive changes over time to these negative conditions, although Davis (1978) did indicate that the introduction of design changes did facilitate local social contact.

In general, issues that researchers felt were of primary concern within student housing were friendship formation, social contact, crowding, achieving a sense of community and privacy, and indicating a sense of satisfaction with the setting. All these features could easily relate to issues of adjustment and may represent an optimal state regarding ideals of social and spatial density, social relationships, and the maintenance of privacy.

Group Identification: Housing and Special Populations

Housing is frequently defined according to the type of group occupying it, and three special groups have accordingly received considerable attention—the elderly, children, and the developmentally disabled. Whereas the emphasis taken by researchers investigating these groups differs considerably, demands for adaptation appear as a consistent theme among the various studies cited.

HOUSING FOR THE ELDERLY

Housing for the elderly services a diverse social group whose expectations are complex and whose needs, goals, and histories vary enormously. One question that arises is whether such housing ought to approximate housing that elderly residents have

left behind, or whether it should represent a radical departure from such dwellings in order to serve more current needs. Even the question of whether to create homogeneous groupings of the elderly in order to achieve a more cohesive sense of neighborhood and community remains unclear.

Moos (1980) noted that out of the 24 million elderly in the United States, 2 million reside in specialized living settings such as residential nursing care facilities, congregate housing, and single-room occupancy hotels. Eight times the number of elderly assumed to be in nursing homes died there, and 3.5 million elderly live in these specialized settings for extended periods. Steinfeld (1982) observed that individuals are concerned to hold onto and live in their houses as they enter old age or when there is income loss or change in marital status. Maintaining independence is critically important, and home ownership is seen as a symbol of this.

The meaning of housing for the elderly comes partially from understanding that such housing is connected with relocation and subsequent adjustment. But, another and perhaps less fluid sense of definition comes from studies of cognitive assessment, behavior needs, and recommendations. For example, cognitive evaluation has been directed toward features that include aspects of hallway design that aid in orientation such as the use of bright colors, carpeting, and sensory experiences (Osterberg, 1981), the preference for retention of particular items of furniture (Kalymun, 1983), a preference for low-rise buildings (Devlin, 1980), and good outdoor space like parks where a variety of activities can take place (Gelwicks, 1970). This list is expanded further by research that emphasizes concern for safety from intruders and threats from fires and elevator mishaps (Devlin, 1980), health and life expectancy, activity levels, social life, morale, satisfaction, and living arrangements (Carp, 1966, 1976), site location, size and attractiveness of development, accessibility to and availability of services, advantages and disadvantages of high-rise buildings, including fear of heights, claustrophobia, exercise of control over building access, and security versus increased companionship (Huttman, 1977), social interaction, participation in activities, and ease in performance of daily routine tasks (Lawton, 1977), and the presence of a variety of socially based factors (Hochschild, 1976).

Lists of needs of the elderly as cited by various researchers add a further dimension to the conceptual definition of housing for this group. These include attending to psychological needs such as safety and comfort, a sense of place, relatedness and environmental mastery; physical needs such as income assistance and cheaper rents, access to services, and those relating to design features and easy maintenance of units including layout, furnishings, and size; and social needs relating to homogeneous and congregate groupings, good landlord relations and tenant contracts, privacy and safety from strangers (Huttman, 1977), needs relating to defensible space, the incorporation of gardens and other aspects of nature among high-rise residents, and the need to achieve a "critical mass" in order for friendship and intimacy to occur satisfactorily among low-rise court residents (Devlin, 1980).

A final component to the definition of housing for the elderly comes from design recommendations made by researchers. Design recommendations have included a need to create a balance between social participation and physical activity as a way of avoiding overloading a residential unit with facilities to make it appear "service rich" (Stephens & Kinney, 1983), the concentration of ethnic grouping rather than a more heterogeneous age-grouping (Steinfeld, 1982), the need to secure recommendations other than those of the U.S. Department of Housing and Urban Development to determine minimum property standards and evaluation of furniture needs (Epp, 1981), the removal of physical barriers and the extension of home range (Moos, 1980), and eliminating the institutional quality of residential settings in order to increase home range and independence (Osterberg, 1981).

Adaptive, coping, and adjustment-type responses have commonly emerged throughout the research quoted. In fact, what most likely occurs here and which is probably more plain to observe among the elderly than for any other group studied is that new housing or drastic changes in housing for the elderly constitute the stimulus basis for an emotional reaction whose initial response first requires some sort of cognitive information search to evaluate the situation. Once such an evaluation occurs, the individual is more able to act in a way that will reduce the emotional state, return the organism to a level of affect that is less emotionally draining, and that will allow energy for further activities in one's daily routine. Most research is organized so that the entire process—from stimulus impact to cognitive assessment to decision making and behavioral action—is never fully evident. Researchers

only present us with a partial view of the process, arguing that environment must include the physical and social but never fully admitting to the dynamic quality of adjustment to a changing residential setting.

CHILDREN AND HOUSING

Descriptions of life among children in various housing settings are rare, although Parke (1978) has emphasized social and cognitive aspects (often descriptive) of children's home environments, and Ahrentzen (1982) offers an annotated bibliography devoted to housing research and children. Most research that mentions children discusses them within the family context, and therefore we find such work embedded in a variety of other sections of this chapter.

Some research has emphasized how adaptable children are to stimulus changes in the home environment. Farley (1978), for example, indicated no negative findings among those children expected to cope with high-density housing. But, in a comparison of the effects of mobile home and single-family dwellings, Landess (1975), Willner, Walkeley, Pinkerton, and Tayback (1962), and Cohen, Glass, and Singer (1973) did find negative effects on children's reading ability in relation to exterior noise and living in high-rise apartments. Also, children have been shown to have much easier access to play areas in low-rise apartments, thus accounting for why parents prefer these settings to high-rise buildings where access to the outdoors and surveillance of children are more difficult to manage (Marcus, 1974).

Although the outdoors is technically not home, there is housing research that views outdoor play as an extension of the dwelling. In fact, Bjorklid-Chu (1977) recommended that all open space in modern high-rise housing estates in Sweden ought to be allocated for children's play. According to Moore and Young (1978), children, in general, play out of doors 22% of the time, although for children aged 5 to 10 years, this figure reaches 30% (Moore & Young, 1978). Outdoor play can certainly serve as an adaptive response to a variety of situations, including overcrowded conditions, need to extend one's boundaries, and need to locate space that can accommodate a large number of children without impinging on parental territory. In the first and last cases, parental concern can provide the motivation to achieve a sense of harmony within the household, whereas the boundary issue is based on the making of adjustments in order to create an optimally centered self.

HOUSING FOR THE DEVELOPMENTALLY DISABLED

Institutional forms of residence, such as are provided for psychiatric patients and those who are broadly classified as developmentally disabled, may serve as the only form of housing these individuals will ever experience. A detailed examination of work in this area of institutional/residential care is undertaken in Chapter 24. Studies exist on the optimization of living environments for a variety of social groups including the physically handicapped (Jeffrey, 1973), psychiatric hospital patients (Ittleson, Proshansky, & Rivlin, 1970; Wolfe, 1975), former psychiatric patients (Smith, 1980), the emotionally disturbed (Birren, 1973; Esser, 1973; Tars & Appleby, 1973), and the mentally retarded (Tognoli, Hamad, & Carpenter, 1978; Valpey, 1982). Other work has centered on evaluation of residential settings for the retarded (McLain, Silverstein, Hubbell, & Brownlee, 1975, 1977; McLain, Silverstein, Brownlee, & Hubbell, 1977) by utilizing measurement tools called Characteristics of the Treatment Environment and Residential Management Survey. In a study by Tars and Appleby (1973), comparison was made of an emotionally disturbed boy at home and in an institutional setting where it was speculated that creativity and initiative were stifled by a stimulus-rich environment in which too much was done for the child. Under these circumstances, adjustment and optimizing behaviors might not obtain unless residents are permitted more control. Well-intentioned modifications in residential institutions might actually undermine residents' motivation to enhance or optimize their living situations. A similar complaint is discussed in the section on housing for the elderly where it was speculated that too many decisions were being made by the staff, thereby co-opting residents' ability to feel in control of their settings. The issue becomes more problematic when providing sheltered housing for the developmentally disabled, though sensitivity to residents' needs may help establish areas where resident participation is both possible and necessary.

Housing and Social Issues: Race and Class

Housing is often linked to social issues—primarily race and class. The stimulus conditions here that will motivate the individual or social group toward adaptation or adjustment might include ones where the group feels itself ill-matched with the residential setting. For example, if a group of urban poor feels alienated or disenfranchised from their housing because of a lack of social life or poor social or health services, adaptation and lethargy may set in, and some neutralization may result, rendering the stimulus conditions less negative. On the other hand, action could be taken to alter the negative conditions to enhance services and social ambience—though this is less likely to occur with groups disadvantaged by race or class or by age, as discussed in the previous section. Although financial limitations might account for the lack of improvements to a large extent, it is also the case that empathic and carefully trained personnel could be hired to work with disadvantaged groups (such as with the Merrill Court/High Heaven high-rises elderly groups [Steinfeld, 1982]) in order to establish greater place attachment and identification as a way of optimizing the social/spatial relationship.

RACE

Studies of race and housing in the United States deal with the ubiquitous conditions of segregation and discrimination. Recent reviews of the historical and contemporary factors that have influenced segregation are presented by Freedman (1969), Freeman and Sunshine (1970), Timms (1971), Forman (1971), Guest (1977), Shumaker and Stokols (1982), and Fairchild and Tucker (1982).

It seems fairly well agreed that mobility among black U.S. citizens is negatively affected by externally imposed conditions rather than by internally imposed family dynamics. These causative factors include restrictive convenants, steering by real estate brokers, fear by white residents that property values will depreciate, discrimination by lending agencies such as the FHA who complicitously support attitudes and practices of realtors including blockbusting, gentrification, community oppression such as the refusal to permit the use of "for sale" signs, and informal pressures (Forman, 1971). Ford and Griffin (1979) include the flight of white residents and attitudes and behaviors of blacks themselves as factors that can also aid in the making of ghettos. Fairchild and Tucker (1982) emphasized the salience of gerrymandered school districts and the creation of suburban white neighborhoods in the 1950s and 1960s through public policy—namely the use of racially restrictive convenants approved by the FHA. Despite the variety of legislative acts such as the Civil Rights acts of 1964 and 1968 and the Model Cities Act, racial discrimination is common. That there is clear-cut prejudice expressed toward blacks seeking housing has also been explored empirically by Johnson, Porter, and Mateljan (1971), Turpin (1971), and Saltman (1975). Although it seems unnecessary for research to point out these rather obvious conditions of discrimination, the data do serve to provide documentation in an area greatly in need of social change.

The provision of good and fair housing for blacks and the poor represents the most urgent of needs, but one has only to examine the research areas of interest to environmental psychologists to note the scant attention devoted to the topic. Solutions to housing problems for blacks where prejudice runs so high seem almost futile and, occasionally, too simplistic. Fairchild and Tucker (1982), for example, note that although there are reports indicating that blacks are satisfied with their housing conditions (Farley & Colasanto, 1980; Ford & Griffin, 1979; West, 1981), there is also indication that whites would be excessively hostile if blacks moved into white neighborhoods (Farley & Colasanto, 1980). Lambert and Filkin (1971) suggest that by not considering moving into these neighborhoods, blacks have avoided facing the discrimination surrounding housing. Heuman (1979) noted that residents of a desegregated community managed to maintain a stable neighborhood when residents were of an equal status, had a common goal, worked cooperatively and interdependently, had the sanction of authority, and were within the laws and customs of that community. In fact, Grunfeld (1982) felt that desegregation would be encouraged under conditions of increased communication and mobility, personal involvement, feeling a part of the community, and under conditions of urban renewal where each settlement was part of an integrated mosaic.

On an equally broad scale, Forman (1971) named a variety of solutions for the provision of adequate housing for blacks and poor people. These were seen as alternatives to large-scale public projects and included small-scale scattered cities, privately built housing sold to a housing authority (turnkey housing), the leasing of privately owned housing moneys that have been provided by HUD to local housing authorities, the provision of various subsidies, urban renewal, and self-help, sweat-equity programs. What are needed in the research literature are accounts of the various attempts to try these solutions along with extensive discussion as to why they do or do not work. Self-help programs represent an area where adjustment and control over setting could be maximally explored and perhaps compared with programs where help is provided primarily from the outside.

There is indication that responses of blacks to negative housing conditions result in more adaptive/coping responses rather than adjustment-type responses because blacks represent a disenfranchized social group. Also, as a result of making adaptive responses, it is more understandable how findings by Schweitzer, Bell, and Daily (1973) might conclude that blacks showed a greater preference for high social density housing over whites. Forced to cope, it is likely that positive attitude change resulted in order to create a cognitively consistent environment–behavior fit.

SOCIAL CLASS

Concern with class issues in housing has generally meant an emphasis on low-income poor and the working classes. Although many housing studies do, in fact, utilize a middle-class population, class is then often actually ignored as an issue. Housing in Third World countries and among displaced refugee groups, although certainly the subject of concern by sociologists and demographers, has also received some attention by environmental psychologists (Appleyard, 1976; Stea, 1980; Turner, 1977; West, 1981; Wheeler, Bechtel, & Ittleson, 1977). On the other hand, homeless refugee groups, such as Palestinians, Cambodians, and Ethiopians, present problems in housing that are more complicated than most researchers are equipped to handle.

One aim of housing research, aside from a concern with studying housing satisfaction, is to try to understand what housing means to individuals who are identified with particular class distinctions. Among the low-income groups studied by Fried and Gleicher (1961) and Yancey (1972), territoriality and social networking were seen to be integral for establishing a satisfactory relationship with dwelling—thus affirming Newman's (1972) argument that defensible space was critical for engendering feelings of security and safety—regardless of social class. For Angrist (1974) and Kalt and Zalkind (1976), issues of physical security, safety, and social networking emerged as important concepts, and Kalt and Zalkind also recommended some forms of rent subsidization and direct housing allowances in order to avoid problems of stigmatization leading to a general downward spiral. Whereas the bulk of research on low-income housing emphasized housing satisfaction, such as with Morrissy and Handal's (1981) study that compared satisfaction among low and high socioeconomic groups, there are studies such as Salling and Harvey's (1981) in which the emphasis is on residential stress. Factors causing stress among the poor seemed more related to situational issues such as income and status and occupation than to personality traits associated with a culture-of-poverty explanation. These low occupational status groups experienced more stress over absence of, or reductions in, social services such as fire and police protection, garbage collection, and schools than issues of neighborhood beauty—a concern of high occupational status groups. These studies all suggest that low-income families might avoid feeling disenfranchised with their housing conditions by articulating a set of requirements that, if met, would improve their adjustment to adverse conditions.

A series of studies on working-class housing (De-Jean, 1976; Servais & Lienard, 1976; Wehrli, Huser, Egli, Bakke, & Grandjean, 1976) has concerned itself with descriptions of differences in terms of how the home space is utilized and also in terms of its providing satisfaction and a sense of well-being. By examining living patterns, it is possible to see how varieties in adjustment have evolved, for example, with respect to needs for entertaining and socializing. One indication is that, although working-class families have been forced to adapt to space restrictions, the space could be allocated in a more flexible manner so as to increase overall satisfaction.

A sociological analysis of housing among two elite social groups in Vancouver provides an unusual contrast to the previously mentioned studies (Pratt, 1982). Low mobility rates and interconnected family and social ties were shown to bind residents of one group together and explain, at least partially, their lack of diversity and slowness to change decorating styles—especially in relation to a second group who were more diverse and loosely connected. The evolution of the home furnishings of the first group suggests that adjustment of (rather than adaptation to) stimulus conditions was typical of them. A broad spectrum of studies of social class, although more urgently needed among the very poorest, can begin to shed some light on issues of concern across class, such as family networking, and the endurance of values shared by family members who have remained in a geographical area for a significant period of time. Rather than feeling at odds with residents because of widely differing class distinctions, knowledge of shared values may help make it easier for designers and planners to implement housing programs for individuals with class backgrounds different from their own.

17.3. CONCLUSIONS

This critical review of research and writing on home and housing integrates two very different areas. Whereas *home* refers to a space, a state of mind, and a set of associations, *housing* concerns itself with the identification and grouping together of a variety of critical issues. On closer examination, one still emerges without a concrete picture of what homes or housing contain, except for the occasional study itemizing the contents of homes as in Kron's (1983) *Home-Psych* and in the research of Csikszentmihalyi and Rochberg-Halton (1981), Altman, Nelson, and Lett (1972) and Tagg (1974), in the work on upper-class Vancouver homes by Pratt (1982), and in the work of Korosec-Serfaty (1984a) on burglary. From such itemizations come fresh ideas concerning approaches to residential environments, perhaps because house contents are so evocative of the past and are laden with rich associations. In order to predict the extent to which residents are capable of optimizing residential settings, more knowledge is needed about home contents in relation to particular residents. For example, in research on relocation, the arrival of the contents of a moving van indicates a tremendous relief from anxiety. But what of individuals whose entire house and contents are destroyed by fire or flood? What is that rebuilding process like? How do various individuals cope with loss, how do they adapt and adjust, and what sorts of things are they likely to miss most or replace first? Refugee populations who are displaced often represent a neglected group greatly in need of attention. How does home for them get defined? After living as refugees for over five years in the same place, what sorts of adaptive and adjustment modes do they consider? And what about the urban homeless, whose place of residence is a doorway or an underground heating shaft?

Research on residential environments has generally ignored Third and Fourth World communities and often has little access to housing research done in socialist countries. Data on housing are dominated by studies from the United States where a lopsided view predominates, emphasizing middle-class populations and ignoring the very poor in both urban and rural settings. Unfortunately, much of this chapter emphasizes research studies published in North America. Studies from West European, Asian, African, Latin American, and socialist and Third World countries are less available and only recently are becoming more widely circulated through the U.K.-

based International Association of Applied Psychology and its affiliate, the International Association for the Study of People in Their Physical Surroundings. In the same way that Western researchers have chosen to study dwelling in a variety of other cultures, it is hoped that non-Western researchers will choose to study residential environments in Western countries.

Although the models of adaptation and adjustment have been shown to be successfully applied to work on home and housing, it is clear that there are many areas still in need of investigation. Future research ought to be directed toward these previously mentioned populations and issues and ought to utilize imaginative approaches for studying how optimal adaptation and adjustment can be achieved.

Although the adaptation model appears simplistic at this point in time, it will necessarily become more complex as exceptions are indicated through continuing research. The areas of research that have received the most attention regarding adaptation theory include those dealing with mobility and relocation, crowding, the elderly, and cognitive evaluation— specifically housing satisfaction. Each of these areas shares two qualities that bear directly on adaptation theory. First, all four areas involve aspects of change and possible disruption. Second, such change will probably give rise to negative affect states among residents and will induce a need to reduce, neutralize, or, it is hoped, to optimize stimulus conditions. This will include making adjustments or adaptations in cognitive states and bringing behaviors into line with perceptions that residents have of their dwellings.

Whereas this theory appears strikingly similar to the essential elements of balance theory (Heider, 1958) and the theory of cognitive dissonance (Festinger, 1957), one should be aware of some primary differences. Research resulting from Heider's and Festinger's work has largely been located in the laboratory and has emphasized a too simplistic method for framing that research. Inquiry and study of housing and home must remain situated in the field— utilizing both descriptive and experimental methodology—especially as such research documents instances of adaptation and adjustment in response to a need to reduce a negative motivational state.

Mobility and relocation, which are seen to be disruptive, involve a variety of cognitive and behavioral modes to bring about adaptation or adjustment. The reason why so much of the research on the elderly utilizes adaptation theory is that the particular target group under consideration is one that has moved or

has been relocated and is thus in need of achieving some reduction in tensions relating to life-style. Crowding, likewise, signifies disruption. Additional family members living in a fixed space can contribute to the negative state as can moving to student housing that must be shared with one or more others.

Whereas these cases all involve housing rather than home, there are clear-cut indications in the chapter that aspects of home also call for adaptation and adjustment. As mentioned in the introduction, when residents experience deficiencies in rootedness, place attachment, continuity, privacy, identity, and family relations in conjunction with home, negative states result such as alienation, dislocation, vulnerability, discontinuity, disunity, and insecurity. How do these states then give rise to a set of cognitions and behaviors within residents that reflect a need to adapt or adjust? To answer this, the process will need to be studied on a longitudinal basis. Currently, research studies provide us with only a partial glimpse of the adaptation process indicating that negative states have resulted or that restoration of some equilibrium is necessary for feeling "at home" in one's dwelling space. Few studies have attempted to research the home on an extensive basis. Hayward's (1975, 1977) study of meaning, although providing an important review of seminal works on home, establishes a set of meaning categories based upon a factor analysis and rating of statements about housing and home generated by middle-class New York City high-rise residents with children. Although the nine categories that emerged provide a broad statement concerning meaning, there is no theoretical position to suggest under which circumstances these meaning categories will be of some use. Happily, Anthony's (1984a) study of memories of home after moving do at least affirm the viability of Hayward's category system. Through the large-scale studies of housing such as those on the elderly by Carp (1966), Carp and Carp (1982), and Huttman (1977), by Rossi (1955, 1980) on relocation and mobility, and by Baum and Valins (1973) on crowding, we derive a sense of how housing can be examined in a variety of applied settings and how various theoretical viewpoints—including adaptation-level theory— can be explored.

There is need to consider housing and home in in-depth treatments according to various subsections outlined and discussed in this chapter, particularly from the vantage point of adaptation-level theory and according to the interests of different researchers. Emphasis ought to be placed both on individual- and group-level resident responses to situational change and should consider the value of utilizing phenomenological and descriptive formats and experimental and correlational procedures for obtaining information. Only then can one continue to assemble the various data bases to affirm a general model of adaptation and adjustment for residential environments.

Acknowledgments

I am grateful to the C.W. Post Research Committee of Long Island University for their award of a writing grant and to Wolfson College (Oxford) and to Michael Argyle and Lawrence Weiskrantz at the Department of Experimental Psychology, Oxford University, for providing space, resources, and a collegial atmosphere in which to write this chapter. I also wish to thank Helen Cooper, Irwin Altman, and Daniel Stokols for their guidance and support through various phases of this project.

REFERENCES

Agnew, J. (1982). Home ownership and identity in capitalist societies. In J.S. Duncan (Ed.), *Housing and identity: Cross-cultural perspectives* (pp. 60–97). New York: Holmes & Meier.

Ahlbrandt, R.S., Jr., & Brophy, P.C. (1976). Management: An important element of the housing environment. *Environment and Behavior, 8*, 505–526.

Ahrentzen, S. (1982). *Children and the built environment: An annotated bibliography of representative research of children and housing, school design and environmental stress.* Architecture Series, No. A-764) Monticello, IL: Vance Bibliographies.

Aiello, J.R., Baum, A., & Gormley, F.P. (1981). Social determinants of residential crowding and stress. *Personality and Social Psychology Bulletin, 7*, 643–649.

Aiello, J.R., & Thompson, D.E. (1980). Personal space, crowding and spatial behavior in a cultural context. In I. Altman, A. Rapoport, & J.F. Wohlwill (Eds.), *Human behavior and environment: Advances in theory and research: Vol. 4. Environment and culture* (pp. 107–178). New York: Plenum.

Alexander, C. (1969). *Houses generated by patterns.* Berkeley, CA: Center for Environmental Structure.

Allott, K.J., & Ladd, F.C. (1976). First marriage and first home. In P. Korosec-Serfaty (Ed.), *Appropriation of space.* Louvain-la-Neuve, Belgium: CIACO, Cooperative Universitaire.

Aloia, A. (1973). Relationships between perceived privacy options, self-esteem and internal control among aged people (Doctoral dissertation, California School of Professional Psychology, 1973). *Dissertation Abstracts International, 34*, 5180B.

Altman, I., & Chemers, M. (1980). *Culture and environment.* Monterey, CA: Brooks/Cole.

Altman, I., & Gauvain, M. (1981). A cross-cultural and dialectic analysis of homes. In L. Liben, A. Patterson, & N. Newcombe (Eds.), *Spatial representation and behavior across the life span: Theory and application* (pp. 283–320). New York: Academic.

Altman, I., Nelson, P.A., & Lett, E.E. (1972, Spring). The ecology of home environments. *Catalog of selected documents in psychology* (No. 150). Washington, DC: American Psychological Association.

Anderson, E.N. (1972). Some Chinese methods of dealing with crowding. *Urban Anthropology, 1*, 143–150.

Anderson, J.R., & Weidemann, S. (1979, December). *Development of an instrument to measure residents' perceptions of residential quality.* Paper presented at the International Conference on Housing, Miami, FL.

Angrist, S.S. (1974). Dimensions of well-being in public housing families. *Environment and Behavior, 6*, 495–516.

Anthony, K.H. (1984a). Moving experiences: Memories of favorite homes. In D. Duerk & D. Campbell (Eds.), *EDRA 15—1984 Proceedings: The challenge of diversity* (pp. 141–149). Washington, DC: Environmental Design Research Association.

Anthony, K.H. (1984b). The role of the home environment in family conflict: Therapists' viewpoints. In D. Duerk & D. Campbell (Eds.), *EDRA 15—1984 Proceedings: The challenge of diversity* (pp. 219–226). Washington, DC: Environmental Design Research Association.

Appleyard, D. (1976). *Planning a pluralist city.* Cambridge, MA: MIT Press.

Argyle, M., & Henderson, M. (1984). The rules of friendship. *Journal of Social and Personal Relationships, 1*, 211–237.

Bachelard, G. (1969). *The poetics of space.* Boston: Beacon.

Barbey, G. (1976). The appropriation of home space: A tentative conceptual definition. In P. Korosec-Serfaty (Ed.), *Appropriation of space* (pp. 215–217). Louvain-la-Neuve, Belgium: CIACO, Cooperative Universitaire.

Barilleau, E.E., & Lombardo, J.D. (1976). Appropriation of space in multifamiliar buildings during the vacation time. Study of a case. In P. Korosec-Serfaty (Ed.), *Appropriation of space* (pp. 329–341). Louvain-la-Neuve, Belgium: CIACO, Cooperative Universitaire.

Baron, R.M., Mandel, D.R., Adams, C.A., & Griffen, L.M. (1976). Effects of social density in university residential environments. *Journal of Personality and Social Psychology, 34*, 434–446.

Barrett, C.L. (1972). *Intentions and expectations in differentiated residential selection.* Paper presented at Allied

Symposium, Indiana University and Purdue University, Indianapolis, IN.

Bateman, M., Burtenshaw, D., & Duffett, A. (1974). Environmental perception and migration: A study of perception of residential areas in south Hampshire. In D. Canter & T. Lee (Eds.), *Psychology and the built environment* (pp. 148–155). New York: Wiley.

Baum, A., Harpin, R.E., & Valins, S. (1975). The role of group phenomena in the experience of crowding. *Environment and Behavior, 7*, 184–198.

Baum, A., & Valins, S. (1973). Residential environment, group size and crowding [Summary]. *Proceedings of the 81st Annual Convention of the American Psychological Association, 8*, 211–212.

Bayazit, N., Yonder, A. & Ozsoy, A.B. (1976). Three levels of privacy behavior in the appropriation of dwelling spaces in Turkish homes. In P. Korosec-Serfaty (Ed.), *Appropriation of space* (pp. 255–264). Louvain-la-Neuve, Belgium: CIACO, Cooperative Universitaire.

Beaux, D. (1976). Attempt at making an overall description of the environment—physical background, activities and psychological factors—as a basis for evaluating background and housing schemes. In P. Korosec-Serfaty (Ed.), *Appropriation of space* (pp. 265–279). Louvain-la-Neuve, Belgium: CIACO, Cooperative Universitaire.

Beckman, J. (1976). A decision model for estimating concurrent school attendance among tribal peoples of Liberia, together with an application regarding differential cognitions toward traditional housing. In A. Rapoport (Ed.), *The mutual interaction of people and their built environment: a cross-cultural perspective* (pp. 275–285). The Hague, Netherlands: Mouton.

Belson, W.A. (1959). *Television and the family.* London: British Broadcasting Corporation.

Belson, W.A. (1967). *The impact of television.* Hamden, CT: Archon.

Berk, S.F. (1980). The household as workplace: Wives, husbands and children. In G.R. Wekerle, R. Peterson, & D. Morley (Eds.), *New space for women* (pp. 65–82). Boulder, CO: Westview.

Bickman, L., Teger, A., Gabriele, T., McLaughlin, C., Berger, M., & Sunaday, E. (1973). Dormitory density and helping behavior. *Environment and Behavior, 5*, 465–490.

Birren, F. (1973). A colorful environment for the mentally disturbed. *Art Psychotherapy, 1*, 255–259.

Bjorklid-Chu, P. (1977). A survey of children's outdoor activities in two modern housing areas in Sweden. In B. Tizard & D. Harvey (Eds.), *Biology of play* (pp. 146–159). London: Spastics International, Lippincott.

Blauw, W. (1982). Moving from old neighborhoods to newtowns. Paper presented at the 10th World Congress of Sociology, Mexico City.

Blum, S.R., & Minkler, M. (1980). Toward a continuum of caring alternatives: Community based care for the elderly. *Journal of Social Issues, 36*, 133–152.

Bochner, S. (1975). The house form as a cornerstone of culture. In R.W. Brislin (Ed.), *Topics in culture learning* (Vol. 3, pp. 9–20). Honolulu: East-West Center.

Brickman, P., & Campbell, D.T. (1971). Hedonic relativism and planning the good society. In M.H. Appley (Ed.), *Adaptation-level theory: A symposium* (pp. 287–302). New York: Academic.

Brower, S., Dockett, K., & Taylor, R.B. (1983). Residents' perceptions of territorial features and perceived local threat. *Environment and Behavior, 15*(4), 419–437.

Burke, R.J., & Weir, T. (1976). Relations of wives' employment to status of husband, wife and pair satisfaction and performance. *Journal of Marriage and the Family, 38*, 279–287.

Burns, S. (1975). *The household economy: Its shape, origins and future.* Boston: Beacon.

Butler, E.W., McAlister, R.J., & Kaiser, E.J. (1973). The effects of voluntary and involuntary residential mobility on females and males. *Journal of Marriage and the Family, 35*, 219–227.

Byrne, D.G., Henderson, S., Duncan-Jones, P., Adcock, S., Scott, R., & Steele, G. (1979). Length of residence, life change and psychiatric morbidity in an Australian urban population. *Australian and New Zealand Journal of Psychiatry, 13*, 7–12.

Campbell, A., Converse, P., & Rogers, W. (1976). *The quality of American life: Perceptions, evaluations and satisfactions.* New York: Russell Sage Foundation.

Canter, D., & Canter, S. (1971). Close together in Tokyo. *Design and Environment, 2*, 60–63.

Canter, D., Gilchrist, J., Miller, J., & Roberts, N. (1974). An empirical study of the focal point in the living room. In D. Canter & T. Lee (Eds.), *Psychology and the built environment* (pp. 29–37). New York: Halsted.

Cantor, M.S. (1978). Where are the women in public broadcasting? In G. Tuchman, A.K. Daniels, & J. Benet (Eds.), *Hearth and home: Images of women in the mass media* (pp. 78–89). New York: Oxford University Press.

Carlisle, S.G. (1982). French homes and French character. *Landscape, 26*(3), 13–23.

Carp, F.M. (1966). *A future for the aged: Victoria Plaza and its residents.* Austin, TX: Hogg Foundation.

Carp, F.M. (1974). Short-term and long-term prediction of adjustment to a new environment. *Journal of Gerontology, 29*, 444–453.

Carp, F.M. (1976). User evaluation of housing for the elderly. *Gerontologist, 16*, 102–111.

Carp, F.M., & Carp, A. (1982). Perceived environmental quality of neighborhoods: Development of assessment scales and their relation to age and gender. *Journal of Environmental Psychology, 2*, 295–312.

Carson, D. (1972). Residential descriptions and urban threats. In J.F. Wohlwill & D. Carson (Eds.), *Environment and the social sciences: Perspectives and applications* (pp. 154–168). Washington, DC: American Psychological Association.

Choldin, H. (1976). Housing standards vs. ecological forces: Regulating population density in Bombay. In A. Rapoport (Ed.), *The mutual interaction of people and the built environment: A cross-cultural perspective* (pp. 287–331). The Hague, Netherlands: Mouton.

Clark, W.A.V., & Cadwallader, M. (1973). Locational stress and residential mobility. *Environment & Behavior, 5*, 29–41.

Clark, W.A.V., & Moore, E.G. (1982). Residential mobility and public programs: Current gaps between theory and practice. *Journal of Social Issues, 38*(3), 35–50.

Cohen, J.F. (1979). Male roles in mid-life. *Family Coordinator, 28*, 465–471.

Cohen, S., Glass, D.C., & Singer, J.E. (1973). Apartment noise, auditory discrimination and reading ability in children. *Journal of Experimental Social Psychology, 9*, 407–422.

Conway, J., & Adams, B. (1977). The social effects of living off the ground. *Habitat, 2*, 595–614.

Cooper, C. (1971, December). St. Francis Square: Attitudes of its residents. *American Institute of Architects Journal, 56*, 22–25.

Cooper, C. (1972). Resident dissatisfaction in multi-family housing. In W.M. Smith (Ed.), *Behavior, design and policy aspects of human habitats* (pp. 119–145). Green Bay: University of Wisconsin-Green Bay Press.

Cooper, C. (1974). The house as symbol of the self. In J. Lang, C. Burnette, W. Moleski, & D. Vachon (Eds.), *Designing for human behavior* (pp. 130–146). Stroudsburg, PA: Dowden, Hutchinson, & Ross.

Couper, M., & Brindley, T. (1975). Housing classes and housing values. *Sociological Review, 23*, 563–576.

Cowan, R.S. (1983). *More work for mother: The ironies of household technology from open hearth to the microwave.* New York: Basic Books.

Cowburn, W. (1966). Popular housing. *Arena, The Architectural Association Journal, 82*(905), 76–81.

Cramer, R.D. (1960, September). Images of home. *American Institute of Architects Journal,* 40–49.

Crull, S.R. (1981). *Housing and neighborhood satisfaction.* Paper presented at the 12th Environmental Design Association Conference, Iowa State University, Ames, IA.

Csikszentmihalyi, M., & Rochberg-Halton, E. (1981). *The meaning of things: Domestic symbols and the self.* Cambridge: Cambridge University Press.

Cunningham, C.E. (1973). Order in the Atoni house. In R. Needham (Ed.), *Right and left: Essays on dual symbolic classification* (pp. 204–238). Chicago: University of Chicago Press.

Danahy, J.W. (1984). Adaptive behaviour in frontyards of residential streetscapes. In D. Duerk & D. Campbell (Eds.), *EDRA 15—1984 Proceedings: The challenge of diversity* (pp. 234–239). Washington, DC: Environmental Design Research Association.

Davis, G.E. (1978). Designing for residential density. In A. Baum & Y.M. Epstein (Eds.), *Human response to crowding* (pp. 353–369). Hillsdale, NJ: Erlbaum.

Deffontaines, P. (1948). *Geographie et Religions* (9th ed.). Paris: Librairie Gallimard.

Dejean, C.H.deL. (1976). Relational systems and their impact on space. In P. Korosec-Serfaty (Ed.), *Appropriation of Space* (pp. 319–328). Louvain-la-Neuve, Belgium: CIACO, Cooperative Universitaire.

Devlin, A.S. (1980). Housing for the elderly: Cognitive considerations. *Environment and Behavior, 12*, 451–466.

Dillman, D.A., & Dillman, J.J. (1981). *The importance of private outdoor space preferences.* Paper presented at the 12th Environmental Design Research Association Conference, Iowa State University, Ames, IA.

Dockett, K., Brower, S., & Taylor, R.B. (1981). Residents' perceptions of site-level features: People, problems, planting and fences. In A.E. Osterberg, C.P. Tiernan, & R.A. Findlay (Eds.), *Design research interactions: Proceedings of the 12th Environmental Design Research Association Conference* (p. 455). Washington, DC: Environmental Design Research Association.

Dovey, K. (1978). Home: An ordering principle in space. *Landscape, 22*(2), 27–30.

Draper, P. (1973). Crowding among hunter gatherers: The !Kung Bushmen. *Science, 182*, 301–303.

Duncan, J.S. (1982a). From container of women to status symbol: The impact of social structure on the meaning of the house. In J.S. Duncan (Ed.), *Housing and identity: Cross-cultural perspectives* (pp. 36–59). New York: Holmes & Meier.

Duncan, J.S. (ed.) (1982b). *Housing and identity: Cross-cultural perspectives.* New York: Holmes & Meier.

Duncan, N. (1982). Home ownership and social theory. In J.S. Duncan (Ed.), *Housing and identity: Cross-cultural perspectives* (pp. 98–134). New York: Holmes & Meier.

Egolf, B., & Herrenkohl, R.C. (1975, July). *Influences on the attractiveness of a residential setting as a place to live.* Paper presented at American Institute of Architects Conference on Human Response to Tall Buildings, Chicago.

Epp, G. (1981). Furnishing the unit from the viewpoint of the elderly, the designer and HUD. In A.E. Osterberg, C.P. Tiernan, & R.A. Findlay (Eds.), *Design research interactions: Proceedings of the 12th Environmental Design Research Association Conference* (pp. 312–317). Washington, DC: Environmental Design Research Association.

Esser, A.H. (1973). Cottage fourteen dominance and territoriality in a group of institutionalized boys. *Small Group Behavior, 4*, 131–146.

Fairchild, H.H., & Tucker, M.B. (1982). Black residential mobility: Trends and characteristics. *Journal of Social Issues, 38*(3), 51–74.

Faletti, M.V. (1979). An experimental investigation of cognitive processing underlying judgments of residential environments by different observer groups (Doctoral dissertation, University of Miami, FL, 1979). *Dissertation Abstracts International, 40*(4), 1924B–1925B.

Farley, J. (1978). High-rise apartment or detached house: What are the implications for children's behavior? In W. E. Rogers & W.H. Ittleson (Eds.), *New directions in environmental design research: Proceedings of the 9th Environmental Design Research Association Conference.* (pp. 145–161). Washington, DC: Environmental Design Research Association.

Farley, R., & Colasanto, D. (1980). Racial residential segregation: Is it caused by misinformation about housing costs? *Social Science Quarterly, 61*, 623–637.

Festinger, L. (1957). *A theory of cognitive dissonance.* Stanford, CA: Stanford University Press.

Festinger, L., Schachter, S., & Back, K. (1950). *Social pressures in informal groups: A study of human factors in housing.* Stanford, CA: Stanford University Press.

Filipovitch, A.J., Juliar, K., & Ross, K.D. (1981). Children's drawings of their home environment. In A.E. Osterberg, C.P. Tiernan, & R.A. Findlay (Eds.), *Design research interactions: Proceedings of the 12th Environmental Design Research Association Conference.* (pp. 258–264). Washington, DC: Environmental Design Research Association.

Fischer, C.S., & Jackson, R.M. (1976). Suburbs, networks and attitudes. In B. Schwartz (Ed.), *The changing face of the suburbs* (pp. 279–307). Chicago: University of Chicago Press.

Fischer, C.S., & Stueve, C.A. (1977). Authentic community?: The role of place in modern life. In C.S. Fischer, R.M. Jackson, C.A. Stueve, K. Gerson, L.M. Jones, & M. Baldassare (Eds.), *Networks and places: Social relations in the urban setting* (pp. 163–186). New York: Free Press.

Foote, N., Abu-Lughod, J., Foley, M., & Winnick, L. (1970). *Housing choices and housing constraints.* New York: McGraw-Hill.

Ford, L., & Griffin, E. (1979). The ghettoization of paradise. *Geographical Review, 69*, 140–158.

Forman, R.E. (1971). *Black ghettos, white ghettos and slums.* Englewood Cliffs, NJ: Prentice-Hall.

Francescato, G., Weidemann, S., Anderson, J., & Chenoweth, R. (1974). Evaluating residents' satisfaction in housing for low and moderate income families: A multimethod approach. In D.H. Carson (Ed.), *Man–environment interactions: Evaluations and application: Vol. 5, Methods and Measures: Proceedings of the 5th Environment Design Research Association Conference* (pp. 285–295). Washington, DC: Environmental Design Research Association.

Francis, M., & Stone, A. (1981). Neighborhood residents as environmental researchers and planners: Methods for community based assessment and planning. In A.E. Osterberg, C.P. Tiernan, & R.A. Findlay (Eds.), *Design research interactions: Proceedings of the 12th Environmental Design Research Association Conference* (pp. 172–182). Washington, DC: Environmental Design Research Association.

Fraser, D. (1968) *Village planning in the primitive world.* New York: Braziller.

Fraser, D. (1974). *African art as philosophy.* New York: Interbooks.

Freedman, L. (1969). *Public housing: The politics of poverty.* New York: Holt, Rinehart & Winston.

Freeman, L.C., & Sunshine, M.H. (1970). *Patterns of residential segregation.* Cambridge, MA: Schenkman.

Fried, M. (1963). Grieving for a lost home: Psychological costs of relocation. In L. Duhl (Ed.), *The urban condition* (pp. 151–171). New York: Basic Books.

Fried, M. (1982). Residential attachment: Sources of residential and community satisfaction. *Journal of Social Issues, 38*(3), 107–120.

Fried, M., & Gleicher, P. (1961, November). Some sources of residential satisfaction in an urban slum. *Journal of the American Institute of Planners, 27*, 305–315.

Gans, H.J. (1962). *The urban villagers: Group and class in the life of Italian Americans.* New York: Free Press.

Gans, H.J. (1967). *The Levittowners.* New York: Pantheon.

Gans, H.J. (1968). Culture and class in the study of poverty: An approach to anti-poverty research. In D.P. Moynihan (Ed.), *On understanding poverty, perspectives from the social sciences* (pp. 201–228). New York: Basic Books.

Gardiner, S. (1974). *Evolution of the house: An introduction.* New York: Macmillan.

Gärling, T. (1972). Studies in visual perception of architectural spaces and rooms: Aesthetic preferences. *Scandinavian Journal of Psychology, 13*(3), 222–227.

Gauvain, M., Altman, I., & Fahim, H. (1983). Homes and social change: A cross-cultural analysis. In N. Feimer & S. Geller (Eds.), *Environmental psychology: Directions and perspectives* (pp. 180–218). New York: Praeger.

Gelwicks, L. (1970). Home range and the use of space by an aging population. In L.A. Pastalan & D.H. Carson (Eds.), *Spatial behavior of older people* (pp. 148–161). Ann Arbor: University of Michigan Press.

Gerson, K., Stueve, C.A., & Fischer, C.S. (1977). Attachment to place. In C.S. Fischer, R.M. Jackson, C.A Steuve, K. Gerson, L.M. Jones, & M. Baldassare

(Eds.), *Networks and places: Social relations in the urban setting*. New York: Free Press.

Gillis, A.R. (1977). High rise housing and psychological strain. *Journal of Health and Social Behavior, 18*(4), 418–431.

Gobster, P.H. (1983). Judged appropriateness of residential structures in natural and developed shoreland settings. In D. Amedeo, J.B. Griffin, & J.J. Potter (Eds.), *EDRA 1983: Proceedings of the 14th International Conference of the Environmental Design Research Association* (pp. 105–112). University of Nebraska-Lincoln.

Goffman, E. (1959). *The presentation of self in everyday life*. New York: Doubleday.

Golan, M.B. (1978, September). Privacy, interaction and self-esteem (Doctoral dissertation, City University of New York, Environmental Psychology Program, 1978). *Dissertation Abstracts International, 39*(3), 1541B.

Golant, S.M. (1982). Individual differences underlying the dwelling satisfaction of the elderly. *Journal of Social Issues, 38*(3), 121–133.

Gove, W.R., Hughes, M., & Galle, O.R. (1979). Overcrowding in the home: An empirical investigation of its possible pathological consequences. *American Sociological Review, 44*(1), 59–80.

Goodey, B. (1970, June). *Social planning in new communities: Some questions for research and practice* (working paper in Planning, Education and Research). Headington, Oxford, England: Oxford Polytechnic.

Graff, C. (1976). Alienation or identification: A function of space in the home. In P. Korosec-Serfaty (Ed.), *Appropriation of space*. Louvain-la-Neuve, Belgium: CIACO, Cooperative Universitaire.

Greenbaum, P.E., & Greenbaum, S.D. (1981). Territorial personalization: Group identity and social interaction in a Slavic-American neighborhood. In A.E. Osterberg, C.P. Tiernan, & R.A. Findlay (Eds.), *Design research interactions: Proceedings of the 12th Environmental Design Research Association Conference* (p. 460). Washington, DC: Environmental Design Research Association.

Grunfeld, F. (1982, August). *The problem of spatial segregation and the preservation of an urban society*. Paper presented at the 10th World Congress of Sociology, Mexico City.

Guest, A.M. (1977). Residential segregation in urban areas. In K.F. Schwirian (Ed.), *Contemporary topics in urban sociology* (pp. 268–336). Morristown, NJ: General Learning Press.

Hamilton, P. (1972, February). *Aspects of interdependence between Aboriginal social behaviour and the spatial and physical environment*. Seminar on low-cost housing for Aborigines in remote areas. Royal Australian Institute of Architects, Canberra, Australia.

Hancock, J. (1980). The apartment house in urban America. In A.D. King (Ed.), *Building and society: Essays on the social development of the built environment* (pp. 151–189). London: Routledge & Kegan Paul.

Hanna, S., & Lindamood, S. (1981). *Components of housing satisfaction*. Paper presented at the 12th Environmental Design Research Association Conference, Iowa State University, Ames, IA.

Hansen, W.B., & Altman, I. (1976). Decorating personal places: A descriptive analysis. *Environment and Behavior, 8*(4), 491–503.

Hart, R. (1978). *Children's experience of place*. New York: Irvington.

Hasselkus, B.R. (1977). Small group home for the elderly. *American Journal of Occupational Therapy, 31*(8), 525–529.

Haumont, N. (1976). Home appropriation practices. In P. Korosec-Serfaty (Ed.), *Appropriation of space* (pp. 226–234). Louvain-la-Neuve, Belgium: CIACO, Cooperative Universitaire.

Hayden, D. (1980). Redefining the domestic workplace. In G.R. Wekerle, R. Peterson, & D. Morley (Eds.), *New space for women* (pp. 101–121). Boulder, CO: Westview.

Hayden, D. (1981). *The grand domestic revolution*. Cambridge, MA: MIT Press.

Hayward, D.G. (1975). Home as an environment and psychological concept. *Landscape, 20*(1), 2–9.

Hayward, D.G. (1977). Psychological concepts of home among urban middle class families with young children (Doctoral dissertation, City University of New York Graduate Center, Environmental Psychology Program, 1977). *Dissertation Abstracts International, 37*(11), 5813B.

Heider, F. (1958). *The psychology of interpersonal relations*. New York: Wiley.

Heidmets, M. (1983). Subject in environment. In H. Lumets, T. Niit, & M. Heidmets (Eds.), *Man in sociophysical environment* (pp. 38–68). Tallinn, Estonian SSR, USSR: Estonian Branch of Soviet Psychological Society Council of Young Scientists & Specialists, Tallinn Pedagogic Institute.

Helphand, K. (1978). *Environmental autobiography*. Eugene: University of Oregon, Department of Landscape Architecture.

Helson, H. (1964). *Adaptation-level theory*. New York: Harper & Row.

Hennessee, J.A., & Nicholson, J. (1972, May 28). N.O.W. says: TV commercials insult women. *New York Times Magazine*, pp. 12–13.

Hesser, G.W., & Moline, L.A. (1982, August). *Mobility, neighborhood interaction, and maintenance: Theoretical and empirical explorations*. Paper presented at the 10th World Congress of Sociology, Mexico City.

Hester, R. (1979, September). A womb with a view—How spatial nostalgia affects the designer. *Landscape Architecture*, 475–481.

Hetherington, E.M., Cox, M., & Cox, R. (1976). Divorced fathers. *The Family Coordinator, 25,* 417–428.

Heuman, L.F. (1979). Racial integration in residential neighborhoods: Towards more precise measures and analysis. *Evaluation Quarterly, 3*(1), 59–79.

Hinshaw, M., & Allott, K. (1972, March). Environmental preferences of future housing consumers. *Journal of American Institute of Planners, 38,* 102–107.

Hobson, R., & Kohn, I. (1973). Utility ratings and 0-1 programming in housing design. In W.E.F. Preiser (Ed.), *Environmental design research: Vol. 1, selected papers. Proceedings of the 4th Environmental Design Research Association Conference* (pp. 440–447). Stroudsburg, PA: Dowden, Hutchinson, & Ross.

Hochschild, A.E.R. (1976). *The unexpected community.* Berkeley: University of California Press.

Hoffman, H. (1972). Monitoring of children's television programming aired by WRC-TV: A comparison of male and female roles. National Organization for Women (Eds.), *Women in the wasteland fight back* (pp. 91–104). Washington, DC: Author.

Holahan, C.J. (1976). Environmental effects on outdoor social behavior in a low-income urban neighborhood: A naturalistic investigation. *Journal of Applied Social Psychology, 6,* 48–63.

Holahan, C.J., & Wilcox, B.L. (1978). Residential satisfaction and friendship formation in high- and low-rise student housing: An interactional analysis. *Journal of Educational Psychology, 70*(2), 237–241.

Hollerorth, B. (1974). *The haunting house.* Boston: Unitarian Universalist Association.

Hollingshead, A.B., & Rogler, L.H. (1963). Attitudes toward slums and public housing in Puerto Rico. In L.J. Duhl (Ed.), *The urban condition* (pp. 229–245). New York: Basic Books.

Horwitz, J., Klein, S., Paxton, L., & Rivlin, L. (1978). Environmental autobiography. *Childhood City Newsletter, 14.* (Available from City University of New York Graduate Center, Program in Environmental Psychology, 33 West 42nd Street, New York, NY 10036.)

Horwitz, J., & Tognoli, J. (1982). Role of home in adult development: Women and men living alone describe their residential histories. *Family Relations, 31,* 335–341.

Howell, S. (1976, April). *Recent advances in studies of the physical environment of the elderly.* Talk given at the Program in Environmental Psychology, City University of New York Graduate Center, New York.

Huttman, E.D. (1977). *Housing and social services for the elderly: Social policy trends.* New York: Praeger.

Hwang, K. (1979). *Coping with residential crowding in a Chinese urban society: The interplay of high density dwelling and interpersonal values. Acta Psychologica Taiwanica, 21*(2), 117–133.

Inman, M., & Graff, C. (1982, July). *Family social climate, house style and life cycle.* Paper presented at the 7th Conference of the International Association for the Study of People and their Physical Surroundings, Barcelona, Spain.

Ittleson, W.H., Proshansky, H.M., & Rivlin, L.G. (1970). Bedroom size and social interaction of the psychiatric ward. *Environment Behavior, 2,* 255–270.

Jacobs, J. (1961). *The death and life of great American cities.* New York: Random House.

Jaulin, R. (1971). Ethnocide: The theory and practice of cultural murder. *The Ecologist, 1,* 12–15.

Jeffrey, D.A. (1973). A living environment for the physically disabled. *Rehabilitation Literature, 34*(4), 98–103.

Johnson, D.A., Porter, R.J., & Mateljan, P.L. (1971). Racial discrimination in apartment rentals. *Journal of Applied Social Psychology, 1*(4), 364–377.

Jones, S. (1972). *When women move: Family migratory patterns as they affect and are affected by the wife.* Paper presented at the Allied Symposium, Indiana University and Purdue University, Indianapolis, IN.

Jung, C.G. (1963). *Memories, dreams and reflections.* New York: Vintage.

Kahana, E. (1975). A congruence model of person-environment interaction. In G. Windley, T.O. Byerts, & F.G. Ernst (Eds.), *Theory development in environment and aging* (pp. 181–214). Manhattan, KA: Gerontological Society.

Kaiser, E.J., Weiss, S.F., Barbey, R.J., III, & Donnelly, T.G. (1970). Neighborhood environment and residential satisfaction: A survey of the occupants and neighborhoods of 166 single-family homes in Greensboro, NC. *Research Reviews, 17*(2), 11–25.

Kalt, N.C., & Zalkind, S.S. (1976). Effects of some publicly financed housing programs for the urban poor. *Journal of Community Psychology, 4*(3), 198–302.

Kalymun, M. (1983). Factors influencing elderly women's decisions concerning living-room items during relocation. In D. Amedeo, J.B. Griffin, & J.J. Potter (Eds.), *EDRA 1983: Proceedings of the 14th International Conference of the Environmental Design Research Association, University of Nebraska-Lincoln* (pp. 75–83). Washington, DC: Environmental Design Research Association.

Kaplan, S. (1977). *The dream deferred: People, politics and planning in suburbia.* New York: Random House.

Kasteler, J.M., Gray, R.M., & Caruth, M.L. (1968). Involuntary relocation of the elderly. *The Gerontologist, 8,* 276–279.

Keith, P.M., & Schafer, R.B. (1980). Role strain and depression in two-job families. *Family Relations, 29,* 483–488.

Klein, K.C. (1976). Housing style preferences and personality (Doctoral dissertation, Illinois Institute of

Technology, 1975). *Dissertation Abstracts International,* *36*(12) 6359B.

Korosec-Serfaty, P. (1979) *Une maison à soi. Determinants psychologiques et sociaux de l'habitat individuel (Vol. 3).* Strasbourg, France: Direction Regionale du Ministère du Cadre de Vie.

Korosec-Serfaty, P. (1984a). Home and the experience of burglary. In *Proceedings of the 8th International Conference on Environment and Human Action, International Association Conference for the Study of People and their Physical Surroundings* (p. 144). West Berlin: International Association for the Study of People in their Physical Surroundings.

Korosec-Serfaty, P. (1984b). The home from attic to cellar. *Journal of Environmental Psychology, 4*(4), 303–321.

Krissdottir, M. (1982). Ingolf's pillars: The changing Icelandic house. *Landscape, 26*(2), 7–14.

Kron, J. (1983). *Home-psych: The social psychology of home and decoration.* New York: Potter.

Ladd, F.C. (1977). Residential history. *Landscape, 21*(2), 15–20.

Lambert, J.R., & Filkin, C. (1971). Race relations research: Some issues of approach and application. *Race, 12*(3), 229–235.

Landess, R.T. (1976). The social-emotional adjustment of children from mobile homes and traditional single-family dwellings: A comparative study (Doctoral dissertation, University of Montana, 1976). *Dissertation Abstracts International, 36*(9), 5651A.

Lansing, J.B. (1966). *Residential location and urban mobility: The second wave of interviews.* Ann Arbor: University of Michigan, Institute for Social Research.

Lansing, J.B., Marans, R.W., & Zehner, R.B. (1970). *Planned residential environments.* Ann Arbor: University of Michigan, Institute for Social Research.

Laudadio, D.M. (1977). An exploratory study to determine relevancy of selected demographic and psychological variables for marketing second-home condominiums (Doctoral dissertation, Michigan State University, 1977). *Dissertation Abstracts International, 37*(9), 6023A.

Lauman, E.O., & House, J.S. (1970). Living room styles and social attributes. *Journal of Social Research, 54,* 321–342.

Lawrence, R.J. (1979). Dual representations of domestic space: Users and architects participating in the design process. In A. Seidel & S. Danford (Eds.), *Environmental design: Research theory and application: Proceedings of the 10th Environmental Design Research Association Conference* (pp. 119–129). Washington, DC: Environmental Design Research Association.

Lawrence, R.J. (1981). The appropriation of domestic space: A cross-cultural perspective, In A.E. Osterberg, C.P. Tiernan, & R.A. Findlay (Eds.), *Design re-*

search interactions: EDRA 12 (pp. 46–55). Washington, DC: Environmental Design Research Association.

Lawrence, R.J. (1982a). A psycho-spatial approach for architectural design and research. *Journal of Environmental Psychology, 2,* 37–51.

Lawrence, R.J. (1982b). Domestic space and society: A cross-cultural study. *Comparative Studies in Society and History, 24*(1), 104–130.

Lawrence, R.J. (1983a). The comparative analysis of homes: Research method and application. *Social Science Information, 22,* 461–485.

Lawrence, R.J. (1983b). Understanding the home environment: Spatial and temporal perspectives. *International Journal for Housing Science and Its Applications, 7*(11), 13–25.

Lawrence, R.J. (1986). The comparative analysis of homes: Research, method and application. In I. Altman & C. Werner (Eds.), *Human behavior and environment: Home environments. Vol. 8.* New York: Plenum, 113–132.

Lawton, M.P. (1975). *Planning and managing housing for the elderly.* New York: Wiley.

Lawton, M.P. (1977). An ecological theory of aging applied to elderly housing. *Journal of Architectural Education, 31*(1), 8–10.

Lawton, M.P., & Cohen, J. (1974). The generality of housing impact on the well-being of older people. *Journal of Gerontology, 29,* 194–204.

Lazarus, R.S. (1966). *Psychological stress and the coping process.* New York: McGraw-Hill.

LeVine, R.A. (1962). Witchcraft and co-wife proximity in southwestern Kenya. *Ethnology, 1,* 39–45.

Lewis, O. (1961). *The children of Sanchez.* New York: Random House.

Lieberman, M.A. (1961). Relationship of mortality rates to entrance to a home for the aged. *Geriatrics, 16,* 515–519.

Lipman, A., & Russell-Lacey, S. (1974). Some social psychological correlates of new town residential location. In D. Canter & T. Lee (Eds.), *Psychology and the built environment* (pp. 139–147). New York: Wiley.

Littlejohn, J. (1967). The Temne house. In J. Middleton (Ed.), *Myth and cosmos: Readings in mythology and symbolism* (pp. 331–347). Austin: University of Texas Press.

Long, L. (1974). *The effects of mobility on the American male as employee.* Paper presented at the Allied Symposium, Temple University, Philadelphia.

Loyd, B. (1982). Women, home and status. In J.S. Duncan (Ed.), *Housing and identity: Cross-cultural perspectives* (pp. 181–197). New York: Holmes & Meier.

Lugassy, F. (1976). The spatialization of identity supported by the body-image and by the dwelling. In P. Korosec-Serfaty (Ed.), *Appropriation of space* (pp. 300–309).

Louvain-la-Neuve, Belgium: CIACO, Cooperative Universitaire.

Lyle, J. (1971). Television in daily life: Patterns of use (Overview). In E. Rubenstein, G. Comstock, & J. Murray (Eds.), *Television and social behavior* (Vol. 4, pp. 1–33). Washington, DC: U.S. Government Printing Office.

Maccoby, E.E. (1951). Television: Its impact on school children. *Public Opinion Quarterly, 15,* 421–444.

Maccoby, E.E., & Jacklin, C.N. (1974). *The psychology of sex differences.* Stanford, CA: Stanford University Press.

Mackintosh, E. (1982). High in the city. In P. Bart, A. Chen, & G. Francescato (Eds.), *Knowledge for design: Proceedings of the 13th Environmental Design Research Association Conference* (pp. 424–434). Washington, DC: Environmental Design Research Association.

Mackintosh, E., Olsen, R., & Wentworth, W. (1977). *The attitudes and experiences of the middle income family in an urban high rise complex and the suburbs.* New York: City University of New York Graduate Center. Center for Human Environments.

Mahler, M.S. (1968). *On human symbiosis and the vicissitudes of individuation, infantile psychosis.* New York: International University Press.

Manning, C. (1981). A simulation of housing adjustment. In A.E. Osterberg, C.P. Tiernan, & R.A. Findlay (Eds.), *Design research interactions: Proceedings of the 12th Environmental Design Research Association Conference* (p. 390). Washington, DC: Environmental Design Research Association.

Marans, R.W. (1976). Perceived quality of residential environments: Some methodological issues. In K.H. Craik & E.H. Zube (Eds.), *Perceiving environmental quality: Research and applications* (pp. 123–147). New York: Plenum.

Marc, O. (1977). *Psychology of the house.* London: Thames & Hudson.

Marcus, C.C. (1974). Children's play behavior in a low-rise inner-city housing development. In D. Carson (Ed.), *Man-environment interactions: evaluation and applications: Vol. 12. Childhood city: Proceedings of the 12th Environmental Design Research Association Conference* (pp. 197–211). Washington, DC: Environmental Design Research Association.

Marmot, A.F. (1982). Flats fit for families: An evaluation of post occupancy evaluation. In P. Bart, A. Chen, & G. Francescato (Eds.), *Knowledge for design: Proceedings of the 13th Environmental Design Research Association Conference* (pp. 224–236). Washington, DC: Environmental Design Research Association.

McAlister, R.J., Butler, E.W., & Kaiser, E.J. (1972). *The adaptation of women to residential mobility.* Paper presented at Allied Symposium, Indiana University and Purdue University, Indianapolis, IN.

McKain, J. (1972). *Geographical relocation and family problems.* Paper presented at Allied Symposium, Indiana University and Purdue University, Indianapolis, IN.

McLain, R.E., Silverstein, A.B., Brownlee, L., & Hubbell, M. (1977). Measuring differences in residential environments among institutions for retarded persons. *Psychological Reports, 41*(1), 264–266.

McLain, R.E., Silverstein, A.B., Hubbell, M., & Brownlee, L. (1975). The characterization of residential environments within a hospital for the mentally retarded. *Mental Retardation, 13*(4), 24–27.

McLain, R.E., Silverstein, A.B., Hubbell, M., & Brownlee, L. (1977). Comparison of the residential environment of a state hospital for retarded clients with those of various types of community facilities. *Journal of Community Psychology, 5*(3), 282–289.

Michelson, W. (1970a). Analytic sampling for design information: A survey of housing experience. In H. Sanoff & S. Cohen (Eds.), *EDRA 1: Proceedings of the first annual Environmental Design Research Association Conference* (pp. 183–197). North Carolina State University, Raleigh.

Michelson, W. (1970b). *Man and his urban environment: A sociological analysis.* Reading, MA: Addison-Wesley.

Michelson, W. (1977). *Environmental choice, human behavior, and residential satisfaction.* New York: Oxford University Press.

Miller, D., & Lieberman, M.A. (1965). The relationship of affected state and adaptive capacity to reactions to stress. *Journal of Gerontology, 20,* 492–497.

Moore, R., & Young, D. (1978). Childhood outdoors: Toward a social ecology of the landscape. In I. Altman & J. Wohlwill (Eds.), *Children and the environment* (pp. 83–130). New York: Plenum.

Moos, R.H. (1980). Specialized living environments for older people: A conceptual framework for evaluation. *Journal of Social Issues, 36*(2), 75–94.

Morgan, L.H. (1965). *Houses and house-life of the American aborigines.* Chicago: University of Chicago Press.

Morris, E.W., Crull, S.R., & Winter, M. (1976). Overcrowding in the home. *Journal of Marriage and the Family, 38,* 309–321.

Morrissy, E., & Handal, P.J. (1981). Characteristics of the Residential Environment Scale: Reliability and differential relationship to neighborhood satisfaction in divergent neighborhoods. *Journal of Community Psychology, 9*(2), 125–132.

Mulvihill, R., & McHugh, S. (1977, December). *A preliminary investigation of housing imagery and the accessibility of innovations in housing estates* (Working Paper No. 2). Dublin: A Foras Forbartha, Planning Division.

Murray, R. (1974). The influence of crowding on children's behavior. In D. Canter & T. Lee (Eds.), *Psychology and the built environment* (pp. 112–117). New York: Wiley.

Nasar, J.L. (1979). The impact of visual aspects of residential environments on hedonic responses, interests, and fear of crime (Doctoral dissertation, Pennsylvania State University, 1979). *Dissertation Abstracts International, 40*(4), 1963B.

Newman, O. (1972). *Defensible space*. New York: Macmillan.

Newman, S.J., & Owen, M.S. (1982). Residential displacement: Extent, nature and effects. *Journal of Social Issues, 38*(3), 135–148.

Newson, J., & Newson, E. (1976). *Seven years old in the home environment*. New York: Halsted.

Norberg-Schulz, C. (1971). *Existence, space and architecture*. New York: Praeger.

Norberg-Schulz, C. (1980a). *Genius loci: Towards a phenomenology of architecture*. New York: Rizzoli.

Norberg-Schulz, C. (1980b). *Meaning in western architecture*. New York: Rizzoli.

Null, R.L. (1979). Determinants of student perceptions of the social and academic climates of suite living arrangements in university residence halls. In A. Seidel & S. Danford (Eds.), *Environmental design: Research, theory and application: Proceedings of the 10th Environmental Design Research Association Conference* (pp. 359–366). Washington, DC: Environmental Design Research Association.

Ofrias, J., & Tognoli, J. (1979). Women's and men's responses toward the home in heterosexual and same sex households: A case study. In A. Seidel & S. Danford (Eds.), *Environmental design: Research, theory and application: Proceedings of the 10th Environmental Design Research Association Conference* (pp. 130–140). Washington, DC: Environmental Design Research Association.

Onibokun, A.G. (1973). Environmental issues in housing habitability. *Environment and Planning, 5*, 461–476.

Ohnuku-Tierney, O. (1972). Spatial concepts of the Ainu of the northwest coast of southern Sakhalin. *American Anthropologist, 74*, 426–457.

Osterberg, A. (1981). Post occupancy evaluation of a retirement home. In A.E. Osterberg, C.P. Tiernan, & R.A. Findlay (Eds.), *Design research interactions: Proceedings of the 12th Environmental Design Research Association Conference* (pp. 301–311). Washington, DC: Environmental Design Research Association.

Parke, R.D. (1978). Children's home environments: Social and cognitive effects. In I. Altman & J. Wohlwill (Eds.), *Children and the environment* (pp. 33–81). New York: Plenum.

Parke, R.D., & Sawin, D.B. (1979). Children's privacy in the home. Developmental, ecological and childrearing determinants. *Environment and Behavior, 11*, 87–104.

Pastalan, L.A. (1973). Involuntary environmental relocation: Death and survival. In W.E.F. Preiser (Ed.), *Environmental design research: Proceedings of the 4th Environmental Design Research Association Conference* Vol. 2 (p. 410). Stroudsburg, PA: Dowden, Hutchinson, & Ross.

Peachey, P. (1981). *Households and the territorial dispersion of human activity systems: A preliminary report on a comparative activity*. Paper presented at the annual meeting of the American Sociological Association, Toronto.

Perin, C. (1977). *Everything in its place: Social order and land use in America*. Princeton, NJ: Princeton University Press.

Pleck, J. (1975, November). *Men's new roles in the family: Housework and child care*. Paper presented at the Ford Foundation/Merrill-Palmer Institute Conference on the Family and Sex Roles, Merrill-Palmer Institute, Detroit, MI.

Pleck, J. (1979). Men's family work: Three perspectives and some new data. *The Family Coordinator, 28*, 481–488.

Pleck, J., & Rustad, M. (1980). *Husbands' and wives' time in family work and paid work in the 1975–76 study of time use* (Research Rep.). Wellesley, MA: Wellesley College, Center for Research on Women.

Pratt, G. (1982). The house as an expression of social worlds. In J.S. Duncan (Ed.), *Housing and identity: Cross-cultural perspectives* (pp. 135–180). New York: Holmes & Meier.

Proshansky, H.M. (1978). The city and self-identity. *Environment and Behavior, 10*, 147–170.

Pynoos, J., Schafer, R., & Hartman, C. (Eds.) (1973). *Housing urban America*. Chicago: Aldine.

Raglan, L. (1964). *The temple and the house*. New York: Norton.

Rahe, R.H. (1969). Life crisis and health change. In P.R.A. May & J.R. Wittenborn (Eds.), *Psychotropic drug response* (pp. 92–125). Springfield, IL: Thomas.

Rapoport, A. (1969). *House form and culture*. Englewood Cliffs, NJ: Prentice-Hall.

Rapoport, A. (1980a). Cross cultural aspects of environmental design. In I. Altman & J. Wohlwill (Eds.), *Human behavior and environment: Culture and environment* (pp. 7–46). New York: Plenum.

Rapoport, A. (1980b). Towards a cross-culturally valid definition of housing. In R. Stough & A. Wandersman (Eds.), *Optimizing environments: Research, practice and policy: Proceedings of the 11th Environmental Design Research Association Conference* (pp. 310–316). Washington, DC: Environmental Design Research Association.

Rapoport, A. (1982). Identity and environment: A cross-cultural perspective. In J.S. Duncan (Ed.), *Housing and identity: Cross-cultural perspectives* (pp. 36–59). New York: Holmes & Meier.

Relph, E. (1976). *Place and placelessness*. London: Pion.

Rent, G.S., & Rent, C.S. (1978). Low-income housing: Factors related to residential satisfaction. *Environment and Behavior, 10*(4), 459–488.

Rivlin, L.G. (1982). Group membership and place meanings in an urban neighborhood. *Journal of Social Issues, 38*(3), 75–94.

Robinson, J. (1980). Images of housing, Minneapolis: A limited study of urban residents' attitudes and values. Unpublished master's thesis, University of Minnesota, Minneapolis.

Rossi, P.H. (1955). *Why families move: A study in the social psychology of urban residential mobility.* Glencoe, IL: Free Press.

Rossi, P.H. (1980). *Why families move* (2nd ed.). Beverly Hills, CA: Sage.

Rykwert, J. (1972). *On Adam's house in paradise: The idea of the primitive hut in architectural theory.* New York: Museum of Modern Art.

Sadalla, E.K., Burroughs, J., & Quaid, M. (1980). House form and social identity: A validity study. In R. Stough & A. Wandersman (Eds.), *Optimizing environments: Research practice and policy: Proceedings of the 11th Environmental Design Research Association Conference* (pp. 201–206). Washington, DC: Environmental Design Research Association.

Sadalla, E.K., Snyder, P.Z., & Stea, D. (1976). *House form and culture revisited.* Paper presented at the 7th Annual Conference of the Environmental Design Research Association, Vancouver, British Columbia, Canada.

Saegert, S. (1980). Masculine cities and feminine suburbs: Polarized ideas, contradictory realities. *Signs: Journal of Women in Culture and Society, 5*(Suppl. 3), 96–111.

Saegert, S., & Hart, R. (1976). *The development of environmental competence in boys and girls.* New York: City University of New York Graduate Center: Center for Human Environments.

Saegert, S., & Winkel, G. (1980). The home: A critical problem for changing sex roles. In G.R. Wekerle, R. Peterson, & D. Morley (Eds.), *New space for women* (pp. 41–63). Boulder, CO: Westview.

Saile, D.G. (1976, March). An English educational program concerned with housing in developing countries. *Arid Lands Newsletter,* University of Arizona, No. 3, pp. 11–12.

Saile, D.G. (1977). Building rituals and spatial concepts: Making a house in the Pueblo Indian world. *Architectural Association Quarterly, 9*(2/3), 72–81.

Saile, D.G. (1986). The ritual establishment of home. In I. Altman & C. Werner (Eds.), *Human behavior and environment: Vol. 8. Home environments.* New York: Plenum, 87–111.

Saile, D.G., Borodah, R., & Williams, M. (1972). Families in public housing: A study of three localities in Rockford, Illinois. In W. Mitchell (Ed.), *Environmental design: Research and practice: Proceedings of the 3rd Environmental Design Research Association.* Los Angeles: University of California.

Salling, M., & Harvey, M.E. (1981). Poverty, personality, and sensitivity to residential stressors. *Environment and Behavior, 13*(2), 131–163.

Saltman, J. (1975). Implementing open housing laws through social action. *Journal of Applied Behavioral Science, 11*(1), 39–61.

Sanford, J. (1984). Designing for privacy, community and control in urban mobile home neighborhoods. In D. Duerk & D. Campbell (Eds.), *EDRA 15—1984 Proceedings: The challenge of diversity* (pp. 150–155). Washington, DC: Environmental Design Research Association.

Sanoff, H. (1973). Youth's perception and categorization of residential cues. In W.E.F. Preiser (Ed.), *Environmental design research, Vol. 1: Proceedings of the 4th Environmental Design Research Association Conference* (pp. 84–97). Stroudsburg, PA: Dowden, Hutchison, & Ross.

Savarton, S., & George, K.R. (1971). *A study of historic, economic and sociocultural factors which influence Aboriginal settlements at Wilcannia and Weilmeringle, New South Wales.* Unpublished thesis, University of Sydney, Sydney, Australia.

Schafer, R. (1974). *The suburbanization of multifamily housing.* Lexington, MA: Heath.

Schweitzer, E., Bell, G., & Daily, J. (1973). A bi-racial comparison of density preferences in housing in two cities. In W.E.F. Presier (Ed.), *Environmental design research, Vol. 1: Proceedings of the 4th Environmental Design Research Association Conference* (pp. 312–323). Stroudsburg, PA: Dowden, Hutchinson, & Ross.

Seamon, D. (1979). *A geography of the life world: Movement, rest and encounter.* London: Croom-Helm.

Seamon, D. (1982). The phenomenological contribution to environmental psychology. *Journal of Environmental Psychology, 2,* 119–140.

Seeley, J.R., Sim, R.A., & Loosley, E.W.(1963). *Crestwood Heights: A study of the culture of suburban life.* New York: Wiley.

Selye, H. (1956). *The stress of life.* New York: McGraw-Hill.

Servais, E., & Lienard, G. (1976). Inhabited space and class ethos. In P. Korosec-Serfaty (Ed.), *Appropriation of space* (pp. 240–246). Louvain-la-Neuve, Belgium: CIACO, Cooperative Universitaire.

Shumaker, S., & Conti, G. (1986). The meaning of home to mobile Americans. In I. Altman & C. Werner (Eds.), *Human behavior and environments: Vol. 8. Home Environments.* New York: Plenum, 237–253.

Shumaker, S.A., & Stokols, D. (1982). Residential mobility as a social issue and research topic. *Journal of Social Issues, 38*(3), 1–19.

Simpson, S., Woods, R., & Britton, P. (1981). Depression and engagement in a residential home for the elderly. *Behaviour Research and Therapy, 19*(5), 435–438.

Smith, C.J. (1980). Optimum living environments for discharged mental patients. In R. Stough & A. Wandersman (Eds.), *Optimizing environments: Research, practice and policy: Proceedings of the 11th Environmental Design Research Association Conference* (pp. 77–84). Washington, DC: Environmental Design Research Association.

Snyder-McKenna, R., & Morris, E.W. (1981). *A dynamic analysis of housing standards*. Paper presented at the 12th Environmental Design Research Association Conference, Iowa State University, Ames, IA.

Sommer, R. (1969). *Personal space*. Englewood Cliffs, NJ: Prentice-Hall.

Sommer, R. (1972). *Design awareness*. San Francisco: Rinehart.

Sonnenfield, J. (1966). Variable values in space and landscape: An enquiry into the nature of environmental necessity, *Journal of Social Issues, 22*, 71–82.

Staines, G.L., & Pleck, J.H. (1983). *The impact of work schedules on the family*. Ann Arbor, MI: University of Michigan, Institute for Social Research, Survey Research Center.

Stea, D. (1980). Psychosocial studies of nomads and squatters: Two applications of cross-cultural environmental psychology. *Revista Interamericana de Psicologia, 14*(1), 1–20.

Stea, D., & Prussin, L. (1978). *Society, settlement, and sex roles in developing areas*. Paper presented at the 9th Environmental Design Research Association Conference, University of Arizona, Tucson.

Steinfeld, E. (1982). The place of old age: The meaning of housing for old people. In J.S. Duncan (Ed.), *Housing and identity: Cross-cultural perspectives* (pp. 198–246). New York: Holmes & Meier.

Stephens, M.A.P., & Kinney, J.M. (1983). Congregate vs. traditional housing for older people: Differential patterns of behavior among residents. In D. Amedeo, J.B. Griffin, & J.J. Potter (Eds.), *EDRA 1983, Proceedings of the 14th International Conference of the Environmental Design Research Association, University of Nebraska-Lincoln* (pp. 84–90). Washington, DC: Environmental Design Research Association.

Stewart, J.N. (1972). *Intention and expectation in differentiated residential selection*. Paper presented at the Allied Symposium, Indiana University and Purdue University, Indianapolis, IN.

Stokols, D. (1978). Environmental psychology. *Annual Review of Psychology, 29*, 253–295.

Stokols, D. & Shumaker, S.A. (1982). The psychological context of residential mobility and well-being. *Journal of Social Issues, 38*(3), 149–171.

Stokols, D., Shumaker, S.A., & Martinez, J. (1983). Residential mobility and personal well-being. *Journal of Environmental Psychology, 3*, 5–19.

Storandt, M., Wittles, I., & Botwinick, J. (1975). Predictors of a dimension of well-being in the relocated healthy aged. *Journal of Gerontology, 30*(1), 97–102.

Suttles, G. (1968). *The social order of the slum*. Chicago: University of Chicago Press.

Tagg, S. (1974). The subjective meaning of rooms: Some analyses and investigations. In D. Canter & T. Lee (Eds.), *Psychology and the built environment* (pp. 65–70). New York: Wiley.

Tallman, I., & Morgner, R. (1970). Life style and differences among urban and suburban blue-collar families. *Social Forces, 48*(3), 334–348.

Tars, S., & Appleby, L. (1973). The same child in home and institution: An observation study. *Environment and Behavior, 5*(1), 3–28.

Taylor, C.C., & Townsend, A.R. (1976). The local 'sense of place' as evidenced in north-east England. *Urban Studies, 13*, 133–146.

Taylor, R.B., Gottfredson, S.D., & Brower, S. (1981). Territorial cognitions and social climate in urban neighborhoods. *Basic & Applied Social Psychology, 2*(4), 289–303.

Taylor, R.B., Gottfredson, S.D., Brower, S.N., & O'Brien, P.N. (1981, August). *Attachment to place and perception of local social problems*. Paper presented at the 89th Annual Convention of the American Psychological Association, Los Angeles.

Thornberg, J.M. (1973). Child's conception of places to live in. In W.E.F. Preiser (Ed.), *Environmental design research, Vol. 1: Proceedings of the 4th Environmental Design Research Association Conference* (pp. 178–190). Stroudsburg, PA: Dowden, Hutchinson, & Ross.

Thorne, B., & Henley, N. (1975). Difference and dominance: An overview of language, gender and society. In B. Thorne & N. Henley (Eds.), *Language and sex* (pp. 5–42). Rowley, MA: Newbury House.

Thorne, R., Hall, R., & Munro-Clark, M. (1982). Attitudes toward detached houses, terraces and apartments: Some current pressures towards less preferred but more accessible alternatives. In P. Bart, A. Chen, & G. Francescato (Eds.), *Knowledge for design: Proceedings of the 13th Environmental Design Research Association Conference* (pp. 435–448). Washington, DC: Environmental Design Research Association.

Tibbetts, S. (1975, December). Sex differences in children's reading preferences. *The Reading Teacher*, 279–281.

Timms, D.W.G. (1971). *The urban mosaic: Towards a theory of residential differentiation*. Cambridge: Cambridge University Press.

Tobey, H.N. (1982). Connotative messages of single family homes: A multidimensional scaling analysis. In P. Bart, A. Chen, & G. Francescato (Eds.), *Knowledge for design: Proceedings of the 13th Environmental Design Research Association* (pp. 449–463). Washington, DC: Environmental Design Research Association.

Tognoli, J. (1980). Differences in women's and men's responses to domestic space. *Sex Roles, 6*, 833–842.

Tognoli, J., & Hornberger, F. (1984, July). Images of household roles in children's television programs. In *Proceedings of the 8th International Conference on Environment and Human Action* (pp. 338–340). West Berlin: International Association for the Study of People and their Physical Surroundings.

Tognoli, J., Hamad, C., & Carpenter, T. (1978). Staff attitudes toward adult male residents' behavior as a function of two settings in an institution for mentally retarded people. *Mental Retardation, 16*(2), 142–146.

Tognoli, J., & Horwitz, J. (1982). From childhood home to adult home: Environmental transformations. In P. Bart, A. Chen, & G. Francescato (Eds.), *Knowledge for design: Proceedings of the 13th Environmental Design Research Association Conference* (pp. 321–328). Washington, DC: Environmental Design Research Association.

Tognoli, J., & Storch, J.L. (1980). Inside and outside: Setting locations of female and male characters in children's television. In R. Stough & A. Wandersman (Eds.), *Optimizing environments: Research, practice and policy: Proceedings of the 11th Environmental Design Research Association Conference* (pp. 288–297). Washington, DC: Environmental Design Research Association.

Tomeh, A. (1964, July). Informal group participation and residential patterns. *American Journal of Sociology, 70*, 28–35.

Tropman, J.E. (1974). *The effects of geographic mobility on the American male as head of the household.* Paper presented at the Allied Symposium, Temple University, Philadelphia.

Tuan, Y. (1977). *Space and place: The perspective of experience.* Minneapolis: University of Minnesota Press.

Tuan, Y. (1979). *Landscapes of fear.* New York: Pantheon.

Tucker, S.M., Combs, M.E., & Woolrich, A.M. (1975). Independent housing for the elderly: The human element in design. *Gerontologist, 15*(1), 73–76.

Turner, J.F.C. (1977). *Housing by people: Towards autonomy in building environments.* New York: Pantheon.

Turpin, D. (1971, April 4). Nineteen of 25 apartment managers display overt bias. *Los Angeles Times,* p. J–1.

Valins, S., & Baum, S. (1973). Residential group size, social interaction and crowding. *Environment and Behavior, 5*, 421–439.

Valpey, D.D. (1982). The psychological impact of 18 years in a board and care home. *Journal of Community Psychology, 10*(1), 95–97.

Vershure, B.E. (1980). Housing symbolism: A study of nonverbal identity communication in home environments (Doctoral dissertation, Arizona State University, 1979). *Dissertation Abstracts International, 40*(10), 5082B.

Vershure, B.E., Magel, S., & Sadalla, E. (1976). House form and social identity. In P. Suedfeld & J. Russell (Eds.), *The behavioral basis of design, Book 2: Proceedings of the 7th Environmental Design Research Association Conference* (pp. 273–278). Stroudsburg, PA: Dowden, Hutchinson, & Ross.

Vinsel, A., Brown, B., Altman, I., & Foss, C. (1980). Privacy regulation, territorial displays, and effectiveness of individual functioning. *Journal of Personality and Social Psychology, 39*, 1104–1115.

Volkman, N. (1981). User perceptions of underground houses and implications for site planning. In A.E. Osterberg, C.P. Tiernan, & R.A. Findlay (Eds.), *Design research interactions: Proceedings of the 12th Environmental Design Research Association Conference* (pp. 277–281). Washington, DC: Environmental Design Research Association.

Voydanoff, P. (1980). Work roles as stressors in corporate families. *Family Relations, 29*, 489–494.

Wagenheim, H.H. (1974). *The effects of mobility on the American male as employee and head of household.* Paper presented at Allied Symposium, Temple University, Philadelphia.

Walker, K., & Woods, M. (1976). *Time use: A measure of household production of family goods and services.* Washington, DC: American Home Economics Association.

Wallis, A. (1982). Mobile homes: A psychological case study of innovation in housing (Doctoral dissertation, City University of New York Graduate Center, Program in Environmental Psychology, 1981). *Dissertation Abstracts International, 42*(9), 3812B.

Ward, B. (1976). *The home of man.* New York: Norton.

Watson, A.J., & Kivett, V.R. (1976). Influences on the life satisfaction of elderly fathers. *The Family Coordinator, 25*, 482–488.

Weber, M. (1981). Model of habitability parameters utilized in study of earth sheltered housing. In A.E. Osterberg, C.P. Tiernan, & R.A. Findlay (Eds.), *Design research interactions: Proceedings of the 12th Environmental Design Research Association Conference* (pp. 272–276). Washington, DC: Environmental Design Research Association.

Wehrli, B., Huser, S., Egli, H., Bakke, P., & Grandjean, E. (1976). Housing conditions, housing activities, and housing attitudes. In P. Korosec-Serfaty (Ed.), *Appropriation of space* (pp. 310–318). Louvain-la-Neuve, Belgium: CIACO, Cooperative Universitaire.

Wekerle, G.R. (1975). *Residential choice behavior, housing satisfaction and future mobility in a singles high rise complex.* Paper presented at Symposium on Human Response to Tall Buildings, American Institute of Architects and Joint Committee on Tall Buildings, Chicago.

Werthman, C. (1968). The social meaning of the physical environment. Unpublished doctoral dissertation, University of California, Berkeley.

West, E.J. (1981). Urban revival and the poor. *The Urban League Review, 5*(2), 12–15.

Wheeler, L., Bechtel, R.B., & Ittleson, W.H. (1977). Environmental psychology and housing: Design in arid urban areas. *Man-Environment Systems, 7*(4), 206–213.

Whiting, B., & Edwards, C.P. (1973). A cross-cultural analysis of sex differences in the behavior of children aged three through 11. *The Journal of Social Psychology, 91,* 171–188.

Wilner, D.M., Walkeley, R.P., Pinkerton, T.C., & Tayback, M. (1962). *The housing environment and family life* Baltimore, MD: Johns Hopkins University Press.

Winnicott, D.W. (1971). *Playing and reality.* New York: Basic Books.

Wohlwill, J.F. (1974). Human adaptation to levels of environmental stimulation. *Human Ecology, 2,* 127–147.

Wolfe, M. (1975). Room size, group size and density: Behavioral effects in a children's psychiatric facility. *Environment and Behavior, 7,* 199–224.

Wolfe, M. (1978). Childhood and privacy. In I. Altman and J. Wohlwill (Eds.), *Human behavior and environment:*

Vol. 3. Children and the environment (pp. 175–222). New York: Plenum.

Women on Words & Images. (1975). *Channeling children: Sex stereotyping in prime time TV.* Princeton, NJ: Author.

Wright, G. (1981). *Building the dream: A social history of housing in America.* New York: Pantheon.

Yancey, W.L. (1972). Architecture, interaction, and social control: The case of a large-scale housing project. In J.F. Wohlwill & D. Carson (Eds.), *Environment and the social sciences: Perspectives and applications* (pp. 126–136). Washington, DC: American Psychological Association.

Zeisel, J. (1973). Symbolic meaning of space and the physical dimension of social relations: A case study of sociological research as the basis of architectural planning. In J. Walton & D. Carns (Eds.), *Cities in change: Studies on the urban condition* (pp. 252–263). Boston: Allyn & Bacon.

Chapter 18

SCHOOL AND CLASSROOM ENVIRONMENTS

Paul V. Gump, *University of Kansas, Lawrence, Kansas*

If we placed ourselves in the midst of a school's operation, a variety of environments could claim our attention. For example, we might focus on the physical provisions for schooling: enclosures, furniture, tools, supplies, and the like, or we could examine the major action structures that represent the patterns of the school's operations: the commuting in hallways, the reciting in classrooms, the playing of games in the gym, the communicating and recording in the office,

and so on. Such selection of environmental components remains the objective or ecological side of the environment. We might become interested in how all of this was being processed by students in their psychological environments, in whether students perceived their situations as nurturant or hostile, as interesting or boring. To some extent, all of these environments will be of importance to us here. However, there is one conception of the environment that will supply the basic organization and the prevailing perspective—that conception is the ecological one.

Schools, or classrooms within schools, are clusters of settings. These settings are objective, out-there behavioral arenas for students and staff. The settings exhibit a physical aspect—site, enclosures, facilities, manipulanda—and they possess a program or action structure. In early elementary school, a standard small setting is the reading circle that has a location usually away from the center of things in the classroom. The circle's chairs face inward around a table or small open space and form a spatial boundary for the activity. Books, charts, and other tools of the educational process are at hand. The reading circle will be occupied by a subgroup of students and a teacher. The participants in the reading circle accept a certain action structure in order to carry out the day's lesson: reading in turn with discussion between turns is a common program, and a discussion and review of previous readings is another type of reading circle program. Reflection will show that the *physical arrangement* of the reading circle and its *program* manifest an interlocking relationship. The program requires much pupil–pupil and pupil–teacher communication so the physical arrangement provides chairs that are reasonably close together and oriented to support face-to-face interaction. The teacher arranges any display items for easy visibility to all reading circle students. The physical arrangement and the program of the reading circle are fitted together. They exhibit what Barker (1968) has labeled *synomorphy* or "similarity of shape." Finally, the reading circle with its beginning and ending times manifests a temporal boundary. Other settings, all of which show a physical milieu, and a program in synomorphic relationship are contained within spatial and temporal boundaries. These settings or environmental segments (Gump, 1982) cluster together to create the ecological environment for a school's staff and students. The quality of school life is heavily determined by the nature of these school settings. Description of the school environment, at the ecological level, then, comes down to the description of school settings.

Manipulation or construction of school environments is directly accomplished only by approach to the ecological environment just described. We can affect events in school by changes in the physical milieu or by changes in the program (including behaviors of program operatives, such as teachers). We cannot create directly the psychological environments, the processed, or "in-the-head," environment of students and staff. We can, of course, arrange the objective things and events (milieu and program) so as to produce changes in the psychological environment.

Although the physical environment of a school and its parts are tightly interfaced with the ongoing action structures or programs, it is possible to consider the physical arrangements as temporarily separated from the programs they are designed to support. Much research on school environments is delivered in this separated fashion. For example, data on open space schools are so reported although it is clear that what actually happens to students in schools depends on whether an open or traditional program operates in the open space schools being investigated. A physical arrangement, such as circular versus row-and-column seating, has been a research target without the program used in the seating facility being given parallel attention.

For heuristic purposes, the following treatment of school settings will begin with consideration of the physical milieu per se, followed by a description of milieu in relation to numbers of people, and then consideration of variations in the program. This separation of aspects of school settings is artificial, but it may provide helpful focuses. In reality, physical qualities of the school environment must be understood in terms of the programs that these environments enclose and support.

18.1. PHYSICAL MILIEU OF SCHOOLS

A useful review of the research available on the physical environment of the school has been provided by Weinstein (1979).

Material on the school's physical environment can be surveyed with a basic question in mind: What is the contribution of particular physical patterns or resources to the ongoing operation of schooling and to the behavior and experience of school inhabitants, its staff, and pupils?

A first milieu consideration for an environmental school unit is the degree of physical enclosure. The open plan school operates on a principle that few internal enclosures, or barriers, are necessary: The traditional "egg-carton" construction assumes that classrooms need to be sealed off from one another so that visual, auditory, or other stimuli cannot travel from one major educational setting to another.

Once the boundary of an environmental part is established, the variable of space inside the boundary can be considered. Although sheer amount of space can be important, the amount of space in relation to the number of users of that space can be an influential variable.

Within the space available, the kind and patterning of the larger facilities become important. The "larger facilities" are those within or on which behavior is enacted. In preschool environments, these range from jungle gyms to small chairs; in academic classrooms, from laboratory counters to tables and desks.

Also of importance within the bounded spaces are the smaller facilities, the things that are used as tools and supplies—the manipulanda.

18.1.1. Within-School Enclosure: Open Space Design

The term *openness* as used in this section refers to the arrangement of physical space within a school building. Traditional school construction provides enclosed, even sealed, spaces for each class. A typical arrangement provides classrooms along each side of a corridor. The term *egg-carton schools* often labels this spatial pattern. Open schools, on the other hand, have larger interior spaces without walls and corridors.

At the outset, it would seem important to emphasize the distinction between "open schools," meaning open space, and "open schools," referring to educational program. Open programs emphasize the children's contribution to their own learning and individualization of instruction. Although open design was advanced to facilitate open education, research reviews have established that no *necessary* relation exists between the two realities (Bennett, Andreae, Hegarty, & Wade, 1980).

Although the construction of open schools has passed its peak, between 1967 and 1970, over half of the schools built were constructed with open patterns (George, 1975). Discussion of why openness became so popular appears elsewhere (Ross, 1979). Economic savings for open construction can be considerable (Gores, 1963), and the economic invitation to open construction remains. It is useful to consider, then, what has been the experience with open school environments.

Fundamental Qualities of the Open Space Arrangement

The most basic quality of open space is nonenclosure. Activity regions that are well sealed in an egg-carton school are without seal in open schools. The basic qualities of openness are (1) space, undivided by walls, is uncommitted, flexible; (2) corridors are not required, and space usually consumed by corridors becomes available; (3) without walls and doors, school inhabitants travel directly between activity regions; and (4) stimuli also travel freely between adjacent activity regions.

Direct Potentialities of Open Space Qualities

Certain kinds of learning arrangements become more feasible with the open space pattern. With easy and direct physical access to spaces, school programs can arrange for students to travel to a variety of sites. In a 4-class pod in a school known to the author, the shift to morning reading sites involved about 85 children moving from 4 base areas to 13 small-group sites. The transit time for any one pupil was less than 20 sec. Several studies have shown open-space schools to be in motion more, to send pupils to more different activity sites (Fisher, 1974; Gump, 1974).

The flexibility of open space makes possible a wide range of pupil-grouping practices. Two or more class-sized groups can be joined for a kind of supergroup presentation (Gump & Ross, 1979). The supergroup can be taught by a team of teachers, or, as seems common, one teacher manages while the rest are freed for other activity—a practice ironically described as "turn teaching," not "team teaching." Related to pupil grouping is the issue of cooperation among teachers. For long periods during the day, teachers in open-space schools can see and hear one another. The old privacy of the self-contained classroom is lost. Teachers' awareness of one another is practically guaranteed in open-space arrangements. This awareness can extend to programmatic cooperation. Team teaching, although not a common arrangement, has been shown to be more likely in the open pattern (Bennett et al., 1980; Gump & Ross, 1979; Meyer, 1971).

With perceptual access across activity regions comes the possibility of visual and auditory distraction. An extensive review of studies by Bennett and colleagues (1980) leaves no doubt that noise and accompanying distraction are very common complaints among open-school inhabitants. A study by Kyzar (1977) recorded sound levels in traditional and open classrooms and found them to be 63 and 70 dB, respectively. Although the effects of noise on children's and teacher's school performances are more fully developed in another chapter of this volume (see Hetz & Wohwill, Chapter 6), the 60–70 dB level may be a crucial range for communication. According to Walsh (1975), at 65 dB, the maximum distance for intelligible communication between teacher and student is only 7 ft.

Decibel intensity is not the only quality of the auditory stimuli related to distraction. Important also is the "message value" of the sound coming from outside a child's activity region. Sounds that indicate interesting events are more interruptive than the same decibel degree of meaningless sound. Talk about others and their activities, laughter, and irritated teacher corrections are examples of messages that invite attention even when their decibel rating may be moderate.

Reactive Potentialities of Open-Space Qualities

The lack of enclosure of basic activity regions can create problems of distraction and intrusion that staffs in open schools will not accept. Staffs' defensive responses include physically changing the openness of the physical environment or altering the program they establish—or both. The problem facing staff moving from a traditional program in an egg-carton school to an open-space school can be pictured as one of dissonance between a continuing traditional program and a new physical milieu. In terms of ecological psychology, the old program and the new milieu are not *synomorphic*, not similar in shape. Forces are set in motion to reestablish synomorphy, to make milieu and program come to terms.

One of the most common practices to bring the traditional program and the open space to terms has been the establishment of markers, screens, barriers, or even specially manufactured partitions between major activity areas. Gump and Ross (1979) measured the original, or "blueprint," physical openness of 21 open elementary schools; they also measured the openness that existed several years after operation. (*Openness* was defined as the ratio of square feet of teaching space to linear partition wall feet.) Employment of partitions (bookcases, cabinets, coat racks, etc.) had substantially reduced openness in these schools. Some open schools provided openness by a movable wall between classrooms. Of 35 such movable walls, 32 were permanently closed. Overall, the average reduction of openness was 38%.

Openness of program and "blueprint openness" were not correlated. However, program openness and modified openness were significantly related. Evidently a kind of " press toward synomorphy" had pushed milieu arrangements close to those of the program.

Although the addition of tall furniture and partitions reestablishes some enclosure, this enclosure can be only partial. Requirements of ventilation and heating will mean that open space must be left below the ceiling for circulation. Although visual stimuli from adjacent activity areas may be sealed off, sounds still cross these screens.

A related defense against physical openness has been the introduction of the quiet room. With sound sealed out (or in), quiet room activities can be undisturbed and nondisturbing. The problem with quiet rooms is that they often are not large enough for a total class. If less than a total class is to use them, the problem of supervision arises. A large-scale English investigation showed that these rooms sat unused 95% of the time (Bennett et al., 1980).

Both the introduction of screening furniture and the provision of quiet rooms can be considered physical defenses employed when open space and the program are not well suited— when they are not synomorphic. Program changes can also be defenses. This approach has not been researched, but interviews conducted by the author indicate some of the ways the program is reshaped to better fit the open space problems.

Teachers who share open spaces will avoid activities that can distract other groups in the same region. Audiovisual equipment will be used only when all groups can share presentations together. Sounds from such equipment carry too well. Musical instruments are not used except in sealed music rooms for the same reason. Outside speakers are not invited for single-class groups because they attract too much attention from adjacent areas. One teacher, when teaching in a self-contained classroom, had cooked samples of Mexican food when that country was studied. In a pod shared by three other teachers, the cooking was abandoned as "too distracting." Class-wide recitation–discussion of social studies issues have been dropped in favor of small group exchanges or seatwork when the class meets as a whole. The principle involved here is that the effects of openness may not show the most direct problems (e.g., distraction). For example, many open schools are not more noisy or distracting than traditional ones. The effects show in efforts taken to avoid the distraction problem.

A kind of tightening reaction in open space can accompany the practice of moving pupils frequently to various sites. Because these sites are shared over time, it is necessary that student arrivals and departures be closely scheduled. Openness that was intended to encourage informality and choice can produce a kind of regimentation not required in traditional self-contained classrooms. Other examples of program rigidity related to openness have been discussed by Evans and Lovell (1979).

Indirect Potentialities of Openness for Student Behavior and Development

What are the potentialities of open space for the behavior and development of schoolchildren? Although the question is clearly central to education, the influence of nonenclosure here is less direct and less predictable than for the relationships between nonenclosure and grouping, or variety of sites, or defensive partitioning. Contradictory or inconclusive research results may be expected.

The potentialities of openness for students may be divided between nonacademic and academic variables. Open space (and perhaps the pupil choice that may be a concomitant) has been associated with increased student autonomy (Meyer, 1971) and with persistence at a task (Reiss & Dydhalo, 1975). Studies on development of a positive self-concept have not yielded consistent results. For example, Weinstein (1979) reports positive effects for three self-concept studies, negative effects from two, and no relationship from three others. A recent metaanalysis of 153 studies (Giaconia & Hedges, 1982) shows that a more positive self-concept is related to certain aspects of open *education*. However, open *space* was *not* one of the effective determining variables in successful open education.

Data on open space and pupil social interaction are sparse. A study by Traub, Weiss, Fisher, Musella, and Kahn (1973) found that elementary children in open-space schools listed fewer peers with whom they might like to play than children in schools of traditional construction. Similarly, O'Neill (1974) found that 8- to 10-year-old boys in open-space schools developed less positive reactions to peers than boys in conventional schools. Although these social effects studies have not all sufficiently been replicated, it is possible that the increased mobility and increased numbers of peers contacted in open-space schools yield less social cohesion than in the enclosed classrooms where children have more associate continuity.

The nonenclosure of students in open schools might be related to task involvement. On the preschool level, Neill (1982) compared matched open design and conventional nursery schools. Openness was associated with more time moving around and "doing nothing," less time on school-related activities. Sheehan and Day (1975) found that some children in open areas were often irritable, noisy, and engaged in "frantic behavior." The addition of partitions and low shelves reduced such reactions.

Moore (1983) compared modified open-plan centers to more fully open and to closed centers. He found the most random behavior in the open center but least in the modified open arrangement. The structural division and partial subdivisions of the modified open plans provided more subsettings, more places for children to be. Modified open plan children did contact more places and were more self-directed, engaged, and exploratory than children in either the fully open or the closed centers.

At the elementary level, a number of studies indicate that open space can be associated with reduced task involvement (Angus, Beck, Hill, & McAtee, 1979; Fisher, 1974). Gump (1974) found that, relative to their counterparts in traditional schools, first- and second-grade children in open-space schools manifested loss of task involvement from two sources: The system was sometimes unready for operation, and the pupils were more often off-task. Although travel to different learning sites was rapid, the time devoted to "getting started" in these changes was relatively long. Interruptions of teaching action by outside persons was also more frequent. These nonsubstance times in open schools reduced the time devoted to academic work. Second, even when the open system was ready for involvement, the children in open space schools were less on-task than those in the conventional schools.

Pupil attributes not favorable for achievement in open schools have been identified as low persistence (Reiss & Dydhalo, 1975), lower IQ (Grapko, 1972), and English as a second language (Traub & Weiss, 1974).

Bell and her associates (1974) showed first-grade children performed more poorly in reading (but not in numbers) if they attended open rather than traditional schools. The investigators suggested that the behaviorally immature child probably could do better in a traditional classroom. However, the Bell research (Bell, Zipursky, & Switzer, 1976) continued into a second year, and the students of the conventional school were still superior in reading. At the end of a third year (Bell, Abrahamsen, & Growse, 1977), the conventional-school students were superior to the open-school students in reading, vocabulary, and in mathematics. The researchers attributed the decreased achievement in the open school to its more informal approach and to the design that failed to protect against distracting stimuli. The Bell research indicates that although certain children (such as the immature) may have special difficulty with open space arrangements, the effects turn out to be more general.

A compilation of studies on school achievement and school design shows either no difference or a difference favoring the conventional school. Giaconia and Hedges (1982) showed that although some aspects of an open *education* were favorable, open *space*—as a part of open education—was not influential in this analysis of 72 studies. Bennett and colleagues (1980) say that the "trends so far favour higher achievement in conventional schools" (p. 49). A scorecard of 28 studies developed by Angus and his researchers (1979) showed academic achievement better for open schools in 3 studies, better in conventional schools in 9 investigations, and no difference in 16 studies. These same investigators carried out the most substantial comparison of open and conventional schools on academic achievement known to the writer. A variety of open constructions was represented in the 70 schools. For comparison, 45 traditional schools were also studied. For the fifth-year students tested, those attending open-space schools scored significantly lower in reading and in mathematics. Scores in written expression tended to be lower but did not reach statistical significance. Achievement results were general and were not dependent on the socioeconomic status of the children.

The burden of the data available on achievement test results for open space versus traditional schools seems to support two conclusions: Certain kinds of students appear to be especially unsuited to the open atmosphere, but it is also possible for the introduction of open space to yield generally negative achievement effects.

Although the links between open space and less academic learning are not all understood, a repeated pattern of staff attempting traditional programs in open spaces appears in many researches. Teachers often maintain their own classes, attempt classwide activities, and rely on their own (not the child's) stimulation to carry much of the activity. The open-space environment is not well-suited to activities of this type. It was designed for more teacher cooperation and student exchange, for small (not class-sized) groups, and for dependence on child initiative and persistence to sustain learning actions. The open environment might be expected to contribute to lowered achievement if the learning activities prescribed are not appropriate to that environment.

18.1.2. Within-School Enclosure: Individual Seclusion

Open-space design can intensify the openness of individuals to stimuli from others. Even the partially secluded areas of traditional classrooms are much reduced in typical open-school arrangements. Consider what becomes of corners: An area of a traditional school might provide 4 classrooms for 100 students; in the open-space school only 1 area is provided. The traditional 4 rooms provide 16 corners, the open area 4.

Privacy opportunities, which are never substantial in traditional schooling, are perceived as even less available in the open areas. Because privacy has been perceived as a contributor to optimum development and adjustment, facilities to increase privacy have been recommended (Mack, 1976; Proshansky & Wolfe, 1974; Sheehan & Day, 1975). Students from fourth, fifth, and sixth grades were reported by Ahrentzen (1982) as less satisfied with open perimeters for their class groups than with wall separation. Students recommended some secluded areas, particularly for reading.

A most thoroughgoing answer to calls for privacy has been the "privacy booth," a classroom niche, perhaps 1 m^2, in which a single student is shielded from outside stimuli and from others' perception of his or her own behavior and person. Elementary students have indicated that they would like to use such a privacy facilitator. Desire for such niches was often expressed when students specified classroom environments they would prefer (Mack, 1976). Further, the niches have been heavily used when first introduced to classrooms (Moffitt, 1974; Weinstein, 1982).

Experience with the booths has provided some surprises. First, complete seclusion is often not desired. Students may enjoy a retreat but not an exclusion. When requested seclusion places have been provided, often they have not been used because, as the young children complained, one "couldn't see what was going on" (Curtis & Smith, 1974). Further, children's attention to a task was longer when the children using the booths could observe activity outside the booths than when such visual access was blocked (Campbell, 1979).

Although students may use the booths heavily when first introduced, popularity can fall off sharply. Weinstein (1982) introduced 2 three-sided cubicles (0.9 m per side) into two fourth-grade classrooms. Each was placed against a wall that furnished the fourth side. Initial pupil demand for use during study periods and free time was so high that additional cubicles were added. However, after about 3 weeks, usage markedly declined until, on the last 6 days of the experiment, visits to privacy booths amounted to less than 0.1 pupil per day. Weinstein provided some booths with windows, but these as well as those with less outward visibility were used infrequently after the initial enthusiasm.

The importance of control in privacy behavior has been pointed out by Altman (1974) who notes that persons seek the power to open and close themselves to others. However, need for privacy, such as that provided by privacy booths, is apparently not a human requirement for most persons in most situations. Sommer (1970) found that about one-half of users of a university library preferred the open or more exposed sitting places to secluded ones. Weinstein did uncover individual differences in use of the privacy booth: Girls who exhibited relatively high privacy behavior at home used the booths relatively more at school. Boys whom teachers rated as easily distracted, aggressive, and not sociable used booths more frequently than boys not so described. And some individuals say they want privacy more than others. However, self-report measures of privacy needs did *not* predict privacy booth usage in the Weinstein study.

Results from privacy booth research are not sufficiently extensive to make firm recommendations on their use in a variety of situations. Booths do provide novelty, "a place different to go" in overly familiar classrooms, but apparently many students do not need them for privacy's sake. Certainly for certain children in certain situations, the privacy booth may provide a useful facility. Sometimes the booths are used as punishment (e.g., a time-out place). Others are employed to reward good behavior. An analysis of these kinds of uses has been provided by Ross (1982).

Other physical arrangements can provide some of the behavioral opportunities that one can infer are sought with privacy booths. Students do often seek seclusion—but not a perceptual cutoff. They might enjoy an out-of-way space but with one or two companions. Students might find security in a place that marks a territory as their own, even if only temporarily. Students doubtless appreciate an environment that provides a variety of places to experience. For such motivations, internal physical differentiations are appropriate, but these can be less enclosing and less restricted to one individual than privacy booths.

18.1.3. Within-School Differentiated Areas

A number of preschool studies have shown that too much open space can have negative effects—that the introduction of internal differentiation can yield better involvement, less distractibility, and aggression (Neill, 1982; Sheehan & Day, 1975). Sometimes the effects of partitioning are indirect. Use of partitioning to bound a play area tended to assist teachers' attempts to restrict the toys to a certain area, and the toy concentration led to increased playing together and less disruptive behavior (Junker, 1976). The degree to which an area is physically enclosed is one aspect of the degree of behavior setting definition of day-care settings. Moore (1983) showed that good definition produced more child exploratory behavior. Definition, functioning with other variables, yielded more child initiation of behavior.

In a kindergarten study, Morrow and Weinstein (1982) developed partially secluded "library" areas (appropriately furnished) to increase the free time that pupils spent in reading. These investigators noted that, if students had come to these areas intending to use the special features, such as felt board stories or story cassettes, and if they found these in use, the students remained in the area looking at books. The small semienclosures "held" them.

In spaces already partitioned, the removal of dividers can become an educational strategy. In a room used by a nursery school and then by kindergarten pupils, Kinsman and Berk (1979) removed the partition between the housekeeping and the block areas. Rather complicated effects were created by this move that was designed to increase cross-sex play. First, the older children reacted by reestablishing the physical division using large toy trucks, an ironing board, a bed, and other props. The nursery-school children let the areas stay open to one another, and this group increased mixed-sex play more than the older one. Finally, play judged irrelevant to the area increased for boys but decreased for girls.

The use of variable height partitions to define and protect activity areas in secondary schools has been described by Evans and Lovell (1979). The target school originally provided an extensive central community area that partially bordered minimally enclosed academic spaces. Manipulation included greater protection for the academic areas and more enclosure definition for central work areas. As a result, interruptions to classroom activity were less frequent. Of special interest was the finding that classroom verbalizations changed to a higher proportion of content questions (questions on substantive issues) rather than process questions (queries dealing with assignment, due dates, etc.). The investigators suggested that increased partitioning directed traffic flow away from the classes, screened out extraneous stimulation, and more emphatically defined academic from nonacademic areas.

At the university level, Holahan (1977) protected one quadrant of a large sitting area of a dormitory cafeteria. Holahan employed partitions with 4-ft-high lower bases and partially open 2-ft upper sections.

Students using the sheltered section reported more satisfaction with dining, and they also engaged in social groupings more frequently than students in the unsheltered quadrants.

Partitioning, thereby defining and sheltering areas in space that are otherwise open, can yield beneficial effects. There are real forces against pressing the partitioning too far. The advantages of keeping space uncommitted and flexible were supports to the open-space movement. Second, teachers in traditional situations seek visual access to all areas where there is student activity. The enclosed rooms in the English open-space schools went mostly unused because of their interference with teacher monitoring (Bennett et al., 1980). Other studies have dealt with the teacher surveillance needs (Neill & Denham, 1982; Twardosz, Cataldo, & Risley, 1974).

Fortunately, some of the effects of partitions or walls can be achieved without permanent and high, vision-blocking screening. Space can be defined and traffic flow diverted by quite low partitions. To provide defined and special places to behave without usual partitions, Leggett, Brubaker, Cohodes, and Shapiro (1977) suggest the use of boxes of various heights that can be pushed together for platforms. Other places can be defined by furniture arrangements that suggest enclosure and shelter but do not prevent the responsible adult from surveying the action.

18.1.4. Spatial Patterns and Paths

The issue of partitioning in preschool environments is related to the larger question of what areas should be separated from others and which should have easy physical access to one another. Nash (1979, 1981) maintains that the young child's distractibility can be employed to yield generalizing behavior. In working out this principle, partitions are used to draw together areas that are complementary. Thus, the construction and the painting areas might be grouped together to encourage the child to make connections, to be "creative." Nash presents data demonstrating that strategic spatial grouping of activities can yield more varied language use, more joinings from different areas, and more expressed confidence in one's capacity to make things.

Some of the most substantial discussions of spatial arrangement at this preschool level come from Kritchevsky, Prescott, and Walling (1977) and from Loughlin and Suina (1982) who make the following points: (1) Space makes invitations to children. Arrival in an extended open space encourages move-

ment, perhaps rough-and-tumble play; and (2) More integrated experiences are likely for children when a fit obtains between these spatial invitations and teachers' expectations for child activity.

The way space is structured determines paths, those "visible broad empty spaces that seem to be going somewhere" (Loughlin & Suina, 1982, p. 63). Paths, in turn, determine child movement or traffic patterns. These patterns influence which areas and facilities will be seen first or most frequently, which will be experienced last, or not at all. The "popularity" of an activity area can be influenced by its relation to paths.

As small children move along their paths and survey the physical environment, their eye level presents them a different visual structuring than the one appearing to adults. From the adults' eye level, the kneehole of a desk is not particularly prominent or important. For a small child, a similar distance away, the same space looms more directly, more seductively. Given the child's size, the space can become a sheltering niche, perhaps a hideaway (Loughlin & Suina, 1982).

Child movement along paths can endanger the security of activity areas. In cases where the borders of activity areas become traffic lanes, the path actions and those of the activity area can interact causing interference, jostlings, and irritations. Similar difficulties arise when activity areas are too close together. A study by Rogers (1976) compared children when they experienced a nursery school setting with planned spatial organization and when they dealt with a setting presenting blocked paths and tight fits between areas. Behavior in the more adequately organized space was more productive, both on the verbal and the activity levels. A method for observing and scoring the adequacy of spatial organization in day-care and preschool environments has been presented by Prescott, Kritchevsky, and Jones (1972).

Issues of spatial organization within classrooms are rarely researched for elementary and high schools. There have been calls for more provision of small-group space (Castaldi, 1977) or for "work turfs" (Leggett et al., 1977). But little research-based material is available. However, another aspect of spatial arrangement, seating patterns, has been investigated.

18.1.5. Classroom Seating

In her article discussing seating arrangements, Weinstein (1985) notes that the traditional classroom with its rows and columns of seats facing a teacher at the front has been a persistent feature of our educational environments for many years. It appears in first grade and in college learning situations, in country and city schools, and even in modern as well as old-fashioned schools. One set of questions for research, then, is the relationship of students' occupancies of various positions within the row-and-column pattern to other variables.

That something about individuals' motivations or psychological situations can be inferred from their positions in space is indicated by the common use of spatial descriptions to describe behavioral conditions. For a female who shrinks to the room's perimeter at a party, we have the appellation "wallflower." For a man whose ideas or behavior seem farfetched, we may say that "he's out in left field." For one who is active and involved, we say "he's right in the center of things." For those who are open about their proposals, we note that "everything is up front." Readers can doubtless supply other examples of spatial imagery that are descriptive of social and psychological situations.

As reported by Weinstein, a correlation between persons' attitudes and their chosen places in classroom space was noted by Waller (1965) over 50 years ago. The front row contained the overdependent, the academically zealous; rebel types, showing their disaffiliation, chose rear seats.

Relations between Selected Seat Positions and Student Attitudes, Participation, and Grades

When students are permitted to select their own classroom positions, the evidence is substantial that position and attitudes are much related. Walberg (1969) found that high school students, if they like school, feel they have the ability to succeed in school and say that they work hard. They also say that they prefer to sit in the front of the room. Millard and Simpson (1980) found that students sitting nearer the teacher found more enjoyment in the classroom than those seated at a distance.

The proposition that teacher–pupil interaction is strongly related to student position in the row-and-column pattern has research support. In their videotape study of teacher and pupil behavior in elementary high school, Adams and Biddle (1970) found that an "action center" in the front and center of the seating area yielded up to six times as much teacher–pupil interaction as the more rear and peripheral areas. Other studies have substantiated the Adams and Biddle finding, although the exact location of the

action center and its degree of advantage for participation have sometimes varied.

One result of the greater participation in a front and center position might be better learning, better grades. Three studies of college classrooms did indeed find better grades for the students seated toward the front of the classes (Becker, Sommer, Bee, & Oxley, 1973; Levine, O'Neal, & McDonald, 1980; Stires, 1980). Failures to find a grade effect in college seating have occurred (see Wulf, 1977).

Choice of a seat position has been related to student personality variables. Thus Totusek and Staton-Spicer (1982) described occupants of the front action zone in an undergraduate course in communication as more creative, more imagination centered, more absorbed in ideas, and more likely to report an unconventional approach to life. Persons may take seats in college classrooms reflective of their marginal or central position in the larger society. Haber (1982) found that blacks or Hispanics in predominately white colleges chose peripheral positions — the blacks coming early to class, apparently to secure these marginal seats.

Because the attitudes of students choosing various positions in the row-and-column seating pattern differ, it can be argued that these positions — in themselves — are not coercive of behavior but merely collect their own special kinds of pupil psychologies. The behavioral differences in the positions are due, then, to "personality differences." Certainly, there is support for this self-selection hypothesis. Even teachers will judge students as more or less motivated depending upon whether they are informed that the students in question chose central or peripheral seating (Daly & Suite, 1982).

If the position effect is carried by the person variables of those individuals occupying the positions, the importance of the position variable is not thereby eliminated. The choice of seating is based on perceptions of what occupant experiences and actions are most likely or feasible in the position. One may assume that the seat position does have qualities, independent qualities, that attract persons with particular motives.

Relations between Assigned Seat Position and Student Attitudes, Participation, and Grades

When seats are assigned, the operation of variables associated with differences in personality cannot account for behavioral and outcome differences associated with the seat position. If certain results are obtained with assigned seating, one could infer experience in the position—apart from personality variables—had important effects.

Although negative evidence exists (Wulf, 1977), it seems likely that student participation in the classroom can be affected by assignment to center versus rear or peripheral seats (Koneya, 1976; Levine et al., 1980). The research of Koneya is instructive because it tests the interaction of person variables and environmental ones in relation to participation. Students were classified as highly, moderately, or lowly verbal prior to assignment to the action zone of the classroom. Such assignment was followed by increases in participation for the highly and moderately verbal students but not for students with low verbal tendency.

Satisfaction with class activity seems higher if one is seated near the front of the room, whether that seat is chosen or assigned (Millard & Simpson, 1980; Weinstein, in press). Whether the increased participation and satisfaction accompanying assignment to more favorable seats leads to better class grades has not been clearly established.

Over 60 years ago, Griffith (1921) provided a well-reasoned account of grade variations related to seating location in large lecture halls. Some 20,000 grades were examined in connection with students assigned a seat number. Although Griffith found that students in rear rows averaged relatively poorer grades, those in the front were not the most successful. Rather, students in the third and fourth rows achieved the highest grades.

The fact that students at the very front as well as those at the back of the lecture audience tested more poorly suggested that "fringe areas," areas separated from the core of the student grouping, were less promising locations. Thus students sitting in the side or rear areas that were separated by aisles from the main group were found to receive lower grades than those in the main body. Griffith employed a "social integration" hypothesis to explain his data. Knowles (1982), who brought the early Griffith work to the attention of contemporary classroom researchers, points out that today the concept of social facilitation might explain Griffith's data. One modern investigator (Stires, 1980) has also found that test scores were higher for those assigned to center seats. However, several others (Millard & Simpson, 1980; Wulf, 1977) found no relationship between assigned seat position and grades.

Relations between Various Seating Arrangements and Student Response

Two physical variables converge when one assesses the quality of a particular seat within a seating ar-

rangement: distance of the seat from significant targets of perception or interaction and orientation of seat with regard to these targets. In large lecture halls and auditoriums, the rear seats put students at sufficient distance that extra concentration is required to track the auditory and visual stimuli at the front (Koneya, 1976). In ordinary-sized classrooms, the distance variable probably cannot operate as coercively. However, orientation can become important. With chairs or chair desks all facing front in the traditional classroom, students and teacher are persistently oriented toward one another. Reciprocally, students, although reasonably close to one another, are not oriented toward one another; instead, they see each other's backs or sides.

Social interaction is encouraged when individuals are able to establish face-to-face contact with its ease of both verbal and nonverbal communication (Steinizor, 1950). Students placed around tables can establish face-to-face contact more easily than those placed in row-and-column positions. Students around tables are not always oriented toward teachers and toward the eye-contact control that teachers employ. These conditions are likely to lead to increased sociality among students around tables and decreased on-task behavior—if the tasks require individual, rather than cooperative, effort.

Several researchers support the preceding analysis. Axelrod, Hall, and Tams (1979) found that the row-and-column seating—as opposed to seating around tables—yielded more on-task and less "talking out" behavior in second and seventh grades, respectively. Similar results were obtained by Wheldall, Morris, Vaughan, and Ng (1981) who placed the 10- and 11-year-old children around tables, then in rows, and finally back at tables. However, this study, like the one by Koneya (1976), shows the interaction of person variables with environmental ones to yield changes in target behavior. Individuals with high task involvement, as measured on the first phase of the experiment, did not change their on-task behavior when in rows. However, students with average or low initial on-task scores increased attentive behavior when placed in rows and reduced it when put again around the tables.

If one wishes to use seating variables to understand or to change classroom events, the following ideas seem reasonable. Students may be saying something about their own needs by the seats they choose. Their behavior in those seats reflects their needs *and* the qualities of that particular position. Assigning different positions to students in a row-and-column arrangement can change the participation and the satisfaction of the changed students. Such alterations may even influence course grades, but this is not assured.

Seating arrangements are a major way the class rooms provide basic spatial structure. It would seem reasonable that this structure should be shaped to match ongoing program qualities. Further, one might speculate that occasional changes in seating patterns over time are useful in themselves. The resulting novelty can temporarily alert participants in a situation that, otherwise, can be repetitive and unexciting.

18.1.6. School Objects

Preceding discussion centered, first, on milieu regions (enclosures and differentiated interior areas) then on milieu positions (seating). This last focus now involves objects or manipulanda. A behavior-enclosing to behavior-enclosed dimension underlies these three categories: (1) Enclosures and regions contain persons and behavior *within* their milieu aspect; (2) Positions provide persons and behavior with a locus; a place to be *at* or *on*; and (3) Manipulanda provide materials for behavior to enclose, to work *with* rather than *within* or *from*. Kind, number, and accessibility of objects interact with enclosure and positions to make certain of the latter more or less frequented by children.

Systematic research, even systematic thinking, regarding the place of objects in school behavior has not been developed. The data that are available demonstrate the importance of this aspect of physical milieu and some of the possibilities in planful manipulation and object provision.

Objects are important on the basis of sheer frequency with which they enter the behavior streams of children. Barker and Wright (1955) analyzed the object transactions for an entire day of a second-grade boy and for a third-grade girl. These children made 1184 and 975 transactions with nonsocial behavior objects. Substantial numbers of these enactments were with things classified as "school objects": the boy, 238 transactions with 116 different objects; the girl, 203 transactions with 103 discrete objects.

That young children truly care about the objects in their behavior streams is indicated by Dawe's study of 200 children's quarrels (1934). Most of these conflicts involved possession or control of things.

The importance of useful educational objects was underlined in a metaanalysis of open education by Gianconia and Hedges (1982). These investigators identified factors associated with "effective open education" (defined as yielding improved self-concept, increased creativity, and more liking for school). Open space was *not* associated with effective open education; scope of instructional objects and materials was so associated.

Objects and Their Utilitarian Function

The fit of objects to children's activity can be understood better with a distinction Prescott (1981) implies between the utilitarian and the evocative use of objects. The utilitarian function is likely when the goal and the means of activity have been decided. Then specific objects are required to carry out the predetermined direction of behavior. In contrast, the evocative function is most likely when persons without predetermined goals and means are open to behavior directions suggested by the intrinsic or culturally developed qualities of the objects they encounter.

The requirement of objects when their utilitarian function is foremost would seem so clear that research in the area would be unnecessary. However, Kounin and Sherman (1979) did find that objects that failed in their utilitarian function (e.g., scissors that would not cut in a cut-and-paste activity) were associated with reduced on-task behavior in nursery school construction activity. Currently, we are simply uninformed about how frequently or how seriously deficiencies in objects interfere with educational activities.

Objects and Their Evocative Function

The capacity of objects to suggest directions of behavior has been labeled "prop seduction" by Redl (personal communication, 1953) who noted that banging is suggested by hammers, throwing by balls, and sword play by long, slender sticks. The evocative function of objects operates most strongly in situations where people are open to the invitations they encounter. For example, a child in preschool free play who is simply looking for something to do would be receptive to objects' evocative influence.

Two main categories of studies can be examined: researches dealing with the degree of availability of a general class of objects (e.g., small manipulanda) and studies focusing on the power of specific kinds of objects to yield specific behavioral directions.

With more toys of various types available to preschool boys, there occurred more activity with the toys and less involvement with teacher-presented core activity (Vlietstra, 1980). The amount of toys was manipulated by Smith and Connolly (1980). A large playroom with some large fixed playthings (e.g., climbing frame) and usual table and chairs was provided with a number of small toys on some occasions and not on others. The lack of toys changed the children's behavior markedly but not necessarily in a negative direction. Without the small manipulanda, children became more physically active, more socially interactive, and made more creative use of furniture (e.g., they created a "chair train").

The addition of toys can certainly increase the amount of play opportunity. Kritchevsky and colleagues (1977) have developed a scale for measurement of the number of play units in a nursery-school environment. For example, a sandbox is one play unit, but the addition of digging tools can increase the units to four. Children's affective and social experience is reported to be more positive when sufficient play units are provided for given numbers of preschoolers (Getz & Brendt, 1982; Prescott, 1981).

The association of specific object types to certain child behaviors has been established in a number of nonexperimental studies. Hendrickson and colleagues (1981) showed that isolate behavior was predominant with puzzles, parquetry, pegboard, legos, tinker toys, and toy animals. Sharing behavior was associated with balls, puppet stages, dress-up materials, blocks, and housekeeping materials. Analogous findings were reported by Shure (1963) and Rosenthal (1973). In an experimental study by Quillitch and Risley (1973), "social toys" (e.g., games) yielded more social interaction than presentation of "isolate toys" (e.g., play-doh, tinker toys, etc.).

Although they do not usually present supportive data, several writers have outlined and illustrated stimulating ideas about what objects should appear in certain educational situations and why. Taylor and Vlastos (1975) suggest use of fixed mirrors to help children discover the relation of points of reflection to changing positions of the sun, the use of tethered mirrors for self-awareness play, and ever-present manipulable gadgets that represent the six basic machines (e.g., level, wheel and axle, pulley, etc.). These authors call for employment of objects in learning centers that are versatile, self-explanatory, capable of corrective feedback or are multisensory, open-ended, and yield novel responses to human action. Description of interesting and instructive objects and educational strategies for their employment has been well-expressed by Nash (1979), Nicholsen (1971), and Volkmor, Langstaff, and Higgins (1974).

Finally, it should be noted that the effectiveness of objects in attracting use and in changing behavior depends not only on their qualities but on their physical context. Weinstein (1977) reported a rare research with physical objects above the preschool level. In a second/third-grade classroom, the use of the game and the science areas was increased by the introduc-

tion of shelving to display objects better and the provision of more surface area for use of the materials.

Storage Issues

Part of the Weinstein success relates to issues of storage. The shelving not only provided display space, it made it easy to remove the clutter of things on the limited surfaces in the center areas. Problems of storage in schools are widely experienced. The more individualized the instructional program, the more the storage problems accelerate. Special activities are likely to require much setup time because materials often are not readily available. The author once timed the setup and the activity periods for a typical second-grade painting lesson. To arrange for oilcloth desk covers, water, paints, brushes, and paper, and the like required 19 minutes; average pupil time spent painting, once everything was set up, was 18 minutes.

Unfortunately, few studies are available to help in decisions about storage. Prescott (1981) reports that whether or not day-care storage was open (available to children) was related to centers' programs offering more or less child choice of activity. Programs that were laissez-faire manifested disorganized storage. Montes and Risley (1975) found that shelf storage as opposed to storage in large toy boxes meant that children spent less time selecting toys and more time actually playing. They did not find that the quality of the play was differentially affected by the storage arrangements.

Enthusiasts for open programs were aware that enrichment and individualization of learning would mean a quantum leap in the number and variety of classroom materials. This leads to problems of storage and retrieval, problems that have been addressed by Leggett et al. (1977). These authors, for example, look forward to unmanned computer-controlled vehicles to provide and remove needed articles.

One issue in storage and retrieval is the autonomy of pupil participants. If students can manage the care of objects themselves, the load on school staff is reduced. Where storage is not available in desks, perhaps tote bags, briefcases, and even fishing tackle boxes (Taylor & Vlastos, 1975) can accommodate pupils' tools and materials. Storage autonomy is furthered by labeling containers to make clear (by drawing or by a "sample") what goes where.

Another problem is finding unused space for storing materials. Hanging shelves (Leggett et al., 1977) and drawers or shelves in space beneath work surfaces are two examples of utilizing often uncommitted space. Vertical space is utilized in a "ferris wheel" display and storage device described by the

Educational Facilities Laboratories (1972). Space is conserved when containers shaped for stacking are employed; thus, labeled shoe boxes can be arranged to store materials for many instructional units. Free-standing, double-sided shelving, or peg boards also conserve linear space (UNESCO, 1979).

The basic "action space" of classrooms can be preserved by using storage elements "that go away" (Educational Facilities Laboratories, 1972). Carts, cupboards on wheels, and portable tool cases (see UNESCO, 1979, Vol. 2, p. 80) are examples of compact storage compartments that can be put elsewhere when not needed. Other useful storage ideas and implementations are available in the references cited.

18.1.7. Why Be Concerned with Qualities of Milieu?

Without certain milieu provisions, particular educational programs cannot operate. If students are to discuss a social issue, a reasonably quiet space for all participants is required. If pupils are to write stories about pioneers, then pencils, papers, writing surfaces, and reference books are necessary. But the very obvious nature of such dependence of program on milieu hardly requires research or even much reflection. What are problems of milieu provision beyond the manifest necessity for minimally appropriate places or objects?

Time and Energy Conservation
The human capacity to "make do" with minimal milieu provisions often means that optimum milieu arrangements are not developed. Human behavior, not milieu elements, can become more intense, can speed up, can apply selective attention to block distractions, can use alternative means, and so on. Children can discuss an issue when seated in an auditorium but should they? Teachers can handle all storage problems by walking back and forth to cabinets at the back of the room, but is that the best use of their time and energy? Teachers or students may function adequately in minimally adequate milieu conditions, but these conditions may need to be inspected, and perhaps changed, to reduce time and energy demands.

Milieu Contribution to Program "Authority"
The qualities of milieu can "state" appropriate behaviors vigorously or vaguely. Where running behavior can and cannot go can be indicated by an imaginary line between two marking trees or by a bright white line laid down between the trees. The placement of chairs in an inward-facing circle, instead of in row-and-column positions, "states" that discussion is to involve attention to one another's persons as well as to their verbal statements. Provision of a reading niche instead of books at student's desks "states" that reading is a valued activity and that it might be attractive or pleasurable. Optimum provisions of place and things can suggest program behaviors and program benefits.

School Sameness
The day-by-day repetition of milieu conditions in schools is well known. The possibility exists that milieu change, for its own sake, can be a stimulating experience. For example, new seating arrangements, introduction of privacy booths, and changed learning centers can freshen experience, can energize behavior. The capacity of novelty to alert and to arouse curiosity in children is well-established (Berlyne, 1963). Further, if a new way of doing, a new orientation to certain subject matter is to be developed, the fact that a change is in progress can be stated by pervasive changes in milieu. In Piagetian terms, the milieu changes can counter prevalent tendencies for students to "assimilate"—to assume that what is about to happen will be just more of the same.

Discussion of the advantages of better fit of milieu provisions to program operations has been provided by Weinstein (1981).

18.2. ISSUES OF SIZE AND DENSITY

How large should a school be? How many children should be assembled in the school's classrooms? Before reviewing ideas and evidence applicable to such questions, the basic phenomena should be clarified.

18.2.1. Basic Realities

Environmental Extent
How large is the environmental unit referred to in the analysis? Various size dimensions have been employed. The most simple and straightforward is amount of *space*. We might use square feet for a classroom or a building; square miles are used for geographical areas.

A second set of dimensions, within environmental extent, refers to *resources*, to behavioral supports and opportunities. Within the general idea of extent of resources as a measure of environmental extent are micro- or macroreferents: We can refer to the extent of supplies, of behavior objects. We can also refer to the number of play places. Even larger resource units, such as settings may be employed. Here the larger environment is the one with the more behavior settings for activity.

Inhabitant Number

The number of persons who occupy a given environmental unit is a fundamental ecological fact. In some cases, the number is broken down into one group of users, customers, or clients and another group of maintainers, such as staff, managers, or service personnel. Thus, a classroom may show 25 students and 1 teacher; a high school, 2000 students and 150 staff members.

The phenomena referred to by inhabitant number and extent of environment would seem to be clear and distinct. In common usage, however, these phenomena and labels are persistently mixed. Classroom "size" is most often not stated as some aspect of environmental extent but number of users in the group. Class "size" is, for example, 15 pupils, and small—or 35 pupils, and large. The same mixing of environmental extent and inhabitant number occurs in measures of urban size. Which is the larger city, New York or Los Angeles? Common understanding has it that New York is larger since it has 7 million inhabitants and Los Angeles has only 3 million. But the spatial extent of Los Angeles is one-and-one-half times that of New York (U.S. Bureau of the Census, 1983).

The use of inhabitant number may be intended to convey the idea that a city has the facilities (domiciles, stores, service operations, etc.) for the stated number of population. But the use of population as a statement of environmental extent makes it impossible to develop a ratio between population and environmental extent and thereby express density.

Density—A Relation between Environmental Extent and Inhabitant Number

In urban measurement, we can take population and relate it to space; then we have an unambiguous statement of density: The density of New York is 23,500 people per square mile, that of Los Angeles, 6,400. In the material to follow, *density* will be taken to mean the relation of inhabitant number to some measure of environmental extent.

In the literature, studies that use inhabitant number and environmental extent as measures of density—but not as a ratio— do exist. High-rise dormitories with more student residents are said to have more density than low-rise dormitories with fewer residents (Nadler, Bar-Tal, & Drukman, 1982). A variant of the problem exists when the major independent variable is inhabitant number and the possible operation of density is not considered. Increase in size of group in day care is said to lead to certain staff and child reactions—but whether the increasing inhabitant number also meant an increasing density is not considered (ABT Associates, 1978).

The discussion to follow will deal with issues of size and density as these have been studied at four levels: preschool, elementary school, high school, and college. As will become clear, not all aspects of the variable set of environmental extent, inhabitant number, and density are dealt with at each level.

18.2.2. Size and Density in Preschool Environments

How many small children should be grouped together in the indoor and outdoor spaces of preschool environments? The question is important because there are both service and profit advantages in enrolling more, rather than less, youngsters in a particular day-care or nursery-school facility. After enough children are accepted to cover basic expenses, the addition of more children costs relatively little. This basic economic reality provides continual pressure to increase enrollments well beyond the "break-even point." Even when the preschool environment is not managed for profit, additional numbers of children mean more children served for the dollar cost.

State authorities were aware of the possible crowding problem long before any definitive data about its effects were available. In 1971, Chapman and Lazar reported on the various spatial requirements laid down by states for day-care centers. For example, the modal amount of square feet per child for indoor environments was set at 35, for outdoor, 75. As one might expect for situations in which no solid data were available, there was considerable variability. One state required 50 ft^2 of indoor space, two others, only 20. Still, all states who supplied data (N = 46) did have requirements, and 33 of these agreed on 35 ft^2 on indoor space per child.

Density Studies

Early research efforts centered on the effects of density on children's social interaction. These investigations seemed to show that increased density was associated with increased negative social behavior (Bates, 1970; Hutt & Vaisey, 1966; Jersild & Markey, 1935). Subsequent researchers, however, did not find a simple positive correlation between density and aggression (McGrew, 1972; Preiser, 1972). The results of experimental studies could differ depending on whether the contrast of densities represented more or less children in the same space (social density) or more or less space for the same number of children (spatial density). Increases in spatial density could lead to less active play but not more aggression (Price, 1971). Increased social density might lead to increased conflict (Loo & Kennelly, 1978).

Whether children become involved in conflict depends on whether they interact socially. One effect of density can be to decrease interaction; then conflict interaction is less likely (Loo, 1972; Loo & Smetana, 1978; McGrew, 1972; Price, 1971).

Helpful reviews of studies dealing with size and density in preschool settings have been provided by Aiello, Thompson, and Baum (1985) and by Prescott (1981). An insightful review and analysis of the problem and considerable research contribution has come from Smith and Connolly (1980). A special value of the Smith and Connolly work is the checking of relationships on a second experimental group. These investigators found that—if play resources per child were maintained—changes of spatial density of 25 to 50 to 75 ft^2 per child did *not* affect child conflict. In the least space conditions, rough-and-tumble play decreased, and use of the climbing frame (similar to a jungle gym) increased. Important changes in social behavior did not arise. In order to determine if more severe restrictions would affect social interaction, Smith and Connolly experimented with a 15-ft^2-per-child arrangement again maintaining resources (i.e., playthings) constant. In the 15-ft^2 condition, physical activity was greatly inhibited, parallel play in large subgroups increased, and more aggressive behavior was observed. These findings, developed in conditions that were not artificial (e.g., children were not strangers to each other or to the setting), deserve considerable attention. Apparently, in a familiar free-play situation, important negative social effects of density may begin when space is less than 25 ft^2 per child.

The Smith and Connolly design also permitted testing effects of reduced play resources with space held constant. This variation tests density as established by the relation of inhabitant number to the resource aspect of environmental extent. Again using children familiar with one another and the setting, these researchers found that reduced play resources (toys and manipulanda) meant that children played in larger groups, were both more sharing of the available equipment, and more aggressive in their interac-

tions. These results were consistent with those of Rohe and Patterson (1974) who found that low density (48 ft^2 per child) and high availability of play resources created less competitive, aggressive, and destructive behavior than high density and low plaything resources.

A related aspect of environmental extent can be amount of play opportunity per child. Sutfin (1982) added jungle gym, guinea pigs and cage, and dramatic play material so that the number of "play spaces" per child rose from 1.5 to 4. Among the results obtained were significant drops in noninvolvement behaviors and in noise and increases in cooperative play and appropriate use of materials. Incidents of conflict did not change, but these were low both in the original and in the changed environment. This study also varied storage arrangements in the effort to make a more optimum environment so that the resulting changes in behavior cannot be certainly ascribed only to the increased play spaces.

Environmental extent can be increased by the addition of more "places to be" by simply adding partitions to a given square footage of space. For example, Rohe and Nuffer (1977) were able to increase cooperative behavior in a given area and with a fixed number of inhabitants by insertion of 4 ft × 4 ft partitions to create five separate activity areas.

Effects of Increase of Inhabitant Number

ABT Associates (1979) studied naturally occurring variations in group size in 67 day-care centers and concluded that both teachers and children are affected by the number of inhabitants variable. In the smaller, as opposed to the larger groups (14 or less v. 15 or more), teachers were more active, social, and less managerial; children were more cooperative, innovative, and involved. Over time, children in the smaller groups scored higher on tests of cognitive development.

The ABT studies indicate that inhabitant number reflected in group size is a powerful variable, probably having more pervasive and decisive effects than number of caretakers per child or training of caretakers. In fact, size effects were observed even when similar child–caretaker ratios were maintained across different-sized groups. It is possible that the increase in group size brings with it decreased resources per child and this, rather than size per se, accounts for the effects. However, there are several cautions against this explanation. First, the fewer resources are less likely to account for differences in staff behavior. Second, ABT Associates suggest that two other correlates of large group size may operate with regard to cognitive gains: Educational activities are less effective because children in large groups are allowed to "tune out," or teachers with large groups are less likely to present educational activities.

Some behavioral effects of group size—when resources per child remain the same—were demonstrated by Smith and Connolly (1980). They found that larger groups yielded less imaginative play and more same-sex play companions. These researchers hypothesized that smaller groups produced more familiarity and ease among participants as was reflected in their willingness to engage in fantasy interaction and in their acceptance of one another, regardless of gender.

The actual size of activity groups in preschool is not only related to staff–child ratios but to how a program is developed when more than one staff person becomes available. One staff member may be responsible for a group of 10 children; when the group is increased to 20, another staff member may be added. Mathematically, a favorable 1:10 ratio has been maintained. However the extra staff person may assume a secondary role of "helping out as needed." The large group size may continue to yield negative effects. Another use may be made of the additional staff person: That person can create a second group from part of the first, a group complete with its own small membership, its own place and behavior objects, and its own possibilities for adult attention. A crucial aspect of staff–child ratios may be not only the numbers but how these numbers are translated into operating group sizes.

Facility Size—Another Aspect of Environmental Extent

Do large day-care centers produce different behaviors and experiences than small ones? The modest amount of reported data available indicate that they do. However, we can infer that the larger facility will not only mean greater environmental extent and increased inhabitant number but possible increases in density. Unfortunately, we do not have studies that systematically isolate these variables to test their separate effects.

In reviewing data from her earlier studies of day-care centers, Prescott (1981) asserts that the variable of facility size affects a range of variables: the program offered, the behavior of teachers, and the behavior and experience of children. The larger facility (one serving over 60 children) maintains more age segregation, offers less choice, is more concerned with rules and order, shows more teacher behavior

that is neutral or distant, and yields more uninvolved, uninterested child behavior. Prescott notes that the large centers had better trained teachers and that crowding was *not* present. This investigator refers to one ABT study (1971) as showing that the larger facilities cost somewhat less per child and offered a variety of resources; however, these centers had difficulty offering quality child care even when they established optimum staff–child ratios.

Prescott reflects that large facilities inevitably mean large numbers of persons to be served. Thus, "decisions must be based on the logistics of getting everyone fed, toileted, and so on" (1981, p. 152).

Several Highlights of Preschool Size and Density Research

Densities as high as 25 ft^2 per child do not seem to create negative behavior, particularly if play resources are maintained. At 15 ft^2, more negative effects can be demonstrated.

Increases in spatial density, however, can create changes in behavior, although these are not necessarily negative.

Provision of fewer play resources can markedly change behavior. If toys and other manipulanda are removed, children may respond with increased interaction—both sharing and conflictful.

Increases in group sizes beyond 15 children, which are likely to develop in day-care centers, are associated with negative effects on teacher interactions with children, on children's social and participatory behaviors, and on cognitive development.

Although several variables beyond size may contribute to this effect, some experimental evidence indicates that group size, per se, can have negative effects.

Finally, data from a few examinations of facility size suggest that the larger facility ($N > 60$) is likely to be concerned more with structure and order and less with providing an open, flexible, child-centered setting.

Size and Density in Relation to the Operating Program

The extent that preschool studies yield consistent findings regarding density probably marks the extent to which similar programs or activity structure operated. The number of persons that can share a space is manifestly related to what the people will do in that space. And one expected effect of density changes will be informal or official changes in activity structures. Elementary-school teachers reported to the author that when their classroom enrollments rose to 30, small groups—which before met in the corner spaces left free of regular seats—had too little space to operate; the teacher responded by establishing total class activities. Material already presented shows how the children themselves change their action structures in dense conditions: with less rough-and-tumble play, less small-group interactive play, and so on (e.g., Smith & Connolly, 1980).

High density with high required physical interaction can lead to reduced task performance: High density with low intrinsic physical interaction may not (Heller, Groff, & Solomon, 1977). Results reported by Loewy (1977) indicated that increased densities in group discussion activities reduce achievement; density did not reduce achievement in lecture formats. Finally, Fagot (1977) failed to find the usual child behavior effects for Dutch 4-year-olds in very dense conditions (1.1 m^2 per child): However, the far-reaching effects of density on the program were obvious if not quantified. Children in the Dutch situation were assigned to areas of the room and did not engage in large motor activities (except outside) and did not have free choice of play activity.

Both the available data and one's intuition about children's preschool environments imply that some of the most important effects of density are not to be found in the analysis of individual child and teacher behaviors but in the kinds of action structures or play forms operating.

18.2.3. Size and Density in the Elementary School

Most density research in the elementary-school period deals with classrooms, but a few studies examine other phenomena.

Playground Density

When the same group of elementary-school boys occupied small versus large playground spaces, they became involved in more fights in the smaller space. However, the conflicts in the small space were of shorter duration than in the large; apparently, other children intervened more frequently in dyadic struggles in the small space (Ginsburg & Pollman, 1975).

Density in Experimental Rooms

Aiello, Nicosia, and Thompson (1979) subjected students in the fourth, eighth, and eleventh grades to conditions of severe density (2.5 ft^2 per child) versus moderate density (7.5 ft^2 per child). Density effects were sharp and pervasive: The crowded children were more physiologically aroused (as shown by skin conductance tests), reported more annoyance, and felt warmer and more uncomfortable. They also engaged in more conflict behavior in a postdensity situation designed to measure cooperation and competition. Density conditions affected boys more negatively than girls. Density affected all age groups similarly.

Loo and Smetana (1978) compared free-play behavior of 10-year-old boys in conditions of 13.6 ft^2 per child versus 52 ft^2. Frequency of positive interaction was not reduced in the higher density condition. Certain avoidance behaviors were more frequent in high density; furthermore, the vigor or activity of play was reduced under high density.

Loo (1978) employed similar conditions to test density effects for 5-year-old boys and girls. At this age level, the higher density did yield more negative social interaction and negative affect; furthermore, children wanted to leave the high-density condition.

The research just cited suggests that density, when marked, can produce negative effects for children ages 5 to 16. However, age and program provisions are important, though they are not yet completely clarified variables. In the Loo comparisons, the youngest children were only 5 years old and did manifest more what might be termed *direct* (as opposed to adaptive) effects of density (aggression, negative affect, need to leave). However, at 10, the boys seemed to employ defenses against the possibility of conflict by more withdrawal and muted play action. The lack of an age effect in the study by Aiello and colleagues (1979) could be related to the fact that the lowest age here was almost as high as the highest age in the Loo and Smetana investigation. However, conditions of the Aiello experiment were severe—children were to sit quietly for 30 min—and were provided little opportunity for overt coping behavior.

Density—or Class Size—of the Classroom

Since 1900, hundreds of classroom studies have focused on the effects of class size on learning and related variables. Almost all of these studies compare the effects of increases in number of pupil inhabitants without comprehensive and complementary increases in the extent of the classroom environment. Therefore, it is appropriate to consider such studies as investigations of classroom density.

In the usual elementary-school situation, a larger number of students in a classroom will increase some densities and not others. Without an increase in space, social density will increase as pupils increase.

Further, the amount of teacher resource available for eliciting, assisting, and evaluating pupils' learning behavior remains relatively unchanged as pupils increase in number. Thus, density with regard to teacher resource also increases. Other aspects of environmental extent may keep pace with additional pupil numbers (number of seats, of textbooks, of supplies, etc.); thus, densities in these areas may remain unaffected.

If research in class size had followed a logical and step-by-step progression, the most direct and immediate effects of ecological variations in class size or density would have been established first, and then the relation of these to outcome measures, such as learning achievement and attitudinal changes, would have followed. The ongoing effects of increases in social density and in density related to teaching resource would have been documented, and then the relationship of such event changes to outcome measures would be pursued. The linkages between density conditions to process variables and then to product variables, such as learning achievement scores, would have been identified.

Research in class size has not been logical, and most of the data available relate to learning or attitudinal outcomes, not to linkages. Accordingly, the outcome data will be summarized first, and then data and reflections on linkages will be considered. Taken one at a time, the multitudinous researches on "class size" yield complicated, even contradictory, results. Past studies by Glass and his associates (1982) have markedly clarified the evidence. These investigators winnowed the existing literature to include only those studies that met minimum criteria for investigative design and control and then performed metaanalyses to determine the thrust of the combined data relating to class size. Although there have been some criticisms of the method (Hedges & Stock, 1983) and some belittling of the findings (Education Research Service, 1980), the findings of Glass and his colleagues are accepted here as representing the best summarization of data available and will be utilized heavily.

With regard to evidence on class size and learning, two conclusions are central. First, smaller class sizes (i.e., lower densities) yield, overall, better scores on learning achievement. The evidence in favor of this assertion is substantial. Further, the better the studies were controlled (e.g., random assignment of pupils to size conditions) and the longer the contrast of conditions was maintained, the stronger the density effect.

The second conclusion is related to, and much moderates the first: When one studies variations between class sizes in the top half of the distribution (sizes 20 and up), size variations seem to make relatively little difference in learning achievement. Inspection of the graph pertaining to pupil numbers and pupil achievement show that reducing class size from 30 to 20 yields an expected gain of about 6 percentile points, whereas a reduction from 20 to 10 yields about 13 points (Glass & Associates, 1982, p. 49). For all data reviewed, reductions in class size begin to make substantial differences in learning achievement somewhere around an enrollment of 15.

The effects of pupil numbers on teacher attitude are more marked and at higher levels. For teachers, class reductions from 30 to 20 yield a 16-percentile improvement in reaction (Glass & Associates, 1982, p. 64).

Student social and emotional effects (attitudes toward teacher, classes, schoolwork, etc.) are also negatively related to numbers in the class. The shape of the number and attitude curve is similar to that for learning achievement. That is, reductions in the lower range (5–20) make much more difference than reductions in the higher range (25–70) (Glass et al., 1982, p. 64).

Two very different questions can arise from the preceding data on the effects of pupil number. On the side of policy, if modest reduction in density in the upper half of the distribution of class sizes makes so little difference, does it pay to attempt size reductions at that level? On the side of understanding the operation of classroom density, why is it that lower density should improve learning and pupil and teacher attitudes? The second issue will be considered first. Reflections here may contribute to answers to the first question.

If one starts with the ecological situation of the classroom with fewer pupils, one finds, on a per-pupil basis, more space available and more teacher resource at hand. The effects of space variation in elementary school have not been well investigated. Data on the involvement of students at the center as opposed to the periphery of student assemblages show disadvantages to those on the peripheries in terms of how much they participate and, in some cases, in how well they learn. With more students in the classroom, peripheries are more extended and more remote. Further, in heavily populated classrooms, the loss of open space to desks can mean less arena available for various small-group activities. Finally, insofar as students simply need some spatial separation from one another, the chronic experience of being too close could lead to negative reactions to the environment and to the learning activity within it.

A major investigation of the *ongoing* effects of substantial density reductions has been reported by Cahen, Filby, McCutcheon, and Kyle (1983). These investigators arranged group-size reductions at midyear for two second grades and traced changes in classroom events as a consequence under reduced pupil numbers. Teachers found that carrying through the daily program involved less behavior management, that matters proceeded more smoothly and quickly and required less energy. Observers reported that teachers used the increased ease of covering academic material to enrich the curriculum or to provide extra activities not integrated with the lessons (instructional games, poetry reading, field trips, etc.). Under reduced group size, there were trends for teachers to attend to waiting students more speedily and to provide more individual attention during seatwork.

With fewer students in the class, significantly less student behavior was involved in downtime, and significantly more student time was invested in academic tasks. An earlier study by Wright, Shapson, Eason, and Fitzgerald (1977) paralleled some of the Cahen findings. This group found that fourth- and fifth-grade children, under conditions of lowered pupil number, experienced more teacher questions directed specifically to them and were more highly involved in class activity.

The preceding investigations illustrate some of the possible intervening events between ecological conditions of small- or large-group size and outcomes of learning achievement and teacher and pupil attitude. However, it is important to note that lowered pupil number did not affect the basic program operations. For example, under reduced class size, teaching formats providing for individual learning activities could have been instituted. (Teachers were encouraged by researchers to make whatever changes they thought appropriate under the reduced size condition.) But program individualization did not occur. The individualization that did occur was more individual contact between student and teacher within the persisting program. The investigators describe this as follows:

> While most of these contacts involved academic work, teachers were also able to take time to just chat with students and find out their feelings and interests. In this way, each teacher acknowledged the individual while still maintaining the group. (Cahen et al., 1983, p. 205)

One implication of the recent studies is that presumably beneficial program innovations are not necessarily produced by group-size reductions. What may be necessary are changes in teachers' vision of what becomes possible when enrollments are reduced and some help in developing measures to enact these visions. (Also, innovations established at midyear may result in less effect than those starting at the beginning of the school term.)

With regard to the feasibility of class-size reduction to around 15, it seems obvious that, for many school districts, such lowered class sizes are not financially possible. The question is whether arrangements to reduce instructional group size within classrooms rather than total class size can be instituted. Such an arrangement would increase the amount of teacher resource per child for the periods during which it was instituted. The investigators of class size (Cahen et al., 1983) emphasize that such arrangements to reduce instructional group size are feasible. They are in operation in various schooling arrangements now. For example, some schools provide for a staggered schedule in which half of the class comes early, perhaps for reading instruction, and this half leaves early so that the remaining half may then have their reading lessons. Other small-group arrangements can be provided by use of aides, parental volunteers, and pupil instructors. The smallest of all groups, the dyad, can be arranged through pupil-to-pupil tutoring. (An example of this arrangement is discussed within the section, Program Units and Participant Action.)

Before leaving the issue of class size, it should be pointed out that findings at this level of schooling are consistent with those established in the preschool and day-care research. Size of instructional group can make a significant difference in children's feelings and those of their teachers. Size can affect the conditions around learning and learning itself.

18.2.4. Size and Density in the High School

The environments of high schools are larger and more varied than those of elementary schools. This larger extent can be expressed by the number of environmental units that make up the school. The unit employed in this discussion is the *behavior setting* that is a bounded, place–time habitat providing individuals with a standing pattern of behavior or a program and an appropriate physical milieu (Barker, 1968). Examples of high-school behavior settings might include Mr. Smith's algebra class, home basketball games, press room operations for the school newspaper, practices of the junior class play, main office, and so forth. In a midwestern city, for 1 year, a single high school maintained 312 behavior settings

(Barker & Gump, 1964); a typical elementary school operated 62 different behavior settings (Kerkman, 1963).

Most of a school's settings can be divided between the curricular and the extracurricular. The curricular settings of high school tend to be more varied than those of elementary school, and they are more likely to be taught by subject matter specialists. In its curricular offerings, the average high school hopes to provide sufficient scope for young people to begin to sort out their academic interests and competencies, their vocational directions.

Perhaps the extracurricular settings of high school provide the greater contrast to elementary school. Such settings are ecologically pervasive. For example, in a survey of 13 high schools in eastern Kansas, 67% of all the settings were, on the average, extracurricular. The average junior student, in a 5-month period, would participate in 20 of these extracurricular settings (Barker & Gump, 1964).

Several investigators have emphasized the social and psychological significance of the high school's extracurricular settings. Coleman (1961) described them as critical to the social system of adolescent peer relationships in high school. Dreeben (1968) has pictured these settings as alternatives to the thorough and probably inhibiting evaluation climate of the classroom. From an ecological point of view, the most fundamental difference between the extracurricular and the curricular settings is the position of the student in each. Most frequently, students in classrooms are similar to clients or customers. Much of the operating effort and most of the action decisions rest with the teacher. In extracurricular settings, most of the operating effort comes from students; for most extracurricular settings students make the majority of the operating decisions. (In athletic and art performances, direction may come from teacher or coaches, but even here, the effort that enables these performances comes from students.) For most extracurricular affairs, teachers are "sponsors," not directors or executives. Students make plans, carry them out, and evaluate their success. Without the student effort and decision making, the extensive extracurricular arrays of high schools could not survive.

High School Size and Undermanning

What will happen to students in their school's extracurricular settings is much affected by the size of the school. The large school presents a different ecological set of conditions than the small one, a difference that is more subtle than simply a matter of more inhabitants and more environment extent. As schools are asked to educate larger numbers of students, they expand both their student bodies and their environmental extent—but not at the same rate. Very small schools in eastern Kansas might have 35 to 50 students and 60 behavior settings; a large school, 2300 students and 500 settings. The number of inhabitants rises much faster than the number of settings. The ratio for the small schools is less than one student per setting; for the large school over four students per setting. Of course, the persons-to-setting ratios are indexes, not direct predictors, of the number of students inhabiting settings. However, the actual numbers are highly correlated to the ratios. The median number of junior class students found in extracurricular settings over a 5-month-period in a small school was 11; for a large school, 36 (Barker & Gump, 1964).

A basic ecological fact about small schools, then is the following: They have relatively few students to carry out the operations of their extracurricular settings. If such settings are to survive, those students that are available will have to work harder, and they will have to take more responsibility than students in the larger high schools. The "undermanning" of the small-school settings will press more effort and more leadership behavior from students than will obtain in the large school (Schoggen, 1984). More thorough explication of undermanning theory can be found in Barker (1968) and refinement and updating of the theory in Wicker (1979). With regard to extracurricular settings, the number of students available per setting—the density—has powerful effects on both behavior and experience in settings. Students in small schools were several times more likely to occupy setting positions of some power and responsibility than were students in large high schools. Students in small high schools were much more likely to report satisfactions in their setting activity that emphasize competence, meeting challenges, and feelings of affiliation with a productive group. In contrast, the large-school students were more likely to emphasize that participation was simply pleasurable or vicarious.

An internal analysis of the school-size study showed that kind of satisfaction was highly determined by the position the respondent held in the extracurricular settings: Satisfactions from being active, from being challenged, were reported by students who occupied some leadership or functionary setting position. This happened in schools regardless of size. However, it is difficult, ecologically, for large schools to offer as many responsibility positions per student as small schools.

Undermanning effects are robust: Wicker (1968) found similar effects in a second major study. Willems (1967) compared academically marginal and nonmarginal students in small and large schools. Small-school students reported considerably more obligations to their school's extracurricular settings than did large-school students. More dramatic were the reactions of the small-schools' academically marginal students compared to large-school marginal students. In the small-school settings, marginal students often had experienced some responsible activity, and they reported just as many feelings of obligation as their small-school nonmarginal peers. In the large school, marginal students had been given little responsible action and reported almost no feelings of obligation to school affairs.

The strong effects of density just described rest on the presence of a substantial arena of extracurricular settings in the high school and on widespread student valuing of this arena. Students' efforts to work harder and take more leadership or functionary action cannot occur unless the settings are both present and prized.

Although such high-school size effects have been replicated (see also Baird, 1969), some studies have reported only insignificant size effects. Most frequently, however, these investigations have compared large schools with still larger ones (Burkhead, 1967; Coleman, 1966). Garbarino (1980), who has provided a useful survey of high school size effects, suggested that a "threshold effect" probably operates such that beyond enrollments of 500, perhaps 700, variations in size make little difference to the variables cited previously. The analysis already explained would make Garbarino's speculation credible. For the small-school effects to operate, there must be undermanning—too few students available per setting optimally to man the settings. For all practical purposes, schools of 1000 have more than sufficient students to sustain their settings just as do schools of 5000.

High School Size and Density Effects Apart from Those of Undermanning

Increasing the number of inhabitants and the number of settings can yield joint effects apart from those associated with how many individuals inhabit an ecological unit. One obvious result of the small-school arrangements is that students interact with many of the same teachers and peers throughout their school experience. Students in large schools go from setting to setting encountering mostly different potential associates in each setting. Put in other terms, *potential*

associate continuity decreases as the number of settings and inhabitants increase.

As students engage in a variety of settings with the same associates, personal development may be enhanced. Bronfenbrenner (1979) refers to the probable advantage of young people's experiencing "cross-sectional dyadic relationships." Of course, associate continuity is pertinent to the issue of security and close feelings. If the aim is to encourage social experience with an increased range of persons, then the large-school variety of associates might be favored. However, it would be important to obtain some depth of interaction with the shifting associates; mere juxtaposition of many persons may not result in truly widened social experience.

To preserve some of the small-school advantages for a large-school organization, the schools-within-a-school plan (sometimes called the *campus plan*) has been instituted (Plath, 1965). In this arrangement, subsets of teachers and students inhabit small buildings and have most of their curricular experiences within this smaller environment. As students go from class to class, they cross one another's paths more frequently than they would in one large-school building. Over the high-school years, a student might experience the same teacher for several classes.

Although the campus school fosters associate continuity and the building of closer peer and teacher relationships, it is important to realize that the arrangement may not duplicate the undermanning conditions of small schools. Here the issue becomes the following: What happens to extracurricular settings in the schools-within-a-school arrangement? If, in order to have "the best," the encompassing school provides one set of football and basketball settings, one group of music and drama performances, one school newspaper, and one student government, and so on, then undermanning will not be obtained. The special press on students to work harder and to engage in more responsible actions in order to sustain their undermanned settings will not operate.

Garbarino (1980) notes that when large numbers occupy an environmental unit, individuals easily become anonymous and, thereby, are released from the informal and interpersonal controls that operate in smaller groups. Deviance can be one result. Plath (1965) reported that the division of a large high school into several smaller ones substantially reduced serious student deviancy. McPartland and McDill (1977) found that larger schools reported more student crime than smaller ones. One reason given was that students in the smaller schools were more visible and subject to greater control.

Garbarino also reported material related to size in relation to school structure and operation. It is a truism that as facilities increase in size (population and environmental extent) they must also change their shape. The larger facility (and school) depends more on formal and impersonal controls. It centralizes operations and places bureaucratic structure ahead of direct responsiveness to inhabitants. Not only are the larger schools likely to lag in their accessibility to students (McPartland & McDill, 1977), they are likely to find school change and innovation difficult (Ford Foundation, 1972).

A final set of effects of school size relates to the context around the school's site. Gold (1975), a facilities planner for the New York City schools, observed that proposals to build large high schools in existing urban neighborhoods now meet with strenuous community opposition. In New York, "the concerns run the gamut from noise to trampled lawns to pilferage in stores, to mugging" (p. 315). Gold adds that construction of large schools in existing neighborhoods will often require large-scale demolition and construction. Not only does this threaten neighborhood stability, it can represent wasted energy investment if it can be shown that renovation of existing buildings for smaller schools is feasible. Gold provides both rationale and options for the establishment of much smaller high schools in highly urbanized areas.

Large high schools impinge on rural areas in a different fashion. Almost inevitably, a proposed larger rural school will be a consolidated one. This requires that one or more small communities lose their existing small high school. Towns stubbornly resist consolidation, then, because the high school is perceived as a crucial feature of the community's identity. Further, the presence of high-school youth in the town enriches many of its settings, some in a direct economical way. (Adolescents are important customers of drug stores, cafes, drive-ins, etc.) The persistent, often acrimonious, effort of some towns to retain their high schools has been impressively detailed by Peshkin (1982).

Reflections on Proposed Solutions to Problems of High-School Size

The description of size effects on the context or the "extrafacility effects," when coupled with the "intrafacility effects" described previously, reminds us that the size issue cuts in varied directions. This fact must be remembered when size solutions are proposed. As size research has become more sophisticated, it has been rightly explained that certain os-

tensible size effects are carried by intermediate conditions. For example, it was shown that small high schools press a much greater proportion of their students into functionary and leadership positions than do large ones. Once in these central positions, the students act and experience the extracurricular arena in terms of hard work, important actions, feelings of responsibility, and obligation. However, if large-school students occupy positions of setting leadership, they, too, have experiences much like their leader counterparts in small schools. Logically, then, a small-school effect could be produced by creating more positions of important function in the large-school settings. However, two considerations limit such a solution. First, the effects of large size go well beyond those produced by undermanning, as the preceding discussion shows. Issues of inaccessibility of administration, of lagging capacity to change, of problems with community context, are not solved by this one manipulation.

A second consideration deals with feasibility of a proposed change. In naturally occurring situations (as opposed to experimental ones), given conditions are supported and constrained by other conditions. The system may very well resist the single change or may not respond in the "logical" fashion. In the case of increasing responsible positions in the school's extracurricular arena, this could only be done in any substantial way by increasing the number of settings. The undermanning effect would operate as students felt press or invitation to sustain these settings. But a large high school already may have all of the settings that students feel should be preserved. The undermanning effect only operates as students strive to maintain desired settings; undesired settings may be left to wither.

The large high school must often be accepted. Some countering of size effects—without seeking smaller schools—is doubtless necessary and should be encouraged. However, consideration of the problem should include respect for the possible embeddedness of intermediate size effects and for the variety of size effects that may exist.

18.3. THE ACTIVITY PROGRAMS OF SCHOOL ENVIRONMENTS

Aspects of physical milieu provide loci and instrumentalities for school environments; aspects of the program offer activity patterns. The program specifies the kinds of sequences of actions in such environ-

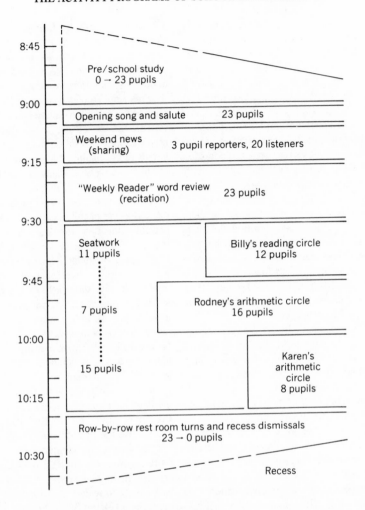

Figure 18.1. A map of Mrs. Carr's classroom segments for one-quarter of a day. Vertical distances show durations; horizontal distances indicate population size. *Source:* Adapted from "School Settings and Their Keeping," by Paul V. Gump, in *Helping Teachers Manage Classrooms* (p. 100), ed. D.L. Duke, 1982, Alexandria, VA: Association for Supervision and Curriculum Development. Reprinted with the permission of the Association for Supervision and Curriculum Development. Copyright © 1982 by the Association for Supervision and Curriculum Development. All rights reserved.

mental units as lessons, opening and closing routines and housekeeping activities, athletic, dramatic, and musical presentations, rituals, celebrations, assemblies, and so on.

18.3.1. Nature of Program Units

The flow of program events over time and across space can be divided into units or segments (Gump, 1967). These units, with their own action patterns,

personnel, space, and facilities, provide the building blocks for operating educational environments. A pattern of such units is provided in Figure 18.1. Represented is about one-quarter of a third-grade classroom day.

From the figure, it can be seen that events for Mrs. Carr's third grade began at about 8:45 a.m. with a preclass "study period" during which students could either study or visit quietly. At the 9:00 a.m. buzzer, the official day began with a segment devoted to a flag salute and group singing. Because this was Monday, Mrs. Carr encouraged sharing of weekend news. Then, after reviewing the vocabulary that would be important in the Weekly Reader, the class (at 9:30) divided into parallel segments for either seat work or a reading circle. Over time, three separate circle segments operated. Last, a structured dismissal routine sent students out to morning recess.

To provide a framework for presentation of program ideas and findings, it will be useful to consider a few segments of Figure 18.1 as these relate to two areas: the kind of action participants take and the action relationships among participants. The content of action for students in seatwork is sedentary and clerical. The actions in the circle activities are also sedentary, but they include verbal input from students and teachers. The action relationships of participants in seatwork is "private"—pupils are not to interact. On the other hand, pupil interdependecy of activity marks the recitation and discussion aspects of the reading and arithmetic circles.

Action structures as used here are socially shared phenomena. They are like task structures but more general in that they are established extraindividual patterns for all kinds of human activities (e.g., worship, recreation, travel, work, etc.).

Action structures depend, for their enactment, on participants' previous common learnings *and* on established signals in the ongoing situation. Once learned and in operation, the requirements of action structures "take over" the content, sequencing, and integration of participants' behavior.

One further aspect of classroom environments is pictured by Figure 18.1—the temporal relationships of the segments of the operating environments. Segments sometimes exist simultaneously, which means that teachers face potentially overlapping situations; for example, the teachers must lead the activity in "Billy's Reading Circle" but monitor and, if necessary, control behavior in "seatwork." Further, children and teachers over time go from one segment to another; these transitions become important aspects of the program environment. Both parallel segment operation and transitions will be discussed later.

18.3.2. Program Units and Participant Action

Some researchers probing the relationships between classroom activities and pupil behavior simply named the activity form. For example, Kowatrakul (1959) found that "illegal behaviors" were more frequent in discussion than in other classroom activities. Later

school researches by Ebmeier and Ziomek (1982), Pintrich and Blumenfeld (1982) and Silverstein (1979) found that such activities as seatwork, boardwork, recitation, and the like were associated with variations in student involvement.

Preschool studies that described activities by simply naming them have been carried out by Rosenthal (1973), Shure (1963), and Warner (1984). The studies often agreed on some activity and pupil behavior relationships. Block play in preschool tended to be relatively socially assertive; seatwork in elementary school yielded relatively less on-task behavior than teacher-led small-group instruction. However, the use of only labels to describe activities is basically unsatisfactory because it does not identify the basic dimensions or genotypic qualities that might account for activity-to-behavior correlations. For example, seatwork activity may be supervised only minimally (the teacher works elsewhere with a small group in reading), and this might account for lower seatwork task involvement. However, a basic dimension of seatwork is its dependence on self-pacing rather than on continuous active external input; perhaps this could account for seatwork's relatively low involvement.

In the search for activity dimensions, teacher-imposed structuredness has been a frequent choice. Preschool study of teacher structure by Huston-Stein, Friedrich-Cofer, and Susman (1977) showed that less structure yielded more prosocial behavior, more aggression, more imaginative play, and increased task persistence. Further structure studies have been provided by Morrison (1979) and Carpenter and Huston-Stein (1980).

Following a review of pertinent literature, Smith and Connolly (1980) undertook an experiment with matched 3- and 4-year-old children using identical materials and identical staff members. Under the "high structure" condition teachers were to involve themselves in children's activity, to talk about play and develop it constructively. Under "low structure" conditions teachers were to be available, answer questions, and protect children but otherwise remain in the background. Low structure resulted in more child–child interaction, more rough-and-tumble play, and more fantasy play. The Smith and Connolly and the Huston-Stein et al. investigations yielded similar results.

The acceptance of the amount of teacher intervention as the operational definition of activity structuredness is a limited approach. Teacher intervention is a common way by which student activity may be highly structured, but the more basic idea is that activity forms—per se—come in various degrees of structuredness. The "visit-or-study" activity in the first segment in Figure 18.1 is low in structure; children's games, however, are very high in structure (in behavioral prescriptiveness)—whether or not the games are led by a teacher.

Development of classroom activity dimensions not defined by their teacher behaviors was accomplished by Gump (1967, 1969) and by Berliner (1983). Details of these systems can be studied by perusal of the references. Only enough will be said here to project the basic ideas of the methods.

First, in each system, the activity determines the action role of the teacher, not the reverse. Second, the kind of input signaling and the kind of child response action are essentials of the activity. Not only do the activity dimensions determine the teacher's action role in the activity and the kind of child action—such dimensions also describe participant-to-participant action relationships. These aspects of activity forms or action structures provide the organization for the research review to follow.

Kind of Participant Activity: Input Aspects

A fundamental dimension of action structures is the extent to which sources in the environment actively and persistently "call for" participant response, as opposed to sources being merely available for perception and for action (Gump, 1982). Active input is high in such classroom activities as lectures, film and audio presentations, recitations and oral tests. On the other hand, seatwork, library sessions, and silent reading periods are examples of passive input action structures. In a third-grade study (Gump, 1967), pupil involvement was significantly higher in the activity segments of active input than in passive input segments (85% vs. 75%). In the study by Kounin, Friesen, and Norton (1966) involving grades 1 through 5, the segments that could be characterized as active input averaged 85% pupil involvement; the passive input segments, 65%.

Because the teacher is often immediately present in active input segments and not in passive input structures, teacher presence might be the more crucial variable. One line of data would deny the possibility: Seatwork with teachers in an ever-present supervisory role yielded lowered pupil involvement just as did seatwork with the teacher functioning elsewhere (Gump, 1967).

Active input is a fundamental and behavior-coercive quality of action structures. However, the active input may, in operation, be clear and continu-

ous, or it may be somewhat faltering or discontinuous. If the latter obtains, the usual higher pupil involvement will not occur. Professionals (teachers and those who construct audiovisual presentations) know how to keep their input clear and forward moving. Child report givers often do not have such skill; as a result, although report giving and listening is an active input segment, child reports in the third grade received the lowest pupil involvement scores of all segment types observed (Gump, 1967).

Preschool research provides an elaboration of these actual input segments with and without good continuity. In short, in small-group "lessons," the active input tends to be continuous when the teacher reads or demonstrates or when a record tells a story. In lessons with much child contribution (e.g., discussions), the input is more faltering and discontinuous. Pupil involvement was significantly lower in the latter kind of action structure (Kounin & Gump, 1977).

Passive input action structures depend on the students' continued interest in, and clarity about, actions to be taken. Because such student orientations are often hard to maintain in passive input segments, these generally show lowered task involvement. But one instructive exception deserves attention. In the Kounin and Gump (1977) study, the class lesson-type with the highest student involvement was *individual construction*. In this action structure, the children lacked any active external elicitation of response. What, then, accounted for the very high student involvement?

In one construction task, children made faces with bits of colored paper on a pie plate. At the start, a black circle may be cut and pasted for an eye; the one-eye appearance suggests another eye that is cut and pasted; now the eyes "call for" a nose, and one is cut and pasted, and so on. In this structure, there is a tight circle of action/feedback-from-action/further action/and the like. The participant responds to immediate narrowed signals and is insulated against distraction. A study by Davenport (1976) showed, for example, that when deviancy occurred in the individual construction lessons, there was relatively little contagion.

The success of the construction lessons could be attributed to children's liking for such activity; however, when children created a *group* construction, the specially high involvement was lost. Group activity required attention to others and to materials as well. The tight and proximate insulating signal cycle of individual construction no longer operated.

The data from the construction lessons turns our attention from the issue of how participant action is signaled to the quality of that action.

Kind of Participant Activity: Response Aspects

A second basic action structure dimension is the extent to which that structure calls for overt, active, "doing" behavior or requires only covert, passive, attending, and information processing. This dimension has been sometimes labeled as *opportunity to respond* (Hall, Delquadri, Greenwood, & Thurston, 1982).

Opportunity to respond is high when participants must locomote, manipulate, or actively communicate. It is low when participants are asked to observe and incorporate or to appreciate. Opportunity to respond tends to be low in such action structures as reading books, listening to stories, lectures, or other audiovisual presentations. Such opportunity is relatively more substantial in writing, in all forms of arts and crafts activities, and in most games. Some action structures provide for opportunity to respond for some people some of the time but require most others to observe and process information passively. Discussion and recitation formats are of this type; here the opportunity to respond is much determined by group size. A discussion group of 4 provides substantial per pupil response opportunity; a full class recitation yields much less response opportunity.

Common experience as well as some empirical work would suggest that low opportunity to respond dominates most school days. In a study of third grades, Gump (1967) found that seatwork, full class recitations, and listening to the teacher— all action structures with low to intermittent opportunity to respond—were the most frequent action structures. The study by Hall et al. (1982) reported that average first and second graders in an innercity school spent only 25% of their classroom day in active academic responding.

The passivity required of students in academic settings seems to increase as they get older. In a high-school study, Harris and Hall (1973) found that classes were built around teacher lectures with active student responding being prescribed only in unit tests that were given about every 10 days.

What classroom arrangement can increase opportunity to respond? In the Harris and Hall (1973) situation, the teachers began to give 5-min quizzes at the end of each session and had them corrected in class. The average unit test grade increased from *D* to *C*. More frequent math testing in upper elementary school increased mastery in multiplication, but even more rapid gains were made when pupils were allowed to play arithmetic games with the principal (Hall et al., 1982).

The effectiveness of frequent tests was not entirely a matter of feedback. Pupils who simply took the tests but received no feedback gained significantly more than pupils in control classes who were not frequently quizzed.

Although frequent quizzing can increase opportunity to respond, it does not represent the most pervasive type of classroom arrangement for this purpose. The anticipation of testing probably alerts and energizes students during the time when the action structure requires only attention and cognitive activity. Students may become more "responsive" even when overt responding was not part of the action structure.

Opportunity to respond in classrooms could be increased if teachers continually elicited answers, reports, and ideas from every student. However, it is manifestly impossible for the teacher to attend to, process, and provide responses for a continuing input of various students' contributions. A major solution was the development of various tutoring arrangements described by Greenwood, Terry, Wade, Dinwiddie, Stanley, Thibideau, and Delquadri (1982). Working with elementary children in the inner city, this group instituted peer tutoring procedures for spelling, arithmetic, and vocabulary learnings. The tutoring pairs of students became part of competing teams. The use of tutors greatly expanded students' active responding and substantially increased scores on weekly tests. Significant gains on standardized tests were obtained for vocabulary and math but not for spelling. Students with previously low classroom performance especially benefited from the tutorial procedures.

Further reviews of student–student tutoring can be found in the work of Devin-Sheehan, Feldman, and Allen (1976) and in Paolitto (1976). Our interest here has been focused on the potentiality for markedly expanded opportunity to respond in the tutorial arrangement. In principle, tutors provide only one set of possibilities for opportunity to respond. Requiring each student to respond to each recitation question is another method that can increase both on-task behavior and academic learning. The use of a computer program provides a variety of ways to increase pupils' actual responding and to maintain adequate feedback to that responding.

Clearly, the actual versus passive input dimension and the passive versus active response dimension must be considered together when analyzing an action structure and in attempting to predict its effects. For example, it is possible that active input, professionally provided, will yield high on-task ratings, yet—because it does not provide opportunities to actively deal with input—does not lead to optimal learning. According to Hall et al. (1982), the limitation in the student participation they observed was not off-task actions but heavy onlooker behavior. And this behavior directly reflected the low opportunity to respond built into the classroom action structures.

Input and Response Dimensions and Teacher Behavior

Although teachers have power to select and shape classroom action structure, they are fundamentally coerced by these structures once they start to operate.

It is easy to see that if the action structure requires continuous active input and if the leader is to be the source of that input, teacher behavior must be much more active in recitation than in seatwork (Gump, 1967). Further, if the active input is to be continuous, interferences from students must be quickly and persistently suppressed. Thus Bossert (1979) found that the same teachers issued more frequent and more public control behaviors in recitation than in other action structures. Kounin (1970) and Kounin and Sherman (1979) have described the teacher managerial behaviors required to obtain high pupil involvement; Gump (1982) traced the relationship between action structures and these teacher behaviors. In brief, the success of active input segments depends on the development and maintenance of activity momentum. Teachers obtain better pupil involvement when they employ group alerting and avoid such interferences with momentum as over-dwelling on one matter, immersing themselves in one child's problem, or otherwise failing to provide the continuous input required.

Management of the passive input segments requires different teacher action. Clarification of goals and means of student participation is crucial if students are to pace themselves. Some challenge in the material may be pointed out, and Kounin (1970) found that, for younger children, introduction of paced seatwork improved pupil involvement. (Novelty was *not* related to pupil involvement in the active input segments.) More detailed coordination of appropriate teacher moves to input types of action structures can be found in the references cited.

The relation of teacher behavior to the issue of actual versus passive responding has not received systematic research attention, but some issues are intuitively obvious. Providing much opportunity to respond means that something needs to be done with all the responses. As noted by Hall et al. (1982, p. 113), "Having pupils increase their rate of responding may prove to be punishing to teachers." Teachers who ask for much written work have to prepare more materials, correct more papers, and provide more feedback. If teachers are not to be overburdened, they must develop arrangements to deal with the high pupil responding. (Peer tutoring is one example.)

18.3.3. Kinds of Participants' Action Relationships

The tutoring action structure provides for more than increased opportunity to respond. The structure places tutor and tutee in a highly interdependent and cooperative action relationship. This and other action formats provide for interdependency on two levels. First, the structure is such that a reward, a success, for one participant in the interdependency pattern is a reward for the other. The tutee gets a good grade on the test, and the tutor gets some credit for making this happen. Second, there is interdependency of task or activity. The tutor queries, the tutee answers, and the tutor evaluates answers and explains or proceeds as is appropriate. The purely cooperative action structure provides for shared rewards and for interlocking and complementary actions. In contrast, the competitive action structure means that the gain of reward for one side or person requires loss of reward for the other; on the activity level, actions are again highly interlocking, but they are antagonistic, blocking, and countering rather than complementary and mutually supportive.

A less participant-interdependent action structure may emphasize individual rewards and actions. Officially, each participating individual can gain a reward without being affected by rewards given or withheld from others. Progress actions toward the reward are neither aided nor blocked by actions of others.

The three action structures defined by participant relationships—cooperative, competitive, and individualistic—are here described in pure form. In actual operation, many structures are combinations. A competitive game also puts even opponents in some basic cooperative relationships: They agree on a game contract that exactly specifies, constrains, and sequences their competitive actions. Further, as noted previously, games with teams put members of the same team into cooperative action relationships.

Appreciation of the action structure's specification of participants' action relationships requires that one decisively separate action relationships from interpersonal and emotional relationships. Participants who agree to share an action structure do not agree necessarily to like one another, to have "a cooperative spirit," and so on. The pitcher and the catcher in baseball maintain an exquisitely cooperative action relationship—regardless of feelings of affiliation or alienation that may exist between them. Good friends, in a game of tennis or of bridge, attack and block one another's actions with acceptance and even zest. Action relationships are logically independent of interpersonal relationships

Having asserted the logical independence of action and interpersonal interrelationships, it is also necessary to recognize that these arenas of human behavior can interact. Persons who, at first merely accept a cooperative structure, may come to feel positively toward those with whom they have shared rewards and complementary behaviors. Conversely, persons who continually experience the loss of a reward through opponents' gain, who are continually countered by opponents, may develop antagonistic feelings.

Not only might interpersonal relationships be improved by interdependent action structures, but, it has been hoped, better learning might be achieved. With students helping one another, their learning could be positively affected by increased action (opportunity to respond), by developing prolearning norms, and by more positive motivations toward their learning situations.

Overview of Action Structures with High Number Interdependency
Past research reviews of cooperative learning methods have been offered by Johnson, Maruyama, Johnson, Nelson, and Skon (1981), Sharan (1980), and by Slavin (1983). Much of what follows especially depends on the Slavin review. When classroom activity groups are formed, three major considerations are relevant: (1) who is grouped with whom?; (2) what are the reward arrangements?; and (3) what are the understood action relationships among participants?

GROUPING ISSUES
As discussed earlier, groups may be small or large. Groups may be homogeneous or heterogeneous with regard to gender, ethnicity, social class, and other person variables. Pupils of contrasting person qualities (ethnicity, etc.) can be grouped together in a cooperative activity. Such a strategy provides action relationships supportive of changed interpersonal relationships.

Of special importance is the issue of heterogeneity with regard to competence in the activity itself. Thus, educational groups may group homogeneously with regard to academic aptitude, an arrangement referred to as *tracking*. On the other hand, grouping may be heterogeneous (see Good & Marshall, 1984, on this issue). When interdependency arrangements involve competition, the necessity to pair competitors of roughly similar competence is fairly obvious. Without some equalization of competitors, certain children must always lose, and others always win.

REWARD ISSUES
Reward here refers to explicit public events around which there is much consensus about their incentive value. Money is such a reward; being "a winner" or being cited as worthwhile or competent are such rewards. *Reward* can be defined as a subjective experience, and it is even possible that the public reward is not personally satisfying. For our purposes here, *reward* will refer to the manifest gains that a participant can achieve in activity participation. Activity arrangements can provide for rewards for the total group, for individuals within the group, or both. Finally, what participants are rewarded for can vary: a product (e.g., presentation to the class) or scores on learning achievement tests.

PROCESS OR ACTIVITY ISSUES
The program may prescribe member actions that are high or low in interdependence. Although interdependent rewards usually entail interdependent actions, this is not an inevitable relationship. Individuals may work apart to yet share rewards. If members do work interdependently, there may or may not be specialization of action roles.

Examples of cooperative arrangements can illustrate the preceding dimensions.

JIGSAW (ARONSON, 1978). The term *jigsaw* refers to a pattern of knowledge for which each group member develops a separate piece to be fitted with other members' pieces, thereby completing the "puzzle." The class is divided into five or six groups, and each group member is given a different topic to develop. The life of Eleanor Roosevelt might be handled by one member, taking her childhood and youth; another, her young-adult years, and so on. Children then leave this group to attend a group where all members will have the same subtopic and will cooperate in developing material. Children return to their original groups, each one now "a specialist" in one phase of Eleanor Roosevelt's life. Presentations are made to the group, and all take a quiz on the topic. In the Jigsaw arrangement, the activity is not only interdependent, but it is also specialized. Each person in the group is significant because each possesses information not held by others.

However, the possible rewards (getting a good grade on the quiz) are individual, not group or interdependent. The grouping issue for Jigsaw is very significant; this action structure has been used to develop better interethnic relationships by systematically mixing the ethnicity in each of the classroom groups. (Research findings are presented later.)

A variant of this format, Jigsaw II (Slavin, 1983), changes the reward structure such that teams are rewarded for individual member scores on quizzes. In this arrangement, it is manifestly important that students help each other understand the material so that the team will do well.

STAD (SLAVIN, 1978). In Student Team Achievement Divisions (STAD), students are assigned to groups to insure both academic aptitude and ethnic balance. Each student studies an assignment using a worksheet for which answers are available. Students are encouraged to help one another learn. They may employ tutoring, quizzing, or discussion as each seems useful. All students then take mastery quizzes. Individual scores on the tests are based on improvement from previous average scores. Teams with the highest scores and students with scores exceeding past performances (or perfect scores) are recognized in the weekly classroom newsletter. In STAD, official specialization is not provided as in Jigsaw. On the other hand, each member is rewarded for gains, and, as a member of a successful team, is rewarded if fellow members are successful.

TGT (DEVRIES & SLAVIN, 1978). The arrangements for Teams-Games-Tournaments (TGT) duplicate those for STAD with regard to grouping, instructional pattern, and worksheets. However, academically matched students of separate teams show their learning by paired competition. The matching of competitors is kept current so that each student always faces a competitor of roughly similar ability. Thus the TGT arrangements provide strong elements of cooperation (as team members help one another get ready for the tournament) and competition. Reward in terms of newsletter recognition go to the highest scoring team and to tournament game winners.

The reader may wish to consult the literature for other forms of group teaching and learning. These forms include Team Assisted Individualization (Slavin, Leavey, & Madden, 1982), Learning Together (Johnson & Johnson, 1975), and Group Investigation (Sharan & Sharan, 1976).

Achievement and Interdependent Action Structures

According to Slavin's analysis (1983) of 41 studies judged methodologically adequate, cooperative approaches produced superior achievement in almost two-thirds. However, simply placing pupils into groups and inviting cooperative study often did not always yield achievement gains over those obtained in the control arrangements. Slavin asserts that group rewards for individual members' learning should be established.

Task specialization without group rewards as in the original Jigsaw program may or may not produce superior achievement. In this connection, arrangements insuring clear individual accountability of group members to one another are important. For example, group rewards for a project in which the contributions of individual members are not checkable may not produce superior learning.

Many cooperative methods establish competitive rewards. (The group can "win," and its members thus become "winners.") Slavin notes that such competition "can increase effectiveness of cooperative learning but only as one among many ways of providing specific group rewards based on member's learning" (Slavin, 1983, p. 53).

Slavin proposed a simple causal chain to explain learning superiorities in properly arranged cooperative groups. Students are placed in a reward and process structure that makes them dependent on one another's learning. As a result, peer norms supportive of learning develop. These then increase individual incentives to learn and to help others learn.

Data from Sharan, Ackerman, and Hertz-Lazarowitz (1979) suggest that cooperative groups may develop more than incentives to learn, that discussion and intellectual exchange may produce learning at a higher cognitive level. To measure the success of their small groups, these investigators devised learning tests at low cognitive levels (basic information, description, simple skills) and high cognitive levels (analysis, evaluation, judgment). On the high-level tests, the small groups were usually significantly higher than the total class groups. On the low-level tests there was usually no difference. Evidently, the peer activity in the Sharan et al. small-group method helps students more deeply engage the material than the whole class didactic teaching approach.

Members' Social Relationships and Interdependent Action Structures

The expectation that shared action relationships and common goals might lead to participant's mutual liking and respect seems quite plausible. To what extent has research confirmed this expectation?

A few studies have dealt with friendships in general. Others have attempted to change interethnic social relationships.

COOPERATIVE ACTION AND FRIENDSHIP

The box score for improved social feeling for various cooperative action structures can be cited from studies summarized by Slavin (1983). Of 19 studies, only 3 reported no positive effects. However, some limits must be placed on this favorable accounting. First, the criteria for the improved social relationships measurement usually were not behavioral. Such questionnaire items as "who's a friend?" or "other students like me as I am" were often used. Second, even self-report measures quite frequently produced positive effects for one dimension of liking and not for another. For example, the investigator might find increased liking for classmates but not more feeling of being better liked by them (Slavin, 1978), and participants might report more friends but not more liking of classmates (Oickle, 1980).

A measure associated with liking of others is the capacity to take the perspective of the other, to see the world, from their point of view. Experience in cooperative activities was found to increase this capacity (Bridgeman, 1977; Johnson, Johnson, Johnson, & Andersson, 1976).

COOPERATIVE ACTION AND CROSS-ETHNIC RELATIONSHIPS

Findings here are important because efforts to improve race relationships by desegregating school environments have often been frustrated by resegregation of the races within their common schools or classrooms. Cooperative learning situations were often devised to counteract this resegregation.

Results presented by Slavin (1983) and by Sharan (1980) show that interdependency formats did increase some aspect of friendship among races. Results appear more consistent, if group rewards as well as process interdependencies are established. The success with friendship across races was not matched by success in changing general racial attitudes. For example, a strong and prolonged cooperative intervention applied by Weigel, Wiser, and Cook (1975) improved Anglo students' attitudes toward Mexican-American classmates (but not blacks). However, the interventions did not reduce generalized prejudice against these groups. Still the fact that cooperative action structures can increase cross-ethnic friendship in a general climate of prejudice is important and encouraging.

Evidence is available (Slavin, 1983) to show that interdependency formats can favorably affect self-esteem, proacademic peer norms, time on task, and desire for cooperative relations in subsequent activities. Generally, it appears that establishing cooperative activities with group rewards is an effective tool to advance interpersonal relationships and other desirable educational goals.

The research on the process between input condition (the official interdependency format) and output (social and achievement gains) is just beginning. Future attempts to exploit the interdependency arrangement should begin by a study of the most recent process literature

Before leaving the issue of action structure and interpersonal relationships, it is important to examine naturally occurring variations in classrooms. In a long-term investigation, Bossert (1979) compared four classrooms that varied in emphasis on recitation and in the practice of single-task versus multitask assignment.

Bossert found that the recitation format hinders close ties between teacher and students. In recitation the teacher must continually direct activity and evaluate responses. Small-group projects, however, permit the teacher to be involved with students in the activity, not simply to oversee their effort.

One effect of recitation is to make clear who is and who is not academically superior. Thus, perceived superiority—or lack of it—becomes a basis for the formation of student associations and friendships. When students worked on a variety of projects in small groups, the need to form associations on the basis of academic skill was reduced. Bossert's data show how both pupil–pupil and pupil–teacher relationships can be affected by variation in activity structures.

Reflections on Interdependency Action Structures

With evidence now available, it is clear that attempts to change pupils' social relationships and achievement can proceed from a substantial research base. However, failures in such efforts have been reported (and many more failures have doubtlessly gone unreported). It is clear that simply establishing groups, rewards, and interdependent actions may not produce the desired effects. Between the official arrangements and derived social and cognitive outcomes is a process, a time when certain events do or do not occur. If cooperative formats are to be successful, mutual encouragement and help during the project must occur. Furthermore, according to Webb and Kenderski (1984), not just any help is associated with learning. Rather, "giving explanations" helps learning; getting manifestly needed explanations may be useful; and "getting answers" or verbatim repetitions of problem directions does *not* help learning.

The research on the process between input condition (the official interdependency format) and output (social and achievement gains) is just beginning. Future attempts to exploit the interdependency arrangement should begin by a study of the most recent process literature.

18.3.4. Relationships among Program Segments

The preceding discussion described qualities of individual segments and their relationship to pupil and teacher responses. Segments actually appear in assemblages as depicted on Figure 18.1. Such groupings display relationships among the segments that may appear as single units over time or operate simultaneously (parallel) at any one time.

Operation of Single versus Parallel (Multiple) Segments

Establishment of small activity groups in the usual cooperative formats will mean simultaneous segments. The multitask classroom emphasis described by Bossert (1979) will often require multiple segment operation. If segments operate in parallel, overlapping situations can develop for teachers. They may face simultaneous calls for their action from two or more separate situations. The effect of overlapping on events in the classroom environment depends upon how the teacher handles the problem. Kounin (1970) noted that pupil deviancy rates were lower and task involvement rates were higher when teachers dealt with both situations without becoming completely immersed in either.

The overlapping situation is particularly important when the teacher is responsible for continuous leadership in one of the segments; the simultaneous reading circle and seatwork arrangement is an example. If the teacher answers demands from the seatwork area with extensive attention, the reading circle operation literally "stalls out." A description of such a classroom problem is described and quantified by Gump (1982) who also suggests some of the ways the overlapping problem might be met. In order to make the operation of the nonteacher-led segment viable, care must be taken to plan activities that children can manage without teacher input. Second, once calls for action come from the nonteacher-led segment, it is important that they not be responded to in a manner which encourages more calls.

Movement from One Segment to Another: The Issue of Transitions

On Figure 18.1, the change from "preschool studying and visiting" to "opening song and salute" marks the first in-class transition of the day. This change will require change in physical position of the visiting students (who must return to their seats), changes in body posture, in attention to behavior objects, and in action relationships from individualistic (study) or dyadic (visiting) to en masse cooperation (singing and saluting and chanting). Present directions of behavior must cease, and new ones become established. Although most classroom research has ignored transitions and focused on segments or activities once they are in operation, several lines of evidence point to the importance of transitions in the classroom habitat.

From the ecological viewpoint, transitions are important because they are very much "there." They are frequent, and they take time. On Figure 18.1, eight transitions are carried out before the morning recess. Up to 30 segments a day can operate in primary elementary classrooms (Gump, 1967; Kounin, 1970), and they require their accompanying transitions.

Prescott (1973) observed children in day-care centers and noted that 26% of child time was required for transitions in "closed centers" and 14% in "open" ones. In elementary school, measurements of transitions have not been reported separately, but time spent in nonsubstance or noninstructional activity has been measured. Researchers are in general agreement that noninstructional time takes up about 20% of the school day, and half or more of this time is devoted to transitions (Bennett et al., 1980; Borg, 1980; Gump, 1974).

Transitions are important also because pupil and teacher behaviors are different in the time between segments. In a study of classes led by student teachers, Arlin (1979) found that off-task behavior was twice as frequent during transitions as during lessons proper. It is not surprising that teacher actions during transitions are more frequent and more directive because many transitions, by their nature, require such teacher activity. However, because deviancy is more likely to be a problem, teacher actions that are counterdeviant also increase at transitions (Gump, 1969).

Finally, data from Kounin (1970) show that how teachers behave around changes in classroom activity is very much related to on-task rates in the nontransitional parts of the day. Briefly, teachers who avoid behaviors that interfere with activity momentum at points of activity change will experience better classroom involvement by pupils.

If transitions are significant portions of the classroom environment, what are considerations for their optimal handling?

Transitions involve three sequential phases: (1) an abandonment of a previous activity with its relevant milieu; (2) a movement toward a second activity; and (3) a "getting into" the second activity with its milieu.

Transitions may be prolonged or difficult because orientations and feelings aroused by the first activity persist to interfere with getting well started in the second. Preparing students for a closedown of the first activity was found by Arlin (1979) to yield more smooth transitions than abrupt cessation of the first activity. If strong feelings or arousals are likely to carry over, a buffer period may be inserted. For example, Krantz and Risley (1977) found that transitions from recess to story time produced 37% off-task behavior in the start of the story time. They then arranged for a short rest period between the two segments, and the off-task rate fell to 14%.

The second phase—movement from first to second activity— has not been researched. One has the impression that it is usually not, of itself, a problem. In open-school research, the author found that although transitions as a whole might easily expand to 6 or 8 min apiece, actual movement from site to site usually required, per child, about 20 sec.

More difficulty occurs in the startup of the second segment. The same open-school research showed that the arena for second segment action was frequently not cleared for use by the group previously using it. However, the most frequent problem was some kind of teacher unreadiness. Most often the unready teacher was conscientiously dealing with other matters: a child with a problem, collection of materials from dispersed points or persons, and so forth. Manifestly, either the teacher must be ready at the opening of the second segment, or some routine about "what to do until the teacher comes" needs to be established. Of course it is possible also to arrange second segments such that teacher signals and beginning suggestions are not required.

For some transitions, this period between structured segments lack action structure; without a guiding structure, children pursue a variety of activities of their own. One obvious solution is the establishment of a structure, a routine, for this time. In Arlin's study (1979), when teachers managed transitions for which a clear routine was operative, they experienced no more pupil off-task behavior than in nontransition periods. Transition routines have been thoughtfully discussed by Yinger (1979).

A trade-off may exist between arrangements that ensure good order during transitions and those that consume less of children's time. The closed centers of Prescott's study used routines, often lineups, to ensure order in change of activity and place; they also used up one-quarter of their children's time. Data from Wallace, Hatfield, Goetz, and Etzel (1976) showed that for one major and frequent nursery-school transition, lineups take more child time than alternative methods.

Underneath the lineup requirement is the program arrangement that transitions must involve relatively simultaneous change by all (or groups) of participants. Transitions can require much time because people, including the teacher, become ready for change at various times, and movement tends to wait for the latest participant. When the teacher or caretaker waits until all are ready and then moves with the group in the next activity, the arrangement has been labeled by LeLaurin and Risley (1972) as *man-to-man defense*. An alternative, *zone defense*, specifies that teachers shall cover settings rather than accompany groups. In this zone defense, the amount of child time in activity engagement was much increased; the time in transition was reduced.

Transition time can also be reduced by reducing the number of major transitions. For example, Gump (1974) found that nonsubstance time in two open-space schools was significantly longer than such time in two traditional ones. Inspection of the data showed that the more frequent major site and teacher transitions in the open-space schools contributed the extra nonsubstance time.

Intuitively, it appears that variations in kinds of transitions must be identified and then evaluated if one is to predict pupil response or recommend changed teacher action. The movement of an entire class from the gymnasium back into spelling would seem a more formidable undertaking than returning a reading circle group to seatwork. Study of transition types is just beginning (Ross, 1984, 1985). The reader may want to check the latest research contributions as these become available.

The preceding discussion of transitions has described school environments in which various en masse and subgroup changes are teacher initiated. Programs do not have to be arranged in this fashion; some are not (Parker & Day, 1972). When pupils work out their own learning plans, they may then proceed from subsetting to subsetting, at their own initiative. To the extent that this is the arrangement, much of the previous discussion is irrelevant. However, the issue now arises of how to help students— no longer contained and supported by similar peer action and teacher signaling—become adequate segment beginners and finishers.

18.4. PSYCHOSOCIAL ENVIRONMENTS MEASURED BY QUESTIONNAIRE: AN OVERVIEW

Many research articles dealing with learning or classroom "environments" have not been included in our discussion. These research contributions have focused on psychological and social variables as these are perceived by students. In contrast, school environments in this chapter have been limited to physical milieus and to programs that form an outside-the-skin context for the behavior and experience of students and staff. The environments in the present discussion have been ecological or "preperceptual" (Barker, 1968, p. 1).

Although the questionnaire measurement of social and psychological variables (for environments) is outside of our primary concern, some explication of these methods and variables might be appropriate. The very bulk of studies labeled *environmental* seems to require some notice in a chapter claiming to deal with school and classroom environments. Further, a clarification of the psychosocial measurement might contribute to an appreciation of the ecological environment as conceived here. Finally, there exists a network of variables proceeding from the objective external context through the psychological and social intervening variables to outcomes of individual behavior and experience. The questionnaire variables might be of interest and utility in researching this network.

Our discussion will be limited, even insufficient, for readers desiring a comprehensive review of the methods and findings of these psychosocial researchers. Only an overview to place them in relation to the ecological position will be attempted.

18.4.1. The Nature of the Psychosocial Questionnaires

Two questionnaires can serve as exemplars of the research methods: Classroom Environment Scale (Moos, 1979) and Learning Environments Inventory (LEI) (Anderson & Walberg, 1974). The latter method has been updated and given an elementary-school version called My Class Inventory (Fisher & Fraser, 1983; Fraser, Anderson, & Walberg, 1982). The LEI probes 15 different dimensions, the CES measures 9. The following outline cluster of sample variables for LEI and CES measurements orders examples of the dimensions into five clusters. (The arrangement is heuristic, not based on a quantitatively derived clustering, nor upon the questionnaire makers' organizations.)

1. Physical provisions: adequacy (LEI)
2. Program quality and implementation: formality (LEI); student contribution (LEI); innovation (CES); order and organization (CES)
3. Teacher-to-student relationship: favoritism (LEI); supportiveness (CES)
4. Student–student relationships: cliqueness (LEI); competition (LEI and CES); affiliation (CES)
5. Student motivation: satisfaction (LEI); apathy (LEI); involvement (CES)

In the preceding outline, physical provision represents an external environmental reality; at the other end of the environment-to-behavior continuum are matters of student motivation. Between these endpoints are the kind and the implementation of program and the relationships of participants. In terms of the orientation of this chapter, the array of the questionnaire variables goes from phenomena that have been parts of the physical milieu (provisions) and activity structure (program quality) and those taken as dependent on these ecological conditions: relationships and on-task or involvement behaviors. Although the questionnaires are sometimes given the simple label of *psychosocial measurements*, the outline makes clear that what would ordinarily be termed *environment* and reactions to and within that environment are all included.

One aspect of the questionnaires that could justify their claim to being environmental measures is the fact that they ask respondents to describe or infer the activity, social, and psychological conditions in which they are immersed. To make these inferences, much subjectivity is involved. Strictly speaking, the whole set of measurements could be called "postperceptual" and therefore completely subjective. In principle, however, it should be possible to use respondents as informants (not "subjects") and gain from them some idea of the ecological environment they inhabit. With the questionnaires, subjectivity, however, is invited because respondents are asked to make "high-inference" judgments about the motivations of others: They are asked to agree or disagree with statements such as "the teacher takes a personal interest in students" or "students feel they must be careful about what they say in class."

With these and other invitations to subjectivity in self-reporting, it would be expected that students sharing the same objective reality—the same classroom—would offer different descriptions of its reality. Such differences do appear (Walberg & Ahlgren,

1970). The contrasts in description are taken by the authors to indicate the sensitivity, even the validity, of the questionnaire. Such differences dismay researchers seeking the ecological or preperceptual environment.

18.4.2. Research with the Psychosocial Questionnaires

Scores obtained on the LEI scale can predict achievement in the classroom (see the preceding references and Haertel, Walberg, & Haertel, 1981). Moos (1979) presented validity data for the CES scale. Not only can measures on the scales predict to student achievement, many are responsive to larger enclosing conditions of the classroom (e.g., kind of school, cultural conditions, etc.). Both Moos (1979) and Trickett (1978) present these kinds of data.

The LEI and CES measures and questionnaires of similar type have been used to measure the somewhat elusive phenomena cluster referred to as *school climate*. The term was suggested by Lewin (1948) to represent aspects of the child's group relationships and may involve such diverse areas as physical environment, organizational structure, participant norms, and their inter- and intrapersonal feelings. A thorough account of the history of climate research has been contributed by Chavez (1984). A thoughtful review of 200 studies and an organization of the many variables into a kind of map of the area has been published by Anderson (1982).

The questionnaires have been seen as useful in going from subjective descriptions of the classroom to motivational and achievement outcomes. They have also provided a set of variables seen as dependent on conditions in which classrooms are embedded.

18.4.3. Ecological Measurements and Psychosocial Questionnaire Measurements

Although the questionnaires provide dimensions that correlate to student achievement, this accomplishment may not advance our understanding in any significant fashion. First, a correlation between involvement and achievement is to be expected. Further, the more basic question for persons in charge of classrooms is: What arrangements lead to optimum scores on both of the correlated variables? Similarly, documented relationship between, for example, affiliation and satisfaction leave us with the more basic issue: How shall condi-

issue: How shall conditions be established to assist gain on both variables?

If one is interested in the preperceptual environment, the questionnaire dimensions properly selected and with some item changes could be helpful in two quite different directions. First, if invitations to subjectivity can be reduced, student descriptions of the physical milieu and of the activity structures that are operative could increase the data yield beyond that feasible with observation alone. Just how the described activity structure or program is implemented (issues of order and organization) is a particular aspect of the classroom reality that requires much observation. Reliable student reports on implementation issues would be quite useful.

Second, the direction of use of the questionnaires involves the questionnaires' potential for economical data collection regarding individual students' behavioral and attitudinal reactions to their preperceptual environments. Here the issue of subjectivity is not a problem; one seeks the individuals' reactions— not their objective reports. We ask, How are the classroom conditions affecting you?

Eventually, one may find development of questionnaires on the classroom that respect the very fundamental difference between ecological and psychological variables, questionnaires that then reliably measure the ecological for coordination to the psychological.

18.4.4. A Note on College Environments

Our discussion does not purport to handle postsecondary- school environments. However, it does seem useful to point out that questionnaire measurements of university residences have been developed that are analogous to the CES (Gerst & Moos, 1972). The University Residence Environment Scale is fully reproduced and research with it has been described by Moos (1979). Ten subscales, with 10 items each, ask about students' perceptions of student interaction, degree of emphasis in the residence upon social versus intellectual activities, the extent of order and of innovativeness, and the range of student influence in making decisions about house operations. Moos (1979) reviews studies dealing with the conditions that influence URES scores (e.g., megadorms v. small residences). He also describes studies that show how URES scores relate to student behavior or attitude.

For the reader interested in assessment and manipulation of college or university environments, one more reference might be valuable. Writing for personnel administrators, Evans (1983) proposes an ecological alternative to the traditional one-on-one remedial approaches to student well-being. The development of this environmental approach includes a brief review of major works in environmental assessment of colleges and a short account of various efforts to improve parts of these institutions.

18.5. RESOURCES AND DIRECTIONS FOR IMPROVEMENT OF SCHOOL ENVIRONMENTS

Inspection of this chapter's references demonstrates how much material has become available since the early 1970s. Researchers and applied professionals have much more empirical material to guide their work than existed earlier. Much of this material investigates long-standing favorites in such research, for example, openness or partitioning, seating arrangements, and class size (i.e., density). New areas have appeared, some of which tend to fill in gaps between some of the more established ones. For example, work on patterns and paths includes milieu areas literally between enclosure and seating. On the program side, vigorous and substantial efforts have gone into arrangements that put participants in various action relationships (cooperative, competitive, or individualistic formats.)

Although energy and productivity have much increased, development of cumulative findings has been retarded because of the heterogeneous frameworks and findings of the various investigators. Without a common framework, examples of the same concept's meaning different things do occur. (The use of *environment* for the psychosocial measurements of a classroom has already been discussed.) Also possible are cases in which the same phenomena are given different names, thus obscuring their basic similarity. For example, are the interdependency formats examples of types of curricula or action structures?

The accumulation of many school environment researches into one array, as in this chapter, makes it possible to test a rudimentary common set of concepts for ordering the ideas' findings. In the present case, it does seem possible to group studies under the *physical milieu* rubric and within that to consider the more extended aspects of the physical habitat first (site, enclosure), then the more intermediary areas (paths and seating), and finally, the most molecular parts (objects). Issues of facility size and of inhabitant number seem reasonably connected to this milieu beginning. On the side of the program, it

has seemed clear that issues regarding the active or passive nature of the input and response modes were fundamental ideas that investigators have dealt with using other concepts. Also basic to any group-living situation are the action relationships established by the program because the interpersonal relationships will take some of their shape from these program patterns.

On the conceptual level, advances in our understanding of school environments could be improved by two developments. First, the present assumption that there is a necessary gap between the physical (milieu) and the behavioral forms (standing pattern of behavior or program) should be reexamined. Although there are questions for which this gap must be respected (human factors research), other questions may require that research arrangements respect the functional togetherness of these aspects of the environment. For example, interdependency formats do not operate merely on a group behavior level: They occur at a time and place with or without enclosure and employ specified behavior objects. It is our belief that, if we want to identify and investigate the more powerful variable sets in the environment, we need units that include both milieu and program. Whatever the effects produced by milieu manipulation, the results depend very much on the operating program. Reciprocally, program effects are always obtained in a physical milieu with certain qualities; variables are often ignored in research reports. Their absence simplifies but impoverishes the research result.

A related conceptual change that is necessary and already developing is the selection of environmental units that are more inclusive, more contextual than stimuli or single-dimension variations. Stodolsky (1983) contends that our difficulties in developing useful research findings in education stems partly from the fragmentary or isolated nature of the pre-yield. She compares the situation to one in which an individual seeking to understand a complex machine is given only a catalog of parts. Stodolsky (1983) and others have come to view instruction as a process of establishing and maintaining activities or classroom segments: "Rather than view instruction as composed of discrete behaviors, I have attempted to capture behavioral patterns and routines at a molar level" (p. 181).

The achievement of relevant contextual units carries an implicit tension: Although one seeks units that represent the environmental reality in some comprehensive fashion, one does not want concepts so broad as to lose anchorage in a firm conception of environment and drift into the phenomena of individual psychology. I fear that *school climate* has become virtually unusable as a clear label for school environment because of such drift.

The development of more inclusive concepts and units and the acceptance of physical milieu and program jointness are logically related; the latter is a major example of the former. Once such matters are advanced, the applied effort will become clearer. Teachers and administrators already think and act in terms of these larger units: activities, classes, meetings, assemblies, and so forth. What is needed is research that informs these efforts. Already, one can survey the varied aspects of researched school environments and encourage practitioners to begin to think about more frequent and more deliberate manipulation of existing environments. The goals would be to introduce more freshness and effectiveness into classroom operations.

The teaching literature, using other words in their titles, is already struggling with matters that require basic understanding of school environments. For example, the third edition of the *Handbook of Research on Teaching* offers for the first time, a chapter, Classroom Management and Organization (see Doyle, 1986). The chapter depends on research from some of the same investigators as have been cited here: Arlin, Berliner, Bossert, Gump, Kounin, Slavin, Stodolsky, and Weinstein. The words *management* and *organization* are action words but still abstractions, which deal with environments, not just students. These words point to how these environments are to be established, maintained, interrelated, and changed.

Eventually, one expects the material on school environments to find its way into all teacher-training curricula so that graduates will know about milieu and program units just as they know about child psychology or curricular development. Education as a craft depends on environmental manipulation. Although there is certainly more to the educational effort than the ecological environment, that environment is an inevitable and extensive part of the endeavor. Scientific information could reshape school environments so that they become increasingly effective and beneficial contexts.

REFERENCES

Abt Associates. (1971). *A study in child care.* Cambridge, MA: Author.

Abt Associates. (1978). *Natural day care study; Preliminary findings and their implications.* Cambridge, MA: Author.

Adams, R.S., & Biddle, B.J. (1970). *Realities of teaching: Explorations with video tape.* New York: Holt, Rinehart & Winston.

Abt Associates. (1979). *Executive summary, children at the center.* Cambridge, MA: Author.

Ahrentzen, S. (1982, Spring). Student responses to openness, softness and seclusion in elementary school classrooms. *Journal of Man-Environment Relations, 1*(3), 42–53.

Aiello, J.R., Nicosia, G., & Thompson, D.E. (1979). Physiological, social and behavioral consequences of crowding on children and adolescents. *Child Development, 50*, 195–202.

Aiello, J.R., Thompson, E., & Baum, A. (1985). Children, crowding and control: Effects of environmental stress on social behavior. In J. Wohlwill & W. van Vliet (Eds.), *Habitats for children: The impacts of density.* Hilsdale, NJ: Erlbaum.

Altman, J. (1974). Privacy: A conceptual analysis. In S.T. Margulis (Ed.), *Privacy.* Milwaukee, WI: Environmental Design Research Association.

Anderson, C.S. (1982). A search for school climate: A review of the research. *Review of Educational Research, 52*, 368–420.

Anderson, G.J., & Walberg, H.J. (1974). Learning environments. In H.J. Walberg (Ed.), *Evaluating Educational Performance.* Berkeley, CA: McCutchan.

Angus, M.J., Beck, T.M., Hill, P.W., & McAtee, W.A. (1979, April). *A summary report of the Australian open area schools project.* Paper presented at the annual convention of the American Education Research Association, San Francisco.

Arlin, M. (1979). Teacher transitions can disrupt time flow in classroom. *American Educational Research Journal, 16*, 42–56.

Aronson, E. (1978). *The jigsaw classroom.* Beverly Hills, CA: Sage.

Axelrod, S., Hall, R.V., & Tams, A. (1979). Comparison of two common classroom setting arrangements. *Academic Therapy, 15*, 29–37.

Baird, L. (1969). Big school, small school: A critical examination of the hypothesis. *Journal of Educational Psychology, 60*, 253–260.

Barker, R.G. (1968). *Ecological psychology.* Stanford, CA: Stanford University Press.

Barker, R.G., & Gump, P.V. (1964). *Big school, small school.* Stanford, CA: Stanford University Press.

Barker, R.G., & Wright, H.F. (1955). *Midwest and its children.* Evanston, IL: Row, Peterson.

Bates, B.C. (1970). Effects of social density on the behavior of nursery school children. *Dissertation Abstracts International, 32*, 537B, (University Microfilms No. 71-16801)

Becker, R.D., Sommer, R., Bee, J., & Oxley, B. (1973). College classroom ecology. *Sociometry, 36*(4), 514–525.

Bell, A.E., Abrahamsen, D.S., & Growse, R. (1977). Achievement and self-reports of responsibility for achievement in informal and conventional classrooms. *British Journal of Educational Psychology, 47*, (Pt. 3), 258–267.

Bell, A.E., Switzer, F., & Zipursky, M.A. (1974). Open area education: An advantage or disadvantage for beginners? *Perceptual and Motor Skills, 39*(1), 407–416.

Bell, A.E., Zipursky, M.A., & Switzer, F. (1976). Informal or open area education in relation to achievement and personality. *British Journal of Educational Psychology, 46*(3), 235–243.

Bennett, N., Andreae, J., Hegarty, P., Wade, B. (1980). *Open plan schools.* Atlantic Highlands, NJ: Humanities. (Original work published 1980).

Berliner, C.D. (1983). Developing conception of classroom environments: Some light on the T in classroom studies of ATI. *Educational Psychologist, 181*(1), 1–13.

Berlyne, D.E. (1963). Motivational problems raised by exploratory and epistemic behavior. In S. Koch (Ed.), *Psychology: A study of a science* (Vol. 5). New York: McGraw-Hill.

Borg, W.R. (1980). Time and school learning. In C. Denlaim & A. Lieberman (Eds.), *Time to learn.* Washington, DC: National Institute of Education.

Bossert, S.T. (1979). *Tasks and social relationships in classrooms. (A study of instructional organization and its consequences).* New York: Cambridge University Press.

Bridgeman, D.L. (1977). The influence of cooperative, interdependent learning on role taking and moral reasoning: A theoretical and empirical study with fifth grade students. *Dissertation Abstracts International, 39*, 1041B. (University Microfilms No. 78-11551)

Bronfenbrenner, U. (1979). *The ecology of human development.* Cambridge, MA: Harvard University Press.

Burkhead, J. (1967). *Input and output in large city high schools.* Syracuse, NY: Syracuse University Press.

Cahen, L.S., Filby, N., McCutcheon, G., & Kyle, D. (1983). *Class size and instruction: A field study.* New York: Longman.

Campbell, F. (1979). Preschool behavior study. *Architectural Psychology Newsletter, 3*(1), 59.

Carpenter, C. Jan, & Huston-Stein, A. (1980). Activity structure and sex-typed behavior in preschool children. *Child Development, 51*(3), 862–872.

Castaldi, B. (1977). *Educational Facilities: Planning, remodeling and management.* Boston: Allyn & Bacon.

Chapman, J., & Lazar, J. (1971). *A review of the present status and future needs in day care research.* Washington, DC: Department of Health, Education, and Welfare, Office of Child Development.

Chavez, R.C. (1984). The use of high-influence measures to study classroom climates. *Review of Educational Research, 54*, 237–261.

Coleman, J.S. (1961). *The adolescent society.* New York: Free Press.

Coleman, J.S. (1966). *Equality of educational opportunity.* Washington, DC: U.S. Government Printing Office.

Curtis, P., & Smith, R. (1974). A child's exploration of space. *School Review, 82*(4), 671–679.

Daly, J., & Suite, A. (1982). Classroom seating choice and teacher perceptions of students. *Journal of Experimental Education, 50*, 64–69.

Davenport, G.G. (1976). The effects of lessons signal system upon the duration and spread of deviancy. (Doctoral dissertation, Wayne State University, 1976). *Dissertation Abstracts International, 37*, 2736A.

Dawe, H.C. (1934). An analysis of two hundred quarrels of preschool children. *Child Development, 5*, 139–157.

Devin-Sheehan, L., Feldman, R.S., & Allen, V.L. (1976). Research on children tutoring children: A critical review. *Review of Educational Research, 46*, 355–385.

DeVries, D.L., & Slavin, R.E. (1978). Teams-Games-Tournaments (TGT): Review of ten classroom experiments. *Journal of Research and Development in Education, 12*(1), 28–38.

Doyle, W. (1986). Classroom organization and managements. In M. Wittrock (Ed.), *Handbook of research on teaching* (pp. 392–431). New York: Macmillan.

Dreeben, R. (1968). *On what is learned in school.* Reading, MA: Addison-Wesley.

Ebmeier, H .H., & Ziomek, R.L. (1982). *Increasing engagement notes of low and high achievers.* Paper presented at the annual meeting of the American Education Research Association, New York.

Educational Facilities Laboratories. (1972). Found spaces and equipment for children. New York: Author.

Education Research Service. (1980). *Class size research: A critique of recent meta analyses.* Arlington, VA: Author.

Evans, G., & Lovell, B. (1979). Design modification in an open-plan school. *Journal of Educational Psychology, 71*, 41–49.

Evans, N.J. (1983). Environmental assessment: Current practices and future directions. *Journal of College Student Personnel, 24*, 293–299.

Fagot, B.I. (1977). Variations in density: Effects on task and social behaviors of preschool children. *Developmental Psychology, 13*, 166–167.

Fisher, C. (1974). *Educational environments in elementary schools differing in architectural and program openness.* Paper presented at the annual convention of the American Educational Research Association, Chicago.

Fisher, D.L., & Fraser, D.J. (1983). Validity and use of the Classroom Environment Scale. *Educational Evaluation & Policy Analysis, 5*, 261–271.

Ford Foundation (1972). *A foundation goes to school.* New York: Author.

Fraser, B.J., Anderson, G.J., & Walberg, H.J. (1982). *Assessment of learning environments: Manual for Learn-*

ing *Environment Inventory (LEI) and My Class Inventory*. Bentley, Australia: Western Australian Institute of Technology.

Garbarino, J. (1980). Some thoughts on school size and its effects on adolescent development. *Journal of Youth and Adolescence, 9*(1), 19–31.

George, P.S. (1975). *Ten years of open space schools: A review of the research*. Gainesville, FL: University of Florida, Florida Educational Research and Development.

Gerst, M., & Moos, R. (1972). Social ecology of university student residences. *Journal of Educational Psychology, 63*, 513–525.

Getz, S.K., & Brendt, E.G. (1982). A test of a method for quantifying amount, complexity, and arrangement of play resources in the preschool classroom. *Journal of Applied Developmental Psychology, 3*, 295–305.

Giaconia, R.M., & Hedges, L.V. (1982). Identifying features of effective open education. *Review of Educational Research52*, 579–602.

Ginsburg, H.J., & Pollman, V. (1975). *Variation of aggressive interaction among male elementary school children as a function of changes in spatial density*. Meetings of the Society for Research in Child Development, Denver, CO.

Glass, G.V., Cahen, L.S., Smith, M.L., & Filby, N.N. (1982). *School class size: Research and policy*. Beverly Hills, CA: Sage.

Gold, A. (1975). The resurgence of the small school in the city. *Phi Delta Kappa, 56*(5), 313–315.

Good, T.L., & Marshall, S. (1984). Do students learn more in heterogeneous or homogeneous groups? In P.L. Peterson, L.C. Wilkinson, & M. Hallinan (Eds.), *The social context of instruction* (pp. 15–37). Orlando, FL: Academic.

Gores, H.G. (1963). Still sits the school house...but less so. *American Institute Architectural Journal, 40*, 83–90.

Grapko, M.G. (1972). *A comparison of open space and traditional classroom structures according to independence measures in children, teachers' awareness of childrens' personality variables, and children's academic progress* (Final Rep.). Toronto: Ontario Department of Education. (ERIC Document Reproduction Service No. ED 088 180)

Greenwood, C.R., Terry, B., Wade, L., Dinwiddie, G., Stanley, S., Thibideau, S., & Delquadri, J. (1982). *An ecological behavioral analysis of instruction: Contexts, student behavior and achievement*. Kansas City: KS: University of Kansas, Bureau of Child Research, Juniper Gardens Children Project.

Griffith, C.R. (1921). A comment upon the psychology of the audience. *Psychological monographs, 30*(136), 36–47.

Gump, P.V. (1967). *The classroom behavior setting: Its nature and relation to student behavior* (Final Rep., Pro-

ject No. 5-0334). Washington, DC: U.S. Office of Education Cooperative Research Branch.

Gump, P.V. (1969). Intra-setting analysis: The third grade classroom as a special but instructive case. In E. Willems & H. Raush (Eds.), *Naturalistic viewpoints in psychological research*. New York: Holt, Rinehart & Winston.

Gump, P.V. (1974). Operating environments in open and traditional schools. *School Review, 84*, 575–593.

Gump, P.V. (1982). School settings and their keeping. In D. Duke (Ed.), *Helping teachers manage classrooms*. Alexandria, VA: Association for Supervision and Curriculum Development.

Gump, P.V., & Ross, R. (1979). What's happening in schools of open design? *JSAS Catalogue Selected Documents in Psychology, 9*(12), 1816.

Haber, G.M. (1982). Spatial relatives between dominants and marginals. *Social Psychology Quarterly, 45*, 219–228.

Haertel, G.D., Walberg, H.J., & Haertel, E.H. (1981). Sociopsychological environments and learning: A quantitation synthesis. *British Educational Research Journal, 7*, 27–36.

Hall, V.R., Delquadri, J., Greenwood, C.R., & Thurston, L. (1982). The importance of opportunity to respond in children's academic success. In E. Edgar, N. Haring, J. Jenkins, & C. Piores (Eds.), *Mentally handicapped children: Education and training* (pp. 107–140). Baltimore, MD: University Park Press.

Harris, J.W., & Hall, R.V. (1973). Effects of systematic reinforcement procedures on performance of underachieving high school pupils. Educational Technology Research (Publication Series No. 51). Englewood Cliffs, NJ: Educational Technology Research.

Hedges, L.V., & Stock, W. (1983). The effects of class size: An examination of rival hypotheses. *American Education Research Journal, 20*, 63–85.

Heller, J.F., Groff, B.D., & Solomon, S.H. (1977). Toward an understanding of crowding: The role of physical interaction. *Journal of Personality and Social Psychology, 35*, 183–190.

Hendrickson, J.M., Tremblay, A., Strain, P.S., & Shores, R.E. (1981). Relationship between toy and material use and the occurrence of socially interactive behaviors by normally developing preschool children. *Psychology in the Schools, 18*, 500–504.

Holahan, C.J. (1977). Consultation in environmental psychology: A case study of a new counseling role. *Journal of Counseling Psychology, 24*, 251–254.

Huston-Stein, A., Friedrich-Cofer, L., & Susman, E.J. (1977). The relation of classroom structure to social behavior, imaginative play, and self-regulation of economically disadvantaged children. *Child Development, 48*, 908–916.

Hutt, C., & Vaizey, M.J. (1966). Differential effects of group density on social behavior. *Nature, 209*, 1371–1372.

Jersild, A.T., & Markey, F.V. (1935). *Conflicts between preschool children*. New York: Columbia University, Teachers' College.

Johnson, D.W., & Johnson, R.T. (1975). *Learning together and alone*. Englewood Cliffs, NJ: Prentice-Hall.

Johnson, D.W., Johnson, R.T., Johnson, J., & Anderson, D. (1976). Effects of cooperative versus individualistic learning. *Journal of Educational Psychology, 68*, 446–452.

Johnson, D.W., Maruyama, G., Johnson, R.T., Nelson, D., & Skon, L. (1981). Effects of cooperative, competitive, and individualistic goal structures on achievement: A metaanalysis. *Psychological Bulletin, 89*, 47–62.

Junker, D.I. (1976). *Structuring toddler's toy use: Areas vs. no areas*. Unpublished master's thesis, University of Kansas, Lawrence.

Kerkman, D.H. (1964). Behavior settings at school in communities differing in size. (Doctoral dissertation, University of Kansas, 1964). *Dissertation Abstracts International, 26*, p. 480.

Kinsman, C.A., & Berk, L.E. (1979, November). Joining the block and housekeeping areas: Changes in play and social behavior. *Young Children*, 66–74.

Knowles, E.S. (1982). A comment on the study of classroom ecology: A lament for the good old days. *Personality and Social Psychology Bulletin, 8*, 357–361.

Koneya, M. (1976). Location and interaction in the row and column seating arrangements. *Environment and Behavior, 8*(2); 265–282.

Kounin, J.S. (1970). *Discipline and group management in the classroom*. New York: Holt, Rinehart & Winston.

Kounin, J.S., Friesen, W.V., & Norton, A.E. (1966). Managing emotionally disturbed children in regular classrooms. *Journal of Educational Psychology, 2*, 129–135.

Kounin, J.S., & Gump, P.V. (1977). Signal systems of lesson settings and the task-related behavior of preschool children. *Journal of Educational Psychology, 66*, 554–562.

Kounin, J.S., & Sherman, L.W. (1979). School environments as behavior settings. *Theory into Practice, 13*, 145–151.

Kowatrakul, Surang (1959). Some behaviors of elementary school children related to classroom activities and subject areas. *Journal of Educational Psychology, 50*, 121–128.

Krantz, P.J., & Risley, T.R. (1977). Behavioral ecology in the classroom. In K. O'Leary & S. O'Leary (Eds.), *Classroom management: The successful use of behavior modification*. New York: Pergamon.

Kritchevsky, S., Prescott, E., & Walling, L. (1977). *Planning environments for young children: Physical space* (2nd ed.). Washington, DC: National Association for the Education of Young Children.

Kyzar, K. (1977). Noise pollution and the schools: How much is too much? *Council of Educational Facility Planners Journal, 4*, 10–11.

Leggett, S., Brubaker, W.C., Cohodes, A., & Shapiro, A.S. (1977). *Planning flexible learning places*. New York: McGraw-Hill.

LeLaurin, K., & Risley, T.R. (1972). The organization of day-care environments: "Zone" versus "man-to-man" staff assignments. *Journal of Applied Behavior Analysis, 5*, 225–232.

Levine, D., O'Neal, E., & McDonald, P. (1980). Classroom ecology: The effects of seating position on grades and participation. *Personality and Social Psychology Bulletin, 6*, 409–416.

Lewin, K. (1948). *Resolving social conflicts*. New York: Harper.

Loewy, J.H. (1977). *Effects of density, motivation, and learning situation on classroom achievement*. Paper presented at the American Psychological Association Convention, San Francisco.

Loo, C.M. (1972). The effects of spatial density upon the social behavior of children. *Journal of Applied Social Psychology, 2*, 372–381.

Loo, C.M. (1978). Density, crowding, and preschool children. In A. Baum & Y.M. Epstein (Eds.), *Human response to crowding* (pp. 371–388). Hillsdale, NJ: Erlbaum.

Loo, C.M. & Kennelly, D. (1978). *Social density: Its effects on behaviors and perceptions of preschoolers*. Paper presented at the American Psychological Association Convention, Toronto.

Loo, C.M., & Smetana, J. (1978). The effects of crowding on the behaviors and perceptions of 10-year-old boys. *Environmental Psychology and Nonverbal Behavior, 2*, 226–249.

Loughlin, C.E., & Suina, J.H. (1982). *The learning environment: An instructional strategy*. New York: Teachers College, Columbia University.

Mack, D. (1976). Privacy: A child's need to be alone in the classroom. *Teacher, 93*(6), 52–53.

McGrew, W.C. (1972). Interpersonal spacing of preschool children. In J.S. Bruner & K.J. Connolly (Eds.), *The development of competence in early childhood*. London: Academic.

McPartland, J.M., & McDill, E.L. (1977). *Violence in schools*. Lexington, MA: Lexington.

Meyer, J. (1971). *The impact of the open space school upon teacher influence and autonomy: The effects of an organizational innovation*. Stanford, CA: Stanford University. (ERIC Document Reproduction Service No. ED 0623 291)

Millard, R., & Simpson, D. (1980). Enjoyment and productivity as a function of classroom seating location. *Perceptual and Motor Skills, 50*, 439–444.

Moffitt, R.A. (1974). The effects of privacy and noise attenuation alternatives on the art-related problem solving performance of third and fourth grade children (Doctoral dissertation, Arizona State University, 1974). *Dissertation Abstracts International, 35*, (3) 1506A-1507A.

Montes, F., & Risley, T.R. (1975). Evaluating traditional day care practices: An empirical approach. *Child Care Quarterly, 4,* 208–215.

Moore, G.T. (1983, April). *Some effects of the organization of the social-physical environment on cognitive behavior in child care settings.* Paper presented at the Society for Research on Child Development, Detroit.

Moos, R.H. (1979). *Evaluating educational environments.* San Francisco: Jossey-Bass.

Morrison, T.L. (1979). Classroom structure, work involvement, and social climate in elementary school classrooms. *Journal of Educational Psychology, 71*(4), 471–477.

Morrow, L.M., & Weinstein, C.S. (1982, November). Increasing children's use of literature through program and physical design changes. *Elementary School Journal, 83*(2), 131–137.

Nadler, A., Bar-Tal, D., & Drukman, O. (1982). Density does not help: Help-giving, help-seeking and help-reciprocating of residents in high and low student dormitories. *Population and Environment, 5,* 26–42.

Nash, C. (1979). *The learning environment: A practical approach to the education of the three, four, and five year old.* Toronto: Collier Macmillan.

Nash, C. (1981). The effects of classroom spatial organization on four- and five-year-old children's learning. *British Journal of Psychology, 51,* 144–155.

Neill, S.R. St. J. (1982). Preschool design and child behavior. *Journal of Child Psychology and Psychiatry, 23*(3), 309–318.

Neill, S.R. St. J., & Denham, E.J.M. (1982). The effects of preschool building design. *Educational Research, 24*(2), 107–111.

Nicholson, S. (1971). How not to cheat children: The theory of loose parts. *Landscape Architecture, 62,* 30–34.

Oickle, E.A. (1980). A comparison of individual and team teaching. *Dissertation Abstracts International, 41,* 3864A-3865A. (University Microfilms No. 8104965).

O'Neill, P. (1974). Creative children in open space and self-contained classroom. In *Educational and Psychological Effects of Open Space Education in Oak Park, Illinois.* Chicago Circle: University of Illinois.

Parker, R.K., & Day, M.C. (1972). Comparisons of preschool curricula. In R.K. Parker (Ed.), *The preschool in action: Exploring early childhood programs.* Boston: Allyn & Bacon.

Paolitto, D.P. (1976). The effects of cross-age tutoring on adolescence: An inquiry into theoretical assumptions. *Review of Educational Research, 46,* 215–237.

Peshkin, A. (1982). *The imperfect union: School consolidation and community conflict.* Chicago: University of Chicago Press.

Pintrich, P.R., & Blumenfeld, P.C. (1982). *Teacher and student behavior in different activity structures.* Paper presented at the annual meeting of the American Educational Research Association, New York.

Plath, K. (1965). *Schools within schools: A study of high school organization.* New York: Teachers College, Bureau of Publications, Columbia University.

Preiser, W. (1972). Behavior of nursery school children under different spatial densities. *Man-Environment Systems, 2,* 247–250.

Prescott, E. (1973). *Who thrives in day care?* Pasadena, CA: Pacific Oaks College.

Prescott, E. (1981). Relations between physical setting and adult/child behavior in day care. *Advances in Early Education and Day Care, 2,* 129–158.

Prescott, E., Kritchevsky, S., & Jones, E. (1972). *The day care inventory.* Unpublished manuscript, Pacific Oaks College, Pasadena, CA.

Price, J.M. (1971). The effects of crowding on social behavior of children. *Dissertation Abstracts International, 33,* 471B (University Microfilms No. 72-19151).

Proshansky, E., & Wolfe, M. (1974). The physical setting and open education: Philosophy and practice. *Social Review, 82,* 557–574.

Quillitch, H.R., & Risley, T.R. (1973). The effects of play materials on social play. *Journal of Applied Behavior Analysis, 6,* 573–578.

Reiss, S., & Dydhalo, N. (1975). Persistence, achievement, and open space environments. *Journal of Educational Psychology, 67,* 506–513.

Rogers, C.O. (1976). *The relationship between the organization of play space and children's behavior.* Oklahoma State University, Stillwater. (ERIC Document Reproduction Service No. ED 127 011)

Rohe, W.M., & Nuffer, E. (1977). *The effects of density and partitioning on children's behavior.* Paper presented at the meeting of the American Psychological Association, San Francisco.

Rohe, W.M., & Patterson, A.J. (1974). The effects of varied levels of resources and density on behavior in a day care center. In D.H. Carson (Ed.), *Man-environment interactions: The evaluations and applications.* Stroudsberg, PA: Dowden, Hutchinson, & Ross.

Rosenthal, B. (1973). *An ecological study of nursery school free play.* Paper presented at the meeting of the American Psychological Association, Montreal.

Ross, R.P. (1979). *Development and application of the openness quotient: A measure of the architectural openness of open plan schools.* Unpublished master's thesis, University of Kansas, Lawrence.

Ross, R.P. (1982, March). *Designing for privacy in the classroom: An ecological perspective.* Address at the meeting of the American Educational Research Association, New York.

Ross, R.P. (1984). *Variations in segment structure and their effects on transitional activities.* Paper presented at theannual meeting of the American Educational Research Association, New Orleans.

Ross, R.P. (1985). Elementary school activity segments and the transitions between them: Responsibilities of teachers and student teachers. (Doctoral dissertation, University of Kansas, Lawrence.)

Schoggen, P. (1984). *Student voluntary participation and high school size.* Address at the meeting of the American Psychological Association, Toronto.

Sharan, S. (1980). Cooperative learning in small groups: Recent methods and effects on achievement, attitudes, and ethnic relations. *Review of Educational Research, 50,* 241–272.

Sharan, S., Ackerman, Z., & Hertz-Lazarowitz, R. (1979). Academic achievement of elementary school children in small group versus whole class instruction. *Journal of Experimental Education, 48,* 125–129.

Sharan, S., & Sharan, Y. (1976). *Small-group teaching.* Englewood Cliffs, NJ: Educational Technology Publications.

Sheehan, R., & Day, D. (1975, December). Is open space just empty space? *Day Care and Early Education, 3,* 10–13.

Shure, M.B. (1963). Psychological ecology of a nursery school. *Child Development, 34,* 979–992.

Silverstein, J.M. (1979). Individual and environmental correlates of pupil problematic and nonproblematic classroom behavior. *Dissertation Abstracts International, 40105A,* 2567A (University Microfilms No. 79-25, 292).

Slavin, R.E. (1978). Student teams and achievement divisions. *Journal of Research and Development in Education, 12*(1), 39–49.

Slavin, R.E. (1983). *Cooperative learning.* New York: Longman.

Slavin, R.E›, Leavey, M., & Madden, N.A. (1982). *Effects of student teams and individualized instruction on student mathematics achievement, attitudes and behaviors.* Paper presented at the annual meeting of the American Education Research Association, New York.

Smith, P.K., & Connolly, K.J. (1980). *The ecology of preschool behavior.* Cambridge, MA: Cambridge University Press.

Sommer, R. (1970). The ecology of privacy. In H.M. Proshansky, W.H. Ittelson, & L.G. Rivlin (Eds.). *Environmental psychology: Man and his physical setting.* New York: Holt, Rinehart & Winston.

Steinizor, B. (1950). The spatial factor in face-to-face discussion groups. *Journal of Abnormal and Social Psychology, 45,* 552–555.

Stires, L. (1980). The effect of classroom seating location on student grades and attitudes: Environment or self-selection? *Environment and Behavior, 12*(2), 241–254.

Stodolsky, S.S. (1983). Classroom activity structures in the fifth grade. (Contract No. 400-77-0094). Washington, DC: National Institute of Education.

Sutfin, H.D. (1982). The effect on children's behavior of a change in the physical design of a kindergarten classroom. *Journal of Man-Environment Relations, 1*(3), 30–41.

Taylor, A.P., & Vlastos, G. (1975). *School zone: Learning environments for children.* New York: Van Nostrand Reinhold.

Totusek, P., & Staton-Spicer, A. (1982). Classroom seating preference as a function of student personality. *Journal of Experimental Education, 505,* 159–163.

Traub, R.E., & Weiss, J. (1974). Studying openness in education: An Ontario example. *Journal of Research and Development in Education, 8,* 47–59.

Traub, R.E., Weiss, J., Fisher, C., Musella, D., & Kahn, S. (1973). *An evaluation study of Wentworth County Roman Catholic Separate School Board Schools.* Toronto: Ontario Institute for Studies in Education, Educational Evaluation Centre.

Trickett, E.J. (1978). Toward a social-ecological conception of adolescent socialization: Normative data on contrasting types of public school classrooms. *Child Development, 49,* 408–414.

Twardosz, S., Cataldo, M., & Risley, T. (1974). Open environment design infant and toddler day care. *Journal of Applied Behavioral Analysis, 7,* 529–546.

UNESCO (1979). *School furniture handbook 1 & 2.* New York: Author.

U.S. Bureau of the Census. (1983). *County and City Data Book.* Washington, DC: U.S. Government Printing Office.

Vliestra, A.G. (1980). Effects of adult-directed activity, number of toys, and sex of child on social and exploratory behavior in young children. *Merrill-Palmer Quarterly, 26*(3), 231–238.

Volkmor, C.B., Langstaff, A.L., & Higgins, M. (1974). *Structuring the classroom for success.* Columbus, OH: Merrill.

Walberg, H.J. (1969). Physical and psychological distance in the classroom. *School Review, 77*(1), 64–70.

Walberg, H.J., & Ahlgren, A. (1970). Predictors of the social environment of learning. *American Educational Research Journal, 7,* 153–167.

Wallace, M.A., Hatfield, V.L., Goetz, E.M., & Etzel, B.C. (1976). Caring efficiently for young children: Control versus freedom. *School Applications of Learning Theory, 8*(3), 20–31.

Waller, W. (1965). *The sociology of teaching.* New York: Wiley.

Waish, D.P. (1975). Noise levels and annoyance in open plan educational facilities. *Journal of Architectural Research, 4,* 5–16.

Warner, R. (1984). *On-task behavior of handicapped and nonhandicapped children in an integrated school.* (Unpublished doctoral dissertation, University of Massachusetts, Amherst, 1984). *Dissertation Abstracts International, 45/01A.*

Webb, N.M., & Kenderski, C.M. (1984). Student interaction and learning in small group and whole class settings. In P. Peterson, L. Wilkinson, & M. Hallinan (Eds.), *The social context of education.* Orlando, FL: Academic.

Weigel, R.H., Wiser, P.L., Cook, S.W. (1975). The impact of cooperative learning experiences on cross ethnic relations and attitudes. *Journal of Social Issues, 31*, 219–244.

Weinstein, C.S. (1977). Modifying student behavior in an open classroom through changes in the physical design. *American Educational Research Journal, 14*, 249–262.

Weinstein, C.S. (1979). The physical environment of the school. A review of the research. *Review of Educational Research, 49*, 577–610.

Weinstein, C.S. (1981). Classroom design as an external condition for learning. *Educational Technology, 21*(8), 12–19.

Weinstein, C.S. (1982). Privacy seeking behavior in an elementary classroom. *Journal of Environmental Psychology, 2*, 23–35.

Weinstein, C.S. (1985). Seating arrangements in the classroom. *International Encyclopedia of Education*. New York: Pergamon.

Wheldall, K., Morris, M., Vaughan, P., & Ng, Y.Y. (1981). Rows versus tables: An example of the use of behavioral ecology in two classes of eleven-year-old children. *Educational Psychology, 1*(2), 171–184.

Wicker, A.W. (1968). Undermanning, performances, and students' subjective experiences in behavior settings of large and small high schools. *Journal of Personality and Social Psychology, 10*, 255–261.

Wicker, A.W. (1979). *An introduction to ecological psychology.* Monterey, CA: Brooks/Cole.

Willems, E.P. (1967). Sense of obligation to high school activities as related to school size and marginality of student. *Child Development, 38*, 1247–1260.

Wright, E.N., Shapson, S.M., Eason, C.T., & Fitzgerald, J. (1977). *Effects of class size in the junior grades.* Toronto: Ministry of Education, Ontario.

Wulf, K.M. (1977). Relationship of assigned classroom seating area to achievement variables. *Educational Research Quarterly, 21*, 56–62.

Yinger, R. (1979). Routines in teacher planning. *Theory into Practice, 18*, 163–169.

Chapter 19

WORK ENVIRONMENTS: OFFICES AND FACTORIES

Eric Sundstrom, *Department of Psychology, University of Tennessee, Knoxville, Tennessee*

This chapter discusses empirical findings on the physical environment in offices and factories. It analyzes the relationships between aspects of the environment and selected outcomes at three levels of analysis: individual, interpersonal, and organizational.

The term *office* refers here to settings where the primary activities comprise the handling of information and the making of plans and decisions. Examples include facilities devoted to accounting, administration, banking, finance, insurance, publishing, or research. By one estimate, half of the U.S. labor force works in offices (Giuliano, 1982). The term *factory* refers to facilities devoted to the conversion of raw materials into marketable products, such as textiles,

electronic equipment, parts, food, clothing, or small appliances. (Other work environments outside the scope of this chapter include "smokestack" facilities, such as steel refineries and chemical plants, as well as retail stores, restaurants, vehicles, farms, mines, and specialized habitats, such as offshore drilling platforms.)

Physical environment refers here to properties of buildings that contain offices and factories, particularly their interior conditions and arrangements. This chapter does not use the broader definitions of *environment* sometimes applied to organizations, which refer to the geographical location or region (see Bass & Bass, 1976) or to the external conditions of an organization, such as competing organizations, natural resources, political conditions, or labor (see Aldrich, 1979; Starbuck, 1983).

This chapter emphasizes *empirical findings* relevant to selected issues in offices and factories. Therefore the coverage of each topic depends in part on the amount of research available. Some topics, such as noise, have been studied extensively and receive more space than others. Less studied topics, such as the role of physical environment in organizations, receive less space but not because they are less important.

The review of empirical research follows the prevailing practice of attempting to link aspects of the physical environment with key *outcomes*. These consist of psychological, social psychological, and organizational variables traditionally regarded as criteria in empirical studies.

The scope is limited by the outcomes chosen. Those emphasized here include individual satisfaction and performance, interpersonal communication, group formation and cohesion, and organizational effectiveness. The discussion does not extend to outcomes involving health or safety.

The chapter consists of six sections and a summary. The first section presents an analytic framework, which provides the basis for the organization of the review. The second section discusses the current status of the empirical research literature. The main body comprises three sections, which discuss findings and theories on the role of the physical environment for individual workers, interpersonal relationships, and organizations. The sixth section discusses the future of offices and factories.

19.1. FRAMEWORK FOR ANALYSIS

The analytic framework used here grows out of a perspective that treats people and their work environments as interdependent elements of systems. The framework rests on three premises. First, an understanding of relationships between people and environments calls for a distinction among levels of analysis: individuals, interpersonal relationships, and organizations. Second, the critical facets of the physical environment differ as a function of the level of analysis. Third, each level of analysis involves different dynamic processes—psychological, social psychological, and organizational—and different outcomes.

A systems analysis suggests that environmental relationships are complex and may change with time (Altman & Chemers, 1980). Such changes involve coping and other forms of adaptation. *Coping* includes any active attempt to alter an unsatisfactory environment or its effects. *Adaptation* includes coping as well as any other response directed toward increased comfort or ease on functioning in an environment (e.g., Dubos, 1980). An analysis of connections between environmental factors and critical outcomes needs to take account of the full range of such adaptive responses, at all levels of analysis.

19.1.1. Levels of Analysis

The three levels of analysis used here include individual workers, interpersonal relationships, and organizations. They overlap, in that events at one level affect the others. For instance, when an organization moves into an unpartitioned office, the workers may experience dissatisfaction with the environment (an individual outcome). Diminished privacy may make them reluctant to talk about confidential matters in the office, which could lead to inadequate communication (interpersonal outcomes). Dissatisfaction and inadequate communication may damage the effectiveness of the organization as a whole (organizational outcome).

Individual Workers
For the individual, analysis focuses on the immediate physical surroundings during work. These include *ambient conditions*: illumination, temperature, air, and sound (Parsons, 1976), which can change from moment to moment. The individual's environment also includes characteristics of the building, its furnishings, and its equipment, particularly those that comprise the work space or work station. *Work station* refers here to an area designed for work by one person. *Work space* refers to a work station assigned to a specific individual.

Interpersonal Relationships
The environment can enter into peoples' choices regarding communication, and the occupants of an environment may adjust their settings to regulate their encounters with each other. For example, an office in which visitors talk with the occupant from across a desk may foster formal encounters. But the occupant may prefer formal encounters and may deliberately arrange the office to foster them. The office can also serve a *symbolic* function, expressing either the occupant's self-identity or status in the organization.

Organizations

An *organization* is defined as a collection of people working in concert toward joint goals, with each person occupying a specific role and position in the hierarchy of authority. An organization also includes the tangible and nontangible resources under its direct control, such as buildings, machinery, equipment, materials, and information. Offices and factories represent components of organizations and resources for attainment of organizational goals. Under ideal circumstances, the environment within an organization is congruent with its other properties.

19.1.2. Facets of the Work Environment

The three levels of analysis deal with the work environment in terms of units of varying size and scale. At the smallest scale, the individual level of analysis focuses on the worker's immediate surroundings—the ambient conditions, the work station or work space, and the supporting environment. The interpersonal level of analysis also addresses work spaces, but concentrates on their convenience for conversation and symbolic capacities. (Symbolic properties of the work space refer to features that visibly differentiate people in terms of status, self-identity, or other characteristics.) The interpersonal level of analysis also focuses on the layout of the work area: proximity of work spaces, enclosure of work spaces, and features of settings used for conversation outside of work spaces. The organizational level of analysis deals with the physical environment at the largest scale, focusing on the internal layout and external configuration of buildings, including such things as the proximity, enclosure, and differentiation of work units.

As the scale of the work environment becomes larger, it becomes more and more difficult to describe its properties in purely physical terms. For the individual, it is possible to define environmental variables, such as ambient temperature and intensity of illumination. However, this is not possible for interpersonal relationships because more than one element of the physical setting can serve the same function, and each element can serve more than one function. For instance, status is symbolized in offices through a wide range of physical features, such as a private office, size of desk, presence of carpeting, and so forth. However, each of these elements serves other functions. So beyond the individual level of analysis, the discussion focuses on social psychological and organizational *processes* and the

ways in which they incorporate the environment, rather than on the environment itself. Table 19.1 shows key facets of the physical environment for the three levels of analysis.

19.1.3. Processes and Outcomes

Each level of analysis involves a separate set of processes, shown in Table 19.1. The individual level of analysis focuses on psychological processes, such as stress and overload. The interpersonal level focuses on social psychological processes, such as choices in communication or regulation of social interaction. At the organizational level the processes comprise the dynamics of the organization.

The outcomes emphasized at each level of analysis appear in the last column. For the individual worker, traditional outcomes include job satisfaction and job performance (e.g., Porter, Lawler, & Hackman, 1975). (*Job satisfaction* is defined here as an individual's general evaluation of the job, considering all of its characteristics.) Another outcome, satisfaction with the physical environment, represents a component of job satisfaction (e.g., Locke, 1983). *Performance* refers to an individual's efficiency, timeliness, accuracy, or other criterion of accomplishment of the job.

At the interpersonal level, outcomes are difficult to separate from processes. Important outcomes include the adequacy of communication and the formation and cohesion of work groups. However, these outcomes are themselves processes. Communication encompasses all of the processes listed for the interpersonal level of analysis.

The organizational level focuses on the general outcome of *organizational effectiveness*, defined here as the extent to which an organization efficiently accomplishes its mission while maintaining continued viability. By this definition, effectiveness encompasses the maintenance of high levels of satisfaction and performance among employees, acceptable levels of productivity, adequate communication, and supportive relationships with the organization's external environment (e.g., Katz & Kahn, 1978). Organizational effectiveness depends on events at the individual and interpersonal levels, as well as events for the organization as a whole.

In sum, the framework for analysis defines three levels of analysis—individual, interpersonal, and organizational—and identifies facets of the physical environment, processes, and selected outcomes for each. This framework guides the remainder of the chapter.

Table 19.1. Levels of Analysis, Facets of the Environment, Processes, and Outcomes

Level of Analysis	Facets of Physical Environment	Key Processes	Outcomes

Individual workers	Ambient Conditions
	  Temperature
	  Air quality
	  Lighting
	  Noise
	  Music
	Work Stations
	  Color
	  Equipment
	  Chair
	  Floor space
	Supporting
	Environment
	Hallways
	Restrooms
	Work areas, etc.
		Adaptation
		Arousal
		Overload
		Stress
		Fatigue
		Attitudes
			Satisfaction
			Performance

Interpersonal relationships	Work spaces
	  Differentiation
	  Room layout
	    Seating
	      arrangements
	    Furniture
	Building layout
	  Inter-work-space
	    proximity
	  Enclosure of
	    work spaces
	  Gathering places
		Self-identity
		Status
		Regulation of
		  immediacy
		Self-presentation
		Choices in
		  communication
		Regulation of
		  interaction
		  (privacy)
			Adequacy of communication
			Group formation
			Group cohesion

Organizations	Buildings
	  Separation of
	    work units
	  Differentiation
	    of work units
		Congruence of
		  organizational
		  structure and
		  physical
		  environment
			Organizational
			  effectiveness

Source: Sundstrom, E., *Work Places*, Cambridge University Press, 1986. Reproduced with permission.

19.2. STATUS OF EMPIRICAL RESEARCH

Empirical research on offices and factories is best described as uneven. Extensive research exists on some topics, but practically none exists on many others. Studies of factories have been rare, and studies of offices have been less than plentiful.

The largest literature exists in the fields of human factors psychology, engineering psychology, and ergonomics, all of which concern the design of equipment and environments. This research is dominated by isolated studies of specific problems, often with minimal ties to theory. Less extensive research exists in industrial and organizational psychology, where studies of the physical environment have been relatively infrequent since World War II. Environmental psychologists have only lately begun to study work environments (Wineman, 1982).

The following section identifies predominant strategies of research and the extent of their application to the work environment.

19.2.1. Strategies of Research

Research on work environments has incorporated four basic strategies: field experiments, laboratory experiments, field studies, and surveys.

Field experiments involve direct interventions in work environments, coupled with systematic measurements to assess their impact. Early field experiments were often primitive; some involved little more than measurements of production before and after a change at a factory (e.g., Luckiesh, 1924). Primitive field experiments allow many threats to the validity of inference (Cook & Campbell, 1979). Field experiments incorporating more sophisticated research designs have been rare.

Laboratory experiments allow researchers to establish causal connections between aspects of the physical environment and participants' responses in artificial settings. Generalizability of the findings to actual work settings is always open to question. Even so, the laboratory has been the principal location for studying the effects of the ambient conditions—particularly noise, temperature, and lighting.

Laboratory experiments on the influence of the environment on performance have used five types of tasks:

1. *Clerical* tasks involve the identification or transcription of symbols, as in typing or checking numbers.

2. *Mental* tasks involve the learning, recall, integration, or transformation of information, as in calculation, proofreading, or coding.

3. *Motor* tasks, like some factory jobs, call for the coordinated manipulation of controls or materials in response to signals, displays, or instructions. Examples include assembly and "tracking."

4. *Vigilance* tasks call for the monitoring of one or more sources of information and the detection of irregularities. The signals are often machine-paced. Vigilance resembles inspection of output or monitoring of machinery in factories.

5. *Dual* tasks call for the simultaneous performance of two tasks, one of which is usually a form of vigilance.

Laboratory experiments have two major limitations. First, their duration is brief—usually only a few minutes to a few hours. So they can only deal with short-term phenomena. Second, they artificially constrain the adaptive responses of participants. In experiments on noise, for instance, people voluntarily endure conditions that they might not ordinarily tolerate in an office or factory. So their capacity to register normal adaptive responses is open to question.

Field studies incorporate measurements of the physical environment, along with psychological or social psychological variables in actual offices and factories. They incorporate no interventions into the environment and seek only the correlations among the variables under study. Although field studies cannot establish a basis for inferring causal connections, they do involve actual work settings.

Surveys involve the systematic asking of questions, either written or oral. A major advantage is the number and diversity of people who can be included. Another advantage is the range of issues that can be covered in one study. Like other techniques, however, surveys allow certain forms of bias (e.g., Babbie, 1975). Furthermore, surveys are limited to the responses to environments that people are able and willing to report, but cannot assess reactions of which people are unaware or unwilling to reveal.

19.2.2. Current Literature

Empirical research on offices and factories cited in the present review appears in Table 19.2, which shows the number of studies of each type, for each topic. Where research is most plentiful, it is dominated by laboratory experiments. For very few topics are there more than a handful of field studies or field experiments.

An important development in research on offices has been the appearance of comprehensive studies that attempt to deal with the physical environment as a whole. Some of the earliest occurred in England (e.g., Langdon, 1966; Manning, 1965) and incorporated surveys of workers' perceptions and direct measurements of the office environment. A similar approach was applied to open-plan offices (e.g., Boyce, 1973; Nemecek & Grandjean, 1973). The few comprehensive office studies in the United States have comprised surveys of office employees (e.g., Buffalo Organization for Social and Technical Innovation, Inc., 1981; Harris & Associates, 1978, 1980).

Comprehensive studies include postoccupancy evaluations or research done to assess the general adequacy of a new building. Such studies generally deal with many facets of the environment. Postoccupancy evaluations typically incorporate surveys but sometimes also include objective measurements (e.g., in offices, Marans & Spreckelmeyer, 1982; Wineman, 1982).

In sum, the empirical research concerning offices and factories involves several disciplines, including environmental psychology, ergonomics, human factors, human engineering, and industrial-organiza-

Table 19.2. Empirical Studies Concerning the Physical Environment in Offices and Factories[a]

Level of Analysis and Topic of Study	Numbers of Studies Cited				
	Laboratory Experiments	Field Experiments	Surveys	Field Studies	Totals
Individual worker					
Lighting	13	1	—	5	19
Windows	—	—	3	1	4
Temperature	27	2	2	8	39
Air quality	4	—	2	1	7
Noise	72	1	1	1	75
Music	9	9	1	—	19
Color	25	—	1	—	26
Work-stations	2	—	5	1	8
Interpersonal relations					
Status	—	—	1	1	2
Personalization and participation	—	1	1	3	5
Ambient conditions and interaction	8	—	—	—	8
Proximity of work spaces and interaction of groups	—	—	—	9	9
Room layout and interaction	11	—	1	9	21
Privacy and enclosure	—	—	4	8	12
Seating arrangement and group discussions	12	—	—	—	12
Organization					
Organization, structural and physical layout	—	—	—	1	1
Comprehensive studies and postoccupancy evaluations	—	2	15	6	23
Totals	183	16	37	54	290

[a]An empirical study is a self-contained report of a research project that involved the collection of original data, with detailed descriptions of methods and results. Each study is counted only once, even if it has multiple experiments. Studies that share a common data base are counted separately if they report separate findings. Studies that deal with more than two of the topics are counted as comprehensive studies.

Source: Sundstrom, E., *Work Places*, New York: Cambridge University Press, 1986. Reproduced with permission.

tional psychology. The literature is uneven, in both the topics studied and the methods used. Of four major methods—field experiment, field study, survey, and laboratory experiment—the laboratory experiment has been most prevalent.

19.3. THE INDIVIDUAL WORKER

This section discusses the relationship between the individual worker and his or her immediate physical environment. It begins by outlining some psychological processes that might mediate the worker's relationships with the environment. Then specific aspects of the work environment are discussed: light-

ing, temperature, air quality, noise, music, windows, color, work stations, and supportive facilities.

19.3.1. Psychological Processes

Hypotheses concerning the relationship between people and environments deal with potential influences on both performance and satisfaction. Proposed sources of influence on performance include arousal, stress, distraction and overload, and fatigue. These may be modified by adaptation. Processes involved in job satisfaction concern the individual's perception of the relative importance of various characteristics of the job, one of which comprises the physical working conditions.

Arousal

The terms *arousal* and *activation* refer to the general level of physiological and psychological excitation or alertness (e.g., Duffy, 1962; Scott, 1966). Arousal is thought to be influenced by temperature, noise, music, and perhaps lighting and color (e.g., Welford, 1973). The *arousal hypothesis* holds that performance is best at moderate levels of arousal but deteriorates when arousal is too high or too low (e.g., Hebb, 1949). Its main corollary concerns the task—optimum arousal for simple tasks is higher than for complex tasks (Yerkes & Dodson, 1908). Similarly, well-learned or familiar tasks are thought to have a higher optimum arousal than new or unfamiliar ones.

According to the arousal hypothesis, a work environment that augments a person's arousal leads to improved performance if it raises the level of arousal to the optimum for the task. However, augmented arousal can degrade performance by raising arousal beyond the optimum. Similarly, an environment that brings arousal below optimum leads to poorer performance. The arousal hypothesis has often been used to account for effects of the work environment, particularly short-term effects (e.g., Broadbent, 1971; Poulton, 1970).

Stress

Stress may be defined as a physiological and psychological response to a perceived threat, demand, challenge, or adversity that includes arousal and active attempts at coping (e.g., Baum, Singer, & Baum, 1981; McGrath, 1970, 1976). Environmental stress depends to a large extent on the individual's appraisal of the environment as containing threats to his or her continued well-being (Cohen, 1980b). Stress could occur in response to many features of an office or factory, especially aversive conditions that occur unpredictably and uncontrollably (e.g., Averill, 1973; Glass & Singer, 1972).

Short-term influences of environmental stress on performance are predicted by the arousal hypothesis. However, one potential effect it does not predict is the *narrowing of attention* (e.g., Saegert, Mackintosh, & West, 1975; Solly, 1969). Furthermore, research on the "aftereffects" of stressors suggests that adverse effects of stress can appear after the stressor is removed (Cohen, 1980a).

Distraction and Overload

The physical environment can create distraction through salient events or through conditions that momentarily draw a person's attention from the task and disrupt his or her concentration. If the environment contains enough distractions, it may create *overload* by occupying more of a person's capacity than can be spared from the task while still maintaining effective performance. Possible sources of overload in the office or factory might include noises, music, flicker from fluorescent lights, uncomfortable temperatures, or poorly designed seating. Events most likely to distract people are sudden, novel events, such as unfamiliar noises, compelling conditions, such as glare, or meaningful events, such as co-workers' conversations. The predicted effect of such conditions on performance depends on the demands of the task. Environmental sources of distraction or overload may only affect people doing tasks so demanding that a temporary diversion of attention leads to poorer performance.

What might be called the "overload hypothesis" applies to people who receive information or stimulation faster or in greater volume than they can handle. One likely response is "ignoring low-priority inputs" (Milgram, 1970; Miller, 1964). If the environment creates or allows events compelling or salient enough to take precedence over the task, then elements of the task itself may become low-priority inputs. On the other hand, with time, people may adapt to sources of distraction in their environments and treat the environment itself as the low-priority input. When adaptation is possible, overload may be a short-term phenomenon.

Fatigue

Aspects of the office or factory may create *fatigue*, which once was defined as including a short-term loss of mental capacity (Blum & Naylor, 1968). The term now refers to the effects of prolonged muscular exertion (Woodson, 1981). Sources of muscular fatigue include features of equipment, such as poorly designed video screens or chairs.

Adaptation

Whether the environment leads to arousal, stress, distraction, overload, or fatigue, these processes may be modified by adaptation (e.g., Dubos, 1980). If so, responses to offices and factories change with time. *Adaptation* is defined here as a response by the occupant(s) of an environment directed toward an increase in comfort or ease of functioning. Adaptation includes (1) metabolic changes, as in acclimatization; (2) automatic physiological responses, as in dilation of the pupils in the dark; (3) changes in perception; (4) changes in habits, such as a slower pace of work; and (5) actions designed to alter an inhospitable environment or its effects, or coping behaviors.

Adaptation through changes in perception, or *perceptual adaptation*, can involve changes in a person's psychological standard of reference, or adaptation level (Helson, 1964). For instance, a new factory worker may find the factory noisy by comparison to familiar settings, but after a while his or her standard of reference may change as he or she comes to regard the factory as less noisy. Such an outcome is predicted by the adaptation-level hypothesis, which has reasonably strong empirical support (Wohlwill, 1975).

Influences on Job Satisfaction

The relationship between the work environment and an individual's job satisfaction depends on the general contribution of the physical environment to job satisfaction and on specific features of the environment. As shown in Figure 19.1, features of the office or factory may be viewed as contributors to satisfaction with the physical environment, which in turn may be regarded as one of many components of job satisfaction. (The figure ignores indirect effects of the environment, such as the influence of temperature on social interaction and in turn on relationships with coworkers.)

The connection of environmental satisfaction with job satisfaction has been addressed in two major theories. Maslow (1943) suggested that the physical environment can help satisfy a person's basic needs but only becomes salient when it threatens not to satisfy them. Once the needs for physical safety, security, and shelter are met, the individual ignores those needs and proceeds to seek satisfaction of higher order needs (higher in the hierarchy of needs). These include needs for social relationships and self-development. The theory has little empirical support (Wahba & Bridwell, 1975). Even so, it has been influential in industrial psychology (e.g., McGregor, 1960).

A later theory by Herzberg (1966; Herzberg, Mausner, & Synderman, 1959) identified two types of job factors—"satisfiers" and "dissatisfiers"—and labeled the physical environment as a dissatisfier. According to this theory, a dissatisfier detracts from job satisfaction through unsatisfactory conditions but only leads to indifference when conditions are satisfactory. In contrast, a satisfier, such as an intrinsically interesting task, contributes to job satisfaction when present but only leads to indifference when ab-

sent. Empirical research on the theory has failed to find a clear-cut distinction between satisfiers and dissatisfiers. However, the research has usually found the physical work environment primarily a source of dissatisfaction (Locke, 1983).

The theories by Maslow and by Herzberg imply that the physical environment may be important for job satisfaction (or at least for the absence of dissatisfaction) but that people tend to overlook it as long as it is minimally adequate. Attribution theory explains the tendency of people to overlook the environment as a consequence of the *fundamental attribution error* or the habit of ascribing feelings and behavior to the influences of other people, rather than the situation (Ross, 1977). If so, workers may routinely underestimate the contribution of their environments to their satisfaction (Taylor, 1982).

Surveys on job satisfaction have provided evidence consistent with the theories—workers have generally identified physical working conditions as one component of their job satisfaction but not one of the most important ones. Early studies asked employees to rank facets of their jobs in terms of importance for their general satisfaction. A review of 20 such studies, including a combined total of over 11,000 workers, found "working conditions" ranked tenth in the list of 14 factors, after such things as job security, interesting work, and wages (Herzberg, Mausner, Peterson, & Capwell, 1957). A survey of 2287 London officer workers included a list of 10 job factors and asked for the two most important ones; the 2 items on the office ranked sixth and seventh (Langdon, 1966). A Swedish survey of 450 office workers asked for ranking of 10 job factors and found the physical environment seventh in importance (Lunden, 1972). A poll of 2300 readers of *Psychology Today*, mostly white-collar workers, found that the physical environment ranked least important of 18 job factors (Renwick & Lawler, 1978). A survey of a sample of 1047 U.S. office workers by Harris and Associates (1978) asked for ratings of importance of 19 job factors and found the two on the office environment fourteenth and seventeenth on the list. The items were rated "very important" by 45% of 37% of the sample.

The results of the surveys on job satisfaction may be misleading. The physical environment often may have been adequate enough to be taken for granted and ignored. If so, workers may have overlooked it and underestimated its importance for their satisfaction, partly because of adaptation or misattribution of their experiences to other people instead of the environment.

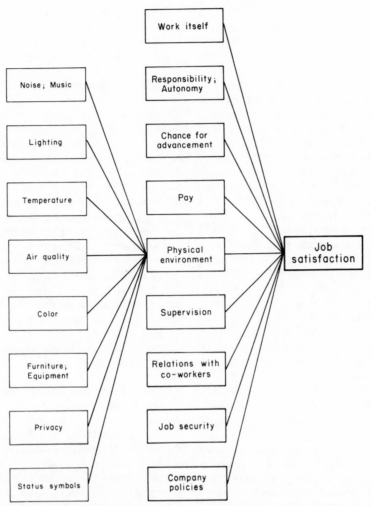

Figure 19.1. Contribution of facets of the physical environment to job satisfaction (from Sundstrom, E. *Work Places,* New York: Cambridge University Press, 1986. Reproduced with permission.)

Surveys concerning job satisfaction typically asked workers how important they believed the physical environment was for their general satisfaction. This approach is based on workers' perception of an association. As an alternative, some researchers assessed employees' satisfaction with the environment, independently assessed their job satisfaction, and investigated the statistical association. This approach does not depend on the accuracy of workers' beliefs concerning the relationship.

At least five field studies have included independent measures of environmental satisfaction and job satisfaction and reported a correlation. Zalesny, Farace, and Kurchner-Hawkins (1983) studied 420 of-fice employees and found job satisfaction correlated with satisfaction with the physical environment as a whole. Similar findings were reported by BOSTI (Buffalo Organization for Social and Technical Innovation, Inc., 1981), Ferguson (1983), Sundstrom, Burt, and Kamp (1980), and Sundstrom, Town, Brown, Forman, and McGee (1982).

The study by BOSTI (1981) included an analysis of office employees' responses before and after changing offices and found corresponding changes in job satisfaction. A total of 389 office employees were questioned about their work environments about 2 months before and 10 months after their offices were either renovated or relocated. (Their jobs and supervisors stayed the same.) Employees showed a general decline in job satisfaction after the change. However, those who reported greater environmental satisfaction after the change showed no decline; those whose environmental satisfaction stayed constant showed decline in job satisfaction; those whose environmental satisfaction declined showed the greatest decrease in job satisfaction (p. 38). This finding is consistent with the idea that the physical environment contributes to job satisfaction.

One psychological process important to the effects of the environment on job satisfaction is *equity*, or the perceived fairness of the exchange between employer and employee (e.g., Adams, 1965). If an employee views the environment as less than he or she deserves by comparison to other people or by reference to a personal standard, then even an apparently adequate environment may lead to job dissatisfaction. On the other hand, a worker may cheerfully tolerate an inadequate environment if he or she feels adequately compensated in other areas, such as wages or satisfying social relationships. (The theory also implies that people should feel dissatisfied in environments they see as excessively nice, but research has usually found very little discomfort in such situations.) Conditions that prompt people to complain about the physical setting because of perceived inequity or to overlook its shortcomings because of compensating benefits apparently remain to be explored.

The contribution of the different facets of the environment to environmental satisfaction has seldom been investigated. The results of studies done in offices suggest that people can easily identify the most and least satisfactory features of their settings (e.g., Boyce, 1974; Harris & Associates, 1978). However, research that has examined multiple facets of the environment has not explored the processes by which an individual arrives at judgments concerning the whole environment. (One untested possibility is that such judgments operate on a "weakest link" principle—the least adequate or most annoying feature of a particular work environment may be the one seen as having the strongest influence.)

In summary, the work environment may have short-term influences on individual performance through arousal, stress, overload, distraction, or fatigue. These effects may be modified by adaptation, which can include changes in perception and behavior. Job satisfaction depends on an individual's evaluation of the relative importance of various characteristics of the job, including the physical environment. However, for several reasons, people may overlook the environment as long as it is minimally adequate. Even so, surveys and field studies show a consistent association between satisfaction with the physical environment and job satisfaction.

19.3.2. Temperature

The influences of temperature are complex for several reasons. First, the sensation of heat or cold depends not only on the ambient air temperature but on relative humidity, speed of air movement, and the presence of radiant sources of heat (Bedford, 1964; McIntyre, 1980). Thermal comfort also depends on the individual's level of activity and the amount of clothing he or she is wearing (Fanger, 1972). Second, even when all of these factors are taken into account, people apparently still exhibit substantial differences in the climatic conditions they find comfortable (e.g., Griffiths, 1975; Grivel & Barth, 1980). Individual differences may be partly attributable to psychological factors, including suggestion (Stramler, Kleiss, & Howell, 1983). Another problem is that there may be no such thing as single comfortable temperature; people may instead prefer variable temperatures (e.g., Gerlach, 1974).

Temperature and Satisfaction

Survey research suggests that temperature represents a major source of discomfort and dissatisfaction in offices and factories. In a national survey, about one-third of office workers and half of factory workers reported unpleasant working conditions, and the foremost complaint concerned the temperature (32% of all problems mentioned; Quinn & Staines, 1979). Similarly, participants in a London survey included 25% who complained of overheating and 21% who complained about the cold (Langdon, 1966). Other surveys have found similar results (Black & Milroy, 1967; Boyce, 1974; Hedge, 1982; Manning, 1965).

One possible reason for discomfort with the temperature in offices is the diversity of conditions that people find uncomfortable. For instance, Harris and Associates (1980) reported that 81% of a sample of U.S. office workers said their ideal temperature was between 68° and 73°F whereas 19% found this range of temperature too warm or too cold. The median "ideal" temperature was 71°F but 4% of employees found this unacceptably warm and 4% found it unacceptably cold. Similarly, Nemecek and Grandjean (1973) found the majority of a sample of Western European office workers comfortable at 72°F (ambient temperature), but even at this temperature, about 20% were either too warm or too cold.

The BOSTI project (1981) linked thermal discomfort in offices with job dissatisfaction. Office workers who changed offices were surveyed before and after moving and were divided into groups for whom excessive temperature fluctuations became more frequent, became less frequent, or remained unchanged. Those whose offices brought more unwanted fluctuations reported a decline in job satisfaction.

Temperature and Performance

The psychological processes most likely to account for the effects of uncomfortably warm temperatures on performance are arousal and distraction. Heat may increase arousal, at least for the first few minutes of exposure, but after a while the body may react with normal or subnormal levels of arousal, depending on the effectiveness of homeostatic mechanisms (Bell, 1981; Poulton, 1980). Elevated or depressed arousal may affect performance. Uncomfortable heat may also be distracting and may affect performance by drawing attention from the task.

Field Studies

Studies in factories have often associated uncomfortable heat with relatively low individual output. The first in the series of studies sponsored by the British Industrial Fatigue Board investigated the correlation of seasonal variation in temperature and output and found summer heat associated with lower output in the manufacture of tinplate. However, in five separate factories, the two without ventilation systems showed the relationship most strongly, and one with a good ventilation system showed it hardly at all. The differences among the factories suggested that ventilation alleviated the adverse effects of heat on performance (Vernon, 1919). Another study found heat (and cold) associated with accidents in a munitions factory (Vernon, 1918). Similarly, an early study of linen weavers found that output declined as temperatures rose above 73°F (wet bulb), even though linen threads are easier to handle in hot, humid conditions (Weston, 1921). At a New Jersey garment factory, individual output declined as temperatures rose from 75°F to 90°F (Link & Pepler, 1970). On the other hand, a study at a Puerto Rican garment factory found no change in output after relocation to an air-conditioned building (Pepler, 1970). And at a welding operation, a cost-based index of average overall production was unrelated to daily ambient temperature, which reached 110°F (Lifson, 1957). (In both studies that found no relationship to heat and output, the indexes of production could have been influenced by other unmeasured factors.)

Laboratory Research

Studies of heat and performance suggest that the influence of temperature varies with the task.

Performance of *mental tasks* has generally been unaffected by heat, with a few exceptions. A review by Wing (1965) concluded that heat produces no reliable effects short of the physiological limits of tolerance. Three laboratory studies found mental performance unaffected by heat, even in temperatures over 92°F (effective temperature) for as long as 7 hours (Chiles, 1958; Fine, Cohen, & Crist, 1960; Pepler & Warner, 1968). One study found an improvement in performance at moderate heat, in relatively brief exposures (Givoni & Rim, 1962), which may reflect short-term arousal. Another study found no effects on one replication but a decrement in performance on another replication (Allen & Fischer, 1978). Four other studies reported decrements in performance of one or more tasks under hot, and sometimes humid conditions (Fine & Kobrick, 1978; Mackworth, 1950; Pepler, 1958; Viteles & Smith, 1946). In all but one of the experiments that showed a decrement, the tasks called for mental calculation plus quick visual searches or fast, coordinated use of the hands. The study with the longest exposures (Fine & Kobrick, 1978) involved the reception of signals over radio headphones. Participants recorded messages by hand and either decoded them or used them as a basis for rapid calculations. The decrement in performance became progressively worse during the last 3 of 7 hours of heat. The decrement could partly reflect the physiological costs in effort required in heat; it could also reflect low levels of arousal (Poulton, 1980).

Performance of *motor tasks* in heat has generally suffered in relevant laboratory experiments. Laboratory experiments found decrements in tracking or similar tasks (Mackworth, 1950; Pepler, 1958, 1959; Pepler & Warner, 1960; Teichner & Wehrkamp, 1954; Vaughn et al., 1968; Viteles & Smith, 1946). Studies that failed to find a decrement included one that found faster reaction time in 10-min exposures to heat, probably due to arousal (Bell, Provins, & Hiorns, 1964) and four others that used brief performance tests interspersed with periods of rest or alternate tasks (Nunnelley, Dowd, Myhre, Stribley, & McNee, 1979; Reilly & Parker, 1968; Russell, 1957). The adverse effect of heat on motor performance seems limited to continuous efforts lasting at least 30 min or so; the effect could reflect the extra physical exertion required by uncomfortable heat.

Laboratory research on the effects of heat on the performance of *vigilance tasks* has been inconsistent. Three studies found decrements using highly demanding tasks (Mackworth, 1950; Pepler, 1958; Reilly & Parker, 1968). For instance, in Mackworth's (1950) clock test, participants watched the hand of a dial as it revolved through 360° in 100 sec in equal 1 sec jumps, occasionally jumping twice the usual arc. The task was to detect the unusual jumps. This required constant attention, as even a 1 sec lapse could bring an error. Errors were more frequent under hot conditions. On the other hand, two studies found no decrement due to heat in moderately demanding tasks (Bell et al., 1964; Colquhoun & Goldman, 1972). The task in Bell et al. allowed up to 30 sec to identify each unusual signal, which was heralded by an oscillating indicator on one of 20 dials. In one study, moderate heat (79°F) facilitated vigilance (Mackworth, 1950). These findings can generally be explained in terms of arousal: an initially stimulating effect of heat or an eventual decline of arousal to subnormal levels in heat.

Studies of *dual tasks*—simultaneous performance of two tasks—have generally found an adverse effect of heat on the task labeled as *secondary*. The decrement usually involved errors of omission. In other words, participants tended to overlook low-priority details in heat, as predicted by theories of overload (e.g., Cohen, 1978).

Four studies reported a decrement in the performance of one of two simultaneous tasks (Azer, McNall, & Leung, 1972; Bell, 1978; Bursill, 1958; Griffiths & Boyce, 1971). Two other studies found a temporary increment in performance in heat, shortly after starting (Poulton & Kerslake, 1965; Provins & Bell, 1970).

Laboratory studies of the effects of cold temperatures on performance have been much less common than those on heat and have given inconsistent results. Pepler and Warner (1968) found that military personnel learned programmed material faster but made more errors in a slightly cool room (62°F) than at a comfortable temperature. Allen and Fischer (1978) found poorer learning of paired associates in one of two experiments in periods of 15 min in a cool room. Two studies found poor tracking at cool temperatures (Russell, 1957; Teichner & Wehrkamp, 1954). Another found poorer vigilance at 67°F than at warmer temperatures (Pepler, 1958). Vaughn, Higgens, & Funkhouser (1968) found no effect of cold (50°F) on tests of manual performance, although colder temperatures can impair manual dexterity (McIntyre, 1980).

In summary, field studies found large percentages of workers dissatisfied with the temperatures in their work places. A few field studies of factories associated uncomfortable heat with relatively low output. Laboratory studies showed that continuous performance of certain types of mental tasks, motor tasks, vigilance, and dual tasks was poorer in heat than at comfortable temperatures. Many adverse effects of heat on performance may be explained in terms of arousal. Sparse research on cold temperatures has yielded mixed results.

19.3.3. Air Quality

The central issue for air quality in offices and factories concerns *air pollution* or unwanted constituents, such as gas, dust, mist, vapor, fiber, or smoke. The relevance of air pollution for health has been well-documented (e.g., Evans & Jacobs, 1981). However, research on the psychological implications of air quality has been rare.

Air pollution does seem to be a problem in offices and factories. In a national survey in which half of factory workers and one-third of office workers reported unpleasant working conditions, over 6% of the complaints concerned the poor ventilation or specific air pollutants (Quinn & Staines, 1977). BOSTI (1981) reported that about one-quarter of office workers in the study said their offices were "too smoky" or "smelly"; this complaint was significantly correlated with dissatisfaction with the physical environment.

Cigarette smoke may represent a common type of air pollution in work environments. Harris and Associates (1980) reported that about one-third of the sample of U.S. office workers said they smoked. Of nonsmokers, 26% said that smoking by co-workers bothered them a great deal. Whereas half of those surveyed believed smoking should be limited to certain areas, 94% of company executives said smoking was not limited in their companies.

19.3.4. Lighting

Lighting in offices and factories lets people see what they are doing and can serve as a source of variety in the ambient environment. Research on lighting has emphasized the effects of its intensity, quality, or distribution on performance and satisfaction.

Lighting and Performance
The most heavily studied question on lighting concerns the influence of intensity or brightness of light on performance by workers. The traditional approach has been more pragmatic than psychological, concen-

trating on the effects of lighting on the visibility of details and on the consequences for performance related to visibility. One of the few exceptions is an early laboratory study that found quicker reaction time, faster multiplication, and quicker responses in a "tapping test" in bright light (Pressy, 1921). This cannot be explained through the visibility of details, but later research has apparently not explored the influences of lighting beyond visibility of details.

Early field research showed that after artificial lighting was added to factories, output sometimes increased substantially. For example, Luckiesh (1924) catalogued cases in which factory managers claimed that added lighting had increased production as much as 79% and decreased accidents as much as 60% (see also Hollingworth & Poffenberger, 1926). In Britain, the Industrial Fatigue Research Board sponsored studies of lighting that linked factory output with the intensity of the light. In a 15-week study of silk weavers, Elton (1920) measured the brightness of the sunlight in the building each day as it changed due to seasonal fluctuation. Output by the silk weavers roughly paralleled the brightness of the natural light, as it declined for 4 weeks and later increased for 10 weeks. Similarly, Weston (1921) recorded the natural illumination in a linen-weaving shop and found that the amount of sunlight declined during the last hours of work. The weavers' efficiency declined with the daylight. A study of typesetters showed similar results (Weston & Taylor, 1926). Similar findings have been reported in a variety of settings (e.g., Sucov, 1973). These field studies leave open the possibility that output was influenced by factors other than lighting, but the results are all consistent with the hypothesis that performance deteriorates when light is insufficient for seeing critical details.

Probably the best known studies of illumination occurred at the Hawthorne Works of the Western Electric Company. They were never reported in detail, but according to the summary by Roethlisberger and Dickson (1941), three experiments failed to link lighting with output by workers. In the first experiment, employees' output in three departments was recorded (small-part inspection, relay assembly, and coil winding), and lighting was varied, but output showed no consistent relationship with it. The second experiment involved the isolation of two groups of coil winders in separate buildings, with the lighting varied in one group. Output increased with lighting in the experimental group, but it also rose in the control group, where lighting was apparently constant.

In the third study, only one group of coil winders took part, isolated in a room illuminated only with artificial light. Their output rose slowly and steadily, despite decreases in lighting, until the experiment ended when the light was so dim that the workers complained of being unable to see what they were doing. One explanation for the increasing output in the Hawthorne Studies is that the researchers unknowingly motivated the workers by giving them detailed knowledge of their own output (Parsons, 1974). A possible reason for the lack of an effect of lighting in the last two studies is that the task of winding coils depends very little on visual cues. In the first study, the lowest level of light was probably sufficient to allow the workers to see the critical details of their tasks (Boyce, 1981).

Soon after the Hawthorne studies, researchers developed sophisticated techniques for studying the effects of lighting on performance in the laboratory. Weston's (1945) approach called for the visual discrimination of stimuli called *Landolt rings* (small circles, each with a gap pointed toward one of the eight points of the compass). Varying the size of the rings, their contrast against their background, and the intensity of lighting, Weston found that speed and accuracy in discriminating Landolt rings improved with added lighting, but improvements became smaller with each increment in lighting. Added light was quite beneficial for difficult versions of the task (small size, low contrast) but had negligible effects in the least difficult versions.

Later research confirmed Weston's findings, especially the diminishing benefits of added light, and found significant differences as a function of *age*. Older people were shown to need more light than younger people to attain equivalent levels of visual performance (Boyce, 1973). (This results from well-documented physiological changes in vision that occur with aging; see McCormick, 1976.)

The "visibility approach" developed in the United States as an extension of earlier laboratory techniques. It sought a single numerical index of visibility applicable to each task, based on size of detail, contrast, and intensity of illumination. Participants in this research watched a translucent screen and identified stimuli flashed onto it for periods as brief as one-hundredth of a second (Blackwell, 1959; Blackwell & Smith, 1970). This research was extrapolated to office and factory work and formed the basis of standards of illumination in offices and factories in the United States. U.S. standards are much higher than those of other industrialized countries, and some researchers have criticized the use of Blackwell's findings to establish them (Faulkner & Murphy, 1973; Murrell, 1965; Rapoport & Watson, 1967).

Some research has continued to use highly artificial measures of performance in simulated office work (e.g., Henderson, McNelis, & Williams, 1975; McNelis, Williams, & Henderson, 1975). However, a few studies have examined realistic measures of performance of office tasks. For example, Smith (1978) varied the lighting as volunteers did seven tasks, including reading, typing, proofreading, and other clerical duties. Results confirmed the earlier finding of diminishing returns of added lighting, though the most difficult tasks probably benefited most from added light. Another study used actual office tasks and confirmed that added light (from 50 to 150 footcandles) benefited older workers but not younger ones (Hughes, 1976).

The sparse research on the quality and distribution of lighting as related to performance has focused primarily on *glare*, or uncomfortably bright light emanating from the task or surrounding area. A laboratory experiment demonstrated that people involuntarily looked away from their tasks when confronted with bright lights in their fields of vision, demonstrating "phototropism" (Hopkinson & Longmore, 1959). Apparently, glare poses a compelling source of distraction, which may be expected to hurt the performance of some tasks in offices and factories.

Lighting and Satisfaction

Much of the limited research on lighting and satisfaction has investigated the intensity of light and found that added light provides successively smaller gains in satisfaction, but only up to a point. Extremely bright light has tended to create discomfort.

Survey research in offices has generally found the lighting to be one of the most satisfactory features of the physical environment (e.g., Harris & Associates, 1978; Langdon, 1966; Manning, 1965). On the other hand, a survey of an English open office found that one-third of participants rated their light as "too bright" (Hedge, 1982).

Some field research has found an increase in average lighting (from about 37 to 74 footcandles) associated with an increase in satisfaction with lighting (Boyce, 1974). However, another field study found reports of eye problems unusually frequent in very bright lighting (93 to 186 footcandles; Nemecek & Grandjean, 1973); these problems may have been due to glare.

A laboratory experiment revealed that people rated moderately intense lighting (35 footcandles)

barely satisfactory, and added light brought successively smaller increments in satisfaction (up to about 157 footcandles), though the increments were almost negligible after about 74 footcandles (Saunders, 1969). This finding agrees fairly well with the office studies and suggests that optimal lighting in offices may be about 40 to 80 footcandles.

Research linking the quality of artificial lighting and employees' satisfaction has been infrequent. Boyce (1974) reported an increase in office employees' perceptions that colors appeared "natural" after moving to an open office where lighting was predominantly artificial, provided by "natural" fluorescent lights. BOSTI (1981) found that reports that work spaces were "dark" and problems with glare or shadows were associated with dissatisfaction with the environment. A laboratory experiment revealed a preference for nonuniform lighting at the periphery of the room (Flynn, Spencer, Martyniuk, & Hendrick, 1973).

In summary, research on lighting suggests that the intensity of lighting can influence performance through its effects on the visibility of details. Field and laboratory research found improvements in performance associated with increased intensity of lighting in tasks involving visual discrimination, especially difficult tasks. However, in laboratory research, gains in performance diminished with each added increment of light. A well-established finding is that requirements for light increase with age. Surveys in offices found a majority of workers satisfied with lighting, but complaints about glare were associated with relatively bright light (over 100 footcandles).

19.3.5. Windows

Windows represent a source of illumination, but they can also affect a worker's ambient environment in other ways. By admitting natural light, windows provide a source of variable lighting, hence variety in the ambient environment. Windows can allow workers to see outside the building, providing a source of stimulation. In some cases they provide ventilation.

Research on windows has generally investigated their connection with employees' satisfaction. Most of the research consists of surveys (Collins, 1975). Several surveys of English office workers found a definite preference for windows (Longmore & Ne'eman, 1974; Manning, 1965; Markus, 1967). Employees whose desks were distant from windows tended to overestimate the contribution of sunlight to their total light (Wells, 1965a) and to express a greater preference for sunlight than those closer to windows

(Markus, 1967). (Reasons for wanting to work near a window generally included references to the view outside as well as to the natural light.)

In the United States, in contrast to England, there is no legal requirement for natural light. One survey among U.S. workers in windowless offices indicated some dissatisfaction (Ruys, 1970; see also Sommer, 1974). (Employees in windowless offices may be dissatisfied partly because of perceived inequity resulting from the lack of an amenity available to others.) In summary, the evidence from surveys suggests a connection between windows and satisfaction with the physical environment.

19.3.6. Noise

Noise usually refers to *unwanted sound* (Kryter, 1970). It is one of the most intensively studied aspects of the physical working environment. Noise has been viewed as a source of dissatisfaction and sometimes as an impediment to performance. It has been the subject of research by psychologists in the laboratory and the office but seldom in the factory.

Noise and Satisfaction

Surveys of office workers indicate that noise represents a prevalent problem. For instance, participants in the survey by Harris and Associates (1978) were asked to identify features of their offices important to getting their jobs done well. They chose from a list of 17 features of the office environment. (This part of the survey dealt only with the office environment, not other features of the job.) Participants chose the "ability to concentrate without noise and other distractions" more frequently than any other item on the list (p. 50). However, ratings of the adequacy of offices on this issue ranked fifteenth out of the 17 features. (In other words, quiet was seen as important but generally not available.) In a second survey, 49% of office workers complained of the lack of quiet in their offices (Harris & Associates, 1980). Similarly, the English study by Langdon (1966) found that noise made 20% of office workers "definitely uncomfortable." In another English survey, noise received lower ratings on "acceptability" than any other feature of the office environment (Keighley, 1970).

Noise apparently poses a particular problem in open-plan offices (e.g., Hedge, 1982; McCarrey, Peterson, Edwards, & Von Kulmiz, 1974). In open offices, walls that might contain the sound are minimal. Of nine studies of employees who moved from conventional to "open" offices, four found that complaints about noise became more prevalent (Boje,

1971; Hanson, 1978; Hundert & Greenfield, 1969; Kraemer, Sieverts, & Partners, 1977); four other studies reported no change in problems with noise, even though some incorporated special measures to combat noise, such as electronic background sound or insulated partitions (Boyce, 1974; Brookes, 1972; Sloan, n.d.; Sundstrom, Herbert, & Brown, 1982). Only one of nine studies found fewer problems with noise after moving to an open office; it, too, incorporated special measures for controlling noise (Riland & Falk, 1972).

Annoyance by noise in offices has been found unrelated to the average level of ambient sound in the open office (Boyce, 1974; Kraemer et al., 1977) and unrelated to the measured level of sound at individual work spaces (Nemecek & Grandjean, 1973). However, a major study found that annoyance was highly predictable from an objective index of noise based on "peak level" of sounds audible above the background sound (Keighley, 1970). Apparently, the average intensity of sound is less important than occasional episodes of sound audible above the background sounds.

The most annoying sources of office noise apparently consist of conversations by co-workers and ringing of telephones. For instance, Boyce (1974) found that over half of the workers in an open office were disturbed by people talking and by phones ringing. Similar findings were reported in other open offices (Brookes, 1972; Kraemer et al., 1977; Nemecek & Grandjean, 1973) and in conventional offices (Langdon, 1966). Noise from co-workers' conversations, although not necessarily loud, may be annoying because of their potential for carrying meaningful information and the resulting tendency to divert attention from one's work to listen. Ringing phones may be annoying because they signal a demand to respond, even if only to ascertain who should answer. (Less disturbing sounds, such as those made by office machines and ventilation equipment, usually carry neither information nor demands.)

Studies that have looked for a link between noise and dissatisfaction in the office have usually found it. Nemecek and Grandjean (1973) reported a strong, inverse relationship between individual disturbance by noise and preference for working in the open office. Sundstrom, Town, Osborn, Rice, Konar, Mandel, and Brill (1982) assessed disturbance by several different sources of noise in a group of office employees. Among workers who were questioned before and after changing offices, people were divided into groups for whom each type of noise increased, decreased, or remained the same after moving. Office workers who reported increases in noise from people talking, telephones, and typewriters expressed lower environmental satisfaction, and those for whom the noises decreased reported higher satisfaction. Noise from people talking was also linked with job dissatisfaction. BOSTI (1981) reported similar findings based on different analyses of the same data.

Noise and Performance

The effects of noise on performance have been studied extensively in the laboratory, with complicated results. One possible reason for the complexity of findings is the variety of psychological processes likely to be evoked by noise.

1. If loud enough, noise might create *arousal* but only until mitigated by adaptation. The brief effect may be beneficial or detrimental, depending on the task.

2. Loud, unfamiliar noise, if unexpected, may create *distraction*, which in turn could disrupt the performance of tasks that call for continued, short-term retention of information.

3. Repeated distraction could lead to *overload* and consequent ignoring of low-priority inputs.

4. Noise could mask sounds made during work that provide useful *feedback*, such as the sounds made by machinery that signal completed cycles or proper operation (Poulton, 1977).

5. Efforts to cope with noise may eliminate adverse effects on performance during exposure, only to deplete capacities and create adverse *aftereffects* that emerge later (Cohen, 1980a).

6. Responses to noise seem to depend not only on its physical properties, such as loudness, but on psychological variables, such as the individual's sense of control or its meaning to the individual.

Laboratory studies of noise have typically introduced one of two types of sounds: *predictable* (constant or repetitive) or *unpredictable* (intermittent, at variable or random intervals for varying durations). The following section first summarizes the findings on predictable noise.

Clerical tasks generally showed no effects of regular noise, except in studies when it changed or served as a signal. Several studies found no effects of continuous noise or repetitive bursts of noise up to 110 dB on such tasks as card sorting, simple coding, and "finding A's" (Glass & Singer, 1972; Obata & Morita, 1934, expt. 1; Schoenberger & Harris, 1965;

Stevens, 1972). Teichner, Arees, and Reilly (1963) found a temporary slowing of letter recognition after a change in the loudness of sound; the effect occurred with a drop in loudness as well as an increase in loudness. Similar findings occurred in Obata and Morita (1934, expt. 2). Harris (1972) reported poorer number searching and transcription in 105-dB noise. On the other hand, two studies found better performance of machine-paced recognition tasks when noise was keyed to the task (Warner, 1969; Warner & Heimstra, 1971). Also Davies (1967) found faster clerical performance using loud noise (95 dB) and a brief test (20 min); this result may reflect short-term arousal.

Mental tasks have typically been unaffected by continuous or regular noise, even as loud as 100 dB. Tasks such as mental arithmetic and reading showed no effects in three studies (Broadbent, 1958; Obata & Morita, 1934; Vernon & Warner, 1932). Samuel (1964) reported a positive effect of 100-dB white noise in 21-min sessions of arithmetic problems in which the numbers were in separate locations. The beneficial effect is consistent with the arousal hypothesis.

The effect of loud, continuous noise on motor performance has often been to increase the frequency of errors. Three studies used the so-called "five-choice" task and found errors increased in continuous noise of 95 dBC or louder (Broadbent, 1953, 1957; Hartley, 1974, expt. 1). (The task has a display of five lights; when one lights up, the participant is supposed to touch the corresponding spot in either the same display or a similar display; then another light goes on as the first goes off, and so on.) Errors during noise could have been partly due to the masking of useful auditory cues (Poulton, 1976, 1977), but this is debatable (Broadbent, 1976). In three other studies, loud, continuous noise resulted in more errors in complex tracking tasks (Eschenbrenner, 1971; Hack, Robinson, & Lathrop, 1965; Stevens, 1972). However, two studies found no effects (Doering, 1977; Plutchik, 1961); another found faster performance of a dexterity test in 100-dB white noise that lasted 25 min (Weinstein & Mackenzie, 1966). Poulton and Edwards (1974) reported a positive effect of low-frequency noise on a manipulation task. These findings could reflect the short-term benefits of arousal; they could also reflect a greater variability of performance after working continuously on the same task in noise (Broadbent, 1979).

Continuous or regular noise louder than 95 dB has been associated with errors in prolonged, difficult vigilance (Broadbent, 1954; Jerison, 1959). However, anything less than a highly demanding vigilance task has not shown such an effect (Blackwell & Belt, 1971; Jerison, 1957). Continuous 100-dB noise has also been associated with a tendency to make more confident judgments in difficult vigilance tasks (Broadbent & Gregory, 1963, 1965). One study found improved vigilance with noise keyed to the task (Watkins, 1964).

Simultaneous tasks have only shown adverse effects of continuous noise when the noise is very loud (100 dB). However, the adverse effects have differed. Hockey (1970a, 1970b) found a "narrowing of attention," in which peripheral or low-priority signals on a secondary vigilance task tended to be ignored. Forster and Grierson (1978) failed to replicate the effect using less intense noise (92 dB) and possibly a less demanding task (See also Forster, 1978; Hockey, 1978). Hamilton and Copeman (1970) found that 100-dB white noise degraded a secondary vigilance task. Loeb and Jones (1978) found their primary tracking task degraded in 105-dB continuous noise, but the secondary task was unaffected. Other studies with less intense, regular noise have found no such difficulties in doing two tasks at once (Finkleman & Glass, 1970; Theologus, Wheaton, & Fleishman, 1974). Adverse effects may be due in part to masking (Poulton, 1977). However, performance in regular, intermittent noise has sometimes been worse than that in continuous noise (e.g., Loeb & Jones, 1978), which contradicts the masking hypothesis. Plausible explanations may be based on overload and/or arousal.

One field experiment found a reduction in errors on a vigilance-type task associated with a reduction in sound level (Broadbent & Little, 1960). This finding is consistent with the masking hypothesis and with findings from the laboratory experiments.

Unpredictable noise has usually had more damaging effects on performance than regular noise. However, clerical performance has generally shown few adverse effects of irregular or unpredictable sounds. Four laboratory studies found no effects on such tasks as number checking, simple coding, and digit transcription (Glass & Singer, 1972; Rabbitt, 1968; Smith, 1951; Wohlwill, Nasar, DeJoy, & Foruzani, 1976). However, one researcher reported a temporary lapse in speed on clerical performance at the onset or offset of noise (Morgan, 1916, 1917).

Motor performance has typically suffered in studies of intermittent noise, in even moderately demanding tasks; the effect has usually been more frequent errors. For instance, Grimaldi (1958) found more errors on a simulated lathe task in 90-dB, high-frequency, irregular tones. Similar findings came from

studies by Eschenbrenner (1971), Laird (1933), Thackray and Touchstone (1970), and Hartley (1974). Even quiet speech disrupted tracking performance (Pepler, 1970). One other study failed to find such decrements, although it incorporated many different tasks for only brief tests (Stevens, 1972). Another study found no effects on simple assembly (Vernon & Warner, 1932).

Laboratory studies suggest that mental performance is disrupted by sudden, unfamiliar noises when the task requires short-term retention of new information. For instance, Woodhead (1964a) found that people doing complex mental subtraction tended to make an unusually large number of errors during the few seconds after loud bursts of rocket noise (100 dB). Woodhead (1969) reported similar results. One study found proofreading for grammatical errors poorer in irregular noise (Weinstein, 1974). Other studies found noise associated with errors in tasks that called for learning and short-term recall (Morgan, 1917; O'Malley & Poplawsky, 1971; Rabbitt, 1968). Harmon (1933) found noise associated with errors in column addition. However, other studies that demanded no new learning or short-term recall found no effects of irregular noise (Hovey, 1928; Park & Payne, 1963; Tinker, 1925). Two studies found that irregular noise led to improved performance on the stroop test, which requires the overlooking of irrelevant cues (Houston, 1969; O'Malley & Poplawsky, 1971, expt. 2).

Difficult, prolonged vigilance tasks have usually shown decrements in irregular noise, even noise of low intensity. Woodhead (1959, 1964b) found temporary lapses of attention during the few seconds after bursts of noise. Similarly, McCann (1969) and McGrath (1963) reported decrements in vigilance. On the other hand, Kirk and Hecht (1963) found that "programmed" noise improved a simple one-signal task. (Also music designed to create arousal aided vigilance; see section 19.3.7.)

Performance of dual tasks has consistently suffered in unpredictable noise. Three studies found a decrement in the secondary task (Boggs & Simon, 1968; Finkelman & Glass, 1970; Theologus et al., 1974). Loeb & Jones (1978) found a decrement in the primary task.

Even in cases where noise has no adverse effect on performance during exposure, it may have aftereffects (S. Cohen, 1980a). However, it is questionable whether the effects of noise found in the laboratory also occur in offices and factories. Industrial studies are few, but they are consistent with the laboratory findings (e.g., Broadbent & Little, 1960).

In summary, surveys suggest that noise is an important source of annoyance and dissatisfaction with the work environment. Studies of offices have found co-workers' conversations and the ringing of telephones the most prevalent sources of annoyance. Laboratory research on performance suggests that regular noise has little effect on clerical and mental performance but sometimes leads to increased errors in motor, vigilance, and dual tasks. Some of the errors may be attributable to the masking of useful sounds that would otherwise give feedback; decrements in performance could also reflect arousal. Laboratory research found no effect of irregular noise on clerical performance, apart from temporary lapses at onset and offset. However, irregular noise was associated with decrements in motor tasks, mental tasks with a requirement for short-term learning and recall, demanding forms of vigilance, and dual tasks.

19.3.7. Music

In contrast to noise, music is sound introduced for enjoyment. Its presence in offices and factories often reflects a desire to boost the morale of workers or otherwise influence the ambient environment through "music conditioning" (e.g., Terry, 1975). Although background music is fairly common, research on its impact on employees has been sparse.

Much of the published research on music consists of experiments done in factories during the 1940s, to discover whether recorded background music aided output.

Studies of actual factories examined the effects of music during inspection, assembly, or finishing. Of nine experiments that involved measurements of production, eight reported at least a marginal increase (Fox & Embrey, 1972, experiments 1 & 2; Kerr, 1944, 1945, experiments 1, 2, 3, & 4; Smith, 1947; Wyatt & Langdon, 1937). However, only in the experiments by Fox and Embrey were the increases in production reported as statistically significant. Two other studies found no effects of music on production (McGehee & Gardner, 1949; Newman, Hunt, & Rhodes, 1966). In studies that measured errors or quality of output, Humes (1941) reported a significant decrease; Kerr (1944, 1945, expt. 2) reported some decreases. Smith (1947) and Kerr (1944, 1945, expt. 2) found an increase, but McGehee & Gardner (1949) and Newman et al. (1966) reported no effects. Of three studies that assessed attitudes, all reported them favorable among 88% or more of the employees questioned (McGehee & Gardner, 1949; Newman et al., 1966; H.C. Smith, 1947).

The results of the experiments in factories are far from compelling. However, the small but consistent increases in output under conditions of music are difficult to dismiss; none of the studies found music associated with a lower rate of output, although quality sometimes suffered.

Research on music in offices includes two studies of music in keypunch rooms, which found no effects on output. Workers did express generally favorable attitudes about the music (Gladstones, 1969; W.A. Smith, 1961).

Laboratory research suggests that the effects of music on performance depend on the task, and the only task for which music has consistently enhanced performance is vigilance. Three experiments showed more correct detections during brief work periods when music was played than in relative silence (Davenport, 1974; Fox & Embrey, 1972, expts. 3 & 4). Three other studies found that music designed to increase arousal had the effect of delaying the unusual decline in performance that occurs with continued vigilance (Davies, Lang, & Shackleton, 1973; McGrath, 1963; Wokun, 1968). Only one experiment found no effects of music on vigilance (Poock & Wiener, 1966).

For other tasks in the laboratory, music has only occasionally shown an effect. Santamaria (1970) found no effects on a clerical task (card filing). Similarly, a mental task involving the comprehension of Russian history showed no effects (Freeburne & Fleischer, 1952). One study found that music enhanced tracking performance when its rhythm was synchronized with the task (Conte, 1966), but another study of tracking found no effects of music (Mikol & Denny, 1955).

Probably the best explanation for positive effects of music on output in the factory and enhanced vigilance in the laboratory is based on arousal. If music does add to arousal, the arousal hypothesis predicts enhanced performance of simple motor tasks. Similarly, music should help overcome the monotony that apparently accompanies continued vigilance. There is some evidence that music does lead to increases in physiological indexes of arousal (see the review in Santamaria, 1970), although it is not entirely consistent. Results of another laboratory experiment suggested that choices regarding music favored increasingly complex melodies among people with more "spare capacity" not occupied by their task (Konecni & Sargent-Pollock, 1976). If so, people in offices and factories may only prefer music to the extent that their capacities are not absorbed by their work. In general, music is probably only desirable for people doing relatively routine jobs.

19.3.8. Color

Color is one of the least studied aspects of the physical environment, but it nevertheless remains the topic of some of the most optimistic claims about morale and efficiency. Most of the limited research on color has examined attitudes and preferences; a few studies have tested the hypothesis that color influences performance. However, there is little evidence that color has any influence on morale or efficiency.

Color Preferences, Perception, and Satisfaction

Most research on attitudes about color has come from the laboratory and has involved judgments regarding small, colored cards of varying hues. For instance, participants in one study were shown color samples; they liked blue and red best, followed by green and violet, and they liked orange and yellow least (Guilford, 1934; Walton, Guilford, & Guilford, 1933). Eysenck (1941) analyzed published results on color preferences by 21,000 people and found the same rank ordering of hues. These findings are consistent with most laboratory research, but much of it is over 30 years old (see reviews by Guilford, 1934; Norman & Scott, 1952). Other research found a preference for lighter colors and pure, "saturated" colors, in contrast with darker shades and colors that represent mixtures of more than one hue (Guilford, 1934; Guilford & Smith, 1959). One study found that preferences for combinations of colors were predictable from preferences concerning the component colors (Allen & Guilford, 1936). Another laboratory experiment has shown that preferences for color depend on the type of lighting and on the hue, lightness, and saturation of the background. Also, a gender difference emerged: Men favored "cool" colors, whereas women favored "warm" ones (Helson & Lansford, 1970). Other research supports the finding that the type of lighting affects perceptions of color (see Boyce, 1981).

One study of office workers found preferences similar to those shown in early laboratory research. BOSTI (1980) reported office employees' preferences regarding several color schemes; they expressed a generally favorable attitude toward "cool" colors, such as blues and greens (72%), "pastel" colors,

such as light blue or pale yellow (67%), and "warm" colors, such as yellows and reds (59%). On the other hand, they generally rejected white (26% favorable), "intense colors like fire engine red or Kelly green" (20%), and grays (10%).

Besides preference, another aspect of color potentially relevant to the satisfaction of office or factory workers is its meaning. However, the meanings associated with colors have varied greatly in the laboratory (e.g., Aaronson, 1970; Schaie, 1961; Wexner, 1954). The only semantic association to emerge with any consistency was the designation of some colors as "cool" (blue and sometimes green) versus "warm" colors (red, orange, and sometimes yellow) (e.g., Birren, 1968; Morgan, Goodson, & Jones, 1975; Newhall, 1941; Tinker, 1938; Wright, 1962).

Office managers have suggested that warm or cool colors can actually lead people to perceive the temperature as correspondingly warm or cool (Wylie, 1958). Such an effect could conceivably occur through suggestion, but only one of four laboratory tests has confirmed it (Fanger, Breum, & Jerking, 1977). Negative findings came from Bennett and Rey (1972), Berry (1961), and Greene and Bell (1980).

Color may also influence workers' satisfaction through perceptions regarding the size of the room. One study found a lighter colored room rated higher on "openness" than a darker colored one (Acking & Kuller, 1972); a similar finding came from a dormitory (Schiffenbauer, Brown, Perry, Schulack, & Zanzola, 1977). Laboratory studies have also shown that brighter colors appear closer than darker ones (e.g., Johns & Sumner, 1948) and that lighter colored objects appear larger than darker ones (Gundlach & Macoubrey, 1931). Whether these findings also apply in offices or factories is an open question.

Color and Performance

Perhaps the most plausible hypothesis linking color with performance is that some colors, such as red, lead to increased arousal (e.g., Munsterberg, 1915). This has apparently not been demonstrated in offices or factories. However, two laboratory studies found a physiological index of arousal elevated during projection of red color slides (Jacobs & Hustmeyer, 1974; Wilson, 1966).

19.3.9. Work Stations

Probably the most important part of the fixed work environment for the individual is the *work station* (an area designed for work by one person). This section discusses the relationship between person and work station, and it selectively reviews research on the work station as a whole and on three aspects of work stations—floor space, equipment, and chairs.

Relationship between Person and Work Station

Whereas the ambient environment can perhaps be analyzed in terms of a few major dimensions, the work station incorporates practically an infinite variety of potentially important features.

For any one component of a work station, many details may be important for the comfort and efficiency of a particular individual. For example, the comfort of a chair depends on the design of the backrest, the seat, the armrests, the casters, and so on (Kleeman, 1981). Furthermore, the relative importance of each feature of a work station depends on unique characteristics of the job and the person, including his or her bodily dimensions. In a chair, comfort also depends on the way it is adjusted, the way the person sits in it, the specific tasks he or she does, and the work routine.

A traditional analysis of the complex relationships between the individual and the work station relies on the model of the *"man–machine system"* (e.g., McCormick, 1976). The system consists of a machine and its human operator (or operators) working in concert. The operator receives "inputs" from displays of information, considers the information, makes decisions, and then manipulates the controls accordingly. The machine produces "output" and provides "feedback," or information about its operation or its output. The operator uses feedback to adjust the controls to produce or maintain a desired effect. This dynamic interchange between person and machine continues over time.

The human–machine system emphasizes the importance of displays and controls. For example, the display portion of a video display terminal (VDT) is a televisionlike screen. The operator's comfort may depend on the height, distance, and tilt of the screen, the presence of glaring reflections, the ambient light, the contrast of the text on the screen, the size, spacing, discriminability, and brightness of the characters, the presence of flicker, and many other features. The adequacy of the controls—the keyboard—depends on the height, tilt, and stability of the keyboard itself, the spacing of the keys, the effort required to depress the keys and so on. (See Cakir, Hart, & Stewart, 1980, on VDT design.)

Besides the displays and controls, the operation of a human–machine system depends on *supportive*

elements of the work station. These include places for the worker to sit, stand, or lean, such as chairs, floormats, footstools, and counters. They also include physical support of the work: work surfaces and storage for materials and supplies.

The work station may be related to the individual's satisfaction and performance through at least three factors: comfort, economy of motion, and fatigue. Comfort may be associated with satisfaction with the environment and ultimately with job satisfaction. To the extent that the work station provides convenient and accessible places for tools, equipment, supplies, and materials, the individual can work efficiently. And to the extent that the design of the work station minimizes fatigue, the worker can maintain comfort and efficiency for relatively long periods.

The Work Station as a Whole

Very little research in offices or factories has explored the connections between the adequacy of the work station as a whole and the individual's satisfaction or performance. Similarly, little research has addressed the adequacy of specific elements of the work station and their relative importance for satisfaction with the work station as a whole or performance while occupying it.

A survey of a sample of U.S. office employees by Harris and Associates (1978) examined the relative importance of elements of the office environment; seven items concerned work stations. Participants were asked to choose the two or three items most "important in helping you to get your job done well" (p. 50). The most frequently chosen feature of the work station was convenient access to tools and equipment (25%). Other features that were selected by more than 10% of participants included the capacity to adjust the work station to fit the job, work-related storage, a comfortable chair, and work surfaces. Less frequently mentioned were back support of the chair (4%) and personal storage (1%). Participants in the survey also rated the adequacy of these seven elements of their work stations, and average scores were all above the midpoint of the rating scale.

The study by Harris and Associates (1978) did not examine the association between ratings of elements of work stations and general measures of satisfaction or performance. However, participants were asked whether they thought they could be more productive under certain conditions, and 62% said they could if their work surfaces, chairs, lighting, and storage space were appropriate for their jobs (p. 23).

A later survey of office workers by Harris and Associates (1980) assessed the relative importance of features of the office environment for employees' comfort. The survey included 12 items on the office environment, of which 4 concerned the work station. These consisted of a comfortable chair (73% said this item influenced their personal comfort "a great deal"), machines and references within easy reach (67%), enough space to move around at the desk (57%), and the ability to change the furniture as the job changed (24%). The study did not assess the association between these features and general measures of satisfaction or performance.

In summary, the result of two surveys suggest that some features of office work stations may be more important than others to employees' satisfaction and performance. Key features of office work stations may include access to tools, equipment, and materials, floor space, work surfaces, and a comfortable chair.

Floor Space

The amount of floor space encompassed by a work station is important for several reasons. First, restricted floor space may be associated with discomfort, if space does not allow occasional stretching and changing of posture. Second, floor space is related to the distance between people in unpartitioned areas and if too restricted may lead workers to get in each other's way. Close proximity among workers might also create conditions for crowding (Sundstrom, 1978). In addition, floor space is a common status symbol.

Langdon's (1966) study of offices included measurements of floor space in 1661 individual offices. Results showed that, independent of the usual differences among offices associated with status, the amount of floor space allocated to each person declined as the number of people in the room increased from one to four people. In rooms with three or more occupants, very few people had more than 60 ft^2 (excluding furniture, which occupied an average of 32% of the floor space). Satisfaction with floor space was associated with its amount. Only about half of the workers with less than 40 ft^2 were satisfied, compared with 68% of those with 40 to 59 ft^2, and 95% of those with 100 ft^2 or more. A smaller study of office employees in the United States found measured floor space correlated with satisfaction with the work space independent of job category (Sundstrom, Town, Brown, Forman, & McGee, 1982). Another study found floor space and distance between work spaces associated with satisfaction with the work space (Sundstrom, Burt, & Kamp, 1980). BOSTI (1981) reported that professional/technical workers who lost 25% or more floor space after changing offices also experienced a decline in job satisfaction.

Furniture

Perhaps the most common item of furniture in offices and factories is the chair. One study on chairs suggests that office workers varied not only in the dimensions of chairs, but also in the ways they sat in them (Burandt & Grandjean, 1963). Other studies found wide differences in ratings of different chairs (Shackel, Chidsey, & Shipley, 1969) and changes over time in habits of sitting in chairs (Branton, 1969). Perhaps as a consequence of such findings, practitioners have developed a complex series of guidelines for the design of chairs that accommodate a wide range of body dimensions and postures (see Ayoub, 1973; Kleeman, 1981; Woodson, 1981). In the survey of U.S. office workers by Harris and Associates (1980), 84% said their chairs were comfortable. However, 26% said they could be "a good deal" more productive in more comfortable chairs.

Equipment

The equipment used in offices and factories varies tremendously, particularly in factories, but there seems to be no research on the prevalence of different types of equipment in either setting. For certain specific pieces of equipment, however, there is considerable research.

For the present review, a single piece of office equipment, the video display terminal (VDT), serves to illustrate the major findings and issues. The VDT is relatively new; it only became common in the 1970s and 1980s. Early studies focused on its design, including such things as the proper height and tilt of the keyboard (see Cakir et al., 1980). Later research began to uncover problems, which is probably not unusual for a new piece of equipment.

According to a review in 1982, the VDT created eyestrain for many workers, along with signs of stress (Wineman, 1982). An extensive review of research published through 1980 concluded that VDTs create eyestrain (Dainoff, Happ, & Crane, 1981; Matula, 1981). Field studies found that clerical operators of VDTs said that they rated their jobs highly on characteristics such as work pressure, supervisory control, workload, and boredom (e.g., Smith, Cohen, Stammerjohn, & Happ, 1981). These job characteristics have been associated with job stress (e.g., Cooper & Payne, 1978). The characteristics may have stemmed from the capacities of the VDT to allow efficient, remote supervision and efficient routing of work.

Findings on the VDT illustrate two important points about the relationship between the individual and the work environment. First, a piece of equipment has the potential to create discomfort as the worker uses it, particularly through characteristics of the displays or controls. Second, a person's job activities depend to some extent upon the design of his or her equipment, and the activities may create stress.

19.3.10. Supporting Facilities

For the individual who works in an office or factory, the physical work environment includes many areas besides a work station. Among others, these include corridors and walkways, foyers, elevators, lounges, cafeterias, copy rooms, mail rooms, locker rooms, meeting rooms, conference rooms, and special work areas. Psychologists have given these aspects of offices and factories very little attention. However, there are hints from a few studies that employees consider them important (e.g., Langdon, 1966; Manning, 1965).

Supporting facilities may be important to individual satisfaction for many of the same reasons that work stations are. For example, a corridor could create positive attitudes through an aesthetically pleasing design or annoyance through narrow width and a circuitous route. Its ambient lighting, sound, air quality, and temperature may temporarily influence the individual's comfort. Whereas it is unlikely that a corridor affects performance, other supportive facilities could do so, including reference rooms and supply rooms. However, the sources and extent of such influences in offices and factories are apparently unknown.

In summary, research and theory suggest that many features of the work environment may contribute to outcomes for the individual worker, including satisfaction and performance. Research indicates that temperature, lighting, noise, and music may be linked with both satisfaction and performance. Windows, air quality, and color have been studied less than other characteristics of the work environment, but they may also be linked to individual outcomes. Features of work stations, such as furniture, equipment, floor space, and supporting facilities may also be important. At the individual level of analysis, key psychological processes that mediate the influences of the work environment may include arousal, stress, distraction, overload, and adaptation.

19.4. INTERPERSONAL RELATIONSHIPS

The second level of analysis concerns interpersonal relationships. This section focuses on the role of the physical environment in social psychological processes and associated outcomes. One issue concerns symbolic properties of work spaces, their relevance to status and self-identity, and their importance for workers' satisfaction. Communication is also discussed, first in relation to physical accommodation of face-to-face conversation and then in relation to privacy and the regulation of accessibility. Finally, connections between the physical environment and the formation and cohesion of groups are explored.

19.4.1. Symbolic Work Spaces

A work space may convey information about the occupant to other people, particularly concerning self-identity and status. *Self-identity* refers to an individual's vision of his or her unique, personal characteristics and values. Expression of self-identity in the office or factory involves visible features of work spaces that differentiate the occupant from others or display attachment to the work space. *Status* refers to a person's relative influence to rank in the organization's hierarchy of authority. A personally assigned work space may contain physical symbols of the occupant's rank.

Expressions of Self-Identity

The principal means by which people can differentiate or express themselves through their work environments include personalization of work spaces, establishment of territories, and participation in the design of their work spaces. *Personalization* refers to the addition of personal items to the work space, such as pictures, posters, calendars, plants, and the like or modification of the work space itself, for instance by painting the walls or rearranging the furniture (e.g., Sommer, 1974). A *territory* is a zone of control and influence (e.g., Altman, 1975). *Participation* in design includes giving information to the designers, choosing colors or styles, and making decisions about issues such as allocation of floor space and furniture (e.g., Becker, 1981; Kleeman, 1981).

PERSONALIZATION

For workers who occupy individually assigned work spaces, the ability to personalize them depends on (1) policies of the organization; (2) decisions made by local executives; and (3) physical limitations of the work spaces.

Among office workers, personalization may be prevalent. BOSTI (1981) reported that 79% of a sample of office workers said they displayed work-related items in their work spaces; 61% said they displayed personal items.

Personalization may also be associated with satisfaction with the physical environment. BOSTI (1981) found that physical accommodation of display was correlated with satisfaction with the work space. Similarly, in a nonwork setting, Hansen and Altman (1976) found that among students living in university dormitories, those who dropped out of school for nonacademic reasons displayed relatively few personal items in their rooms. In contrast, a follow-up study found that dropouts showed relatively more personalization but that the items they displayed tended to concern places besides the university (Vinsel, Brown, Altman, & Foss, 1980).

If personalization is related to satisfaction with the environment, it could be because it fosters a sense of individuality among workers. One study of factors related to job satisfaction found that feeling like an individual, not a "cog in a machine," was ranked fifth in importance among 19 job factors (Harris & Associates, 1978). Other research on job satisfaction has identified "recognition" as an important factor (Locke, 1983).

WORK SPACE AS TERRITORY

A *territory* represents a zone of control. According to Altman's (1975) theory, territories contribute to the individual's ability to regulate social interaction. A work space may constitute a territory for the individual if the occupant can exercise substantial control over it. The ability to personalize a work space may be important as a demonstration of control, and, therefore, may be a component of territoriality in work environments.

A small study of office employees found them highly satisfied in "nonterritorial" work spaces. A group of product engineers occupied conventional offices with small rooms for one or two people each, until their office was made into an open office in which nobody was assigned to a specific place and in which no personal belongings were to be left overnight. The new office had few walls, though it had a conference room and a separate "quiet" area. The researchers expected the engineers to stake territorial claims on specific work locations, but systematic observations revealed a tendency to use varied locations. (None spent more than half of his time in the office in any one location.) Satisfaction with the office environment remained as high as before and as high as that of a comparable group of engineers at a different location who retained the conventional arrangement (Allen & Gerstberger, 1973). This finding casts doubt on the generality of the tendency of office workers to form attachments to specific work stations.

Another study treated territoriality as a personality trait. In a group of office workers, Sloan (1972) classified some as "territorial" and others "nonterritorial" and designed work spaces accordingly, with boundaries for the territorial people. Responses to a survey suggested that the workers were satisfied with work spaces tailored to their territorial inclinations.

PARTICIPATIVE DESIGN

Whereas personalization allows self-expression within an existing work space, participative design potentially allows self-expression through any facet—its layout, furnishing, or decoration. However, by some accounts, the typical office worker has practically no influence in the design of work spaces (Becker, 1981; Dickson, 1975). Experts have called for more participative design (e.g., Kleeman, 1981; Sommer, 1974).

Participation in the design of work spaces may lead to a relatively high level of satisfaction with the physical environment, but research on this question is scarce. In a survey by Harris and Associates (1978), 72% of office workers believed their participation in the design of their own offices would have a "good effect" on it (p. 87). Sloan (n.d.) studied the renovation of the Seattle FAA building, which involved substantial participation by the employees. Results of a survey showed that about half of the employees said they participated "moderately actively" or "very actively" in the design on the new office. A larger fraction of employees was satisfied with the Seattle building (34%) than with a comparable building in Los Angeles that involved less participation (23%). Improved environmental satisfaction among people who participated in the design of their environments has been reported in other settings (e.g., Wandersman, 1979a, 1979b). It could reflect the higher quality of participatively planned environments or a greater sense of involvement and autonomy by the occupants, or both.

BOSTI (1981) assessed participation by office workers in the design of six aspects of their work spaces. The most common form of participation was to give an opinion or information. Nearly one-third of employees made decisions about the location of their equipment, but less than 10% decided on color schemes, graphics, or plants. People with supervisory responsibility participated more than non-supervisors. Participation was significantly correlated with both environmental satisfaction and job satisfaction. (Another analysis of the same data by Town [1982] found the association even after statistically controlling for job-type, gender, and government versus private sector.)

Status Markers

The physical environment in offices has traditionally symbolized status in the hierarchy of authority. Many organizations have written policies regarding the characteristics of work spaces for people at various ranks (e.g., Duffy, 1969; Konar & Sundstrom, 1986).

Status markers, or characteristics of work spaces that signify rank, seem to evoke ambivalent reactions. On the one hand, anecdotes suggest that employees want symbols of rank and complain when people of lesser or equal rank have things they lack (e.g., Steele, 1973). On the other hand, people often downplay the importance of status markers. In one study, people were reluctant to explicitly recognize the role of status symbols, preferring instead to explain the visible differences among ranks in terms of their importance for their jobs (Lipman, Cooper, Harris, & Tranter, 1978).

Status markers seem to serve several important functions. They visibly communicate an individual's rank, providing co-workers and visitors with explicit information. They can serve as incentives, if tied to promotion, or as compensation, if tied to performance. They may also supply props for the job, as in the case of a chief executive officer with a private conference room attached to her or his office.

According to Adams's (1953) theory of "status congruency," people strive for agreement among different hierarchies in a social system. The theory implies that people seek consistency between formal rank and physical amenities and experience dissatisfaction with inconsistency. Predictions of the theory agree with the practice of denoting status through traditional status markers.

COMMON STATUS MARKERS

Research on offices has found higher rank associated with greater floor space and fewer people per room (Langdon, 1966) and greater physical enclosure of work spaces (Sundstrom, Town, Brown, Forman, & McGee, 1982). Participants in the survey of office workers by Harris and Associates (1978) identified a variety of status markers actually in use. More than

20% said that each of the following things differentiated executives: the style and material of desks, tables, and chairs, amount of privacy, the amount of space, paintings and wall decorations, materials used in furniture, and types of floor coverings (p. 59). The survey by BOSTI (1981) asked office workers what they would like if they got a promotion. More than 20% identified each of the following: more space (65%), a privileged location (50%), more furnishings (30%), higher quality furnishings and finishes (28%), and controlled access (24%). In brief, studies of office workers indicate that many features of work spaces are recognized as status markers.

STATUS MARKERS AND SATISFACTION

In one study, the perceived accuracy of the work space in reflecting status was called *status support*, which correlated with environmental satisfaction. Konar, Sundstrom, Brady, Mandel, and Rice (1982) analyzed the responses of 529 office workers (those in BOSTI, 1980) and reported that status support was correlated with the presence of many customary status symbols. These included private office, limited accessibility, capacity to personalize, desk size, and distance from neighboring work spaces. (These items were defined as status symbols in that people with supervisory responsibility were more likely than others to have them.) For people with supervisory responsibility, status support was more closely associated with environmental satisfaction than it was for other employees.

BOSTI (1981) reported similar findings for a larger group of office workers. Furthermore, among workers who changed offices, an increase in status support was associated with an increase in environmental satisfaction. Also, those with supervisory responsibilities gained more status support after changing offices.

In brief, limited evidence supports the idea that people are most satisfied in work spaces with physical amenities consistent with their ranks in the organization.

19.4.2. Communication

This section discusses the role of the physical environment in communication, focusing upon the convenience and quality of face-to-face conversations. A common hypothesis holds that environments facilitate communication, particularly face-to-face conversation, by placing people in close proximity with their counterparts (e.g., Lorenzen & Jaeger, 1968). If so, it is probably because people make choices regarding communication partly on the basis of expediency. If the convenience and comfort of face-to-face conversation influence choices in communication, these factors may also play a part in the general adequacy of communication.

This section first advances some hypotheses on the role of the work environment in communication. Then it reviews research on the connection between physical accessibility and interpersonal relationships and the research on the association between environmental factors and the quality of conversations.

Physical Settings and the Adequacy of Communication

For an individual in an office or factory, any communication involves one or more *recipients* and certain *messages* sent through a particular *medium*, such as face-to-face conversation, telephone, written letter, and so on. Messages can be "formal" (job-related) or "informal" (not explicitly connected with the parties' jobs).

Choices in communication may follow a "principle of least effort" (Gerstberger & Allen, 1968). In other words, people may tend to choose the most convenient form of communication that minimally serves their purposes. If so, the physical accessibility of coworkers—proximity or the lack of barriers between them—may enter into choices regarding communication about which the initiator has discretion.

Specifically, the following hypotheses are suggested.

1. Physical accessibility is a factor in the *medium of a formal communication* directed to a particular co-worker. (For example, a supervisor who must contact a certain subordinate can choose a face-to-face conversation, a phone call, or a written note.)
2. Accessibility is a factor in the choice of the *recipient of informal conversation*. (For example, an office worker may choose to chat informally with the person at a neighboring desk rather than go across the building to visit an acquaintance.)

Through its role in choices in communication, the physical environment may enter into the adequacy of communication. For a given individual, this depends on the congruence between the individual's goals and his or her communications with others. These in turn depend on reaching desired recipients, using media that provide satisfactory fidelity of communication, maintaining sufficient frequency of exchange for the relationships, and exchanging appropriate information or messages.

When communication occurs as face-to-face conversation, its adequacy may also depend on other factors: the conversants' comfort, psychological closeness, and resources for self-presentation. These in turn may be influenced by the ambient environment or arrangement of the room. Research on these issues is reviewed after a discussion of studies on physical accessibility.

Physical Accessibility and Communication

Two field studies sought, but failed to find, a connection between *formal* communication and physical proximity of work spaces within the same building. Duffy (1974a, 1974b, 1974c) surveyed 361 people in 16 small organizations (about 30 people each) and found an index of physical accessibility of neighbors unrelated to the average frequency of communication or to the average number of daily contacts within the organization. (The study did not include an assessment of the correlation of distances between specific pairs of people with communication in those pairs.) Farbstein (1975) surveyed 185 employees in three small London organizations about their face-to-face conversations. He measured the average distance separating pairs of persons and reported no correlation of average distance and average time spent in contact. However, the average distance traveled for conversations was correlated with the "distance to be moved," suggesting that people went as far as necessary for formal conferences in the same building.

A field study at a corporate office found indirect evidence of an association between proximity and contact between supervisor and supervisee (Szilagyi & Holland, 1980). A total of 96 people changed offices and were divided into groups of whom the number of neighbors within 50 ft (walking distance) increased, decreased, or stayed the same. Results of a survey of job characteristics given before and after the change showed people who experienced an increase in the number of neighbors nearby reported less "autonomy" in their jobs and more "feedback" regarding their performance. If supervisors were among the neighbors who moved closer, perhaps they visited more often. Closer supervision could account for the lower autonomy and greater feedback.

Evidence is scarce for the idea that physical proximity increases the chances of people's choosing face-to-face conversation over other means of formal communication with a specific person. A review of six studies on choices regarding the medium of communication found face-to-face conversation preferred over "teleconferencing" in situations involving brief travel time or journey. However, "teleconferencing" was preferred for communication involving longer travel times (Galitz, 1980). Tolerable travel time probably depends on the importance attached to the meeting and the acceptability of a teleconference in its place.

One field study linked proximity of work spaces with face-to-face communication of all kinds, formal and informal. Conrath (1973) collected records of all contact among 30 employees of a Canadian utility, including face-to-face conversations, telephone calls, and personally addressed letters. Physical proximity between pairs of people was highly correlated with occurrence and frequency of face-to-face contact and with telephone calls within the pairs. (However, these workers probably were located near the people with whom they had the most need to talk.) Telephone calls paralleled the "task structure" of the organization, defined by interdependent jobs. Written messages paralleled the "authority structure." These findings agree with the idea that for job-related contact, people choose face-to-face conversation more often when their work spaces are physically close. (The findings also agree with the idea that organizations place people near their counterparts.)

A few field studies link proximity of work spaces with *informal* communication. At an automobile plant, an increase in the distance between work stations 10 to 20 ft was associated with a drop in reports of conversations between neighbors (Faunce, 1958). Similarly, two studies of offices found that clerical employees tended to choose neighbors for friendly conversation (Gullahorn, 1952; Homans, 1954). Other studies found an association between proximity of work spaces and friendships (Szilagyi & Holland, 1980; Wells, 1965b).

Open-plan offices created visual accessibility and were expected to facilitate communication (e.g., Lorenzen & Jaeger, 1968). However, evaluation studies of open offices did not consistently find the expected increases in communication. One study by Brookes (1972a; 1972b; Brookes & Kaplan, 1972) reported an increase in "sociability." Hundert and Greenfield (1969) found face-to-face conversation increased. Ives and Ferdinands (1974) reported a general increase in "communication." Boyce (1974) reported interdepartmental contact more frequent in an open office than in earlier conventional ones. On the other hand, several studies reported no differences in communication (Boje, 1971; Sloan, n.d.; Sundstrom, Herbert, & Brown, 1982). Furthermore, Boyce (1974) found a decrease in supervisory contact, and Oldham and Brass (1979) found decreases in "feedback" and "friendship opportunity." Clearwater

(1979) found a decrease in "face-to-face talking." Hundert and Greenfield (1969) reported that people spend less time on the phone and in meetings. Hanson (1978) found no change in "opportunities to confer" but a decrease in privacy for confidential conversation.

The case study of the "nonterritorial" office showed a substantial increase in communication among engineers whose offices were converted from conventional to open with unassigned work spaces. After the change, the engineers reported contacting an average of 6.3 people within the office per day, compared with 3.6 before (Allen & Gerstberger, 1973). This increase could reflect a habit of talking with immediate neighbors, whose numbers probably increased with the greater mobility and more varied locations of people in the nonterritorial office.

Another aspect of the layout of a building important to communication concerns the existence of *gathering places* outside of individual work spaces. Such places may correspond to what Bechtel (1976) called "activity nodes," or areas where peoples' paths cross during routine activities. However, to develop into a gathering place, an area of a building probably needs to be convenient to individual work spaces (e.g., Markus, 1970), centrally located (Steele, 1973), and comfortable for conversation (e.g., Mehrabian, 1976). These hypotheses are based on anecdotes and they need to be tested.

Ambient Conditions and Social Interaction

Research from social psychology suggests that ambient conditions can influence face-to-face encounters in several ways. For instance, noise can lead to insensitivity to social cues (Cohen & Lezak, 1977; Korte, Ympa, & Toppen, 1975; Mathews & Canon, 1975). This effect could represent a response to overload, an effect of distraction, or a narrowing of attention under stress. Noise may also lead to negative reactions to others. In a laboratory simulation, people exposed to loud noise assigned lower salaries to fictitious job applicants than in quiet conditions (Sauser, Arauz, & Chambers, 1978). This finding is consistent with laboratory studies that found uncomfortable heat associated with lower attraction to a fictitious stranger (Griffitt, 1970; Griffitt & Veitch, 1971). However, other laboratory research suggests that environmental stress may only lead to negative responses to people who are not present at the time. Environmental stress may even create positive responses to other people in the same setting through "shared stress" (Kenrick & Johnson, 1979). Whether aversive environmental conditions in offices and factories lead to insensitivity or to liking or disliking is an open question.

One well-established influence of the ambient conditions in offices and factories concerns interference by background noise with conversation. As background noise increases, people either have to stand closer to each other or talk louder to be heard (McCormick, 1976). A typical factory may have a sound level of about 78 dB (Dreyfuss, 1966); the average worker in such a background would probably have to shout to be heard farther away than 4 or 5 ft and probably could not be heard at all at 20 ft.

Other plausible hypotheses have apparently not been tested in offices or factories: (1) People in aesthetically pleasant surroundings may respond more favorably to each other than in less pleasing settings (e.g., Maslow & Mintz, 1956; Mintz, 1956; see the review by Sundstrom, 1984); and (2) people in physically uncomfortable settings may have relatively brief conversations.

Seating Arrangements and Psychological Distance

Most studies on the arrangement of rooms in work environments concern the placement of desk and chairs in individual offices. Perhaps the most frequently studied hypothesis is that in an office with a desk between occupant and visitor, greater psychological distance exists than with no desk between them. In consequence, the "desk-between" layout is thought to be preferred by people who want distance from visitors. Joiner (1976) found desk-between arrangements prevalent among people in government and commercial organizations, but "open" arrangements were more common among academics (also Campbell, 1980). Another study found that professors whose offices had a desk-between arrangement were perceived as less accessible to students, but these professors tended to be the older and more senior faculty (Zweigenhaft, 1976). Students who viewed photos of offices thought they would feel more comfortable and welcome in open arrangements (Campbell, 1978; Morrow & McElroy, 1981). On the other hand, a study that involved structured interviews in open versus desk-between arrangements failed to find any differences in the durations of the interviews (Campbell, 1979). Widgery and Stackpole (1972) found that anxious visitors to an office were more comfortable with the desk-between arrangement, whereas less anxious visitors preferred the open layout. On the whole, the findings suggest that a conversation across a desk involves greater psychological distance than exists in a conversation with no intervening barrier.

19.4.3. Privacy

This section continues the discussion of the relationship between the physical environment and interpersonal relationships, focusing on privacy and the ability to regulate social contact. After exploring the concept of privacy and its application in work environments, research is reviewed on the link of physical enclosure of work spaces with privacy and the link of privacy with satisfaction.

The Concept of Privacy

Theorists have generally defined privacy in one of three ways: as a retreat from people, as management of information, or as regulation of interpersonal interaction. Definitions based on retreat suggest that privacy occurs when a person or group deliberately withdraws from contact with others (e.g., Bates, 1964; see the review by Altman, 1975). Definitions based on management of information suggest that privacy exists when a person or group can decide how and to whom information about them is communicated (e.g., Margulis, 1979; Westin, 1970). When people cannot control the flow of information about themselves, it becomes possible for others to exert influence over them by judging their activities against norms and calling forth sanctions when the activities do not conform (Kelvin, 1973). The definition of privacy based on regulation of interaction derives from the idea that people strive to maintain an optimum level of interaction with others. Privacy exists as long as an individual or group has "selective control over access" by other people (Altman, 1975, 1976). When control over interaction fails, possible consequences include crowding (too much social stimulation) or isolation (too little). Altman suggested that when people experience too much or too little social interaction, they attempt to correct the situation through "privacy-regulation mechanisms." These mechanisms comprise verbal and nonverbal behaviors, including use of the physical environment to regulate contact with others.

Privacy in Work Environments

Uses of the term *privacy* at work generally correspond with its definition in terms of retreat, information management, and regulation of interaction. For example, Justa and Golan (1977) asked 40 business executives to describe what privacy meant in the context of the office. Many listed more than one situation, including being able to work without distractions (69%), controlling access to information (35%), freedom to do what they want to do (35%), controlling access to space (35%), being alone (25%), and other meanings.

Office planners and designers distinguish specific types of privacy. *Speech privacy* refers to the ability to converse in a work space without being understood outside it (Cavanaugh, Farrell, Hirtle, & Watters, 1962; Sundstrom, Herbert, & Brown, 1982). The term *conversational privacy* is synonymous. *Acoustical privacy* usually means speech privacy plus isolation from noise. *Visual privacy* refers to isolation from unwanted observers. Visual privacy is available in environments that obstruct direct visibility and that render unlikely the sudden appearance of observers. A private office with a closable door may provide complete visual privacy, but with less enclosure an individual may be seen or approached and may be accessible to surprise observation (Archea, 1977).

In summary, privacy in work environments generally implies some form of limited accessibility to other people. It usually connotes intentional retreat from observation or audition or from unwanted interruption, distraction, or interaction. Definitions of "privacy" in offices or factories suggest that people use their ability to manage information and regulate interaction to delimit exchanges with other people.

Enclosure and Privacy

The physical enclosure required for an employee to maintain a balance between privacy and communication may vary considerably from one person to the next. Research on preferred numbers of people in an office suggests that only a minority of office workers want a fully enclosed work space. Canter (1968) surveyed a group of 1180 English office workers and found that only 44% said they wanted to be in a room or partitioned area with one to four people. BOSTI (1980) reported that only about one-third of a sample of U.S. office workers wanted a room alone, and nearly half wanted a room shared by two to seven people. However, most participants in the BOSTI study worked in rooms with more people than they preferred.

Surveys among employees who work in open-plan offices suggest that the lack of enclosure makes privacy a major problem (Hedge, 1982; Marans & Spreckelmeyer, 1982; McCarrey et al., 1974; Nemecek & Grandjean, 1973; Wolgers, 1973). Evaluation studies have examined employees' perceptions of privacy after moving from conventional offices (or having their facilities converted) to open arrangements with fewer walls. Of seven studies that solicited employees' reports on privacy after changing to open offices, four registered a decline in privacy or an increase in complaints of its lack (Boyce, 1974; Brookes, 1972b; Hanson, 1978; Hundert & Green-

field, 1969). Others found mixed results. Riland and Falk (1972) reported a decline in privacy for telephone calls but not in privacy for conversations, which was already low. Sloan (n.d.) found privacy lower at one location but greater at another, where partitions were used extensively to separate work spaces. Sundstrom, Herbert, and Brown (1982) found a decline in privacy, primarily among managers who left private offices. (The lower privacy reflected a loss of speech privacy among managers; their perceptions were supported by acoustical measurements that indicated lower levels of conversational privacy.) Other studies reported a general decline of conversational privacy in open offices (Hanson, 1978) and among managers in particular (Ives & Ferdinands, 1974). Most of the evaluation studies were limited in that they did not assess the enclosure of individual work spaces, which usually varied. Instead, most of these studies reported the average perceptions of entire office staffs.

Field studies that did include assessments of enclosure in each work space have consistently found it associated with privacy. Sundstrom et al. (1980) used as an index of enclosure the number of sides of a work space bounded by walls or partitions at least 6 ft tall (this number varied from 0 to 4, as work spaces were approximated by rectangles). People in managerial and professional/technical jobs had more enclosure. The number of enclosed sides was correlated with occupants' ratings of privacy of the work spaces. A later field study showed similar results (Sundstrom, Town, Brown, Forman, & McGee, 1982).

Other studies found evidence that the connection of physical enclosure with privacy varies with the individual's job. Sundstrom, Town, Rice, Konar, Mandel, and Brill (1982b) predicted on the basis of the earlier studies that physical enclosure satisfies different needs for people in clerical, professional/technical, and managerial jobs. Office employees in these three job groups completed a questionnaire on their environments before and after changing offices. Enclosure was defined in terms of the number of sides of a work space enclosed by high partitions or walls; those in clerical jobs had least enclosure, and managers had most. Participants were divided into groups for whom enclosure had increased, decreased, or stayed the same after the change. Enclosure was strongly associated with ratings of control over accessibility and conversational privacy among managers and with isolation from intrusion among professional/technical employees. However, enclosure was not associated with any form of privacy among clerical employees. (BOSTI, 1981, using a different index of enclosure and the same database, reported similar findings.)

Another field study assessed perceptions of privacy and physical enclosure of work spaces among 288 office workers at eight organizations. Privacy decreased as an index of physical "openness" increased (Ferguson, 1983). The index of openness was also associated with "aural distractions." The work spaces were most open at the lowest job levels, and openness decreased with increasing job levels. Privacy also increased with job level.

In summary, field studies have generally found enclosure of work spaces associated with privacy. However, some studies found differences among job categories. Managers, professional/technical employees, or people with high ranks had more enclosure and more privacy than people in clerical jobs or lower ranks.

Privacy, Satisfaction, and Performance

Privacy has the potential to contribute to satisfaction with the physical environment by helping people maintain adequate control over information or interaction. Speech privacy may be particularly important among managers. Privacy may aid performance by contributing to the ability to limit interruptions during complex work or to conduct confidential conferences. On the other hand, privacy may detract from performance by shielding people from the motivating effects of social facilitation or visibility to co-workers (e.g., Geen & Gange, 1977; Knowles, 1983).

One field study assessed privacy and satisfaction with the environment, job satisfaction, and job performance. Office workers completed a survey in which they rated three aspects of privacy: control over accessibility, isolation from intrusions, and speech privacy. A total of 389 employees in clerical, professional/technical, and managerial jobs completed the questionnaire before and after changing offices. For each type of privacy, they were divided into groups whose privacy increased, stayed the same, or decreased. All three types of privacies were linked with satisfaction with the physical environment but not with job satisfaction or performance. The association of the three types of privacies with satisfaction with the physical environment held for all three job categories, but the strength of the connections varied by job category. Speech privacy was particularly associated with environmental satisfaction among managers; freedom from intrusions was strongly related to satisfaction among professional/technical employees. On the other hand, control over access was

only weakly related to satisfaction among clerical employees (Sundstrom, Town, Rice, Konar, Mandel, & Brill, 1982a). A later study of 288 office workers also found privacy associated with satisfaction with the work space (Ferguson, 1983).

In summary, some evidence suggests that privacy is associated with satisfaction with the physical environment. However, one study found that the relationship depended to some extent on the job. Among professional/technical employees, isolation from interruptions was strongly related to environmental satisfaction; among managers speech privacy was strongly related to satisfaction with the physical environment.

19.4.4. Small Groups

A *group* is defined here as two or more people who interact in such a way as to influence each other (following Shaw, 1981). Properties of a group also often include interdependence, shared goals, shared perceptions of group membership, and interaction (Cartwright & Zander, 1968). A *small group* is arbitrarily defined as fewer than 20 to 30 people. The physical environment may play a role in the formation and cohesion of a group and in the pattern of interactions within it.

Development of Small, Informal Groups

One common hypothesis holds that physical proximity among work spaces encourages the development of social ties among the occupants—as an outgrowth of the informal communication associated with proximity. A study in a factory found that informal groups sometimes developed among people whose work stations were close enough to allow conversation, but only among a few of the workers (Walker & Guest, 1952). However, many neighbors failed to form groups, suggesting that physical proximity provided an *opportunity* for social ties to develop, and only workers who were compatible developed them. A study at Western Electric's Hawthorne Works also documented the development of informal groups among people in neighboring work spaces, among people who appeared compatible (Homans, 1950). Similarly, clerical employees who worked in one room of an accounting office formed informal ties that apparently reflected common socioeconomic backgrounds (Homans, 1954). Gullahorn (1952) found mutual friendships among only a fraction of office workers who occupied neighboring work spaces and routinely conversed. These four small studies suggest that proximity of work spaces may predispose the development of an informal group in an office or factory, but only among compatible people.

Enclosure and Cohesion

A common hypothesis holds that the enclosure of a group gives people a reason to focus their interactions within the group and limit their contacts outside it, which fosters internal cohesion (e.g., Melcher, 1976, p. 138). *Cohesion* refers to the strength of the social ties that hold a group together (e.g., Cartwright, 1968). Evidence from work environments is apparently limited to a field study of employees in an insurance office that found more mutual friendships in enclosed areas containing about 30 people than in a large, open area containing about 200 people (Wells, 1965b).

Enclosure of a group may also contribute to cohesiveness by shielding it from observation and interference from outside, allowing personal exchanges and unique norms to proceed without interference. Evidence consistent with this idea comes from a case study of a group of clerical employees. They worked in an enclosed area surrounded by steel mesh walls that were lined with file cabinets; the area was entered through closable doors. The group was cohesive and had developed habits not shared by the rest of the company, such as sending out for afternoon snacks. Morale was high, and the group had a record of efficient performance. When the group was moved to a new location that made its activities visible to others, the unconventional practices were quickly noticed and prohibited. Morale plummeted, and the group eventually dissolved as its members were dispersed (Richards & Dobyns, 1957). In effect, privacy allowed the group to develop and maintain norms that could not survive in an exposed setting.

Patterns of Interaction within Groups

Apart from field studies that associate physical proximity of work spaces with the likelihood of conversation between the occupants, research relevant to group dynamics comes almost exclusively from the laboratory. Studies of group discussions suggest that conversations follow lines of eye contact (Steinzor, 1950), and leadership tends to emerge in positions that afford eye contact with the largest proportion of the group's members (e.g., Hearn, 1957; Strodtbeck & Hook, 1961; see Sundstrom, 1984, for a review).

Laboratory research on "communication networks" within groups shows that centralization of communication influences several aspects of group process. Networks are created by artificially restricting who can contact whom. The most "centralized" network forces all messages to flow through one central person, who resembles the hub of a wheel. Centralized communication networks have been associated with restriction in the numbers of messages sent, emergence of a leader in the central position, a centralized procedure for decision making, dissatisfaction in peripheral positions, and a performance differential that favors centralized networks for simple tasks and decentralized ones for complex tasks (see Shaw, 1981, for a review). However, there is evidence that in experienced groups, networks may eventually cease to have an effect on performance (Burgess, 1968). Anyway, the generalizability of laboratory finding on group dynamics to work environments remains to be shown.

19.5. ORGANIZATIONS

For the organization, the physical environment of its offices and factories represents one of many resources to be molded and controlled in the service of its goals. A perspective useful at this level of analysis treats the organization as a system and the physical environment as one of many interrelated components that contribute to organizational effectiveness. The physical environment may have a role by reinforcing the structure or climate of the organization. However, its role also hinges on processes and outcomes at the interpersonal and individual levels of analysis. This section first discusses the treatment of offices and factories in theories of organizations, then explores organizational effectiveness and its potential links with the work environment at three levels of analysis.

19.5.1. Work Environments and Theories of Organizations

Theories of organizations fall into three broad categories. *Classical* theories deal with formal rules and roles. *Humanistic* theories focus on the social and psychological effects of the roles and rules. *Systems* theories depict organizations as dynamic entities whose components exert mutual influence. In all three types of theories, the work environment has had a relatively minor role.

Classical Theories

These theories include Weber's concept of bureaucracy, Taylor's "scientific management," and their derivatives (Howell, 1976; Katz & Kahn, 1978; Tausky, 1978).

Weber's (1947) theory dealt with the structural characteristics of organizations, primarily the hierarchy of authority and the definition of roles. Weber depicted organizations as formal structures of specialized, interlocked roles, each with a position in the hierarchy of authority and a specific set of duties. Role and rank comprised the incumbent's *office* or position. Weber emphasized the necessity for a unitary line of authority, uniform practices, rewards based on performance, and separation of jobs from personal lives. Weber's theory apparently had no explicit place for the physical environment but implicitly supported the use of status symbols. The concept of "office" included a room designated for the incumbent, appropriate to the person's rank.

F.W. Taylor (1911) took the idea of role specialization to its logical extreme in his *Scientific Management*. He argued that jobs need to be broken down into their smallest elements, analyzed for the most efficient procedures, and done accordingly to the "one best way." His methods of "motion study" suggested modifications of tools and equipment in the interest of efficiency. Taylor's theory focused more on the design of tasks than on the physical environment, but the emphasis on efficiency had a powerful influence on factories and offices. Taylor suggested designs for tools and work stations based on economy of motion. He also emphasized supervision, which called for an environment that allowed visual accessibility—or "oversight"—of workers.

In Taylor's theory, the relationship between person and environment can best be described by analogy to the relationship of a cog to a machine. The problem addressed in the theory was to keep the human components of an organization operating at peak efficiency. This and other so-called machine theories (Katz & Kahn, 1978) overlooked employees' needs and perceptions and provided an impetus for humanistic theories.

Humanistic Theories

Two groups of theories from the Human Relations movement in management have particular relevance to the work environment: theories relevant to job satisfaction, such as those by Maslow and Herzberg, and theories on interpersonal relations in organizations, such as those by Likert and Homans.

In an early theory related to job satisfaction, Maslow (1943) suggested that each person has a "hierarchy of needs," including needs for social relationships and personal growth, which were neglected in the classical theories. Maslow pictured the physical environment as satisfying basic needs for shelter and se-

curity. Once these needs are satisfied, the individual attends to the "higher-order" needs and ignores the physical environment. Herzberg's (1966) theory of "satisfiers" and "dissatisfiers" depicted the physical environment as dissatisfier—a source of dissatisfaction or indifference, but not satisfaction (see the section on Influences on Job Satisfaction). According to Herzberg, people gain satisfaction from such things as interesting work and autonomy.

Among theories of organizations that emphasized interpersonal relationships, Likert's (1961) *"linking pin" model* pictured each manager and his or her subordinates as a group or "family." The organization was viewed as a pyramid of overlapping families, interconnected through their common members, or "linking pins." Unlike the classical theories, this model explicitly recognized the importance of groups or teams.

Likert's theory had no overt role for the physical environment. However, an earlier theory by Homans (1950) contained an idea at least implicit in many humanistic theories: patterns of interaction are associated with physical proximity among workers. Homans also hypothesized that the more frequent interactions between people, the more positive their sentiments are toward each other. By implication, cohesive groups form among people whose jobs and physical environments create opportunities for frequent interaction.

Burolandschaft, and later the open plan office, rested on the assumption that open, undivided offices promote communication, particularly among coworkers whose desks are close to each other (e.g., Lorenzen & Jaeger, 1968). The open office was supposed to promote interpersonal relationships by maximizing communication. Burolandschaft also drew on systems theory in its premise that efficient communication creates beneficial effects throughout the organization.

Systems Theories

Systems theories explicitly recognized the interdependence among the components of organizations. Homans (1950) suggested that a change in one part of an organization produces corresponding changes in other parts. Others argued that an organization represents an "open" system in which the relationships among components depend on external surroundings of the organization (e.g., Katz & Kahn, 1966).

The physical environment had a relatively prominent role in the theory of *sociotechnical systems* (Trist, Higgins, Murray, & Pollack, 1963; see also Cooper & Foster, 1971). The theory emphasized the importance of the fit between technology and the social structure of an organization. It suggested a general principle—that technology (task characteristics, physical layout, and equipment) complements relationships among workers and jobs.

In summary, theories of organizations have depicted the work environment in offices and factories in terms of formal roles and symbols of office, individual efficiency and job design, satisfaction or dissatisfaction of individual needs, interpersonal interaction, or the fit between environment and organization.

19.5.2. Organizational Effectiveness

Theorists disagree on the definition of organizational effectiveness but agree that it includes more than productivity. Some definitions are multidimensional (see Nadler, Hackman, & Lawler, 1979; P.C. Smith, 1983; Steers, 1975). For example, Schein (1972) defined effectiveness in terms of communication, flexibility, creativity, and commitment within the organization. Other definitions use broad criteria based on the effective use of resources (Argyris, 1964; Katz & Kahn, 1978). *"Effectiveness"* is defined here as an organization's success in maintaining (1) satisfaction and commitment among its members; (2) communication and coordination among individuals and work units; (3) adequate production or output; and (4) a mutually supportive relationship with external surroundings. The work environment may contribute to the first three.

Individual Level of Analysis
Two outcomes for the individual—job satisfaction and performance—represent key components of organizational effectiveness. An individual's satisfaction with the job is not consistently related to performance but does show a consistent association with low rates of absence and turnover (see, for example, Davis, 1977).

Evidence discussed earlier suggests a clear link between satisfaction with the physical environment and job satisfaction. In turn, other research suggests that a variety of environmental factors are related to satisfaction with the physical environment. These include the ambient conditions—lighting, temperature, and noise, and probably music and air quality. Features of the work station or work space, such as color, floor space, equipment, chair, and capacities for personalization and enclosure are also linked with satisfaction with the physical environment. However, the connection of the work place with an individual's job satisfaction depends upon many factors and probably varies greatly from person to person. The contribution of the physical environment to organizational effectiveness through job satisfaction depends on the extent to which each person's physical environment satisfies his or her unique needs.

As for performance, the research evidence suggests that the physical environment exerts an influence through several psychological processes, especially arousal, distraction, overload, and stress. These processes are apparently influenced by ambient conditions, especially noise or heat. Performance may be improved or degraded depending upon the task. Most of the demonstrated links between the physical environment and performance represent short-term effects, which may not persist in offices or factories because of *adaptation*. However, adaptation itself may affect performance over the long term, through changes in work habits or allocation of effort.

Interpersonal Level of Analysis
To the extent that the work environment has a role in interpersonal relations, it may make indirect contributions to organizational effectiveness. These might occur in physical environments that support employees' relationships or communications with co-workers. For instance, there is evidence of satisfaction with work spaces that appropriately display status, or express occupants' self-identities through personalization, or provide privacy. It is possible (but not empirically demonstrated) that in work spaces that allow comfortable conversation, occupants perform more effectively if their jobs require frequent conversations. Similarly, in work spaces conducive to informal conversation, workers may gain satisfaction from friendly relations with co-workers.

An hypothesis advanced by the advocates of "office landscape" held that open offices enhance communication, and that improved communication leads in turn to improved productivity or effectiveness of the organization (e.g., Planas, 1978). However, the evidence on communication suggests that only some types of communication improved, in some facilities, and that some types of communication sometimes became more difficult. At the same time, people in open offices have complained about noise and lack of privacy. Direct tests of the claim that open offices lead to improved productivity have been hampered by the lack of an unambiguous criterion. However, a few postoccupancy evaluations of open offices incorporated ratings by employees of their performance after changing from conventional offices. Mixed results came from two large German studies (Boje, 1971; Kraemer, Sieverts, & Partners, 1977) and one U.S. study (Sloan, n.d.). Another U.S. study showed no change in self-rated output (Zeitlin, 1969); one more showed a decline (Hundert & Greenfield, 1969). In short, some employees in some locations rated their own performance better after changing to open plan offices, but others saw no change or worse performance.

To the extent that open plan offices failed to increase productivity, the failure may reflect the complexity of the relationship between various types of communication and features of the physical environment. Even if increased accessibility did lead to an increase in communication, the result would not necessarily be a more productive organization, for at least two reasons. First, change in an organization rarely occurs as a consequence of change in only one element (such as the physical layout) while others remain unchanged (Katz & Kahn, 1978). In the studies of open offices, employees' jobs and their interrelations often stayed the same—only the physical layout changed. Forces toward stability probably compensated for the new offices. Second, an organization can only benefit from greater communication when it is insufficient in the first place; in some cases communication may have been adequate before changing offices.

The work environment may contribute to organizational effectiveness through symbolic messages about status. For instance, physical status markers may prevent confusion. However, the role of the work place as a symbolic medium may be limited to conveying information about existing properties of the organization. Work groups may be designated through arrangements of furniture, enclosure by partitions or walls, or locations in separate buildings. However, the designation of work groups can contribute to the effectiveness of an organization only where work groups are desired.

Links of the work environment with organizational effectiveness through interpersonal relations may depend on characteristics of the organization. Work environments can symbolize status or group identity, and may figure in communication. Whether these influences in turn contribute to the effectiveness of the organization depends on which qualities are symbolized, which types of communication are facilitated, and how consistent these symbolic messages or types of communication are with other elements of the organization. In effect, the role of the work environment in interpersonal relations is a problem for the organizational level of analysis.

Organizational Level of Analysis

A premise of this level of analysis holds that the work environment reflects or supports the structure and/or climate of the organization. This view has precedent in both practice and theory (e.g., Duffy, 1974a; Trist et al., 1963). Systems theories imply that organizations generate internal forces toward congruence between properties of the organization and properties of the physical environment (Sundstrom, 1986).

ORGANIZATIONAL STRUCTURE

The term "structure" applied to an organization refers to relatively stable characteristics, such as roles, work units, and their interrelationships (see, for example, Payne & Pugh, 1983). Researchers have attempted to identify dimensions of organizational structure and have converged on a fairly consistent list. One review of the literature identified seven dimensions (James & Jones, 1976):

1. *Size* of the organization (total number of people and net assets).
2. *Centralization* of decision making and authority in the highest ranking positions.
3. *Configuration* of roles and work units, including the numbers and sizes of subdivisions; the number of hierarchical levels, the "span of control" (number of supervisees per supervisor); and a "tall" versus "flat" shape (*tall* means many levels of authority and relatively narrow spans of control).
4. *Formalization* of roles, including role specification, emphasis on status, and emphasis on formal communication.
5. *Specialization*, or the number of different specialities.
6. *Standardization* of procedures.
7. *Interdependence* among tasks or components of the organization.

These seven dimensions agree fairly closely with the list identified in another review by Payne and Pugh (1983).

Duffy (1974a, 1974b, 1974c) presented a theory on the connections between organizational structure and the office environment. He suggested that two qualities of organization—bureaucracy and interaction—are associated with two qualities of office environments—differentiation and subdivision. *Bureaucracy* referred to the "tightness with which members of an organization are bound together" (1974c, p. 221), including the degree of centralization, the predominance of professional employees, the importance of authority, the specification of rules, and other features. *Interaction* referred to the frequency and importance of communication among co-workers or with visitors. (Duffy's *bureaucracy* encompassed centralization, specialization, formalization, standardization, and elements of configuration. *Interaction* resembled interdependence.) Duffy's *differentiation* of the physical environment referred to variety among individual work spaces, as opposed to uniformity. *Subdivision* of the office referred to the presence of screens, partitions, or walls between work spaces.

Duffy theorized that organizations with a high degree of bureaucracy have highly differentiated office environments and that a high degree of interaction is associated with low subdivision. An empirical study generally failed to confirm the hypothesis. Duffy surveyed 361 office employees from a total of 16 small organizations and recorded properties of their work spaces. As expected, organizations with a high frequency and importance of internal communication had relatively unsubdivided offices. However, several other indexes of communication were unrelated to subdivision. And contrary to expectations, highly centralized organizations had relatively open and undifferentiated layouts.

The unexpected association of centralization with open and undifferentiated layouts was apparently due to the tendency of people with professional training or high rank to have enclosed, differentiated work spaces. Organizations with a large proportion of professionals or high-status employees were relatively decentralized. Most of the correlations between properties of organizations and properties of office environments could be traced to the proportion of people with professional training.

In retrospect, Duffy's hypothesis probably used overinclusive dimensions of organizational structure. *Bureaucracy* included several important structural dimensions, some of which may be related to different features of the work environment in different ways. The physical variables also may have been too inclusive. For instance, *subdivision* referred to the enclosure of individual work spaces as well as the separation of subgroups of the organization.

An alternative hypothesis holds that each of eight structural dimensions of an organization is reflected in one or more physical properties of its work environment, such that the physical structure is congruent with the organizational structure. The congruence hypothesis derives from Michelson (1970) and is consistent with ecological psychology (Wicker, 1979). Table 19.3 represents an elaborate hypothesis from Sundstrom (1986); it lists dimensions of organizational structure and proposes parallel dimensions of the physical environment. The proposed relationships are as follows:

Table 19.3. Dimensions of Organizational Structure and Properties of Physical Environments Hypothesized as Parallel

Dimensions of Organizational Structure	Properties of the Physical Environment
Size (total number of people and net assets)	*Space* (amount of floor space in buildings of the organization)
Technology (extent to which processes in the organization incorporate technology)	*Automation* (proportion of space devoted to machinery and equipment)
Configuration (including numbers and sizes of subdivisions and the number of levels in the hierarchy)	*Delineation of subdivisions and subgroups* (through location, enclosure, and physical boundaries)
	Differentiation by rank (of groups or individual work spaces, using status markers)
Interdependence (among work units and tasks, including work flow)	*Proximity of work units* adjacent in work flow in the organization
Specialization (the number of different jobs and tasks included in the organization)	*Differentiation by job or task* (of work areas for subdivisions or individuals)
	Enclosure of task areas or work spaces (for specific tasks or jobs)
Centralization (of decision making, authority, and control to the highest ranking members of the organization)	*Uniformity of work spaces* (within ranks and jobs)
	Visual accessibility of work spaces (within subdivisions, for supervision)
Formalization of roles (including role specification, emphasis on status, emphasis on formal channels)	*Differentiation by rank* of work spaces
	Uniformity of work spaces within ranks
Standardization of procedures and specification of tasks	*Rigidity of layout* within buildings and subdivisions

Source: Sundstrom, E., *Work Places*, Cambridge University Press, 1986. Reproduced with permission.

1. The size of an organization (number of people and amount of assets) may be reflected in its space — the numbers and sizes of its buildings.

2. The greater the extent to which an organization incorporates technology, the more it incorporates automation, and the greater the share of its space devoted to machines and equipment.

3. The configuration of an organization may be mirrored in its physical configuration, in that subdivisions are delineated through buildings or locations in different buildings.

4. The status hierarchy may be reflected in status markers for individuals and groups.

5. The interdependence among work units or tasks within an organization depends on the nature of its products and the details of its internal processes. If interdependence calls for face-to-face exchange of information or rapid movement of materials or products, efficient operation depends on *work flow*. A congruent physical work environment accommodates work flow with maximum economy of motion, so that work units or individuals adjacent in the work flow (or interdependent in their tasks) are physically accessible. Where work flow involves physical objects or face-to-face contact, interdependence may be associated with accessibility among work units.

6. For organizations with a high degree of specialization, a congruent work environment contains a corresponding diversity of work spaces. Specialization may also call for physical separation of tasks (Bechtel, 1976).

7. In highly centralized organizations, work environments may contain clusters of highly uniform work spaces in open areas. Uniform work spaces reflect minimal latitude in decisions about the work environment; open work areas allow convenient supervision.

8. In highly formalized organizations, a congruent environment emphasizes and symbolizes formal roles, ranks, and rules. Roles may be symbolized in work spaces differentiated by jobs. Ranks may be conveyed through work spaces differentiated by status, and rules may be symbolized by uniformity of work spaces within jobs and ranks.

9. In an organization with a high degree of standardization, a congruent environment may have a rigidly fixed arrangement. For instance, an office with closely specified rules may also have a fixed layout delineated by structural walls.

These hypothetical parallels between organizational structure and the work environment have apparently not been tested. However, they are generally consistent with guidelines offered for the design of offices (e.g., Moleski & Lang, 1982). Some of the parallels seem to be emphasized in at least some office buildings (e.g., Duffy, 1977, 1978; Jockusch, 1982). Similarly, some factories exhibit congruence between layout and the designation of work groups and the physical layout of buildings (e.g., Dowling, 1973).

ORGANIZATIONAL CLIMATE

Whereas *structure* refers to the formal characteristics of an organization, *climate* is broader and less precisely defined. It often refers to the unique values, style, culture, or collective personality of an organization. According to Porter et al. (1975), climate means "the typical or characteristic day-to-day properties of a particular work environment — its nature as perceived and felt by those who work in it or are familiar with it" (p. 456). However, definitions differ. In some cases, climate is defined as collective perception within an organization of the quality of life there (e.g., Tagiuri & Litwin, 1968). In other cases, it is defined as a property of an organization independent of individual perceptions (e.g., Payne & Pugh, 1983). Researchers have sometimes argued that climate is not even a property of the organization but of individual perceptions (e.g., Schneider, 1975). Some have argued that if climate is psychological, it is difficult to distinguish from other perceptions related to work, such as job satisfaction and job characteristics (e.g., Guion, 1973). *Climate* refers here to perceptions of the quality or style of an organization shared among its members. (This definition includes shared perceptions of the structure of an organization along with collective perceptions of jobs.)

Researchers and theorists have defined dimensions of organizational climate similar to those defined for organizational structure but with less agreement. A review of research gives a list that represents a reasonable synthesis (Campbell, Dunnette, Lawler, & Weick, 1975, p. 306):

1. *Individual autonomy*, or freedom and responsibility in decision making.

2. *Degree of structure imposed* on the position, including the closeness of supervision and the specification of jobs.

3. *Reward orientation*, including general satisfaction and orientation toward profit, promotion, and achievement.

4. *Consideration, warmth, and support*, particularly in supervisory practices.

5. *Cooperative interpersonal relations among peers*, including presence of conflict, tolerance of con-

flict, and cooperation among peers. (The authors only considered adding this fifth dimension to their list.)

There are apparently no empirical studies of the connection between climate and properties of the work environment. However, Steele and Jenks (1977) provided a practical perspective on the use of the physical environment to stimulate change in organizational climate. They identified their own dimensions of climate: (1) "stimulating energy," (2) "improving the distribution of energy," (3) "increasing pleasure," and (4) "improving growth possibilities" (p. 132). To stimulate energy, they suggested visual stimulation (e.g., colors or graphics), central gathering places and meeting places, and changing the sizes of spaces to fit "task needs." To improve the distribution of energy, they advocated reducing the "boundary barriers" between groups, reducing actual and functional distances, reducing the "status function" (i.e., status symbols), and building in flexibility. To increase pleasure, they recommended support for personalization, livening up "dead zones" (such as corridors and supply rooms), and avoiding "sterility." To improve the possibilities of "growth" (psychological development of individuals), they recommended creating "demand qualities" (by leaving parts of the settings unfinished), sharing decisions about the physical environment, and providing technical support for "tinkering" with settings. These ideas remain to be tested in research.

A general hypothesis on the connection of the work environment with climate is that organizations express their values in their offices and factories. If so, climate is reflected in the work environment (but the environment does not necessarily dictate the climate). For instance, an organization with little orientation toward general satisfaction may provide less comfortable accommodations and pay less attention to individuals' needs. (Even so, a lavish office with every work space tailored to its occupant may not guarantee a positive climate—though it would probably be associated with a high level of satisfaction with the environment.) However, the connection between the work place and organizational climate remains largely unstudied.

19.6. FUTURE WORK ENVIRONMENTS

This section considers some possible changes in the work environment and related technology and speculates about future offices and factories.

19.6.1. Changes in the Office

Discussions of the "office of the future" generally focus on the advent of small, powerful computers, advanced forms of electronic communication, and the associated possibilities for electronic handling of information. Technology now exists for a "paperless office," in which people work through video display terminals attached to computers, which allow practically instant storage and retrieval of information, composition and editing of written text, and transfer of messages (e.g., Giuliano, 1982; Ruff & Associates, 1978). Technology also exists for advanced telecommunications, including the picture phone and other innovations (Sundstrom, 1986). Issues for the future of the office concern three questions: (1) to what extent will office work occur in employees' homes?, (2) to what degree will electronic communication replace personal meetings?, and (3) will employees participate more than they do now in the design of their offices?

Office Work at Home?

Toffler (1980) advanced the concept of the "electronic cottage" and predicted that a large fraction of office workers will eventually spend substantial amounts of their time working at home. On the other hand, Naisbett (1982) argued that while working at home, people miss the social stimulation of the work place and may therefore resist the "electronic cottage." At present, office work at home apparently occurs mainly among the self-employed, rarely among employees of large organizations. However, a few companies have publicized the results of successful experiments with electronic cottage work (Becker, 1981; Sundstrom, 1986).

One impetus in favor of office work at home is employees' convenience (they could avoid some commuting). A major counterforce is the requirement for organizational change. Jobs and supervisory relationships would have to be revised, with employees exercising greater autonomy and responsibility. Consequences of the electronic cottage could include the disappearance of some personal work spaces in office buildings and the weakening of symbolic ties between people and places, which now include the use of work spaces to signal status, express self-identity, and reflect the organization's values. Organizations would lose control over employees' working conditions and might focus more on the results of work. The electronic cottage could eventually change the role of employee to that of contractor and the role of the office building to that of conference center (Sundstrom, 1986).

Electronic Meetings?

New technology creates the potential for future office workers to communicate with practically anyone, practically anyplace, by way of electronic media. A shift toward electronic communication and away from face-to-face meetings could lead to change in the office environment. In the most extreme scenario, people would work at home from video terminals, do all of their communicating electronically, and have no need of central office buildings. More likely, however, people may rely on electronic media for a share of their communications.

The question is, to what extent will electronic communication replace face-to-face meetings? Anecdotes suggest that electronic communication represents an acceptable substitute for a meeting only when travel makes the meeting difficult or impossible. Telephone calls and video conferences represent choices of expediency, perhaps selected when meetings are not important enough to warrant the time and expense of travel but still have high enough priority for an exchange involving voice or visual communication. One expert suggested that office workers use video conferences for "lower level lower risk" meetings (Gottschalk, 1983).

Reliance on electronic communications could lead to changes in the office environment. One likely change is the appearance of video-conference centers in office buildings. Advancing technology may also create the possibility of an inexpensive picture phone on every desk. However, this may give people more communication than they want. Even so, it is conceivable that computers and video display terminals could incorporate a visual channel. The "picture phone" could become a commonplace feature of the desk-top computer. If it does, though, it appears unlikely to replace more than a fraction of face-to-face meetings.

Participation by Employees in the Design of Work Environments?

Some experts foresee a greatly expanded role of employees in the design of offices and factories of the future. Dickson (1975) described some experiments in which workers exercised substantial responsibility in the design of new buildings. Kleeman (1982) noted that "participatory design" offers potential solutions to problems experienced by office workers confronted with changing technology. Becker (1981) criticized traditional practices of giving workers a minor part of decisions concerning their office environments.

Under ideal circumstances, participative design allows the work environment to be tailored to its users. To the extent that office workers have a voice in decisions about the size, furnishing, color, arrangement, lighting, or layout of their work spaces, the environment may meet their needs better than otherwise. And participation itself could be a source of satisfaction for employees. On the other hand, barriers to participative design could come from the lack of an organizational vehicle for incorporating employees in the planning of their environments, the need for organizational change to create one, and possibly resistance by professional architects, planners, and designers who now design offices. Participative design may augment employees' satisfaction or efficiency, but it would carry costs.

Some developments seem to favor participative design. One is a wider trend toward participative management (e.g., Zager & Rosow, 1982). Another is the increasing use of modular work spaces, in which partitions and furniture are portable and easily rearranged. This furniture allows the layout of an office to be changed quickly and inexpensively. However, it remains to be seen whether work environments of the future will involve greater participation by workers.

19.6.2. Changes in the Factory

Potential changes in the factory stem from *automation*, or the use of machines to do operations formerly done by hand. Automation seems likely to touch practically every facet of manufacturing. With the advent of computerized controllers and robots, it is technically possible to manufacture many products untouched by human hands (Forester, 1980).

Advances in microelectronics, computers, and associated equipment allow the automation of at least six facets of manufacturing (Bessant, Braun, & Moseley, 1980; Toffler, 1980): (1) transfer of materials, parts, and products; (2) regulation of the physical conditions in production, such as temperature and humidity; (3) automation of operations, such as machining, welding, mixing, and painting (Zermeno, Moseley, & Braun, 1980); (4) small-batch production through computer-controlled machines that make customized items (Toffler, 1980); (5) advanced sampling and quality control through robots, sensors, and other methods; and (6) integration and coordination of manufacturing processes (Gold, 1982).

As a consequence of automation, the physical environment of the factory has the potential to be as comfortable as an office. Many of the most dirty and hazardous jobs are being automated. Many remaining jobs in factories involve the programming, monitoring, and control of machines in clean, well-lit, climate-controlled, quiet production lines.

Speculation on the future of environments in factories is chancy because factories are highly varied and because their configuration depends on their products, labor, materials, markets, and other factors. In the context of volatile conditions in manufacturing, at least three questions arise concerning the relationship between factory workers and their physical environments: (1) will the factory incorporate a rising standard of physical comfort for workers?, (2) to what extent will factories be designed to accommodate work groups or teams?, and (3) to what extent will factory work be done in workers' homes?

A Rising Standard of Comfort?

One reason for increasing comfort in factories may be the need to attract highly skilled employees, whose importance may grow. A higher standard of comfort in factories may also arise out of the need for special conditions in certain industrial processes, as in food or beverage processing, that require constant temperatures and humidities. Where factories have the means to monitor and control the ambient environment, these may be used to regulate the environment of people.

Accommodation of Work Groups?

If the current trend toward the design of jobs for groups continues (e.g., Zager & Rosow, 1982), it seems likely that factories will be designed accordingly. If so, more factories may incorporate separate areas designed for groups (e.g., Dowling, 1973). However, trends toward the use of work groups could abate. One reason for the use of groups is to add variety, autonomy, and cooperation to otherwise monotonous jobs (Hackman & Oldham, 1980). If the monotonous jobs now being given groups begin to disappear, so could the need for work groups. It remains to be seen whether the next generation of factories will be designed for work groups.

Cottage Industry?

Factory work could conceivably begin to move into workers' homes. The availability of inexpensive computers and industrial machines may allow people to produce and market certain products from home. Traditional cottage industry has often involved cloth-

ing, foods, and handicrafts. Advances in communication could even create more possibilities for marketing out of the home than ever before. Electronic communications, in combination with robots, could even create a new type of cottage industry based on the remote monitoring or operation of factory machines. However, although the potential for remote factory work probably exists now, it may be slow to develop, as organizations may have to change to incorporate it. And organizations would need reasons to change. Cottage work would have to either save money or promote satisfaction among employees.

In summary, changes in both office and factory could stem from automation and new technology. However, the extent and the pace of change seem to depend on the requirement for change in the organization as a whole.

19.7. SUMMARY

This chapter provides a selective review of the environmental psychology of offices and factories. It describes empirical findings and related theory within an analytic framework based on a conception of person–environment relationships as a system. The framework defines three levels of analysis: individual, interpersonal, and organizational. At each level of analysis, the review focuses on different facets of the physical environment and on different, but interrelated, outcomes. Relationships among facets of the physical environment and key outcomes are explored in terms of psychological, social psychological, and organizational processes.

For the individual worker, the physical working environment consists of ambient conditions (temperature, air, light, and sound), a work station, and supportive facilities, such as hallways, lounges, restrooms, and other shared areas. Key outcomes include the individual's satisfaction with the physical environment, satisfaction with the job, and performance. The environment may influence these outcomes through psychological arousal, stress, distraction, overload, or fatigue. However, the influences may change over time, through adaptation.

Research on the individual worker includes mainly field studies, surveys, and laboratory experiments. The evidence suggests that all of the ambient conditions, and some aspects of work stations can influence individual satisfaction and performance. However, these influences depend on long-term adaptation of individuals in work environments, which has seldom been studied. Individual satisfaction is also associated with aspects of the work space that accurately symbolize the occupant's status, express his or her self-identity, or provide privacy appropriate for the job.

At the interpersonal level, key outcomes include the adequacy of communication and the formation and cohesion of small groups. An analysis of environmental factors in communication suggests that the environment influences workers' accessibility for face-to-face conversations and regulates their social contact.

Research in offices and factories suggests that informal, face-to-face conversation is associated with proximity among work spaces. Physical proximity has also been associated with the formation of small groups under some conditions; cohesion may be associated with physical enclosure of a group. Research in nonwork environments suggests that conversations are most comfortable that allow people to select an interpersonal distance and choose whether or not a desk or the like is between them. Interaction in group discussions is associated with lines of eye contact.

For an organization, the key outcome is organizational effectiveness, which subsumes a variety of criteria. Research linking it with the work environment in offices and factories is sparse. However, the work environment may serve important functions for organizational effectiveness through the individual and interpersonal relationships, as well as through the organization as a whole. A hypothesis consistent with current thinking is that organizations strive for congruence between physical environments and structure and climate.

In the future, as offices and factories evolve, technology will probably bring major changes in workers' equipment and work stations that call for different job activities, a redistribution of jobs, and changes in organizational structure. The physical environment itself may also change. For offices of the future, key questions concern the possibilities of work in employees' homes via computer terminals and the substitution of telecommunication for face-to-face meetings. For factories of the future, key issues concern the introduction of computerized production lines and the use of robots to perform repetitive jobs. Another question concerns the extent to which factories of the future will accommodate the work group as a principal work unit.

Acknowledgments

This chapter was written especially for the Handbook of Environmental Psychology *but drew heavily on a* book written concurrently on the same topic—E. Sundstrom, with M.G. Sundstrom, Work Places: Psychology of the Physical Environment in Offices and Factories *(New York: Cambridge University Press, 1986).*

This chapter benefited greatly from comments on an earlier draft by Stephen Margulis of BOSTI, Buffalo, NY.

REFERENCES

Aaronson, B.S. (1970). Some affective stereotypes of color. *International Journal of Symbology, 2*(1), 15–27.

Acking, C.A., & Kuller, R. (1972). The perception of an interior as a function of its color. *Ergonomics, 15*(16), 645–654.

Adams, J.S. (1965). Inequity in social exchange. In L. Berkowitz (Ed.), *Advances in Experimental Social Psychology* (Vol. 2; pp. 267–299). New York: Academic.

Adams, S. (1953). Status congruency as a variable in small group performance. *Social Forces, 32*(1), 16–22.

Aldrich, H.E. (1974). *Organizations and environments.* Englewood Cliffs, NJ: Prentice-Hall.

Allen, E.C., & Guilford, J.P. (1936). Factors determining the affective values of color combinations. *American Journal of Psychology, 48*(4), 643–648.

Allen, M.A., & Fischer, G.J. (1978). Ambient temperature effects on paired associate learning. *Ergonomics, 21*(2), 95–101.

Allen, T.J., & Gerstberger, P.G. (1973). A field experiment to improve communications in a product engineering department: The nonterritorial office. *Human Factors, 15*(5), 487–498.

Altman, I. (1975). *The environment and social behavior.* Monterey, CA: Brooks/Cole.

Altman, I. (1976). Privacy: A conceptual analysis. *Environment and Behavior, 8,* 7–29.

Altman, I., & Chemers, M. (1980). *Culture and environment.* Monterey, CA: Brooks/Cole.

Archea, J. (1977). The place of architectural factors in behavioral theories of privacy. *Journal of Social Issues, 33*(3), 116–137.

Argyris, C. (1964). *Integrating the individual and the organization.* New York: Wiley.

Averill, J.R. (1973). Personal control over aversive stimuli and its relation to stress. *Psychological Bulletin, 80*(4), 286–303.

Ayoub, M.M. (1973). Work place design and posture. *Human Factors, 15*(3), 265–268.

Azer, N.Z., McNall, P.E., & Leung, H.C. (1972). Effects of heat stress on performance. *Ergonomics, 15*(6), 681–691.

Babbie, E.R. (1975). The practice of social research. Belmont, CA: Wadsworth.

Bass, B.M., & Bass, R. (1976). Concern for the environment: Implications for industrial and organizational psychology. *American Psychologist, 31*(2), 158–166.

Bates, A. (1964). Privacy—A useful concept. *Social Forces, 42*, 429–434.

Baum, A., Singer, J., & Baum, C. (1981). Stress and the environment. *Journal of Social Issues, 37*(1), 4–35.

Bechtel, R.B. (1976). *Enclosing behavior.* Stroudsburg, PA: Dowden, Hutchinson, & Ross.

Becker, F.D. (1981). *Workspace: Creating environments in organizations.* New York: Praeger.

Bedford, T. (1964). *Basic principles of ventilation and heating.* London: H.K. Lewis.

Bell, C.R., Provins, K.A., & Hiorns, R.W. (1964). Visual and auditory vigilance during exposure to hot and humid conditions. *Ergonomics, 7*(3), 279–288.

Bell, P.A. (1978). Effects of noise and heat stress on primary and subsidiary task performance. *Human Factors, 20*(6), 749–752.

Bell, P.A. (1981). Physiological, comfort, performance and social effects of heat stress. *Journal of Social Issues, 37*, 71–94.

Bennett, C., & Rey, P. (1972). What's so hot about red? *Human Factors, 14*(2), 149–154.

Berry, P.C. (1961). Effect of colored illumination upon perceived temperature. *Journal of Applied Psychology, 45*(4), 248–250.

Bessant, J., Braun, E., & Moseley, R. (1980). Microelectronics in manufacturing industry: The rate of diffusion. In T. Forester (Ed.), *The microelectronics revolution* (pp. 198–218). Oxford: Blackwell.

Birren, F. (1968). Color for interiors. New York: Whitney Library of Design.

Black, F.W., & Milroy, E.A. (1967). Experience of air-conditioning in offices. *Arena, 82*, 157–163.

Blackwell, H.R. (1959). Development and use of a quantitative method for specification of interior illumination levels on the basis of performance data. *Illuminating Engineering, 54*, 317–353.

Blackwell, H.R., & Smith, S.W. (1970). Additional visual performance data for use in illumination specification systems. *Illuminating Engineering, 65*, 389–410.

Blackwell, P.J., & Belt, J.A. (1971). Effect of differential levels of ambient noise on vigilance performance. *Perceptual and Motor Skills, 32*, 734.

Blum, M.L., & Naylor, J.C. (1968). *Industrial Psychology.* New York: Harper & Row.

Boggs, D.H., & Simon, J.R. (1968). Differential effects of noise on tasks of varying complexity. *Journal of Applied Psychology, 52*, 148–153.

Boje, A. (1971). *Open plan offices.* London: Business Books. (Original work published 1968)

BOSTI (1980, 1981). See Buffalo Organization for Social and Technological Innovation.

Boyce, P.R. (1973). Age, illuminance, visual performance, and preference. *Lighting Research and Technology, 5*, 125–144.

Boyce, P.R. (1974). Users' assessments of a landscaped office. *Journal of Architectural Research, 3*(3), 44–62.

Boyce, P.R. (1981). *Human factors in lighting.* London: Applied Science Publishers.

Branton, P. (1969). Behaviour, body mechanics and discomfort. *Ergonomics, 12*(2), 316–327.

Broadbent, D.E. (1953). Noise, paced performance, and vigilance tasks. *British Journal of Psychology, 44*(4), 295–303.

Broadbent, D.E. (1954). Some effects of noise on visual performance. *Quarterly Journal of Experimental Psychology, 6*, 1–5.

Broadbent, D.E. (1957). Effects of noises of high and low frequency on behavior. *Ergonomics, 1*, 21–29.

Broadbent, D.E. (1958). Effect of noise on an "intellectual task." *Journal of the Acoustical Society of America, 30*, 824–827.

Broadbent, D.E. (1971). *Decision and stress.* London: Academic.

Broadbent, D.E. (1976). Noise and details of experiments: A reply to Poulton. *Applied Ergonomics, 7*(4), 231–235.

Broadbent, D.E. (1979). Human performance and noise. In C.M. Harris (Ed.), *Handbook of noise control* (2nd ed.). New York: McGraw-Hill.

Broadbent, D.E., & Gregory, M. (1963). Vigilance considered as a statistical decision. *British Journal of Psychology, 54*, 309–323.

Broadbent, D.E., & Gregory, M. (1965). Effects of noise and signal rate upon vigilance analyzed by means of decision theory. *Human Factors, 7*, 155–162.

Broadbent, D.E., & Little, E.A. (1960). Effects of noise reduction in a work situation. *Occupational Psychology, 34*(1), 133–140.

Brookes, M.J. (1972a, January). Changes in employee attitudes and work practices in an office landscape. In W.J. Mitchell (Ed.), *Proceedings of the 1972 Conference of the Environmental Design Research Association.* Los Angeles: University of California Press.

Brookes, M.J. (1972b). Office landscape: Does it work? *Applied Ergonomics, 3*(4), 224–236.

Brookes, M.J., & Kaplan, A. (1972). The office environment: Space planning and affective behavior. *Human Factors, 14*(5), 373–391.

Buffalo Organization for Social and Technological Innovation (BOSTI). (1980). *The impact of office environment on productivity and quality of working life: First interim report.* Buffalo. NY: Author.

Buffalo Organization for Social and Technological Innovation. (1981). *The impact of office environment on productivity and quality of working life: Comprehensive findings.* Buffalo, NY: Author.

Burandt, U., & Grandjean, E. (1963). Sitting habits of office employees. *Ergonomics, 6*(2), 217–228.

Burgess, R.L. (1968). An experimental and mathematical analysis of group behavior within restricted networks. *Journal of Experimental Social Psychology, 4*, 338–349.

Bursill, A.E. (1958). The restriction of peripheral vision during exposure to hot and humid conditions. *Quarterly Journal of Experimental Psychology, 10*, 113–129.

Cakir, A., Hart, D.J., & Stewart, T.F.M. (1980). *Visual display terminals: A manual covering ergonomics, workplace design, health and safety, task organization.* Chichester, England: Wiley.

Campbell, D.E. (1978). *The effects of different office arrangements on visitors.* Unpublished paper presented at the 86th annual conference of the American Psychological Association, Toronto.

Campbell, D.E. (1979). Interior office design and visitor response. *Journal of Applied Psychology, 64*(6), 648–653.

Campbell, D.E. (1980). Professors and their offices: A survey of person-behavior-environment relationships. In R.R. Stough & A. Wandersman (Eds.), *Optimizing environments: Research, practice and policy.* Washington, D.C.: Environmental Design Research Association.

Campbell, J.P., Dunnette, M.D., Lawler, E.E., & Weick, K.E. (1975). Environmental variation and managerial effectiveness. In R.M. Steers & L.W. Porter (Eds.), *Motivation and work behavior.* New York: McGraw-Hill.

Canter, D. (1968). Office size: An example of psychological research in architecture. *Architect's Journal, 147*(7), 881–888.

Cartwright, D. (1968). The nature of group cohesiveness. In D. Cartwright & A. Zander (Eds.), *Group dynamics: Research and theory* (3rd ed.). New York: Harper & Row.

Cartwright, D., & Zander, A. (1968). *Group dynamics: Research and theory* (3rd ed.). New York: Harper & Row.

Cavanaugh, W.J., Farrell, W.R., Hirtle, P.W., & Watters, B.G. (1962). Speech privacy in buildings. *Journal of the Acoustical Society of America, 34*(4), 475–492.

Chiles, W.D. (1958). Effects of elevated temperatures on performance of a complex mental task. *Ergonomics, 2*(1), 89–96.

Clearwater, Y.A. (1979). *Social-environmental relationships in open and closed offices.* Unpublished doctoral dissertation, University of California, Davis.

Cohen, S. (1978). Environmental load and the allocation of attention. In A. Baum, J.E. Singer, & S. Valins (Eds.), *Advances in environmental psychology.* Hillsdale, NJ: Erlbaum.

Cohen, S. (1980a) The aftereffects of stress on human performance and social behavior: A review of research and theory. *Psychological Bulletin, 88*(1), 82–108.

Cohen, S. (1980b). Cognitive processes as determinants of environmental stress. In I. Sarason & C. Spielberger (Eds.), *Stress and anxiety* (Vol. 7). Washington, D.C.: Hemisphere Press.

Cohen, S., & Lezak, A. (1977). Noise and inattentiveness to social cues. *Environment and Behavior, 9*, 559–572.

Collins, B.L. (1975). *Windows and people: A literature survey.* Washington, DC: U.S. Department of Commerce, National Bureau of Standards, Building Science Series #70.

Colquhoun, W.P., & Goldman, R.F. (1972). Vigilance under induced hyperthermia. *Ergonomics, 15*(6), 621–632.

Conrath, C.W. (1973). Communication patterns, organization structure, and man: Some relationships. *Human Factors, 15*(5), 459–470.

Conte, J.A. (1966). A study of the effects of paced audio rhythm on repetitive motion. *Journal of Industrial Engineering, 17*(31), 163–169.

Cook, T.D., & Campbell, D.T. (1979). *Quasi-Experimentation.* Chicago: Rand-McNally.

Cooper, C.L., & Payne, R. (Eds.). (1978). *Stress at work.* Chichester, England: Wiley.

Cooper, R., & Foster, M. (1971). Sociotechnical systems. *American Psychologist, 26*, 467–474.

Dainoff, M.J., Happ, A., & Crane, P. (1981). Visual fatigue and occupational stress in VDT operators. *Human Factors, 23*(4), 421–438.

Davenport, W.G. (1974). Arousal theory and vigilance: Schedules for background stimulation. *Journal of General Psychology, 91*(4), 51–59.

Davies, D.R. (1967). Physiological and psychological effects of exposure to high intensity noise. *Applied Acoustics, 1*(3), 215–233.

Davies, D.R., Lang, L., & Shackleton, V.J. (1973). The effects of music and task difficulty on performance at a visual vigilance task. *British Journal of Psychology, 64*(3), 383–389.

Davis, K. (1977). *Human behavior at work* (5th ed.). New York: McGraw-Hill.

Dickson, P. (1975). *The future of the workplace: The coming revolution in jobs.* New York: Weybright & Talley.

Doering, J.R. (1977). *Combined effects of noise, illumination and task complexity on task performance.* Unpublished master's thesis, University of Wisconsin, Oshkosh.

Dowling, W.F. (1973, Autumn). Job redesign on the assembly line: Farewell to blue collar blues? *Organizational Dynamics*, 51–67.

Dreyfuss, H. (1966). *The measure of man: Human factors in design.* New York: Whitney Library of Design.

Dubos, R. (1980). *Man adapting* (2nd ed.). New Haven, CT: Yale University Press.

Duffy, E. (1962). *Activation and behavior.* New York: Wiley.

Duffy, F.C. (1969). Role and status in the office. *Architectural Association Quarterly, 1*, 4–13.

Duffy, F.C. (1974a). Office design and organizations: 1.

Theoretical basis. *Environment and Planning B, 1,* 105–118.

Duffy, F.C. (1974b). Office design and organizations: 2. The testing of a hypothetical model. *Environmental and Planning B, 1,* 217–235.

Duffy, F.C. (1974c). *Office interiors and organizations: A comparative study of the relation between organizational structure and the use of interior space in sixteen office organizations.* Unpublished doctoral dissertation, Princeton University, Princeton, NJ.

Duffy, F.C. (1977, May 18). Appraisal (of Hillingdon Civic Center). *Architects' Journal,* pp. 939–943.

Duffy, F.C. (1978, March 29). Three offices: Reading. *Architects' Journal,* pp. 593–604.

Elton, P.M. (1920). A study of output in silk weaving during winter months (Rep. No. 9). London: His Majesty's Stationery Office, Industrial Fatigue Research Board.

Eschenbrenner, A.J. (1971). Effects of intermittent noise on the performance of a complex psychomotor task. *Human Factors, 13,* 59–63.

Evans, G., & Jacobs, S.V. (1981). Air pollution and human behavior. *Journal of Social Issues, 37*(1), 95–125.

Eysenck, H.J. (1941). A critical and experimental study of color preferences. *American Journal of Psychology, 54,* 385–394.

Fanger, P.O. (1972). Improvement of human comfort and resulting effects on working capacity. *Biometeorology, 5*(2), 31–41.

Fanger, P.O., Breum, N.O., & Jerking, E. (1977). Can color and noise influence man's thermal comfort? *Ergonomics, 20*(1), 11–18.

Farbstein, J.D. (1975). *Organization, space and activity: The relationship of task and status to the allocation and use of space in certain organizations.* Unpublished doctoral dissertation, University of London, London.

Faulkner, T.W., & Murphy, T.J. (1973). Lighting for difficult visual tasks. *Human Factors, 15*(2), 149–162.

Faunce, W.A. (1958). Automation in the automobile industry: Some consequences for in-plant social structure. *American Sociological Review, 23,* 401–407.

Ferguson, G.S. (1983). Employee satisfaction with the office environment: Evaluation of a causal model. In D. Amedeo, J.B. Griffin, & J.J. Potter (Eds.), *EDRA 1983: Proceedings of the 14th International Conference of the Environmental Design Research Association.* Washington, DC: Environmental Design Research Association.

Fine, B.J., Cohen, A., & Crist, B. (1960). Effects of exposure to high humidity at high and moderate ambient temperature on anagram solution and auditory discrimination. *Psychological Reports, 7,* 171–181.

Fine, B.J., & Kobrick, J.L. (1978). Effects of altitude and heat on complex cognitive tasks. *Human Factors, 20*(1), 115–122.

Finkelman, J.B., & Glass, D.C. (1970). Reappraisal of the relationship between noise and human performance by means of a subsidiary task measure. *Journal of Applied Psychology, 54*(3), 211–213.

Flynn, J.E., Spencer, T.J., Martyniuk, O., & Hendrick, C. (1973). Interim study of procedures for investigating the effect of light on impression and behavior. *Journal of the Illuminating Engineering Society, 3*(2), 87–94.

Forester, T. (Ed.) (1980). *The microelectronics revolution.* Oxford: Basil Blackwell.

Forster, P.M. (1978). Attentional selectivity: A rejoinder to Hockey. *British Journal of Psychology, 69,* 505–506.

Forster, P.M., & Grierson, A.T. (1978). Noise and attentional selectivity: A reproducible phenomenon? *British Journal of Psychology, 69,* 489–498.

Fox, J.G., & Embrey, E.D. (1972). Music—An aid to productivity. *Applied Ergonomics, 3*(4), 202–205.

Freeburne, C.M., & Fleischer, M.S. (1952). The effect of music distraction upon reading rate and comprehension. *Journal of Educational Psychology, 43,* 101–109.

Galitz, W.D. (1980). *Human factors in office automation.* Atlanta, GA: Life Office Management Association.

Geen, R.G., & Gange, J.J. (1977). Drive theory of social facilitation: Twelve years of theory and research. *Psychological Bulletin, 84*(6), 1267–1288.

Gerlach, K.A. (1974). Environmental design to counter occupational boredom. *Journal of Architectural Research, 3*(3), 15–19.

Gerstberger, P., & Allen, T. (1968). Criteria used by research and development engineers in the selection of an information source. *Journal of Applied Psychology, 52*(4), 272–279.

Giuliano, V.E. (1982). The mechanization of office work. *Scientific American, 247*(3), 149–164.

Givoni, B., & Rim, Y. (1962). Effects of the thermal environment and psychological factors upon subjects, responses and performance of mental work. *Ergonomics, 5*(1), 99–114.

Gladstones, W.H. (1969). Some effects of commercial background music on data preparation operators. *Occupational Psychology, 45,* 213–222.

Glass, D.C., & Singer, J.E. (1972). *Urban stress: Experiments on noise and social stressors.* New York: Academic.

Gold, B. (1982). CAM (Computer Aided Manufacturing) sets new rules for production. *Harvard Business Review, 60*(6), 88–94.

Gottschalk, E.C. (1983, June 26). Firms are cool to meeting by television. *Wall Street Journal,* p. 35ff.

Greene, T., & Bell, P.A. (1980). Additional considerations concerning the effects of "warm" and "cool" wall colours on energy conservation. *Ergonomics, 23,* 949–954.

Griffiths, I.D. (1975). Thermal comfort: A behavioral approach. In D. Canter & P. Stringer (Eds.), *Environmental interaction: Psychological approaches to our physical surroundings*. New York: International Universities Press.

Griffiths, I.D., & Boyce, P.R. (1971). Performance and thermal comfort. *Ergonomics, 14*(3), 457–468.

Griffitt, W. (1970). Environmental effects on interpersonal affective behavior. Ambient effective temperature and attraction. *Journal of Personality and Social Psychology, 15*, 240-244.

Griffitt, W., & Veitch, R. (1971). Hot and crowded: Influences of population density and temperature on interpersonal affective behavior. *Journal of Personality and Social Psychology, 17*, 92–98.

Grimaldi, J.V. (1958). Sensori-motor performance under varying noise conditions. *Ergonomics, 2*(1), 34–43.

Grivel, F., & Barth, M. (1980). Thermal comfort in office spaces: Predictions and observations. In E. Fernandes, J. Woods, & A. Faist, (Eds.), *Building energy management*. Oxford: Pergamon.

Guilford, J.P. (1934). The affective value of color as a function of hue, tint, and chroma. *Journal of Experimental Psychology, 17*, 342–370.

Guilford, J.P., & Smith, P.C. (1959). A system of color preferences. *American Journal of Psychology, 72*(4), 487–502.

Guion, R.M. (1973). A note on organizational climate. *Organizational Behavior and Human Performance, 9*, 120–125.

Gullahorn, J.T. (1952). Distance and friendship as factors in the gross interaction matrix. *Sociometry, 15*, 123–134.

Gundlach, C., & Macoubrey, C. (1931). The effect of color on apparent size. *American Journal of Psychology, 43*, 109–111.

Hack, J.M., Robinson, H.W., & Lathrop, R.G. (1965). Auditory distraction and compensatory tracking. *Perceptual and Motor Skills, 20*, 228–230.

Hackman, J.R., & Oldham G.R. (1980). *Work redesign*. Reading, MA: Addison-Wesley.

Hamilton, P., & Copeman, A. (1970). The effects of alcohol and noise on components of tracking and monitoring tasks. *British Journal of Psychology, 6*(2), 149–156.

Hansen, W.B., & Altman, I. (1976). Decorating personal places: A descriptive analysis. *Environment and Behavior, 8*(4), 491–504.

Hanson, A. (1978). Effects of a move to an open landscape office. *Dissertation Abstracts International, 39*(6), 3046B.

Harmon, F.L. (1933). The effects of noise upon certain psychological and physiological processes. *Archives of Psychology, 23*(147), 1–84.

Harris, C.S. (1972). Effects of intermittent and continuous noise on serial search performance. *Perceptual and Motor Skills, 35*, 627–634.

Harris, L. & Associates, Inc. (1978). *The Steelcase national study of office environments: Do they work?* Grand Rapids, MI: Steelcase.

Harris, L. & Associates, Inc. (1980). *The Steelcase national study of office environments No. 2: Comfort and productivity in the office of the 80's*. Grand Rapids, MI: Steelcase.

Hartley, L.R. (1974). Performance during continuous and intermittent noise and wearing ear protection. *Journal of Experimental Psychology, 102*, 512–516.

Hearn, G. (1957). Leadership and the spatial factor in small groups. *Journal of Abnormal and Social Psychology, 54*, 269–272.

Hebb, D.O. (1949). *Organization of behavior*. New York: Wiley.

Hedge, A. (1982). The open-plan office: A systematic investigation of employee reactions to their work environment. *Environment and Behavior, 14*(5), 519–542.

Helson, H. (1964). *Adaptation-level theory: An experimental and systematic approach to behavior*. New York: Harper & Row.

Helson, H., & Lansford, T. (1970). The role of spectral energy source and background color in the pleasantness of object colors. *Applied Optics, 9*, 1513–1562.

Henderson, R.L., McNellis, J.F., & Williams, H.G. (1975). A survey of important visual tasks in offices. *Lighting Design and Application, 5*, 18–25.

Herzberg, F. (1966). *Work and the nature of man*. Cleveland, OH: World.

Herzberg, F., Mausner, B., Peterson, R., & Capwell, D. (1957). *Job Attitudes: Review of Research and Opinion*. Pittsburgh: Psychological Service.

Herzberg, F., Mausner, B., & Snyderman, B. (1959). *The motivation to work*. New York: Wiley.

Hockey, G.R. J. (1970a). Effects of loud noise on attentional selectivity. *Quarterly Journal of Experimental Psychology, 22*, 28–36.

Hockey, G.R.J. (1970b). Signal probability and spatial locations as possible bases for increased selectivity in noise. *Quarterly Journal of Experimental Psychology, 22*, 37–42.

Hockey, G.R. (1978). Attentional selectivity and the problems of replication: A reply to Forster & Grierson. *British Journal of Psychology, 69*, 499–503.

Hollingworth, H.L., & Poffenberger, A.T. (1926). *Applied psychology*. New York: Appleton.

Homans, G.C. (1950). *The human group*. New York: Harcourt, Brace & World.

Homans, G.C. (1954). The cash posters: A study of a group of working girls. *American Sociological Review, 19*, 724–733.

Hopkinson, R.G., & Longmore, J. (1959). Attention and distraction in the lighting of workplaces. *Ergonomics, 2,* 321–334.

Houston, B.K. (1969). Noise, task difficulty and Stroop color-word performance. *Journal of Experimental Psychology, 82,* 403–404.

Hovey, H.B. (1928). Effects of general distraction on the higher thought processes. *American Journal of Psychology, 40,* 585–591.

Howell, W.C. (1976). *Essentials of industrial and organizational psychology.* Homewood, IL: Dorsey.

Hughes, P.C. (1976). Lighting the office. *The Office, 84,* 127ff.

Humes, J.F. (1941). The effects of occupational music on scrappage in the manufacture of radio tubes. *Journal of Applied Psychology, 25,* 573–587.

Hundert, A.J., & Greenfield, N. (1969). Physical space and organizational behavior: A study of an office landscape. Proceedings of the 77th annual convention of the American Psychological Association, Washington, DC.

Ives, R.S., & Ferdinands, R. (1974). Working in a landscaped office. *Personnel Practice Bulletin, 30*(2), 126–141.

Jacobs, K., & Hustmeyer, F.E. (1974). Effects of four psychological primary colors on G.S.R., heart rate and respiration rate. *Perceptual and Motor Skills, 38,* 763–766.

James, L.R., & Jones, A.P. (1976). Organizational structure: A review of structural dimensions and their conceptual relationships with individual attitudes and behavior. *Organizational Behavior and Human Performance, 16,* 74–113.

Jerison, H.J. (1957). Performance on a single vigilance task in noise and quiet. *Journal of the Acoustical Society of America, 29,* 1163–1165.

Jerison, H.J. (1959). Effects of noise on human performance. *Journal of Applied Psychology, 43*(2), 96–101.

Jockusch, P. (1982). *Towards a redefinition of standards for the quality of working life.* Paper presented at the 20th Congress of the International Association of Applied Psychology, Edinburgh.

Johns, E., & Sumner, F.C. (1948). Relation of the brightness differences of colors to their apparent distances. *Journal of Psychology, 26,* 25–29.

Joiner, D. (1976). Social ritual and architectural space. In H. Proshansky, W. Ittelson, & L. Rivlin (Eds.), *Environmental psychology* (2nd ed.). New York: Holt, Rinehart & Winston.

Justa, F.C., & Golan, M.B. (1977). Office Design: Is privacy still a problem? *Journal of Architectural Research, 6*(2), 5–12.

Katz, D., & Kahn, R.L. (1966). *The social psychology of organizations.* New York: Wiley.

Katz, D., & Kahn, R.L. (1978). *The social psychology of organizations, 2nd ed.* New York: Wiley.

Keighley, E.C. (1970). Acceptability criteria for noise in large offices. *Journal of Sound and Vibration, 11*(1), 83–93.

Kelvin, P. (1973). A social psychological examination of privacy. *British Journal of Social and Clinical Psychology, 12,* 248–261.

Kenrick, D.T., & Johnson, G.A. (1979). Interpersonal attraction in aversive environments: A problem for the classical conditioning paradigm? *Journal of Personality and Social Psychology, 37,* 572–579.

Kerr, W.A. (1944). Psychological research in industrial music and plant broadcasting. *Journal of Psychology, 17,* 243–261.

Kerr, W.A. (1945). Experiments on the effects of music on factory production. *Applied Psychology Monographs, 5,* 1–40.

Kirk, R.E., & Hecht, E. (1963). Maintenance of vigilance by programmed noise. *Perceptual and Motor Skills, 16,* 553–560.

Kleeman, W.B. (1981). *The challenge of interior design.* Boston, MA: CBI Publishing.

Kleeman, W.B. (1982). The future of the office. *Environment and Behavior, 14*(5), 593–610.

Knowles, E.S. (1983). Social physics and the effects of others: Tests of the effects of audience size and distance on social judgments and behavior. *Journal of Personality and Social Psychology, 45*(6), 1263–1279.

Konar, E., & Sundstrom, E. (1986). Status demarcation in the office. In J. Wineman (Ed.), *Behavioral issues in office design.* New York: Van Nostrand.

Konar, E., Sundstrom, E., Brady, C., Mandel, D., & Rice, R. (1982). Status markers in the office. *Environment and Behavior, 14*(3), 561–580.

Konecni, V.J., & Sargent-Pollock, D. (1976). Choice between melodies differing in complexity under divided-attention conditions. *Journal of Experimental Psychology: Human Perception and Performance, 2*(3), 347–356.

Korte, C., Ypma, I., & Toppen, A. (1975). Helpfulness in Dutch society as a function of urbanization and environmental input level. *Journal of Personality and Social Psychology, 32*(6), 996–1003.

Kraemer, Sieverts & Partners. (1977). *Open-plan offices: New ideas, experience and improvements.* London: McGraw-Hill.

Kryter, K.D. (1970). *The effects of noise on man.* New York: Academic.

Laird, D.A. (1933). The influence of noise on production and fatigue as related to pitch, sensation, level and steadiness of noise. *Journal of Applied Psychology, 17,* 320–330.

Langdon, F.J. (1966). *Modern offices: A user survey* (National Building Research Paper No. 41). London: Her Majesty's Stationery Office.

Lifson, K.A. (1957). Production welding in extreme heat. *Er-*

gonomics, 1(1), 345–346.

Likert, R. (1961). *New patterns of management.* New York: McGraw-Hill.

Link, J.M., & Pepler, R.D. (1970). Associated fluctuations in daily temperature, productivity and absenteeism. *ASHRAE Transactions, 76*(Pt. 2), 326–337.

Lipman, A., Cooper, I., Harris, R., & Tranter, R. (1978). Power: A neglected concept in office design? *Journal of Architectural Research, 6*(3), 28–37.

Lippencott, J.G., & Margulies, W.P. (1958). Physical environment. In H.L. Wylie (Ed.), *Office management handbook* (2nd ed.). New York: Ronald.

Locke, E. (1983). The nature and causes of job satisfaction. In M. Dunnette (Ed.), *Handbook of industrial and organizational psychology.* New York: Wiley.

Loeb, M., & Jones, P.D. (1978). Noise exposure, monitoring and tracking performance as a function of signal bias and task priority. *Ergonomics, 21*(4), 265–272.

Longmore, J., & Ne'eman, E. (1974). The availability of sunshine and human requirements for sunlight in buildings. *Journal of Architectural Research, 3*(2), 24–29.

Lorenzen, H.J., & Jaeger, D. (1968). The office landscape: A "systems" concept. *Contract, 9*(1), 164–173.

Luckiesh, M. (1924). *Light and work.* New York: Van Nostrand.

Lunden, G. (1972, March-April). Environment problems of office workers. *Build International, 1*, 90–93.

Mackworth, N.H. (1950). *Researches on the measurement of human performance* (Special Rep., Series 268). London: Her Majesty's Stationery Office, Medical Research Council.

Manning, P. (Ed.), (1965). *Office design: A study of environment.* Liverpool, England: University of Liverpool.

Marans, R.W., & Spreckelmeyer, K.F. (1982). Evaluating open and conventional office design. *Environment and Behavior, 14,* 333–351.

Margulis, S.T. (1979). *Privacy as information management: A social psychological and environmental framework* (Rep. No. NBSIR 79-1793). Washington, DC: U.S. National Bureau of Standards, National Engineering Laboratory, Center for Building Technology.

Markus, T.A. (1967). The function of windows — A reappraisal. *Building Science, 2,* 97–121.

Markus, T.A. (1970). Building appraisal: St. Michael's Academy, Kilwinning. *Architects' Journal, 7,* 9–50.

Maslow, A.H. (1943). A theory of human motivation. *Psychological Review, 50,* 370–396.

Maslow, A.H., & Mintz, N.L. (1956). Effects of esthetic surroundings: I. Initial effects of three esthetic conditions upon perceiving "energy" and "well-being" in faces. *Journal of Psychology, 41,* 247–254.

Mathews, K.E., & Canon, L.K. (1975). Environmental noise level as a determinant of helping behavior. *Journal of Personality and Social Psychology, 32,* 571–577.

Matula, R.A. (1981). Effects of visual display units on the eyes: A bibliography (1972–1980). *Human Factors, 23*(5), 581–586.

McCann, P.H. (1969). The effects of ambient noise on vigilance performance. *Human Factors, 11*(3), 251–256.

McCarrey, M.W., Peterson, L., Edwards, S., & Von Kulmiz, P. (1974). Landscape office attitudes: Reflections of perceived degree of control over transactions with the environment. *Journal of Applied Psychology, 59*(3), 401–403.

McCormick, E.J. (1976). *Human factors in engineering and design.* New York: McGraw-Hill.

McGehee, W., & Gardner, J. (1949). Music in a complex industrial job. *Personnel Psychology, 2*(3), 405–417.

McGrath, J.E. (Ed.) (1970). *Social and psychological factors in stress.* New York: Holt, Rinehart & Winston.

McGrath, J.E. (1976). Stress and behavior in organizations. In M.E. Dunnette (Ed.), *Handbook of industrial and organizational psychology.* Chicago: Rand McNally.

McGrath, J.J. (1963). Irrelevant stimulation and vigilance performance. In D.N. Buckner & J.J. McGrath (Eds.), *Vigilance: A symposium.* New York: McGraw-Hill.

McGregor, D. (1960). *The human side of enterprise.* New York: McGraw-Hill.

McIntyre, D.A. (1980). *Indoor climate.* London: Applied Science Publishers.

McNelis, H.G., Williams, P.E., & Henderson, R.L. (1975). A survey and analysis of important visual tasks in offices (Pt. 2). *Lighting Design and Application, 5,* 16–23.

Mehrabian, A. (1976). *Public places and private spaces: The psychology of work, play and living environments.* New York: Basic Books.

Melcher, A.J. (1976). *Structure and process of organizations.* Englewood Cliffs, NJ: Prentice-Hall.

Michelson, W. (1970). *Man and his urban environment: A sociological approach.* Reading, MA: Addison-Wesley.

Mikol, B., & Denny, M.P. (1955). The effect of music and rhythm on rotary pursuit performance. *Perceptual and Motor Skills, 5,* 3–6.

Milgram, S. (1970). The experience of living in cities. *Science, 167,* 1461–1468.

Miller, J.G. (1964). Adjusting to overloads of information. *Disorders of Communication, 42,* 87–100.

Mintz, N.L. (1956). Effects of esthetic surroundings. II. Prolonged and repeated experience in a "beautiful" and an "ugly" room. *Journal of Psychology, 41,* 459–466.

Moleski, W., & Lang, J. (1982). Organizational needs and human values in office planning. *Environment and Behavior, 14*(3), 319–332.

Morgan, G.A., Goodson, F.E., & Jones, T. (1975). Age differences in the association between felt temperatures and color choices. *American Journal of Psychology, 88*(1), 125–130.

Morgan, J.J. (1916). The overcoming of distraction and other resistances. *Archives of Psychology, 24*(4), No. 35, 1–84.

Morgan, J.J. (1917). The effect of sound distraction upon memory. *American Journal of Psychology, 28,* 191–208.

Morrow, P.C., & McElroy, J.C. (1981). Interior office design and visitor response: A constructive replication. *Journal of Applied Psychology, 66*(5), 646–650.

Munsterberg, H. (1915). *Business psychology.* Chicago, IL: La Salle Extension University.

Murrell, K.F.H. (1965). *Human performance in industry.* New York: Reinhold.

Nadler, D.A., Hackman, J.R., & Lawler, E.E. (1979). *Managing organizational behavior.* Boston: Little, Brown.

Naisbett, J. (1982). *Megatrends: Ten new directions transforming our lives.* New York: Warner.

Nemecek, J., & Grandjean, E. (1973). Results of an ergonomic investigation of large-space offices. *Human Factors, 15*(2), 111–124.

Newhall, S.M. (1941). Warmth and coolness of colors. *Psychological Record, 4*(15), 198–212.

Newman, R.I., Hunt, D.L., & Rhodes, F. (1966). Effects of music on employee attitude and productivity in a skate board factory. *Journal of Applied Psychology, 50*(6), 493–496.

Norman, R.D., & Scott, W.A. (1952). Color and affect: A review and semantic evaluation. *Journal of General Psychology, 36,* 185–223.

Nunneley, S.A., Dowd, P.J., Myhre, L.G., Stribley, R.F., & McNee, R.C. (1979). Tracking-task performance during heat stress simulating cockpit conditions in high performance aircraft. *Ergonomics, 22*(5), 549–555.

Obata, J., & Morita, S. (1934). The effects of noise upon efficiency. *Journal of the Acoustical Society of America, 5,* 255–261.

Oldham, G.R., & Brass, D.J. (1979). Employee reactions to an open-plan office: A naturally occurring quasi-experiment. *Administrative Science Quarterly, 24,* 267–284.

O'Malley, J.J. & Poplawsky, A. (1971). Noise-induced arousal and breadth of attention. *Perceptual and Motor Skills, 33,* 887–890.

Park, J.F., & Payne, M.C. (1963). Effects of noise level and difficulty of task in performing division. *Journal of Applied Psychology, 47*(6), 367–368.

Parsons, H.M. (1974). What happened at Hawthorne? *Science, 182,* 922–932.

Parsons, H.M. (1976). Work environments. In I. Altman & J.F. Wohlwill (Eds.) *Human behavior and environment: Advances in theory and research.* New York: Plenum.

Payne, R., & Pugh, D.S. (1983). Organizational structure and climate. In M.D. Dunnette (Ed.), *Handbook of industrial and organizational psychology.* New York: Wiley.

Pepler, R.D. (1958). Warmth and performance: An investigation in the tropics. *Ergonomics, 2*(1), 63–88.

Pepler, R.D. (1959). Extreme warmth and sensorimotor coordination. *Journal of Applied Physiology, 14,* 383–386.

Pepler, R.D. (1970). Associated fluctuations in daily temperature, productivity and absenteeism. *ASHRAE Transactions, 76,* 326–337.

Pepler, R.D., & Warner, R.E. (1960). Warmth, glare and a background of quiet speech: A comparison of their effects on performance. *Ergonomics, 3*(1), 68–73.

Pepler, R.D., & Warner, R.E. (1968). Temperature and learning: An experimental study. *ASHRAE Transactions, 74*(2), 211–224.

Planas, R. (1978, March). Perfect open plan priority: The human element. *Buildings,* 74–75.

Plutchik, R. (1961). Effect of high intensity intermittent sound on compensatory tracking and mirror tracing. *Perceptual and Motor Skills, 12,* 187–194.

Poock, G.K., & Wiener, E.L. (1966). Music and other auditory backgrounds during visual monitoring. *Journal of Industrial Engineering, 17*(6), 318–323.

Porter, L.W., Lawler, E.E., & Hackman, J.R. (1975). *Behavior in organizations.* New York: McGraw-Hill.

Poulton, E.C. (1970). *Environment and human efficiency.* Springfield, IL: Thomas.

Poulton, E.C. (1976). Continuous noise interferes with work by masking auditory feedback and inner speech. *Applied Ergonomics, 7*(2), 79–84.

Poulton, E.C. (1977). Continuous intense noise masks auditory feedback and inner speech. *Psychological Bulletin, 84*(5), 977–1001.

Poulton, E.C. (1980). *The environment at work.* Springfield, IL: Thomas.

Poulton, E.C., & Edwards, R.S. (1974). Interactions and range effects in experiments on pairs of stresses: Mild heat and low frequency noise. *Journal of Experimental Psychology, 102*(4), 621–628.

Poulton, E.C., & Kerslake, D. (1965). Initial stimulating effect of warmth upon perceptual efficiency. *Aerospace Medicine, 36,* 29–32.

Pressy, S.L. (1921). The influence of color upon mental and motor efficiency. *American Journal of Psychology, 32,* 326–356.

Provins, K.A., & Bell, C.R. (1970). Effects of heat stress on the performance of two tasks running concurrently. *Journal of Experimental Psychology, 85,* 40–44.

Quinn, R.P., & Staines, G.L. (1979). *The 1977 quality of employment survey.* Ann Arbor, MI: University of Michigan, Institute for Social Research.

Rabbitt, P. (1968). Recognition and memory for words correctly heard in noise. *Psychonomic Science, 6*(8), 383–384.

Rapoport, A., & Watson, N. (1967). Cultural variability in physical standards. *Transactions of the Bartlett Society, 6,* 63–83.

Reilly, R.E., & Parker, J.F., Jr. (1968). *Effect of heat stress and prolonged activity on perceptual-motor performance* Rep. No. NASA CR-1153. U.S. National Aeronautics and Space Administration.

Renwick, P.A., & Lawler, E.E. (1978, May). What you really want from your job. *Psychology Today*, pp. 53–65.

Richards, C.B., & Dobyns, H.F. (1957). Topography and culture: The case of the changing cage. *Human Organizations, 16,* 16–20.

Riland, L.H., & Falk, J.Z. (1972, April). *Employee reactions to office landscape environment.* Rochester, NY: Eastman Kodak Company, Personnel Relations Department, Psychological Research & Services.

Roethlisberger, F.J., & Dickson, W.J. (1941). *Management and the worker.* Cambridge, MA: Harvard University Press.

Ross, L. (1977). The intuitive psychologist and his shortcomings: Distortions in the attribution process. In L. Berkowitz (Ed.), *Advances in experimental social psychology* (Vol. 10). New York: Academic.

Ruff, C. & Associates. (1978). Tomorrow's working environment. *Fortune, 97*(10), 23ff.

Russell, W. (1957). *Effects of variations in ambient temperature on certain measures of tracking skill and sensory sensitivity* (Rep. No. 300). Fort Knox, KY: U.S. Army Medical Research Laboratory.

Ruys, T. (1970). *Windowless offices.* Unpublished master's thesis, Seattle: University of Washington.

Saegert, S., Mackintosh, B., & West, S. (1975). Two studies of crowding in urban public spaces. *Environment and behavior, 7*(2), 159–184.

Samuel, W.M.S. (1964). Noise and the shifting of attention. *Quarterly Journal of Experimental Psychology, 16,* 264–267.

Santamaria, A. (1970). *Background music on a mental task: Influence of playing time on performance and heart variability.* Unpublished master's thesis, Kansas State University, Manhatten, KS.

Saunders, J.E. (1969). The role of the level and diversity of horizontal illumination in an appraisal of a simple office task. *Lighting Research and Technology, 1*(1), 37–46.

Sauser, W.I., Arauz, C.G., & Chambers, R.M. (1978). Exploring the relationship between level of office noise and salary recommendations: A preliminary research note. *Journal of Management, 4*(1), 57–63.

Schaie, K.W. (1961). Scaling the association between colors and mood tones. *American Journal of Psychology, 74,* 266–273.

Schein, E.H. (1972). *Organizational psychology* (2nd ed.). Englewood Cliffs, NJ: Prentice-Hall.

Schiffenbauer, A.I., Brown, J.E., Perry, P.L., Schulack, L.K., & Zanzola, A.M. (1977). The relationship between density and crowding: Some architectural modifiers. *Environment and Behavior, 9,* 3–14.

Schneider, B. (1975). Organizational climates: An essay. *Personnel Psychology, 28,* 447–479.

Schoenberger, R.W., & Harris, C.S. (1965). Human performance as a function of changes in acoustic noise levels. *Journal of Engineering Psychology, 4,* 108–119.

Scott, W.E. (1966). Activation theory and task design. *Organizational Behavior and Human Performance, 1,* 3–30.

Shackel, B., Chidsey, K.D., & Shipley, P. (1969). The assessment of chair comfort. *Ergonomics, 12*(2), 269–306.

Shaw, M. (1981). *Group dynamics: The psychology of small group behavior* (3rd ed.). New York: McGraw-Hill.

Sloan, S.A. (1972, January). Translating psycho-social criteria into design determinants. In W.J. Mitchell (Ed.), *Environmental design: Research and practice. Proceeding of the 1972 Conference of the Environmental Design Research Association.* Los Angeles, CA: University of California Press.

Sloan, S. (undated). Tenant/G.S.A./landlord/Maslov/love/ participation/satisfaction/ offices/personal space/work production/social needs/designers/users/product/process. Spokane, WA: People Space Architecture Company.

Smith, H.C. (1947). *Music in relation to employee attitudes, piecework, and industrial production.* Stanford, CA: Stanford University Press.

Smith, K.R. (1951). Intermittent loud noise and mental performance. *Science, 114,* 132–133.

Smith, M.J., Cohen, B.G.F., Stammerjohn, L.W., & Happ, A. (1981). An investigation of health complaints and job stress in video display operations. *Human Factors, 23*(4), 387–400.

Smith, P.C. (1983). Behaviors, results, and organizational effectiveness: The problem of criteria. In M. Dunnette (Ed.), *The handbook of industrial and organizational psychology.* New York: Wiley.

Smith, S. (1978, July). Is there an optimum light level for office tasks? *Journal of the Illuminating Engineering Society,* 255–258.

Smith, W.A. (1961). Effects of industrial music in a work situation requiring complex mental activity. *Psychological Reports, 8,* 159–162.

Solly, C.M. (1969). Effects of stress on perceptual attention. In B.P. Rourke (Ed.), *Explorations in the psychology of stress and anxiety.* Don Mills, Ontario, Canada: Longmans.

Sommer, R. (1974). *Tight spaces.* Englewood Cliffs, NJ: Prentice-Hall.

Starbuck, W.H. (1983). Organizations and their environments. In M. Dunnette (Ed.), *Handbook of industrial and organizational psychology.* New York: Wiley.

Steele, F.I. (1973). *Physical settings and organization development.* Reading, MA: Addison-Wesley.

Steele, F.I., & Jenks, S. (1977). *The feel of the work place: Understanding and improving organizational climate.* Reading, MA: Addison-Wesley.

Steers, R.M. (1975). Problems in the management of organizational effectiveness. *Administrative Science Quarterly, 20,* 546–558.

Steinzor, B. (1950). The spatial factor in face to face discussion groups. *Journal of Abnormal and Social Psychology, 45,* 522–555.

Stevens, S.S. (1972). Stability of human performance under intense noise. *Journal of Sound and Vibration, 21*(1), 35–56.

Stramler, C.S., Kleiss, J.A., & Howell, W.C. (1983). Thermal sensation shifts induced by physical and psychological means. *Journal of Applied Psychology, 68*(1), 187–193.

Strodtbeck, F. & Hook, H. (1961). The social dimensions of a 12-man jury table. *Sociometry, 24,* 397–415.

Sucov, E.W. (1973, February). European research. *Lighting Design and Application,* 39-43.

Sundstrom, E. (1978). Crowding as a sequential process: Review of research on the effects of population density on humans. In A. Baum & Y. Epstein (Eds.), *Human response to crowding.* Hillsdale, NJ: Erlbaum.

Sundstrom, E. (1984). Physical environment and interpersonal behavior. In K. Deaux & L. Wrightsman, *Social psychology in the eighties* (4th ed.). Monterey, CA: Brooks/Cole.

Sundstrom, E. (1986). *Work places: The psychology of the physical environment in offices and factories.* New York: Cambridge University Press.

Sundstrom, E., Burt, R., & Kamp, D. (1980). Privacy at work: Architectural correlates of job satisfaction and job performance. *Academy of Management Journal, 23*(1), 101–117.

Sundstrom, E., Herbert, R.K., & Brown, D.W. (1982). Privacy and communication in an open plan office: A case study. *Environment and Behavior, 14*(3), 379–392.

Sundstrom, E., Town, J., Brown, D., Forman, A., & McGee, C. (1982). Physical enclosure, type of job, and privacy in the office. *Environment and Behavior, 14*(5), 543–559.

Sundstrom, E., Town, J., Osborn, D., Rice, R., Konar, E., Mandel, D., & Brill, M. (1982). *Office noise, satisfaction, and performance.* Unpublished paper presented at the annual conference of the American Psychological Association, Washington, DC.

Sundstrom, E., Town, J., Rice, R., Konar, E., Mandel, D., & Brill, M. (1982a). *Privacy in the office, satisfaction, and performance.* Unpublished paper presented at the annual conference of the American Psychological Association, Washington, DC.

Sundstrom, E., Town, J., Rice, R., Konar, E., Mandel, D., & Brill, M. (1982b). *Physical enclosure of workspaces and privacy in the office.* Unpublished paper presented at the Congress of the International Association of Applied Psychology, Edinburgh.

Szilagyi, A., & Holland, W. (1980). Changes in social density: Relationships with functional interaction and perceptions of job characteristics, role stress, and work satisfaction. *Journal of Applied Psychology, 65*(1), 28–33.

Tagiuri, R., & Litwin, G.H. (1968). *Organizational climate: Explorations of a concept.* Boston, MA: Harvard University.

Tausky, C. (1978). *Work organizations: Major theoretical perspectives.* Itasca, IL: Peacock.

Taylor, F.W. (1911). *Scientific Management.* New York: Harper & Row.

Taylor, R.B. (1982). On ignoring the physical environment. *Population and Environmental Psychology Newsletter, 9*(3), 20–22.

Teichner, W.H., Arees, E., & Reilly, R. (1963). Noise and human performance: A psychophysiological approach. *Ergonomics, 6*(1), 83–97.

Teichner, W.H., & Wehrkamp, R.F. (1954). Visual-motor performance as a function of short-duration ambient temperature. *Journal of Experimental Psychology, 47,* 447–450.

Terry, G.R. (1975). *Office management and control.* Homewood, IL: Irwin.

Thackray, R.I., & Touchstone, R.M. (1970). Recovery of motor performance following startle. *Perceptual and Motor Skills, 30,* 279–292.

Theologus, G.C., Wheaton, G.R., & Fleischman, E.A. (1974). Effects of intermittent moderate-intensity noise stress on human performance. *Journal of Applied Psychology, 59,* 539–547.

Tinker, M.A. (1925). Intelligence in an intelligence test with an auditory distraction. *American Journal of Psychology, 36,* 467–468.

Tinker, M.A. (1938). Effect of stimulus-texture upon apparent warmth and affective value of colors. *American Journal of Psychology, 51,* 532–535.

Toffler, A. (1980). *The third wave.* New York: Bantam.

Town, J.P. (1982). *Effects of participation in office design on satisfaction and productivity.* Unpublished doctoral dissertation, University of Tennessee, Knoxville.

Trist, E., Higgins, G., Murray, H., & Pollack, A. (1963). *Organizational choice.* London: Tavistock.

Vaughn, J.A., Higgins, E.A., & Funkhouser, G.E. (1968). Effects of body thermal state on manual performance. *Aerospace Medicine, 39*(12), 1310–1315.

Vernon, H.M. (1918). *An investigation of the factors concerned in the causation of industrial accidents* (Memo No. 21). London, His Majesty's Stationery Office, British Ministry of Munitions, Health of Munition Workers Committee.

Vernon, H.M. (1919). *The influence of hours of work and of ventilation on output in tinplate manufacture.* Industrial Fatigue Research Board, Report #1. London, England: His Majesty's Stationery Office.

Vernon, H.M., & Warner, C.G. (1932). Objective and subjective tests for noise. *Personnel Journal, 11,* 141–149.

Vinsel, A., Brown, B.B., Altman, I., & Foss, C. (1980). Privacy regulation: Territorial displays and effectiveness of individual functioning. *Journal of Personality and Social Psychology, 39*, 1104–1115.

Viteles, M.S., & Smith, K.R. (1946). An experimental investigation of the effect of change in atmosphere conditions and noise upon performance. *Heating, Piping and Air Conditioning, 18*, 107–112.

Wahba, M.A., & Bridwell, L.G. (1975). Maslow reconsidered: A review of research on the need hierarchy theory. In K. Wexley & G. Yukl (Eds.), *Organizational behavior and industrial psychology: readings with commentary* (p. 5–11). New York: Oxford University Press.

Walker, C.R, & Guest, R.H. (1952). *The man on the assembly line*. Cambridge, MA: Harvard University Press.

Walton, W.E., Guilford, R.B., & Guilford, J.P. (1933). Color preferences of 1,279 university students. *Journal of Psychology, 45*, 322–328.

Wandersman, A. (1979a). User participation: A conceptual framework. *Environment and Behavior, 11*, 465–482.

Wandersman, A. (1979b). User participation: A study of types of participation, effects, medicators, and individual differences. *Environment and Behavior, 11*, 185–208.

Warner, H.D. (1969). Effects of intermittent noise on human target detection. *Human Factors, 11*(3), 245–250.

Warner, H.D., & Heimstra, N.W. (1971). Effects of intermittent noise on visual search tasks of varying complexity. *Perceptual and Motor Skills, 32*, 219–226.

Watkins, W.H. (1964). Effect of certain noises upon detection of visual signals. *Journal of Experimental Psychology, 67*(1), 72–75.

Weinstein, A., & Mackenzie, R.S. (1966). Manual performance and arousal. *Perceptual and Motor Skills, 22*, 498.

Weinstein, N.D. (1974). Effect of noise on intellectual performance. *Journal of Applied Psychology, 59*(5), 548–554.

Welford, A.T. (1973). Stress and performance. *Ergonomics, 16*(5), 567–580.

Wells, B.W.P. (1965a). Subjective responses to the lighting installation in a modern office building and their design implications. *Building Science, 1*(1), 57–68.

Wells, B.W.P. (1965b). The psycho-social influence of building environments: Sociometric findings in large and small office spaces. *Building Science, 1*, 153–165.

Westin, A. (1970). *Privacy and freedom*. New York: Atheneum.

Weston, H.C. (1921). *A study of efficiency in fine linen weaving* (Rep. No. 20). London: His Majesty's Stationery Office, Industrial Health (Fatigue) Research Board.

Weston, H.C. (1945). *The relation between illuminance and visual performance* (Rep. No. 87). London: His Majesty's Stationery Office, Industrial Health Research Board.

Weston, H.C., & Taylor, A. (1926). *The relation between illumination and efficiency in fine work*. London: His Majesty's Stationery Office, Industrial Fatigue Research Board and Illumination Research Committee.

Wexner, L.B. (1954). The degree to which colors (hues) are associated with mood-tones. *Journal of Applied Psychology, 38*, 432–435.

Wicker, A.W. (1979). *An introduction to ecological psychology*. Monterey, CA: Brooks/Cole.

Widgery, R., & Stackpole, C. (1972). Desk position, interview anxiety, interviewer credibility: An example of cognitive balance. *Journal of Counseling Psychology, 19*(3), 173-177

Wilson, G.D. (1966). Arousal properties of red versus green. *Perceptual and Motor Skills, 23*, 947–949.

Wineman, J. (1982). Office design and evaluation: An overview. *Environment and Behavior, 14*(3), 271–298.

Wing, J.F. (1965). *A review of the effects of high ambient temperature on mental performance* (Rep. No. AMRL-TR-65-102). Aerospace Medical Research Laboratories, Wright-Patterson Air Force Base, Ohio.

Wohlwill, J.F. (1975). Behavioral response and adaptation to environmental stimulation. In A. Damon (Ed.), *Physiological anthropology*. Cambridge, MA: Harvard University Press.

Wohlwill, J.F., Nasar, J.L., DeJoy, D.M., & Foruzani, H.H. (1976). Behavioral effects of a noisy environment: Task involvement versus passive exposure. *Journal of Applied Psychology, 61*(1), 67–74.

Wokoun, W. (1968). *Effects of music on work performance*. Technical Memo. #1–68. Aberdeen Proving Grounds, MD: U.S. Army Human Engineering Laboratories.

Wolgers, B. Study of office environment-attitudes to office landscapes and open-plan offices. *Build International, 6*, 143–146.

Woodhead, M.M. (1959). Effect of brief loud noise on decision making. *Journal of the Acoustical Society of America, 31*, 1329–1331.

Woodhead, M.M. (1964a). The effect of bursts of noise on an arithmetic task. *American Journal of Psychology, 77*, 627–633.

Woodhead, M.M. (1964b). Searching a visual display in intermittent noise. *Journal of Sound and Vibration, 1*(2), 157–161.

Woodhead, M.M. (1969). Performing a visual task in the vicinity of reproduced sonic bangs. *Journal of Sound Vibrations, 9*(1), 121–125.

Woodson, W.G. (1981). *Human factors design handbook*. New York: McGraw-Hill.

Wright, B. (1962). The influence of hue, lightness and saturation on apparent warmth and weight. *American Journal of Psychology, 75*, 232–241.

Wyatt, S., & Langdon, J.N. (1937). *Fatigue and boredom in repetitive work* (Rep. No. 77). London: His Majesty's Stationery Office, Industrial Health Research Board.

Wylie, H.L. (1958). *Office management handbook* (2nd ed.). New York: Ronald.

Yerkes, R.M., & Dodson, J.D. (1908). The relation of strength of stimulus to rapidity of habit formation. *Journal of Comparative Neurology and Psychology, 18,* 459–482.

Zager, M., & Rosow, M.I. (Eds.). (1982). *The innovative organization: Productivity programs in action.* New York: Pergamon.

Zalensny, M., Farace, R.V., & Kurchner-Hawkins, R. (1983). *Perceived work environment and organizational level as determinants of employee work perceptions and attitudes.* Unpublished paper presented at the confer-ence of the American Psychological Association, Anaheim, CA:

Zeitlin, L.R. (1969, April). *A comparison of employee attitudes toward the conventional office and the landscaped office* (Tech. Rep.). New York: Port of New York Authority.

Zermeno, R., Moseley, R., & Braun, E. (1980). The robots are coming—slowly. In T. Forester (Ed.), *The microelectronics revolution.* Oxford: Basil Blackwell.

Zwiegenhaft, R.L. (1976). Personal space in faculty office: Desk placement and the student-faculty interaction. *Journal of Applied Psychology, 61,* 529–532.

Chapter 20

HUMAN BEHAVIOR, COGNITION, AND AFFECT IN THE NATURAL ENVIRONMENT

Richard C. Knopf, *The North Central Forest Experiment Station, St. Paul, MN*

20.1. INTRODUCTION

How do humans relate to the natural environment? The answer we get, it seems, depends on the investigator we ask. Differences in perspective abound. Perhaps the only point that enjoys consensus in the literature is that our understanding of the character of transactions between people and the natural environment remains remarkably incomplete.

It is not as if the matter has not been considered by either the intuitive or scientific literature. Interest in the relations between people and nature is pervasive—indeed, it seems to have been a preoccupation of virtually every culture in recorded history (Kluckhohn, 1953). We have at our disposal a massive—if not unwieldy—body of literature on the topic, scattered across a diverse array of literary worlds and scientific disciplines. Competing for our attention are philosophical essays on the meaning of nature, (e.g., Eiseley, 1957; Thoreau, 1854); scholarly examinations of patterns of attitudes toward nature throughout history (e.g., Glacken, 1967; Nash, 1973) and across cultures (e.g., Altman & Chemers, 1980; Tuan, 1974), content analyses of graphic art (e.g., Clark, 1976; Gussow, 1972) and popular literature (e.g., Jackson, 1975; Marx, 1964) to determine values ascribed to nature, edited volumes designed to assemble the works of scientists investigating people–nature transactions (e.g., Altman & Wohlwill, 1983; Childs & Melton, 1983; Laurie, 1979), integrative reviews of the scientific literature amassed on this topic in recent decades (e.g., Driver & Greene, 1977; Zube, Sell, & Taylor, 1982), and, thoughtful reflections on the implications that such revelations may have for environmental management and design (e.g., Appleton, 1975; Kaplan & Kaplan, 1978). Indeed, at least three major symposiums have been convened to encourage a dialogue between social scientists and environmental policymakers on the role of nature in the human life space (Elsner & Smardon,

1979; U.S. Department of Agriculture, 1977a; U.S. Department of Interior, 1968).

The literature on people–nature relations is largely intuitive. Most of its tenets have not been subjected to validation through the scientific process (R. Kaplan, 1983; Ulrich, 1983; Wohlwill, 1983). Yet the past decade has witnessed some aggressive data-building efforts in such unlikely fields as sociology, forestry, marketing, leisure sciences, and economics— not to mention the disciplines of environmental psychology and geography. Our purpose here is to transcend these disciplinary lines and sort through the accumulating maze of detail in an attempt to extract themes, principles, and concepts of value in constructing theoretical perspectives on how people relate to nature.

The analysis develops through four phases. First, the chapter begins by synthesizing the major philosophical and theoretical positions relating to the broad question of how people relate to nature. Second, the major disciplines fostering research on the question are delineated, and the issues driving the varied emphases of each are highlighted. Third, the chapter presents a cross-disciplinary analysis of these emerging data bases to establish what is being revealed about the character of people–nature transactions. And finally, having established what is known and the limitations thereof, the chapter sets forth needed directions for future research.

20.2. PHILOSOPHICAL AND THEORETICAL PERSPECTIVES

20.2.1. Preference as an Innate Response

One disposition in the literature is to construe nature as a human requirement. Under this orientation, humans are posed as organisms evolving over millions of years in the natural environment—growing and organizing in response to it and, indeed, becoming fascinated by it (Berrill, 1955; Butzer, 1977; Dubos, 1968; Iltis, Loucks, & Andrews, 1970; S. Kaplan, 1977; Ulrich, 1977). To survive, it is argued, humans not only had to be efficient in assimilating information about the natural environment, but they had to develop a predilection for doing so (Ulrich, 1973). In short, natural selection would work against members of the species who did not find stimulation from their natural surroundings to be of gripping significance.

The evolutionists, then, see the contemporary human as an organism typically operating in non-natural worlds but saddled with senses and psyche genetically programmed for operation in the natural world. Most evolutionists stop short of the argument that humans cannot operate effectively in nonnatural worlds. But they do suggest that humans are more likely to function effectively in those environments that possess attributes similar to the natural settings in which they evolved.

One such attribute, for example, might be *legibility* (S. Kaplan, 1976; Ulrich, 1983). The logic here is that the evolving human gained preference for settings that served his or her need to efficiently comprehend and predict. Thus a preferred setting would be one offering information that is readily identifiable and grasped—such as one with an uncluttered sense of depth and smooth-textured features (Ulrich, 1977). Another attribute might be *mystery* (Cullen, 1961; R. Kaplan, 1977a). Here, the belief is that the evolving organism gained preference for settings that served its knowledge-hungry state— settings that promised new information with a change in vantage point. Thus a preferred setting would include the trail that bends, the road that turns, or the vista temporarily hidden from view but accessible through a simple shift in position. Yet another attribute might be *refuge* (Appleton, 1975; Edney, 1976). Here the evolving organism is conceived of as developing preference for settings that provided shelter from elements of the environment that threatened its comfort and survival. Hence a preferred setting would include vantage points that would maximize security and seclusion.

An overall picture emerges of humans who, as products of a long evolutionary journey, are better adapted to locales that are comprehensible yet invite further exploration and are open, yet offer seclusion (Appleton, 1975). But beyond such abstractions, the evolutionists have something even more pointed to suggest: Humans have an innate preference for the particular *patterns* of stimulation that natural environments carry. Thus the curvilinear forms and edges, the continuous gradations of shape and color, the blending of textures, the lunar and seasonal cycles, and the other features that distinguish natural from artificial environments (Wohlwill, 1983) are all-important to an organism whose sensory mechanisms were developed in response to them. Some see traces of our evolutionary path in our fascination with wild animals (S. Kaplan, 1977), Japanese gardens (Orians, 1980), and assiduously groomed parks and backyards (Balling & Falk, 1982). Each of these is purported to reflect a pattern of stimulation originally dominant on the East African savanna, where our biological apparatus is supposed to have evolved (Leakey, 1976).

Others point to our innate physiological rhythms, which are synchronized with rhythms in nature (Driver & Greene, 1977; Dubos, 1965), or to our reduced capacities to function when natural air ion ratios are changed through artificial electric fields (Krueger, 1973; Logan, 1974). Still others turn to studies demonstrating the heritability of habitat preferences among animals (Partridge, 1978; Wecker, 1963) as evidence for genetically determined biases that affect environmental preferences (Balling & Falk, 1982; S. Kaplan, 1977).

The position of this evolutionary perspective, then, is that people are closely tied to the natural environment. It is felt that the human design—and the human capacity—will be better understood only as these linkages with the natural environment are better understood. Humans, so the argument runs, are best suited for acting in the environment that wrote the script.

20.2.2. Preference as a Learned Response

The literature also nourishes an alternate tradition that disputes the implied essentiality of nature. The belief is that natural environments, like all environments, hold different values for people with different life experiences (Moore, 1979; Tuan, 1977). If nature has meaning, proponents argue, it is because society has conditioned us to ascribe meaning to it.

Proponents of this view quickly point to the impressive number of cross-cultural and historical analyses that proclaim the absence of consistent orientation toward nature (Glacken, 1967; Jackson, 1975; Kluckhohn, 1953; Lowenthal & Prince, 1976; Marx, 1964; Nash, 1973; Shepard, 1967; Stillman, 1975; Tuan, 1974). At some points in history, natural environments were the personification of evil, harboring the temptations, the physical dangers, and the uncontrollable forces that victimized humankind. Cities were revered as sanctuaries for the full pursuit of the human potential. At other points in history, the opposite held true (Nash, 1973; Tuan, 1974). Cities were the anomalies of the world, whereas natural environments were the havens for insight, integration, and spiritual and physical restoration. But one need not rely on history to paint a picture of attitudinal differences: Even contemporary societies show clear contradictions in orientations to nature (Stainbrook, 1968). In Western societies, people have tended to operate as if natural environments need to be controlled, domesticated, and subjected to their service. In Eastern societies, nature is more typically perceived as a nonexploitable ally—a phe-

nomenon to seek unity with, to draw on for spiritual perspective. Kluckhohn (1953), an anthropologist, describes three fundamental orientations toward nature that have been displayed at various times in the cultural record: (1) people feeling subjected to nature, construing it as a harsh and powerful force; (2) people feeling in control of nature, viewing it as a resource to dominate and exploit; and (3) people showing reverence to nature, as an ally to live in harmony with. Tuan (1971), in turn, categorizes six distinct sets of attitudes. The message from such analyses seems to be that people's relations with nature are relatively fluid and culture-bound. Dramatic cultural shifts can even accrue during the course of a generation (Altman & Chemers, 1980), particularly if there are rapidly shifting religious dogmas (Glacken, 1967) or advances in technology (Nash, 1973).

Writings in this genre further suggest that culture affects not only the values ascribed to nature but also the manner in which we represent its physical character. Nomadic cultures, for example, conceive of space as being more fluid and less bounded than do nonnomadic cultures (Rapoport, 1972). Cultures oriented to survival in wildland environments possess more highly differentiated vocabularies describing natural processes (Cole, 1975; Vanstone, 1962). Aivilik Eskimos are reputed to have at least a dozen different terms to describe the various winds and an equally rich vocabulary to describe different snow conditions (Tuan, 1974).

Indeed, argue the culturists, whether we like nature or not depends on little more than whether we are familiar with it. If nature is innately important to people, they ask, why is it that people not raised in natural settings feel so threatened during their first encounters with them (S. Kaplan & Talbot, 1983; Lewis, 1978)? Why is it that strongly urbanized children actually show less preference for play areas with natural surfaces (soil and grass) than for play areas with human-made surfaces such as concrete and asphalt (Marcus, 1974)? And especially, why is it that people seem to prefer the kinds of landscapes to which they are accustomed (Wohlwill, 1983)? Arctic peoples, for example, seem to actually prefer barren, arid scenes, whereas temperate-climate peoples seem to prefer landscapes they are used to (Sonnenfeld, 1968). What accounts for these differences, ask the culturalists, if preferences for certain patterns of natural stimulation have been instilled through years of evolution on the African savanna, as the evolutionists would argue?

Many culturists believe that value ascription develops during early childhood (Tuan, 1977). They suggest that preschoolers, unlike older children and adults, are neutral to the presence of nature as they sort photographs; they are more strongly influenced by other attributes, such as size of photographs, color, or type of weather represented (Holcomb, 1977). They also suggest that young children demonstrate remarkable indifference to flower fragrances and charnel or fecal odors (Tuan, 1977). And they suggest that adults are forceful in instilling their values in young children. Aiello, Gordon, and Farrell (1974), for example, found neighboring families of similar economic and educational backgrounds differing markedly in their feelings about the suitability of natural areas for their children's play. Although some parents actively encouraged their children to play in the woods or about the pond, other parents who were unfamiliar with nearby natural areas strongly encouraged their children to stay clear of these areas. Other authors have examined the process by which adult values are transmitted through the value-laden characterizations of plants, animals, and landscapes in children's reading materials (Marcus, 1977; More, 1977). Children's impressions of nature, it seems, depend on what books they read. As Tuan (1977) might suggest, if people agree on what nature has to offer, it is because they have been taught in the same school.

This line of thinking prompts yet another assertion by those subscribing to the cultural perspective: Substantial diversity among individual views of nature can exist even *within* cultures. One common suggestion is that positive affect for nature is essentially an upper-class phenomenon (Foresta, 1980; Sills, 1975). Maslowian psychologists infer, and political analysts confirm, that appreciation for natural stimuli and environmental aesthetics emerges only after more basic material needs and interests are satisfied (Banovitz, 1971; Springer & Constantini, 1974). And, lest this position fall into dispute, we are quickly directed to consider the possibility that one's appreciation for nature is mediated by other individual-bound variables, such as gender (Macia, 1979), ethnicity (Peterson, 1977), age (Balling & Falk, 1982), and personality structure (Craik, 1975; Sonnenfeld, 1968). Further, it is intuitively acceptable to propose that purely situational forces, such as stress levels (Knopf, 1983; Ulrich, 1979) and frustrated achievement or exploratory needs (Adams & Stone, 1977; Knopf, Driver, & Bassett, 1973) would alter one's perception and valuation of natural stimuli.

In the face of all these arguments, strong advocates of the cultural perspective would suggest that the search for rules to describe how certain patterns of natural stimuli evoke certain kinds of emotions is futile indeed. The basic dilemma, they maintain, is that people respond to their environments not as mere collections of physical attributes but as storehouses of past experiences and repositories of accumulated emotions and meanings (Ittelson, Franck, & O'Hanlon, 1976; Jacques, 1980; Moore & Golledge, 1976; Tuan, 1974). In their view, the way people perceive an environment depends upon the way they have experienced it. And so it is with natural environments. It is not the trees, bushes, and grasses per se that generate affect; it is the set of symbols people hang on them. Culturalists taking these positions to the extreme would suggest that humans require natural stimulation no more than any other form of stimulation. Humans, they would conclude, can reach full potential in its absence (Holcomb, 1977; Krieger, 1973).

20.2.3. Purported Values of Nature

Whether one construes response to nature as innately driven, as learned, or as a fusion of both processes (Ulrich, 1983), the prevailing sentiment is that nature is a useful resource for people. Even the culturalists, who discount the role of nature as an innately required stimulus, are quick to expound upon its virtues. Four broad themes have emerged within the literature: (1) nature restores; (2) nature facilitates competence building; (3) nature carries symbols that affirm culture or the self; and (4) nature offers, if nothing more, a shift in the stimulus field—inherently pleasing to an organism fueled by a need to investigate.

Nature as Restorer
Perhaps the most emphatic assertion is that natural environments offer respite from overly complex, chaotic stimulation in everyday life spaces (Knopf, Driver, & Bassett, 1973; Stainbrook, 1968). The notion that natural settings are more peaceful and subdued than urban areas dominates the writings of outdoor essayists throughout the history of Western civilization (e.g., Eiseley, 1957; Leopold, 1949; Thoreau, 1854; Walton, 1793). The earliest advocates for urban parks in America believed that natural parks were sources of tranquility—havens to escape the hectic pace, material orientation, and environmental degradation of daily settings (LeCorbusier & DePierrefeu, 1948; Rutledge, 1971; Sax, 1980; Wright, 1941). This conviction continues with contemporary park leaders, landscape architects, and urban planners (Alexander, Ishikawa, & Silverstein, 1977; Lewis, 1977).

Stephen Kaplan (1977), posing the evolutionary perspective, suggests that because patterns in nature are inherently gripping, people are not required to expend energy suppressing distracting stimuli. In nature, he suggests, we do not have to pay attention to less than interesting stimuli. Our distraction–suppression mechanisms can rest, and our energy reserves can be restored. Therefore, we are more effective in coping with competing and distracting stimulus sources on reentry to our normal life spaces (Lazarus, 1966). Wohlwill (1983), adhering to a less evolutionary stance, attributes the restorative powers of nature to its relative absence of gross movement. For whatever reason, few would deny that natural environments are important for escape. Stillman (1975, 1977), in a provocative historical study of values ascribed to nature, drew one primary conclusion: As stress levels within a culture escalate, so does the significance attached to natural environments as places of solace.

Nature as Competence Builder

Other writers suggest that natural environments are valued because they heighten the individual's sense of control, competency, and esteem (Houston, 1968; Lewis, 1977). This theme is particularly pronounced in the therapeutic recreation and group-camping literature, which poses nature as a powerful therapeutic tool for enhancing self-reliance, self-confidence, and mental health (Bernstein, 1972; Burch, 1977; Gibson, 1979; Hanson, 1977; Lundegren, 1975). A typical observation is that of Rachel Kaplan (1974), who found wilderness program participants emerging with stronger concern for others, more realistic assessments of personal strengths and weaknesses, greater self-sufficiency in the use of time and talents, and positive views of the self.

If natural environments offer these benefits, how are they generated? The following points summarize the kinds of positions offered in response to this query. They are conceptually neither cumulative nor lacking in contradiction, for they are outgrowths of a diversity of theoretical perspectives.

First, nature is viewed as being particularly effective in moving people beyond their self-perceived limits. For most, it presents a new world to master, where accustomed behavior patterns, resources, and problem-solving styles are no longer appropriate. Nature in general, and therapeutic wilderness programs in particular, force individuals to successfully master new experiences, thus enlarging the perceived bounds to their own potential and promising continued growth and achievement (Barcus & Bergeson,

1972). This, in turn, evokes perceptions of self-reliance, self-determination, and responsibility. The individual discards impressions that he or she is a victim of, or subjected to, the whims of the environmental milieu and emerges with a heightened sense of competency and destiny control (Hobbs & Shelton, 1972).

Second, nature is seen as being largely devoid of negative feedback, thus providing relief from the kinds of feedback normally associated with interchanges in nonnatural environments. In this sense, natural environments are relatively innocuous: They rarely argue, fight back, or otherwise respond to us (Lewis, 1973; Wohlwill, 1983). To cite Lewis (1977), nature is relatively nonthreatening and nonjudgmental in a world that is constantly judgmental. There is a relative absence of feedback that demands counterresponse. This attribute, according to Wohlwill (1983), might account for the frequently reported feeling of oneness with nature. There can be so little counterresponse from an individual's presence, he argues, that the boundaries between self and the environment become muted and lose definition. The same sensation—loss of distinction between self and environments—occurs in other (primarily recreation) settings (Csikszentmihalyi, 1975a). There, as in nature, the sensation seems to be precipitated by escalated control and accompanying absence of negative feedback.

A third (and perhaps contradictory) position is that natural settings are both manipulatable and predictable. Hart (1973) suggests that natural settings better provide the manipulative environment that Piaget describes as essential to the development of human intelligence. So nature is responsive—quite a distinction from the physical, social, and institutional settings that people normally contend with. And how it responds is typically predictable. There are few surprises in nature. According to Bernstein (1972), it is this dual property of responsiveness and predictability that allows one to focus on growth-oriented behaviors rather than being consumed with defensive, coping behaviors.

Fourth, because nature is responsive, it serves as an important vehicle for the expression of self-identity. Urban gardens, for example, appear to be an important means of self-expression for those who feel cut off from such opportunities in other aspects of life (Lewis, 1977). The garden becomes a highly visible means for displaying one's own personality and values, and in so doing, it affirms one's importance. It becomes one's own territory, an affirmation of involvement and belonging (R. Kaplan, 1978; Lee,

1972). Natural environments as a whole probably function in the same way. They stand, relative to the inflexible or otherwise uncontrollable forces in other settings, quite ready to respond to one's will. They are, in short, self-confirming environments (Stainbrook, 1968).

A fifth position holds that experiences in nature generally evoke the sensation that control has shifted to the self. Relative to more formally structured situations, people in nature have more personal discretion in behavioral choice. People can be more concerned with mastering skills of their own choosing rather than trying to conform to social or institutional constraint. Because of this self-chosen character of behavior in natural environments and because natural environments are inherently responsive, an individual operating in nature is more likely to be rewarded for his or her actions (Bernstein, 1972). This sharpened ability to control reward flow translates into heightened self-concept (Harris, 1975).

Although each of these arguments is witness to the therapeutic power of nature, none implies that this vehicle is different than any other that provides sensations of control and mastery (Csikszentmihalyi, 1975b). Indeed, most of play behavior reflects the drive to gain control and mastery (Barnett & Storm, 1981; Ellis, 1973). In this sense, nature as a therapeutic tool is no different than chess, archery, dancing, tennis, golf, football, basketball, and a host of other activities (Abrahams, 1970; Catton, 1969; Csikszentmihalyi, 1975a; Pierce, 1980).

Nature as Symbol

Here the value of nature is described in terms of its capacity to carry meaning. Under this view, nature represents a construct—a product of the mind—that endows nature with the ability to represent or emanate the meaning of life itself (Lowenthal, 1967; Wohlwill, 1983). Water, for example, is purported to have attractive power because it symbolizes the beginnings of life, either in utero (Ryback & Yaw, 1976) or in the evolutionary amniotic fluid (Thoreau, 1864). Historians have frequently noted how parks and other natural reserves assume significance as symbols of national pride, bygone treasured eras, and optimism for the future (Sax, 1980). The writings of outdoor essayists undeniably reflect the rich overlay of meanings we thrust on nature—and suggest that these meanings serve as an affirmation of both the self and culture (Blomberg, 1982).

What is it that nature symbolizes? Four broad dimensions can be constructed from the philosophical writings. At one level, nature seems to emerge as a symbol of life itself. It is seen as a symbol of the basic vitality of life and its capacity for growth and change (Wohlwill, 1983). People seem to see in nature an affirmation that life has an importance, an order, a destiny, a purposiveness in the cycles of living and dying—and an inherent goodness (Blomberg, 1982). At another level, nature seems to emerge as a symbol of continuity or enduringness. For those who perceive the world to be in a state of rapid and uncontrollable change, nature becomes revered as something stable, timeless, and universal (Scheffer, 1977). At a third level, nature symbolizes a force greater than, and impervious to, human action. In this sense, it represents an innocent purity, a cleansing power, the right not to be subjugated—in short, "the way things are supposed to be" (Stillman, 1975). At a fourth level, nature emerges as a symbol of mystery and spirituality. It becomes a symbol of the ability to experience new forms of reality that are unbounded by the structures, laws, and limitations of the physical world (Lowenthal & Prince, 1976). It is not surprising, given this propensity, that nature plays a pervasive role throughout the religious writings of diverse cultures (S. Kaplan & Talbot, 1983).

Some investigators suggest that the concept of nature is so invested with symbolic elaborations and transformations that it defies scientific analysis (Blomberg, 1982; Lowenthal & Prince, 1976). Others, however, flatly disagree, in turn suggesting that objective bases for whatever is perceived can be found in stimulus attributes of the physical array (Wohlwill, 1976, 1983). These alternate views notwithstanding, most people agree that nature is an important carrier of symbols—symbols that serve to confirm the basic values of those who create them.

Nature as Diversion

It may also be possible that people turn to nature simply for diversity. It is clear that the information-hungry human is fueled by the need to investigate. Indeed, a lack of textural and cultural diversity is quite unappealing (Mehrabian & Russell, 1974; Wohlwill, 1976).

The intuitive literature is riddled with suggestions that, as stimulus-rich as urban settings are, life can become monotonous (Iltis, 1973; Lieberman, 1970; Parr, 1965). Nature then injects diversity into the urban experience both through direct encounter and vicarious experience. Even without making the presumption that urban settings are monotonous, one cannot discount the power of nature to lure us with its promise of information (R. Kaplan, 1977a) and stimulation that departs from the routine (Watt, 1972).

20.2.4. Is Nature Important?

Although there are a variety of positions on how people relate to nature, there is clear agreement that nature as a stimulus source is important. We have, on the one hand, evolutionists arguing that the needs for nature run deep: that they are, in effect, innately wired into our basic design. Their writings dwell on the character of human perceptual and cognitive processes and suggest that natural stimuli play an important role in the effective functioning of these processes. Others might not dismiss the notion of innate response but emphasize the powerful roles of culture or other experiential forces in shaping how people respond to nature. In this view, natural stimulation—because it becomes filtered through layers of experience—has the potential for generating either positive or negative affect.

On the other hand, we have numerous culturists, essayists, and historians who would argue that nature as a stimulus source is inherently neutral. Their writings dwell on the character of affective response to nature, which shows clear inconsistencies across cultures and over time.

Perhaps a more integrative view is to propose that response to nature emerges from an interaction of both innate and experiential forces. It seems logical to propose that perceptual and cognitive tendencies are strongly innately prescribed, whereas affective tendencies are strongly experientially prescribed. In this sense, the evolutionary and cultural perspectives are both correct—each addresses a different aspect of people–nature transactions.

Regardless of their position, most writers emphasize the utility of nature as a resource humans can draw on in their quest for optimality. Those adhering strongly to the evolutionary perspective might suggest that the kinds of stimuli associated with natural environments uniquely contribute to effective functioning. Those subscribing to the cultural perspective might suggest that nature as a stimulus source is functionally indistinct from other vehicles that can deliver restoration, actualization, symbolic meaning, or diversion—such as music, art, and travel (Mehrabian, 1976). Just like these other vehicles, they assert, nature can generate both positive and negative affect. But just like these other vehicles, they are quick to add, nature more likely than not tends to be useful for the goal-striving human.

The general population seems to agree. In nearly every study of visual preference, natural scenes are consistently preferred over other scenes (R. Kaplan, 1983; Kaplan, Kaplan, & Wendt, 1972; Wohlwill, 1976). And, in urban settings, scenes with vegetation tend to be preferred over those lacking it (Lansing, Marans, & Zehner, 1970; Thayer & Atwood, 1978). Yet these findings do not stand incontrovertible. Some writers have suggested that such studies have presented an unrealistically sanitized version of nature. Notoriously missing, for example, are the biting insects, the uncomfortable temperatures, the bothersome winds, the repertoire of negative experiences people associate with known environments, and other unattractive features (Aiken, 1976; Driver & Greene, 1977; Tuan, 1979). Still others might suggest that these findings do nothing more than echo current positive views toward nature—that contradictory results would emerge if the studies could be replicated in different eras (Altman & Chemers, 1980).

Although some point to exploding participation rates in outdoor recreation as evidence of people's need for nature in face of increasing urbanization, others point to the fact that significant blocks of the population avoid participating altogether as evidence that the desire for nature is culturally defined (contrast Duncan, 1978; U.S. Department of the Interior, 1979). Yet those who never leave urban settings may receive the benefits of nature through urban greenery, reading materials, and other media.[1] As. R. Kaplan (1978, 1983) suggests, nature can be the tree outside the window, the garden in the backyard, or the greenery near a factory worker on an outdoor lunch break. Exactly what nature is and what nature is not defies precise definition (Carson, 1970; Wohlwill, 1983) and is a lively topic for debate. Witness how Iltis (1973), for example, refutes Krieger's (1973) suggestion that technologically modified environments can replicate whatever kinds of stimulation are desired from nature.

So where do the philosophical and theoretical writings lead us? We are left with a series of logical and plausible arguments, but few of them have been empirically verified (Wohlwill, 1976, 1983). As Wohlwill (1983) suggests, the individual's response to nature has not been a principal focus of psychological inquiry, even among environmental psychologists. Yet there is increasing recognition that nature *is* different as a stimulus—and that its properties and effects are worthy of scientific attention (Bernaldez & Parra, 1979; Wohlwill, 1983; Zube, 1974). With that recognition, data are now beginning to emerge in a variety of disciplines that have bearing on the problem. We now turn to the task of analyzing the lines of empirical activity that are evolving and examining the issues that are being addressed on a discipline-by-discipline basis. Having benefited from that overview, we will then turn to the task of integrating the empirical and conceptual revelations emerging from these varied disciplines.

20.3. EMPIRICAL PERSPECTIVES

20.3.1. Origins of Empirical Activity

Recognition that people's response to nature is an important issue for research spills well beyond the bounds of psychological inquiry. Indeed, human response to nature has stimulated interest within virtually every scientific discipline bearing a social emphasis. Although environmental psychologists continue to lament over the apparent lack of activity, numerous lines of inquiry have been aggressively evolving elsewhere in such diverse disciplines as forestry, leisure sciences, sociology, economics, geography, and marketing. Each discipline brings unique perspective to the problem of defining the character of relations between people and nature. These perspectives not only temper conceptions of what these relations are, but they also shape what kinds of data are generated and even how the data are interpreted. So in constructing an adequate model of people–nature transactions, it becomes imperative that we build an appreciation of how these perspectives have shaped the very character of the data available to us.

The following analysis should not be taken to imply that particular investigators can possess heritage from but one discipline. Such an inference would discount the contributions of those with multiple-disciplinary orientations, an obvious error. Rather, the intent is to demonstrate how the varying disciplines, being fueled by different kinds of issues, have generated different forms of research activities and theoretical perspectives. What the analysis does imply is that one's disciplinary heritage—be it single or multiple— will influence one's conception of how people relate to nature.

Forestry and Natural Resources Management

Following World War II, recreational visits to natural areas in the United States dramatically outpaced population growth, reaching billions of visits annually (Catton, 1971). Nearly 600 million visits are received each year on federal lands alone in the United States, an increase of more than 60% over the past 15 years (Cordell & Hendee, 1982; U.S. Department of the Interior, 1979). During the same period, the population expanded by a mere 17%.

Faced with the pressures of swelling use, federal land managers responded by constructing new facilities and other support services. But these added services, in turn, began to entice even more people into outdoor areas. Policymakers began to realize that, unwittingly, they had begun to create a whole new form of recreation experience. Signals began to appear that veteran nature-oriented and crowd-sensitive users were being displaced by a new breed of socially oriented, facility-dependent visitors (Clark, Hendee, & Campbell, 1971). And a plethora of new problems began to emerge, such as visitor conflict (Driver & Bassett, 1975), congestion (Nash, 1977), exceeded site capacity (Stankey, 1973), vandalism (Alfano & Magill, 1976), theft (Hadley, 1971), assaults (Kendzie, 1983), vegetational and soil impact (Cole, 1982), and, in general, changes in the overall character of backcountry experiences (Schreyer & Knopf, 1984). The weakness of traditional management approaches was being revealed—the complex issue of recreation quality was not being addressed (Schreyer, 1976).

In response, resource management agencies began to switch from a policy of passively accommodating increasing volumes of use to one of determining and offering appropriate mixes of desired experiences (Brown, Driver, & McConnel, 1978). A call was extended to the research community to (1) quantify what these experiences might be and (2) identify management practices that would guarantee these experiences while minimizing visitors' perception of being regulated. The latter has spawned numerous studies of visitor attitudes toward management options ranging from those that are subtle and lighthanded (e.g., providing people with information about alternatives) to those that are authoritarian and accompanied by sanctions (e.g., rationing access, restricting behavior).[2] The former has created a preponderance of research on motives for visiting the outdoors (Knopf, 1983), on outdoor recreation satisfaction (Propst & Lime, 1982), and on the need-satisfying properties of particular outdoor locales (Brown & Ross, 1982). It is this research that bears most directly on our interest in defining the character of transactions between people and nature.

The earliest research activities concentrated on

identifying, through informal observation and unstructured interviews, the reasons why people visited natural environments for recreation (e.g., Burch, 1965; Catton, 1969). The message was that motives were diverse: Escape, achievement, affiliation, social recognition, exploration, self-actualization, spiritual rejuvenation, exercise, and nature appreciation were all cited (Hendee, 1974; Knopf, 1972). By the early 1970s, attention focused on developing psychometric scales to describe motive strengths along these identified themes (Hendee, Catton, Marlow, & Brockman, 1968; Knopf et al., 1973).[3] In the mid-1970s, a common feature of research was to construct and compare motive profiles for recreationists engaging in different outdoor studies (Driver, 1976; Tinsley, Barrett, & Kass, 1977). Such studies revealed that motive structures were activity-dependent—that is, people doing different things in the out-of-doors seemed to be pursuing quite different goals (Driver & Brown, 1978). There appeared to be no single or common motivation propelling people into these backcountry areas.

As research progressed into the late 1970s, it became clear that motive profiles also lacked homogeneity even among recreationists participating in the same activity. It was discovered that recreationists engaging in the same activity—even those in the same recreation setting—could be divided into motivationally distinguishable groups. Brown, Hautaluoma, and McPhail (1977), for example, found a Colorado deer-hunting population to be comprised of eight motivationally distinguishable groups and found differences in hunting style, degree of support for specific management practices, and socioeconomic makeup. Similarly, Bowley (1979) described five motive types among a population of Pennsylvania backcountry trail hikers and found differences in crowding perception, satisfaction level, and degree of support for a variety of trail management practices—even though all were sampled from the same setting. These segmentation-based motivational analyses have since been performed for numerous other outdoor populations, including wilderness users (Brown & Haas, 1980), cross-country skiers (Ballman, 1980), vacation tourists (Knopf & Barnes, 1980), anglers (Driver & Cooksey, 1977), and interpretive center visitors (Brown, Bester, & Knopf, 1978). What was being revealed was that people with different motives were reacting to the same environmental features in different ways and feeling differently about what kinds of settings managers should be offering.

By the 1980s, increased sensitivity to the diversity of outdoor recreation goals generated strong interest in understanding how different environmental settings help people meet their desired psychological outcomes (Brown & Ross, 1982). Interest surged in building measures of environmental performance in the form of satisfaction scales (Propst & Lime, 1982; Schomaker & Knopf, 1982) that could be used to assess the degree to which particular settings were fulfilling particular outcomes (Ditton, Fedler, & Graefe, 1982; Shelby, 1980).

At the same time, resource management agencies became intrigued with the notion that different kinds of lands might service different kinds of motive profiles. They became interested in developing a land classification system that would distinguish among locales serving different forms of human needs (U.S. Department of Agriculture, 1980; U.S. Department of the Interior, 1980). The most recent generation of social research in forestry has responded to these interests—attempting to establish, mostly through correlational studies, the association between desired psychological outcomes from the recreational engagement and preferred patterns of environmental stimuli (Ballman, 1980; Brown & Ross, 1982; Manfredo, 1979; McLaughlin & Paradice, 1980). The primary theoretical position of this literature assumes strong linkage between the character of the physical setting and the experience generated (Brown, Driver, & McConnel, 1978), although conceptual and empirical evidence to the contrary has been offered (Allen, 1979; Knopf, Peterson, & Leatherberry, 1983).

Emerging from the nearly two decades of empirical work are hundreds of analyses of outdoor motives and studies of how these motives relate to environmental perception and satisfaction. In addition to the plethora of analyses on virtually every form of outdoor recreation (Knopf, 1983), entire symposia have examined the goal orientations of participants in particular forest-based activities, most notably hunting (Shaw & Zube, 1980), river floating (U.S. Department of Agriculture, 1977b), organized educational camping (van der Smissen, 1976), snowmobiling, and cross-country ski touring (Knopp & Merriam, 1980). The dominant theme continues to be that people are in search of multiple goals during outdoor pursuits and the character of these goals has bearing on how people respond to the environmental features.

Foresters, then, who have a strong tradition of research into the question of how people respond to nature, bring two important perspectives to the problem. First, they subscribe to the notion that people migrate to nature not for a universal cause but for a diversity of goals that vary greatly from individual to individual. Second, they focus on the physical setting as being an important determinant of response. The goal-striving human, they maintain, cares much about the precise character of his or her physical surroundings.

Health, Recreation, and Leisure Studies

Specialists in the health, recreation, and leisure fields have traditionally stressed the important influence of leisure on mental health (Tinsley, 1978). People are seen as using leisure to raise self-esteem, establish identity, facilitate self-actualization, and enhance life satisfaction. Maslow's (1962) theory is popular, with the assumption that leisure can help gratify higher order needs that cannot be met in more restrictive, nonleisure environments (M. Kaplan, 1975; Tinsley & Tinsley, 1982). And, after White (1957), many leisure theorists equate play behavior with competence behavior—whereby leisure is used persistently and pervasively to help one gain mastery over life events (Barnett & Storm, 1981; Ellis, 1973). People in truly recreative experiences, it is argued, experience a sharp sense of control over action and the environment, a loss of the sensation of time, a harmony and union between self and the environment, a lessening of personal problems, and a more positive self-appreciation (Csikszentmihalyi, 1975a). This assertion is not new: Philosophers from Plato to Sartre have suggested that individuals are most whole, creative, and in control when at play (Schiller, 1884). The thrust of leisure science has been to acknowledge the importance of leisure pursuits, through emphasis on detailed knowledge of leisure activities and the functions these activities perform for the individual.

One of the first tasks of the early leisure scientists was to describe leisure behavior and sociodemographic correlates of it. Much of this work is pertinent to our understanding of outdoor activity, in that the description, classification, and prediction of outdoor recreation behavior was a common focus, particularly in the 1960s (Outdoor Recreation Resources Review Commission, 1962; Sessoms, 1963). It was then that researchers began to notice the influences on outdoor behavior of culture (Burch, 1970), gender (Brewer & Gillespie, 1966), age (Green & Wadsworth, 1967), income (Sessoms, 1963), occupation (Bishop & Ikeda, 1970), life cycle (Burch, 1966), race (Outdoor Recreation Resources Review Commission, 1962), place of residence (Hendee, 1969), family life-style (Kenyon & McPherson, 1970), childhood experiences (Yoesting & Burkhead, 1973), and other sociocultural variables. Although much of this research was later denounced as superficial, it

brought attention to the diversity and pervasiveness of outdoor behavior. And, for our purposes, it suggests the powerful role sociocultural forces play in determining actions in the outdoors.

As empirical activity in leisure research matured, investigators turned to the more fundamental question of what forms of leisure are optimal. They were being pressed by leisure counselors to create trait and factor tests that could be administered to people to help them decide what forms of leisure activities they should pursue (McKechnie, 1974). Three broad lines of inquiry emerged from this emphasis that bear on the problem of assessing behavior in natural settings.

First, a spurt of activity centered on defining the psychological payoffs of particular activities (Crandall, 1980; Hawes, 1978a; London, Crandall, & Fitzgibbons, 1977; Tinsley et al., 1977). This research paralleled in substance the motive research being done in forestry, but due to its broader scope, it provided the capacity to analyze motives for outdoor activity in relation to motives for other forms of activities (Knopf et al., 1983; Pierce, 1980). And, echoing research in forestry, activities were classified according to the kinds of needs they serve (Tinsley & Kass, 1979). There was interest, too, in defining the relative substitutability of different activities (Becker, 1976; Chase & Cheek, 1979), with much of the attention focused on outdoor activities because of the problem of land resource scarcity (Hendee & Burdge, 1974; O'Leary, Field, & Schreuder, 1974).

Second, there was focus on the individual, and on what shapes individual preference. In particular, attention turned to personality as a potential mediator of leisure needs and satisfaction. Much of the early work was housed in sport psychology, where trait studies blossomed in the late 1960s and early 1970s (Alderman, 1974). This activity was fueled primarily by counselors in educational settings who believed that recreational sports programming needed to be better keyed to specific personalities of students (Morgan, 1974). As theoretically logical correlations between personality inventory scores and sport activity preferences emerged, interest grew in exploring relationships between personality and preferences for other forms of recreation—including outdoor recreation. And, with regard to the latter, a powerful message was emerging: Trait scores are powerful forecasters of not only what people do but also what they attend to, in the outdoors (Driver & Knopf, 1977; Howard, 1976; Macia, 1979; Martin & Myrick, 1976; Moss & Lamphear, 1970).

Third, interest arose in understanding the mediating effects of nonleisure experience, particularly work place conditions, on recreation preference (Champoux, 1975; Grubb, 1975). Useful predictors included stress level (Grubb, 1975), the character of social role demands (Cheek & Burch, 1976), mood state (Lewissohn & Graf, 1973), stimulation level (Loy & Donnelly, 1976), achievement opportunity, (Adams & Stone, 1977), and rate of prior energy expenditure (Witt & Bishop, 1970). This activity forces us to consider that recreational preferences—including those related to behavior in natural settings—are neither pervasive nor consistent but fluctuate according to daily experience.

Thus the conceptual orientation of leisure research contributes two broad sensitivities that are important as we construct a model of people–nature relations. First, we must consider that many of the benefits ascribed to natural environments (self-revelation, competence building, esteem enhancement, person–environment fusion) are also ascribed to people's recreational experiences *in general*. We must entertain—at least temporarily—the notion that recreational experiences in the outdoors may be functionally indistinguishable from recreational experiences elsewhere. Second, we again must consider the possible fluidity of relations with nature; that responses are not generic but individualistic—shaped by the interacting forces of personality and experience. Indeed numerous authors have suggested that predictive powers in recreation choice models will be strengthened only as we begin to adopt the interactionist (Mischel, 1973) perspective—thereby forcing ourselves to address the confounding influences of personality and setting (Iso-Ahola, 1980; Knopf, 1983; Levy, 1979). Although this literature does not dispute the contention that humans have innate preferences for nature, it does argue that much of behavior and sensation in the outdoors is shaped by experience, forces, and events outside the realm of nature.

Environmental Sociology

People in the outdoors do not act in void of a social context. They act in response to the regulatory principles and adjustment mechanisms of a larger society (Burch, 1971; M. Kaplan, 1960), and they respond to the will of the group with whom the experience is shared (Field & O'Leary, 1973; Kelly, 1976). And, indeed, they even actively pursue social stimulation that they can draw upon to affirm self-identity, confirm personal values and world views, and establish bonds of friendship (Cheek & Burch, 1976).

The outdoor experience is clearly a group experience (Cheek, 1971; Field & O'Leary, 1973). Cheek and Burch (1976, p. 24) found 96% of visitors to such outdoor areas as parks, beaches, rivers, and lakes were participating as members of a group. Even the image of the solitary wilderness journeyer proves to be false—fewer than 2% of visitors to the wilderness are alone (Lee, 1977; Stankey, 1973). And, to complicate our picture, it may well be that many of the people we describe as "flocking to nature" are in fact doing little more than responding to social obligation. Cheek and Burch (1976, p. 12) found that over half of the visitors they sampled at outdoor recreation sites were there at the wish of someone else. Similarly, Kelly (1976) found 26% of recreation ventures performed under "some obligation to others," with an additional 29% performed under "considerable obligation."

For these reasons, analysis of behavior and preference in natural environments is seen by many primarily as a sociological problem (Burch, 1971; Cheek, Field, & Burdge, 1976; Dunlap & Catton, 1979). Under this perspective, social exchange is the fundamental variable around which behavior is organized. Any single behavior is only part of a larger set of social transactions and cannot be understood in isolation of them (Altman, 1977). What people do and what is gained will depend on the people participating and the interchanges that transpire (Field, Burdge, & Burch, 1975; Lee, 1972). To a sociologist, the "environment" for a person in the outdoors is likely to be construed as the group one is associated with, the character of other social stimulation present, the community in which one resides, the institutions to which one belongs (economic, work, educational, religious, and family), and the culture one is reared within (Catton & Dunlap, 1980). This stands in sharp contrast to the concept prevailing within other disciplines, where *environment* is understood in terms of one's physical surroundings. And this concept strongly influences what it is that sociologists feel people are responding to during outdoor experiences (Cheek et al., 1976).

The revelations of sociological inquiry related to natural environments research have been analyzed by several sources (Cheek & Burch, 1976; Cheek et al., 1976; Dunlap & Catton, 1979; Knopf, 1983). Three insights are particularly noteworthy.

First, individuals seem to rely heavily on the social environment for cues on how to behave. Behavioral choice—whether during the initial selection of outdoor behavior or during the actual experience—is strongly attuned to the expectations of others (Bultena & Field, 1980; Lee, 1972; Schreyer & Nielson, 1978; West, 1977). Second, each outdoor locale carries its own normative order—what is socially acceptable behavior in one setting may not be in another (Heberlein, 1977; Jacob & Schreyer, 1980). Individuals who do not fit in receive cues that direct them to more appropriate settings (Lee, 1972). It is common in outdoor recreation areas to find groups with potentially conflicting values purposively and voluntarily segregating into distinct territories (Westover & Chubb, 1980). Third, social exchange may be an end in itself. Observations of behavior in parks have led sociologists to conclude that orientation to the group overshadows orientation to the physical setting. Family groups interact differently with the environment than friendship groups, even in the same setting (Burch, 1965; Cheek, 1971). An individual shifting from one social group to another is likely to participate in a wholly different stream of activity (Field, 1976). And what is important is that the expressed satisfactions would differ (Buchanan, Christensen, & Burdge, 1981; Hendee, Clark, & Dailey, 1977). Thus many sociologists conclude that behavior and meaning in the outdoors is linked less to the physical array than to the configuration of the group. The physical setting may be important to people, but it is important because it offers an arena for social interaction, reinforcement, and bonding (Cheek & Burch, 1976, p. 167).

Sociologists also have been attracted to a variety of other natural environment-related topics through interest in the social dynamics of public policy formulation. Such topics include the dynamics of organizational, institutional, and governmental response to environmental problems (Dunlap & Catton, 1979); social impact assessment of planned environmental change (Finsterbusch & Wolf, 1977; McEvoy & Dietz, 1977); bureaucratic impediments to sound assessment of such impacts (Andrews, Burdge, Capener, Warner, & Wilkinson, 1973); public resistance to environmental policy change (Field, Barron, & Long, 1974; Shelby, 1981); techniques for obtaining citizen input (Fairfax, 1975; Heberlein, 1976); organizational impacts of alienated publics emerging from controversial environmental policy decisions (Alston & Freeman, 1975; Twight & Paterson, 1979); schisms between users' and managers' images of public land resources and political implications of this dichotomy (Bultena & Taves, 1961; Twight & Catton, 1975); the dynamics of membership in conservation organizations and how they influence individual action (Hendee, 1971; Mitchell & Davies, 1978); and evolution of cultural and individual environmental attitudes (bibliographies are offered by Buttel & Morrison, 1977; Dunlap & Van Liere, 1978).

In summary, the foregoing sociological research forces us to consider action in the outdoors as being highly responsive to, even oriented to, social stimula-

tion. It suggests that our attempts to model choice in natural environments will be woefully inadequate without analysis of the social context of decision making (Ajzen & Fishbein, 1973; Altman, 1977). It also prompts us to abandon the intuitive preconception that the physical setting is necessarily the dominant producer of sensation during outdoor experiences. And finally, it moves us to pose the outdoor actor not as a passive victim of whatever the natural setting has to offer but as an active creator of optimal flows of stimulation, primarily through active manipulation of the social context (Dunlap & Catton, 1979).

Environmental Psychology

Whereas other disciplines tend to focus on behavior and needs while investigating the character of people–nature transactions, environmental psychologists tend to focus on the cognitive processes. Trends in natural environments research within environmental psychology tend to parallel those in the discipline as a whole (Stokols, 1978), with research being conducted not only by environmental psychologists proper (S. Kaplan & R. Kaplan, 1978; Ulrich, 1983; Wohlwill, 1983) but also by investigators in other disciplines, such as forestry, who are strongly influenced by the perspectives of environmental psychology (Driver, 1972; Knopf, 1983; Peterson, 1973). Areas of study include emotional consequences of exposure to nature (More, 1980; Ulrich, 1979); therapeutic values of wilderness (R. Kaplan, 1974; S. Kaplan & Talbot, 1983); territorial behavior and attachment to place (Jacob & Schreyer, 1980; Lee, 1972); orientations toward privacy in nature and response to social densities (Gramman, 1982; Hammitt, 1982); consequences of environmental stress and the role of nature in its mediation (Driver & Knopf, 1976; Ulrich, 1977); need-satisfying properties of natural objects, experiences, or locales (R. Kaplan, 1973b; Lewis, 1977); formation and utility of cognitive maps in natural environments (R. Kaplan, 1976; Knopf, 1981); cognitive representation of natural environments (Beaulieu & Schreyer, 1982; Feimer, 1983); role of experience or familiarity in shaping preference (Bryan, 1979; Hammitt, 1979), perception (Newby, 1979; Peterson, 1977) and the cognitive structuring process (Schreyer & White, 1979; Williams & Schreyer, 1982); behavioral ecology, particularly in relation to littering and vandalism (Crump, Nunes, & Crossman, 1977; Gold, 1977); and behavioral control, particularly in relation to managerially undesirable behavior (Clark, Hendee, & Burgess, 1972; Clark, 1976).

One important thrust of environmental psychology research has been to examine the properties of nature that differentiate it from other stimuli acting on people (Wohlwill, 1983). This interest has been spurred by the consistent finding that people pay attention to nature as they cognitively organize their world (Ward & Russell, 1981). Studies of how people internally represent their environment reveal that degree of naturalness is an important, if not fundamental, dimension by which settings are differentiated (Bernaldez & Parra, 1979; Craik, 1970; Herzog, Kaplan, & Kaplan, 1982; Palmer & Zube, 1976; Ullrich & Ullrich, 1976; Ward, 1977; Zube, 1976). And it has also been spurred by the consistent finding in photojudgment studies that people prefer natural scenes over partly natural or built scenes (Bernaldez & Parra, 1979; R. Kaplan, 1983; Kaplan, Kaplan, & Wendt, 1972; Thayer & Atwood, 1978; Wohlwill, 1976; Zube, 1976).

So the quest began to determine how nature is distinguishable from nonnature or how certain scenes are preferred over others, using predictors, such as complexity (Kaplan, Kaplan, & Wendt, 1972; Wohlwill, 1976), coherence (Kuller, 1972; Kwok, 1979), mystery (Appleton, 1975; R. Kaplan, 1973a), diversity (Bernaldez & Parra, 1979; Gustke & Hodgson, 1980), legibility (Kaplan, Kaplan, & Wendt, 1972; Lee, 1979), texture (Rabinowitz & Coughlin, 1970; Ulrich, 1977), spaciousness (R. Kaplan, 1983; Patey & Evans, 1979), and focality (Lee, 1979; Ulrich, 1977). Interest also emerged in quantifying the optimal composition of forest landscapes in terms of such properties as species composition, species distribution, vegetational density, color contrast, and other readily identifiable attributes (Daniel & Boster, 1976; Zube, Sell, & Taylor, 1982). And interest emerged in identifying variables influencing the degree to which human-made elements or facilities are congruous with the patterns of stimulation found in nature (Steinitz & Way, 1959; Wohlwill & Harris, 1980).

This wave of inquiry has not been spared the continuing debate in environmental psychology over the saliency of the linkage between physical properties of an environment and human response to it (Ward & Russell, 1981; Wohlwill, 1976). Some investigators focus on the purely physical properties of nature as powerful determinants of experience (Wohlwill, 1983), whereas others avoid specifying variables in terms of objective referents and emphasize the extreme subjectivity of the natural experience (Lowenthal & Prince, 1976; Tuan, 1974). The debate has spilled over into forestry-based outdoor recreation research, as it struggles with the question of how the physical environment shapes experience (Knopf et al., 1983). Proponents of the subjective paradigm have sparked a new generation of research on the symbolic functions of nature (Lee, 1977; White & Schreyer, 1979) and the role of image or personal schemata in influencing preference and choice (Hodson & Thayer, 1980; Schreyer, Jacob, & White, 1982; Veal, 1973).

Another pertinent contribution of environmental psychology rises from its quest to develop measures of environmental personality (Craik, 1976). Primarily through the influence of Hendee (1967), Sonnenfeld (1969), and McKechnie (1970), interest began to grow in developing measures that differentiate people according to the ways they comprehend or make use of the physical environment. The logic is that people relate to the physical environment in stable, consistent ways, just as they relate to themselves and others in predictable ways. Hendee's (1967) "wildernism–urbanism" scale, for example, describes the degree to which individuals have a general disposition toward urban amenities during outdoor experiences. Scale scores have been predictive of both recreation site selection (Loder, 1978; Wohlwill & Heft, 1977) and management preferences (Schreyer, Roggenbuck, McCool, Royer, & Miller, 1976; Stankey, 1972). Similarly, scale scores on the McKechnie Environmental Response Inventory have been linked to patterns of recreation activity (McKechnie, 1974) and have been used to account for value differences between resource managers and resource users (Peterson, 1974a). More recent activity has successfully showed relationships between outdoor preferences and measures of general disposition, such as privacy orientation (Twight, Smith, & Wissinger, 1981), sensation-seeking tendency (Loy & Donnelly, 1976), and external versus internal locus of control (Kleiber, 1979). This literature, although yet being neither abundant nor pervasive, does prompt us to consider the notion that relationship to the environment is a matter of personal style.

So despite the relative lack of attention devoted to people–nature transactions in environmental psychology (Wohlwill, 1983), the contributions nonetheless are important. We are sensitized to the distinguishing properties of nature and witness evidence of apparent human proclivity for these properties. At the same time, we are sensitized to the power of the mind in being able to organize, filter, adapt, adjust, enrich, and indeed even overrule stimuli from the surrounding physical array for its own purposes. We are forced to consider that the way in which people respond to a natural environment will depend on their goals, their personalities, and their repertoire of past experiences (Knopf, 1983). So we find here a theme that is strikingly similar to that advanced by sociology: Environmental experience is not wholly defined by the physical array. Certainly there is evidence that the inherent properties of nature have an influence on the individual and his or her behavior. But there also is evidence that prior experience can modulate what the character of that influence will be.

Natural Resource Economics

The discipline of economics concerns itself with the matter of how scarce resources, such as the flow of services from natural environments, may be allocated among competing demands. Natural environments, for the most part, are managed for a multiplicity of objectives (see Pitt and Zube, Chapter 27, this volume). This requires decision makers to gauge the importance of each service relative to the others and establish the acceptable degree of trade-off between mutually conflicting services (e.g., timber production and wilderness preservation). The dilemma is that many of the services rendered by natural environments—such as outdoor recreation experiences and landscape aesthetics—have no market values because they are subsidized public goods. There is, then, no obvious basis for comparison with alternative services that do bear market values—such as timber and minerals. The standard research problem, addressed by many environmental economists, is to measure the values of environmental commodities for which no market prices exist (Krutilla & Fisher, 1975; Maler, 1974).

Economists approach the problem by assuming that the values attached to an object are reflected in the costs a person is willing to incur to experience it (Dwyer & Bowes, 1979; Fischer, 1975). Two general methodologies have been employed to estimate this willingness to pay—one direct, the other indirect. The direct approach involves querying people directly about what they would be willing to pay through surveys or bidding games (Price, 1979; Sinden & Smith, 1975). The indirect approach involves generating estimates of the expenditures people make while gaining access to the object in question (Ulph & Reynolds, 1979). In the case of valuing a recreational facility, for example, data would be compiled on the costs incurred while traveling to, staying at, and returning from the site (including the cost of time). Value could be established by summing expenditure data across all utilizers, yielding a common dollar measure for comparing with otherwise incommensurate commodities (Cesario & Knetsch, 1976).

These valuation methodologies have been widely used by land management agencies for the calculation of benefit–cost analyses to guide resource allocation decisions (Dwyer, Kelly, & Bowes, 1977). In-

deed, studies of individual and social value attached to various environmental commodities comprise one of the most prolific areas in natural environments research (Waggener & Ceperley, 1978). We have, at our disposal, measures of the relative social utility of such resources as national parks, water reservoirs, wildlife sanctuaries, wilderness areas, urban parks, ski areas, campgrounds, and other outdoor recreation areas (see O'Rourke [1974] and Lavery [1975] for surveys of work in outdoor recreation). We also have indexes of the relative values of specific outdoor behaviors—such as fishing, hunting, swimming, cross-country ski touring, and backpacking (e.g., Doling & Gibson, 1979; Hammack & Brown, 1974; McConnell, 1977; Stynes, 1980a).

In recent years, numerous economists have become concerned with defining the optimal capacity of recreation sites and have studied the relationship between number of visitor encounters and willingness to pay for the experience (Cesario, 1980; Menz & Mullen, 1981; Miller, Prato, & Young, 1977). Fisher and Krutilla (1972) have represented congestion as a series of distinguishable demand curves at various levels of crowding. In backcountry areas, most empirical accounts show an inverse relationship and willingness to trade extra visits for less crowded opportunities (Price, 1979). Economists have also introduced the concepts of existence and option values; the premise is that calculation of value of an environmental resource must include (1) values ascribed by those who may never intend to visit it but find it a valued vicarious experience, and (2) values that would accrue to future generations from maintaining its current state (Bishop, 1982; Kreiger, 1973; Krutilla, 1967). Other significant contributions of economists include evaluations of the effects of entrance fees, energy costs, and other expenses of access on demand for an outdoor experience (Burke & Williams, 1979; Clawson, 1959; Peterson, Anderson, & Lime, 1982); the impacts of new recreation sites on demand for existing ones (Mansfield, 1971); the influence of added facilities or services on demand for a locale (Doling & Gibson, 1979); the demand consequences of introducing changes in access through rationing or site modification (Workman, 1981); and econometric studies of the relative substitutability of alternate recreation opportunities (Kurtz & King, 1980). Of particular interest to environmental psychology is the economists' recent use of willingness to pay methodology in examining the psychological utility of varied combinations of elements in the physical array (Miller et al., 1977).

The perspectives of economists benefit those concerned with the psychological functions of natural environments in several ways. First, they demonstrate the value and potential of behavioral analysis in yielding insights into individual and societal preference. Many economists eschew the use of intrapsychic measures and their attendant problems entirely, yet still draw inferences about the nature of human preference in relation to matters of environmental quality (Fisher & Krutilla, 1972; Goldin, 1971). Second, they demonstrate that values accrued from an outdoor experience emerge from more than the within-setting experience. People are oriented to, and derive benefits from, an outdoor experience while traveling to it and returning from it, while anticipating it, while recollecting it, and even while vicariously experiencing it (Clawson & Knetsch, 1966; Krutilla, 1967). Although vicarious experience of the outdoors has captured the attention of some psychologists (Ulrich, 1983) and certainly the authors of intuitive literature on nature, as a whole it has been avoided as a topic of research. Finally, the economic perspective sensitizes us to the need to construe individual preference for one environment over another or one object over another, as a function of both the rewards *and* costs perceived in gaining access to it. Many environmental choice models, especially recreation choice models, are based upon measures of rewarding experiences alone, whereas measures of associated costs are ignored (Cooksey, Dickinson, & Loomis, 1982). The thrust of economics research forcefully points out the inadequacies of these models.

Geography

Geography is yet another spawning ground for the study of outdoor places and the meanings of these places. Much of the research follows the traditional orientation of the field: mapping, simulating, and predicting behavioral flows in response to resources and impediments that limit access to resources (Coppock, 1982).

This emphasis has fostered the development of several lines of behavioral simulation research related to use of outdoor areas. Most of the activity has concentrated on simulating use patterns in outdoor recreation areas (Shechter & Lucas, 1978). Early analyses of these areas showed that visitors concentrate in narrow spatial fields, whereas larger nearby locales receive very little use—even though both areas are physically alike (Stankey, Lucas, & Lime, 1976). Resource managers, interested in reducing use at congested locations and avoiding excessive encounters at other locations, began to ask how they could accomplish these goals without reducing total use levels. Researchers responded by developing use

simulation models capable of forecasting the consequences of various management policies (Shechter & Lucas, 1980).

Although travel simulation models are common, particularly in the larger fields of geography and engineering, those being produced for outdoor recreation areas are distinguished by their focus on encounters.[4] There is interest in visual encounters as well as physical encounters and overtaking encounters (where faster parties pass slower parties) as well as meeting encounters (face-to-face encounter by travel in opposite direction). Models have been developed to account for such phenomena among wilderness users (Shechter & Lucas, 1978), backcountry trail hikers (Romesburg, 1974), recreational river floaters (Carls, 1978), hunters (Stynes, 1980a), lake boaters (Hammon, 1974), state and regional park users (Penz, 1975), and national park auto tourists (Devine, Borden, & Turner, 1976). Simulation methodology in a gaming format has also been developed to enhance land managers' understanding of use management principles (Mitchell & Schomaker, 1980).

Geographers have also mapped behavioral flows in natural environments from a regional perspective (Lavery, 1974). They have learned, for example, how outdoor behavior is distributed in response to such mediating forces as weather (Van Lier, 1973), energy availability (Corsi & Harvey, 1978), distribution of recreation sites (Aldskogius, 1977), knowledge of recreation sites (Baxter, 1979), attractiveness of recreation sites (Peterson et al., 1982), features of the microscale physical environment, such as mountains, rivers, and transportation corridors (Aldskogius, 1967; Ewing, 1980; Patmore, 1974), and features of the macroscale physical environment, such as fences, ridges, and parking lots (Eastwood & Carter, 1981; Hecock, 1970).

Although the traditional focus has been behavioral, many geographers interested in natural environments research are now emphasizing the cognitive perspective (Aldskogius, 1977; Tuan, 1975). Perception of crowding in natural environment and how it influences user dispersion has been of particular interest (Lime, 1977; Lucas, 1964). Considerable attention has also been devoted to perception of, and behavioral response to, natural hazards, such as floods, droughts, tornadoes, and earthquakes (Feimer, 1983; Heathcoate, 1969; Kates, 1976; White, 1974). And, to a lesser extent, just as in environmental psychology, there has been interest in the cognitive representation of outdoor locales (e.g., Ewing & Kulka, 1979; Goodrich, 1977; Perry, 1975).

Geographers have introduced to natural environments research the methodological capacity to describe behavioral flows and simulate the behavioral consequences of management intervention. Its potential will be better realized as simulation models are developed to monitor the psychological as well as the behavioral consequences of environmental stimuli or management action. This potential has been largely untapped, although its rudiments may be reflected in studies that fuse traditional behavioral geography with cognitive psychology. Noteworthy illustrations include the simulation research of Becker, Niemann, and Gates (1981) that correctly construes response to backcountry crowding experiences as having behavioral as well as psychological consequences, and the research of Aldskogius (1977) that demonstrates how regional recreation behavior patterns can be better simulated when psychological variables (e.g., cognitive image, individual preferences) are incorporated into the models.

Market Research

Personal expenditures for outdoor recreation total over $100 billion annually in the United States alone (Cordell & Hendee, 1982). Outdoor product manufacturers and retailers have, naturally, turned to market research for pricing, product, promotion, and location decisions to help them capture greater shares of these expenditures (Stynes, in press). The intent is to develop product offerings with a sharpened public image and more widespread appeal (Kotler, 1976). At the same time, resource administrators have become interested in market research as a tool for predicting trends in recreation equipment consumption. In this way, recreation sites and facilities now under construction can be designed to accommodate future equipment requirements.

Of the seven disciplines we have focused on, marketing perhaps is the least developed empirically in focusing on the broad theme of natural environments utilization. But three distinct lines of inquiry are emerging that have bearing on the problem.

First, there is interest in modeling or predicting the life cycle of particular recreational products. The goal is to understand patterns of diffusion of products across different market segments, and the expected rate of growth and total market life in each. Brand-specific analyses are abundant in industry, but consumption life cycles have also been analyzed for broader activities, such as snowmobiling (Stynes & Szcodronski, 1980), cross-country skiing (Stynes, 1980b), boating (Seneca & Davis, 1976), fishing (Allen & Dwyer, 1978), downhill skiing (Stynes & Mahoney, 1980), and use of tourist areas (Baron, 1975; Butler, 1980). A thoughtful review of the potential this research holds for the administration of recreation resources is offered by Crompton and Hensarling (1978).

Second, there is interest in applying traditional market segmentation techniques (Kotler, 1976) to populations of outdoor recreationists to identify groups differing in recreation goals, behavior patterns, disposable incomes, equipment portfolios, and other variables of interest in marketing. The premise is that marketing efforts will be more effective if they are keyed toward specific, well-defined market segments (Stynes, in press). The State of Michigan, for example, has segmented its tourist population into six categories—sightseer, young sports, winter/water, outdoorsman, resort, and night life—and has developed specialized promotional campaigns targeted to each segment (Bryant & Morrison, 1980). Three general classes of segmentation studies in outdoor recreation and tourism can be identified: (1) those that differentiate market segments by population background variables, such as age, income, or equipment (e.g., Tantham & Dornoff, 1971; Stynes, in press); (2) those differentiating on the basis of benefits sought (e.g., Goodrich, 1980; Hawes, 1978b)[5]; and (3) those differentiating on the basis of current activity or product involvement (e.g., LaPage, 1979; Stynes & Mahoney, 1980). The latter has been identified as holding the most promise for outdoor retailers or resource planners (LaPage, 1968). The typical model segments the market for a particular product into active consumers, inactive consumers, potential consumers, and past consumers no longer interested in consumption—as was done by LaPage (1979) in a national study of camping behavior and Stynes and Mahoney (1980) in a statewide study of downhill skiing activity. The point of this research is to identify background features that distinguish the four groups, so that promotional materials can be designed to maximize the population of active consumers (LaPage, 1974).

Third, there is growing interest in identifying the criteria people employ in choosing among alternate recreation products or locales. The research to date has primarily employed the traditional multibrand, multiattribute marketing models and has focused on tourism where there is great interest in developing travel destination models (Scott, Schewe, & Frederick, 1978; Woodside & Ronkainen, 1980). And, expectedly, there is particular interest in the role of product or resource image in affecting choice (Hunt, 1975; Mayo, 1973), and the role information plays in changing the image or otherwise affecting choice (Johnson, 1978; Perry, 1975).

Thus market research is yet another disciplinary focus that points to the dynamic character of people's involvement with nature. Although the number of empirical studies it has fostered relating to the broad theme of people–nature transactions is limited compared with other disciplines, the existing evidence implies that action and preference in the outdoors are strongly tied to variables outside the natural domain.

20.3.2. The Need for an Integrative Perspective

The problem of how people relate to natural environments, then, seems to be a germane one to science. At least seven disciplines find the topic worthy of pursuit. And, as the preceding analysis makes clear, each discipline contributes a unique perspective to the matter. Foresters emphasize the diversity of values associated with experiences in natural environments and prompt us to respect the power of the physical environment in defining those experiences. Activity in the leisure sciences causes us to wonder whether, from the standpoint of need gratification, natural environments are indeed offering unique contributions to the human life space. Moreover, it points to the powerful role of personality in particular and prior experience in general in affecting how people respond to nature. Environmental sociology research makes us wonder whether people have need for anything other than social reinforcement, effectively deflating our image of the physical array as the primary determinant of meaning. Work in environmental psychology restores our faith in nature as a cognitively distinguishable and important stimulus, but it also reminds us that the mind is not a passive victim of whatever the physical array has to offer—it has, to the contrary, a powerful capacity to create its own experience. Economists force us to consider that transactions with nature involve more than on-site experiences, and they, like geographers, remind us of the power of behavioral analysis as a complement to intrapsychic analysis in building appreciation of how people relate to nature. Finally, market research fixes our attention on variables external to the natural environment as primary determinants of response to it, prompting us to recognize the extreme fluidity of relations with nature.

In one sense, we value the uniqueness of each disciplinary perspective. For when fused together, we find ourselves equipped with a more holistic and accurate model of people–nature transactions than the limited perspective of any one discipline would allow. But in another sense, these same disciplinary perspectives lock individual investigators into a limited view of reality—which distorts how research problems are conceptualized, how specific constructs are defined, and even how data are interpreted.

Consider, for example, the problem of building environmental taxonomies. This problem is of fundamental interest to outdoor recreation planners, who are relying on researchers to develop a recreation resource classification system that distinguishes among locales servicing different forms of human needs (Driver & Brown, 1978). Taxonomies emerging from the forestry perspective tend to presume strong linkage between the physical character of the recreation setting and the experience generated. The currently popular Recreation Opportunity Spectrum (ROS) land inventory system[6] is an outgrowth of this perspective, implying that variation in response to outdoor recreation settings is strongly linked to variation along the primitive-urban continuum (Brown, Driver, & McConnel, 1978). In sharp contrast, taxonomies emerging from the sociological perspective have classified outdoor locales in terms of their abilities to facilitate different forms of social transactions (Cheek & Burch, 1976, p. 155; Lee, 1972). Also in sharp contrast, taxonomies emerging from the leisure sciences perspective pay less attention to the physical or social character of a locale and dwell more on the styles of personal involvement that are evoked—employing such dimensions as active–passive, participant–spectator, control–noncontrol, and association–disassociation (de Grazia, 1962; M. Kaplan, 1960). And taxonomies emerging from the perspective of cognitive psychology eschew objective measures altogether and classify resources on the basis of subjective judgments of functional variation (Ritchie, 1975; Ullrich & Ullrich, 1976). Although the differences are intriguing, they also cause confusion—both to the outdoor planner in search of an appropriate inventory methodology and to the scientist in search of an understanding of what is important to people in nature.

Even such a fundamental and relevant construct as "outdoor recreation quality" is not spared the tainting effects of disciplinary focus. Those with backgrounds in forestry tend to define outdoor recreation quality as the degree to which the environment facilitates goal accomplishment (Wagar, 1966). But, following forestry's historical emphasis, *environment* has been largely construed as the surrounding physical array. So we find virtually every conception of outdoor quality being offered dwelling heavily upon the physical setting as a primary determinant of what is extracted from the outdoor experience (e.g., Brown,

Driver, & McConnel, 1978; Peterson, 1974b; Rossman & Ulehla, 1977).[7] On the other hand, those with backgrounds in sociology tend to define outdoor recreation quality as the degree to which the setting promotes a shared scheme of social order (Lee, 1977). Under this conception, the essential ingredient for a quality experience is linked not to the physical constituency of the environment but to the perception that other users of an area carry similar definitions of appropriate behavior (Jacob & Schreyer, 1980; Lee, 1972). Such differences in perspective are, once again, intriguing. But we surmise that both perspectives fail in offering an adequate view of how the outdoor recreator evaluates the quality of his or her experience.

Even the meaning ascribed to particular data can be influenced by disciplinary perspective. For example, those who strongly emphasize the power of the physical setting in affecting response might observe people in nature, make note of accompanying sensations (e.g., self-environment fusion; loss of awareness of time; heightened self-sufficiency; expanded personal insight and identity), and conclude that the natural environment was instrumental in evoking them (e.g., Bernstein, 1972; Gibson, 1979; Hanson, 1977). However, leisure scientists would not be likely to agree. They have repeatedly documented the same sensations for virtually all forms of recreative activity—not just those in the outdoors (Csikszentmihalyi, 1975a; Panzarella, 1980). Rather than attributing the cause to the natural environment per se, they would be more likely to conclude that there simply was greater congruence between environmental demands and the skills of the individuals in question (Csikszentmihalyi, 1975b; Ellis, 1973). On the other hand, sociologists observing the same data might attribute the cause to shifted group dynamics and patterns of social reinforcement (Burch, 1977).

So, at least while the study of people–nature transactions remains in its primordial state, there is no assurance that the propositions that now frequent the literature are not mere artifacts of the disciplinary perspective that generated them. To build an acceptable theory of how people relate to natural environments, we need to draw simultaneously from all perspectives—putting the insights we glean from each in relation to those available from the others. But it seems we have been reluctant to do so. Only infrequently is there collaboration across these differing perspectives; it is rare to find cross-citation among the seven bodies of literature. We need a process of aggressive critique and debate on the people–nature issue that transcends disciplinary lines. We need to better clarify the fundamental dif-

ferences of view, to better articulate the issues requiring research attention, and to generate alternatives to the present independent courses of inquiry.

In the meantime, while awaiting the debate, we can search through the accumulating data to highlight those principles and concepts governing human response to natural stimuli that seem to stand across disciplinary lines. We now turn to that task. Our analysis will examine in sequence three general dimensions of the problem of defining the character of transactions between people and the natural environment. First, we will focus on the question of meaning, with the intent of elucidating the goals that seem to underlie people's involvement with nature. Second, we will focus on the cognitive process, considering the role natural stimuli play as people process information about their worlds and considering how people mentally represent natural environments. And third, we will focus on affective response, addressing the question of whether exposure to natural stimuli results in altered emotional states.

20.3.3. The Character of Transactions

Questing
What are people searching for when they migrate to natural environments? The study of meaning spans disciplines, but each discipline views meaning in a slightly different context. Foresters are interested in aspects that have implications for land management (Hendee, 1974); leisure scientists are interested in aspects that have implications for personal growth (Tinsley & Kass, 1979); sociologists are interested in aspects that reveal something about the dynamics of social group processes (Lee, 1972); environmental psychologists are interested in aspects that bear on how environmental stimuli are processed (Kaplan & Kaplan, 1978); geographers are interested in aspects that bear on the shaping of behavior (Aldskogius, 1977); and market researchers are interested in aspects that are useful in developing locational choice models (Woodside & Ronkainen, 1980).

Collectively, the empirical studies of meaning ascribed to natural environments are generating at least eight major points.

First, people value the psychological consequences of an outdoor behavior more than the behavior itself. For example, anglers do not go fishing as much for the food as for the opportunity to relax, achieve, and socialize (Hendee et al., 1977; Knopf et al., 1973). Hunters tend to be more interested in escape, companionship, and exercise than in harvesting or displaying game (More, 1973; Potter, Hendee, & Clark, 1973). Floaters appear to be more concerned with maintaining an optimum flow of social reinforc-ers than with experiencing the water itself (O'Leary et al., 1974). And the recent surge of interest in high-risk outdoor activities would not appear to be very rational unless some substantial psychological rewards were forthcoming (McAvoy & Dustin, 1981; Schreyer & White, 1979).

Second, any outdoor activity is pursued to extract a *range* of psychological consequences. People are not fixed on a single goal (Hendee, 1974). One "kayaks" a river not only to gain a sense of achieve-ment but also to affiliate, escape, explore, exercise, be autonomous, gain status, or have a spiritual or aesthetic experience (Schreyer & Roggenbuck, 1978). Motives for participating in other outdoor ac-tivities are similarly diverse (Driver, 1976; Rossman & Ulehla, 1977). Within this broader package of goals, however, some indeed are more important than others for a particular individual in a given situa-tion (Knopf et al., 1973).

Third, people engaging in different outdoor ac-tivities appear to be searching for different mixes of psychological outcomes (Driver, 1976; Tinsley et al., 1977). Fourth, people visiting different *kinds* of out-door settings seem to be searching for different mixes of psychological outcomes (Brown & Ross, 1982).

Fifth, although differences across activities and settings are significant, the goals of individuals par-ticipating in the same outdoor behavior even in the same outdoor locale are not entirely homogeneous (Brown et al., 1977; Brown & Haas, 1980). Sixth, people vary in their level of commitment to outdoor activity. Significant portions of the populace, in the United States at least, rarely or never participate in outdoor recreation activities (Cordell & Hendee, 1982; Pierce, 1980). It is also possible that signifi-cant numbers of people who use natural environ-ments for recreation may be there strictly out of so-cial obligation (Cheek & Burch, 1976, p. 12). Then too, even some of those who freely choose natural environments for recreation may be merely seeking "something to do while passing time" (Hendee et al., 1977), whereas others, in contrast, are expressing a central life interest (Jacob & Schreyer, 1980). The data seem to be informing us that not all people are aligned to the natural environment with equal inten-sity.[8]

Seventh, the meaning derived from an outdoor ex-perience is related to the personality of the deriver (Knopf, 1983).[9]

And eighth, the meaning derived is also related to one's repertoire of prior experience—both with the particular locale or activity in question (Bryan, 1979;

Tuan, 1974) and with the character of antecedent en-vironmental experience in general (Knopf, 1983; Ul-rich, 1983). Goals for outdoor activity seem closely tied to the nature of conditions experienced at work (Grubb, 1975), in the home (Knopf, 1976), in the neighborhood (Wellman, 1979), and in the communi-ty at large (Bultena & Field, 1980; Driver & Knopf, 1976).

These eight points converge to reinforce a recur-ring theme of this chapter: The meanings that people attach to nature and the goals they pursue therein are fluid and individualistic. Indeed, the goals are varied, but one may wonder if they have a certain kind of common substance. Integrative reviews of the outdoor recreation literature lead one to conclude that the range of goals pursued in nature is no less rich than the range of goals pursued elsewhere (Bryan, 1980; Driver, 1976; Knopf, 1972). But the data also suggest that certain goals are more recur-ring or pervasive than others. These goals relate to the broad themes of escape, social reinforcement, competence building, and aesthetic enjoyment.

The Quest for Tranquility

A large share of outdoor behavior appears to be, in fact, coping behavior. Virtually every motive analysis that has been conducted is riddled with testimony about desires to reduce tension (Knopf, 1983). Al-though most motives are found to vary widely across activities and settings, the escape motive remains conspicuously stable and dominant (Davis, 1973; Knopf, 1972; Wellman, Dawson, & Roggenbuck, 1982). And people seem to have a specialized notion of what they are escaping from. They appear to be less inclined to escape from things in general but rather to escape from very specific, identifiable sources of stress such as noise (Lucas, 1964), crowd-ing (Lime & Cushwa, 1969), the city (Foresta, 1980), unpredictability (Catton, 1969), stimulus overload (Rossman & Ulehla, 1977), social restriction (Etzkorn, 1965), and social threat (Campbell, Hen-dee, & Clark, 1968). People have identified nature as a place where they can have more control over their actions (Downing & Clark, 1978), a place where they are not accountable for the consequences of their ac-tions (Catton, 1969), a place where there are rela-tively few humanly imposed demands (S. Kaplan & Talbot, 1983), and a place where stimulation intensity can be more tightly controlled (Twight et al., 1981).

Perhaps the most convincing data emerged on a national outdoor recreation survey conducted by Mandell and Marans (1972). They asked household heads to rate the relative importance of 12 reasons for wanting to participate in their favorite outdoor activity. The most important reason was "to relieve my tensions." An impressive 60% of the sample, representive of the United States' populace, rated this reason "very important."

Some investigators have argued that such revelations, derived largely from self-report questionnaires, are merely reflecting psychometric artifact. The data have been challenged as being subject to social desirability bias (Wellman, 1979) or distortion arising from loaded or leading questions inadvertently so designed by a biased investigator (Bryan, 1979). However, these data are supported by findings that the disposition to view nature as a vehicle for escape rises as stress levels experienced in everyday environments rise (Knopf, 1983). Knopf (1973), for example, found campers from more urbanized environments showing greater orientation toward privacy, toward experiencing a threat-free social environment, and toward escaping physical stressors such as noise, bright lights, and crowds. Elsewhere, he found people experiencing high levels of crime and density in their home neighborhoods were more likely to engage in outdoor recreation for purposes of escape (Knopf, 1983). And Wellman (1979) discovered that higher levels of housing unit density at summer lakeshore residences were related to displays of escape-oriented outdoor behavior. Elsewhere, Grubb (1975) found escape-oriented behavior linked to on-the-job stress levels experienced by auto assembly workers, and Bishop and Ikeda (1970) found people in occupations requiring high energy expenditures tending to seek activities requiring low expenditure. Other, more generalized studies have demonstrated how specific kinds of escape-oriented goals can be linked to rather specific sources of job or home stress—such as noise, deadline pressures, family pressures, and neighborhood upkeep (Driver & Knopf, 1976; Knopp, 1972; Mandell & Marans, 1972).

Does nature provide the only setting within which stressed individuals can achieve tranquility? Clearly not, but there is some intriguing evidence of its particularly potent role. Feingold (1979) found wilderness vacationers substantially more likely to report "mental relaxation" as an outgrowth of their experience than city vacationers. Similarly, Rossman and Ulehla (1977) found that Colorado students strongly associated "tranquility" with outdoor recreation areas in natural settings but not with outdoor recreation areas in and around cities.

The point of these varied analyses is that there is indeed substance to the intuitive belief that nature serves as a haven for restoration. There appears to be more to natural environments than pure aesthet-

ics; people seem driven to them in a calculated effort to cope with an unsatisfactory life situation. Action in the outdoors, it seems, is strongly influenced by the state of affairs in environments left behind.

THE QUEST FOR SOCIAL AFFIRMATION

If a principal function of nature is to provide solace from social stress, one might surmise that nature attracts people interested in social withdrawal. This, however, is hardly the case. Running pervasively through the outdoor motive studies are themes such as companionship (Bryan, 1980), fellowship (Bultena & Klessing, 1969), intimacy (Pierce, 1980), sociability (Etzkorn, 1965), sharing (R. Kaplan, 1973b), meeting new people (McCay & Moeller, 1976), and status recognition (Schreyer & Roggenbuck, 1978). The data clearly are affirming a fundamental position of environmental sociology: People in the outdoors are not only influenced by social interaction, but they actively seek it out (Cheek & Burch, 1976; Cheek et al., 1976; Knopf, 1983). Even when visitors to the outdoors report that they wish to shun social interaction, their behavior suggests otherwise. Hancock (1973), for example, found auto campers expressing a preference for campsites that offered visual seclusion from other campers. However, this preference was not reflected in choices actually made as campsites were experimentally manipulated to reduce screening. Similarly, Lee (1977) found wilderness users expressing a preference for privacy. However, the obvious lack of even attempting avoidance or withdrawal behavior as strangers were encountered did not bear out their stated preference for being alone. It seems as though people expressing an interest in withdrawing from social stress are not so much interested in social isolation as they are in having control over the kinds of social stimulation they experience and over the demands placed on them to accommodate that stimulation (Hammitt, 1982).

People seem fixed on the social group and the stimulation it provides (Field, 1976). Once again, then, we are faced with the question of the role nature plays during this fixation on social exchange. As we have seen, the tenets of sociology would hold that commitment to any kind of transaction with the natural environment would be low, relative to commitment to the group. And, the data support this view. Field (1976) noted how recreating groups in parks moved freely from activity to activity during their outings. The focus clearly was on group interchange, and the behavioral vehicle for accomplishing it seemed relatively unimportant. O'Leary et al. (1974) demonstrated that for particular social groups a wide variety of activities were considered acceptable and interchangeable. But a change in the nature of the group brings a corresponding change in the perception of what kinds of activities are appropriate (Cheek, 1971; Field & O'Leary, 1973). If, for example, members of a family group return to an outdoor setting as members of a friendship group, they are likely to participate in a completely different repertoire of activities (Burch, 1965; Field, 1976). These data suggest that outdoor activity is less an end in itself and more a means to facilitate exchange among members of the group.

Bearing on this point are Lee's (1974) comparative analyses of social exchange patterns for densely populated urban beaches and sparsely visited wilderness areas. He found both the style and intensity of social exchange in both areas to be similar, despite common sense interpretations to the contrary. His research raises the possibility that, from a functional perspective, there is more commonality than disparity between urban beach behavior and wilderness behavior. Although the setting may indeed be important to people, perhaps establishing predictable (Lee, 1977) and useful (Cheek & Burch, 1976, p. 183) patterns of social exchange is even more important.

Although the data clearly establish social exchange as an essential focus of outdoor behavior, empirical analyses of the content and dynamics of such exchanges are conspicuously absent in the literature. There does seem to be general agreement among sociologists that the voluntary outdoor group is an important source of self-affirmation used to reinforce confidence in the rightness of one's values, perspectives, and life-style (Burch, 1969; Cheek & Burch, 1976, p. 167). But real insight into the kinds of social exchange practiced during outdoor experiences and the reasons underlying such exchanges must await further research.

THE QUEST FOR COMPETENCE
It seems possible that the search for social affirmation through outdoor experiences is related to the more basic need for affirmation and enhancement of one's sense of competence. Humans are driven by a quest for competence (S. Kaplan, 1976; White, 1957), and the data suggest that natural environments—like all environments—are called on to serve the drive. Themes such as mastery (Barcus & Bergeson, 1972), achievement (Brown & Haas, 1980), skill development (Wellman et al., 1982), challenge (Schreyer & Nielson, 1978), self-testing (Young, 1982), self-expression (Lewis, 1973), self-sufficiency (R. Kaplan, 1974), problem solving (Catton, 1969), control (S. Kaplan & Talbot, 1983), and

fitness (Mandell & Marans, 1972), riddle the empirically based outdoor motive literature. And, as noted earlier, empirical analyses of the benefits accruing from competence-building behavior in outdoor settings are abundant (Barcus & Bergeson, 1972; Gibson, 1979; S. Kaplan & Talbot, 1983). But the intuitive views described earlier about why natural environments may be particularly effective for competence enhancement have not been subjected to empirical test.

Feelings of competency are maximized when there is congruence between skill level and environmental demands (Michelson, 1977; White, 1957). There emerges a sort of transcendental state—where the individual experiences total involvement, relevancy, and control, and where there is little distinction between self and environment, between stimulus and response, and between past, present, and future (Csikszentmihalyi, 1975a; Maslow, 1962; Panzarella, 1980). It is clear that such experiences are both sought and gained from behavior in the outdoors (Outdoor Recreation Resources Review Commission, 1962; S. Kaplan & Talbot, 1983; Rossman & Ulehla, 1977). But it is not clear whether natural settings hold unique properties that make them more effective in evoking such experiences (Csikszentmihalyi, 1975a).

THE QUEST FOR NATURAL STIMULI
Motivational studies of recreational behavior in the outdoors often posit that the desire "to experience nature" is the most important reason for participating (Driver & Knopf, 1976). This holds true for analyses across a wide spectrum of outdoor locales, from wilderness (Brown & Haas, 1980; Haas, Allen, & Manfredo, 1979) to rural settings (Clark et al., 1971; Knopf et al., 1973) to urban green space areas (Driver, Rosenthal, & Peterson, 1978; Foresta, 1980).

It is not clear what can be safely concluded from such information. Can the findings be attributed to social desirability or investigator bias (Bryan, 1979; Wellman, 1979)? Do they suggest that people value the intrinsic, aesthetic properties of nature? Or do they merely reflect the fact that people perceive nature as important—not for its own sake but for purposes of accomplishing the more fundamental goals of withdrawal, social interaction, and competence building? Certainly, the data imply that nature is important to people—but they do not address the more challenging question of whether people perceive in nature unique and beneficial properties that cannot be attributed to any other stimulus. We now turn to that question.

Knowing

One of the least contested points in the literature on human–nature transactions is that people pay attention to natural stimuli as they process information about their world (Wohlwill, 1983). This point is supported by research on how people spontaneously organize photographs of varied environmental stimuli, which consistently reveals that the distinction between natural and artificial is important to people as they differentiate among environments.

Research by Palmer & Zube (1976), who employed Q-sort methodology to develop a perceptually based land classification scheme for a New England river valley, illustrates the point. They found that people differentiated landscape photos into seven fundamental groups: forested hills, wetlands and streams, open water, meadows and open areas, farms, towns, and industry. The findings suggest that judgment was made along a continuum ranging from purely natural through various stages of human modification to the totally built environment (Zube, 1976). A parallel effort to identify a perceptually based classification scheme for urbanized environments has been successful (Herzog et al., 1982). A nonmetric factor analysis of preference ratings for 140 urban scenes yielded five groupings: contemporary buildings, older buildings, unusual architecture, alleys and factories, and urban nature. Again, nature seemed to be an important discriminating variable. Ullrich and Ullrich (1976) performed a multidimensional scaling analysis on perceived similarities of western rivers and concluded that rivers are differentiated on the basis of relative naturalness (pristine versus developed) and scale (physical breadth of the river). These same dimensions were identified as dominant in Ward's (1977) more generalized analysis of environmental differentiation. Although environmental meaning clearly cannot be represented by a limited set of one or two such dimensions, naturalness does appear to consistently emerge as salient (Ward & Russell, 1981). To be sure, some perceptual differentiation studies, notably in architecture, do not identify naturalness as a discriminating variable (e.g., Betak, Brummel, & Swingle, 1974; Hershberger, 1972). But, more likely than not, this can be attributed to limited ranges of stimuli for the variable in question (Ward, 1977).

Disagreement has been registered over whether use of such a criterion for perceptual categorization is a learned or innate response. Research on the matter—which is a most appropriate focus for developmental psychology—has been sparse. Holcomb's (1977) study is frequently cited in support of the former alternative—preschoolers were documented as sorting photographs along dimensions other than those relating to the presence of nature. The study, however, was self-indicted as only exploratory, involving a small sample and unsystematic procedures. In the meantime, Wohlwill (1983) has produced evidence that 6-year-olds do rely on the artificial/natural distinction as a criterion for dichotomously sorting environmental scenes. In fact, the results of spontaneous sorting were consistent across age—at least through the study population range of 6 through 14 years. Curiously enough, explanations rendered by the youngest children for their responses were more exemplar-specific and inconsistent, whereas the older children's responses were more group-encompassing and consistent, with specific references to the natural/artificial dichotomy. Perhaps, as Wohlwill suggests, this is indicative of how we attend to natural stimulation even before the culturally induced symbolic or affective components of response have had a chance to become overlayed upon it.

Not only do people pay attention to natural stimuli, they seem to prefer them. Natural scenes are consistently rated higher than built scenes in studies of aesthetic preference, and degree of naturalness consistently emerges as a powerful predictor of environmental preference in correlational analyses (Herzog et al., 1982; Kaplan, Kaplan, & Wendt, 1972; Nassauer, 1979; Wohlwill, 1976; Zube, 1976). The effect is so powerful that even unspectacular or subpar natural scenes elicit higher levels of preference than all but a small fraction of urban scenes. Ulrich (1981) proved this to be true even when comparing everyday rural scenes and picturesque Scandinavian townscapes. Even the slightest amount of vegetation significantly heightens preference for a built scene (Thayer & Atwood, 1978; Ulrich, 1983). Conversely, even the slightest evidence of a built feature within a natural scene substantially lowers preference (Carls, 1974; Wohlwill & Harris, 1980).

It seems as if people respond fundamentally differently to the nature content per se. Attempts to explain the preferential differences in terms of other predictors of information content, most notably complexity, have failed (Kaplan, Kaplan, & Wendt, 1972; Wohlwill, 1976; Ulrich, 1983). So the ultimate basis for this differentiation is still unknown (Wohlwill, 1976).

Perhaps the only research addressing this question is that guided by the evolutionary perspective described earlier and best articulated by S. Kaplan (1976) and Ulrich (1983). According to their models, preferred environments are those that serve the knowledge-hungry human by (1) having attributes that facilitate perception and comprehension (legibility); (2) conveying the notion that additional information can be gained if the setting is explored (mystery); and (3) being free of threat (refuge). And, according to their models, preferred environments would have attributes that approximate those of the settings experienced during the long evolutionary journey—namely the savannas of East Africa (Balling & Falk, 1982). In this context, the preferred setting would be open and spacious, be punctuated by scattered treelike vegetation, and contain a relatively smooth ground surface. As. R. Kaplan (1983) articulates, a large, undifferentiated open space, treeless and homogeneous, is likely to be boring—but equally unpreferred would be an overgrown and impenetrable tangle, for it does not offer security or comprehendability. The optimal setting, it is suggested, provides clarity, mystery, and refuge simultaneously.

There is empirical support for these views. The visual preference research of Zube and associates in New England (Zube, Pitt, & Anderson, 1975; Zube, 1976) concluded that after controlling for the effects of water, the highest preference was for pastoral scenes—open areas of meadows or abandoned fields with woods surrounding them—as opposed to either more completely forested areas or entirely open areas. Research by Daniel and Boster (1976) on preferences attached to various coniferous forest scenes in the western United States concluded that the most preferred scenes tended to be of open woods, with an absence of underbrush and downed wood, and an abundance of grass cover. Patey and Evans (1979) found that forest scenes vegetationally manipulated to create a low understory shrub density were aesthetically preferred over more natural forest scenes with dense understories. Other studies confirm that landscapes with large, open areas of mowed grass and scattered groves of closely planted vegetation are most pleasing (Gallagher, 1977; R. Kaplan, 1977b; Rabinowitz & Coughlin, 1970). As R. Kaplan (1978) suggests, there seems to be an interest in orderliness. The most preferred settings in her study of urban streams, creeks, and drains were those with sharply defined boundaries between water and land and those with finely textured grassy areas (R. Kaplan, 1977b). But as she further suggests, orderliness must be accompanied by mystery in order to be compelling (R. Kaplan, 1983). Her analyses of preferences for photographs of roadside views vividly illustrate this point. Scenes showing open farmlands interrupted by a nearby screen of trees elicited significantly higher levels of preference than compara-

ble scenes without the trees. Similarly, Hammitt (1980) found that aesthetic responses to interpretive trail scenes escalated as the forward view became partially screened.

Ulrich (1983), interpreting available data in the context of evolutionary theory, cites several properties of most preferred natural scenes. First, complexity must be moderate to high (Kaplan, Kaplan, & Wendt, 1972; Wohlwill, 1976). Second, the complexity must be patterned and have structural properties that establish a focal point (Kuller, 1972; Kwok, 1979). Third, depth must be moderate to high and must be perceived unambiguously (Brush, 1978; Craik, 1970). Fourth, the ground texture must be homogeneous and even and be perceived as conducive to movement (Rabinowitz & Coughlin, 1970; Ulrich, 1973). Fifth, an element of mystery must be present (Hammitt, 1980; R. Kaplan, 1973a). Sixth, appraised threat must be low (Ulrich & Zuckerman, 1981). And seventh, a water feature must be present (Brush & Shafer, 1975; Zube, Pitt, & Anderson, 1975). Given these properties, Ulrich (1983) cautions against narrow definitions of what constitutes natural stimulation. Indeed, these properties can hold for strongly human-influenced settings such as golf courses, urban outdoor parks, residential backyards, and rural farmlands. And the data suggest such settings are at least as preferred, if not more, than many purely natural settings (Gallagher, 1977; R. Kaplan, 1977b; Rabinowitz & Coughlin, 1970). Preference, it seems, relates not so much to whether a setting is purely natural as to whether the setting has predominant vegetation or water and an absence of built features (Ulrich, 1983).

Perhaps the most scintillating data in support of the evolutionary perspective are offered by Balling and Falk (1982). Subjects of six different age groups (ranging from elementary-school age to senior citizens) were asked to rate preferences for five types of natural biomes—tropical rain forest, temperate deciduous forest, coniferous forest, savanna, and desert. Elementary-school children preferred savanna over all other biomes. The differential preference for savanna and more familiar environments evaporated for older age groups.

Although the Balling and Falk data, indeed, seem to indicate the likelihood of innate landscape preferences, they also simultaneously point to the powerful role of personal experience, culture, and adaptive processes in the mediation of preference. And this is precisely the point being raised by alternate research paradigms in cognitive psychology and geography emphasizing the extreme subjectivity of environmental experience (Ittelson et al., 1976; Jacques, 1980; Moore & Golledge, 1976; Tuan, 1974). Under that perspective, the individual is posed not as a passive victim of external stimulation but as an active operator upon it (Stokols, 1978). The basic premise is that people transform reality by imposing their own order on incoming stimuli. The mind is seen as the creator of environmental experience. The physical array may be a resource employed in the process— but it is not necessarily the determinant of experience. Different people, it is argued, can look at the same physical array and sense different things. The same urban neighborhood can be seen by one person as a slum and by another as a positive source of stimulation and a haven from fear (Gans, 1962). A wilderness area can be seen as a source of inspiration and tranquility by one and as a threatening wasteland by another (Nash, 1973). So under this perspective, the environments that people actually are responding to are not the same environments that experimental researchers are striving to objectively define. Rather, "environment" is an entity structured by the mind.

Research on the mental representation of natural environments, like research on environmental representation in general, is in its infancy. From the limited data that do exist, however, a few principles can be constructed that confirm the preceding position (Knopf, 1983).

First, people actively impose information on the environment. They construct images of what each setting has to offer, and the image creates more information about the external environment than the external environment actually carries. They see more than is there. Image definition can be shifted substantially by something as simple as a single linguistic cue. Designation of a locale as "wilderness," "national park," or "wild river" generates imagery and visitation rates on these areas that are not conferred on contiguous resources that are physically indistinguishable (Nash, 1973). Reed (1973) showed how symbolic labels, such as *national park* and *national forest* prompt images of desirability even when nothing else is known about the environment. Hodson and Thayer (1980) found that forest scenes identified as wilderness elicited higher attractiveness ratings than when the same scenes were identified as tree farms. Buhyoff and Leuschner (1978) demonstrated how preference ratings of forest scenes are lowered as people are informed of insect damage. More and Buhyoff (1979) described how visitation skyrocketed at a West Virginia recreation locale when its name was changed from "North End of Wilburn Ridge" to "Rhododendron Gap." People do not, however, rely solely on linguistic cues to differentiate outdoor places. Stankey (1973) found that trail hikers mentally differentiate the wilderness into three zones: portal, travel, and destination. Even though all zones were essentially homogeneous in physical character, the hikers perceived more crowding upon encountering others in the destination zones than in the transitory zones. Lee (1972) found that urban residents mentally distinguish urban parks as serving different ethnic, age, and socioeconomic populations. The physical resources may be functionally equivalent, but the images of these resources are not.

Second, mental representations of outdoor locales can be highly individualistic and frequently distorted. This point is most powerfully demonstrated in the market research literature, especially in tourism, which is keenly interested in how image distortion affects travel behavior and how personal images are vulnerable to reconstitution through advertising campaigns (Hawkins, Shafer, & Rovelstad, 1980; Hunt, 1975; Mayo, 1973; Perry, 1975). In forestry research, correlations between perceived and objective measures of physical conditions in outdoor recreation areas are consistently weak (Knudson & Curry, 1981; Lucas, 1979; Merriam & Smith, 1974). The same campsite can be viewed as too secluded or too open, depending on the visitor (Foster & Jackson, 1979). The same recreation locale can be seen by some visitors as a natural reserve and by others as an arena for social interaction (Driver & Bassett, 1975; Knopf & Lime, 1984; McCool, 1978). And images of wilderness fluctuate profoundly with differences in experience, life-style, and recreation activity interests (Beaulieu & Schreyer, 1982; Lucas, 1964).

Third, use history is an important determinant of how an outdoor setting is represented. Repeated interaction with a setting forms an affective bond that sets the resource apart from others (Jacob & Schreyer, 1980; Lee, 1972; McDonough, 1982; Newby, 1979). As the bonding process develops, the environment becomes represented less by its physical character and more by the record of past experiences it has bestowed (Tuan, 1974). At the same time, the individual begins to make more subtle environmental differentiation (R. Kaplan, 1977b; Williams, 1980), to develop a more complex, well-defined set of expectations from the environment (Bryan, 1979; Schreyer & White, 1979), to adopt a narrower definition of what forms of behaviors are appropriate (Jacob & Schreyer, 1980; Lee, 1972), and to formulate less flexible opinions about how the area should be managed (Katz, 1979; O'Leary, 1976). These forces may be powerful and salient as mediators of response to outdoor settings: A roadside survey of backcountry recreationists in the northwestern United States revealed that most have specific, favorite places to recreate and that they return to them repeatedly (Downing & Clark, 1978). Use history is also important in building the frame of reference visitors employ while evaluating how an environment is performing. Veteran users of an area tend to evaluate the quality of an area not only in terms of what it offers but also in terms of what it has offered in the past (Nielsen, Shelby, & Hass, 1977; Schreyer et al., 1976). First-time visitors evaluate an environment more in terms of its present state, accepting what they see as normal and appropriate for that place (Heberlein, 1977). It is probably due to these conflicting images that, in areas of escalating use, veteran users feel more crowded and perceive more environmental damage than first-time users (Knopf & Lime, 1984; Schreyer et al., 1976; Vaske, Donnelly, & Heberlein, 1980).

Finally, the mental representation of an outdoor locale can often be construed in parameters other than those related to the physical array. It may be, as many sociologists would suggest, that outdoor locales are largely represented—and differentiated— by the character of social transactions that transpire (Cheek & Burch, 1976; Lee, 1972). It may be, as many leisure researchers would suggest, that a major portion of visitors to the outdoors construct images of outdoor locales more in terms of the activities that transpire there rather than in terms of the character of the physical settings (Schreyer et al., 1982; Shafer & Burke, 1965; Williams & Schreyer, 1982). There seem to be at least three fundamental sources of stimulation people are attending to in outdoor locales—the physical setting (Brown et al., 1978), the social setting (Cheek & Burch, 1976), and the activity pursued (Bryan, 1979). Correspondingly, the data imply that images of outdoor locales are constructed with information from each of these three arenas (Williams, 1983). What the limited data do not yet make clear is the relative contribution of each source in the internal representation of, and response to, outdoor locales. What they do make clear is that more information is being carried, and more information is being responded to, than that emerging from the physical array.

So how do humans come to know the natural environment? It seems that part of the knowing may be innate; people seem to be equipped with a disposition toward sensing and preferring nature. But it also seems that much of our knowing, particularly as we gain experience, is shaped by forces that have little to do with the character of nature itself. The mind is wired to respond, but it also has the capacity to create its own environmental experience. What is the nature of this experience? It is to this question that we now turn.

Responding

It would seem improbable that, with the prevailing interest in emotional response to natural environments in all forms of literatures, practically no research has been conducted on the topic. But that is certainly the case. There are, of course, numerous accounts of the power of nature in inducing positive mood shifts based on informal observation or content analyses of visitor diaries (Burch, 1977; Gibson, 1979; S. Kaplan & Talbot, 1983). However, experimental research clearly establishing the link between patterns of stimulation and emotional response is scarce (Ulrich, 1983).

A particularly illuminating exception is research by Ulrich (1979), who found that stressed individuals felt better after exposure to natural scenes than after exposure to urban scenes matched for complexity. Slides of unspectacular natural scenes reduced fear arousal and induced greater overall positive affect— including feelings of playfulness, friendliness, affection, and elation. Urban scenes, in contrast, increased sadness. In subsequent research, Ulrich (1981) demonstrated that one need not be stressed to experience emotional benefits of nature. Unstressed individuals were found to have significantly higher alpha wave amplitudes and lower heart rates while viewing natural scenes, both of which are physiological indicators of a more relaxed state. More and Payne (1978) found that people leaving natural areas had less negative moods than when they entered them, but they were surprised to find positive affect lowered as well. They speculated in retrospect that positive moods should, indeed, be higher at entry than at termination because the full effects of anticipation are still being reaped, whereas the negative effects of withdrawal are not yet acting (More, 1980). Support for this position is offered by Hammitt (1981), who tracked positive mood levels as people moved through five phases of interaction with a natural bog environment in Michigan: anticipation, travel to, on-site visitation, travel from, and recollection at home. Mood scores increased steadily during the anticipation through on-site phases, decreased substantially during the travel-from phase, but increased again as subjects were asked to reflect on the experience several weeks later. So, true to the speculations of More (1980), nature does seem to have ameliorating effects, although the overall manifestation of these effects may be less obvious than we might surmise.

Such data are enticing, but they do not equip us with the ability to make meaningful inferences about the influence natural stimuli have upon affective states. We need to eliminate the paucity of research on the topic, employing both subjective and neurophysiological measures, and evaluating one in the context of the other as a means for validating results (Ulrich, 1983). The enduring as well as situational effects of exposure to nature need to be documented, and the behaviors motivated by these effects need to be evaluated (Driver et al., 1978). In studying these effects, research needs to abandon its strict reliance on visual stimulus material—for many affective ties are built through auditory and olfactory experience (Tuan, 1977). And nature must be represented more appropriately as a dynamic entity, with variable effects from changing weather, wildlife, lighting, colors, seasons, solar phenomena, and other regular and irregular forces of change (Aiken, 1976; Buhyoff & Wellman, 1979; Sonnenfeld, 1969b). Nature's ephemeral qualities—the stuff around which the popular literature is largely built—are the qualities most ignored by research.

20.4. CONCLUSIONS AND NEEDED RESEARCH DIRECTIONS

How do humans relate to nature? Intuitive notions abound, but empirically verified laws do not. Perhaps the most informed conclusion we can draw is one that enjoys consensus in the literature: It is much too early to tell.

The data do make clear, however, that people are oriented to nature. They find it important, and they seem to like it—at least in terms of its visual properties. But is this liking prewired as an outgrowth of the human evolutionary journey, or is it a learned response? Both forces seem to be at work. There is evidence that the disposition toward nature is innate. Yet it is clear that people in the outdoors respond to things in addition to nature itself, such as the weight of a social milieu, the dictates of their personality, the influence of their home environment, their record of prior experience, and cognitive structures that impose their own interpretation of what the environment is offering. The values people ascribe to outdoor experiences are diverse, and they vary across individuals, activities, and time. Even beyond the question of whether preference for nature is innate or learned lies the more fundamental question of whether nature is required. As Wohlwill (1983) suggests, having an innate preference for natural stimuli does not imply that humans cannot

thrive in purely artificial surroundings. Definitive insight on this matter, however, must await future research.

In what directions should research proceed? At least four new lines of inquiry need to emerge. First, research must more clearly define what constitutes "environment" for a person in the outdoors. Much of current research reflects the influence of classical utility theory—humans are posed as rational decision makers, making interattribute comparisons among alternatives and selecting behaviors that maximize net return (Arrow, 1958; Mitchell & Biglan, 1971). The theoretical position itself may be of virtue, but it has tended to be represented incompletely and perhaps erroneously in much of the research on outdoor behavior, particularly in forestry and marketing. The typical research scenario involves (a) obtaining ratings of the relative desirability of potential physical attributes of an outdoor setting; (b) measuring the perceived presence of each in alternate locales; and (c) predicting preference by evaluating congruence between the two sets (Harris, 1982; Peterson, 1974b). The broader conception of "attributes," so it seems, becomes narrowly construed as properties of the physical array. Such a perspective presumes that people pay attention only to the properties of the physical array while acting in the outdoors. And it presumes that people function strictly by being acted upon by the external environment, rather than acknowledging their abilities to *act on* the external array to create the environmental experience they desire (Ittelson et al., 1976; Stokols, 1978). The data suggest both perspectives are wrong. Rather, people arrive at outdoor settings under the influence of an entire repertoire of stimulus sets—the social group they are with, the equipment they have brought, the culture that shaped them, the home and work conditions they have experienced, and, indeed, the mind that supplements, supplants, and otherwise mediates stimulation from the external array (Knopf, 1983). People draw on these sources of stimuli as well as the physical setting.

More research is needed, then, on the psychological representation of outdoor places—both in terms of physical features and in terms of the meaning overlayed upon these features (Tuan, 1974). We need to understand how outdoor places are cognitively organized not only as places to experience nature but as places representing security, action, social reinforcement, control, collective awareness, and satisfying and unsatisfying memories (Aiken, 1976; Jackson, 1973). Many questions remain unanswered. What do people attend to as they discriminate among outdoor places? How might we develop a classification scheme that best distinguishes locales providing differential contributions to the human life space? Do people image particular locales differently as a result of different life experiences? How does an individual's history of use with a setting moderate his or her representation of it? Answers to such questions will emerge only after we abandon strict preoccupation with objective analyses of environmental attributes and begin looking at the environment from the eyes of the experiencer.

Second, and an outgrowth of the first, research must more forcefully address the role of individual differences in preference formation. Personality measures now rampant in the environmental psychology literature are drastically underutilized in outdoor research. Potentially powerful forecasters include locus of control, cognitive flexibility, cognitive complexity, privacy orientation, and arousal or sensation-seeking tendencies, all of which may be linked to preferred environmental arrays, on-site behavior, and response to situations, such as congestion and intergroup conflict (Knopf, 1983; Ulrich & Zuckerman, 1981). And the role of prior experience in shaping relations with nature has not been adequately examined. At one level, we need to more completely understand the generalized effect of everyday environmental stimulation upon preference. Wohlwill (1976), for example, suggests that what one prefers may be related to the adaptation levels one has built up during his or her prior experience. At another level, we need to more thoroughly understand the effect of immediately prior stimulation or arousal levels upon preference. Trail hikers, for example, apparently are most visually involved at points where the scenery shifts, suggesting that the character of stimulus change may be as important as the character of stimulus composition in affecting preference (Cherem, 1972; Gustke & Hodgson, 1980; Ulrich, 1983). Prior experience seems to be an important mediator of response, but this variable has captured surprisingly little attention in research on outdoor aesthetics.

Third, research must more adequately treat nature as a complex, multidimensional stimulus. The stimulus must be visual as well as nonvisual (Tuan, 1977); it must represent undesirable environmental features (e.g., biting insects, dampness) as well as desirable ones (Driver & Greene, 1977); and it must imply the harboring of unpleasant human connotations (e.g., hate, fear) as well as pleasant ones (Jackson, 1973). Only as nature becomes more realistically represented can research begin to adequately document how humans relate to it.

Finally, research needs to more directly examine the relative importance of innate tendencies as op-

posed to learning in the formation of response to nature. It may well be, as Ulrich (1977) suggests, that both forces are at work in shaping response. But insight must await the results of cross-cultural experimental research, which is currently almost nonexistent. The rare exceptions, involving comparisons of European and American groups, show remarkable similarity in preference ratings for diverse landscapes (Shafer & Tooby, 1973; Ulrich, 1977). Perhaps through such analyses, research can address the broader question of what patterns of stimulation are optimal for people. Identifying what constitutes optimality for people is a fundamentally different research problem than identifying how people make use of and respond to particular scenes or environments. The latter, which has been the focus of traditional research, has given us the ability to describe the needs and responses salient in various settings, but it has not enabled us to address the broader question of what forms of experiences are most important to people. We are confronted once again with numerous challenging questions. How do we operationalize the concept of optimality (Stokols, 1978)? What are the relevant dimensions? What shapes its character? Is the character stable or situationally defined? What bearing does prior experience have? What are the indicators of optimality? Is expressed preference a valid indicator? Having first answered these questions, the remaining task is to define how natural environments fit in the optimization process.

By approaching inquiry at this level, research on the character of human–nature transactions will be germane not only to those with a specialized interest in nature but to the whole of the environment–behavior field. As a field, we must turn to the broader question of what humans are striving for, so that the effects of any one kind of environmental transaction can be evaluated in the context of this larger quest. This is precisely the information being demanded by environmental planners, who need to know the relative contribution of various kinds of environmental experiences in facilitating progress toward optimality (Knopf, 1983). Speculation abounds and the data to date confirm that natural stimuli play an important role in the optimization process. Should future research affirm this role, it would imply the need for scientists and planners alike to explicitly recognize the natural/artificial distinction as a principal underlier of environmental meaning.

NOTES

1. Indeed, the mere presence of trees on urban residential lots inflates the value of the property by as much as 12%

(Morales, Boyce, & Fausette, 1976; Payne & Strom, 1975).

2. Reviews of this line of inquiry are offered by Brown, Driver, and Stankey; 1976, and Peterson and Lime, 1979.

3. Methodological issues underlying the development of outdoor recreation motive scales have continued to be a salient focus of research (Graefe, Ditton, Roggenbuck, & Schreyer, 1981; Tinsley, Kass, & Driver, 1981; Wellman, Dawson, & Roggenbuck, 1982).

4. The typical program for these models generates visiting parties who arrive at the recreation area at various simulated dates and times, enter the area at particular points, select paths of travel and move along them (Shechter & Lucas, 1978). By having data on existing patterns of arrival, routes followed, and travel speeds, the models can establish encounter levels experienced by specific visitor groups at particular places. The models then can be used to predict encounter levels that would result from spatial or temporal redistribution of use at the area's access points, assignment of campsite locations, or other use redistribution techniques (Stankey et al., 1976).

5. This line of research is parallel to the previously described motive segmentation research underway in the forestry and natural resources management disciplines. The difference is related to goals. Whereas forestry focuses on empirically defining and accommodating all benefit segments, marketing in general focuses on defining and accommodating those segments that maximize financial flow to the research sponsor (LaPage, 1968).

6. The ROS planning methodology has been adopted by the two principal land management agencies in the United States and is being considered for adoption by other agencies internationally (Buist & Hoots, 1982). It presumes there are six fundamental classes of outdoor recreation locales, organized along a spectrum: primitive, semiprimitive, nonmotorized, semiprimitive motorized, roaded natural, rural, and urban. The six classes are seen as delivering distinguishable forms of human experience. Indeed, it is argued that the same overt recreation activity, carried out in different settings along this primitive-urban continuum, will produce different experiences (Brown, Driver, & McConnel, 1978; Clark & Stankey, 1979).

7. To be sure, the role of social stimulation is acknowledged within these conceptions. But, adhering to the forestry discipline's conception of "environment," those with forestry backgrounds tend to dwell heavily on measures of its physical properties (e.g., density) rather than addressing the character of transactions occurring between individuals or social systems (contrast Brown, Driver, & McConnel, 1978 with Cheek & Burch, 1976).

8. This conclusion raises a philosophical dilemma for public land managers as they struggle with the issue of equity in the distribution of scarce outdoor resources (Schreyer & Knopf, 1984).

9. The full potential of personality research will be realized only when investigators abandon their strong reliance on trait models and begin to subscribe to the increasingly popular interactionist perspective being developed by mainstream personologists (Bowers, 1973; Mischel, 1973).

Certainly, what we do know is that individuals have tendencies for relating to the natural environment in enduring, personal ways (Hendee, 1967; McKechnic, 1970). But what we do not yet know is how these tendencies are situationally mediated or induced (Iso-Ahola, 1980; Knopf, 1983).

REFERENCES

Abrahams, G. (1970). *The chess mind.* London: Penguin.

Adams, A.J., & Stone, T.H. (1977). Satisfaction of need for achievement in work and leisure time activities. *Journal of Vocational Behavior, 11,* 174–181.

Aiello, J.F., Gordon, B., & Farrell, T.S. (1974). Description of children's outdoor activities in a suburban residential area: Preliminary findings. In D.H. Carson (Ed.), *EDRAS: Man-Environment Interactions: Evaluations and Applications—The State of the Art in Environmental Design Research* (Vol. 12) (pp. 157–196). Stroudsburg, Pa.: Dowden, Hutchinson, and Ross.

Aiken, S.R. (1976). Towards landscape sensibility. *Landscape, 20,* 20–28.

Ajzen, I., & Fishbein, M. (1973). Attitudinal and normative variables as predictors of specific behaviors. *Journal of Personality and Social Psychology, 27,* 41–57.

Alderman, R.B. (1974). *Psychological behavior in sport.* Philadelphia: Saunders.

Aldskogius, H. (1967). Vacation house settlement in the Siljan Region. *Geografiska Annaler, 49,* 69–95.

Aldskogius, H. (1977). A conceptual framework and a Swedish case study of recreational behavior and environmental cognition. *Economic Geography, 53,* 163–183.

Alexander, C., Ishikawa, S., & Silverstein, M. (1977). *A pattern language.* New York: Oxford University Press.

Alfano, S.S., & Magill, A.W. (Eds.). (1976). *Vandalism and outdoor recreation: Symposium proceedings* (General Tech. Rep. PSW-17). Berkeley CA: U.S. Department of Agriculture Forest Service, Pacific Southwest Forest and Range Experiment Station.

Allen, A.T., & Dwyer, J.F. (1978). *A cross-sectional analysis of hunting, fishing, and boating in Illinois.* (Forestry Research Rep. No. 78-8). Urbana: University of Illinois, Agricultural Experiment Station.

Allen, D.J. (1979). *Wilderness user preferences for psychological outcomes and setting attributes.* Unpublished doctoral dissertation, Colorado State University, Ft. Collins.

Alston, R.M., & Freeman, D.M. (1975). The natural resources decision-maker as political and economic man. *Journal of Environmental Management, 3,* 167–183.

Altman, I. (1977). Research on environment and behavior: A personal statement of strategy. In D. Stokols (Ed.), *Perspectives on environment and behavior: Theory, research, and applications.* New York: Plenum.

Altman, I., & Chemers, M. (1980). *Culture and Environment*. Monterey, CA: Brooks/Cole.

Altman, I., & Wohlwill, J.F. (Eds.). (1983). *Human Behavior and Environment: Vol. 6. Behavior and the natural environment*. New York: Plenum.

Andrews. W.H., Burdge, R.J., Capener, H.R., Warner, W.K., & Wilkinson, K.P. (Eds.). (1973). *The social well-being and quality of life dimension in water resources planning*. Logan: Utah State University, Council on Water Resources.

Appleton, J. (1975). *The experience of landscape*. New York: Wiley.

Arrow, K.J. (1958). Utilities, attitudes, choices: A review note. *Econometrica, 26*, 1–23.

Balling, J.D., & Falk, J.H. (1982). Development of visual preference for natural environments. *Environment and Behavior, 14*, 5–28.

Ballman, G. (1980). Operationalizing the cross-country skiing opportunity spectrum. In T.B. Knopp & L.C. Merriam (Conference coordinators), *Proceedings, North American Symposium on dispersed winter recreation* (Educational Series No. 2-3). St. Paul: University of Minnesota, Office of Special Programs.

Banovitz, J. (1971). *Managing the modern city*. Washington. DC: International City Management Association.

Barcus, C., & Bergeson, R. (1972). Survival training and mental health: A review. *Therapeutic Recreation Journal, 6*, 3–7.

Barnett, L.A., & Storm, B. (1981). Play, pleasure and pain: The reduction of anxiety through play. *Leisure Sciences, 4*, 161–175.

Baron, R.R.V. (1975). *Seasonality in tourism: A guide to the analysis of seasonality and trends for policy making* (Tech. Series No. 2). London: The Economist Intelligence Unit.

Baxter, M.J. (1979). The application of logit regression analysis to production constrained gravity models. *Journal of Regional Science, 19*, 171–179.

Beaulieu, J., & Schreyer, R. (1982). An initial examination of environmental categorization by recreationists. In S. Iso-Ahola (Ed.), *Proceedings of the 1982 Symposium on Leisure Research* (p. 55). Washington, DC: National Recreation and Parks Association.

Becker, B.W. (1976). Perceived similarities among recreational activities. *Journal of Leisure Research, 8*, 112–122.

Becker, R.H., Niemann, B.J., & Gates, W.A. (1981). Displacement of users within a river system: Social and environmental tradeoffs. In D.W. Lime & D.R. Field (Tech. Coordinators), *Some Recent Products of River Recreation Research* (pp. 33–38), (General Tech. Rep. NC-63). St. Paul: U.S. Department of Agriculture, Forest Service, North Central Forest Experiment Station.

Bernaldez, F.G., & Parra, F. (1979). Dimensions of landscape preferences from pairwise comparisons. In G.H.

Elsner & R.C. Smardon (Eds.), *Proceedings of Our National Landscape Conference* (pp. 256–262). (General Tech. Rep. PSW-35). Berkeley, CA: U.S. Department of Agriculture, Forest Service, Pacific Southwest Forest and Range Experiment Station.

Bernstein, A. (1972). Wilderness as a therapeutic behavior setting. *Therapeutic Recreation Journal, 6*, 160–161, 185.

Berrill, N.J. (1955). *Man's emerging mind*. New York: Dodd, Mead.

Betak, J.F., Brummell, A.C., & Swingle, P.G. (1974). An approach to elicit attributes of complex visual environments. In D. Carson (Ed.), *EDRA 5: Man-environment interactions: Evaluations and applications—The state of the art in environmental design research* (Vol. 9). Shroudsburg, PA: Dowden, Hutchinson, and Ross.

Bishop, D.W., & Ikeda, M. (1970). Status and role factors in the leisure behavior of different occupations. *Sociology and Social Research, 44*, 190–208.

Bishop, R.C. (1982). Option value: An exposition and extension. *Land Economics, 58*, 1–15.

Blomberg, G. (1982). Coastal amenities and values: Some pervasive perceptions expressed in the literature. *Coastal Zone Management Journal, 10*, 53–77.

Bowers, K.B. (1973). Situationism in psychology: An analysis and critique. *Psychological Review, 80*, 307–336.

Bowley, C.S. (1979). *Motives, management, preferences, and perceptions of crowding of backcountry hiking trail users in the Allegheny National Forest of Pennsylvania*. Unpublished master's thesis, University Park, PA: Pennsylvania State University.

Brewer, D., & Gillespie, G.A. (1966). *Socioeconomic factors affecting participation in water-oriented outdoor recreation* (Publication No. ERS-403). Columbia: University of Missouri, Missouri Agricultural Experiment Station.

Brown, P.J., Bester, N.L., & Knopf, R.C. (1978). *Audience preferences at Flaming Gorge National Recreation Area and Cranberry Mountain Visitor Center facilities* (Recreation Research Project Paper No. 16-437-CA). Ft. Collins: U.S. Department of Agriculture, Rocky Mountain Forest and Range Experiment Station.

Brown, P.J., Driver, B.L., & McConnel, C. (1978). The opportunity spectrum concept and behavioral information in outdoor recreation resource supply inventories: Background and application. In *Proceedings, Integrated inventories of renewable natural resources workshop* (pp. 73–84). (General Tech. Rep. RM-55). Ft. Collins: U.S. Department of Agriculture Forest Service, Rocky Mountain Forest and Range Experiment Station.

Brown, P.J., Driver, B.L., & Stankey, G.H. (1976). Human behavior science and recreation management. In *XVI International Union of Forestry Research Organization World Congress Proceedings, Division 6* (pp. 53–63). Washington, DC: International Union of Forestry Research Organizations.

Brown, P.J., & Haas, G.E. (1980). Wilderness recreation experiences: The Rawah case. *Journal of Leisure Research, 12*, 229–241.

Brown, P.J., Hautaluoma, J.E., & McPhail, S. (1977). Colorado Deer Hunting Experiences. In *Transactions, 42nd North American Wildlife and Natural Resources Conference* (pp. 216–225). Washington, DC: Wildlife Management Institute.

Brown, P.J., & Ross, D.M. (1982). Using desired recreation experiences to predict setting preferences. In *Forest and river recreation: Research update* (pp. 105–110). (Misc. Publication No. 18). St. Paul: University of Minnesota, Agricultural Experimental Station.

Brush, R.O. (1978). Forests can be managed for aesthetics: A study of forest landowners in Massachusetts. In *Proceedings of the National Urban Forestry Conference* (pp. 349–360). Washington, DC: U.S. Department of Agriculture, Forest Service.

Brush, R.O., & Shafer, E.L., Jr. (1975). Application of a landscape preference model to land management. In E.H. Zube, R.O. Brush, & J.G. Fabos (Eds.), *Landscape assessment: Values, perceptions and resources* (pp. 168–182). Stroudsburg, PA: Dowden, Hutchinson, & Ross.

Bryan, H. (1979). *Conflict in the great outdoors: Toward understanding and managing for diverse sportsmen preferences* (Sociological Studies No. 4). Birmingham: University of Alabama, Bureau of Public Administration.

Bryan, H. (1980). Sociological and psychological approaches to assessing and categorizing wildlife values. In W.W. Shaw & E.H. Zube (Eds.), *Wildlife Values*. (Institutional Series Rep. No. 1). Tucson: University of Arizona, Center for Assessment of Noncommodity Natural Resource Values.

Bryant, B.E., & Morrison, A.J. (1980). Travel market segmentation and the implementation of market strategies. *Journal of Travel Research, 18*, 2–8.

Buchanan, T., Christensen, J.E., & Burdge, R.J. (1981). Social groups and the meanings of outdoor recreation activities. *Journal of Leisure Research, 13*, 254–266.

Buhyoff, G.J., & Leuschner, W.A. (1978). Estimating psychological disutility from damaged forest stands. *Forest Science, 24*, 424–432.

Buhyoff, G.J., & Wellman, J.D. (1979). Seasonality bias in landscape preference research. *Leisure Sciences, 2*, 181–190.

Buist, L.J., & Hoots, T.A. (1982). Recreation Opportunity Spectrum approach to resource planning. *Journal of Forestry, 80*, 84–86.

Bultena, G.L., & Field, D.R. (1980). Structural effects in national parkgoing. *Leisure Sciences, 3*, 221–240.

Bultena, G., & Klessing, L. (1969). Satisfaction in camping: A conceptualization and guide to social research. *Journal of Leisure Research, 1*, 348–354.

Bultena, G.L., & Taves, M.J. (1961). Changing wilderness images and forestry policy. *Journal of Forestry, 59*, 167–171.

Burch, W.R., Jr. (1965). The play world of camping: research into the social meaning of outdoor recreation. *American Journal of Sociology, 70*, 604–612.

Burch, W.R., Jr. (1966). Wilderness—The life cycle and forest recreational choice. *Journal of Forestry, 64*, 606–610.

Burch, W.R., Jr. (1969). The social circles of leisure: Competing explanations. *Journal of Leisure Research, 1*, 125–147.

Burch, W.R., Jr. (1970). Recreation preferences as culturally determined phenomena. In B.L. Driver (Ed.), *Elements of outdoor recreation planning* (pp. 61–88). Ann Arbor, MI: University Microfilms.

Burch, W.R., Jr. (1971). Daydreams and nightmares: A sociological essay on the American environment. New York: Harper & Row.

Burch, W.R., Jr. (1977). Urban children and nature: A summary of research on camping and outdoor recreation. In *Chilren, nature and the urban environment* (pp. 101–112), (General Tech. Rep. NE-30). Upper Darby, PA: U.S. Department of Agriculture Forest Service, Northeastern Forest Experiment Station.

Burke, J.F., & Williams, P.W. (1979). Gasoline prices and availability: What do they mean for tourism? *Utah Tourism and Recreation Review, 8*, 1–8.

Butler, R.W. (1980). The concept of a tourist area cycle. *The Canadian Geographer, 24*, 5–12.

Buttel, F.H., & Morrison, D.E. (1977). The environmental movement: A research bibliography with some state-of-the-art comments. (Exchange Bibliography No. 1308). Monticello, IL: Council of Planning Librarians.

Butzer, K.W. (1977). Environment, culture and human evolution. *American Scientist, 65*, 572–584.

Campbell, F.L., Hendee, J.L., & Clark, R. (1968). Law and order in public parks. *Parks and Recreation, 3*, 28–31, 51–55.

Carls, E.G. (1974). The effects of people and man-induced conditions on preference for outdoor recreation landscapes. *Environment and Behavior, 4*, 447–470.

Carls, E.G. (1978). A simulation model of wild river use. *Leisure Sciences, 1*, 209–218.

Carson, D.H. (1970). Natural landscape as meaningful space for the aged. In L.A. Pastalan & D.H. Carson (Eds.), *Spatial Behavior of Older People* (pp. 194–210). Ann Arbor: University of Michigan Press.

Catton, W.R., Jr. (1969, December). Motivations of wilderness users. *Pulp and Paper Magazine of Canada*, pp. 121–126.

Catton, W.R., Jr. (1971). The wildland recreation boom and sociology. *Pacific Sociological Review, 14*, 339–359.

Catton, W.R., Jr., & Dunlap, R.E. (1980). A new ecological paradigm for postexuberant sociology. *American Behavioral Scientist, 24*, 15–47.

Cesario, F.J. (1980). Congestion and the valuation of recreation benefits. *Land Economics, 56*, 329–338.

Cesario, F.J., & Knetsch, J.L. (1976). A recreation site demand and benefit estimation model. *Regional Studies, 10,* 97–104.

Champoux, J.E. (1975). *Work and nonwork: A review of theory and empirical research* (Tech. Rep. No. 31). Irvine: University of California, Graduate School of Administration.

Chase, D.R., & Cheek, N.H. (1979). Activity preferences and participation: Conclusions from a factor analytic study. *Journal of Leisure Research, 11,* 92–101.

Cheek, N.H. (1971). Toward a sociology of not-work. *Pacific Sociological Review, 14,* 245–258.

Cheek, N.H., & Burch, W.R. (1976). *The social organization of leisure in human society.* New York: Harper & Row.

Cheek, N.H., Field, D.R., & Burdge, R.J. (1976). *Leisure and recreation places.* Ann Arbor: Ann Arbor Science.

Cherem, G.J. (1972). *Visitor responsiveness to a nature trail environment.* Unpublished doctoral dissertation, University of Michigan, Ann Arbor.

Childs, A.W., & Melton, G.B. (Eds.). (1983). *Rural Psychology.* New York: Plenum.

Clark, K. (1976). *Landscape into art.* London: Harper & Row.

Clark, R.N. (1976). Control of vandalism in recreation areas—Fact, fiction, or folklore? In S.S. Alfano & A.W. Magill (Eds.), *Vandalism and outdoor recreation: Symposium proceedings* (pp. 62–72), (General Tech. Rep. PSW-17). Berkeley, CA: U.S. Department of Agriculture, Forest Service, Pacific Southwest Forest and Range Experiment Station.

Clark, R.N., Hendee, J.C., & Burgess, R.L. (1972). The experimental control of littering. *Journal of Environmental Education, 4,* 22–28.

Clark, R.N., Hendee, J.C., & Campbell, F.L. (1971). Values, behavior, and conflict in modern camping culture. *Journal of Leisure Research, 3,* 143–159.

Clark, R.N., & Stankey, G.H. (1979). *The recreation opportunity spectrum: A framework for planning, management and research* (General Tech. Rep. PNW-98). Seattle: U.S. Department of Agriculture Forest Service, Pacific Northwest Forest and Range Experiment Station.

Clawson, M. (1959). *Methods of measuring the demand for and the benefits of outdoor recreation* (Reprint No. 10). Washington, DC: Resources for the Future.

Clawson, M., & Knetsch, J.L. (1966). *Economics of outdoor recreation.* Baltimore: John Hopkins University Press.

Cole, D.N. (1982). *Wilderness campsite impacts: Effects of amount of use.* (Research Paper INT-284). Ogden, UT: U.S. Department of Agriculture Forest Service, Intermountain Forest and Range Experiment Station.

Cole, D.P. (1975). *Nomads of the nomads.* Chicago: Aldine.

Cooksey, R.W., Dickinson, T.L., & Loomis, R.J. (1982). Preferences for recreational environments: Theoretical considerations and a comparison of models. *Leisure Sciences, 5,* 19–34.

Coppock, J.T. (1982). Geographical contributions to the study of leisure. *Leisure Studies, 1,* 1–27.

Cordell, H.K., & Hendee, J.C. (1982). Renewable resources recreation in the United States: Supply, demand, and critical policy issues. Washington, DC: American Forestry Association.

Corsi, T.M., & Harvey, M.E. (1978). Toward a causal model to explain differing household vacation patterns as a result of higher fuel prices. *Journal of Leisure Research, 10,* 298–310.

Craik, K.H. (1970). *A system of landscape dimensions: Appraisal of its objectivity and illustration of its scientific application.* Berkeley: University of California, Institute of Personality Assessment and Research.

Craik, K.H. (1975). Individual variations in landscape description. In E.H. Zube, R.O. Brush, & J.G. Fabos (Eds.), *Landscape assessment: Values, perceptions, and resources* (pp. 130–150). Stroudsburg, PA: Dowden, Hutchinson, & Ross.

Craik, K.H. (1976). The personality research paradigm in environmental psychology. In S. Wapner, S.B. Cohen, & B. Kaplan (Eds.), *Experiencing the environment* (pp. 55–79). New York: Plenum.

Crandall, R. (1980). Motivations for leisure. *Journal of Leisure Research, 12,* 45–54.

Crompton, J.L., & Hensarling, D.M. (1978). Some suggested implications of the product life cycle for public recreation and park agency managers. *Leisure Sciences, 1,* 295–306.

Crump, S.L., Nunes, D.L., & Crossman, E.K. (1977). The effects of litter on littering behavior in a forest environment. *Environment and Behavior, 9,* 137–146.

Csikszentmihalyi, M. (1975a). Play and intrinsic rewards. *Journal of Humanistic Psychology, 15,* 41–63.

Csikszentmihalyi, M. (1975b). *Beyond boredom and anxiety.* San Francisco: Jossey-Bass.

Cullen, G. (1961). *Townscape.* New York: Reinhold.

Daniel, T.C., & Boster, R.S. (1976). *Measuring landscape aesthetics: The scenic beauty estimation method* (Research paper No. RM-167). Ft. Collins, CO: U.S. Department of Agriculture, Rocky Mountain Forest and Range Experiment Station.

Davis, R.L. (1973). *Selected motivational determinants of recreational use of Belle Isle Park in Detroit.* Unpublished master's thesis, University of Michigan, Ann Arbor.

deGrazia, S. (1962). *Of time, work and leisure.* New York: Twentieth Century Fund.

Devine, H.A., Borden, F.Y., & Turner, B.J. (1976). *A simulation study of the Cades Cove visitor vehicle flow* (Occasional Paper No. 4). Washington, DC: U.S. Department of the Interior, National Park Service.

Ditton, R.B., Fedler, A.J., & Graefe, A.R. (1982). Assessing recreational satisfaction among diverse participant groups. In *Forest and river recreation: Research update* (pp. 134–139), (Miscellaneous Publication No. 18). St. Paul: The University of Minnesota, Agricultural Experiment Station.

Doling, J., & Gibson, J.G. (1979). The demand for new recreational facilities: A coventry case study. *Regional Studies, 13,* 181–190.

Downing, K., & Clark, R.N. (1978). Users' and managers' perceptions of dispersed recreation impacts: A focus on roaded forest lands. In R. Ittner, D.R. Potter, J.K. Agee & S. Anschell (Eds.), *Recreational Impact on Wildlands* (pp. 18–23), (Report No. R-6-001-1979). Portland, OR: U.S. Department of Agriculture, Forest Service R-9.

Driver, B.L. (1972). Potential contributions of psychology to recreation resource management. In J. Wohlwill & D.H. Carson (Eds.), *Environment and the social sciences: Perspectives and applications* (pp. 233–244). Washington, DC: American Psychological Association.

Driver, B.L. (1976). Quantification of outdoor recreationists' preferences. In B. van der Smissen (Ed.), *Research, camping and environmental education* (pp. 165–188). State College: Pennsylvania State University, College of Health, Physical Education and Recreation.

Driver, B.L., & Bassett, J.R. (1975). Defining conflicts among river users: A case study of Michigan's AuSable River. *Naturalist, 26,* 19–23.

Driver, B.L., & Brown, P.J. (1978). The opportunity spectrum concept and behavioral information in outdoor recreation resource supply inventories: A rationale. In H. G. Lund, V. J. LaBau, P. F. Ffolliott, D. W. Robinson (Tech. coordinators), *Proceedings, Integrated inventories of renewable natural resources workshop* (pp. 24–32), (General Tech. Rep. RM-55). Ft. Collins, CO: U.S. Department of Agriculture, Forest Service, Rocky Mountain Forest and Range Experiment Station.

Driver, B.L., & Cooksey, R.W. (1977). Preferred psychological outcomes of recreational fishing. In *Catch-and-Release Fishing as a management tool: A national sport fishing symposium* (pp. 27–40). Arcata, CA: Humbolt State University.

Driver, B.L., & Greene, P. (1977). Man's nature: Innate determinants of response to natural environments. In *Children, nature, and the urban environment* (pp. 63–72), (General Tech. Rep. NE-30). Upper Darby, PA: U.S. Department of Agriculture Forest Service, Northeastern Forest Experiment Station.

Driver, B.L., & Knopf, R.C. (1976). Temporary escape: One product of sport fisheries management. *Fisheries, 1,* 21–29.

Driver, B.L., & Knopf, R.C. (1977). Personality, outdoor recreation and expected consequences. *Environment and Behavior, 9,* 169–193.

Driver, B.L., Rosenthal, D., & Peterson, G. (1978). Social benefits of urban forests and related green spaces in cities. In *Proceedings of the National Urban Forestry Conference* (Vol. 1) (pp. 98–113), (Publication No. 80-003). Syracuse: State University of New York, College of Environmental Science and Forestry.

Dubos, R. (1965). *Man adapting.* New Haven: Yale University Press.

Dubos, R. (1968). *So human an animal.* New York: Scribner's.

Duncan, D.J. (1978). Leisure types: Factor analyses of leisure profiles. *Journal of Leisure Research, 10,* 113–125.

Dunlap, R.E., & Catton, W.R., Jr. (1979). Environmental sociology. *Annual Review of Sociology, 5,* 243–273.

Dunlap, R.E., & VanLiere, K.D. (1978). *Environmental concern: A bibliography of empirical studies and brief appraisal of the literature* (Public Administration Series Bibliography P-44). Monticello, IL: Vance Bibliographies.

Dwyer, J.F., & Bowes, M.D. (1979). Benefit-cost analysis for appraisal of recreation alternatives. *Journal of Forestry, 77,* 145–148.

Dwyer, J.F., Kelly, J.R., & Bowes, M.D. (1977). *Improved procedures for valuation of the contribution of recreation to national economic development.* (Report No. 128). Urbana: University of Illinois, Water Resources Center.

Eastwood, D.A., & Carter, R.W.G. (1981). The Irish dune consumer. *Journal of Leisure Research, 13,* 273–281.

Edney, J.J. (1976). Human territories: Comment on functional properties. *Environment and Behavior, 8,* 31–47.

Eiseley, L. (1957). *The immense journey.* New York: Watts.

Ellis, M.J. (1973). *Why people play.* Englewood Cliffs, NJ: Prentice-Hall.

Elsner, G.H., & Smardon, R.C. (Eds.). (1979). *Proceedings of Our National Landscape: A conference on applied techniques for analysis and management of the visual resource* (General Tech. Rep. PSW-35). Berkeley, CA: U.S. Department of Agriculture, Forest Service, Pacific Southwest Forest and Range Experiment Station.

Etzkorn, K.R. (1965). Leisure and camping: The social meaning of a form of public recreation. *Sociology and Social Research, 49,* 76–81.

Ewing, G.O. (1980). Progress and problems in the development of recreational trip generation and trip distribution models. *Leisure Sciences, 3,* 1–24.

Ewing, G.O., & Kulka, T. (1979). Revealed and stated preference analysis of ski resort attractiveness. *Leisure Sciences, 2,* 249–276.

Fairfax, S. (1975). Public involvement and the Forest Service. *Journal of Forestry, 73,* 657–659.

Feimer, N.R. (1983). Environmental perception and cognition in rural contexts. In A.W. Childs & G.B. Melton (Eds.), *Rural Psychology* (pp. 113–149). New York: Plenum.

Feingold, B.H. (1979). *The wilderness experience: The interaction of person and environment.* Unpublished doctoral dissertation, University of California, Los Angeles.

Field, D.R. (1976). The social organization of recreation places. In N.H. Cheek, D.R. Field, & R.J. Burdge (Eds.), *Leisure and recreation places.* Ann Arbor, MI: Ann Arbor Science.

Field, D.R., Barron, J.C., & Long, B.F. (Eds.). (1974). *Water and community development: Social and economic perspectives.* Ann Arbor, MI: Ann Arbor Science.

Field, D.R., Burdge, R.J., & Burch, J.S. (1975). *Sex roles and group influences on sport fishing behavior.* Paper presented at the annual meeting of the Rural Sociological Society, San Francisco.

Field, D.R., & O'Leary, J.T. (1973). Social groups as a basis for assessing participation in selected water activities. *Journal of Leisure Research, 5,* 16–25.

Finsterbusch, K., & Wolf, C.P. (Eds.). (1977). *Methodology of social impact assessment.* Stroudsburg, PA: Dowden, Hutchinson, & Ross.

Fisher, A.C., & Krutilla, J.V. (1972). Determination of optimal capacity of resource-based recreation facilities. *Natural Resources Journal, 12,* 417–444.

Fischer, D.W. (1975). Willingness to pay as a behavioral criterion for environmental decision-making. *Journal of Environmental Management, 3,* 29–41.

Foresta, R.A. (1980). Comment: Elite values, popular values and open space policy. *Journal of the American Planning Association, 46,* 449–456.

Foster, R.J., & Jackson, E.L. (1979). Factors associated with camping satisfaction in Alberta Provincial Park campgrounds. *Journal of Leisure Research, 4,* 292–306.

Gallagher, T.J. (1977). Visual preference for alternative natural landscapes. Unpublished doctoral dissertation, University of Michigan, Ann Arbor.

Gans, H.J. (1962). The urban villagers: Group and class in the life of Italian-Americans. New York: Free Press.

Gibson, P.M. (1979). Therapeutic aspects of wilderness programs: A comprehensive literature review. *Therapeutic Recreation Journal, 13,* 21–33.

Glacken, C.H. (1967). *Traces on the Rhodian shore: Nature and culture in Western thought from ancient times to the end of the eighteenth century.* Berkeley, CA: University of California Press.

Gold, S.M. (1977). Neighborhood parks: Non-use phenomenon. *Evaluation Quarterly, 1,* 319–328.

Goldin, K.D. (1971). Recreational parks and beaches: Peak demand, quality and management. *Journal of Leisure Research, 3,* 81–107.

Goodrich, J.N. (1977). Differences in perceived similarities of tourism regions: A spatial analysis. *Journal of Travel Research, 16,* 10–13.

Goodrich, J.N. (1980). Benefit segmentation of U.S. international travelers: An empirical study with American Express. In D.E. Hawkins, E.L. Shafer, & J.M. Rovelstad (Eds.), *Tourism marketing and management issues* (pp. 138–140). Washington, DC: George Washington University Press.

Graefe, A.R., Ditton, R.B., Roggenbuck, J.W., & Schreyer,

R. (1981). Notes on the stability of the factor structure of leisure meanings. *Leisure Sciences, 4,* 51–65.

Gramman, J.H. (1982). Toward a behavioral theory of crowding in outdoor recreation: An evaluation and synthesis of research, *Leisure Sciences, 5,* 109–126.

Green, B.L., & Wadsworth, H.A. (1967). Boaters, fishermen, hunters: What affects participation and what do they want? (Research Bulletin No. 829). Lafayette, IN: Purdue University, Agricultural Experiment Station.

Grubb, E.A. (1975). Assembly line boredom and individual differences in recreation participation. *Journal of Leisure Research, 7,* 256–269.

Gussow, A. (1972). *A sense of place: The artist and the American land.* New York: Saturday Review Press.

Gustke, L.D., & Hodgson, R.W. (1980). Rate of travel along an interpretive trail: The effect of an environmental discontinuity. *Environment and Behavior, 12,* 53–63.

Haas, G.H., Allen, D.J., & Manfredo, M. (1979). Some dispersed recreation experiences and the resource settings in which they occur. In *Assessing amenity resource values* (pp. 21–26), (General Tech. Rep. No. RM-68). Ft. Collins: U.S. Department of Agriculture, Forest Service, Rocky Mountain Forest and Range Experiment Station.

Hadley, L.C. (1971). Perspectives on law enforcement in recreation areas. In *Recreation symposium proceedings.* Upper Darby, PA: U.S. Department of Agriculture, Forest Service, Northeastern Forest Experiment Station.

Hammitt, J., & Brown, G.M. (1974). Waterfowl and wetlands: Toward bioeconomic analysis. Baltimore, MD: Johns Hopkins University Press.

Hammitt, W.E. (1979). Measuring familiarity for natural environments through visual images. In G.H. Elsner & R.C. Smardon (Eds.), *Proceedings of Our National Landscape conference* (pp. 217–226), (General Tech. Rep. No. PSW-35). Berkeley, CA: U.S. Department of Agriculture, Forest Service, Pacific Southwest Forest and Range Experiment Station.

Hammitt, W.E. (1980). Designing mystery into trail experiences. *Journal of Interpretation, 5,* 16–19.

Hammitt, W.E. (1981). *Outdoor recreation: Is it a multiphase experience?* Unpublished manuscript. Knoxville: University of Tennessee, Department of Forestry, Wildlife and Fisheries.

Hammitt, W.E. (1982). Cognitive dimensions of wilderness solitude. *Environment and Behavior, 14,* 478–493.

Hammon, G.A. (1974). *Capacity of water based recreation systems* (Report No. 90). Chapel Hill, University of North Carolina, Water Research Institute.

Hancock, H.K. (1973). Recreation preference: Its relation to user behavior. *Journal of Forestry, 71,* 336–337.

Hanson, R.A. (1977). An outdoor challenge program as a means of enhancing mental health. In *Children, nature and the urban environment,* (pp. 171–174), (General

Tech. Rep. No. NE-30). Upper Darby: U.S. Department of Agriculture, Forest Service, Northeastern Forest Experiment Station.

Harris, C.C. (1982). Experiences as a decision-making process. In *Forest and river recreation: Research update,* (pp. 160–163), (Misc. Publication No. 18). St. Paul: University of Minnesota, Agricultural Experiment Station.

Harris, D.V. (1975). Perceptions of self. In B. van der Smissen (Ed.), *Research, camping, and environmental education* (pp. 153–164). State College: Pennsylvania State University, College of Health, Physical Education and Recreation.

Hart, R. (1973). Adventures in a wood wonderland. *Natural History, 82,* 67–69.

Hawes, D.K. (1978a). Satisfactions derived from leisure-time pursuits: An exploratory nationwide survey. *Journal of Leisure Research, 10,* 247–264.

Hawes, D.K. (1978b). Empirically profiling four recreational vehicle market segments. *Journal of Travel Research, 14,* 13–20.

Hawkins, D.E., Shafer, E.L., & Rovelstad, J.M. (Eds.). (1980). *Tourism marketing and management issues.* Washington, DC: George Washington University Press.

Heathcoate, R.L. (1969). Drought in Australia: Problem of perception. *Geographical Review, 59,* 175–194.

Heberlein, T.A. (1976). Some observations on alternative mechanisms for public involvement. *Natural Resources Journal, 16,* 197–212.

Heberlein, T.A. (1977). Density, crowding, and satisfaction: Sociological studies for determining carrying capacities. In *Proceedings, River Recreation Management and Research Symposium,* (pp. 67–76), (General Tech. Rep. No. NC-28). St. Paul: U.S. Department of Agriculture, Forest Service, North Central Forest Experiment Station.

Hecock, R.D. (1970). Recreation behavior patterns as related to site characteristics of beaches. *Journal of Leisure Research, 2,* 237–250.

Hendee, J.C. (1967). *Recreation clientele—The attributes of recreationists preferring different management agencies, car campgrounds or wilderness in the Pacific Northwest.* Unpublished doctoral dissertation, University of Washington, Seattle.

Hendee, J.C. (1969). Rural-urban differences reflected in outdoor recreation participation. *Journal of Leisure Research, 1,* 333–341.

Hendee, J.C. (1971). Membership in conservation groups and outdoor clubs. In *Recreation Symposium Proceedings.* Upper Darby, PA: U.S. Department of Agriculture Forest Service, Northeastern Forest Experiment Station.

Hendee, J.C. (1974). A multiple-satisfaction approach to game management. *Wildlife Society Bulletin, 2,* 104–113.

Hendee, J.C., & Burdge, R.J. (1974). The substitutability concept: Implications for recreation research and management. *Journal of Leisure Research, 6,* 157–162.

Hendee, J.C., Catton, W.R., Jr., Marlow, C.O., & Brockman, C.F. (1968). *Wilderness users in the Pacific Northwest—Their characteristics, values, and management preferences* (Research Paper No. PNW-61). Portland, OR: U.S. Department of Agriculture, Forest Service, Pacific Northwest Forest and Range Experiment Station.

Hendee, J.C., Clark, R.N., & Dailey, T.E. (1977). *Fishing and other recreation behavior at high-mountain lakes in Washington State* (Research Note PNW-304). Portland, OR: U.S. Department of Agriculture, Forest Service, Pacific Northwest Forest and Range Experiment Station.

Hershberger, B.G. (1972). Toward a set of semantic scales to measure the meaning of architectural environments. In W.S. Mitchell (Ed.), *Environmental Design: Research and practice (EDRA (Environmental Design Research Association III) 3) (pp. 6-4.1—6-4.10).* Los Angeles: University of California.

Herzog, T.R., Kaplan, S., & Kaplan, R. (1982). The prediction of preference for unfamiliar places. *Population and Environment, 5,* 43–59.

Hobbs, T., & Shelton, G. (1972). Therapeutic camping for emotionally disturbed adolescents. *Hospital and Community Psychiatry, 23,* 298–301.

Hodson, R.W., & Thayer, R.L. (1980). Implied human influence reduces landscape beauty. *Landscape Planning, 7,* 171–179.

Holcomb, B. (1977). The perception of natural vs. built environments by young children. In *Children, nature, and the urban environment* (pp. 33–38), (General Tech. Rep. No. NE-30). Upper Darby, PA: U.S. Department of Agriculture Forest Service, Northeastern Forest Experiment Station.

Houston, C.S. (1968). The last blue mountain. In S.Z. Klausner (Ed.). *Why man takes chances* (pp. 52–58). New York: Doubleday.

Howard, D.R. (1976). Multivariate relationships between leisure activities and personality. *Research Quarterly, 47,* 226–237.

Hunt, J.D. (1975). Image as a factor in tourism development. *Journal of Travel Research, 13,* 1–7.

Iltis, H.H. (1973). Can one love a plastic tree? *Bulletin of the Ecological Society of America, 54,* 5–7, 19.

Iltis, H.H., Loucks, D.L., & Andrews, P. (1970). Criteria for an optimum human environment. *Bulletin of the Atomic Scientists, 25,* 2–6.

Iso-Ahola, S.E. (1980). *The social psychology of leisure and recreation.* Dubuque, IA: Brown.

Ittelson, W.H., Franck, K.A., & O'Hanlon, T.J. (1976). The nature of environmental experience. In S. Wapner, S.B. Cohen, & B. Kaplan (Eds.), *Experiencing the en-*

vironment (pp. 187–206). New York: Plenum.

Jackson, J.B. (1973). Commentary: Visual blight—Civic neglect. In *Visual blight in America* (Resource Paper No. 23). Washington, DC: Association of American Geographers, Commission on College Geography.

Jackson, J.B. (1975). The historic American landscape. In E.H. Zube, R.O. Brush, & J.G. Fabos (Eds.), *Landscape assessment: Values, perceptions, and resources* (pp. 4–9). Stroudsburg, PA: Dowden, Hutchinson, & Ross.

Jacob, G.R., & Schreyer, R. (1980). Conflict in outdoor recreation: A theoretical perspective. *Journal of Leisure Research, 12,* 368–380.

Jacques, D.C. (1980). Landscape appraisal: The case for a subjective theory. *Journal of Environmental Management, 10,* 107–113.

Johnson, R.C. (1978). An evaluation of information dissemination systems in municipal parks and recreation departments. *Recreation Research Review, 6,* 33–38.

Kaplan, M. (1960). *Leisure in America: A social inquiry.* New York: Wiley.

Kaplan, M. (1975). *Leisure: Theory and policy.* New York: Wiley.

Kaplan, R. (1973a). Predictors of environmental preference: Designers and clients. In W.F.E. Preiser (Ed.), *Environmental Design Research* (pp. 265–274). Stroudsburg, PA: Dowden, Hutchinson, & Ross.

Kaplan, R. (1973b). Some psychological benefits of gardening. *Environment and Behavior, 5,* 145–162.

Kaplan, R. (1974). Some psychological benefits of an outdoor challenge program. *Environment and Behavior, 6,* 101–116.

Kaplan, R. (1976). Way-finding in the natural environment. In G.T. Moore & R.G. Golledge (Eds.), *Environmental Knowing: Theories, research and methods* (pp. 46–57). Stroudsburg, PA: Dowden, Hutchinson, & Ross.

Kaplan, R. (1977a). Down by the riverside: Informational factors in waterscape preference. In *Proceedings: River recreation management and research symposium* (pp. 285–289), (General Tech. Rep. No. NC-28). St. Paul, MN: U.S. Department of Agriculture, Forest Service, North Central Forest Experiment Station.

Kaplan, R. (1977b). Preference and everyday nature: Method and application. In D. Stokols (Ed.), *Perspectives on environment and behavior: Theory, research, and application* (pp. 235–250). New York: Plenum.

Kaplan, R. (1978). The green experience. In S. Kaplan & R. Kaplan (Eds.), *Humanscape: Environments for people* (pp. 186–193). North Scituate, MA: Duxbury.

Kaplan, R. (1983). The role of nature in the urban context. In I. Altman & J.F. Wohlwill (Eds.), *Human Behavior and Environment: Vol. 6. Behavior and the natural environment.* New York: Plenum.

Kaplan, S. (1976). Adaptation, structure and knowledge. In G.T. Moore & R.G. Golledge (Eds.), *Environmental knowing: Theories, research and knowledge* (pp. 32–45). Stroudsburg, PA: Dowden, Hutchinson, & Ross.

Kaplan, S. (1977). Tranquility and challenge in the natural environment. In *Children, nature and the urban environment* (pp. 181–186), (General Tech. Rep. No. NE-30). Upper Darby, PA: U.S. Department of Agriculture, Forest Service, Northeastern Forest Experiment Station.

Kaplan, S. (1982). Where cognition and affect meet: A theoretical analysis of preference. In P. Bart, A. Chen, & G. Franscescato (Eds.), *Knowledge for design* (pp. 183–188). Washington, DC: Environmental Design Research Association.

Kaplan, S., & Kaplan, R. (Eds.). (1978). *Humanscape: Environments for people.* North Scituate, MA: Duxbury.

Kaplan, S., Kaplan, R., & Wendt, J.S. (1972). Rated preference and complexity for natural and urban visual material. *Perception and Psychophysics, 12,* 334–356.

Kaplan, S., & Talbot, J.F. (1983). Psychological benefits of a wilderness experience. In I. Altman & J.F. Wohlwill (Eds.), *Human Behavior and Environment: Vol. 6. Behavior and the natural environment.* New York: Plenum.

Kates, R.W. (1971). Human perception of the environment. *International Social Science Journal, 22,* 648–663.

Kates, R.W. (1976). Experiencing the environment as hazard. In S. Wapner, S.B. Cohen & B. Kaplan (Eds.), *Experiencing the environment* (pp. 133–156). New York: Plenum.

Katz, M. (1979). Fishing survey results. *Theodore Gordon Flyfishers Bulletin, 6,* 2–4.

Kelly, J.R. (1976). *Two orientations of leisure choices.* Paper presented at the annual American Sociological Association Convention, New York.

Kendzie, A. (1983). Packing iron: Is it time you carried a gun? *Backpacker, 20,* 15–17.

Kenyon, G.S., & McPherson, B.O. (1970). *An approach to the study of sport socialization.* Paper presented at the seventh World Congress of Sociology, Varna, Bulgaria.

Kleiber, D.A. (1979). Fate control and leisure attitudes. *Leisure Sciences, 2,* 239–248.

Kluckhohn, F.R. (1953). Dominant and variant value orientations. In C. Kluckhohn, H.A. Murray & D.M. Schneider (Eds.), *Personality in nature, culture and society* (pp. 342–357). New York: Knopf.

Knopf, R.C. (1972). *Motivational determinants of recreation behavior.* Master's thesis, University of Michigan, Ann Arbor. (University Microfilms Photocopy No. M-4224)

Knopf, R.C. (1973). *Uses of outdoor recreation resources in the Northeastern lower peninsula of Michigan for purposes of stress mediation.* Rogers City, MI: Northeast Michigan Regional Planning and Development Commission.

Knopf, R.C. (1976). *Relationships between desired consequences of recreation engagements and conditions in home neighborhood environments.* Unpublished doctoral dissertation, The University of Michigan, Ann Arbor.

Knopf, R.C. (1981). Cognitive map formation as a tool for facilitating information transfer in interpretive programming. *Journal of Leisure Research, 13,* 232–242.

Knopf, R.C. (1983). Recreational needs and behavior in natural settings. I. I. Altman & J.F. Wohlwill (Eds.), *Human Behavior and Environment: Vol. 6. Behavior and the Natural Environment* (pp. 204–233). New York: Plenum.

Knopf, R.C. & Barnes, J.D. (1980). Determinants of satisfaction with a tourism resource: A case study of visitors to Gettysburg National Military Park. In D.E. Hawkins, E.L. Shafer, and J.M. Rovelstad (Eds.), *Tourism, Marketing and Management Issues* (pp. 217–238). Washington, DC: George Washington University Press.

Knopf, R.C., Driver, B.L., & Bassett, J.R. (1973). Motivations for fishing. In *Transactions, 38th North American Wildlife and Natural Resources Conference.* Washington, DC: Wildlife Management Institute.

Knopf, R.C., & Lime, D.W. (1984). A recreation manager's guide to understanding river use and users. (General Technical Report No. W.-38). Washington, DC: U.S. Department of Agriculture, Forest Service.

Knopf, R.C., Peterson, G.L., & Leatherberry, E.C. (1983). Motives for recreational river floating: Relative consistency across settings. *Leisure Sciences, 5,* 231–255.

Knopp, T.B. (1972). Environmental determinants of recreational behavior. *Journal of Leisure Research, 4,* 129–138.

Knopp, T.B., & Merriam, L.C. (Eds.). (1980). *Proceedings, North American Symposium on dispersed winter recreation.* (Educational Series 2-3) (pp. 31–35). St. Paul: University of Minnesota, Office of Special Programs.

Knudson, D.M., & Curry, E.B. (1981). Campers' perceptions of site deterioration and crowding. *Journal of Forestry, 79,* 92–94.

Kotler, P. (1976). *Marketing management.* Englewood Cliffs, NJ: Prentice-Hall.

Krieger, M. (1973). What is wrong with plastic trees? *Science, 179,* 446–455.

Krueger, A. (1973). Are negative ions good for you? *New Scientist, 58,* 668–670.

Krutilla, J.V. (1967). Conservation reconsidered. *American Economic Review, 57,* 777–786.

Krutilla, J.V., & Fisher, A.C. (1975). *The economics of natural environments: Studies in the valuation of commodity and amenity resources.* Baltimore, MD: Johns Hopkins University Press.

Kuller, R. (1972). *A semantic model for describing perceived environment.* Stockholm: National Swedish Institute for Building Research.

Kurtz, W.B., & King, D.A. (1980). Evaluating substitution

relationships between recreation areas. In D.E. Hawkins, E.L. Shafer, & J.M. Rovelstad (Eds.), *Tourism, Marketing and Management Issues* (pp. 391–404). Washington, DC: George Washington University Press.

Kwok, K. (1979). Semantic evaluation of perceived environment: A cross-cultural replication. *Man-Environment Systems, 9,* 243–249.

Lansing, J.B., Marans, R.W., & Zehner, R.B. (1970). *Planned residential communities.* Ann Arbor: University of Michigan, Institute for Social Research.

LaPage, W.F. (1968). *Campground marketing—The heavy half strategy.* (Research Note No. NE-93). Broomall, PA: U.S. Department of Agriculture, Forest Service, Northeastern Forest Experiment Station.

LaPage, W.F. (1974). Market research: The missing link in resource-development planning for outdoor recreation. In *Outdoor recreation research: Applying the results* (pp. 107–113). (General Tech. Rep. NC-9). St. Paul, MN: U.S. Department of Agriculture, Forest Service, North Central Forest Experiment Station.

LaPage, W.F. (1979). *Growth potential of the skier market in the national forests.* (Research Paper WO-36). Washington, DC: U.S. Department of Agriculture, Forest Service.

Laurie, I.C. (Ed.). (1979). *Nature in cities.* New York: Wiley.

Lavery, P. (Ed.). (1974). *Recreational geography.* New York: Wiley.

Lavery, P. (1975). The demand for recreation: A review of studies. *Town Planning Review, 46,* 185–200.

Lazarus, R.S. (1966). *Psychological stress and the coping process.* New York: McGraw-Hill.

Leakey, R.E.F. (1976). Hominids in Africa. *American Scientist, 64,* 174–178.

LeCorbusier, C.E.J., & DePierrefeu, F. (1948). *The home of man.* London: Architectural Press.

Lee, M.S. (1979). Landscape preference assessment of Louisiana river landscapes. A methodological study. In G.H. Elsner & R.L. Smardon (Eds.), *Proceedings of Our National Landscape Conference* (pp. 572–580). (General Tech. Rep. No. PSW-35). Berkeley, CA: U.S. Department of Agriculture, Forest Service, Pacific Southwest Forest and Range Experiment Station.

Lee, R.G. (1972). The social definition of outdoor recreation places. In W.R. Burch, N.H. Cheek, & L. Taylor (Eds.), *Social behavior, natural resources and the environment* (pp. 68–84). New York: Harper & Row.

Lee, R.G. (1974, August). *Social groups as behavioral entities on public beaches.* Paper delivered at the annual meeting of the Rural Sociological Society, Montreal, Canada.

Lee, R.G. (1977). Alone with others: The paradox of privacy in wilderness. *Leisure Sciences, 1,* 3–19.

Leopold, A. (1949). *A Sand County almanac.* New York: Oxford University Press.

Levy, J. (1979). A paradigm for conceptualizing leisure behavior: Towards a person-environment interaction analysis. *Journal of Leisure Research, 11,* 48–60.

Lewis, C.A. (1973). People-plant interaction: A new horticultural perspective. *American Horticulturist, 52,* 18–25.

Lewis, C.A. (1977). Human perspectives in horticulture. In *Children, nature, and the urban environment* (pp. 187–192). (General Tech. Rep. No. NE-30). Upper Darby, PA: U.S. Department of Agriculture, Forest Service, Northeastern Forest Experiment Station.

Lewis, C.A. (1978). Nature city. In S. Kaplan & R. Kaplan (Eds.), *Humanscape: Environments for people* (pp. 448–453). North Scituate, MA: Duxbury.

Lewissohn, P., & Graf, M. (1973). Pleasant activities and depression. *Journal of consulting and clinical psychology, 41,* 261–268.

Lieberman, M. (1970). Parks and mental health. *Park Practice Trends, 7,* 30–32.

Lime, D.W. (1977). When the wilderness gets crowded. *Naturalist, 28,* 1–5.

Lime, D.W., & Cushwa, C.T. (1969). *Wildlife aesthetics and auto campers in the Superior National Forest* (Research Paper No. NC-32). St. Paul, MN: U.S. Department of Agriculture, Forest Service, North Central Forest Experiment Station.

Loder, A.W. (1978). *Relationship of camper characteristics and choice of a campground.* Unpublished master's thesis. Pennsylvania State University, State College.

Logan, H.L. (1974). Light and the human environment. *Fields Within Fields, 5,* 58–64.

London, M., Crandall, R., & Fitzgibbons, D. (1977). The psychological structure of leisure: Activities, needs, people. *Journal of Leisure Research, 2,* 252–263.

Lowenthal, D. (1967). Introduction: Environmental perception and behavior. In D. Lowenthal (Ed.), *Environmental perception and behavior* (Research Paper No. 109). Chicago: University of Chicago, Department of Geography.

Lowenthal, D., & Prince, H.C. (1976). Transcendental experience. In S. Wagner, S.B. Cohen & B. Kaplan (Eds.), *Experiencing the environment* (pp. 117–132). New York: Plenum.

Loy, J.W., & Donnelly, P. (1976). Need for stimulation as a factor in sport involvement. In T.M. Craig (Ed.), *Humanistic and mental health aspects of sports, exercise, and recreation.* Chicago: American Medical Association.

Lucas, R.C. (1964). *The recreational carrying capacity of the Quetico-Superior area* (Research Paper No. LS-15). St. Paul, MN: U.S. Department of Agriculture, Forest Service, North Central Forest Experiment Station.

Lucas, R.C. (1979). Perceptions of non-motorized recreational impacts: A review of research findings. In R. Ittner, D. R. Potter, J. K. Agee, & S. Anschell (Eds.), *Recreational impact on wildlands* (pp. 24–31), (Report No. R-6-001-1979). Portland, OR: U.S. Department of

Agriculture, Forest Service Region 9.

Lundegren, H.M. (1975). Self-concepts of special populations. In B. van der Smissen (Ed.), *Research, camping and environmental education* (pp. 253–274). State College: Pennsylvania State University, College of Health, Physical Education and Recreation.

Macia, A. (1979). Visual perception of landscape: Sex and personality differences. In G.H. Elsner & R.C. Smardon (Eds.), *Proceedings of Our National Landscape Conference* (pp. 279–285), (General Tech. Rep. PSW-35). Berkeley, CA: U.S. Department of Agriculture, Forest Service, Pacific Southwest Forest and Range Experiment Station.

Maler, K. (1974). *Environmental economics: A theoretical inquiry.* Baltimore, MD: Johns Hopkins University Press.

Mandell, L., & Marans, R. (1972). *Participation in outdoor recreation: A national perspective.* Ann Arbor, MI: Institute for Social Research.

Manfredo, M.J. (1979). *Wilderness experience opportunities and management preferences for three Wyoming wilderness areas.* Unpublished doctoral dissertation. Colorado State University, Ft. Collins.

Mansfield, N.W. (1971). The estimation of benefits from recreation sites and the provision of a new recreation facility. *Regional Studies, 5,* 55–69.

Marcus, C. (1974). Children's play behavior in a low-rise inner city housing environment. In D.H. Carson (Ed.), *Man-environment interaction: Evaluations and applications— The state of the art in environmental design research* (Vol. 12). Stroudsburg, PA: Dowden, Hutchinson, & Ross.

Marcus, L.S. (1977). Within city limits: Nature and children's books about nature in the city. In *Children, nature and the urban environment* (pp. 83–88), (General Tech. Rep. No. NE-30). Upper Darby, PA: U.S. Department of Agriculture, Forest Service, Northeastern Forest Experiment Station.

Martin, W.S., & Myrick, F.L. (1976). Personality and leisure time activities. *Research Quarterly, 47,* 246—253.

Maslow, A.H. (1962). *Toward a psychology of being.* Princeton, NJ: Van Nostrand.

Marx, L. (1964). *The machine in the garden.* New York: Oxford University Press.

Mayo, E.J. (1973). Regional images and regional travel behavior. In *Proceedings of the Fourth Annual Conference of the Travel Research Association* (pp. 211–218). Washington, DC: Travel Research Association.

McAvoy, L.H., & Dustin, D.L. (1981). The right to risk in wilderness. *Journal of Forestry, 79,* 150–152.

McCay, R.E., & Moeller, G.H. (1976). *Compatibility of Ohio trail users* (Research Note No. NE-225). Upper Darby, PA: U.S. Department of Agriculture, Forest Service, Northeastern Forest Experiment Station.

McConnell, K.E. (1977). Congestion and willingness to pay: A study of beach use. *Land Economics, 53,* 185–195.

McCool, S.F. (1978). Recreational activity packages at water-based resources. *Leisure Sciences, 1,* 163–174.

McDonough, M.H. (1982). The influence of place on recreation behavior: An ecological perspective. In D.W. Lime (Tech. coordinator), *Forest and river recreation: Research update* (pp. 120–123), (Misc. Publication No. 18). St. Paul: University of Minnesota, Agricultural Experiment Station.

McEvoy, J., & Dietz, T. (Eds.). (1977). *Handbook for environmental planning: Social consequences of environmental change.* New York: Wiley.

McKechnie, G.E. (1970). Measuring environmental dispositions with the Environmental Response Inventory. In J. Archea & C. Eastman (Eds.), *Proceedings, Second Annual EDRA Conference Pittsburgh, PA.* Stroudsburg, PA: Dowden, Hutchinson, & Ross.

McKechnie, G.E. (1974). The psychological structure of leisure: Past behavior. *Journal of Leisure Research, 6,* 27–45.

McLaughlin, W.J., & Paradice, W.E.J. (1980). Using visitor preference information to guide dispersed winter recreation management for cross-country skiing and snowmobiling. In *Proceedings, North American Symposium on dispersed winter recreation* (pp. 64–72), (Educational Series 2-3). St. Paul: University of Minnesota, Office of Special Programs.

Mehrabian, A. (1976). *Public places and private spaces: The psychology of work, play and living environments.* Cambridge, MA: MIT Press.

Mehrabian, A., & Russell, J. (1974). An approach to environmental psychology. Cambridge, MA: MIT Press.

Menz, F.C., & Mullen, J.K. (1981). Expected encounters and willingness to pay for outdoor recreation. *Land Economics, 57,* 33–40.

Merriam, L.C., Jr., & Smith, C.K. (1974). Visitor impact on newly developed campsites in the Boundary Waters Canoe Area. *Journal of Forestry, 72,* 627–630.

Michelson, W. (1977). From congruence to antecedent conditions: A search for the basis of environmental improvement. In D. Stokols (Ed.), *Perspectives on environment and behavior: Theory, research, and applications.* New York: Plenum.

Miller, R.R., Prato, A.A., & Young, R.A. (1977). Congestion, success and the value of Colorado deer hunting experiences. In *Transactions, 42nd North American Wildlife Conference* (pp. 129–136). Washington, DC: Wildlife Management Institute.

Mischel, W. (1973). Toward a cognitive social learning reconceptualization of personality. *Psychological Review, 80,* 252–283.

Mitchell, C.C., & Schomaker, J.H. (1980). *Wilderness travel simulator: A GPSS/360 user's manual with exercises* (Contribution No. 134). Moscow: University of Idaho, Forest, Wildlife and Range Experiment Station.

Mitchell, R.C., & Davies, J.C. (1978). *The United States environmental movement and its political context: An overview* (Discussion Paper No. D-32). Washington, DC: Resources for the Future.

Mitchell, T.R., & Biglan, A. (1971). Instrumentality theories: Current uses in psychology. *Psychological Bulletin, 76,* 432–454.

Moore, G.T. (1979). Knowing about environmental knowing: The current state of theory and research on environmental cognition. *Environment and Behavior, 11,* 33–70.

Moore, G.T., & Golledge, R.G. (1976). Environmental knowing: Concepts and theories. In G.T. Moore & R.G. Golledge (Eds.), *Environmental knowing: Theories, research and methods* (pp. 3–24). Stroudsburg, PA: Dowden, Hutchinson, & Ross.

Morales, D., Boyce, B.N., & Fausetti, R.J. (1976). The contribution of trees to residential property values. *Valuation, 23,* 27–43.

More, T.A. (1973). Attitudes of Massachusetts hunters. In J.C. Hendee & C. Schoenfeld (Eds.), *Human dimensions in wildlife programs* (pp. 72–76). Rockville, MD: Mercury.

More, T.A. (1977). An analysis of wildlife in children's stories. In *Children, nature and the urban environment* (pp. 89–94), (General Tech. Rep. NE-30). Upper Darby, PA: U.S. Department of Agriculture, Forest Service, Northeastern Forest Experiment Station.

More, T.A. (1980). *Emotional responses to recreation environments* (Research Paper No. NE-461). Broomall, PA: U.S. Department of Agriculture, Forest Service, Northeastern Forest Experiment Station.

More, T.A., & Buhyoff, G.J. (1979). *Managing recreation areas for quality user experiences: A theoretical framework* (Research Paper No. NE-432). Broomall, PA: U.S. Department of Agriculture, Forest Service, Northeastern Forest Experiment Station.

More, T.A., & Payne, B. (1978). Affective responses to natural areas near cities. *Journal of Leisure Research, 10,* 7–12.

Morgan, W.P. (1974). Selected psychological considerations in sport. *Research Quarterly, 45,* 374–387.

Moss, W.T., & Lamphear, S.C. (1970). Substitutability of recreational activities in meeting stated needs and drives of the visitor. *Journal of Environmental Education, 1,* 129–131.

Nash, R. (1973). *Wilderness and the American mind.* New Haven: Yale University Press.

Nash, R. (1977). River recreation: History and future. In *Proceedings, River Recreation Management and Research Symposium* (pp. 2–7), (General Tech. Rep. No. NC-28). St. Paul, MN: U.S. Department of Agriculture, Forest Service, North Central Forest Experiment Station.

Nassauer, J. (1979). Managing for naturalness in wildland and agricultural landscapes. In G.H. Elsner & R.C.

Smardon (Eds.), *Proceedings of Our National Landscape Conference* (pp. 447–453), (General Tech. Rep. No. PSW-35). Berkeley, CA: U.S. Department of Agriculture, Forest Service, Pacific Southwest Forest and Range Experiment Station.

Newby, P.T. (1979). Towards an understanding of landscape quality. *Landscape Research, 4*, 11–17.

Nielsen, J.M., Shelby, B., & Hass, J.E. (1977). Sociological carrying capacity and the last settler syndrome. *Pacific Sociological Review, 20*, 568–581.

O'Leary, J.T. (1976). Land use redefinition and the rural community: Disruption of community leisure space. *Journal of Leisure Research, 8*, 263–274.

O'Leary, J.T., Field, D.R., & Schreuder, G. (1974). Social groups and water activity clusters: An exploration of interchangeability and substitution. In D.R. Field, J. C. Barron, & B.F. Long (Eds.), *Water and community development: Social and economic perspectives.* Ann Arbor, MI: Ann Arbor Science.

Orians, G. (1980). Habitat selection: General theory and applictions to human behavior. In J. Lockhard (Ed.), *Evolution of human social behavior* (pp. 49–66). New York: Elsevier.

O'Rourke, B. (1974). Travel in the recreational experience: A literature review. *Journal of Leisure Research, 6*, 140–156.

Outdoor Recreation Resources Review Commission. (1962). *Participation in outdoor recreation: Factors affecting demand among American adults.* Washington, DC: U.S. Government Printing Office.

Palmer, J., & Zube, E.H. (1976). Numerical and perceptual landscape classification. In E.H. Zube (Ed.), *Studies in landscape perception* (pp. 43–57). Amherst: University of Massachusetts, Institute for Man and Environment.

Panzarella, R. (1980). The phenomenology of aesthetic peak experience. *Journal of Humanistic Psychology, 20*, 69–85.

Parr, A.E. (1965). City and psyche. *Yale Review, 55*, 71–85.

Partridge, L. (1978). Habitat selection. In J.R. Krebs & N. B. Davies (Eds.), *Behavioral ecology: An evolutionary approach* (pp. 351–376). Sunderland, MA: Sinaver.

Patey, R.C., & Evans, R.M. (1979). Identification of scenically preferred forest landscapes. In G.H. Elsner & R.C. Smardon (Eds.), *Proceedings of Our National Landscape Conference* (pp. 532–538), (General Tech. Rep. No. PSW-35). Berkeley, CA: U.S. Department of Agriculture, Forest Service, Pacific Southwest Forest and Range Experiment Station.

Patmore, J.A. (1974). Routeways and recreation patterns. In P. Lavery (Ed.), *Recreational Geography* (pp. 70–96). New York: Wiley.

Payne, B., & Strom, S. (1975). The contribution of trees to the appraised values of unimproved residential lots. *Valuation, 22*, 36–45.

Penz, C.H. (1975). Outdoor recreation areas: Capacity and the formulation of use policy. *Management Science, 22*, 139–147.

Perry, M. (1975). Planning and evaluating advertising campaigns related to tourist destinations. In S.P. Ladany (Ed.), *Management science applications to leisure-time operations* (pp. 116–123). New York: American Elsevier.

Peterson, G.L. (1973). Psychology and environmental management for outdoor recreation. In W.F.E. Preiser (Ed.). *Proceedings, Environmental Design Research Association Conference IV* (pp. 161–173). Stroudsburg, PA: Dowden, Hutchinson, & Ross.

Peterson, G.L. (1974a). A comparison of the sentiments and perceptions of wilderness managers and canoeists in the Boundary Waters Canoe Area. *Journal of Leisure Research, 6*, 194–206.

Peterson, G.L. (1974b). Evaluating the quality of the wilderness environment: Congruence between perception and aspiration. *Environment and Behavior, 6*, 169–193.

Peterson, G.L. (1977). Recreational preferences of urban teenagers: The influence of cultural and environmental attributes. In *Children, nature and the urban environment* (pp. 1–6), (General Tech. Rep. No. NE-30). Upper Darby, PA: U.S. Department of Agriculture, Forest Service, Northeastern Forest Experiment Station.

Peterson, G.L., Anderson, D.H., & Lime, D.W. (1982). Multiple-use site demand analysis: An application to the Boundary Waters Canoe Area Wilderness. *Journal of Leisure Research, 14*, 27–36.

Peterson, G.L., & Lime, D.W. (1979). People and their behavior: A challenge for recreation management. *Journal of Forestry, 80*, 343–346.

Pierce, R.C. (1980). Dimensions of leisure. III: Characteristics. *Journal of Leisure Research, 12*, 273–284.

Potter, D.R., Hendee, J.C., & Clark, R.N. (1973). Hunting satisfaction: Games, guns or nature? In J.C. Hendee & C. Schoenfeld (Eds.), *Human dimensions in wildlife programs* (pp. 62–71). Rockville, MD: Mercury.

Price, C. (1979). Public preference and the management of recreational congestion. *Regional Studies, 13*, 125–139.

Propst, D.B., & Lime, D.W. (1982). How satisfying is satisfaction research—A look at where we are going. In *Forest and river recreation: Research update* (pp. 124–133), (Misc. Publication No. 18). St. Paul: University of Minnesota, Agricultural Experiment Station.

Rabinowitz, C.B., & Coughlin, R.E. (1970). *Analysis of landscape characterictics relevant to preference* (Discussion Paper Series No. 38). Philadelphia: Regional Science Research Institute.

Rapoport, A. (1972). Australian Aborigines and the definition of place. In W.J. Mitchell (Ed.), *Environmental design: research and practice* (Vol. 3), (pp. 3.1-3.14). Los Angeles: University of California, School of Architecture and Urban Planning.

Reed, H.P. (1973). *A prestige hierarchy of recreation land classification*. Unpublished master's thesis, Utah State University, Logan.

Ritchie, J.R.B. (1975). On the derivation of leisure activity types: A perceptual mapping approach. *Journal of Leisure Research, 7,* 128–140.

Romesburg, H.C. (1974). Scheduling models for wilderness recreation. *Journal of Environmental Management, 2,* 159–177.

Rossman, B.B., & Ulehla, Z.J. (1977). Psychological reward values associated with wilderness use: A functional-reinforcement approach. *Environment and Behavior, 9,* 41–66.

Rutledge, A.J. (1971). *Anatomy of a park*. New York: McGraw-Hill.

Ryback, R.S., & Yaw, L. (1976). The magic of water. *Man-Environment Systems, 6,* 81-83.

Sax, J. (1980). *Mountains without handrails: Reflections on the national parks*. Ann Arbor: University of Michigan Press.

Schiller, C.F. (1884). *Essays—Aesthetical and philosophical*. London: Bell.

Scheffer, V.B. (1977). *Messages from the shore*. Seattle: Pacific Search Press.

Schomaker, J.H., & Knopf, R.C. 1982). Generalizability of a measure of visitor satisfaction with outdoor recreation. *Applied Psychological Measurement, 6,* 173–183.

Schreyer, R. (1976). Sociological and political factors on carrying capacity decision-making. In *Proceedings, Third Resource Management Conference* (pp. 228–258). Santa Fe, NM: National Park Service Southwest Regional Planning Office.

Schreyer, R., Jacob, G.R., & White, R.G. (1982). Environmental meaning as a determinant of spatial behavior in recreation. In J. Frazier & B. Epstein (Eds.). *Proceedings of Applied Geography Conferences*, (Vol. 4) (pp. 294–300). Binghamton: State University of New York.

Schreyer, R., & Knopf, R.C. (1984). The dynamics of change in ourdoor recreation environments—Some equity issues. *Journal of Park and Recreation Administration, 2,* 9–19.

Schreyer, R., & Nielson, M.L. (1978). *Westwater and Desolation Canyons: Whitewater river recreation study*. Logan: Utah State University, Institute for the Study of Outdoor Recreation and Tourism.

Schreyer, R., & Roggenbuck, J.W. (1978). The influence of experience expectation on crowding perceptions and social-psychological carrying capacities. *Leisure Sciences, 4,* 373–394.

Schreyer, R., Roggenbuck, J.W., McCool, S.F., Royer, L.E., & Miller, S. (1976). *The Dinosaur National Monument Whitewater river recreation study*. Logan: Utah State University, Department of Forestry and Outdoor Recreation, Institute for the Study of Outdoor Recreation and Tourism.

Schreyer, R., & White, R. (1979). A conceptual model of high risk recreation. In *First Annual National Conference on recreation planning and development* (Vol. 1, pp. 191–194). New York: American Society of Civil Engineers.

Scott, D.R., Schewe, C.D., & Frederick, D.G. (1978). A multi-brand/multi-attribute model of tourist state choice. *Journal of Travel Research, 17,* 23–29.

Seneca, J.J., & Davis, R.K. (1976). a cross-section analysis of state recreation activity. *Journal of Leisure Research, 8,* 88-97.

Sessoms, H.D. (1963). An analysis of selected variables affecting outdoor recreation patterns. *Social Forces, 42,* 112–115.

Shafer, E.L., Jr., & Burke, H.D. (1965). Preferences for outdoor recreation facilities in four state parks. *Journal of Forestry, 63,* 512–518.

Shafer, E.L., Jr., & Tooby, M. (1973). Landscape preferences: An international replication. *Journal of Leisure Research,5,* 60–65.

Shechter, M., & Lucas, R.C. (1978). *Simulation of recreational use for park and wilderness management*. Baltimore, MD: Johns Hopkins University Press.

Shechter, M., & Lucas, R.C. (1980). Validating a large scale simulation model of wilderness recreational travel. *Interfaces, 10,* 11–18.

Shaw, W.W., & Zube, E.H. (Eds.). (1980). *Wildlife values*. (Institutional Series Report No. 1). Tucson: University of Arizona, Center for Assessment of Noncommodity Natural Resource Values.

Shelby, B. (1980). Crowding models for backcountry recreation. *Land Economics, 56,* 43-55.

Shepard, P. (1967). *Man in the landscape*. New York: Knopf.

Sills, D. (1975). The environmental movement and its critics. *Human Ecology, 3,* 1–40.

Sinden, J.A., & Smith, R.K. (1975). The analysis and management of forest landscapes: Exotics, eucalypts and solitude. *Australian Forestry, 38,* 183–200.

Sonnenfeld, J. (1968). Variable values in space and lanscape: An inquiry into the nature of environmental necessity. *Journal of Social Issues, 22,* 71–82.

Sonnenfeld, J. (1969). Personality and behavior in environment. In *Proceedings of the 1969 American Association of Geographers* (Vol. 1) (pp. 136–140). Washington, DC: American Association of Geographers.

Springer, J., & Costantini, E. (1974). Public opinion and the environment: An issue in search of a home. In S. Nagel (Ed.), *Environmental Politics* (pp. 195–224). New York: Praeger.

Stainbrook, E. (1968). Human needs and the natural environment. In *Man and nature in the city*. Washington, DC: U.S. Department of the Interior, Bureau of Sport Fisheries and Wildlife.

Stankey, G.H. (1972). A strategy for the definition and management of wilderness quality. In J.V. Krutilla (Ed.), *Natural environments: Studies in theoretical and applied analysis*. Baltimore, MD: Johns Hopkins University Press.

Stankey, G.H. (1973). *Visitor perception of wilderness recreation carrying capacity* (Research Paper No. INT-142). Ogden, Utah: U.S. Department of Agriculture, Forest Service, Intermountain Forest and Range Experiment Station.

Stankey, G.H., Lucas, R.C., & Lime, D.W. (1976). Crowding in parks and wilderness. *Design and Environment, 7*, 38–41.

Steinitz, C., & Way, D. (1959). A model for evaluating the visual consequences of urbanization. In C. Steinitz & P. Rogers (Eds.), *Qualitative values in environmental planning: A study of resource use in urbanizing watersheds* (Sect. 3). Washington, DC: U.S. Department of the Army, Office of the Chief of Engineers.

Stillman, C.W. (1975). This fair land. In E.H. Zube, R.O. Brush, & J.G. Fabos (Eds.), *Landscape assessment: Values, perceptions, and resources* (pp. 18–30), Stroudsburg, PA: Dowden, Hutchinson, & Ross.

Stillman, C.W. (1977). On the meanings of nature. In *Children, nature and the urban environment* (pp. 25–32), (General Tech. Rep. No. NE-30). Upper Darby, PA: U.S. Department of Agriculture, Forest Service, Northeastern Forest Experiment Station.

Stokols, D. (1978). Environmental psychology. *Annual Review of Psychology, 29*, 253–295.

Stynes, D.J. (1980a). An economic model of deer hunting. *Leisure Sciences, 3*, 99–119.

Stynes, D.J. (1980b). Interrelationships among three outdoor winter sports. In *Proceedings, North American symposium on dispersed winter recreation*. (Educational Series 2-3). St. Paul: University of Minnesota, Office of Special Programs.

Stynes, D.J. (in press). Tourism market segmentation. *Leisure Today.*

Stynes, D.J., & Mahoney, E.M. (1980). *Michigan downhill ski marketing study: Segmenting active skiers*. (Research Rep. No. 391). East Lansing: Michigan State University, Agricultural Experiment Station.

Stynes, D.J., & Szcodronski, K. (1980). Predicting trends in Michigan snowmobiler populations using product life cycle and diffusion of innovations theories. In T.B. Knopp, & L.C. Merriam (Conference coordinators), *Proceedings, North American symposium on dispersed winter recreation* (pp. 148–153), (Educational Series No. 2-3). St. Paul: University of Minnesota, Office of Special Programs.

Tantham, R.L., & Dornoff, R.J. (1971). market segmentation for outdoor recreation. *Journal of Leisure Research, 3*, 5–15.

Thayer, R.L., & Atwood, B.G. (1978). Plants, Complexity and pleasure in urban and suburban environments. *Environmental Psychology and Nonverbal Behavior, 3*, 67–76.

Thoreau, H.D. (1950). *Walden and other writings*. New York: Modern Library. (Original work published 1854).

Thoreau, H.D. (1951). *Cape Cod*. New York: Norton, (Original work published 1864).

Tinsley, H.E.A. (1978). The ubiguitous question of why. In D.J. Brademas (Ed.), *New thoughts on leisure* (pp. 43–62), Champaign, Il: University of Illinois Press.

Tinsley, H.E.A., Barrett, T.C., & Kass, R.A. (1977). Leisure activities and need satisfaction. *Journal of Leisure Research, 9*, 110–120.

Tinsley, H.E.A., & Kass, R.A. (1979). The latent structure of the need satisfying properties of leisure activities. *Journal of Leisure Research, 11*, 278–291.

Tinsley, H.E.A., Kass, R.A., & Driver, B.L. (1981). Reliability and concurrent validity of the recreation experience preference scales. *Educational and Psychological Measurement, 41*, 897–907.

Tinsley, H.E.A., & Tinsley, D.J. (1982). A holistic model of leisure counseling. *Journal of Leisure Research, 14*, 100–116.

Tuan, Y.F. (1971). *Man and nature*. (Commission on college geography resource paper No. 10). Washington, DC: Association of American Geographers.

Tuan, Y.F. (1974). Topophilia: A study of environmental perception, attitudes, and values. Englewood Cliffs, NJ: Prentice-Hall.

Tuan, Y.F. (1975). Place: An experiential perspective. *Geographical Review, 65*, 151–165.

Tuan, Y.F. (1977). Experience and appreciation. In *Children, nature, and the urban environment*. (General Tech. Rep. No. NE-30). Upper Darby, PA: U.S. Department of Agriculture, Forest Service, Northeastern Forest Experiment Station.

Tuan, Y.F. (1979). *Landscapes of fear.* New York: Pantheon.

Twight, B.W., & Catton, W.R., Jr. (1975). The politics of images: Forest managers vs. recreation publics. *Natural Resources Journal, 15*, 297–306.

Twight, B.W., & Paterson, J.J. (1979). Conflict and public involvement: Measuring consensus. *Journal of Forestry, 77*, 771–776.

Twight, B.W., Smith, K.L., & Wissinger, G.H. (1981). Privacy and camping: Closeness to the self versus closeness to others. *Leisure Sciences, 4*, 427–441.

Ullrich, J.R., & Ullrich, M.F. (1976). A multidimensional scaling analysis of perceived similarities of rivers in Western Montana. *Perceptual and Motor Skills, 43*, 575–584.

Ulph, A.M., & Reynolds, I.K. (1979). An activities model of consumer behaviour with special reference to outdoor recreation. *Scottish Journal of Political Economy, 26*, 33–60.

Ulrich, R.S. (1973). *Scenery and the shopping trip: The roadside environment as a factor in route choice* (Michigan Geographical Publication No. 12). Ann Arbor: University of Michigan.

Ulrich, R.S. (1977). Visual landscape preference: A model and application. *Man-Environment Systems, 7,* 279–293.

Ulrich, R.S. (1979). Visual landscapes and psychological well-being. *Landscape Research, 4,* 17–23.

Ulrich, R.S. (1981). Natural versus urban scenes: Some psycho-physiological effects. *Environment and Behavior, 13,* 523–556.

Ulrich, R.S. (1983). Aesthetic and affective response to natural environments. In I. Altman & J.F. Wohlwill (Eds.), *Human Behavior and Environment: Vol. 6. Behavior and the natural environment.* New York: Plenum.

Ulrich, R.S., & Zuckerman, M. (1981). Preference for landscape paintings: Differences as a function of sensation-seeking. Newark: University of Delaware, Department of Geography.

U.S. Department of Agriculture. (1977a). *Children, nature and the urban environment.* (General Tech. Rep. No. NE-30). Upper Darby, PA: Author, Forest Service, Northeastern Forest Experiment Station.

U.S. Department of Agriculture. (1977b). *Proceedings, River recreation management and research symposium.* (General Tech. Rep. No. NC-28). St. Paul, MN: Author, Forest Service, North Central Forest Experiment Station.

U.S. Department of Agriculture. (1980). *Planning for recreation opportunities.* Forest Service Manual 2300, Recreation Management, Chapter 2310. Washington, DC: Author, Forest Service.

U.S. Department of the Interior. (1968). *Man and nature in the city.* Washington, DC: Author, Bureau of Sport Fisheries and Wildlife.

U.S. Department of the Interior. (1979). *The third nationwide outdoor recreation plan: The assessment.* Washington, DC: Author, Heritage Conservation and Recreation Service.

U.S. Department of the Interior. (1980). *Recreation planning* (Manual 8320). Washington, DC: Author, Bureau of Land Management.

van der Smissen, B. (Ed.). (1976). *Research, camping and environmental education.* State College: Pennsylvania State University, College of Health, Physical Education and Recreation.

Van Lier, H.N. (1973). *Determination of planning capacity and layout criteria of outdoor recreation projects.* Wageningen, The Netherlands: Centre for Agricultural Publishing and Documentation.

Vanstone, J.W. (1962). *Point Hope: An Eskimo village in transition.* Seattle: University of Washington Press.

Vaske, J.J., Donnelly, M.P., & Heberlein, T.A. (1980). Perceptions of crowding and resource quality by early and more recent visitors. *Leisure Sciences, 3,* 367–381.

Veal, A.J. (1973). *Perceptual capacity: A discussion and some research proposals* (Working Paper No. 1). Birmingham: University of Birmingham, Center for Urban and Regional Studies.

Wagar, J.A. (1966). Quality in outdoor recreation. *Trends in Parks and Recreation, 3,* 9–12.

Waggener, T.R., & Ceperley, L. (1978). *Economics of outdoor recreation demand: A bibliography of analytical and demand related literature* (Publication No. S-78-2). Seattle: University of Washington, Cooperative Park Studies Unit.

Walton, I. (1793). *The compleat angler or contemplative man's recreation.* London: Hawkins.

Ward, L.M. (1977). Multidimensional scaling of the molar physical environment. *Multivariate Behavioral Research, 12,* 23–42.

Ward, L.M., & Russell, J.A. (1981). The psychological representation of molar physical environments. *Journal of Experimental Psychology, 110,* 121–151.

Watt, K.E.F. (1972). Man's efficient rush toward deadly dullness. *Natural History Magazine, 81,* 74–82.

Wecker, S.C. (1963). The role of early experience in habitat selection by the prairie deer mouse *Peromyscus maniculatis bairdi. Ecological Monographs, 33,* 307–325.

Wellman, J.D. (1979). Recreational response to privacy stress: A validation study. *Journal of Leisure Research, 11,* 61–73.

Wellman, J.D., Dawson, M.S., & Roggenbuck, J.W. (1982). Park managers' predictions of the motivations of visitors to two National Park Service areas. *Journal of Leisure Research, 14,* 1–15.

West, P.C. (1977). A status group dynamics approach to predicting participation rates in regional recreation demand studies. *Land Economics, 53,* 196–211.

Westover, T., & Chubb, M. (1980). Crime and conflict in urban recreation areas. In *Proceedings of the Second Conference on Scientific Research in the National Parks: Vol. 6. Sociology* (pp. 408–425). Washington, DC: U.S. Department of the Interior, National Park Service.

White, G.F. (Ed.). (1974). *Natural hazards: Local, national, global.* New York: Oxford University Press.

White, R.G., & Schreyer, R. (1979). Nontraditional uses of the national parks. *Leisure Sciences, 4,* 325–341.

White, R.W. (1957). Motivation reconsidered: The concept of competence. *Psychological Review, 66,* 297–333.

Williams, D.R. (1980). *Relationship to place as a determinant of outdoor recreation preferences.* Unpublished master's thesis. Utah State University, Logan.

Williams, D.R. (1983). *Cognitive dimensions of recreation engagements: A developmental analysis of recreation participation.* Unpublished doctoral dissertation, University of Minnesota, Minneapolis.

Williams, D.R., & Schreyer, R. (1982). Characterizing the person-environment interaction for recreation resource planning. In J. Frazier & B. Epstein (Eds.), *Proceed-*

ings of Applied Geography Conferences (Vol. 4), (pp. 294–300). Binghamton: State University of New York.

Witt, P.A., & Bishop, D.W. (1970). Situational antecedents to leisure behavior. *Journal of Leisure Research, 2,* 64–77.

Wohlwill, J.F. (1976). Environmental aesthetics: The environment as a source of affect. In I. Altman & J.F. Wohlwill (Eds.), *Human behavior and the environment* (Vol. 1) (pp. 37–86). New York: Plenum.

Wohlwill, J.F. (1983). The concept of nature: A psychologist's view. In I. Altman & J.F. Wohlwill (Eds.), *Human behavior and environment: Behavior and the natural environment (Vol. 6)* (pp. 1–34). New York: Plenum.

Wohlwill, J.F., & Harris, G. (1980). Response to congruity or contrast for man-made features in natural recreation settings. *Leisure Sciences, 3,* 349–365.

Wohlwill, J.F., & Heft, H. (1977). A comparative study of user attitudes towards development and facilities in two contrasting natural recreation areas. *Journal of Leisure Research, 9,* 264–280.

Woodside, A.G., & Ronkainen, I.A. (1980). Tourism management strategies for competitive vacation destinations. In D. E. Hawkins, E. L. Shafer, & J. M. Rovelstad (Eds.), *Tourism, marketing and management issues* (pp. 3–19). Washington, DC: George Washington University Press.

Workman, W.G. (1981). Wilderness recreation: Some management and research challenges. *Recreation Research Review, 6,* 17–22.

Wright, F.L. (1941). *Frank Lloyd Wright on architecture: Selected writings 1894–1940.* New York: Duell, Sloan and Pearce.

Yoesting, P.R., & Burkhead, D.L. (1973). Significance of childhood recreation experience and adult leisure behavior: An exploratory analysis. *Journal of Leisure Research, 5,* 25–36.

Young, J.G. (1982). Psychic freedom in creative persons. *Journal of Creative Behavior, 15,* 179–182.

Zube, E.H. (1974). Cross-disciplinary and intermode agreement on the description and evaluation of landscape resources. *Environment and Behavior, 6,* 69–89.

Zube, E.H. (1976). Perception of landscape and land use. In I. Altman & J.F. Wohlwill (Eds.), *Human Behavior and Environment (Vol. 1).* New York: Plenum.

Zube, E.H., & Pitt, D.G. (1987). Management of natural environments. In D. Stokols & I. Altman (Eds.), *Handbook of Environmental Psychology.* New York: Wiley.

Zube, E.H., Pitt, D.G., & Anderson, T.W. (1975). Perception and prediction of scenic resource values of the Northeast. In E. H. Zube, R. O. Brush, & J. G. Fabos (Eds.), *Landscape assessment: Values, perceptions and resources* (pp. 151–167). Stroudsburg, PA: Dowden, Hutchinson, & Ross.

Zube, E.H., Sell, J.L., & Taylor, J.G. (1982). Landscape perception: Research, application and theory. *Landscape Planning, 9,* 1–33.

THE COMMUNITY PSYCHOLOGY PERSPECTIVE IN ENVIRONMENTAL PSYCHOLOGY

Charles J. Holahan, *Department of Psychology, University of Texas at Austin, Austin, Texas*

Abraham Wandersman, *Department of Psychology, University of South Carolina, Columbia, South Carolina*

21.1. THE NATURE OF THE COMMUNITY PSYCHOLOGY PERSPECTIVE

The community psychology perspective in environmental psychology represents the concerns of a wide field of study that is attempting to understand and solve human problems in the context of the interlocking forces of the social community and the physical environment. At a general level, the community perspective in environmental psychology has come to reflect a merging of the conceptual and methodological concerns of environmental psychology with the social intervention skills and models of community psychology. More specifically, the community perspective informs and broadens environmental psychology with (1) an intervention *goal* that focuses on quality of life, (2) an intervention *target* that encompasses social processes at a variety of levels, and (3) an intervention *method* that relies on primary and secondary prevention. This chapter discusses the body of research, theory, and social intervention efforts that has evolved in the two decades that scientists and professionals have attempted to treat the human contexts where people live and work as a target for social intervention efforts.

In this chapter, we apply an overarching conceptual framework developed by Wandersman, Andrews, Riddle, and Fancett (1983) that serves to link environmental psychology, community psychology, and efforts at preventive interventions (see Figure 21.1). The framework relates the physical environment, perception of the environment, and efforts to cope with environmental demands to the eventual human effects of the environment. In addition, the framework suggests points for preventive interventions in the environment–behavior chain. Environmental psychologists have focused less directly on factors affecting stress and coping than have community psychologists. The framework emphasizes that stress-producing environmental conditions will initiate coping efforts and that these coping attempts may be successful or unsuccessful, culminating in either positive or negative outcomes.

Environmental psychologists have also typically adopted an individual perspective in examining en-vironmental effects, focusing on how the environment affects an individual's behavior. The framework contributes an awareness that group and community effects can also be shaped by environmental influences, including, for example, effects at the social network level, on the demographic makeup of the community, or in organizational patterns and practices. Similarly, resources that can be utilized in the coping process include professional support and social networks and social support, as well as individual resources. Coping attempts, too, may include citizen participation at the group or neighborhood scale, as well as individually based adaptive efforts.

In Figure 21.1, variables traditionally examined in environmental psychology are shown in closed boxes. These involve the environmental antecedents as well as outcome and mediating variables at the individual level. Variables contributed to the framework by the community psychology perspective are shown in hatched boxes. These include social characteristics of facilities or communities, along with outcome and mediating variables that reflect social process at a

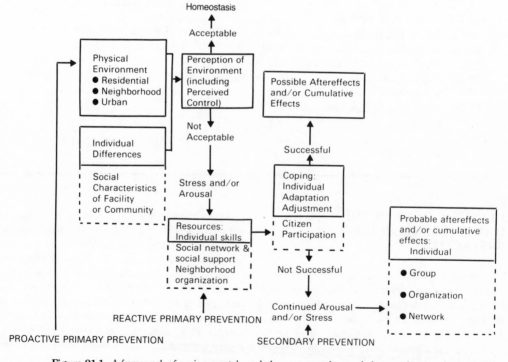

Figure 21.1. A framework of environmental psychology, community psychology, and prevention.

variety of levels. The variables and accompanying arrows at the base of the model identify strategic points for primary and secondary preventive interventions in the environment and behavior chain. The distinction between reactive primary prevention and secondary prevention involves the point in the arousal–stress experience at which the intervention is initiated.

In this chapter, we begin by examining the defining characteristics of the community psychology perspective in environmental psychology at a general level, discussing in turn quality of life, social process, and preventive interventions. Next, we turn to a consideration of specific examples of research and intervention efforts that reflect a merging of the community psychology and environmental psychology viewpoints. Finally, we conclude by exploring future directions for research and social intervention programs within the framework we have presented.

21.1.1. Quality of Life

The community psychology focus in environmental psychology is characterized by a concern with applying psychological knowledge in attempting to resolve the major problems of our society. Since its inception, community psychology has been inherently an applied discipline with a social intervention focus. Community psychology emerged largely as a reaction to limitations in the perspective and practice of clinical psychology. Community psychologists have been critical, for example, of clinical psychology's focus on deficits rather than health, on treatment instead of prevention, and on individuals in contrast to social institutions (Heller & Monahan, 1977). At the same time, however, community psychologists have tended to maintain the *intervention tradition* of clinical psychology, especially as it has been informed by developments in the epidemiology of disease and in the refinement in public health models.

Environmental psychology, in contrast, was motivated by concerns about limitations in the concepts and methods of social psychology and the tendency of social psychologists—as well as other experimentally oriented psychologists—to ignore the role of the physical environment in shaping behavior (Altman, 1976). While broadening their investigative interests to encompass aspects of the molar physical environment, many environmental psychologists have been strongly influenced by the *empirical mode* of mainstream social psychology. Environmental psychology is "problem-oriented" in that it attempts to answer a wide range of practical questions asked by architects, interior designers, and city planners about the social and psychological effects of their designs (Proshansky, 1972). The problem focus in environmental psychology is balanced, however, by an equally strong commitment to theoretically oriented research.

The community perspective reinforces and broadens the problem-focused side of environmental psychology. First, it brings to environmental psychology a guiding commitment to applied problems that stem from its own roots in clinical work and the community mental health movement. In addition, the community perspective contributes a combination of intervention models and skills that have been shaped over a long history of intervention experience. Finally, the community emphasis brings to environmental psychology a set of values that are informed by the commitment to social change, including values relating to "habitability" and "optimization."

Central to the community perspective's interest in social change is a concern with the *habitability* of the built environment, with its "livability" in social and psychological terms. This concern is consistent with environmental psychology's historical roots in the environmental movement of the 1960s (Proshansky & Altman, 1979). The quality of the physical environment and the long-term consequences on the environment of industrial pollution, careless waste disposal, and poor resource management were topics of heated public debate. Earth Day in 1970 represented a dramatic expression of the social consciousness around environmental issues that typified this period. Proshansky and Altman explained that the social concern with people's effects on the environment grew to encompass a similar concern with the long-term effects of the physical environment on human beings. As people became more sensitive to surrounding environmental conditions, they came to recognize more fully the many subtle ways in which the environment can affect human functioning. Similarly, people came to appreciate the important role of social and cultural diversity in person–environment "fit" as well as the community's need for a sense of environmental influence or "empowerment" in dealing with concerns about quality of life at the residential and neighborhood scale (Holahan, 1978).

21.1.2. Social Process and Social Ties

A defining characteristic of the community perspective in environmental psychology in an emphasis on social process as a mediating link in understanding the effects of the physical environment on the behavior and experience of individuals. Community psychology is inherently concerned with examining the ties between the individual and the broader social context and with employing social systems interventions to effect behavioral change (Reiff, 1970). In applying this social process view to environmental psychology, Moos (1976) argued that an adequate conceptualization of the role of the physical environment as a shaper of human behavior needs to take account of a broad array of organizational and societal factors as well as physical ones. The community perspective strives to bring a societal awareness into psychology as well as a psychological appreciation to the conventional study of societal processes. The community perspective represents a domain of inquiry where psychology meets sociology and political science, where the individual interfaces with society (Heller, Price, Reinharz, Riger, & Wandersman, 1984).

This concern with social process and social ties is reflected in the definition of community itself. The community perspective emphasizes a social as well as a physical or geographic definition of community. Bernard (1973) pointed out:

> "Community," as distinguished from "the community," emphasizes the common-ties and social-interaction components of the definition. It is characterized not so much by locale as by "a high degree of personal intimacy, emotional depth, moral commitment, social cohesion, and continuity in time." (Bernard, 1973, p. 2)

In a similar vein, Sarason (1974) suggested that a concern with a "psychological sense of community" is the overarching value that provides direction and justification for community psychology. He defined the sense of community as:

> The perception of similarity to others, as acknowledged interdependence with others, a willingness to maintain this interdependence by giving to or doing for others what one expects from them, the feeling that one is part of a larger dependable and stable structure. (p. 157) (cf. Yankelovich, 1981).

Summarizing an extensive literature relating to sense of community, McMillan and Chavis (in press) identified four key elements in the sense of community. *Membership* involves a sense of belonging and identification with the group, a feeling of relatedness and personal investment in the group. *Influence* involves the individual's ability to affect the group as well as the power of the group to influence the larger systems that encompass it. *Sharing of values* involves the fulfillment of the individual's personal values and needs by the group. *Shared emotional connection* involves an identification with a shared history, fostering a common spiritual bond or "community of spirit."

An appreciation of the complex nature of social process has led community-oriented environmental psychologists to study expressions of social behavior at a variety of levels (see Altman, 1975). This view in environmental psychology parallels Bronfenbrenner's (1977) analysis of the ecology of human development in developmental psychology. According to Bronfenbrenner, an understanding of human development demands going beyond the immediate situation containing the individual to envision the ecological environment as a nested arrangement of contexts that surround the immediate settings in which the person participates. The *microsystem* represents the complex of relations between the developing person and the environment in the immediate setting such as the residential environment. The *mesosystem* involves the interrelations among the major settings containing the developing person, for example, interactions between the family and the school. The *exosystem* represents formal and informal social structures that impinge on the person's immediate settings such as the neighborhood environment. The *macrosystem* reflects the overarching institutional patterns or general prototypes of the culture of which the micro-, meso-, and exosystems are concrete manifestations.

An appreciation of the multilevel complexity of behavior may be applied at a number of points in the environment and behavior chain, including the antecedent environmental conditions, the behavioral outcomes, and the social processes that mediate between environment and behavior. For example, research in environmental psychology has traditionally encompassed environmental factors at the residential, neighborhood, and urban levels, which correspond roughly to the micro-, exo-, and macrosystems discussed by Bronfenbrenner. The community perspective extends this appreciation to encompass the behavioral consequences of physical settings at a variety of social levels that go beyond effects on individual behavior, including effects on the group (Stokols, 1981), organizational (Moos, 1976), and social network (Gottlieb, 1981) levels. The community perspective further broadens this appreciation to include more dynamic social processes such as social support and citizen participation, among the explanatory variables that are seen to mediate the effects of environment on behavior.

21.1.3. Preventive Interventions

The approach to social intervention that characterizes the community focus reflects an underlying concern with *prevention* (Felner, Jason, Moritsugu, & Farber, 1983). Cowen (1980) cites two major factors that have encouraged an interest in prevention among community psychologists:

> The frustration and pessimism of trying to undo psychological damage once it had passed a certain critical point; the costly, time-consuming, culture-bound nature of mental health's basic approaches, and their unavailability to, and ineffectiveness with, large segments of society in great need. (p. 259)

The ultimate goal of prevention, according to Cowen, is "to engineer structures, processes, situations, events, and programs that maximally benefit, both in scope and temporal stability, the psychological adjustment, effectiveness, happiness, and coping skills of large numbers of individuals" (p. 264). According to Catalano and Dooley (1980), *proactive primary prevention* attempts to prevent the occurrence of risk factors, whereas *reactive primary prevention* aims to improve coping resources following exposure to stressors. *Secondary* prevention efforts are initiated when initial coping attempts have been unsuccessful and are directed toward helping individuals cope with continued stress.

Proactive primary prevention in environmental psychology attempts to eliminate or modify environmental stressors or aspects of the built environment that are provoking stress. Interventions might involve, for example, interior and outdoor spaces in public housing environments, high-rise student housing environments, and nursing home design. The utilization of knowledge about physical environments and interventions aimed at physical environments are among the most powerful approaches to proactive primary prevention available for meeting Cowen's criteria of maximum benefit in scope and stability. Swift (1980) noted, for instance, that

> Through application of current knowledge about such stressors as noise, crowding, economic fluctuations, cultural and linguistic alienation and social isolation, the community mental health professional can be instrumental in preventing negative outcomes and promoting healthy environments for persons who will otherwise remain outside the community mental health system. (p. 226)

Reactive primary prevention in environmental psychology is directed toward helping people cope with stress early in the stress process before it produces harmful effects. Secondary preventive efforts are oriented toward helping individuals cope with continued arousal and stress when initial coping efforts prove unsuccessful. Both reactive primary prevention and secondary prevention might be targeted on the mediating processes of social support and personal control that link (or moderate) the stress-adjustment relationship.

Social Support

The prospect of utilizing natural sources of social support as a strategy for helping individuals to deal with existing stresses has been discussed by Caplan (1974). A social support system incorporates an enduring pattern of ties (Caplan, 1974) or a network of relationships (Sarason, 1976), which are an individual's link to essential resources. In times of psychological need, it has been suggested that social support networks can provide emotional sustenance and informational guidance as well as tangible assistance (Caplan, 1974).

Researchers believe that social support serves a particularly important role in enabling the individual to sustain positive psychological adjustment during periods of high "stress" (Dohrenwend, 1978; Moos, 1981). The report of the President's Commission on Mental Health (1978) pointed out that people faced with psychological stresses typically turn first to informal networks of social support, including family, neighbors, and community organizations. A number of research studies have, in fact, indicated that persons experiencing a high level of stress in their lives are protected from harmful psychological consequences when the stress occurs in the presence of adequate levels of social support (Antonovsky, 1979; Berkman & Syme, 1979; Caplan, 1974; Dean & Lin, 1977; Wilcox, 1981).

Personal Control

Strategies to maximize personal control can also be utilized as preventive interventions. Investigators have argued that the negative psychological effects of environmental stressors can be reduced when individuals achieve personal control over the stressful situation (Averill, 1973; Moos, 1981). Wandersman and associates (Wandersman, Andrews, Riddle, & Fancett, 1983) explained that efforts to maximize personal control generally fall into three categories: (1) designing or modifying environments so that they are "responsive" to users' goals, particularly though user and citizen participation in the design process (Carr & Lynch, 1968; Leff, 1978), (2) providing users with information, skills, or resources for coping with the environment (Baron & Rodin, 1978; Cohen & Sherrod, 1978), and (3) increasing users' freedom of choice regarding selection (Korte, 1978) or allowing periodic escapes from environments (Cohen & Sherrod, 1978).

Cohen and Sherrod (1978) suggested that the concept of personal control may be the most significant element in understanding the effects of stressful environments on human behavior. They reasoned that perceived control affects an individual's self-perceptions, expectancies, and motivation, fostering a sense of competence in dealing with the environment. Low levels of personal control, in contrast, result in expectations of ineffectiveness and eventually in learned helplessness (Seligman, 1974, 1975). Laboratory studies of personal control have, in fact, consistently found that personal control attenuates the adverse psychological effects of stressful situations. Empirical evidence that perceived control over aversive events significantly modifies stress reactions has been demonstrated for noise (Glass & Singer, 1972), crowding (Baron & Rodin, 1978; Cohen & Sherrod, 1978), traffic (Novaco, Stokols, Campbell, & Stokols, 1979), and train commuting (Singer, Lundberg, & Frankenhaeuser, 1978).

21.2. AREAS OF COMMUNITY RESEARCH AND INTERVENTION

In this section, we discuss a variety of research and intervention efforts that are characteristic of the community psychology perspective in environmental psychology. The section is organized according to the three levels of physical environment shown in the first block of Figure 21.1 — the residential, neighborhood, and urban environments. Because work on the residential environment has been especially diverse, we have further divided the residential environment subsection into "housing" (e.g., public housing and urban tenement housing) and "specialized residential settings" (e.g., psychiatric hospitals and nursing homes). The section on the neighborhood environment examines both social networks and citizen participation at the neighborhood level. Under the urban environment, we consider urban stressors such as noise, crowding, and forced relocation, along with new town development. Because the extensive literature on crowding encompasses both residential

crowding (e.g., dormitory crowding) and urban stress (e.g., population size and heterogeneity), we deal with aspects of crowding in both of these sections. Each section concludes with an evaluative summary of the research and intervention efforts in that domain.

21.2.1. The Residential Environment

Housing

PUBLIC HOUSING
Based on the awareness that social support plays a key role in psychological adjustment, especially during periods of stress, community-oriented environmental psychologists have engaged in a variety of environmental studies and interventions focused on social support and social networks in residential settings. Because the residential environment can be a stressful setting as well as the context for a variety of interlocking social networks (Fried & Gleicher, 1961; Kelly, 1964), it has been the target for a number of such studies. Of special concern has been the stress associated with high-rise public housing.

One of the most thoroughly investigated case studies of the breakdown of social interaction and social support in high-rise public housing involved the Pruitt-Igoe housing project in St. Louis. The Pruitt-Igoe project consisted of approximately 40 11-story buildings, with a total of almost 3000 apartments. From its inception, the project failed overwhelmingly to meet the social and psychological needs of its residents. Pruitt-Igoe became notorious for its rampant vandalism and constant sense of fear and distrust (Rainwater, 1966).

Yancey (1971) conducted a series of interviews with residents of Pruitt-Igoe in an effort to uncover why the project failed as a human habitat. Yancey discovered that Pruitt-Igoe lacked the cohesion and mutual support that have been found to characterize many central city neighborhoods. In analyzing the cause of this breakdown in natural social support, Yancey concluded that the physical design of the Pruitt-Igoe project had exerted an "atomizing" effect on the informal social networks that typify many inner city neighborhoods. Yancey strongly criticized the philosophy behind Pruitt-Igoe's design that encouraged minimizing "wasted space," that is, semipublic space within the buildings that was outside of individual apartments. He pointed out that an initial review of the Pruitt-Igoe architecture (*Architectural Forum*, 1951) praised the architects for limiting semipublic space between apartments.

Yancey, however, argued for a different design philosophy. He suggested that the designers of multi-family housing for low-income residents, rather than seeing the space between apartments as something to be avoided, should strive to provide an appropriate amount of space between dwelling units. At the core of the problem, he argued, was a lack of adequate "defensible space"—physical space that is characterized by a high level of social responsibility and personal safety. Yancey explained that defensible space is achieved when the semipublic space between apartments is actively used by a large number of residents who assume some personal responsibility and interest in keeping the area safe. The defensible space notion is particularly compelling because it incorporates aspects of both social networks and personal control. He noted that such semipublic space and facilities would offer areas that smaller and identifiable groups of residents could organize with a sense of personal "turf." He emphasized that designers should minimize space in the residential setting that belongs to no one and foster the development of spaces between dwelling units over which groups of residents will share a feeling of informal control.

One feature of high-rise public housing that produces dissatisfaction is the height of the building. A central problem with height involves the high-rise tenants' lack of control over their environments. In his interviews with residents of the Pruitt-Igoe complex, Yancey (1971) found that the architectural design of the building was such that as soon as the child left the confines of the apartment unit, he or she was "out of mother's sight and direct control." Similarly, Heimstra and McFarling (1978) noted that mothers in high rises are not able to supervise their children as well as mothers in ground-level row housing or single-family units. Often the mother restricts her children's activity to the apartment, which reduces her opportunities for social interaction. This decrease in opportunity for social interaction is in sharp contrast to those mothers who live in single-family dwellings or row housing and have an enclosed yard and thus have increased opportunity for informal contact and surveillance. These problems of height have led Cappon (1971) to conclude that high rises are poor environments for families due to the alienation, withdrawal, and psychosomatic symptoms they foster.

Newman (1972) has further developed the notion of defensible space in high-rise public housing environments, emphasizing that by improving the social functioning of public housing the level of crime in these settings can be significantly reduced. Like Yancey, Newman's analysis of the social psychological fail-ure of public housing is related to the social network level. Newman explained that defensible space is a characteristic of housing environments that inhibit criminal activity by presenting a physical setting that gives the impression of an underlying social order that can defend itself. He proposed that central to defensible space is the natural surveillance of the setting by its residents. He defined *natural surveillance* as the ability of residents to observe the public areas of the residential environment while they are engaged in their daily activities. Again, it is clear that natural surveillance depends on both the presence of a social network and the exercise of personal control.

Newman suggested that natural surveillance can be best achieved by designing the residential setting in such a way that people will naturally view the common paths, entry and lobby areas, and outdoor areas in the residential environment. When natural surveillance is achieved, an intruder will perceive that his or her activities are under observation by residents and that unlawful activity will be easily recognized and dealt with. Newman advanced a number of design criteria for achieving natural surveillance. For example, he recommended dividing corridor space within buildings into distinct zones, each with its own small cluster of apartments. This might be done by placing unlocked swinging doors at strategic points along the corridor. Newman also proposed designing buildings so that their lobbies faced toward rather than away from the surrounding city streets and included several apartments near the lobby area in order that their residents might oversee activity in the lobby area.

Newman provided evidence for his hypothesis about the role of defensible space in crime prevention in a comparison of housing projects across the street from each other in New York City that were matched in population characteristics relating to socioeconomic status, family composition, and ethnic background. The high-rise Van Dyke project was "totally devoid of defensible space qualities," whereas the low-rise buildings of the Brownsville project had comparatively more defensible space qualities. The high-rise apartments were found to have 50% more total crime incidents, including over three and one half times as many robberies and 64% more felonies and misdemeanors than the low-rise apartments. Despite Newman's effort to account for the role of population characteristics, his research findings have been criticized on methodological grounds by a number of investigators (see Adams, 1973; Kaplan, 1973; Patterson, 1977).

McCarthy and Saegart (1979) lend some support

to Newman's findings. They found that people in low-rise structures expressed a willingness to prevent vandalism within their buildings, whereas those in high rises indicated minimal willingness, even when the vandalism was on their floor. In addition, those in high-rise structures felt no one would help if they were attacked within their building as contrasted to the low-rise residents who felt someone would respond.

At the primary proactive prevention level, designs incorporating defensible space concepts may reduce alienation, fear, and crime as well as increase residents' sense of control over their residential environment. Dingemans and Schinzel (1977) indicate that several cities and states have adopted policies requiring that plans for new public housing be examined by boards or police departments in light of security design principles. Noting, however, that the "vast majority of new housing being built today is neither high-rise, nor public housing," Dingemans and Schinzel (1977) indicate that preventive design principles must be applied to the design of the most rapidly increasing type of housing—low-rise garden apartments and suburban townhouses. Based on a survey of 75 townhouse developments in northern California, the authors make several recommendations to ensure that "defensible space defects" will not be repeated. These recommendations could be applied to public housing as well. Their suggestions include:

> Subdivide the homes into small clusters of houses that are clearly labeled and share a definite area of open space and parking....Provide better surveillance of the garage entrances and parking spaces....Provide private space around the front and rear of each house, even if it requires subdividing part of the greenbelt....Provide outdoor recreation areas for children that are within the view and territorial domain of individual homes....Place the windows and home face to face with the greenbelts in such a way that residents will actually look out of their windows on a regular and casual basis without feeling that anyone's privacy is being invaded....Establish and use a design bank of superior design ideas. (pp. 35–36)

Research by Zeisel (1971, 1973) involving low-rise tenement housing for a low-income urban population may be extended to consider planning needs in low-rise public housing. Zeisel suggested that a chief problem with urban housing is the design of low-rise tenement housing environments that are inconsistent with the social characteristics of their residents. He argued that a chief cause of such incompatibilities in housing design is the discrepancy in ethnic and social

class background between most architects and the low-income urban populations they design for. Implicit in Zeisel's criticism is the lack of personal control that low-income urban residents are able to exert in the housing design decisions that affect their lives. Zeisel has developed an alternative strategy for reaching decisions in planning urban housing for low-income residents that greatly enhances the control of the residents themselves in the design choices. In a primary proactive intervention design, he designed two tenement buildings for Puerto Rican families in New York City based on a series of detailed observations and in-depth discussions with the future residents themselves. The intervention was oriented toward improving the match between the residential design and social group processes among the users as well as toward allowing users control over the design decisions.

Zeisel found that for these Puerto Rican families, the kitchen tended to serve as a "turnstile" to and from the apartment, with the person in the kitchen acting as the controller. Based on this observation, he designed the new setting so that the person in the kitchen would be the first person to see who entered the apartment and the last person to see who left the apartment. In addition, he discovered that the Puerto Rican residents used the kitchen and living room areas for very different and distinct functions; the kitchen was used for informal gatherings and eating, whereas the living room served more formal functions. For these reasons, Zeisel clearly separated the kitchen and living room in his design. Finally, he found that the families used apartment windows for the observation of, and communication with, ongoing street activities. He thus arranged the new apartment plan so that both the kitchen and living room had windows facing the street. Zeisel contrasted his new plan for a three-bedroom apartment with that of an architect whose design plan reflected his own preconceptions as a middle-class white American. In sharp contrast to Zeisel's plan, the middle-class architect's plan allowed visitors to pass the bedroom area before reaching the kitchen, had the kitchen and living room sharing an open-space area, and had no kitchen windows facing the street. It is clear that the middle-class architect's assumptions about housing were out of step with the spatial needs and behavior patterns of the user group he was designing for.

Finally, we should point out that not all public housing is bad. Good public housing can positively influence health, behavior, and attitudes and can thus be a preventive intervention. Wilner, Walkley, Pinkerton, and Tayback (1962) compared 300 black families who recently moved from substandard private housing (i.e., a slum) to new public housing with 300 families who continued to live in the slum. The researchers found some improvement in those who had moved to new housing, including better relations with neighbors and somewhat higher self-esteem. In addition, children's illnesses were less severe, resulting in better school attendance and better grades.

RESIDENTIAL CROWDING

A particular social psychological problem in housing environments is residential crowding (see also Chapter 10). Because many of the laboratory studies of personal control have involved stresses that are common in overcrowded residential environments such as high levels of density and noise, community-oriented research and interventions involving personal control have focused heavily on residential crowding. Often these interventions have been carried out in a setting that provides an *analog* of the stressful condition of urban residential life — high density student housing.

Research evidence has demonstrated that high levels of crowding in student housing designs that involve long double-loaded corridors and common facilities shared by large numbers of residents, when coupled with an inability on the part of residents to control effectively their social contacts at the group level with other residents, have negative social and psychological effects on residents' functioning (Baum, Aiello, & Calesnick, 1978; Baum, Harpin, & Valins, 1975; Baum & Valins, 1977). Baum and Valins (1977) noted that the architectural design of a college dormitory can affect the residents' perception of crowding and consequently their patterns of interaction. Their hypothesis was that if the architectural design of the dormitory provided semiprivate spaces, small-group formation would be facilitated, and the individual's ability to control unwanted social interaction would be strengthened. The investigators compared students living in a suite design (six people, two in a room, share a bathroom and a lounge) versus a hall or corridor design (17 double-occupancy rooms share a central bathroom and an end hall lounge).

Baum and Valins's findings indicated that residents of suite-designed housing, a design that included more semiprivate space, experienced greater feelings of privacy, less sense of crowding, and less desire to avoid other hall residents. In contrast, the members of corridor design dormitories, with little or no provision of semiprivate space, experienced more feelings of lack of privacy, more sense of crowding, and an increased desire to avoid other hall residents. In addition to residents' self-reports, data from behavioral mapping provided evidence for social withdrawal by the corridor residents. Baum and Valins proposed that "crowding is experienced when high density inhibits individuals' ability to regulate the nature and frequency of their social interaction with others" (1979, p. 138).

Karlin, Epstein, and Aiello (1978) investigated students who had been randomly assigned by the housing office to live in doubles or triples (i.e., two people living in rooms designed for two people vs. three people living in rooms designed for two people) due to a lack of dormitory space. The investigators made assessments early in the first semester and at the end of the semester. Results showed that students living in triples had lower grades and lower performance on complex tasks. Tripled women had more physical and psychological problems than students living in doubles or than tripled men, and all of the female triples dissolved by the end of the first semester. Other researchers have found at the social-group level that students living in socially dense university housing were less willing to mail a stamped letter that had been lost and less willing to join in cooperative group projects than were residents of less dense settings (Bickman, Teger, Gabriele, McLaughlin, Berger, & Sunaday, 1973; Jogenson & Dukes, 1976).

In a field study, Rodin (1976) studied black 6- and 9-year-old boys who lived in a low-income housing project. She reasoned that increases in social density would be related to reduced personal control over such things as achieving desired quiet and going to sleep at a chosen hour. She speculated further that long-term residence in a low-control housing environment would generate symptoms of learned helplessness assessed at the individual level. Rodin found in an experimental game that the low-control youngsters exerted *behavioral control* (using a "choice" key associated with candy or marble rewards on a prearranged schedule) less frequently than children from high-control environments. Moreover, the low-control children were more inclined to use the key to earn experiment-administered candy rather than self-selected candy.

Rodin conducted a follow-up study with a sample of junior-high-school students, some of whom lived in high-density residential environments, whereas others did not. First she asked the youngsters to solve a problem that was either solvable (the control condition) or unsolvable (a condition that can induce learned helplessness). Then she asked both groups to solve a second problem that was solvable. When the first problem had been unsolvable, however, the youngsters from high-density environments performed more poorly on the second problem than youngsters from low-density environments. Rodin concluded that the youngsters from high-density environments had come into her laboratory with learning histories that already included extensive helplessness conditioning. In effect, the high-density subjects began the task with a well-learned expectation that their ability to control events would be low and that they would perform poorly.

Epstein (1981) noted further that the effects of density in residential settings are ameliorated by control and the interpersonal orientation of the group (e.g., competition vs. cooperation) and thus group factors can moderate the effects of density. Baum and Davis (1980) conducted an environmental intervention involving primary proactive prevention designed to prevent crowding stress at the group level by allowing residents in a high-rise dormitory more behavioral control over their social contacts with other residents. They were interested in learning how a crowded long-corridor dormitory at a small liberal arts college might be improved through relatively simple design modifications. Initially, the dormitory consisted of a long corridor shared by a single group of over 40 residents. The investigators pointed out that the double-loaded long corridor led to a general loss of personal control over social contacts in the hallway and other shared spaces. They explained that the dormitory's design resulted in students' meeting other residents in the hallway when interaction was unwanted such as when a student desiring to use the bathroom or study lounge encountered another resident with whom he or she was not comfortable.

Baum and Davis carried out a design modification on one floor of the dormitory that involved converting three central bedrooms to lounge space, creating two separate social groups of about 20 students each. In order to evaluate the effects of this design modification, Baum and Davis systematically assessed residents' behavior and experiences during a 3-month period on the modified floor, on another long corridor in the same dormitory that was not changed, and on a short corridor in a comparable dormitory. The investigators found that the design modification in the long corridor significantly improved the social psychological functioning of residents on the remodeled floor.

Students living in the bisected dorm corridor had more positive interaction on the floor, more confidence in their ability to exert control over their social interactions in the dormitory, and less withdrawal in both residential and nonresidential settings. This positive experience was equivalent to the *short*-corridor dorm. The results showed more symptoms of stress, withdrawal, and helplessness on the long corridor. The authors (1980) concluded:

> Direct architectural intervention prevented crowding stress and post stressor effects. In the long run a preventive strategy of the kind taken in the present research may be more beneficial to residents of high-density settings than treatment programs instituted after the problem has been identified. (p. 480)

Another shared space in high-rise student housing where students' behavioral control over their social contacts with other students is limited is the dining commons. Holahan and Wilcox (Holahan, 1977; Holahan & Wilcox, 1977) conducted a primary proactive environmental intervention at the organizational level involving the dining commons of a high-rise dormitory housing 3000 students oriented toward enhancing students' personal control. The investigation allowed student residents to play an active role in determining the nature of the intervention. The researchers began by surveying residents of the dormitory to learn how satisfied or dissatisfied they were with their residential environment. They found that students were especially dissatisfied with the dormitory's lack of privacy and that a particular area of dissatisfaction involved the communal dining area, which students felt was too institutional in appearance and too uncomfortable for socializing.

Based on this information about user dissatisfaction in the setting, the investigators met with student representatives and residence-hall staff in planning design improvements in the dining commons. Attractive and colorfully designed partitions were added to part of the previously open dining room to allow students more personal control over their contacts with other students. Depending on the level of privacy sought, students could join a large group of other students in the traditional open-space areas or select a more private area behind the new partitions to eat alone or engage in a personal conversation with one or more fellow students.

Holahan and Wilcox evaluated the effects of the design changes by systematically observing the behavior of students in the dining area during the semester before and the semester after the intervention. They found that there was significantly more small-group conversation in the dining commons after the design changes were implemented. In addition, to assess students' attitudes about the intervention, the investigators surveyed them during the semester after the design changes had been completed. They found that students were significantly more satisfied with the new dining commons environment than with the previously undifferentiated dining area. Even more important was the fact that the researchers were able to establish a lasting participation process at the organizational level, with the dormitory's administrative staff agreeing to meet regularly with student representatives to discuss students' residential needs.

EVALUATIVE SUMMARY

Research on housing provides an excellent example of work at the interface of community and environmental psychology. This research encompasses all three levels of social process represented as possible outcomes in our framework (see Figure 21.1) — social groups (e.g., Baum & Valins, 1977), social organizations (e.g., Holahan & Wilcox, 1977), and social networks (e.g., Yancey, 1971). The social change focus of the community perspective is evident in the choice of public housing and residential crowding as central research interests, and research in dormitory settings has produced some real environmental change (e.g., Baum & Davis, 1980; Holahan, 1977).

In addition, housing research has addressed particular attention to the processes of social support and personal control that are viewed as key mediating links in our framework. In fact, much of this research focuses simultaneously on support and control, including work on defensible space (e.g., Newman, 1972; Yancey, 1971), social overload in dormitories (e.g., Baum & Davis, 1980), and subcultural needs in tenement housing (e.g., Zeisel, 1971, 1973). Moreover, this research generally includes sound empirical data, though the empirical methods are more rigorous in residential-crowding work (e.g., Rodin, 1976) than in public housing studies (e.g., Newman, 1972).

At the same time, research on housing has notable limitations. A limitation of work directed toward both interior space and outdoor space in high-rise public housing is that the evaluations have focused on the social and psychological limitations of *existing* projects (e.g., McCarthy & Saegert, 1979; Newman, 1972; Yancey, 1971), but the recommendations for change in public housing design have been directed only generally toward architects and urban decision makers for applications in *future* designs. There have been no efforts that we are aware of in environmental psychology to alter the physical environment in existing public housing settings as part of an ongoing evaluation and social change program. Also, although research in high-rise student housing (e.g., Baum &

Valins, 1977; Baum et al., 1978), suggests important directions for applications in urban settings, the differences between the residents of the two types of settings in age, income, education, family composition, and mobility makes generalizations to urban high-rise housing difficult.

It is clear that it is important to consider the moderating effects of the social characteristics of the residents before we develop general principles on the effects of environmental design. Residential design must conform to the behavioral and cultural characteristics of its residents (e.g., Zeisel, 1971, 1973). In addition, group dynamics can play an important role in influencing the effects of a residential environment. Baum and Valins (1977), after reviewing a number of studies on crowding, suggested that the effects of tripling in dorms may be due to the social dynamics of a triad as well as to density.

Finally, in considering intervention strategies, the *process* of designing and implementing the intervention is critical. Although the Baum and Davis (1980) intervention, which bisected a crowded long-corridor dormitory, was designed by experts, the Holahan and Wilcox (1977) intervention in a high-rise dormitory relied on resident input to develop the intervention. This type of participatory process might produce more widespread effects, including increases in social support and social networks among residents as a result of working together on the intervention.

Specialized Residential Settings

PSYCHIATRIC HOSPITALS

Community-oriented research and interventions have also focused on social processes in psychiatric hospital settings. Ironically, many psychiatric hospital environments inhibit the very social behaviors that are the expressed goals of the hospitals' therapeutic programs. Interventions in this area have involved efforts to alter the interior design or furniture arrangements in ongoing psychiatric ward settings in an effort to encourage more social contact and group cooperation on the part of patients. These studies are relevant to secondary prevention and may have important implications for future efforts at primary prevention.

A definitional issue arises with preventive interventions in treatment settings such as mental hospitals. Although traditional definitions of prevention (e.g., Caplan, 1974) relegate all preventive interventions with mental patients as tertiary prevention, these definitions assume interventions at the individual level. However, the community psychology focus on interventions at the organizational and institutional levels creates the possibility for higher order preventive interventions even in traditional treatment settings. Treatment can adversely affect the healing process. An institutionalized atmosphere, ambient and crowding stressors, the disruption of ongoing social relationships, and the inherent dependency of the patient role can aggravate existing illnesses as well as subject individuals to new psychological and physical health threats. Reducing aspects of the hospital environment that exacerbate *existing* illnesses or thwart the recovery process offers a key intervention point for secondary prevention efforts. Eliminating factors in the hospital environment that can precipitate *new* health problems such as physical agitation from hospital crowding and noise or depression from the loss of personal control associated with the patient role, represents a unique opportunity for primary prevention (Winkel & Holahan, 1985).

Goffman (1961) described in poignant terms the almost total loss of personal privacy faced by mental patients. In the hospital, he observed, patients were stripped of personal possessions, physical examinations, and property inspections were conducted at the staff's will, many toilets were without doors, and patients' activities were constantly observed throughout the day. In addition, not only are many total institutions designed without safe, personal territories where users can retreat from the bustle and activity of institutional life, but even articles of personal property may be confiscated to achieve a standardized institutional life. Schwartz (1968) explained that strong feelings of "social nakedness" are experienced by mental patients who are confronted with the total surveillance of their lives.

Sommer and Kroll (1979) conducted a survey study at the institutional level to assess the suitability of the physical environment of a California psychiatric hospital in meeting the social and psychological needs of its patients and staff. A recurring area of discontent with the hospital environment reported by patients concerned their inability to control privacy. Patients felt that the lack of privacy in their sleeping areas and bathrooms was among the worst features of the hospital. Particular complaints concerned the lack of shower curtains and toilet doors in the bathrooms. Similarly, patients were upset about a bathroom design that placed tubs, showers, and open toilets in direct line of sight of the bathroom entrance.

Sommer and Ross (1958) were asked to increase social interaction at the group level among female patients on a geriatric ward in a psychiatric hospital in Saskatchewan, Canada. Although, as part of a recent remodeling, the ward has been cheerfully painted and new furniture had been added in the dayroom, the dayroom was remarkable for its lack of social interaction. The experimenters noted that the chairs there had been arranged in a highly unsocial manner, with most seating shoulder to shoulder along the walls of the room. In a small-scale secondary intervention, the investigators rearranged the chairs in a more social manner in small groupings around tables situated throughout the dayroom. Behavioral observations conducted in the dayroom before and after the change in seating revealed that the amount of social interaction between patients was twice as high under the social arrangement as under the unsocial one.

Holahan (1972) replicated Sommer and Ross's findings in an experimental dayroom in a psychiatric hospital where extraneous environmental influences could be carefully controlled and patients could be randomly assigned to experimental conditions. In an unsocial dayroom arrangement, chairs were placed shoulder to shoulder along the walls of the room in a manner that approximated the unsocial atmosphere that is so often typical of psychiatric hospitals. In contrast, in a social arrangement chairs were situated around small tables in the middle of the room in an effort to environmentally facilitate social interaction among patients. Behavioral observations in the contrasting dayroom settings demonstrated that patients in the social arrangement engaged in significantly more group-level interaction and conversation than did those in the unsocial arrangement. The most pronounced difference between the settings was in conversations that involved more than two persons. Although such multiperson conversations were frequent under the social arrangement, they almost never occurred in the unsocial setting.

Holahan and Saegert (1973) planned and conducted a large-scale secondary prevention involving the physical remodeling of a psychiatric ward in a New York hospital. The remodeling was intended to encourage social involvement and cooperation among patients and to discourage the high level of social withdrawal that had become typical of the ward as well as to engender personal control on the part of the ward staff in the change process. The remodeling involved repainting the ward in bright attractive colors, adding comfortable modern furniture to the ward dayrooms and bedrooms, and creating semiprivate areas in the dormitorylike bedrooms by installing 6-ft-high partitions to divided the bedroom space into two-bed sections.

To evaluate the effects of the design changes at the group level, Holahan and Saegert carried out systematic behavioral observations on the remodeled ward 6 months after the renovation had been completed. In comparison to an unchanged control ward that was identical to the remodeled ward before renovation and that had a similar sample of patients, the newly designed ward showed significantly more social interaction among patients and ward staff members, as well as more socializing between patients and visiting family members and friends.

Holahan (1976a) examined the effects of the ward remodeling in terms of its broader effects at an institutional level on the social system in the hospital. He noted that social effects of the renovation were evident in a number of important, though unanticipated, areas, including role relationships and job investment on the part of ward staff. For example, after the remodeling, ward physicians became more open to feedback from other staff members and more responsive to staff and patient needs. In addition, nurses' aides gained the right to contribute suggestions to therapeutic planning and to openly express their attitudes about ward functioning and patient care to other staff members at all levels.

Whitehead, Polsky, Crookshank, and Fik (1982) also described a secondary prevention intervention involving the redesign of a 30-bed psychiatric unit in an aging federal hospital. In this project, rooms were redesigned to provide a more flexible use of space, ranging from relatively private to relatively public use. In addition, several spaces were designed to encourage and focus social interaction around recreation, work, and other ward activities. Observations of behavior and measures of satisfaction were obtained before and after the ward redesign. Both subjective and objective measures at the individual and group levels indicated that "structural changes were accompanied by increased staff–patient contacts,...a redistribution of patients to areas for socializing and some reduction in the psychopathological behavior exhibited by patients" (Whitehead et al., in press).

The preceding studies focused on the manipulation of furniture and physical space as a means of increasing the social interaction of psychiatric patients and thus preventing isolated, socially withdrawn behavior. Ittelson, Proshansky, and Rivlin (1970), however, approach the problem of passive, withdrawn behavior from the perspective of personal control, asserting that the issue underlying increased social interaction is the patient's "freedom of choice." They discovered sharp behavioral differences between patients of single- and multiple-occupancy rooms. Those patients who occupied a single-occupancy room exhibited a wider range of behavior and less

withdrawn behavior than those patients assigned to multiple-occupancy rooms. Residents who shared rooms were observed spending almost one-half of their time lying on their beds, either asleep or awake. The investigators accounted for this behavior by suggesting that patients within the multiple-occupancy room see their behavioral options as limited and thus are constrained to choose isolated, passive behavior over any other. Some caution should be exercised in interpreting these findings because, as the investigators pointed out, patients' room assignments were not entirely random.

Knight, Zimring, Weitzer, and Wheeler (1978) found similar results in a secondary prevention effort to redesign the living environment in a large state training facility for the developmentally disabled. Two types of renovations of large, open living quarters were performed: one renovation created single or double rooms with doors that could be locked; the second renovation maintained the large sleeping room but 4-1/2-ft partitions were built around the beds. The experiment consisted primarily of sampling social behaviors at the group level of residents both before and after renovation. In addition, residents' behaviors on the renovated wards were compared to the behaviors of residents from an unrenovated control ward. Preliminary reports indicate that residents recognized and used their private spaces when such spaces were well-defined. "Residents were more alert, interacted more with other residents, and used their own space more. These changes were seen despite the very low functional ability of the residents" (Zimring, 1981, p. 154). Zimring suggests that this was due to the environmental design's allowing residents to control their social interaction and their ambient environment (heat, noise, light). Also, an increase in various socially valued activities such as appropriate use of space and respect for the privacy of others occurred both during and following renovation, especially for the occupants of one- and two-person bedrooms.

SHELTERED CARE SETTINGS

Another focus for community-oriented research and interventions has been sheltered care settings for the elderly. Elderly persons are especially vulnerable to the negative social psychological effects of total institutions. The effects of aging on perceptual acuity, physical strength and endurance, and ease of mobility make many environmental features that younger persons may cope with easily a source of special challenge and frustration for the elderly (Carp, 1976; Lawton, 1977). Investigators have been particularly distressed by the debilitating social and psychological consequences for elderly residents of the almost total loss of individual responsibility and personal control that is characteristic of life in many nursing homes and geriatric hospitals (Lawton, 1977; Moos, 1980). Environmental interventions in sheltered-care settings have been directed both toward designing settings that foster personal control and toward helping residents to gain more personal control in traditionally designed settings.

In a primary proactive effort, Lawton (1971, 1979) has encouraged a design philosophy at the institutional level in the Philadelphia Geriatric Center that is oriented toward enhancing residents' sense of personal control. Lawton explained that residents' control can be enhanced by creating designs that generate a range of social options within the setting. For instance, a geriatric setting might be designed with a large communal space for active group participation, a smaller lounge area where more personal conversation might be pursued, and private or semiprivate bedrooms where residents might think, meditate, or read by themselves.

In addition, Lawton suggested that a variety of spaces might be planned in institutional environments that would allow residents to maintain and practice personal skills and competencies and to pursue personal interests or hobbies. For instance, a setting might include facilities for cooking and planning meals; washing, drying, and ironing clothes; and personal activities, crafts, and hobbies. Lawton also encouraged design features that would facilitate recognition and orientation in the environment, permitting residents to function more independently in traveling about the setting. For instance, he noted that at the Philadelphia Geriatric Center's Weiss Institute, which was designed for the needs of older persons with serious behavioral deficits, residents' rooms are color-coded to facilitate recognition, elevator-area colors are different on each floor, large-sized, three-dimensional room numbers are located outside each room, large-lettered names of occupants are affixed to room doors, and large signs and maps indicating the location of important areas are situated on each floor.

Lipman and Slater (1979) have provided architectural plans appropriate for a primary proactive intervention in nursing homes that are intended at the institutional level to minimize residents' dependence on staff and to encourage independent functioning and a sense of personal control. Their plans favor small, group living units that are physically separated from staff accommodations. Staff services are minimized,

and the plans encourage residents to care for themselves in carrying out their daily functions. The authors explained that they sacrificed large communal areas such as a lounge for 20 persons or a dining room for 30 persons, in favor of smaller, dispersed accommodations. For example, a group living unit for 7 persons provides appropriate spaces for residents to engage in a variety of normal day-to-day activities such as preparing their food, eating or socializing in small groups, and toileting and bathing themselves in privacy. The authors noted that in conventional nursing homes, built on an institutional scale, residents need to ask for staff assistance, even for such a simple activity as preparing a cup of tea. In addition, the small-group design separated from staff accommodations encourages residents to provide mutual assistance to one another when help is required instead of relying exclusively on staff support.

Additional interventions have been aimed at fostering policy changes that can enhance residents' feelings of personal control in traditionally designed nursing homes. In a primary reactive intervention conducted in a nursing home in Connecticut, Langer and Rodin (1976) compared a group of residents whose personal control was enhanced with a group whose control remained low. Residents in an *enhanced control* condition were given a talk that emphasized that they were responsible for themselves and were offered plants they could care for themselves. Persons in a *low-control* condition, in contrast, were told that the nursing home staff were responsible for them and then were given plants that were cared for by the staff. Behavioral measures and survey ratings at the individual level revealed that residents in the enhanced control condition, in comparison to the low-control condition, were more improved after 3 weeks in terms of alertness, active participation, and general sense of well-being. In a follow-up evaluation, Rodin and Langer (1977) assessed the long-term effects of their manipulation of personal control in the nursing home 18 months after the initial study. They reported that the positive effects of control on residents' functioning found in the earlier study persisted over the 18-month period.

In a similar primary reactive intervention, Schulz (1976) investigated the effects of increases in both personal control and predictability on the well-being of residents in a retirement home in North Carolina. In a field experiment, he had college students visit the residents under three conditions: (1) residents in a *no-control* condition were visited on a random schedule, (2) persons in a *predictability* condition were informed when a visit would occur and how long it would last, and (3) individuals in a *behavioral control* condition were allowed to determine the frequency and duration of visits. In addition, residents in a fourth condition were not visited and served as a baseline *comparison* group. Schulz found that both the behavioral control and predictability conditions had positive effects assessed at the individual level on the well-being of the elderly residents. Residents in the behavioral control and predictability conditions were more healthy physically, more positive psychologically, and more active than those in the no-control and comparison conditions.

Schulz and Hanusa (1978), however, in evaluating the long-term effects (up to 3-1/2 years) of their intervention program, discovered that the initial beneficial effects of control and predictability on residents' well-being did not persist after the initial study was terminated. To explain the differences in long-term effects between their intervention and that of Langer and Rodin, Schulz and Hanusa drew on recent reformulations of learned helplessness theory that have explained the learned helplessness syndrome in terms of the underlying *attributions* individuals make about the cause of the effectiveness or ineffectiveness of their behavior (Abramson, Seligman, & Teasdale, 1978; Miller & Norman, 1979). They explained that the Langer and Rodin manipulation emphasizing residents' *responsibility for themselves* probably encourages residents to make internal, stable, and global attributions. In contrast, the Schulz manipulation involving a *particular visiting program* probably led residents to make external, unstable, and specific attributions. The authors concluded that, according to the attributional model of learned helplessness, we would expect that the beneficial effects of the Langer and Rodin study would endure after the initial study was terminated, whereas those from the Schulz study would not.

Moos (1980) has developed a comprehensive assessment instrument called the Multiphasic Environmental Assessment Procedure (MEAP), which can be used to evaluate the overall environmental context of institutions for the elderly. The MEAP includes measures of an institution's architectural features, policy orientation, social environment, and resident and staff characteristics. It is appropriate for use in planning for and evaluating the types and levels of resident control that may characterize a setting.

The MEAP's resident control scale affords an assessment of the degree of "behavioral" control available to residents in a facility. This scale measures the extent to which the institution allows residents formal and informal input in running the facility (e.g., resi-

dents help to plan menus and play a role in making the rules about attendance at activities). An index of policy choice assesses the level of "decisional" control residents have by measuring the degree to which the institution provides options from which residents can select individual patterns for daily activities (e.g., residents can choose the times they get up, have meals, and go to bed).

In a study using the MEAP at the institutional level in 93 sheltered-care settings, David, Moos, and Kahn (1981) found that the most notable correlates of community integration (resident participation in activities in the community) were aspects of program social climate such as perceived resident independence and influence, and program policies such as providing mechanisms for resident control of decision making. In contrast, aspects of the physical environment such as neighborhood location, demonstrated little relationship to integration. These results suggest that social rather than physical environmental factors may be the most important barriers to community participation, and they imply that such participation is potentially within the control of facility administrators and staff. In a further application of the MEAP, Moos (1981) found that in facilities that were high in resident choice and control and that had residents with greater functional resources, the cohesion, organization, and pleasantness of the facilities was enhanced beyond what could be expected from relevant environmental and personal factors alone. This interaction between resident choice and control with functional abilities suggests that an increase in resident choice and control may not have beneficial effects in a setting populated by poorly functioning residents who neither want nor are prepared for more responsibility.

EVALUATIVE SUMMARY
Research on specialized residential settings is most impressive for the amount and scope of the environmental change it has produced. Investigators have altered dayroom seating arrangements (Sommer & Ross, 1958), ward physical design (Holahan & Saegert, 1973; Knight et al., 1978; Whitehead, et al., 1982) and physical design at the institutional level (Lawton, 1971, 1979) in real treatment settings. It should be noted, though, that investigators are not in complete agreement on the effects of institutional design and that some discrepancies are apparent such as Lawton's (1971, 1979) encouragement of large communal spaces and Lipman and Slater's (1979) avoidance of them. Design alterations in psychiatric settings have also received strong empirical evalua-

tions (e.g., Holahan & Saegert, 1973), though architectural innovations in sheltered-care settings have often not been systematically evaluated (e.g., Lipman & Slater, 1979).

The chief shortcoming of work in specialized residential settings is in the conceptual scope of the research. Although our framework emphasizes the need for outcome data at multiple levels of social process, the work in psychiatric settings has been almost uniformly restricted to the small-group level (e.g., Holahan, 1972; Holahan & Saegert, 1973; Knight et al., 1978; Sommer & Ross, 1958; Whitehead, et al., 1982). What is even more disappointing is that research evaluating the effects of enhanced personal control in sheltered-care settings has relied solely on outcome data at the individual level (e.g., Langer & Rodin, 1976; Schulz, 1976) as opposed to the group or organizational levels. Moreover, work directed toward enhancing group interaction in psychiatric settings has failed to examine or even to theorize about the underlying psychological needs such as social support that may be met through increased group interaction (e.g., Holahan, 1972; Holahan & Saegert, 1973; Sommer & Ross, 1958).

What is more important is that the community psychology perspective suggests that the effects of architectural interventions in hospital and sheltered-care environments need to be viewed through the complex lens of a broader framework. Wandersman and Moos (1981) discussed how the social characteristics of a treatment environment (program and policy, resident and staff characteristics, and social climate) as well as architectural features can influence outcomes. For example, the issue of control in a hospital environment is complex, involving control by the staff as well as by patients. Because patient control can conflict with staff control, the staff may sometimes resist allowing patients increased control. Holahan (1976a) found that the nursing staff actively resisted an architectural innovation on a psychiatric ward designed to enhance patient privacy because it reduced staff surveillance of patients. Similarly, Curtiss (1976) discussed a token economy program where the hospital staff found it very difficult to allow patients increased control because of a fear that it might weaken the program's effectiveness.

21.2.2 The Neighborhood Environment

Nisbet (1962) indicated that an intermediate structure between the home and the city is needed that would allow individuals to feel meaningfully related to the larger society and would give rise to "the quest for community." The urban neighborhood stands as such an intermediate structure and has received considerable attention in the social science literature—though relatively little from psychology. In this section, although our discussion will include the traditionally defined or macroneighborhood, much of our discussion will focus on a smaller and more local entity—the microneighborhood.

The microneighborhood is a small grouping of houses on one or two blocks. (A block generally refers to both sides of a resident's street; cross streets serve as block boundaries.) The block is a resident's immediate environment, and many residential concerns are located there. Because macroneighborhoods are larger, they are often varied in population, and the boundaries of the neighborhood are often unclear (Taylor, 1982). There may be very different concerns, needs, and interests in different parts of the macroneighborhood. The block is immediate, relatively homogeneous, and its boundaries are clear. It is easy for residents to identify with.

Neighborhoods can be described in terms of their *physical characteristics* such as neighborhood size and area, type and condition of housing, and location and pattern of placement of amenities (Taylor, 1982). Research has related neighborhood physical environment characteristics to crime (e.g., Greenberg, Rohe, & Williams, 1982) and to neighborhood satisfaction (e.g., Lansing, Marans, & Zehner, 1970). Neighborhoods can also be described in terms of their *social organization*. Warren and Warren (1977; Warren, 1981) have developed a typology of neighborhoods based on social organization. The typology has three dimensions: interaction (the degree of social exchange within a neighborhood), identification (the degree of individual identification with the neighborhood), and connections (linkages to the larger community). They found that the social organization of a neighborhood was related to both helping among neighbors and to general well-being.

The physical characteristics of the microneighborhood encompass housing type, quality and design, and street traffic. Several studies have found relationships between characteristics of the physical environment at the microneighborhood level and social interaction. In their classic study, Festinger, Schacter, and Back (1950) found that friendships are influenced by physical (nearness) and functional (shared paths) distance. Similar findings were obtained by Caplow and Forman (1950). However, this relationship is mediated by perceived homogeneity of residents and by their need for friendships (Gans, 1967). Michel-

son (1976) provides a detailed discussion of the relationship of environments, social composition, and
·mutual assistance.

Appleyard and Lintell (1972) found that street traffic at the microneighborhood level was associated
with less social interaction among neighbors, more
territorial withdrawal, and more concerns about
safety. Several studies have found relationships between characteristics of the neighborhood physical
environment and crime-related outcomes. In a study
of 63 housing sites, Newman and Franck (1980) found
that building size and accessibility were related to
crime as well as to fear about crime. A study of
blocks in Baltimore by Taylor, Gottfredson, and
Brower (1980) found that the pressure of real and
symbolic barriers such as fences was related to lower
crime and fear. (See Taylor, 1982, and Chapter 25 in
this volume for a detailed review of neighborhood
physical characteristics and crime.)

Relationships and Networks

The close spatial location of neighbors makes them
particularly unique to perform functions that other
network members would find difficult (Warren, 1981).
According to Unger and Wandersman's (1984) review,
neighboring relations still have a very important place
in many individuals' lives. Several social roles of
neighbors have been described (Keller, 1968; Warren, 1981). Neighbors often serve as support systems for individuals, providing emotional and material
aid. Neighbors have been viewed as natural helpers.
They can provide direct aid such as helping to watch
children or lending tools. Neighbors also provide a
sociability function. The extent to which neighbors
are willing to greet and visit with each other can
serve as a source of social belonging and reduce feelings of social isolation that is fostered in cities.
Neighborhoods and their informal leaders may provide residents with a link to numerous organizations
and services in their larger community. Such aid as
day care may be provided on an informal basis by a
neighbor, or neighbors may serve as referral agents
to existing child-care services. Neighbors may also
join together to exercise their political skills and to
better the quality of their living environment.

Jacobs's (1961) anecdotal observations suggested
an important social psychological role of casual social
contacts among neighbors in the lives of urban residents. A vital aspect of urban social life consists of
casual social contacts between people who meet one
another accidentally, in outdoor public settings, while
they are engaged in daily errands. Jacobs suggests,
in fact, that such informal social contacts in public

settings offer an ideal type of social interchange for
city people, providing a necessary balance between a
highly accessible form of social contact and the individual's need for privacy. Despite the casual nature of
such street contacts, they form an extremely important part of the urbanite's social life, and casual
"sidewalk acquaintanceships" can endure for many
years and even decades. A survey study by Fried and
Gleicher (1961) in Boston's West End offers some
empirical support for Jacobs's views. They found that
a central aspect of residents' attitudes toward their
neighborhood was their feelings of psychological
closeness to their neighbors. Additional empirical
support for Jacobs's position is provided by an observational study in Baltimore's inner city by Brower and
Williamson (1974). Their observations revealed that a
significant amount of social interaction among residents occurred in the area's outdoor public spaces. In
fact, like Jacobs, they discovered that most outdoor
social recreation occurred in informal spaces, mostly
along the street.

At a reactive primary prevention level, an example
offered by Harshbarger (1976) in describing the
psychological effects of a crisis suggests the need to
consider the neighborhood social network in planning
treatment interventions. Harshbarger notes that following the Buffalo Creek flood in which hundreds of
families suddenly lost their homes, priorities among
emergency personnel were (1) clear the debris and
(2) locate quasi-permanent shelter for persons who
lost their homes. The Department of Housing and
Urban Development provided mobile homes to the
survivors. However, when families were assigned to
mobile homes, no attempt was made to cluster residents according to their former neighborhoods; thus
social groupings among the survivors were further
splintered. Harshbarger notes such action, which
impeded natural processes of social support at the
network level, probably negatively affected the individuals' adaptation to the stress. By planning the environment to accommodate existing social networks,
adaptation costs may have been prevented.

Citizen Participation

The community perspective's interest in enhancing
personal control has encouraged research and intervention programs focusing on citizen participation.
Citizen participation is a process in which individuals
share in decision-making roles in the institutions, programs, and environments that affect their lives (Heller et al., 1984). Although citizen participation is relevant to environmental planning (e.g., Wandersman,
1979b) and at the building and urban scales (Rohe,

1985) as well as the neighborhood context, we will concentrate here on citizen participation at the neighborhood level. Increasingly, neighbors are joining together by participating in neighborhood and block organizations to enhance their neighborhood support systems, exercise their political skills to solve neighborhood problems, and as a consequence, better the quality of their living environment (Ahlbrandt & Cunningham, 1979; Boyte, 1980; Rich, 1979, 1980). Minimal estimates of the number of active neighborhood associations existing range from 4000 to 8000 groups. These neighborhood organizations have been successful in tackling such issues as neighborhood preservation, zoning and land use, and crime and safety (Perlman, 1976, 1978). Wandersman (1979b, 1981) has developed frameworks that attempt to systematize theory and research on participation in planning environments and participation in community organizations.

In many cities, block organizations as well as neighborhood organizations are common. The National Commissions on Neighborhoods compiled a list of 8000 neighborhood organizations, and there are 10,000 block organizations in New York City alone (Perlman, 1978). The potential responsivity of a block organization is illustrated in the techniques often used to develop one. Yates (1976) investigated several types of decentralized community structures such as block organizations, advisory boards, multiservice centers, model cities programs, community corporations, and community school boards. He found that block organizations had a higher impact than did other community structures because of several characteristics of the block organizations: (1) task orientation for block organizations is specific but flexible enough to allow block leaders to choose whatever tasks are appropriate to their skills and resources, (2) tasks are usually uncomplicated and their solutions relatively clear-cut, (3) the small scale of block organizations allows for maximum participation and attracts participants because involvement can be perceived to have meaning and importance. Yates (1976, p. 173) concludes that "block associations come closest to resolving the contradiction in collective action by developing small, problem-solving organizations with widespread participation among block residents."

Heller and associates (1984) suggest that community psychology can increase the understanding of citizen participation, community organization, and neighborhoods that is provided by political science, sociology, and social work by applying psychological perspectives, concepts, and methods. The Neighborhood Participation Project (NPP) conducted by Wandersman and his colleagues (Chavis, Stucky, & Wandersman, 1983; Wandersman, 1981; Wandersman & Florin, 1981; Wandersman, Jakubs, & Giamartino, 1981; Unger & Wandersman, 1983) illustrated this contribution. The NPP was a longitudinal study of citizen participation in block organizations that used several levels of analysis. One of the questions investigated concerned identifying the individual characteristic that predict whether or not a resident becomes involved in citizen participation. The literature suggested that traditional demographic and personality variables have limited ability to predict behavior and limited potential for application. Florin and Wandersman (1984) operationalized a Person X situation approach to predicting behavior, based on Mischel's (1973) cognitive social-learning variables. They compared the predictive power of 15 demographic and personality variables with five cognitive social-learning variables (CSLVs) and found that the CSLVs predicted more of the variance. Florin and Wandersman also suggested that the CSLVs are more useful to citizens and professionals interested in increasing participation.

At the organizational level, Giamartino and Wandersman (1983) assessed the relationship between social climate and satisfaction and involvement with the block organization. The results suggested that five aspects of social climate measured by the Group Environment Scale (Moos & Humphrey, 1974) (cohesiveness, task orientation, leader support, leader control, and order and organization) were related to satisfaction and involvement with the organization. In addition, the same social climate variables were strongly related to whether or not the block organization was still meeting 1 year later.

The research knowledge gained through the NPP was later made available by the researchers as feedback to neighborhood residents through a carefully planned workshop format (Chavis et al., 1983). The feedback process enabled the residents to help themselves, engendering a sense of personal control while at the same time facilitating natural processes of social support among neighbors. The education of citizens about social science research may also enhance their competence and lead to empowerment (Rappaport, 1981).

In terms of the preventive focus of our framework, participation as a strategy incorporates a number of prevention principles, including (1) early intervention before symptoms of disorder appear, (2) the potential to affect and involve large numbers of people, (3) belief in the competence of people to help themselves and solve problems, (4) basis in a growth model that assumes that people can change, particularly in response to educative intervention, environments are dynamic, and person–environment interactions can be targeted for positive change; and (5) intervention into natural systems because people are continuously interacting with their environments.

Participation meets Caplan's (1974) criteria for social action as part of a prevention program by (1) attenuating hazardous circumstances (e.g., removing the stress-inducing properties of environments through more satisfactory designs), and (2) providing services to foster healthy coping (e.g., allowing citizens to develop competencies and positive feelings through the process of participation). In addition, participation fosters a sense of personal control over the environment, providing a key strategy for optimizing environments. It enables citizens to influence, plan, and affect the environment, increasing the congruence of the environment with individual needs and values, and fostering satisfaction, responsibility, positive self-concept, and positive behaviors. Finally, participation operates as an expressive force for creating a sense of community and dispelling feelings of social alienation (Chavis, 1983; Langton, 1978).

Naparstek and Biegel (Biegel & Naparstek, 1982; Biegel & Sherman, 1979; Naparstek, Biegel, & Spiro, 1982) developed a neighborhood empowerment program—the Neighborhood and Family Services project—which involved reactive primary prevention in the central city areas of Baltimore and Milwaukee. The project involved ethnic neighborhoods and used social networks to encourage neighborhood-based community mental health services. The neighborhood plays a centrally important role in the project, serving as a vehicle for strengthening lay and professional support networks, human service programming, and citizen–client involvement. In each neighborhood, the project worked through a local community organization. Outgrowths of the project included seminars for clergy, agency, and community, brown-bag luncheons, a "neighborhood and family" picnic, a hotline run by community volunteers, family workshops on coping with stress, family communication workshops, "rap groups" for teenagers, and self-help groups for separated, divorced, and widowed persons. The project was able to simultaneously strengthen both social support and personal control.

Evaluative Summary

Research on the neighborhood environment has appropriately collected outcome data at the social network level (e.g., Biegel & Naparstek, 1982; Wan-

dersman, 1981). Unfortunately, though, although our framework emphasizes the link between physical environment and social processes, much of this work has tended to define neighborhoods in primarily social terms, failing to deal explicitly with the physical properties of neighborhoods at either the conceptual or measurement levels. Although neighborhood participation offers an excellent context for preventive interventions, very little work has been done by community-oriented environmental psychologists in this area. The paucity of empirical work is understandable in light of the physical and temporal complexity of the problem, and the few carefully conducted longitudinal studies that have been undertaken are noteworthy (e.g., Wandersman's Neighborhood Participation Project).

Finally, social intervention efforts involving citizen participation have often reflected an overly optimistic view of people and community change. Constraints that can prevent cooperation and consensus from achieving constructive change may arise from organized opposition as well as from the constraints of time, money, energy, and ability. Those who become involved in community development projects are but a handful of the potential participants available from the citizenry (Biddle & Biddle, 1965). Furthermore, those with severe financial or physical deficits (a problem in any poor community) may be unable to participate (see Heller et al., 1984, for a detailed discussion of the potential and problems of citizen participation).

21.2.3. The Urban Environment

The community psychology perspective's concern with habitability has focused particular concern on the problem of environmental stress. Common views of the city conclude that it fosters negative behavior. Cities are places of stress, tension, fear, complexity, confusion, crime, pollution, and crowding. Empirical evidence verifies that many stimuli identified as potential environmental stressors are more prevalent in cities than in nonurban areas such as noise and density (Stokols, 1979). Yet some social scientists have suggested that the positive social psychological features of cities may have been overlooked (Fischer, 1976; Proshansky, 1978).

Urban Noise

An extensive body of literature in environmental psychology has investigated noise as an urban stressor (Glass & Singer, 1972; see also Chapter 11 in this volume). Researchers have been interested in learning about the potential effects on people's health and behavior of long-term exposure to the noise of heavy traffic, building construction, wailing sirens, and street repair that characterize the urban environment. People's subjective reactions to noise have typically been assessed by community surveys oriented toward particular noise problems such as noise from traffic or from aircraft. Community surveys have generally focused on subjects' reports of "annoyance" as a result of noise. Several surveys have focused on residents' annoyance with traffic noise. Surveys in Great Britain (McKennell & Hunt, 1966) and in the United States (Bolt, Beranek, & Newman, Inc., 1967) have indicated that automobile traffic noise is the most bothersome and most frequently mentioned source of noise in urban settings. In a before/after study in Great Britain, residents were significantly more annoyed by traffic noise after the opening of a nearby highway than they had been before (Lawson & Walters, 1974). Other surveys have been conducted in the general vicinity of major airports throughout the world, including Great Britain (Stockbridge & Lee, 1973), Sweden (Rylander, Sorenson, & Kajland, 1972) and Los Angeles (Burrows & Zamarin, 1972). McLean and Tarnopolsky (1977) conclude that annoyance is related to level of exposure to aircraft noise; 60 to 70% of residents report annoyance in areas of high aircraft noise and only 3 to 4% register annoyance in areas of low aircraft noise.

A growing body of research has shown that aversive noise has deleterious effects on many aspects of social behavior. When Ward and Suedfeld (1973) played taped traffic noise over loudspeakers at selected sites on the campus of Rutgers University, they found that students' classroom participation and attention declined. In a survey of residents of San Francisco, Appleyard and Lintell (1972) discovered that there was little social participation among residents on a street noisy with traffic and a marked tendency to withdraw from the street socially. On a relatively quiet street with light traffic, in contrast, residents had three times as many friends and twice as many acquaintants and showed a strong inclination to engage in the social life of the street. Additional research has shown that noise reduces people's willingness to engage in helping behavior. Matthews and Canon (1975) found that subjects exposed to loud noise were less willing than those who experienced low noise to help an individual pick up accidentally dropped materials in a laboratory setting. When they used a field experimental design, the investigators found that people were less inclined to help

someone pick up accidentally dropped books when a loud lawn mower was running than under quiet conditions. Page (1977) also found that under noisy conditions students were significantly less willing to help another student who had dropped packages or to offer change for a quarter to a student who wanted to make a phone call than were students under low-noise conditions.

Additional research has examined the effects of noise on the learning and performance of school-age children. Cohen, Glass, and Singer (1973) investigated the effects of highway noise on children living in high-rise apartments. Children on the lower (noisier) levels performed significantly more poorly on auditory discrimination and reading tests than children on higher floors. A similar pattern of difficulties was found in children whose classrooms were next to a railroad compared to those whose classes were on the other side of the building (Bronzaft & McCarthy, 1975). Cohen, Evans, Krantz, and Stokols (1980) investigated the effects of airplane noise on children in terms of feelings of personal control, attentional strategies, and physiological processes related to health. They compared children attending schools under the airport corridor of a busy metropolitan airport versus children in quiet schools. The schools were matched for race and social class variables. Students from the noisier schools had higher blood pressure, were more likely to fail on a cognitive task, and were more likely to "give up" before the time to complete the task had elapsed than the children from quiet schools. Some expected differences were not found (e.g., reading scores).

The most obvious, but by no means the easiest, preventive programs involving primarily proactive prevention with urban environmental stressors are efforts to remove the stressor. For example, Bronzaft (1981) evaluated the effects of a noise abatement program in a school located adjacent to a railroad track. She found that reading scores improved after noise control devices were implemented. At the urban scale, such interventions often involve the need to influence the formulation of public policy as it relates to zoning, building codes, and environmental regulations and standards.

The development and application of community surveys of noise annoyance, noise-reduction zoning legislation, and noise-abating design strategies create opportunities for both proactive and reactive primary prevention. For example, Weinstein (1976) argues for the systematic application of psychological measures of noise annoyance in communities that might be adversely affected by a new project such as a highway extension. When an established community stands to be disrupted by a new noise source, he contends, the decision to build or not to build should be based on the needs of the community in question and not on fixed noise standards developed in other settings. Baranek (1966) encouraged the use of zoning legislation to place buffer zones between residential areas and noisy superhighways and airports. He also suggested design strategies that would more effectively insulate against noise such as thicker or multilayered walls, "floating" floors, acoustically insulated ceilings, and better designed ventilation ducts that would reduce the transmission of noise. He notes that many European countries have developed excellent acoustical building codes that have been applied in the major rebuilding programs since World War II. Baranek adds, however, that similar acoustical standards will not be easy to achieve in the United States because each local community establishes its own building codes and because builders in a competitive housing market are often more interested in economic shortcuts than in qualitatively better designs.

Southworth (1969) proposes the innovative design strategy of masking or distracting people's attention from moderate noise by overlapping it with interesting sounds. Southworth points out that the shapes of structures and the wall materials employed along the street can either reduce and absorb noise or create a resounding chamber of amplified noise if they are poorly designed. The use of new types of road surfaces can also serve to reduce traffic noise. Beranek (1966) and Southworth (1969) have urged improvements in the design of transportation equipment that would help to reduce noise. Motor vehicle noise might be reduced by the improved design of engines, mufflers, tires, and noise-dampening housing for engines. Such improvements would be especially beneficial in trucks and buses. Airplane noise might be reduced through the improved design of engines and wings and by silencing devices fitted to the exhaust ports of jet engines. Beranek cautions, however, that such costly design changes will probably not be undertaken until the responsible government agencies establish noise standards for the various transportation modes.

Urban Crowding

The largest body of research on urban stress has focused on the psychological stresses associated with crowding (see also Carp, Chapter 10, this volume). Milgram (1970) discussed information overload as a theoretical model for explaining how city residents cope with urban crowding. In presenting his argument, Milgram drew on and extended the sociological theories of urban life of Wirth (1938) and Simmel (1950). Milgram proposed that urbanites are exposed to information overload from three sources: (1) a large number of people, (2) high population density, and (3) a greatly heterogeneous population. These three features of urban life provide a flood of informational inputs whose rate and quantity exceed the individual's capacity to process them. Milgram argued that the urbanite's effort to adapt to information overload leads to the socially aloof and interpersonally unresponsive stance that often characterizes social life in the city. Long-term adaptation to information overload leads to the development of generalized social norms that curtail and minimize the breadth and intensity of urban social contacts.

A number of environmental psychologists have advanced models of crowding that are based on the notion of information overload. Desor (1972) viewed crowding as excessive stimulation from social factors. Similarly, Esser (1972) suggested that crowding results from information overload from unfamiliar or inappropriate social sources. Rapoport (1975) also envisioned crowding in terms of information processing, proposing that crowding is caused by excessively high social or sensory stimulation. Saegert and associates (Saegert, 1973; Saegert, Mackintosh, & West, 1975) have used the notion of information overload to explain the psychological consequences of social and spatial density. Their own research in a Manhattan department store demonstrated that when social density is high, customers are able to recall fewer details about the store's merchandise and physical layout than when density is low.

Saegert and colleagues (1975) proposed that clear orientation in design elements is essential in overloaded high-density environments. The number of choice points in high-density settings should be low, and paths should be especially clear. The number of signs and messages should not be excessively high in environments that are already overloaded. Stokols (1976) added that the potential negative effects of crowding can be reduced through architectural features that allow people optimum flexibility in coping with changing densities such as movable walls and ceilings.

Rapoport (1975) has suggested several physical properties of settings pertaining to density that affect the likelihood that they will be perceived as crowded. His proposals were based on a belief that certain types of information tend to be interpreted as indications that an environment is densely populated. He noted, for example, that tall buildings tend to indicate a higher density than low buildings even when other information indicates that the two types of settings are equal in density. Rapoport also suggested that the availability of adjacent nonresidential spaces such as parks, pubs, and shops tends to make a residential area seem less dense. Density will also appear to be lower in residential areas where "defenses" are available to control social interaction such as fences, compounds, and courtyards. Finally, settings with natural greenery will be judged as less dense than areas without natural greenery.

Langer and Saegert (1977) carried out a primary reactive preventive intervention aimed at reducing crowding stress in a consumer environment through enhancing people's personal control in the setting. Rather than altering the environment itself, the intervention focused on reducing crowding stress by enhancing people's feelings of cognitive control in the overcrowded context. Drawing on available research concerning stress and health, Langer and Saegert suggested that people can be helped to cope with the stress of crowding by being provided with accurate information about the likely physiological and psychological reactions to crowding. They reasoned that providing people with prior knowledge about the physiological and psychological effects of crowding would help them to develop anticipatory adjustments to the crowded situations.

Langer and Saegert evaluated the effectiveness of this cognitive coping strategy in a field study conducted in New York City supermarkets. They recruited 80 female shoppers and assigned them a task of selecting the most economical product for each item on a prearranged grocery list. The shoppers completed the assigned task under conditions of high and low social density. In addition, half of the subjects were provided with increased cognitive control in the situation by being informed beforehand that the crowded situation might cause them to feel aroused or anxious. Using measures at the individual level, Langer and Saegert found that the aversiveness of the high-density situation was reduced through increased cognitive control. The shoppers who were provided with increased cognitive control felt more comfortable and were able to successfully complete more of the assigned tasks than were subjects who were not provided with prior information.

Urban Renewal and Forced Relocation

Investigators using the community perspective have been interested in evaluating the social psychological consequence of planned urban change. Urban renewal has been suggested as a way of ameliorating

urban stressors such as crowding and noise. Duhl (1963) cautioned, however, that the natural supports that are available to urban residents in their own communities can sometimes be destroyed by slum clearance and urban relocation projects. Fried (1963) interviewed more than 500 residents in Boston's West End both before their move from the West End and after they had been relocated to make room for urban renewal. He had anticipated that residents would report short-term psychological discomfort in response to the crisis of being forced to move. Using measures at the individual level, he discovered instead that they experienced a severe grief reaction, similar to the grief and mourning people experience for a lost loved one. And rather than being transitory, this grief reaction persisted for a long time after residents had resettled in a new neighborhood. In fact, almost 50% of respondents reported feeling sadness or depression up to a year after the move, and 25% of residents still felt sad or depressed 2 years after relocation.

Fried interpreted this grief reaction as a response to the loss of the stable neighborhood social networks that had been a central ingredient in residents' community life. Dislocation from the old neighborhood had fragmented the established networks of easily accessible and familiar interpersonal contacts that were essential to the social life of the West End. Fried found that severe grief reactions were most common among residents who had the most positive feelings about their West End neighbors and was most pronounced among persons who reported that their five closest friends had lived in the West End. The grief reaction that Fried observed in West Enders who were forced to leave their neighborhood is especially understandable because the loss of their established sources of social support occurred simultaneously with the loss of personal control in being forced to move from a familiar setting to a new and unfamiliar residential environment.

Because forced relocation presents a serious psychological threat to a resident's psychological health, patterns of relocation that are oriented toward maintaining and reinforcing the locatee's feeling of social identity should be encouraged. Young and Willmott (1957) encouraged planners to attempt to move residents one block at a time, as established social groups, to avoid destroying the social cohesiveness of the central city. Fried (1963) proposed that rather than demolishing an entire neighborhood at one time, planners might redevelop small parcels of the neighborhood in sequence. This strategy would help the neighborhood to retain its identity during the demolition period and would allow relocated residents to re-settle more easily within the old neighborhood. Hartman (1975) argued that as an alternative to the demolition and rebuilding of inner-city neighborhoods, more effort might be directed toward rehabilitating the already existing housing. This strategy would offer residents the option of remaining in the inner city in decent housing conditions. What is more important is that displacement and relocation stresses could be avoided and a continued sense of neighborhood and community identity could be maintained. Similarly, Swanson and her colleagues (Swanson, Swanson, & Dukes, 1980) encourage the development and systematic evaluation of publicly sponsored programs oriented toward neighborhood rehabilitation and preservation in an effort to minimize the human costs of forced relocation.

The issue involved here is moral and political as well as psychological. Marris (1963) has pointed out that urban renewal typically displaces the poorest of the city's population— cultural and ethnic minorities and immigrant groups. Because relocated families are usually poor, they cannot afford the new housing that replaces their old homes. Most relocated families move to neighborhoods that are similar to the neighborhood that was cleared, to live in substandard housing, usually at higher rents. Hartman (1975) has addressed considerable attention to the human impact of the forced relocation associated with urban renewal. In a scholarly critique of federal housing policy, he concludes that

> Urban renewal...might more properly be labeled a de-housing program. This program was introduced in the 1949 Housing Act as "slum clearance," but was taken over at the local level by those who wished to reclaim urban land occupied by the poor for commercial, industrial, civic, and upper-income residential uses. Over half a million households, two-thirds of them nonwhite and virtually all in the lower income categories, have been forcibly uprooted. A substantial percentage of these persons were moved to substandard and overcrowded conditions and into areas scheduled for future clearance, at a cost of considerable personal and social disruption. (p. 107)

Holahan (1976b) naturalistically observed street life at the social network level in New York City's Lower East Side to investigate the social effects of high-rise housing projects on the social viability of a renewed neighborhood. Based on his findings, Holahan advanced a number of design suggestions of a secondary preventive nature for encouraging outdoor social activity and neighborhood-based social support in urban renewal programs involving high-rise housing projects. He asserted that even an aesthetically attractive environment is not sufficient to encourage outdoor socializing among adults unless the environmental setting is able to support a range of diverse functional activities. He suggested a design approach that would integrate the project with the natural patterns of urban life in the surrounding city environment. Holahan explained that such a design philosophy might include both mixed functional uses of the outdoor space and appropriate design features to facilitate socializing. For example, the design of project space might encourage mixed functional uses—recreational, leisure activities, consumer behaviors, and task-oriented activities— that would attract project residents to use available outdoor space. Then innovative design features in the outdoor setting, such as nooks, benches, tables, and recreational equipment, might be added to support the informal social contact likely to occur between residents who meet accidentally while pursuing diversified tasks in such multifunctional space.

Although large urban renewal projects causing forced relocation of intact neighborhoods have become less frequent, a new form of forced relocation appears to be taking its place— forced relocation due to toxic wastes. The Love Canal community in New York is the most famous case of toxic waste threats to a community (see Levine, 1982). Lois Gibbs (1983), a concerned resident of Love Canal, in a reactive primary prevention effort at the social network level, helped form a neighborhood organization to cope with the problems confronting the community. The organization provided social support and gave the community some power and control over the decisions by local, state, and federal government affecting their lives. More research is needed to study the physical and psychological threats to many other communities caused by toxic wastes as well as the communities' attempts to cope with such threats, as underscored by a recent news item:

> Wednesday, the cheering stopped. The people of Times Beach learned Tuesday that the Reagan administration will spend $33 million to move them away from their contaminated community, but now they face a problem money can't solve.
> They face the death of their town and a future among strangers. (*The State*, February 27, 1983, p. 14-B)

New Towns

Although interventions related to urban renewal typically involve reactive primary prevention and secondary prevention, planned urban change also offers an opportunity for primary prevention. A unique context for proactive primary prevention at the social network level involves the development of new towns and planned communities. In the 1960s and 1970s, there was strong interest in "new towns" and planned communities as an alternative to urban growth and urban sprawl. The urban society was viewed as a cold, impersonal, hectic, polluted, and noisy environment that led to alienation, powerlessness, and lack of a sense of community (e.g., Fromm, 1968; Packard, 1972; Reich, 1970; Slater, 1970). Many urban and social planners (e.g., Hoppenfeld, 1967) attributed these consequences to the piecemeal, haphazard, and impersonal fashion in which many of the environments developed and suggested that comprehensive planning with humanitarian values could alleviate many of these problems.

Planned communities offered an opportunity to start fresh without having to correct the mistakes of the past. New towns were proposed in which thousands of acres of rural land would be built into towns and cities of 15,000 to 100,000. The new towns would incorporate the advanced ideas of physical planning and social planning. The visions for new towns were grand, as described by the developers of the two best known new towns in the United States. According to James Rouse, the developer of Columbia, Maryland:

> Our cities grow by accident, by whim of the private developer and public agencies....By this irrational process, non-communities are born—formless places, without order, beauty or reason, with no visible respect for people or the land....The vast, formless spread of housing, pierced by the unrelated spotting of schools, churches, stores, creates areas so huge and irrational that they are out of scale with people—beyond their grasp and comprehension—too big for people to feel a part of, responsible for, important in....There really can be no other right purpose of community except to provide an environment and an opportunity to develop better people. The most successful community would be that which contributed the most by its physical form, its institutions, and its operation to the growth of people. (Hoppenfeld, 1967, p. 399)

Robert Simon (the developer of the new town of Reston, Virginia) described his plans for the new town of Riverton:

> Picture a community where the homes touch on tree-lined walkways on which you can stroll or jog or bicycle in safety. This unique network of byways leads to shops, schools, parks, and community centers where people of all ages can find opportunities

of many kinds. You are free to pick and choose and experience the good life as you envision it. Baseball, basketball, tennis, golf, swimming, boating and nearly all active pursuits are here to be enjoyed. So are the opportunities for participation in music, drama, dance, crafts, the visual arts, and special study courses. Then there are paths to explore, flowers to grow, shrubs to trim, and the good earth to feel flowing through your fingers....I invite you to discover for yourself what makes Riverton more than just a new place to live...what makes it the way to live. (In Riverton brochure, 1972).

However, the well-intentioned plans of developers and professional planners can go awry. For example, in designing the new town of Columbia, Maryland, the planners wanted to promote interaction, neighboring, and a sense of community. Each house was part of a defined neighborhood, and each neighborhood was to have a neighborhood center, swimming pool, and convenience (grocery) store. The convenience store was to be a 5-min walk or bike ride away that could safely be reached by walkways and bike paths. Therefore, automobile usage could be reduced, interaction between neighbors increased, and children could play a useful role by picking up groceries. However, when people moved in, many preferred a 5-min car ride to the village center that had a large shopping center and supermarket rather than a 5-min walk, and many of the convenience stores went broke. In addition, the planners decided that all of the mailboxes should be centrally located on a block. Social interaction was to have increased when people collected their mail. However, many residents hated the "gang" mailboxes because they preferred privacy and could not go outside in their robes. They protested bitterly, but the planners thought it was a good idea and kept the gang mailboxes. The "expert" design had not taken into account some of the life-style preferences of residents. These examples suggest that well-intentioned plans developed by experts may not work and that the participation of citizens in planning the new town may have avoided problems.

Do new towns actually make a difference in how people live? The amount of research on new towns, in comparison to hype and hope, is small. Burby, Weiss, and colleagues (1975) conducted the most comprehensive study of new communities. They studied 36 communities; 17 were new communities of which 13 were nonfederally assisted (including Columbia, Maryland, and Reston, Virginia), 2 were federally assisted, and 2 were retirement communities. Each of the federally assisted and nonfederally assisted new communities was paired with a significantly less planned conventional community in terms of age, price range, type of housing, and location. The study involved over 7000 interviews with residents, developers, and government officials. The study found generally that new communities provide better facilities but that there were few differences in satisfaction. Specifically, new communities had advantages in the following areas: (1) better land use planning and access to community facilities, (2) reduction in car travel, (3) better recreational facilities, (4) higher ratings of the overall community, and (5) better living environments for low and moderate income households, blacks, and the elderly. There was relatively little difference between new communities and conventional communities in (1) satisfaction to key family goals such as a good place to raise children and convenience to work, (2) evaluations of housing and neighborhood livability, (3) residents' social perceptions (community identity, neighboring) and participation in community life, (4) satisfaction with the quality of life, and (5) satisfaction with public services and government.

The lack of differences in major aspects of quality of life between planned and conventional communities is important to consider because it implies that the effects of physical and social design may be more limited than many planners hope. It is possible that conventional communities may have adopted many of the amenities of planned communities, and that is why there were few differences. However, it is in the area of satisfaction with amenities that differences *do* show up between planned and conventional communities. Rather, Burby, Weiss, and colleagues found that quality of life was most heavily influenced by economic security, family life, personal strengths and values, and friendships. These factors were not heavily influenced by the physical and social design of the new communities.

In the late 1970s, new towns faced two major obstacles. The more concrete problem was economic. First, there was a cash flow gap between investment of money and slow returns from sales of lots and houses. The second was a gap between raised expectations about life in a new community and the actual reality of people's lives. By 1983, many of the 16 federally assisted new communities had defaulted and were sold to private developers who scaled-down plans and dreams (Underhill, 1983, personal communication).

Evaluative Summary

A significant amount of research on the urban environment has appropriately viewed behavioral out-

comes at the social network level (e.g., Gibbs, 1983; Holahan, 1976b; Weinstein, 1976). In terms of our framework, it is disappointing that a large number of studies have also examined the consequences of urban stress only at the level of individual behavior, including research on noise (e.g., Bronzaft, 1981), crowding (e.g., Langer & Saegert, 1977), and forced relocation (e.g., Fried, 1963). Also, although urban stress has received considerable psychological attention (e.g., Glass & Singer, 1972), many of the interventions in this area involve only secondary prevention (e.g., Fried, 1963; Holahan, 1976b), and the only macrointervention that has been examined from the perspective of proactive primary prevention—new town planning—has fallen disappointingly short of its social goals. The new towns represent a bold social experiment that has taught us much about the economic and social realities of building communities. Many of the successful features of new towns can be and have been adopted by smaller communities. Community planners wishing to achieve larger effects on quality of life may need to look at more "radical" designs of community such as the Israeli kibbutz that has communal child rearing and equal sharing of economic resources.

Although our framework emphasizes the importance of the interaction between social characteristics of communities and the physical environment, there has been a surprising tendency to disregard the sociocultural diversity of urban populations in psychological research in this area. For example, investigators proposing noise-abatement programs at the community level (e.g., Beranek, 1966; Southworth, 1969) have not dealt adequately with the need for, and the difficulty of, balancing competing community needs and preferences. Cohen and Weinstein (1981) point out that actual sound level accounts for only 10 to 25% of the variance in measures of noise annoyance, and individual variation in reported annoyance is considerable. McLean and Tarnopolsky (1977) point out that even at the lowest levels of aircraft noise, some people report being annoyed, whereas at the highest noise levels, some people are not annoyed at all. Moreover, competing community needs influence the psychological response to noise such as when a noisy industrial site is perceived as providing jobs for local people.

21.3. FUTURE DIRECTIONS

What are the needs for future research and intervention efforts within the community psychology perspective in environmental psychology? We will address this issue by considering the type of future research that will be needed to increase our understanding of each of the conceptual blocks in our organizing framework (see Fig. 21.1). We will begin by looking at the "input" blocks in the framework (physical environment and social characteristics of the community), move through the "mediating" blocks (perception of environment, resources, and coping), and finally proceed to the "outcome" blocks (aftereffects and cummulative effects). We will conclude by raising a broader issue about the *process* of future research in the community psychology perspective, considering the nature of the relationship between the researcher and the researched.

21.3.1 Broadening Our View of Environment

In the "physical environment" block, we feel that work at the sociological level needs to be more fully represented in community and environmental psychology. Sociological analyses of urban life sometimes coincide and sometimes contrast with psychological views. Much research by environmental psychologists on environmental stressors commonly associated with urban areas such as noise, crowding, and air pollution has generally shown that these stressors cause negative effects. On the other hand, sociologists such as Fischer (1976) and Srole (1976) have suggested that the evidence relating to urban stress is less clear-cut. Fischer (1976) argued that the available research had produced little evidence that the city alters people's basic psychological condition. Srole (1976) compared the data on psychiatric impairment in the classic Midtown Manhattan study with a study of impairment in a rural county in Nova Scotia and found more impairment in the rural area. It is clear that urban environments are highly complex and that a combination of psychological and sociological perspectives will be needed in future research.

The importance of the neighborhood or community as a place also contains divergent sociological and psychological views. Several sociologists have suggested that, as technology, communication, transportation, and life-styles have advanced, neighborhoods, as geographical places, may be losing some of the importance they once had (e.g., Wellman, 1979). Many of the relationships people have and many of the activities people engage in can and do take place outside of the neighborhood. Relatives, friends, work settings, and associations are often located outside

the neighborhood. Keller (1968) has suggested that

> More typical of the realities of this century are those individuals and families seeking more space, better jobs, higher status, or greater amenities. For these people local areas or neighborhoods are but stepping stones—not necessarily devoid of sentimental value—in the pursuit of happiness. Perhaps future research will tell us that twentieth century urban man had a utilitarian rather than a sentimental attitude to the areas in which he resides. (p. 123)

Psychologists Unger and Wandersman (1985), however, offered a somewhat different view in a review of pertinent literature in environmental psychology, community psychology, and sociology. According to them:

> Neighboring involves the social interaction, the symbolic interaction, and the attachment of individuals with the people living around them and the place in which they live. Therefore, while controversies about the importance or lack of importance of the urban neighborhood in today's society are taking place, it is clear that neighboring plays an important role in people's lives. Neighboring shapes perceptions of neighbors, influences social interaction or social isolation, and affects problem solving and neighborhood viability, *whether or not people are actively interacting with their neighbors.* (p. 34)

Unger and Wandersman suggested the need for future research examining the relationships among aspects of the physical environment, social relationships, symbolic cues, and affective attachment to the neighborhood.

21.3.2. The Importance of Culture

In the "social characteristics" block, there is a need to better account for cultural, subcultural, economic, and regional differences in communities. For example, Merry (1981), in her discussion of the defensible space concept, noted that although architectural design is necessary to create spaces that can be defended, it may not be *sufficient* to ensure safety or prevention of crime. Using anthropological participant observations of a small inner-city housing project that conformed to the defensible space design, she observed that several factors are essential for effective defense in addition to design. Within the project she investigated, there was *ethnic heterogeneity* as well as a lack of interaction across ethnic lines. Consequently, each group was unfamiliar and puzzled about the family structure and friendship patterns of the other groups, often resulting in their being unable to identify those who "belonged," and misinterpreting interactions. In addition, defensible space often remained undefended due to fear of retaliation and a sense of futility about calling the police.

At a broader scale, cross-cultural similarities and influences in how people affect their environments and how the physical environment affects people need to be investigated. Although negative effects of noise have been established cross-culturally, other variables such as privacy, crowding, and social interaction are manifested differently and have different meanings in different cultures (Altman & Chemers, 1980). It is important that research be performed to determine the extent to which results found in the United States on environmental characteristics, control, coping, and outcomes are valid for other cultures. To the extent that there are differences, caution tempers our understanding of social process and attempts at intervention.

21.3.3. Types of Personal Controls

In regard to the "perception of the environment" block, it is clear that perception of control is a central concept in much of the literature we have reviewed. Yet control has many meanings, and there are different types of controls. For example, Kaplan and Kaplan (1983) clarify different meanings that have been included under the concept of control. They distinguish between personal control and things being under control (rather than haphazard or random). Kaplan (1982) cites evidence that suggests that it is the latter meaning that is the most critical. Future research is needed to systematically compare different types of perceived controls and to assess their potentially differing effects on people.

Another important distinction involves the level of control. Although research on personal control has demonstrated the important mediating role of perceived control in the human response to stress, the personal control construct in the community perspective is essentially psychological and needs to be broadened to include related constructs at the *sociological* level. For example, the concept of "social control" has increasingly become a focus for studies of urban community development and neighborhood security. Social control is the ability of residents of an area to regulate events and conditions in their neighborhood. Research on the dynamics of neighborhood stability indicates that where social control is weak, communities tend to fall victim to rapid population turnover, loss of local businesses, physical deterioration, and rising crime. By contrast, where residents can exercise some control over the physical develop-

ment of their neighborhood and the behavior of persons in the neighborhood, communities tend to avoid the syndrome of decline because residents have greater confidence in the future of the neighborhood (Ahlbrandt & Brophy, 1975; Ahlbrandt & Cunningham, 1979; Clay, 1979; Goetze, 1979; Henig, 1982; Schoenberg & Rosenbaum, 1980).

The social control perspective has gained increasing acceptance as an approach to understanding the sources and impacts of crime and designing ways in which crime can be prevented by residents themselves (Merry, 1981; Podolefsky & Dubow, 1981; Taylor & Shumaker, 1982). The social control perspective is clearly articulated by Lewis and Salem (1980, 1981). They suggest that crime is just one of a number of social problems that may invade an area, as that area and adjacent areas undergo social change. Neighborhood change results from large-scale social and economic forces that are continually at work in urban areas. This invasion, which can signal a decay of the existing, underlying civic order in the neighborhood, is reflected in the physical decay of property and social disorganization in the community. As fear of victimization increases, residents may withdraw from the very social contact with one another that is necessary for social control, creating a vicious circle in which fear of crime leads to greater opportunities for crime and even higher levels of fear (Garofolo & Laub, 1979).

21.3.4. Measuring Social Support

In the "resources" block, there is a need for stronger methodological procedures for studying social support. Although research on social support confirms its important role in psychological health, research in this area is subject to criticism on methodological grounds (Heller & Swindle, 1983; L. Wandersman, 1982). Measures of social support have typically been developed in an ad hoc fashion to meet the needs of particular studies, resulting in idiosyncratic indexed without established reliability or validity (Andrews, Tennant, Hewson, & Vaillant, 1978; Dean & Lin, 1977). Also little is known about how alternative sources of social support relate to health for different groups of persons. There is a need for reliable and valid measures of different sources of social support.

The availability of stronger indexes of social support might also increase the predictive strength of the social support domain, which has tended to be relatively weak. In addition, a limitation of many studies of social networks and mental health is an inability to exclude the alternative causal explanation that poor adjustment may lead to a breakdown in social contacts (c.f., Heller, 1979; Ilfeld, 1976). Prospective study designs are needed, where the conjoint and separate variability of adjustment and social contacts can be assessed in a longitudinal framework (see Holahan & Moos, 1981).

21.3.5. Steps Toward Environmental Competence

In the "coping" bloc, our framework suggests focuses for future research and interventions directed toward fostering individual and group *coping* efforts in stressful environments. For example, knowledge concerning the ways in which the environment relates to human functioning can be used to teach people how to create, select, and transcend environments; that is, to enhance *environmental competence*. People can be sensitized to the characteristics of varied behavior settings and be taught what to expect and how to cope in these settings. Also those responsible for selecting the environments of others such as social workers who make decisions about community placements, can do so with a greater awareness of the traits or behaviors that alternative environments demand.

At a primary prevention reactive level, strategies to promote positive coping include the targeting of situations or populations for which risk of mental disorder is high. Levi and Anderson (1975) address the issue of high-risk urban situations by calling for a policy that created an "early warning system" that would alert program administrators to the possibility that negative effects may result from impending changes in the population and/or environment. High-risk populations would include those with high rates of generalized low control, including the elderly, the young, the poor, or groups undergoing rapid change such as newcomers from rural or foreign areas.

Research is also needed on citizen participation as it relates to the physical environment. As Wandersman (1979b, 1981) and Heller and colleagues (1984) point out, there is a considerable gap between the positives of participation proposed by the proponents of citizen participation and the empirical evidence of the effects of such participation. Data pertaining to the effects of citizen participation on the development of personal and social controls would be especially relevant to our framework.

21.3.6. A Dynamic View

In the "outcome" blocks of our framework, work in the community psychology perspective has generally succeeded in encompassing social processes at the group, organization, and network levels. Yet there has often been a "static" character to the outcomes studied. Although our framework may appear to have a linear quality, we encourage a *systems oriented* perspective in which the relationship between parts of the framework are dynamic, interactive, and often reciprocal. For example, a feedback loop might go from "outcomes" to "coping" and then back to "physical environment" to reflect *optimization*, which has really not been examined empirically in environmental research. Similarly, in the "physical environment" block, *mesosystem* influences might be represented by reciprocal arrows between the residential, neighborhood, and urban levels. There is also a need for research designs reflecting the dynamic quality of *temporal change* at the residential, neighborhood, and urban levels.

21.3.7. Responsibility and the Research Process

There is a strong tradition in environmental psychology that research be useful and that bridges be built between researchers and practitioners (Altman, 1975). This tradition is influenced by the continued requests of environmental designers and architects for information that can be used to design better environments. However, the methodology of environmental psychology has not fully recognized the values and process of performing research in a community. Except in the area of user participation, it has not explicitly discussed the relationship between the researchers and the researched. For example, what is the obligation of the researcher who has performed a postoccupancy evaluation for the owners of an office building to the workers in the building? Although community psychology does not have definitive answers, several community psychologists have formulated values, principles, and guidelines regarding the research process and the relationship between the researchers and the researched.

The quality of the relationship between the researcher and the participants of a study affects the success of the researchers in collecting reliable and valid data (Heller et al., 1984). The term *experimental colonialism* has sometimes been used to characterize the traditional relationship of scientists to many host communities. Subjects in research can often feel exploited; their time and resources are used in the research, and they often receive little in return (Blauner & Wellman, 1973; Chavis, Stucky, & Boyd, 1980; Montero & Levine, 1977). Some minority and poor communities have concluded that research has brought them little benefit and at times has actually been harmful (Williams, 1980).

Researchers need to find ways to balance their relationship with the participants; they need to give resources and information as well as to take them. For example, Chavis and colleagues (1983) suggested that returning basic research to the community from which it was obtained has the potential for (1) improving the quality of social science research, (2) increasing the potential for the use of research findings, (3) encouraging public support for social science research, and (4) helping people to help themselves.

Research, even nonintervention research, has an impact on the immediate setting and perhaps the broader environment (Trickett, Kelly, & Vincent, 1985). The research can set in motion social occasions, settings, and informal interactions. According to Kelly (1979), "the process of our work is fully as important as the content" (p. 245). Systematic investigation of the process of research (e.g., entry into the system, collection of data) can be important in interpreting results and in illuminating the phenomenon being investigated and the system in which it operates (Cowen & Gesten, 1980). Community and environmental field research will eventually need a systematic body of research that empirically investigates alternative procedures in the research process.

Individually, environmental psychology and community psychology represent some of the most exciting developments in psychology in recent years. The domain of shared inquiry and concern between the two fields identifies a conceptual terrain of uniquely rich potential for investigation and social action. We have presented a framework that may serve to suggest possibilities for cooperative research and social intervention programs. A major goal of this chapter has been to stimulate the curiosity and interest of new investigators who might further the collaborative efforts between environmental and community psychologies.

REFERENCES

Abramson, L.Y., Seligman, M.E.P., & Teasdale, J.D. (1978). Learned helplessness in humans: Critique and reformulation. *Journal of Abnormal Psychology, 87,* 49–74.

Adams, J.R. (1973). Review of defensible space. *Man-Environment Systems, 3,* 267–268.

Ahlbrandt, Jr., R.S., & Brophy, P. (1975). *Neighborhood Revitalization: Theory and Practice.* Lexington, MA: Lexington Books.

Ahlbrandt, Jr., R.S., & Cunningham, J.V. (1979). *A new public policy for neighborhood preservation.* New York: Praeger.

Altman, I. (1975). *The environment and social behavior.* Monterey, CA: Brooks/Cole.

Altman, I. (1976). Privacy: A conceptual analysis. *Environment and Behavior, 8,* 7–31.

Altman, I., & Chemers, M. (1980). *Culture and environment.* Monterey, CA: Brooks/Cole.

Andrews, G., Tennant, C., Hewson, D.M., & Vaillant, G.E. (1978). Life events stress, social support, coping style, and risk of psychological impairment. *Journal of Nervous and Mental Disease, 166,* 307–316.

Antonovsky, A. (1979). *Health, stress and coping.* San Francisco: Jossey-Bass.

Appleyard, D., & Lintell, M. (1972). The environmental quality of city streets: The resident's viewpoint. *Journal of the American Institute of Planners, 38,* 84–101.

Architectural Forum. (1951, April). Slum surgery in St. Louis, pp. 128–136.

Averill, J. (1973). Personal control over aversive stimuli and its relationship to stress. *Psychological Bulletin, 80,* 286–303.

Baron, R.M., & Rodin, J. (1978). Personal control as a mediator of crowding. In A. Baum, J. Singer, & S. Valins (Eds.), *Advances in environmental psychology: Vol. 1. The urban environment.* Hillsdale, NJ: Erlbaum.

Baum, A., Aiello, J.R., & Calesnick, L.E. (1978). Crowding and personal control: Social density and the development of learned helplessness. *Journal of Personality and Social Psychology, 36,* 1000–1011.

Baum, A., & Davis, G.E. (1980). Reducing the stress of high-density living: An architectural intervention. *Journal of Personality and Social Psychology, 38,* 471–481.

Baum, A., Harpin, R.E., & Valins, S. (1975). The role of group phenomena in the experience of crowding. *Environment and Behavior, 7,* 185–198.

Baum, A., & Valins, S. (1977). *Architecture and social behavior: Psychological studies in social density.* Hillsdale, NJ: Erlbaum.

Beranek, L.L. (1966). Noise. *Scientific American, 215,* 66–76.

Berkman, L.F., & Syme, S.L. (1979). Social networks, host resistance, and mortality: A nine-year follow-up study of Alameda County residents. *American Journal of Epidemiology, 109,* 186–204.

Bernard, J. (1973). *The sociology of community.* Glenview, IL: Scott, Foresman.

Bickman, L., Teger, A., Gabriele, T., McLaughlin, C., Berger, M., & Sunaday, E. (1973). Dormitory density and helping behavior. *Environment and Behavior, 5,* 465–490.

Biddle, W.W., & Biddle, L.J. (1965). *The community development process: The rediscovery of local initiative.* New York: Holt, Rinehart & Winston.

Biegel, D., & Naparstek, A. (1982). The neighborhood and

family services project: An empowerment model linking clergy, agency professionals and community residents. In A. Jeger & R. Slotnik (Eds.), *Community mental health and behavioral ecology: A handbook of theory, research and practice*. New York: Plenum.

Biegel, D., & Sherman, W. (1979). Neighborhood capacity building and the ethnic aged. In D. Gelfand & A. Kutzik (Eds.), *Ethnicity and Aging*. New York: Springer.

Blauner, R., & Wellman, D. (1973). Toward the decolonization of social research. In J.A. Ladner (Ed.), *The death of white sociology*. New York: Vintage.

Bolt, Baranek, & Newman, Inc. (1967). *Noise environment of urban and suburban areas*. Washington, DC: Federal Housing Administration.

Boyte, H.C. (1980). *The backyard revolution*. Philadelphia: Temple University Press.

Bronfenbrenner, U. (1977). Toward an experimental ecology of human development. *American Psychologist, 32*, 513–531.

Bronzaft, A.L. (1981). The effect of a noise abatement program on reading ability. *Journal of Environmental Psychology, 1*, 215–222.

Bronzaft, A.L., & McCarthy, D.P. (1975). The effect of elevated train noise on reading ability. *Environment and Behavior, 7*, 517–529.

Brower, S.N., & Williamson, P. (1974). Outdoor recreation as a function of the urban environment. *Environment and Behavior, 6*, 295–345.

Burby, R., Weiss, S.F., et al. (1975, September). *New communities USA: Results of a national study* (Executive Summary). Washington, DC: U.S. House of Representatives, Subcommittee on Housing of the Committee on Banking, Currency and Housing.

Burrows, A.A., & Zamarin, D.M. (1972). Aircraft noise and the community: Some recent survey findings. *Aerospace Medicine, 43*, 27–33.

Caplan, G. (1974). *Support systems and community mental health: Lectures on concept development*. New York: Behavioral Publications.

Caplow, T., & Forman, R. (1950). Neighborhood interaction in a homogeneous community. *American Sociological Review, 15*, 357–366.

Cappon, D. (1971). Mental health in the high rise. *Canadian Journal of Public Health, 62*, 426–431.

Carp, F.M. (1976). Housing and living environments of older people. In R.H. Binstock & E. Shanas (Eds.), *Handbook of aging and the social sciences*. New York: Van Nostrand Reinhold.

Carr, S., & Lynch, K. (1968). Where learning happens. *Daedalus, 17*, 1281–1286.

Catalano, R., & Dooley, D. (1980). Economic change in primary prevention. In R.H. Price, R.F. Ketterer, B.C. Bader, & J. Monahan (Eds.), *Prevention in mental health: Research, policy, and practice*. Beverly Hills, CA: Sage.

Chavis, D.M. (1983). *Sense of community in the urban environment: Benefits for human and neighborhood development*. Unpublished doctoral dissertation, Vanderbilt University, Nashville, TN.

Chavis, D.M., Stucky, P.E., & Boyd, T. (1980). Returning research data: Getting away from experimental colonialism. In R.R. Stough & A. Wandersman (Eds.), *Optimizing environments: Research, practice, and policy*. Washington, DC: Environmental Design Research Association.

Chavis, D.M., Stucky, P.E., & Wandersman, A. (1983). Returning basic research to the community: A relationship between scientist and citizen. *American Psychologist, 38*, 424–434.

Clay, P.L. (1979). *Neighborhood renewal*. Lexington, MA: Lexington Books.

Cohen, S., Evans, G.W., Krantz, D.S., & Stokols, D. (1980). Physiological, motivational and cognitive effects of aircraft noise on children: Moving from the laboratory to the field. *American Psychologist, 35*, 231–243.

Cohen, S., Glass, D.C., & Singer, J.E. (1973). Apartment noise, auditory discrimination, and reading ability in children. *Journal of Experimental Social Psychology, 9*, 407–422.

Cohen, S., & Sherrod, D.R. (1978). When density matters: Environmental control as a determinant of crowding effects in laboratory and residential settings. In L. Severy (Ed.), *Crowding: Theoretical and research implications for population-environment psychology*. New York: Human Sciences Press.

Cohen, S., & Weinstein, N. (1981). Nonauditory effects of noise on behavior and health. *Journal of Social Issues, 37*, 36–70.

Cowen, E.L. (1980). The wooing of primary prevention. *American Journal of Community Psychology, 8*, 253–284.

Cowen, E.L., & Gesten, E.L. (1980). Evaluating community programs: Tough and tender perspectives. In M.S. Gibbs, J.R. Lachenmeyer & J. Sigal (Eds.), *Community Psychology*. New York: Gardner.

Curtiss, S. (1976). Humanism and behaviorism in a state mental hospital. In A. Wandersman, P. Poppen, & D. Ricks (Eds.), *Humanism and behaviorism: Dialogue & growth*. Elmsford, NY: Pergamon.

David, T.G., Moos, R.H., & Kahn, J.R. (1981). Community integration among elderly residents of sheltered care settings. *American Journal of Community Psychology, 9*, 513–526.

Dean, A., & Lin, N. (1977). The stress-buffering role of social support: Problems and prospects for systematic investigation. *Journal of Nervous and Mental Disease, 165*, 403–417.

Desor, J.A. (1972). Toward a psychological theory of crowding. *Journal of Personality and Social Psychology, 21*, 79–83.

Dingemans, D.J., & Schinzel, R.H. (1977). Defensible space design of housing for crime prevention. *Police Chief*, 34–36.

Dohrenwend, B.S. (1978). Social stress and community psychology. *American Journal of Community Psychology, 6*, 1–14.

Duhl, L.J. (Ed.). (1963). *The urban condition*. New York: Basic Books.

Epstein, Y.M. (1981). Crowding stress and human behavior. *Journal of Social Issues, 37*, 126–144.

Esser, A.H. (1972). *A biosocial perspective on crowding*. In J.F. Wohlwill & D.H. Carson (Eds.), *Environment and the social sciences: Perspectives and applications*. Washington, DC: American Psychological Association.

Felner, R.D., Jason, L.A., Moritsugu, J.N., & Farber, S.S. (1983). *Preventive psychology: Theory, research and practice*. New York: Pergamon.

Festinger, L., Schacter, S., & Back, K. (1950). *Social pressures in informal groups*. New York: Harper.

Fischer, C.S. (1976). *The urban experience*. New York: Harcourt Brace Jovanovich.

Florin, P., & Wandersman, A. (1984). Cognitive social learning variables and participation in community development. *American Journal of Community Psychology, 12*, 689–708.

Fried, M. (1963). Grieving for a lost home. In L.J. Duhl (Ed.), *The urban condition*. New York: Basic Books.

Fried, M., & Gleicher, P. (1961). Some sources of residential satisfaction in an urban slum. *Journal of the American Institute of Planners, 27*, 305–315.

Fromm, E. (1968). *The revolution of hope: Toward a humanized technology*. New York: Bantam.

Gans, H.J. (1967). *The Levittowners*. New York: Pantheon.

Giamartino, G., & Wandersman, A. (1983). Organizational climate correlates of viable urban block organizations. *American Journal of Community Psychology, 11*, 529–541.

Gibbs, L.M. (1983). Community response to an emergency situation: Psychological destruction and the Love Canal. *American Journal of Community Psychology, 11*, 116–125.

Glass, D.C., & Singer, J.E. (1972). *Urban stress*. New York: Academic.

Goetze, R. (1979). *Understanding neighborhood change*. Cambridge, MA: Ballinger.

Goffman, E. (1961). *Asylums: Essays on the social situation of mental patients and other inmates*. Garden City, NY: Anchor.

Garofolo, J., & Laub, J. (1979). The fear of crime: Broadening our perspective. *Victimology, 3*, 242–253.

Gottlieb, B.H. (1981). *Social networks and social support*. Beverly Hills, CA: Sage.

Greenberg, S.W., Rohe, W.M., & Williams, J.R. (1982). *Safe and secure neighborhoods: Physical characteristics and informal territorial controls in high and low crime neighborhoods. Final report*. Washington, DC: National Institute of Justice.

Harshbarger, D. (1976). An ecological perspective on disaster intervention. In H.J. Parad, H.L. Resnick, & L. Parad (Eds.), *Emergency and disaster management: A mental health service book*. Bowie, MD: Charles Press.

Hartman, C. (1975). *Housing and social policy*. Englewood Cliffs, NJ: Prentice-Hall.

Heimstra, N.W., & McFarling, L.H. (1978). *Environmental psychology* (2nd ed.). Monterey, CA: Brooks/Cole.

Heller, K. (1979). The effects of social support: Prevention and treatment implications. In A. Goldstein & F. Kanfer (Eds.), *Maximizing treatment gains: Transfer enhancement in psychotherapy*. New York: Academic.

Heller, K., & Monahan, J. (1977). *Psychology and community change*. Homewood, IL: Dorsey.

Heller, K., Price, R., Reinharz, P., Riger, S., & Wandersman, A. (1984). *Psychology and community change* (2nd ed.). Homewood, IL: Dorsey.

Heller, K., & Swindle, R.W. (1983). Social networks, perceived social support, and coping with stress. In R. Felner, L.A., Jason, J. Moritsugu, & S. Farber (Eds.) *Preventive psychology: Theory, research and practice*. Elmsford, NY: Pergamon.

Henig, J.R. (1982). *Neighborhood mobilization: Redevelopment and response*. New Brunswick, NJ: Rutgers University Press.

Holahan, C.J. (1972). Seating patterns and patient behavior in an experimental dayroom. *Journal of Abnormal Psychology, 80*, 115–124.

Holahan, C.J. (1976a). Environmental change in a psychiatric setting: A social systems analysis. *Human Relations, 29*, 153–166.

Holahan, C.J. (1976b). Environmental effects on outdoor social behavior in a low-income urban neighborhood: A naturalistic investigation. *Journal of Applied Social Psychology, 6*, 48–63.

Holahan, C.J. (1977). Consultation in environmental psychology: A case study of a new counseling role. *Journal of Counseling Psychology, 24*, 251–254.

Holahan, C.J. (1978). *Environment and behavior: A dynamic perspective*. New York: Plenum.

Holahan, C.J., & Moos, R.H. (1981). Social support and psychological distress: A longitudinal analysis. *Journal of Abnormal Psychology, 49*, 365–370.

Holahan, C.J., & Saegert, S. (1973). Behavioral and attitudinal effects of large-scale variation in the physical environment of psychiatric wards. *Journal of Abnormal Psychology, 82*, 454–462.

Holahan, C.J., & Wilcox, B.L. (1977). Ecological strategies in community psychology: A case study. *American Journal of Community Psychology, 5*, 423–433.

Hoppenfeld, M. (1967, November). A sketch of the planning-building process for Columbia, Maryland. *Journal of the American Institute of Planners, 33*.

Ilfeld, F. (1976). Methodological issues in relating psychiatric symptoms to social stressors. *Psychological Reports, 11,* 213–218.

Ittelson, W.H., Proshansky, H.M., & Rivlin, L.G. (1970). Bedroom size and social interaction of the psychiatric ward. *Environment and Behavior, 2,* 255–270.

Jacobs, J. (1961). *The death and life of great American cities.* New York: Random House.

Jorgenson, D.O., & Dukes, F.O. (1976). Deindividuation as a function of density and group membership. *Journal of Personality and Social Psychology, 34,* 24–39.

Kaplan, S. (1973). Review of defensible space. *Architectural Forum, 138,* 8.

Kaplan, S. (1983). A model of person-environment compatibility. *Environment and Behavior, 15,* 311–332.

Kaplan, S., & Kaplan, R. (1982). *Cognition and environment: Functioning in an uncertain world.* New York: Praeger.

Karlin, R.A., Epstein, Y.M., & Aiello, J.R. (1978). Strategies for the investigation of crowding. In A. Esser & B. Greenbie (Eds.), *Design for community and privacy.* New York: Plenum.

Keller, S. (1968). *The urban neighborhood: A sociological perspective.* New York: Random House.

Kelly, J.G. (1964). The mental health agent in the urban community. In *Urban America and the planning of mental health services.* New York: Group for the Advancement of Psychiatry.

Kelly, J.G. (1979). "T'aint what you do; it's the way you do it." *American Journal of Community Psychology, 7,* 244–260.

Knight, R.C., Zimring, C.M., Weitzer, W.H., & Wheeler, H.C. (1978). Effects of the living environment on the mentally retarded. In A. Friedman, C. Zimring, & E. Zube (Eds.), *Environmental design evaluation.* New York: Plenum.

Korte, C. (1978). Helpfulness in the urban environment. In A. Baum, J. Singer, & S. Valins (Eds.), *Advances in environmental psychology: Vol. 1. The urban environment.* Hillsdale, NJ: Erlbaum.

Langer, E.J., & Rodin, J. (1976). The effects of choice and enhanced personal responsibility for the aged: A field experiment in an institutional setting. *Journal of Personality and Social Psychology, 34,* 191–198.

Langer, E.J., & Saegert, S. (1977). Crowding and cognitive control. *Journal of Personality and Social Psychology, 35,* 175–182.

Langton, S. (Ed.). (1978). *Citizen participation in America.* Lexington, MA: Heath.

Lansing, J.B., Marans, R.W., & Zehner, R.B. (1970). *Planned residential environments.* Ann Arbor: University of Michigan, Institute for Social Research.

Lawson, B.R., & Walters, D. (1974). The effects of a new motorway on an established residential area. In D.

Canter & T. Lee (Eds.), *Psychology and the built environment.* New York: Wiley.

Lawton, M.P. (1971). The human being and the institutional building. In C. Burnette, J. Lang, & D. Vaschon (Eds.), *Architecture for human behavior: Collected papers from a mini-conference.* Philadelphia: American Institute of Architects, Philadelphia Chapter.

Lawton, M.P. (1977). The impact of the environment on aging and behavior. In J.E. Birren & K.W. Schaie (Eds.), *Handbook of the psychology of aging.* New York: Van Nostrand Reinhold.

Lawton, M.P. (1979). Therapeutic environments for the aged. In D. Canter & S. Canter (Eds.), *Designing for therapeutic environments: A review of research.* Chichester, England: Wiley.

Leff, H.L. (1978). *Experience, environment, and human potentials.* New York: Oxford University Press.

Levi, L., & Anderson, L. (1975). *Psychological stress: Population, environment, and the quality of life.* New York: Spectrum.

Levine, A. (1982). *Love Canal: Science, politics, and people.* Lexington, MA: Lexington Books.

Lewis, D., & Salem, G. (1980). Crime and urban community: Towards a theory of neighborhood security (Final Rep.). Center for Urban Affairs, Northwestern University, Evanston, IL.

Lewis, D., & Salem, G. (1981). Community crime prevention: An analysis of a developing strategy. *Crime and Delinquency, 43,* 405–421.

Lipman, A., & Slater, R. (1979). Homes for old people: Towards a positive environment. In D. Canter & S. Canter (Eds.), *Designing for therapeutic environments: A review of research.* Chichester, England: Wiley.

Marris, P. (1963). A report on urban renewal in the U.S. In L.J. Duhl (Ed.), *The urban condition.* New York: Simon & Schuster.

Matthews, K.E., & Canon, L.K. (1975). Environmental noise level as a determinant of helping behavior. *Journal of Personality and Social Psychology, 32,* 571–577.

McCarthy, D.P., & Saegert, S. (1979). Residential density, social overload, and social withdrawal. In J.R. Aiello & A. Baum (Eds.), *Residential crowding and design.* New York: Plenum.

McKennell, A.C., & Hunt, E.A. (1966). *Noise annoyance in central London.* London: Building Research Station.

McLean, E.K., & Tarnopolsky, A. (1977). Noise, discomfort and mental health: A review of the socio-medical implications of disturbance by noise. *Psychological Medicine, 7,* 19–62.

McMillan, D., & Chavis, D. (in press). A theory of sense of community. *Journal of Community Psychology.*

Merry, S.E. (1981). Defensible space undefended: Social factors in crime control through environmental design. *Urban Affairs Quarterly, 16,* 397–422.

Michelson, W. (1976). *Man and his urban environment: A sociological approach*. Reading, MA: Addison-Wesley.

Milgram, S. (1970). The experience of living in cities. *Science, 167*, 1461–1468.

Miller, III, I.W., & Norman, W.H. (1979). Learned helplessness in humans: A review and attribution-theory model. *Psychological Bulletin, 86*, 93–118.

Mischel, W. (1973). Toward a cognitive social learning reconceptualization of personality. *Psychological Review, 80*, 252–283.

Montero, D., & Levine, G.N. (Eds.). (1977). Research among racial and cultural minorities: Problems, prospects, and pitfalls. *Journal of Social Issues, 33*, 1–222.

Moos, R.H. (1976). *The human context: Environmental determinants of behavior*. New York: Wiley.

Moos, R.H. (1980). *The environmental quality of residential care settings*. Paper presented at the annual conference of the Environmental Design Research Association, Charleston, SC.

Moos, R.H. (1981). A social-ecological perspective on health. In G. Stone, F. Cohen, & N. Adler (Eds.), *Health Psychology*. San Francisco: Jossey-Bass.

Moos, R.H., & Humphrey, B. (1974). *Preliminary manual for Group Environment Scale*. Palo Alto, CA: Consulting Psychologists Press.

Naparstek, A., Biegel, D., & Spiro, H. (1982). *Neighborhood networks for humane mental health care*. New York: Plenum.

Newman, O. (1972). *Defensible space: Crime prevention through urban design*. New York: Macmillan.

Newman, O., & Franck, K.A. (1980). *Factors influencing crime and instability in urban housing developments*. Washington, DC: National Institute of Justice.

Nisbet, R.A. (1962). *Community and power: A study in the ethics of order and freedom*. New York: Oxford University Press.

Novaco, R.W., Stokols, D., Campbell, J., & Stokols, J. (1979). Transportation, stress, and community psychology. *American Journal of Community Psychology, 7*, 361–380.

Packard, V. (1972). *A nation of strangers*. New York: McKay.

Page, R.A. (1977). Noise and helping behavior. *Environment and Behavior, 9*, 311–335.

Patterson, A.H. (1977). Methodological developments in environment-behavioral research. In D. Stokols (Ed.), *Perspectives on environment and behavior*. New York: Plenum.

Perlman, J. (1976). Grassrooting the system. *Social Policy, 7*, 4–20.

Perlman, J. (1978). Grassroots participation from neighborhood to nation. In S. Langton (Ed.), *Citizen participation in America*. Lexington, MA: Heath.

Podolefsky, A., & Dubow, F. (1981). *Strategies for community crime prevention*. Springfield, IL: Thomas.

President's Commission on Mental Health. (1978). *Report to the President from the President's Commission on Mental Health*. Washington, DC: U.S. Government Printing Office.

Proshansky, H.M. (1972). For what are we training our graduate students? *American Psychologist, 27*, 205–212.

Proshansky, H.M. (1978). The city and self-identity. *Environment and Behavior, 10*, 147–170.

Proshansky, H.M., & Altman, I. (1979). Overview of the field. In W. P. White (Ed.), *Resources in environment and behavior*. Washington, DC: American Psychological Association.

Rainwater, I. (1966). Fear and the house-as-haven in the lower class. *Journal of the American Institute of Planners, 32*, 23–31.

Rapoport, A. (1975). Toward a redefinition of density. *Environment and Behavior, 7*, 133–158.

Rappaport, J. (1981). In praise of paradox: A social policy of empowerment over prevention. *American Journal of Community Psychology, 9*, 1–25.

Reich, C. (1970). *The greening of America*. New York: Random House.

Reiff, R. (1970). The need for a body of knowledge in community psychology. In I. Iscoe & C.D. Spielberger (Eds.), *Community psychology: Perspectives in training and research*. New York: Appleton-Century-Crofts.

Rich, R.C. (1979). The roles of neighborhood organization in urban service delivery. *NASPAA Urban Affairs Papers, 1*, 2–23.

Rich, R.C. (1980). The dynamics of leadership in neighborhood organizations. *Social Science Quarterly, 60*, 570–587.

Riverton brochure. (1972). Riverton, VA.

Rohe, W. (1985). Urban planning and mental health. In A. Wandersman & R. Hess (Eds.), *Beyond the individual: Environmental approaches and prevention*. New York: Haworth.

Rodin, J. (1976). Crowding, perceived choice and response to controllable and uncontrollable outcomes. *Journal of Experimental Social Psychology, 12*, 564–578.

Rodin, J., & Langer, E.J. (1977). Long-term effects of a control relevant intervention with the institutionalized aged. *Journal of Personality and Social Psychology, 35*, 897–902.

Rylander, R., Sorensen, S., & Kajland, A. (1972). Annoyance reactions from aircraft noise exposure. *Journal of Sound and Vibration, 24*, 419–444.

Saegert, S. (1978). High-density environments: Their personal and social consequences. In A. Baum & Y.M. Epstein (Eds.), *Human response to crowding*. Hillsdale, NJ: Erlbaum.

Saegert, S., Mackintosh, E., & West, S. (1975). Two studies of crowding in urban public spaces. *Environment and Behavior, 10*, 159–184.

Sarason, S.B. (1974). *The psychological sense of community: Prospects for a community psychology.* San Francisco: Jossey-Bass.

Sarason, S.B. (1976). Community psychology, networks, and Mr. Everyman. *American Psychologist, 31,* 317–328.

Schoenberg, S.P., & Rosenbaum, P.L. (1980). *Neighborhoods that work: Sources for viability in the inner city.* New Brunswick, NJ: Rutgers University Press.

Schulz, R. (1976). Effects of control and predictability on the physical and psychological well-being of the institutionalized aged. *Journal of Personality and Social Psychology, 33,* 563–573.

Schulz, R., & Hanusa, B.H. (1978). Long-term effects of control and predictability-enhancing interventions: Findings and ethical issues. *Journal of Personality and Social Psychology, 38,* 1194–1201.

Schwartz, B. (1968). The social psychology of privacy. *American Journal of Sociology, 73,* 741–752.

Seligman, M.E.P. (1974). Depression and learned helplessness. In R.J. Friedman & M.M. Katz (Eds.), *The psychology of depression: Contemporary theory and research.* New York: Wiley.

Seligman, M.E.P. (1975). *Helplessness.* San Francisco: Freeman.

Simmel, G. (1950). Secrecy and group communication. In K.H. Wolff (Ed. and Trans.), *The sociology of Georg Simmel.* New York: Free Press.

Singer, J., Lundberg, U., & Frankenhaeuser, M. (1978). Stress on the train: A study of urban commuting. In Baum, A., Singer, J., & Valins, S. (Eds.), *Advances in environmental psychology: Vol. 1. The urban environment.* Hillsdale, NJ: Erlbaum.

Slater, P. (1970). *The pursuit of loneliness.* Boston: Beacon.

Sommer, R., & Kroll, B. (1979). Personal privacy in a psychiatric ward setting. *Environment and Behavior, 11,* 114–129.

Sommer, R., & Ross, H. (1958). Social interaction on a geriatrics ward. *International Journal of Social Psychiatry, 4,* 128–133.

Southworth, M. (1969). The sonic environment of cities. *Environment and Behavior, 1,* 49–70.

Srole, L. (1976). The city versus town and country: New evidence on an ancient bias. In L. Srole & A.K. Fischer (Eds.), *Mental health in the metropolis.* New York: Harper.

Stockbridge, H.C.W., & Lee, M. (1973). The psycho-social consequences of aircraft noise. *Applied Ergonomics, 4,* 44–45.

Stokols, D. (1976). The experience of crowding in primary and secondary environments. *Environment and Behavior, 8,* 49–86.

Stokols, D. (1979). A congruence analysis of human stress. In I.G. Sarason & C.D. Spielberger (Eds.), *Stress and anxiety* (Vol. 6). Washington, DC: Hemisphere.

Stokols, D. (1981). Group x place transactions: Some neglected issues in psychological research on settings. In D. Magnusson (Ed.), *Toward a psychology of situations.* Hillsdale, NJ: Erlbaum.

Swanson, D., Swanson, L.A., & Dukes, M.J. (1980). *The evaluation and design of neighborhood preservation strategies to minimize the negative aspects of displacement.* Paper presented at the annual conference of the Environmental Design Research Association, Charleston, SC.

The State (1983, February 27). p. 14-B.

Swift, C. (1980). Primary prevention. In R.H. Price, R.F. Ketterer, B.C. Bader, & J. Monahan (Eds.), *Prevention in mental health: Research, policy and practice.* Beverly Hills, CA: Sage.

Taylor, R.B. (1982). Neighborhood physical environment and stress. In G. Evans (Ed.), *Environmental stress.* Cambridge, England: Cambridge University Press.

Taylor, R.B., Gottfredson, S.D., & Brower, S. (1980). The defensibility of defensible space. In T. Hirschi & M. Gottfredson (Eds.), *Understanding crime.* Beverly Hills, CA: Sage.

Taylor, R.B., & Shumaker, S. (1982). Community crime prevention in review: Questioning implicit assumptions. Paper presented at the Law and Society Association meeting, Toronto, Canada.

Trickett, E., Kelly, J., & Vincent, T. (1985). Community research: Methods, paradigms, and applications. In D. Klein & E. Susskind (Eds.), *Knowledge building in community psychology.* New York: Praeger.

Unger, D.G., & Wandersman, A. (1983). Neighboring and its role in block organizations: An exploratory report. *American Journal of Community Psychology, 11,* 291–300.

Unger, D.G., & Wandersman, A. (1985). The importance of neighboring: The social, cognitive, and affective components of neighboring. *American Journal of Community Psychology, 13,* 139–169.

Wandersman, A. (1979a). User participation: A study of types of participation, effects, mediators and individual differences. *Environment and Behavior, 11,* 185–208.

Wandersman, A. (1979b). User participation in planning environments: A conceptual framework. *Environment and Behavior, 11,* 465–482.

Wandersman, A. (1981). A framework of participation in community organizations. *Journal of Applied Behavioral Science, 17,* 27–58.

Wandersman, A., Jakubs, J., & Giamartino, G. (1981). Participation in block organizations. *Journal of Community Action, 1,* 40–47.

Wandersman, A., Andrews, A., Riddle, D., & Fancett, C. (1983). Environmental psychology and prevention. In R. Felner, L. Jason, J. Moritsugu, & S. Farber (Eds.), *Preventive psychology: Theory, research, and practice.* Elmsford, NY: Pergamon.

Wandersman, A., & Florin, P. (1981). A cognitive social learning approach to the crossroads of cognition, social behavior and the environment. In J. Harvey (Ed.), *Cognition, social behavior and the environment*. Hillsdale, NJ: Erlbaum.

Wandersman, A., & Moos, R.H. (1981). Assessing and evaluating residential environments: A sheltered living environments example. *Environment and Behavior, 13*, 481-508.

Wandersman, L. (1982). An analysis of the effectiveness of parent-infant support groups. *Journal of Primary Prevention, 3*, 99–115.

Ward, L.M., & Suedfeld, P. (1973). Human responses to highway noise. *Environmental Research, 6*, 306–326.

Warren, D.I. (1981). *Helping networks*. Notre Dame, IN: University of Notre Dame Press.

Warren, R., & Warren, D.I. (1977). *The neighborhood organizer's handbook*. Notre Dame, IN: University of Notre Dame Press.

Weinstein, N.D. (1976). Human evaluations of environmental noise. In K.H. Craik & E.H. Zube (Eds.), *Perceiving environmental quality: Research and applications*. New York: Plenum.

Wellman, B. (1979). The community question: The intimate networks of East Yorkers. *American Journal of Sociology, 84*, 1201–1231.

Whitehead, C., Polsky, R.H., Crookshank, C., & Fik, E. (1982). *An ethological evaluation of psychoenvironmental design*. Unpublished manuscript, Los Angeles: University of California, Department of Psychiatry.

Wilcox, B.L. (1981). Social support, life stress, and psychological adjustment: A test of the buffering hypothesis. *American Journal of Community Psychology, 9*, 371–386.

Williams, R.L. (1980). The death of white research in the black community. In R.L. Jones (Ed.), *Black psychology* (2nd ed.), New York: Harper & Row.

Wilner, D.M., Walkley, R.P., Pinkerton, T.C., & Tayback, M. (1962). *The housing environment and family life*. Baltimore, MD: Johns Hopkins Press.

Winkel, G.H., & Holahan, C.J. (1985). The environmental psychology of the hospital: Is the cure worse than the illness? *Prevention in Human Services, 4*, 11–33.

Wirth, L. (1938). Urbanism as a way of life. *American Journal of Sociology, 44*, 1–24.

Yancey, W. (1971). Architecture, interaction and social control. *Environment and Behavior, 3*, 3–21.

Yankelovich, D. (1981). *New rules in American Life: Searching for self-fulfillment in a world turned upside down*. New York: Random House.

Yates, D. (1976). Political innovation and institution building—The experience of decentralization experiments. In D. Yates (Ed.), *Theoretical perspectives on urban politics*. Englewood Cliffs, NJ: Prentice-Hall.

Young, M., & Willmott, P. (1957). *Family and kinship in East London*. New York: Free Press.

Zeisel, J. (1971). Fundamental values in planning with the non-paying client. In C. Burnette, J. Lang, & D. Vaschon (Eds.), *Architecture for human behavior: Collected papers from a mini-conference*. Philadelphia: American Institute of Architects, Philadelphia Chapter.

Zeisel, J. (1973). Symbolic meaning of space and the physical dimension of social relations: A case study of sociological research as the basis of architectural planning. In J. Walton & D. Carns (Eds.), *Cities in change: Studies on the urban condition*. Newton, MA: Allyn & Bacon.

Zimring, C.M. (1981). Stress and the designed environment. *Journal of Social Issues, 37*, 145–171.

Chapter 22

EXTREME AND UNUSUAL ENVIRONMENTS

Peter Suedfeld, *Department of Psychology, University of British Columbia, Vancouver, BC*

Paradoxically environmental psychologists have, to a great extent, ignored the most fascinating environments: those that lie outside the common everyday situations encountered by most of us. Descriptions of how people cope with such conditions attract a much wider and more enthusiastic readership than the painstaking analysis, the meticulous research, and the ingenious theories published in professional journals. As a matter of fact, I suspect that many environmental psychologists themselves enjoy the tales of solitary sailors, polar explorers, and deep-sea divers more than they do the monthly issue of even their favorite scientific periodical.

22.1. RELEVANT DIMENSIONS

The first major problem encountered by anyone who tries to review the literature in this area is that of definitions. It is easy enough to find examples of "extreme and unusual environments"; but both adjectives imply at least quantitative, and perhaps qualitative, characteristics. Many of the situations that we would label this way are in fact customary and moderate for some individuals, and even for entire cultures.

In this section, I shall identify some of the constructs and variables with which the rest of the chapter deals. A consideration of the terms *extreme* and *unusual* will be followed by a look at three kinds of parameters that can be used to delineate how a particular environment fits those terms. Then, four major categories of extreme and unusual environments will be described. As the next section of the chapter will show, previous environmental taxonomies overlap with mine; the essential difference is in how different writers have decided to subdivide the phenomena.

Let us look at some dimensions that appear to be particularly relevant in the consideration of extreme and unusual environments. One relevant point is the common distinction between the "actual" and the "perceived" situations (Magnusson, 1981). The perception of extremeness and unusualness is perhaps an inescapable component of these dimensions; but in general, the perceptions appear to be closely related to reality—that is, to objectively definable parameters. We can separate *extremeness*, which refers to the presence of physical characteristics related to danger and discomfort, from *unusualness*, the novelty of the environment. Both must be evaluated with regard to some specified reference individual or group at some specified time. Both *are* dimensions, along which all environments can be scaled. This chapter will concentrate on those situations that are near the high end of either or both continua.

22.1.1. Physical Parameters

One set of specific categories can be derived from physical characteristics of the environment: temperature, air composition and pressure, humidity, terrain features, day–night (light–dark) cycles, the availability of food, water and shelter, and the presence of toxic objects or substances. Categorization can also proceed along general types of environments, such as natural versus built and rural versus urban (see Sells, 1963).

The extremeness and unusualness of physical features can be grossly ranked as follows:

1. Environments in which survival is impossible without advanced technology, which are highly hazardous, and which are inhabited only on experi-

mental or exploratory bases (e.g., outer space, the ocean floor).

2. Environments in which survival requires special equipment and techniques but which (or counterparts of which) serve as the natural habitat of some human groups (e.g., the Arctic, high mountains, deserts).

3. Environments during and immediately after drastic disruption of their normal attributes that involve a high degree of danger and a major alteration in physical characteristics (e.g., familiar and safe environments transformed by earthquake, hurricane, or battle). This category, related to the study of natural and other disasters, will not be covered in this chapter except to illustrate or reinforce other parts of the relevant literature.

22.1.2. Interactive Parameters

Other factors are related to person–environment interactions. Examples are the availability of information, ease of communication, mobility or physical restriction, degree of complexity in the environment, both at any particular time and as an aspect of environmental change, ease of communication with other people both within and outside the environment, the degree of mobility or physical restriction, status implications of being in the environment, degree of isolation from other members of one's group and from other groups, whether the individual is there voluntarily, actual and expected duration, control, predictability, privacy and territorial integrity, and the extent to which the environment pervades the individual's life.

22.1.3. Psychological Parameters

The last set of dimensions is more individual and internal. These dimensions describe how the individual perceives and copes with the environment, rather than the environment itself. These include such things as how the people in the environment perceive themselves, their degree of preparation, training, and fitness, personality characteristics, affective interactions, group and individual morale, motivation, and cohesiveness, group structure and leadership, and so on.

22.2. ENVIRONMENTAL CATEGORIES

It may be useful here to differentiate four other categories that are related to the antecedents of the individual's encounter with the situation. Note that any combination of the physical, interactive, and psychological parameters described before may be present in specific situations falling into any of the types of antecedents listed next.

A *normal* environment is one where the environment forms the everyday traditional surroundings of a particular group and is designated as extreme because of physical or resource availability characteristics that militate against comfort and survival. Some of *our* accustomed surroundings fit this category. For example, we know that situations characterized by high social density and stimulus input are often stressful and can be both aversive and damaging (Baum & Valins, 1978; Calhoun, 1962; Lipowski, 1971; Suedfeld, 1980; Zuckerman, Persky, Miller, & Levin, 1969). Some such situations, for example in prisons, have attracted research attention. It has also been established that excessive stimulation is the major factor in "brainwashing" or coercive persuasion (Farber, Harlow, & West, 1957; Schein, 1961). But in general, these conditions also describe modern city living, an experience shared by most psychologists. They may therefore not be unusual enough—nor, perhaps because of their familiarity, extreme enough—by our norms to be included in the chapter.

An *instrumental* environment is one where the environment (sometimes physically the same as that mentioned before) is entered by a group or individual in order to achieve some specific substantive goal. As a rule, the participants are either volunteers or at least accede to participation. They know what is going to be encountered; they may be specially selected, trained, and equipped; and to a greater or lesser extent they share a value system that considers the goal to be worth reaching despite discomfort and danger. Examples of these are wintering over in a polar scientific station, exploring unknown territory, or seeking religious enlightenment as a hermit.

A *recreational* environment is one where the environment is voluntarily chosen because it satisfies a desire to achieve something remarkable (climbing Mount Everest or sailing around the world single-handed), or at least gratifying: meeting a challenge successfully, experiencing unspoiled nature, and exploring new sensations and situations. This category cannot always be clearly distinguished from the previous one because motives are often mixed, and the appropriate category for a given environment may depend on circumstances. For example, going on a wilderness hunting trip would be classified as instrumental for a backwoodsman but recreational for a trophy hunter. Unusual events or experiences and unusual environments are also difficult to untangle here (as in some other parts of this chapter).

A *traumatic* environment is one that includes extreme and unusual conditions imposed on an unwilling individual. Again, environments and experiences are mixed together. Because the most dramatic aspects tend to be unrelated to the place per se, however, the coverage of the chapter will not bear heavily on these situations.

I shall distinguish between traumatic environments of two major kinds. "Natural" situations include natural disasters (fire, flood, famine, earthquake, volcanic eruption, tidal wave, tornado, hurricane, etc.) and natural environments into which the individual is precipitated through some disaster (shipwrecked sailors adrift on the ocean or passengers in a crashed airplane isolated in a remote wilderness area). "Man-made" environments are made extreme or unusual through human means—industrial accidents, pollution, explosion, fire. Some medical environments also belong to this category: intensive care units for patients recovering from open heart surgery or the complete immobilization involved in treatment for burns or bone injuries. The last group involves deliberate and hostile environmental designs: concentration camps, war zones, and the like. Because these may differ along the experience, rather than the environment, parameter, the chapter will not treat them in detail.

22.3. ALTERNATIVE TAXONOMIES

Other writers have proposed environmental taxonomies, some of which overlap or cut across the parameters and categories listed before. Others are only partly, if at all, relevant to the topic of the chapter.

Some proposed environmental taxonomies have components relevant to extreme or unusual situations. For example, Sells (1963) listed four major categories: natural aspects of the environment, man-made aspects, task factors, and characteristics of the individuals within the situations. Each of these categories includes dimensions that overlap with ours.

In a 1973 version, Sells concentrated on environments involving social isolation, confinement, or sensory restriction. Although he felt that it was impossible to list all relevant variables, he did note three major dimensions: characteristics of the situation, of the social system, and of individual personality. The first of these is most closely related to our taxonomic area. It includes a mixture between features of the physical environment and others that I categorize as interactive.

Magnusson (1981) considers nine properties of actual situations, most of which I would call interactive, and five person-bound (psychological) properties. He offers another scheme as well: structural characteristics versus content characteristics, the former being more general and quantitative. In the same book, Block and Block (1981) provide one of the few nonintuitive analyses, based on the factorial analysis of a test battery—the California Situational Q-set. Again, what I have called interactive characteristics appear to be the most salient.

Bachrach (1982), dealing specifically with extreme environments, defines them as being hot, dry, wet, cold, high, or characterized by high or low pressure. He also equates extremeness with potential danger and with stressfulness. I would argue that stimulation level should join the physical variables proposed by Bachrach (Suedfeld, 1979).

Stressfulness may be a feature of extreme and unusual environments, as Bachrach suggests, but is clearly an emergent characteristic of particular transactions involving persons and both the physical and nonphysical aspects of situations (Gauvain, Altman, & Fahim, 1983). Even the harshest physical surroundings may not produce stress in a person who is capable of coping with them.

22.4. PLAN OF THE CHAPTER

The great mass of literature in this area is not scientific but autobiographical, historical, anecdotal, and sometimes mythical. It is difficult to feel the impact of the environment on human beings without reading this kind of material. But the personal and the scientific approaches must shed light on each other, rather than being viewed as competing or incompatible. This chapter provides the nomothetic counterpart to the idiographic literature (Allport, 1937).

A case-by-case look at extreme and unusual environments would have to be very long. It would also involve considerable redundancy because of common features. For example, many extreme and unusual environments are geographically remote from more accustomed milieux. The consequences of this fact include difficulty in communicating with one's normal social network and the removal of familiar perceptual and cognitive anchors. Another common characteristic is the involvement of a small group, which must stay together for long periods of time in an essentially monotonous location. The location may be entirely or mostly enclosed because of life-support requirements. These features are experienced by the crews of space capsules, nuclear submarines, small sailing boats, polar scientific stations, and life rafts.

It might be useful to consider an approach other than examining the psychological consequences of a long list of situations. My preference is to examine how basic psychological processes may be modified in environments that are clearly extreme and unusual. The point of this approach is that, as psychologists, we are primarily interested in the interaction between the physical environment and the individual. Perhaps the best way to understand this interaction is by taking the psychological process (dependent variable), rather than the specific environment (independent variable), as the basic unit of analysis.

The processes of interest correspond to broad subdivisions of psychology: the relationship between extreme and unusual environments and aspects of psychophysiology, perception, cognition, emotion, social processes, personality, and mental health. In considering these matters, we should differentiate between experiences and environments, or between events and places. When the consequences, adaptations, and reactions are not place-specific (cf. Russell & Ward, 1982), the appropriate noun to follow the adjectives *extreme* and *unusual* is "experience," not "environment." This chapter will for the most part focus on *environments*. I will ignore extreme and unusual experiences that occur in the normal, modal, or accustomed settings of our society. This is why there is but little mention of prisons and prison camps, war zones, and sites hit by natural disasters. Further I will refer to research with infrahuman animals only when its relevance to human reactions is very clear. The last rule of thumb is a primary focus on environments that exist in the world outside the laboratory.

22.5. PHYSIOLOGICAL AND PSYCHOPHYSIOLOGICAL EFFECTS

These effects must be placed within the context of the extremely wide adaptability and stress resistance of the human species. Some extreme and unusual environments have attributes to which no human group in the history of this species has had to adapt (e.g., weightlessness in space). Other factors have characterized the habitat of various human societies: the ecosystems of the Arctic, of high mountains, of arid lands, of grasslands, and of the humid tropics (Moran, 1979). Some physiological coping mechanisms are common among populations inhabiting particular areas and were presumably enhanced through generations of biological selection. Others represent individual reactions that are evoked by situational factors regardless of the person's ethnic or racial heritage.

22.5.1. Polar and Circumpolar Environments

The Arctic Inuit "must cope with extreme cold, low biological productivity of the terrestrial ecosystem, periods of prolonged light and darkness, and the dangers of working on snow and ice" (Moran, 1979, p.110). Because of the snow, high winds, and bulky polar clothing, they expend about twice as much energy in outdoor activity as would be needed for the same actions in a temperate environment. Skin disorders can result from the necessary clothing and from limited washing facilities. Hypothermia and frostbite are constant dangers, and there is danger of retinal damage from intense glare reflecting off the ice unless goggles are worn. The terrain is dangerous (crevasses, rapidly rising fogs, ice breaking up). A host of minor problems, some interacting with pre-existing health status, can also occur (Koerner, 1982; Shurley, 1970). During the constant darkness of midwinter, sleep and activity rhythms are disrupted. As a result, loss of sleep and physical fatigue increase the spread of contagious diseases. Disorientation of rhythms also occurs in the summer, with a prolongation of diurnal activity and loss of a sense of time (Condon, 1983). Nutritional problems may arise from the restricted nature and tenuous availability of food sources, particularly in winter. Although this has been ameliorated to some extent by contact with Western technology, some critics have suggested that the new diet causes deficiency diseases. In at least one case, osteoporosis, paleopathological evidence shows that the condition long antedated the change in diet (Zimmerman, 1985).

Physiological adaptive mechanisms are relevant but are probably less important than cultural ones. Contrary to the stereotype, Inuit have less subcutaneous fat than most Caucasians. Adaptation seems to be based more on changes in blood flow and metabolic rate. The same is true of Australian aborigines, whose desert environment can become very cold and whose material ways of coping with that problem have traditionally been limited. For Caucasian newcomers, physiological adaptation takes about 6 weeks to develop.

The subarctic region of North America is less stark than the polar areas but is marked by extreme cold and poor soil productivity. Cultural adaptations are very important. Some researchers have argued that cold may not even be a significant stressor for Algonquian Indian groups living in the area. This is because artifacts and folkways protect the group from the adverse effects of low temperature to the point where neither frostbite nor freezing is a major danger. Among the Indians who range this area, there appear to be no major physiological adaptations (Steegmann, 1983). It is worth noting that in spite of cold, wind, radiation, photocyclic changes, and the like, mortality rates in subarctic European communities do not seem to be negatively affected by the environment (Linderholm, 1981).

22.5.2. Hot Climates

The physiological reaction to hot environments is characterized by an increase in body temperature and more rapid air and fluid movement. Adaptation progresses rapidly, probably because human beings evolved in the tropics. Only about 2 weeks are required to acclimatize from a temperate to a tropic environment (Sloan, 1979). It is useful to differentiate between hot-dry and hot-humid milieux. The former is typified by deserts but also includes some seasonally hot and dry areas. The latter is typified by jungle and various other tropical environments.

Hot-Dry Environments

Desert environments involve extreme changes from daytime heat to nighttime cold. One principal hazard is not being prepared for these two extremes. Inhabitants must adapt not only to alternating heat and cold but also to low availability of food and water (Hanna & Brown, 1983). Low humidity leads to clear skies and, as a rule, sparse vegetation, so that there is little shade. Sunburn becomes a problem. The supply of water is usually limited: Excessive sweating leads to dehydration and salt deficiency. These, in turn, may result in heat cramps, heat stroke, and heat exhaustion.

Hot-Humid Environments

Because of leaf canopies and cloud cover, solar radiation is less of a problem in hot-humid than in hot-dry areas. On the other hand, high humidity reduces the effectiveness of sweating in reducing body heat. As a result, the culturally and personally appropriate amount of clothing is much less than in the desert. Sweat evaporates with reduced loss of electrolytes (Moran, 1979). There may be a lower proportion of body mass to skin area; however, there is a wide range of body dimensions among tropical tribes (e.g., from the Watusi to the Pygmies). Dark skin is less susceptible to sunburn and protects the underlying tissues from excessive ultraviolet light but absorbs 30 to 40% more sunlight than white skin. The balance may be in favor of dark skin in hot-dry and light skin in hot-humid environments, but the difference is probably outweighed by other adaptive mechanisms (Blum, 1961). Jungle environments also tend to harbor a multitude of predators and parasites. In fact, once acclimatization has occurred, the frequently observed problem of low energy level may be due more to endemic low-grade illness than to any climatic factor.

22.5.3. Natural High-Altitude Environments

In high mountains, the major problems are hypoxia, cold, dehydration, and ultraviolet radiation leading to sunburn and snow blindness. Physiological adaptation focuses on increasing the efficiency of oxygen flow. Various changes occur in lung and blood physiology and action. Changes in body weight, glucose metabolism, and other biochemical alterations have been reported at 6300 m (West, 1984). The adaptive physical characteristics of indigenous mountaineers (e.g., larger chest capacity) are not inherited and do not appear in the infants of mountain families that have moved to sea-level communities. Such individuals, and those who move to low altitudes and then return to the mountains, must acclimatize themselves in the same way as do first-time arrivals. This is done by climbing up gradually or by using an artificial source of oxygen.

Failure to acclimatize can lead to altitude sickness at 3000 m or higher (*soroche*, first described in 1590). The symptoms are breathlessness, giddiness, headache, insomnia, weakness, vomiting, and loss of appetite. More serious consequences are edema, pneumonia, and thrombosis. Psychological symptoms, similar to those of high-altitude fliers whose oxygen equipment malfunctions, include irresponsibility and euphoria.

Although acute mountain sickness passes in about 3 days, a chronic version does exist. It has even been known to develop in people who have lived in the mountains all their life (Moore & Regensteiner, 1983). These patients must be removed from the environment. A degenerative syndrome, high-altitude deterioration, is characterized by depressed appetite and thirst, resulting in loss of weight and energy. The onset of this occurs at 5500 m, so that any climbing above that should be done rapidly and if possible with

the use of extra oxygen. Above 6000 m, life expectancy is only about 3 months and at 9000 m only about 2 days (Ross, 1975).

22.5.4. Artificial Environments

In extreme and unusual environments other than natural, long-term habitats, psychophysiological adaptation obviously occurs in a more episodic fashion. In space, for example, zero gravity provides an environment that cannot be achieved anywhere else, although the condition can be duplicated very briefly during some aerobatic maneuvers and approximated through flotation in water.

Space Flight
Money (1981) has identified weightlessness as the source of the four major biological problems of space flight. These are (1) the movement of fluids to the upper part of the body (one problem here is that when the gravity field is reestablished, the rapid draining of blood from the head may cause unconsciousness); (2) cardiovascular decompensation (low blood pressure, decreased capacity for physical work, and lowered cardiac output); (3) loss of minerals from bone (calcium, phosphorus, potassium, and nitrogen, which apparently can result in permanently fragile bones); and (4) problems involving the organ of balance in the inner ear (particularly space motion sickness).

Problems other than weightlessness are radiation, abnormal temperature and humidity, acceleration, disruption of circadian rhythms, noise and vibration, and abnormal atmospheric composition. High levels of noise may lead to disturbances of sleep and communication and possibly hearing loss. However, good insulation can alleviate these problems (Garriott, Parker, Lichtenberg, & Merbold, 1984). The loss of white blood cells increases susceptibility to infections. Rapid acceleration and radiation sickness may be a danger both here and in high-altitude flight.

Flying and Diving
In high-altitude flying and in deep-sea diving, the danger of uncontrolled rapid change in air pressure is added to the problem of obtaining sufficient oxygen. Increases in pressure that are not equalized can lead to "squeeze": Depending on the part of the body that is affected, symptoms may be as trivial as bruises and blood blisters or as serious as burst eardrums. If the inner ear is affected, vertigo poses life threats to divers and flyers. Abrupt decreases in pressure during ascent may lead to burst lungs, pos-

sibly fatal air embolisms, and the bends (Lanphier, 1974). Although these are usually perceived as primarily hazardous to divers (Bachrach, 1982), the death of three Russian cosmonauts in 1971 was caused by air embolisms that resulted from a leaky hatch in the re-entering spacecraft (Ross, 1975).

Hypoxia and nitrogen narcosis, with their symptoms of euphoria and carelessness, have been identified as the causes of death for fliers whose oxygen supply failed without their awareness as well as for divers going below 30 m without special precautions. Further problems are caused by low temperature, leading to rapid loss of energy and work efficiency (Bachrach, 1982). In some underwater environments—submarines and artificial habitats such as Sealab—there may be loud machinery noise and a progressive accumulation of toxic gases. When anxiety and stress are added, performance (including performance of tasks required for survival) may be seriously impaired. Destruction of the long bones and near the joints (necrosis of the bone), apparently caused by the repeated blockages of small arteries by gas bubbles, is also a hazard.

Experimental Environments

Early experiments using laboratory sensory deprivation, now usually referred to as the restricted environmental stimulation technique or REST (Suedfeld, 1980), reported a pattern of physiological changes. In effect, this pattern was a combination of central nervous system deactivation and increasing autonomic arousal (Zubek, 1969).

More recent studies have begun to establish the components of the phenomenon. Flotation REST in a tank of saline solution is associated with both electrophysiological and biochemical indices of deep relaxation (e.g., Jacobs, Heilbronner, & Stanley, 1984). Barabasz and Barabasz (1985) demonstrated that when subjects are given a non-anxiety arousing orientation to REST, the traditional physiological signs of increasing anxiety do not emerge. Other researchers are investigating the use of telemetric apparatus, but no data are available as yet.

This may be one area where studies of infrahuman animals should be mentioned. Experiments in which infant animals are brought up in sensory deprivation (Tees, 1980) show some physiological and behavioral deficits. These may occur because the relevant organ atrophies or fails to develop. There is, however, little evidence for such effects either in human infants or in animals reared under social isolation conditions (Holson & Sackett, 1984; Kagan, 1976).

Unusual environments can be dangerous even if they are not particularly extreme. Heroin addicts are much more likely to die from "overdoses" when the drug was taken in an environment not usually associated with ingestion. Environmental cues usually related to taking the drug may become conditioned stimuli that elicit an anticipatory response attenuating the drug effect. In a novel environment, this response and attenuation do not occur, and the physiological impact of the drug is potentiated. The same difference in mortality occurs among rats that receive a dose either in the presence or absence of environmental cues previously associated with drug administration (Siegel, Hinson, Krank, & McCully, 1982).

22.6. SENSATION AND PERCEPTION

Some of the environments we are considering clearly do cause major shifts in perceptual functioning. Occasionally adaptation to the environment affects perception. Space suits and diving suits hamper movement and also reduce the visual field, auditory acuity, tactile sensations, and the like. Perhaps less dramatic, but more common, are similar problems caused by bulky cold-weather clothing; the fur lining of the Inuk parka, for instance, cuts off peripheral vision. In the dangerous world of the Arctic, this can be a fatal occurrence. It becomes necessary to move the entire upper body in order to scan the visual field.

Vision is affected by changes in the force of gravity and by climatic conditions in mountain climbing. Additional factors relevant to high-altitude flying and deep-sea diving are the absence of size and distance cues as well as excessively or insufficiently bright light. Under experimental conditions, high ambient temperature has been shown to result in reduced visual sensitivity within 30 min. (Hohnsbein, Piekarski, & Kampmann, 1983). The generalizability of this finding is brought into question by the complex nature both of the procedure and of the results.

Visual distortions occur in environments where the normal spatial cues are removed or changed. Distances are overestimated under water and sometimes across a far vista outdoors. In the latter situation, mirages may represent a psychologically disturbing phenomenon. Distance and the nature of the intervening medium also affect color perception. These effects are perhaps most dramatic under water. Among other phenomena, a drastic shift toward the bluish-green end of the color spectrum greatly increases the monotony of the perceived environment

(Bachrach, 1982). The degree of this effect can be seen by comparing the undersea visual percept with photographs using good flash equipment.

In addition, unusual viewing conditions distort the perceived size of objects, their slope, and other attributes (Ross, 1975). The reader may recall the case of the African forest Pygmy who was removed for the first time from the dense forest in which he lived. Taken to the (for him) unusual environment of an open area, he completely misinterpreted novel size and distance relationships. For example, he perceived distant cattle as insects that became larger as he came closer to them (Turnbull, 1961). Conversely individuals who live in the open spaces of deserts or snow fields are more likely to see short lines as long ones extending back into the distance (Binnie-Dawson, 1982). The apparent lack of discriminable stimuli troubles some people when they first enter unfamiliar environments such as the wilderness.

Experimental REST studies show many sensory and perceptual effects (Zubek, 1969). Most of these appear to be due to one of three factors: lowered sensory thresholds because of the prolonged lack of input, residual stimuli in the environment, and an increased level of attention to stimuli produced by one's own body. The widely cited hallucinations reported by early investigators have turned out to be a jumble of endogenous stimuli, dreams or daydreams, and elaborated cognitive imagery (Suedfeld, 1980). However, reliably interesting perceptual phenomena remain in the case of cross-receptor and cross-modal effects and the sequence of lack of sensitivity followed by supersensitivity (Bross, 1985).

In many environments, perceptual effects can be largely ignored because they appear to be trivial. This is true of space flight. The prediction based on research in restricted environmental stimulation (e.g. National Academy of Sciences, 1972) was that nothing particularly dramatic would occur. This has indeed been true.

22.7. PROBLEM SOLVING

Two major categories of performance have been tested in research on extreme and unusual environments. The more important of the two consists of tasks that have to be performed in the "real" environment and are an integral part of the mission. These may be specific, time-bounded problems or the general process of coping with the environment. Following scarce and elusive prey through miles of jungle or living through a polar ice storm presents a series of

tasks and problems. Although performance may not be objectively scorable, a rough ordinal scale of degree of success can usually be developed. The adaptation of a society to its environment is also relevant. Unfortunately, very little psychological literature has been produced on this topic, although, of course, it is a major concern of archaeology and anthropology. The interested reader may want to look at Jochim (1981) and Vayda (1969) for scholarly treatments of several such interactions or at Harris (1974, 1977) for very readable, stimulating, and controversial nontechnical versions.

The other category is performance on tasks that are specifically presented in order to measure how environmental factors affect efficiency. These tasks tend to be quantifiable, objective, clear-cut, and usually brief. Frequently they are administered in analogue environments. To contrast them with the first group, we can compare a task measuring vigilance and reaction time to visual stimuli, performed as part of a test battery, with the actual efficiency of an operator tracking blips in an Arctic radar station.

22.7.1. Field Studies

Temporary Sites
Performance in "instrumental" extreme situations seems to show relatively little deterioration, except under conditions of very high danger and severe deprivation. However, some decreases in memory, vigilance, and the ability to concentrate have been reported (Mullin, 1960). Memory and alertness suffered most in Soviet aquanauts undergoing 16 to 18 days under high pressure in a chamber (Gulyr & Sirota, 1974). At very high altitude, motor behavior, learning, and memory on experimental tasks deteriorates, as does expressive language (West, 1984). Both task duration and severity of hypoxia lead to decreased efficiency in signal detection (Cahoon, 1970). On the other hand, polar crew members tested on experimental cognitive tasks at base after "wintering-over" or in the field after a summer expedition show stability or slight improvement (Gregson, 1978; Rivolier, Goldsmith, Lugg, & Taylor, in preparation).

Any performance deterioration that is found, either in field or experimental confinement, may be more a reflection of motivational than of cognitive loss (Smith, 1969; Suedfeld, 1969). One implication of this is that when the task has clear survival implications or for some other reason is seen as important, performance is not likely to be worse than under normal environmental conditions.

Even in traumatic situations, many survivors do adapt to the situation and tolerate both the physical privations and psychological problems (e.g., Cooke, 1960; Trumbull, 1942). For example, castaways have spent as much as 5 years alone, on deserted and barren islands, solving series of life-threatening problems effectively (e.g., Neider, 1952).

In many cases, traumatic insertions are into what I have called "extreme experiences," not environments. War zones, communities suffering natural disasters, and various types of prison camps come under this heading. Because of the limitations of the chapter, I want to mention only briefly the resiliency of the human being shown by the ability to cope with such circumstances. This kind of stress can lead to high morale, cooperativeness, creative problem solving, and self-sacrifice. As a result, rates of psychiatric problems and even death rates are sometimes much lower than expected and are lower than those of otherwise comparable groups in normal settings (Bloom & Halsema, 1983; Janis, 1951). Nor is there evidence of cognitive deterioration in such settings as prisons (Wormith, 1984) or even solitary confinement units within prisons (Gendreau, 1984; Suedfeld, Ramirez, Deaton, & Baker-Brown, 1982).

Active coping, meeting the challenge, can take a variety of psychological and behavioral forms. Several authors (e.g., Janis, 1951; Sonnenfeld, 1969) have discussed what is commonly called *adjustment* (changing the environment) as opposed to *adaptation* (a shift in adaptation level so as to make the environment more tolerable). Suedfeld (1979) differentiated reactions to stressful environments as positive or negative tropism, passive or active adaptation, and destruction. Of these, only active adaptation would alter the environment. Active adaptation might also involve cognitive and affective tactics; for example, concentrating on "good" occurrences; dedicating oneself to a mission, to religion, or to one's fellow prisoners; playing elaborate jokes on each other or on the captors; and concentrating on the will to live or the meaningfulness of life (Dimsdale, 1977; Frankl, 1963; Hunter, 1958).

Other behavioral and social mechanisms include increasing one's mastery over the environment, collaboration or resistance, identification and affiliation with a mutually helping group, and, of course, attempts at physical escape. These tactics improve the chances of prisoner survival. Except for behaviors that are specifically directed toward interaction with captors, they are also appropriate in situations where the extreme and unusual environment is not imposed deliberately by enemies.

Permanent Communities

Studies in "normal" extreme and unusual environments present a confounding problem. This chapter is not the place for a thorough discussion of cultural ecology—the view that environmental factors either determine particular cultural behaviors (the strong version) or at least are functionally interdependent with them (the weak version; see Berry, 1975). But the relationship between the two is important and can obviously be viewed as one example of environmental adaptation. Every facet of cultural behavior is involved in adjusting to the challenges, demands, and opportunities provided by the physical setting (Altman & Chemers, 1980).

Groups whose homes are in the polar regions or in arid deserts differ widely from each other and from the ethnocentric norms of psychologists, on many dimensions. These range from the genetic to the cultural (including language and education). Although differences in cognitive performance and cognitive style have been found between such groups (e.g., Berry, 1976; Cole & Scribner, 1974; Taylor & Skanes, 1975), the role—if any—played by features of the global environment in the development of these differences cannot even be estimated.

To untangle genetic and environmental characteristics, we need research on populations that live in unusual environments but whose background is from a mainstream culture. Isolated farm communities, lumber or mining camps, and the like serve as good models. Very little systematic research has been done on cognitive processes in such situations. The landmark work is that of Haggard (e.g., 1973), who compared Norwegian children living on remote farms with matched urban controls. The isolated children showed greater dispersion around the mean on a number of measures and lower scores on indices requiring knowledge of interpersonal skills and verbal fluency. However, most measures showed no consistent differences, and the longer the isolates stay in school the smaller the differences are.

22.7.2. Experimental Results

Analogue or experimental task performance is the least relevant to our considerations here. Simulations indicate that members of isolated groups show little if any performance deterioration over time (Beare, Biersner, Bondi, & Naitoh, 1981; Brady & Emurian, 1978; Flinn & Hartman, 1961). The same is true of isolated subjects in reduced stimulation laboratories (Rasmussen, 1973; Suedfeld, 1980). Within these general findings, there are changes as a function of such mediating factors as stress level and type of task.

Many research, training, and selection programs have used experimental isolation situations as an analogue. If the environment is designed to approximate the eventual "real" counterpart closely, and the number and the types of individuals, the tasks and work schedules imposed, and so on are also realistic, this appears to be a useful procedure. Altman and Haythorn (e.g., 1967; summarized in Haythorn, 1973) showed that confined dyads did better on a number of cognitive tasks than controls who were not confined. This finding agrees with data on naturally restricted groups, for example, in polar stations.

Parallels between group confinement studies and experiments in profound sensory restriction (one person in complete darkness, silence, and immobility) are probably farfetched and not very informative (Suedfeld, 1980; Vernon, 1963). Animals reared under conditions of sensory or social deprivation show some deficits in learning and other performance measures (Harlow, 1959; Holson & Sackett, 1984; Tees, 1980). These are neither irreversible nor universally severe. Among human adults, the cognitive effects of REST are mediated by the type of problem presented. Performance on such simple tasks as rote learning and memory frequently improves, whereas arithmetic problems, IQ test items, logical deductions, and the like show no consistent pattern. Problems requiring some creativity (telling a story, making up novel uses) show decrements, but anecdotal evidence reports improvements in highly creative thought, a lead that is worth pursuing systematically (Suedfeld, 1969, 1980). It is possible that the established effectiveness of REST in fostering desired habit changes and other health-related adaptations is related to this effect (Suedfeld & Kristeller, 1982).

22.8. EMOTIONAL REACTIONS

Affective states are widely believed to be responsive to even such mundane environmental conditions as the weather (Jorgenson, 1981). By extension, emotional reactions to extreme and unusual environments should be among the most psychologically interesting aspects of this topic.

22.8.1. Positive Emotions

Affective responses vary widely. They include fear, excitement, transcendental bliss, boredom, withdrawal or emotional flatness, aggressiveness, and a composite that represents the elation of meeting a challenge. This last emotion perhaps synthesizes pride, fear, excitement, and intense concentration, and it appears to be particularly important in situations voluntarily chosen by participants. Although experimenters have found positive evaluations of stressful situations (Houston, Blom, Burish, & Cummings, 1978), the topic has not been studied much by psychologists. However, it has certainly been reflected in many of the writings about individuals facing environmental challenges (e.g., Taylor, 1984; Wolfe, 1979), even under extremely traumatic circumstances (Frankl, 1963).

Humor is probably one of the most easily available methods for reducing stress and aversive arousal. Anecdotal reports of individuals in even the most extreme circumstances attest to its usefulness (e.g., Hunter, 1958). Real wit and humor abound in some recent Antarctic groups (Hankinson, 1984) and in the transcriptions of astronaut communications. In spite of such examples, psychologists have paid amazingly little attention to humor as a factor in dealing with environmental adversity. Nelson (1973) feels that in long-term confined groups, humor is eroded because increasing familiarity eliminates the possibility of surprises. But systematic considerations of this and other humor-related hypotheses are missing, in contrast to the attention paid to fear, boredom, aggression, and other negative affects.

Other positive characteristics may be either affective states, affective–cognitive approaches, or stable personality traits. I include them under the heading of positive emotional reactions somewhat arbitrarily.

Emotional Tendencies: At the State–Trait Boundary

One dimension is what Apter (1984) calls *paratelic dominance*: seeing the environment in terms of challenges to be met. When the affect aroused is interpreted more as excitement than as fear, coping behavior is more probable. Some of the biographical literature indicates that individuals taking this position can come through terrible ordeals relatively unscathed (Jackson, 1974), whereas those who feel helpless may suffer considerably more (Jacobson, 1973).

A related concept is *framing* (Kahneman & Tversky, 1984). If an experience is cognitively framed as a possible loss, the individual is motivated by the desire to avoid it; if as a possible gain or fair trade, the preparatory response may be a readiness to enjoy and benefit from it. In training people to cope with extreme–unusual environments, a deliberate inculcation of particular "frames" may be an effective tactic.

Courage is another positive characteristic that may be perceived either as an emotional state or a personality trait. Unlike its intuitive opposite—fear—courage has not attracted much psychological research. Here I will only note that courageous behavior is common in dangerous situations and that people frequently take it for granted (Rachman, 1984). More research obviously needs to be done. One area of particular interest may be to contrast cold with hot forms of courage. *Cold courage* is exemplified by the bomb-disposal personnel studied by Rachman and by such people as Raoul Wallenberg, who over a period of months in 1944 invented a variety of methods for circumventing the Nazi extermination of Hungarian Jews. *Hot courage* describes the actions of a soldier who performs heroically in combat or someone who jumps into a torrent to save a drowning child.

Related to courage is altruism and self-sacrifice. Again categorization as an affective state is relatively arbitrary but seems appropriate. There are many such examples in extreme and unusual environments: L.E.G. Oates, of Scott's Antarctic expedition, emulating Inuit elders who walk off into the ice to die so as not to burden their fellows; people who give up scarce food to others who seem to need it more; health and other professionals who give up comfort, rest, or chance of escape to help their patients.

22.8.2. Fear

Obviously one salient emotional reaction to extreme and unusual environments is *fear* or *anxiety*. I shall use the terms interchangeably because in many environments it is difficult to separate realistic fears from what may be unfounded ones.

Physiological arousal precedes and accompanies exposure to danger. High arousal, in turn, increases the probability of simple, previously learned responses (Spence, 1953). If these responses are appropriate to the situation, they enhance the probability of success and survival. This is the rationale for intensive drill in training people to cope rapidly with hazardous circumstances. But the highly aroused fearful person—even, or perhaps especially, if thoroughly drilled—is at increased risk when previously dominant responses become self-defeating and novel or complex strategies are needed.

Longitudinal and cross-sectional studies show that physiological responsivity to danger diminishes as the individual becomes more experienced and self-confident (e.g., Ursin, Baade, & Levine, 1978). Individuals who do not show such habituation may never reach a high level of competence in coping with the problems posed by the situation (Fenz, 1975). The realization that one is not improving can maintain high levels of apprehension. Conversely the failure of some physiological mechanism to adapt may prevent coping skills from developing. That old theoretical standby, excessive arousal, may be involved. Like emotional reactions, arousal can be reinstated by conditions that increase the perceived danger (e.g., decreased visibility under water or the fear that a parachute may not be properly packed).

Passive adaptation may take the form of the extreme apathetic withdrawal called *Musselmanism* among German concentration camp prisoners and *give-up-itis* among American POWs in Korea. Affected prisoners are unwilling to get up in the morning, wash, work, or even eat. The reaction is partly due to physical weakness from illness, hunger, and fatigue. Another causal factor may be learned helplessness (Seligman, 1975)—the psychological exhaustion that comes from going through one's entire coping repertoire without success in solving the problem. The affective basis of the condition is shown by the fact that its cure lies in evoking some emotion in victims, sometimes by insulting or slapping them and sometimes by appealing to them to help a sick or injured comrade.

22.8.3. Aggression

It has been argued that aggression is triggered or facilitated by various aspects of the macroenvironment, either as a function of general arousal or more specifically. Ambient heat is perhaps the most frequently cited parameter. Researchers (Boyanowsky, Calvert, Young, & Brideau, 1981–1982) have built on references to the "long, hot summers" supposedly associated with urban riots. Other implicated factors have been noise, air pollution, and social-environmental aspects including crowding and violations of territory or personal space (Mueller, 1983).

Interpersonal conflict in isolated groups appears to be the rule rather than the exception, although in some cases of great danger and general discomfort, such reactions may be suppressed. When intragroup hostility does occur in highly selected teams such as aquanauts (Radloff & Helmreich, 1968), it is usually not expressed through direct aggression. It may instead take the form of horseplay, teasing, or practical jokes (Hunter, 1958; Mullin, 1960; Taylor, 1969). Direct aggression is also suppressed in nonelite groups undergoing extreme hazard and deprivation, as among concentration camp prisoners (Radil-Weiss, 1983) and on a societal level among groups such as the Arctic Inuit.

Although there is no systematic research, "daily hassles" (e.g., Lazarus, 1984), discomforts, and frustrations may lead to more aggressive behavior than situations that are dangerous or that demand attention and coping behavior. Under circumstances of prolonged but not extreme deprivation, social monotony, fatigue, or confinement, some small groups do not suppress or disguise such feelings. Expeditions mapping new territories chronically exhibit squabbling, rebellion against the leader, the development of hostile subgroups, and the like (Tikalsky, 1982). Although direct aggressive behavior is rare, space data also indicate that hostility develops within crews and on the part of the crew toward ground controllers (Bluth, 1980). This can be exacerbated by the need of a commander to assert himself (Foushee, 1982) and may reflect poor personnel selection practices. But it also occurs in situations where hierarchical group structure is deliberately de-emphasized and where psychological selection procedures are carefully applied (Helmreich, 1983).

Conflict emerged as a consequence of prolonged subacute stress in the Peace Corps as well. There were disagreements between volunteers and natives. More serious resentments occurred between volunteers and their immediate Peace Corps superiors (country directors or area representatives), between rural and urban volunteers, between those assigned to community development versus those assigned to education, and among volunteers with different ideological and motivational commitments (Pallanich, 1968; Textor, 1966).

22.8.4. Boredom

Boredom is a major problem in long-duration situations after adaptation to novelty and extremeness has occurred. As the environment and the task become routinized and increasingly automatic, attention turns elsewhere. In an attempt to maintain relatively high levels of stimulation, the individual may become hypersensitive to the habits and characteristics of coworkers, leading to social stress and hostility; focus more on internal stimuli, giving rise to withdrawal, introspection, daydreaming, and possibly to hypochondria; or turn to such behaviors as alcohol and drug abuse, vandalism, or compulsive rituals. In extreme cases, more serious problems such as hallucinations

may occur. Those who design extended missions should try to set continuing challenges that require cooperative behavior toward superordinate goals (Sherif & Sherif, 1956). This is particularly important if day-to-day survival is not a constant problem. Experimental research (Brady & Emurian, 1978; Rasmussen, 1973) and field studies of more mundane work environments such as assembly lines (e.g., Frankenhaeuser, 1978) and remote mining camps (Veno & Dufty, 1982a) have generated very similar data.

An interesting review related to this issue (Thackray, 1981) came to the conclusion that whereas boredom and monotony do not necessarily produce physiological signs of stress (Lazarus & Cohen, 1977), such signs emerge when a monotonous environment is combined with a need to maintain high levels of alertness. This may explain why lone sailing is much less stressful since the need for constant vigilance has been reduced by automatic steering mechanisms and the radio (Heaton, 1976; Henderson, 1976). Unfortunately many dangerous environments (and some work situations, such as those of air traffic controllers) still feature just this combination.

22.8.5. Transcendental Experiences

One emotional reaction, not well understood, is a feeling of transcendence, which can take various forms. One is a submergence of the self in, or union with, the universe as a whole or supernatural entities. Another variant is a general feeling of exaltation or grandeur, sometimes paradoxically coupled with a realization of personal insignificance. Such reports have come primarily from individuals who are completely isolated for a relatively long period of time in a natural environment (e.g., hermits, single-handed sailors or fliers, wilderness hikers). The spate of Western visitors to Zen temples and Yogic ashrams reflects a similar pattern.

Anthropological, religious, and other writings have for millennia indicated that communion with the divine can be obtained under such conditions. Examples include such major figures in the history of religion as Moses, Jesus, Buddha, and Mohammed as well as many thousands of less known individuals. In many cultures, this environmental *Gestalt* is a routine part of the rites through which an adolescent male about to enter adulthood identifies his spiritual guides and protectors. Transcendence, coupled with the joy of overcoming a novel environmental challenge, also forms a theoretical basis for such programs as Outward Bound and the variety of "wilderness therapies" initiated within the past decade (Harrison, 1982; Katz, 1973). As in the vision quest, the experience is supposed to generalize and produce self-confidence that carries over into the participant's everyday life.

No systematic study has brought together all of these data to study the conditions under which the altered states of consciousness occur. However, there are some common features. One is solitude over a relatively prolonged period. Another is physical hardship, which may be provided by inadequate nourishment and fatigue. In some rites of passage, physical pain is produced by torture before and during the wilderness quest. A relatively unchanging and monotonous environment is also standard. The expectation that transcendence will occur may be crucial, particularly if all of the purely environmental criteria are not met (Suedfeld, 1980). Hood (1977) reported that the experience most likely to induce such states was the anticipation of low stress in a situation that actually turned out to be highly stressful. Jilek (1982) speculates that the combination of focused attention, pain, and alternating high and low levels of stimulation and mobility combine to induce transcendental altered states through the secretion of endogenous opioid polypeptides.

22.9. GROUP DYNAMICS

Small groups confined together for relatively prolonged periods have been studied intensely. They include the crews of exploratory expeditions, polar stations, space vehicles, submarines, underwater habitats, far-voyaging ships and aircraft, and small combat teams as well as groups of victims of natural and other disasters (hostages, prisoners, castaways, survivors of shipwrecks, plane crashes, earthquakes, and the like). It appears that in long-term isolated groups, factors related to remoteness may be among the major stressors. Boredom, unchanging group membership, and the absence of accustomed sources of gratification are particularly important.

22.9.1. Leadership

The survival and success of the group are closely linked with the emergence and acceptance of competent leadership and the development of appropriate divisions of labor and responsibility (Altman, Smith, Meyers, McKenna, & Bryson, 1962; Kinkead, 1959; Torrance, 1954). Mutually supportive group practices emerge in most such situations. Popular literature

has overemphasized supposed selfishness and lack of mutual help in some of these, including Nazi concentration camps (Luchterhand, 1970) and Chinese POW camps in the Korean War (Biderman, 1963).

One recurring event among isolated groups is the development of conflict between the head of the group and other members (Braun, 1961). Feelings of anger toward one's own leaders are common among passive victims, for example, of air raids or natural disasters (Hibbert, 1983; Huntford, 1980; Janis, 1951; Reid, 1980). Mutual hostility also occurs between the leader and a "key man," a person whose task specialty is central to the success of the group (Fiedler, 1955). The head–key man controversy may be a matter of rivalry for the leadership and in fact sometimes results in the development of schismatic subgroups.

The optimal type of leadership in such situations needs to be studied systematically. Nelson (1973) has reported that team members in the Antarctic want their leader to behave democratically on routine matters, to consult with technical experts on specialized issues, and to act decisively and quickly in emergencies. This implies a flexible leadership style, whose relationship to established theories of leader characteristics and behaviors is not obvious. We do not know how successful such a style would be, nor how these preferences fit in with those of other groups in extreme and unusual environments.

22.9.2. Group Morale and Cohesiveness

The parallels between the group deterioration shown by Arctic explorers, Antarctic crews, concentration camp prisoners, and other inhabitants of long-duration extreme environments indicate that there are common factors. The most obvious is isolation from other environments and people. Physical privation and discomfort also play a part. Some social factors show decrements among military units operating in a cold, high-altitude environment. Although the general level of adjustment may remain adequate, such soldiers show feelings of loneliness and homesickness, depression, anxiety, boredom, and decreased interpersonal communication (Sharma, Vaskaran, & Manhotra, 1976). These adaptation problems resemble those found toward the end of an Antarctic winter. However, polar crews show an end spurt when their assignment is almost over: increased sociability, conversation, self-disclosure, and so on. The difference is probably related to imminent return, to the group's more careful selection and training, and to their self-perception as elite volunteers.

Most confined groups show a progressive decrease in interpersonal liking and communication as time goes on. These can lead to serious problems in task success. Cooperative behavior may be replaced by less appropriate solitary work. Regressive—sometimes infantile—actions (Gunderson, 1973) can further detract from performance. A lack of adequate communication, noted by the famous military historian S.L.A. Marshall (1961) as one of the most serious problems in ground combat, also appears to be instrumental in many aviation accidents (Foushee, 1982).

In some cases—for example, when normally abhorred behavior such as cannibalism is adopted (e.g., Read, 1974)—negative repercussions may result when the group returns to a less extreme environment. As in the case of the Donner party, these may lead to mutual accusations on the part of the survivors and a complete breakdown of group feeling.

Intergroup conflict is common—for example, between scientists and naval personnel in U.S. Antarctic stations that have groups of both. As one might expect, high workload or danger appears to decrease the incidence of adaptation problems (Natani & Shurley, 1974). No such conflicts were found among the aquanauts of the Tektite II program, who were divided into scientists and engineers. But these groups were much closer to each other in values and goals than the two groups in the Antarctic stations. Even in Tektite, relations were better when members of each group participated in some of the work activities of the other so that they gained understanding of the others' concerns and approaches (Helmreich, 1971).

It would be interesting to do a systematic study of the interpersonal problems arising during expeditions, to investigate whether in fact there is a pattern as to the behavior of the participants and the causes and outcomes of the problems. We should also compare these events with inter- and intragroup relationships in other environments.

Extreme deprivation can, in relatively short periods, lead to massive and possibly irreversible societal change. Some people and cultures adapt adequately to permanent or temporary hardships (e.g., the Inuit; invaded and bombed countries in wartime). A contrast is the dramatic case of the Ik, a Central African tribe that in the 1930s was displaced from its traditional hunting ground. Food became extremely scarce, and no good alternative source was found. By the 1970s the tribe had no norms of mutual help, no moral code, and no observable social bonds. Not only religion but also sexual activity and child bearing had to a great extent disappeared from the normal life of the people (Turnbull, 1972). Furthermore one small group that migrated to a new environment with abundant food retained the norms of complete selfishness.

Simulations show that compatibility on such traits as dogmatism and needs for achievement, affiliation, and dominance is related to lower subjective stress and symptomatology, less personal friction, but surprisingly, poorer task performance (Altman & Haythorn, 1967). Other group confinement studies in simulated capsules, cabins, and bomb shelters bear out the importance of interpersonal compatibility. Just as in the field, group relations deteriorate throughout periods of confinement, with subjects withdrawing from group activity and preferring solitude. Territoriality and fairly impersonal interactions become the norm (Smith, 1969).

22.10. RELEVANT PERSONALITY CHARACTERISTICS

Investigators have spent considerable time and effort to identify personality characteristics related to good or poor adaptation, social cooperativeness versus destructiveness, and the like in space flight or polar weather-station operations. The way in which people react to the environment is conceived of as being to a great extent personality-based.

I do not intend to deal in any detail with selection factors for extreme and unusual environments. Although much effort has been expended on research in this area, the findings have been essentially those predicted by common sense. Individuals who are self-reliant, have high social skills and high autonomy, who are goal-oriented and competent at their tasks, and so on are repeatedly identified as the most effective in such environments. The search for a challenge may be related to high levels of sensation seeking (Zuckerman, 1979). There is no doubt that personality and situational factors affect the degree to which people are willing to expose themselves to dangerous situations (Klausner, 1968), but the ability to take such experiences in stride can be amazing (see, e.g., Rachman, 1984).

It is now generally accepted that behavior during and after catastrophic events will be primarily a function of the event itself rather than of pretrauma personality (e.g., Dimsdale, 1977). The idea that disasters cause permanent damage only to those who are predisposed toward neurosis is a beautiful psychiatric example of what social psychologists call the fundamental attribution error: ascribing behavior to transsituational personality traits rather than to the impact of the environment. Of course, personality factors do matter. Among the most important ones related to survival and adaptation may be those that lead to positive perceptions of difficult tasks and environments, to a strong and favorable self-concept, and to an ability to function well under conditions of high stress. But even individuals with the best possible combination of traits will eventually succumb if the environment is harsh enough. Personality differences may become essentially irrelevant to adaptation in truly extreme environments.

22.11. EFFECTS ON MENTAL HEALTH

22.11.1. Destructive and Self-Destructive Behaviors

Extreme and unusual environments present many objective hazards to life. These are, to a large extent, fairly obvious. In any case, they lie outside the focus of this chapter. More germane are instances where the individual dies or commits suicide for reasons that may at least be related to environmental factors. In a recent case, a lone 'round-the-world yacht racer was widely presumed to have been driven into suicidal psychosis by isolation and monotony. In actuality his death was probably due to another factor—the inevitable and imminent discovery that he had attempted to cheat in the race (Bennet, 1974). Stress arising from this and other personal problems may have been exacerbated by the environmental conditions of the long voyage. Many "single-handers" do experience periods of loneliness and anxiety. The latter are well-founded, given the dangers in which they sometimes find themselves. As one writer indicates: "No one will ever know how many vessels have disappeared without a trace...because of judgments influenced by mental aberrations" (Holm, 1974, p. 396). Psychological aberrations may be caused by physical problems, which thus indirectly lead to the loss of the vessel. Even modern circumnavigators sometimes set out without appropriate food and medication. Some of them are in a physical condition that would deter most people from any arduous activity. Cancer, diabetes, and incipient blindness are some examples (Holm, 1974).

Adverse reactions to similar conditions occurring traumatically are more validly attributed to the situation itself. Shipwreck survivors in lifeboats and air crash survivors in remote areas show a high mortality rate within the first few days, even though they may not be injured and may have sufficient food and water (Bombard, 1953; Suedfeld, 1980). The degree to which state of health, hardihood, previous training in

survival techniques, familiarity with the ocean, and similar factors enter into the equation has not been systematically evaluated. Contributing factors include shock, fear, and the objective hazards of the environment.

Long-term dwellers in extreme environments are not immune to dramatic behavioral disturbances. "Cabin fever" produces uncontrolled acting out after people have been confined indoors for a long time because of snow, strong winds, or extreme cold. *Cafard*—hysterical behavior often culminating in homicide and/or suicide—is found among soldiers of the French Foreign Legion stationed in small desert outposts under conditions of heat, sandstorms, crowding, severe discipline, and frequent danger. "Arctic hysteria" afflicts the Inuit, with symptoms varying somewhat among cultural units (Moran, 1979). Another possible example is the Windigo cannibal–witch syndrome of the northern Algonquians, although the very existence of this condition has been questioned (Marano, 1982; Pelto & Pelto, 1979).

Environmental monotony and response restriction may be implicated in all of these patterns. The difficulties caused by isolation and boredom are often exacerbated by unfavorable climate and terrain. Other aggravating factors may be changes in the light–dark cycle, extremely high or low ambient temperatures, and malnutrition. Under more modern circumstances, with better food, temperature control, and the like, such reactions may disappear.

22.11.2. Psychosomatic Problems

Psychosomatic complaints are frequent among individuals isolated in polar situations as well as among those who undergo prolonged confinement in the course of research (e.g., Gunderson, 1973). The most common symptoms are sleep disturbances, headache, fatigue, sore muscles, and gastrointestinal dysfunction. Such symptoms are most likely to occur when danger is not acute and neither survival nor the tasks to be performed require constant alertness. Relatively high levels of discomfort because of boredom or crowding exacerbate the occurrence of complaints (Cox, Paulus, McCain, & Schkade, 1979).

Among the most frequently reported adverse reactions to long isolation in polar stations are insomnia, depression (including loss of motivation), and poor adjustment to the group. The relative lack of serious problems may be due to the careful selection of well-adjusted personnel. Those who serve repeatedly in Antarctic stations are the most self-sufficient of all (Taylor, 1970).

22.11.3. Hallucinations

Another common symptom reported by isolates is hallucinations, which are sometimes attributed to the organism's attempt to maintain an acceptable level of stimulation in a monotonous environment. This would explain their occurrence among Arctic voyagers and immobilized orthopedic patients. Some cases seem to be related to physical causes such as a reaction to toxic substances (Byrd, 1938; Slocum, 1900/1958) or malnutrition (Mawson, 1725). Hallucinations have also been ascribed to cold stress, especially in combination with fatigue; anecdotes about mountain climbers, castaways, and hikers seem to have these factors in common (Lloyd, 1981).

One interesting feature, which to my knowledge has not been emphasized in previous treatments of this phenomenon, is the prevalence in these hallucinations of other people or superhuman entities, usually felt to be helpful, supportive, and capable of saving the hallucinator. The similarity of these beings to those encountered on vision or spirit quests—ancestral spirits, totemic animals, and other guides and protectors—is striking. It also supports a more psychologically oriented explanation for the experience than one based exclusively on neurochemical changes.

22.11.4. Community Mental Health

The high rate of individual and group symptomatology among dwellers in remote communities, particularly in harsh environments, has been noted frequently. Limited recreational and other resources, restricted mobility, and sensory and social monotony are implicated. So are physical discomfort due to climate and arousal dysfunctions caused by photocyclic changes. In many of the environments that we have discussed, there are no real communities involved; it would be interesting to see more such. For example, there may be intriguing data from the Argentine and Chilean Antarctic bases, which have recently added families to the usual crews of scientists, technicians, and support workers.

The problems of people living in remote resource-extraction settlements are exacerbated by the fact that most of them are used to more urban communities. Boredom, restlessness, and unfamiliar environmental factors such as those noted previously lead to high rates of alcoholism and other substance abuse, violence, vandalism, and worker turnover. As a result, some employers have tried having their labor force commute, either from a major city or a nearby town; alternate relatively long periods on site

with long periods of leave in a city; or live near the site in a company town (Veno & Dufty, 1982b). The last of these replaces formerly all-worker campsites with communities where spouses and children reside. This, to some extent, allays the problem of the worker but puts in its place equivalent problems of spouses who do not even have the distraction of following clear-cut work schedules. A high rate of symptomatology and marital and social breakdown can result. Some attempts are now being made both in community planning and health-care planning to deal with these problems.

22.11.5. Posttraumatic Stress Disorder

Survivors of many types of disasters—shipwrecks, floods, air raids, concentration camps—show common symptoms that may persist throughout life. Because the majority of precipitating events are what I would call *extreme experiences*, rather than *extreme environments*, I shall not treat this topic here. But it is interesting to note the proliferation of terms such as *posttraumatic stress disorder, KZ (concentration camp) syndrome, disaster syndrome, shell shock, combat veteran syndrome*, and so on. This variety should not be allowed to swamp the overwhelming evidence that the symptoms themselves appear to be similar among survivors of very different traumatic environments.

The most recent edition of the definitive psychiatric diagnostic manual (American Psychiatric Association, 1980) lists posttraumatic stress disorder (acute, delayed, and chronic) as a specific syndrome. The diagnostic criteria include intrusive memories and dreams of the event, numbing of responsiveness, survivor guilt, impaired memory, sleep disturbances, and avoidance of activities that remind the individual of the traumatic situation. This category, so prominently applied to veterans of the Vietnam War (Figley, 1978), obviously describes the most common set of symptoms found as the aftermath of a wide range of experiences.

22.12. CONCLUSION

22.12.1. Summary of Results

It is somewhat difficult to produce a meaningful summary of such a wide variety of data. In my opinion, the most striking aspect of the literature is the ability of human beings to adapt, individually and socially, to the harshest of naturally or artificially occurring conditions. Another reliable finding is that psychological deterioration of various kinds tends to occur primarily when there is a long period of subacute frustration, privation, and confinement. In contrast, cognitive and social performance can remain high in dealing with extreme danger. The chronic conditions themselves can also be surmounted adaptively in cultures whose traditional folkways are shaped to such environments.

Physiologically, the cardiovascular system seems to be the most salient locus of change. In varying the flow of blood closer to or further from the skin, it regulates internal temperature in reaction to ambient heat or cold; it adjusts the rate of flow to deal with abnormal air pressures and oxygen availability; and, of course, it responds to shifting levels of arousal. The limits of its adaptability are usually fairly clear. Other adverse effects are more subtle, as in the case of the loss of bone minerals among astronauts. Among indigenous populations, some features that at first glance seem to be genetic adaptations turn out on closer examination to be either inaccurate stereotypes or not in fact inherited. These mechanisms need to be investigated systematically. Perhaps the most important area in which we have to be content for the time being with speculation rather than data is the role of neurochemicals in the reaction and adaptation to extreme and unusual environments. Endorphin secretion must be responsive to ambient conditions, and the interaction between it and characteristics of the psychological–behavioral response must be elucidated.

Sensory and perceptual reactions are affected by the environment, but the extremeness or novelty of the situation does not seem to be a crucial variable. Rather the same parameters as in any other perceptual field determine the response: threshold changes; cues as to size, distance, direction, and the like; the quality of light; ambient noise; clothing and equipment as they facilitate or impede acuity; and so on.

Problem solving and cognitive processes show complex patterns. To begin with, cultural adaptations to adverse environments obviously work. Any group that through generations survives in the Arctic, the Amazon, or the High Andes has clearly solved some very difficult problems. But there are striking cultural differences among groups that live in superficially similar milieux—for example, Sherpas and Andean Indians. An elucidation of such differences might shed light on subtle aspects of the environments and identify powerful determinants. In other types of extreme and unusual environments, the most striking finding is the lack of universality. Cognition and problem solving do not generally deteriorate unless the conditions are so severe that there is physiological damage; otherwise, any decrement seems to be more a function of loss of motivation rather than of ability to perform the task (Rasmussen, 1973; Suedfeld, 1969). A last important point is that efficacy sometimes actually improves, although the individuals themselves may be unaware of that fact.

In the case of affective reactions, we again have a surprise in the degree to which positive consequences are found. Perhaps because aversive ones are more striking or because of the professional perspective of much of psychology, fear and other negative emotions have had more attention than courage, altruism, and humor. But the historical evidence supports the importance and frequency of the latter. It is time for psychologists to explore these reactions in more depth.

The social fabric is one area where negative consequences of extreme and unusual environments are common, except in cultures that have been used to such an environment over a long period. Societies where such conditions appear rapidly seem to suffer, as do small groups in remote work and living sites. Conflict within the group, problems of leadership, and loss of cohesiveness and morale are common. Groups of elite volunteers in relatively short-duration situations are most likely to resist this deterioration.

Individual differences have been studied mostly in the context of selection. The existing literature offers few surprises. As one author has said, the usual procedure of measuring the characteristics of people in the situation and correlating them with performance gives the same results as if we turned it around: from an examination of the situation, generating a list of what seem to be adaptive characteristics (Haggard, 1973). However, the work has concentrated on rather traditional and general personality measures and traits, and recent developments in personality theory might fruitfully be applied in this area.

Most groups and individuals appear to come through even fairly traumatic circumstances without major symptoms of mental illness. However, some symptoms are fairly common among people whose experiences have been extremely harsh, particularly when these conditions were imposed deliberately by a hostile source rather than the individual's having volunteered with knowledge of what to expect. Natural disasters can also have this effect, implying that voluntariness, training, and perceived ability to cope may be crucial determinants. The symptoms of "posttraumatic stress disorder" include nightmares, hyperreactivity to stimuli associated with the experience, psychosomatic illnesses, apathy, and guilt feelings.

It should be obvious that "extreme and unusual environments" are not very difficult to find among the encounters that human beings have with the world. What is interesting is that psychologists should have devoted so little attention to studying them. After all, some of the most interesting human groups live in such situations. Many other people experience them at some time in their life, sometimes with significant, long-lasting aftereffects. The number of participants is increasing with every worker on an offshore oil rig and with every patient who has to lie still for hours in the restricted environment of a medical imaging unit. Reactions to all of these settings could tell us much about basic psychological processes.

22.12.2. Problems of the Literature

There are glaring gaps in our knowledge. One is that researchers have addressed themselves to only a tiny proportion of extreme and unusual environments in any systematic way. Rigorous studies have concentrated on those situations where such research is relatively easy to do because of the availability of funds, organizational support, preparation time, and so forth. Most of these situations involve governmental or industrial staffs trying to solve specific mission-related problems in space, in the polar regions, under the ocean, or at isolated encampments. Psychologists have done relatively little systematic research even about what I have called "normal" extreme situations—for example, among peoples who dwell in such conditions—although physiologists and anthropologists have collected considerable data there.

Aside from its lack of general coverage, psychological research in these areas has other flaws. Subjects are frequently nonrepresentative, whether self-selected or possessing some set of characteristics that lead to their being in the environment. Usually, there is only one treatment group. Even when there are several, people are almost never assigned to them randomly. Experimental and control groups, comparison between similar groups in normal and extreme environments, or even pre- and postenvironment comparisons on the same group are very rare indeed except in simulation research and in a few examples of polar work. Some of these problems are inherent in the research context, but others could be avoided if sponsoring agencies could be convinced of the need for rigorous studies.

In field studies, there are usually so many intricately interrelated independent variables as to be only very grossly specified. Dependent variables are usually chosen on an intuitive, shotgun basis rather than with a view toward coherence or generalizable significance. Very seldom do we get a clear statement of any but obvious hypotheses; even more rarely, hypotheses derived from a coherent theory; and almost never a strong hypothesis-testing design allowing us to evaluate opposing predictions drawn from different theories.

22.12.3. Research Suggestions

A basic necessity is for comprehensive literature reviews. We should have an overview of the many extreme and unusual environments about which we now only have partial information, usually based on fortuitous access to specific occurrences. For example, there is no thorough analysis of the types and roles of vision quests in tribal societies or of the experiences and reactions of castaways and lone voyagers.

Aside from correcting the design and methodological problems noted earlier, there is a major need for applying some nontraditional research methods to the study of extreme and unusual environments. The psychological literature here is based mostly on experimental analogues, interviews, and paper-and-pencil measures. Although these have provided much information and will doubtless continue to do so, they cannot give us access to all of the relevant facts. I think we can do much better using not only psychological research methods but also some borrowed from anthropology, archaeology, economics, history, and political science. Nor do I suggest that this is an exhaustive list.

One obvious method, common in anthropology and with a long history in social psychology, is participant observation. With the shining exception of polar research, we have not had much of that—and even there, most psychologists have not wintered over. It seems obvious that to be on location for a fairly long period, interacting with others and experiencing the environment for oneself, is an important way to collect information. It is, however, time-consuming, uncomfortable, and sometimes dangerous. Furthermore there are logistical problems and perhaps difficulties in gaining the cooperation of the people who customarily inhabit the locale.

On the other hand, the prospects may be improving. The U.S. space program is accepting scientists to fly in the space shuttle, and many psychologists have been involved in polar activities. Many psychologists are pilots, scuba divers, mountain climbers, or cave explorers. Thus at least the recreational and some of the instrumental occasions can be scientifically explored. And with travel being considerably less arduous than a few decades ago, the remote areas of the earth have become accessible enough for such explorations as well.

Another desirable addition to the repertoire is the use of documentary and archival sources. There is a massive literature of autobiographies, diaries, letters, logbooks, newspaper and magazine articles, work reports, and the like that have been produced by people who had lived in environments of interest. Among native groups there are some of these same materials plus folktales, local histories, family records, and so forth. As economic historians have shown, records of how material resources are obtained and used can shed light on the relative importance of various activities and goals as well as on the nature of day-to-day life. Demographers and sociologists as well as health scientists use census data, vital records, and various indices of community characteristics.

All of these sources of information have been neglected in our research. Documents call for systematic content analyses such as those used in political science, political psychology, and related areas (Knutson, 1973). Quantitative techniques include the scoring of affects, motives, cognitive characteristics, interrelationships among individuals, groups, and activities. Qualitative analyses could provide insights to be explored with other methods. Both with these and with some of the other kinds of data mentioned in this section, multivariate and time-series analyses could lead to new realizations.

Unobtrusive measures (Webb, Campbell, Schwartz, & Sechrest, 1966) could be of great value. Among obvious applications would be those regarding group structure and culture, territoriality, interpersonal relationships, changes in motivation, interests, and effectiveness. All are derivable from observing items of decoration, personal belongings, the arrangement of furniture and equipment, artifacts produced on site, and signs of accretion and erosion. Nelson (1973), in a perceptive discussion of this kind of datum, points to the significance of the "site visit" in our understanding of the last moments of Scott and his teammates: Where Scott's diary (which was found with his body) could be read to show decreasing cohesiveness among the group, the position of the bodies was strong evidence to the contrary.

Observations using modern technology would also be helpful. If the psychologist cannot enter the environment, perhaps video and audio recording equipment can. This technique was used successfully in gathering data during the saturation diving projects

of the U.S. government (the Sealab and Tektite series; Radloff, 1973). Information was gathered about the use of space, activity patterns and levels, group and individual work habits, and the like. Once again we can borrow from historians: The use of recorded oral histories, going far beyond the usual limited interview, can provide novel perspectives from people who have lived the experience.

22.12.4. Theoretical Considerations

The research should also be theory-oriented. At the moment, it is difficult to make sense of the data because of the absence of theoretical guidance. The time is ripe to remedy the situation now that environmental psychology as a whole is developing such bases. The data generated by one experimental situation, REST, have been viewed in the light of some dozen formulations (Suedfeld, 1980). It is not likely that all, or even a large proportion, of the variables involved in reactions to the whole variety of extreme and unusual environments will be explicable by any one model. There are two ways of incorporating theories in this field. One is to use the theory to explain and predict environmental effects, and the other is to use extreme and unusual environments to test hypotheses derived from the theory.

At the moment, arousal theory (e.g., Hebb, 1955) is probably the most widely cited and most frequently applied concept in this area. It is particularly attractive because many extreme and unusual environments intuitively seem to raise or lower the level of arousal. The theory links an unusually wide range of processes (psychophysiological, cognitive, and emotional) to a common substrate (see Rasmussen, 1973). However, it also has significant flaws. For one thing, measures—and even definitions—of arousal are often inconsistent with each other, making predictions vague and disconfirmation unlikely. Second, arousal theory fails to explain some phenomena that fall within its purview. For example, there are theoretically paradoxical reversals in hedonic tone within any area of the arousal curve such as between boredom and relaxation or excitement and anxiety (Apter, 1984).

Critical experiments contrasting hypotheses derived from arousal theory, Apter's reversal theory, and other candidates should be high in priority. For those who believe in the arousal-labeling model of affect (Schachter & Singer, 1962), the extreme environment should provide an exacting test of the hypothesis. Conversely theorists who consider the affect as primary (Tomkins, 1962; Zajonc, 1980) have an unusually good selection of situational cues related to emotional involvement.

A related issue is that of stress. The comparative impact of major threat and daily hassles and frustrations, long-term changes as stress continues, and what happens when stressful periods are successfully survived are questions of basic as well as applied significance. Sources of stress could be identified, separated by looking at a variety of selected environments, and compared. Issues related to stress management or resistance — significant life events, individual differences, social support networks — could be examined in situations where they really matter.

Personality theories could also be given a good test here. As the most obvious example, what individual characteristics will predict adaptation to these environments? Many established theories have been applied, but not all; still, perhaps newer constructs are more promising. Among obvious candidates are hardiness (Kobasa, 1979), self-efficacy (Bandura, 1977), paratelic dominance (Apter, 1984), risk taking (Knowles, Cutter, Walsh, & Casey, 1973), and sensation seeking (Zuckerman, 1979). No one knows the degree to which any of these would really work, nor whether some cluster of them would be an appropriate thing to look for. The relationship of any such measures to the range of relevant dependent variables may also be interesting. After all, there is no reason to assume that a high level of problem solving in an emergency will necessarily be associated with the same personal traits as the ability to remain congenial in long confinement.

Coping with extreme and unusual environments is also an interesting subject. The interplay of affect and thinking, or hot and cold cognition, as they influence success, should be tested. Then we might think about the adaptiveness of different behavior patterns. For example, I have referred to Musselmanism as a form of learned helplessness and as being self-defeating. But there is the possibility that learned helplessness (i.e., freezing and immobility) leads to heightened secretion of beta endorphin, which reduces pain. Thus the withdrawal syndrome might at least reduce phenomenological suffering, even if it does not meet our cultural preferences about how to cope with danger. Analyses of facial expressions of people in extreme environments could shed some light on affective differences and their behavioral consequences.

The whole issue of the neurophysiological effects of extreme environments is intriguing. Apparently some of the reactions are characterized by gaiety and happiness. Chemical effects are obviously relevant to nitrogen narcosis ("rapture of the deep"), anoxic euphoria in high-altitude mountain sickness and flying, and hypothermic euphoria, the reputed happiness that overcomes people who are freezing to death. Are these emotional states related directly to chemical aspects of the environment–body interchange, or to endogenous opioids, or is cognitive–affective interpretation involved?

Another related example: I have mentioned that lone voyagers under circumstances of extreme fatigue, danger, deprivation, and pain often encounter a spiritual helper. This is so common, across so many types of travelers — Western sailors, Inuit hunters, native Indian adolescents — that it demands attention. There would appear to be some interplay among neurophysiology, perception–cognition, and affect. No one has yet attempted to offer a full theoretical explanation of this dramatic phenomenon, but one can envisage concepts including changes in hemispheric dominance under stress or psychodynamic mechanisms by which stimuli are reinterpreted.

The interaction within small groups is perhaps more intense and more long-lasting here than in almost any comparable situation. Theories dealing with group dynamics — friendship formation, group structure and communication, leadership, conformity — could clearly provide interesting hypotheses. As an illustration, I have referred to Nelson's (1973) idea that flexible leadership style can be important in isolated groups. How does this tie in with Fiedler's (1971) model of leader effectiveness, or with the trait versus interactional approach to authoritarian leadership (e.g., Suedfeld, 1983)?

Other research is suggested by constructs dealing with influence and persuasion: types of social power, public commitment, the structure of persuasive arguments, minority influence, reinforcement and modeling, and cognitive consistency — to name a few. Proxemic research might also be tried. What are the effects of extreme environments on nonverbal communication, territoriality, personal space, and interaction distance, and the like? Because we are considering many cultures and ethnic groups, the relevance of cross-cultural comparisons is obvious. Adaptive folkways, small group structures, and work patterns may be related to concepts of social and individual development and even to sociobiology.

I am not attempting anything more than a listing of relevant theoretical issues that are particularly salient to my own interests. Any reader can supply an alternate or supplementary roster and is urged not only to do so but to consider actually collecting some relevant data. Work on the problems posed by extreme and unusual environments can help to solve serious real-life problems and to elucidate important questions of scientific research and theory. And an interest in the area can result in exposure to new literatures, stimulating facts and ideas, and much fun.

REFERENCES

Allport, G.W. (1937). *Personality: A psychological interpretation*. New York: Holt.

Altman, I., & Chemers, M. (1980). *Culture and environment*. Monterey, CA: Brooks/Cole.

Altman, I., & Haythorn, W.W. (1967). The ecology of isolated groups. *Behavioral Science, 12*, 169–182.

Altman, J.W., Smith, R.W., Meyers, R.L., McKenna, F.S., & Bryson, S. (1962). *Psychological and social adjustment in a simulated shelter: A research report*. Washington, DC: Office of Civil Defense.

American Psychiatric Association. (1980). *Diagnostic and statistical manual of mental disorders* (3rd ed.). Washington, DC: Author.

Apter, M.J. (1984). Reversal theory and personality: A review. *Journal of Research in Personality, 18*, 265–288.

Bachrach, A.J. (1982). The human in extreme environments. In A. Baum & J.E. Singer (Eds.), *Advances in environmental psychology: Vol. 4. Environment and health*. Hillsdale, NJ: Erlbaum.

Bandura, A. (1977). Self-efficacy: Toward a unifying theory of behavior change. *Psychological Review, 84*, 199–215.

Barabasz, A., & Barabasz, M. (1985). Effects of restricted environmental stimulation: Skin conductance, EEG alpha and temperature responses. *Environment and Behavior, 17*, 239–253.

Baum, A., & Valins, S. (1978). *Architecture and social behavior: Psychological studies in social density*. Hillsdale, NJ: Erlbaum.

Beare, A.N., Biersner, R.J., Bondi, K.R., & Naitoh, P. (1981). *Work and rest on nuclear submarines* (Rep. No. 946). Groton, CT: Naval Submarine Medical Research Laboratory.

Bennet, G. (1974). Psychological breakdown at sea: Hazards of single-handed ocean sailing. *British Journal of Medical Psychology, 47*, 189–210.

Berry, J.W. (1975). An ecological approach to cross-cultural psychology. *Netherlands Journal of Psychology, 30*, 51–84.

Berry, J.W. (1976). *Human ecology and cognitive style*. Beverly Hills, CA: Halsted.

Biderman, A.D. (1963). *March to calumny*. New York: Macmillan.

Binnie-Dawson, J.L.M. (1982). A bio-social approach to environmental psychology and problems of stress. *International Journal of Psychology, 17*, 397–435.

Block, J., & Block, J.H. (1981). Studying situational dimensions: A grand perspective and some limited empiricism. In D. Magnusson (Ed.), *Toward a psychology of situations*. Hillsdale, NJ: Erlbaum.

Bloom, M., & Halsema, J. (1983). Survival in extreme conditions. *Suicide and Life-Threatening Behavior, 13*, 195–206.

Blum, H.F. (1961). Does the melanin pigment of human skin have adaptive value? *Quarterly Review of Biology, 36*, 50–63.

Bluth, B.J. (1980, May). *Social and psychological problems of extended space mission*. Paper presented at the meeting of the American Institute of Aeronautics and Astronautics, Baltimore, MD.

Bombard, A. (1953). *The voyage of the Heretique*. New York: Simon & Schuster.

Boyanowsky, E.O., Calvert, J., Young, J., & Brideau, L. (1981–82). Toward a thermo-regulatory model of violence. *Journal of Environmental Systems, 11*, 81–87.

Brady, J.V., & Emurian, H.H. (1978). Behavior analyses of motivational and emotional interactions in a programmed environment. *Nebraska Symposium on Motivation, 26*, 81–122.

Braun, J.R. (1961). *Notes on the literature: The relation of isolation, cold, and stress to behavior at remote sites*. Paper presented at the Tri-Service Conference on Research Relevant to Behavior Problems of Small Military Groups under Isolation and Stress, Fort Worth, TX.

Bross, M. (1985). The application of sensory restriction techniques in the study of sensory threshold regulation. In T. Fine, J. Stanley, & K. Johnson (Eds.), *REST and Self-Regulation: Proceedings of the First International Conference*. Toledo: Medical College of Ohio.

Byrd, R.E. (1938). *Alone*. New York: Ace.

Cahoon, R.L. (1970). Vigilance performance in hypoxia. *Journal of Applied Psychology, 54*, 479–483.

Calhoun, J.B. (1962). Population density and social pathology. *Scientific American, 206*, 139–148.

Cole, M., & Scribner, S. (1974). *Culture and thought*. New York: Wiley.

Condon, R.G. (1983). Seasonal photoperiodism, activity rhythms, and disease susceptibility in the central Canadian Arctic. *Arctic Anthropology, 20*, 33–48.

Cooke, K. (1960). *Man on a raft*. New York: McGraw-Hill.

Cox, V.C., Paulus, P.B., McCain, G., & Schkade, J.K. (1969). Field research on the effects of crowding in prisons and on offshore oil platforms. In J.R. Aiello & A. Baum (Eds.), *Residential crowding and design*. New York: Plenum.

Dimsdale, J.E. (1977). The coping behavior of Nazi concentration camp survivors. In J.E. Dimsdale (Ed.), *Survivors, victims, and perpetrators: Essays on the Nazi Holocaust. Washington, DC: Hemisphere.

Farber, I.E., Harlow, H.F., & West, L.J. (1957). Brainwashing, conditioning and DDD (debility, dependency and dread). Sociometry, 20, 271–285.

Fenz, W.D. (1975). Strategies for coping with stress. In I. Sarason & C. Spielberger (Eds.), Stress and anxiety (Vol. 1). Washington, DC: Hemisphere.

Fiedler, F.E. (1955). The influence of leader-keyman relations on combat crew effectiveness. Journal of Abnormal and Social Psychology, 51, 227–235.

Fiedler, F.E. (1971). Validation and extension of the contingency model of leadership effectiveness: A review of empirical findings. Psychological Bulletin, 76, 128–148.

Figley, C.R. (Ed.). (1978). Stress disorders among Vietnam veterans. New York: Brunner/Mazel.

Flinn, D.E., & Hartman, B.O. (1961). Performance data in space cabin simulators. Paper presented at Supreme Headquarters Allied Powers in Europe Medical Conference, Paris.

Foushee, H.C. (1982, November). The role of communications, sociopsychological, and personality factors in the maintenance of crew coordination. Aviation, Space, and Environmental Medicine, pp. 1062–1066.

Frankenhaeuser, M. (1978). Coping with job stress: A psychobiological approach. Stockholm: University of Stockholm, Department of Psychology.

Frankl, V. (1963). Man's search for meaning. New York: Washington Square Press.

Freedman, J. (1975). Crowding and behavior. New York: Viking.

Garriott, O.K., Parker, R.A.R., Lichtenberg, B.K., & Merbold, U. (1984). Payload crew members' view of Spacelab operations. Science, 225, 165–167.

Gauvain, M., Altman, I., & Fahim, H. (1983). Homes and social change: A cross-cultural analysis. In N. Feimer & S. Geller (Eds.), Environmental psychology: Directions and perspectives. New York: Praeger.

Greene, W.A. (1966). The psychosocial setting of the development of leukemia and lymphoma. Annals of the New York Academy of Sciences, 125, 794–801.

Gregson, R.A.M. (1978). Monitoring cognitive performance in Antarctica. New Zealand Antarctic Record, 1, 24–32.

Gulyr, S.A., & Sirota, S.S. (1974). [State of human higher nervous activity during long stay in limited space under a pressure of 3 and 5 atm]. Fiziolohichneji Zhurnal (Kiev), 20, 440–448.

Gunderson, E.K.E. (1973). Individual behavior in confined or isolated groups. In J.E. Rasmussen (Ed.), Man in isolation and confinement. Chicago: Aldine.

Haggard, E.A. (1973). Some effects of geographic and social isolation in natural settings. In J.E. Rasmussen (Ed.), Man in isolation and confinement. Chicago: Aldine.

Hankinson, K.W. (1984). Interim report: JSE Brabant Island, 1983–85. England: RAF Finningley.

Hanna, J.M., & Brown, D.E. (1983). Human heat tolerance: An anthropological perspective. Annual Review of Anthropology, 12, 259–284.

Harlow, H.F. (1959). The development of learning in the rhesus monkey. American Scientist, 47, 479–485.

Harris, M. (1974). Cows, pigs, wars and witches: The riddles of culture. New York: Random House.

Harris, M. (1977). Cannibals and kings: The origins of cultures. New York: Random House.

Harrison, H. (1982). Wilderness therapy. Wilderness Psychology Newsletter, 6, 4–5.

Haythorn, W.W. (1973). The miniworld of isolation: Laboratory studies. In J.E. Rasmussen (Ed.), Man in isolation and confinement. Chicago: Aldine.

Heaton, P. (1976). The singlehanders. London: Joseph.

Hebb, D.O. (1955). Drives and the C.N.S. (conceptual nervous system). Psychological Review, 62, 243–254.

Helmreich, R.L. (1971). TEKTITE II Human Behavior Program (Tech. Rep. No. 14). Austin: University of Texas.

Helmreich, R.L. (1983). Applying psychology in outer space: Unfulfilled promises revisited. American Psychologist, 38, 445–450.

Henderson, R. (1976). Singlehanded sailing. Camden, ME: International Marine Publishing.

Hibbert, C. (1983). Africa explored: Europeans in the dark continent 1769–1889. New York: Norton.

Hohnsbein, J., Piekarski, C., & Kampmann, B. (1983). Influence of high ambient temperature and humidity on visual sensitivity. Ergonomics, 26, 905–911.

Holm, D. (1974). The circumnavigators. Englewood Cliffs, NJ: Prentice-Hall.

Holson, R., & Sackett, G.P. (1984). Effects of isolation rearing on learning by mammals. Psychology of Learning and Motivation, 18, 199–254.

Hood, R.W., Jr. (1977). Eliciting mystical states of consciousness with semistructured nature experiences. Journal for the Scientific Study of Religion, 16, 155–163.

Houston, B.K., Blom, L.J., Burish, T.G., & Cummings, E.M. (1978). Positive evaluations of stressful experiences. Journal of Personality, 46, 205–214.

Hunter, E. (1958). Brainwashing: The story of men who defied it. New York: Pyramid.

Huntford, R. (1980). Scott & Amundsen: The race to the South Pole. New York: Putnam.

Jackson, G. (1974). Surviving the long night. New York: Vanguard.

Jacobs, G.D., Heilbronner, R.L., & Stanley, J.M. (1984). The effects of short term flotation REST on relaxation: A controlled study. Health Psychology, 3, 99–112.

Jacobson, S.R. (1973). Individual and group responses to

confinement in a skyjacked plane. *American Journal of Orthopsychiatry, 43,* 459–469.

Janerich, D.T., Stark, A.D., Greenwald, P., Burnett, W.S., Jacobson, H.I., & McCusker, J. (1981). Increased leukemia, lymphoma, and spontaneous abortion in western New York following a flood disaster. *Public Health Reports, 96,* 350–356.

Janis, I.L. (1951). *Air war and emotional stress.* New York: McGraw-Hill.

Jilek, W.G. (1982). Altered states of consciousness in North American Indian ceremonials. *Ethos, 10,* 326–343.

Jochim, M.A. (Ed.) (1981). *Strategies for survival: Cultural behavior in an ecological context.* New York: Academic.

Jorgenson, D.O. (1981). Perceived causal influences of weather: Rating the weather's influence on affective states and behaviors. *Environment and Behavior, 13,* 239–256.

Kagan, J. (1976). Emergent themes in human development. *American Scientist, 64,* 186–196.

Kahneman, D., & Tversky, A. (1984). Choices, values, and frames. *American Psychologist, 39,* 341–350.

Katz, R. (1973). *Preludes to growth: An experiential approach.* New York: Macmillan.

Kinkead, E. (1959). *In every war but one.* New York: Norton.

Klausner, S.Z. (Ed.) (1968). *Why man takes chances.* Garden City, NY: Doubleday.

Knowles, E.S., Cutter, H.S.G., Walsh, D.H., & Casey, N.A. (1973). Risk-taking as a personality trait. *Social Behavior and Personality, 1,* 123–136.

Knutson, J.N. (Gen. Ed.) (1973). *Handbook of political psychology.* San Francisco: Jossey-Bass.

Kobasa, S.C. (1979). Stressful life events, personality and health: An inquiry into hardiness. *Journal of Personality and Social Psychology, 37,* 1–11.

Koerner, F.C. (1982). *Polar biomedical research: An assessment.* Washington, DC: National Academy Press.

Lanphier, E.H. (1974). Medical aspects of diving: Underwater physiology. In B.E. Empleton, E.H. Lanphier, J.E. Young, & L.G. Goff (Eds.), *The new science of skin and scuba diving* (rev. ed.). Chicago: Follett.

Lazarus, R.S. (1984). Puzzles in the study of daily hassles. *Journal of Behavioral Medicine, 7,* 375–390.

Lazarus, R.S., & Cohen, J.B. (1977). Environmental stress. In I. Altman and J. Wohlwill (Eds.), *Human behavior and environment* (Vol. 1). New York: Plenum.

Linderholm, H. (1981). Arctic exploitation. In B. Harvald & H. Hansen (Eds.), *Circumpolar 81: Proceedings of the International Symposium on Circumpolar Health* (pp. 533–539), Copenhagen.

Lipowski, Z.J. (1971). Surfeit of attractive information inputs: A hallmark of our environment. *Behavior Science, 16,* 461–471.

Lloyd, E.L. (1981). Hallucinations and misinterpretations in hypothermia and cold stress. In B. Harvald & H. Hansen (Eds.), *Circumpolar 81: Proceedings of the International Symposium on Circumpolar Health* (pp. 612–616), Copenhagen.

Luchterhand, E. (1970). Early and late effects of imprisonment in Nazi concentration camps: Conflicting interpretations in survivor research. *Social Psychiatry, 5,* 102–110.

Magnusson, D. (1981). Wanted: A psychology of situations. In D. Magnusson (Ed.), *Toward a psychology of situations.* Hillsdale, NJ: Erlbaum.

Marano, L. (1982). Windigo psychosis: The anatomy of an emic-etic confusion. *Current Anthropology, 23,* 385–412.

Marshall, S.L.A. (1961). *Men against fire.* New York: Apollo.

Mawson (1725). *Journal excerpt.* Cited in Neider, C. (Ed.) (1952). *Great shipwrecks and castaways.* New York: Harper.

Money, K.E. (1981). Biological effects of space travel. *Canadian Aeronautics and Space Journal, 27,* 195–201.

Moore, L.G., & Regensteiner, J.G. (1983). Adaptation to high altitude. *Annual Review of Anthropology, 12,* 285–304.

Moran, E.F. (1979). *Human adaptability: An introduction to ecological anthropology.* North Scituate, MA: Duxbury.

Mueller, C.W. (1983). Environmental stressors and aggressive behavior. In R. Geen & E. Donnerstein (Eds.), *Aggression: Theoretical and methodologic issues* (Vol. 2). New York: Academic.

Mullin, C.S., Jr. (1960). Some psychological aspects of isolated Antarctic living. *American Journal of Psychiatry, 117,* 323–325.

Natani, K., & Shurley, J.T. (1974). Sociopsychological aspects of a winter vigil at South Pole station. In E.K.E. Gunderson (Ed.), *Human adaptability to Antarctic conditions.* Washington, DC: American Geophysical Union.

National Academy of Sciences. (1972). *Human factors in long-duration spaceflight.* Washington, DC: National Academy of Sciences.

Neider, C. (Ed.). (1952). *Great shipwrecks and castaways.* New York: Harper.

Nelson, P.D. (1973). The indirect observation of groups under confinement and/or isolation. In J.E. Rasmussen (Ed.), *Man in isolation and confinement.* Chicago: Aldine.

Pallanich, J. (1968). Fighting frowned on [Letter]. *Peace Corps Volunteer, 6*(6), 28–29.

Pelto, G.H., & Pelto, P.J. (1979). *The cultural dimension of the human adventure.* New York: Macmillan.

Rachman, S.J. (1984). Review article: Fear and courage. *Behavior Therapy, 15,* 109–120.

Radil-Weiss, T. (1983). Men in extreme conditions: Some medical and psychological aspects of the Auschwitz concentration camp. *Psychiatry, 46*, 259–269.

Radloff, R.W. (1973). Naturalistic observations of isolated experimental groups in field settings. In J.E. Rasmussen (Ed.), *Man in isolation and confinement*. Chicago: Aldine.

Radloff, R.W., & Helmreich, R. (1968). *Groups under stress: Psychological research in SEALAB II*. New York: Appleton-Century-Crofts.

Rasmussen, J.E. (Ed.). (1973). *Man in isolation and confinement*. Chicago: Aldine.

Read, P.P. (1974). *Alive*. New York: Avon.

Reid, A. (1980). *Discovery and exploration: A concise history*. London: Gentry.

Rivolier, J., Goldsmith, R., Lugg, D., & Taylor, A. (in press). *Man in the Antarctic: The international biomedical expedition to the Antarctic*. London: Taylor-Francis.

Ross, H.E. (1975). *Behavior and perception in strange environments*. New York: Basic Books.

Russell, J.A., & Ward, L.M. (1982). Environmental psychology. *Annual Review of Psychology, 33*, 651–688.

Schachter, S., & Singer, J.E. (1962). Cognitive, social and physiological determinants of emotional state. *Psychological Review, 69*, 379–399.

Schein, E.H. (1961). *Coercive persuasion*. New York: Norton.

Seligman, M.E.P. (1975). *Helplessness*. San Francisco: Freeman.

Sells, S.B. (1963). Dimensions of stimulus situations which account for behavior variance. In S.B. Sells (Ed.), *Stimulus determinants of behavior*. New York: Ronald.

Sells, S.B. (1973). The taxonomy of man in enclosed space. In J.E. Rasmussen (Ed.), *Man in isolation and confinement*. Chicago: Aldine.

Sharma, V.M., Vaskaran, A.S., & Malhotra, M.S. (1976). Social compatibility under prolonged isolation and high altitude. *Indian Journal of Applied Psychology, 13*, 11–15.

Sherif, M., & Sherif, C.W. (1956). *An outline of social psychology* (rev. ed.). New York: Harper & Row.

Shurley, J.T. (Ed.). (1970). Symposium on man on the South Polar Plateau. *Archives of Internal Medicine, 125*, 625–659.

Siegel, S., Hinson, R.E., Krank, M.D., & McCully, J. (1982). Heroin "overdose" death: Contribution of drug-associated environmental cues. *Science, 216*, 436–437.

Sloan, A.W. (1979). *Man in extreme environments*. Springfield, IL: Thomas.

Slocum, J. (1958). *Sailing alone around the world*. New York: Macmillan. (Original work published 1900)

Smith, S. (1969). Studies of small groups in confinement. In J.P. Zubek (Ed.). *Sensory deprivation: Fifteen years of research*. New York: Appleton-Century-Crofts.

Sonnenfeld, J. (1969). Equivalence and distortion of the perceptual environment. *Environment and Behavior, 1*, 83–100.

Spence, K.W. (1953). Learning and performance in eyelid conditioning as a function of the intensity of the UCS. *Journal of Experimental Psychology, 45*, 57–63.

Steegmann, A.T. (Ed.). (1983). *Boreal forest adaptations*. New York: Plenum.

Suedfeld, P. (1969). Changes in intellectual performance and susceptibility to influence. In J.P. Zubek (Ed.), *Sensory deprivation: Fifteen years of research*. New York: Appleton-Century-Crofts.

Suedfeld, P. (1979). Stressful levels of environmental stimulation. In I.G. Sarason & C.D. Spielberger (Eds.), *Stress and anxiety* (Vol. 6). New York: Halsted.

Suedfeld, P. (1980). *Restricted environmental stimulation: Research and clinical applications*. New York: Wiley.

Suedfeld, P. (1983). Authoritarian leadership: A cognitive-interactionist view. In J. Held (Ed.) *The cult of power*. Boulder, CO: East European Monographs.

Suedfeld, P., & Kristeller, J.L. (1982). Stimulus reduction as a technique in health psychology. *Health Psychology, 1*, 337–357.

Suedfeld, P., Ramirez, C., Deaton, J., & Baker-Brown, G. (1982). Reactions and attributes of prisoners in solitary confinement. *Criminal Justice and Behavior, 9*, 303–340.

Taylor, A.J.W. (1969). Ability, stability and social adjustment among Scott Base personnel, Antarctica. *Occupational Psychology, 43*, 81–93.

Taylor, A.J.W. (1970). Professional isolates in New Zealand's Antarctic Research Programme. *International Review of Applied Psychology, 18*, 135–138.

Taylor, A.J.W. (1984). Socioticism: The trinity of adversity. *Recent Developments in World Seismology*.

Taylor, L.J., & Skanes, G.R. (1975). Psycholinguistic abilities of children in isolated communities of Labrador. *Canadian Journal of Behavioural Science, 7*, 30–39.

Tees, R.C. (1980). The effects of sensory deprivation on the behavior of infrahuman organisms. In P. Suedfeld, *Restricted environmental stimulation: Research and clinical applications*. New York: Wiley.

Textor, R.B. (Ed.). (1966). *Cultural frontiers of the Peace Corps*. Cambridge, MA: Massachusetts Institute of Technology.

Thackray, R.I. (1981). The stress of boredom and monotony: A consideration of the evidence. *Psychosomatic Medicine, 43*, 165–176.

Tikalsky, F.D. (1982, Winter). Historical controversy, science, and John Wesley Powell. *Journal of Arizona History*, pp. 407–422.

Tomkins, S.S. (1962). *Affect imagery consciousness*. New York: Springer.

Torrance, E.P. (1954). The behavior of small groups under the stress conditions of "survival." *American Sociological Review, 19,* 751–755.

Trumbull, R. (1942). *The raft.* New York: Holt.

Turnbull, C.M. (1961). Some observations regarding the experiences and behavior of the Bambuti pigmy. *American Journal of Psychology, 74,* 304–308.

Turnbull, C.M. (1972). *The mountain people.* New York: Simon & Schuster.

Ursin, H., Baade, E., & Levine, S. (1978). *Psychobiology of stress: A study of coping men.* New York: Academic.

Vayda, A.P. (Ed.). (1969). *Environment and cultural behavior: Ecological studies in cultural anthropology.* Garden City, NY: Natural History Press.

Veno, A., & Dufty, N.F. (1982a). *Mine towns in Australia's North-West: Options for operation and quality of life.* Paper read at the meeting of the Australia and New Zealand Association for the Advancement of Science, Sydney, NSW, Australia.

Veno, A., & Dufty, N.F. (1982b). Planning mining operations in remote Australia. *Professional Psychology, 13,* 722–727.

Vernon, J. (1963). *Inside the black room.* New York: Potter.

Webb, E.J., Campbell, D.T., Schwartz, R.D., & Sechrest, L. (1966). *Unobtrusive measures: Nonreactive research in the social sciences.* Chicago: Rand McNally.

West, J.B. (1984). Human physiology at extreme altitudes at Mount Everest. *Science, 223,* 784–788.

Wilson, H. (1942). Mental reactions to air raids. *Lancet, 1,* 284–287.

Wolfe, T. (1979). *The right stuff.* New York: Farrar, Straus & Giroux.

Wormith, J.S. (1984). The controversy over the effects of long-term incarceration. *Canadian Journal of Criminology, 26,* 423–437.

Zajonc, R.B. (1980). Feeling and thinking: Preferences need no inferences. *American Psychologist, 35,* 151–175.

Zimmerman, M.R. (1985). Paleopathology in Alaskan mummies. *American Scientist, 73,* 20–25.

Zubek, J.P. (Ed.). (1969). *Sensory deprivation: Fifteen years of research.* New York: Appleton-Century-Crofts.

Zuckerman, M. (1979). *Sensation seeking: Beyond the optimal level of arousal.* Hillsdale, NJ: Erlbaum.

Zuckerman, M., Persky, H., Miller, L., & Levin, B. (1969). Contrasting effects of understimulation (sensory deprivation) and overstimulation (high stimulus variety). *Proceedings of the 77th Annual Convention of the APA, 88,* 319–320.

Author Index and Subject Index appear at the end of Volume Two.